HYMNAL COMPANION

to the

Lutheran Book of Worship

HYMNAL COMPANION

to the

Lutheran Book of Worship

MARILYN KAY STULKEN

FORTRESS PRESS   Philadelphia

Library of Congress Cataloging in Publication Data

Stulken, Marilyn Kay, 1941–

    Hymnal companion to the Lutheran book of worship.
    Bibliography: p. 575
    Includes index.
    1. Hymns—History and criticism. 2. Lutherans
—Hymns—History and criticism. 3. Hymns—Instruction and study. 4. Lutherans—Hymns—Instruction and study. I. Lutheran Church in America. Lutheran book of worship. II. Title.
    ML3168.S85   783.9   81–707
    ISBN 0-8006-0300-1   AACR2

REF.

31,129

7976B81   Printed in the United States of America   1–300

To My Parents
Leon and Lenora Stulken

Contents

Introduction

Modern hymnals provide access to the language of devotion and praise of Christian people across the ages and throughout the world. Similarly they enable singing the differing melodies which have given those words wing. A rich diversity is revealed as one puts side by side texts from the Bible, St. Ambrose, Martin Luther, Charles Wesley, Ray Palmer, and John Arthur, or as one compares plainsong tunes with chorale melodies, psalm tunes, English hymns, and spirituals. Any hymnal is an anthology of the breadth and imagination of Christian expression.

American hymnals embody this diversity in a special sense. American hymnological traditions, most of them, were brought from Great Britain or Europe and have since added a uniquely American accent to the imported heritage they preserve and further. In recent decades a sample of hymns from all over the world often has been added to that fundamental mix.

It should not be surprising, then, if a modern Lutheran hymnal presents the most variegated collection of all, since the European heritage of Lutheranism is so diverse: German, Danish, Swedish, Finnish, Norwegian, Icelandic, Slovak. The *Lutheran Book of Worship* contains hymns from all these sources and then adds items from the Anglo-American, European Reformed, Scottish and Irish, and American folk traditions. To complete its ecumenical circle, it also includes a sampling of hymns from Asia, Africa, and Latin America.

A cardinal virtue of good hymns is their immediate accessibility to the worshiper. But lovers of hymns and those who select hymns for services desire and need greater understanding of the development of the various traditions as well as information about specific texts and tunes, and about hymnists and composers. This book was prepared for them.

This book's primary purpose is to enable a fuller and more informed use of the hymnal half of the *Lutheran Book of Worship*. It provides answers to many questions raised by the presentation of the hymns themselves, and it offers background information on all its hymn texts and tunes. Information about hymnists and composers which can be useful in teaching and preaching is also to be found.

The careful reader will note occasional discrepancies in the sources of texts or tunes between the *Lutheran Book of Worship* and this book. They evidence the vitality of hymnology as a scholarly discipline where new discoveries are continually made. As this *Companion* goes to press, hymnological research has advanced beyond its status when the *Lutheran Book of Worship* manuscript was finished.

For those who do not actually use the *Lutheran Book of Worship* in services, the *Companion* offers the most comprehensive introduction to the various traditions of Lutheran hymnody presently available in English. The initial sections deal not only with the familiar Anglo-American tradition and the classic German hymns; they also lead the reader into the lesser known Scandinavian and Central European traditions. In so doing this *Companion* makes its unique contribution to hymnological literature. The hymnologist and musician will, of course, find the complete set of indexes of special interest and value.

A modern hymnal without a companion is like a gallery without a catalog: one can enjoy the paintings, but only on a relatively superficial level. The *Companion* can whet one's appetite for as yet unknown hymns as well as heighten one's appreciation of more familiar ones.

This *Hymnal Companion* together with the *Manual on the Liturgy* (1979) place the *Lutheran Book of Worship* into the larger context of liturgical and musical research and experience.

EUGENE L. BRAND

Preface

One does not write a book such as this alone. This work owes its existence to the labors of many persons, past and present, whose research and assistance have made the present volume possible. Forming the foundation for this companion are the other companions, handbooks, and hymnological references which can be found listed in the Bibliography on p. 575. Additional material has been made available by a number of hymnologists, researchers, and librarians in this country and abroad, and by the many contributors to the *Lutheran Book of Worship* who have been so cooperative in providing biographical and background information. To all of these I am enormously indebted.

There are many to whom I extend a special word of gratitude—to those who contributed the fine articles on the history contained in the front pages of this book; to M. Alfred Bichsel, whose assistance with my dissertation, *A Handbook to the Service Book and Hymnal of the Lutheran Church in America,* helped to make the present companion a possibility; to Karen Walhof and Theodore DeLaney, whose answers to my many questions helped get this companion off the ground; to those more knowledgable than I in the hymnody of various countries— Mandus Egge (Norwegian), Edward Hansen (Danish), Toivo Harjunpaa (Finnish), Joel Lundeen (Swedish), and Jaroslav Vajda (Slovak-Bohemian); to W. Thomas Smith and Harry Eskew of The Hymn Society of America and Bernard S. Massey of The Hymn Society of Great Britain and Ireland for their assistance; to those who volunteered their help with translation—my brother-in-law, Bruce Brolsma, and Alice Johnson who assisted with Swedish; Toini Landis who gave so many hours in the translation of Danish and Norwegian; and to Rudy Zuiderveld for assistance with Dutch; to my sister, Imogene Stulken, my sister-in-law, Carol Stulken, and my good friend, Janis Altorfer, who donated typing services; to my copy editor, Linda Olson Peebles, whose eagle eye has been invaluable; and last, but by no means least, to my parents and other members of my family and to my friends for their continuing prayers and support throughout this project.

MARILYN KAY STULKEN

The Use of Hymns in Worship

"And when they had sung a hymn, they went out to the Mount of Olives." Thus Matthew and Mark record the use of a "post-communion canticle" at the first Eucharist. The "hymn" sung by Jesus and his disciples was possibly from Psalms 115–118, as it was customary to use those Psalms after the Passover meal. The Hebrew Psalms of Old Testament times continued to play an important role in the worship of the early Christian community, together with the Old and New Testament canticles.

Hymnody as we know it originated during the fourth century, and developed not as a part of the Mass, but within the prayer offices.[1] Prayers at dawn and at dusk, derived from ancient Jewish tradition, were continued and expanded by the early Christian church. Worship at the third, sixth, and ninth hours was established by the end of the fourth century. In 529 St. Benedict, in his *Regula monasteriorum,* written for the monks at Monte Cassino, set forth a complete schedule of eight daily prayer offices (see p. 13) and enjoined the singing of hymns at these services. Except for the services at dawn and at dusk, which were at first attended by the laity, the prayer offices were held primarily within the monastic community.

DE TEMPORE HYMNS[2]

The concept of a cycle of hymns assigned to specific times and seasons of the church year is ancient. In the very earliest lists of hymnody for the prayer offices there was a delineation between hymns for Easter and those for the rest of the year. By the end of the sixth century a yearly cycle of hymns, presumably in general use within the Benedictine Order throughout Western Europe, consisted of some sixty hymns designated for specific hours and/or seasons—Nativity, Epiphany, Lent, and Easter.[3]

In the ninth century a new cycle of hymns superceded the older one. The ninth and tenth centuries were marked by liturgical reform and vigorous development in the hymn cycles. The Church calendar expanded to include not only the festivals of Nativity, Epiphany, Palm Sunday, Easter, Ascension, Pentecost, and Trinity, but also an ever-increasing number of feasts of the Apostles, Biblical saints, early Christian martyrs, and local saints. This expansion called forth a corresponding expansion in the cycle of hymns appropriate to the various festivals and feasts. These cycles were eventually arranged as follows:[4]

[1] The word "office" as used here means service of worship.

[2] *De tempore* is a Latin term meaning "of the time or circumstance."

[3] Four hymns included in this cycle can be found in the LBW: "Aurora lucis rutilat" (LBW 154), "Ad cenam agni providi" (LBW 210), "Splendor paternae gloriae" (LBW 271), and "Christe qui lux es et dies" (LBW 273).

[4] The uses of the various Latin hymns contained in the LBW are given with the discussion of those hymns in this companion.

Commune de tempore hymns for the daily prayer services
Proprium de tempore hymns for the annual festivals
Commune sanctorum general hymns for martyrs, virgins, and confessors
Proprium sanctorum hymns for the feasts of individual saints

The *de tempore* hymn (also known as the "Hymn of the Day," "Hymn of the Week," or "Gradual Hymn") as used within Lutheranism was developed by Martin Luther out of the Gradual. Historically the Gradual (the *responsorium graduale,* so named because it was sung from the *gradus* or step of the altar or ambo) was a responsorial Psalm—one in which each verse of the Psalm was sung by a soloist, with the congregation (and later the choir) responding with a short affirmative statement. Over the centuries the length was drastically reduced, and the music became highly ornate.[5] The Gradual, which came between the Epistle and the Gospel, was one of the Propers of the Mass, that is, it used a cycle of texts which changed according to the Church calendar.

While retaining the Gradual in the form then current in his Latin Mass of 1523, Luther substituted a congregational hymn for the Gradual in his German Mass of 1526, hence the term, "Gradual Hymn." Many church orders of the Reformation era followed Luther's lead, and a fixed yearly cycle of hymns, based on Luther's suggestions, was established for every Sunday and festival of the Church year. While this order of hymns varied slightly from one region to another it displayed considerable uniformity over all.

By tradition the theme of the Gradual was closely related to the Gospel (using the old One-Year Pericopes). The Gradual Hymn, which replaced the Gradual, was the chief hymn of the service, reflecting the dominant theme of the day—usually contained in the Gospel—and often relating it to the entire plan of salvation. It was frequently sung antiphonally, or in alternation, as were many of the ancient Psalms. The congregation, singing in unison, alternated with a choir singing in unison (the *schola* or *chorus choralis*), a choir singing polyphonic settings of the chorales (the *figural* choir), the organ playing chorale settings such as those contained in Samuel Scheidt's *Görlitzer Tabulaturbuch* (1650), or an instrumental ensemble. Thus an entire treasury of church music was brought into play to interpret and illuminate the content and meaning of the hymn for the congregation, and genuinely artistic music was an integral part of corporate worship.

The Gradual Hymn remained in general use for two centuries until the philosophies of Pietism and later of Rationalism obscured the meaning of worship as understood by the early Reformers. Some liturgical and hymnological scholars attempted to reintroduce the use of the Gradual Hymn during the nineteenth century, but without success. The plan was finally reestablished in Germany by Christhard Mahrenholz, Wilhelm Thomas, Konrad Ameln, and others who prepared the *Evangelisches Kirchengesangbuch* of 1950. Similar plans came into use in Holland, Switzerland, and the Scandinavian countries, and in 1961 Ralph Gehrke compiled a Hymn of the Week series for the United States, using hymns available in *The Lutheran Hymnal,* 1941. Since that time a number of official and unofficial "Hymn of the Week" listings have been prepared. A contemporary adaptation of the traditional Lutheran *de tempore* series is

---

[5]It was out of the alleluia following the Gradual that the sequence developed (see p. 14).

indicated by hymns marked with an asterisk under HYMNS FOR THE CHURCH YEAR, pp. 929 ff, of the LBW. In current usage the *de tempore* hymn or Hymn of the Day follows, or occasionally precedes, the sermon.

HYMN SELECTION

In his article on German Hymnody (p. 19), Carl Schalk notes that "Luther viewed the congregational hymn or chorale as an integral and vital part of the liturgy." The careful selection of hymns to relate to the day's Scriptures is of great importance. Hymns are specified for two points in the LBW liturgy—the Entrance Hymn and the Hymn of the Day. Hymns may also be used as the Hymn of Praise, as a Psalm paraphrase, at the Offertory, during Communion, and as a Post-communion Canticle. Although possible, it is not necessary for a service to be monothematic; hymns and service music might be chosen to reflect various emphases found in the lections.

A list entitled "Hymns for the Church Year" is included on pp. 577–601 of this book. This provides a number of suggestions to assist in the choice of congregational hymns, as well as hymn-based choir music and organ works. Suggestions are made for each of the Sundays and Principal Festivals, the Lesser Festivals, and the Occasions. Some hymns are appropriate for all three series—A, B, and C—and some relate to the individual series. Sometimes a hymn ties in with an entire Scripture lesson; more often a single stanza of a hymn picks up a single verse of Scripture. Such is the richness of both Scriptures and the hymns.

EXPANDING A CONGREGATION'S HYMN REPERTOIRE

In order to use fully the resources of the LBW, a congregation needs to become familiar with as many of the hymns as possible. It is helpful, when planning an on-going program of hymn introduction, to start with a list, *by tune name,* of hymns currently familiar to the congregation—including hymns from the previous hymnal. For example, if "Guide me, O thou great Jehovah" (SBH 520), first tune, was familiar, the tune name "Cwm Rhondda" would be listed. The index on page 946 of the LBW gives "Cwm Rhondda" as the setting for two hymns in the LBW—#343 and #415. Either of these hymns could be sung easily.

Once a list of familiar hymns has been established plans can begin to expand it. In the case of easier tunes, frequent repetitions will be sufficient to eventually add a hymn to those that a congregation can sing with confidence. Careful selection of hymns to tie in with the service has an added advantage, in that congregations are more eager to pitch in and give their best on a less familiar hymn if it has a specific reason for being included.

A more intensified approach to hymn learning is a Hymn of the Month program, which allows a congregation to focus on a specific hymn, getting to know something of its background, and becoming thoroughly familiar with it by hearing and/or singing it each Sunday for a month. Various teaching approaches are possible and can include the use of the hymn as an anthem; singing it in alternation with the choir, a soloist, or an instrumental ensemble; or, after it has become somewhat familiar, simply incorporating it as one of the hymns in the service. Bulletin inserts and/or brief announcements of the background of the hymn will add special interest. In this, as in any program of hymn teaching, it is important to include also the children of the Sunday school, and the children's choir, which can be very helpful in teaching new hymns to the congregation. Hymns selected should be generally appropriate to the season of the church year in which they are used. (It might be necessary occasionally to limit the hymn of the month to the first three Sundays, or to begin it later in the month, when it does not mesh with the liturgical emphasis of a whole month.) Once a hymn has been learned as a hymn of the month, it should reappear in the service from time to time to refresh people's memory.

EFFECTIVE HYMN PLAYING

A congregation's full participation in hymn singing can often be encouraged or discouraged by the quality of leadership provided by the organist. A check list for careful preparation of the hymns includes

—correct notes.

—correct rhythm—full-value long notes, uncrowded triplets, crisply-played dotted rhythms without a hint of triplet feeling, and eighth notes without a hint of unevenness.

—steady tempo—from phrase to phrase and from stanza to stanza.

—correct tempo—not so fast as to leave a congregation breathless and not so slow as to leave them asleep. The tempo of a hymn will be determined to some degree by the text of the hymn. A slower tempo is sometimes necessary in a large, resonant room. If a hymn tune seems dreary or doesn't seem to "get off the ground," a quicker tempo might be needed.

—clean technique in which all vertical sounds are played precisely together.

—clearly-separated repeated notes. As a general rule, all repeated notes in the soprano and bass, and all notes repeated from a weak to a strong beat in the inner parts, should be separated by half-value rests. (In the case of longer notes, a rhythmic separation of less than half value can often be used.)

—proper phrasing for breathing. Most hymns have longer notes at the ends of phrases. A clear rhythmic separation at these points will allow the congregation to breath and enable them to know where the next phrase begins. In hymns with a long expanse of seemingly no place to breath, the problem can sometimes be solved by the use of a slightly slower tempo, or a slight delay of the beginning of the next phrase which will allow a catch breath without destroying the rhythm.

—good sense of the rhythmic accents. A hymn such as "O God, our help in ages past" (LBW 320) is clearly in $\frac{4}{4}$ meter, and in one such as "Detroit" (LBW 240) the meter is $\frac{3}{2}$. Some melodies, especially those from the Reformation, however, are often more flexible rhythmically, and contain delightful shifts of rhythm. An excellent sample of such a tune is "Herzlich tut mich erfreuen" (LBW 141), where the pattern of accents is as follows:

```
4   1  2  3  4  1  2  3  4
```
The day of res-ur - rec - tion!

```
1 2   1 2 3 1 2 3   1 2 (etc.)
```
Earth, tell it out a-broad

—good registration. Organ sound should be clear and capable of leading the congregation. The best organ tone for hymn accompaniment is the Principal (other stop names might include Open Diapason, Diapason, Prestant, Octave, or Super Octave). To this might be added mixtures or reeds as noted below. The tremolo or vibrato as well as celeste or Unda Maris stops should not be used to accompany singing; and such specially-tuned stops as Tierce 1 3/5 or Sequialtera are best used only as part of a solo sound when the melody is soloed out.

VARIETY IN HYMN SINGING
AND ACCOMPANIMENT

Variety of tone color and/or harmony or texture can often increase the vitality of singing. All choices of variation should, of course, begin with a consideration of the text and be appropriate to it.

Changes of Tone Color

The simplest means of achieving variety in hymn accompaniment is through changes of organ registration. To a basic registration of Principal 8,' 4,' and 2' one can add brilliance and assertiveness with the use of mixtures, or fire, warmth, or power by the use of a reed or reeds. A stirring beginning or crowning climax of a hymn might include both reeds and mixtures. Simpler registrations, such as Principal 8' and 4' (with or without the 16' in the pedal), are in order for more contemplative texts. (For very personal stanzas, such as stanza 3 of "O sacred head, now wounded" [LBW 116, 117] or stanza 4 of "Ah, holy Jesus" [LBW 123], it can be effective for the organ to play the first two or three chords quietly and stop, leaving the congregation to sing unaccompanied.) On organs with adequate resources, soloing out the melody can also provide variety, and can be especially helpful if the congregation is singing a less-than-familiar hymn. The simplest method is to play the melody in the right hand on a louder registration, the bass in the pedal, and the inner parts with the left hand on a softer registration.

Variety of timbre or tone color can also be achieved by the use of other instruments with organ. (The use of other instruments can be especially welcome where the organ is limited, or where a piano is used for worship.) Instrumental descants can be a joyous experience, but instruments need not be limited to descants. Playing together with the organ straight from the hymnal, a string quartet adds a wonderful sheen to the sound; a single cello on the bass line gives it definition; a violin gives a singing quality to the melody which cannot be achieved on the organ alone. Brass instruments can provide power and a festive air. Each of the woodwind instruments lends its own special and unique timbre when played together with the organ. Some of these instruments can read directly from the hymnal; others must be transposed. The following table will be of assistance to those unfamiliar with the various transpositions:

Strings

Violin—Range: 1st G below Middle C to 3rd B above
   Transposition: None required

Viola—Range: first C below Middle C to second C above
   Transposition: None required (Uses alto and treble clef)

Cello—Range: second C below Middle C to first C above
   Transposition: None required

Double Bass—Range: third E below Middle C to first A below
   Transposition: None required (Sounds an octave lower than written)

Woodwinds

Flute—Range: first D above Middle C to second B^b above
   Transposition: None required

Oboe—Range: Middle C to second D above
   Transposition: None required

English Horn—Range: first E below Middle C to second E^b above
   Transposition: Up a perfect fifth

Clarinet in B^b—Range: first D below Middle C to second G above
   Transposition: Up a major second

Clarinet in A—Range: C below Middle C to second F above
   Transposition: Up a minor third

Bass Clarinet—Range: second D below Middle C to second D above
   Transposition: Up a major second for bass clef or up a major ninth for treble clef

Brass

Horn in F—Range: second D below Middle C to C above
   Transposition: Up a perfect fifth

Trumpet in B^b—Range: G below Middle C to second A^b above
   Transposition: Up a major second

Trumpet in C—Range: first A below Middle C to second B^b above
   Transposition: None required

Tenor Trombone—Range: first F below Middle C to first C above
   Transposition: None required (Uses bass and tenor clef)

Bass Trombone—Range: second C below Middle C to first F above
   Transposition: None required

Tuba—Range: 3rd F below Middle C to first A below
   Transposition: None required

Recorders

Soprano (Descant)—Range: C above Middle C to 4th D above

Alto (Treble)—Range: F above Middle C to third G above

Tenor—Range: Middle C to third D above

Bass—Range: F below Middle C to second F above
                     Transposition: None required

Changes of Harmony and/or Texture

It is immediately apparent as one pages through the LBW hymns that there is a good bit of harmonic variety built in; not all the hymns are set in four-part harmony. Plainsong and chorale melodies, as well as many folksongs, were historically sung in unison. A number of twentieth-century melodies have also been conceived to be sung in unison. In the LBW these unison settings have often been provided with accompaniments in a keyboard, rather than four-part choral, idiom. Frequently, although not always, these settings have been printed with the unison melody above and the accompaniment below.

Some organists have the gift and the background to improvise different harmonizations for a given tune. Most, however, will need to depend on other sources. In some cases, these "other sources" are right in the LBW. For example, three different harmonizations are available for the tune "Lobt Gott, ihr Christen"—at LBW 47, 300, and 351. Using the hymn tune index which begins on page 945 of the LBW, one can easily determine whether a tune appears more than once in the LBW, and if so, note whether the settings are different. Other hymnals, including the two immediate predecessors to the LBW—the *Service Book and Hymnal*, 1958, and *The Lutheran Hymnal*, 1941—can also be a good source of different settings. (In some cases tune names have been changed. The various names by which tunes have been known are given in the discussions of the hymns in this companion.) Alternate harmonizations of the Lutheran chorales can be found especially in the various chorale books such as the *Wurttembergisches Choralbuch* listed on page 929 of the LBW index, or the *Choralbuch zum evangelischen Kirchengesangbuch*, 1969, published by Bärenreiter. Also useful is the *Australian Lutheran Hymnbook*, 1978, available through Augsburg Publishing House.

When using settings from other collections it will be necessary to check the melody to see that it is identical with the LBW.

Various Ways of Singing

All hymns can be sung in unison, and many can also be sung in parts. One simple but effective way of achieving variety is having various stanzas sung by women or men alone, or by the left or right half of the congregation. Many of the hymns can also be sung in canon. The classic hymn of this type is the "Tallis Canon" (LBW 278), where the tenor part is written to begin the melody one measure after the soprano. A new tune, "Laurel," by Dale Wood (LBW 268), has followed suit, with the tenor melody beginning two beats after the soprano. Several other melodies can also be sung in canon, including "St. Columba" (LBW 456), "Noel Nouvelet" (LBW 148), and many of the early American tunes such as "Twenty-fourth" (LBW 122, 126), "Lord, revive us" (LBW 290), "Beach Spring" (LBW 423), "Holy Manna" (LBW 463), and others. "Ah, holy Jesus" (LBW 123), sung in canon with the second group beginning one measure after the first, creates a series of sharp dissonances especially appropriate for the second stanza. Where the canon is not included in the harmony as it is in LBW 268 and 278, the accompaniment will need to be adjusted if one is used.

Further variety can be achieved through alternation of the choir (singing in unison or in parts) with the congregation, or with the use of organ alone on a stanza or stanzas of a hymn while the congregation reads the text. This *alternatum* practice has a long tradition in Christian worship and, as noted earlier, is especially appropriate for use with the Hymn of the Day. Several Bach harmonizations, which would be especially useful for choir stanzas, are readily available in the *Service Book and Hymnal*. Numerous hymntune-based organ and choir works, dating from the Reformation to the present, are available through the three major Lutheran publishers, as well as various other publishing houses.

xix

Descants and Free Organ Accompaniments

In some cases a descant can be created by raising one of the inner voices an octave. The tenor line of "All glory be to God on high" (LBW 166), for example, played an octave higher with a recorder while a soprano soloist sings a stanza, works very well. Some imagination and experimentation will bring out a good deal of descant material available in the LBW.

Numerous collections of descants and free organ accompaniments are also available from various publishers. Collections containing choir anthems based on hymn tunes can also be a good source of descants, as well as varied harmonizations. As with other settings, free accompaniments and descants should be appropriate to the text. Also, the congregation must be familiar enough with the tune that they can "hold their own" against whatever the organ, instruments, or choir might do.

SERVICE MUSIC BASED ON HYMN TUNES

The explosion of hymns and tunes which accompanied and followed the Lutheran Reformation touched off a parallel explosion of organ and choral works based on these hymn tunes, leaving for future generations a vast wealth of high-quality service music. The profound and beautiful chorale-based compositions of Johann Sebastian Bach (LBW 219) remain unexcelled. Among the numerous other composers of works based on early Lutheran hymn tunes are such as Dietrich Buxtehude (1637–1707), Johann Pachelbel (1653–1706), Michael Praetorius (1571–1621), Samuel Scheidt (1587–1654), Jan Petersoohn Sweelinck (1562–1621), George Philipp Telemann (1681–1767), and Johann Gottfried Walther (1684–1748). A source of great rejoicing, especially among church musicians, is the fact that many of the classical Lutheran hymns are once more available to all Lutherans in North America,[6] and the works based on them can again become an integral part of the service. Early Lutheran hymns and tunes new to those who used the *Service Book and Hymnal* are:

    215 O Lord, we praise you
    297 Salvation unto us has come
    299 Dear Christians, one and all, rejoice
    308 God the Father, be our stay
    317 To God the Holy Spirit let us pray
    335 May God bestow on us his grace
    350 Even as we live each day
    395 I trust, O Christ, in you alone
    519 My soul, now praise your maker!

[6] The shift from German to English in North American Lutheran worship, which began around 1800, occurred at a time of liturgical decline and before the existence of the many fine English translations prepared during the nineteenth century, with a resulting loss of much of our Lutheran hymnological heritage (see pp. 93ff). While the situation had improved with later hymnals, the LBW contains by far the best representation of early Lutheran hymnody to date for a large segment of Lutheranism. The Lutheran Church—Missouri Synod, having its roots in later German immigrations, retained many of these hymns, which congregations have loved and sung with great enthusiasm.

Additional tunes from early Reformation collections include the settings for:

  28   Savior of the nations, come
  48   All praise to you, eternal Lord
  85   When Christ's appearing was made known
       and 512   Oh, blest the house
 105   A lamb goes uncomplaining forth
 141   The day of resurrection!
 273   O Christ, you are the light and day
 284   Creator Spirit, heavenly dove
       and 473   Come, Holy Ghost, our souls inspire
 349   I leave, as you have promised, Lord

The tune, "Vater unser" (LBW 442) is now associated with a paraphrase of the Lord's Prayer, as it was originally. The *Liedmesse* or chorale service, represented in the *Service Book and Hymnal* by the Gloria in excelsis ("All glory be to God on high") and the Agnus Dei ("O Lamb of God most holy"), is completed in the LBW with the addition of the Kyrie (LBW 168), the Creed (LBW 374), and the Sanctus (LBW 528).

Among the "second generation" Reformation hymns and tunes are "Who trusts in God, a strong abode" (LBW 450) and "From God can nothing move me" (LBW 468), and the setting for "O Trinity, O blessed Light" (LBW 275).

Two early Lutheran hymns and tunes not included in either *The Lutheran Hymnal,* 1941, or the *Service Book and Hymnal* are "To Jordan came the Christ, our Lord" (LBW 79) and "The only Son from heaven" (LBW 86).

Written or adapted by Martin Luther and his contemporaries, the vigorous hymns of the Reformation formed the nucleus of European Lutheran hymnody. Many are decidedly useful in Lutheran worship still today, and continue to form the basis for twentieth-century compositions.

Compositions based on other types of hymn tunes are also abundant—plainsong (especially by composers from France, Italy, and Spain), Psalm tunes, and English and American hymn tunes. Along with the renewed interest in the early American folk melodies has come a surge of compositions based on these tunes. Brand-new compositions are based on the tunes newly-written for the LBW.

There is, clearly, an abundance of hymntune-based service music available. For choirs this can provide hymn stanzas to be sung in alternation with the congregation, Psalm settings, and offertories, as well as anthems. Hymntune-based organ works can serve as introductions and organ stanzas of congregational hymns, and works based on the hymns used in a service can also be used as preludes, music at the offering, and postludes, serving to highlight these hymns. Other organ works based on appropriate hymns can also be meaningful.

As with the selection of congregational hymns, the careful selection of hymn-based organ and choral works to tie in with the Scriptures of the day can help point up these lections. The list of hymn selections (p. 577) can be helpful in choosing service music as well as congregational hymns. For organists, especially, a listing—by tune name rather than by title[7]—of organ works contained in one's library can be very useful.

[7]Listing by tune name allows one to relate many organ settings to more than one hymn. "Wie schön leuchtet," for example, is the tune used for five hymns in the LBW—Nos. 43, 73, 76, 138, and 459.

Of great assistance in relating organ works—especially those of European composers—to LBW tunes of European origins is the fact that the tune name given is that of the first line of the hymn with which it was originally associated. The tune associated with "Glory be to God the Father!" (LBW 167), for example, had been called "St. Nicholas" in English-language hymnals. It has now been returned to "Herr, ich habe misgehandelt," under which title German organ settings of the tune would most likely appear.

"O come, let us sing unto the Lord!"

—Psalm 95:1a

INFORMATION CONTAINED IN THE
LBW HYMN SECTION

A good bit of information on the hymns can be found in the LBW itself. The sources of the words and music are listed below the hymn on the left-hand side. The tune name and meter are given at the right. (Meter indicates the number of syllables per line of verse, and a metrical index begins on p. 949 of the LBW.) The following abbreviations are used in the LBW:

adapt.	adapted
alt.	altered
attr.	attributed to
b.	born
c.	*circa* or about
©	copyright[1]
cent.	century
composite	a combined translation from the works of various authors
d.	died
hymnal version *hymnal translation*	prepared for the LBW
para.	paraphrased by
st.	stanza
tr.	translated by

---

[1]Questions regarding copyright can be answered by referring to the acknowledgments that begin on p. 922 of the LBW.

HISTORICAL ESSAYS

Greek and Latin Hymnody

M. Alfred Bichsel

Greek Hymns

The term *hymn* is derived from the Greek word *hymnos,* which in classical Greek from Homer on meant a song of praise in honor of the gods, of heroes and conquerors. In the Scriptures, however, it is used to define a song of praise in honor of God.

But as we look at certain passages in the New Testament, more specifically in the Pauline epistles, we find the word used with two other terms as well. The first of these is the term *psalmos.* In his letter to the Ephesians (5:19) St. Paul writes:

λαλοῦντες ἑαυτοῖς ψαλμοῖς καὶ ὕμνοις καὶ ᾠδαῖς πνευματικαῖς, ᾄδοντες καὶ ψάλλοντες τῇ καρδίᾳ ὑμῶν τῷ κυρίῳ . . .

(Addressing one another in psalms and hymns and spiritual songs, singing and making melody to the Lord with all your heart . . .)

In this passage we see the word *psalmos* which was already used by the translators of the Septuagint for the Hebrew Book of Psalms (the *Sefer tehilim*). In classical Greek the word *psalmos* meant "a pulling and twanging musical strings with the fingers" and later, a song sung to the accompaniment of a stringed instrument. No doubt this was found by the translators to be the most satisfactory Greek equivalent because of the instrumental implications of the superscriptions to many of the Psalms. There is a similar passage in Paul's letter to the Colossians (3:16).

This brings us to a consideration of the other term used by St. Paul: the ᾠδὴ πνευματική, the "spiritual song" as most English translations have it, although *Good News for Modern Man* uses "sacred song." The Greek word ᾠδή means a song, a lay, a strain, an ode, the last of which is the English derivative. In the plural it means lyric poetry.

While these terms might be considered synonymous, there must be some distinction, be it ever so slight, for it is not likely that so sharp a mind as Paul's would be likely to admonish his fellow Christians that they should teach one another with songs, and songs, and spiritual songs, or hymns, and hymns, and so on.

To this writer the term ode or song is generic. The fact that Paul feels the need to add the adjective πνευματική (spiritual) seems to corroborate this view. It was not an ordinary or secular, pagan, heathen song that they were to use, but a spiritual one, that is, one that had Christian orientation.

The other two terms, *hymnos* and *psalmos* then, are specific, the latter taking the characteristics of the Old Testament Psalms if not the Psalms themselves. It is to be remembered that Jewish Christians were accustomed to using the *sefer tehilim* in the synagogue and Gentile converts had the Psalter available from the Septuagint which had been translated during the reign of Ptolemy III (247–222 B.C.) Besides the Psalms themselves, there were the Old Testament Canticles or songs as, for example, the song of Moses (Exodus 15:1–18), the song of Deborah and Barak (Judges 5), and the Song of Hannah (1 Samuel 2:1–10), to name but a few. In addition there are the New Testament Canticles such as the

3

Magnificat (Luke 1:46–55), the *Benedictus* (Luke 1:68–79), and the *Nunc Dimittis* (Luke 2:29–32), which bear close poetic resemblance to the Psalms.

Hymnologists are agreed that these New Testament Canticles were inspired by older poems, for example, the *Magnificat* by the Song of Hannah, and the *Benedictus* by the language used by the Old Testament prophets and by the eighteen benedictions used in the Temple Service. In his article on "Hymnology" in the *New Catholic Encyclopedia* (New York, 1967), the noted hymnologist, Joseph Szöverffy, indicates that "with few exceptions, early Christian hymns were not written down but were very often the product of sudden inspiration. They probably resembled Hebrew Psalms and Canticles, using parallelism in structure, long enumerations of the attributes of the Deity, etc."

Many hymnological scholars also believe that there are to be found fragments of primitive hymns throughout the New Testament. This certainly harmonizes with Szöverffy's assertion regarding momentary and sudden inspiration and an attempt to recapture the thought later. Most of these fragments seem to be found in the Pauline epistles and one might conclude that he was quoting from them as he was writing to the various congregations he had founded, and he might even have heard them there originally.

In general these fragments fall into two categories. The first category includes those that are doctrinal or didactic or liturgical in scope. Many of the early teachings of the Christian church seem to be found in some of these hymn fragments. It needs to be remembered that outside the Old Testament Scriptures there were no written documents in the church of the Apostolic Age except those that appeared and were circulated either as general epistles such as those of John, James, and Peter, or the specific letters of Paul. The Gospels began to appear later. It must also be born in mind that many other documents were circulated and that controversy and conflict already appear at this early time as a result of conflicting views being circulated by those who opposed the Apostles. Paul, the great Jewish convert, zealous missionary, and champion of orthodoxy, seems to have an abundance of these primitive hymn fragments. Some examples of this first category can be found in Ephesians 5:14; 1 Timothy 3:16 and 6:15–16; 2 Timothy 2:11–13; Titus 3:4–7; Philippians 2:6–11; and Revelation 22:17.

In the second category are those that are doxological in content. These are all from the book of Revelation: 1:4–8; 4:8; 4:11; 5:9–10; 5:12; 11:15; 11:17–18; and 15:3–4.

While these passages are not strophic as are later Greek and Latin hymns, they are nevertheless in metrical prose as is the *Te Deum* (LBW 3) of a later date, and they certainly meet the standards of good poetry; there is music in their very sound.

We also gain information, though very little, from a pagan document written shortly after the close of the Apostolic Era. This is the famous letter of Pliny the Younger to the Emperor Trajan. At that time the former was governor of Bithynia and Pontus. In asking the emperor how he should deal with the Christians, he makes brief mention of their assembly. This he had been able to find out from those questioned. Here is the pertinent portion of that letter: ". . . quod essent soliti stato die ante lucem convenire carmenque Christo quasi deo dicere secum invicem . . ." ("that they were accustomed to come together on a regular day [probably Sunday] before dawn and to sing a song alternately to Christ as to a god").

4

The Apostolic Constitutions which were completed before the end of the fourth century mention a number of primitive Greek hymns which may very well have been the "carmen Christo"—the hymn to Christ to which Pliny makes reference in his letter, which was written some time between 107 and 115 A.D.

One of these hymns is the *hymnos eothinos* or morning hymn. The hymn is found in a number of ancient sources besides the Apostolic Constitutions. It is also found at the end of the Codex Alexandrinus (fifth century). These anonymous hymns (*hymni adespoti*) had considerable influence in shaping the liturgy of the early church. The morning hymn is an expansion of the greater doxology, *Doxa en ypsistis theo* (Glory to God in the highest). Closer examination reveals that one verse is later found toward the end of the *Te Deum*.

Another hymn mentioned in the Apostolic Constitutions is an evening hymn (*Hymnos esperinos*). There are three noteworthy sections to this hymn: 1) The beginning seems to be taken from the opening of Psalm 113: "Praise the Lord! Praise, O servants of the LORD, praise the name of the LORD!" 2) The next portion paraphrases the *Gloria in Excelsis* section of the Morning Hymn. 3) The last portion consists of the Canticle of Simeon, the *Nunc Dimittis*.

Numerous other hymns are to be found in these documents, but we shall restrict our discussion to those which have been retained in present-day liturgies. One of these is the *Tersanctus* or Thrice Holy taken from the opening verses of Isaiah 6. This is the *Kadosh* of the Hebrew liturgy. In the Clementine liturgy it appears in this form: "Holy, holy, holy Lord of Sabaoth. Heaven and earth are full of your glory. Praise to all ages. Amen." The liturgy of St. Mark, St. James, and St. John Chrysostom have slight alterations to this basic text, the latter two including the "hosanna" section: "Hosanna in the highest. Blessed is He that cometh in the Name of the Lord. Hosanna in the highest."

In passing, we should also make mention of another Trinitarian hymn which is so important to the Eastern churches. This is the *Trisagion*, which should not be confused with the *Tersanctus*. In the Eastern liturgies it is a short hymn verse sung after the Little Entrance. The text is as follows: *Agios o Theos, Agios ischyros, agios athanatos, eleison imas* (Holy God, Holy Mighty, Holy Immortal, have mercy on us). It is also found in the old Roman Good Friday liturgy both in Latin and Greek, sung antiphonally by the choirs. In the latter language it seems to be a vestigial remain from the days when the liturgy was still done in Greek.

A final early hymn is the lesser doxology, *Doxa Patri,* which is identical with the Latin *Gloria Patri.*† It was already in use at the time of Basil (*c.* fourth century). In Rome it was already in use at the time of Clement (*c.* 91). In the East it is used after each so-called *stasis,* that is, a subdivision consisting of two or more Psalms. In the Western Usage of St. Benedict (480) it was to be used after each Psalm, a practice which has persisted to the present day. The purpose of the lesser doxology was to give a Christian Trinitarian orientation to the Hebrew Psalter and Canticles. The same applies to the three Lukan Canticles of the New Testament which do not actually contain such an orientation.

The use of hymns varied in certain localities especially in the East. A certain reserve with regard to hymns not of Scriptural source in the liturgy persisted as late as the fourth and fifth centuries. This is note-

---

†Glory be to the Father, and to the Son, and to the Holy Ghost: as it was in the beginning, is now, and ever shall be, world without end. Amen.

worthy because of a similar attitude on the part of John Calvin many centuries later (see below, page 58). There is evidence that hymns were in use at Antioch in the middle of the third century (269). It was primarily because of the activity of certain heretics that hymns gradually found more favorable acceptance in order to combat heresy with truth.

Ancient Greek hymnody appears in two distinct and somewhat different categories and styles. First, there are those hymns written in the decaying classical meters frought with an ever increasing disregard for the classical rules of quantity. Second, the larger and more important body of hymns are those found in the Service Books of the Eastern Orthodox Church issuing from hymns of the Old and New Testament. These later developed into the highly elaborate canons of the ninth and tenth centuries.

Some of the authors of the first epoch were: Clement of Alexandria (170–220), whose hymn, "Shepherd of tender youth," was included in the *Service Book and Hymnal,* 1958, No. 179; Methodius (d. 313); Gregory of Naziensis (323–389); Synesius of Cyrene (LBW 309); and Sophronius of Jerusalem (629).

The most important, most brilliant, and most prolific period of Greek or Byzantine hymnody is the period of the odes and canons. It was a period in which monasticism flourished. The Holy Land was in the hands of the Mohammedans since Jerusalem had been captured in 636. It was during this period that the Eastern Church was rocked by the Iconoclastic Controversy. This unfortunate and, at times, most bloody and scandalous state of affairs lasted over a century, *c.* 726–842. The chief defenders of the orthodox faith were the monks. Through their daily hours of prayer and through their devotion to their icons, there blossomed the greatest period of Byzantine hymnody.

Most of the Greek hymns that have come down to us in translation come from some of these canons. Probably the most prolific translator was John Mason Neale (LBW 34). A canon consists of nine (eight) odes, each of which contains any number of stanzas or strophes from three to twenty or more. The canons are modeled after the Scriptural canticles which were sung at the daily office called the *orthros* (comparable to Lauds of the Western Church). Since there were nine of these canticles, the number of odes should comply. The canticles were:

1. The Song of Moses in Exodus 15:1–18.
2. The Song of Moses in Deuteronomy 32.
3. The Song of Hannah in 1 Samuel 2:1–10.
4. The Song of Habakkuk in Habakkuk 3:1–19.
5. The Song of Isaiah in Isaiah 26:9–20.
6. The Song of Jonah in Jonah 2:2–9.
7. The Song of the Three Children in Apocryphal Daniel 3:27–33.
8. The Benedicite in Apoc. Daniel 3:34–67.
9. The Magnificat and Benedictus in Luke 1:46–55; 68–79.

Since the second canticle of the *orthros* is used only in Lent, no odes were composed for it. Hence there are actually only eight odes in number, but typical Greek logic insists on numbering them in such a way that nine result: 1, 3, 4, 5, 6, 7, 8, 9, (a' γ' δ' ϵ' ς' ζ' η' θ').

Opposite page: Original Greek version of "The day of resurrection!" (LBW 141) showing the eight odes.

ᾠδὴ αʹ.

Ἀναστάσεως ἡμέρα, | λαμπρυνθῶμεν λαοί·
  πάσχα κυρίου, πάσχα·
ἐκ γὰρ θανάτου πρὸς ζωὴν | καὶ ἐκ τῆς πρὸς οὐρανὸν
  Χριστὸς ὁ θεὸς
ἡμᾶς διεβίβασεν, | ἐπινίκιον ᾄδοντας.

Καθαρθῶμεν τὰς αἰσθήσεις | καὶ ὀψόμεθα
  τῷ ἀπροσίτῳ φωτὶ
τῆς ἀναστάσεως Χριστὸν | ἐξαστράπτοντα, καὶ
  «χαίρετε» φάσκοντος
τρανῶς ἀκουσόμεθα, | ἐπινίκιον ᾄδοντες.

Οὐρανοὶ μὲν ἐπαξίως | εὐφραινέσθωσαν,
  γῆ δὲ ἀγαλλιάσθω·
ἑορταζέτω δὲ κόσμος | ὁρατός τε ἅπας
  καὶ ἀόρατος·
Χριστὸς γὰρ ἐγήγερται, | εὐφροσύνη αἰώνιος.

ᾠδὴ γʹ.

Δεῦτε πόμα πίωμεν καινὸν
  οὐκ ἐκ πέτρας ἀγόνου τερατουργούμενον,
ἀλλ' ἀφθαρσίας πηγὴν | ἐκ τάφου ὀμβρήσαντος Χριστοῦ,
  ἐν ᾧ στερεούμεθα.

Νῦν πάντα πεπλήρωται φωτός,
  οὐρανός τε καὶ γῆ καὶ τὰ καταχθόνια·
ἑορταζέτω δὲ πᾶσα κτίσις | τὴν ἔγερσιν Χριστοῦ,
  ἐν ᾧ στερεούμεθα.

Χθὲς συνεθαπτόμην σοι, Χριστέ,
  συνεγείρομαι σήμερον ἀναστάντι σοι·
συνεσταυρούμην σοι χθές· | αὐτός με συνδόξασον, σωτὴρ,
  ἐν τῇ βασιλείᾳ σου.

ᾠδὴ δʹ.

Ἐπὶ τῆς θείας φυλακῆς | ὁ θεηγόρος Ἀββακοὺμ
  στήτω μεθ' ἡμῶν καὶ δεικνύτω
φαεσφόρον ἄγγελον | διαπρυσίως λέγοντα·
σήμερον σωτηρία τῷ κόσμῳ,
  ὅτι ἀνέστη Χριστὸς ὡς παντοδύναμος.

Ἄρσην μὲν ὡς διανοίξας | τὴν παρθενεύουσαν νηδὺν
  πέφηνε Χριστός· ὡς βροτὸς δὲ
ἀμνὸς προσηγόρευται· ἄμωμος δὲ ὡς ἄγευστος
κηλῖδος τὸ ἡμέτερον πάσχα,
  καὶ ὡς θεὸς ἀληθὴς τέλειος λέλεκται.

Ὡς ἐνιαύσιος ἀμνὸς | ὁ εὐλογούμενος ἡμῖν
  στέφανος Χριστὸς ἑκουσίως
ὑπὲρ πάντων τέθυται | πάσχα τὸ καθαρτήριον,
καὶ αὖθις ἐκ τοῦ τάφου ὡραῖος
  δικαιοσύνης ἡμῖν ἔλαμψεν ἥλιος.

Ὁ θεοπάτωρ μὲν Δαυῒδ | πρὸ τῆς σκιώδους κιβωτοῦ
  ἥλατο σκιρτῶν· ὁ λαὸς δὲ
τοῦ θεοῦ ὁ ἅγιος, | τὴν τῶν συμβόλων ἔκβασιν
ὁρῶντες, εὐφρανθῶμεν ἐνθέως,
  ὅτι ἀνέστη Χριστὸς ὡς παντοδύναμος.

ᾠδὴ εʹ.

Ὀρθρίσωμεν ὄρθρου βαθέος
  καὶ ἀντὶ μύρου τὸν ὕμνον | προσοίσομεν τῷ δεσπότῃ,
καὶ Χριστὸν ὀψόμεθα | δικαιοσύνης ἥλιον,
  πᾶσι ζωὴν ἀνατέλλοντα.

Τὴν ἄμετρόν σου εὐσπλαγχνίαν
  οἱ ταῖς τοῦ ᾅδου σειραῖς | συνεχόμενοι δεδορκότες
πρὸς τὸ φῶς ἠπείγοντο, | Χριστέ, ἀγαλλομένῳ ποδὶ,
  πάσχα κροτοῦντες αἰώνιον.

Προσέλθωμεν λαμπαδηφόροι
  τῷ προϊόντι Χριστῷ | ἐκ τοῦ μνήματος ὡς νυμφίῳ,
καὶ συνεορτάσωμεν | ταῖς φιλεόρτοις τάξεσι
  πάσχα θεοῦ τὸ σωτήριον.

ᾠδὴ ϛʹ.

Κατῆλθες ἐν τοῖς κατωτάτοις τῆς γῆς
  καὶ συνέτριψας μοχλοὺς | αἰωνίους κατόχους
πεπεδημένων, Χριστέ, | καὶ τριήμερος
  ὡς ἐκ κήτους Ἰωνᾶς | ἐξανέστης τοῦ τάφου.

Φυλάξας τὰ σήμαντρα σῶα, Χριστέ,
  ἐξηγέρθης τοῦ τάφου, | ὁ τὰς κλεῖς τῆς παρθένου
μὴ λυμηνάμενος | ἐν τῷ τόκῳ σου,
  καὶ ἀνέῳξας ἡμῖν | παραδείσου τὰς πύλας.

Σωτήρ μου τὸ ζῶν τε καὶ ἄθυτον
  ἱερεῖον ὡς θεὸς | σεαυτὸν ἑκουσίως
προσαγαγὼν τῷ πατρὶ | συνανέστησας
  παγγενῆ τὸν Ἀδάμ, | ἀναστὰς ἐκ τοῦ τάφου.

ᾠδὴ ζʹ.

Ὁ παῖδας ἐκ καμίνου ῥυσάμενος
  γενόμενος ἄνθρωπος
πάσχει ὡς θνητὸς | καὶ διὰ πάθους τὸ θνητὸν
ἀφθαρσίας ἐνδύει εὐπρέπειαν,
ὁ μόνος εὐλογητὸς τῶν πατέρων
  θεὸς καὶ ὑπερένδοξος.

Γυναῖκες μετὰ μύρων θεόφρονες
  ὀπίσω σου ἔδραμον·
ὃν δὲ ὡς θνητὸν | μετὰ δακρύων ἐζήτουν,
προσεκύνησαν χαίρουσαι ζῶντα θεόν,
καὶ πάσχα τὸ μυστικὸν σοῖς, Χριστέ,
  μαθηταῖς εὐηγγελίσαντο.

Θανάτου ἑορτάζομεν νέκρωσιν,
  ᾅδου τὴν καθαίρεσιν,
ἄλλης βιοτῆς | τῆς αἰωνίου ἀπαρχήν,
καὶ σκιρτῶντες ὑμνοῦμεν τὸν αἴτιον,
τὸν μόνον εὐλογητὸν τῶν πατέρων
  θεὸν καὶ ὑπερένδοξον.

Ὡς ὄντως ἱερὰ καὶ πανέορτος
  αὕτη ἡ σωτήριος
νὺξ καὶ φωταυγής, | τῆς λαμπροφόρου ἡμέρας
τῆς ἐγέρσεως οὖσα προάγγελος,
ἐν ᾗ τὸ ἄχρονον φῶς ἐκ τάφου
  σωματικῶς πᾶσιν ἐπέλαμψεν.

ᾠδὴ ηʹ.

Αὕτη ἡ κλητὴ καὶ ἁγία ἡμέρα,
  ἡ μία τῶν σαββάτων, | ἡ βασιλὶς καὶ κυρία,
ἑορτῶν ἑορτὴ | καὶ πανήγυρίς ἐστι πανηγύρεων,
  ἐν ᾗ εὐλογοῦμεν | Χριστὸν εἰς τοὺς αἰῶνας.

Δεῦτε τοῦ καινοῦ τῆς ἀμπέλου γεννήματος,
  τῆς θείας εὐφροσύνης, | ἐν τῇ εὐσήμῳ ἡμέρᾳ
τῆς ἐγέρσεως | βασιλείας τε Χριστοῦ κοινωνήσωμεν,
  ὑμνοῦντες αὐτὸν | ὡς θεὸν εἰς τοὺς αἰῶνας.

Ἆρον κύκλῳ τοὺς ὀφθαλμούς σου, Σιών, καὶ ἴδε·
  ἰδοὺ γὰρ ἥκασί σοι | θεοφεγγεῖς ὡς φωστῆρες
ἐκ δυσμῶν καὶ βορρᾶ | καὶ θαλάσσης καὶ ἕῳα τὰ τέκνα σου,
  ἐν σοὶ εὐλογοῦντα | Χριστὸν εἰς τοὺς αἰῶνας.

Πάτερ παντοκράτορ καὶ λόγε καὶ πνεῦμα,
  τρισὶν ἑνιζομένη | ἐν ὑποστάσει φύσις,
ὑπερούσιε | καὶ ὑπέρθεε, εἰς σὲ βεβαπτίσμεθα
  καὶ σὲ εὐλογοῦμεν | εἰς πάντας τοὺς αἰῶνας.

ᾠδὴ θʹ.

Φωτίζου, φωτίζου ἡ νέα Ἱερουσαλήμ·
  ἡ γὰρ δόξα κυρίου | ἐπὶ σὲ ἀνέτειλε·
χόρευε νῦν καὶ ἀγάλλου, Σιών·
  σὺ δέ, ἁγνή, | τέρπου, θεοτόκε,
ἐν τῇ ἐγέρσει τοῦ τόκου σου.

Ὦ θείας! ὦ φίλης! ὦ γλυκυτάτης σου φωνῆς!
  μεθ' ἡμῶν ἀψευδῶς γὰρ | ἐπηγγείλω ἔσεσθαι
μέχρι τερμάτων αἰῶνος, Χριστέ·
  ἣν οἱ πιστοὶ | ἄγκυραν ἐλπίδος
κατέχοντες ἀγαλλόμεθα.

Ὦ πάσχα τὸ μέγα | καὶ ἱερώτατον, Χριστέ·
  ὦ σοφία καὶ λόγε | τοῦ θεοῦ καὶ δύναμις,
δίδου ἡμῖν ἐκτυπώτερον
  σοῦ μετασχεῖν | ἐν τῇ ἀνεσπέρῳ
ἡμέρᾳ τῆς βασιλείας σου.

The ode itself consists of two integral parts:

1. The *Hirmos* is the stanza which is the model after which all the succeeding strophes are patterned.
2. The *Troparia* (singular *troparion*) are the stanzas that are modeled after the *hirmos*.

Invariably the canons are acrostic in structure. At times the acrostic is alphabetical, at others it spells out a verse of poetry or a quotation of some sort, and at other times it reveals the name of the author.

Among the authors of canons which have come down to us in translation are the following: John of Damascus (d. *c.* 780), Andrew of Crete (660–732), Cosmos of Jerusalem surnamed the Melodist (d. *c.* 760), Theophanes (759–818), Methodius (d. 846), Joseph the Hymnographer (*c.* 810–883), and Theodore (759–826). The last three were all connected with the Studium Monastery in Constantinople. Of these, only John of Damascus is represented in the LBW: "Come, You Faithful, Raise the Strain" (LBW 132) and "The Day of Resurrection!" (LBW 141).

Since these translations were made during the nineteenth century and cast into the poetic concepts of that time, it was only natural that hymn tunes of that era were either created for them or others were used that were metrically suitable. None of the original Byzantine melodies have been used in either English or American hymnals.

Yet since there is some connection between the modal system of Gregorian Chant and the *echoi* of Byzantine Chant, we must devote some time to its discussion. In addition, there are a number of Greek-American musicians who are attempting to use the Byzantine melodies with new English translations. Among these is Anna Gallos, a graduate of the Eastman School of Music.

Byzantine Chant, the official music of the Eastern Greek Orthodox Church, mirrors the evolution of its dogmatic ideas and doctrines from the early days of the Eastern Empire to the full splendor of the service at the height of its development. When we hear Byzantine Chant, we realize that we are listening to tonal, poetic, and lingual combinations which reflect the character of Byzantine civilization, for the poetic forms were Syrian and Palestinian in their origin, while the melodies or tonal elements were based on the chant heard in the Jewish synagogue. The language used, however, to express this unique form of vocal art was and still is Greek.

The chant derives its name from the Byzantine Empire, the capital of which was Constantinople, now Istanbul. When Constantine rebuilt it in 330, he referred to it as New Rome, the capital of his reunited Roman Empire. After the permanent division in 395, it remained the capital of the Eastern Empire for over a thousand years until its capture by the Turks in 1453. During much of this time, Byzantium was the seat of a flourishing culture which blended Hellenistic and Oriental elements.

Byzantine hymn melodies are made up of melodic formulae which are linked together by short transitional passages. The construction of the melody of a hymn was based on the combination and linking together of a certain number of melodic formulae characteristic of the mode in which the hymn was composed. The mode, known in Greek as *echos*, is not a scale in the Western sense, but the sum of all of those themes or formulae which constitute the quality of the *echos*; or, as Archbishop Chrysanthos has expressed it: "*Echos* is the scheme or idea of the melody arranged according to the practice of the expert musician, who knows which tones should be omitted, which chosen, on which tone one should begin, and on which tone one should end." (*Great Music Theory,* 1815)

In *A History of Byzantine Music and Hymnography* (Oxford, 1949) Egon Wellesz, a noted authority on Byzantine music and hymnography, sums it up in this manner: "It is obvious that the oldest versions of both Byzantine and Gregorian melodies go back to a common source, the music of the Churches of Antioch and Jerusalem which, in turn, were derived from the Jews. On the pattern of these melodies both Eastern and Western Churches developed their own ecclesiastical music, adding and transforming the originals as the necessities of their different rites demanded."

While the function of the modes between the two systems differs, the structure of the Byzantine *echoi* is similar to the Gregorian modes. There is even some relationship in the nomenclature. Some textbooks on Gregorian Chant even indicate that the Byzantine nomenclature is the parent of the Gregorian. The best way to examine them is by a comparative table:

Byzantine			Gregorian
ἦχος α′	echos protos	1	Dorian
ἦχος πλ. α′	echos plagios protos	2	Hypodorian
ἦχος β′	echos deuteros	3	Phrygian
ἦχος πλ. β′	echos plagios deuteros	4	Hypophrygian
ἦχος γ′	echos tritos	5	Lydian
ἦχος βαρύς	echos barys	6	Hypolydian
ἦχος δ′	echos tetrardos	7	Mixolydian
ἦχος πλ. δ′	echos plagios tetrardos	8	Hypomixolydian

In the enumeration of the Gregorian column, it must be remembered that musical scholars prefer the numerical designation which reflects the Byzantine division rather than the pseudo-Greek names which are used primarily in Germany, England, and the United States.

The music of the Eastern Church was transmitted to posterity by two systems of notation: 1) Ecphonetic and 2) Neumatic. Both types are derived from the three basic prosodic accents of the Greek language: the acute ′, the grave ‵, and the circumflex ^. It is generally believed that these marks were invented by the grammarian Aristophanes of Byzantium (*c.* 180 B.C.) and were used as a guide for declamation when Greek became the predominant language in the East.

The ecphonetic signs were used for the cantillation of the pericopes of the time: the *Prophetologion,* the *Apostoleos,* and the *Evangelarion.* The signs are found in the official lectionaries and are placed above and below the text in order to indicate the proper inflection of the voice in declaiming the lection.

Unlike ecphonetic notation, neumatic notation clearly indicates pitches and intervals. Numerous symbols are given to indicate the starting note, a repeated note, and various intervals (ascending or descending). An interesting symbol is the *ison* which also has simple harmonic connotations characteristic of Byzantine Chant. This consists of sustaining the mode center (or occasionally its dominant) by one voice while the other voices sing the hymn melody.

This monodic form of Byzantine Chant remained until the latter part

9

of the nineteenth and early twentieth century, when three and four part homophonic harmonizations for male voices appeared for the liturgy only.

Perhaps the great schism of 1054 in which the Eastern and Western church separated, anathematized and excommunicated each other, had an effect on the normal development of ecclesiastical music. There are some who feel that the Byzantine chant with its characteristic sustained *ison* could very well have been the early germ which started *organum,* the development of which took place in the West from the ninth to the thirteenth centuries. The schism between the Greek and Roman Church occurred just as *organum* began to develop. Perhaps it is a far-fetched but perfectly feasible theory to speculate that Byzantine Chant might have followed the trend of Roman liturgical music had not the schism occurred.

Latin Hymns

The hymns of the Western or Latin Church are very important, not only because of their own intrinsic worth, but also because in translation they furnish an important source of pre-Reformation as well as Reformation hymnody. The study may be divided into three periods: 1) the formative, from the fourth to the eighth centuries; 2) the period of florescence in the Middle Ages from the Carolingian period to the Reformation; and 3) the period of decline from the Reformation to the present.

As was the case with the Eastern Church, the music of the Western Church can trace its origin to the Jewish worship in the synagogue. Since Greek was the international and predominant language of the first three centuries of the Christian era, it was only natural that the hymns of the Eastern Church would have an important influence on those of the West, and that some of them would even find a place in the western rites.

It was noted earlier (p. 5) that one of the most ancient Greek hymns was the anonymous morning hymn found in numerous ancient sources. Examination revealed that the first part of this hymn is the source of the *Gloria in Excelsis,* and the second part that of the *Te Deum.* As it is well known, the Angelic Hymn, the *Gloria in Excelsis* later became one of the important hymns of the Mass (see LBW pages 58–59, 79–80, or 100–101 for a translation).

While Ambrose of Milan (LBW 28) is generally regarded as the father of Latin hymnody, there were a number of lesser precursors. One of these was Marius Victorinus (*c.* 360) who wrote three Trinitarian hymns of an apologetic nature that were strongly influenced by Scripture and the Psalms.

Damasus I, 36th Bishop of the Roman See in 366, found himself in the midst of the Arian controversy against which he wrote epigrams. In light of what was to follow during the days of Ambrose, some mention of this controversy should be made.

In about the year 318, Arius of Alexandria taught that Christ was the highest human being, the *Logos* through whom everything was created, but He was not true God; He was dissimilar in essence from the Father—"a god junior grade" as Martin Marty puts it in his *Short History of Christianity.* Arius was excommunicated by the Council of Alexandria, but he kept propagating his views in sermons, poems, and folklike hymns. As the heresy grew and spread, it was necessary to achieve some agreement or semblance thereof before the church would be split. Thus the Emperor Constantine had the Council of Nicaea summoned which in 325 condemned the rank Arian heresy of dissimilar natures as well as the semi-Arian view of similar nature, and accepted the view that Christ was of the same substance with the Father. (Out of this council came the Nicene Creed.)

The first Latin hymnwriter in the traditional sense was St. Hilary, Bishop of Poitiers (c. 310–366), who brought his inspiration to the West from his eastern exile. Except for three hymn fragments that were discovered in 1844 by G. F. Gamurrini, his *Liber Hymnorum* is entirely lost. Two of these acrostic hymn fragments contain mostly didactic material against the Arians. He did so much polemic writing and preaching against the Arians that he earned for himself the title of *Malleus Arianorum* (Hammer of the Arians).

The strophic Latin hymn as it is known today came into being in the fourth century. From a textual point of view, the impetus occasioning this hymnody came as a result of the Arian heresy, the proponents of which used popular songs to promulgate their false teaching. Responding in kind, Ambrose (340–397) and his followers wrote and used hymns to stir up and inspire the faithful to withstand the church's enemies. In view of this heresy, it is understandable that the tradition of closing each hymn with a doxology to the Holy Trinity was already established in these earliest Latin hymns. For example, the last stanza of Ambrose's "Splendor Paternae Gloriae" (LBW 271) reads:

> Deo Patri sit gloria,
> Ejusque soli Filio,
> Cum Spiritu Paraclito,
> Nunc et per omne saeculum.

> All Laud to God the Father be;
> All praise, eternal Son, to thee;
> All glory, as is ever meet,
> To God the Holy Paraclete.

> (tr. Robert Bridges)

It can be assumed that the texts and melodies of the Ambrosian hymns had immediate congregational appeal, for they were written with congregational participation in mind. In the first place, they were written in simple Latin, the *Lingua Vulgata,* which would have been readily understood by the common people, not in Greek, the language of the learned. Secondly, the hymns drew liberally from Scriptural sources and stressed orthodox faith and pious living. Finally, the simple meter used (iambic dimeter) could be rendered easily by a congregation and must have added to the hymns' effectiveness.

The number of authentic Ambrosian hymns is still greatly a matter of conjecture. Samuel W. Duffield lists only four which are of undoubted authorship. These are: "Deus, Creator Omnium"; "Aeterne rerum conditor"; "Jam surgit hora tertia, Qua"; "Veni, Redemptor Gentium." The authenticity of the first three have been attested by St. Augustine (LBW 146), and the last by St. Celestine (c. 340). Undoubtedly Ambrose wrote many more, and Duffield has attempted to place them into a number of categories which would attempt to indicate their decreasing order of authenticity. Without laboring the point, let us merely indicate that there were many imitators who wrote in the same style and are simply classed as "Ambrosiani."

Probably the best known of Ambrose's hymns because of Martin Luther's (LBW 48) translation ("Nun komm, der Heiden Heiland") is "Veni, Redemptor Gentium" (LBW 28):

11

Veni Redemptor Gentium,
Ostende partum virginis;
Miretur omne saeculum
Talis decet partus Deum.

Savior of the nations, come,
Virgin's Son, make here Thy home!
Marvel now, O heav'n and earth,
That the Lord chose such a birth.

(Tr. from German by William M. Reynolds)

The meter is the typical popular iambic dimeter, and the tune that Luther used is an adaptation of the tune found for the original Latin hymn in a twelfth-century source.

Aurelius Clemens Prudentius (LBW 42) has been called the First Christian Poet by some writers on hymnology. After a life of jurisprudence, he cultivated the art of literature and gave himself over especially to hymns in honor of God and the saints, and against paganism. Probably the most important of his hymn collections is the *Cathemerinon* (Book of Hours) since it is from this book that most of the hymns still in use are taken. The work contains hymns for dawn and morning; before and after meals; evening (lamp-lighting); before retiring; before and after fasts; burial of the dead; Christmas and Epiphany.

Well known to most Christians is the Christmas hymn "Of the Father's Love Begotten" ("Corde natus ex Parentis," LBW 42). Two other favorites were "Despair Not, O Heart," ("Jam moesta," included in the *Service Book and Hymnal,* 1958, #297) and "O Chief of Cities, Bethlehem" ("O sola magnarum urbium," LBW 81).

Another hymnwriter from this early period is Coelius Sedulius (LBW 64), best known to us through his acrostic hymn "A solis ortus cardine" which Luther translated as "Christum wir sollen loben schon." This hymn had formerly been attributed to Ambrose. All twenty-three of the letters of the alphabet figure in this hymn. (The Latin alphabet did not include J, U, and W.) Sedulius was also the author of a commentary on the four Gospels which he called *Carmen Paschale.* He wrote it as an epic in the style of Virgil.

Another hymnist from the Western Church represented in the LBW is Venantius Honorius Clementianus Fortunatus (LBW 118). (At times he added another to his four names—Theodosius.) Though a Roman, he became Bishop of Poitiers in 597. Scholars of his style feel that he represents the last expiring effort of the Latin Muse in Gaul, an effort to retain something of the "old classical culture amid the advancing tide of barbarism." That this is true can be seen from the fact that he did not write some of his hymns in the usual popular iambic dimeter. His best known hymn, "Pange, lingua, gloriosi," ("Sing my tongue the glorious battle") is in trochaic tetrameter:

Pange, lingua, gloriosi
Lauream certaminis,
Et super Crucis trophaeo
Dic triumphum nobilem:
Qualiter Redemptor orbis
Immolatus vicerit.

(see LBW 118 for translation)

Music historians have assumed that these hymns of Fortunatus give some idea of the style of Gallican chant; they are among the few remnants that survived the Carolingian attempts at its suppression.

Another of his hymns found in the LBW is "Vexilla regis prodeunt":

> Vexilla Regis prodeunt:
> Fulget Crucis mysterium
> Qua vita mortem pertulit,
> Et morte vitam protulit.
>
> (see LBW 124 for translation)

Although Rome was slow to adopt the hymn, it became the task of the monasteries to preserve and further develop the hymnody of the Latin church. The establishment of the canonical hours in the Benedictine Rule helped foster the use of hymns of the Ambrosian type along with the singing of the Psalter. Latin hymns gradually developed into cycles for the entire church year. They commemorated the great feasts of the year, as well as the feasts of the saints. The canonical office hours were as follows: Matins: midnight; Lauds: 3 A.M.; Prime: 6 A.M.; Terce: 9 A.M.; Sext: 12 noon; None: 3 P.M.; Vespers: 6 P.M.; Compline: 9 P.M. (In practice the times of these services varied with the seasons of the year. Matins was often held sometime after midnight, or just before daybreak, when it was followed by Lauds at sunrise. Vespers occurred at sunset, and Compline at nightfall or before retiring for the night.)

The Pope and Doctor of the Western church whose name was given to the music of that church should certainly not be overlooked, even though scholars disagree on the number of hymns that might be attributed to him. As Abbot of the Benedictine Monastery of St. Andrew which he founded in Rome, St. Gregory the Great (540–604) (LBW 101) certainly must have had more than a passing interest in the office hymn.

Born in Rome at about the time that St. Benedict had reformed monasticism by founding the order which bears his name, Gregory eventually became praetor of that city. He became interested in the famous Abbey of Monte Cassino and eventually withdrew from the world and secular life. He was a man of considerable wealth, and in 575 he endowed six new monasteries in Sicily and, in his own palatial residence in Rome, established a seventh dedicated to St. Andrew. He eventually became Abbot of this establishment and then succeeded to the papacy in 590.

The two Gregorian hymns in the *Service Book and Hymnal,* 1958, are also included in the LBW: "O Christ, Our King, Creator, Lord" (LBW 101) and "Father, We Praise You" (LBW 267).

Another important writer of this period was Rhabanus Maurus, to whom is attributed "Veni, Creator Spiritus" (LBW 472). Perhaps there is no Latin hymn that is so celebrated as this one. There are more than sixty English translations alone. While its strict liturgical use is that of the hymn at Vespers from Whitsunday until the following Friday, and at Terce till Saturday, both inclusive, it has also been used on many other solemn occasions in extra-liturgical functions. Luther translated it as "Komm, Gott Schöpfer" (LBW 284).

Purely for musical reasons we should not forget Paul the Deacon. One of his claims to fame is the fact that he was the biographer of Gregory the Great. He was a monk at the Abbey of Monte Cassino and he lived *c.* 730–799. He is known, however, only for the hymn which became famous because of its musical connotation. The title of this hymn is "Ut queant laxis" and it is a hymn dedicated to St. John the Baptist. It is this hymn which Guido of Arezzo (*c.* 995–1050) used to develop his solmization system based on the ascending steps of the scale

13

as part of his theoretical system of dividing the entire tonal system into its component seven hexachords. The pertinent stanza (with the solmization syllables italicized) follows:

> *Ut* queant laxis
> *re*sonare fibrix
> *Mi*ra gestorum
> *fa*muli tuorum,
> *Sol*ve polluti
> *la*bii reatum
> Sancte Ioannes.

We cannot speak of Latin hymnody without the mention of Theodulph of Orleans (760–821) (LBW 108). His hymn has become one that is beloved of all Christians: "Gloria, laus, et honor" ("All Glory, Laud, and Honor"). In Roman liturgical usage it was the Palm Sunday processional hymn. Its meter is elegiac.

> Gloria, laus, et honor tibi sit, Rex Christe Redemptor:
> Cui puerile decus prompsit Hosanna pium.

Up to this point the type of hymns that we have been discussing are the type that have been designated as monostrophic, that is, each strophe or stanza is sung to one or the same melody. The polystrophic hymns came into being about the eighth or ninth centuries. They were called sequences (a special type of trope†) and were developed from the florid *jubilus* of the final vowel of the *Alleluia*. Thus the original sequences had no text. The practice of adding a text seems to have originated in the Benedictine Abbey of Jumièges, and was brought to St. Gall by a monk who managed to flee from the monastery as it was being sacked by the Normans. It was Notker (Balbulus) of the Benedictine monastery of St. Gall who further developed the French method of textual addition in order to render the style syllabic. As the sequence developed as a form, new melodies were composed. The reason for calling it polystrophic is that groups of melodies were set to pairs of verses giving us a pattern somewhat like this: aa bb cc dd ee ff, etc. Sometimes groups were repeated giving us the pattern: aa bb cc dd ee ff, cc dd ee ff, gg hh, etc. Some also begin and end with unpaired verses and phrases: x, aa bb cc dd . . . . . y.

This form became very popular and spread throughout Europe. Probably the best known and most prolific writer of sequences was Adam of St. Victor (d. 1192). Luther anticipated the action later taken by the Council of Trent (1545–1563) by eliminating them from his *Formula Missae* (1523) with a couple of possible exceptions. Among other liturgical reforms, the Council banned the sequence with the exception of these four: "Victimae Paschali Laudes" by Wipo of Burgundy (*c.* 1000–50) (LBW 137), "Veni sancte spiritus" attributed to Innocent III (1164–1216), "Lauda Sion salvatorem" by St. Thomas Aquinas (*c.* 1261), "Dies irae" by Thomas of Celano (*c.* 1200). In 1727 the sequence "Stabat Mater" by Jacopone da Todi (*c.* 1306) was reinstated.

Probably the best known sequence is the "Victimae Paschali" from which the pre-Reformation vernacular hymn "Christ ist erstanden"

---

†The practice of "troping," that is, of making additions to the authorized text and/or music of the liturgy, developed during the Middle Ages. One example can be found at LBW 168. The use of tropes and sequences expanded greatly throughout Europe until the Council of Trent, when all tropes and all but the five sequences mentioned below were abolished.

(LBW 136) is derived as well as Luther's "Christ lag in Todesbanden" (LBW 134). Unrhymed, it begins and closes with an unpaired phrase. This certainly would make for its antiquity, and it would be well to see it in its entirety, together with an example of a monostrophic hymn by Gregory the Great, "Audi, benigne Conditor." (See pages 16 and 17.)

From the sixteenth century onward, Latin hymnody was on the decline. One reason advanced for this is the fact that Latin was no longer a "mother tongue" for the clergy, even among the religious orders. Another reason given is the fact that the Renaissance passion for classical purity overemphasized form to the detriment of thought and content. In his article on "Hymnology" in the *Catholic Encyclopedia* (New York, 1907-1922), Clemens Blume depicted the situation in these words: "The humanists abominated the rhythmical poetry of the Middle Ages from an exaggerated enthusiasm for ancient classical forms and meters. Hymnody then received its death blow as, on the revision of the Breviary under Urban VIII (1568-1644), the medieval rhythmical hymns were forced into more classical forms by means of so-called corrections." Hundreds of "corrections" were made by Urban and a commission of scholars appointed by him. Fortunately the Breviaries of some monastic orders, such as the Benedictine, did not adopt the changes, and in many cases the melodies or tunes remained the same.

Yet, even the period of decline of the Latin hymn, from the Renaissance to the present, is not completely devoid of pieces of poetic and musical inspiration. Notwithstanding the fact that in the Roman church it is not in liturgical usage, there is no hymn more beloved by all Christians than the Christmas "Adeste Fideles" (LBW 45), ascribed to John Francis Wade (1711-1786).

In addition, Father Charles Coffin (1676-1749) (LBW 22), rector of the University of Paris, was among those commissioned to revise the Paris Breviary of 1736. The revision included a number of his Latin hymns of which two Advent hymns are remarkable: "Jordanis oras praevia" and "Instantis adventum Dei," both of which are found in all recent Lutheran hymn books. The opening stanza of each is well worth reading in John Chandler's translations as they are found in the LBW, Nos. 36 and 22 respectively.

There remains but to say a word about the music. While no examples of Byzantine chant can be found in the LBW (see above, page 8), a number of translated Latin hymns are given with their plainsong melodies.

Plainsong or plainchant, often called "Gregorian chant," in its original form is monophonic (a single melodic line without harmony or accompaniment) and rhythmically free. Some scholars trace its origins to Greek music, others to Hebrew. During the early Christian era, additional melodies were incorporated into the body of chant from a number of sources. It is doubtful whether Gregory the Great contributed to the liturgical music that bears his name. It is certain that he instituted a number of liturgical reforms during his pontificacy (590-604) which included the codifying and assembling of the chants then in existence.

Authorities on the chant generally divide it into four categories: 1. Monologue and dialogue; 2. Psalmodic; 3. Strophic (our present discussion); 4. Commatic.

Although we are primarily interested in No. 3, it might be well to say a word about the others. The first consists of formulae for chanting the pericopes and formulae for versicles and responses. The second also consists in numerous formulae for the chanting of the Psalter and Canticles.

V Ictimae paschá-li láudes * ímmolent Christi- áni.

Agnus redémit óves : Chrístus ínnocens Pátri   reconci-

li- ávit peccatóres. Mors et ví-ta du-éllo   conflixére mirán-

do : dux vítae mórtu-us, régnat vívus. Dic nóbis Marí- a,

quid vidísti   in ví- a? Sepúlcrum Chrísti vivéntis,   et gló-

ri- am vídi resurgéntis : Angé-licos téstes,   sudá-ri- um, et

véstes. Surréxit Chrístus spes mé- a : praecédet sú-os in Ga-

lilaé- am. Scímus Chrístum surrexísse   a mórtu- is vere :

tu nóbis, víctor Rex,   mi-se-ré-re.   Amen. Alle-lú-ia.

Udi, be-nígne Cóndi-tor, Nóstras pré-ces cum flé-

tibus, In hoc sácro jejúni- o Fúsas quadragená- ri- o.

2. Scru-tá-tor álme córdi-um, Infírma tu scis ví-ri- um : Ad

te revérsis éxhibe Remissi- ó-nis grá- ti- am. 3. Multum

quidem peccávimus, Sed párce confi-téntibus : Ad nómi-

nis láudem tú-i, Cónfer medé-lam lánguidis. 4. Concéde

nóstrum cónteri Córpus per abstinénti- am, Cúlp*ae* ut

re-línquant pábulum Jejú-na córda críminum. 5. Praésta

be- áta Tríni-tas, Concéde símplex Uni-tas : Ut fructu-ó-

sa sint tú- is Jejuni- ó-rum mú-nera. Amen.

The fourth is the developed art form of the chant—highly ornate, florid and melismatic. Stylistically they can be described as follows:

Categories 1 and 2 have many syllables to few notes.

Category 4 has many notes to one syllable.

Category 3 is syllabic and has mostly one note to each syllable.

As was the music of the Eastern church, the chant is modal in tonality. There are eight modes corresponding to the *echoi* (cf. chart on page 9). Within the eight modes there are four pairs having the same *finalis* or key center, but different melodic dominants, as given below. In the case of modes 1 and 2, for example, the *finalis* for both is *d,* but each has a different melodic dominant—mode 1 has *a* and mode 2 has *f.* The melodic range for mode 1 is from *d* to *d,* and for mode 2 is from *a* to *a.*

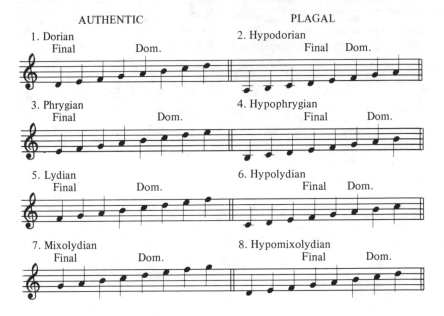

German Hymnody

Carl F. Schalk

The Early Reformation Period (c. 1517–1577)

One of the significant contributions of the Reformation to the Christian Church was the restoration of popular song to the people. While the popular singing of religious hymns and songs was not unknown in the Middle Ages, its use in connection with the liturgy was infrequent, sporadic, and—except in certain circumstances—often proscribed by the church. The tradition of popular religious song was, however, nourished up to the sixteenth century through such varied vehicles as the medieval *Leisen*; popular songs in the Minnesinger and Meistersinger traditions, some of which infiltrated the church in unofficial ways; songs of the Flagellants and other enthusiasts of the thirteenth and fourteenth centuries; the songs produced by mystics of the fourteenth century; and the general movement toward the vernacular in worship evident already in the fifteenth century. By the time of the six-teenth-century Reformation there was available to Luther and his followers not only a variety of popular liturgical, devotional, and ecstatic hymnody, but there existed a climate in which it was possible to involve the people in liturgical congregational song in a more significant way than in the preceding centuries.

Since Martin Luther (1483–1546) (LBW 48) stood at the center of the German Reformation and its encouragement of popular congregational song, it is crucial that his view of congregational song and its role in worship be clearly understood. Luther's view of congregational song was centered in a view of music as a gift of God, a gift which found its highest fulfillment in the proclamation of God's Word. While it is a commonplace to note that Luther's restoration of congregational song to a place of prominence was a significant contribution of the Reformation to the entire church, what is less commonly observed is that Luther viewed the congregational hymn or chorale as an integral and vital part of the *liturgy* and not merely as a general Christian song loosely attached to worship. It was *liturgical hymnody*—in which doxa and dogma were united in doxological proclamation, and in which the people joined together in praise, mutual expression of the faith, and in the simple, practical, and liturgical demonstration of the universal priesthood of all believers—that was the genius of the developing hymnody of the early Lutheran Reformation.

In the development of a body of material for use in congregational song, the early Reformation, led by Luther's own example, explored five chief sources.

1) The first source was the treasury of Gregorian chant, the melodies of which were often simplified melodically thus making them more readily ac-cessible for congregational singing, and the texts of which were often cor-rected, altered, or "improved" theologically where they were contrary to the Reformation's understanding of the Gospel. Chants taken from both the Ordinary and Proper of the Mass as well as from the repertoire of Latin of-fice hymns became part of the people's song in this manner. Thus the chant melody of the office hymn "Veni, Creator Spiritus" (LBW 472) became "Komm, Gott Schöpfer" (LBW 284, 473); "Veni Redemptor gentium" gave birth to at least three tunes—"Erhalt uns, Herr, bei deinem Wort"

19

(LBW 230), "Nun komm, der Heiden Heiland" (LBW 28), and "Verleih uns Frieden gnägdiglich" (LBW 471); "A solis ortus cardine" (LBW 64) became "Christum wir sollen loben schön"; and so on. Certain Reformation tunes developed from the repertoire of sequence hymns (see above, p. 14): "Christ lag in Todesbanden" (LBW 134) from the "Victimae paschali laudes" (LBW 137) via "Christ ist erstanden" (LBW 136), and "Gott sei gelobet und gebenedeiet" (LBW 215) which was drawn from the "Lauda Sion Salvatorem." Chants from the Ordinary of the Mass served as a source for still other melodies such as the "Kyrie Gott Vater in Ewigkeit" (LBW 168), an adaptation of the "Kyrie fons bonitatis," and "Allein Gott in der Höh sei Ehr" (LBW 166) drawn from a Gregorian *Gloria.* Even Luther's "Jesaia, dem Propheten das geschah" (LBW 528) has a marked similarity to a Gregorian *Sanctus* as does Nikolaus Decius' "O Lamm Gottes unschuldig" (LBW 111). The early Reformation's use of the Gregorian repertoire, freely adapted in this way, was not only an eminently practical matter, utilizing a large body of material already at hand; it also underscored the Reformation church's concern for catholicity by continuing to root the people's song in the traditional melodies which had nourished Christians for centuries.

2) A second source of early Reformation hymnody was the *Leisen,* a

Title page from the Etlich Christlich lider *("Achtlieder-buch") printed in Wittenberg in 1524. Two tunes from this earliest of Lutheran hymnals are included in the LBW: "Es ist das heil" (LBW 194, 297) and "Nun freut euch" (LBW 299).*

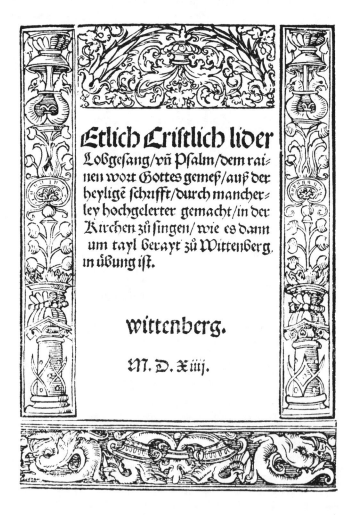

body of sacred, pre-Reformation German folk hymns characterized by the use of some form of "Kyrie eleison" as the conclusion of each stanza. *Leisen* were sung in processions, by pilgrims, at other special religious occasions, and occasionally at Mass. In the later Middle Ages certain *Leisen* associated with particular festivals were sometimes sung by the people in the vernacular alternating with the Latin verses of the sequences sung by the choir. Some of the early *Leisen* included the twelfth-century "Christ is arisen" ("Christ ist erstanden," LBW 136), "We journey in the name of God" ("In Gottes Namen fahren wir"), and "To God the Holy Spirit let us pray" ("Nun bitten wir den Heiligen Geist," LBW 317). Other popular *Leisen* included "All praise to you, eternal Lord" ("Gelobet seist du, Jesu Christ," LBW 48), "These are the holy Ten Commands" ("Dies sind die heiligen zehn Gebot"), "Man, wouldst thou live all blissfully" ("Mensch, willst du leben seliglich"), "Even as we live each day" ("Mitten wir im Leben sind," LBW 350), and "Jesus Christ, our Savior true" ("Jesus Christus unser Heiland, der den Tod").

3) Another source of early Reformation hymnody was the *Cantios,* Latin spiritual songs of pre-Reformation times which although religious in content were not directly associated with the liturgy. These included the macaronic song "Good Christian friends, rejoice" ("In dulci jubilo," LBW 55) and the "He whom shepherds once came praising" ("Quem pastores laudavere") which when joined with "The glorious angels came today" ("Nunc angelorem") and the "God's own son is born a child" ("Magnum nomen Domini") form the Quempas carol (LBW 68).

4) Another source was that group of songs which were the result of the process of contrafaction. Generally, this process consisted of providing a sacred text to an already existing popular secular melody. The classic example is Luther's children's song for Christmas, "From heaven above to earth I come" ("Vom Himmel hoch da komm ich her," LBW 51) based on the secular song "Good news from far abroad I bring" ("Aus fremden Landen komm ich her"). Other examples of melodies originally associated with secular texts which were supplied by the Reformation church with sacred texts include not only the well-known "O Welt, ich muss dich lassen" (taken into the church with Paul Gerhardt's text "Now rest beneath night's shadow," LBW 276, 282) and "Herzlich tut mich verlangen" (originally associated with the secular love song "Mein G'müt ist mir verwirret" and used in the church with the text "O sacred head, now wounded" LBW 116, 117), but also such tunes as "Auf meinem lieben Gott" (originally associated with the text "Venus, du und dein Kind sind alle beide blind"), "O Herre Gott, dein göttlich Wort" (originally associated with "Weiss mir ein Blümlein blaue"), and many others. Such a free use and adaptation of secular melodies for sacred purposes was made possible in part because the distinction between sacred and secular musical styles as we think of it today was for most practical purposes nonexistent. The Reformation church was by no means alone in the use of contrafacta; the Catholic church also utilized this device, although with less frequency.

5) A final source of hymnody for the Reformation church was newly-composed hymns. Luther encouraged Christian poets to prepare new songs which the people could make their own and with which they could praise their God and proclaim the Gospel. In his "Order of Mass and Communion for the Church at Wittenberg" (1523) Luther expressed just such encouragement.

I also wish that we had as many songs as possible in the vernacular which the people could sing during mass, immediately after the gradual and also after the Sanctus and Agnus Dei. For who doubts that originally all the people sang these which now only the choir sings . . . (*Luther's Works,* Vol. 53, p. 36)

Luther himself set the example, and a careful examination of the kinds of hymns which Luther wrote is rewarding for what it tells of his view of the role of hymnody in worship.

Noteworthy among Luther's original hymns is a group based on the Psalms. These include his "Out of the depths I cry to you" ("Aus tiefer Not schrei ich zu dir," LBW 295) based on Psalm 130, and "May God bestow on us his grace" ("Es wolle Gott uns genädig sein," LBW 335) based on Psalm 67. The idea of writing such German Psalms was continued by other writers such as Johann Graumann in his "My soul, now praise your maker!" ("Nun lob, mein Seel, den Herren," LBW 519) based on Psalm 103. Other hymns by Luther include his "We all believe in one true God" ("Wir glauben all an einen Gott," LBW 374), a paraphrase of the Nicene Creed, and "Isaiah in a vision did of old" ("Jesaia dem Propheten das geschah," LBW 528), a paraphrase of the *Sanctus.* Both of these hymns are generally acknowledged as the work of Luther, both text and tune. Other hymns for which Luther either wrote the text or corrected, adapted, or wrote additional stanzas to other texts include a variety of church year hymns and six catechism hymns: "These are the holy Ten Commands" ("Dies sind die heiligen zehn Gebot") and "Man, wouldst thou live blissfully" ("Mensch, willst du leben seliglich"), Luther's long and short versions of the Ten Commandments; "We all believe in one true God" ("Wir glauben all an einen Gott," LBW 374), a paraphrase of the Nicene Creed; "Our Father in the heaven who art" ("Vater unser im Himmelreich"), Luther's version of the Lord's Prayer; "To Jordan came the Christ, our Lord" ("Christ unser Herr zum Jordan kam," LBW 79), a hymn of Baptism; and "Jesus Christ, our God and Savior" ("Jesus Christus, unser Heiland"), a hymn for Holy Communion. Leupold* lists thirty-five hymns with which Luther was involved in one way or another which were intended for congregational singing in addition to his first song "A new song here shall be begun" ("Ein neues Lied wir heben an"), which was a ballad protesting the martyrdom of two young men in Brussels in 1523, and "To me she's dear, the worthy maid" ("Sie ist mir lieb, die werte Magd"), a courtly air also not intended for congregational singing. Luther also wrote or assisted in the preparation of a number of liturgical chants (*Agnus Dei, Te Deum, Magnificat, Gloria in excelsis*).

Luther's example and encouragement inspired a number of writers of his time to provide new hymns for congregational use. Among these were Justus Jonas (1493–1555) who wrote "Wo Gott der Herr nicht bei uns Hält"; Paul Eber (1511–1569) who wrote such texts as "When in the hour of deepest need" ("Wenn wir in höchsten Nöten sein," LBW 303), "To God the anthem raising" ("Helft mir Gottes Güte preisen"), and "Lord God, we all to Thee give praise" ("Herr Gott dich loben alle wir," Eber's German translation of Philipp Melanchthon's Latin text); Lazarus Spengler (1479–1534) who wrote "All mankind fell in Adam's fall" ("Durch Adams Fall ist ganz verderbt"); Albrecht of Brandenburg (1522–1557) to whom is attributed "The will of God is always best" ("Was mein Gott will, das g'scheh allzeit," LBW 450); Paul Speratus (1484–1551) whose text "Salvation unto us has come" ("Es ist das Heil uns kommen her," LBW 297) is recognized as among the greatest of the early Reformation hymns; Johannes Schneesing (?–1567) who wrote "I trust, O Christ, in you alone" ("Allein zu dir, Herr Jesu Christ," LBW 395); and Nikolaus Decius (*c.* 1485–?) who wrote both text and tune for two great Lutheran classics, "All glory be to God on high" ("Allein Gott in der Höh sie Ehr," LBW 166) and "Lamb of God, pure and sinless" ("O Lamm Gottes, unschuldig," LBW 111). Nikolaus Herman (*c.* 1480–1561) is remembered not only for such hymn texts as "Let all together praise our God" ("Lobt Gott, ihr Christen," LBW 47), "The radiant sun shines in the sky" ("Die helle Sonn' leuchtet herfür"), and "When my last hour is close at hand" ("Wenn mein Stundlein vorhanden ist"), but also for such exemplary tunes as "Lobt Gott, ihr Christen" (LBW 47, 300, 351), "Erschienen ist der herrlich Tag" (LBW 154), and "O heilige Dreifaltigkeit" (LBW 275).

Luther and many of the early Reformation hymnwriters stood in the tradition of the Meistersingers in which poet and tune-maker were the same person. This is reflected in the frequent use of the barform, a favorite device of the Meistersingers, in many of the newly-composed chorales of this period. In essence the barform was a three-part poetic and musical structure consisting of a *Stollen,* the repetition of the *Stollen,* and an *Abgesang.* Each *Stollen* ordinarily consisted of two parts, the *Abgesang* of three. Thus the normal barform could be schematized as: A(ab)—A(ab)—B(cde). Such hymns as "Dear Christians, one and all, rejoice" ("Nun freut euch, lieben Christen gmein," (LBW 299), "A mighty fortress is our God" ("Ein feste Burg ist unser Gott," LBW 228, 229), and "All glory be to God on high" ("Allein Gott in der Höh sei Ehr," LBW 166) all reflect the use of this textual and musical structure.

The Lutheran chorale (the word chorale reflects its origin in the German word *Choral* meaning the Gregorian chant), as the congregational song of this period came to be known, reflected a variety of roots and origins. Its texts spoke directly of sin and salvation, of man's fall and his redemption through Christ's victory over death and the devil. Its melodies were popular, vigorous, and filled with rhythmic life. They were sung in unison without accompaniment, the people frequently alternating with choir and instruments in their presentation, especially in the *de tempore* or Gradual hymn (Hymn of the Day). These songs were essentially *liturgical* songs, songs not simply to involve the people but to involve them in *singing the liturgy.* All of this was tied directly to Luther's concern for the hymn as the proclamation of the Good News, as the "living voice of the Gospel" (*viva vox evangelii*). Leupold* stresses this same theme as he remarks that "Luther's hymns were not meant to create a mood, but to convey a message. They were a confession of faith, not of personal feelings." (p. 197) This then was the mood of early Lutheran hymnody, a vigorous proclamation of doxological praise in texts which spoke the Good News plainly and directly, and melodies which matched in their strength and vigor the proclamation of that same Gospel.

This renewed interest in congregational song resulted in the publication of numerous hymn collections during the early Reformation period. The earliest of these collections and the first collection of Lutheran hymns to be identified as such was the *Etlich Christlich lider* (1524), the so-called *Achtliederbuch* because of the eight hymns which it contained (four by Luther, three by Speratus, one by an unnamed author). It contained only five melodies. The *Geystliche gesangk Buchleyn* (1524), edited by Luther's friend and musical advisor Johann Walther (LBW

350), was not a hymnbook in the modern sense of the word but rather a collection of polyphonic motets for choir based on many of the old and newer chorales and hymns. Other early collections include the *Enchiridion oder Handbuchlein* (1524) from Erfurt (which contained 25 texts with 15 melodies), *Eyn gesang Buchleyn* (1525) from Zwickau (containing 24 texts with 17 melodies), *Teutsch Kirchenampt mit lobgesengen vn götlichen psalmen* (1525) from Straszburg (containing 14 melodies), *Enchiridion geistlicher gesenge vnd Psalmen* (1528) published by Michael Blum in Leipzig (containing 63 texts and 27 melodies), Michael Weisse's (LBW 37) collection of the Bohemian Brethren, *Ein New Gesengbuchlen* (1531) (containing 157 texts and 112 melodies), Joseph Klug's (LBW 85) hymnal published in Wittenberg (1529, a second edition published in 1533), Valentin Schumann's *Geistliche Lieder* (1539), and what is probably the finest hymnal of this period, the *Geystliche Lieder* (1545), the so-called Babst hymnal named after the printer of the collection, and generally considered to be the most representative German hymnal of this period. It contained 89 hymns with an additional 40 in an appendix. The proliferation of hymn collections throughout Germany and beyond attests to the continued popularity of the chorale and its rapid spread throughout the areas where the Reformation reached. From 1524 to Luther's death in 1546 it is estimated that almost 100 hymnals were produced in Germany.

It should not be overlooked that German Catholicism also produced several important hymnals during this time, among them Vehe's *Ein New Gesangbuchlein Geistlicher Lieder* (1537) and, later in the century, Johann Leisentritt's *Geistliche Lieder und Psalmen* (1567) which bears a striking resemblance to the earlier Babst hymnal of 1545.

The Period of Lutheran Orthodoxy or Lutheran Scholasticism (c. 1577–c. 1617)

The signing of the Formula of Concord in 1577 (and the subsequent appearance of the Book of Concord in 1580) serves as a convenient if somewhat arbitrary date in noting the continuing development of German hymnody. The Formula of Concord was important in that it settled a number of bitter theological controversies which developed among the Lutherans following Luther's death in 1546. Many of these controversies developed from the later views of Philipp Melanchthon, Luther's coworker and leading humanist of the Reformation. While the Formula of Concord rejected much of Melanchthon's theology, it made use of his Aristotelian methodology to systematize Luther's theological thought, introducing logic and rationalism into a period known variously as the age of Orthodoxy or as the period of Lutheran Scholasticism.

It is clear in retrospect that the vigorous hymnic production of the early years of the Reformation was giving way to a transitional period in which the future shape of German hymnody was not yet quite clear. By the 1550s such early hymnwriters as Speratus, Jonas, Decius, Spengler, and Albrecht of Brandenburg had passed from the scene. The 1560s saw the deaths of Johann Hermann, Schneesing, and Eber, and a new generation of hymnwriters was appearing on the scene, many of whom had been involved in one way or another in the various controversies which shook Lutheranism in the latter 1500s.

It was inevitable that these controversies would have their effect on the hymnody written during those years. "Dry, dogmatic, didactic, and often bombastic verse became the vogue. There were rhymed Epistles and Gospels; the poetic expression became weak and unyielding." (Fred

Precht, *Church Music* 66.1, p. 9) One poet, Ludwig Helmbold, even produced a metrical version of the Augsburg Confession.

While most of the poorer hymnody of these times has passed out of use, there still remain hymns from this time which in their popular objectivity and often childlike naiveté were warmly received and continue to be so still today. Hymns by such writers as Nikolaus Selnecker (1532–1592), a student at Wittenberg and favorite pupil of Melanchthon and one of the writers of the Formula of Concord, who wrote "Let me be yours forever" ("Lass mich dein sein und bleiben," LBW 490), and such other texts as "Lord Jesus Christ with us abide" ("Ach bleib bei uns, Herr Jesu Christ"), "O faithful God, thanks be to thee" ("Wir danken dir, o treuer Gott"), and "O Lord, my God, I cry to thee" ("O Herre Gott, in meiner Not"); Bartholomäus Ringwaldt (1523–1599) who contributed "The day is surely drawing near" ("Es ist gewisslich an der Zeit," LBW 321) and "O Holy Spirit grant us grace" ("Gott Heil'ger Geist, hilf uns mit Grund"); Martin Schalling (1532–1608) who wrote the masterful hymn of comfort, "Lord, thee I love with all my heart" ("Herzlich Lieb hab ich dich, O Herr," LBW 325); and Ludwig Helmbold (1532–1598) whose metrical version of the Augsburg Confession is now forgotten but whose timeless "From God can nothing move me" ("Von Gott will ich nicht lassen," LBW 468) and such other hymns as "Lord, help us ever to retain" ("Herr Gott, erhalt uns für und für") and "Ye parents, hear what Jesus taught" ("Höret, ihr Eltern, Christus spricht") continue to be sung.

Somewhat later writers, all born in the decade or two following Luther's death, contributed significant hymns which continue to find a place in hymnals today: Martin Behm (1557–1622) who wrote "O Jesus King of glory" ("O König aller Ehren"), "Lord Jesus Christ, my life, my light" ("O Jesu Christ, mein's Lebens Licht"), and "O blessed Holy Trinity" ("O heilige Dreifaltigkeit"); Valerius Herberger (1562–1627) who wrote "Farewell I gladly bid thee" ("Valet will ich dir geben"); and Philipp Nicolai (1556–1608) who contributed two of the finest hymns of this or any period, the king and queen of chorales: "Wake, awake, for night is flying" ("Wachet auf, ruft uns die Stimme," LBW 31) and "O Morning Star, how fair and bright!" ("Wie schön leuchtet der Morgenstern," LBW 76) for which Nicolai wrote both text and tune. This period marks the beginning of the transition from a more objective and confessional hymnody (*Bekenntnislieder*) to hymnody of a somewhat more personal, devotional character (*Erbauungslieder*). While this new emphasis was to come into much greater prominence by the mid-seventeenth century, its beginnings can be seen already in the more introspective hymnody which developed from the personal trials and tribulation associated with the doctrinal controversies of the latter 1500s.

The last quarter of the sixteenth century and the first quarter of the seventeenth century was also the great period of the cantionals, collections of hymns and chorales for choir in four or five parts in which the melody was placed in the upper part (in contrast to the Renaissance practice of placing the cantus firmus in the tenor), the remaining voices proceeding in homorhythmic fashion. While intimations of this new practice may be seen earlier in the sixteenth century, it was Lucas Osiander's *Fuenfzig geistliche Lieder und Psalmen* (1586) which set forth for the first time in a clear and consistent fashion the basic characteristics of cantional style. Osiander's title, "Fifty sacred songs and psalms arranged so, that an entire Christian congregation can sing along," indicated both the purpose and the intent of the collection. Osiander's collection inspired the publication of numerous cantional collections, most notable among them being Hans Leo Hassler's (LBW 116) *Kirchengesaenge, Psalmen, und geistliche Lieder . . . simpliciter gesetzt* (1608) and Michael Praetorius' (LBW 36) *Musae Sioniae* (Pts. VI-VIII, 1609–10). Other similar collections were published by Andreas Raselius (1588), Seth Calvisius (1597), Johann Eccard [LBW 124] (1597), Bartholomäus Gesius [LBW 455] (1601), Melchior Franck [LBW 348] (1602), Melchior Vulpius [LBW 115] (1604), and many others.

These cantional collections were generally intended to be used by the choirs (singing in parts), the congregation singing the chorale melodies simultaneously, or as settings for choir alone alternating with the congregation in the singing of the chorales. In this period the organ began to assume a more dominant position in accompanying congregational singing by first doubling the choir's parts in the cantional collections and, by the later seventeenth century, ultimately replacing the choir and accompanying the congregation alone. One of the early references to the use of the organ to accompany congregational singing is found in the *Hamburger Melodey-Gesang-buch* (1604). With the publication of Johann Hermann Schein's (LBW 123) *Cantional oder Gesangbuch Augsburgischer Confession* (1627) which included figured bass, the development of the cantional takes a new turn in which the organ gradually assumes an increasingly important role and in which the history of the cantional collection becomes the history of the organ chorale book.

Among the hymn tunes which developed in this period the tunes of Melchior Vulpius (*c.* 1560–1615) deserve special mention. Among them are "Lobt Gott den Herren, ihr" (LBW 542), "Christus, der ist mein Leben" (LBW 263), "Gelobt sei Gott" (LBW 144), "Jesu Kreuz, Leiden und Pein" (LBW 115), and "Die helle Sonn leucht" (LBW 292). Melchior Franck's "Jerusalem, du hochgebaute Stadt" (LBW 348) has also continued in use in many hymnals, as has Bartholomäus Gesius' "Machs mit mir, Gott" (LBW 455).

The Period of Paul Gerhardt, the Thirty Years' War, and the Development of New Literary Concerns (c. 1618–c. 1675)

This period encompasses the time of the Thirty Years' War and the development of new literary concerns in German hymnody. Its most prominent representatives are Paul Gerhardt (LBW 23) and Johann Crüger (LBW 23), two imposing figures, one a writer of texts and the other a writer of melodies, whose work played such an important part in this period of hymnody.

It is difficult to underestimate the importance of the Thirty Years' War (1618–1648) on the development of hymnody of this time. The privation and distress which was the lot of countless people caught up in this war was a significant factor in the development of a new kind of hymn. Johannes Riedel (*The Lutheran Chorale; Its Basic Traditions,* Minneapolis, 1967) characterizes the times as follows: "Confronted with the horrible killing and pillaging of the Thirty Years' War, the individual sought enlightenment, self-understanding, comfort, and consolation in a personal and subjective approach to God." It was inevitable that the hymnody which developed in this period increasingly sought to relate more closely to the life situations in which people found themselves, a fact particularly evident in the many so-called "cross and comfort" hymns which played a prominent part in the story of this period's hymnody.

While the Thirty Years' War had a profound effect on the content of

26

the hymnody of these times, an equally important factor was the matter of stylistic changes in the German language influenced in large part by the work of Martin Opitz (1597-1639) whose *Buch der Deutschen Poeterey* (1624) exemplified the new approach to language. It was Opitz who, in leading a reform in the art of German poetry, introduced into hymnody a greater concern for metrical regularity and purity of language. The overall impact of these reforms was to give the German hymnody of the time a smoother and more polished character both rhythmically and poetically. This development, together with a theological content which was warmer and more closely tied to the everyday situations of the people, served to give a decidedly new character to the hymns of this period.

Another important development of the time is seen in the increasing separation of the roles of poet and composer. The Meistersinger tradition in which text and tune were the creation of a single person—the basic tradition of the early Reformation—increasingly gave way to a situation in which the poet wrote words which were then set by another, the hymn tune composer. No longer is the pattern that of a Luther or a Nicolai who wrote both text and tune, but hymnists are seen more and more as separated into text writers or tune writers. Nevertheless, use of the old barform as a structural principle continues to be seen in such great hymns from this period as "Now thank we all our God" ("Nun danket alle Gott," LBW 533, 534), "Soul, adorn yourself with gladness" ("Schmücke dich, o liebe Seele," LBW 224), and "Jesus, priceless treasure" ("Jesu, meine Freude," LBW 457, 458). With the gradual abandonment of the modal system (in which most of the early chorales had been conceived) and the growing importance of tonality, melodies of this time are increasingly cast in either major or minor keys.

The transition to this new approach to hymnody is seen not only in Martin Opitz's own "Arise and shine in splendor" ("Brich auf und werde lichte") but perhaps most clearly in the work of Johann Heermann (1585-1647) who was among the first to adopt the new approach to poetry. His hymns—among which the best and most sung are perhaps "Ah, holy Jesus" ("Herzliebster Jesu, was hast du verbrochen," LBW 123), "O God, my faithful God" ("O Gott, du frommer Gott," LBW 504), and "O Christ, our light, O Radiance true" ("O Jesu Christe, wahres Licht," LBW 380)—combine the objective character of the earlier Reformation with the cleaner poetic approach of his own time.

Other hymnists of this time, born in the late sixteenth century, include Matthäus von Löwenstern (1594-1648) remembered for his texts "Lord of our life and God of our salvation" ("Christe, du Beistand deiner Kreuzgemeine," LBW 366) and "Now let all loudly sing praise" ("Nun preiset alle"); Johann Meyfart (1590-1642) who wrote the text for "Jerusalem, whose towers touch the skies" ("Jerusalem, du hochgebaute Stadt," LBW 348); Josua Stegmann (1588-1632) who wrote "Abide with us, our Savior" ("Ach bleib mit deiner Gnade," LBW 263); and Martin Rinkart (1586-1649) remembered for his "Now thank we all our God" ("Nun danket alle Gott").

Somewhat later hymnwriters include Heinrich Held (1620-1659) who wrote "Come, oh, come, O quick'ning Spirit" ("Komm, o komm, du Geist des Lebens," LBW 478) and "Let the earth now praise the Lord" ("Gott sei Dank durch alle Welt"); Josua Wegelin (1604-1640) who wrote "On Christ's ascension I now build" ("Auf Christi Himmelfahrt allein"); Simon Dach (1605-1659) whose "Through Jesus' blood and merit" ("Ich bin bei Gott in Gnaden") and "Oh, how blest are ye whose toils are ended" ("O wie selig seid ihr doch, ihr Frommen") continue to be sung; and Johann Rist (1607–1667), a prolific writer of hymns which include "Arise, sons of the kingdom" ("Auf, auf, ihr Reichsgenossen"), "O darkest woe" ("O Traurigkeit"), "Lord Jesus Christ, Thou living Bread" ("Du Lebensbrot, Herr Jesu Christ"), "O living bread from heaven" ("Wie wohl hast du gelabet," LBW 197), and "Help us O Lord! Behold we enter" ("Hilf, Herr Jesu, lass gelingen").

The person who above all others represented the spirit, turmoil, and promise of the times was Paul Gerhardt (1607–1676), preacher and poet who had personally suffered the ravages of the Thirty Years' War and who stood as a staunch representative of Lutheran orthodoxy often in difficult circumstances. Gerhardt wrote 123 hymns in all, and even the hymns of Martin Luther have hardly attained the popularity of Gerhardt's hymns as they have been translated into the English language. With Gerhardt we can see most clearly the transition to a more personal and subjective hymnody. Certainly among his most popular and significant hymns are "O Lord, how shall I meet you" ("Wie soll ich dich empfangen," LBW 23), "Once again my heart rejoices" ("Fröhlich soll mein Herze springen," LBW 46), "A Lamb goes uncomplaining forth" ("Ein Lämmlein geht und trägt die Schuld," LBW 105), "Awake, my heart, with gladness" ("Auf, auf, mein Herz, mit Freuden," LBW 129), and his masterful "O sacred head, now wounded" ("O Haupt voll Blut und Wunden," LBW 116, 117) based on the Latin poem by Bernard of Clairvaux. Not to be overlooked, however, are such other masterpieces as "If God himself be for me" ("Ist Gott für mich, so trete," LBW 454), "Evening and morning" ("Die güldne Sonne," LBW 465), "Commit what ever grieves thee" ("Befiehl du deine Wege"), "We sing, Immanuel, Thy praise" ("Sollt ich meinem Gott nicht singen"), the tender Christmas hymn "O Jesus Christ Thy manger is" ("O Jesu Christ dein Kripplein ist"), and many others.

Pertinent to Gerhardt's contribution to hymnody is the partnership which he enjoyed with Johann Crüger, his organist and choirmaster at the Nicolaikirche in Berlin. Crüger brought many of Gerhardt's hymns into more common use by publishing eighteen of them in his *Praxis Pietatis Melica* (1644). By the fifth edition the number of Gerhardt's hymns included in this significant collection had grown to eighty-one. This partnership was continued by Crüger's successor, Johann Ebeling (1637–1676), and resulted in such hymns as "Evening and morning," ("Die güldne Sonne") and "Why should cross and trial grieve me" ("Warum sollt ich mich denn grämen") for which Gerhardt provided the words and Ebeling the music.

Another writer of texts from this time who contributed several hymns still in wide use is Johann Franck (1618–1677). His "Soul, adorn yourself with gladness" ("Schmücke dich, o liebe Seele," LBW 224) and "Jesus, priceless treasure" ("Jesu, meine Freude," LBW 457, 458) were also provided with tunes by Johann Crüger and are among the hymnic treasures which continue to be sung by many Christians throughout the world.

The most significant collection of hymns published during this period was Johann Crüger's *Praxis Pietatis Melica* (1644), one of five collections which he published during the 1640s and 1650s. Its title ("The Practice of Piety Through Music") was indicative of the direction in which German hymnody was moving. Texts which spoke more directly of personal and more subjective concerns of the Christian life with its joys and trials, coupled with melodies which were smoother, cleaner, more regular metrically, and which breathed a more intense, personal, at times even mystical spirit, were welcomed into the circle of Christian song. This was a direction which was paralleled by the development of a body of intensely personal devotional literature which was widely circulated and used at this time. This direction was to come full flower with the age of Pietism, but it was in the first three quarters of the seventeenth century that the bases for the hymnody of Pietism were clearly being laid.

The Period of Pietism (c. 1675–c. 1750)

The pietistic movement in Germany in the late seventeenth and first half of the eighteenth centuries is largely associated with the names of Philip Jacob Spener (1635-1705) and August Hermann Francke (1663-1727). The movement was largely a reaction against an orthodox formalism in which the Christian life was seen largely as a matter of passive subscription to closely defined dogmas, reception of the sacraments, and participation in the ordinances of the church. Pietism sought to restore the vigorous spiritual life which Luther had preached by emphasizing personal Bible study, prayer, and works of Christian charity. Spener urged the formation of gatherings (*collegia pietatis*) in which the laity might study, pray, discuss the Sunday sermons, and in general deepen their spiritual life. In contrast to what many considered a "dead orthodoxy" Pietism, in Carl Mirbt's words, emphasized "the duty of striving after personal and individual religious independence and collaboration, and declared that religion is something altogether personal, and that evangelical Christianity is present only when and in so far as it is manifested in Christian conduct."† While the movement is here dated somewhat arbitrarily from the appearance of Spener's book *Pia desideria* (1675), which contained his attack on the established church and his recommendations for restoring spiritual life to what he considered a sterile and formalized church, its roots can clearly be seen even earlier in the century. Francke established a center for the Pietistic movement at the University of Halle to which he went in 1698 and especially emphasized a zeal for mission work. It was from Halle, incidentally, that Heinrich Melchior Muhlenberg was sent to America some years later to establish and more effectively organize Lutheranism there.

The effect of Pietism on the hymn texts written during these times was to place an ever greater emphasis on the personal, subjective aspects of the Christian life. Individualistic, privatistic, and even mystical aspects of religion received ever greater stress in hymn texts often intended for private devotional use but which increasingly found their way into hymnals to be used in corporate worship.

These emphases were reinforced by a new and different concept of edification. Edification, which the New Testament and early church understood as the building up of the Christian *community,* increasingly became a more privatistic and personal matter; Spener's phrase was the "edification of the inner man." In this new piety music was increasingly seen as a means of stirring up feelings of devotion, and the individual was effectively edified as his emotions were indeed stirred and as he felt himself being edified. The simple hymn style became the model, and through the stately, somber, and dignified execution of the music the hearer was able to absorb what was useful in the text. That such an approach often lapsed into an irreverent sentimentalism was an indication

---

†Quoted in the article on "Pietism," *The Westminster Dictionary of Church History,* Jerald C. Brauer, editor (Philadelphia: Westminster Press, 1971).

of the dangers to which such extreme personal subjectivism could lead.

Musically, many of the hymns of this period were characterized by melodies of a lighter nature, the occasional use of triple or waltz-like meters, the emergence of the *Geistliche Arien,* and the altering of the rugged, uneven rhythms of the Reformation chorales to melodies which were isorhythmic in character, the tunes proceeding largely in equal-note values often underlayed with a richer harmonic foundation than had been known previously. Such developments, exemplified by J. S. Bach's (LBW 219) chorale harmonizations, were completely in harmony with a view which saw a slow, stately, somber execution of hymns as a means for stirring up religious feelings.

While the poorer examples from this period have thankfully fallen out of use in most present-day hymnals, many fine examples from this time still remain and reflect in varying degrees this new understanding of the role of the hymn in Christian worship. Some of the more important hymn text writers of this time include Johann Jakob Schütz (1640–1690) who wrote "Sing praise to God, the highest good" ("Sei Lob und Ehr dem höchsten Gut," LBW 542); Wolfgang Dessler (1660–1722) who wrote "My soul's best friend, what joy and blessing" ("Wie wohl ist mir, o Freund der Seelen"); Johann J. Rambach (1693–1735) whose "Baptized into your name most holy" ("Ich bin getauft auf deinen Namen," LBW 192), "My Maker, be Thou nigh" ("Mein Schöpfer, steh bei mir"), and "O Thou love unbounded" ("Unumschränkte Liebe") are frequently sung; Karl Bogatzky (1690–1774), author of "Awake, O Spirit of the watchmen" ("Wach auf, du Geist der ersten Zeugen," LBW 382); and Laurentius Laurenti (1660–1722) who wrote "Rejoice, rejoice, believers" ("Ermuntert euch, ihr Frommen," LBW 25). Adam Drese (1620–1701), also from this earlier period, wrote the tune "Seelenbräutigam" (LBW 341) which is widely sung.

Several German Reformed hymnists of this period include Joachim Neander (1650–1680) who wrote the texts "Praise to the Lord, the Almighty" ("Lobe den Herren, den mächtigen," LBW 543), "Wondrous King all-glorious" ("Wunderbarer König"), and the tunes "Unser Herrscher" (LBW 182, 250) and "Wunderbarer König" (LBW 249); Gerhard Tersteegen (1697–1769), a mystic, who wrote "God himself is present" ("Gott ist gegenwärtig," LBW 249); and Ludwig von Zinzendorf (1700–1760), author of "Jesus, still lead on" ("Jesu, geh voran," LBW 341) and "Jesus, your blood and righteousness" ("Christi Blut und Gerechtigkeit," LBW 302).

Other hymnists of the period who must not be overlooked are Erdmann Neumeister (1671–1756) who wrote "Jesus sinners will receive" ("Jesus nimmt die Sünder an," LBW 291) and "I know my faith is founded" ("Ich weiss, an wen ich glaube"); and Benjamin Schmolck (1672–1737), author of "Open now thy gates of beauty" ("Tut mir auf die schöne Pforte," LBW 250), "Dearest Jesus, we are here" ("Liebster Jesu, wir sind hier," LBW 187), "My Jesus as Thou wilt" ("Mein Jesu, wie du willst"), and "What our Father does is well" ("Was Gott tut, das ist wohl getan").

Perhaps the most significant hymnal of Pietism was Johann Anastasii Freylinghausen's *Geistreiches Gesangbuch* (1704) and his *Neues Geistreiches Gesangbuch* (1714). These two books, subsequently bound together and reissued as one book (1741), were known as the "Freylinghausen Gesangbuch" or the "Halle hymnal" (after the Halle Orphanage which published and distributed it throughout Germany). The influence of this book also extended to America through the many immigrants who brought this book with them in the 1700s. Freylinghausen's hymnal contained 1581 hymns with 597 melodies, the music consisting simply of melody with figured bass. Tunes from Freylinghausen's hymnal which have continued to find their way into today's hymnals include "Macht hoch die Tür" (LBW 32), "Gott sei Dank" (LBW 379), and "Dir, dir, Jehova" (LBW 382).

A second characteristically Pietistic hymnal of the period was Georg Christian Schemelli's *Musikalisches Gesangbuch* (1736). Published to counter and diminish the Pietistic leanings of the German hymnody of the times, this book itself reveals a strong pietistic orientation. J. S. Bach served as musical editor for this book which contained melodies "in part newly composed, and in part improved in the figured bass" by Bach. The collection was intended for private devotions in the home and its contents are not congregational hymns in the strict sense of the term. They belong to that category of *Geistliche Arien,* sacred ariettas, or spiritual songs. It contained 954 such songs, among them "Come, soothing death," ("Komm, süsser Tod"), "Jesus, Jesus, Thou art mine," ("Jesu, Jesu, du bist mein"), and "Come, souls, behold this day" ("Kommt, Seelen, dieser Tag"). Typical of the texts in this collection and also reflecting the intense personalism of much of the hymnody of Pietism is a hymn of Wolfgang Dessler ("Ich lass dich nicht") set to a melody from a collection entitled "Herzensmusik" (1727):

> I hold Thee fast
> Be Thou my Jesus ever
> Though earth and hell or death at last
> Should strive to win me or my faith to sever.
> So fast I cleave to Thee,
> My Champion ever be.
> Hear Thou my spirit's plea:
> Be Thou my Savior ever,
> I cleave to Thee,
> I cleave to Thee.
>
> (tr. Henry S. Drinker, alt.)

The Period of Rationalism (c. 1750–c. 1816)

While German Pietism at its best maintained a link, however tenuous, with a confessional Lutheran hymnody—the basic core of confessional hymns from the sixteenth-century Reformation was at least to be found in the over 1500 hymns in the Freylinghausen hymnal—this basic core of confessional hymnody was largely submerged in the flood of Pietistic hymnody. Pietism's lack of intellectual strength and vigor resulting from the strong emphasis on human feeling soon left the field open for the movement known as the Enlightenment or Rationalism.

Reason, science, naturalism, and a humanism not grounded in the Christian faith shook the very foundations of the church. Neither music nor hymnody were spared as hymns and liturgies were rewritten and altered to conform to the demands of human reason. Editors rewrote and revised hymns to conform to the tenor of the times; frequently stanzas which spoke too clearly or directly of matters of faith which could not be aligned with reason were simply deleted. While perhaps originally well-meant, this process gradually led to the abandonment of the clear proclamation of the Gospel in much of the hymnody of the time. As Philip Schaff put it:

31

Conversion and sanctification were changed into self-improvement, piety into virtue, heaven into the better world, Christ into Christianity, God into Providence, Providence into fate. Instead of hymns of faith and salvation, the congregations were obliged to sing rhymed sermons on the existence of God, the immortality of the soul, the delights of reunion, the dignity of man, the duty of self-improvement, the nurture of the body, and the care of animals and flowers.

(Julian,* p. 417)

In the hymnody of this period which retained a strong and clear statement of the Christian faith one name stands out above all others: Christian Fürchtegott Gellert (1715–1769) whose "Jesus lives! The victory's won!" ("Jesus lebt, mit ihm auch ich," LBW 133) is a forthright declaration of the Easter faith. Other hymnody of this time includes Matthias Claudius' (1740–1815) text "We plow the fields and scatter" ("Wir pflügen und wir streuen," LBW 362) and the J. A. P. Schulz (1747–1800) tunes "Wir pflügen" (LBW 362) and "Her kommer dine arme Smaa" (LBW 52).

Efforts Toward Recovery (c. 1817–1900)

The Confessional Revival, which began largely as a reaction against the rationalism which held sway in the latter eighteenth and early nineteenth centuries, may be conveniently dated as beginning with the reissuing of Luther's Ninety-Five Theses together with other theses of his own by Claus Harms, archdeacon of St. Michael's church in Kiel in 1817 on the occasion of the 300th anniversary of the Reformation. In his theses Harms clearly pointed out the dangers of rationalism, also in the church's hymnody, a fact clearly in evidence in the hymnals of the time.

The impact of the Confessional Revival on the church's song was significant in two specific ways. Concerning the liturgy of the church the Confessional Revival sought to reestablish the norms and structures of the sixteenth-century Reformation. In terms of hymn texts it sought to restore the unaltered texts of Reformation hymnody, texts which had been rewritten, altered, and edited in the preceding century so as to bring them into line with the thinking of the time as it was determined by a rationalistic approach to theology. In terms of hymn melodies the Confessional Revival sought to restore the original, unaltered, rhythmic form of the chorale melodies of the Reformation time which had been reduced to even-note melodies in the centuries following the Reformation. Such a restoration, it was believed, would not only be more faithful to the spirit of Luther and the Reformation but would also reinvigorate congregational singing which had fallen to a sad state of affairs. A contemporary account of congregational singing in mid-nineteenth century reflected an all-too-common situation.

Each syllable is sung without distinction for a period of about four beats; on the last syllable of each line or at the end of the melodic phrase there follows a long fermata lasting 8–12 beats, the last part of which is incorporated in a more or less intricate organ interlude. So all of the melodies follow one line after the other in this repetitious manner, whether sad or joyous, mournful or exultant, all performed in a creeping dragging fashion. The hymns of Luther have had their wings clipped and have put on the straight-jacket of 4/4 time. And so it came about that the more inflexible the singing of the chorale was, the more solemn it was thought to be.†

†*Ev. Kirchenzeitung,* 1847, No. 84. Quoted in Johann Daniel von der Heydt, *Geschichte der Evangelischen Kirchenmusik in Deutschland,* Berlin: Trowitzsch and Son, 1926, p. 195.

Results of historical research by such men as Philip Wackernagel (1800–1877), Hoffman von Fallersleben (1798–1874), Karl von Winterfeld (1786–1852), Johannes Zahn* (1817–1895), Albert Fischer (1829–1896), Friedrich Layriz (1808–1859), and many others provided the basis for the recovery of the German hymnody of the Reformation. One of the central concerns of the Confessional Revival in terms of hymnody was to restore to use that basic core of Reformation hymnody which had been submerged in the flood of pietistic and rationalistic hymnody of the preceding period. This central core of Reformation hymnody (*Kernlieder*) was perhaps best exemplified in the Babst Gesangbuch of 1545.

Among the various books which attempted to set a standard for the time were the *Berliner Gesangbuch* (1829), Karl von Raumer's *Sammlung Geistlicher Lieder* (1831) which included a representative core of Reformation hymnody together with the original form of the melodies, Friedrich Layriz' *Kern des deutschen Kirchengesangs* (1844–55), the *Eisenach Choralebuch* (1852), together with other collections by Gregor Lange, August Vilmar, Christian K. J. von Bunsen, and Wilhelmi which appeared in the second quarter of the century.

Among the hymnwriters of the time must be mentioned Karl J. P. Spitta (1801–1859), perhaps the greatest German hymnist of the nineteenth century and author of "We are the Lord's" ("Wir sind des Herrn, wir leben oder sterben," LBW 399) and "O happy home where Thou art loved most dearly" ("O selig Haus, wo man dich aufgenommen"); and Albert Knapp (1798–1864), one of the editors of the *Wuerttemberg Gesangbuch* (1842) and author of "Dear Father, who hast made us all" ("O Vaterherz, das Erd' und Himmel schuf") and "It is not death to die" ("Nein, nein, das ist kein sterben"). Tunes still sung from this period include Layriz's "Eins ist Not" and Friedrich Filitz's (1804–1876) "Wem in Leidenstagen" (LBW 95).

While the period of the German Confessional Revival was not especially rich in numbers of hymnwriters, its contribution of the restoration of the earlier Reformation hymnody was a significant one which continues, in a variety of ways, to affect and inform present-day Lutheran hymnody in Germany, Scandinavia, and in the United States.

Scandinavian Hymnody

DENMARK

Edward A. Hansen

Denmark, a predominantly Lutheran country, has a great treasure in its hymns of Christian faith. Danish immigrants came to the United States following the American Civil War, bringing with them their Bible and hymnal. Transplanted in the new land, they continued to sing their hymns in church and home. When the language of worship and preaching gradually shifted to English, translations were made of many Danish hymns, which became the heritage of a new generation when published in successive editions of the *Hymnal for Church and Home* (1927–1949). In the LBW seventeen translations of hymns by Danish hymnwriters were selected to appear.

The flowering of Danish hymnody spans three centuries. Chief contributors to the wealth of Danish church song are four churchmen: Thomas H. Kingo (LBW 102), Hans A. Brorson (LBW 52), Nicolai F. S. Grundtvig (LBW 62), and Bernhardt S. Ingemann (LBW 355). In addition to this "big four," one Danish woman hymnwriter, Birgitte Boye (LBW 43), has two hymns in the LBW.

Although the Nordic peoples were lovers of song from ancient times, there was little singing in church prior to the Reformation except the Mass chanted by the priests in Latin.

The first Danish hymnal, *Det kristelige Messeembede,* was published by Hans Mortensen at Malmö in 1528. It contained ten hymns. Later collections circulated for a time until a compilation by Bishop Hans Tausen was issued in 1544. This was replaced in 1569 by *Den danske Psalmebog,* compiled by Hans Thomissön (LBW 227), head pastor of the Church of our Lady in Copenhagen. This book contained 268 hymns and served through many reprints as the hymnal of the Danish church for more than 150 years. By royal decree, it was used in all churches—a copy was to be chained to the chair of the parish clerk!—and in all schools.

After the religious renewal brought by the Reformation, Danish church life in the latter part of the sixteenth and the first half of the seventeenth centuries was characterized by a rather staid and unimaginative orthodoxy. The poems and hymns of Thomas Hansen Kingo (1634–1703) stand out against the literary barrenness of this period as an exceptional phenomenon.

Kingo, Denmark's first great hymnwriter, is often referred to as "the singer of orthodoxy," yet no one can read his soul-stirring hymns with their profound sense of sin and grace without feeling that he had a deeper concept of life in Christ than a mere dogmatic training could give him. The king, to whom Kingo had dedicated a volume of his hymns, appointed him bishop of Fynn when he was only forty-two years of age. He continued to write hymns, while serving his diocese with earnestness and ability.

In 1683 King Christian V commissioned Thomas Kingo to prepare and publish a new church hymnal for Denmark and Norway. His commission directed him to eliminate present undesirable hymns, to revise antiquated rhymes and expressions, and to adopt two new hymns by himself or another for every pericope of the church year. Kingo attacked the project assiduously, and in six years produced a hymnal draft containing 267 hymns, of which 137 were his own. This however was rejected, on the basis that too many of the old familiar hymns had been changed or eliminated. The final book prepared by a committee, which came to be known as "Kingo's Hymnal," contained 297 hymns, of which eighty-five were by Kingo. This hymnal served the church for more than a hundred years.

The LBW has four of Kingo's hymns: "All who believe and are baptized" (LBW 194), "O Jesus, blessed Lord" (LBW 220), "On my heart imprint your image" (LBW 102), and "Praise and thanks and adoration" (LBW 470).

The movement born in Halle, Germany, which came to be termed Pietism (see above, p. 29) spread north in the middle of the eighteenth century to Scandinavia. Stressing the individual's need of repentance, conversion, and an intimate personal relationship with Christ, it found a welcome among Danish people famished through the years of dry preaching which, while doctrinally correct, had lacked the spiritual nourishment of Bible study and prayer.

The son of a Lutheran pastor, with two brothers also in the ministry, Hans Adolph Brorson (1694–1764) was an ardent Pietist. Serving in neighboring parishes in the southern part of Jutland, the three clergy brothers labored zealously to increase church attendance, revive family devotions, encourage Bible reading and hymn singing, and minimize the worldly amusements which led Christians astray. A revival took place with such effectiveness that its spirit could still be marked in the parish for two centuries afterward.

In 1732 Brorson produced a small booklet of ten hymns, seven of which were for the Christmas season. This collection of lyrical hymns served to establish his place among the greatest of the Scandinavian hymnwriters. Encouraged by the good reception which these hymns received, he continued to write and also translate hymns from German. A volume of his hymns was published in 1739. These were of varying quality, but many of them continued to be sung in succeeding generations, and earned him the title of "the sweet singer of Pietism."

Two of Brorson's hymns appear in the LBW: one of his Christmas hymns, "Your little ones, dear Lord" (LBW 52), and his great hymn based on Revelation 7:9–17, "Who is this host arrayed in white" (LBW 314).

Brorson's hymns achieved great popularity during the first half of the eighteenth century, and there was great demand to have them included in the official hymnbook. Commissioned by the king to prepare a new book, Erik Pontoppidan published his *Den nye Psalmebog* in 1740. The hymnal, which was a revision of Kingo's with the addition of Brorson's hymns, never enjoyed widespread acceptance.

The LBW also contains two hymns by a Danish woman hymnwriter of this period, Birgitte Katerine Hertz Boye (1742–1824). Each consists of a single stanza. They are: "He is arisen! Glorious Word!" (LBW 138), and "Rejoice, rejoice this happy morn" (LBW 43). Boye contributed 124 hymns and 24 translations to a collection prepared by Ludvig Harboe and Ove Guldberg. This collection, however, like Pontoppidan's, failed to replace the Kingo hymnal.

A third hymnal, Bishop C. Balle's *Evangelisk-Kristelig Salmebog,* 1797, also failed to take the place of Kingo's. Out of reaction to Balle's book, which was criticized as being rationalistic and having omitted a large number of Kingo's and Brorson's hymns, appeared the *Roskilde Konvents Salmebog* (1855, with subsequent editions in 1873 and 1890).

A towering giant in Danish church life during the nineteenth century was Nicolai Frederik Severin Grundtvig (1783–1872). He was the youngest of five children who grew up in a Lutheran parsonage at Udby, a country parish in Sjælland. He appeared on the scene during a period when Rationalism was rampant, and many pastors were preaching an emasculated version of the gospel. Like his father before him, the young Grundtvig studied for the ministry. He entered a vigorous challenge to the prevailing spirit of his time with an eloquent probation sermon connected with his application for ordination. He denounced the Rationalist clergy with his question, "Why has the Word of God disappeared from His house?" As a result, he became involved in a series of lengthy and difficult controversies with the church authorities.

The limits of this article do not allow a delineation of the struggles and triumphs which at last brought him acclaim in the Nordic countries and beyond as a historian, poet, educator, preacher, religious philosopher, hymnologist, and folk leader. Perhaps he will be remembered most, however, for his hymns. When his fiftieth anniversary as a pastor was celebrated in 1861, the king conferred upon him the title of bishop. Money was presented to him to finance a popular edition of his *Sang-Värk til den Danske Kirke.*

His masterful hymns still dominate the Danish hymnbook. He sang for all seasons of the Christian year, but he is known above all as the poet of Pentecost. He wrote a number of hymns lifting up the work of the Holy Spirit. Professor Martensen caught the essence of Grundtvig's legacy when he paid tribute to "his conception of the spiritual as the reality besides which all other things are nothing but shadows, and of the spirit-inspired word as the mightiest power in human life."[†]

The LBW has included an assortment of seven hymns by Grundtvig: "Bright and glorious is the sky" (LBW 75), "Built on a rock" (LBW 365), "Cradling children in his arm" (LBW 193), "God's Word is our great heritage" (LBW 239), "Peace, to soothe our bitter woes" (LBW 338), "Spirit of God, sent from heaven abroad" (LBW 285), and "The bells of Christmas chime once more" (LBW 62).[‡]

A contemporary of Grundtvig was Bernhardt Severin Ingemann (1789–1862). A teacher and writer of historical novels, he also wrote hymns which have enjoyed widespread popularity in Denmark. While they lack the theological depth of Kingo, Brorson, or Grundtvig, they nevertheless breathe a spirit of childlike trust in the goodness and love of God. Ingemann is represented in LBW with a hymn rather untypical of his style, "Through the night of doubt and sorrow."

Danish Hymn Tunes

While the Mortensen (1528) and Tausen (1544) collections contained some tunes, Thomissön's ambitious *Psalmebog* of 1569 provided 203 melodies for its 268 hymns, drawn primarily from German chorale tunes and Danish folksong. Containing the first music printed with movable

[†]Jens Christian Aaberg, *Hymns and Hymnwriters of Denmark* (Des Moines, Iowa: Committee on Publication of the Danish Evangelical Lutheran Church in America, 1945), 157.

[‡]"O day full of grace" (LBW 161) is not a translation of Grundtvig's hymn with the same opening line, but is a new translation of a version of the pre-Reformation Nordic "day song" which also inspired Grundtvig's hymn.

type in Denmark, this hymnal is today the oldest source of a number of tunes. Originally planned for release in the same year as Thomissön's *Psalmebog,* Niels Jesperson's *Gradual. En Almindelig Sangbog* of 1573 contained melodies for the hymnals in use at the time. The sixty Danish hymns in the *Gradual* were arranged according to the church year. In addition there were Latin Introits and Alleluias for the entire liturgical year.

Thomissön's and Jesperson's books were replaced in 1699 by "Kingo's Hymnal," and his *Gradual.* At the hand of Kingo, many of the older melodies were extensively altered to achieve the rhythmic variety he desired.

The first publication of Pontippidan's *Psalmebog* (1740), which was patterned after Johann Freylinghausen's (LBW 32) *Geistreiches Gesang-Buch,* included seventy-six tunes in the appendix to a text edition. The second edition, 1742, which had one hundred melodies printed over the words, was the last official hymnal printed with music in Denmark. Thereafter the music was published separately in books for the organist.

The first such chorale book was F. C. Breitendich's *Fuldstaendig Choral-Bog,* 1764. Containing 196 melodies with figured bass, it drew on the 1699 *Gradual,* as well as various Pietist collections such as Frey-linghausen's. The "reform" movement toward the isometric chorale in vogue throughout Europe at the time can be seen clearly in Breitendich's chorale book, and the development was brought to completion in the *Kirke-Melodierne,* 1781, and *Choral-Bog,* 1783, of Niels Schiorring and the *Koral-Melodier,* 1801, of Harnock Otto Conrad Zinck. Melodies in these latter collections were in strictly regular rhythm with fermatas at the end of each phrase.

Grundtvig's new popular and national tone led to a revolution in Danish church song, and melodies were written in the new Romantic style by such composers as C. E. F. Weyse (LBW 161), A. P. Berggren (LBW 298), J. P. E. Hartmann, and A. Winding, and were included in chorale books such as those published by Henrik Rung (1857) and Christian Barnekow (1892).

NORWAY

Mandus A. Egge

Norwegian hymnody, separate from Scandinavian hymnody, particularly that of Denmark, did not develop until after Norway became an independent nation in 1814. Being a part of the Kingdom of Denmark until that time, and with the church being a state church, the hymn and chorale books from Hans Thomissön's (LBW 227) *Den danske Psalmebog* of 1569 to H. O. C. Zinck's *Koral-Melodier,* 1801, were used in both countries. The history of Norwegian hymnody, separate from that of Denmark, really begins about the middle of the nineteenth century. Norway, however, had been a Christian nation since the year one thousand, and a Lutheran nation since shortly after the Lutheran Reformation, and so there were at least some Christian songs among the people other than those of the great Danish hymnwriters. Among these were poems by Petter Dass (1647–1707, LBW 244), whose catechism songs set to old church melodies became very popular, and by Johan Nordahl Brun (1745–1816, LBW 227).

In 1834, Wilhelm Andreas Wexels (LBW 351), catechist at Our Savior's Church in Oslo, produced a small volume of hymns for use in schools and homes, and in 1840 a collection of 714 hymns titled, in

English translation, *Christian Hymns*. Only fifteen hymns were original however, the majority being translations from Swedish and German sources as well as Danish. Wexels produced additional books later, and in 1849 proposed that his latest collection of 504 hymns be considered for a church hymnal. His collection was severely criticized and was not approved by the Church of Norway. He continued his work and in 1859 submitted another edition of *Christian Hymns* containing 850 hymns. His work was again rejected. One of his hymns, "Oh, happy day when we shall stand," is included in the LBW.

(Wexel's niece, Maria Wexelsen [1832–1911], is also represented by a hymn in the LBW: "I am so glad each Christmas Eve" [LBW 69].)

The tunes from Thomas Kingo's (LBW 102) 1699 hymnbook were well-established throughout Norway, supplemented by Pietist tunes. Because of Norway's special geographic conditions, however, traditions varied greatly, and melodies were sung very differently from one locality to another. One writer noted in 1857 that in outlying regions parishioners sang from memory, adding ornaments to the melody as each felt inspired. Organists, when there was an organ in the church, filled in the slow tempos with their own trills and interludes.

The first authorized Norwegian chorale book, Ole A. Lindeman's 1835 *Choralebog,* was based largely on that of Zinck, supplemented with tunes from F. C. Breitendich's and Niels Schiorring's collections, all from Denmark. Lindeman's four-part harmonizations were quite modern and he initiated the Norwegian custom of harmonizing repetitions differently. Like the collections on which it was patterned, however, the *Choralebog* gave all the tunes in strictly regular rhythm.

It remained for two competent hymnists, one a poet and the other a musician, to provide the Church of Norway with a hymnal that was more representative of the Norwegian people, a collection which has essentially remained the church's hymnal until now. The poet was Magnus Brostrup Landstad (LBW 310), a son of a pastor and himself a pastor, and the musician was Ludvig Matthias Lindeman (LBW 285), a son of a church organist (Ole A. Lindeman) and himself a church organist.

Landstad, whom E. E. Ryden calls "a bard of the frozen fjords," was born in 1802 in Måsøy, Finnmarken, Norway, where his father was pastor of the northernmost church in the world. In the 1840s, while he was serving a parish at Seljord in the beautiful Telemark area, the Department of Church Affairs asked Landstad to prepare a national hymnal. Not until 1852, however, after moving to a parish in Fredrikshald and being provided an assistant pastor, did he accept the assignment. In 1861 he submitted his proposal for the contents of a hymnal. Though his work was generally well received, one of Norway's leading newspapers, *Morgenbladet,* criticized particularly the omission of certain hymns and the language used in the book. Landstad replied by writing "Om Salmebogen" (About the Hymnal) which was published in *Morgenbladet,* and later in book form. A few sentences will indicate his attitude:

> "If we are to get a new hymnal we must meet on the common ground of faith in love. We must not cling to our preconceived notions; not let ourselves be influenced too strongly by our own tastes, nor by our own desires, as though we were the only ones entitled to a hearing. We must concede that others may also have well-founded demands that ought to be considered . . . . A church hymnal has the lofty mission of serving as the medium of confession, of prayer, and of praise, during the service in the sanctuary, as well as in the home."

Concerning certain hymns which were omitted he wrote,

> "But the sickly subjectivity, which 'rests' in the varying moods of pious feelings and godly longings, and yet does not possess any of the boldness and power of true faith—such as we find in Luther's and Kingo's hymns—this type of church hymn must be excluded."†

Landstad revised his work several times, and finally in 1869 the book was authorized for use in public services. By the end of 1870 Landstad's *Kirkesalmebog* had been introduced into 648 of the 923 parishes in Norway.

J. N. Skaar wrote in *Norsk Salmehistorie* in 1879, "Landstad's work in folk-song gave a decidedly Norwegian ring to his hymns, but he did not succeed in liberating himself entirely from his Danish patterns. . . . His hymns are marked by a popular tone, but they also possess pure warmth and earnestness and a churchly spirit. . . . In a masterly manner he restored the old hymn. Altho his hymns, in poetic flight, cannot rank with Kingo's, still in depth of feeling, in truth and sobriety of sentiment, in simplicity, in clear and open confession of that which is most precious to the heart of the Christian, in these Landstad's hymns rank equal to, if not above, the best in the possession of our Church." (Dahle, p. 196)

Three of Landstad's hymns are included in the LBW: "To you, omniscient Lord of all" (LBW 310), "A multitude comes from the east and the west" (LBW 313), and "I know of a sleep in Jesus' name" (LBW 342).

When Landstad demanded in 1857 that the authorization of Ole Lindeman's *Choralebog* be withdrawn, a discussion concerning the rhythmic principles of hymn melodies arose which was to last for twenty years. Among those advocating that the Reformation chorales be restored to their original rhythmical forms were J. D. Behrens, Erik Hoff (LBW 256), and O. Winter-Hjelm, whose *37 aeldre Salmemelodier,* 1876, was an important essay on the development and character of the Lutheran chorale. Opposing them was the Romanticist of Norwegian church music, Ludvig M. Lindeman.

Lindeman (1812–1887), who became a recognized organist in the Scandinavian countries and throughout Europe and England, is remembered and honored primarily for his work in collecting and compiling folk melodies of the Norwegian people and for his *Koralbog*. He began his work in folk music in 1840 and that year published a book of melodies for Wexels' hymnal and a few small collections of folk tunes. That year, also, he began a series of journeys throughout Norway, into the valleys and among the fjords, to listen to people sing old songs. On one of these journeys, during the summer of 1848, he traveled through Valders, a valley toward the northwest from Oslo, which resulted in three collections, one of 86 old hymn tunes, one of 83 ancient folk tunes, and one of 13 "melodies." He avoided the wealthy and the elite and visited primarily the poor and the uneducated because these people were least affected by education and culture and the melodies were therefore pure. The melodies were most frequently secured from the elderly, and from "spillemenn" (fiddlers). Each melody was written down to be reworked later. One of the difficulties was that these people did not always follow the tempered scale, and so it was difficult to determine which of two notes they were singing, that is, a quarter tone higher or lower. Lindeman tried to get the singer to decide which of the two tones was

†John Dahle, *Library of Christian Hymns.* Translated by M. Casper Johnshoy (Minneapolis: Augsburg Publishing House, 1925), 193–194.

correct, the higher or the lower. Other difficulties were that the singers did not always sing rhythmically and that verses and lines were of varying lengths. Tunes were made to conform to the words. Patience was of the essence, but Lindeman succeeded remarkably well.

After working out the melodies, Lindeman harmonized them. With remarkable skill he succeeded in carrying the character of the melody into the harmonization, giving the harmonizations a distinctly Norwegian flavor. His first collection, *Aeldre og Nyere Norske Fjeldmelodier* ("Older and Newer Norwegian Folkmelodies"), was published in 1853. One of the melodies included in this publication was "Den store hvide Flok" (LBW 314). Several other collections followed.

Lindeman's most important contribution was the *Koralbog* which was published in 1872 and authorized for use in the churches in 1877. This book contains the melodies with accompaniment for Landstad's hymnal. The book includes old chorales in use in the churches in Norway at the time together with many new melodies, mostly folktunes Lindeman had found. Although he did not favor the return to the original rhythmic forms of the chorale tunes, Lindeman put new life into the singing of hymns in the church by replacing the deadly uniform rhythms and slow tempos with dotted rhythms, more rapid tempos, and rests at the ends of phrases rather than fermatas. The introduction of many new folk tunes was also important. His harmonizations were radical, which made for greater interest, but also led to criticism. At Lindeman's funeral, however, it was said that "He taught the Norwegian people to sing."[†]

Seven tunes by Lindeman are included in the LBW: "Fred til Bod" (LBW 147, 338), "Du som gaar ud" (LBW 285), "Naar mit Öie" (LBW 301), "I Himmelen, I Himmelen" (LBW 330), "Kirken den er et gammelt Hus" (LBW 365), "Gud skal alting Mage" (LBW 458), and "Her vil ties" (LBW 481).

Also represented in the LBW are the composer Peder Knudsen (1819–1863) whose tune "Jeg er saa glad" is at LBW 69, and Ulrik Koren (1826–1910), a Norwegian-born pastor whose hymn "Al verden nu raabe for Herren med fryd" (LBW 256) was published in the United States in 1874.

ICELAND

Shirley McCreedy

Migration to Iceland had taken place beginning in the year 870 A.D. when Norwegian noblemen and chieftains rejected the tyrannical rule of the first Norwegian monarch. Other groups came from England, Scotland, and Ireland, descendants of Vikings who had settled earlier in the British Isles.

The art of music has been practiced in Iceland since the time of that most famous of all her sons, Leifur Eiriksson, who sailed for Greenland in the tenth century and landed on the coast of New England. The teaching of singing began at Hólar in 1107, with the first bishop instigating its practice. A French priest, Father Richini, was brought to Hólar to serve as chaplain and, more especially, to teach music.

The early bishops became noted for their singing. The common people

---

[†]E. E. Ryden, *The Story of Christian Hymnody* (Rock Island, Ill.; Augustana Book Concern, 1959), 231.

learned the responses to the liturgy. Much antiphonal and responsive music was composed to Latin texts. As time went on they translated the psalms and canticles and other songs into their native tongue. The Roman Catholic Era had brought the Gregorian Chant across the water; the Reformation added its own song, and so it continued. It was folk-music in the purest sense of the word, as indigenous to Iceland as the falcon or the ptarmigan.

Like Norway, Iceland was under sovereignty of the Danish crown at the time of the Reformation. Gizur Einarsson, who had studied with Martin Luther (LBW 48) and Philipp Melanchthon at Wittenberg, introduced the Reformation to Iceland. Made bishop of Skalholt at age twenty-five, Einarsson replaced the Roman Mass with the liturgy prepared by Johannes Bugenhagen (LBW 103) in 1527 for worship in Denmark. The earliest Lutheran hymnbook seems to have consisted of a few hymns translated into Icelandic from *Det kristelige Messeembede* published by Hans Mortensen at Malmö in 1528.

Oddur Gottskalksson's translation of the New Testament was published in Skalholt in 1540—ten years before the victory of the Reformation in Iceland was certain. It was Bishop Gudbrandur Thorlaksson who secured the position of Lutheran doctrine and rite in Iceland and prepared the first Icelandic translation Bible, published at Hólar in 1584. The printing of the Bible in Icelandic was immensely significant in the preservation of the language.

Thorlaksson's hymnal, *Ein ny Psalma Bok,* 1589, and service book, *Graduale. Ein Almenneleg Messusöngs Bok* (called *Grallarinn*), 1594, were patterned to some degree after two Danish books—Hans Thomissön's *Den danske Psalmebog* (1569) and Niels Jesperson's *Gradual* (1573). The *Psalma Bok* and the *Grallarinn,* which preserved church song in the ancient modes, were used by Icelanders for well over two hundred years.

The prolific publications of the period immediately following the Reformation set the tone for an intense personal and communal piety throughout Iceland. A strong religious tradition gradually became the heritage of every farm family, and by the mid-1700s regular religious exercises—church attendance and daily prayers with reading and singing, especially during Lent—had become universal.

This fervent personal devotion found expression in a number of fine literary works written in the best Icelandic tradition. Among these were Hallgrimur Petursson's (1614–1674) *Passiusalmer*—fifty passion hymns completed in 1659 and printed at Hólar in 1666. Written to be sung to sixteenth-century German chorale tunes, these hymns consisted of fifteen to twenty stanzas each.

> During the three centuries that have passed since their first appearance, they have been reprinted sixty-five times. . . . The common people of Iceland have taken these poems closely to their hearts . . . finding in them consolation and strength, . . . the child turning to them for its first words of prayer. . . . In the battle of life with its trials and tribulations their lines have sprung to the lips; . . . in the last conflict they have served best to strengthen and console, and were unfailingly used when loved ones were laid to their final rest. The Hymns of the Passion . . . were sung or read during Lent in every Icelandic home; one hymn each evening. Today they are broadcast throughout Lent on the radio. Thus Hallgrimur has been the companion of every child of Iceland, from the cradle to the grave, for three centuries. His contribution to

the religious life of the nation and its spiritual endurance in the hard days gone by can never be fully estimated.†

Charles Venn Pilcher was the first to translate the *Passion-Hymns of Iceland* into English (London, 1913). This publication contains short versions of fourteen of Hallgrimur Petursson's hymns. Ten years later an enlarged and revised edition, *Icelandic Meditations on the Passion,* was published in New York.

We are also indebted to C. Venn Pilcher for his translations from the hymns of Valdimar Briem, another giant of Icelandic hymnody. One hundred forty-two of Briem's texts appeared in the 1886 Icelandic Hymnal. "How marvelous God's greatness" is included in the LBW (#515).

Until the mid-nineteenth century, Iceland seems to have depended largely on Denmark for its hymns, especially those of Thomas Kingo (LBW 102). The first comprehensive Icelandic hymnal, *Nyr vidbaetir vid hina evangelisku salmabok,* 1861, was based on the official Danish hymnal of the time, the *Roskilde Konvents Salmebog,* 1855, and contained, in addition to some Icelandic texts, a large number of hymns by Kingo, as well as those of Hans A. Brorson (LBW 52), Birgitte K. Boye (LBW 43), Nicolai F. S. Grundtvig (LBW 62), and Bernhardt S. Ingemann (LBW 355).

The nineteenth century saw the rise of a number of gifted native poets. In his *Passion-Hymns of Iceland,* Pilcher singles out Helgi Halfdanarson (1826-1894), former principal of the Theological Seminary in Reykjavik and noted translator who contributed 211 hymns to the 1886 Hymnal; Dr. Matthias Jochumsson (1835-1920), author of the Icelandic Millennial Hymn ("O Gud Vors Lands"), the national anthem; Pall Jonsson (1812-1889), a priest at Vikvak, Skag.; Arnor Jonsson (1771-1853) of Vatnsfirdi; and Bjorn Halldorsson Sr. (died 1841) from Gardi. Other nineteenth-century poets include Steingrimur Bjarnason Thorsteinsson (1831-1913), author of many works in praise of his country and its beauty of nature who was represented in the *Service Book and Hymnal,* 1958 ("The fading day adorns the west," #236); Stefan Thorarensen (1831-1892); Bjorn Halldorsson (1823-1882); and Fridrik Fridriksson (1868-1961). The 1886 *Salmabok* was the first to contain a large proportion of native Icelandic hymns.

The most comprehensive treatise on Icelandic music was written by Bjarni Thorsteinsson, author of *Islensk Pjodlog.* A minister in Siglufirdi, Thorsteinsson spent twenty-five years gathering music from all over Iceland, and compiled a 950-page thesis (musical scores included). Beginning with the liturgical music of the first Icelandic bishops, it follows through the development with technical data and musical scores chronologically arranged. He reveals how some of the hymns were taken from Icelandic folk songs, the *Vikivakar,* for example, and tells how the *Rimur* developed from the liturgical chanting. Thorsteinsson points out that the Danish composer, A. P. Berggren (LBW 298), had collected many folk songs from Iceland and used them in his hymn book in Denmark.

Through the centuries an elaborate paraphrasing of hymn tunes developed in Iceland. The melodies were often sung as *Tvisöngur*—a

†Sigurbjorn Einarson, Introduction to *Hymns of the Passion.* Translated by Arthur Charles Gook. (Reykjavik, 1966).

Coincidentally, Arthur Charles Gook completed the English translations of the entire fifty Passion Hymns (a formidable task) shortly before his death in 1959, and they were published in 1966, exactly three hundred years after the beloved poet-priest had completed and published (respectively) the original Passion Hymns.

kind of two-part organum in slow tempo which combined parallel fifths and contrary motion with unisons, octaves, and thirds. This popular tradition was retained in some localities until the beginning of the present century.

Influenced by Christoph E. F. Weyse (LBW 161), Pétur Guðjonsson edited a hymnbook with unison tunes in 1861, which he followed with a three-part chorale book (published posthumously in 1878). Jónas Helgason continued in the Weyse tradition with his chorale book of 1884 (supplement, 1886), Iceland's first four-part chorale book.

Iceland's earliest recognized composer was Sveinbjorn Sveinbjornsson, who wrote the music for "O Gud Vors Lands." Other famous and well-loved composers, all born before the turn of the century, have written both sacred and secular volumes—Sigfus Einarsson, Sigvaldi Kaldalons, Bjorgvin Gudmundsson, and Sigurdur Thordarson.

SWEDEN
Joel W. Lundeen

The hymn tradition of the Church of Sweden is probably unique in several ways. It is doubtful that in any other church official hymnals were used for so long a period of time or had such a great influence on national culture. The "Old Psalmbok"† of 1695 was used for 125 years and more; the 1819 "Wallin Psalmbok" for 118 years. The Psalmbok, especially the 1819 one, came to be regarded as a national treasure, a cultural classic much in the same way as *The Book of Common Prayer* has been regarded in English-speaking lands. The core of the 1937 Psalmbok is still the 1819 Psalmbok, as can be expected of any Psalmbok of the future. For Swedes the Psalmbok became much more than a collection of hymns for use in public worship; it became the people's prayer book and chief devotional resource, as the diary of Dag Hammarskjöld and much of Swedish literature attests.

Sweden's Reformer, Olavus Petri (1493–1552), like Martin Luther (LBW 48) in Germany, saw the need for evangelical hymnody in the vernacular and became himself his country's first vernacular hymnist. In 1526, only two years after Luther's publication of his first small collection of hymns, Olavus published in Stockholm his *Svenske Songer eller Wijsor* ("Swedish Hymns and Songs") of which no copy is today in existence. It probably contained eight to twelve hymns. Enlarged editions of the book were published in 1530 and 1536. Although much of the contents of these books consisted of translations of Latin and German hymns (the *Te Deum,* for instance) and paraphrases of the Old Testament Psalter, some seems to have been original with Olavus. Several hymns still in use in Sweden are attributed to him.

But it is Olavus' brother, Laurentius Petri, the first evangelical archbishop of the kingdom, who is usually called "the father of Swedish hymnody." Although himself the author of several hymns, it is chiefly as the editor and promoter of the most widely-used sixteenth-century hymnals that he deserves that honor. His hymnbooks of 1543, the first to have the title *Then Swenska Psalmboken,* and of 1549, 1567, and 1572— each much enlarged from its predecessor—were all, however, based on

---

†"Psalmbok" or "Psalmebog" in the Scandinavian languages means "Hymnal"; "psalm" in those languages equals "hymn" in English—it has no reference to the Old Testament Psalter. For convenience, however, the term "Psalmbok" will be used throughout this article.

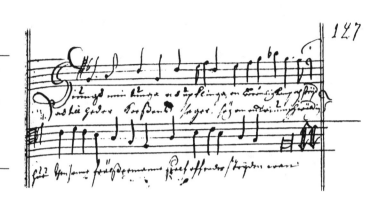

Right: "Upp min tunga" (LBW 155) as it appeared in the Riddar-holmskyrkans handskrivna koralbok, *1694. Below: Title page of* Then Swenska Psalmboken, *Stockholm, 1697, and "Upp min tunga" as it appeared in that collection.*

157.

Vp min tunga at lofsiunga   En berömlig kamp och strijd/ Hwilken wärfde
Som sigh hände när Gudh sände Oß til hielp sin Son här nidh.

At wij ärfde Seger och en ewig frijd.

1. VP min tunga at lofsiunga
   En berömlig kamp och strijd/
   Som sigh hände när Gudh sände
   Oß til hielp sin Son här nidh.
   Hwilken wärfde At wij ärfde
   Seger och en ewig frijd.
2. Ormen rådde och förmådde

Ewa

Olavus' earlier books and form a direct continuity from them to the first officially authorized hymnal, that of 1643 (usually called "The Upsala Psalmbok"); it in turn was a revision of a 1622 book (commonly called "The Old Upsala Psalmbok").

During the Reformation, congregational singing caught on slowly in Sweden. Except in Stockholm and the other larger cities the process seems to have been much more gradual there than in Germany. During the sixteenth and seventeenth centuries, while the desire for a uniform official book for the whole realm grew increasingly strong, many unofficial books, either private or diocesan, were published; these added greatly to the store of hymnody which could eventually be included in the officially authorized books.

Then Swenska Psalmboken, 1695, was the first both to be officially authorized and to have its use required in all churches of the land. It was largely the work of Bishop Jesper Svedberg of Skara (LBW 440). His chief collaborators were Bishops Haquin Spegel and Isaac Kolmodin, considered to be along with him among Sweden's greatest hymnwriters. Svedberg had published in 1694 at his own expense a "Proposed Psalmbok," which was criticized for being too subjective, perhaps unorthodox, and was rejected by the national church. It was this proposed hymnal, nevertheless, which was sent to America for the use of the Swedish churches in the Delaware Valley. But the officially accepted book of 1695 turned out, after all, to be basically Svedberg's Psalmbok, after the excision of a number of his hymns and the alteration of others. (Many of these hymns were included in later Psalmboks.) This book served the Church of Sweden for 124 years (from 1695 to 1819), and in some places even longer. On the whole, it could be said of it that it expresses excellently both the theological and the devotional essence of the Period of Orthodoxy in Sweden.

The adoption of the 1695 Psalmbok coincided roughly with the beginning of Pietism in Sweden's religious life. Because the Pietists felt it did not allow enough expression for the subjective side of religious life, they began to publish supplementary hymn collections, for use at private religious gatherings, which were soon known widely throughout the land. The song book of the conservative Pietists, *Mose och Lambens wisor* ("Songs of Moses and the Lamb"), was published in its first edition in 1717 and had many subsequent editions well into the nineteenth century. Similar books were published by the more radical Pietists beginning in 1732 (containing Swedish versions of the hymns of Gerhard Tersteegen [LBW 249]), by the Moravians in 1743–45 (with many new hymns by Anders Carl Rutstrom, some of which are now generally accepted), and others. These made contributions to later, official hymnbooks.

Language, poetic taste, and religious needs changed much in the century and a quarter during which the "Old Psalmbok" of 1695 was in use. Many efforts at revising it failed, though again all contributed to later hymn books. Finally in 1819 Sweden's second and greatest official hymnal, commonly called "Wallin's Psalmbok," was authorized and appointed for use in the churches.

The 1819 book was largely the work of Johan Olaf Wallin (LBW 73), later Archbishop of Upsala, Sweden's greatest hymnwriter. It contained some 130 original texts and 150 translations or major revisions by him. Among his chief collaborators were Bishop Frans Mikael Franzén (LBW 26), Samuel Johan Hedborn (LBW 247), and the writer and historian, Eric Gustav Geijer. The book represented both the high-point in classic

45

Swedish literary style and the blending of a new idealist romanticism with the older strict Lutheran orthodoxy. In time it came to win such a secure place in the hearts of the Swedish people that no other book could completely replace it.

At the time, however, it was different. It was no easier then to change from an old hymnal to a new one than it is for us today. Many congregations and groups of conservative Pietists, especially in the north of Sweden, clung tenaciously to "the old books" (including the old edition of Luther's Small Catechism with explanations, the old form of the liturgy—especially its direct form of Absolution after Confession of Sins —as well as the old hymnal). The old book continued to be reprinted into the twentieth century. Several groups of immigrants to America from Sweden (among them the founders of the present Bethel Lutheran Church in Willmar, Minnesota) came to this country expressly so that they could continue to use "the old books."

In Sweden the 1819 book was at first sharply criticized in many quarters for signs of the influence of rationalism and for disrespect for the old classic, orthodox tradition. Many efforts were made to revise or supplant it. The most successful of them was a revision in the direction of stricter orthodoxy by Bishop J. H. Thomander and Dean Peter Wieselgren in 1849. Although rejected in Sweden, this revised Psalmbok was adopted in 1893 as the official hymnal in Swedish for the Augustana Lutheran Church in North America.

Although the 1819 book was a literary masterpiece, touched by the idealism and subjective mood of that age's poetic style, it did not wholly satisfy the Pietists either. Just as in the previous century, unofficial song books began to appear, often new editions of the eighteenth-century books. About the middle of the nineteenth century a new wave of revivalism, commonly called "the new evangelicalism," began to sweep the country. Its leader was the famous lay preacher, Carl Olof Rosenius (LBW 371). Because of close connections with similar Anglo-American movements, hymns from such sources, including the Gospel songs of Ira Sankey, William J. Kirkpatrick, William B. Bradbury (LBW 293), and others, became very popular in revivalist circles in Swedish translations. New hymns, more subjective in nature and lighter in style than those in the Psalmbok, were written in great profusion by Rosenius himself and by many of his followers. Among the most prolific and popular of these was Karolina ("Lina") Sandell Berg (LBW 474), "the Fanny Crosby of Sweden." The simple, rhythmic, and singable tunes of Oskar Ahnfelt (LBW 371), who traveled the country singing these songs to the accompaniment of his guitar, helped greatly to spread them. They began to be published in a collection called *Andeliga Sånger* ("Spiritual Songs") in constantly enlarging editions beginning in 1850 to our own time. Similar song books were also published by the more radical "free church" groups which tried more sharply to disassociate themselves from the national church. All these also have contributed something to the latest official hymnals. Again an American note: the first hymnal of any kind authorized by the Augustana Lutheran Church was a compilation of this type of hymn; called *Hemlandssånger* ("Homeland Songs"),† it was first published in 1891. This collection was expressly *not* intended for use at Sunday morning worship.

---

†A double reference to the Christian pilgrim's longing for his heavenly "homeland" and the Swedish immigrants' understandable nostalgia for the earthly "homeland" from which they had come.

46

Swedish Hymn Tunes

The preceding paragraphs deal primarily with the texts of Swedish hymns, not their tunes. The 1572 edition of *Then Swenska Psalmboken* contained four manuscript tunes, and the 1586 edition had the first printed tunes—for the Credo in Swedish and Latin. With the exception of the "Old Upsala Psalmbok" of 1622, which provided the melody line for a few of its hymns, no music was printed in the usual editions of the Psalmbok. The music, provided primarily for the use of the organist or cantor, was printed in a separate volume, as was generally customary in Germany and the other Scandinavian countries. This volume was called the "Koralbok" (Chorale book). Until the late seventeenth century these were often found only in handwritten (manuscript) form. Important manuscript collections were those from Kalmar, *c.* 1640; Mönsterås, 1646; and Riddarholm, 1694. Often collections from other lands—from Germany (Rostock, Stralsund, etc.) or Denmark (both Hans Thomissön's *Den danske Psalmebog* and Niels Jesperson's *Gradual,* for instance)—were used. But the preservation of the old traditions in church music from the Reformation and even before is clearly evident in the first official printed tune book, Harold Vallerius' *Koralpsalmboken* of 1697, a music edition of the 1695 Psalmbok, containing 254 tunes. Here are found the great Reformation chorales in their original rhythmic and modal forms together with traditional Swedish tunes and those inherited from the plainsong period—most with just a melody line and figured bass.

The eighteenth century saw many attempts to "modernize" the Koralbok, but without much success. This occurred with a vengeance in the 1820–1821 *Svensk Choralbok,* I & II, of C. J. F. Haeffner, intended to accompany the 1819 Psalmbok; here the tunes are harmonized in strict four-part choral style, triple and irregular meters are almost entirely deleted, the modal character of most tunes is lost, and the more florid, melismatic phrases in the melodies are severely truncated. This became the usual music used in Swedish churches until recent decades. Although altered, these tunes remained basically those used in earlier books and have kept that heritage alive.

Many were dissatisfied with Haeffner's approach. Olof Åhlström's 1832 chorale book attempted to strike a middle ground in the controversy between rhythmic and non-rhythmic chorales. A movement began to revive the older traditions in church music and to combine it with the best of the new. A book known as *Pettersson's Koralpsalmboken,* 1858, which was the first *Koralpsalmboken* to have both words and full music setting since Valerius' 1697 publication, included a number of tunes in the older rhythmic forms, and reached its tenth edition in 1901. C. E. Södling's *Svensk Folkets Choralmelodier,* 1878, employed rhythmic versions from the 1697 hymnbook. In the late nineteenth century a vigorous attempt was made by "The Friends of Church Music" society, led by Richard Norén and John Morén, to restore the older rhythmical and more melismatic form of traditional tunes and to write new, more appropriate music.

FINLAND

Toivo K. Harjunpaa

A partial use of vernacular hymnody was by no means unknown in the Latin services during the later Middle Ages. Clear evidence for this

47

comes also from Scandinavia. It is likely that in Finland, too, on major festivals the people were taught to join in brief responsorial stanzas in Finnish; some very archaic texts which survive may go back to this period. Conclusive evidence for this, however, so far has not been found. A number of Latin liturgical hymns, sequences, and school songs, serving the specific needs of the medieval Finnish Church, have been written and composed in Finland. An oral tradition of Finnish folk poetry, some of it with Christian themes, came into being before the end of the Middle Ages, and some of it of touching beauty. But the Reformers rejected it wholesale (including its indigenous meters) as "devil's work."

From the Middle Ages until 1809, Finland was politically united with Sweden. Thus the progress of the Reformation in Sweden had an influence on Finland, including worship. This was further aided by the fact that part of the population of Finland is Swedish-speaking.

Most of the books necessary for worship in Finnish were written by Michael Agricola (c. 1510–1557), the Finnish Reformer and "father of the Finnish literary language." His translations included the whole New Testament (1548) and large portions of the Old including the Psalter. He also published the Mass (1549) and a manual of occasional services as well as material for the divine office (Prayer Book). He did not issue a separate hymnal, but scattered among his other works are some thirty liturgical hymns, canticles, sequences, and antiphons, nearly all translated from Latin. This fact characterizes well Agricola's cautious and conservative nature as a Reformer. Though he had studied in Wittenberg, he did not include any of Martin Luther's (LBW 48) hymns among his translations. The Reformation hymnody is represented only by Nicolaus Decius' "Agnus Dei" paraphrase (LBW 111).

By at least 1540, a number of Agricola's contemporaries were also translating hymns and other liturgical texts for Finnish worship. Nineteen hymns not found among Agricola's translations are included in a Codex, named after its original compiler, M. J. Westh. This Codex included the first two of Luther's hymns in Finnish: his metric creed (LBW 374) and the Pentecost hymn "Nun bitten wir den Heiligen Geist" (LBW 317).

In 1578, the Swedish King John III authorized Jacob Finno (d. 1588), principal of the Cathedral School of Turku (Abo), to prepare necessary Finnish religious books. These included a hymnal. The King was keenly interested in the enrichment of worship, hoping to promote the reunion of Christendom through a return to the ideals and practices of the Patristic age. This first Finnish hymnal was published in 1583. Finno made ample use of the already existing hymnic material in Finnish which he further increased and improved. As a pattern and resource in his work, he used one of the more recent Swedish hymnals (1572). Though the number of hymns in both was the same (101), Finno's work was not a mere Finnish version of the Swedish original. Many of the hymns Finno translated directly from German. Lutheran hymnody was well represented in this hymnal and included sixteen hymns of Luther. Worship needs played a decisive part in the selection of hymns. Finno also wrote a few original hymns of his own, probably seven in all. Some of these and a substantial portion of his hymnal have remained in use through many revisions to this day. Several of these hymns served the catechetical needs of the Lutheran Church. By the time the hymnal appeared, King John had already given up his earlier overtures to Rome.

Mention must also be made of a collection of Latin hymnody and school songs which Jacob Finno is known to have assembled and revised theologically. It was published by his former student Theodoric Petri Rutha in Greifswald in 1582. This was the celebrated *Piae Cantiones,* a collection of seventy-four songs of medieval origin sung in the Cathedral school of Turku. Many were of continental origin; several have been traced to Bohemian sources. Others originated in Finland and some in Sweden. Since the 1850s several of the *Piae Cantiones* tunes have found their way to Anglo-American hymnals and collections of carols. In the *Service Book and Hymnal,* 1958, the second tune of "Divinum Mysterium" (#17) comes from *Piae Cantiones.*

After Finno, the foremost Finnish hymnodist was Hemming of Masku (d. 1619), a parish pastor near Turku. He was the author of the greatly enlarged second Finnish hymnal of 242 hymns, probably published in 1605. It included the whole Finno hymnal, only slightly revised, and over one hundred new hymns, mostly German, next Swedish, Latin, and for the first time, ten hymns of Danish origin. About twenty were written by Hemming. They and his translations manifest his superior poetic and literary qualities when compared with the work of Finno. This hymnal expressed well the theology and ethos of the emerging Lutheran orthodoxy. For most of that century, the Finnish hymnal remained substantially larger than any used in Sweden. Several enlarged editions appeared until 1700, the largest containing 300 hymns (1693). Hemming, too, was interested in *Piae Cantiones* and brought out his own Finnish translation (1616). In 1625, an enlarged Latin edition of *Piae Cantiones* appeared in Rostock for the Cathedral school of Viipuri (Viborg) in eastern Finland. Also, a revised and shorter version of Hemming's hymnal was published in 1621 by Olavus Elimaeus, the Bishop of Viipuri.

Even a Swedish hymnal of quality and substantial size appeared in Finland in 1673. Its author was the Bishop of Turku, Johan Gezelius. At a time when there was not yet a single, authorized hymnal in Sweden, this "Abo Hymnal" was also used in Sweden. But all such diocesan hymnals were superseded in 1695 by the royally authorized Swedish national hymnal (music edition, 1697). A corresponding authorized Finnish hymnal was published in 1701; both were in use in Finland until 1886. Little is known of the preparation of this new Finnish hymnal. The task was no doubt supervised by Bishop Gezelius, Jr. (d. 1718). It had the same number of hymns as the Swedish authorized version (413). But though it expressed the same manly and robust spirit of Lutheran orthodoxy as did the Swedish hymnal, it was far from a mere translation. With great tenacity and with only minor revisions, all but four of the earlier Finnish hymns were retained in 1701. On the other hand, almost all new hymns were translations from the 1695 hymnal. About 120 hymns in Finnish had no equivalent in the Swedish book. Comparison of the tunes produces similar results: some fifty tunes are found only in the Finnish music edition (1702). Some of these tunes are of Finnish origin. The common body of the tunes was quite large, numbering nearly 200. The 1702 music edition was the first of its kind in Finland. Previously—and long after 1702 —hand-written collections of tunes were used.

The new century brought a new type of hymnody to Finland through Sweden: the spiritual songs of an individualist type, unauthorized and sung in the illegal conventicles of Pietists and Moravians. Almost two centuries elapsed before these songs found their way to the authorized hymnals in Finland. The best known of the new collections was *Sions Sånger* (Songs of Zion), which appeared in Sweden in 1743–45 and as a Finnish translation in 1790. A leading contributor to the original edition was Johan Kahl whose hymn, "Arise, My Soul, Arise," is in our new

LBW (516). Pietism became a powerful religious factor in Finland, especially since the early nineteenth century. A number of separate movements gradually arose, most of them also institutionally organized, and with their separate collections of spiritual hymnody. However, as they all belong to the national Lutheran Church, they also use the authorized liturgy and hymnal.

The need for a new, both theologically and linguistically, more contemporaneous hymnal was felt in Finland in the early nineteenth century. A hymnal committee was appointed in 1817. Its intensive work under the able leadership of Archbishop J. Tengström created much interest, though the committee's large proposal (1836) was not adopted for public use. The new hymnal authorized in 1819 in Sweden was also partly used in the Swedish congregations in Finland.

New committees were appointed after the middle of the century to prepare hymnals in Finnish and Swedish. A significant feature now was the prominent way in which the nation's foremost cultural leaders participated in this work. On the Finnish committee were Elias Lönnrot, the publisher of the national epic *Kalevala,* and Julius Krohn who is represented in the LBW by hymn number 319. The leading lights in the Swedish committee were J. L. Runeberg (*Service Book and Hymnal,* 1958, #396), the "national poet of Finland"; Z. Topelius; and L. Stenbäck. Both committees published several proposals before satisfactory results were achieved. The Church Assembly authorized both hymnals in 1886. The Finnish had 536 hymns, the Swedish 500. Both books kept in revised form most of the contents of the previous hymnals. The final musical editor, Richard Faltin, closely followed the German choral tradition in the choice of needed tunes and in harmonization. This fourth Finnish hymnal did not find an enthusiastic reception among many of the rural people who belonged to the various revival movements; its distinguished creators knew better the rules of grammar and poetry than the heartbeat of earnest, popular piety. The old, robust hymnal (1701) was often found a truer friend in times of real need, and has not totally disappeared from use even today.

Dissatisfaction with the fourth hymnal was also gradually directed against the excessively German character of its music (The Faltin Choral Book, 1888; revised ed., 1903). Since 1890, a large number of beautiful folk melodies, long-used by various revival groups, had been "discovered." Voices were raised for their inclusion in the official hymnal as alternate melodies. Beginning in 1903, many of these tunes were gradually adopted for official use. In the LBW, the hymns 384 and 516 have tunes which represent Finnish religious folk music, melodically rooted in old chorales.

Slovak Hymnody

Jaroslav J. Vajda

The Slavs—and especially the Slovaks, who have adopted the ninth-century missionary brothers, Cyril and Methodius, as their patron saints—trace the beginnings of their literary and spiritual identity to those two Macedonian emissaries. Their legacy included translations into Old Slavonic of the four Gospels, the Book of Acts, the Epistles, a hymnal and breviary. The orginal manuscripts have been preserved only in copies dating from the tenth and eleventh centuries.

The earliest Slovak songs are found in the *Codex protoslavus Hankensteinianus,* an eighth-century manuscript, and they are religious in nature. The oldest Czech hymn, a Kyrie dating from the tenth century, is said to have been composed by St. Vojtech (Adalbert), the second bishop of Prague:

Hospodyne pomiluy ny	Lord, have mercy!
Ihu Xpe pomiluy ny	Christ, have mercy!
Ty spase wsseho mira	You Savior of the world
Spasyz ny y uslyss	save us and hear,
Hospodyne hlassy nassye	O Lord, our voices!
Day nam vssyem Hospodyne	Grant to us all, O Lord,
zzizn a mir vzemi	harvest and peace throughout the land!
Krles Krles Krles.	Kyrie eleison: :/: :/:

After the fall of Great Moravia in 907 to the Hungarians and the Battle of Pressburg (Bratislava), the Slavic nations were split; the Western Slavs, the Czechs, Slovaks, and Poles were separated from the Southern Slavs (the Bulgarians, Croats, and Serbs). Slovakia fell under the political domination of Hungary until 1918, and together with the Czechs, under the spiritual control of the German bishops until the Hussite and Lutheran Reformations. Latin became the dominant language in the church. The heritage of Cyril and Methodius was mocked and scorned by the new German and Hungarian masters, and it was only as a gesture of defiance and of national survival that the Slovaks and their Czech brothers maintained their vernacular traditions. This explains why the Czech reformers succeeded in gaining the support of their people when they pitted the power of the vernacular against the official Latin of their opponents. Hymns composed in the language of the people became the intimate expression of their national and religious convictions.

Prior to the Lutheran Reformation, several Bohemian collections of hymns had appeared with numerous hymns written by Czech authors. The first such known hymnal is one published January 13, 1501, containing eighty-nine hymns, of which twenty-one are by Matthias Kunvaldský (1460-1500), Ján Taborský (d. 1495), and Lucas of Prague (c. 1460-1528). The Bohemian Brethren produced a *Kancionál* of their own in 1505, which seems to have contained some 400 hymns. A second edition of still another hymnal by the Brethren was printed in 1519, and was supposed to have been edited by Lucas of Prague. Jan Roh (Horn)

(LBW 132) and his co-workers produced the hymnal in 1561 which contained 744 hymns, including sixty from the hymnbook of 1501, and whose title is identical with that of the unavailable hymnal of 1541.

These collections, though coinciding with the life and career of Martin Luther (LBW 48) in some cases, nevertheless attest to the explosive creativity of hymns in the vernacular prior to and apart from the Lutheran hymnody which soon caught up with and surpassed it. The exploration of this new terrain was accomplished by the time Luther was a youth of eighteen and some twenty-two years before he produced his "Achtliederbuch." In fact, Luther drew upon these sources as he rewrote the Czech reformers' Latin originals in German, and later Lutheran hymnodists and hymnal compilers drew upon the compositions of such writers as Michael Weisse (LBW 37), Jan Roh (Horn), and other Bohemian or Silesian hymnwriters.

It was in Moravia that the first hymnals of a Lutheran character appeared, those of Jakub Kunvaldský in 1572 and Tobiáš Závorka in 1602. Prior to the appearance of Tranovský's *Cithara Sanctorum* (1636), Slovak Lutherans made use of the Czech hymnbooks of the Brethren and Calixtenes. For one thing, they understood the language of the Czechs and had no need to produce hymnals of their own; for another, there was a dearth of Slovak Lutheran hymnwriters who were able to produce hymns in the Slovak language. Only after the disaster at the Battle of White Mountain, November 8, 1620, when the supply of hymnals from Bohemia dried up and numerous scholars emigrated from Bohemia, Moravia and Silesia to Slovakia, did Slovak hymnody develop.

If the Reformation required only fourteen days to spread throughout Germany, it took only a year or two to take root in Slovak lands. In Lubic already in 1520, the priest Thomas Preisner read Luther's 95 Theses from the pulpit to a large assembly of the faithful. As early as 1521, the Reformation claimed adherents in the Slovak mining towns, and the reformer of Bardejov and its vicinity was the well-known pupil of Luther, Leonard Stoeckel.

Slovakia was prepared for the Reformation when it broke upon Europe. Jan Hus's (1369?-1415) teaching was widespread and had conditioned the people for such a Reformation as Luther's. German merchants traveling and doing business in Slovakia brought with them some of the new religious concepts as well as books and particularly the Bible. Furthermore, many Slovak students attended German universities. For example, from 1522 to 1564 some 200 Slovak students were studying in Wittenberg alone. When they came home, they zealously spread Luther's teaching. In Hungary Calvinism took root rather than Lutheranism. As Bohemia came under the full control of the Catholics, and Hungary was busy fending off the Turks and could leave the Lutherans alone to practice their religion, Slovakia became the only Slavic land to develop and preserve Lutheranism in domesticated form.

The Lutherans in Slovakia were relatively free to practice their religion from the time of the Hungarians' defeat at the Battle of Mohacs in 1526 until the onset of the Counter-Reformation around 1604 under the direction of the Hapsburgs. As the Counter-Reformation grew in strength, it pushed the Protestants before it toward the East, toward Slovakia and Hungary and the Turks. Ahead of this wave a Lutheran pastor, Juraj Tranovský (LBW 96), born of Polish parents in Silesia, arrived in Slovakia to find his Wartburg in the Orava Castle where he produced the most important Slovak Lutheran book, his classic hymnal of 1636, the *Cithara Sanctorum,* known as the "Tranoscius."

52

Tranovský was not the first Slovak Lutheran hymnwriter, however, nor was his the first Slovak hymnal. Clearing the path to the "Tranoscius" were such hymnwriters and collectors as Ján Silvan (1493–1573), Juraj Banovský (d. 1561), Ján Pruno of Frăstak (1555–1586), Vavrinec Benedikt (1555–1615), Eliáš Láni (1570–1617), and Daniel Pribiš (c. 1580–c. 1645).

Silvan is called the first Slovak lyric poet. He wrote numerous hymns, several of which appeared in later hymnals. Benedikt, a professor of mathematics, wrote a Czech grammar and was the first to conform the long and short syllables of his hymn texts to the equivalent qualities of the musical notes. Láni, a beloved and distinguished church superintendent, was the outstanding hymnwriter prior to Tranovský. Eight of his hymns were preserved in Pribiš's *Catechism.*

Daniel Pribiš's *Catechism* of 1634 is an important source of Slovak hymnody before Tranovský. Pribiš added a supplement of 112 hymns to his translation of Luther's Catechism, the majority of which were taken over into the *Cithara Sanctorum.* Among the hymns of identifiable origins, there are eight hymns by Láni, seven by Pribiš, one by Cengler, and about sixty Old-Czech hymns. The remainder are of apparent Slovak origin. This collection is noteworthy also because Pribiš altered many Czech expressions in favor of their Slovak equivalents. Although this is the largest collection of Slovak/Czech hymns before the *Cithara,* Tranovský did not use this hymnal as a basis for his own because his hymnal was already completed by that time. Later editions of the *Cithara* did, however, draw upon Pribiš's *Catechism.*

Older than Pribiš's supplement is the hymn collection of Ján Pruno Fraštacký, whose primary purpose was to offer the first Slovak translation of Luther's *Small Catechism,* eleven pages of hymns being included incidentally. It is not likely that Tranovský considered this slender collection in compiling the *Cithara,* since it was quite antiquated by 1635, having been published in 1584.

The third and oldest collection is found in the *Bystrická Agenda,* actually the Czech Agenda of 1571 and 1581, consisting of fourteen chapters, to each of which were added appropriate hymns in order to save the pastor the trouble of having to hunt out hymns from larger collections. There are forty-two pages of hymns, many of which found their way into the *Cithara.* A number of Luther's hymns appear here for the first time in translations made on Slovak soil. In addition, there are a number of Latin medieval hymns in Czech translation and adaptations of Czech hymns. Sixteen of nineteen funeral antiphons are of Slovak Lutheran origin. It is from this treasure that Tranovský gleaned.

The *Cithara Sanctorum* ("Tranoscius")

Ján Mocko, Tranovský's biographer and student of his work, notes that as a hymnodist and pray-er Juraj Tranovský is unsurpassed in Slovakia to this day. That his contributions to the sacred literature of the Slovak Lutheran Church are monumental is beyond question. Only his early death prevented him from leaving a still greater heritage.

Tranovský prepared two other collections before the *Cithara Sanctorum.* His 150 Latin odes and hymns were published as *Odarum Sacrarum* in 1629. That the hymns in this collection were intended by Tranovský for use in congregational worship is confirmed by the inclusion of twenty harmonized melodies (in four parts) composed by Tranovský himself, with a melody for each metrical pattern. The use of Latin hymns in Lutheran churches, especially where Germans were more numerous, was not unusual even at this late date. The book was received with high respect by the learned and with delight by the general public.

Tranovský's *Phiala Odoramentorum,* an especially fine collection of prayers for public and private worship, was published in either 1631 or 1635. Beginning in 1653 these prayers were added to the *Cithara Sanctorum.* Tranovský intended for this work to be a temporary agenda until a more adequate one could be composed, but this was not realized until 1734!

Tranovský had scarcely completed this important work when he set himself to the still more important production of a hymnal. The Slovak Church had no hymnal of its own before 1636, but had to rely on Bohemian printed or manuscript hymnals, some of which contained Slovak hymns. After the White Mountain disaster, no more hymnals were forthcoming from Bohemia. Tranovský's enterprise therefore was eagerly anticipated by his fellow Lutherans. Their hopes were not unfulfilled, for when the *Cithara Sanctorum* ("Tranoscius") appeared in 1636, published by Vavrinec Brewer in Levoča, it was acclaimed by Lutherans near and far. More than any other work, it laid the foundation for a subsequent abundance of sacred literature of a high quality. It stood head and shoulders above any comparable book of its day. Tranovský did not live long enough to witness the acclaim his hymnal received from clergy and laity alike.

Mocko advances four reasons which led Tranovský to publish a separate hymnal for the Slovak Lutherans. 1) The dissatisfaction of Slovak Lutherans, after the Synod of Zilina, with Czech hymnody growing out of a theology based on the compromising Czech Confession of 1575. 2) The desire of Slovak Lutherans for more hymns by Luther than their Czech hymnals offered. 3) The immediate needs of his parishioners and exiles for an orthodox hymnal. 4) The confidence of Slovak Lutheran pastors and noblemen who loved the purity of the Word that Tranovský was the man to fulfill this particular destiny.

The first edition of the *Cithara Sanctorum* appeared in 1636 although the preface was written December 1, 1635.

The text of the title page reads:

> Old and new spiritual songs which the Christian Church can use with much benefit during the Seasons and on Festivals as well as in all its general and particular needs, to which are added hymns of Dr. M. Luther, all translated from the German into our Slovak language.
>
> By Pastor Juraj Tranovský, minister of the Lord in the church of Sv. Mikuláš in Liptov. Printed in Levoča, 1636. In addition to the foreword and index, containing 700 numbered pages.

Since Tranovský had found only four Slovak translations of Luther's hymns, he translated all the rest which were admittedly Luther's, and added them to these four. Nor did he exclude the longer hymns from the hymnal, as he saw them serving the purpose of "pilgrimage" hymns on long travels to the churches, and also as containing very worthwhile thoughts, although their quality did not necessarily match their length.

Of the 414 hymns, slightly more than 150 were from Tranovský's pen, either as translations or original. Not all can be traced accurately, because Tranovský in his modesty did not identify himself as the author or translator, although scholarship has established most of his compositions.

The *Cithara Sanctorum* was supplied with melody lines for the hymns, and Tranovský was concerned that all the hymns fit their melodies metrically. He revised certain texts in order to get the best reading of several extant versions, and to correct departures from the Scriptures.

The body of the hymnal was followed by lengthy and detailed instructions to the cantors for leading the singing of the hymns.

Subsequent Editions of the *Cithara Sanctorum*

A second edition of the *Cithara* appeared shortly after Tranovský's death. Published again by Vavrinec Brewer in Levoča, it bears the date 1638 on its title page, and 1639 in its colophon. This is an unaltered reprint of the first edition, except that the foreword, instructions to the cantors, the Latin salutatory verses, and the melodies are omitted.

Other editions followed rapidly, so that by the end of the seventeenth century, the *Cithara* had gone into ten editions, each one adding or subtracting elements of the earlier editions. The edition of 1696, or the tenth, published by Samuel Brewer in Levoča, became a definitive edition for subsequent editors. In the seventeenth edition (1768) the heading, "Of the Opposition and Temptations to the Church," and the twelve hymns beneath it had to be removed because of Jesuit censorship, and replaced with others of the same length.

The eighteenth edition had appeared by the Edict of Toleration of 1781, by which time the number of hymns had increased to 998–1001.

By the time the Edict of Toleration permitted the confession of Protestantism, the building of Lutheran churches where there were at least one hundred Lutheran families, and the calling of pastors and teachers, the climate within Lutheranism had deteriorated. Rationalism sought to "correct" the *Cithara* by adding supplementary hymns, which however always remained distinct from the closed body of the hymnal of 998 (or 1001) hymns. The first edition of this period (Vienna, 1786) and the next are replete with "corrections," extending even to the prayers.

Various editions were printed in Bratislava (Pressburg) some in Budin, others in Pest. Seeing the publication of the *Cithara* as a profitable enterprise, two Budapest publishers sought a monopoly on its printing. To control the integrity of the book, the Lutheran Church in Slovakia assumed the responsibility for its publication. The book was subsequently printed inside Slovakia and outside, in Germany as well as Hungary.

The edition of 1895, under the editorship of the foremost Tranovský scholar, Ján Mocko, is the most critical edition to date. It is by no means the last edition, for it was followed by six more editions in Hungary, one in Slovakia, and four in America.

All in all, since the *Cithara Sanctorum* appeared in 1636, it has gone through at least 113 editions in three and a half centuries.

Slovak Hymnwriters after Tranovský

Although Tranovský was the greatest and most prolific of Slovak hymnwriters, he was by no means the last. The doubling of the contents of the *Cithara* came from the addition of more original hymns and many more translations from German hymnwriters who lived during or after Tranovský's lifetime. Paul Gerhardt's (LBW 23) hymns are among the most popular in Slovak Lutheran churches, but he was just beginning to write his magnificent hymns when the *Cithara* was published. It remained for Samuel Hruškovic and others of his skill to render these jewels in Slovak.

Next to Tranovský, Hruškovic (1694–1748) was the best translator of German chorales, and has been called the Slovak Catherine Winkworth (LBW 29). A student of great scholars in Wittenberg, he was later elevated to the position of superintendent of the Banska district. Twice called before the court to be deprived of his pastorates, he died after much tribulation. Among his published works were Luther's Catechism and the expanded *Cithara* of 1745.

Others who enriched various editions of the *Cithara* with their hymns and/or translations were Juraj Zábojnik (1608–1672); Adam Plintovic (*c.* 1650); Daniel Sinapius-Horčička (1640–1688), editor of the 1684 edition of the *Cithara;* Jeremiáš Lednický (d. 1685); Daniel Krman (1663–1740); Eliáš Mlynarovič (*c.* 1700); Ján Glozius Pondelský (1675–1724); Juraj Ambrozius (d. 1746); Ján Blazius Sr. (1684–1763); Pavel Jakobei (1695–1752); Ján Blazius Jr. (1708–1773); Michal Inštitoris Mošovský (1733–1803), editor of the 1787 edition of the *Cithara;* and Pavel Teslák (1759–1801).

The Age of Rationalism and the *Zpěvník*

After the major revision and expansion of the *Cithara* by Hruškovic in 1745, the hymnal became bulkier and more expensive, the number of hymns quickly reaching a thousand. The *Cithara* was faulted for its lack of hymns dealing with certain doctrines, and numerous pastors and congregations began to agitate for a smaller and more contemporary hymnal. The *Rúčny kancionalík* ("Pocket Hymnal") of Mošovský, rather than solving the problem, merely created more confusion, without eliminating the archaisms of the *Cithara* or filling its gaps.

Unsuccessful attempts to produce a new hymnal were made by Martin Hamaljar in 1796 and by Stefan Leška in his *Nová kniha zpěvu* ("New Book of Hymns") published in Prague in the same year. An appeal was issued in 1834 and again in 1836 for revised and new hymns that would be considered for a new hymnal. A committee was appointed early in 1841 to review the submitted hymns and to establish criteria for a new worship book. The committee, composed of the district superintendents of the Lutheran Church and other experts, began its work energetically on September 21, 1841, but soon discovered that it would have to meet often and for longer periods of time in order to complete the task. The preface to the book was written on June 16, 1842. It was named *Zpěvník,* "The Hymnal," and contained 842 hymns, of which only 332 were retained from the *Cithara,* and of this number only 55 were left unaltered by the compilers of the *Zpěvník.* Though not much fewer in number, most of the longer hymns were shortened in order to reduce the size of the hymnal.

The *Zpěvník* was compiled by the most illustrious writers and theologians of their day: Michal Miloslav Hodža (1811–1870), Ján Chalupka (1791–1871), Samuel Chalupka (1812–1883), Ján Kollár (1793–1852), and Karol Kuzmány (1806–1866). It is not without significance that Ján Chalupka, Kollár, and Kuzmány studied at Jena in the early 1800s whereas just about all the hymnwriters and compilers before Hruškovic studied in Wittenberg. The contributors to the *Zpěvník* were apostles of the Enlightenment and their product betrays the theology of the day. Both books were influenced by the prevailing Lutheran theology of the German universities.

When Slovak Lutherans came to America they arrived with both books, and a division occurred among them on the basis of their use. The conservative Lutherans insisted on using and republishing the *Cithara,* whereas the moderate Slovak Lutherans opted for the *Zpěvník.* Among the charges leveled against the *Zpěvník* were inferiority of hymnic quality and false doctrine.

56

The Music of the *Cithara Sanctorum*

The melodies to which the Slovak Lutherans have sung their hymns and liturgies derive from a variety of sources, the earliest being the Old Slavonic and Glagolitic liturgies with their single melody line. This liturgical music has survived chiefly in the Eastern Orthodox areas of Slavic Europe where it is still used today. The Slovak Christians, coming under the jurisdiction of Rome, adopted the Roman rite and with it the Gregorian chant. However, alongside the official Gregorian idiom, various independently composed sequences, hymns, tropes, and religious songs were directly connected to the Old Slavonic cultus, although they were written to conform to Latin forms.

A number of early hymns trace the Gregorian influence, although among Lutherans in Slovakia the Old Czech melodies were used with their Czech texts. These in turn were derived chiefly from Czech folk songs. The German Lutheran chorale became a part of Slovak Lutheran hymnody not only by virtue of translation of the texts but also because of the numerous German settlements throughout present-day Czechoslovakia, whose services were often conducted by bilingual Slovak pastors.

To meet and halt the popularity of the *Cithara,* the Roman Catholics produced their own hymnal in Slovakia, the *Cantus Catholici* in 1655 compiled by Benedikt Szolosi, a Jesuit from Trnava. In content and music, the *Cantus Catholici* drew upon the medieval pre-Reformation hymnody, although it did contain many melodies of Reformation hymns. Following this first Counter-Reformation hymnal, numerous individual hymns were composed by cantors and priests, and many printed hymnbooks appeared in addition to those that remained only in manuscript form.

The arrival of Protestantism in Slovakia resulted in the creation of schools and musical training. Choirs were organized to sing polyphonically, and concerts were present in all the major Slovak cities. Although their repertory drew heavily upon German compositions, their existence and performances challenged the creativity of a long list of composers whose works are only now being recognized, performed, and recorded.

As the editions of the *Cithara* multiplied, the need for accompaniment books grew. In the preparation of the most recent *Partitúra* (accompanist's score) by Julius Letňan and Karol Wurm in 1955, more than twenty-five extant "choralebooks" were consulted, many of them in manuscript form, dating from the sixteenth century. Among the most important were: the Kunvaldský *Kancional* of 1675, Závorka's *Kancionál* of 1602, the *Tranoscius* of 1636, 1674, and 1684, the *Cantus Catholici* of 1655, the Glosius *Kanionál* of *c.* 1730, a manuscript *Partitúra* of *c.* 1750, the M. Grylus manuscript *Partitúra* of 1790, the Adam Škultéty *Partitúra* of 1798, and the *Veíká Partitúra* ("The Large Partitura") of 1935 by Juraj Chorvát and Julius Batel. In the United States, Ján Murček produced a *Partitúra* in 1913 and Jozef Kucharik compiled his *Duchovná Cithara* ("Spiritual Harp") in 1933. The latter two have provided the accompaniment for most of the American and Canadian Slovak Lutherans.

Among the domestic composers of sacred music in the peak classical period was Anton Zimmermann of Bratislava. Others of significance were Johann Nepomuk Hummel, Anton Aschner, Richter and Hrdina, and others.

Metrical Psalmody

Carol Ann Doran

Religious poetry of the Jews forms a considerable portion of the Old Testament. The poetry of the Psalms in particular became an important part of Jewish Temple worship. They were sung by choirs, accompanied by instruments, and chanted by priests and people responsorially.

The Jews who became Christians naturally continued singing Psalms, for they served well to praise both the God of Abraham and their risen Lord. And although vast outpourings of religious poetry intended for singing have been born out of Christian faith and experience, no other body of hymns has been assimilated so fully into Christian liturgies. The Proper of the Mass and the Daily Offices glow with selections from the Psalms.

People sang Psalms both inside and outside the services of worship in the early centuries of the Church's life. As services became longer and more ornate, however, trained choirs began to assume increasing responsibility for music, just as clergy, in the role of celebrant, were superseding the people as principal participant. By the twelfth century, all the choral parts in the service were sung exclusively by either clergy or the choir.

By the time of the Reformation in Europe, the people's participation in worship had become an issue of urgent concern. In 1523, Martin Luther (LBW 48) wrote, "I also wish that we had as many songs as possible in the vernacular which the people could sing during Mass, . . . for who doubts that originally all the people sang these which now only the choir sings or responds to while the bishop is consecrating?"[†]

It was a question not only of hymns in a proper devotional style for use in the new Mass and Communion services, but of songs in the vernacular through which the people might express their faith and carry it to others. Luther dearly loved the ritual of the old church, and he knew the power of folk music in the home and the ale-hall. He urged capable followers to write hymns and he wrote many himself. He utilized with great enthusiasm the means well-known to reformers of ages past—hymnody as ammunition for the battle and nourishment for those fighting it.[‡]

The Reformed Church in Geneva, Switzerland, however, was led by one whose conviction it was that folk song of the time was "frivolous" and who wanted no association with its tunes to intrude on worship. John Calvin was a man of disciplined and solid scholarship. While he was not himself a musician, he paid careful attention to the details of public worship and was convinced that psalmody—inspired songs of Scripture—was the only fit body of poetry appropriate to be sung in the church. In fact, he allowed nothing in Reformed practice which was not authorized by Scripture.

He also rejected the elaborate polyphony of the Roman church, which

---

[†]Ulrich S. Leupold, *Luther's Works,* Vol. 53 (Philadelphia: Fortress Press, 1965), 36.

[‡]Hilary, Bishop of Poitiers (*c.* 310–366), for example, wrote hymns emphasizing Trinitarian doctrines in the effort to combat the Arian heresy, and Ephraem Syrus (b. 307) battled the Gnostic poets through hymns.

58

he considered a purely human contrivance, and the use of the Tones for chanting the Psalms. Calvin chose, instead, French translations in metrical verse—that verse which has a regular recurring pattern of stressed and unstressed syllables—as opposed to the prose form.

In English, for example, this may be seen in the difference between the prose translation of Psalm One from the New English Bible (1970) and the metrical form used in the Ainsworth Psalter of 1612.

English Bible:

> Happy is the man who does not take the wicked for his guide.
>> nor walk the road that sinners tread
>> nor take his seat among the scornful.

Ainsworth:

> O Blessed man, that doth not in
>> the wickeds counsell walk:
> Nor stand in sinners way; nor sit
>> in seat of scornful folk.

This device of setting a metrical text to music traditionally has been useful in assisting the memory and, in fact, was the prevalent form of popular song in Calvin's time. The lines, accents, and rhyme patterns were arranged in the same way for each stanza so that a single melody could be used over and over again. Ecclesiastical poetry of preceding centuries took this form, as have folk songs of various countries.

In a work of such gravity as a metrical setting of the Psalms for Reformed worship, excellence of translation obviously would require a gifted spirit, for paraphrase frequently is involved. Fortunately, one of France's most talented poets had begun this work even before Calvin issued his famous *Institutes* (1536), in which the plan for Reformed worship was outlined.

Clément Marot (*c.* 1497–1544), a well-known writer and favored friend of French royalty, had translated some of the Psalms into French verse in 1532 or 1533 as a project of his own. Members at court were fascinated by these paraphrases and shared them in ever-widening circles. They were eagerly received, for many people had no other access to the Bible in the vernacular. In fact, a version of some of Marot's Psalms, *Aulcunes pseaulmes et cantiques mys en chant* (Strassburg, 1539) was authorized by Calvin for use in worship at Geneva.

But upon publication of these verses in 1542, the poet was charged with heresy and forced to flee to Geneva to protect his life. He was welcomed by Calvin and encouraged to continue working on the Psalm translations. Unfortunately, after completing only nineteen more, he died under mysterious circumstances while traveling. Other editions of Marot Psalms are *Psalmes de David, translatez de plusieurs autheurs et principallement Cle. Marot, Anvers* (Antwerp), 1541, and *La Manyere de faire prières aux églises francoyses . . . ensemble pseaulmes et cantiques, c.* 1542. This last volume was called "the Pseudo-Roman" because the unexpected note, "Imprimé à Rome par la Commandement du Pape," was added at the end by the printer, apparently in an effort to increase sales among Roman Catholics.

The significance of Marot's contribution to metrical psalmody at this critical period in its development is amplified by Waldo Pratt in a paper delivered before the Hymn Society. He reminds us that the excellence of Marot's verse undoubtedly was in no minor way responsible for its wide acceptance and use by large numbers of people in varied stations of life.

59

"The contagion of Geneva spread far and wide," he says, and "everywhere the French Psalter flew like a flag at the head of aggressive Calvinism."†

The work of translating the Psalms was not completed until the arrival in Geneva in 1547 of Théodore de Besze or de Bèze or, as Latinized, Beza (1519–1605). Calvin assigned him responsibility for completing the full Psalter and gradually drew him higher into leadership of the Reformed Church.

The completed French Psalter, *Pseaumes de David mis en rime francaise par Clement Marot & Theodore de Beze,* was published in Paris in 1562. It contained 125 tunes, seventy of which were written by Louis Bourgeois (LBW 29), who was musical editor of earlier editions of the Psalter. Some of these make use of first lines of secular songs. Some may be traced to Strassburg, where the earliest versions of Marot's Psalms had appeared, and are thought to have originated under the influence of Lutheran hymnody heard there. Matthaus Greitter, a Lutheran since 1524 living in Strassburg, is named as the originator of the tunes for Psalms thirty-six and ninety-one. The origins of many of the tunes remain to be discovered.

The wide variety of poetic meters is one of the most outstanding characteristics of this 1562 French Psalter (sometimes called the "Genevan" Psalter). Each Psalm seems to have been given an individual treatment in both text and tune, although twenty-one melodies were assigned to more than one poem. Their enthusiastic adoption by the people for use both inside and outside worship services might have been a direct consequence of this, for each possessed a distinctive character and was, therefore, easier to remember as a unique creation. Within the 125 tunes of the French Psalter, there are 110 different poetic meters, each of which requires a certain form of tune. Douen suggests that the tunes may be divided into three types: "Gregorian," "Approaching the modern minor," and "fully major."‡

The significance of this French Psalter of 1562 might be stated in terms of its influence on publications throughout the history of metrical psalmody. Pratt lists 225 separate publications during the formal existence of Huguenotism in France (through 1685), but the full extent of this Psalter's influence through translation and free adaptation cannot easily be known. (Julian* chronicles new editions and revisions down through 1863.)

The first publication of English metrical Psalms was within a volume frequently described as Lutheran in origin. The music, all in unison, was based on Lutheran chorale melodies and Gregorian chant. The volume was titled *Goostly psalmes and spirituall songs,* and was printed by Myles Coverdale around 1543. Because it was banned by Henry VIII only three years later, however, it had little influence on the development of English psalmody. It is interesting as an early example of English versification, for it contained metrical versions of the *Magnificat, Nunc Dimittis,* the Lord's Prayer, Creed, and Ten Commandments as well as German and Latin Hymns along with thirteen metrical Psalms.

The "landmark" English collection of metrical Psalms was published in 1562 (the same year as the completed French Psalter) by John Day

†Waldo Selden Pratt, "The Significance of the Old French Psalter," Hymn Society Paper IV, pp. 5–6.

‡E. O. Douen, *Clément Marot et la psaultier hugenot* (Paris: l'Imprimeri Nationale, 1877–1878).

IL faut que de tous mes efprits Ton

los & pris l'exalte & prife, Deuant les

grãs me prefenter Pour te châter l'ay faiĉt em-

prife. En ton faiĉt tẽple ado reray, Ce-

lebreray Ta renommée, Pour l'amour de ta

grãd' bonté, Et fe au te Tant e fti mée.

> *The tune "Mit freuden zart"*
> *(LBW 140) as it appeared with Psalm*
> *138 in the Genevan Psalter, 1551.*

(LBW 234) in London: *The whole Book of Psalmes, collected into English metre by T. Sternhold, John Hopkins, and others: conferred with the Ebrue with apt notes to sing them withal. Faithfully perused and allowed according to th' ordre appointed in the Quene's Maiesties Iniunctions. Very mete to be used of all sorts of people privately for their solace & comfort; laying apart all ungodly songes and ballades, which tende only to the norishing of vyce, and corrupting of youth.* In another parallel with the Geneva publication, this English Psalter was the culmination of work accumulated through many editions prior to 1562.

Thomas Sternhold's metrical Psalms initially were his own effort, begun to provide an attractive musical alternative to the amorous and obscene songs sung at the court of Henry VIII. Sternhold was groom to the king's robes and is said to have gained Henry's favor through his poetic compositions. The first edition of his works, which is undated, was dedicated to young King Edward and is titled: *Certayne Psalmes, chose out of the Psalter of David and drawen into Englishe metre by Thomas Sternhold, grome of ye kynge's Maiesties roobes;* it contains nineteen Psalms.

After his death a larger collection of thirty-seven Psalms appeared (in 1549) which claimed to be all that Sternhold "did in his lyfe tyme drawe into English metre." All were in the old Ballad meter (Common Meter, which is 8,6,8,6, doubled or tripled)† with only two exceptions. The 1551 edition of Sternhold's Psalms included seven Psalms by his disciple, John Hopkins.

In 1553, the accession of Mary Tudor to the English throne caused

---

†These numbers indicate the number of syllables in each line of poetry.

61

many to flee to Geneva to escape religious persecution. In this atmosphere, their embryonic Sternhold and Hopkins Psalter was subjected to the strong influence of the developing French translations and tunes. By that time, the Geneva Psalter contained eighty-three Psalms, each with its own tune.

The 1556 edition of Sternhold and Hopkins is noteworthy not only because it is the first version to contain music, but also because it is included as a separate but central section of a "rival" prayer book used by the exiles in Geneva, who strongly disliked the English Prayer Book. Commonly referred to as the "Anglo-Genevan Psalter," this edition formed the second section of *The forme of prayers and ministration of the Sacraments, Etc. used in the Englishe Congregation at Geneva; and approved by the famous and godly learned man, John Calvyn*. By this time, fifty-one Psalms were available, including seven new versions and a metrical form of the Ten Commandments. These additions were probably the work of the leader of the English at Geneva, William Whittingham, who was a Hebrew scholar.

Not only the old ballad meter, but also Long Meter (8,8,8,8) doubled, and Short Meter (6,6,8,6) doubled, were used. Reflecting a characteristic of the French Psalter, the 1556 English collection assigned each Psalm its own proper tune—a practice not continued in subsequent English editions, however. Whittingham also adapted at least one French tune to fit a corresponding English Psalm in his book.

Unfortunately, however, all this was accomplished without outstanding musical success, so it is not surprising that few of the 52 tunes of this first musical edition survived the versions of 1558 and 1561. The less popular and weaker ones were omitted along with some that were strongly modal. As a consequence, by the year 1562, when both Psalters were published in their completed forms, the French collection contained 125 tunes for the 150 Psalms; the English, fifty tunes.

Through the 1561–1562 editions of Sternhold and Hopkins, the titles contain these words: *"Very mete to be used of all sorts of people privately."* In 1566 the title reads: *Newlye set foorth and allowed to bee soong of the people together, in Churches, before and after Morning and Evening prayer, as also before and after the Sermon, and moreover in private houses*. . . . The eminent American hymnologist, Louis Benson, suggests that these paraphrases were not intended to be used in divine service of the English church, but easily crept in as a result of their enormous popularity outside it, and their convenience as a substitute for chanting the Psalms. John Jewel, Bishop of Salisbury, wrote to Peter Martyr from London in 1560:

> Religion is now somewhat more established than it was. The people are everywhere exceedingly inclined to the better part. The practice of joining in church music has very much helped this; for as soon as they had once begun singing in public, in only one little church in London, immediately not only the churches in the neighborhood, but even the towns far distant, began to vie with each other in the same practice. You may now sometimes see at Paul's cross, after the service, 6000 persons, old and young, of both sexes, all singing together and praising God.†

Following the appearance of the first complete Sternhold and Hopkins in 1562, at least one reprint or revised edition appeared each year for nearly a century. The demand for this book increased so greatly that be-

†Peter LeHuray, *Music and the Reformation in England* (New York, 1967), p. 375.

tween 1620 and 1640 more than one hundred new printings were made available—without copyright restriction, of course.

The first harmonized Sternhold and Hopkins Psalter was published by John Day in 1563 and was entitled, *The whole psalmes in foure partes, which may be song to al musicall instrumentes, set forth for the encrease of vertue: and abolishyng of other vayne and triflyng ballades.* More than 140 tunes are harmonized in a simple chordal style, the four voices printed in separate part-books labeled "medius," "contratenor," "tenor," and "bassus." The melody is almost always in the tenor, but in the bass or treble in a few cases. More than half of the harmonizations are by a William Parsons, but other composers are represented as well.

Other harmonized versions of Sternhold and Hopkins were later published for varying numbers of voice parts and instruments, the last of which was the notable, *Whole Booke of Psalmes,* published by Thomas Ravenscroft in 1621. By this time most of the contributors were professional church musicians, and the preface is addressed "to all that have skill or will unto sacred music."

In addition to the publications based on words and music of the standard Sternhold and Hopkins, many other volumes appeared to accommodate public enthusiasm for these Psalms. There were free polyphonic settings of verse by Sternhold and Hopkins, a group of which used popular secular tunes with English Psalms, and a composition based on the first fourteen chapters of the Acts of the Apostles set in English verse —words and music by Thomas Tye. Later polyphonic settings of the Psalms and instrumental works using Psalm tunes as thematic material are found useful even today, and assist in making known to contemporary Christians the music which was so important to the early life of the Reformed Churches.

Scotland's earliest psalter, by J. and R. Wedderburn, was titled *Gude and godlie Ballatis* and probably was published before 1546. In 1564 a psalter was attached to the *Book of Common Prayer* in which over half of the Psalms were from the Anglo-Genevan psalter, and the remainder were from the 1562 English Psalter or were written by Scottish authors. The 1615 edition of the Scottish Psalter (*The Psalmes of David*) introduced the "Common Tunes"—tunes not associated with particular Psalms but available to any of appropriate meter. Harmonizations of the tunes came in the 1635 Scottish Psalter.

In America, the Psalters were used faithfully by those who had so carefully transported them to this new land. The French collection reached this country first with the Huguenot expeditions of 1562–1565 in Florida and Psalms were sung by both the French and the Indian natives. In his book, *History of the Huguenot Emigration to America,* Charles Baird writes,

> Long after the breaking up of Laudonnière's colony, the European, cruising along the coast or landing upon the shore, would be saluted with some snatch of a French Psalm uncouthly rendered by Indian voices, in strains caught from the Calvinists. (I, p. 68)

The Dutch settlers in New Amsterdam brought with them the official music of the Reformed Church in the Netherlands—a direct translation of the French Psalter by Peter Dathleen, using Bourgeois tunes. The chaplain of Sir Francis Drake's famous voyage around the world in 1577 records the practice of Psalm-singing on board ship during the long trip, undoubtedly from the Sternhold and Hopkins Psalter.

The Ainsworth Psalter is another collection which must be noted in connection with metrical psalmody used early in American colonial history. It was published in 1612 in Amsterdam and brought to the New World aboard the Mayflower. The Separatist Puritans, who were called Pilgrims, had fled to Holland before sailing for America, and, while there, had adopted use of the French tunes which were being sung by the Dutch. Henry Ainsworth's Psalter incorporated nineteen of these Bourgeois tunes and was used with notably high musical standard at Plymouth as late as 1692.

The first book of *any* kind printed in the English-speaking colonies on this continent was the Bay Psalm Book printed in Cambridge, Massachusetts, in 1640. In no way connected to the Old World, this was the work of thirty colonial ministers who desired a metrical translation of the Psalms which expressed the meaning of the original Hebrew as precisely as possible. The completed volume of 296 pages was welcomed by those who had been critical of the "humane composure" which was the nature of the versifying process used by European editions. Within a short period of practical usage, however, the awkwardness of its "close-fitting" translation became apparent. The preface to the Bay Psalm Book argues:

> If therefore the verses are not always so smooth and elegant as some may desire or expect; let them consider that Gods Altar needs not our pollishings; . . . for we have respected rather a plaine translation, than to smooth our verses with the sweetnes of any paraphrase, and soe have attended Conscience rather than Elegance, fidelity rather than poetry, in translating the hebrew words into english language, and Davids poetry into english meetre.

This version of the twenty-third Psalm is an example of the contents of the Bay Psalm Book:

> "The Lord to mee a shepheard is,
>   want therefore shall not I
> Hee in the folds of tender-grasse,
>   doth cause me down to lie:
> To waters calme me gently leads
>   Restore my soule doth hee:
> he doth in paths of righteousness:
>   for his names sake leads mee. . ."

The early editions of the Bay Psalm Book contained no music, possibly because no one in the colony was capable of engraving it. Instead, at the end of the volume, an "Admonition" refers singers to tunes found in other well-known English psalters by listing the Psalm number within each collection. By the 1698 edition, a number of tunes had been included in the back of the book, in two-part harmony, crudely engraved from woodcuts.

In London, Sternhold and Hopkins became the "Old Version" in 1696 with the appearance of *A New Version of the Psalms of David, fitted to the tunes used in Churches,* by Nahum Tate (LBW 452), Poet Laureate, to William III, and Dr. Nicholas Brady (LBW 452), a Royal Chaplain. From this time forward, the prefix, "Old," as in, "Old Hundredth," for example, was added to designate tunes identified with Psalms in the Sternhold and Hopkins collection.

Critics of the "New Version" expressed concern at "The Poetry, the Style, the Running of the Verse . . .", for Tate and Brady, both of whom were poets, had succeeded in what they had set out to do; they had considered literary and poetical excellence (within the style of the time) a valid principle of translation.

Not everyone agreed, of course. Those who valued literal translation were not pleased and expressed doubt that this "New Version" by Tate and Brady, "was ever conferred with the Hebrew as the other [Old Version by Sternhold and Hopkins] was . . . ." Although many parish churches in England and America did adopt this "New Version," its usage was never that enjoyed by the "Old Version."

Louis Benson views the appearance of this Tate and Brady Psalter as an important development in the outgrowth from English metrical psalmody toward the English hymn.† From the root of metrical psalmody, which probably will always continue to be practiced in some form, the new shoot began as a freer paraphrase and finally blossomed in a form which was so free as to resemble only basically the original stock.

By the early eighteenth century, the evolution of this metrical psalmody appeared to have reached a standstill. One English writer describes the "dull indifference, the neglect and the thoughtless air that sits upon the faces of a whole assembly while the Psalm is on their lips. . . ." What some describe as the "cultus" of psalmody eventually had a stifling effect over the period of several generations in which people had neglected other kinds of church music.

The Psalms, after all, are a closed body of material. Those committed to their use cannot anticipate additions to the repertoire—only new translations. And of even greater concern to some was the inability of the Psalms to satisfy the needs of Christian devotion. Nowhere is the name of Christ mentioned within them. Benson (p. 52) has written, "The Canonical Psalms represented one dispensation and the worshippers, another."

In addition, serious difficulties with musical practice had arisen, particularly for English-speaking people. Whereas the French Psalter had utilized a great variety of meters, the English collections tended to reduce the numbers of tunes to a group which were formed in Common Meter, a fact which Pratt suggests laid a "paralyzing hand on English hymnodic verse for at least three centuries."

Psalmody had depended heavily on oral tradition, for some Psalters contained no printed tunes within them. In the transmission much had become imprecise. The disorder experienced by colonial Psalm-singers was so widespread that it resulted in the "Singing School movement" of the early 1700s, instituted by a group of New England divines to prevent the continuance of these abuses.

Metrical psalmody was by definition a congregational experience. The leadership of professional musicians was neither needed nor sought. As a result, the efforts to raise musical standards usually exerted by those educated in music was not present to balance the influence of the untrained.

What leadership there was came from the parish clerk both in England and America. Where the practice of "lining out" was allowed, it was the clerk who decided the tune to be used and then "gave it out" line by line, singing words and music for the people to repeat. This disjointed pattern was another source of dissatisfaction, for the sense and meaning of lines sung separately from the whole were sometimes, at the least, unedifying. In the case of verse three of Psalm fifty, the clerk would have sung, "The Lord will come and He will not," and the people would have repeated it,

---

†Louis Benson, *English Hymn* (Richmond, Virginia, 1962).

going on to apply the same process to the second line, "Keep silent, but speak out."

In time, however, it was the parish clerk, unintentionally, who strengthened moves toward less restricted expression, for it eventually became the accepted privilege of the clerk to prudently alter or omit any portion of the Psalm which he regarded as inopportune. Benson (p. 51) says the "remedy was irregular, inconvenient to those who could read, and dependent at best upon the discretion and readiness of a class of officials not characteristically gifted with either."

By this and other practices, however, the previous basic principle of strict adherance to Scripture was further deserted so as to be of little consequence to those who were leaders in the next developments toward English hymnody.

The Psalm was expanded from strict translation through paraphrase and then freer paraphrase. There was imitation of Scripture and exposition of Scripture and finally a hymn more or less suggested by Scripture. This growth allowed expression of the human impulse to write devotional poetry and accommodated a need for songs of an advanced stage of revelation.

The work of Dr. Isaac Watts (1674–1748) (LBW 39) is esteemed for excellence in "accommodating" the Psalms, but the work of John Patrick, "Preacher to the Charter-House, London," is an earlier example of this practice. In 1679 Patrick published *A Century of Select Psalms and Portions of the Psalms of David, especially those of praise.* In this book, published many years before Tate and Brady, he introduced the name of Christ and addressed Him specifically. Watts himself later praised Patrick's work, which was well received by Nonconformists, saying, ". . . he hath made use of the present language of Christianity in several Psalms, and left out many of the Judaisms." When Watts's *The Psalms of David imitated* was published in 1719, its author openly states (in the preface) his intention to "exceed" Dr. Patrick by applying his method to every Psalm and by improving his verse.

The story is told of Watts's first hymn composition being a response to his father's challenge to him to improve on the psalmody in use, which the younger Watts thought uncouth and lacking beauty and dignity. He believed that church song should be evangelical in the sense of reflecting New Testament theology, freely-composed rather than strictly Scriptural, and expressive of the thoughts and feelings of those singing in the present time. In "A Short Essay toward the Improvement of Psalmody," Watts expresses his belief that congregational song should represent our word to God, not God's to us. His convictions systematically were put into practice with no effort to soothe those who clung to strict Psalm-singing. The five arguments explained in Watts's "Essay" are pertinent to our consideration of the decline in use of metrical Psalms. Benson (p. 112) summarizes them in these words:

1. A Psalm properly translated for Christian use is no longer inspired as to form and language: only its materials are borrowed from God's word. It is just as lawful to use other Scriptural thoughts, and compose them into a spiritual song.

2. The very ends and design of psalmody demand songs that shall respond to the fullness of God's revelation of Himself. God's revelation in Christ, and our own devotions responding to it, require Gospel songs.

3. The Scriptures themselves, especially Ephesians 5:19–20, and Colossians 3:16–17, command us to sing and give thanks in the name of Christ.

66

Why shall we pray and preach in that name, and sing under terms of the Law?

4. The Book of Psalms does not provide for all occasions of Christian praise, or express all Christian experiences.

5. The primitive "Gifts of the Spirit" covered alike preaching, prayer and song. It is admitted by all that, under the present administration of Grace, ministers are by study and diligence to acquire and cultivate gifts of preaching and prayer. Why shall they not also seek to acquire and cultivate the capacity of composing spiritual songs, and exercise it along with the other parts of worship, preaching and prayer?

The unusually large number of editions of Watts's hymns gives us an idea of the demand for his works. The process by which congregations became hymn-singers often included use of Watts's "Psalm Imitations." Following that initial experience of free Christian song, the hymn was easily welcomed. People developed strong loyalties for the work of their beloved Dr. Watts which lasted through the middle of the nineteenth century both in America and abroad.

In spite of those who opposed Isaac Watts, accusing him of "burlesquing" the Psalter, hymnody was beginning to prevail. Psalmody gradually weakened its hold on the faithful, particularly as hymns of an increasingly higher quality were made available to the people.

While texts from both the Old Version (LBW 245, "All people that on earth do dwell") and the New Version (LBW 452, "As pants the hart for cooling streams"), as well as the Scottish Psalter of 1650 (LBW 451, "The Lord's my shepherd") are to be found, the primary contribution of metrical psalmody to the LBW is its tunes. From the French Psalters we have such melodies as "Old Hundredth" (which is included five times), "Freu dich sehr" (LBW 29/470), "Wenn wir in höchsten Nöten sein" (LBW 303), "Mit Freuden zart" (LBW 140/421). "Old 124th" (LBW 376), "Donne secours" (LBW 493), "O Seigneur" (LBW 545), and "Old 107th" (LBW 318/431). Settings from the Old Version include "Windsor" (LBW 114), "Southwell" (LBW 309), "St Flavian" (LBW 234), and "Winchester Old" (LBW 264); and among those from the New Version are William Croft's "St. Anne" (LBW 320) and "Hanover" (LBW 548). The Scottish Psalter of 1615 has given us "Dundee" (LBW 464/524) and the 1635 Scottish Psalter, "Caithness" (LBW 99).

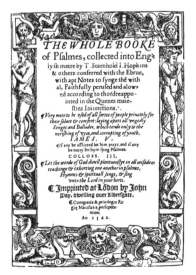

Title page of the English Psalter, 1562 (see pp. 62f).

English and American (Non-Lutheran) Hymnody

Stanley E. Yoder

IN ENGLAND

Compared with Lutheran Germany and Scandinavia, the development and acceptance of vernacular hymnody in England was somewhat delayed. It was not until the turn of the eighteenth century that a serious hymnic challenge to metrical psalmody prevailed, and it was well after the turn of the nineteenth century before its acceptance could be called general. The first part of this chapter will survey that period of challenge, development, and acceptance, which is important to us because so many of Britain's hymnwriters and composers are represented in and sung from contemporary hymnals of English-speaking Christendom (including the LBW, more than one-fourth of whose hymns are eighteenth- or nineteenth-century English in origin).

The Grip of Metrical Psalmody

At the onset of the English Reformation, under Henry VIII and Archbishop Cranmer, there was at least a possibility that England would go Lutheran. In worship, the first Book of Common Prayer (that of Edward VI, 1549) paralleled the Lutheran respect for the western liturgical tradition. However, it all proved transient. Edward's second Prayer Book three years later reveals the domination of the English Reformation by Reformed (Calvinist) theology and practice—an influence that became even more pervasive when British divines returned from exile in Calvin's Geneva and other Reformed centers on the Continent, whither they had fled from Queen "Bloody Mary" (the Roman Catholic daughter of Henry VIII and Catherine of Aragon).

The implications for hymnody of a Calvinist Church of England stem from the Reformer himself, who wrote in his preface to the 1543 Genevan psalter:

> Therefore, when we have looked thoroughly, and searched here and there, we shall not find better songs nor more fitting for the purpose, than the psalms of David which the Holy Spirit made and spoke through him.†

This "Scriptural Principle"—as it may be called—ruled congregational song in Britain for 150 years (from the Reformation to Isaac Watts) in the form of metrical psalmody. That subject has been treated in the preceding chapter.

The Scriptural Principle permeated the worship song not only of the Church of England, but also English and Scottish Presbyterians, Congregationalists (all more or less Calvinists in theology), and the English Baptists. As a result, metrical psalmody was ubiquitous. Only the small Roman Catholic constituency (much suppressed and occasionally persecuted from Elizabeth I's reign until the eighteenth century) would have sung anything else—when they dared sing at all.

---

†Transl. by Charles Garside in "Calvin's Preface to the Psalter: a Reappraisal," *Musical Quarterly,* XXXVII (1951), pp. 570–71.

While at least a hundred other partial or complete metrical psalters appeared during the seventeenth century, few of these were any real challenge to the Old Version in congregational worship, as distinguished from private devotional use. Not even the so-called "New Version" (1695) of Nahum Tate and Nicholas Brady (LBW 452) broke the grip, except in some of the larger city churches, and in New England. In fact the Old Version continued as the norm in much of the Church of England until well into the nineteenth century.

The Stirrings of Hymnody

Nonetheless, the seventeenth century saw increasing dissatisfaction with metrical psalmody in general, and the Old Version in particular. The complaints revolved about three issues: 1) textual accuracy *vis-à-vis* the Hebrew; 2) intelligibility; and 3) elegance of expression.

The first two of these reflected Puritan concerns for faithfulness to the Biblical text and for clarity of communication, both in the interest of edification. The Old Version was found wanting in these virtues, primarily because the severe constraints of meter and rhyme often muddled both meaning and grammar. These same constraints led others with literary interest to criticize the Old Version for being graceless and inelegant. In this regard, the metrical psalters ran a distant second (if even that) to the Authorized ("King James") Version of the Bible (1611).

Resolution of these issues proved difficult. Improving accuracy and intelligibility tended to make the style even more wooden. Attempts toward gracefulness of expression usually fell into paraphrasing the biblical text —a sin to Puritans. The result was increasing frustration with the whole tradition of metrical psalmody, and with the Scriptural Principle underlying it.

It was in this milieu that English hymnody was born, "hymnody" here meaning congregational song with texts other than the Psalms or Psalm paraphrases. To be sure, there had always been a few "hymns" appended to the Old Version, such as "The humble suit of a sinner," "Thanksgiving after receiving the Lord's Supper," a versified *Magnificat* (LBW 6) and *Nunc Dimittis,* and so forth. Also, the "Veni, Creator Spiritus" was sung in English at ordinations (in the same translation by Bishop Cosin as is used in the LBW at 472 and 473).

The presence of such items suggests two influences: 1) versifications of liturgical texts, in the manner of Martin Luther's (LBW 48) *Deutsche Messe:* and 2) Lutheran/Reformed piety picked up by the Genevan exiles. That such hymns were permitted, thus slightly stretching the Scriptural Principle, came about through a loop-hole in the Elizabethan royal/ecclesiastical strictures on church music, in which a "hymn or such-like song" could be sung at the beginning or end of Morning or Evening Prayer. The vagueness of the phrase was the key, and to this day the use of non-psalmic or non-scriptural hymnody has not been explictly permitted in the Church of England (though mention will be made later of an ecclesiastical court case which was interpreted as permission). There has never been an official hymnbook of the Church of England; instead, several commercially-published books have been and are in use.

In any case, the twenty or so "hymns" variously included in editions of the Old Version proved to be the thin end of the wedge. It was driven further in the seventeenth century by a few men such as George Wither (1588–1667), who wrote additional hymns to supplement the Old Version. Wither wrote ninety, some biblically-based, but others of his own composition for the major feasts and seasons of the church year. These efforts have not survived in our hymnals, but some of the tunes he persuaded the well-known Orlando Gibbons (1583–1625) to compose for his texts are still sung (LBW 206, 257, 373, 438, and 505).

There seemed to be a growing conviction that congregational song was not only a medium of God's Word to his people in worship, and not only of their response of praise to that Word in biblical language—the Psalms—but also of the church's or individual Christian's experience. Put another way, congregational song could be not only didactic and proclamatory, but interpretive, commentative, and expressive of feeling (response). The accompanying fact that they were New Testament Christians responding to the Gospel was not lost on these people either: in this way, too, confinement to the Psalms was frustrating.

It was for Isaac Watts (LBW 39), however, to consolidate these frustrations, feelings, and first stirrings of hymnody into a definite challenge to the Scriptural Principle and its vehicle, metrical psalmody.

Isaac Watts—the "Father" of English Hymnody

In English church history, Watts (1674–1748) belonged to the Independent tradition. Independents stemmed from those in the sixteenth century who dissented from both the established Church of England and from those Puritans who hoped to reform (or re-reform) that Church along Presbyterian lines. In exile in Holland, these "separatists" divided into Baptists and Independents (or Congregationalists).

During the seventeenth century, the Baptists and Independents (collectively referred to as "Dissenters"), although returned to England, were persecuted and driven underground by both Anglicans and Puritans. It was out of all this that the Pilgrim emigration to New England took place. But by Watts's time these privations had been eased somewhat, though Dissenters could not hold civil office or attend the universities.

Theologically, Independency was moderately Calvinist. Ecclesiastically, the local congregation was the highest authority in both faith and practice. Sociologically, it tended to a middle-class constituency in the cities (a class then rising), and the poor in the rural areas. The popular distinction was that Anglicans attended "church" or "parish," while Dissenters went to "chapel."

More strongly than Wither and the other seventeenth-century hymnists, but for all the same reasons, Watts felt that congregational song must be freed from the tyranny of metrical psalmody, which dominated Independent as throughly as Anglican and Puritan/Presbyterian worship.

So Watts, too, set his pen to paper. He first decided to make "David speak the common sense and Language of a Christian";† that is, he began his own metrical psalter, which was eventually published in 1719 as *The Psalms of David Imitated in the Language of the New Testament.* It contains 332 versifications of 138 Psalms, mostly in the three dominant meters of the Old Version: Common, Long, and Short. Some psalms were cast in two or all three meters.

Quite a number of these have endured, and some are now "classics." While Watts was generally much freer in his paraphrasing than his predecessors, he selectively "Christianized"; "Give to our God immortal praise" (Psalm 136, LBW 520), "Jesus shall reign" (Psalm 72, LBW 530), the everpopular "Joy to the world" (Psalm 98, LBW 39), and others contain direct or allusive references to Christ. Other psalms he

---

†Watts, *Psalms of David Imitated,* preface.

was content to leave in their Old Testament ambience; for example, "O God, our help in ages past" (Psalm 90, common meter version, LBW 320), "From all that dwell below the skies" (Psalm 117, LBW 550), and "Before Jehovah's awesome throne" (Psalm 100, LBW 531). This last is interesting in that its original first stanza had as its third line, "the British Isles shall send the noise"—free paraphrase indeed! The familiar first stanza is an alternate provided later by John Wesley (LBW 302).

Yet, in spite of the license he took, Watts realized that the Psalms could not be bent to his basic concept of congregational song without violating their integrity altogether, for what he wanted was the singer's personal involvement in the content and action of his or her singing—a Christian's response of adoration before a wonderful God and His Gospel.

Thus, concurrent with the work on the Psalms, Watts began *Hymns and Spiritual Songs,* which was first published in 1707—twelve years before the *Psalms of David Imitated.* As the title suggests, Watts was no longer limiting himself to the Psalms, but paraphrased the New Testament and (more radically) wrote according to his own inspiration (though certainly biblically informed).

Hymns and Spiritual Songs contains 351 hymns in three sections, or books: "Collected from the Scripture," "Compos'd on Divine Subjects," and "Preparation for the Lord's Supper." From the first book the LBW has "Come, let us join our cheerful songs" (Revelation 5:11–13, LBW 254). Book II yields "Alas! And did my Savior bleed" (subject "Godly sorrow arising from the sufferings of Christ", LBW 98). The famous "worm" in stanza one ("for such a worm as I?") has since yielded to "sinners," for while "worm" was a very conventional reference for fallen humanity in the eighteenth century, in the twentieth it is not. It is one of a number of words that have "lost caste" since Watts's time, and thus sometimes make Watts appear quaint or even crude. From the small (25 hymns) Book III, the LBW has three. "When I survey the wondrous cross" (LBW 482) and "Nature with open volume stands" (LBW 119) are among the best of Watts's entire output, though no longer associated exclusively with the Sacrament. The third hymn is "It happened on that fateful night" (LBW 127), also appropriate for Maundy Thursday.

In these hymns we see how Watts realized his intent to remedy the deficiencies of metrical psalmody through 1) the explicitly Christian ambience; 2) the personal (but not sentimentalized) response of the individual to the Gospel; and 3) concern for literary integrity and grace (remembering that Watts wrote in an essentially seventeenth-century style, before Addison began the "purification" of English in the eighteenth century). Not every hymn by Watts exhibits all three traits, nor did they succeed every time; but those that did remain beloved and sung. And rightly so.

Did Isaac Watts succeed in breaking the grip of metrical psalmody? In the long term, yes; but in his own time, he might be compared with Daimler or Ford and their first automobiles: when the latter appeared, they looked like and only slowly replaced horse-drawn carriages. But eighty years later. . .! So with *Hymns and Spiritual Songs* in the old meters and sung to the old psalm tunes: they gained ground only slowly in the Dissenting churches and hardly at all in the Church of England. But by the mid-eighteenth century, most of English Dissent was singing hymns (Watts's and others') with a frequency that has led some to observe that hymns *are* the liturgy of dissent. In a practical sense then, if

not in a strictly chronological one, Isaac Watts was indeed the father of
English hymody.

The Later Eighteenth Century

Within a Church of England which had become diluted in doctrine and
arid in practice as a result of the Enlightenment, there arose the
Evangelical Revival. This was a multi-faceted movement which combined the moderate Calvinism of Dissent with the piety and enthusiasm
of the Methodists; yet its followers could not bring themselves to
separate from the established church, with its claims to historical con-
tinunity and tradition. They continue to this day, informally called
"Anglican Evangelicals."

The Anglican Evangelicals were hospitable to hymnody, which they
found to be an ideal vehicle for the expression of their faith and piety.
The most enduring hymnwriters of the movement are undoubtedly John
Newton (1725–1807, LBW 261) and William Cowper (pronounced
"Cooper," 1731–1800, LBW 483) who produced the *Olney Hymns* in
1779. Most of its 348 hymns have fallen out of use, but the best remain
from both authors (see the LBW indices). It should be noted that Cowper
was one of very few major figures in English literary history who inten-
tionally wrote hymns, as distinguished from poetry from which hymns
were later derived. (The great Puritan poet John Milton [LBW 318] was
another.) But the rigidity of meter and rhyme required by congregational
hymnody does not make it an attractive genre to people of letters.

The Methodist movement, founded by John and Charles Wesley
(LBW 302 and 27), was another part of the Evangelical Revival. The
brothers always intended the movement to remain within Anglicanism,
adding evangelical fervor and individual piety to its classical doctrine.
Eventually, however, the Methodists were forced out of the Church of
England, and formed the Methodist Church, complete with episcopal
polity. Interestingly, Charles Wesley remained an Anglican priest until
his death in 1788.

Like the Anglican Evangelicals, the Methodists were most receptive to
hymnody. Moravianism, both European and English, had developed a
substantial body of hymnody, and had been an early influence upon the
Wesleys. John's contribution was to translate some of it into English,
along with hymns by Paul Gerhardt (LBW 23), Johann Scheffler (LBW
455), Johann Freylinghausen (LBW 32), and others. However, it was
Charles who brought Methodist hymnody into its own. He himself wrote
upwards of 6000 hymns (the number depending upon where one draws
the line between hymns and devotional poetry, and in any case many of
them spur-of-the-moment texts for specific occasions or meetings), and
inspired others to write also, such as John Cennick and Edward Perronet
("All hail the power of Jesus' name!", LBW 328/329).

By this time, the English language had become more refined, less
angular, as initiated by Joseph Addison (LBW 264). That, combined
with Charles's flair for classical (Latin) vocabulary and style, and his
command of classical Christian doctrine, gives his hymns a flavor
altogether different from those of Isaac Watts. This is revealed in atten-
tive reading of examples such as "Hark! The herald angels sing" (LBW
60) or "Victim Divine, your grace we claim" (LBW 202) being respectively distillations of the doctrines of the Incarnation and the Holy Communion. The other side of the Wesleyan coin—a refined personal fervor
—is revealed in a hymn such as "Oh, for a thousand tongues to sing"
(LBW 559).

It is somewhat of a paradox that Charles's opulent style and beautiful vocabulary were employed in a popular movement addressed to an often illiterate public. Methodist music provided a meeting ground. By the time of the Wesleys, a German musician trained in Italy had come to England and revolutionized music there: George Frideric Handel (LBW 39). Compared with the older tunes used for metrical psalmody, Methodist tunes, developing under the Handelian influence, had a melodic rhythm which tended to dominate the verbal rhythm of the text: the words now had to fit the music, often one syllable to several notes. The tune "Helmsley" (LBW 27) illustrates this well.

In the hands of a Handel, such a style could provide a musical commentary on the text. In later Methodism, with composers of lesser stature, the connection became weaker, and the Wesley brothers were distressed at what they viewed as irresponsible vulgarity in the music of the movement. But there was no doubt that it had popular appeal, and further weakened the grip of metrical psalmody on English Christendom.

The Nineteenth Century

If eighteenth-century English hymnody was the preserve of Dissent, both without and within the Church of England, the next century saw the belated but massive turning of the latter from metrical psalmody to hymnody.

All along, moderate and high-church Anglicans had felt constrained by the old sixteenth-century royal/ecclesiastical prohibitions against anything but psalmody. Thus the Old Version, and to a limited extent the Tate and Brady New Version of 1696, with a repertoire of tunes from the musical editions of these psalters (culminating in Henry Playford's of 1677) formed the staple of their congregational song. At least musically, it was not a totally static tradition, for new tunes kept appearing, such as "Darwall's 148th" (LBW 261), "Duke Street" (LBW 352), and "Truro" (LBW 363).

By the later eighteenth century, however, many Anglicans were becoming restive with psalmody and envious of Dissent and its growing hymnody. Watts's paraphrases and even hymns were beginning to creep into their worship. The legal aspect was resolved in 1820 when the Archbishop of York sided with hymnody in adjudicating a complaint from the parishioners of St. Paul's, Sheffield, whose rector Thomas Cotterill (LBW 547), assisted by the journalist James Montgomery (LBW 50), had introduced hymns. Montgomery (1771–1854) was to become a major figure in nineteenth-century English hymn-writing.

A few years earlier, Reginald Heber (1783–1826, LBW 84), a priest from Shropshire who was to become a missionary bishop in India, had assembled a collection of hymns for the church year. Most were his own, such as "Holy, holy, holy" for Trinity Sunday (LBW 165); but he also enlisted others like Henry Hart Milman, who contributed a hymn for Palm Sunday, "Ride on, ride on in majesty!" (LBW 121).

Heber's work brings three new dimensions to English hymnody:

1) Hymnody breaks into the established church. At first—as with Heber—it tended to occur in middle-of-the-road Anglicanism, where both doctrine and tradition were observed less rigidly than in the "high church" wing. But by mid-century, even the latter was singing hymns, though preferably translations of the Latin office hymns. It was the beginning of the end for metrical psalmody in England (though not in Scotland, where metrical psalmody is still employed side by side with hymnody).

73

2) Hymnody is intended for and incorporated into liturgical worship, remembering that in the eighteenth century hymnody was employed in Dissenting non-liturgical worship, prayer meetings of the Anglican Evangelicals, and Methodist society meetings (which the Wesleys never intended should replace Anglican parochial worship).

3) With Heber we move in literary style from Watts's seventeenth-century quaintness and Charles Wesley's classical opulence into romanticism, for this was the age of William Wordsworth and Sir Walter Scott in Britain. The word-imagery characteristic of the romantic movement is epitomized in the first line of Heber's familiar "From Greenland's icy mountains, from India's coral strand." At times, the imagery was too highly-colored for the truth: another Heber hymn begins "By cool Siloam's shady rill"—a line accused of containing a maximum of misstatement in a minimum of space, as biblical Siloam was probably neither cool, shady, nor furnished with rills! But it sounds so beautiful on the tongue of the singer!

This poetic allusiveness (which was to continue into Victorian hymnody), along with Wesley's classicism and Watts's metaphors, while congruent with their respective periods, strike many today as incongruous in our period, and even embarrassing to sing. In an age of high technology, there is a tendency to demand of language more and more designative precision. Furthermore, many feel that words are cheap, and used so often to deceive, manipulate, or obscure. The results are an impatience with past styles, and a general "flattening" of language.

As with Isaac Watts in eighteenth-century Independency, Heber's venture did not open the floodgates immediately. It took the Cotterill-Montgomery affair and especially the Tractarian ("Oxford") Movement to do that. The latter, which began in 1833, was initially an effort to alert the Church of England to a threat to its internal authority by Parliament (the reorganization of the [Anglican] Church of Ireland). It soon became a call to renewal of the Church's historical and catholic tradition—"high church" in more than the liturgical sense. However Anglicans viewed the movement, it did serve to bestir their Church, and this included hymnic interest and usage.

Tractarians (the most famous of them being John Henry Newman, later to become a priest and cardinal in the Roman Church) rediscovered the Latin hymns, and set about translating them into English. By far the most prolific translator was John Mason Neale (1818–1866, LBW 34), many of whose efforts appear in the LBW. Early leaders of the movement, including John Keble, Newman, and Philip Pusey (LBW 366), wrote original hymns. In their footsteps came a whole generation of both Tractarian and Evangelical hymnwriters: bishops like William W. How (LBW 77), Christopher Wordsworth (LBW 90), and Edward H. Bickersteth (LBW 491); clergy like Henry F. Lyte (LBW 272), John S. B. Monsell (LBW 131), John Ellerton (LBW 262), and Samuel J. Stone (LBW 369); laity like Frances Ridley Havergal (LBW 260), Anne Steele (LBW 240), and Robert Grant (LBW 91); Roman Catholics like Frederick W. Faber (LBW 290) and Edward Caswall (LBW 37). Some wrote many hymns; and many wrote only one or a few. The translation of Latin hymns was paralleled by an interest in German hymnody, particularly by Catherine Winkworth (1829–1878, LBW 29), many of whose translations have continued in use.

How did this gathering flood of hymnody find its way into the parish churches? Until the middle of the nineteenth century, hymnbooks were either single-author volumes (such as Watts's *Hymns and Spiritual*

Songs) or local collections (such as Cotterill's in Sheffield). But about 1860, the clergyman and hymnwriter Sir Henry W. Baker (1821–1877, LBW 414) gathered a committee to assemble a hymnal for general Anglican use (though not to be an "official" hymnal—the Church of England has never had such). Thus, in 1861 *Hymns Ancient and Modern* was published, the first modern English hymnal: eclectic, multiple-authored, liturgically arranged, committee-edited, and with music. At the time it was labeled "high church," but by 1900 (and revised/expanded) it had become regarded as "low" to "middle," the "high" position to be filled in 1906 by the *English Hymnal*. Similar books, formally or informally "official," appeared for Congregationalists, Baptists, and others. Specialized books, such as those by Neale and Winkworth, were also published. The Church of Scotland (Presbyterian) produced its official *Church Hymnary* in 1898.

While all this writing and publishing activity continued throughout the Victorian era in Britain, the Victorian hymn tunes are an equally important contribution of the period. If the reader has formed an impression that the musical side of English hymnody has lagged behind the textual side in development, he or she is correct. Congregations (of whatever tradition) had an active repertoire of texts far in excess of tunes; indeed, the total number of tunes was somewhat less than that of texts. This was feasible because for so long most of the meters used were the relatively few of metrical psalmody; thus, for example, a common meter tune could be used for almost any common-meter text the congregation knew. The concept of fixed text-tune "marriages" characteristic of German hymnody did not begin until Charles Wesley began to expand the list of meters, thus requiring new, "custom" tunes. Later, in the nineteenth century, more tunes were composed for specific texts, and "marriages" of older ones were ordained by *de facto* usage, or by appearing together in a book such as *Hymns Ancient and Modern*; for example, Watts's "O God, our help in ages past" to Croft's "St. Anne" (LBW 320).

In the nineteenth century, popular interest in music was increasing, due to Novello's cost-lowering revolution in music publishing, Hullah's singing-class movement, and the advent of the romantic period in music—Carl Maria von Weber, Felix Mendelssohn (LBW 60), and others. This interest created a fertile field for hymn tune composers in the Victorian period.

The most familiar name in this large group is surely John Bacchus Dykes (1823–1876), creator of "Nicaea" for Heber's "Holy, holy, holy" (LBW 165). But the list also includes Authur Sullivan (LBW 153), Samuel Sebastian Wesley (LBW 197), Henry J. Gauntlett, Edward J. Hopkins (LBW 262), Joseph Barnby (LBW 280), John Stainer (LBW 56), Henry Smart (LBW 50), John Goss (LBW 549), George Elvey (LBW 170), and William H. Monk (LBW 272, first music editor of *Hymns Ancient and Modern*).

Now, a century later, retrospective views of the Victorian era have tended to be negative. It is seen as having been complacent, secure in the *status quo,* and desirous of avoiding tension and controversy in life. Whether or to what extent this assessment is accurate, Victorian hymn tunes on the whole lack the rhythmic and melodic tension and strength of the older Psalm tunes and the best of the Methodist tunes. Instead, melodies make much use of repeated notes, bass lines tend to stagnate, trite rhythmic patterns are used, and tunes which begin hopefully enough often come to a dull end.

This analysis notwithstanding, many Christians today love the Victorian tunes, and some texts have become so firmly wedded to them that they are undoubtedly assured a secure place in our books for some time to come.

Welsh Hymnody

In the eighteenth century, Wales was strongly affected by the Methodist movement, which took and continues to exhibit there a definite Calvinistic flavor. From this there flowed, well into the nineteenth century, a hymn tune tradition that did not make significant headway outside of Wales or Welsh enclaves until our own century.

Those tunes which have become relatively popular are well represented in the LBW. Most of them convey a characteristic intensity, sonority, and rhetorical power which can strongly move a congregation. This effect is achieved with several devices: repetition of a text phrase ("Bryn Calfaria," LBW 156/172, "Cwm Rhondda," LBW 343/415); an insistent rhythmic figure ("Ebenezer," LBW 233/355); economy of melodic form ("Aberystwyth," LBW 91); and overall an apt sense of tune architecture.

If all this is a mirror of the Welsh character and Welsh Christianity, then once again hymnody proves itself a remarkably sensitive and accurate reflection of the people who create it and use it.

Accompaniment of Hymn-singing

We are so accustomed to our own hymn-singing being accompanied by an organ (or piano, or guitar) that we may be tempted to assume that the same was true in seventeenth- and eighteenth-century England.

Generally, organs were found only in the larger churches and cathedrals, and many of these were either silenced or destroyed by Puritan militants in the seventeenth century. Thus, metrical psalmody was basically unaccompanied, the singing being led by the parish clerk.

In the eighteenth century, there arose the parish "band" to support the singing. It was typically a motley collection (one could not say "ensemble") of whatever players and instruments were available: string, woodwind, and/or brass. Historians of the time often wrote in despair at the resulting sound.

Only in the nineteenth century did the organ return in significant numbers, whether with a human player or in the form of the "barrel organ," in which the pipe valves were actuated by pins on a revolving drum (as in the musical clock), the pins being set to play a Psalm tune. This was, of course, another reason why parishes had such a limited tune repertoire.

In Scotland, unaccompanied singing was a matter of conviction, and in the nineteenth century a great "organ controversy" erupted. While organs were eventually accepted in many "kirks," unaccompanied singing is still found today, especially in the highlands and islands of Scotland.

What, then, has this condensed recital of the British experience with hymnody up to 1900 shown? In common with the Lutheran countries, hymnody in Britian went through a process of evolution in style and content as it responded to varied movements and controversies within the Church, understandings of worship, and perceptions of the personal *vis-à-vis* the corporate dimensions of Christianity. That evolution continues, as any tradition must if it is not to stagnate.

At the same time, however, the British were wrestling with the very idea of a hymnody other than the metrical Psalms, beginning as they did with a strictly interpreted Scriptural Principle. It took the better part of three centuries before the acceptance of hymnody was truly general. That struggle was partly of theology and partly of human inertia, but in any case without parallel in the Lutheran lands because, unlike John Calvin, Martin Luther had no qualms about hymnody.

Once won to hymnody, though, the British rapidly built a sizable hymnic tradition, which is an important element in our American experience, to which we next turn.

IN AMERICA

The use of Psalmody in the New World has been discussed in the previous chapter, pp. 63ff. The Bay Psalm Book, published in Cambridge, Massachusetts, in 1640, soon came to be used as far south as Philadelphia and even enjoyed a publishing history in England and Scotland until 1754. The 1651 revision contained some "hymns"—versified Scripture other than the Psalms (Isaiah, Song of Solomon, Revelation, and so forth)— which became the thin end of the wedge for hymnody as in seventeenth-century England. The popularity of the Bay Psalm Book was unchallenged until the New Version of 1696 and Watts's *Psalms of David Imitated* and *Hymns and Spiritual Songs* came on the American scene. The New Version was printed in New York as early as 1710 and became fairly popular in urban churches, especially Episcopal and Presbyterian.

The introduction of Isaac Watts to America was facilitated by his previous literary and theological reputation by correspondence with various New England clergy, including the eminent Cotton Mather, who warmly endorsed *Hymns and Spiritual Songs*, though for private/family devotional use only. In addition, the visiting English evangelist George Whitefield (LBW 522) and the American preacher Jonathan Edwards both championed Watts's hymns in worship. Together, the New Version and Watts brought the Bay Psalm Book era to a close by about 1760, but in gentle steps, such as Prince's revision of 1758 that also included hymns of Watts; the publication of Watts's Psalm paraphrases and hymns together (*Watts Entire*); and the American editions of *Psalms of David Imitated* such as Timothy Dwight's of 1801, with additions such as Dwight's own paraphrase of Psalm 137, "I love Thy kingdom, Lord" (LBW 368), probably the oldest American text still in common use.

It should be noted that the Wesleys' hymns and translations made slower headway in America than did Watts's, largely because they had strong competition within Methodism from camp meeting/revival hymnody.

The Improvement of Musical Practice

During the Bay Psalm Book period, music suffered a decline in the colonies. This was not because of an oft-alleged Puritan suspicion of the arts (not true), but simply because the rigors of making a new life in a new world pushed music well down the priority list. Thus, the well-testified musicality of the original colonists became diluted. Many congregations had a repertoire of only a half-dozen Psalm tunes, and these often adulterated. Their singing was disorganized, and a leader had to "line out" the psalm; that is, he sang one line at a time, repeated by the congregation, often at a dirge-like tempo.

Attempts to remedy this dismal state of affairs took several forms: new tune books, the itinerant singing school movement, and later, more formal music education.

The ninth edition (1698) of the Bay Psalm Book contained a thirteen-tune supplement. In 1721 John Tufts published a book of twenty tunes, and in 1770 the *New England Psalm Singer* was published, with original tunes (many in the imitative "fuguing" style) by the famous William Billings (see LBW 426). Oliver Holden published *The Union Harmony* in 1793 containing the tune "Coronation" (LBW 328), the earliest American tune still in common use.

These and other tune books used both staff notation and syllables; however, there were only four syllables for the octave (fa-sol-la-fa-sol-la-mi), a simplification borrowed from England. Most of these books also contained an introduction describing some method for learning how to read musical notation. In 1801, William Little and William Smith published *The Easy Instructor,* an excellent tune book whose "method" introduced a simple additional device destined to become famous: the "shape note," in which the shape of the note heads on the staff corresponded with the four solmization syllables—a triangular note for "fa," oval for "sol," square for "la," and diamond for "mi."

This system was taken up by singing teachers who itinerated around the young nation from about 1770 to 1830. Arriving in a town, the teacher would first enlist funding, students, and a hall (often the tavern). The school term was three to four weeks, during which the students learned the rudiments of reading and were taught songs by syllable, usually in three parts. Words were added only when parts were fully learned. A final concert displayed the group's accomplishments to the townspeople.

This phenomenon greatly improved the level of singing in churches. It also spawned many more tune books. Some of the latter became classics of the genre, and their tunes are appearing in contemporary hymnbooks as a re-appreciation of this distinctive American contribution to hymnody has developed.

The singing school/shape note movement (termed "fasola") made its most enduring impact in rural Appalachia, especially in the South. There it became a tradition among the white settlers, lasting through the nineteenth century into the twentieth.

Among the most famous fasola books are John Wyeth's *Repository of Sacred Music,* 1813 (LBW 33, 499); Ananias Davisson's *Kentucky Harmony,* 1816 (LBW 220,246); *Missouri Harmony,* 1820; William Walker's *Southern Harmony,* 1835 (LBW 30, 61, 217, 347, 360, 372, 385); and B. F. White's *The Sacred Harp,* 1844 (LBW 392, 423).

What these books display is a bringing together of the older Yankee singing-teacher tunes (of English Psalm-tune lineage), and folk music of a generally Anglo-Scottish-Irish style, including dance rhythms, fiddle tunes, and ornamentation. This music was set to "standard" hymn texts (Watts and Newton especially), and to secular or semi-secular moral ballads, songs of experience, national history narratives, and so on.

However, as the nation matured during the nineteenth century, the singing teachers and then the shape notes were challenged by advocates of more sophisticated musical taste, pedagogy, and practice, first in the urban centers of the East, then westward. The name of Lowell Mason (1792–1872, LBW 353), sometimes reckoned as the "father" of music education in the United States, is perhaps the best known of these educators. Eventually, alongside the folk hymn tunes of the fasola tradition, there emerged composed American hymn tunes.

The Nineteenth Century

As the nineteenth century dawned, American authors increasingly appeared alongside the English in hymnbooks. Some landmark volumes are:

1821, William A. Muhlenberg's *Church Poetry* for Episcopalians, following their inclusion of some hymns in the American *Book of Common Prayer*.

1824, Asahel Nettleton's *Village Hymns* for Congregationalists and Presbyterians. Both the above contained English texts, now including Heber and Montgomery, and American texts by writers such as Bishop George W. Doane (LBW 464) and Francis Scott Key (LBW 243). Nettleton also furnished a separate tune book for his hymnal, with specific text-tune recommendations—a harbinger of things to come.

1831, *The Christian Lyre*, more revival-oriented, but including James W. Alexander's translation of "O sacred head, now wounded" (LBW 116/117).

1831ff, various books by Lowell Mason, reacting to *The Christian Lyre*. He included many of his own tunes, along with those of his colleague Thomas Hastings (LBW 327).

1855, *The Plymouth Collection* by Henry Ward Beecher, which went Nettleton one better by printing text and tune together, six years before *Hymns Ancient and Modern* did the same in England. Beecher included texts by his sister, Harriet Beecher Stowe.

1858, *Sabbath Day Hymn Book*. Notable for original hymns and translations from the Latin by Ray Palmer (LBW 479).

From 1836 onwards, American Methodists published books which show a delayed appreciation of the hymnic output of the Wesley brothers.

Also active in the ante-bellum years were Unitarian and liberal Congregationalist hymnwriters such as Samuel Longfellow (LBW 257), John Greenleaf Whittier (LBW 506), Oliver Wendell Holmes, James Russell Lowell, Julia Howe (LBW 332), and Frederick H. Hedge.

The above list only highlights the obvious fact that hymnody was as much in floodtide in the United States as in England during the nineteenth century. Dozens of books and hundreds of authors and composers contributed to the flood.

After the trauma of the War between the States, the remaining years of the century were used by American Christianity to assimilate the large corpus of English and American hymnody which had become available. More and more, hymnody took on an ecumenical aspect, as denominations borrowed from each other's hymnic traditions. Then, too, denominations which were not originally English-speaking were becoming increasingly Americanized, in the process translating their own hymnody and beginning selectively to utilize the Anglo-American tradition.

These years also witnessed the appearance of two new phenomena: the Black "spiritual" folk hymn, and the "gospel" hymnody that accompanied the revival movement dominated by Moody and Sankey.

In 1867 *Slave Songs of the United States* appeared, the first concerted effort to commit to paper and thus preserve an oral tradition among the African people brought to the United States as slaves. Subsequently, the famed Jubilee Singers of Fisk University presented the songs to the public, and inspired other Blacks and Black schools to collect and sing the several hundred known spirituals.

This folk-art-form reflected both the religious and the social experience of an enslaved people. Because they had been largely Christianized, the texts of the spirituals were biblically-based. Some of the most well-known were derived from the Old Testament, frequently telling of oppressed people and their liberation by God, situations with which the Negro in America could readily identify. On the other hand, the New Testament was the obvious source for "Were you there" (LBW 92), and "Go tell it on the mountain" (LBW 70). Not a few have a similarity to the Anglo-American ballad form, as in the setting of Joshua and the battle of Jericho.

The music of the spirituals (LBW 70, 92, 212, 359) has been the subject of some musicological controversy. It seems safe to say that while there are African elements in the background, the melodies of the spirituals are American-born, influenced by the white environment, especially the hymnody of the camp meetings.

As a hymnic tradition for liturgical worship, the Black spirituals have made only slow headway; and indeed, their textual content, together with the unique ethos in which they arose, make their broader use genuinely problematic for many. Nonetheless, when the external setting is appropriate, the spiritual can be a powerful and moving medium of hymnic expression by a congregation.

The other hymnic phenomenon of the nineteenth century is the "gospel hymn" tradition. Its antecedents were the camp meeting songs and revival hymnody of earlier years, followed by the songs of the Sunday School movement. The more immediate background began in 1863 with William B. Bradbury's (LBW 293) *Pilgrim's Songs*, intended to meet the need for hymns to enliven religious meetings. Other hymnists of this time and style were Joseph Gilmore (LBW 501), William W. Walford, Robert Lowry, and Philip P. Bliss (LBW 346).

When Dwight L. Moody and Ira D. Sankey returned from their mission to England in 1873, the latter's *Sacred Songs and Solos* was combined with Bliss's *Gospel Songs* (1874) as the famous *Gospel Hymns and Sacred Songs*, which eventually became a series of six books that sold over fifty million copies. Perhaps the most well-known gospel hymnwriter in the years that followed was Fanny Crosby (1820–1915), blind from infancy, who wrote over 8,000 songs, many under a host of pseudonyms.

A century later, we are still close enough to this tradition that many older Christians today were reared on it; for them it is the norm for hymnody. Also, present-day revival and evangelistic leaders and groups continue to depend on it, because the easily-remembered words and tunes (especially the omni-present refrains), coupled to a strong appeal to personal/private feelings and to a nostalgia for the faithstyle of a former time, can have great psychological impact. However, for Christians with a more corporate understanding of faith and worship, and an awareness of the dangers of fugitive religion, the use of the gospel hymns is problematic.

In America, then, we have traced the same evolution from metrical psalmody to hymnody as occurred in England. At first Americans simply imported English hymnic developments; it was not until the later eighteenth century that original American hymnody appeared in significant quantity and the evolution could become more self-generating and contained.

Further, the very newness of the nation imposed phenomena such as the decline of music and the unique efforts to reverse that decline, and the continuing influence of frontier-style revival hymnody. Racial pluralism has contributed the Negro spiritual, and religious/ethnic pluralism an ecumenical variety to our hymnody. The result has been, and continues to be, vital and interesting resources for congregational song in our worship.

Lutheran Hymnody in North America

R. Harold Terry

The story of Lutheran hymody in North America begins some 350 years ago. It recalls explorers and colonists who challenged the dangers of the sea in their search for a new world. It deals with pioneer pastors and their long, difficult journeys on horseback through poorly-marked wilderness trails as they served the needs of scattered congregations. It involves immigrants who fled war-torn or economically-depressed homelands of central and northern Europe in desperate hopes for a new life.

Europe had suffered a century of war beginning in 1618. Armies had ravaged farmlands and homes, confiscating livestock, burning villages and cities, and demolishing churches. Roads were blackened with the wretched of all ages fleeing for their lives. Those who did not die of cold and starvation filled up the cities of Europe with lean and squalid beggars, who had once been thriving farmers and shopkeepers. Many of the refugees made their way along the Rhine to the Netherlands. Some continued across the channel into England. The English government sent many of them to the American colonies, especially to New York and Pennsylvania. Thus began waves of migrations from Europe to the New World including a significant number of Lutherans, members of "the singing church."

Lutherans brought their Bibles and hymnals from their homelands along with their meager belongings. When the best land of New York and Pennsylvania was claimed, they kept moving, some westward across the Alleghenies, others southward through the Shenandoah Valley of Virginia and into North and South Carolina. Out of the faith of these people the Lutheran churches in America were built.

The church expresses its faith through its hymns. The hymnal is an anthology of praise and devotion. Martin Luther (LBW 48) had given the German people both the Bible and the hymn book in their own language. To pioneer peoples the hymnal was a valuable possession. A will dated May 21, 1792 and still preserved in Rowan County, North Carolina, records the wishes of a Lutheran settler, Peter Troutman Sr., who after the payment of all his just debts, gives and bequeaths unto his wife Ann Elizabeth:

> her bed and furniture, one sorrel horse, one cow, her spinning wheel, one large iron pot, and one small ditto, one frying pan, one pewter dish, two plates, two spoons, one ink tray, *one psalm book*, one smoothing iron, five sheep, and one swarm of bees, and also her maintenance in my house for as long as she lives, the same to be provided for her by my son Jacob. . . .†

Pilgrims

Lutheran hymnody came to America with the Pilgrims in 1620. When they landed at Plymouth Rock they brought with them the *Booke of Psalms; Englished Both in Prose and Metre* which Henry Ainsworth had published for them in Holland in 1612. Ainsworth had broken with the

---

† Hugh George Anderson, ed., *Foundations of Lutheranism in North Carolina* (Salisbury: North Carolina Synod, LCA, 1973) 13. (Italics added).

Church of England and fled to Holland where he met the English Separatists in Amsterdam. Among the thirty-nine melodies in the Ainsworth Psalter are some German chorale tunes. "Vater Unser" (LBW 310, 442), which had been used with Luther's hymn paraphrase of the Lord's Prayer since 1539, was assigned by Ainsworth to Psalms 34, 82, 133, and 149. The Ainsworth book with its Lutheran melodies is the volume that Henry W. Longfellow (LBW 279) describes in "The Courtship of Miles Standish," in his portrayal of Priscilla singing at home:

> Open wide in her lap lay the well-worn psalm-book of Ainsworth,
> Printed in Amsterdam, the words and the music together,
> Rough-hewn, angular notes, like stones in the wall of a churchyard,
> Darkened and overhung by the running vine of the verses.

The melodies in the Ainsworth book are for unison singing, printed in the customary diamond-shaped notes of the period, and without bar lines to indicate measures. In *America's Music: From the Pilgrims to the Present* (New York, 1966), Gilbert Chase points out that the singing of the Pilgrims was by no means dull and solemn but was done with great verve and gusto in considerable rhythmic freedom.

New Denmark

The first Lutheran hymns to be sung in North America were probably Danish hymns at the time of Jens Munck's expedition in 1619. Rasmus Jensen, thought to be the first Lutheran pastor to set foot in the New World, accompanied the expedition which had been authorized by King Christian IV of Denmark. The settlers sailed through the Labrador Sea north of Newfoundland and Quebec and across the Hudson Bay to what is now Churchill, Manitoba. They named their new home "Nova Dania" (New Denmark). Munck's diary records their Christmas observance:

> The Holy Christmas Day was celebrated in customary Christmas fashion. We had a sermon and Communion; and our offerings to the minister after the sermon were in accordance with our means. The crew had very little money, nevertheless they gave what they had; some gave white fox furs, so that the minister had enough wherewith to line a coat.†

Unfortunately, the New Denmark settlement was short-lived. Early next year, scurvy attacked the group and sickness spread until some forty had died. Only Munck and two sailors managed to get back to their homeland. First they reached Norway where "having taken care of the ship and being again in a Christian country, we all broke down and cried thanking God for His wonderful assistance." (Wolf, p. 3)

The LBW calendar of commemorations appoints February 20 as the date for honoring the memory of Rasmus Jensen.

Presumably, Pastor Jensen used the hymnal *Den Danske Psalmebog*, 1569 (LBW 227). This hymnal, widely used throughout Denmark at that time, was a deeply evangelical expression of the Lutheran faith. From the original edition the book had a distinctive Lutheran flavor, including at least three-fourths of Luther's hymn texts.

New Amsterdam

The first permanent Lutheran settlers in the New World were the Dutch. The Dutch West India Company settled some forty families near Albany

---

† Richard C. Wolf, *Lutherans in North America* (Philadelphia: Lutheran Church Press, 1965), 2.

(called Fort Orange) in 1623 and some two hundred persons on Manhattan Island (named New Amsterdam) in 1625. They came for commercial purposes. Lutherans had been living in the Netherlands for some fifty years and many of them had become traders and merchants. Some of these Lutherans were a part of the first Dutch settlements in the New World.

Dutch Lutherans had a heritage of hymnody and liturgy which went back to the Reformation. Their church order of 1566 was the work of Illyricus Flacius (1520–1575) who had personally conferred with Luther.

Lutherans in the new settlements, however, were not allowed freedom of worship. Unlike the Dutch government, the Dutch West India Company was intolerant of any religion except that of the Dutch Reformed church. Lutherans were expected to attend the Reformed services and have their children baptized and instructed by Reformed pastors. Under Governor Stuyvesant's enforcement of these policies, it was difficult and dangerous for the Lutherans even to hold informal worship services in their homes.

Years later, in 1657, the Lutheran churches in Amsterdam sent a Lutheran pastor to New Amsterdam. He was John Ernst Götwasser. But the religious intolerance had not changed and the Reformed pastors made it uncomfortable for the new Lutheran pastor and had him deported within two years.

Finally, in 1664 the Dutch Lutherans found religious freedom. The English conquered New Amsterdam, which they renamed New York, drove out the Dutch government, and granted religious toleration to its inhabitants.

Five years later the Lutheran pastor, Jacob Fabritius, was sent from Holland to serve the Dutch Lutherans in New York. With him he brought the Lutheran hymnody and church order of the church in Amsterdam, which he used in the congregations in New York and Albany. Once again Lutherans could worship according to their distinctive heritage. The Amsterdam church order served as a model for Henry Melchior Muhlenberg when he prepared the first American liturgy in 1748, and also, by way of the Savoy Church in London, influenced the church orders of the Georgia and Carolina Lutherans. In addition, the organization of the General Synod in 1820 was patterned after that of the Lutheran church in the Netherlands. Thus Dutch Lutherans made a significant contribution to Lutheranism in the New World.

New Sweden

In 1682 William Penn sailed up the Delaware River with plans to establish a colony in the New World where independence and religious toleration could permanently prevail. He discovered that Swedish Lutherans had already arrived there a generation before him and had set villages and churches. Moreover they had established friendly relations with the Indians which laid the foundation for Penn's own friendly negotiations with them.

King Gustavus Adolphus had planned a Swedish colony in the New World. Although he didn't live to see his dream come true, Lutherans from Sweden came in 1638 to a site on the Delaware River and called it New Sweden (now Wilmington, Delaware). Here they built Fort Christina and Holy Trinity ("Old Swedes") Church, the oldest Protestant church in America.

Reorus Torkillus, a Lutheran pastor, came from Sweden in 1639 or 1640 with a second expedition and served the Fort Christina colonists.

Under his leadership the colonists built a temporary chapel and organized a congregation. He is thus recognized as the first Lutheran pastor to organize a congregation in the New World. He died in 1643 and is buried in the cemetery of "Old Swedes" church.

A year later a second Lutheran pastor came from Sweden. His name was John Campanius. He joined the second colony of Swedes located at Tinicum Island, nine miles southwest of what is now Philadelphia. (A highway south of the Philadelphia International Airport honors the first Swedish governor of this colony, John Printz—Governor Printz Boulevard.)

Campanius not only ministered to the Swedes but also did missionary work among the Indians. He translated Luther's Small Catechism into the Indian language, although it was not published for fifty years.

The hymnal used by the early Swedish colonists was the "Old Upsala Psalmbok," 1622, the standard book of worship in Sweden at that time.

In 1655 Governor Stuyvesant of New Amsterdam seized control of the Swedish colonies and ended the power of the Swedish crown in the New World. Many Swedes returned to their homeland. Contact with the mother country came virtually to an end for those settlers who remained. Lacking spiritual leadership, the Swedes suffered in their church life. Pastor Lars Lock had succeeded Campanius but his ministry became ineffective due to an unhappy marriage and physical disabilities. Another pastor, Jacob Fabritius, came from the Dutch church at New Amsterdam to serve the Swedes but within a few years he became blind. Lay persons sought to hold things together in the churches but spiritual life continued to deteriorate.

Finally some help came after Andrew Printz, a nephew of the former governor, visited the Swedish settlements in 1690 and reported their spiritual plight to authorities in the motherland. King Charles XI of Sweden was persuaded to send pastors and spiritual resources. Pastors Andrew Rudman, Erick Bjoerk, and Jonas Aureen reached the Delaware settlements in June 1697 and an era of spiritual renewal began. They brought Bibles and other books to the colonists. Campanius' translation of the Catechism of fifty years earlier was published. New churches were built. Holy Trinity at Wilmington was dedicated June 4, 1699. Gloria Dei Church in Philadelphia was dedicated in 1700. Both of these churches are still standing today and are called "Old Swedes" Church. Both became Episcopalian, however, when they were unable to secure Lutheran pastors any longer.

In 1700 Andrew Rudman had two hymns printed as a New Year's gift to the Gloria Dei congregation at Wicaco in Philadelphia. These are the earliest Lutheran hymns known to have been printed in the New World. Copies are in the univeristy libraries of Helsingfors and Uppsala, Sweden. Also extant is an undated pamphlet of six hymns by Rudman, possibly written and published about 1701. Both pamphlets contained words only without music.†

Rudman left the Swedes on the Delaware in 1701 in order to accept a call from the Lutherans of New York to be their pastor. He served effectively here but due to the climate returned to Pennsylvania in 1703 where he ordained Justus Falckner to be his successor in New York.

One of the resources received from the homeland was a supply of

---

† See Edward C. Wolf, "Lutheran Hymnody and Music Published in America 1700–1850: A Descriptive Bibliography," *Concordia Historical Institute Quarterly* (Vol. 50, N. 4. Winter 1977), 165f.

Bishop Jesper Svedberg's (LBW 440) hymnal of 1694. Violently attacked and charged with being heretical, the book was confiscated by order of the king and not allowed in Swedish churches. Yet this hymnal, with its alleged heresies, was sent to the colonists in America for their use.

A "History of New Sweden" was written by Israel Acrelius who came to Wilmington as pastor in 1749. This is a primary source of knowledge concerning the history of the Swedish settlement.

Charles Magnus Wrangel came from Sweden in 1759 and became a friend and associate of Henry Melchior Muhlenberg. He assisted Muhlenberg in training American candidates for the ministry. It is estimated that there were about 3,000 Swedes in the Swedish congregations of this time.†

The First Ordination in the New World

Justus Falckner (LBW 182) and his brother Daniel came to America and worked for the William Penn colony. In 1701 they helped negotiate the sale of 10,000 acres of land in Pennsylvania to the Reverend Andrew Rudman, pastor of the Swedish settlement at Wicaco and Tinicum on the Delaware River southwest of Philadelphia. Encouraged by Pastor Rudman, Justus Falckner decided to enter the ministry. His historic service of ordination was held on November 24, 1703 in the Gloria Dei ("Old Swedes") Lutheran Church in Wicaco. Representing the Archbishop of Sweden, Pastor Rudman conducted a full Latin service assisted by the Swedish pastors, Erik Björk and Andreas Sandel.

Musicians for the ordination service included some of the Brethren of the Wissahickon, a group of mystics who had come to Philadelphia from different sections of Germany in search of religious liberty.‡ For the ordination service these Wissahickon Brethren came with a small portable organ along with viols, oboes, trumpets, and kettledrums. This is possibly the first use of a church organ in any Protestant church in the New World. The service began with an organ prelude played from the gallery and supplemented by the other instrumentalists. The Wissahickon musicians intoned "Veni, Creator Spiritus" (LBW 472) in Latin and later in the service, "Veni Sancte Spiritus" (*The Lutheran Hymnal,* 1941, #227; *Service Book and Hymnal,* 1958, #121). They also intoned Psalm 114, *Non nobis dominus* ("Not unto us, Lord").#

Justus Falckner succeeded Andrew Rudman as pastor in New York. His parish stretched some 200 miles from Long Island to Albany, including settlements on both sides of the Hudson. While he is known today chiefly for his hymn, "Rise, O children of salvation," and for his historic ordination service, he provided very effective pastoral leadership to the colonists during a twenty-year ministry. He wrote a book on the basic doctrines of Christianity which is the first theological work pub-

---

† Abdel Ross Wentz, *The Lutheran Church in American History* (Philadelphia: Fortress Press, 1933), 46.

‡ Led by 21-year-old Johannes Kelpius, the Wissahickon Brethren settled along the banks of the Wissahickon Creek which flows into the Schuylkill River above Philadelphia. Here they meditated, studied, played music, and engaged in works of mercy. Some of them were accomplished musicians credited with bringing the first organ to the New World. Some were hymnwriters, the best-known being their leader, Kelpius. His book of original hymns was perhaps the first such collection in the colonies.

See also *5 Hymns from the Hymn Book of Magister Johannes Kelpius,* translated by Dr. Christopher Witt and edited by Robert Bornemann (Philadelphia: Fortress Press, 1976).

Edward T. Horn III, "German Hymnody in Colonial Philadelphia," lecture at the Hymn Society of America national convocation, Philadelphia, Pa., May 8, 1976.

lished in America. His church records and devotional writings provide valuable accounts of the church life of his time.

Justus' brother, Daniel, returned to Germany in 1698 to be ordained, and then returned to Pennsylvania where in 1703 he organized a number of German Lutherans into the first German Lutheran congregation in the New World—at Falckner's Swamp, New Hanover, about thirty miles northwest of Philadelphia.

"One Church, One Book"—A New Dream

The American colonies were growing in numbers and expanding geographically. Wentz notes that from 1690 to 1750 their population had increased from a quarter of a million to a million and a half. Still politically dependent upon England, they were developing a self-consciousness and a spirit of independence as European migrations continued, bringing to American shores tens of thousands in search of religious liberty and economic opportunity.

With the increasing influx of new settlers, a sizeable proportion of them being Lutherans from the north European countries, the supply of pastors and lay catechists could not keep up with the demand for church leadership. Consequently, churches suffered spiritual deterioration, confusion, and conflict. Some churches faced lack of any leadership at all; others suffered the wrong kind of leadership—self-appointed, incompetent, worldly-minded and unauthorized preachers.

This was the situation when Henry Melchior Muhlenberg at age 31 arrived in Philadelphia on November 25, 1742. The churches at Philadelphia, New Hanover, and Trappe had requested Lutheran church authorities in London and Halle to send them a pastor. Professor Francke, the Pietist leader at Halle, had chosen young Muhlenberg for the task. Muhlenberg had received a thorough education in Germany including a theological degree at the University of Göttingen and had acquired considerable skills in languages and music. While he was a schoolmaster in Halle, Johann Sebastian Bach (LBW 219) was only twenty miles away at St. Thomas Church, Leipzig, pouring forth his musical and spiritual creativity.

Muhlenberg became pastor of the three congregations which had made the request for a pastor from Germany, and with the motto *Ecclesia Plantanda* ("The church must be planted"), he began to organize additional congregations. He received financial support from Halle for a church building program and in 1745 the Lutheran Church in Halle also sent three helpers: Pastor Peter Brunholtz and lay catechists John Nicholas Kurtz and John Helfrich Schaum. In April 1745, Muhlenberg married Anna Mary Weiser, the daughter of the Indian agent Conrad Weiser.

Two highlights of Muhlenberg's career both came in 1748. He organized the first Lutheran synod in America, the Ministerium of Pennsylvania, and he prepared the first American liturgy for the Lutheran church in the New World. It was adopted by the first synodical convention in 1748. His dream for American Lutheranism was "One church, one book," a goal yet to be fully realized.

The structure of the 1748 liturgy and its hymnody indicate Muhlenberg's adherence to the historical liturgical traditions of the Lutheran churches in Germany and Scandinavia and his faithfulness to evangelical Lutheran principles. Following is the order of service for the Holy Communion:

A hymn of invocation to the Holy Spirit, "Nun bitten wir den Heili-
gen Geist" ("To God the Holy Spirit let us pray," LBW 317) or
"Komm, Heiliger Geist, Herre Gott" ("Come, Holy Ghost and
Lord," LBW 163)

Confession of Sins—Exhortation, Confession, Kyrie

Gloria in Excelsis in the metrical hymn paraphrase, "Allein Gott in
der Höh sei Ehr" ("All glory be to God on high," LBW 166)

Salutation and Collect for the Day

Epistle

A Hymn substitute for the Gradual

Creed or the metrical hymn version, "Wir glauben all an einen Gott"
("We all believe in one true God," LBW 374)

Hymn before the sermon, "Liebster Jesu, wir sind hier" ("Dearest
Jesus, at your word," LBW 248) or "Herr Jesus Christ, dich zu uns
wend" ("Lord Jesus Christ, be present now," LBW 253)

Sermon

General Prayer and the Lord's Prayer

Hymn

Salutation, responses, and closing collect

Aaronic benediction with the closing invocation, "In the Name of the
Father, and of the Son, and of the Holy Ghost"

The First German Lutheran Hymnal
Published in America

When Muhlenberg arrived in America, the most commonly-used hymnbook among Lutherans was the *Marburger Gesang-Buch,* published in
Marburg, Germany. Muhlenberg drew upon the resources of his hymnal
in the preparation of his liturgy of 1748. The historic series of collects
and the lectionary from the Marburg hymnal were included in
Muhlenberg's litgurgy. Also, of course, the basic structure is that of the
historic liturgical rite of the western church.

The Marburg hymnal was first published in 1549 as a modest collection of 80 hymns. By 1747 it had gone through a number of editions until
it contained 615 hymns and psalm paraphrases.

An American edition of the Marburg hymnal was published by
Christopher Sauer, the colonial Germantown printer, in 1759.† (There
were no copyright laws to worry about in those days.) This was the first
Lutheran hymnal published in America.

Sauer, probably a member of the Church of the Brethren, had set up
his printing shop in Germantown in 1731, having learned the printing
trade at the Ephrata Cloister where Conrad Beissel, another hymnwriter
and musician and onetime member of the Wissahickon Brethren in
Philadelphia, had organized a Protestant monastic community.‡ Sauer

---

† Reed and Ryden do not date the first edition early enough. Ryden's date, 1759 *(The Encyclopedia of the Lutheran Church,* p. 1084), is the date of the second edition. Reed's date,
1762 *(The Lutheran Liturgy,* p. 167), is the date of the third edition. Edward T. Horn III
(op. cit.) and Edward C. Wolf (op. cit., p. 166f.) correctly identify 1757 as the date of the
first edition. Sauer reprinted the Lutheran Marburg hymnal (not to be confused with a
Reformed Marburg hymnbook which he also printed) in 1759, 1762, 1770, 1774, and 1777.
As late as 1799 Carl Cist, a Philadelphian, published a pocket edition. In 1774, Ernst Ludwig Baisch of Philadelphia published another version of the Marburg hymal under the title
Neu-vermehrt und vollstaendiges Gesangbuch zur Uebung der Gottseligkeit; Wolf (op. cit.,
p. 167) mentions the possibility that the book itself may have been printed in Germany and
shipped to Pennsylvania for distribution.

‡ The buildings of this community are still maintained by the Commonwealth of Pennsylvania and are open to the public with guided tours.

was *the* printer of church hymnals in his day. He published the Ephrata hymnal (621 hymns), the Mennonite *Ausbund* (822 pages containing some 60 hymns, most with especially long stanzas, and also containing accounts of the Swiss Mennonite brethren), the Moravian hymnal, and also hymnals for the German Reformed church and the Schwenckfelders. Sauer also published Luther's translation of the Psalms, for the German Lutherans in Pennsylvania.

After the Battle of Germantown in 1777, Christopher Sauer was accused of collaboration with the British. He was arrested and forced to walk barefoot from Germantown to Valley Forge. There he appeared before General George Washington and could have been convicted of treason and shot except for the intercession of Henry Melchior Muhlenberg's son, General Peter Muhlenberg, a prominent member of Washington's staff. Sauer was banished from Germantown and his property and printing presses were confiscated and sold at a United States Marshall's sale for 10,000 pounds. Sauer died pennyless in 1783 at the home of a married daughter near Trappe, Pennsylvania. (Horn, op. cit.)

Another hymnal in common use during Muhlenberg's time was the Freylinghausen "Halle book," 1741. Johann Anastasius Freylinghausen (1670–1739, LBW 32), was one of the influential leaders of the Pietistic movement at the University of Halle. Along with effective preaching, teaching, and theological writing, Freylinghausen was interested in hymnody as a means of communicating the evangelical Lutheran faith. He edited the *Geistreiches Gesangbuch* in 1704, containing 683 hymns with 174 melodies. In 1705 he published a second edition, this time enlarged to 758 hymns and 195 melodies. In 1714 came an additional section entitled *Neues Geistreiches Gesang-buch* with 815 hymns.

In 1741 both sections were combined into one volume, the "Halle book," with 600 melodies, seventeen of them new. This is our oldest source for some 269 hymn tune melodies. Walter Buszin characterizes the Freylinghausen melodies as soft, charming, and appealing; they often resemble arias rather than hymn melodies. Their melodies frequently have musical ornamentation, and the accompanist fills in the harmony from figured bass notations.†

Other German hymnals used by the Lutherans in the American colonies during the time of Muhlenberg include the Württemberg collection of 1742 and the Wernigerode and Cöthen hymnbooks. The Wernigerode collection, which went through nine editions between 1712 and 1766, was used by the Salzburg Lutherans who settled in Georgia in 1734. John and Charles Wesley (LBW 302 and 27) were on the ship which brought the Salzburgers to Savannah and were especially moved by the singing of Moravians on the ship. It is likely that the Wesleys also heard the Lutherans singing from their hymnbooks but there doesn't seem to be any historical record of this.

In 1751 Muhlenberg visited the Lutheran congregations in New York as a peacemaker. Language controversies were acute because the congregations consisted of Dutch and German Lutherans each wanting to worship in their own language, while others preferred to worship in the English language. Muhlenberg preached three times on Sunday, in Dutch, English, and German. His visit stretched out to six months during 1751 and he visited again for three months the following year.

---

† Walter E. Buszin, "J. A. Freylinghausen," *The Encyclopedia of the Lutheran Church,* ed., Julius Bodensieck (Minneapolis:Augsburg Publishing House, 1965) 889.

Muhlenberg's journal entries provide an interesting account of church life at this time, including the level of musical attainment of the congregation.

> July 20, Saturday (1751). Again had many visitors, but also had time for meditation since I was to preach once in Dutch and once in English the next day. The deacons and elders had published it far and wide that a Lutheran preacher from Pennsylvania and New York was to preach. Some had replied that they did not want to hear any more Lutherans because they were squabblers and wranglers and most of them were vagabonds. Others had heard that it was to be in German and said they could not understand that crooked German language anyhow, etc.†

Muhlenberg comments on the next day's service and its hymnsinging as follows:

> July 21, Sunday. I preached in Dutch in the morning. The church was not quite filled with Lutherans and Reformed. The people paid attention with eyes, ears, mouth, and nose, and numbers shed tears. Our poor Lutherans in this locality have been very much dispersed and driven away by the long-standing quarrels of the preachers and their bad example. They have a fine church built of massive stone, and also a parsonage. Some of them still stick together, go to the church on Sundays, and read a sermon, but the singing has gone wholly to ruin. They are not able to sing even the best-known hymns, and the miserable and lamentable noise they make sounds more like a confused quarrel than a melody. In the afternoon the church was too small and large numbers had to stand outside around the doors and windows. I preached in English on the Prodical Son, Luke 15, and we sang *"Jesu, deine tiefe Wunden,"* from our (Lutheran) English hymn book. The hymn and melody were unknown, so I read each verse aloud and sang it for them. Several women with soft, melodious voices joined in and made a pleasing harmony which quite enraptured the people. Never in my life did I see such attentive listeners!'' (*Journals*, 296f.)

On June 7, 1752 Muhlenberg preached twice to the Lutheran congregation in New York City. In his journal entry for that day he refers to the use of the Marburg Hymnal and also to the language problem faced in the services:

> June 7. In the forenoon preached a Dutch sermon and in the afternoon a German sermon. . . .
>
> The Dutch people still have old editions of psalters and hymnals which do not include many of the excellent Lutheran hymns; the Germans meanwhile use the Marburg Hymnal. It is aways difficult to find a suitable hymn which is included in both books and whose melody is familiar, for the Germans and the Dutch always sing together. For this reason I translated the beauitful hymn *"Jesu deine tiefe Wunden"* into Dutch and had the people sing it in both languages today for the first time, which they did with great enthusiasm and joy. The Germans could sing it from their books, but I had to give out a line at a time to the Dutch people. Many were greatly pleased because, as they said, nothing quite so harmonious has been heard in the church for many years. (*Journals,* 331.)

The English hymnal which Muhlenberg mentions is the first English hymnbook used in America: *Psalmodia Germanica* (the sub-title continues: "or the German Psalmody, translated from the High Dutch, together with their Proper Tunes and Thorough Bass"), London, 1732. This is the second edition. It had previously appeared in parts in 1722 and 1725. It had been prepared and published by John Christian Jacobi,

---

†*The Journals of Henry Melchior Muhlenberg,* edited and translated by Theodore G. Tappert and John W. Doberstein, 3 vols. (Philadelphia: Fortress Press, 1942-57), 296.

organist and keeper of the Royal German Chapel at St. James' Palace in London from 1708 to 1750. Queen Anne had married Prince George of Denmark, a Lutheran. In order to provide German services, the Royal Chapel had Lutheran chaplains from Germany.

Jacobi translated a number of German hymns into English, including eleven by Luther and eight by Paul Gerhardt (LBW 23). The first edition included sixty-two hymns together with fifteen chorales. Three of the hymns and the first stanza of a fourth were by Isaac Watts (LBW 39).

Muhlenberg owned a copy of *Psalmodia Germanica* and brought it with him to America. He found this hymnal being used at Trinity Church in New York City and also in the Lutheran church in Hackensack, New Jersey.

Luther Reed commented that the literary style of *Psalmodia Germanica* is "so deficient, indeed often so ludicrous," that it was not possible to include any of its translations in the *Service Book and Hymnal.*†

The translation of "Ein feste Burg" (LBW 228) appears in *Psalmodia Germanica* as follows:‡

> God is our Refuge in Distress,
>   Our strong Defence and Armour,
> He's present, when we're comfortless,
>   In Storms he is our Harbour;
>   Th' infernal Enemy
>   Look! how enrag'd is he!
>   He now exerts his Force
>   To stop the Gospel-Course;
> Who can withstand this Tyrant?

The First English Lutheran Hymnal Printed in America

Psalmodia Germanica was reprinted in New York City in 1756 for the use of English-speaking Lutherans. Albert Weygandt was pastor of Trinity Church at the time. He was prominent in the community and was a trustee of King's College (now Columbia University) from 1755 until his death in 1770. Responding to the demand for instructional and worship materials in English, he had translated Luther's Catechism in 1755 for his congregation. Then in 1756 he persuaded Hugh Gaine, the prominent publisher of the *New York Mercury,* to reprint *Psalmodia Germanica* from the second London edition of 1732. This reprint also contained an undated London supplement and, contrary to its full title, it contained no music. Its 120 hymns are mostly of German origin but with several by Watts.

This was the first Lutheran hymnal printed in America. It was still a British product, simply reproduced on American soil for continued use by English-speaking Lutherans. It was this American edition which was widely used along the east coast for several generations as more and more Lutheran congregations turned to the English language for their worship of God.

---

† Luther D. Reed, *Worship: A Study of Corporate Devotion* (Philadelphia: Fortress Press, 1959) 149.

‡ Edward T. Horn III, *A Colonial Liturgy in English* (Philadelphia: Fortress Press, 1976). This liturgy also includes translations from *Psalmodia Germanica* of "Komm Heiliger Geist, Herre Gott," "Allein Gott in der Hoh sei Ehr," and "Liebster Jesu, wir sind hier." A copy of *Psalmodia Germanica* is in the rare book collection of the Philadelphia Seminary Library.

The First Official Synodical Hymnal
in America

In 1782 the Ministerium of Pennsylvania appointed a committee to prepare an official synodical hymnal. The committee consisted of H. M. Muhlenberg, his son Henry Ernst (pastor of Trinity Church, Lancaster, the first president of Franklin College, and an eminent botanist), John Christopher Kunze (the elder Muhlenberg's son-in-law and a pastor in New York), and J. H. C. Helmuth (a prominent pastor in Philadelphia). In 1786 the committee brought out the first edition of the first official synodical hymnal in America, the *Erbauliche Liedersamlung,* printed in Germantown by Leibert and Billmeyer. This was also the first German-language hymnal produced in America. The first edition included 592 pages with 706 hymns and followed closely the arrangement of hymns in the Freylinghausen hymnal, with 361 hymns in common between the two. It also had 236 hymns in common with the 1757 Sauer reprint of the Marburg hymnal.

The *Erbauliche Lieder-Sammlung* (the second "m" was added to "Sammlung" in later editions) carefully retained the old standard hymns such as those of Luther and Gerhardt. It was a popular hymnal and was reprinted or published in enlarged editions in 1795, 1803, 1805, 1811, 1812, 1814, 1817, 1818, with about a dozen more reprints until 1850. The first edition included thirteen original hymns by Dr. Helmuth and approximately ten more of his texts appeared in later editions. Many German hymnals produced during the nineteenth century drew heavily upon this hymnal for their contents.

A companion volume, the *Choral-Buch für die Erbauliche Lieder-Sammlung,* 1813, provided tunes with figured bass for Muhlenberg's hymnal, and is apparently the first chorale book published in the United States. Produced by the congregations of St. Michael and Zion Lutheran Churches in Philadelphia, it utilized the rather monotonous isometric forms of the melodies found in Europe at the time.

The First Native American English Hymnal

In 1795 John Christopher Kunze published *A Hymn and Prayer-Book,* subtitled "for the use of such Lutheran Churches as use the English language." This was the first Lutheran hymnal in the English language to be produced in America. Kunze (1744–1807) was born in Neufeld, Germany, and came to America in 1770. A man of scholarly attainments, especially in Hebrew, he taught Semitic languages at the University of Pennsylvania and at King's College (later Columbia University) in New York. He helped organize the Lutheran seminary in Philadelphia, served as an official translator for the United States Congress, and was the first Lutheran in the New World to receive the Doctor of Divinity degree. He served as pastor in Pennsylvania and New York.

A son-in-law of Henry Melchior Muhlenberg, Kunze was senior of the Lutheran clergy in the state of New York and pastor of Trinity Church, New York City. He published *A Hymn and Prayer-Book* in order to provide worship materials in English for the youth of his church, many of whom had become Episcopalians in order to worship with the use of the English language.

The hymnal contains 240 hymns, 70 of English origin such as those of Isaac Watts (LBW 39), Charles Wesley (LBW 27), John Newton (LBW 261), William Cowper (LBW 483), Philip Doddridge (LBW 35), and Augustus M. Toplady (LBW 327). In his preface, Kunze states that many of the hymns had come from *Psalmodia Germanica* and from a Moravian Brethren collection printed in London in 1789. About 150 hymns were rather inferior translations of German originals. The translation of "O Sacred Head" (LBW 116/117) begins, "O Head, so full of bruises," and another hymn reads:

> Jehovah, Thy wise government
> And its administration,
> Is found to be most excellent
> On due consideration.†

An appendix includes hymns by Kunze, John Frederick Ernst, and George Strebeck. The hymnal contains no music; a tune index lists sixty chorale melodies for the entire hymnal, many of which failed to fit the English texts comfortably.

Kunze included in his 1795 hymnal his translation of the German liturgy then in use. This liturgy was an official revision of the original Muhlenberg liturgy of 1748 which had never been printed, only copied by hand and circulated to pastors. The Ministerium of Pennsylvania authorized an official revision in 1786. "This revision was a decided injury to the pure Lutheran type of the older service. It showed that the liturgical taste of the leaders in the church was suffering a decline." (Wentz, 306).

In 1778 Kunze had also published a German collection of thirteen poems and thirty-one original hymns or sacred song texts. Entitled *Einige Gedichte und Lieder nebst einer vorangesezten Abhandlung von dem rechten Gebrauch der Dichtkunst,* this volume was intended primarily for use in the home.

Two other English-language hymnals followed the 1795 hymnal in rapid order, both prepared by assistants of Kunze. In 1797 George Strebeck, a Methodist minister and assistant of Kunze, published *A Collection of Evangelical Hymns,* subtitled "made from different authors and collections, for the English Lutheran Church in New-York." Containing 299 hymns, this hymnal was a radical departure from its predecessor. Strebeck included only forty-eight texts from Kunze's hymnal; of these, only thirteen were of German origin as compared to 150 in the earlier book. The remaining 186 hymns were mostly Anglican. A few years later, Strebeck led a number of members of the Lutheran congregation to join him in becoming Episcopalian.

In 1806, Ralph Williston, another Methodist assistant of Kunze, published a third English-language hymnbook entitled *A Choice Selection of Evangelical Hymns, from Various Authors:* "for the use of the English Evangelical Lutheran Church in New-York." This hymnal also ignored Lutheran heritage hymns, although Kunze wrote in the introduction that the book had nothing "dissonant to our doctrine or incompatible with the spirit of genuine godliness."‡ The Williston volume included 437 hymns, 188 by Watts and 112 by Wesley. The liturgy and lectionary occupied some one hundred pages. Like his predecessor, Williston also left the Lutheran Church to become an Episcopalian, taking much of the congregation with him.

In 1814 the New York Synod published an official English hymnbook, F. H. Quitman's *A Collection of Hymns and a Liturgy,* commonly

---

† Reed, *Worship,* 149.
‡ Ernest E. Ryden, "Hymnbooks,"*The Encyclopedia of the Lutheran Church.* (Minneapolis: Augsburg Publishing House, 1965), 1085.

known as "The New York Synod's Hymn Book." For fifty years and more it was widely used in New York, Pennsylvania, and New Jersey. It included some two hundred hymns of Watts and seventy of Anne Steele (LBW 240), but Wesley was largely ignored. Completely putting aside the core of confessional hymnody from Reformation times, the book reflected the rationalistic thinking and emphasis on natural religion then prevalent throughout the church. It has been described as having little that would offend a Unitarian or high Arian. In 1834 a supplement of 180 hymns was added in a new edition, including texts of James Montgomery (LBW 50), Reginald Heber (LBW 84), John Kelly (LBW 129), and John Bowring (LBW 104).

The General Synod and Its Hymnody

The United Lutheran Church in America was organized in 1917 in New York City as a result of the merger of three general church bodies, the General Synod, the General Council, and the United Synod South. Each of these predecessor bodies had a distinct development of its liturgical and hymnic traditions. The earliest of the three bodies was the General Synod. It was organized in Hagerstown, Maryland, in 1820 by representatives of four constituent synods: Pennsylvania, New York, North Carolina, and Maryland-Virginia. The North Carolina Synod had suggested that the synods could be strengthened by such an organization and resolved that "in its judgment it would be well if the different Evangelical Lutheran Synods in the United States were to stand, in some way or other, in true union with one another." (Wentz, 129). The General Synod established Gettysburg Seminary in 1826 in order to insure a supply of trained pastors for the needs of the congregations.

The General Synod sought to provide a hymnal to serve the worship needs of all English-speaking Lutheran congregations in America. A committee appointed in 1825 published *Hymns Selected and Original, for Public and Private Worship* (Gettysburg, 1828) which was influenced by Quitman's 1814 *Collection*. The General Synod had approved the committee's work at its meeting in October 1827. The first edition included 766 hymns. Revisions in 1841 and 1852 increased the number to 965 and 1024 respectively.

E.E. Ryden (LBW 186) says of its theological and literary character:

> *Hymns Selected and Original* reveals many of the doctrinal aberrations which characterized the General Synod of that period. The book failed to reflect the true genius of the Lutheran Church. Moreover, the few Lutheran hymns it contained had been poorly translated. Despite these shortcomings, however, it found wide acceptance, and was probably used by at least four-fifths of the English-speaking congregations in the United States. By 1856, no less than 69 editions of the volume had been printed.†

† Ryden, 1085.

A copy of an 1854 printing of this hymnal came to the author's attention some twenty years ago. It belonged to a parishioner in North Carolina who said it had been in his family for a hundred years. The book measured 2-1/4 by 3-1/4 inches, was bound in brown leather, and contained 692 pages with 1004 hymns plus additional "Dismissions and Doxologies" bringing the total to 1024. The title page indicated that it was printed and sold by T. Newton Kurtz, No. 151 West Pratt Street, Baltimore. The editorial committee as of the May 16th, 1828 publication date in Gettysburg was listed as:

S. S. Schmucker, Professor of Theology in the Theological Seminary of the General Synod of the Evangelical Lutheran Church

C. P. Krauth, Pastor of the Second English Lutheran Church, Philadelphia

G. Shober, Pastor of the Lutheran Church, Salem, N.C.

J. G. Schmucker, D.D., Pastor of the Lutheran Church, York, Pa.

B. Keller, Pastor of the Lutheran Church, Germantown, Pa.

Samuel S. Schmucker, whose influence was felt strongly in the preparation and revisions of *Hymns Selected and Original,* was one of the principal leaders of the General Synod during this time. He was a vigorous leader of the so-called American Lutheranism movement which advocated a departure, to some degree, from the historic principles of Lutheranism as formulated in the Augsburg Confession and other confessional documents. He was the chief proponent for the establishment of Gettysburg Theological Seminary, became its first professor, and taught systematic theology there for some forty years. His career was a stormy and controversial one during which he definitely left the influence of his personality on more than five hundred men whom he helped to prepare for the Lutheran ministry.

The *Church Book* of the General Council

The American Civil War tragically disrupted both the nation's life and the church's life as well. In 1863 Lutherans in the South withdrew from the General Synod to form the United Synod of the South. The Ministerium of Pennsylvania, due to doctrinal difference, withdrew also and in 1867 organized the General Council, a union of synods committed to historic principles of confessional Lutheranism. During the course of this movement toward confessionalism, the Philadelphia Seminary was established in 1864 and Muhlenberg College in 1867.

The Ministerium had published a new English liturgy in 1860, based largely on the Muhlenberg liturgy of 1748 and in addition restoring basic features of the historic Lutheran liturgy. This service laid the foundations for the preparation of the Common Service of 1888.

After receiving the new liturgy in English, people's thoughts turned to the need of a new hymnal. In 1862 at the convention in Allentown, Dr. William J. Mann in his president's report to the Ministerium expressed the need for "an improved English Hymn Book. . . . more fully in harmony with the spirit of our Church."†

The *Church Book* of the General Council was ready for use at the Council's second convention in 1868 and was favorably received as the most significant book of worship produced thus far by Lutherans in America. It included 167 translations from the Latin, eleven from the Greek, and a considerable representation from recent English hymnody since the compilers had been able to draw upon the outstanding new hymnal from England, *Hymns Ancient and Modern,* 1861. Louis F. Benson (LBW 200) commented on the *Church Book*; "There was at the time no American hymnal so fully representative of the development of hymnody, so discriminating in selection, so scholarly in treatment."‡

The excellence of the *Church Book* can be attributed directly to the exceptional competence and scholarship of the compilers. Especially outstanding among the committee members were Dr. Charles P. Krauth (1823–83), Dr. Beale M. Schmucker (1827–88), and the Rev. Frederick M. Bird. Krauth (LBW 62) graduated from Gettysburg Seminary in 1841 and was a vigorous opponent of the "American Lutheranism" movement of Gettysburg's professor, Dr. Samuel S. Schmucker. Krauth became professor of systematic theology at the Philadelphia Seminary at the time of its establishment in 1864. He edited *The Lutheran, The Missionary,* and the *Lutheran Church Review.* His major theological publication was *The Conservative Reformation and Its Theology,* 1871.

† Reed, *The Lutheran Liturgy* (Philadelphia: Fortress Press, rev. ed., 1960), 177.
‡ Louis Fitzgerald Benson, *The English Hymn* (New York: Doran, 1915), 561.

Two of Krauth's translations appear in the LBW: "The bells of Christmas chime once more" (LBW 62) and "Wide open are your hands" (LBW 489).

Beale M. Schmucker was the son of S. S. Schmucker and graduated from Gettysburg Seminary in 1847 where his father was professor of systematic theology. Influenced by Charles P. Krauth, however, the younger Schmucker departed from his father's "American Lutheranism" theology to become a leader in conservative, confessional Lutheranism. Beale Schmucker became a prominent leader in the General Council, a skilled liturgist and parliamentarian, and played an active role in liturgical renewal, hymnology, and compiling and editing worship resources. He had one of the most prominent roles in the creation of the Common Service, 1888, as we shall see.

The Reverend Frederick Mayer Bird, grandson of a Lutheran pastor, contributed significantly to the *Church Book* from his knowledge and expertise in hymnology. Graduate of the Univeristy of Pennsylvania and Union Theological Seminary, he served as a U.S. Army chaplain and in 1868 left the Lutheran church to become an Episcopal minister. He later became a professor at Lehigh University, editor of *Lippincott's Magazine,* and contributed articles to Julian's *Dictionary of Hymnology.**

Luther Reed (*Worship*, 61f.) comments:

> The *Church Book* was significant as a scholarly and native American liturgy and hymnal in the language of the land. Its strength lay not only in its definitely confessional character, but equally in the depth of its historic foundations and the breadth of its ecumenical sympathies. . . . The one great weakness of both the liturgy and the hymnal of the *Church Book* was the fact that its editors made no provisions for musical rendition of the texts. This lack had to be supplied by the often uneven efforts of private individuals.

This musical deficiency was later overcome by the publication of the *Church Book with Music,* 1893, prepared by Harriet Reynolds Krauth Spaeth (LBW 52).

The General Council also authorized a hymnal to meet the needs of its German congregations. A committee consisting of Drs. Adolf Spaeth, Conrad Sigmund Fritschel (professor at Wartburg Seminary, Dubuque, Iowa), and B. M. Schmucker prepared the *Kirchenbuch für Evangelisch-Lutherische Gemeinden* which was published in Philadelphia in 1877. This German book resembled the English *Church Book* in scope and contents but went a step further in restoring for the first time the full orders of Matins and Vespers for the benefit of Lutherans in America.

John Endlich's *Choralbuch mit Liturgie und Chorgesänge zum Kirchenbuch der Allgemeinen Kirchenversammlung* (Philadelphia, 1879), provided music for the liturgy and hymns, as well as choral selections. While Endlich retained the rhythmic patterns of the old chorale melodies, he attempted to express them in modern notation, which was often less than totally successful.

Hymnody in the South

A small collection of thirty-six hymns was published in 1797 in Salisbury, North Carolina, entitled *Sammlung von erbaulichen Gesängen bey dem öffentlichen Gottesdienste, für die deutschen Gemeinen in Nord-*

Carolina. All of its contents were from German sources. This book was prepared for use by Lutheran, Reformed, and Moravian congregations and appears to have been used mostly within the Carolinas. Its texts reflect the theology of the eighteenth-century German Enlightenment.

One of the most influential families in the southern states was the Henkel family, publishers of church hymnals and other books of theology and Christian instruction. Paul Henkel, a prominent Lutheran pastor and descendant of Lutheran pastors from colonial times, was born in Rowan County, North Carolina, in 1754 and served in the Revolutionary War. After becoming a minister, he was appointed by the Ministerium of Pennsylvania to be an itinerant missionary in Virginia, North and South Carolina, Kentucky, Tennessee, and Ohio. He founded numerous churches and was instrumental in the organization of the North Carolina Synod in 1803, the Ohio Synod in 1813, and the Tennessee Synod in 1820.

Paul Henkel's children also became prominent leaders in the Lutheran church. Solomon was a physician and printer. Philip, a pastor, helped organize the Tennessee Synod. Ambrose, a pastor, became a publisher at New Market, Virginia. Andrew was a pastor in Ohio. David was a pastor in North Carolina, Kentucky, and Indiana. Charles, a gifted preacher, was a pastor in Ohio.

Paul Henkel established a printing business in New Market, Virginia, and from the Henkel press came significant theological publications including the first English edition of the *Book of Concord,* 1851.

In 1810 Paul Henkel published a collection of German hymns entitled *Das neueingerichtete Gesangbuch.* Its purpose was to serve the needs of small congregations which did not need the large *Erbauliche Lieder-Sammlung.* The Henkel book had 246 hymns. A second edition came from the New Market press in 1812.

In 1816 the *Church Hymn Book* appeared, perhaps the first Lutheran hymnal in English to be published in the South. It contained 347 hymns. The North Carolina Synod endorsed Henkel's book in 1817, giving it an official synodical status. The hymnal contains both original texts by Paul Henkel and English translations from German originals.

A second edition of the *Church Hymn Book* appeared in 1838, prepared by Paul's son Ambrose, who states in the preface that he was commissioned by the Tennessee Synod. It was enlarged to 679 hymns; of these, Paul Henkel contributed 303 (translations, paraphrases, or originals). Later editions came in 1850 and 1857.

The Tennessee Synod published its own liturgy in 1840. This was used until 1872 when the synod adopted the *Church Book* of the General Council.

The Tennessee Synod included churches in North and South Carolina, Virginia, and Tennessee. Paul Henkel led in the establishment of the Tennessee Synod in 1820 because he felt the North Carolina Synod was failing to uphold the doctrinal standards of confessional Lutheranism. For a century Tennessee Synod congregations existed side by side with other synodical congregations within adjoining states.

The North Carolina
Book of Worship, 1868

After the Civil War many Lutherans in the southern states were being influenced by the revivalistic practices of neighboring denominations. In order to combat this trend and to encourage a move to more formal worship, the North Carolina Synod sponsored a new *Book of Worship* in

1868. Worship had previously been highly informal and centered on the ministers. According to a contemporary account,

> Many will breathe a silent prayer, then look about to see who is there. Every time the door opens all look around, perhaps awaiting the minister. Presently the minister enters and immediately ascends the pulpit. Whilst he is finding his text and the hymns, the choir sings an introductory. He arises, gives out his hymn, reads a portion of Scripture. He then prays and all are silent from the fact that no one knows what he intends to pray about or pray for. He then gives out another hymn, after the singing of which he announces his text and preaches the sermon, prays again, sings another hymn, and dismisses.†

The new hymnal and service book involved the congregation in singing liturgical responses. Some congregations resisted the new hymnal with violent opposition; others used only the hymnal portion of the book. The Tennessee Synod gave the book mild approval but recommended the *Church Book,* 1868, of the northern General Council for its own congregations.

The Common Service, 1888

The Common Service produced by the General Council, the General Synod, and the United Synod of the South in 1888 was a significant step in the direction of Henry Melchior Muhlenberg's dream of "one church, one book." The idea had been revived at various times over the years. Gottlieb Schober, a North Carolina synod pastor, echoed Muhlenberg's idea in correspondence to the Ministerium of Pennsylvania at the time of the founding of the General Synod in 1820. In 1870, the eighty-year-old Dr. John Bachman of Charleston, for fifty-six years the pastor of St. John's Church in that city, wrote to the General Synod meeting in Winchester, Virginia (quoted in Reed, *Liturgy,* 182f.):

> We cannot fail in the course of time to become one of the largest denominations, in point of membership, on this Continent. . . . We have, however, too many Synods and the shades of difference that are formed in our doctrines have prevented such a union as ought to exist in the Church of the Reformation.
> I have ventured to suggest to our Synod the appointment of delegates to meet those of other Synods in consultation, for the purpose of promoting a greater uniformity in our Books of Worship, than at present exists. . . . If this object could be accomplished, our Church would, in my opinion, be more respected at home and abroad, and would accomplish a far greater amount of good.

In 1876 the General Synod, South in effect invited the General Synod, North and the General Council to consider "the feasibility of adopting but one Book containing the same hymns and the same order of services and Liturgic forms to be used in the public Worship of God in all the English-speaking Evang. Lutheran Churches of the United States." (Reed, *Liturgy,* 183) The idea met with a favorable response from both of the other bodies and a joint committee began its work in 1884. Dr. B. M. Schmucker was chosen chairman and the Reverend Edward T. Horn of Charlestown, South Carolina, became secretary. It is believed that the term "Common Service" was first used by Edward Traill Horn

---

† H. George Anderson, *The North Carolina Synod Through 175 Years (1803–1978)* (Salisbury, North Carolina: Sponsored by the Historical Committee of the North Carolina Synod, 1978) 16f.

(1850-1915) in an article entitled "Feasibility of a Service for all English-speaking Lutherans" published in the *Lutheran Quarterly Review* in 1881.†

In *Worship* (p. 62) Luther Reed observes:

> The chief architects of the Common Service were Drs. Beale M. Schmucker, Edward Traill Horn, and George U. Wenner. Other more or less active members of the joint committee were Drs. E. J. Wolf, Joseph A. Seiss [LBW 518], Henry E. Jacobs [LBW 225], Adolph Spaeth, and F. W. Conrad. Dr. Horn at thirty-four years of age was the youngest member of the committee and, as events developed, the most influential. A graduate of the Philadelphia Seminary, he was pastor of historic St. John's Church in Charleston, South Carolina. His initiative, taste, and judgment gave him the balance of power in the entire enterprise.

The General Council in 1879, meeting in Zanesville, Ohio, proposed the rule that should decide all questions related to the preparation of the Common Service: "The common consent of the pure Lutheran liturgies of the sixteenth century, and when there is not an entire agreement among them the consent of the largest number of greatest weight."‡

The Common Service of 1888 was a liturgy only, without musical settings and without a hymnal. The three sponsoring bodies then prepared their own hymnbooks containing the Common Service along with their own separate collections of hymns. The General Council authorized a new and enlarged edition of the *Church Book* to include the Common Service. On October 15, 1888, Dr. B. M. Schmucker, having prepared the copy for the printer, ran with the completed manuscript in his handbag to catch a train from Pottstown to Philadelphia and died from overexertion on the train. After further delays, the revised *Church Book* finally appeared in 1892.

Eventually the Common Service appeared in the service books of nearly every Lutheran body in America.

The *Common Service Book*, 1917

In 1909 the General Council proposed to the General Synod and the United Synod in the South that the three groups produce a common hymnal and a standard form of the Common Service. Each of the three bodies had made its own revisions in the text so that there was no uniformity among them.

The joint committee began its work in Philadelphia on November 1, 1910. Luther D. Reed lists the membership in the original edition (1947) of *The Lutheran Liturgy*. (It is omitted in the revised edition.) Chairman was Charles S. Albert until his death in 1912 when John A. Singmaster succeeded him. Secretary was Edward Traill Horn until 1914, and then Luther D. Reed.

A full list of the membership is as follows:

From the General Synod—Charles S. Albert, David H. Bauslin, Ezra K. Bell, Jacob A. Clutz, William E. Fischer (LBW 171), George A. Getty, Frederick H. Knubel, Harold Lewars, Junius B. Remensnyder, John A. Singmaster, and George U. Wenner.

---

† Reed, *Liturgy*, 184. Dr. Horn's grandson, Edward T. Horn III, had a prominent role in the preparation of the *Service Book and Hymnal*, 1958, and is the translator of "Come, oh, come, O quickening Spirit," (LBW 478).

‡ Dr. B. M. Schmucker's *Preface to the Common Service*, 1888.

From the United Synod in the South—Eli C. Cronk, Luther A. Fox, M. G. G. Scherer, and Andrew G. Voigt.

From the General Council—Ernst F. Bachman, C. Theodore Benze, Charles M. Esbjorn, Michael E. Haberland, Ludwig Holmes, Edward Traill Horn, William L. Hunton, Charles M. Jacobs, Henry Eyster Jacobs, Fritz Jacobson, Edwain F. Keever, John C. Mattes, C. Armand Miller, Jeremiah F. Ohl, Luther D. Reed, Gomer C. Rees, Albert Reichert, Theodore E. Schmauk, Carl B. Schuchard, Adolf Spaeth (active in preliminary studies of the Church Book Committee of which he was chairman until his death in 1910), August Steimle, Paul Z. Strodach (LBW 143), and John E. Whitteker.

Liturgical texts chairman was John A. Singmaster; hymnal texts chairman and music chairman (presumably for both hymns and liturgy) was Jeremiah H. Ohl.

The committee completed its work in time for the *Common Service Book* to appear in 1917, the four hundredth anniversary of the Reformation. Out of the work of a joint committee for the celebration came the impetus for the merger of the three general bodies to form the United Lutheran Church in America. In November 1918 the new church came into being in New York City and immediately had a *Common Service Book* with hymnal and full musical settings.

> When the music edition of the *Common Service Book* came from the presses in 1917 it was hailed as one of the most significant events of the quadricentennial observance of the Protestant Reformation. But it also had far-reaching practical results. The spirit of fellowship engendered by thirty-three years of joint liturgical and hymnological studies on the part of the three general bodies was undoubtedly one of the most potent factors which led to their organic union in 1918 as the United Lutheran Church in America. The merger brought together the oldest Lutheran churches in American life, groups which had become completely identified with the American scene and thoroughly imbued with its ideals. The *Common Service Book,* by the same token, represented the highest point thus far attained by Lutheran scholarship and culture in the New World, and was so recognized by all communions.†

Norwegian Hymnody in America

From 1846 to 1918 there were at least seventeen different synods of the Norwegian Lutherans who had come to America. As early as 1870 Norwegians were questioning the need for so many Norwegian Lutheran bodies.

Some of the hymnals brought by early Norwegian settlers, such as those by Thomas H. Kingo (LBW 102) and Magnus Brostrup Landstad (LBW 310), contained hymns that are still being used today. The first Norwegian hymnal to be published in America was primarily the work of Ulrik Vilhelm Koren (1826–1910), president of the Norwegian Lutheran Synod of America from 1894 to 1910, a group in fellowship with the Missouri Synod. Still used today is Koren's hymn "Oh, sing jubilee to the Lord" (LBW 256), a paraphrase of Psalm 100. The first Norwegian pastor to settle west of the Mississippi, Koren also taught at Luther College, Decorah, Iowa. Koren's hymnal was published in 1874, containing 515 hymns (115 by Landstad and 27 original texts and 21 translations by Koren).

In 1893 the United Lutheran Norwegian Church (which operated St. Olaf College, Northfield, Minnesota) and the Hauge Synod united in the

† Ryden, 1086.

100

publication of Landstad's hymnal. They added to it 96 hymns, making a total of 730. The hymns were in Norwegian and were so predominantly European and Norwegian that only one hymn had been translated from English.

The first Norwegian hymnal printed in English was the *Hymnbook* of 1879 sponsored by the Norwegian Synod and printed by the Lutheran Publishing House in Decorah, Iowa. It was prepared by August Crull (LBW 24), a Missouri Synod pastor, and was also used by Missouri Synod congregations. Of 130 hymns, eighty-two were German translations and seven from Danish and Norwegian sources.

Five years after publishing the Landstad hymnal in Norwegian, the United Norwegian Church brought out its first English hymnbook, *The Church and Sunday School Hymnal* of 1898. It included 316 texts, only two of which were translations from the Danish and Norwegian.

In 1905 the Norwegian Synod, which had fellowship with the Missouri Synod and the Synodical Conference, published an English hymnal containing 309 hymns, of which nine were Scandinavian translations.

The official hymnal most widely used by Norwegians in the twentieth century was *The Lutheran Hymnary,* 1912. It was jointly produced by the United Church, the Norwegian Synod, and the Hauge Synod. John Dahle was head of the committee and F. Melius Christiansen (1871-1955), founder of the St. Olaf Choir, was music editor. This hymnal recovered treasures of the Norwegian heritage in its 262 translations from the Norwegian, along with 118 translations from German sources. In 1917 the Norwegian Synod, the United Norwegian Lutheran Church, and the Hauge Synod merged to form the Norwegian Lutheran Church of America, later known as the Evangelical Lutheran Church. This new body adopted *The Lutheran Hymnary* as its official hymnal. In 1960 the Evangelical Lutheran Church, the United Evangelical Lutheran Church (Danish), and the American Lutheran Church (German) merged to form the national body also known as the American Lutheran Church, with headquarters in Minneapolis.

An unofficial hymnal entitled *Concordia* was published in 1916, in both English and Norwegian, for youth and Sunday school use. In 1932 it appeared in a revised edition with an increase in the number of hymns from 250 to 434. The large number of Scandinavian folk songs, some with lyrical harmonizations by F. Melius Christiansen, won an enthusiastic reception for this book, and in many Norwegian congregations it rivaled *The Lutheran Hymnary* in popularity.

Danish Hymnody

Danish Lutherans were slower to organize into church bodies than were Swedes and Norwegians. For one thing, the Danish immigration during the nineteenth century was much smaller by comparison. Also for many years the Danes shared their church life with the Norwegians with whom they had much in common. The first Danes to organize a congregation of their own were apparently those in Indianapolis, Indiana in 1868. The first Danish church body to be organized was the Danish Evangelical Lutheran Church, formed in 1874 out of a church mission society. It was conservative in theology and followed the traditions of Nikolai F. S. Grundtvig (LBW 62), the great folk hero, church leader and hymnwriter of Denmark. The Lutheran Danes in America were undoubtedly singing the original versions of the popular hymns of Grundtvig such as ''Built on a rock'' (LBW 365), ''Bright and glorious is the sky'' (LBW 75), and others.

Danish immigrants undoubtedly brought their hymnals from their homeland which would have included collections by Thomas H. Kingo (LBW 102), C. C. N. Balle (LBW 62) and the Guldberg-Harboe *Psalmebog* (LBW 43).

Danish Lutheranism in America developed around two church organizations eventually called the United Evangelical Lutheran Church and the American Evangelical Lutheran Church. With their limited numerical strength, neither group was able to produce any significant hymnals in the Danish language. In 1927 they jointly produced an English collection entitled *Hymnal for Church and Home,* with revisions in 1938 and 1949. In 1932 they also jointly produced *The Junior Hymnal.* The AELC also published a collection of folk songs and hymns entitled *A World of Song.*

The Virgin Islands belonged to Denmark until the United States purchased them in 1917. The Lutheran church in Denmark supplied pastors during the time of their possession of the islands and in 1872 provided an English-language hymnbook published in Copenhagen and entitled *Hymns, Liturgy, and Prayers for the use of the Evangelical Lutheran Church of the Danish Westindia Islands.* Containing 520 hymns, the book also includes an order of service with the traditional epistles and gospels, and other liturgical rites. The hymns are predominantly Anglican with scarcely a dozen coming from Lutheran sources.

In 1960 the UELC with 183 congregations participated in the merger of the new American Lutheran Church, and in 1962 the AELC with 182 congregations became a part of the Lutheran Church in America. Both of these new church bodies were then using the recently-produced *Service Book and Hymnal* of 1958.

Augustana Hymnody

Ryden (p. 1089) notes that Swedish Lutherans who participated in the founding of the Augustana Lutheran Church in 1860 "cherished Wallin's [LBW 73] psalmbook of 1819 as their dearest treasure next to the Bible." Johan Olof Wallin's masterpiece was so highly-regarded by Swedish Lutherans that no change was made in it for more than a century.

In 1856 Tuve Nilsson Hasselquist (1816–1891) published *Femtio Andliga Sanger* (Fifty Spiritual Songs). Born in Sweden and educated at the University of Lund, he was a pastor in Sweden from 1839 until 1852 when he came to Galesburg, Illinois. He was a founder and the first president of the Augustana Synod (1860–70), president of Augustana College and Theological Seminary (1863–91), and editor of the church paper *Augustana* (1855–91).

Following soon after the Hasselquist songbook was a collection entitled *Salems Sanger* by Eric Norelius (1833–1916), Swedish-born pastor in America who helped found the Augustana Synod and was its president (1874–81; 1899–1910), editor of the *Augustana* periodical, and a distinguished historian of the Augustana church.

In 1892 the church authorized a new Swedish hymnal entitled *Hemlandssånger* (Songs of the Homeland) intended for use in Vespers and other informal occasions. Of its 500 hymns, nearly 100 were by Sweden's prolific poet and hymnwriter Carolina ("Lina") Sandell Berg (1832–1903), whose popular hymn "Children of the heavenly Father" is in the LBW, no. 474.

In 1895 the Augustana Synod authorized the theological faculty of Augustana Seminary to prepare a new English hymnal. With Dr. C. W.

Foss as editor, the committee submitted a text edition of 355 hymns to the synod meeting in 1899. The synod approved their work and ordered a music edition. In 1901 the English hymnal entitled *Hymnal* appeared with 355 hymns in a music edition. This book was considered an interim hymnal, to serve until a more adequate book could be prepared.

In 1910 a hymnal committee was appointed whose work finally resulted in *The Hymnal* of 1925. In 1917 E. W. Olson (LBW 474), secretary of literature at Augustana Book Concern, Rock Island, Illinois, joined the committee; it is his translation of "Children of the heavenly Father" which has been used in American hymnals. Added to the committee in 1920 was C. A. Wendell, who is represented in the LBW with stanza 2 of "Wondrous are your ways, O God!" (LBW 311). Joining the committee in 1922 was E. E. Ryden who played an influential role in selecting the tunes and editing the liturgical music for *The Hymnal*, 1925. Ryden served also as secretary of the commission on the hymnal for the *Service Book and Hymnal* and is represented in the LBW with four original texts (186, 339, 354, 516) and two translations (319, 384).

The 1925 *Hymnal* contains 663 hymns of which 73 are translations of Swedish originals. The preface to *The Hymnal* lists about 42 texts written for the book and 33 music settings newly composed or arranged.

The liturgical section includes an English translation of the Swedish liturgy with variable musical settings of certain parts following the practice of the Church of Sweden. It also contains a three-year lectionary with texts written out in the American Standard version of the Bible. Along with occasional services, a psalter, and other miscellaneous items, the Common Service, Matins, and Vespers with musical settings are reproduced from the *Common Service Book* of the United Lutheran Church in America.

Finnish Hymnody in America

"More than half of the 900 colonists in 'New Sweden,' the Swedish seventeenth-century settlement along the Delaware River, had been Finns."† These colonists and their congregations became Episcopalian when they could no longer secure pastors from Sweden.

Lutherans from Finland began large-scale immigrations to America after 1850, settling in the northern states from coast to coast, with concentrations in Minnesota, the iron mining regions of northern Michigan, and Canada.

At first the Finns affiliated with Norwegian or Swedish congregations but after 1867 Finnish congregations began to be organized. In 1876 the first Finnish pastor in America, Alfred E. Backman, came to serve three congregations in Hancock, Calumet, and Allouez, Michigan. With an increase in congregations, the Finnish Evangelical Lutheran Church of America, known as the Suomi Synod, was organized in 1890 with J. K. Nikander as its first president. Six years later Suomi College and Theological Seminary were established at Hancock, with Nikander serving as president until his death in 1919.

One group broke away and founded the Finnish National Church in 1898. Another group had started the Finnish Apostolic Lutheran Church of America around 1873.

The first hymnal used by the Finns in America was the *Suomalainen Virsikirja* (Finnish Hymnbook) published in Helsinki in 1886 with the

† Armas K. E. Holmio, "Suomi Synod," *The Encyclopedia of the Lutheran Church* (Minneapolis: Augsburg Publishing House, 1965), 1373.

103

sub-title: "For the Evangelical Lutheran Congregations under the Grand Duke of Finland." In 1909 the Finnish Lutheran Book Concern in Hancock reprinted this book in the original language.

Another valuable resource for Finnish congregations was the chorale book, *Koraalikirja,* by G. J. Vogler, published in Helsinki in 1909.

A growing interest in preserving the heritage of Finnish hymnody for congregations in America led to the publication in 1925 of *Siionin Lauluja* (Songs of Zion) by the Book Concern in Hancock. The contents were mostly Finnish, but the addition of an English section in the back reveals a trend toward the growing use of the English language in the church. The hymnal committee consisted of John Wargelin, then president of Suomi College and later president of Suomi Synod (1950–55), Victor Kuusisto, Hugo Hillila, S. V. Autere, Alpo Setala, and Matt Luttinen.

A Sunday school hymnal, *Pyhakoulun Laulukirja,* was published in Hancock in 1923. Approximately three-fourths of the hymns were in the Finnish language with the remainder in English.

Until 1930 the Suomi Synod had used a version of the Church of Finland liturgy which had been translated into English and published in Hancock. After 1930, by synod authorization, congregations used *The Hymnal* of the Augustana Church which had been published in 1925 in Rock Island, Illinois. This hymnal included the Common Service of the United Lutheran Church in America as well as the traditional Swedish liturgy. Finnish congregations originally used *The Hymnal* for the sake of the hymns, but for the order of service they used the English translation of the liturgy of the Church of Finland. Eventually some of the Finnish congregations began to use the Common Service as well. Finnish Sunday schools also made use of the Augustana *Junior Hymnal.*

The Suomi Synod assumed a responsible role within American Lutheranism and in ecumenical relationships. In 1962 the synod, with 153 congregations, merged with the United Lutheran Church in America, the Augustana Lutheran Church, and the American Evangelical Lutheran Church to form the Lutheran Church in America.

The Joint Synod of Ohio and Its Hymnody

The Joint Synod of Ohio, one of the antecedent bodies of the American Lutheran Church, was founded in 1818. Its congregations consisted of German Lutherans of Pennsylvania who had crossed the Allegheny Mountains in the late 1700s to settle the Northwest Territory.

For several decades it was content to use German-language hymnals. These included the popular *Erbauliche Lieder-Sammlung* of 1786 and many of its subsequent editions. Pual Henkel, a home missionary in Springfield, Ohio in 1810, prepared *Das Neu Eingerichtete Gesang-Buch* containing 249 more or less familiar German hymns. Possibly used also was *Das Neue Gesangbuch,* 1816, authorized by the Pennsylvania Ministerium's Lutheran Conference in western Pennsylvania and the Ministerium's conservative *Deutsches Gesangbuch* of 1849.

The *Gesangbuch* appeared in 1870, authorized by the Joint Synod of Ohio and containing 532 hymns. Printed in Columbus, Ohio, this hymnal went through at least fourteen editions and included a later supplement of fifty-four texts.

The Synod produced an English hymnal in 1845 entitled *A Collection of Hymns and Prayers, for Public and Private Worship,* containing 453 hymns and printed at Zanesville, Ohio. The contents reflect a strong position of Lutheran orthodoxy. Many hymns came from the General

Synod's *Hymns, Selected and Original* and a few, from the Episcopal hymnal. The Ohio collection was revised in 1855, 1858, and 1863.

In 1880 the Ohio Synod brought out *The Evangelical Lutheran Hymnal.* It enjoyed widespread use for decades, with a music edition appearing in 1908. One of the influential synodical leaders well represented in this hymnal through original texts and translations was Matthias Loy (LBW 490). Three of his hymns or translations were in the *Service Book and Hymnal* (518, 260, 506), and one of these, his translation of "Let me be yours forever," is in the LBW (490).

The Buffalo Synod and Its Hymnody

The Buffalo Synod was one of the three German synods which merged in 1930 to become the American Lutheran Church with headquarters in Columbus, Ohio. (The other two were the Joint Synod of Ohio and the Iowa Synod.) The Buffalo Synod was organized in 1845 by Johannes A. A. Grabau (1804–1879), a German-born pastor who opposed the decree of King Frederick William III enforcing union of Lutherans and Reformed. After being deposed and arrested in Germany, he came to America with about a thousand followers and settled in Buffalo, New York, where he was pastor for nearly forty years. He founded the Martin Luther Seminary in Buffalo in 1840 and taught there.

In 1842 Grabau published the *Evangelisch-Lutherisches Kirchengesang-Buch* in Buffalo. Its 491 hymns represented a strong expression of the German heritage with a conservative theological stance. A liturgy was included with the hymns which, in an 1848 revision, added the historic Gospels and epistles. The Grabau hymnal was revised again in 1865 and later.

When the need developed for worship in the English language, the Buffalo Synod used *The Evangelical Lutheran Hymnal,* 1880, produced by the Joint Synod of Ohio.

The *American Lutheran Hymnal,* 1930

Efforts to produce an intersynodical hymnal were begun in 1921 when representatives of eight Lutheran bodies met in Chicago at the invitation of the Iowa Synod. An intersynodical hymnal committee worked during that decade and produced the *American Lutheran Hymnal* in 1930. The book was accepted only by the American Lutheran Church which was formed also in 1930 out of the merger of the Joint Synod of Ohio, the Iowa Synod, and the Buffalo Synod.

Containing 651 hymns, the 1930 book sought to be an ecumenical collection of Christian hymnody, drawing freely upon existing Lutheran hymnals to provide a representation of both English sources and also traditional German and Scandinavian chorales. Emmanuel Poppen headed the intersynodical hymnal committee. Hermann Brueckner (LBW 249), a professor at Hebron College, Hebron, Nebraska, provided seventy translations from German hymns, three from French, and four original hymns. Others well-represented by original and translated hymns were Paul E. Kretzmann, professor at Concordia Seminary, Saint Louis; William H. Lehmann, home missions executive of the American Lutheran Church; and A. F. Rohr, a pastor in Fremont, Ohio. For the liturgical section of the book, the Common Service, Matins, and Vespers along with musical settings were reproduced from the United Lutheran Church in America's *Common Service Book* of 1917.

The *American Lutheran Hymnal* served the needs of the American Lutheran Church until the 1958 arrival of the *Service Book and Hymnal.*

Even then a number of congregations continued to use the 1930 book.

A new merger of Lutheran bodies in 1960 created the new American Lutheran Church, with headquarters in Minneapolis, out of the former ALC, the Evangelical Lutheran Church (Norwegian), and the United Evangelical Lutheran Church (Danish). In 1963 the Lutheran Free Church also merged with the new ALC.

The Lutheran Church—Missouri Synod and Its Hymnody

The German Evangelical Lutheran Synod of Missouri, Ohio, and Other States, now known as the Lutheran Church—Missouri Synod, was organized in 1847 by Lutherans from Saxony who had fled their native land to escape rationalism and religious coercion. C. F. W. Walther (1811–1887) had arrived with the group of some 700 immigrants in 1839 and became their spiritual leader a few years later. In 1841 he became pastor of Trinity Church, St. Louis, the "mother church" of the Missouri Synod and in 1844 began *Der Lutheraner,* a widely-circulated periodical. In 1847 he published a German hymnbook for his congregation, the *Kirchengesangbuch für Evangelisch-Lutherische Gemeinden.* It contained 437 texts representative of the orthodox and confessional periods of the sixteenth and seventeenth centuries plus a few eighteenth-century texts. An initial printing of 1,500 copies for Trinity Church was quickly subscribed and additional printings followed.†

"Walther's hymnbook" or the "St. Louis hymnal," as it was called, remained the property of the St. Louis congregation for over fifteen years but then became the official book of worship of the Missouri Synod, officially transferred to the general body on March 31, 1862.‡

The Walther book went through various editions and reprints until the final edition of 1917, sharing honors with the *Erbauliche Lieder-Sammlung* for its longevity among American Lutheran hymnals. (E.C. Wolf, p. 174)

The criteria for the hymn selection were described in the June 15, 1848 issue of *Der Lutheraner,* probably written by Walther himself:

> In the selection of the adopted hymns the chief consideration was that they be pure in doctrine; that they have found almost universal acceptance within the orthodox German Lutheran Church and have thus received the almost universal testimony that they have come forth from the true spirit (of Lutheranism); that they express not so much the changing circumstances of individual persons but rather contain the language of the whole church, because the book is to be used primarily in public worship; and finally that they, though bearing the imprint of Christian simplicity, be not merely rhymed prose but the creations of a truly Christian poetry.#

The first hymnal in English used by Missouri Synod congregations was the *Hymnbook,* 1879, sponsored by the Norwegian Synod, prepared by August Crull, a Missouri Synod pastor, and printed by the Lutheran Publishing House in Decorah, Iowa.

Between 1882 and 1905 three small hymnals appeared that helped pave the way for the first official English hymnal of the synod. *Lutheran Hymns. For the Use of English Lutheran Missions* appeared in 1882 with

---

† Edward C. Wolf, "Lutheran Hymnody and Music Published in America 1700-1859—A Bibliography," *Concordia Historical Institute Quarterly* (Vol. 50, no. 4, Winter 1977), p. 174.

‡ Carl Schalk, *The Roots of Hymnody in the Lutheran Church—Missouri Synod.* (St. Louis: Concordia Publishing House, 1965), p. 17.

#Schalk, 15.

eighteen familiar hymns set to fifteen melodies. *Hymns of the Evangelical Lutheran Church,* also for the use of English Lutheran missions, was published by Concordia Publishing House in 1886, compiled and edited by August Crull. In 1905 *Hymns for Evangelical Lutheran Missions,* known as the "Grey Hymnal," appeared, the work of F. Bente of Concordia Seminary, St. Louis.

In 1888 the English Lutheran Conference of Missouri authorized an English hymnal. Crull prepared the book and the following year it was published in Baltimore under the title *Evangelical Lutheran Hymn Book* with 400 hymns, text only. Liturgical material included morning and evening worship, and the three ecumenical creeds, along with the Augsburg Confession. In 1891 a new edition appeared with the addition of fifty hymns plus the Common Service, Matins, and Vespers, the liturgical orders having been approved by the General Council, General Synod, and the United Synod in the South. This edition was known as the Pittsburgh hymnal.

Encouraging the use of the *Evangelical Lutheran Hymn Book,* the president of the English Conference, F. Kügele, wrote in *Der Lutheraner,* "If we desire to build a true English Lutheran church for our descendants, then we must also be concerned, before it is too late, for a true English hymnal." (Schalk, 42)

The need for a music edition was met in 1912 with an enlarged edition of the *Evangelical Lutheran Hymn-book* with tunes. Published by Concordia Publishing House in St. Louis, it became the official English hymnal of the entire Missouri Synod. Along with 567 hymns, it contained a liturgical section of 112 pages with the Common Service, Matins, Vespers, doxologies, and chants.

In 1929 the Missouri Synod authorized the revision of the *Evangelical Lutheran Hymn-Book* and an intersynodical committee of the Synodical Conference began its work the following year. Under the chairmanship of W. G. Polack (LBW 168), the committee completed its work on a hymnal and service book in ten years and *The Lutheran Hymnal* was published in 1941. Its 660 hymns include 347 translations from the following sources: German, 248; Latin, 46; Scandinavian, 31; Greek, 9; Slovak 6; French, 2; Italian, 2; Dutch, Welsh, and Finnish, 1 each. The appearance of this book brought to English-speaking Lutherans "the treasure of the confessionally orthodox and musically vital hymnody of Reformation times. . . rooted in sound doctrine." (Schalk, 46f.)

The Lutheran Hymnal includes an Easter hymn by its distinguished pioneer leader and theologian, C. F. W. Walther: "He's risen, He's risen, Christ Jesus, the Lord" (no. 198). Another pioneer pastor, Herman Fick, is represented with a missionary hymn, "Rise, Thou Light of Gentile nations" (no. 498). W. G. Polack, chairman of the hymnal committee, contributed nine translations and three original hymns; one of the originals, "God the Father, Son and Spirit," was written to commemorate the centennial of the Saxon migration to America and was sung in nationwide anniversary services on June 19, 1938.

The liturgical section of *The Lutheran Hymnal* included the Common Service, Matins, and Vespers with musical settings, plus introits, collects, and graduals for the church year, collects and prayers, and the psalter.

Valuable companion volumes are *The Handbook to the Lutheran Hymnal* by W. G. Polack (St. Louis: Concordia Publishing House, 1942) and the *Concordance to The Lutheran Hymnal* by E. V. Haserodt (St. Louis: Concordia, 1956).

In 1969 the LC—MS Commission on Worship brought out the *Wor-*

ship Supplement containing ninety-three new hymns. These included traditional hymns revised for modern use and newly-written hymns relevant to Christian living in today's world. From the original material included in the *Worship Supplement* the LBW has the following texts: "From shepherding of stars that gaze" (LBW 63), "Lord of all nations, grant me grace" (LBW 419), "O God, O Lord of heaven and earth" (LBW 396), and "Thy strong word did cleave the darkness" (LBW 233); also the text and tune of "Now the silence" (LBW 205) and the tune of "Sing, my tongue, the glorious battle" (LBW 118).

Contemporary forms of liturgical materials included in the *Worship Supplement* were three orders for Holy Eucharist, three forms of confession and absolution, three services of prayer and preaching, new musical settings for Matins and Vespers, and offices for Prime, Noonday, and Compline. Liturgical music settings were prepared by Paul Bunjes (LBW 38) and Richard Hillert (LBW 63). The *Worship Supplement* provides a pew edition with text and melodies, and an organist's edition with accompaniments.

The *Service Book and Hymnal,* 1958

During the first half of the twentieth century, Lutheran churches in America and Canada were divided into a confusing assortment of districts, synods, and general or national church bodies. From colonial times the immigrant church had perpetuated its original linguistic, ethnic, cultural, and theological differences into separate organizational structures from shore to shore. The multiplicity of Lutheran groups and especially the alphabetical abbreviations by which they were known were largely incomprehensible not only to non-Lutherans but also to the vast majority of Lutheran pew sitters.

The differences, of course, extended to the worship practices and hymnals and service books of the various Lutheran bodies. By mid-century, "A Mighty Fortress" appeared in six different text versions and four different tune variations in the Lutheran hymnals currently in use. It was indeed time to move closer to Muhlenberg's dream of "one church, one book."

The United Lutheran Church in America, meeting in convention in Minneapolis in 1944, was about to accept the report of its *Common Service Book* committee concerning six years of work on proposals for hymnal revision. In a moment with far-reaching implications, Dr. Oscar Blackwelder, pastor of the Lutheran Church of the Reformation in Washington, D.C., introduced an amendment that instructed the committee, in completing the hymnal revision, "to seek the fullest possible cooperation with other Lutheran bodies, in the hope of producing, as nearly as proves feasible, a common Lutheran hymnal in America." (Reed, *Worship,* 66) The convention responded positively and the way was prepared for two-thirds of the Lutherans in America to have a common hymnal and service book.

The Joint Commission on the Hymnal began its work in Pittsburgh June 19–21, 1945. Eight months later the Joint Commission on the Liturgy was organized in Chicago. Both commissions worked independently during the coming decade. Dr. Luther D. Reed served as chairman of both commissions. Ultimately eight church bodies participated in the project. Four of these groups merged in 1960 to form the American Lutheran Church: the largest group, also called the American Lutheran Church which had formed in 1930 from three German groups, the Iowa Synod, the Joint Synod of Ohio, and the Buffalo Synod; the

Evangelical Lutheran Church in America (Norwegian), the United Evangelical Lutheran Church (Danish), and (in 1963) the Lutheran Free Church (Norwegian) united with the other merged group.

The other four entered into union in 1962 to form the Lutheran Church in America. These were the Augustana Lutheran Church (Swedish), the American Evangelical Lutheran Church (Danish), the Suomi Synod (Finnish), and the United Lutheran Church in America (predominantly German).

Early in its work the hymnal commission surveyed the four hymnals used by the participating churches and discovered 153 hymns in common; 192 of the same hymns were included in three of the four hymnals.

The Lutheran Church—Missouri Synod declined the invitation to participate for reasons stated by President John W. Behnken in his reply of August 17, 1946: "Our Synod recently published a new Hymnal. . . (and) would not be interested now in effecting another change." (Reed, *Worship,* 67)

Dr. Ernest E. Ryden, secretary of the hymnal commission, explained to synodical representatives at the national assembly in Chicago, November 6-7, 1957:

> Although no set of rules or principles were ever established by the Commission on a Common Hymnal, the members of the Commission soon arrived at a common understanding relative to the requisites that should be met by every hymn included in the collection. Three of these were constantly kept in the foreground:
> A. It must be Scriptural in language or thought.
> B. It must be devotional in character.
> C. It must be lyrical in quality and exalted in poetic expression.
> In its first report to the eight cooperating churches, the Commission stated: "We have no call to preserve mediocrity, triviality or sentimentality, but should provide our people with hymns that are noble in thought and distinguished in form."
> In general, the Commission sought to make the hymnal a true companion of the liturgy, providing for the full round of the Christian Year and all aspects of the Christian life. It also endeavored to produce a hymnal truly ecumenical in character which would give expression to the continuity and catholicity of the church's life. The ultimate touchstone of a good hymn is not Lutheran authorship, but faithfulness to Scriptural truth. It should meet the spiritual needs of contemporary America.†

The SBH contains 602 hymns, covering 710 pages (often two tunes are provided and occasionally three). Liturgical material and indexes require 314 additional pages producing a total of 1,024 pages.

The collection contains some eighty hymns from classical Greek and Latin sources. It is well represented with Lutheran heritage hymns, including Scandinavian. Almost two-thirds of the hymns are of English or American origin. More than fifty American authors are represented, many of whom had not appeared in earlier Lutheran hymnals.

The music of the hymnal includes sixteen plainsong melodies, some eighty German chorales (with fifteen Bach harmonizations), twelve Swedish chorales and folk tunes, twelve Norwegian tunes, and ten from the Danish. English hymn tunes are in abundance, including recent composers such as Ralph Vaughan Williams (LBW 101), Martin Shaw (LBW 541), and Gustav Holst. Canadian composers or arrangers include

---

† Ryden, "Review of the Hymns in the New Service Book and Hymnal," in *Program of Introduction for the Service Book and Hymnal of the Lutheran Church, 1957-1958* (unpublished manual), pp. 12-13.

109

Graham George (LBW 121), Healey Willan (LBW 125) (in the liturgical music), and Ulrich S. Leupold (LBW 516). Twenty previously unpublished hymn tunes appear as a result of a tune competition conducted by the Commission.

The *Common Service Book* of 1917 had expressed the heritage of approximately one-third of American Lutheranism. The *Service Book and Hymnal* blended the traditions of German, Swedish, Danish, Finnish, and Norwegian groups representing two-thirds of the Lutherans in America.

Dr. Ryden commented in 1965:

> Although the *Service Book and Hymnal* may be rightly regarded as a spiritual and cultural triumph in American Lutheranism, its creators do not look upon it as the final word in a common book of worship. That ideal, they feel, will not be achieved until the other one-third of the Lutherans in the new world cooperate in the creation of such a volume.†

The membership of the Joint Commission on the Liturgy and Hymnal was as follows:

> L Commission on the Liturgy
> H Commission on the Hymnal
> + deaths during the twelve-year working period

American Lutheran Church

L. O. Burry + H
Albert Jagnow + H
  Secretary of music committee
Hans Knauer H
H. C. Leupold L
Lawrence S. Price H
Samuel F. Salzman L

American Evangelical Lutheran Church

A. C. Kildegaard L

Augustana Evangelical Lutheran Church

G. Everett Arden L
Conrad Bergendoff L
Otto H. Bostrom + L
Clifford A. Nelson H
E. W. Olson H
Oscar N. Olson L
E. E. Ryden H
  Secretary
C. J. Sodergren + H
C. A. Wendell + H

Evangelical Lutheran Church

Selmer A. Berge L & H
Lawrence N. Field L & H
Herman A. Preus L & H
Gabriel Tweet L & H

Finnish Evangelical Lutheran Church of America (Suomi Synod)

Alvar Rautalahti L & H
Raymond Wargelin H

Lutheran Free Church

T. O. Burntvedt L & H
Leland B. Sateren H

United Evangelical Lutheran Church

Fred C. M. Hansen L & H
Adolph Kloth L & H
C. Scriver Kloth L & H
C. M. Videbeck

United Lutheran Church in America

Emil E. Fischer L
Harvey D. Hoover L & H
Edward T. Horn III L & H
  Chairman of subcommittee on music of both commissions
Ulrich S. Leupold H
  Music editor of German chorales
Luther D. Reed L & H
  Chairman of both commissions
William R. Seaman H
  Secretary of Joint Editorial Committee
George R. Seltzer L & H
  Chairman of subcommittee on text of both commissions
Paul Z. Strodach + L & H

---

† Ryden, "Hymnbooks," 1090.

Lutheran Book of Worship, 1978

The Lutheran Hymnal, 1941, represented the basically German heritage and tradition of the Lutheran Church—Missouri Synod, approximately one-third of American Lutheranism. The *Service Book and Hymnal,* 1958, represented the combined German and Scandinavian heritage of the American Lutheran Church (formed in 1960) and the Lutheran Church in America (formed in 1962), both churches constituting approximately the other two-thirds of Lutheranism in America. The *Lutheran Book of Worship,* 1978, prepared by representatives of the above three bodies plus the Evangelical Lutheran Church of Canada, incorporates and expresses for the first time in history the liturgical and hymnological heritage of virtually 100 percent of North American Lutheranism. It is indeed a "hymnal for all Lutherans."

In 1945 the Lutheran Church—Missouri Synod had declined the invitation from other Lutheran bodies to participate in a common hymnal and service book, having so recently produced their own hymnal in 1941. In 1965, however, feeling the need to replace *The Lutheran Hymnal,* the Missouri Synod voted "to pursue a cooperative venture with other Lutheran bodies as soon as possible in working toward, under a single cover: (a) a common liturgical section in rite, rubric, and music; (b) a common core of hymn texts and musical settings; (c) a variant selection of hymns, if necessary."

In 1966 the Inter-Lutheran Commission on Worship was formed by the American Lutheran Church, the Lutheran Church in America, the Lutheran Church—Missouri Synod, and the Synod of Evangelical Lutheran Churches (Slovak). The latter group subsequently merged with the Lutheran Church—Missouri Synod, and the Evangelical Lutheran Church of Canada (formerly the Canadian district of the American Lutheran Church) became a participant in the ILCW.

The ILCW organized into working committees on liturgical texts, liturgical music, hymn texts, and hymn music. Each committee was augmented by specialists in the respective areas in addition to a core of ILCW members so that its membership was marked by professional competence as well as being broadly representative of the various strands of Lutheran tradition within the participating church bodies.

Officers, ILCW members, and members of the working committees were as follows:

ALC American Lutheran Church
ELCC Evangelical Lutheran Church of Canada
LCA Lutheran Church of America
LCMS Lutheran Church—Missouri Synod
†   deaths during the twelve-year working period

Inter-Lutheran Commission on Worship

ALC

Louis Accola 1975-78
Eugene L. Brand 1966-71
Mandus A. Egge 1966-78
Paul Ensrud 1966-68
Carl Fischer 1968-74
Edward A. Hansen 1966-78

Richard P. Hermstad 1975-78
Hans F. Knauert† 1966-68
Theodore S. Liefeld 1966-78
  Vice-Chairperson 1966-68,
    1970-72
  Secretary 1968-70
Harold W. Moench 1968-74
Alf Romstad 1966-67
Leland B. Sateren 1966-78
Clifford J. Swanson 1971-78
  Chairperson 1972-78

ELCC

L. R. Likness   1966-78
   Vice-Chairperson   1969-70
   Chairperson   1970-72

LCA

John W. Arthur   1966-78
Ruth Becker   1972-73
Eugene L. Brand   1972-75
Edgar S. Brown Jr.   1966-70
L. Crosby Deaton   1966-72
   Secretary   1966-68
   Chairperson   1968-70
Gilbert E. Doan Jr.   1970-78
   Secretary   1970-78
Toivo K. I. Harjunpaa   1970-78
Edward T. Horn III   1966-72
Frederick F. Jackisch   1966-78
Ulrich S. Leupold†   1966-70
Shirley McCreedy   1974-78
Daniel Moe   1966-78
Constance Parvey   1972-78
Krister Stendahl   1966-70
Ralph R. Van Loon   1970-71,
   1975-78

LCMS

Henry C. Abram   1976-78
Paul G. Bunjes   1966-72
Walter E. Buszin†   1966-68
E. Theodore DeLaney   1969-76
Paul Foelber   1969-78
   Vice-Chairperson   1972-78
Herbert Kahler   1966-75
   Treasurer   1966-70
A. R. Kretzmann   1966-69
Herbert F. Lindemann   1966-69
   Chairperson   1966-68
   Vice-Chairperson   1968-69
Paul K. Peterson   1972-78
Fred L. Precht   1966-76
Warren G. Rubel   1968-74
   Treasurer   1970-72
Rodney Schrank   1974-78
Ralph C. Schultz   1969-72
Martin L. Seltz†   1966-67
   Secretary   1966
Jaroslav J. Vajda   1966-78
   Treasurer   1972-78
Willis Wright   1972-78

ILCW Staff

Eugene L. Brand
   Project Director 1975-78
Robert A. Rimbo
   Project Assistant   1976-78

Hymn Music Committee

ALC

Paul Christiansen   1967-69
Jerry A. Evenrud   1975-78
Ronald Nelson   1974-78
Ruth Olson   1969-74
Leland B. Sateren   1967-78
Dale Warland   1967-74

LCA

Charles R. Anders   1967-78
Larry Houff   1974-78
Frederick F. Jackisch   1967-78

LCMS

Jan Bender   1967-70
Walter E. Buszin   1967-69
Paul Foelber   1970-78
Edward Klammer   1967-78
Ludwig Lenel   1967-74
Carl Schalk   1968-78

Hymn Texts Committee

ALC

Bessie Coleman   1970-73
Gracia Grindal   1973-78
Edward A. Hansen   1967-78
John Milton   1967-68
Gerald Thorson   1968-78
George Utech   1967-70

LCA

L. Crosby Deaton   1968-70
Gilbert E. Doan Jr.   1967-78
Edward T. Horn III   1967-69
Joel W. Lundeen   1967-78
Marilyn Waniek   1970-72
Stanley Yoder   1973-78

LCMS

E. Theodore DeLaney   1967-78
Hilton C. Oswald   1967-78
Martin L Seltz†   1967
Jaroslav J. Vajda   1967-78

Liturgical Music Committee

ALC

Gerhard M. Cartford   1967-78
Paul Ensrud   1967-68
Carl Fischer   1968-78
Richard P. Hermstad   1975-78
Reuben G. Pirner   1967-75

LCA

Robert A. Bornemann   1967-71
L. Crosby Deaton   1967-68
Donna Zierdt Elkin   1973-78
Donald Hinkle   1971-78

Ulrich S. Leupold† 1967-70
Daniel T. Moe 1967-78
Stanley Yoder 1970-72

LCMS

Paul G. Bunjes 1967-72
Richard W. Hillert 1967-78
Carlos R. Messerli 1967-78
Fred L. Precht 1973-78

Liturgical Texts Committee

ALC

Eugene L. Brand 1967-71
Ralph Quere 1971-78
Clifford J. Swanson 1967-73
Johan A. Thorson 1967-78

ELCC

L. R. Likness 1973-78

LCA

John W. Arthur 1967-78
Charles A. Ferguson 1968-78
Edward T. Horn III 1967-68
Philip Pfatteicher 1968-78
Krister Stendahl 1967-68

LCMS

Hans C. Boehringer 1967-78
A. R. Kretzmann 1967-69
Herbert F. Lindemann 1967-78
Paul K. Peterson 1973-78
Fred L. Precht 1969-72

Beginning in 1969 the ILCW produced the *Contemporary Worship* series, nearly a dozen booklets of hymns and liturgical resources for trial use by congregations. Additional evaluation was secured through conferences with theological faculties, programs for testing proposed materials, surveys of hymn usage in congregations, questionnaires to pastors and church leaders, and reviews by official committees in the participating churches. Never before in the preparation of hymnals have such extensive measures been taken to insure a worship book that is both responsive and responsible in meeting the needs of the church.

In its 1975 annual report the ILCW included a statement about the nature of the new hymnal for approval by the participating church bodies. "The new hymnal ought to serve at least the following purposes:
—as a full hymnic resource for Lutherans in America today,
—as a repository of hymnological treasures of the church of all ages and modes of expression,
—as an educational tool of high quality,
—as a worship book for all Lutherans, serving not only immediate needs but also probing into the future through the introduction of some new items,
—as a practical book that can find use in practically all situations—in church, in school, at home,
—as a resource that holds high promise for a unifying effect among Lutherans,
—most of all, a 'people's book.' "

No other hymnal has ever been as representative of the various cultural and geographic traditions within world Lutheranism. German, Swedish, Norwegian, Danish, Finnish, Icelandic, Slovak-Bohemian—these historic hymnic traditions are blended with the distinctively American patterns and developments which belong to English-speaking Lutherans in North America today. While preserving the hymnic treasures of the past, the LBW also expresses and introduces exciting new statements of the church's life and faith today as created by its leading poets and musicians.

The LBW contains 537 hymns. The hymn texts committee screened a total in excess of 2300 texts in the process of finalizing the collection. The numerical total in the hymnal comes to 569 because (a) the opening 21 are a collection of canticles and (b) hymn texts with more than one tune are separately numbered.

113

The committee sought to use responsible judgment in updating the language of the hymns wherever possible, eliminating archaic pronouns and phraseology, and removing sexist and discriminatory allusions. In some cases the original archaic version of a hymn was retained due to historical considerations or to rhyming requirements within the poetic structure.

The hymn music committee sought to obtain the most effective hymn tune and musical setting for each text. Within the traditions of the Lutheran chorales, the committee had to choose between the original, more syncopated rhythmic version and the later, more even-rhythmed isometric versions which often developed within Scandinavian Lutheranism. In many instances, today's members of "the singing church" will now have the opportunity to sing the chorales in the more vigorous and exciting original versions. Where different tunes are used for the same text in the various hymnals previously in use among Lutherans, the committee had to decide which tune to use, or whether an entirely different tune should be selected. In some instances, sensing that a tune association had become overly familiar and dull, the committee purposely created a new wedding of text and tune in order to present the text in a stimulating new musical dress. The committee recovered many of the musical treasures of our early American tradition and also commissioned entirely new settings from distinguished, contemporary composers.

Two hundred years ago, Henry Melchior Muhlenberg, the patriarch of American Lutheranism, voiced the hope for "one church, one book." With the *Lutheran Book of Worship*, the Lutherans of America have come closer to this goal than ever before. We now have "one book" that draws together the multi-dimensional richness of historic and contemporary Lutheranism. And because of the well-documented unifying influence of hymnals throughout the church's history, we can eagerly anticipate the realization of the other half of Muhlenberg's dream as we work and pray "that the Church may be one."

THE CANTICLES AND HYMNS

Derived from the salutation of John the Baptist, "Behold, the Lamb of God, who takes away the sin of the world!" (John 1:29), the ancient Latin chant, "Agnus Dei, qui tollis peccata mundi, miserere nobis" (Lamb of God, you take away the sin of the world, have mercy on us), was introduced into the liturgy during the time of Pope Sergius I (687–701) and ordered to be sung three times at the Communion of the priest and people. Later, during the eleventh century, the last clause of the third repetition was changed to "dona nobis pacem" (grant us peace). Two LBW hymns (103 and 111) are based on the *Agnus Dei.*

The text was prepared by the International Consultation on English Texts (ICET), a group consisting of representatives of English-speaking churches all over the world which met for the first time in London in 1969. Working for six years, the International Consultation on English Texts created the common texts now in use in Roman Catholic, Episcopalian, and Lutheran liturgies, and in the orders of worship of various other English-speaking denominations. (See also: Philip H. Pfatteicher and Carlos R. Messerli, *Manual on the Liturgy,* Augsburg Publishing House, 1979, p. 8.)

The music, by Richard W. Hillert (LBW 63), was composed for the LBW.

2   BLESSED BE THE LORD *(Benedictus)*

The song of Zacharias, father of John the Baptist, comes from Luke 1:68–79, and in the Middle Ages was used as the canticle for Lauds (at sunrise). This is an ICET text (see LBW 1).

The music, by Richard W. Hillert (LBW 63), was composed for the LBW.

3   YOU ARE GOD; WE PRAISE YOU *(Te Deum laudamus)*

The *Te Deum laudamus,* one of the greatest of Christian hymns, was used extensively during the Middle Ages and was considered by Martin Luther (LBW 48) to be second only to the Apostles' and Athanasian Creeds as a symbol of faith. An extended article on the *Te Deum laudamus* is given in Julian,* pages 1119-1134.†

Consisting of three sections—two hymns and a litany—it is of unknown authorship. According to an eighth-century legend, alternate phrases were sung spontaneously by Ambrose (LBW 28) and Augustine (LBW 146) at the latter's baptism in 387 A.D. Scholars have found some of the lines in Cyprian's *De Mortalitate,* 272 A.D. The hymn is felt to be a composite. Some attribute the collection of the lines into their present form to Nicetas, Bishop of Remesiana (in present-day Yugoslavia), contemporary of Jerome (*c.* 340–420) and friend of Prudentius (LBW 42). The *Te Deum* has been in use since the sixth century as a hymn for Matins (after midnight). This is an ICET text (see LBW 1). Hymn paraphrases of the *Te Deum* can be found at LBW 432, 535, and 547.

The music, by Richard Hillert (LBW 63), was composed for the LBW.

†An asterisk indicates that a reference is included in the Bibliography, p. 575.

4   COME, LET US SING TO THE LORD *(Venite exultemus)*

This version of Psalm 95 is from *The Book of Common Prayer,* 1977, of the Episcopal Church.

Richard Hillert's (LBW 63) music, composed for the LBW, provides an alternate setting to that found in Morning Prayer, LBW p. 132.

5   LET MY PRAYER RISE BEFORE YOU AS INCENSE
(Domine clamavi)

This version of Psalm 141 is from *The Book of Common Prayer,* 1977, of the Episcopal Church.

Gerhard Cartford's (LBW 466) music, composed for the LBW, provides an alternate setting to that found in Evening Prayer, LBW p. 145.

6   MY SOUL PROCLAIMS THE GREATNESS OF THE LORD
(Magnificat)

The Song of Mary (Luke 1:46–55), as a Latin canticle beginning "Magnificat anima mea Dominum," has been sung at Vespers (sunset) in the Western Church since at least the sixth century. (In the Eastern church it is used as a morning canticle.) It is chanted to all eight of the Gregorian psalm tones. Vespers being the principal sung office of the day, many fine polyphonic settings of the *Magnificat* have been composed throughout the centuries, including those by Heinrich Schütz (LBW 180) and J. S. Bach (LBW 219). Giovanni Pierluigi da Palestrina (LBW 135) wrote two settings in each of the eight modes; Orlando di Lasso (1532–1594) wrote at least fifty settings; and César Franck (1822–1890) completed sixty-three of the one hundred he had planned. Numerous organ settings, many of them intended to be used in alternation with singers, have also been written.

This ICET text (see LBW 1) has been set to music by Gerhard Cartford (LBW 466) for the LBW. Another setting is given in Evening Prayer, LBW p. 147, and a hymn paraphrase can be found at LBW 180.

7   CLIMB TO THE TOP OF THE HIGHEST MOUNTAIN (Advent)

8   THE PEOPLE WHO WALKED IN DARKNESS
(Christmas/Epiphany)

9   I CALLED TO MY GOD FOR HELP (Lent)

10   SING PRAISE TO THE LORD (Easter)

11   NOW LISTEN, YOU SERVANTS OF GOD (General)

12   GOD, WHO HAS CALLED YOU TO GLORY (General)

Canticles 7–12, with texts by John W. Arthur (LBW 387) and music by Richard W. Hillert (LBW 63), were first published in *Contemporary Worship–5,* 1972.

This text from 2 Timothy 2 was set to music by Lucien Deiss and published in *Biblical Hymns and Psalms,* Vol. I, Cincinnati, 1965.

Father Lucien Deiss of Vaucresson (a suburb of Paris), France, was born September 2, 1921, in Alsace-Lorraine. Educated at the Universitas Gregoriana in Rome, he has served as director of the Grand Scholasticat of Chevilly, Paris, where he taught Scripture and theology. He was engaged in the liturgical movement, working for reforms as a member of the Consilium of Liturgy of Vatican II, and was also involved in the Biblical movement, assisting in the preparation of the French ecumenical Bible. A noted scholar, liturgist, author, composer, and pastor, he conducts Biblical and liturgical workshops around the world. He is co-founder of the Association of St. Ambrose and editor of the journal, *Assemblée Nouvelle.* Among his many books are titles such as *Spirit and Song of the New Liturgy,* 1970; *Biblical Prayers,* 1976; *The Christian Celebration,* 1977; *Be Reconciled With God,* 1977; *Springtime of the Liturgy,* 1979 (a new edition of his *Early Sources of the Liturgy*); and *Dance as Prayer,* 1979. In addition he has prepared several music collections—*Biblical Hymns and Psalms,* Vol. I (1965) and Vol. II (1970); *A Child is Born,* 1974; *Sing for the Lord,* 1977; and a Spanish hymnal, *Gloria al Señor,* 1978, as well as a large number of records. His musical awards include the Grand Prix du Disque, the Prix Madame, René Coty, and an honorary Doctor of Music degree from Duquesne University.

14 LISTEN! YOU NATIONS

John W. Arthur's (LBW 387) text, set to music by J. Bert Carlson (LBW 113), was included in *Contemporary Worship–5,* 1972.

15 SEEK THE LORD (*Quærite Dominum:* Song of Isaiah)

This text from Isaiah 55 is pointed for singing, and can be sung to psalm tones, such as those found at LBW p. 291.

16 I WILL SING THE STORY OF YOUR LOVE

Drawn from Psalm 89 and Jeremiah 33, this text was set to music by Daniel Moe (LBW 427), and included in *Contemporary Worship–3,* 1972.

17 HOW BLEST ARE THOSE WHO KNOW THEIR NEED OF GOD
(Beatitudes)

Jan O. Bender's (LBW 396) setting of the Beatitudes (Matthew 5) was included in *Contemporary Worship–5,* 1972.

18 ALL YOU WORKS OF THE LORD *(Benedicite, omnia opera)*

Taken from verses 35–65 of the Song of the Three Young Men, this canticle was sung at Lauds (sunrise) on Sunday in many medieval rites.

19 I WILL SING TO THE LORD
(Cantemus Domino: **Song of Moses and Miriam)**

Text from Exodus 15.

20 CHRIST JESUS, BEING IN THE FORM OF GOD
(Song of Christ's Humiliation and Exaltation)

Text from Philippians 2.

21 O RULER OF THE UNIVERSE
(Magna et mirabilia: **Song of the Redeemed)**

Text from Revelation 15.

Canticles 18–21 are pointed for singing and can be sung to psalm tones, such as those found at LBW p. 291.

22 THE ADVENT OF OUR GOD *(Instantis adventum Dei)*
Tune: Franconia

Charles Coffin, a distinguished scholar and Latin author, was born in 1676 at Buzancy in the Ardennes in northern France and studied at Duplessis College of the University of Paris. In 1701 he became a faculty member of the College of Beauvais, and later became its principal, succeeding the historian Charles Rollin. He became rector of the University of Paris in 1718, but returned after a few years to his former position at Beauvais. He died in Paris, June 20, 1749.

Some of Coffin's Latin poems were published in 1727, and in 1736 his *Hymni Sacri Auctor Carolo Coffin* contained one hundred hymns. Most of his hymns, including "Instantis adventum Dei" and "Jordanis oras praevia" (LBW 36), were also published in the 1736 *Paris Breviary,* a collection ordered by the Archbishop of Paris, designed to replace the ancient Latin hymns with more modern ones, and containing the work of several French writers. In 1755 Coffin's collected poems were published in two volumes by Lenglet of Paris.

Translation of this hymn is by John Chandler. Born in England on June 16, 1806, at Witley, Godalming in Surrey, Chandler attended Corpus Christi College at Oxford, receiving a Bachelor of Arts degree in 1827, and a Master of Arts degree three years later. Ordained in 1831, he succeeded his father in 1837 as vicar of Witley and later was appointed rural dean. He died at Putney, July 1, 1876.

Chandler became interested in accompanying the ancient prayers of the Anglican Church with hymns from the same period. Some translations from the *Paris Breviary,* published by Isaac Williams in the *British Magazine* along with their Latin originals, attracted Chandler's attention. He immediately secured a copy of the *Paris Breviary* and also a copy of George Cassander's *Hymni Sacri* of 1556 and set to work

120

translating the hymns. In 1837 he published his volume which he titled *The Hymns of the Primitive Church,* as he was unaware that some of the hymns he had translated were little more than a hundred years old. Chandler also wrote a *Life of William of Wykeham,* 1842, and *Horae sacrae, prayers and meditations from the writings of the divines of the Anglican Church,* 1854, as well as sermons and devotional materials.

This hymn, which was included in his *Hymns,* 1837, as the "Nocturn for Advent," has undergone several alterations in the present form.

FRANCONIA. Johann Balthasar König was baptized January 28, 1691, at Waltershausen, near Gotha, in Thuringia, Germany, and became a chorister at Frankfurt-on-Main in 1703. He became a choirmaster under Georg Phillip Telemann at St. Katherine's Church, Frankfurt, and later succeeded him at St. Katherine's, and as municipal director of music. He died March 31, 1758, in Frankfurt.

König's *Harmonische Lieder-Schatz,* 1738, containing nearly two thousand tunes, including a number of French melodies, was one of the largest and most influential collections of tunes of the eighteenth century.

Originally set to G. W. Wedel's "Was ist, das mich betrübt," in König's *Lieder-Schatz,* this tune appeared as given below (Zahn* #2207).

The present form appeared in William Henry Havergal's (LBW 406) *Old Church Psalmody,* 1847, where it was marked "German Melody, circa. 1720."

23   O LORD, HOW SHALL I MEET YOU
(Wie soll ich dich empfangen)

Tune: Wie soll ich dich empfangen

Paul Gerhardt ranks with Martin Luther (LBW 48) as a writer of German hymns. While Luther's hymns are objective, and sometimes militant in their tone, Gerhardt's are more subjective, reflecting the quiet strength of the unwavering faith and trust in God's love which were a part of Gerhardt's very being.

Gerhardt, son of the mayor of Gräfenhayniches, near Wittenberg, Germany, was born on March 12, 1607. He entered Wittenberg University in 1628, but the Thirty Years' War (1618–1648) apparently disrupted matters for him, both in regard to completing his studies and to his locating a parish, so that he was still at Wittenberg around 1642. After that time he went to Berlin where he served for several years as tutor in the house of the lawyer Andreas Barthold, whose daughter, Anna Maria, he married in 1655. He seems to have preached from time to time in Berlin, and there he was in contact with Johann Crüger (see below), in whose hymnal many of Gerhardt's hymns appeared. Crüger's successor, Johann Georg Ebeling (LBW 465), brought out the first edition of Gerhardt's over one hundred hymns in 1666 and 1667. In 1651 Gerhardt took his first parish, becoming chief pastor at Mittenwalde, near Berlin, where he remained until 1657 when he returned to Berlin as third assistant pastor of St. Nicholas' Church. However, Elector Friedrich Wilhelm, a Calvinist, sought to have the Lutheran clergy in Berlin sign a statement that they would not preach on doctrinal differences. Gerhardt refused and was removed from his post there in 1666. Two years later he was called to the church at Lübben on the Spree, where he ministered to a congregation described in Julian* as "a rough and unsympathising people." There he died on May 27, 1676.

Not only Gerhardt's professional life, but also his personal life, met with many difficulties. His wife bore five children, but only one survived. His wife also died at the time he lost his fourth child, leaving him with a boy six years of age. Gerhardt's portrait at Lübben bears the inscription, "Theologus in cribo Satanae versatus" ("A theologian sifted in a sieve"). Yet in the midst of all, Gerhardt composed well over one hundred hymns, many of them the finest and most beloved of Christian hymnody.

"Wie soll ich dich empfangen" first appeared in 1653 in Christoph Runge's (LBW 340) *D. M. Luthers und anderer vornehmen geistreichen und gelehrten Männer geistliche Lieder und Psalmen,* a hymnal published in Berlin, of which Crüger was music editor. A composite translation, based on Catherine Winkworth's (LBW 29) *Chorale Book for England,* 1863, was prepared for *The Lutheran Hymnal,* 1941. Subsequent alterations consist mainly of updated second person pronouns. Another translation, "O how shall I receive Thee?", was used in the *Service Book and Hymnal,* 1958.

WIE SOLL ICH DICH EMPFANGEN was written for this text by Johann Crüger, and included with it in the original 1653 publication.

Johann Crüger, son of an innkeeper, was born April 9, 1598, at Gross-Breesen, near Guben in Prussia. At fifteen he went off to school, at Sorau, Breslau, Olmütz, and finally at Regensburg, where he attended a "Poet's School." There he studied music under Paul Homberger who had been a pupil of Giovanni Gabrielli. After traveling in Austria, Hungary, Bohemia, and Moravia, Crüger returned to Freiberg in Saxony and then went in 1615 to Berlin, where he became a tutor to the children of Christoph von Blumenthal, captain of the guard of Elector Frederick Wilhelm I. He entered Wittenberg University as a theological student in 1620, but two years later became cantor of St. Nicholas' Church in Berlin and a teacher in the *Gymnasium* of the Grey Cloister, and in these positions he remained until his death on February 23, 1662.

Crüger published several hymnals during his lifetime. His *Newes volkkömliches Gesangbuch Augsburgischer Confession,* 1640, contained 161 hymns in four parts; his *Geistliche Kirchenmelodien,* published in 1649, contained the same number of hymns, 109 of which were given with instrumental accompaniment; his *Geistliche Lieder und Psalmen* was a collection of ninety-two tunes without texts; and his *Psalmodia Sacra,* 1657, which contained Ambrosius Lobwasser's Psalms, had 184 tunes with instrumental accompaniments. Crüger's major contribution to hymnody was his *Praxis Pietatis Melica,* first published in 1644. This work, the principal collection of seventeenth-century hymnody, underwent numerous revisions and enlargements, until the final edition, published nearly a hundred years later, contained over thirteen hundred hymns.

24 COME, O PRECIOUS RANSOM *(Komm, du wertes Lösegeld)*
Tune: Meinen Jesum lass ich nicht

Based on Matthew 21:5-9, this Advent hymn first appeared in Johann Gottfried Olearius' book *Jesus! Poetische Erstlinge an geistlichen Deutschen Liedern und Madrigalen,* published in Halle in 1664.

Olearius, son of the pastor of St. Ulich's Church in Halle, Germany, was born September 25,1635. In 1653 he entered the University of Leipzig, and following studies there and at other German universities, he received a Master of Arts degree from Leipzig University in 1656. Two years later he was ordained as assistant to his father at St. Mary's Church in Halle. In 1685 he became pastor and also superintendent of the second portion of the district of Saale; and in 1688 he was appointed chief pastor, superintendent, and member of the consistory at Arnstadt, as well as professor of theology in the *Gymnasium* there. He died in Arnstadt on May 21, 1711, having been totally blind for some years.

Olearius wrote a number of devotional works and composed the melodies to several of his own hymns. His *Jesus! Poetische Erstlinge* was enlarged and revised and published in Arnstadt in 1697 as *Geistliche Singe-Lust.*

Translation of the hymn is by August Crull, and was included with the opening line, "Come, *Thou* precious Ransom, come," in the *Evangelical Lutheran Hymn-Book,* 1889. The second stanza was altered extensively in *The Lutheran Hymnal,* 1941, and subsequent alterations have been made for the LBW.

The son of a lawyer, Crull was born January 27, 1845, in Rostock, Germany, and attended the *Gymnasium* there. Soon after he entered the *Gymnasium,* his father died and his mother married Albert Friedrich Hoppe, who later became the editor of the St. Louis edition of *Luther's Works.* Crull came to the United States with his family and attended Concordia College at St. Louis and Fort Wayne, graduating in 1862. Three years later he graduated from Concordia Seminary, St. Louis. After serving as assistant pastor of Trinity Church, Milwaukee; director of the Lutheran High School, Milwaukee; and pastor of the Lutheran Church in Grand Rapids, he became professor of the German language and literature at Concordia College, Fort Wayne in 1873. There he remained until his retirement in 1915, when he returned to Milwaukee, where he died February 7, 1923.

Crull was married twice. His first wife, *née* Sophie Biewend, and three of their four children preceded him in death. His second marriage was to Katharina John, who survived him by many years.

A distinguished hymnologist, Crull prepared translations that appeared in four hymnals: *The Lutheran Hymnary,* 1879; the *Evangelical Lutheran Hymnal,* 1880; *Hymns of the Evangelical Lutheran Church,* 1886; and the *Evangelical Lutheran Hymnbook,* 1889. His publications also included a German grammar and two volumes of German poetry.

MEINEN JESUM LASS ICH NICHT, one of several tunes for that

hymn by Christian Keimann, appeared in the *New verfertigtes Darm-städtisches Gesangbuch,* 1699 (Zahn* #3455). It is by an unknown composer. Another setting for "Meinen Jesum lass ich nicht" can be found at LBW 291.

25 REJOICE, REJOICE, BELIEVERS *(Ermuntert euch, ihr Frommen)*
Tune: Haf trones lampa färdig

Laurentius Laurenti, considered to be one of the best hymn writers of the Pietistic period, based this hymn on Matthew 25:1–13, the Gospel for the Twenty-seventh Sunday after Trinity (old pericopes), and included it in his *Evangelia Melodica,* 1700, a set of texts and tunes for the entire church year. It was also included, along with thirty-four others by Laurenti, in Johann Freylinghausen's (LBW 32) *Geistreiches Gesang-Buch.*

Son of a burgess of Husum in Schleswig (a duchy ruled by Denmark), Lorenz Lorenzen was born June 8, 1660. His father was a music lover who made sure that his son had a sound music education. He entered the University of Rostock in 1681, and after a year and a half, went to Kiel to study music. There he Latinized his name to Laurentius Laurenti. In 1684 he became cantor and music director of the cathedral church in Bremen and remained there until his death on May 29, 1722.

This is the finest of Laurenti's hymns, most of which were based on lessons of the Church Year. Sarah Borthwick Findlater's translation, opening "Rejoice, *all ye* believers," appeared in *Hymns from the Land of Luther,* first series, 1854. A few alterations have been made for the LBW.

Sarah Borthwick, daughter of the manager of the North British Insurance Office, was born in Edinburgh, Scotland, on November 26, 1823. She became the wife of the Reverend Erick John Findlater, pastor of the Free Church of Scotland at Lockhernhead, Perthshire, and their family, although poor, was later described by one of their daughters as a very happy one. With her sister, Jane Borthwick (LBW 147), she prepared *Hymns from the Land of Luther,* to which she contributed fifty-three of the 122 translations. The translations in *Hymns from the Land of Luther,* which was published in four series (1854, 1855, 1858, and 1862), are considered to be second in quality and popularity only to those of Catherine Winkworth (LBW 29). Sarah died at Torquay, Devonshire, England, on Christmas Day, 1907.

HAF TRONES LAMPA FÄRDIG (also called "Vigil"), a Swedish folk melody associated with the Swedish version of this hymn, was included as the setting for Sarah Findlater's translation in the *Hymnal,* 1901, of the Augustana Synod. A new harmonization has been prepared by Ronald Nelson (LBW 258).

26 PREPARE THE ROYAL HIGHWAY *(Bereden väg för Herran!)*
Tune: Bereden väg för Herran

Frans Mikael Franzén was born February 9, 1772, at Uleåborg, Finland, of Swedish parentage. In 1785, at the age of thirteen, he passed the entrance examinations to the Åbo Academy. When his father died two years later, he went home and for a while worked at his father's occupation—that of a salesman—but soon realized that it did not suit him. He returned to his studies at Åbo, where he earned a Master's degree. In 1790 he entered the University of Uppsala to pursue philosophical studies, returning in 1791 to Åbo to prepare his dissertation for the Doctor of Philosophy degree. He became academic librarian at Åbo in 1794, and four years later, professor in history of literature as well. From 1794, also, he was editor of the newspaper, *Åbo Tidningar.* Ordained in 1803, he left his academic position to become pastor at Pemars. During the Napoleonic wars Sweden lost Finland to Russia, and many of the Swedes living in Finland returned to their native land, among them Franzén, who accepted a pastoral call to the Kumla parish in Sweden in 1810. Kumla was a rural parish, and serving there was a great adjustment for Franzén after his years at the university. However, it was during this time that his abilities as a poet, which had shown themselves when he was a young man, now had a chance to blossom, and he wrote some of his finest hymns. Franzén became associated with Archbishop Johan Olof Wallin (LBW 73) in the preparation of the *Svenska Psalm-Boken* of 1819, described by Ryden* as a hymnic masterpiece from the golden age of Swedish hymnody. To this work he contributed twenty-nine hymns. Already in 1808 Franzén had been elected to the Swedish Academy. When in 1825 he became pastor of Klara Church in Stockholm, he was elected the academy's secretary. In 1834 he was appointed bishop of the diocese of Härnösand, a domain which extended into Lapland. He worked tirelessly in his diocese until his death on August 14, 1847, especially concerned with the problem of intemperance which was so detrimental to the nomads of the North.

This hymn first appeared in Franzén and Wallin's 1812 *Prof-Psalmer,* but met with criticism in the *Litteratur-Tidningar.* In a review in the June 10, 1817, issue of the *Stockholms Posten* Franzén published it in a revised form, and it was thus included in the *Psalm-Boken* of 1819. The translation has been prepared by the Inter-Lutheran Commission on Worship.

BEREDEN VÄG FÖR HERRAN was included in *Then Swenska Psalmboken ("Koralpsalmboken"),* 1697, the tune edition of the 1695 *Psalmboken.* Often called the "Svedberg Hymnal," the 1695 *Psalmboken* was a revision of a hymnal completed a year earlier by Jesper Swedberg (LBW 440). (The earlier hymnal, confiscated by the Swedish Church, was used nevertheless by the Swedish Lutheran colonists along the Delaware.) The tune was also included in the *Riddarholmskyrkans handskrivna koralbok,* 1694, a manuscript forerunner of the 1697 publication, containing basically the same material. The form of the melody used here is noted in the 1939 *Koralbok för Svenska Kyrkan* to be that found in the manuscript of Ovikens Church in Jämtland from the last half of the eighteenth century. The harmony is a somewhat simplified version of that given in the 1939 *Koralbok.*

27   LO! HE COMES WITH CLOUDS DESCENDING
Tune: Helmsley

This hymn by Charles Wesley was included in *Hymns of Intercession for all Mankind,* 1758, designated for the Second Sunday in Advent. The final lines of the first and fourth stanzas have been altered.

Wesley, one of the great hymnwriters of the ages, is represented by twelve hymns in the LBW. His total output was over six thousand, the best of which rank with the finest of the English language.

Wesley was the eighteenth and last child of Samuel and Susanna Wesley, born December 18, 1707, at the Epworth rectory, Lincolnshire. He received a Master of Arts degree in 1730 from Christ Church College, Oxford, where he had become one of the first group of "Oxford Methodists," and after graduation he became a tutor at the college. In 1735 he was ordained and immediately came to America where he worked for some months as a missionary in Georgia. Soon afterwards he came in contact with the Moravians, who also had a strong influence on his brother John (LBW 302); and on Whitsunday, May 21, 1738, he is said to have found "rest to his soul." The same year he became curate at Islington, London, but soon resigned and joined his brother John as an itinerant preacher. He was married in 1749, and his wife, the former Sarah Gwynne, accompanied him on his journeys. In 1756 he ceased his travels and lived first in Bristol, and after 1771, in London, ministering to Methodist Societies in those places. He died in London on March 29, 1788, and was buried in Marylebone churchyard, an Anglican church, as he considered himself to have lived and died a member of the Church of England. A list of the poetical works of John and Charles Wesley is given in Julian,* pages 1259–1260.

HELMSLEY. Born in 1725 at Tregynon near Newtown, Montgomery-shire, in Wales, Thomas Olivers was orphaned at the age of four and grew up rather uncared for and with little education. He was apprenticed to a shoemaker in 1743 and followed that trade throughout his life. Compelled to leave his native place at eighteen because of the "ungodliness" of his life, he traveled from place to place until he chanced to hear the preaching of George Whitefield (LBW 522) at Bristol and subsequently joined the Methodist Society at Bradford-on-Avon. In 1753 he became an evangelist under John Wesley and continued in that work, first at Cornwall, and then at various places in England and Ireland until his sudden death in March, 1799, in London. He was buried in Wesley's tomb in City Road Chapel burial ground.

"Helmsley" is said to have been adapted to this hymn from a melody Olivers heard whistled on the street. The first line bears a resemblance to a tune in Thomas Arne's *Thomas and Sally,* published in 1761, which began:

Called "Olivers," the tune was included in John Wesley's *Sacred Melody,* 1765, in the form shown on the next page. In Martin Madan's *Collection of Hymn and Psalm Tunes* for Locke Hospital, 1769, the tune had its present shape and the name "Helmsley." Frost* notes that the Mandan collection originally appeared in sections before 1769, and there is a possibility the tune appeared there before it appeared in Wesley's collection.

28 SAVIOR OF THE NATIONS, COME *(Veni, Redemptor gentium)*
Tune: Nun komm, der Heiden Heiland

According to Julian* this hymn is one of twelve definitely ascribed to Ambrose, as it is clearly attributed to him by Augustine (LBW 146) in 372, Pope Celestine in 430, and other early writers. It is found in several eighth- and ninth-century manuscripts.

Ambrose of Milan, the father of Latin hymnody, was for the first part of his life in the legal profession. Son of a prefect of the Gauls, he was born, probably at Treves, in 340 A.D. When he was thirteen years old, his father died and his mother moved with her children to Rome. There he received his education and so distinguished himself as a lawyer that he was appointed consul of Liguria and Aemilia in 374, for which position he moved to Milan. At the end of the same year, although he was only a layman and a catechumen, he was elected bishop of Milan, taking office a week after his baptism. As bishop of Milan, he found himself in direct conflict with the Arian heresy, especially since Justina, wife of Emperor Valentinian I, had herself subscribed to Arianism. His unflinching defense of the faith also led him at one point to refuse the Emperor Theodosius entrance into the church until he had repented for a general massacre he had ordered at Thessalonica. Exhausted from his labors, Ambrose died on April 4, Easter Eve, in 397.

Ambrose's hymns, written in *iambic dimeter,* are characterized by their simplicity and austerity; "the great objects of faith in their simplest expression are felt by him so sufficient to stir all the deepest affections of the heart, that any attempt to dress them up, to array them in moving languages, were merely superfluous."† Like the hymns of Luther many centuries later, Ambrose's hymns were written for congregational use, for the strengthening of faith in a period of adversity. Immediately popular, Ambrose's hymns were soon imitated by others, creating a collection of over ninety "Ambrosian hymns." A few of these hymns are definitely ascribed to Ambrose by his contemporaries and a few more are very probably his. The remainder have for one reason or another been ascribed to Ambrose, but more likely were written by an anonymous author in the style of Ambrose. (See also p. 11.) The practice of antiphonal singing is also said to have been introduced to the West by Ambrose.

In 1523 Martin Luther (LBW 48) prepared a quite literal translation, beginning "Nun komm, der Heiden Heiland," which was included the following year in the Erfurt *Enchiridia* and in Johann Walther's (LBW 350) *Geystliche gesangk Buchleyn,* Wittenberg.

†Richard Chenivix Trench, *Sacred Latin Poetry* (London: MacMillan and Co., 1864), p. 86.

The English text found here is the work of several persons. Stanzas 1–2 and 5–7 represent an altered version of a text submitted by Gracia Grindal (LBW 32); stanza 3a is from a translation beginning "Come, thou Savior of our Race," by William Morton Reynolds, published in *Hymns, Original and Selected, for Public and Private Worship, in the Evangelical Lutheran Church,* 1851, of which he was an editor; and stanzas 3b–6, by Martin Seltz, were included in the *Worship Supplement,* 1969, to *The Lutheran Hymnal.*

Son of a former captain in the Revolutionary War, Reynolds was born March 4, 1812, and graduated in 1832 from Jefferson College at Canonsburg, Pennsylvania. After teaching for a year in New Jersey, he was appointed principal of the preparatory department of Pennsylvania College. Fearing, however, that his position as a militant abolitionist might alienate the southern patronage of the college, he resigned and became pastor of a Lutheran congregation at Deerfield, near Allowaystown, in New Jersey. In 1836 he was recalled to his former post at Pennsylvania College where he remained until 1850 when he began three years as president of Capitol University, Columbus, Ohio. From 1853 to 1857 he served two academies in eastern Pennsylvania, and from 1857 to 1860 he was president of Illinois State University, Springfield. Ordained a minister of the Protestant Episcopal church in 1864, he served as rector of St. Paul's Church, Warsaw, Illinois, 1865–1871, and Christ Church, Harlem (Oak Park), Illinois, from 1872 until his death on September 15, 1876.

Martin Louis Seltz, born December 20, 1909, near Gibbon, Minnesota, graduated in 1928 from Concordia College, St. Paul, Minnesota, and in 1934 from Concordia Seminary, St. Louis, Missouri. From 1928 to 1932 he was an instructor at Concordia College. As a vicar he served St. John Lutheran Church, Hoboken, New Jersey (1933–1934); and as a pastor, Trinity, Hill City, Minnesota (1934–1940); St. Paul, Waseca, Minnesota (1940–1946); Trinity, Boone, Iowa (1946–1961); Immanuel, Elmhurst, Illinois (1961–1965); and Concordia, South St. Paul, Minnesota, from 1965 until his untimely death on October 5, 1967. Seltz was married to Helen Louise Spittler in 1945 and was the father of four children. A musician as well as a pastor, he served for three summers beginning in 1932 as music director of Lutherland, Pennsylvania, and was a choral union director in Minnesota and Iowa. He edited *The North Star Song Book,* 1945, 1956, which was published by the Minnesota district of the Walther League. In the Lutheran Church—Missouri Synod he served on the board of directors of the Minnesota district from 1943 to 1946, and the Iowa West district from 1954 to 1960, and from 1962 was a member of the Commission on Worship, serving as its secretary after 1965. After 1965, also, he was a member of the Inter-Lutheran Commission on Worship.

NUN KOMM, DER HEIDEN HEILAND is an adaptation of a plain-song melody, proper to the original Latin text, which is first found in the Einsiedeln *Hymnal* of the twelfth or thirteenth century. The LBW form of the melody was included in the Erfurt *Enchiridia,* 1524. Jan Bender (LBW 396) has prepared the harmonization. J. S. Bach (LBW 219) wrote four organ settings of this tune—three for the *Clavierübung* and one for the *Orgelbüchlein*—and used it also in Cantatas 36 and 62.

The tune, "Erhalt uns, Herr" (LBW 230), is patterned after the original plainsong melody.

29   COMFORT, COMFORT NOW MY PEOPLE
(Tröstet, tröstet, meine Lieben)

Tune: Freu dich sehr

Clearly expressing Isaiah 40:1-5, this hymn was originally written for St.
John the Baptist's Day, June 24, but is also appropriate to the Advent
Season. It was first included in Olearius' *Geistliche Singe-Kunst,* published in Leipzig in 1671. This collection, one of the largest and most important German hymn books of the seventeenth century, contained more
than twelve hundred hymns, over three hundred by Olearius.

Johannes Olearius was born September 17, 1611. His father, also a
hymnwriter, was pastor of St. Mary's Church and superintendent of
Halle, in Saxony, Germany. Johannes received a Master of Arts degree
in 1632 and a Doctor of Divinity degree in 1643 at the University of
Wittenberg, where from 1635 he was a member of the philosophical
faculty. From 1637 to 1643 he served as superintendent of Querfurt,
after which he was appointed court preacher to Duke August of Sachsen-
Weissenfels and private chaplain at Halle, becoming a member of the
consistory in 1657 and general superintendent in 1664. When the administration changed in 1680, Duke Johann Adolf gave Olearius similar
appointments at Weissenfels, where he remained until his death on April
24, 1684. In addition to his collection of hymns, he also published devotional books and a commentary on the entire Bible.

The translation by Catherine Winkworth was included in her *Chorale
Book for England,* 1863. The first stanza has been considerably altered.

The LBW contains thirty translations by Winkworth, a translator of
German hymns whose English versions were faithful to the text and spirit
of the original, as well as good English verse. Born at Ely Place,
Holborn, London, in England, on September 13, 1829, Catherine spent
most of her early life in the neighborhood of Manchester until she moved
in 1862 with her family to Clifton near Bristol. A devout and well-
informed woman, Winkworth devoted much of her energy to the higher
education of young women, serving as secretary of an association for
promotion of higher education of women; governor of Red Maids'
School, Bristol; promoter of Clifton High School for Girls; and a
member of the Cheltenham Ladies' College. She died suddenly of heart
disease on July 1, 1878, at Monnetier in Savoy, France.

Her *Lyra Germanica,* published in two series, 1855 and 1858, was very
well received, the first series going to twenty-three editions and the second, to twelve. In 1863 she published the *Chorale Book for England*
which contained not only translations of German hymns, but also the
tunes belonging to them. Her *Christian Singers of Germany,* 1869, contains the biographies of German hymnwriters.

FREU DICH SEHR (also "Psalm 42"), adapted by Louis Bourgeois,
was included in *Trente quatre Pseaumes de David,* Geneva, 1551, as a
setting for Theodore de Beze's version of the forty-second psalm, "Ainsi
que la biche ree." It was associated with the German funeral hymn,
"Freu dich sehr, o meine Seele," in J. Rhamba's *Harmoniae sacrae,*
Gorlitz, 1613 (Zahn* #6543). Originally the melody was associated with
a French folksong, "Ne l'oseray je dire," which dates from 1505.
J. S. Bach (LBW 219) used the melody in Cantatas 13, 19, 25, 30, 32, 39,
70, and 194.

For fifteen years, beginning in 1542, Louis Bourgeois was entrusted
with writing, selecting, and arranging the music for the French psalters.

Bourgeois, who seems to have been born sometime between 1500 and 1510 in Paris, became a follower of Calvin and went with him to Geneva in 1541. There, in 1545, he became choirmaster at St. Pierre and St. Gervais. The citizens of Geneva regarded him highly for his contributions to the psalter, as well as for his high character and his teaching of the children, and granted to him special rights and privileges. His musical skills seem to have been considerable. In 1551 he was imprisoned for a day by the city council for making unauthorized changes in some of the tunes. His alterations were accepted later, nonetheless. Bourgeois prepared two collections of harmonizations of the psalm tunes, one in 1547, and a second in 1561. He also prepared a textbook on singing, *Le droit chemin de musique,* 1550. In 1557 he left Geneva and returned to Paris where, after his 1561 publication mentioned above, he vanished from sight.

30 COME, THOU LONG-EXPECTED JESUS
Tune: Jefferson

See LBW 27 for Charles Wesley. This text appeared in *Hymns for the Nativity of our Lord,* 1744.

JEFFERSON was included in William Walker's *Southern Harmony,* 1835, as the setting for "Glorious things of Thee are spoken" (LBW 358). The tune bears some resemblance to "Pleading Savior" found at LBW 243.

Son of a Welsh immigrant, William Walker was born near Cross Keys, South Carolina, on May 6, 1809, and received an elementary education. When he was eighteen he went with his family to live near Spartanburg. He became associated with the Welsh-Baptist church when he was about twenty years old, and soon thereafter began teaching music. For the rest of his life "Singin' Billy" Walker taught singing in North and South Carolina, Georgia, and eastern Tennessee, and devoted his life to collecting and organizing Southern Appalachian folk hymns and tunes. Many of these were of Welsh, Scotch, Irish, and English origins. At the age of twenty-four he married Amy Golightly, and they became the parents of ten children. Together with Benjamin Franklin White, who married Amy's sister Thurza, Walker prepared a collection of hymns which he took to New Haven for printing. When *Southern Harmony* came out in 1835, however, the title page mentioned only William Walker. Thereafter he always signed his name "William Walker, A. S. H." ("author of *Southern Harmony*"). B. F. White subsequently moved to Harris County, Georgia, and in 1844 published *The Sacred Harp* (LBW 423), which contained some of the same material and became equally famous. *Southern Harmony* was immensely popular among the southern rural people and, before the Civil War, could be purchased in the general store. Going through four editions (the last in 1854) it sold 600,000 copies during the first twenty-five years. William Walker died September 24, 1875.

The LBW harmonization was done by Donald A. Busarow, a teacher of organ, theory, composition, and church music courses at Wittenberg University since 1975. Born April 10, 1934, in Racine, Wisconsin, Busarow graduated from Concordia Teachers College, River Forest, Illinois, in 1956, and continued music studies at the University of Michigan and Cleveland Institute (Master of Music) and Michigan State University (Doctor of Philosophy). Composition study has been with Marcel Dick, Jere Hutcheson, and Jan Bender (LBW 396). He has taught in Lutheran elementary schools and served as parish musician in Detroit and Cleveland. From 1972 to 1975 he taught at Concordia College, Milwaukee, Wisconsin, where he was also chairman of the department of sacred music. He is now head of the organ and church music department at Wittenberg University. In addition, he serves as organist and choirmaster at St. Matthew Evangelical Lutheran Church, Huber Heights, Ohio. He has published over twenty compositions for choir and organ, and conducted numerous church music clinics and hymn festivals.

31 WAKE, AWAKE, FOR NIGHT IS FLYING
(Wachet auf, ruft uns die Stimme)
Tune: Wachet auf

Philipp Nicolai, writer of both the text and tune of two monuments of German hymnody (this hymn and LBW 76), was born at Mengeringhausen in Waldeck, August 10, 1556, the son of a Lutheran pastor. He entered the University of Erfurt in 1575, and the next year went to Wittenberg, graduating in 1579. Later, in 1594, he received a Doctor of Divinity degree from Wittenberg University. For four years after his graduation he assisted his father at Mengeringhausen and then was appointed Lutheran pastor at Herdecke. The town council at Herdecke being Roman Catholic, however, Nicolai found many difficulties there and was forced to leave when Spanish troops invaded the city in 1586. He went to Niederwildungen, and two years later became chief pastor to Countess Margaretha of Waldeck and tutor to her son, Wilhelm Ernst. In this position he found himself in disagreement with the Calvinists on the meaning of the Lord's Supper, and took part in having the Formula of Concord adopted by the clergy of the principality. He went to Unna in Westphalia in 1596 where he again was involved in controversy with the Calvinists; in addition, the city fell victim in 1597 and 1598 to the plague, which took the lives of a great number of its inhabitants. During this time Nicolai prepared his *Frewden-Spiegel dess ewigen Lebens,* 1599, which he composed, according to his preface, "to leave behind me (if God should call me from this world) as a token of my peaceful, joyful, Christian departure, or (if God should spare me in health) to comfort other sufferers whom He should also visit with the pestilence. . . ." Three hymns were included in this work, two being "Wachet auf" and "Wie schön leuchtet der Morgenstern," both texts and tunes. Nicolai was forced to leave Unna in 1598, again in the face of a Spanish invasion, and returned the following year. His final charge was St. Catherine's Church, Hamburg, where he served from 1601 until his death of a fever on October 22, 1608. In Hamburg he gained great fame for his influential preaching, being hailed as a "second Chrysostom."

"Wachet auf," the "King of Chorales," is based on Matthew 25:1-13, the parable of the Wise and Foolish Virgins, and also on Revelation 19:6-9, 21:21; 1 Corinthians 2:9; Ezekiel 3:17; and Isaiah 3:8. The German text is a reversed acrostic, with the opening letters of the stanzas reading "W. Z. G." for Graf zu Waldeck, Nicolai's former pupil.

Catherine Winkworth's (LBW 29) translation is from her *Lyra Germanica,* second series, 1858. The text has been altered for the LBW.

WACHET AUF was also published in the *Frewden-Spiegel,* 1599. It appears to be based on the "Silberweise" (about 1513) by Hans Sachs, the cobbler-poet of Nuremburg (1494-1576).

Johann Sebastian Bach (LBW 219) based Cantata 140 on Nicolai's hymn, and also rearranged a movement of that cantata as one of the *Schübler Chorales* for organ. Mendelssohn (LBW 60), in his oratorio, *St. Paul,* used the tune in the overture and as one of the choruses.

The harmonization is from the *Neues Choralbuch,* Basel and Kassel, 1970.

32 FLING WIDE THE DOOR *(Macht hoch die Tür)*
Tune: Macht hoch die Tür

The son of a judge, Georg Weissel was born at Domnau near Königsberg, East Prussia, in 1590, and studied for three years at the University of Königsberg, after which he studied for brief periods at Wittenberg, Leipzig, Jena, Strasbourg, Basel, and Marburg. He served as rector of the school at Friedland near Domnau beginning in 1614, but resigned his post after three years to return to Königsberg University to resume theological studies. He became pastor of the newly-built Altrossfahrt Church at Königsberg in 1623 and remained there until his death on August 1, 1635. His hymn, "Macht hoch die Tür," was first published seven years after his death, in *Preussische Fest-Lieder,* 1642. A new translation has been prepared by Gracia Grindal, associate professor of English at Luther College, Decorah, Iowa.

Born in Powers Lake, North Dakota, on May 4, 1943, Grindal lived also at Tioga and Rugby, North Dakota, during her childhood. When she was twelve years old, her family moved to Salem, Oregon, where she graduated from high school. Following her graduation from Augsburg College in 1965, she spent a year in Oslo, Norway, before entering the University of Arkansas. There she completed a Master of Fine Arts degree in 1969. For two summers, in 1967 and 1969, she worked as an editorial assistant at Augsburg Publishing House. Since 1968 she has been at Luther College where she teaches poetry and writing courses. Her poems and articles have appeared in *Christian Century, The Cresset, Lutheran Standard, Decorah Public Opinion, Lutheran Women, College English, Dialog,* and several other publications. In 1976 she wrote the text for the cantata, *Dream of Shalom.* She has been a judge for writing contests of the National and the International Council of Teachers in English, and has given several lectures on the language of worship and hymnody. In 1977 she was a workshop leader for the Lutheran World Federation–USA Committee Consultation on Women and Worship. From 1973 to 1978 she was a member of the hymn text committee of the Inter-Lutheran Commission on Worship, and after 1975 was also on the editorial policies committee.

MACHT HOCH DIE TÜR appeared with this text in Freylinghausen's *Geistreiches Gesangbuch,* Halle, 1704, a significant hymnbook of the Pietists which had a great deal of influence on church song of the eighteenth century.

Johann Anastasius Freylinghausen, son of the mayor of Gandersheim, Brunswick, Germany, was born December 2, 1670. He entered the

University of Jena in 1689, but became attracted to Pietism and left the university. He went first to Erfurt, and then to Glaucha, a suburb of Halle, where he served for twenty years without salary as assistant to August H. Francke (a leading Pietistic preacher), declining all other offers. In 1715 Freylinghausen married Francke's daughter and moved with his father-in-law to his new parish, St. Ulrich's in Halle. On the death of Francke in 1727, Freylinghausen became pastor of St. Ulrich's and carried on the various institutions (schools, orphanage, printing press, Bible society, etc.) which had been started by his predecessor. Freylinghausen himself died February 12, 1739.

The harmonization is from the *Orgelchoralbuch,* 1952.

33 THE KING SHALL COME

Tune: Consolation

This hymn, so full of the emphasis on light characteristic of early Greek hymnody, was first published in 1907 in John Brownlie's collection of translations, *Hymns from the East, being Centos and Suggestions from the Service Books of the Holy Eastern Church.* No Greek source for this hymn has ever been found, however, and it is believed to be an original poem by Brownlie, reflecting his intimate knowledge of Greek hymnody. Stanza 4 has been considerably altered.

Through his research, his translations from Greek and Latin, and his original hymns, John Brownlie made an extensive contribution to hymnody. Included among his publications, in addition to that above, are *Hymns of Pilgrimage,* 1889; *Hymns of the Early Church,* 1896; *Hymns of the Greek Church,* 1900–1906; and many more. In 1899 he published *Hymns and Hymn Writers of the Church Hymnary,* a commentary on hymns contained in *The Church Hymnary,* 1898, the hymnal of the Presbyterian Church of the United Kingdom.

Born in Glasgow, Scotland, on August 6, 1859, Brownlie was later educated at the university there, and at the Free Church College. From 1885 he served as assistant minister to the Free Church, Portpatrick, Wigtownshire, until he took full charge there in 1890. He became involved also in the education system and served first as governor, from 1897, and after 1901, as chairman of governors of Stranraer High School. He died in 1925 at Crieff, Perthshire.

CONSOLATION, sometimes also called "Morning Song," first appeared in John Wyeth's *Repository of Sacred Music: Part Second,* published at Harrisburg, Pennsylvania, in 1813. There it was the setting for Isaac Watts's (LBW 39) "Once more my soul, the rising day." In the index of Ananias Davisson's *Kentucky Harmony,* 1816 (LBW 220), and in several later collections, the tune was credited to "Dean." Some have suggested that "Dean" might be a misspelling of "Dare"—the Rev. Elkanah Kelsay Dare (1782–1826), a Methodist minister, Freemason, and musician, who for a time was dean of boys at Wilmington College, Wilmington, Delaware. However, although Dare is credited with a number of other tunes in the index to Wyeth's *Repository,* there is no source given for this tune. The melody is related to "Bourbon" (LBW 127) and to "Hiding Place" (LBW 537).

John Wyeth, born in Cambridge, Massachusetts, on March 31, 1770, was not a musician at all, but an enterprising printer. After a youth filled with adventure, including a stay on Santo Domingo, he settled in Harrisburg, where he was editor of the Federalist paper, *Oracle of the Dauphin*. His first *Repository of Sacred Music,* published in 1810, drew entirely from earlier collections of standard psalm and fuguing tunes. Printed as late as 1834, this book sold some 25,000 copies. The *Repository of Sacred Music: Part Second* (1813) was designed to supply the market for folk-style music created by the camp-meetings and revivals so prevalent in Pennsylvania at the time, and was aimed primarily at Methodist and Baptist use, although Wyeth himself was an active Unitarian. Since Wyeth was not a musician, it was necessary for another person to have assisted in the preparation of the work, and it is possible that Elkanah Dare was entrusted with this task. The *Part Second* is a considerably more important collection than the original *Repository,* in that it contains a number of new tunes, and served as a source for several succeeding collections. Wyeth died in Philadelphia on January 23, 1858.

The harmonization was prepared by Theodore A. Beck for the *Worship Supplement,* 1969, to *The Lutheran Hymnal.* Born in 1929, Beck received a Bachelor of Science in Education degree at Concordia Teachers College, River Forest, Illinois, and Master of Music and Doctor of Philosophy degrees from Northwestern University, Evanston, Illinois. Since 1953 he has been a member of the faculty at Concordia College, Seward, Nebraska.

34   OH, COME, OH, COME, EMMANUEL *(Veni, veni, Emmanuel)*

Tune: Veni, Emmanuel

The antiphons on which this hymn is based date back to the ninth century and possibly earlier. Seven in number, they are often referred to as the "O" Antiphons as each opens with an "O," addressing the Messiah with one of his scriptural titles, and closing with a petition appropriate to the title. The fifth antiphon, for example, has been translated by Matthew Britt in *The Hymns of the Breviary and Missal* (New York, 1955) as follows: "O Dayspring, Brightness of the Eternal Light and Sun of Justice: come, and enlighten those who sit in darkness and in the shadow of death." The seven antiphons open as follows:

> "O Sapientia, quae ex ore altissimi. . ." (O Wisdom from on high. . .)

> "O Adonay et dux domus Israel. . ." (O Lord and leader of the house of Israel. . .)

> "O Radix Jesse qui stas in signum populorum. . ." (O Root of Jesse who stood as a standard of the people. . .)

> "O Clavis David et sceptrum domus. . ." (O Key of David and scepter of our home. . .)

> "O Oriens, splendor lucis aeternae. . ." (O Dayspring, splendor of eternal light. . .)

> "O Rex gentium et desideratus. . ." (O longed-for King of the nations. . .)

> "O Emmanuel, rex et legifer noster. . ." (O Emmanuel, our king and law-giver. . .)

These antiphons were sung, one each day, at Vespers before and after the Magnificat from Decemer 17 to 23.

Later, probably during the twelfth century, an unknown author collected the antiphons into Latin verse, and it is from this verse that John Mason Neale made his translation. The earliest available source of the verse is the Appendix of *Psalteriolum Cantionum Catholicarum,* 1710. Appearing originally as "Draw nigh, draw nigh, Emmanual" in Neale's *Medieval Hymns,* 1851, the translation was included in a considerably altered version in the Original Edition of *Hymns Ancient and Modern,* 1861. That form is used here with some further revisions.

Born January 24, 1818, in London, England, John Mason Neale was educated at Shelborne Grammar School and by private tutors before entering Trinity College, Cambridge, in 1836. There he earned a number of prizes, including (no fewer than eleven times) the Seatonian Prize for sacred poetry. While at Cambridge he became involved with the Church Movement and became one of the founders of the Ecclesiological or Cambridge-Camden Society. He was married in 1842 to Sarah Norman Webster, and in the following year, due to his High Church views, was presented only with a small incumbency at Crawley in Sussex. Soon thereafter lung disease made it necessary for him to spend some time in Madiera. There a remarkable library enabled him to read and gather material for books he was to write later. In 1846 he was presented with the wardenship of Sackville College in East Grimstead, a refuge for needy old men. Neale remained in this position (held before and after him by a layman) for the rest of his life, the only other preferment offered him being the provostship of St. Ninians, Perth, which he was unable to accept because his poor health would not have tolerated the cold climate. His condition worsened in 1866, and after five months of suffering he died on the Feast of the Transfiguration, August 6, 1866, at the age of forty-eight.

From external appearances, Neale's brief life might be judged a failure, kept as he was by Church politics to an obscure and low-paying position for his entire career. But judged in other terms it was a complete success. First, his contributions to humanity during his years at Sackville College were considerable. In addition to ministering to the men there, he established the Sisterhood of St. Margaret, a group dedicated to going to the homes of the poor, the sick, the needy, and the suffering and to ministering to their bodily and spiritual needs. Out of this organization grew other institutions: an orphanage, a middle class school for girls, and a house for fallen women (which later had to be shut down due to opposition from the community). Second, perhaps if he had risen to high church positions, the duties and concerns of such positions would have crowded his time and he would not have been able to make his outstanding contribution to church history and hymnology. A listing of Neale's prose writings, hymns, and translations covers several pages in Julian* (pp. 786–790). It is said that he could read, write, and think in twenty-one different languages, and his extensive reading and intimate knowledge of Latin and Greek equipped him better than anyone else to create his immortal translations of hymns in those languages. Through his *Hymnal Noted,* 1851, he brought to the English-speaking world the hymns of the *Sarum Breviary,* a collection of pre-Renaissance office hymns; he made known the Latin sequence; and he prepared the first English versions ever made of Greek hymns. One success he lived to see: the Church revival—the reinstatement of the great liturgical, hymnological, and musical heritage of the Church, to which he had devoted his

135

career—was taking hold in England. The LBW includes eighteen translations by Neale, as well as three of his original hymns.

VENI, EMMANUEL. Until some twenty years ago the origins of this beautiful and well-known melody remained a mystery. The tune could not be traced back farther than *The Hymnal Noted,* Part II, 1856, where it was marked "From a French Missal in the National Library, Lisbon." Since the source could not be found, it was assumed by many that the tune was created, possibly from fragments of *Kyrie* melodies, by Thomas Helmore, a priest and musician who collaborated with Neale in the production of *The Hymnal Noted* and other publications. In 1959, however, Bernarr Rainbow published an article in *The Musical Times* quoting a statement by Helmore in John Stainer (LBW 56) and George S. Barrett's *Dictionary of Musical Terms* (1881) that the tune was indeed "copied by the late J. M. Neale from a French Missal," and that Neale, in his *Handbook of Portugal,* had described a situation of great disorganization in the Bibliotheca Publica at Lisbon, with many manuscripts in the course of distribution and exchange. Rainbow raised the intriguing possibility that the melody was still awaiting discovery. That discovery was reported by Mother Thomas More in the September, 1966, issue of *The Musical Times.* The melody had been found in a small fifteenth-century *Processional* which belonged to a community of French Franciscan nuns. Originally it served as the tune for a series of additional verses, beginning "Bone Jesu dulcis cunctis," to the funeral responsory, "Libera me."

The harmonization is by C. Winfred Douglas (LBW 498) from *The Hymnal 1940* of the Episcopal Church.

35   HARK, THE GLAD SOUND!
Tune: Chesterfield

Philip Doddridge, son of an oil merchant and a member of a large (twenty children) and devout family, was born in London, England, June 26, 1702. His maternal grandfather was a Lutheran minister and his paternal grandfather was one of the ministers who had been ejected in 1662 under the Commonwealth because he refused to comply with the Act of Uniformity. Doddridge attended Kingston Grammar School, and since he was orphaned at an early age, the Duchess of Bedford offered to send him to Cambridge to prepare for ministry in the Church of England. Philip declined her offer, however, and went instead to the Nonconformist Academy at Kibworth in 1719, becoming an Independent minister at Kibworth in 1723. Four years later he was appointed to Castle Hill Meeting, Northampton, a parish made up of poor, hardworking people. There he opened an academy for those preparing for the Nonconformist ministry. The wide range of subjects, taught mostly by Doddridge himself, included Hebrew and Greek, philosophy, logic, algebra, trigonometry, and theological subjects. Young men from all over England and from the Continent came to attend the school. Doddridge became a victim of tuberculosis, and left for Lisbon in 1751 in hope of regaining his health, but died there October 26.

A friend and admirer of Isaac Watts (LBW 39) and a supporter of the work of John Wesley (LBW 302) and George Whitefield (LBW 522), Doddridge wrote over four hundred hymns, none of which were published during his lifetime. His hymns were written mainly for use in his parish and given out freely, and were first published in 1755 by Job Orton in *Hymns, Founded on Various Texts in the Holy Scriptures,* a volume arranging the hymns as they relate to and express various Scripture texts from Genesis to Revelation. There this hymn was included under "Christ's Message," Luke 4:18–19. He was also the author of *Rise and Progress of Religion in the Soul* and *The Family Exposition.*

CHESTERFIELD (also known as "Richmond" and "Spa Fields Chapel") is attributed to Thomas Haweis. Born January 1, 1734, at Redruth, Cornwall, in England, Haweis first undertook an apprenticeship in medicine, but turned instead to theology, studying at Christ Church, Oxford, and then at Magdalen Hall. Ordained in 1757, he became chaplain to the Earl of Peterborough, after which he served as curate of St. Mary Magdalen's Church at Oxford. Removed from there by the bishop because of his Methodist leanings, he became an assistant to Martin Madan at the Locke Hospital in London. Later, in 1764, he became rector to the Parish of Aldwinkle, Northamptonshire, and in 1768, chaplain to Lady Huntingdon's Chapel at Bath and manager of the college she established at Trevecca in Wales. Robert McCutchan, in his *Hymn Tune Names* (Nashville, 1957), notes that "Chesterfield" refers to Lord Chesterfield, a statesman and author who frequently visited Selina Hastings, Countess of Huntingdon, while Haweis was chaplain to her. Haweis published a number of prose works in addition to *Carmina Christo, or Hymns to the Saviour,* 1792, the collection in which this tune was contained. Haweis died February 11, 1820, in Bath, Somersetshire.

As the setting for "O Thou from whom all goodness flows," a text also by Haweis, this tune originally had a more elaborate fourth phrase, as given below.

Called "Pierce" or "Aldwinkle" the tune appears frequently in early American collections. The present form of the melody is by Samuel Webbe Jr. (son of the composer of LBW 388), and was included in *Webbe's Psalmody,* 1853, a collection of tunes by father and son.

The younger Webbe, born in London, England, about 1770, studied music first with his father and later with the famous Italian pianist and composer, Muzio Clementi. He was organist at a Unitarian church in Liverpool in 1798, but later returned to London to teach music, and in 1817 succeeded his father as organist at the Spanish Embassy Chapel. Going once more to Liverpool, he served two Roman Catholic churches —St. Nicholas' and then St. Patrick's. A skillful composer of songs, motets, catches, and glees, Webbe also wrote on music theory. He published the *Collection of Psalm Tunes* in 1808 and earlier, with his father, the *Collection of Motetts and Antiphons* in 1792.

36 ON JORDAN'S BANKS THE BAPTIST'S CRY
(Jordanis oras praevia)

Tune: Puer nobis

This Latin hymn by Charles Coffin appeared in his *Hymni Sacri* and in the *Paris Breviary,* both published in 1736, and was translated in Chandler's *Hymns of the Primitive Church,* 1837. See LBW 22 for Charles Coffin and John Chandler. The LBW uses four stanzas from Chandler, with considerable alteration. The doxology is from the Original Edition of *Hymns Ancient and Modern,* 1861.

PUER NOBIS. The Latin hymn, "Puer nobis nascitur," which had the form of a trope (see p. 14) on the Benedicamus Domino, was the first text used with this tune. The earliest source of the tune itself is a fifteenth-century manuscript from the Trier library, where it appeared as follows (Bäumker*, I, #95).

The tune underwent a number of variations and the text was translated, appearing in German as "Uns ist geborn ein Kindelein." Another form of the melody, from the *Piae Cantiones,* 1582, can be found in *The Hymnal 1940* of the Episcopal Church, with the English text, "Unto us a boy is born! The King of all creation."

Michael Praetorius, whose name is a latinized form of "Schulz" or "Schulze," was born at Kreutzberg in Thuringia, Germany, on February 15, 1571. His father was a Lutheran pastor who had studied with Johann Walther (LBW 350). Although he died on his fiftieth birthday, Praetorius accomplished much during his lifetime, including the publication of three major works: *Musae Sioniae,* sixteen volumes, five in Latin and eleven in German, published between 1605 and 1612; *Syntagma Musicum,* a three-volume encyclopedia of music (1615-1619); and *Musa Aonia* (1619), a secular work in nine volumes. The second volume of *Syntagma Musicum* deals with instruments and instrumental music, and contains rare and valuable descriptions and illustrations of instruments of his day, including organs. Three volumes of *Musae Sioniae* (VI, VII, and VIII) contained chorale melodies in four-part harmony and simple counterpoint. His adaptation of "Puer nobis nascitur" was included in volume VI, 1609.

Praetorius attended the University of Frankfurt an der Oder and held other organ positions before becoming organist in 1604, and later *Kapellmeister* and private secretary to the court of Bishop Heinrich Julius of Halberstadt, who was later duke of Brunswick and Lüneburg. He was also appointed honorary prior of the Ringelheim Monastery near Goslar, but was not compelled to reside there. In 1594 he went with the duke to Wolfenbüttel and there had his own home from 1612.

The harmonization was prepared by George Ratcliffe Woodward (LBW 149).

37 HARK! A THRILLING VOICE IS SOUNDING!
(En clara vox redarguit)

Tune: Freuen wir uns all in ein

The original form of this Latin hymn, "Vox clara ecce intonat," is occasionally ascribed to Ambrose (LBW 28), although most sources consider it to be anonymous, and date it variously from the fifth to the tenth century. Based on Romans 13:11 and Luke 21:25, the hymn is well-suited for use throughout Advent, and from the tenth century was assigned to Lauds (sunrise) for the first Sunday in Advent and then daily until Christmas Eve. In the Mozarabic rite it was used at Vespers (sunset) on Wednesdays. During the seventeenth century the hymn was revised (see p.15). Edward Caswall's translation of the remodeled hymn, "En clara vox redarguit," from the *Roman Breviary*, 1632, appeared in his *Lyra Catholica,* 1849, beginning "Hark, *an awful* voice is sounding." The opening line was soon changed to "a thrilling voice," and in the Original Edition, 1861, of *Hymns Ancient and Modern,* several other revisions were made. A few further changes have been made for the LBW.

Edward Caswall's English translations of Latin hymns are considered second only to those of John Mason Neale (LBW 34), and number about two hundred in all. Born July 15, 1814, the son of the vicar of Yately, Hampshire, in England, Caswall attended Brasenose College, Oxford, and graduated with honors (Bachelor of Arts, 1836; Master of Arts, 1838), having won for himself a reputation as a humorist with his satire *Art of Puck* while there. Ordained a priest of the Church of England in 1839, he became curate of Stratford-sub-Castle, Wiltshire, near Salisbury the following year, and remained there until his resignation in 1847. Caswall became caught up in the Tractarian Movement, with its interest in things of the ancient church, and he and his wife went to Rome in 1847 where they were both received into the Roman Catholic Church. Following his wife's death of cholera in 1849, Caswall entered the Oratory of St. Philip Neri at Edgbaston, Birmingham, joining Dr. John Henry Newman, whose writings had influenced his conversion and with whom he developed a close friendship. He was re-ordained in 1852, and spent the remainder of his life at the oratory where he devoted himself to his clerical duties and to service to the poor and the sick, and to little children. It was during this period that his devotional material, hymns, and Latin translations were written. Beside *Lyra Catholica,* his poetic works were included in *The Masque of Mary and Other Poems,* 1858; *A May Pageant and Other Poems,* 1865; and *Hymns and Other Poems,* 1873. He died January 2, 1878.

FREUEN WIR UNS ALL IN EIN. Michael Weisse, born about 1480 in Neisse, Silesia, entered Cracow University in 1504. He became a priest, and later a monk in Breslau. Deeply moved by the writings of Martin Luther, however, he and two other monks left the convent in 1518 and joined the Bohemian Brethren in their house at Leitomisch in Bohemia. He soon became an important and influential member of the group, founding German communities of the Brethren at Landskron in Bohemia, and at Fulnek in Moravia. Twice he was sent, in 1522 and 1525, to discuss the views of the Brethren with Luther (LBW 48). He died March 19, 1534 at Landskron.

In 1531 Weisse prepared the first German hymn book for the Brethren, entitled *Ein New Gesengbuchlen,* in which this tune was the setting for the hymn "Freuen wir uns all in ein." This hymnal, which contained 155 hymns either written or translated by Weisse, was very influential in Lutheran hymnody, with over three-quarters of the hymns entering German Lutheran hymnbooks in the sixteenth and seventeenth centuries.

The setting was prepared by Richard Hillert (LBW 63) for *The Worship Supplement,* 1969, to *The Lutheran Hymnal.*

38   O SAVIOR, REND THE HEAVENS WIDE
(O Heiland, reiss die Himmel auf)
Tune: O Heiland, reiss die Himmel auf

This German hymn first appeared in *Ausserlesene Catholische Geistliche Kirchengesäng* printed by Peter von Brachel in Cologne, 1623 (Bäumker* IV, #24). The translation by Martin L. Seltz (LBW 28) was included in the *Worship Supplement,* 1969, to *The Lutheran Hymnal,* and has been slightly altered for the LBW.

O HEILAND, REISS DIE HIMMEL AUF. When this hymn first appeared in 1623 it was sung to a version of "Conditor alme siterum" (LBW 323). The present anonymous tune is found in the *Rheinfelsisches Deutsches Catholisches Gesangbuch,* Augsburg, 1666, the second edition of a hymnal printed originally by Johan Jacob Körner in Vienna in 1660. Johannes Brahms has written a set of variations for choir based on this hymn. Paul Bunjes prepared the harmonization, which was included in the *Worship Supplement,* 1969, to *The Lutheran Hymnal.*

Born in Frankenmuth, Michigan, on September 27, 1914, Bunjes attended Concordia Teachers College, River Forest, Illinois, from 1933 to 1936. He received a Bachelor of Arts degree from Valparaiso University, Valparaiso, Indiana, in 1941, a Master of Music degree from the University of Michigan in 1944, and in 1966, a Doctor of Philosophy degree from Eastman School of Music of the University of Rochester, New York. He has attended several other universities for course work and enrichment, including a half-year in Germany and other European countries. While in Europe he was engaged in a research project on polyphonic music of the Reformation time, specifically editing Georg Rhau's (LBW 398) *Postremum Vespertini Officii Opus,* which was published by Bärenreiter as *Musikdrucke Rhau V* in 1970. He spent sixteen years in teaching and administration on the elementary level at St. Lorenz, Frankenmuth, and at Zion in Wausau, Wisconsin. Since 1951 he has been a member of the faculty at Concordia Teacher's College, River Forest, and since 1961, chairman of the music department. From 1948 to the present he has designed over seventy organs for churches and for college and university chapels. His compositions include numerous works for organ, chorus, and orchestra. Author of *The Service Propers Noted, The Formulary Tones Annotated, The Praetorius Organ,* and *Postremum Vespertini,* all published between 1960 and 1970, he has also contributed articles to *Lutheran Education* and to *Church Music,* and since 1965 has served on the editorial staff of the *Journal of Sacred Music.* He is a member of a number of professional organizations.

Tune: Antioch

Born July 17, 1674, Isaac Watts learned Greek, Latin, French, and Hebrew under the Reverend John Pinhorne, rector of All Saints' and master of the Free-School at Southampton. Like Philip Doddridge (LBW 35), Watts's spiritual and literary descendant, Isaac was offered an education at one of the universities by a wealthy member of the community, but he went instead to a Nonconformist academy at Stoke Newington in 1690. These "academies," which paralleled the universities in their education, were created because the Church of England would not allow Dissenters to attend the universities. On completion of his academy education in 1694, Watts returned home where he spent the next two years, and where he wrote a large number of the hymns contained in *Hymns and Spiritual Songs,* 1707–1709. His first hymn, "Behold the Glories of the Lamb," was written on the suggestion that he write something better, when Watts had complained that the Psalm versions were harsh and uncouth. In 1696, Watts went to the home of Sir John Hartopp where he served as tutor for the next six years. Three years later he preached his first sermon to the congregation at Mark Lane, an aristocratic Dissenting meeting in London, where he became an assistant to Dr. Isaac Chauncy, the son of President Charles Chauncy of Harvard College. During these years Watts undertook intensive study and writing to such a degree that he permanently weakened his health. Ordained in 1702, he succeeded Chauncy as minister to the Mark Lane congregation, and in the same year moved to the home of Thomas Hollis in the Minories. Under Watts's leadership the Mark Lane congregation grew so that it became necessary to call an assistant minister and to move the congregation twice, the second time being to its own building on Bury Street. Watts soon became a prominent and influential London minister. When he became seriously ill in 1712, he was invited to become a guest in the home of Sir Thomas Abney, alderman and one-time Lord Mayor of London. There he remained for the rest of his life, becoming a volunteer tutor to Abney's children and chaplain to his family when it became evident that his stay would be permanent. In 1739 Watts suffered a paralytic stroke which left him permanently disabled, and nine years later, November 25, 1748, he died.

As London's leading Dissenting minister, Watts was in close contact with other spiritual leaders of his day, including Nicolaus L. von Zinzendorf (LBW 302). In 1728 the Universities of Aberdeen and Edinburgh made him a Doctor of Divinity. In addition to numerous volumes, including *The World to Come, Catechism, Scripture History, The Improvement of the Mind,* and a book on logic which became a standard textbook at Oxford, Watts wrote over six hundred hymns. The majority of these appeared in four publications: *Horae Lyricae,* 1706–1709; *Hymns and Spiritual Songs,* 1707–1709; *Divine and Moral Songs,* 1715; and *The Psalms of David,* 1719. The fourth-named publication consisted of paraphrases of the Psalms—hymns based on the Psalms but given New Testament emphasis.

"Joy to the World" is from *The Psalms of David,* Psalm 98, second part, headed "The Messiah's Coming and Kingdom."

ANTIOCH. The opening measures of two movements from Handel's *Messiah,* "Glory to God in the Highest" and "Comfort Ye My People," (shown on the next page), served as the basis for this tune.

Glo - ry to God, glo - ry to God in the high -

In Lowell Mason's (LBW 353) works, the tune first appeared in his *Occasional Psalms,* 1836, marked "Arr. from Handel." There it had a first and second ending and some variation in the second phrase. In *The National Psalmist,* 1848, it was in its present form.

George Frideric Handel, known by all for his *Messiah,* was born in Halle, Germany, on February 23, 1685. He was the son of a barber-surgeon whose business-mindedness could not allow for his son's study of music. On a trip with his father to Saxe-Weissenfels, however, Handel had opportunity to play the chapel organ there, and so impressed the duke that Handel's father changed his mind and arranged music study for him with Friedrich Wilhelm Zachau at Liebfrauenkirche in Halle in 1693. After three years of studying counterpoint, harmony, organ, harpsichord, violin, and oboe, Handel went to Berlin for a year and then in 1697 became organist at the cathedral church at Halle. He studied law at the University of Halle for a year (1702–1703) but gave it up and went to Hamburg where he began his career as an opera composer. From 1706 until 1710, he was in Italy—in Naples, Rome, Venice, and Florence—where he composed a number of works in the Italian language. In 1710, he took a position in Hanover, but after a few weeks went on a visit to London. A second visit to that city in 1712 was extended indefinitely. Becoming a naturalized citizen of England, he remained there to become a very successful composer of Italian opera which was in vogue there at the time. In all, he composed forty-six operas during his lifetime. When interest in Italian opera began to wane, Handel turned his attention to oratorios. *Saul* and *Israel in Egypt* were performed in 1739, and three years later in Dublin, *Messiah* was heard for the first time. Handel's twenty-six English oratorios were full of dramatic music and grand choruses and set the pattern in oratorio for two centuries to follow. In addition, Handel composed instrumental music, harpsichord and organ works, and other sacred and secular choral and solo vocal music. His works, in an edition by Friedrich Chrysander, fill ninety-seven volumes (1858–1867). In 1751 his sight began to fail and by 1753 he was entirely blind. On April 6, 1759, he presided at the organ for a performance of the *Messiah* at Covent Garden and eight days later he died. He was buried with public honors at Westminster Abbey.

Tune: Greensleeves

William Chatterton Dix was born June 14, 1837, the son of a surgeon in Bristol, England. Educated at Bristol Grammar School, he went on to enter the business world, becoming the manager of a marine insurance company. Also a gifted writer, Dix made many fine contributions to hymnody which were published in his *Hymns of Love and Joy,* 1861; *Altar Songs, Verses On the Holy Eucharist,* 1867; *Vision of all the Saints,* 1871; and *Seekers of a City,* 1878. His writings include also translations of hymns from Greek and Abyssinian sources, two devotional works, and a book of instruction for children. He died September 9, 1898, at Cheddar in Somerset.

"What Child Is This" is taken from "The Manger Throne," written about 1865, one of many of his Christmas and Easter Carols.

GREENSLEEVES came on the scene suddenly, appearing twice the same day in September, 1580—in a license to Richard Jones to print "A new Northern Dittye of the *Lady Greene Sleeves,*" and in a license to Edward White to print "A ballad, being the Ladie Greene Sleeves *Answere* to Donkyn his frende." Twelve days later it appeared with a sacred text as "*Greene Sleves* moralised to the Scripture, declaring the manifold benefites and blessings of God bestowed on sinful man." William Shakespeare, in *The Merry Wives of Windsor,* mentions it in a line by Falstaff and in Mrs. Ford's ". . . I would have sworn his disposition would have gone to the truth of his words: but they do no more adhere and keep pace together, than the Hundredth Psalm to the tune of Green Sleeves." Although the first mention we have of the tune is in 1580, it was no doubt popular by then since it made several appearances within a short time.

The present setting of the tune is from Henry Ramsden Bramely and John Stainer's (LBW 56) *Christmas Carols New and Old,* London, 1871, and was included also in James Murray's (LBW 67) *Joyful Songs,* Cleveland, 1875.

41 O LITTLE TOWN OF BETHLEHEM

Tune: St. Louis

Born in Boston, Massachusetts, December 13, 1835, Phillips Brooks attended Boston Latin School and Harvard University. After returning to Boston Latin School to teach, a venture which was clearly unsuccessful, Brooks went to the Episcopal Theological Seminary at Alexandria, Virginia, to prepare for the ministry. Ordained in 1859, he began his ministry at the Church of the Advent in Philadelphia, where his preaching and his personality made such an impression that he was called in 1861 to Holy Trinity Church in Philadelphia. When Bishop Eastburn resigned in 1868 from Trinity Church in Boston, the congregation called Brooks. Brooks, however, was not easily convinced to come to Boston, and nearly an entire year passed between the first call and his final acceptance. It was during this winter, in December of 1868 while Brooks was still in Philadelphia, that "O Little Town of Bethlehem" was written. No doubt a trip to Palestine two years earlier provided inspiration and material for the hymn. In October of 1869 Brooks preached his first sermon at Trinity Church, Boston, and began his distinguished twenty-seven-year ministry to that church. Within a short time his sermons, his Wednesday evening lectures, and his magnanimous personality had begun to fill the pews of the old church on Summer Street and in 1871 the site of the present Trinity Church (Copley Square) was purchased. Before the building could be erected, however, the Boston fire in 1872 destroyed the old church and the congregation had to worship in an auditorium until 1877. Nevertheless, the congregation continued to grow and Brooks's fame continued to spread. He published the first volume of sermons in 1878 and it sold over 200,000 copies. He preached regularly at the Episcopal Theological School and at Harvard University. His lectures on preaching delivered at Yale were published and were widely circulated in America and also in England. In England he also preached widely, forming a warm friendship in that country with Arthur Stanley, Dean of Westminster Abbey. One who always enjoyed travel, Brooks frequently visited England, and went twice to Asia, once to India, and once to Japan. On the death of Bishop Paddock in 1891, Phillips Brooks was elected bishop of the diocese of Massachusetts, a position he held briefly until his sudden death on January 23, 1893.

ST. LOUIS. Lewis Henry Redner was born in Philadelphia December 14, 1831, and was educated in the public school system there. At age sixteen he entered real estate, a venture in which he was extremely successful, eventually owning his own business and becoming very wealthy. He served four other churches as organist before going to Holy Trinity Church, where he remained as official organist from 1861 to 1864. After that he resigned to have more time for other enterprises of the church. In 1858 Holy Trinity Church had opened a Chapel to provide additional space for worship and to offer church membership to those who did not wish to pay pew rents. It was to the Sunday school of this Chapel that Redner devoted much of his time, serving as organist, superintendent, and precentor, and in nineteen years expanding its rolls from thirty-six to over a thousand. It was Redner's suggestion that Brooks write a hymn for which he himself would compose a tune. This melody came to him during the night before Christmas, and he got out of bed and quickly jotted it down, filling in the harmony the next morning before going to church. "O Little Town of Bethlehem" was sung for Christmas morning services in 1868; and text and tune were published six years later in *The Church Porch,* a hymnal for Episcopal Sunday schools prepared by William R. Huntington of Worcester, Massachusetts. It was he who named the tune "St. Louis." Redner continued to work for Holy Trinity Church for many years, serving as a member of the vestry for thirty-seven years. Through his support an endowment fund was started which still supports the work of Holy Trinity Church in the center city today. He died in Atlantic City, where he had gone to recuperate from an illness, on August 29, 1908.

42 OF THE FATHER'S LOVE BEGOTTEN (*Corde natus ex Parentis*)
Tune: Divinum Mysterium

Marcus Aurelius Clemens Prudentius, a great Christian poet of the early days of Christianity, was born in northern Spain in 348 A.D. He received a good education, after which he was first a lawyer, and then a judge, before he was appointed by the Emperor Theodosius to a court office. At age fifty-seven, convinced of the vanity and impermanence of most of life, he retired to a life of poverty and seclusion, and began to write the works which were so widely read and influential during the Middle Ages, and from which many fine Christian hymns have been drawn. He died about 413.

Both of his hymns included in the LBW (see also LBW 81) are taken from the *Cathemerinon,* Prudentius' most important work. *Cathemerinon* contains twelve extended poems, one for each hour of the day. "Corde natus" is taken from the ninth poem beginning "Da puer plectrum, choreis ut canam fidelibus."

John Mason Neale (LBW 34) translated the hymn in the meter of the original in his *Hymnal Noted,* 1851, beginning "Of the Father, sole begotten." In the Original Edition of *Hymns Ancient and Modern,* 1861, the text was revised by Henry Williams Baker (LBW 414) who also included a translation of the Latin doxology which had been added to Prudentius' text at a later date. Baker's version, with very slight alteration, has been taken into the LBW.

DIVINUM MYSTERIUM is a plainsong melody used as a setting for Neale's "Of the Father sole begotten" in *The Hymnal Noted.* There it was marked "Melody from a manuscript at Wolfenbütel of the XIIIth century." However, that source has never been identified, and most of the information on the subject agrees that the tune is probably from a copy of the *Piae Cantiones Ecclesiasticae et Scholasticae* which came into the hands of Thomas Helmore (LBW 34), music editor of *The Hymnal Noted.* This important collection was published in 1582 by Theodoricis Petri (Didrik Pedersen) of Finland, with the object of preserving the medieval songs and carols then current in Sweden.

Originally the melody was a Sanctus trope (see p. 14) and it can be found in tropers of the twelfth to the fifteenth centuries in Italy and Germany with the words "Divinum Mysterium." The harmonization is by Carl Schalk (LBW 118).

43 REJOICE, REJOICE THIS HAPPY MORN
(Os er i dag en Frelser född)
Tune: Wie schön leuchtet

Birgitte Katerine, daughter of Jens Johansen, was born in Gentofte, Denmark, March 7, 1742. Betrothed at an early age to Herman Hertz, a game-keeper in the service of the king, she was married in 1763 when he became forester of the district of Vordingborg. Although she became the mother of four children, she still found time to learn German, French, and English in order to read poetry in its original language, and to translate numerous hymns into Danish. When in 1773 the Society for the Advancement of Liberal Arts solicited for sacred poetry, she contributed twenty hymns, eighteen of which were later included in a hymnal issued by Bishop Ludvig Harboe and state secretary Ove Guldberg. When the office of forester was abolished the family found themselves in reduced financial circumstances. Birgitte brought the matter to Guldberg who relayed the concern to Prince Fredrik. The two sons of the Hertz household were, consequently, educated at the Prince's expense. When Birgitte's husband died, the Prince maintained the family until she was remarried three years later, in 1778, to Hans Boye, an employee at the customhouse in Copenhagen. Guldberg, dissatisfied with the existing official hymnal, secretly prepared a collection of his own, and requested Birgitte to contribute to it. When Harboe and Guldberg's *Psalmebog* was published in Copenhagen in 1778 it contained 124 of her original hymns as well as twenty-four translations. Her own *Davids Psalmer i en fri Oversættelse*, containing Psalms 1–89, appeared in three volumes, 1781–1785. She also wrote nationalistic poetry, and dramatic works, many of which were performed for special royal events. She died October 17, 1824, having also survived her second husband.

This single stanza, based on the Benedictus (Luke 1:76–79), was included in the 1778 *Psalmebog*, and has been traditionally sung on Christmas Day in Danish and Norwegian churches and in many Scandinavian churches in America.

The translation of the hymn was prepared by Carl Doving in 1911 and included in *The Lutheran Hymnary*, 1913. Doving, who served on the *Lutheran Hymnary* committee and did extensive hymnological research, was born in Norddalen, Norway, March 21, 1867. He immigrated to the United States in 1890 and attended Luther College (Bachelor of Arts, 1903) and Luther Seminary. After serving as pastor of churches in Red Wing, Minnesota; Montevideo, Minnesota; and Brooklyn, New York, he became city missionary to Chicago. He died October 2, 1937.

WIE SCHÖN LEUCHTET, the melody always used with this hymn, is a rhythmically simplified form of the tune found at LBW 76.

44 INFANT HOLY, INFANT LOWLY *(W zlobie lezy)*
Tune: W zlobie lezy

The origins of this Polish carol are unknown. Edith Reed's translation appeared in two publications during December of 1925: *Music and Youth* and *Panpipes*. Alterations to the text are few.

Edith Margaret Gellibrand Reed was born March 31, 1885, at Islington, Middlesex, London, in England. She attended St. Leonard's School in St. Andrew's, and the Guildhall School of Music in London. An associate of the Royal College of Organists, she assisted Percy Scholes in editing *The Music Student* and *Music and Youth* (also known as *Piano Student*). From 1923 to 1926, she also edited *Panpipes*, a music magazine for children. Other publications include two mystery plays for Christmas and *Story Lives of the Great Composers*. She died June 4, 1933, at Barnet, Herfordshire.

W ZLOBIE LEZY, the Polish folk melody traditionally associated with this text, has been harmonized by Richard Hillert (LBW 63).

45 OH, COME, ALL YE FAITHFUL *(Adeste fideles)*
Tune: Adeste fideles

Text and tune are united in the history of this widely-known Christmas hymn. Both appear in several manuscripts signed by John Francis Wade:

a)   In the possession of the Rev. Maurice Frost, *c.* 1743, the "Jacobite" manuscript

b)   At Clongowes Wood College, Kildare, Ireland, 1746 or 1749, recently lost or stolen

c)   At the Henry Watson Music Library, Manchester, England, *c.* 1750

d)   At Stonyhurst College, Lancashire, 1751

e) and f) At St. Edmund's College, Old Hall, Ware, England, 1760, a *Graduale* and a *Vesperal*

g)   At Princethorpe Priory, 1761

The hymn and tune first appeared in print in the *Essay or Instruction for Learning the Church Plain Chant,* 1782, and were repeated, with a four-part setting of the tune, in Samuel Webbe's (LBW 388) *Collection of Motetts or Antiphons,* 1792.

The melody, often called "Portuguese Hymn" because of its having been introduced as such when it was sung in 1785 in the Portuguese Chapel in London, was ascribed by Vincent Novello (1781–1861) to John Reading, organist of Winchester Cathedral from 1675 to 1681. During the nineteenth century the melody, so named, was set to a wide variety of texts other than "Adeste fideles."

In his extensive discussion of the Wade manuscripts, *Adeste Fideles: A Study of Its Origin and Development* (Buckfast Abbey, 1947), Dom John Stéphan draws the conclusion that both text and tune were written by John Wade himself. The earliest of the manuscripts listed above is believed by Stéphan to have been the original since it contains some variations in both text and tune which were altered in all later manuscripts. The tune, for instance, was in 3/4 rhythm in the first manuscript, as given below.

John Francis Wade was an Englishman who lived at Douay in northern France. Douay, which had an English college, was a haven for Roman Catholic refugees during the Jacobite rebellion of 1745. There he prepared beautiful copies of plain chant and other music, and also taught Latin and church song. He died August 16, 1786, at the age of seventy-five.

Early in the nineteenth century, Abbé Etienne Jean François Borderies rewrote some of the orginal four stanzas. To these he added three more (including our present stanza 3), producing the form of the Latin hymn used on the Continent. The hymn, in its orginal form in England and in the altered form on the Continent, very soon became widely popular among Catholics.

Frederick Oakeley's translation beginning "Ye faithful, approach ye," based on the English form of the Latin hymn, was written in 1841 for use at the Margaret Street Chapel (now called All Saints, Margaret Street). An altered version beginning, "O come, all ye faithful, joyfully triumphant," with stanzas 4 and 5 translated by William Mercer (LBW 281) and others from the Continental form of the Latin hymn, was printed in F. H. Murray's *A Hymnal for Use in the English Church,* 1852.

Oakeley, whose father was at one time governor of Madras, was born September 5, 1802, at Shrewsbury, England, and received a Bachelor of Arts degree from Christ Church, Oxford, in 1824. He took holy orders and was prebend of Lichfield Cathedral and preacher at Whitehall before going in 1839 as a minister to Margaret Chapel, London. There Richard Redhead (LBW 109) was organist and the two men gave great attention to the worship services and to the music and the choir.

Oakeley became interested in the Tractarian Movement, and in 1845 joined John Henry Newman at Littlemore and was received into the Roman Catholic communion. For years he worked among the poor of Westminster, and became canon of Westminster in 1852 on the establishment of the new Roman hierarchy. He died in Islington, London, on January 29, 1880.

46   ONCE AGAIN MY HEART REJOICES
    (Fröhlich soll mein Herze springen)
    Tune: Fröhlich soll mein Herze springen

Paul Gerhardt's (LBW 23) joyful, tender Christmas hymn first appeared in Johann Crüger's (LBW 23) *Praxis pietatis melica,* 1653. These stanzas from Catherine Winkworth's (LBW 29) translation, given in her *Lyra Germanica,* second series, 1858, are altered only slightly.

FRÖHLICH SOLL MEIN HERZE SPRINGEN was composed by Johann Crüger (LBW 23) for this hymn, and published together with it.

47   LET ALL TOGETHER PRAISE OUR GOD
    (Lobt Gott, ihr Christen allzugleich)
    Tune: Lobt Gott, ihr Christen

Both text and tune of this hymn are by Nikolaus Herman. The words, written about 1554, were first published in 1561 at Wittenberg in *Die Sonntags Euangelia vber das gantze Jar.* It was the first of "Three Spiritual Christmas Songs of the newborn child Jesus, for the children in Joachimsthal."

The translation by F. Samuel Janzow (LBW 63) was included in the *Worship Supplement,* 1969, to *The Lutheran Hymnal.*

LOBT GOTT, IHR CHRISTEN appeared together with this hymn in 1561, but was originally written for Herman's children's hymn on the life and work of John the Baptist, "Kommt her, ihr liebste Schwesterlein," in *Ein Christlicher Abentreien,* Leipzig, 1554 (Zahn * #198). It is possibly based on the ancient Christmas antiphon, "Puer est natus nobis." The harmonization is from the *Würtemberg Choralbuch,* 1953.

Herman's birth date is not known with any certainty, but seems to have been around 1480. He was born in Altdorf near Nüremberg in Bavaria. By 1518, he had gone to St. Joachimsthal in Bergstadt, Bohemia, where he became a teacher in the Latin school and organist and choirmaster of the Lutheran Church under Pastor Johann Mathesius, a pupil and friend of Martin Luther (LBW 48) who had at one time lived as a member of Luther's household. Many of the hymns written by Herman were inspired by Mathesius' sermons. Deeply concerned with the Christian education of children and young people, Herman wrote most of his hymns for them, and wrote a book on the subject: *Eyn gestreng vrteyl Gottes,* published about 1526. In 1554 and 1558, he published two volumes of poetry, titled *Cantica Sacra.* Herman, who was also a good organist, frequently composed the melodies for his hymns. A number of these were very singable and came into common use. He published another hymnal, *Die Historien von der Sintflut* in 1562. His death at St. Joachimsthal is given in different sources as May 3 or May 15, 1561.

J. S. Bach (LBW 219) used the tune in Cantatas 151 and 195, and included two settings in the *Choralgesänge.* One of his organ settings is in the *Orgelbüchlein* and the other two are among his Miscellaneous Chorales.

48 ALL PRAISE TO YOU, ETERNAL LORD
(Gelobet seist du, Jesu Christ)
Tune: Gelobet seist du

A single German stanza, one of the few popular vernacular songs used in Pre-Reformation church services (see also LBW 136 and 317), is first found in a manuscript from around 1370. There it is introduced by a stanza (slightly altered) from an eleventh-century Latin sequence, quoted in Julian* (p. 408) thus:

> Hinc oportet ut canamus cum angelis septem gloria in excelsis:—
>> Louet sistu ihū crist,
>> dat du hute ghebaren bist
>> van eyner maghet. Dat is war.
> Des vrow sik alde hemmelsche schar. Kyr.

On Christmas Day it was often sung as the people's response to the sequence "Grates nunc omnes." With its Kyr [ie Eleison] at the end, it is one of the medieval German hymns called "Leise." Dating back to the ninth century, these German hymns were still found in the Reformation period, with a number of Lutheran chorales belonging to the category.

Wackernagel* (III, 9) gives the following form of the stanza from the sixteenth century:

> Gelobet seystu, Jesu Christ,
> das du mensch geboren bist
> Von eyner youngfraw, das ist war,
> des frewet sych der engel schar.

To this Martin Luther added six stanzas and published the hymn first on a broadsheet, possibly Christmas 1523, or early in 1524, and then in the Erfurt *Enchiridia,* 1524.

Martin Luther, son of Hans Luther, a miner, and his wife Margarete, was born November 10, 1483, in Eisleben. He was educated at

Magdeburg and Eisenach and received a Master of Arts degree from the University of Erfurt. Following his university education he entered the Augustinian convent at Erfurt and was ordained a priest in 1507. The following year he began to lecture at Wittenberg University and in 1512 received a Doctor of Divinity degree. During a visit to Rome in 1511 he had become aware of some of the corruptions of the Church, and his feelings were brought to a climax when the Dominican friar Tetzel came to Wittenberg selling indulgences. On October 31, 1517, he nailed ninety-five theses on the door of the Wittenberg Castle Church, denouncing some of the Church's practices. He was called to Rome to answer to his theses, but was kept by his university and the Elector of Saxony from going. When his *The Babylonian Captivity of the Church* brought a papal bull against him, he publicly burned it, for which he was excommunicated in 1520. In 1521 he was summoned to the Diet at Worms where he refused to recant his beliefs, and was placed under Imperial ban. On his way back to Wittenberg he was "kidnapped" by the Elector who feared for Luther's life, and he was kept for a year at Wartburg. There he began his German translation of the Bible, a work which was completed in 1534. In 1522, he returned to Wittenberg and immediately set about preparing a German Mass and hymns for the use of his followers. The first hymnal, *Etlich Cristlich lider Lobgesang uñ Psalm,* 1523/1524—called the "Achtliederbuch" because it contained eight hymns (four of which were by Luther)—was published by the Nürnberg printer, Jobst Gutknecht. In 1524, also, appeared the Erfurt *Enchiridia* in which this hymn was included. A number of hymnals followed, the last being *Geystliche Lieder,* published by Valentin Babst in Leipzig in 1545. Luther drew from several sources for his hymns—translations from Latin hymns, versifications of the Psalms and other parts of Scripture, and revisions of pre-Reformation German popular hymns—and also wrote his own originals. He died February 18, 1546, in Eisleben.

An anonymous translation in a different meter was included in *The Sabbath Hymn Book,* 1858, published by the Mason Brothers in New York. This text was used in the *Service Book and Hymnal,* 1958, and has been adapted here to fit the meter of the original German tune.

GELOBET SEIST DU appeared with the text on the broadsheet and in the 1524 Erfurt *Enchiridia,* and is possibly the tune associated with the original German stanza, although no pre-Reformation source exists. Jan Bender (LBW 396) prepared the harmonization for the *Worship Supplement,* 1969, to *The Lutheran Hymnal.* J. S. Bach (LBW 219) used this hymn in his Cantatas 64 and 91, and also in his *Christmas Oratorio.* A setting for organ is given in his *Orgelbüchlein* and four settings are found among his Miscellaneous Preludes.

49   O SAVIOR OF OUR FALLEN RACE *(Christe Redemptor omnium)*
Tune: Christe Redemptor

This Christmas Vesper (sunset) hymn dates from the ninth or tenth century, or possibly earlier, and was found in the Sarum, York, and Aberdeen *Breviaries,* and in the *Roman Breviary* before 1525. There were two major revisions of the text, one in the *Roman Breviary* of 1632 and a second in Charles Coffin's (LBW 22) *Hymni Sacri* and the *Paris Breviary,* both of 1736.

Several English translations of all three Latin versions can be found. Gilbert E. Doan's (LBW 99) text is based on the original, and was prepared for the LBW.

CHRISTE REDEMPTOR is the tune proper to this text, and also long associated with "Jesu dulcedo memoria" (LBW 316). It is considered to date from the end of the twelfth or from the thirteenth century. Forms of the melody differ widely from one locality to another; the one used here is the Sarum (Salisbury, England) form. The harmonization is by Richard Hillert (LBW 63).

50   ANGELS, FROM THE REALMS OF GLORY

Tune: Regent Square

James Montgomery ranks with Charles Wesley (LBW 27) and Isaac Watts (LBW 39) in his contribution to English hymnody. Although intended by his parents to enter the Moravian ministry, Montgomery was fascinated with the writing of poetry from age ten and, with only a few years of formal education, entered on a life-long literary career, in which he made a considerable Christian witness. In addition to his hymns, Montgomery wrote much poetry which raised a strong voice against slavery.

Born November 4, 1771, in Irvine, Ayrshire, Scotland, Montgomery was sent at the age of six or seven to a seminary of the Brethren at Fulneck in Yorkshire. A few years later his parents went as missionaries to the West Indies, where they both died. His parents' missionary zeal was later reflected in many of Montgomery's own hymns. He did not remain at the seminary after 1787, but went out and worked for a while in a retail shop, first at Mirfield near Wakefield, then at Wath near Rotherham. Although he remained with his second employer for only a year, the man thought highly of Montgomery and sought him out many years later to give him aid and consolation at the time of his imprisonment. Montgomery went to London to try to publish his poems, but was unsuccessful, and after returning briefly to Wath, he went to Sheffield in 1792. There he became assistant to Joseph Gales, auctioneer, bookseller, and printer of the newspaper, the *Sheffield Register*. Two years later Gales left England in the face of possible prosecution for libel, and Montgomery took over the paper, immediately changing the name to the *Sheffield Iris*. He himself was imprisoned twice, once for reprinting a song in commemoration of the fall of the Bastille, and once for publishing an account of a riot in Sheffield. For the rest of his life he remained in Sheffield, working on the paper and publishing his many hymns and poems. His poetic gifts were widely recognized as time went on and he lectured on poetry in Sheffield and at the Royal Institution in London. During the last twenty-one years of his life he received a Royal pension of two hundred pounds a year. Montgomery's fine home in Sheffield was located on "The Mount," a lovely hill in the west end of the city. There he died in his sleep on April 30, 1854.

The list of Montgomery's poetical works includes *Prison Amusements* (written during a stay in prison), *The West Indies, Greeland and other Poems, The Christian Psalmist* (1825) and *Original Hymns for Public, Private, and Social Devotion* (1853). "Angels, from the realms of glory," one of the author's most popular hymns, appeared in the *Shef-*

field Iris, December 24, 1816. LBW stanzas 1–3 are Montgomery's; the fourth stanza is a doxology added in the *Salisbury Hymn Book,* 1857.

REGENT SQUARE was included as the setting for "Glory be to God the Father" (LBW 167) in *Psalms and Hymns for Divine Worship,* 1867, of the English Presbyterian Church. It was named for Regent Square Church, the cathedral of English Presbyterianism in London, where Dr. William Hamilton, editor of the book, was minister.

The composer, Henry Thomas Smart, was the son of Henry Smart, music publisher, orchestra director, and accomplished violinist, and a nephew of Sir George Thomas Smart. Born in London, England, on October 25, 1813, Henry Thomas was educated at Highgate. During his boyhood he spent his leisure hours at the Robson organ factory and was also able to attend scientific lectures at the Royal Institution. At the age of twelve he showed remarkable skill at mechanical drawing. He studied law, but after four years in the legal profession he devoted himself entirely to music. Having received his early music training from his father, he continued on his own, working diligently in organ study until he was considered a very accomplished organist. His organ appointments included Blackburn Parish Church, 1831–1836; St. Giles, Cripplegate, 1836–1838; St. Philip's, Regent Street, 1838–1839; St. Luke's, Old Street, 1844–1864; and St. Pancras Church, 1865–1879. He designed the organs at Leeds Town Hall, 1858, and in St. Andrew's Hall, Glasgow, 1877, and at the Great Exhibition in 1851 was one of five organists asked to perform.

Shortly after he took his post at St. Philip's, Regent Street, Smart also became music critic to the *Atlas,* a weekly journal. He was music editor of the *Chorale Book,* 1865, and the *Presbyterian Hymnal,* 1875, and contributed tunes also to *Hymns Ancient and Modern,* 1861, and to *Psalms and Hymns,* 1867. In addition to a large number of vocal pieces—part-songs, trios, duets, songs—Smart also composed an opera, an oratorio, services, organ music, and a large number of hymn tunes. After he became completely blind at age fifty-two (his eyesight had begun to fail already when he was eighteen years old), his daughter took down all his compositions for him. His ability to extemporize, for which he had long had a reputation, served him well in his blindness. He died in London, July 6, 1879.

The harmonization of the tune is by Paul O. Manz, cantor of Mount Olive Lutheran Church, Minneapolis, Minnesota. Born May 10, 1919, in Cleveland, Ohio, Manz has studied with Albert Reimenschneider, Edwin Arthur Kraft, Edwin Eigenschenck, and Arthur Jennings, and received a Master of Music degree from Northwestern University, Evanston, Illinois. He was awarded a Fulbright grant to study organ, improvisation, and composition at the Royal Flemish Conservatory of Music in Antwerp, Belgium, where he worked with Flor Peeters and earned the first prize with highest distinction. An extension of the grant permitted him to continue his studies in Frankfurt, Germany, with Helmut Walcha. Before going to Mt. Olive Church, he held posts at Winnebago Academy, Fond du Lac, Wisconsin; Emanuel Lutheran Church, St. Paul, Minnesota; University of Minnesota, Minneapolis, Minnesota; Macalester College, St. Paul, Minnesota; and Concordia College, St. Paul, Minnesota. His position as cantor of Mount Olive Church extends his ministry beyond the bounds of his local parish (where he serves as minister of music) and enables him to serve the whole Church as composer, recitalist, teacher, lecturer, and leader in worship. He has concertized extensively in the United States, Canada, and Europe, including a three-month tour with the Roger Wagner Chorale in 1964 as guest organist, and has become especially well-known for his exciting and inspiring hymn festivals. He has participated in many organ clinics and liturgical seminars, has appeared as lecturer and recitalist at regional and national conventions of the American Guild of Organists, and served as organist for the Third Assembly of the World Federation of Lutherans. In 1968 he was invited to be the American recitalist at festivities in Antwerp honoring Flor Peeters' retirement from active teaching, and in 1973 he was conference chairman of an International Youth Music Festival in Berlin. He is the recipient of several honors, including a Doctor of Letters from Concordia College, Seward, Nebraska; a Doctor of Music from Carthage College, Kenosha, Winsconsin; and a St. Caecilia Medal from Boys' Town, Omaha, Nebraska. In addition to his series of chorale improvisations for organ, his compositions include a number of choral works, and some compositions for choir and congregation with organ and instruments. His four albums of organ improvisations have received considerable acclaim. He is past president of the Lutheran Society for Worship, Music, and the Arts. Married in 1943, Manz and his wife, Ruth *née* Mueller, are the parents of three children of their own, and four by adoption after the death of their parents, the Rev. and Mrs. Herbert J. Mueller.

51 FROM HEAVEN ABOVE *(Vom Himmel hoch da komm ich her)*
Tune: Vom Himmel hoch

Leupold* notes that Martin Luther (LBW 48) used an old garland song which consisted of a single stanza (actually a refrain) as the basis for the first stanza of this hymn. In a popular singing game of Luther's day, a young man would sing this refrain and then give out a riddle to one of the girls in the circle. If she could not solve the riddle she had to give the singer her wreath or garland. Konrad Ameln in *The Roots of German Hymnody* (St. Louis: Concordia Publishing House, 1964) gives the German of both:

> *Original garland song*
>
> Aus Fremden Landen komm ich her
> und bring euch viel der neuen Mär,
> der neuen Mär bring ich so viel,
> mehr den ich euch hie sagen will.

> *Luther's stanza*
>
> Vom Himmel hoch da komm ich her,
> ich bring euch gute neue Mär;
> der guten Mär bring ich so viel,
> davon ich singen und sagen will.

A translation of the garland song is given by Leupold:

> Good news from far abroad I bring
> Glad tidings for you all I sing,
> I bring so much you'd like to know,
> Much more than I shall tell you though.

Written for his family's celebration of Christmas Eve, Luther's hymn included fourteen stanzas in addition to the one rearranged from the folk song. It was printed in Joseph Klug's (LBW 85) *Geistliche Lieder,* Wittenberg, 1535. A translation from Catherine Winkworth's (LBW 29) *Lyra Germanica,* first series, 1855, served as the basis for this English text prepared by the Inter-Lutheran Commission on Worship for the LBW.

VOM HIMMEL HOCH. Originally Luther's words were sung to the folk melody which accompanied "Aus fremden Landen komm ich her"; but the tune was later replaced with the present one, which is believed to have been written by Luther himself. This tune, which first appeared in Valentin Schumann's *Geistliche lieder auffs new gebessert und gemehrt,* published in Leipzig in 1539, soon entered a number of other Lutheran hymnals, and was also found in many Roman Catholic hymnals after 1567. In Schumann's hymnal the melody originally had an eighth-note upbeat at the beginning, rather than the half note used here. J. S. Bach (LBW 219) used the tune in his Christmas Oratorio, and as the basis for several organ works—a set of canonic variations, four settings among his Miscellaneous Preludes, and one·in the *Orgelbüchlein.*

52 YOUR LITTLE ONES, DEAR LORD
(Her kommer, Jesus, dina smaa)
Tune: Her kommer dine arme Smaa

This hymn by Hans Adolf Brorson was very possibly sung for the first time around a nativity scene at a prayer meeting at Emmerle in the Tønder parish. It was published in *Nogle Jule-Psalmer,* Tønder, 1732, a small collection (ten hymns) with a large title, which translated reads, *Some Christmas Hymns, Composed to the Honor of God, the Edification of Christian Souls and, in Particular, of my Beloved Congregation during the Approaching Joyful Christmastide, Humbly and Hastily Written by Hans Adolph Brorson.*

Brorson, one of Denmark's greatest hymnwriters, was born June 20, 1694, at Randerup, and spent his childhood on the western coast of Sønderjylland. His family had been well-to-do farmers for many generations until the line was broken by his grandfather who became a pastor. Hans's father, also a pastor, died when Hans was barely ten years old, leaving behind a heavy indebtedness. His mother, for the sake of her three sons, married their father's predecessor, and Hans was able to attend the Latin school at Ribe, and in 1712 entered the University of Copenhagen. He gradually lost interest in theology, his major field, however, and broadened his course of study to include philology, philosophy, and history, and in 1715 was also appointed to Borch's collegium. Here he fell sick due to over-exertion, and had to abandon his studies and leave Copenhagen. He spent some time in Sønderjylland with his brother Nicolai, a pastor and an enthusiastic proponent of pietism; and in Randerup, where he was an assistant to his stepfather. For four years beginning in 1717 he was a tutor in the home of his uncle Clausen, during which time his health greatly improved. His stepfather died in 1721, and Brorson was offered the calling. After completing his finals at Copenhagen he was ordained in 1722, and in the same year was married to Cathrine Steenbeck Clausen. He served in Randerup until 1729 when he was transferred to Tønder, a mixed Danish and German parish. There he worked closely with the German pastor, pietist, and hymnwriter, Johan Herman Schräder. Brorson's own talent for hymnwriting soon revealed itself. At the Tønder parish, both German and Danish services were held, but the hymns were sung in German. Brorson set about to provide the congregation with some Danish hymns. In addition to *Nogle Jule-Psalmer,* his first publication, he prepared several other collections, including ones for Advent, Passion, Easter, Pentecost, and the minor festivals. All of these were gathered into a single volume, *Troens rare Klenodie,* 1739, which went through six editions during his lifetime. In 1737 he was appointed district superintendent, and in 1741, bishop of Ribe. In the same year that he was appointed bishop, his wife died while giving birth to their thirteenth child, and the following year he was married to Johanne Christine Riese. As a bishop Brorson was greatly loved and respected, and was an active proponent of public education. During his last years, in spite of pain and suffering due to ill health, he wrote seventy more hymns which his son published in 1765 in a collection titled *Svane-Sang.* Brorson died at Ribe on June 3, 1764.

All told, Brorson's hymns and translations number in the hundreds. *Den ny Salmebog,* a revision of Thomas Kingo's (LBW 102) hymnal, which Brorson projected and to which he contributed extensively, was published in 1740 by Erik Pontoppidan.

Harriet Reynolds Krauth, daughter of Charles Porterfield Krauth (LBW 62), was born September 21, 1845, in Baltimore, Maryland. She attended the Girls' School in Philadelphia, and in 1879, became the second wife of the Reverend Adolph Spaeth, who later became president of the General Council of the Lutheran Church in America, and a professor at the Lutheran Theological Seminary, Mt. Airy, Philadelphia. She is said to have been a model wife, and mother to the children of her adoption as well as the five of her own. Her son, Sigmund, became a well-known writer, lecturer, and music critic. Harriet Spaeth was a musician, and served for many years as organist at St. Stephen's Church, West Philadelphia. In addition to providing translations for the *Church Book,* 1868, and *The Sunday School Hymnal,* 1901, she also was responsible for the music edition of the *Church Book,* 1872. She translated *The Deaconess and Her Works* and *Pictures from the Life of Hans Sachs,* and was the author of a biography of her husband. Together with her husband she also prepared a biography of her father. Many of her articles appeared in *The Lutheran.* She worked zealously for the founding of Krauth Memorial Library at the seminary, and was active in the work of the Mary J. Drexel Home, the Lankenau Hospital, and the Lutheran Orphans' Home in Germantown. She died in Philadelphia on May 5, 1925.

Her translation, "*Thy* little ones, dear Lord, are we," was written in 1898 and included in the *Lutheran Hymnary,* 1913. The alterations are very minor ones.

HER KOMMER DINE ARME SMAA (also "Paedia"), composed by Johann A. P. Schulz, was included in the collection *Religiose Oden und Lieder,* Hamburg, 1789, where it was the setting for the children's hymn, "Den süssen Schlaf erbitten wir."

Johann Abraham Peter Schulz, the son of a baker, was born March 31, 1747, in Lüneberg, Germany. Like many other talented boys of his time, he was discovered through his singing in the church. He studied in Lüneberg with the organist Schmügel, who had been a pupil of Georg

Phillip Telemann, and at the age of fifteen, set out for Berlin to study with Johann Philipp Kirnberger, the noted theorist, then at the height of his fame as a teacher. From 1768 to 1773, as accompanist and piano teacher to the Polish countess Sapieha, he traveled in Italy, France, and Austria, during which time he came to know Franz Joseph Haydn (LBW 358). On his return to Berlin, he assisted Kirnberger with his treatise on composition, and together with Kirnberger and J. G. Sulzer, published *Allgemeine Theorie der schönen Künste*, 1771-1774. From 1775 he was director of the Royal French Theater in Berlin. It closed in 1778, and he became director of music to the crown princess. In 1780 he assumed the prestigious position of director of music to Prince Heinrich of Rheinsberg in Prussia, and the following year was married to Wilhelmina F. C. Flügel. When she died three years later, he married her sister, Louise. During the 1780s he achieved considerable fame as a composer, especially with his songs, in which he paid very careful attention to text setting. His sacred songs published in 1784 were translated into Danish and published in Denmark the following year. Thus, when the Royal Danish theater was going to choose a new director, Schulz's name was already well-known, and he was hired in 1787. He was well-liked by the Danes, and became involved in social and political issues, and in the introduction of music to the schools of Denmark. In 1788 he established his annual Holy Week concerts to provide funds for the widows of musicians and other benevolent societies. When the royal palace burned in 1794 Schulz destroyed his health in his attempt to save the irreplaceable music archives. He resigned in 1795 and boarded a boat to Lisbon, hoping to find relief from his pneumonia. A storm carried the ship to Norway, however, and Schulz returned to Germany. After living for a while in Lüneberg, Berlin, Rheinberg, and Stettin, he died at Schwedt an der Oder on June 10, 1800.

Schulz's works include *Lieder im Volkston,* 1785-1790 (a collection of sacred and secular German songs), operas, oratorios, and instrumental music. His compositions set the tone in Danish music, and greatly influenced C. E. F. Weyse (LBW 161) who studied with him.

53 COLD DECEMBER FLIES AWAY *(Lo desembre congelat)*

Tune: Lo desembre congelat

Both words and music of this carol come to us from Catalonia, an area in northeastern Spain. The original language of the carol, Catalan, is related to both French and Spanish, but is closer to Latin than either. The language has its own body of literature and is spoken today in parts of southwestern France, Valencia, the Balearic Islands, and in Sardinia, as well as in Catalonia. Howard Hawhee, who prepared the English text in 1975, notes that "the Catalonians were very much influenced by the troubadours in their lyric writing, and this song is no exception; the vivid imagery is very much in the troubadour tradition."

Born in Cresco, Iowa, on July 27, 1953, Howard Hawhee attended Luther College, Decorah, Iowa, where he was a student of Gracia Grindal (LBW 32) at the time this text was prepared. He received a Bachelor of Arts degree in 1975, and enrolled in the comparative literature program at the University of Iowa, working toward a Doctor of Philosophy degree. He has held various scholarships, including National Merit Finalist and Luther Regents' Scholar in 1971, State of Iowa Scholar, 1971-1973, and Helen K. Fairall Scholar, 1977-1978.

The tune, LO DESEMBRE CONGELAT, like the original Catalonian words, is of unknown origin. The present setting was prepared by Walter C. Ehret for the *International Book of Christmas Carols,* 1963.

A native of New York City, Ehret is district coordinator of music for the Scarsdale Public Schools, Scarsdale, New York. He holds a Bachelor of Science degree from Juilliard School of Music and a Master of Arts degree from Teacher's College, Columbia University, and has taught for over twenty-five years in New Jersey and New York. His choral groups have performed in Carnegie Hall and Madison Square Garden, as well as on radio and television. As a lecturer, conductor, and clinician, he has conducted clinics, workshops, and festivals in seventeen states. He has held offices in numerous music education associations, including the presidency of the Bergen and Nassau County Music Educators Association. Over one thousand of his choral arrangements are in print, as well as several collections of choral music. Author of the *Choral Conductor's Handbook* (1959), *Music for Everyone* (1960), and *Time for Music* (1960); and co-author of *Functional Lessons in Singing* (1960), and *Growing with Music,* Ehret has also produced several educational records.

54   IT CAME UPON THE MIDNIGHT CLEAR

Tune: Carol

Edmund Sears wrote this Christmas hymn while he was minister to the Unitarian congregation in Wayland, Massachusetts, and it was printed in the *Christian Register* for December 29, 1849. The hymn reflects the emphasis of Unitarianism of the time on the social implications of the Gospel.

Born in western Massachusetts, in the town of Sandisfield, on April 6, 1810, Edmund Hamilton Sears attended Union College, Schenectady, New York, graduating in 1834. After graduation from Harvard Divinity School in 1837 he served Unitarian congregations in the environs of Boston: Wayland, Lancaster, and Weston, Massachusetts. Among his publications were *Regeneration,* 1853; *Pictures of the Olden Time,* 1857; *The Fourth Gospel, the Heart of Christ,* 1872; and *Sermons and Songs of the Christian Life,* 1875. He died January 16, 1876, at Weston.

CAROL. Richard Willis' *Study Number 23* was included in his *Church Chorals and Choir Studies,* New York, 1850, for "See Israel's gentle shepherd stand." His adaptation of the tune to its present form for "While shepherds watched their flocks by night" was published separately in 1860, and consisted of a new third phrase and the repetition of the second phrase as the closing phrase.

Born in Boston, Massachusetts, on February 10, 1819, Richard Storrs Willis was the son of the founder of *The Youth's Companion* and the brother of a poet. Following his graduation in 1841 from Yale, where he had been active in various musical organizations, he went to Germany. There he became a student and close friend of Felix Mendelssohn (LBW 60), whose biography he later published. On his return to New York in 1848 he planned to teach colloquial German at Yale, but was advised to enter journalism, which he did. He served as music critic for *The Albion,* the *New York Tribune,* and *The Musical Times,* and from 1852 to 1864 was editor of *The Musical Times, The Musical World,* and *Once a*

Month. In addition to *Church Chorals* he published *Our Church Music,* 1856, a handbook for ministers and musicians; *Waif of Song,* 1876; and *Pen and Lute,* 1883. His compositions included church anthems and secular songs. After 1861 he lived in Detroit, except for the years 1874–1878 during which he lived in Nice, Italy, where his daughter was in school. He died in Detroit, May 7, 1900.

55 GOOD CHRISTIAN FRIENDS, REJOICE *(In dulci jubilo)*

Tune: In dulci jubilo

Text and tune of this medieval carol have come down through the centuries together. The original text is "macaronic," that is, a combination of Latin with a vernacular language. The earliest existing form of the carol is at Leipzig University Library, Codex 1305, which dates from around 1400. There the first of four stanzas reads as follows:

> *In dulci jubilo*
> Singet und sit vro.
> Aller unser wonne
> Layt in presepio,
> Sy leuchtet vor dy sonne
> *Matris in gremio*
> *Qui alpha est et O.*
> *Qui alpha est et O.*

Earliest mention of the carol is by a fourteenth-century writer who relates a vision of Heinrich Suso, a mystic who died in 1366, in which angels drew him into a dance and sang this carol to him. The carol is one of a group of related Christmas songs (see also LBW 68).

Published in an early Lutheran hymnal, Joseph Klug's (LBW 85) *Geistliche Lieder,* Wittenberg, 1533, "In dulci jubilo" entered countless Protestant and Roman Catholic collections thereafter. The LBW form of the tune is identical with that in Klug's hymnal. *Piae Cantiones,* 1582, contained the text in Latin and Swedish; and in 1646 an entirely German version, beginning "Nun singet und seid froh," appeared in the Hannover *New Ordentlich Gesang-Buch.*

An interesting early English translation, retaining the macaronic identity of the text, appeared in 1540 in John Wedderburn's *Gude and Godlie Ballatis:*

> In dulci jubilo,
> Now let us sing with mirth and jo,
> Our hartis consolation
> Lyis in praesepio
> And schynis as the Sone,
> Matris in gremio.
> Alpha es et O.
> Alpha es et O.

John Mason Neale's (LBW 34) translation was included in *Carols for Christmas-tide,* 1853, a book containing twelve carols intended to be an inexpensive collection available to all church choirs, which he edited with Thomas Helmore. Originally the translation opened "Good Christian *men* rejoice," and the exclamations "News! News!" "Joy! Joy!" and

"Peace! Peace!" followed the third line in the first, second, and third stanzas respectively.

Richard Hillert's (LBW 63) harmonization of the tune was prepared for the LBW.

56 THE FIRST NOEL

Tune: The First Nowell

The word "Noel" (Old English: "Nowell") derives from the Latin word "Natalis," meaning birthday or birth. Related words are found in many languages—"Noël" in French, "Nadal" in Provençal, "Natal" in Spanish, "Natale" in Italian. It has long been sung or shouted in expressing joy over the birth of Christ. As far back as "The Franklin's Tale" in Chaucer's *Canterbury Tales* (fourteenth century) one reads:

> Biforn him stant braun of the tusked swyn,
> And "Nowel" cryeth every lusty man.

The words of this carol are first found in Davies Gilbert's *Some Ancient Christmas Carols,* second edition, published in London in 1823. Gilbert wrote in his preface that until recently [1823] in the Protestant West of England, people gathered on Christmas Eve for cakes and cider or beer and sang these carols until late into the night. Then on Christmas Day, the carols took the place of the Psalms in the church services, especially the afternoon service, with the whole congregation joining in.

It is not known how long the carol has been in existence. Some feel that it is no older than the seventeenth century; others believe that the fanciful treatment of the Star motif suggests an earlier date.

THE FIRST NOWELL. The tune first appeared together with an altered version of the text in 1833 in *Christmas Carols, Ancient and Modern,* published by a London lawyer, William Sandys. This collection of carols is an important one, with an extensive introduction and a large number of texts. Among the eighteen tunes given one finds the first written versions of eleven carols, including also "I saw three ships."

Although the tune is traditional with this carol, some authorities point out that the repetitive nature of the tune, and the fact that it lies mostly between the third of the scale and the upper octave, would indicate that it was originally a descant or a portion of another tune. Patrick* believes that it was a descant to Jeremiah Clark's "An Hymn for Christmas Day," an elaborated form of the tune "St. Magnus" (LBW 173). In *The English Carol* (New York: Oxford University Press, 1958), Erik Routley notes that the tune fits as a descant to "Rejoice and be merry," and in the *Companion to Congregational Praise** he comments that the melody "is so familiar that it is seldom realised what a very peculiar tune it in fact is." Ann G. Gilchrist, in the *Journal of the Folk Song Society,* V, quotes a manuscript tune-book, dated 1820, from Orton, Westmorland, in which a phrase of "The First Nowell" serves as the treble part of the Christmas hymn "Hark, hark what news the angels bring."

The harmonization by John Stainer is from *Christmas Carols New and Old,* 1871, which he edited with Henry Ramsden Bramley.

Stainer was born June 13, 1840, at Southwark, London, England, and from 1847 to 1856 was a chorister at St. Paul's Cathedral. In 1854 he began his career as an organist in the church of St. Benedict and St.

Peter's, Paul's Wharf, and two years later succeeded F. Gore Ouseley as organist of St. Michael's, Tenbury. In 1859 he was appointed organist at Magdalen College, and entered Christ Church, Oxford, where he received a Bachelor of Music degree. Afterwards he went to St. Edmund's Hall, receiving a Bachelor of Arts degree in 1863, a Doctor of Music degree in 1865, and a Master of Arts degree in 1866. He succeeded Sir John Goss (LBW 549) at St. Paul's Cathedral in 1872, where he reorganized the musical life of the cathedral, raised the standards of the choir to one of the finest in the nation, and carefully trained the choristers, making St. Paul's Choir School a model for all others in the country. In 1888 he was knighted by Queen Victoria, and shortly afterwards, due to failing eyesight, discontinued his cathedral work. From 1889 to 1899 he was a professor of music at Oxford University, and in 1900 became Master of the Company of Musicians. He died at Verona on March 31, 1901.

Besides his hymn tunes, Stainer also wrote other church music, including cantatas and anthems. He published textbooks on organ, harmony, composition, and musical terms, and with H. R. Bramley prepared one of the early collections related to the revival of carol singing. He did editorial work for *The Church Hymnary,* 1898, and was also connected with the earlier stages of *Hymns Ancient and Modern.*

57 LET OUR GLADNESS HAVE NO END *(Narodil se Kristus Pán)*
Tune: Narodil se Kristus Pán

Dating probably from the early fifteenth century, this Bohemian carol was included in Tobias Zavorka's *Kancional* of 1602.

An English text, "Christ the Lord to us is born," by Vincent Pizek and John Bajus was included in *The Lutheran Hymnal,* 1941; and a translation by Herman Breuckner (LBW 249), "Be ye joyful, earth and sky," was given in *The Concordia Hymnal,* 1932. The present translation is of unknown origins.

NARODIL SE KRISTUS PÁN is the anonymous fifteenth-century tune associated with this carol. Named "Salvator natus" in *The Lutheran Hymnal,* the melody is given here with a new harmonization by Richard Hillert (LBW 63).

58 LO, HOW A ROSE IS GROWING *(Es ist ein Ros entsprungen)*
Tune: Es ist ein Ros

The poetic prophecy of Isaiah 11:1, "There shall come forth a shoot from the stump of Jesse, and a branch shall grow out of his roots," found expression in hymnody as early as the eighth century. A hymn by the Greek writer, Cosmas the Melodist, as translated by John Mason Neale (LBW 34), begins "Rod of the Root of Jesse, Thou, Flower of Mary born." The present German carol is believed by some to date from as early as the fifteenth century. The earliest source of the text is a manuscript from St. Alban's Carthusian monastery in Trier, which is preserved in the municipal library of Trier. According to the owner's mark on the inside cover, this manuscript is a prayer book which belonged to the procurator, Brother Conrad the Carthusian of Mainz, and was written down between 1582 and 1588. As first published in the *Alte Catholische Geistliche Kirchengeseng* (*Speierischen Gesangbuch*), Cologne, 1599, the text consisted of twenty-three stanzas and related the events of Luke 1 and 2, and Matthew 2.

The translation is by Gracia Grindal (LBW 32).

ES IST EIN ROS. The earliest source of this melody, which is believed by some to date from the fifteenth or even the fourteenth century, is the *Alte Catholische Geistliche Kirchengeseng,* Cologne, 1599. Segments of the tune have been noted in other melodies, including the setting for Psalm 91 in the Uhlenberg Psalter, 1582, and for "Wer Gott will recht vertrauen" in Philipp von Winnenbergh's *Christliche Reuterlieder,* Strassburg, 1582. The opening phrase can also be seen in the first phrase of a fifteenth-century spinning song given below.†

The beautiful setting found in the LBW is from Michael Praetorius' (LBW 36) *Musae Sionae,* VI, published in 1609.

59 WHEN CHRISTMAS MORN IS DAWNING
(*När Juldagsmorgon glimmar*)
Tune: Wir hatten gebauet

This hymn was published in *Andelig Örtegård för Barn,* Jönköping, 1851, numbers 13 and 14, a Swedish periodical edited by G. Berggren, a school teacher in Kalmar. In this publication the text is credited to Abel Burckhardt, a German author, about whom nothing further is known. Because it appeared in 1856 in Betty Ehrenborg-Posse's *Andliga sånger för barn,* volume II, it has sometimes been attributed to her.

Joel W. Lundeen (LBW 146) prepared the translation for the LBW.

WIR HATTEN GEBAUET, used as the setting for this hymn both in Sweden and in North America, is a German folk melody. Considered by some to be a Thuringian folksong, it was known at least as early as 1819, when it was sung on November 29 with August von Binzer's text, "Wir hatten gebauet." Johannes Brahms used the melody in his *Academic Festival Overture.*

60 HARK! THE HERALD ANGELS SING
Tune: Mendelssohn

See LBW 27 for Charles Wesley. This hymn of ten four-line stanzas, which was published in *Hymns and Sacred Poems,* 1739, originally began

> Hark, how all the welkin rings
> Glory to the King of kings.

---

†A detailed discussion of the sources of the text and tune can be found in Herbert Vossebrecher, *Die Gesänge des Speyerer Gesangbuchs (Köln 1599),* Cologne, 1968.

161

The present opening lines are from George Whitefield's (LBW 522) *A Collection of Hymns for Social Worship,* 1753. Details of other alterations are given in Julian* (p. 487). The Inter-Lutheran Commission on Worship has also made a few slight revisions.

MENDELSSOHN, which has also been called "Jesu Redemptor," "Bethlehem," "St. Vincent," "Berlin," "Festgesang," and "Nativity," was written in 1840 to celebrate the 400th anniversary of printing. It is the second movement, "Vaterland, in deinem Gauen," of Mendelssohn's *Festgesang an die Künstler,* Op. 68. The melody is taken unaltered from this work for male chorus and brass, except for the third line where the voices in unison were accompanied as given below.

Gu - ten - berg, _____ der deutsche Mann, _____

Brasses:

Although Mendelssohn expressed the desire to find another text for his music, he felt that the setting would never be appropriate to a sacred text. In 1855, however, William H. Cummings adapted the music to Charles Wesley's hymn, and the combination, which has proved to be a good one indeed, was published in Richard R. Chope's *Congregational Hymn and Tune Book,* 1857.

Felix Mendelssohn-Bartholdy, a member of a Christian-Jewish family, was born February 3, 1809, in Hamburg, Germany. His grandfather was the great Jewish philosopher Moses Mendelssohn, his father was a wealthy banker, and his mother was an exceptionally refined and cultured woman. Mendelssohn grew up under ideal conditions, beginning his music training at an early age and studying with the best of teachers. An exceptionally gifted young man, he became proficient not only in music—as pianist, organist, conductor, and composer—but in linguistics and painting as well. His overture to *Midsummer Night's Dream* was written when he was seventeen; and his later work—his *Songs without Words,* his organ sonatas, his oratorios *Elijah* and *St. Paul,* his *Reformation Symphony,* and many other works—is well-known to music lovers. His grandmother's Christmas gift to him in 1823 was a manuscript copy of J. S. Bach's (LBW 219) *St. Matthew Passion.* This work he conducted in Berlin in 1829, one hundred years after its original performance. After traveling and giving concerts in England, Italy, and France, he settled for a while in Düsseldorf, where from 1833 to 1835 he was director of music for the city. Thereafter he made his home in Leipzig, where he built the Gewandhaus Orchestra into the first of the great modern symphony orchestras, and in 1843 established the Leipzig Conservatory. He died in Leipzig, November 4, 1847.

William Hayman Cummings, born August 22, 1831, in Sidbury, Devonshire, England, served as a boy chorister at St. Paul's Cathedral, and later in the Temple Church. In 1847 he took a position as organist at

Waltham Abbey, and soon thereafter became a tenor in the Temple, and also at Westminster Abbey and the Chapel Royal. At the age of sixteen he sang in the premiere performance of Mendelssohn's *Elijah,* conducted by the composer. Widely acclaimed as a tenor soloist, he sang for the Birmingham Festival in 1864, and sang some concerts in the United States. He was noted for his singing of the principal parts of Bach's Passions, as well as other works. From 1879 to 1896 he was professor of singing at the Royal Academy of Music. For a time, also, he was conductor of the Sacred Harmonic Society and precentor at St. Anne's, Soho. In 1896 he succeeded Joseph Barnby (LBW 280) as principal of the Guildhall School of Music, where he remained until his retirement in 1911. In 1900 he received an honorary Doctor of Music degree from the University of Dublin. He died June 6, 1915.

Also an antiquarian, Cummings was one of the founders of the Purcell Society, and in 1882 prepared a biography of Henry Purcell. He contributed also to *Grove's Dictionary of Music and Musicians.* His compositions include a cantata, "The Fairy Ring," 1873, as well as church music, glees, and part songs.

61 THE HILLS ARE BARE AT BETHLEHEM

Tune: Prospect

At Christmastime Pastor Royce J. Scherf and his wife, Frieda, send greetings to the members of their congregation in the form of an original Christmas hymn and tune. This hymn was written for such a greeting in 1973.

Scherf was born October 19, 1929, in Garnavillo, Iowa, and was a member of St. Paul Lutheran Church there. In 1951 he received a Bachelor of Arts degree from the University of Iowa, and three years later, completed a Bachelor of Divinity degree at Chicago Lutheran Theological Seminary, Maywood, Illinois (now the Lutheran School of Theology at Chicago). He served a dual parish in Nebraska—St. Peter's, Pilger, and St. Luke's, Stanton—from 1954 to 1956, after which he was at St. John's, Alliance, Nebraska, from 1957 to 1960, and St. John's, Maywood, Illinois from 1960 to 1971. Since 1971 he has been the pastor of Immanuel Lutheran Church, Evanston, Illinois. Married to Frieda Konig, he is the father of two sons.

Scherf's hymn texts have been written in the context of local congregational worship, and many have been supplied with tunes by Frieda Scherf.

PROSPECT appeared in William Walker's (LBW 30) *Southern Harmony,* 1835, where it was the setting for Isaac Watts's (LBW 39) "Why should we start and fear to die?" The composer of this pentatonic melody is unknown. Wilbur C. Held has prepared the harmonization for the LBW.

Held, born August 20, 1914, in Des Plaines, Illinois, attended the American Conservatory of Music in Chicago, where he received a Bachelor of Music degree in 1937, and a Master of Music degree in 1941. While at the American Conservatory he studied organ with Frank Van Dusen and theory and composition with John Palmer, and was for seven years assistant to Leo Sowerby (LBW 195) at St. James Episcopal Church, where he played a number of Sowerby's own works. He has also studied briefly with Marcel Dupré, André Marchal, Vernon de Tar, Normand Lockwood, and Wallingford Riegger. Before World War II he taught privately and held church positions in the Chicago area, and played a number of recitals. Drafted as a conscientious objector during the war, he served in the Michigan forests and later in a nutritional laboratory in Minneapolis. While in Minnesota he was organist for two years at the First Baptist Church in St. Paul and one year at Christ Episcopal Church in St. Paul, and also served for a year as dean of the Twin Cities Chapter of the American Guild of Organists. He was married to Virginia Starrett, also of Des Plaines, in 1944. Two years later he went to teach at Ohio State University, Columbus, Ohio, and in 1949 was also appointed organist-director at Trinity Episcopal Church in Columbus. He remained in these two positions until his retirement as professor of music from Ohio State University in 1977. In 1978 he also retired from Trinity Church, and is now living in southern California.

Active in the American Guild of Organists, Held has both an associateship and a fellowship in that organization, and has served on the National Council. He has presented numerous recitals, lectures, and workshops, and his published compositions include organ and choral works as well as hymn tunes.

62 THE BELLS OF CHRISTMAS *(Det kimer nu til Julefest)*

Tune: Det kimer nu til Julefest

Like Karl Spitta (LBW 399) a generation later in Germany, Nikolai Frederik Severin Grundtvig lived during the Rationalistic period during which orthodox Christianity was at a low ebb, he attended university under rationalistic theologians, and later found himself in opposition to the existing system. Grundtvig, the greatest Danish hymnwriter of the nineteenth century, was born September 8, 1783, the son of a Lutheran pastor at Udby. He attended the University of Copenhagen and graduated in 1803. For a while thereafter he spent his time tutoring for a wealthy family and later teaching at a school for boys. During this time also he became interested in Danish literature and history and Nordic mythology, and began to write poetry. When Grundtvig's father became ill he asked his son to come to assist him at his church at Udby. Nikolai's trial sermon for ordination, however, contained such scorching charges against the contemporary rationalistic theology that he was reprimanded and his ordination forestalled until the following year. The intervening year was spent in intensive soul-searching which led to a temporary nervous collapse. In 1811 he was ordained, but for ten years was a pastor without a parish, and was not even permitted to confirm his own children. As time went on, however, he began to gain popularity, not only by his preaching, but especially through his hymns and his poetry. His hymnal, *Sang-Värk til den Danske Kirke,* published in 1837, was well received by the people. In 1839 he was fully reinstated and was appointed pastor in Vartov. Champion of a movement to raise the intellectual standards of the Danish people, he established folk schools in Rödding, opening the first in 1844. These schools spread quickly in Denmark, and also in Sweden, Finland, and Norway, so that Grundtvig became known as the "father of the public school in Scandinavia." His greatness came to be recognized fully during the last part of his life. When Denmark became a constitutional monarchy in 1848, Grundtvig served as a member of the constitutional assembly. When he celebrated his golden jubilee as a pastor, representatives from all departments of church and state, as well as many persons from the other Scandinavian countries, were present for the celebration. In the same year the king appointed him a bishop. He died September 1, 1872, just one week short of his eighty-ninth birthday.

Grundtvig began work on this hymn in 1810, and it was first published in his *Nyeste Skilderie af Kjøbenhagen,* December 23, 1817. Translated in 1867 by Charles Porterfield Krauth, the hymn was included in *The Lutheran Hymnary,* 1913.

Krauth, an eminent Lutheran pastor, was born in Martinsburg, Virginia, on March 17, 1823. His mother died the following year, and he spent his childhood in the home of his grandmother. He was educated at Pennsylvania College (of which his father was the first president) and at Gettysburg Theological Seminary, graduating in 1841. For the next twenty years he served a number of parishes, including a mission at Canton, in Baltimore (1841-1842); Second English Lutheran Church, Baltimore (1843-1847); Shepherdstown, Jefferson County, Virginia (1847-1852); and Winchester, Virginia (1848-1852); English Lutheran Church at Pittsburgh (1855-1859); and St. Mark's, Philadelphia (1859-1861). After 1861 Krauth was editor of the *Lutheran and Missionary,* and served various churches in Philadelphia when they were in need of a pastor. He had a prominent part in the General Council throughout its existence, helping to formulate its constitution and serving for ten years as president. In 1865 he and Joseph Seiss (LBW 518) became part of the committee which was preparing the *Church Book,* 1868, to which he contributed a great deal of time and energy in the preparation of the liturgy. In 1844 Krauth was married to Susan Reynolds, and two sons and a daughter were born to them. Susan Krauth died of a lung disease in 1853 and Krauth was remarried two years later to Virginia Baker. His daughter, Harriet Reynolds Spaeth, is also represented in the LBW (52). Philadelphia College conferred the Doctor of Divinity degree on him in 1856. When the Theological Seminary at Philadelphia was established in 1864, Krauth was one of the first professors. In 1868 he became professor of mental and moral philosophy at the University of Pennsylvania, and five years later, vice-provost of the university. Towards the end of his life he was professor of history, and served as acting provost. When his health began to fail, he took a trip to Europe in hopes of recovering, but died on January 2, 1883.

DET KIMER NU TIL JULEFEST (also "Emmanuel") was written by Carl Christian Nicolai Balle, a Danish pastor and amateur musician. Born in Copenhagen in 1806, Balle served churches in Vesterbølle and later in Nebsager. He died in 1855.

63 FROM SHEPHERDING OF STARS

Tune: Shepherding

A native of Calgary, Alberta, F. Samuel Janzow was born July 17, 1913, and attended Concordia College, St. Paul, Minnesota (1930-1932) and Concordia Seminary, St. Louis (1932-1936). Following his ordination, he served from 1936 to 1947 as pastor of Luther-Tyndale and Holy Trinity churches in London, England. He continued his education at the

University of Minnesota, completing a Master of Arts degree in 1948. Thereafter he was pastor of Trinity Lutheran Church, Trimont, Minnesota, until 1954 when he was appointed to his present position—professor of English and theology at Concordia Teachers College, River Forest, Illinois. During the summer of 1965 he returned to England where he attended Oxford University, and in 1968 he completed a Doctor of Philosophy degree at the University of Chicago. In addition to his articles which have appeared in *The Campus Pastor, Lutheran Education, Concordia Journal,* and *Costerus,* he has published *Psalms for the Church Year,* and has two works in process of publication—*The Hymns of Martin Luther,* and versification of portions of the *Acts of the Apostles.* From 1961 to 1978 he was editor of *Motif: A Literary Journal.* His hymns and hymn translations have appeared in several journals and hymn collections. Married to Lydia Marie *née* Pieper, he is the father of two children.

"From shepherding of stars" was first published in the November, 1963, issue of *Lutheran Education,* and was included four years later in *A New Song.* Its first hymnal appearance was the *Worship Supplement,* 1969, to *The Lutheran Hymnal.*

SHEPHERDING was written for this text at the request of the editors of *Lutheran Education.* Included also in *A New Song,* it received its name in the *Worship Supplement,* 1969, to *The Lutheran Hymnal.*

The composer, Richard W. Hillert, has been a professor of music at Concordia College, River Forest, Illinois since 1959. Born March 14, 1923, in Granton, a small farming community in Clark County, Wisconsin, he received a Bachelor of Science in Education degree in 1951 from Concordia Teachers College, River Forest, and also holds Master of Music (1955) and Doctor of Music (1968) degrees in composition from Northwestern University, Evanston, Illinois. He has studied composition with Matthew Nathaniel Lundquist, Anthony Donato, and at the Berkshire School of Music, Tanglewood, Massachusetts, with Goffredo Petrassi. He served as teacher and director of music at Bethlehem Lutheran Church, St. Louis, Missouri, from 1951 to 1953, and at Trinity, Wausau, Wisconsin, from 1953 to 1959. In addition to his position at Concordia College, he has been director of music at Christ Lutheran, Chicago, 1959–1960, and Faith Lutheran, Westchester, Illinois, 1964–1969. Associate editor of *Church Music* since its beginning in 1966, he has contributed numerous articles to that journal, as well as to various other publications. He is also represented in *Keywords in Church Music* and in the *Handbook of Church Music,* both published in 1977. The list of his compositions, many of which are for church use, is extensive and includes choral works, Gospel motets, hymn tunes and carols, and chamber music, as well as works for piano and for organ with instruments. Most recently he has turned his talents toward preparing music for the LBW. A member of the Liturgical Music Committee from its beginning in 1966, he is the composer of Setting One of the Holy Communion, as well as of settings of portions of Matins, three canticles, two original hymn tunes, and numerous harmonizations. Previously he was music editor of *Worship Supplement,* 1969, to *The Lutheran Hymnal,* for which he prepared a setting of the Holy Eucharist, canticles for Matins and Vespers, and hymn tunes and harmonizations. (See also "Composers for the Church: Richard Hillert" in *Church Music,* 72:1.)

Tune: A solis ortus cardine

Coelius Sedulius' *Paean Alphabeticus de Christo* ("Hymnus de Christo") is, as the title suggests, an acrostic. In the original poem, which gives the life of Christ in verse, each of the twenty-three stanzas begins with one of the letters of the alphabet. From this poem, a hymn consisting of the first seven stanzas came into use. In Roman and Sarum rites, where the hymn was assigned to Lauds (sunrise) on Christmas Day, as well as to various other Offices, a doxology was added which was not part of the original. Used extensively in England, the hymn was in general Latin use including Mozarabic, although it did not come into Ambrosian use.

Little is known of Sedulius' life. It is felt that he was probably born in Rome, and lived during the early part of the fifth century. It has been derived from his two letters to Macedonius that in his early life he devoted himself to heathen literature, and only late in life was he converted to Christianity. Once he became a Christian, however, he turned his talents to his new faith, and wrote two poetic settings and one prose rendering of the Gospel story, in addition to other writings.

A German translation by Martin Luther (LBW 48), "Christum wyr sollen loben schon," was included in 1524 in the Wittenberg *Geystliche gesangk Buchleyn* and the Erfurt *Enchiridia.*

John Ellerton (LBW 262) prepared a Common Meter translation of Sedulius' hymn and published it in his *Church Hymns,* 1871. His Long Meter form, based on the earlier translation, was included in the 1889 Supplement to the 1875 edition of *Hymns Ancient and Modern.* It is this second version which is used in the LBW with only two slight changes in the final stanza.

A SOLIS ORTUS CARDINE is the plainsong melody which has been associated with Sedulius' Latin hymn both in England, since Anglo-Saxon times, and on the Continent. The form of the melody used in the LBW is from the *Antiphonale Sarisburiense* and was included by John Mason Neale (LBW 34) in his *Hymnal Noted,* 1851.

The harmonization of the melody is by Roger Tyrone Petrich, who was born July 26, 1938, in Fargo, and grew up in Grand Forks, North Dakota. After two years at the University of North Dakota, where he majored first in engineering, then in liberal arts, he went to St. Olaf College, Northfield, Minnesota, and studied organ with Paul Ensrud and David N. Johnson (LBW 558), and choral conducting with Olaf Christiansen and Kenneth Jennings. He received a Bachelor of Music degree magna cum laude in 1961. Further education included study of composition with Leo Sowerby (LBW 195) at the American Conservatory of Music, Chicago; and organ with Paul Callaway, liturgics with Leonard Ellinwood, and continued work with Sowerby at the College of Church Musicians, Episcopal National Cathedral, Washington, D.C. For two years beginning in 1963 he was director of music at Christ Lutheran Church, Bethesda, Maryland. After a year at the Spandauer Kirchenmusikschule, Berlin, Germany, where he received instruction in composition, choral conducting, and organ design from Ernst Pepping, Helmuth Rilling, and Karl Theodore Kühn, he went in 1966 to the University of Iowa, Iowa City. There he studied organ with Gerhard Krapf and choral literature with Daniel Moe (LBW 427), receiving a Master of Arts degree in 1968 and a Master of Fine Arts degree two years later, and continuing with further work toward a Doctor of Musical Arts degree. In 1971 he became director of music at Luther Memorial Church in Madison, Wisconsin, where he established a weekly recital series and a Bach cantata series, and founded a parish chamber orchestra. Since 1977 he has been director of music at Our Lady of the Assumption, Beloit, Wisconsin. His assignment has been to teach new music to the congregation and build up congregational singing in this Roman Catholic parish. He has composed much music for use in his last two parishes, a small amount of which has been published.

65 SILENT NIGHT, HOLY NIGHT! *(Stille Nacht, heilige Nacht)*
Tune: Stille Nacht

This beloved Christmas carol was written for the Christmas Eve service on December 24, 1818, at St. Nikolaus Church in Oberndorf in the Austrian Alps. As the organ had ceased to function on the day of the service, Father Joseph Mohr, assistant parish priest, decided to write a new hymn for the service. He took it to Franz Gruber, parish organist and teacher in the village school, who wrote the tune. The two sang the hymn that evening, with Gruber accompanying on the guitar, and the choir repeating the last two lines in four-part harmony. The carol was not published for twenty years, but in the meantime it came to be widely known. Karl Mauracher of Zillerthal who came to repair the St. Nikolaus Church organ secured a copy and spread it throughout Tyrol as a "Tyrolian folksong." The Strasser brothers and sisters, glovemakers of Zillerthal, sang the carol at the Leipzig fair in 1831. Franz Alscher, a Leipzig organist, copied it down; and a year later a musician named Friese, from Dresden, heard the Strasser family sing it and took a copy to Berlin. Another touring family, the Rainers, sang it for the Emperor of Austria, the Czar of Russia, Queen Victoria of England, Napolean III, and Johann Wolfgang von Goethe, and in 1839 sang it in New York City at the Alexander Hamilton monument. Mohr himself prepared a manuscript arrangement for chorus, organ, and orchestra in 1833. Finally, in 1838, "Stille Nacht" was published in Leipzig in the *Katholisches Gesang-und Gebetbuch für den öffentlichen und häuslichen Gottesdienst zunächst zum Gebrauche der katholischen Gemeinden im Königreiche Sachsen* (the "Leipziger Gesangbuch"). For a time the music was attributed to others, including Mozart and Michael and Joseph Haydn (LBW 252 and 358), but in 1854 Gruber sent a letter to Berlin with a detailed account of the writing of the hymn, establishing its correct origins.

Joseph Mohr was born in Salzburg on December 11, 1792, the son of Anna Schoiberin, a Salzburg seamstress, and Joseph Mohr, a mercenary who spent most of his time as a musketeer in the archbishop's army. A parish priest took an interest in Joseph and eventually became a foster father to him. Joseph became a chorister at the Salzburg Cathedral where the Mozarts had served a generation earlier, and later attended Salzburg University. Ordained a priest in 1815, he served a number of parishes in the Salzburg diocese, including Ramsau and Laufen, Kuchl, Golling, Vigaun, Adnet, Authering, and Hof. It was during his service as assistant priest at St. Nikolaus Church in Oberndorf, where he remained from August 25, 1817, to October 19, 1819, that he wrote "Stille Nacht." From 1828 he was vicar at Hintersee, and from 1837 until his death on December 5, 1848, was a vicar at Wagrein.

Franz Xaver Gruber, son of a poor linen weaver, was born at Unter-weizberg near Hochburg, Austria, on November 25, 1787. His father discouraged his going into music, as he wanted him to take up a more lucrative vocation. Franz, however, studied violin secretly and later studied organ with Georg Hartdobler of Burghausen. He became a school teacher and held his first position at Arnsdorf where he taught from 1807 until 1829. He was also organist at St. Nikolaus Church in nearby Oberndorf from 1816. Afterwards he taught at Berndorf, where he became headmaster in 1833, and also held a music position at Halleim, near Salzburg. He died June 7, 1863. Although he wrote over ninety compositions, he is remembered today for this one hymn tune. A son, Felix, succeeded him at Halleim, and a grandson, Franz, became *Kapellmeister* at the Salzburg Cathedral.

The translator of this hymn remained unknown for nearly a century until Byron E. Underwood, in an article in *The Hymn* (October, 1957), revealed him to be Bishop John Freeman Young. The three English stanzas in common use today (the first, sixth, and second of the original) appeared in *The Sunday-School Service and Tune Book: Selected and arranged by John Clark Hollister,* a small book published by Mason Brothers of New York and Boston in 1863. There it is headed "From the Third (unpublished) Part of 'Hymns and Music for the Young.' By permission of the author." This unpublished hymnal was prepared by John Freeman Young, and in a later collection, *Great Hymns of the Church,* 1887, the translation was attributed to him.

Young was born October 30, 1820, at Pittston, Kennebec County, Maine. He received his secondary education at Wesleyan Seminary in Readfield, Maine, and then entered Wesleyan University at Middleton, Connecticut. Following his conversion to the Episcopal Church he entered Virginia Theological Seminary, graduating in 1845. Ordained a deacon at St. Michael's Church, Bristol, Rhode Island, he went immediately to St. John's Church, Jacksonville, Florida, where he served from 1845 to 1848. He was ordained a priest in 1846. In 1848 he resigned from St. John's and began mission work in Bragoria County, Texas. Thereafter he moved to Livingston, Madison County, Mississippi, and in 1853 he went to Napoleonville, Louisiana, where he established Christ Church. In 1860 he went to New York City, where he became assistant rector of Trinity Church, and subsequently married Harriet Ogden. Consecrated bishop of the Diocese of Florida in 1867, he remained there until his death of pneumonia on November 15, 1885.

Bishop Young took office at the time of the Reconstruction. An enormously energetic prelate, he reopened and strengthened a number of older parishes and founded numerous missions, made efforts to win back some of the Negroes who had joined more fundamentalist African sects, and helped to reestablish a number of parochial academies. In addition he established several missions to Cuban immigrants in Key West, and later went to Cuba itself where he laid the foundations of the missionary district there. In 1865 Columbia College honored him with a Doctor of Sacred Theology degree.

66 COME REJOICING, PRAISES VOICING *(Čas radosti, veselosti)*
Tune: Čas radosti

This hymn is based on a medieval Latin carol, "Omnis mundus iucundetur." The Bohemian text, by an unknown author, was included in the sixth edition, 1674, of the "Tranoscius" (LBW 96). Jaroslav Vajda's (LBW 159) English translation was prepared for *Slovak Christmas,* Cleveland, 1960.

ČAS RADOSTI appears to be based on the melody of the original Latin hymn, and perhaps dates from the twelfth century. It was harmonized for the LBW by Roger Petrich (LBW 64).

67   AWAY IN A MANGER
Tune: Away in a Manger

Although frequently called "Luther's Cradle Hymn," this children's hymn is actually a product of nineteenth-century America. Richard S. Hill, in his article "Not so far away in a manger: Forty-one settings of an American Carol" in *Music Library Association Notes* of December, 1945, discusses his research into the authorship of the text and the many tunes with which it has been used at one time or another. There he notes that the hymn appears nowhere in Martin Luther's (LBW 48) works; indeed the only known German version is in a collection published in 1934 in Missouri. However, "although Luther himself had nothing to do with the carol, the colonies of German Lutherans in Pennsylvania almost certainly did."

The earliest source found to date is the *Little Children's Book for Schools and Families* published in Philadelphia in 1885 under the Evangelical Lutheran Church in North America. Two anonymous stanzas appear there, set to a tune by J. E. Clark entitled "St. Kilda." The second appearance of the text is in J. R. Murray's *Dainty Songs for Little Lads and Lasses,* 1887, Cincinnati. There it appears with the present tune initialed "J. R. M." Murray is no doubt the composer of the tune, but has no one but himself to blame for going so long unrecognized; for it was here in his collection that "Away in a Manger" was headed "Luther's Cradle Hymn. Composed by Martin Luther for his children, and still sung by German mothers to their little ones."

James R. Murray was born March 17, 1841, in Andover, Massachusetts, his parents having arrived from Scotland the year before. His music education was received from Lowell Mason (LBW 353), George F. Root, George J. Webb (LBW 389), and William B. Bradbury (LBW 293), and at the Musical Institute in North Reading, Massachusetts. He was a Union Army soldier in the Civil War. Afterwards he was a music editor for the Root and Cady firm in Chicago from 1868 until 1871, when the Chicago fire destroyed the building, and he returned to Andover to teach music in the public schools. In 1881 he went to Cincinnati where he worked with the John Church Company until his death on March 10, 1905. He also published a number of Sunday school hymnals which contained a large number of his tunes, most of which have been deservedly forgotten.

The third stanza, also anonymous, is found in Charles H. Gabriel's *Vineyard Songs,* 1892. Gabriel, who lived for some time in Wilton Junction, Iowa, was a composer whose success with gospel songs was equivalent to that of Irving Berlin in the area of commercial songs.

The tune has also been called "Mueller" because of its attribution to a mysterious Carl Mueller in a collection of the 1920s. Richard Hillert (LBW 63) prepared the harmonization for the LBW.

(Quem pastores laudavere)

Tune: Quem pastores/Nunc angelorum/Resonet in laudibus

This hymn is made up of three carols from a group of related fourteenth-century German Christmas songs (see Zahn* #'s 8573-75, 8580 and Baumker* I, #'s 45-50). (Also included in the group is "In dulci jubilo" [LBW 55].) A number of these carols are preserved in the Hohenfurth Abbey manuscript 20, dated 1410. In addition to their Latin texts, each of the tunes has been coupled with at least one German text, and the tunes with their several texts were included in numerous Catholic and Lutheran hymnals of the sixteenth and seventeenth centuries.

QUEM PASTORES appeared in print for the first time in Valentinum Triller's *Ein Schlesich Singebüchlein aus Göttlicher Schrifft,* 1555, with the text, "Preiss sey Gott im höchsten Throne." It was found also with the text "Den die Hirten lobeten sehr," and in the *Mainzer Cantional* of 1605, with "Geborn ist uns ein König der ehre." The term "Quempas," derived from the first two syllables of this text, had, by the sixteenth century, come to be used as a generic designation for Christmas carols. Martin Luther (LBW 48) himself participated in the *"Quempas Singen,"* the singing of carols by students in Latin school.

NUNC ANGELORUM was printed in Joseph Klug's (LBW 85) 1543 *Geistliche Lieder zu Wittemberg.* The text "Heut ist der Engel glorischein" was also used with this tune.

RESONET IN LAUDIBUS was also published in Klug's 1543 *Geistliche Lieder.* The fourteenth-century words, "Joseph lieber, Joseph Mein," like "Resonet in laudibus," were sung as a part of mystery plays which took place around a crib in the church. Other German texts of later date include: "Singen wir mit fröligkeit," "Es miess erklingen uberall," and "Lobent und dankent dem Kindelein." The portion of the melody used here with "God's own Son, is born a child" is actually a separate melody which was the setting for "Magnum nomen Domini," made up of material from the first and last lines of "Resonet in laudibus" and often attached to it.

The English translation is from the *Worship Supplement,* 1969, to *The Lutheran Hymnal.* Martin Seltz's (LBW 28) text is based on a translation of "Quem pastores laudavere" by C. Winfred Douglas (LBW 498), included in *The Hymnal 1940* of the Episcopal Church. Herbert Bouman's translation, beginning "The glorious angels came today," was prepared for the *Worship Supplement.*

Herbert J. A. Bouman, the son of a Lutheran pastor, was born July 21, 1908, in Freeman, South Dakota. Following his graduation from Concordia College, St. Paul, Minnesota, he went to Concordia Seminary, St. Louis, where he received Master of Divinity and Master of Sacred Theology degrees. Further studies were undertaken at Indiana University, and he holds a Doctor of Divinity degree from Concordia Theological Seminary, Springfield, Illinois. As a Lutheran pastor, he has served Our Savior, Canton, Ohio; St. John, Geneva, Ohio; St. John, Decatur, Indiana; and Immanuel, Sheboygan, Wisconsin. He has also taught at Bethlehem Lutheran School, Richmond, Virginia; Concordia College, Fort Wayne, Indiana; and Concordia Seminary, St. Louis, Missouri. He has lectured at theological conferences in Germany, England, France, and Brazil; and has held several church offices, in-

cluding chairman of the Board of Appeals of the Lutheran Church
—Missouri Synod, and Secretary to the Commission on Theology and
Church Relations (LC–MS); and has served with the Division of
Theological Studies of the Lutheran Council in the USA, and participated in the Lutheran-Reformed Dialogs. In addition to sermons,
devotional literature, and articles in various professional theological
journals, his publications include several translations: four volumes of
the American edition of Luther; Edmund Schlink, *Theology of the
Lutheran Confessions . . . The Doctrine of Baptism;* Hans-Werner Gen-
sichen, *We Condemn;* and Walter V. Loewenich, *Luther's Theology of
the Cross.*

The harmonization is by Ronald Nelson (LBW 258).

69 I AM SO GLAD EACH CHRISTMAS EVE
(Jeg er saa glad hver Julekveld)
Tune: Jeg er saa glad

Marie Wexelsen, a Norwegian hymnwriter whose mother was a sister of
Wilhelm Wexels (LBW 351) and whose father was a cousin, began
writing poetry at the age of twenty. Born September 20, 1832, at Ostre
Toten, Norway, she lived for many years in Trondhjem, where she died
in 1911. Her hymns were known throughout Norway.

This hymn was included in the *Nynorsk Salmebog,* 1926. Peter
Andrew Sweeggen's English translation, written in 1931, was included in
The Concordia Hymnal, 1932. The first line has been altered from "*How
glad I am* each Christmas eve," and there are several other changes in the
text as well.

Born June 30, 1881, in South Dakota, Peter Andrew Sveeggen (also
Sveegen) graduated from the University of Minnesota and completed
his Master of Arts degree there in 1909. After teaching for four years at
the university, he taught at Decorah High School, Decorah, Iowa, and
for another year at Ellsworth College in Iowa Falls, Iowa. From 1915 to
1952 he was chairman of the English department at Augsburg College,
Minneapolis, Minnesota. He died October 29, 1959.

JEG ER SAA GLAD (also called "Christmas Eve"), long considered to
be a German or Norwegian folksong, is now known to have been written
by Peder Knudsen.

Knudsen, son of a parish singer in Voga, Norway, was born in 1819.
His musical ability became evident when he was still young, and he was
accepted as a member of the Pre-military Musical Organization in Christiania (now Oslo). He studied several instruments, especially violin, and
was later secured by Johann Behreus as a choral director in
Holinestraud. In 1854 he was appointed civic music director and school
music administrator in Kragerö, where he organized the Midsummer Eve
music festivals. Five years later he became organist and choirmaster in
Olesund, during which time he composed "Christmas Eve." He died
shortly before Christmas in 1863.

70 GO TELL IT ON THE MOUNTAIN
Tune: Go Tell It

The traditional stanzas of this Negro spiritual read:

When I was a seeker
I sought both night and day,
I asked the Lord to help me,
And he showed me the way.

He made me a watchman
Upon a city wall,
And if I am a Christian,
I am the least of all.

The present three stanzas were written by John Wesley Work Jr., and included in *American Negro Songs and Spirituals,* New York, 1940.

Born August 6, 1871 (some sources give 1872 or 1873), in Nashville, Tennessee, Work majored in history and Latin at Fisk University, Nashville. While he was a student there, he also studied voice with Jennie Asenath Robinson, and sang in the Mozart Society, where he became interested in Negro spirituals. After graduation in 1895 he spent a year teaching in the Tullahoma, Tennessee, public schools; a year studying at Harvard University; and a year working as a library assistant at Fisk University. He completed a Master's degree at Fisk in 1898 and was appointed instructor of Latin and Greek there. In 1906 he was made chairman of the History and Latin Department. Throughout the time that Work taught at Fisk University, he was a leader in the movement to preserve, study, and perform Negro spirituals. Together with his brother, Frederick Jerome Work (1879-1942), he collected, harmonized, and published several collections of slave songs and spirituals, the earliest of which was *New Jubilee Songs as Sung by the Fisk Jubilee Singers,* 1901. His treatise, *Folk Song of the American Negro,* 1907, is one of the earliest extensive studies of Black folk music undertaken by a descendant of an ex-slave. In addition, he lectured throughout the country and wrote several articles in leading periodicals on the subject of folk music. For eighteen years he trained and performed with both professional and student groups of the Jubilee Singers, and in 1909 he organized the Fisk Jubilee Quartet which later made recordings for the Victor Talking Machine Company. As a tenor soloist he appeared at Fisk University and throughout the country. After 1916, with a change in the administration, there were strong negative feelings toward Black folk music at the university, and it finally became necessary for Work to resign in 1923. He served for two years as president of Roger Williams University in Nashville until his sudden death on Labor Day, September 7, 1925.

GO TELL IT is the tune traditionally associated with this Negro spiritual. In his *White and Negro Spirituals* (New York: J. J. Augustin, 1944), George Pullen Jackson notes that the melody used for the stanzas is closely related to "We'll March around Jerusalem," from the *Revivalist,* Troy, New York, 1868. The tune is also similar to several others, including the opening lines of Stephen Foster's "Oh, Susanna." The refrain has been noted to bear similarities to George F. Root's "Tramp, tramp, tramp, the boys are marching."

The harmonization was written in 1958 by Hugh Porter, who served from 1945 until his death on September 23, 1960, as director of the School of Sacred Music, Union Theological Seminary, New York City. Born in 1897 at Heron Lake, Minnesota, Porter served in the Student Army Training Corps at the University of Chicago during World War I and later received a Bachelor of Music degree with honors from the

American Conservatory of Music in Chicago. He completed a Bachelor of Arts degree at Northwestern University in Chicago in 1924, and a Master's degree from Union Theological School of Sacred Music six years later. In 1944 the School of Sacred Music conferred a doctorate on him. While at Northwestern he served as organist there, and in New York City he served as organist of Calvary Episcopal Church and the Church of the Heavenly Rest (Episcopal), and organist-choirmaster of St. Nicholas Reformed Church and Second Presbyterian Church. He taught at New York University, the David Mannes Music School, and the Juilliard School of Music, and was for several years organist of the Chautauqua, New York, Institution, and organist of the Oratorio Society of New York. As a concert organist he appeared frequently with the New York Symphony Orchestra, and gave recitals throughout the United States. With his wife, Ethel Flentyre Porter, he was a musical editor of the *Pilgrim Hymnal,* 1958. (Ethel Porter was also one of the editors of the *Guide to the Pilgrim Hymnal.**)

71   ANGELS WE HAVE HEARD ON HIGH
(Les anges dans nos campagnes)
Tune: Gloria

Considered by Jan R. H. de Smidt in *Les Noels et al tradition popularie,* 1932, to date from the eighteenth century, text and tune of this French carol were first published in 1855 in the *Nouveau recueil de cantiques.* The translation used here is from Henri Frederick Hemy's (LBW 500) *Crown of Jesus Music,* Part II, London, 1862, a Roman Catholic collection. (There the tune was designated an "English Air.") Several alterations of the 1862 text are more or less standard to present-day usage. Neither the author of the French text nor of the English translation is known.

GLORIA, also known as "Iris," is the French melody traditionally associated with these words. The harmonization is from a setting by Edward Shippen Barnes included in *The New Church Hymnal,* New York, 1937.

Barnes was born at Seabright, New Jersey, on September 14, 1887, and received a Bachelor of Arts degree from Yale, where he studied with Horatio Parker, Harry Benjamin Jepson, and David Stanley Smith. Continuing his education in Paris, he worked with Vincent d'Indy, Abel Decaux, and Louis Vierne. He served as organist and choirmaster of the Church of the Incarnation and Rutgers Presbyterian Church in New York City, and at St. Stephen's Church, Philadelphia, before going in 1938 to First Presbyterian Church in Santa Monica, California. In 1954 he retired to Idyllwild, California, where he donated a small organ and played services for the church there until his death on February 14, 1958. During the First World War, he served in 1918 and 1919 in the Naval Reserve. In addition to his *Method of Organ Playing,* Barnes has written a number of organ and choral works as well as anthems and services for the Episcopal Church.

(Estennialon de tsonue Jesus ahatonnia)
Tune: Une jeune pucelle

This hymn, the earliest Canadian carol in existence, is attributed by tradition to Jean de Brébeuf, a Jesuit priest who started a mission among the Hurons in the early seventeenth century. According to Osborne,* a collection of songs and chants of the Hurons prepared by Father Chaumonot, a contemporary of Brébeuf, has been lost, and the text has come to us via another priest, Father de Villeneuve, who from 1747 to 1794 was stationed at Lorette. Its first appearance in print was in Ernest Myrand's *Noëls Anciens de la Nouvelle France* (Quebec: Dussault & Proulx, 1899).

Brébeuf, who is said to have counted among his ancestors William the Conqueror and St. Louis, king of France, was born March 25, 1593, at Condé-sur-Vire in Lower Normandy. In 1617 he entered the Jesuit noviciate in Rouen, and two years later was appointed a teacher in a secondary school. From 1620 to 1621 he taught at the Collège in Rouen, and in 1622 he received the priesthood at Pontoise. He remained at Rouen as a steward of the Collège until 1625, when he was chosen for mission work in New France and sailed to Quebec. In the summer of 1626 he traveled by canoe the eight hundred miles from Quebec to Huron country, where he lived among the Bear tribe. Returning to France he served as a preacher and confessor at the church in Rouen. In 1630 he took his final vows as a Jesuit and from 1631 to 1633 was steward, minister, and confessor at the Collège in Eu. Returning to New France in 1633, he went again to Huron country the following year. Although the Hurons had had good trade relations with France for some time, feelings of good will faded during the 1630s when European viruses reduced their population by nearly two-thirds. The missionaries' presence became odious to the Hurons, and for the next several years Brébeuf and his fellow priests endured repeated persecutions. The Iroquois, seeing that the Hurons' numbers were reduced, seized the opportunity to annihilate them. One by one the missionaries fell victim to Iroquois massacres, and on March 16, 1649, Brébeuf was captured and taken to Saint-Ignace, where he was cruelly tortured and put to death. Although the Huron mission came to an end with Brébeuf's death, the seeds for further mission work were sown when the Hurons scattered to the neighboring tribes. Brébeuf also made a significant contribution with his writings on his canoe trip into the wilderness in 1626 and his descriptions of the Hurons.

Osborne* notes that the English version of this carol, by Jesse Edgar Middleton, is really an interpretation, coming from the original Huron via French, and tailored to fit this melody. Stanzas 1 and 3 were included in *The International Book of Christmas Carols,* 1963; Stanza 2 was prepared by Gilbert E. Doan Jr. (LBW 99). Middleton was born November 3, 1872, in Pilkington Township, Wellington County, Ontario. He attended Ottawa Normal School and taught school from 1892 to 1895. Turning to journalism, he was first a proofreader, then a copyist, and finally a correspondent for the Montreal *Herald.* After working as a special writer for the Toronto *Mail and Empire,* he accepted, in 1942, a position as writer for *The Saturday Night.* For nearly forty years, also, he served as choirmaster at Centennial United Church in Toronto. His publications include a collection of poetry, four historical books, and two novels, as well as several plays which have been produced in Toronto and Banff. He died in Toronto May 27, 1960.

UNE JEUNE PUCELLE is a sixteenth-century French folk song which is closely related to the tune "Von Gott will ich nicht lassen" found at LBW 468. It served as the basis for organ noëls composed by Claude Daquin (1695–1772) and Nicholas LeBegue (1631–1702). Blume* (p. 33) suggests that it has pre-Protestant origins, probably from popular sources. The harmonization is by Frederick Jackisch (LBW 236).

73 ALL HAIL TO YOU, O BLESSED MORN!
(Var hälsad, sköna morgonstund)

Tune: Wie schön leuchtet

Johan Olof Wallin, Sweden's foremost hymnwriter, was born at Stora Tuna, Dalarna, October 15, 1779, the son of a poor sergeant major in the Dalarna regiment. He studied at Falun, Västeros, and finally at Uppsala, where he received a Doctor of Philosophy degree at the age of twenty-four. Ordained in 1806, he became a theological assistant at Karlberg War College in 1807, and the following year passed the pastor's examination brilliantly and was appointed lecturer at the college as well as pastor in Solna. By the time he began his service in these positions, he was a doctor of theology and a member of the Swedish Academy. In 1812 he became pastor of Adolf Frederik Church in Stockholm, and six years later took the position of dean of Västeros. Returning to Stockholm in 1821 he assumed the pastorate of Storkyrkan, and three years later was made a bishop. Appointed chief royal preacher in 1830, he became archbishop of Sweden in 1837. He died in Uppsala on June 30, 1839.

Wallin's great poetic gift was recognized already in 1805 and 1809 when he received the highest prize for poetry from the Swedish Academy. During that period also, he began to publish collections of hymns, both his own and those of others. When, in 1809, the Swedish parliament appointed a commission to prepare a new hymnbook to replace the one which had been in use since 1695, Wallin was a member of the committee. The 1811 hymnal was prepared in haste, and met with severe criticism. Wallin recommended at least one year's postponement of approval, and he himself was called upon to revise the work, which afterwards was to be examined by a pastoral committee. The resulting 1819 *Svenska Psalm-Boken* clearly reflects Wallin's high standards: "a new hymn, aside from the spiritual consideration, which must never be compromised in any way, should be so correct, simple, and lyrical in form, and so free from inversions and other imperfections in style, that after a lapse of a hundred years, a father may be able to say to his son, 'Read the hymnal, my boy, and you will learn your mother tongue!'" (Ryden*, p. 176) Of a total of 500 hymns, 128 were originals by Wallin, and well over 150 were revisions or translations by him. The 1819 *Psalm-Boken* remained in use for more than a hundred years, with an appendix added in 1920. In the 1937 *Psalmbok* replacing it, over a third of the 600 hymns were originals, translations, or revisions by Wallin.

"Var hälsad, sköna morgonstund" was written for this tune and included in the 1819 *Psalm-Boken*. Using a translation by Ernest William Olson (LBW 474) from the Augustana *Hymnal,* 1901, as a starting point, the Inter-Lutheran Commission on Worship has prepared a new English text for the LBW.

WIE SCHÖN LEUCHTET. This tune is the same as that found at LBW 43.

176

Tune: Tollefson

Richard Purdy Wilbur, one of the leading poets in the United States today, was born in New York City on March 1, 1921, and received a Bachelor of Arts degree from Amherst College in Massachusetts in 1942. After completing a Master of Arts degree at Harvard in 1947, he remained there as a member of the Society of Fellows for three years, and was an assistant professor of English from 1950 to 1954. He went to Rome for a year and returned to an appointment as associate professor of English at Wellesley College, Wellesley, Massachusetts, following which he was professor of English at Wesleyan University, Middletown, Connecticut, until January of 1978. Since then he has been writer in residence at Smith College, Northampton, Massachusetts. He has received many honors, including Pulitzer and Bollingen Prizes and the National Book Award, and is chancellor of the American Academy of Arts and Letters. He is the author of numerous works, including *The Mind-Reader* (poems, 1976), *Responses* (prose pieces, 1976), and *The Learned Ladies* (translation from Molière, 1978).

This Christmas hymn was written around 1959 at the invitation of Professor Richard Winslow of Wesleyan University for their annual Christmas concert, and was published in *Advice to a Prophet and Other Poems,* 1961.

TOLLEFSON. Paulette Tollefson was born April 25, 1950, in Marion, Indiana, and grew up in the Minneapolis–St. Paul area. In 1968 she entered St. Olaf College as a science major, but soon switched to music theory and composition. She was elected to Phi Beta Kappa during college and graduated in 1972 with a Bachelor of Arts degree magna cum laude. While at St. Olaf she played tenor saxophone in the St. Olaf band and sang with the Manitou Singers and the Chapel Choir. Since her graduation from college she has worked in Minneapolis, first in merchandise display design at Dayton's department store, then as assistant to an ingredient merchandiser for the Pillsbury Company. Currently she is systems engineer for IBM, marketing large computer systems. She pursues her music interest through involvement in a small swing band, in several dance groups, and in the Bethlehem Lutheran Church Choir, which under the direction of Dr. Richard Sieber has had opportunity to work with people such as Chad Mitchel and Dave Brubeck. Her civic involvement is through the Minneapolis JAYCEE's, in which she holds an office.

"Tollefson" was composed during her freshman year at St. Olaf when she was studying music theory with Charles Anders (LBW 386), and was among several tunes submitted to the Inter-Lutheran Commission on Worship for approval. It was composed in simple folk style (it is a pentatonic tune within the compass of an octave) both to complement Richard Wilbur's poem, and so that she, a guitarist and not a pianist, could make use of it. It was first published in *Contemporary Worship–1,* 1969, and two years later was included in *The Hymn Book* of the United Church and the Anglican Church of Canada.

75 BRIGHT AND GLORIOUS IS THE SKY *(Dejlig er den Himmel blaa)*

Tune: Dejlig er den Himmel blaa

See LBW 62 for Nikolai Grundtvig. This hymn, one of Grundtvig's earliest, was composed for Christmas 1810. First printed in Knud Lyhne Rahbek's *Sandsigeren* in April 10, 1811, it was included in 1815 in *Kvaedlinger eller Smaakward.*

A translation beginning "Splendid are the heavens high" by Jens Christian Aaberg was included in the *Hymnal for Church and Home,* 1927, and the *American Lutheran Hymnal,* 1930. LBW stanzas 3, 4, and 5, as well as the last half of stanza 1, are from Aaberg's translation. The remaining lines are the work of the commission which prepared the *Service Book and Hymnal,* 1958, especially Fred C. M. Hansen and Thorvald Olsen Burntvedt.

Aaberg, author of *Hymns and Hymnwriters of Denmark,* 1945, and editor of *Favored Hymns and Songs,* 1961, translated some eighty hymns and songs from Danish and served on the committees which compiled the *American Lutheran Hymnal,* 1930; the *Hymnal for Church and Home,* 1927; the *Junior Hymnal for Church and Home,* 1932; and the revised *Hymnal for Church and Home,* 1938. Born November 8, 1877, in Moberg on the West coast of Denmark, he came to the United States in 1901. He went to Minneapolis, Minnesota, to join his brother who was then studying for the ministry at Augsburg College and Seminary. After attending St. Ansgar's College, and Grand View College and Seminary in Des Moines, Iowa, 1904–1908, he was ordained to the ministry of the Danish Evangelical Lutheran Church in America. His first call was to Marinette, Wisconsin, after which he was pastor from 1912 to 1926 of St. Peder's Lutheran Church, Dwight, Illinois. From 1926 until his retirement in 1946 he served in Minneapolis. He held various offices throughout the synod, and in 1947 received the Knight Cross of Denmark from King Frederick. In 1908 he was married to Elsie Cathrine Raun. He died June 22, 1970.

DEJLIG ER DEN HIMMEL BLAA (also "Celestia"). According to Ole Mørk Sandvik in *Norsk Koralhistorie* (Oslo, 1930), this tune was included in Andreas Berggren's (LBW 298) *Melodier til den af Roeskildes Praesteconvent udgivne Psalmebog,* Copenhagen, 1853, and is said to have been composed about 1840 by an old man who had never before given himself to composition.

76 O MORNING STAR, HOW FAIR AND BRIGHT!
(Wie schön leuchtet der Morgenstern)

Tune: Wie schön leuchtet

See LBW 31 for Philipp Nicolai. This "Queen of Chorales" was, like "Wake, awake," included in Nicolai's *Frewden-Spiegel dess ewigen Lebens* (1599), and here again Nicolai composed both tune and text. The original seven stanzas (given in Polack* #343) formed an acrostic. The opening letters of the stanzas are W, E, G, U, H, Z, and W, referring to *Wilhelm Ernst, Graf und Herr zu Waldeck,* a former student of Nicolai's. Based on Psalm 45, this hymn is believed to have been written in 1597. It quickly became a favorite in Germany where it was used for many occasions, especially weddings, where it was considered almost indispensable. The translation has been prepared by the Inter-Lutheran Commission on Worship for use in this hymnal.

WIE SCHÖN LEUCHTET is believed to be a reconstruction of "Jauchzet dem Herren, alle lande," Psalm 100, included in Wolff Köphel's *Psalter,* 1538, where the tune reads as given below.

Except for a slight change in the rhythm of the second phrase, the melody appears here as it did in the *Frewden-Spiegel.* The even rhythm as found at LBW 43 is a later development.

J. S. Bach used this tune in Cantatas 1, 36, 37, 49, 61, and 172, and included a harmonization in his *Choralgesänge.* He also based one of his Miscellaneous Preludes for organ on the melody.

77   O ONE WITH GOD THE FATHER

Tune: Thornbury

William Walsham How, son of an English solicitor, attended Wadham College, Oxford, and was ordained a priest in 1847. He was successively curate of St. George's, Kidderminster; curate of Holy Cross, Shrewsbury; rector of Whittington; rural dean of Oswestry; honorary canon of St. Asaph; and beginning in 1865, chaplain of the English Church in Rome. In 1879 he became rector of St. Andrew's Undershaft, London, and suffragan bishop for East London; and in 1888, bishop of Wakefield. Remembered as the "poor man's bishop," How was well-known as a dynamic leader of work for the poor in the East End of London. Honorary doctorates were bestowed on him, by the Archbishop of Canterbury in 1879, and by Oxford in 1886. Born in Shrewsbury, England, December 13, 1823, he died while on vacation in Ireland, in Leenane, County Mayo, on August 10, 1897.

How was the author of several theological and pastoral works and was the editor, with Thomas Baker Morrell, of *Psalms and Hymns,* 1854. He was also one of the editors of *Church Hymns,* published in 1871 by the Society for the Promotion of Christian Knowledge, in which this hymn appeared.

THORNBURY. Basil Harwood, born April 11, 1859, in Woodhouse, Olveston, Gloucestershire, England, was educated at Charterhouse and at Trinity College, Oxford, receiving a Bachlor of Music degree in 1880 and a Bachelor of Arts degree the following year. He completed a Master of Arts degree in 1884, and a Doctor of Music degree in 1896. His education also included study with Carl Reinecke and Jadassohn at the Leipzig Conservatory. He served as organist at Trinity College (1878–1881), St. Barnabas, Pimlico (1883–1887), Ely Cathedral (1887–1892), and Christ Church, Oxford (1892–1909). In addition he served as precentor of Keble College, as conductor of the Oxford Bach Choir, and as choragus of the University of Oxford. After 1909 he retired to devote his time to composition. He died April 3, 1949.

Harwood was musical editor of the *Oxford Hymn Book,* 1908, and the composer of much sacred music including services, communion settings, anthems, cantatas, and organ works. His hymn tunes numbered about ninety, but only a few have remained. "Thornbury" was written for Edward Hayes Plumptre's "Thy hand, O God, has guided" and sung at the twenty-fifth Annual Festival of the London Church Choir Association in 1898. It first appeared in the Association's Festival Book, November 17, 1898, and was later published in Harwood's *Hymn Tunes Original and Selected,* 1905.

78   ALL PRAISE TO YOU, O LORD
Tune: Garelochside

Hyde Wyndham Beadon was born in England in 1812 and attended St. John's College, Cambridge, receiving a Bachelor of Arts degree in 1835 and a Master of Arts degree four years later. Ordained in 1836, he became vicar of Haselbury Plucknett, near Crewkerne, in 1837, and the following year was appointed vicar of Latton, Wiltshire. Later he was made honorary canon of Bristol, and also served as rural dean. Together with Greville Phillimore and James Russell Woodford he edited *The Parish Hymn Book,* 1863 and 1875. He contributed four hymns to this collection in 1863, including the present hymn, which had the opening line "*Glory* to *thee,* O Lord." The alteration of the first line to "All praise to thee, O Lord" occurred soon afterward and was found in several hymnals. Beadon died May 12, 1891 at Latton.

GARELOCHSIDE, composed by Kenneth George Finlay, was first published in *Christian Praise,* 1957.

Born in Marylebone, London, England, in 1882, Finlay was the son of a professor at Aberdeen. He studied at Robert Gordon's College, Aberdeen, and the Merchiston Castle School in Edinburgh, and became a famous naval architect. He published a number of papers and was made a member of the Royal Institute of Naval Architects. In 1928 he changed the course of his life entirely and entered the Royal College of Music, where he studied with Ralph Vaughan Williams (LBW 101). The following year he went to the Teacher's Training College at Jordonhill in Glasgow, and in 1930 was appointed teacher of class singing at Irvine under the Ayrshire County Council. There he taught for seventeen years until he retired to his sister's home in Cobham, Kent. He later went to Glasgow, where he died April 15, 1974. His works include two cantatas, choral works, a prelude for strings, and some forty hymn tunes.

79   TO JORDAN CAME THE CHRIST, OUR LORD
(Christ unser Herr zum Jordan kam)
Tune: Christ unser Herr

See LBW 48 for Martin Luther. With this baptism hymn Luther completed his hymns on parts of the Catechism. Leupold* cites a Low-German hymnal published in Lübeck in 1556 which dates this hymn 1541. It seems probable that it was published as a broadsheet that year. Within the next two years it appeared in Christian Rödinger's *Ein schön Geistlich Sangböck,* Magdeburg, 1542?, and in three hymnals published in 1543: Joseph Klug's (LBW 85) *Geistliche Lieder su Wittemberg,* Johann Walther's (LBW 350) *Geystlike leder uñ Psalmen,* and an Appendix to Valentin Schumann's *Geistliche lieder auffs new gebessert und gemehrt* (first published in Leipzig in 1539).

Several English translations have been made. Julian* mentions one as early as 1568, in *Gude and Godly Ballates,* beginning "Christ baptist was be Johne in Jordan flude." Elizabeth Quitmeyer's translation was prepared at the request of Carl Schalk (LBW 118) and submitted to the Lutheran Church—Missouri Synod Commission on Worship. The LC–MS commission later joined with the Inter-Lutheran Commission on Worship in 1965, and the hymn appears in print here for the first time.

Elizabeth Quitmeyer was born in Detroit on June 20, 1911, and majored in home economics at school. She suddenly became very ill, however, and states that she "chased the cure" for fifteen years, five of which were spent in the hospital. Realizing that her activities would always be limited, she changed her plans for a profession and prepared for and then worked in a business office for twenty-two years. Failing health necessitated her retirement in 1974.

Her gift for poetry-writing was discovered when she was in the hospital, where she wrote verses for family and friends' birthdays and anniversaries, as well as for the hospital paper. She continued to write for special occasions at the office, and began also to write more serious verse. Several of her hymns and translations have appeared in various Missouri Synod periodicals. A special old German book in her library, dating from 1680, provided the source for a translation which appeared in *This Day* and was later set to music for use on the Lutheran Hour. Although she has retired from the business office, she has not retired from hymn-writing; her verses continue to appear in print from time to time.

CHRIST UNSER HERR was first published in Johann Walther's (LBW 350) *Geystliche gesangk Buchleyn,* Wittenberg, 1524, with Martin Luther's "Es wollt uns Gott genädig sein" (LBW 335) (Zahn* #7246). It became associated with the present text in 1543, however, and has been firmly bonded to it since then. J. S. Bach (LBW 219) prepared two harmonizations of the melody, including the chorale at the close of Cantata 176. The LBW harmonization was prepared by Richard Hillert (LBW 63).

80   OH, WONDROUS TYPE! OH, VISION FAIR
(Caelestis formam gloriae)
Tune: Deo gracias

"Caelestis (also 'Coelestis') formam gloriae" is an anonymous Latin hymn written for the Feast of the Transfiguration when that observance came into common use in the fifteenth century. Its appearance in the *Sarum Breviary* of 1495 indicates that it has been used at Salisbury from the beginning. John Mason Neale (LBW 34) included his translation, beginning "A type of those bright rays on high," in *The Hymnal Noted,* 1851. A somewhat altered version, given in *The Hymnal 1940* (Episcopal), is used here with a further change in the final stanza.

DEO GRACIAS. This fine, strong tune was the setting for a ballad commemorating the victory of King Henry V of England over the French at Agincourt in 1415, the first stanza of which reads:

> Owre kynge went forth to normandy.
> with grace and myzt of chyvualry
> ther god for hym wrouzt mervelusly.
> Wherfore Englonde may calle and cry. Deo gratias.

Early English sources in which "Deo gracias" is found include a parchment roll at Trinity College, Cambridge, dating from the first half of the fifteenth century (transcribed with a quotation of the full ballad text in J. A. Fuller-Maitland's *English Carols of the Fifteenth Century,* 1891) and a manuscript in the Bodleian Library at Oxford, coming probably from the mid-fifteenth century (transcribed with extensive notes in John Stainer's [LBW 56] *Early Bodleian Music,* 1901).

Carl Schalk's (LBW 118) harmonization was included in the *Worship Supplement,* 1969, to *The Lutheran Hymnal.*

81 O CHIEF OF CITIES, BETHLEHEM *(O sola magnarum urbium)*
Tune: Truth from Above

See LBW 42 for Marcus Prudentius. Consisting of a total of 208 lines, "Quicumque Christum quaeritis" (the twelfth poem of Prudentius' *Cathemerinon*) provided four separate hymns for the Roman Church. This hymn, "O sola magnarum urbium," begins at line 77 and is included in Roman use for Epiphany at Lauds (sunrise). It did not come into liturgical use until after the Council of Trent, when it was included in the *Roman Breviary* of 1570.

The English version used here is the work of several translators. Stanzas 1, 2, and 4 are from Nathaniel B. Smithers' *Translations of Latin Hymns of the Middle Ages,* 1879; stanza 3 is from Charles Winfred Douglas' (LBW 498) *The Monastic Diurnal,* 1932; and stanza 5 is from a four-volume translation of *The Roman Breviary,* 1879, by John Patrick Crichton-Stuart, third Marquis of Bute.

Smithers, who cast Delaware's vote for Abraham Lincoln at the 1860 Presidential Convention in Chicago, was born in Dover, Delaware, on October 8, 1818. A life-long member of the Methodist Church, he counted some of the earliest followers of Methodism among his ancestors. At the age of five, Smithers is said to have been "repeating passages from Virgil, when most children are prattling nursery rhymes," and his later command of Latin was so complete that he was able to perpetrate a hoax—his "discovery" of the "Latin original" of a poem by Bret Harte, which he published in the *New York Herald,* went unchallenged until he revealed himself to be the author. Before he was six years old his mother died, and when he was about eleven he moved with his father to Bohemia Manor in Cecil County, Maryland, where he was placed in the West Nottingham Academy. He graduated from Lafayette

College, Easton, Pennsylvania, in 1836 at the age of seventeen and entered the law school of Judge Reed at Carlisle, Pennsylvania. In 1840 he was admitted to the bar of Cumberland County, Pennsylvania, and the following year, to the bar of Kent County, Delaware. A brilliant and hard-working man with strong Christian principles, he took only cases which he felt were just, and soon became one of the leading lawyers in the state of Delaware. In 1845 he was elected clerk of the House of Representatives of the State Assembly, and three years later served as a delegate to the Whig National Convention in Philadelphia. Smithers was a staunch anti-slavery man and a prohibitionist. When the Whig party enacted legislation with which he could not concur, he joined an independent party and later cast his lot with the Republican party. In 1853 he was married to his cousin, Mary Elizabeth Smithers. On the death of William Temple, Delaware's Representative in 1863, Smithers was elected a member of the Thirty-eighth Congress under President Lincoln, but was not reelected in 1864 because of his stand on Negro equality and the draft. He continued as a political leader, however, and represented his state in the 1864, 1868, and 1880 national conventions; and in 1895 he served briefly as Delaware's Secretary of State. Mrs. Smithers died of tuberculosis in 1867, leaving him with two young children. His daughter also died in 1875. In 1882 he married Mary Townsend, who brought some much-needed happiness to his home life. Smithers' son, a bright and promising young lawyer, also died at the age of thirty, and Smithers himself died on January 16, 1896.

John, Marquis of Bute, was born September 12, 1847, at Mount Stuart in County Bute, Scotland, and was educated at Christ Church, Oxford. Renouncing Presbyterianism he entered the Roman Catholic Church in 1868. Four years later he was married to Gwendolyn Mary Anne Fitzalan-Howard. He was rector of St. Andrews, 1892–1898, and provost of Rothesay, 1896–1899, and for some time also was president of University College, Cardiff, in Wales. In 1892 he became lord lieutenant of the county of Bute. The Doctor of Laws degree was bestowed on him by Glasgow University (1879), Edinburgh University (1882), and St. Andrews (1893). He died October 9, 1900, at Dumfries House, and his heart was buried at the Mount of Olives.

TRUTH FROM ABOVE is the tune from the English carol, "This is the truth sent from above." In 1823 it was referred to by Hone as one of the carols "now annually published." Ralph Vaughan Williams (LBW 101) noted it as sung by Mr. W. Jenkins of King's Pyon, Herefordshire, in July, 1909, and included a four-part setting in his *Eight Traditional English Carols,* which is found here. He also used the melody in his *Fantasia on Christmas Carols.* Note that the meter shifts between $\frac{5}{4}$ and $\frac{6}{4}$.

82 AS WITH GLADNESS MEN OF OLD

Tune: Dix

This hymn, included by William Dix (LBW 40) in his *Hymns of Love and Joy,* 1861, was also published the same year in the Original Edition of *Hymns Ancient and Modern.* Some sources give the date of its composition as 1860, and Fred G. Healy* notes that it appeared in A. H. Ward's *Hymns for Public Worship and Private Devotion,* published for St. Raphael's Church in Bristol during that year. Percy Dearmer* says that it was written during an illness in Epiphany about 1858, after Dix read the Gospel for the day, and that it was included in the trial copy of *Hymns Ancient and Modern,* 1859.

Because the Wise Men came to a house and not to a stable (Matthew 2:11), two slight changes were made in the 1875 Revised Edition of *Hymns Ancient and Modern,* which were approved by Dix. The *Service Book and Hymnal,* 1958, uses the original text; the 1875 revision is used in the LBW.

DIX, also called "Treuer Heiland," was included as the setting for "Treuer Heiland, wir sind hir" in Conrad Kocher's *Stimmen aus dem Reiche Gottes,* published in Stuttgart in 1838 (Zahn* #4809) and repeated in his *Zionsharfe,* 1855, a large collection of tunes "from all centuries and all confessions of the Christian Church."

The last two phrases were originally three as given below.

When the tune was included with "As with gladness" in the Original Edition of *Hymns Ancient and Modern,* 1861, the melody was given its present form by William Henry Monk (LBW 272).

Kocher was born in Ditzingen, near Leonberg in Würtemberg, Germany, on December 16, 1786. At age seventeen he went to St. Petersburg as a tutor, but became impressed with the music of Mozart and Haydn (LBW 358); and a friendship with Muzio Clementi confirmed his decision to go into music. After studying piano and composition for a while at St. Petersburg, he returned to Germany and went to Stuttgart in 1811. The Cotta publishing house published some of his works, and seeing that Kocher had special ability, sent him to Rome to study music. Kocher came to know the works of Palestrina (LBW 135) in Rome, and became enthusiastic about a general reform of church music in Germany. He founded a School of Sacred Song in Stuttgart in 1821 which popularized four-part singing in churches and spread its influence throughout Würtemberg. From 1827 until his retirement in 1865, he was organist and choirmaster of the Stiftskirche in Stuttgart. In 1852 he received an honorary Doctor of Philosophy degree from the University of Tübingen. He died March 12, 1872.

Besides editing chorale books, to which he contributed a number of tunes, Kocher wrote an oratorio and some operas and sonatas, and published a treatise on church music, *Die Tonkunst in der Kirche,* 1823.

83 FROM GOD THE FATHER, VIRGIN-BORN *(A Patre Unigenitus)*
Tune: Deus tuorum militum

This anonymous Latin hymn is found in several eleventh-century manuscripts, and is considered by some sources to date from the tenth, or possibly even the ninth, century.

John Mason Neale's (LBW 34) translation, included in his *St. Margaret's Hymnal,* 1875, is given in the LBW with considerable alterations in stanzas 2 and 3, and some slight changes in stanza 4. Stanzas 5 and 6 have been completely rewritten.

DEUS TUORUM MILITUM. During the sixteenth and seventeenth centuries, concurrent with the "modernization" of the Breviaries (see p. 15), there arose in France a new kind of church tune. Although generally not clearly cast in a regular rhythmic meter, these tunes were more measured than the older plain-chant and were also in the modern major and minor modes. Some of the tunes were adapted from older plainsong melodies, others from secular tunes; but the origins of most of the melodies have not as yet been discovered. These French melodies made their way into England when a number of them were taken from La Feillée's *Méthode de Plain-Chant* (published in 1750 and later in 1782 and 1808) into *The Hymnal Noted,* 1851, a work prepared by John Mason Neale (LBW 34) and Thomas Helmore. From there they entered *The English Hymnal,* 1906, and later English collections.

This tune is found as the setting for the Latin Office hymn for martyrs, "Deus tuorum militum," in the *Grenoble Antiphoner,* 1753. Basil Harwood's (LBW 77) harmonization was prepared for *The Hymn Book,* 1971, of the United Church and the Anglican Church of Canada.

84 BRIGHTEST AND BEST OF THE STARS OF THE MORNING
Tune: Morning Star

Reginald Heber's *Hymns Written and Adapted to the Weekly Church Services of the Year,* published in London and in New York in 1827, was a landmark, being the first modern English hymnal arranged according to the Church Year and one of the hymnals ushering in the distinctive Literary Movement in English hymnody. Although published after his death, the hymnal was being planned several years earlier, for in 1820 Heber had tried without success to obtain authorization of his manuscript collection. *Hymns Ancient and Modern,* 1861, later followed his example, providing Sundays, Holy Days, and seasons with appropriate hymns.

Heber was born August 21, 1783, at Malpas, Cheshire, in England. His career at Brasenose College, Oxford, brought prizes for his poetic endeavors. Ordained in 1807, he became vicar of the family estate of Hodnet, Shropshire. In 1823 he was appointed bishop of Calcutta, a see which at the time included the whole of India. The next three years included ceaseless travel and enthusiastic service, and the ordination of the first native Anglican minister. The burden of his responsibilities was too great, however, and he died suddenly in Trichinopoly on April 3, 1826.

All of Heber's hymns were written before he went to India; many were published between 1811 and 1816 in the *Christian Observer.* "Brightest and Best" was included in the November, 1811, issue of that publication, and in Heber's *Hymns,* 1827.

MORNING STAR is part of an anthem written in 1892 for the Gifford Hall Mission. It was included two years later in *The Church Hymnal* (Episcopal), edited by Charles Hutchins, as a setting for Heber's hymn.

James Procktor Harding was born May 19, 1850, at Clerkenwell, London. An amateur musician, he served thirty-five years as organist and choirmaster of St. Andrew's Church, Thornhill Square, Islington, in London. He also worked for many years in the English civil service as a clerk in the internal revenue department. He and his brother devoted much time and money to the spiritual and physical well-being of the poor through the Gifford Hall Mission in Islington. Harding wrote a number of services, anthems, and part songs, many of which were for children's festivals at the mission. He died February 21, 1911.

85 WHEN CHRIST'S APPEARING WAS MADE KNOWN
(Hostis Herodes impie)
Tune: Wo Gott zum Haus

This hymn is a continuation (stanzas 8, 9, 11, and 13) of the hymn found at LBW 64. The doxology is from a later source. The hymn was in general use for Epiphany in the Roman and Sarum rites, and was found also in the Mozarabic rite, but not in the Ambrosian.

John Mason Neale's (LBW 34) translation from *The Hymnal Noted,* 1851, with the first line "The Star proclaims the King is here," was used in *The Lutheran Hymnal,* 1941. LBW stanzas 2–5 are from Neale's text; stanza 1 was newly prepared by the compilers of *The Hymn Book,* 1971, of the United Church and the Anglican Church of Canada.

WO GOTT ZUM HAUS (Zahn* #305) was included in Joseph Klug's *Geistliche Lieder,* 1533, as the setting for "Wo Gott zum Haus nicht gibt sein' Gunst," a hymn based on Psalm 127 and ascribed to Johann Kohlross.

Klug, together with Michael Lotter, Hans Lufft, and Georg Rhau (LBW 398), was one of four Wittenberg publishers who printed Lutheran books, tracts, etc., at the time of the Reformation. Little is known of his life. His independent activity apparently began at the end of the year 1523 when he made use of a title-page border formerly in the possession of the Kranach-Böringschen press. His most important publication, the *Geistliche Lieder,* edited by Martin Luther (LBW 48), first appeared in 1529 (all copies of which are now lost), with altered new editions coming in 1533, 1535, and 1543. This hymnal served as the model for subsequent hymnals for a number of years. Klug seems to have been held in high esteem by Luther, whose coat of arms appears within the title-page border of *Geistliche Lieder,* and it is highly probable that he assisted Luther in the selection of the hymns included. Besides the works of Luther and his co-workers, Klug also published academic works, including discussions of contemporary political issues, of other writers. His activities continued until 1552.

86 THE ONLY SON FROM HEAVEN
(Herr Christ, der einig Gotts Sohn)
Tune: Herr Christ, der einig Gotts Sohn

Both the German text and the tune of this hymn appeared in the Erfurt *Enchiridia* of 1524. Elizabeth Meseritz was born about 1500, a descendant of Polish nobility. Due to persecutions of Protestants during those days, her parents had sought refuge in Wittenberg. There, in 1524, she married the son of a Leipzig burgess, Caspar Cruciger (Kreutziger), a student at Wittenberg. Her husband, whom Martin Luther (LBW 48) accounted to be his most hopeful student and treated as his own son, became rector of St. John's School and preacher in St. Stephen's Church, Magdeburg, in 1525. Three years later he was called to the philosophical faculty at Wittenberg, but in accord with the wishes of Luther, was made a professor of theology instead. Elizabeth is known to have been a friend of Katherine Luther, a lover of music, and an affectionate wife and mother. She died in May of 1535.

Wackernagel* lists three hymns written by Elizabeth Cruciger. Highly regarded by hymnologists, the present hymn bears some resemblance, especially in its first stanza, to "Of the Father's Love Begotten" (LBW 42).

Translation of the hymn is by Arthur Tozer Russell, and appeared in 1851 in his *Psalms and Hymns, partly Original, partly Selected, for the Use of the Church of England.*

Russell was born March 20, 1806, at Northampton in England. The son of the Reverend Thomas Clout (who later changed his surname to Russell), he was educated at St. John's College, Cambridge, and was ordained in 1829. He served as vicar of Caxton from 1830 to 1852; of St. Thomas, Toxteth Park, Liverpool, in 1866; and of Wrockwardin Wood from 1867 to 1874. For a few months before his death (on November 18, 1874) he was rector of Southwick near Brighton.

In the earlier years of his professional life he was an extreme high churchman. The study of Saint Augustine altered his views, however, and he became and remained a moderate Calvinist. Author of numerous theological books and biographical works, as well as composer of some hymn tunes, Russell published, in addition to *Psalms and Hymns* mentioned above, *Hymn Tunes, Original and Selected, from Ravenscroft and other old Musicians,* 1840, and *Hymns for Public Worship,* 1848.

HERR CHRIST, DER EINIG GOTTS SOHN is a folk tune attached to the secular text, "Mein Freud möcht sich wohl mehren," in the *Lochamer Liederbuch,* a manuscript collection written down by different persons between 1455 and 1460. Containing forty-seven anonymous pieces of music, forty-four of which are songs, the *Lochamer Liederbuch* originally came from in or near Nuremberg, and is the most important source of early German folk song. Elizabeth Cruciger wished her hymn to be sung to this tune, and both were published in the Erfurt *Enchiridia,* 1524.

J. S. Bach (LBW 219) used the tune in his Cantatas 96 and 164, and as the basis for organ works found in the *Orgelbüchlein* and in his Miscellaneous Preludes.

Jan Bender's (LBW 396) harmonization was prepared for the LBW.

87   HAIL TO THE LORD'S ANOINTED

Tune: Freut euch, ihr lieben

See LBW 50 for James Montgomery. From its first appearance this hymn has had widespread popularity. Written to be sung as a Christmas ode at the Moravian Settlement in 1821, it was sent the next month with George Bennett on his mission tour to the South Seas. In the spring of

1822 it was read at the close of an address which Montgomery delivered at a missionary meeting in the Pitt Street Wesleyan Chapel in Liverpool. Dr. Adam Clarke, present at the meeting, was so impressed with it that he asked for a copy, and printed it in his *Commentary on the Bible,* 1822. In the same year, also, it was printed in the May issue of the *Evangelical Magazine,* and was included in Montgomery's *Songs of Zion, being Imitations of the Psalms* as Psalm 71.

FREUT EUCH, IHR LIEBEN appeared in Leonhart Schröter's *Neuwe Weynachtliedlein,* 1587, with the anonymous sixteenth-century Christmas hymn, "Freut euch, ihr lieben Christen" (Zahn* #'s 5374, 5375a).

Schröter was born in Torgau, Germany, in 1532. His father had at one time sung in Johann Walther's (LBW 350) choir at Torgau, and Schröter himself received his early music training from the local *Kantor.* He later succeeded Gallus Dressler and Martin Agricola as *Kantor* of the school at Magdeburg, achieving considerable eminence as composer of settings for both Latin and German texts. With others, including Bartholomaus Gesius (LBW 455), Melchior Vulpius (LBW 115), Michael Praetorius (LBW 36), Hans Leo Hassler (LBW 116), and Melchior Frank (LBW 348), Schröter was a leader in bringing the music of personal expression, as practiced by the Italian Orlando di Lasso, into Germany. In dealing with Latin texts, however, such as his *Hymni Sacri* of 1587, he was known to write very strictly in the older polyphonic tradition. In addition to his *Hymni Sacri,* Schröter's publications include *Geistliche Lieder,* 1562; *Cantiones suavissimae,* 1576 and 1580; and his four- and eight-voice Christmas songs, 1586–1587, for which he has become particularly well-known. He died in 1601.

A translation of the original German text, "Freut euch, ihr lieben Christen," along with Schröter's harmonization, was published as an anthem in 1967 by Concordia Publishing House. The harmonization found here was prepared for the LBW by Carl Schalk (LBW 118).

88 OH, LOVE, HOW DEEP *(O amor quam exstaticus)*
Tune: Deo gracias

Described by Julian* as one of the precursors of Christmas and Epiphany carols, this anonymous Latin hymn consists of twenty-three stanzas, beginning "Apparuit benignitas." It has sometimes been attributed to Thomas à Kempis on the strength of its affinity to some of his works. Benjamin Webb's translation of eight stanzas (2, 4, 6, 9, 10, 11, 12, and 23 of the original) was included in *The Hymnal Noted,* Part II, 1854. The text has received several alterations along the way. The final stanza as given here is a completely different translation from Webb's, and is found in *The Pilgrim Hymnal,* 1962.

Born in 1379 or 1380 to peasant parents, Thomas Hammerken was sent at age twelve to a poor-scholars' house attached to the Brothers' House of the Brethren of the Common Life in Deventer, Holland. There he became known as Thomas from Kempen (Thomas à Kempis). After six years at Deventer, Thomas joined the community at Mount St. Agnes near Zwolle, and in 1413 was ordained a priest. He remained at Mount St. Agnes until his death in 1471, writing, copying manuscripts, and doing editorial works. Among his works are a chronicle of St. Agnes, several biographies, tracts, and hymns.

Founded in 1375 by Gerald Groote, whose biography is among Thomas' writings, the community of the Brethren of the Common Life was a lay fellowship dedicated to Christian service as exemplified by the life of Christ. The aims of the organization were set down in *The Imitation of Christ* (first printed in 1471), a work of which Thomas was most probably editor and compiler. It was one of the earliest books printed, and has been translated into more languages than any other book except the Bible.

Benjamin Webb was born November 28, 1819, in London, England, and was educated at St. Paul's School, at Trinity College, Cambridge, where he was a friend of John Mason Neale (LBW 34). He received a Bachelor of Arts degree in 1842 and a Master of Arts degree in 1845. In 1842, also, he was ordained a deacon, and in the following year, a priest. He served as assistant curate of three parishes before his appointment in 1851 as curate of Sheen in Staffordshire. Later, in 1862, he became vicar of St. Andrews, Wells Street, London, where Joseph Barnby (LBW 280) was organist and choir director. The church gained considerable fame for its excellent musical services during his stay there. In 1881 he was appointed prebend of Portpool in St. Paul's Cathedral.

Webb's church publications were numerous. He was also the author of several anthems published by Novello. Some of his hymn translations were included in *The Hymnal Noted,* of which he was one of the editors. The *Hymnary,* 1872, which he edited in conjunction with the Reverend Canon W. Cooke, contained five original hymns. He also served as editor of the *Church Quarterly Review* from 1881 until his death on November 27, 1885, in London.

DEO GRACIAS is discussed at LBW 80.

89   HOW GOOD, LORD, TO BE HERE!

Tune: Potsdam

Originally beginning "'*Tis* good, Lord, to be here," this hymn was written at Cambridge, England, on the feast of the Transfiguration in 1888, and was first published in the 1904 edition of *Hymns Ancient and Modern.*

Born January 9, 1858, at Keynsham, England, Joseph Armitage Robinson was educated at Christ's College, Cambridge, receiving a Bachelor of Arts degree in 1881, a Master of Arts degree in 1884, a Bachelor of Divinity degree in 1891, and a Doctor of Divinity degree in 1896. From 1881 to 1899 he was a fellow of the college, and in 1904 was made an honorary fellow. Ordained a deacon in 1881 and a priest in 1882, he served from 1883 to 1884 as domestic chaplain to the Bishop of Durham; from 1884 to 1890 as dean of Christ's College; from 1888 to 1892 as assistant curate at Great St. Mary's in Cambridge; and from 1893 to 1899 as Norrisian Professor of Divinity. Beginning in 1899 he was rector of St. Margaret's, Westminster, for one year and Canon of Westminster for three years. He was dean of Westminster from 1902 to 1922, and in 1911 became Dean of Wells, where he served until his death at Upton Noble on May 7, 1933.

Robinson made an important contribution to theological study and criticism in England, and received numerous honorary degrees both in England and on the continent. Among his many publications are the

Cambridge Texts and Studies, of which he was originator and first editor in 1891, and a commentary on *Ephesians,* 1903.

POTSDAM is taken from the subject of the second fugue in E major of J. S. Bach's (LBW 219) *Forty-eight Preludes and Fugues* (The Well-Tempered Clavier), completed in 1742. Adaptation of the fugue subject for a hymn tune is from William Mercer's (LBW 281) *The Church Psalter and Hymn Book,* 1854. The tune name, "Potsdam," apparently refers to an event which occurred near the end of Bach's life: Bach's son, Karl Philipp Emmanuel, had been appointed *Kapellmeister* and panist to King Frederick "the Great" of Prussia in 1740. In 1747 Bach went to visit his son, and the king, learning that he had come, received him graciously and invited "Old Bach," as he called him, to perform on the various organs at Potsdam, as well as to try out the new Silbermann pianofortes at the palace. So impressed was the king with Bach's ability to improvise, that he offered Bach a subject, on which Bach not only improvised at the time, but which, on his return home, he developed into elaborate contrapuntal compositions. These he sent to the king as a *Musikalische Opfer,* or "Musical Offering."

90 SONGS OF THANKFULNESS AND PRAISE
Tune: Salzburg

Christopher Wordsworth, nephew of the poet William Wordsworth, was born at Lambeth in England on October 30, 1807. His father was rector of Lambeth and later master of Trinity College, Cambridge. Wordsworth studied at Trinity College, where he won a great number of prizes and graduated with honors in classics and mathematics, and afterwards became a fellow and classical lecturer at his college. He was ordained in 1833, and in 1836 became public orator at the university and head master at Harrow School. Two years later he was married to Susan Hatley Freere. From 1844 to 1850 he was canon at Westminster, and for nineteen years thereafter ministered to a small country parish, Stanford-in-the-Vale-cum-Goosey, in Berkshire. In 1869 he was consecrated bishop of Lincoln, a position he held until one month before his death. He died at Harewood on March 20, 1885.

Wordsworth wrote voluminously, including a commentary on the entire Bible and a work on church history. His *Holy Year: or Hymns for Sundays, Holidays, and Other Occasions throughout the Year* was published in 1862. "Songs of Thankfulness and Praise" was included in the *Holy Year,* where it was headed "Sixth Sunday after Epiphany. A Recapitulation of the successive Epiphanies or Manifestations of Christ, which have been already presented in the Services of the former weeks."

SALZBURG was included in the nineteenth edition of *Praxis Pietatis Melica* (LBW 23), edited by Christoph Runge (LBW 340) at Berlin in 1678 (Zahn* #6778). There it was a setting for J. G. Albinus' "Alle Menschen müssen sterben" (translated in *The Lutheran Hymnal,* 1941, #601). (See LBW 97 for another of at least thirteen tunes used with Albinus' hymn at one time or another.)

In the 1690 edition of *Praxis Pietatis Melica* this tune is attributed to J. Hintze. Jakob Hintze, born September 4, 1622, at Bernau, near Berlin, Germany, served as court-musician to the Elector of Brandenburg at

Berlin from 1666 to 1695. After Johann Crüger's death he undertook the editing of *Praxis Pietatis Melica,* to which he contributed a total of sixty-five new melodies. He died May 5, 1702, in Berlin.

The tune, titled "Salzburg," was attached to "At the Lamb's high feast" (LBW 210) in the Original Edition of *Hymns Ancient and Modern,* 1861. The harmonization is a simplified form of J. S. Bach's (LBW 219) setting in his *Choralgesänge.*

91 SAVIOR, WHEN IN DUST TO YOU

Tune: Aberystwyth

First printed in *The Christian Observer,* November 1815, this hymn was later included in *Sacred Poems, by the late Rt. Hon. R. Grant,* 1839. Meanwhile, three American Episcopalian collections included it: *The Hymnal,* 1826; Wainwright's *Music of the Church,* 1828; and *Psalms, in metre selected from The Psalms of David,* 1833.

Robert Grant was born in 1779 in Bengal; his father, sometime member of Parliament for Inverness, was director of the East India Company and an Indian philanthropist. Robert was educated at Magdalen College, Oxford, and was called to the Bar in 1807. As a member of Parliament he represented in succession Elgin Burghs, Inverness Burghs, Norwich, and Finsbury. In 1831 he was made a member of the Privy Council; in 1832 he became Judge Advocate General; and in 1834 he was knighted on the occasion of his becoming governor of Bombay. He died on July 9, 1838 at Dalpoorie, Western India.

His hymns were contributed to *The Christian Observer* and to H. V. Elliott's *Psalms and Hymns,* 1835, and were collected and published by his brother in 1839.

ABERYSTWYTH, named for a Welsh sea resort city on Cardigan Bay, was first published in Stephens' *Ail Lyfr Tonau ac Emynau,* 1879. There it was the setting for the Welsh hymn later sung at Parry's funeral, "Beth sydd i mi yn y byd."

Joseph Parry was born May 24, 1841, at Merthyr Tydfil, Wales. Like many other young boys in his region, he was working in the iron foundery by the age of ten. In 1854 he came with his family to the United States and settled at Danville, Pennsylvania, where he continued to work in an iron foundry. He learned music in a class organized by fellow iron-workers, who later collected money to send him to study at Geneseo, New York. On a visit to Wales he so impressed the Welsh musicians there that the Eisteddfod Council raised funds for his study at the Royal Academy of Music in London. There he studied composition with William Sterndale Bennett and voice with Manuel Garcia, and took organ lessons. He went on to complete a Bachelor of Music degree at Cambridge in 1871, and a doctorate in 1878. Returning briefly to the United States from 1871 to 1873, he conducted a music school at Danville, and served as organist of one of the leading churches there. The remainder of his life was spent in Wales. He was professor of music at the newly-opened University College, Aberystwyth, for six years, after which he conducted his own music schools first at Aberystwyth, then at Swansea, before going in 1888 as lecturer and head of the music department at University College, Cardiff. At Cardiff, also, he set up another of his own music schools. During the last dozen years of his life he knew the bitter disappointment of the loss of two sons, as well as the rewards of national renown. In 1896 the Welsh Eisteddfod in Llandudno gave him 600 pounds for his services to Welsh music. A final tour of the United States took him as far as Salt Lake City. He died February 17, 1903.

Parry's compositions included oratorios, contatas, operas, choral and instrumental works, and over four hundred hymn tunes. A biography in Welsh and English has been prepared by Owain T. Edwards, 1970.

92   WERE YOU THERE

Tune: Were You There

The first printed version of this Negro spiritual is found in William E. Barton's *Old Plantation Hymns,* published in Boston in 1899, with the text: 1. "Were you there when they crucified my Lord?" 2. ". . . they nailed him to the cross?" 3. ". . . they pierced him in the side?" and 4. ". . . the sun refused to shine?" There the melody had the form given below.

Similar songs have been found among white spirituals, such as "Saw ye my Savior" and "Have you heard how they crucified our Lord?" which have been recorded by George Pullen Jackson. Little was done to write down Negro spirituals until after the Civil War, the first definite step being *Slave Songs of the United States,* published in 1867. They were first introduced to the American public and to Europe by the Jubilee Singers of Fisk University in the 1870s, and other schools soon followed the example.

Spirituals such as "Were you there" represented more than simple Biblical narrative. Distances of time and space were removed, and the worshiper became personally related to and involved in the events. The use of the word "tree" no doubt had special significance to those who had witnessed lynchings.

The only Negro spiritual included in the *Service Book and Hymnal,* 1958, this hymn is found in most major denominational hymnals today, and is one of four spirituals selected for the LBW. The fourth stanza has been altered by the Inter-Lutheran Commission on Worship. C. Winfred Douglas' (LBW 498) harmonization was prepared for *The Hymnal 1940* of the Episcopal church.

Tune: O du Liebe meiner Liebe

This Italian hymn was written by Girolamo Savonarola and published by Fra Serafino Razzi in *Laudi Spirituali,* Venice, 1563.

Savonarola, born in Ferrara, Italy, in 1452, was intended for the medical profession, but the cultural upheaval of the Italian Renaissance, together with an unhappy love affair, turned his thoughts to the monastery. There he became concerned with the paganism emphasized in the study of the early pagan writers such as Plato, Seneca, and Ovid, and in some of the paintings and writings of the Renaissance. His *Laudi spirituali* were written to replace the objectionable secular songs in use during his time. He spoke out boldly against the immorality and the worldly conquests of Pope Alexander VI. His preachings against the vices of his day soon gained him many supporters. When Lorenzo the Magnificent died in 1492, Savonarola gained great power during the political confusion which followed until, by 1497, he was virtually dictator of the city of Florence. He organized groups of boys and girls to gather up and burn in public bonfires all "vanities," from cosmetics to indecent and pagan books, paintings, song collections, etc. Savonarola's activities soon incurred the wrath of Alexander VI and others of the city, and the ecclesiastical and secular courts condemned him a heretic. On May 23, 1498, he was hanged and his body burned.

Jane Francesca Wilde's translation was contributed to R. R. Madden's *Life and Martyrdom of Savonarola,* published in 1853, and repeated in her *Poems by Speranza,* 1864. Several alterations have been made in the text which originally consisted of ten four-line stanzas.

Jane Francesca Elgee, the daughter of an archdeacon, was born in 1826 at Wexford on the southeast coast of Ireland. In 1851 she married Dr. William Wilde, a Dublin oculist, and later became the mother of Oscar Wilde. Although her family was Protestant and conservative, she became caught up in the Irish nationalist movement and, beginning in 1847, sent poetry to *The Nation* signed "Speranza" ("Hope"). She published several secular works including *The American Irish* and books on old Irish customs, legends, and folkways. She died February 3, 1896, at Chelsea.

O DU LIEBE MEINER LIEBE is based on a secular folk song, "Sollen nun die grünen Jahre," which dates from around 1700. In 1732, a version of the tune, as given below, was included in a Catholic hymnal, the *Bambergisches Gesang-Buch,* with the text "Ach wie kan doch sorgen ich" (Bäumker,* III, #223).

The form of the melody found in the LBW was included in a manuscript chorale book of the Moravian Brethren, compiled in Herrnhut around

1735, as the setting for Matthäus Gottfried Hehl's "Unergründliches Regieren." It was first printed in Johann Thommen's *Erbaulicher Musicalischer Christen-Schatz oder 500 Geistliche Lieder,* Basel, 1745, where it was the tune for the anonymous hymn, "O du Liebe meiner Liebe" (Zahn* #6699).

Johann Thommen, born in Basel on January 6, 1711,was a tailor who later set up his own oilcloth factory. He also cultivated music, and was cantor of St. Peter's Church, Basel, from 1738 and established a singing school for the study of church music. He died February 5, 1783.

94   MY SONG IS LOVE UNKNOWN

Tune: Rhosymedre

Samuel Crossman was one of the first English writers of hymns (as opposed to metric psalms) preceding Isaac Watts (LBW 39). Born about 1624 in Bradfield Monachorum in Suffolk, England, he attended Pembroke College, Cambridge, receiving a Bachelor of Divinity degree in 1660. As vicar of All Saints, Sudbury, he served his Anglican congregation, and ministered to a Puritan congregation as well. When the Act of Uniformity was imposed in 1662, he was deposed from the ministry due to his Puritan leanings, but he later conformed and became one of the King's chaplains. In 1667 he was appointed prebendary of Bristol and vicar of St. Nicholas Church, and in 1683, a few weeks before he died, became dean of Bristol. He died on February 4, 1683, and was buried in the Cathedral Church.

Crossman's hymns were published in a book of nine poems: *The Young Man's Meditations, or some few Sacred Poems upon Selected Subjects, and Scriptures,* London, 1664. His seven stanzas are given here complete and unaltered.

RHOSYMEDRE, originally called "Lovely" and ending with an extended "Halleluia," was included in *Original Sacred Music Composed and Arranged by the Revd John Edwards, B. A., Jesus College, Oxford,* published about 1840.

John David Edwards, born in 1805 or 1806, received a Bachelor of Arts degree from Oxford University, and was ordained a priest three years later. After 1843 he served for some years as vicar of Rhosymedre, Ruabon, in North Wales. He died November 14, 1885, at Llanddoget Rectory, Denbighshire. Although he wrote a considerable amount of music, he is chiefly remembered for this tune.

The harmonization by Richard Hillert (LBW 63) is from the *Worship Supplement,* 1969, to *The Lutheran Hymnal.*

95   GLORY BE TO JESUS *(Viva! Viva! Gesù! che per mio bene)*

Tune: Wem in Leidenstagen

This hymn, one of four Italian originals in the LBW, is the work of an unknown author. The source of the hymn is the *Raccolta di Orazioni de Pie Opere colle Indulgenze,* compiled, according to an 1880 translation of the collection, by a Roman priest, Telesephoems Galli, who died in 1845. Since Pope Pius VII already in 1815 granted indulgences of one hundred days "to all the faithful who say or sing" this hymn, it is believed to date from the eighteenth century.

The translation is by Edward Caswall (LBW 37). The first two lines of the sixth stanza were altered to their present form in the Original Edition of *Hymns Ancient and Modern,* 1861.

WEM IN LEIDENSTAGEN. Also called "Filitz," or "Caswall" for its association with this hymn, this tune by Friedrich Filitz was included in his *Vierstimmiges Choralbuch zu Kirchen und Hausgebrauch,* published in 1847. There it was set to Heinrich Siegmund Osswald's hymn for mourners, "Wem in Leidenstagen" (Zahn* #1127.)

Filitz was born March 16, 1804, in Arnstadt, Germany, and his education culminated in a Doctor of Philosophy degree. From 1843 he lived in Berlin and worked together with Ludwig Christian Erk, with whom he published *Vierstimmige Choräle der vornehmsten Meister des 16. und 17. Jahrhunderts* in 1845. This was one of the early nineteenth-century collections which marked a return to the use of the Reformation chorales after a decline in their use during the previous century. He also prepared a chorale book for Christian K. Josias von Bunsen's *Allgemeines Gesang-und Gebetbuch,* published in 1846, and in the next year issued his *Vierstimmiges Choralbuch.* In 1848 he went to Munich where he remained for the rest of his life. He died December 8, 1876.

96   YOUR HEART, O GOD, IS GRIEVED *(Známe to, Pane Bože náš)*
Tune: Známe to, Pane Bože náš

The Slovak Lutheran church uses a number of different Kyrie settings including seasonal ones for Advent, Christmas, Lent, Easter, Ascension, and Pentecost, and an additional one for Sundays and festivals. The present hymn is a non-festival Kyrie. It was originally a nine-fold Kyrie, with each of the bids followed by an appropriate stanza. These stanzas, by Jiři (Juraj) Tranovský, were included in his *Pisne duchovni stare i move . . . cili Cithara Sanctorum,* known among Slovak Lutherans as the "Tranoscius," published in Levoca in 1636.

Tranovský, of Polish descent, was born in a village near Tešín in Silesia, where his forbears had lived for generations as farmers. (His birth date is sometimes given as 1592, but Jaroslav Vajda notes that Tranovský's own acrostic fixes the date of his birth as April 9, 1591.) Following studies at Kolberg (1605–1607), Tranovský proceeded to Wittenberg University. Already during his student days he was writing poetry both in Czech and Latin. About 1612 he went to Bohemia, which at that time was united with Silesia, Tranovský's native land, and which enjoyed freedom of worship for Lutherans. There in Prague he accepted a teaching position at the *Gymnasium* near Sv. Mikuláš (St. Michael). In 1613 he took a similar position at Holesov, a small town in Moravia near the Hungarian border. Two years later he went to Medziriečie, where he was a teacher in the school and a leader of the local singing society, a position which provided sufficient economic stability to allow him to marry Anna Polani of Polansdorf. In 1616 he was ordained a Lutheran pastor. With the ascension to power of Ferdinand II of Bohemia, in 1617, toleration of Lutheranism came to an end, and Tranovský and his congregation were called upon to endure the trials of the Thirty Years' War. For a time in 1621 he, along with the entire population of the city, was forced to flee to Tešín, and in the following years Medziriečie and the surrounding area were repeatedly plundered. Tranovský himself was imprisoned in 1624. Famine and pestilence took the lives of some two thousand persons, including three of Tranovský's children, and during this time he buried half his congregation. The following year he was exiled and returned to his native Silesia, where he was called as court preacher to the castle in Bielsko, where he became a friend of the Szúnyogh family who were staunch supporters of Lutheranism. After the occupation of upper Silesia, he was again forced to move, and went as court preacher to Orava Castle in 1628. His health was beginning to fail. Convinced that he would not live to the age of fifty, he set to work gathering, arranging, and completing his Latin hymns. His *Odarum Sacrarum,* 1629, contained 150 Latin texts for congregational singing, together with several tunes of his own composition. His final call was to Sväty Mikuláš in 1631, where he became senior pastor and so received the judgeship of the consistory. Here he produced his two greatest works, the *Phiala Odoramentorum* and the "Tranoscius." Tranovský became ill in the fall of 1636, and died on May 29, 1637.

The translation of this hymn was prepared in 1969 by Jaroslav Vajda (LBW 159) for *Laudamus,* the hymnal of the Lutheran World Federation, fourth edition, 1970.

ZNÁME TO, PANE BOŽE NÁŠ was also included in the "Tranoscius," 1636, and is given here in an arrangement by Michal Kútsky from the *Kuckarik Partitura.*

Kútzky, a Slovak choirmaster, was baptized on November 21, 1828 in Skalica. He received his fundamental piano instruction in the Regenschor in Skalica, and following studies in the *Gymnasium* in Komarno, he continued his piano studies with J. Kumlík while attending the lyceum in Bratislava. He undertook the study of theology in Vienna, where after the death of J. Kollár in 1852 he served as organist. For two years he served as teacher and organist in Skalica, and for three years was a professor of mathematics and music at the Lutheran lyceum in Banská Švtiavnica. From 1857 to 1863 he was teacher and cantor in Bekeščaba. In 1863 he was called by the Brezová pod Bradlom congregation as teacher and cantor. There he served until his death on March 18, 1899, greatly elevating Lutheran congregational singing and music. In 1873 he founded a forty-voice mixed church choir which performed at various religious and national festivals. In the 1880s he also organized a small string ensemble. He composed a number of hymn tunes and compiled a choralebook for the Lutheran hymnal, which his son-in-law, Bohumil Fiala, published in 1902 as *Chorále do stvorhlasu vypracované.*

The second and third phrases of this tune bear a resemblance to the opening and closing phrases of "Wie schön leuchtet" (LBW 76).

97 CHRIST, THE LIFE OF ALL THE LIVING
(Jesu, meines Lebens Leben)
Tune: Jesu, meines Lebens Leben

Ernst Christoph Homburg was born in 1605 at Mihla (Miller, Mühla) near Eisenbach, Germany, and practiced law at Naumburg in Saxony. He was a highly-regarded secular poet in his younger days and in 1648 became a member of the Fruitbearing Society, and later was a member of the Elbe Swan Order which was founded in 1660 by Johann Rist (LBW 197). Domestic troubles, including his illness and that of his wife, led him to turn to God; he wrote nearly 150 hymns intended primarily for his own private use to strengthen his faith and trust. They were published in his *Geistliche Lieder* which was printed in two parts in 1659 at Jena and Naumburg. "Jesu, meines Lebens Leben" was published in the first part, which had the engraved title "Naumberg," 1658. Homburg died June 2, 1681, in Naumberg.

Catherine Winkworth's (LBW 29) translation appeared in her *Chorale Book for England,* 1863.

JESU, MEINES LEBENS LEBEN was originally the setting for J. G. Albinus' "Alle Menschen müssen sterben" (see *The Lutheran Hymnal,* 1941, #601) and appeared in *Das grosse Cantional: oder Kirchen-Gesangbuch,* published in Darmstadt in 1687 (Zahn* #6779a). It later became associated with the present text in *Anhang, An das Gothaische Cantional,* 1726.

The harmonization was prepared for the LBW by David Herman, associate professor of organ, church music, and music theory at Drake University, Des Moines, Iowa. A native of Williamsport, Pennsylvania, Herman was born November 24, 1944, and began his study of music with Frederick A. Snell. His Bachelor of Music degree is from Wittenberg University, Springfield, Ohio where he studied organ with Elmer Frederick Blackmer and Frederick Jackisch (LBW 236), and composition with Jan Bender (LBW 396). At the University of Michigan he worked with Robert Glasgow (organ), and Percival Price (carillon), and received a Master of Music degree. In 1974 he was awarded the Doctor of Musical Arts degree from the University of Kansas, where he studied organ with James Moeser. His doctoral thesis was later expanded into a book on the life and music of Jan Bender. Before taking his present position at Drake in 1972, he taught organ and harpsichord at the University of Kansas, and served as organist and choirmaster at churches in Kettering, Ohio, and Detroit, Michigan. In addition to his teaching, he has been organist and choir master at Trinity Lutheran Church, Des Moines, and since 1978 has held the same position at Messiah Lutheran Church.

Herman is a member of the Lutheran Society for Worship, Music, and the Arts; the Hymn Society of America; the American Guild of Organists; the Guild of Carillonneurs in North America; and Pi Kappa Lambda. He has played recitals on many of the significant organs and carillons of North America, and given a number of workshops in organ literature and service playing. He and his wife, Lauri, have two daughters.

98   ALAS! AND DID MY SAVIOR BLEED

Tune: Martyrdom

See LBW 39 for Isaac Watts. This hymn was included in his *Hymns and Spiritual Songs,* 1707. Except for the last line of stanza 1, which originally read, "For such a worm as I," the alterations are minor and few.

MARTYRDOM has also been known as "Avon," "Fenwick," "All Saints," and "Drumclog." The source of the tune seems to be a Scottish folk melody, identified by Anne Gilchrist in *The Choir,* 1934, as the ballad "Helen of Kirkconnel." Toward the end of the eighteenth century it was printed on leaflets where it appeared in duple meter. When Robert Archibald Smith included it in his *Sacred Music sung in St. George's Church,* Edinburgh, 1825, it was in the triple meter form that we use today, and designated an "Old Scottish Melody" harmonized by Mr. Smith. Two years later it appeared in *The Seraph, a Selection of Psalms and Hymns,* Glasgow, attributed to Hugh Wilson. A dispute over copyright ensued, out of which Wilson was declared owner.

Hugh Wilson was born in Fenwick, Ayrshire, in 1766 (some sources give 1764). After some education in the village school, he joined his father in the shoemaking trade. However, he continued to study music, mathematics, and sundial design in his spare time, and eventually became a calculator and draughtsman to a mill in Pollokshaws, and later held a similar post in Duntocher. He died August 14, 1824, and was buried at Old Kilpatrick. A member of the Secession Church, he sometimes led the psalmody in his home town, and in Duntocher was a manager and co-founder of the first Sunday school in that church.

Robert Archibald Smith, born November 16, 1780, was the son of a weaver. His musical talent showed itself when he was young and he became an accomplished violinist and cellist and, by 1803, a music teacher. From 1807 he was precentor and session clerk at the Abbey Church in Paisley; in 1823 he went to Edinburgh as the leader of psalmody under Dr. Andrew Thomson at St. George's Church. There he edited his *Sacred Music.* A teacher, editor, composer, and performer, he also compiled a six-volume collection, *The Scottish Minstrel,* 1820–1824. He died at Edinburgh January 3, 1829.

99   O LORD, THROUGHOUT THESE FORTY DAYS

Tune: Caithness

This hymn by Gilbert E. Doan is a paraphrase of "Lord, who throughout these forty days," which was written by Claudia Frances Hernaman and included in her *Child's Book of Praise,* 1873.

Gilbert E. Doan Jr., who served as chairman of the hymn texts committee of the Inter-Lutheran Commission on Worship from 1967 to 1978, was born at Bethlehem, Pennsylvania, on September 14, 1930. After receiving a Bachelor of Arts degree in geology at Harvard College in 1952, he went on to complete a Bachelor of Divinity degree at the Lutheran Theological Seminary, Philadelphia, in 1955, and a Master of Arts degree in American Civilization at the University of Pennsylvania in 1962. From 1955 to 1961 he served as a campus pastor in Philadelphia. Since that time he has been Northeastern Director of National Lutheran Campus Ministry, taking a year's leave of absence (1965–1966) to study at Princeton Theological Seminary. He has completed all the requirements for the Doctor of Theology degree in homiletics and liturgics, except for his dissertation. Married in 1957 to Janice Yelland of Havertown, Pennsylvania, he is the father of four children. He was married in 1976 to Roberta McKaig McAlaine and now lives in Ardmore, Pennsylvania.

Doan's publications include *Renewal in the Pulpit,* 1966, *Sermons on Peace and War, Preaching to College Students*, and *Worship in Campus Ministry,* as well as several devotional guides. He has contributed numerous reviews, articles, and sermons to *The Lutheran, The Lutheran Forum, The Lutheran Quarterly, Una Sancta, The Princeton Seminary Bulletin, Luther Life, Frontiers, Time Out,* etc. In addition he was editor of *The Preaching of Frederick W. Robertson,* 1964, and of the August, 1969, issue of *The Lutheran Quarterly.* He has presented a number of lectures, and is listed in *Who's Who in the East.*

Claudia Frances Ibostson was born at Addlestone, Surrey, England, on October 19, 1838, and in 1858 was married to the Reverend J. W. D. Hernaman, an inspector of schools. Her intense interest in the religious education of children led her to prepare 150 original hymns and translations from Latin for children. These she published in her *Child's Book of Praise, Christmas Carols for Children* (1884 and 1885), and in various collections of other editors. She died in Brussels, Belgium, on October 10, 1898.

CAITHNESS. A discussion of psalters can be found on pp. 58ff. While the 1615 edition of the Scottish Psalter, *The CL Psalms of David . . . ,* published by A. Hart in Edinburgh, had twelve unharmonized "Common tunes," the 1635 edition, *The Psalmes of David in Prose and Meeter,* had thirty-one tunes, provided with harmonizations. This collection, which according to Millar Patrick in his *Four Centuries of Scottish Psalmody* (London: Oxford University Press, 1949) "represents the high-water mark of the psalmody of the Reformation in Scotland," was edited by Edward Millar who had graduated from Edinburgh University in 1624. "Caithness," called "Cathnes Tune" in the 1635 psalter, is considered to be of Scottish origin, and derives its name from Caithness County in northeastern Scotland.

100 DEEP WERE HIS WOUNDS
Tune: Marlee

Regarding the origin of this hymn, William Johnson writes:

> "Deep Were His Wounds" was not written on a sudden impulse. From childhood at home and in church school I have been deeply impressed by the Biblical accounts of the suffering, death and resurrection of Christ. The words of my hymn were a result of a pondering of Isaiah 53, especially the words "By his stripes we are healed." At that time I was still unmarried and had my home with a married brother and his family. Our 86-year-old father also shared the home and was at that time quite feeble both in body and mind. The evening of February 13 it happened that I was alone at home with him. He retired early and was soon asleep and it was thus in a setting of silence and solitude that I was able to find the words to express my thoughts about "His stripes" and "our healing." I remember that at the completion of my poem I had an experience of deep joy and peace.

Written on February 13, 1953, the hymn was included as a Lenten poem the next month in *The Lutheran Companion.* Ernest E. Ryden (LBW 186), editor of *The Lutheran Companion,* took note of the poem and later brought it to the *Service Book and Hymnal,* 1958.

Johnson was born March 28, 1906, on a small farm near Center City, Minnesota, the fifth of seven children, and attended Chisago Lake Lutheran Church, where he later continued to be active, teaching the adult Bible Class. His home, church, and community were bilingual, using both Swedish and English. Although he had only an eighth grade public school education, Johnson has enjoyed reading poetry from his childhood, and has published two collections, *Wild Flowers* in 1948, containing ninety poems, and in 1969 two hundred poems titled *Bill's Poems.* In addition he has published numerous individual poems since 1937 when his first, "He makes it white," appeared in *The Lutheran Companion.* Besides his poetry, Johnson also wrote a number of prose contributions for the congregational paper of Chisago Lake Church.

As a young man Johnson worked for his father in masonry, bricklaying, and cement work, and thereafter worked as a farm laborer until 1955 when he became supervisor of the milk testing program of the Chisago County Dairy Herd Improvement Association. Married in 1957 to Viola Loftness of rural Hector, Minnesota, he lived in Center City, Minnesota, until his wife's death in 1969. In 1970 he married Inez Jones and the couple have retired to Hinckley, Minnesota, where Johnson is active in the First Presbyterian Church. Since his retirement he has made a trip to Sweden and has prepared some translations from both Swedish and Norwegian.

MARLEE was written for William Johnson's text in the *Service Book and Hymnal,* 1958.

Leland Bernhard Sateren was born at Everett, Washington, on October 13, 1913, of Norwegian extraction. After receiving a Bachelor of Arts degree from Augsburg College in 1935, he was for three years director of music of the public schools at Moose Lake, Minnesota. In 1937 he traveled to Europe to research choral literature. He received a Master of Arts Degree from the University of Minnesota in 1943, and during his years at the university served as director of music of the university radio station, KUOM. Following three years as educational director in the Civilian Public Service, he went in 1946 to Augsburg College, where since 1950 he has been professor of music and director of the Augsburg Choir which in 1965 and 1975 toured Norway and Central Europe. From 1950 to 1973 he was chairman of the music department of Augsburg College. Twice he has made major studies of choral organizations; in 1961 a sabbatical leave allowed him to study thirty-four major college and university choirs in northeastern United States, and in 1966 he observed and studied fourteen European choirs. Sateren is the conductor of the Sateren Choral Workshops, and serves as adjudicator and director at music festivals and contests; and as teacher, lecturer, and director at various choral schools, music institutes, and clinics. For three summers (1971, 1973, and 1974) he also conducted choral schools in Oslo, Norway and Göteborg, Sweden. He is a member of various professional associations, including the Music Educators National Conference and the Hymn Society of America, and served on the Inter-Lutheran Commission on Worship from 1967 to 1978.

As a composer, Sateren has written over three hundred choral works, and published a large number of works for treble voices, including *Cantate Domino.* He has also published works on choirs and choral music and contributed articles to professional magazines. Honors include a Doctor of Humane Letters from Gettysburg College and a Doctor of Music from Lakeland College, both in 1965; the St. Olaf Medal conferred by King Olav of Norway in 1971; and the first F. Melius Christiansen Memorial Award of the Minnesota chapter of the American Choral Directors Association, 1974. Sateren and his wife live in Minneapolis and are the parents of five children.

101   O CHRIST, OUR KING, CREATOR, LORD
(Rex Christe, factor omnium)
Tune: Oakley

The son of a patrician family, Gregory I (the Great), was born about 540 and received an excellent education, especially in law, which prepared him for public office. He served as a member of the Senate, and around 570 became prefect of Rome, presiding over the Senate, and having also responsibility for the city's defense, and for financial and social matters. After his father's death, Gregory became a Benedictine monk; and around 575 he established six monasteries on family lands in Sicily and turned his own home into a monastery. In 577 he was named one of seven cardinal deacons of Rome and soon thereafter spent six years in Constantinople as a representative of Pope Pelagius II. From 590 until his death on March 12, 604, he was pope.

Gregory, who viewed himself as the "Servant of the Church's servants," made his influence felt throughout a vast territory. Through his missionaries and representatives he converted the Arian Visigoths and weakened the Donatists in North Africa. He himself held the Lombards from invading Rome by paying them a large sum of money. When he saw some fair-haired children from Britain being sold as slaves in Rome, he determined to evangelize that land, and sent Augustine (who became the first Archbishop of Canterbury) with forty other monks. Gregory is credited with making revisions in the liturgy, including the extending of the singing of the Alleluia from Easter to all nonpenitential days, and the present placement of the Lord's Prayer. To him is also attributed the establishment of the Schola Cantorum (although this was probably a reorganization rather than a founding, as such schools for singing had existed in Rome before), and the revision or simplification of the chant, which seems to have contained excessive melismas at the time. Gregory's reforms went out with his missionaries to all points, in most cases completely replacing what had been in use before, and "Gregorian chant" became standard in all Western churches.

The earliest sources of this hymn are several eleventh-century manuscripts. Julian* notes that during medieval times it was often used in the Good Friday Tenebrae service, and that it survived in its original Latin form in the Lutheran church for a long time. As late as 1748 it was included in Latin in the Lutheran *Gesangbuch* of Dresden.

Ray Palmer's (LBW 479) translation from the *Sabbath Hymn Book,* 1858, was included in the *Service Book and Hymnal,* 1958. That translation has been extensively reworked by the Inter-Lutheran Commission on Worship.

OAKELY was written for Thomas Browne's (LBW 541) "The night is come like to the day," in *Songs of Praise,* 1925. Vaughan Williams' familiarity with folksong is evident in this pentatonic tune, which shows a similarity, not only in mode, but also in shapes and relative heights of phrases, to "Consolation" (LBW 33).

Ralph Vaughan Williams, the outstanding figure in English church music during the first half of the twentieth century, was the son of the vicar of Christ Church in Down Ampney. Born October 12, 1872, he entered the Royal College of Music in 1890. There he studied with Walter Parratt, Charles Hubert Hastings Parry (LBW 283), and Charles Villiers Stanford (LBW 189). He received a Bachelor of Music degree from Trinity College, Cambridge, in 1894. The following year he received a Bachelor of Arts degree and returned to the Royal College of Music, where he established a life-long friendship with Gustav Holst. For three years beginning in 1896 he was organist at South Lambeth Parish Church. After travels to Berlin, where he studied with Max Bruch, and to Paris, where he was a student of Maurice Ravel, he returned to England and completed a Doctor of Music degree at Trinity College in 1901. He joined the Folk-Song Society in 1904 and spent a number of years collecting English folksongs. These folksongs influenced all his composition and served as a rich source of tunes for the collections he edited: *The English Hymnal,* 1906, *Songs of Praise,* 1925, and the *Oxford Book of Carols,* 1928. During the First World War he enlisted in the army and served in Macedonia and France. On his return he became professor of composition at the Royal College of Music.

Included in his compositions are sacred and secular works—songs, choral works, operas, orchestral works, etc. He came to the United States in 1922 to conduct his *Pastoral Symphony* at the Norfolk, Connecticut, Festival. In 1935 he was awarded the Order of Merit. He died August 26, 1958, at St. Marylebone.

102 ON MY HEART IMPRINT YOUR IMAGE
(Skriv dig, Jesus, paa mit Hjerte)
Tune: Der am Kreuz

Thomas Hansen Kingo, the first great hymnwriter of Denmark, was the son of a weaver, and the grandson of a Scottish tapestry weaver who had emigrated to Denmark. He was born December 15, 1634, in Slangerup. After spending several years at a Latin school where the teaching was poor and the discipline cruel, Kingo transferred to a school in Hillerød, near Frederiksborg. There he was taken into the home of the rector, Albert Bartholin. Surrounded by some of the finest beauty and splendor in Denmark—Frederiksborg Lake and Castle—he studied Danish literature, an unusual choice, since the upper classes at that time were studying German. After completing theological studies at the University of Copenhagen in 1658, he worked for a time as a private tutor. Ordained in 1661, he served first as pastor of a country parish near Vedby, and in 1668 returned to his home town, Slangerup, as parish pastor. The following year he received a Master of Arts degree, and was married to Sille Lambertsdotter. In 1677 he was consecrated bishop of Odense in the island of Fyen. He was made a member of the Danish nobility in 1679, and honored with a doctor of theology degree three years later. He died October 14, 1703.

Kingo was married three times. Since his first two wives were widows with children, he inherited a large family of step-children. After the death of his second wife, he married a young lady of nobility. This was a singularly happy marriage, in which his wife accompanied him on all his pastoral visits.

Kingo discouraged the use of translated hymns and created a body of Danish hymns which were indigenous to his homeland and expressed a sentiment native to his people. His first hymnal, *Aandeligt Sjunge Chor,* was published in two parts in 1673 and 1681. In 1683 he was appointed by King Christian V to prepare a new hymnal for the Danish Church. The *Vinterparten* ("Winter part," containing hymns for Advent to Easter) was completed in 1689, and included a total of 267 hymns, half of them by Kingo, and many others altered by him. It met with strong disapproval and the king immediately appointed Søren Jonassen, dean of Roskilde, to take over the work. His hymnal, finished in 1693, did not contain a single hymn by Kingo. It, too, was rejected. Finally the king set up a committee to compile the hymnal. The resulting collection, approved in 1699, contained eighty-five of Kingo's original hymns.

Popularly known as "Kingo's Hymnal," it served the Danish church for over one hundred years.

"Skriv dig, Jesus" is the fifteenth stanza of a twenty-nine stanza hymn on Christ's crucifixion and death beginning "Bryder frem, I hule Sukke." It was published in the *Vinterparten,* Odense, 1689. The translation, prepared in 1898 by Peer Olsen Strömme, was included in the *Lutheran Hymnary,* 1913. Originally beginning "On my heart imprint *Thine* image," the text is given here with several alterations.

Strömme, a talented lecturer and writer, was born September 15, 1856, at Winchester, Wisconsin. He completed a Bachelor of Arts degree at Luther College, Decorah, Iowa, in 1876, and three years later graduated from Concordia Seminary. From 1879 to 1886 he served as a parish pastor at Mayville, North Dakota; Ada, Minnesota; and Nelson, Wisconsin. He also served as superintendent of schools in Norman County, Minnesota, and in 1887, became a teacher at St. Olaf College, Northfield, Minnesota. Six years later he took a post as principal of the Mt. Horeb Academy, Mt. Horeb, Wisconsin. He died on his birthday in 1921.

Author of numerous poems and hymns, Strömme also served as editor of *Norden,* 1887-1889; *Daglige Tidende,* 1889; *Amerika,* 1895-1898; *Minneapolis Tidende,* 1899-1903; *Politiken,* 1904; and *Vor Tid,* 1904-1905. His *Hvorledes Halvor Blev Prest,* the story of student and faculty life at Luther College in Decorah, went through many editions, both in Norwegian and in English translation as *How Halvor Became a Pastor.*

This hymn was included in the *Service Book and Hymnal,* 1958, in Jens Christian Aaberg's (LBW 75) translation, "Print Thine image pure and holy."

DER AM KREUZ. This tune by Johann B. König (LBW 22) was the setting for the Lenten hymn attributed to Johann Mentzer, "Der am Kreuz ist meine Liebe," in the *Harmonischer Liederschatz,* Frankfurt, 1738 (Zahn* #6641). The harmonization is by Frederick Jackisch (LBW 236).

103 O CHRIST, THOU LAMB OF GOD *(Christe, du Lamm Gottes)*
Tune: Christe, du Lamm Gottes

See LBW 1 for a discussion of the Agnus Dei. The English text, "O Lamb of God that takest away the sins of the world . . . ," was included in the English Litany, 1544, and the first Prayer Book of Edward VI, 1549. The use of the word "Christ" is unique to Lutheranism, and first appeared in Low German as "Christe, du lam Gades" in Johannes Bugenhagen's *Der Erbarn Stadt Brunswig Christlike ordeninge,* 1528. A High German translation was published in Nürnberg in 1531. (The entire Brunswick order, with an English translation, can be found in Reed's* *Lutheran Liturgy.*)

CHRISTE, DU LAMM GOTTES, the melody that appeared with this text in Bugenhagen's *Brunswig Christlike ordeninge,* 1528, is related to the "Kyrie" setting (based on Gregorian Psalm Tone I) in Martin Luther's (LBW 48) German Mass of 1526. Leupold* suggests that since Bugenhagen was a close friend and co-worker of Luther's the latter might himself have had a hand in arranging this hymn.

Johannes Bugenhagen was born June 24, 1485, at Wollin in Pomerania, and from 1502 to 1504 studied at Greifswald. After serving as rector of the city school in Treptow on the Rega, he was ordained a priest in 1509 and became a vicar of St. Mary's Church in Treptow. Through study of Erasmus he became interested in Bible study, and in 1517 he became a lecturer on the Bible and the Church fathers at the convent school in Belbuck. The following year, at the request of his prince, he prepared a history of Pomerania. Influenced by the writings of Luther, he went to Wittenberg in 1521 to study theology, and there gained the respect and friendship of Luther and Philipp Melanchthon, and was the first among the reformers to marry. He assisted Luther in the preparation of a translation of the Bible, and prepared his own Low German version. As pastor in Wittenberg he often substituted as lecturer or preacher for Luther, and on Luther's death, preached his funeral sermon. Having completed a Doctor of Theology degree at Wittenberg in 1533, he became a professor there two years later. Bugenhagen had a special gift for organization, and from 1528 to 1544 ordered church affairs in North Germany and in Denmark, where after the arrest of the Roman Catholic bishops in 1536 he ordained new superintendents the following year. In addition to his Braunschweig (Brunswick) church order, he prepared services for Hamburg (1529), Lübeck (1531), Pomerania (1535), Denmark (1527), Schleswig-Holstein (1542), Brunswick-Wolfenbüttel (1543), and Hildesheim (1544), all of which were influenced by Luther's German Mass of 1526. His *Passionsharmonie* and *Historia des Leidens und der Auferstehung,* 1526, compilations from the four Gospels of the Passion and Resurrection stories respectively, provided texts for composers for many years to come. He died April 20, 1558.

See LBW 111 for another form of the Agnus Dei used in early Lutheran services. Harmonization of this tune is by Carl Schalk (LBW 118).

104   IN THE CROSS OF CHRIST I GLORY
Tune: Rathbun

John Bowring, an extremely versatile and gifted man, was born in Exeter, England, October 17, 1792. After school he entered a merchant's office and during the ensuing four years laid the groundwork for his literary achievements, learning six languages: French, Italian, Spanish, Portuguese, German, and Dutch. He continued the study of languages until, near the end of his life, he had studied two hundred languages and could converse in one hundred. His literary output includes translations from works in at least twenty-two languages, in addition to original writings in the areas of finance, economics, history, travel, biography, poetry, natural science, religion, and slavery. In 1811 he joined the firm of Milford and Company and for several years he traveled extensively on the Continent for this company. His marriage to Maria, daughter of Samuel Lewin of Hackney, took place in 1816. Intense literary interests led him to devote himself extensively to writing after 1822. Two volumes of sacred poetry appeared shortly: *Matins and Vespers with Hymns and Occasional Devotional Pieces* in 1823 and *Hymns: as a Sequel to Matins* in 1825. It is from the latter collection that the hymn, "In the Cross of Christ I Glory," was taken. During this time, also, he served as co-editor of the *Westminster Review*. His devotion to literature had a bad effect on business, however, and he was induced to turn for employment to government. Beginning in 1828 he worked as a political economist in Holland (where he received an honorary Doctor of Laws degree from the University of Groningen, one of many such honors he was to receive during his life), and in France and Belgium. From 1835 to 1837 and again from 1841 to 1849 Bowring served in Parliament, and in 1849 began his nine years of service to China, first as consul at Canton, then as minister plenipotentiary to China, and finally as governor of Hong Kong. He was knighted by Queen Victoria in 1859. Near the end of his stay in China, an attempt was made to poison him and his family by putting arsenic in their bread. His wife died as a result, and Bowring was remarried in 1860. After his retirement from his work in China, he returned to England and maintained a full schedule of writing, lecturing, and serving as a member of several associations until shortly before his death at Claremont, Exeter, on November 23, 1872.

RATHBUN, written in 1849, was named for Mrs. Beriah S. Rathbun, the leading soprano of the choir of Central Baptist Church, Norwich, Connecticut. It was included in H. W. Greatorex's *Collection of Psalm and Hymn Tunes, Chants, Anthems, and Sentences,* published in Boston in 1851, where it was set to "Saviour, who Thy flock art feeding."

Ithamar Conkey, of Scotch ancestry, was born in Shutesbury, Massachusetts, on May 5, 1815. After serving as organist and choir director at Central Baptist Church in his native town, he went to New York City. There he was bass soloist at Calvary Episcopal Church, then a member of the choir of Grace Church, and finally, after 1861, bass soloist and conductor of the quartet-choir of the Madison Avenue Baptist Church. He died April 30, 1867, at Elizabeth, New Jersey.

105 A LAMB GOES UNCOMPLAINING FORTH
(Ein Lämmlein geht und trägt de Schuld)
Tune: An Wasserflüssen Babylon

See LBW 23 for Paul Gerhardt. This hymn was first published in Johann Crüger's (LBW 23) *Praxis Pietatis Melica,* third edition, 1648. The translation was prepared by the Inter-Lutheran Commission on Worship.

AN WASSERFLÜSSEN BABYLON. This melody, which is generally ascribed to Wolfgang Dachstein, originally appeared with Dachstein's metric version of Psalm 137, "An Wasserflüssen Babylon," in the third part of *Teutsch Kirchenampt mit lobgsengen,* Strasbourg, 1525.

Born about 1487, Dachstein was a monk at Strasbourg and organist of the cathedral there. In 1524 he espoused the cause of the Reformation and became organist and assistant preacher at St. Thomas' Church. With his friend, Matthäus Greitter, he edited the *Teutsch Kirchenampt,* and he is also credited with several melodies in the Genevan Psalter. He died in 1553.

J. S. Bach (LBW 219) used this melody as the basis for organ works in his Eighteen Chorales and his Miscellaneous Preludes, and a setting is included in his *Choralgesänge*. The harmonization used here is from the *Württembergische Choralbuch,* 1953.

106 IN THE HOUR OF TRIAL
Tune: Penitence

See LBW 50 for James Montgomery. This hymn, dated October 13, 1834, was distributed in manuscript form to twenty-two of Montgomery's friends. It was first printed in his *Original Hymns for Public, Private, and Social Devotion,* 1853. The text was considerably altered in Mrs. Frances A. Hutton's *Supplement and Litanies,* and further revised in Godfrey Thring's (LBW 170) *The Church of England Hymnbook,* revised edition, 1882.

PENITENCE was composed by Spencer Lane one Sunday noon in 1875 to be used with this text at the evening service at St. James's Episcopal Church, Woonsocket, Rhode Island.

Lane, born April 7, 1843, in Tilton, New Hampshire, served in the Union Army during the Civil War. Afterwards he studied at the New England Conservatory of Music, and then became an instructor in vocal and instrumental music and ran a music store in New York City. For thirteen years he was organist and choir director at St. James's Church in Woonsocket, Rhode Island, after which he was music director of the Congregational Church at Monson, Massachusetts. He spent some time also in Richmond, Virginia, before going finally to Baltimore, Maryland, where he was an associate of the Sanders and Stayman music firm and organist and choirmaster of All Saints' Church. He died of a stroke on August 10, 1903, at Reedville, Virginia.

107 BENEATH THE CROSS OF JESUS
Tune: St. Christopher

Elizabeth Cecilia Clephane, daughter of the sheriff of Fife and Kinross, was born in Edinburgh, Scotland, June 18, 1830. After her father's death she and her two sisters went first to Ormiston, East Lothian, then to Bridgend, Melrose, where the old bridge stands to which Sir Walter Scott refers in his *The Abbot and The Monastery.* The sisters, members of the Free Church of Scotland, devoted their lives to charity in the Melrose community. Elizabeth died February 19, 1869. Her hymns were published after her death in the *Family Treasury,* this hymn appearing in 1872.

ST. CHRISTOPHER. Edited by Alfred Stone, *The Bristol Tune Book* was first published in Bristol, England, in 1863. A "Second Series" with many new tunes appeared in 1876, and a further supplement of thirty-seven tunes was added in 1881. To this 1881 supplement Frederick C. Maker was invited to contribute, and "St. Christopher" was one of seven of his tunes accepted for the book.

Frederick Charles Maker (1844–1927), who spent his entire life in Bristol, Gloucestershire, England, trained as a chorister at the Cathedral there. He served as organist of Milk Street Methodist Free Church, then of Clifton Downs Congregational Church, and from 1882, of Redland Park Congregational Church, where he remained until 1910. Besides hymn tunes, he published anthems, cantatas, and piano pieces. He accompanied the Bristol Festival Choirs, directed by Alfred Stone, and for twenty years was visiting professor of music at Clifton College. He also conducted the Bristol Free Church Choir Association.

Tune: Valet will ich dir geben

During the Middle Ages it was customary for the clergy and choirs to process within the church and also into the church square and the streets of the town, singing the appropriate processional hymns. This hymn represents a *genre* of processional hymns which had verses and a refrain, with the refrain having a separate melody from the verses. The Latin hymn and its plainsong melody can be seen in the *Liber Usualis* (Tournai: Desclée & Co., 1961), p. 586.

Theodulph, born about 750 or 760, probably in Spain or Italy, was of a noble Gothic family. He entered a monastery at Florence and was brought by Charlemagne to France in 781, where he was first made abbot of Fleury and then bishop of Orleans. Accused of conspiring against King Louis the Pious, he was imprisoned at Angers in 818 where he probably wrote this hymn. In his *Medieval Hymns,* 1851, John Mason Neale (LBW 34) relates the legend that King Louis passed the prison in the Palm Sunday procession, and Theodulph sang this hymn from his window and so delighted the king that he was immediately liberated. However, the unfortunate truth is that he probably remained imprisoned until his death in 821, possibly of poisoning.

The original poem was seventy-eight lines long, but only a portion of it was used as a Palm Sunday hymn. Neale included a translation beginning "Glory, and honour, and laud be to Thee, King Christ the Redeemer!" in his *Medieval Hymns.* A second translation beginning "Glory, and laud, and honour" was included in his *Hymnal Noted,* 1854, and was slightly revised when it was included in the Original Edition of *Hymns Ancient and Modern,* 1861. This last form has been further altered for the LBW.

VALET WILL ICH DIR GEBEN is also known as "St. Theodulph" because of its association with this hymn.

The composer, Melchior Teschner, was born April 29, 1584, at Fraustadt in Silesia. His father was a chief steward. A gifted child, Melchior studied under Johann Klee at the *Gymnasium* of Zittau, and in 1602 entered the University of Frankfurt-an-der-Oder, where he studied philosophy and theology, and music under Bartholomäus Gesius (LBW 455). From 1605 to 1608 he was cantor and teacher in the village of Schmiegel, where he saved money to go to Wittenberg for further studies. Afterwards he seems to have gone to Helmstedt for a short time. In 1609 the council of his home town of Fraustadt called him as *Kantor* and teacher at the school and church of the Kripplein Christi. Valerius Herberger, who had been teacher there since 1584, and pastor since 1590, had had a new church built in 1604 to replace a larger one appropriated by the Roman Catholics. Three years later a new school was also built. Teschner also substituted occasionally for the ailing Pastor Adam Krause in the village of Oberpritschen, a suburb of Fraustadt. When Krause died, Teschner was called as pastor of Oberpritschen. These were the years of the plague, and from July to November, 1613, over two thousand people died in Fraustadt alone, including Krause, and Teschner's teacher, Gesius. (The following year another teacher, Johann Klee, also died.) At this time Herberger composed his famous hymn for the dying, "Valet will ich dir geben." Teschner composed two melodies for the hymn. During the seventeenth century, the tune found in the LBW was adopted in all the Lutheran churches (and in many Catholic churches as well) in Germany, Switzerland, Holland, France, Sweden, and Finland. Teschner provided both tunes with five-voice settings and published them as *Ein andechtiges Gebet,* Leipzig, 1614 (Zahn* #5404). In 1616 he married Elisabeth Klee, daughter of his former teacher, and to this union three sons and four daughters were born. He was called upon in 1627 to officiate at the burial of his friend and colleague, Herberger, to whom he dedicated an *Epicedium.* Teschner himself died December 1, 1635, as a result of an attack by the Cossacks, and was thus spared witnessing the burning of Kripplein Christi Church in 1644. One of his sons and also a grandson succeeded him as pastor of Oberpritschen.

Some writers have noted a resemblance between this tune and "Sellinger's Round," a sixteenth-century round dance which, in the *Fitzwilliam Virginal Book* (early seventeenth century), appeared as given below.

Blume* notes that the Genevan Psalter setting for Psalm 3 is also related.

J. S. Bach (LBW 219) made use of the melody in the St. John Passion and Cantata 95, and prepared two harmonizations for the *Choralgesänge.* Two organ settings are included among his Miscellaneous Preludes. The harmonization found here is from the *Neues Choralbuch,* 1970.

109 GO TO DARK GETHSEMANE

Tune: Gethsemane

See LBW 50 for James Montgomery. Montgomery wrote two versions of this hymn. The first appeared in Thomas Cotterill's (LBW 547) *A Selection of Psalms and Hymns for Public and Private Use,* ninth edition, London, 1820; the second, with stanzas 2-4 considerably altered, in a collection edited by E. Parsons, *et al.,* titled *A Selection of Hymns for the Use of the Protestant Dissenting Congregations of the Independent*

Order in Leeds, 1822. The second version was repeated in Montgomery's own *Christian Psalmist,* 1825, and, with a few changes, is the form used here. Both the 1820 and 1825 texts can be found in Julian*, p. 430.

GETHSEMANE ("Petra," "Ajalon," or "Redhead No. 76"). Richard Redhead, born at Harrow, England, March 1, 1820, was in his youth a chorister of Magdalen College, Oxford. He held only two organ positions in his life: Margaret Street Chapel (which in 1859 became All Saints' Church), Cavendish Square in London, from 1839 to 1864; and St. Mary Magdalene, Paddington, until 1894. He died April 27, 1901, at Hellingly, Sussex. Leaning strongly in favor of the Oxford Movement, he published several collections which were important on the musical side of the Catholic revival. Together with Frederick Oakley (LBW 45) he edited the first Gregorian psalter, the *Laudes Diurnae,* 1843.

This tune was number LXXVI in Redhead's *Church Hymn Tunes, Ancient and Modern, for the Several Seasons of the Church Year,* 1853. The harmony has been altered since the first publication.

110   AT THE CROSS, HER STATION KEEPING
(Stabat Mater dolorosa)
Tune: Stabat Mater

For a discussion of sequences, see page 14.

Authorship of the Stabat Mater has not been finally established. Among those credited with having written it are Pope Gregory the Great (LBW 101), Bernard of Clairvaux (LBW 116), Bonaventura (d. 1274), Pope John XXII (d. 1334), and Pope Gregory XI (*c.* 1378). The two persons most commonly credited with the authorship, however, are Pope Innocent III, who died in 1216, and Jacaponi di Benedetti, with the latter being more widely accepted as the possible author. Jacaponi, a lawyer born in Todi in Umbria, entered a Franciscan monastery around 1278 and died there in 1306 at an advanced age. Originally intended for devotional use, the poem was popular among the Flagellants in the fourteenth century and came into several Missals in the fifteenth century. Its use in the Roman liturgy dates from 1727. The text has been set to music by a number of composers and translated into many languages. The English text which appears in the LBW is the work of Edward Caswall (LBW 37) and Richard Mant (LBW 176), with revisions by several others.

STABAT MATER, also known as "Mainz," first appeared in the *Maintzisch Gesangbuch,* published in Mainz and Frankfurt in 1661, in the form given below (Bäumker*, I, #476).

In the earliest of the John Wade manuscripts (LBW 45), it appeared in a form similar to that found here; and in 1784 it was published in the *Evening Office of the Church According to the Roman Breviary.*

111   LAMB OF GOD, PURE AND SINLESS
(O Lamm Gottes, unschuldig)

Tune: O Lamm Gottes, unschuldig

See LBW 103 for another version of the Agnus Dei.

Nikolaus Decius (also Nicolaus à Curia, von Hofe, or Hovesch) was born about 1485, in Hof, in Upper Franconia, Bavaria. He attended the University of Leipzig, receiving first a Bachelor of Arts degree in 1506, and later also a *Baccalaureus utrius que iuris*. After his studies he entered a cloister; it is not known where—possibly it was the Franciscan cloister in Hof where his brother was prior. He went in 1515 to Braunschweig, where he was a teacher, and where he learned Low German. In 1519 he became prior of the Benedictine nunnery at Steterburg near Wolfenbüttel. Having been attracted by the teachings of Martin Luther (LBW 48), he served briefly in 1522 as rector of the lyceum in Hanover, but returned in the fall of that year to Braunschweig where he became a master in the St. Katherine and Egidien School. At this time the city of Braunschweig had become a part of the Reformation. Decius published his *Summula,* containing selections from the Gospel of Matthew, Latin authors, and Low German poetry. In addition he produced Low German substitutes for the Gloria in Excelsis, Sanctus, and Agnus Dei, two of which, "Aleyne God yn der Höge sy eere" (LBW 166) and "O Lam Godes unschüllich," are found in the LBW. These hymns pre-date Luther's first hymnal by a year. In 1523 Decius entered Wittenberg University to study Reformation theology, and completed a Master of Arts degree. Luther recommended him as assistant pastor to Paulus von Rhode at St. Nicholas Church in Stettin, where he remained until 1527. It appears that he married the following year. In 1532 he was assistant pastor in the East Prussian town of Liebstadt, but two years later was forced to leave, and went to Mühlhausen near Elbing, which had been settled by Dutch religious refugees, with whom he sympathized. A capable musician (a harpist), he was appointed cantor in Bartenstein, south of Königsberg, and also teacher in the village Latin school. Meanwhile he had come to the attention of Margrave Albrecht, and in 1540 was invited to become senior pastor and assistant cantor in Königsberg, where Johann Kugelmann (LBW 519) was chief cantor. His leanings toward Calvinism did not disturb the broad-minded Albrecht. In 1543 Decius returned to Mühlhausen, where the Calvinist settlement was growing. In April of 1546 he prepared a successor to perform his duties in Mühlhausen. After this we have no record of him; the date and place of his death are unknown.

The three hymns from the liturgy were published in Low German in *Geystlyke Leder,* Rostock, 1531, and in High German in Valentin Schumann's *Geistliche lieder, auffs new gebessert und gemehrt,* 1539.

Joel W. Lundeen's (LBW 146) translation was prepared for the LBW.

O LAMM GOTTES, UNSCHULDIG is an adaptation by Decius of a plainsong Agnus Dei which dates from the thirteenth century, or possibly earlier. The original plainsong can be found in Mass nine, "Cum jubilo," for the feast of the Blessed Virgin in *The Liber Usualis* (Tournai: Desclee Company, 1963), p. 18. The form of the melody used here was included in Anton Corvinus' *Christliche Kirchen-Ordnung,* Erfurt, 1542. This publication, which had a preface by Elisabeth Duchess of Brunswick-Lüneburg, was prepared for use in the principalities of Calenberg and Göttingen of which she was regent. A later form of the melody, published in the Eisleben *Gesangbuch,* 1598, was used in the *Service Book and Hymnal,* 1958. The 1542 form of the melody was more widely used in southern Germany, while the 1598 version was preferred in northern Germany. The hymn and tune were in Roman Catholic use by 1631 when they were included in David Gregor Corner's (LBW 200) *Gross Catolisch Gesangbuch* (Bäumker*, I, 456).

J. S. Bach (LBW 219) used the tune in the *St. Matthew Passion* and included a setting in his *Choralgesänge.* His settings for organ are included in the *Orgelbüchlein* and in his Eighteen Chorales.

112   JESUS, IN THY DYING WOES

Tune: Ack, vad är dock livet här

Thomas Benson Pollock was born May 28, 1836, at Strathallan, Isle of Man, in England. At Trinity College, Dublin, he received the vice-chancellor's prize for English verse in 1855, and graduated with a Bachelor of Arts degree in 1859. Four years later he also received a Master of Arts degree. For a while he had studied medicine, but in 1861 was ordained, and served as curate at St. Luke's, Leek, Staffordshire, and at St. Thomas', Stamford Hill, Middlesex, London. In 1865 he joined his brother at St. Alban's Mission in Birmingham. The district was poor, but the two brothers soon gathered a large congregation and built one of the finest churches in the city. Their church became a High Church stronghold, for which they were at first strongly criticized; but their devotion and their educational and social work among the poor gained them respect and admiration. Thomas' brother died in December, 1895, and Thomas himself died the following year on December 15.

Pollock wrote a number of metrical litanies which he published in *Metrical Litanies for Special Services and General Use,* Oxford, 1871. "Jesus, in thy dying woes" is from that collection. He also served from 1895 to 1896 on the committee of *Hymns Ancient and Modern,* to which he contributed some hymns and a number of his litanies.

ACK, VAD ÄR DOCK LIVET HÄR was included in *Then Swenska Psalmboken,* Stockholm, 1697, as the setting for "Ack, vad är dock livet här." Originally it was in triple meter, as given below.

The melody made its way, titled "Swedish litany," into *The Hymnal 1940* (Episcopal) as the setting for Pollock's hymn, and from there into the *Pilgrim Hymnal* and the *Service Book and Hymnal,* both 1958.

113   JESUS, IN THY DYING WOES

Tune: Ack, vad är dock livet här

See LBW 112 for this text (given here in shortened form) and tune. The alternate harmonization was written for the LBW by J. Bert Carlson.

Carlson, pastor of St. Luke's Lutheran Church in West Collingswood, New Jersey, was born in Chicago, Illinois, on September 6, 1937. He completed a Bachelor of Music degree at the American Conservatory of Music in Chicago in 1958, and in 1963, graduated from the Lutheran School of Theology in Maywood, Illinois, and was ordained. Six years later he completed a Master of Music degree at Duquesne University of Pittsburgh, Pennsylvania. He has served parishes in Richmond, Indiana (1963-1964); Erie, Pennsylvania (1964-1966); and Pittsburgh, Pennsylvania (1966-1970). Since 1970 he has been in West Collingswood. He and his wife Nancé, *née* Willis, are the parents of three sons.

Carlson served from 1970 to 1973 on the Commission on Worship of the Lutheran Church in America. His choral and solo music has been published by a number of companies. A book of *Sacred Solos,* 1977, with texts by Nancé, was also published as duets two years later. His opera, *Lazarus!,* commissioned by Wittenberg University, was first performed in March of 1979.

114   THERE IS A GREEN HILL FAR AWAY

Tune: Windsor

Cecil Frances Humphreys was born in 1818 (a few older sources give 1823) in Ireland, in Redcross parish, Wicklow County. Around 1835 the family moved to Miltown House in Tyrone County. There she wrote a number of hymns and published what is perhaps her most important volume: *Hymns for Little Children,* 1848. Two years later she married the Reverend William Alexander, rector of the county of Tyrone, who later became bishop of Derry and Raphoe, and finally, archbishop of Armagh and primate of all Ireland. Before her marriage, she and her sister established a school for the deaf. Later, she was known to walk miles daily, ministering to the sick and taking food to the poor, irrespective of their creed. When she and her husband went to Londonderry, she founded a Girls' Friendly Society. She died in Londonderry on October 12, 1895.

As a little girl Mrs. Alexander had begun to write poetry, and she later published several collections including *Verses from the Holy Scripture* (1846), *Narrative Hymns for Village Schools* (1853), *Poems on Subjects in the Old Testament* (in two parts, 1854 and 1857), and *Hymns Descriptive and Devotional* (1858). In addition she contributed a number of poems to current hymn collections, such as *Psalms and Hymns* (published by the Society for the Promotion of Christian Knowledge), *Hymns Ancient and Modern,* and the *Irish Church Hymnal.* Although many of her hymns were written for children, she was of the opinion that "a namby-pamby, childish style is most unpleasing to children," and that "it is surprising how soon they can understand and follow a high order of poetry." Her *Hymns for Little Children* (in its 67th edition by 1888) contained, in addition to a morning and evening hymn and a hymn on the Trinity, hymns to illuminate and expand the Catechism—on Baptism, the Creed, the Commandments, Prayer, and the Lord's Supper. Written at the bedside of a sick child, "There is a green hill far away" was given in *Hymns for Little Children* as one of the hymns on the Creed following "Suffered under Pontius Pilate, was crucified, dead, and buried." The hymn was sung at the funeral of Archbishop Alexander, who survived his wife by sixteen years. Two other well-known hymns from *Hymns for Little Children* are "Once in royal David's city" and "All things bright and beautiful."

WINDSOR ("Dundee") was included as the setting for Psalm 116 in *The Booke of the Musicke of M. William Damon, late one of her maiesties Musitions: conteining all the tunes of David's Psalmes, as they are ordinarily soung in the Church: most excellently composed into 4 parts.* This collection, printed by Thomas Este (LBW 264) in 1591, was the second book of psalm settings Daman prepared, an earlier book having been published in 1579 (see LBW 309). The melody seems to be based on one by Christopher Tye in his *Actes of the Apostles,* 1533, Chapter III:

Daman's melody originally appeared as given below.

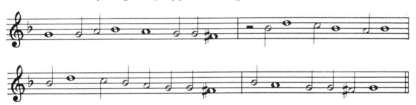

Born about 1500, Tye holds an important place in English church music. As a boy and a young man he was a singer at King's College, Cambridge, where he was a lay clerk in 1537. His education included a Bachelor of Music in 1537 and a Doctor of Music in 1545 from Cambridge; and in 1548 Oxford honored him with a second Doctor of Music degree. From 1541 to 1561 (although possibly not continuously) he was master of the choristers at Ely Cathedral. He took holy orders in the Reformed Church in 1560, and ministered at Doddington-cum-Marsh, Newton-cum-Capella, and Wilbraham Parva. During his later days he was organist to Queen Elizabeth's Chapel. He died at Doddington on the Isle of Ely in March of 1573.

Tye's church music forms the bridge between pre-Reformation and post-Reformation times, and had considerable influence on Elizabethan and Edwardian composers. His pre-Reformation compositions had Latin texts, but like William Byrd and Thomas Tallis (LBW 278), he also used Latin texts from time to time during the reign of Elizabeth. Some twenty Latin motets and four masses survive, including a mass based on the English folksong, "The Western Wynde." It is possible that Tye was also music master to Prince Edward VI, for in his play, "When You See Me You Know Me" (1605), William Rowley has Edward say to Tye:

Doctor, I thank you and commend your cunning.
I oft have heard my Father merrily speake
In your hye praise and thus his Highnesse sayth,
England one God, one truth, one Doctor hath
For Musicks Art and that is Doctor Tye.

William Daman (also Damon), born about 1540, apparently in Liège, Belgium, went to England with Thomas Sackville, Lord Buckhurst, in 1562. After 1579 he was one of Queen Elizabeth's musicians. He was married and was the father of five children. He died at his home in Broad Street Ward, St. Peter-le-Poore parish, in London, late in 1591. His *Booke of Musicke,* published in 1591 after his death, was one of the most famous and influential psalters published for the next fifty years. The collection was published as a pair of books. One had the melodic interest in the tenor, as was the custom of the day; the second was exceptional in placing the melody in the soprano. In addition to his psalm tunes he composed some motets, an anthem, and some instrumental music.

115 JESUS, I WILL PONDER NOW *(Jesu, deine Passion)*
Tune: Jesu Kreuz, Leiden und Pein

Sigismund von Birken, son of the pastor of Wildstein, near Eger in Bohemia, was born April 25 or May 5, 1626. Three years later his father, along with the other Evangelical pastors, was forced to flee from Bohemia, and the family took up residence in Nürnberg. Sigismund attended the Egidien *Gymnasium* at Nürnberg, and then went to the University of Jena to study law and theology. In 1645 he returned to Nürnberg, having completed neither course, and became tutor at Wolfenbüttel to the princes of Brunswick-Lüneburg for a year. The same year, on account of his poetical gifts, he was admitted to the Pegnitz Shepherd and Flower Order and crowned as a poet. Following a three-year tour (during which he was admitted by Philipp von Zezen as a member of the German Society or Patrotic Union) he returned to Nürnberg as a private tutor. Ennobled by the Emperor Ferdinand III for his poetic gifts in 1654, he became a member of the Fruitbearing Society in 1658, and on the death of Harsdörffer in 1662, became Chief Shepherd of the Pegnitz Order, to which he imparted a distinctly religious cast. Various sources give his death date as June 12, or July, 1681.

This hymn was first published in Nürnberg in the *Heilige Karwochen,* 1653. The translation by August Crull (LBW 24) was included in the *Evangelical Lutheran Hymn-Book,* Baltimore, 1889.

JESU KREUZ, LEIDEN UND PEIN was the setting for that hymn by Petrus Herbert in Melchior Vulpius' *Ein schön geistlich Gesangbuch,* Jena, 1609 (Zahn* #6288a).

Vulpius, composer of some of the finest melodies of the Lutheran church, was born about 1560 at Wasungen, Henneberg, in Thuringia. Appointed cantor at Weimar in 1602, he remained in that position until his death in August of 1615. In addition to his *Gesangbuch* of 1609, he published *Cantiones sacrae* in 1602 and *Kirchengesänge und geistliche Lieder Dr. Luthers* in 1604. The *Cantional,* published in 1646, some thirty years after his death, contained tunes which had not been published before. His works also include a setting of the Passion according to St. Matthew, 1612–1614.

Tune: Herzlich tut mich verlangen

Richard C. Trench, in his *Sacred Latin Poetry* (London: MacMillan and Co., 1864, p. 136), spoke of Bernard of Clairvaux as "the stayer of popular commotions, the queller of heresies, the umpire between princes and kings, the counsellor of popes, the founder, for so he may be esteemed of an important religious Order, the author of a crusade." Martin Luther (LBW 48) held Bernard in highest esteem.

Bernard was born in what is now France—at Fontaines, near Dijon—in 1091. His father, Tecelin or Tesselin, who lost his life in the First Crusade, was a knight, a friend and vassal of the Duke of Burgundy. Bernard's mother also died during his youth. Following a university education he entered a Cistercian monastery at Citeaux. Writers unanimously ascribe great persuasive powers to him. From the day he entered the monastery, taking several of his friends and family members with him, he never ceased to use that power. Shortly after entering Citeaux, Bernard headed twelve monks in the establishment of a new monastery at Clairvaux in the Wormwood Valley of France. From there he made his tremendous influence felt until his death. His intense devotion and his strength of character led many to seek his council, including high church and state officials. When the College of Cardinals was divided on the election of a pope, some choosing Innocent II and others, Anacletus II, Bernard's judgment was sought. Choosing Innocent II, Bernard secured the support of King Henry I of England and Lothar, the German emperor, in his decision. Bernard also had influence in the filling of other church posts, and one of his monks of Clairvaux later became Pope Eugene III. A true mystic, whose personal love of Jesus and devotion to His Passion were based on a direct experience of Christ's love, Bernard came into sharp conflict with the rationalistic ideas of such men as Peter Abelard (LBW 337), whose condemnation Bernard personally instigated in Sens in 1140. In 1146 Bernard turned his magnetic powers to gathering forces for the ill-fated Second Crusade. Hordes of people answered his call, including King Louis VII of France and King Conrad III of Germany, but only about a tenth of them reached the Holy Land. Most died in Asia Minor, and those who did arrive in Palestine found their efforts sabotaged by local lords who feared the newcomers might take over. Bernard was blamed. The apology he wrote is among his works still extant today. He died shortly thereafter, in 1153.

The five hymns in the LBW ascribed to Bernard of Clairvaux have been drawn from two larger poems. "Wide open are your hands" (LBW 489) and "O sacred head, now wounded" are two portions of a poem beginning "Salve mundi salutare" which has seven sections in all, each addressed to a member of Christ's body on the Cross: the feet, the knees, the hands, the side, the breast, the heart, and the head. Authorship of the verses has not been established with any certainty. Some writers attribute them to Arnulf von Loewenn, but there is definitely a strong tradition, dating back as far as 1450, in favor of Bernard of Clairvaux. A German version of the entire hymn was prepared by Paul Gerhardt (LBW 23), and the seventh section, "O Haupt voll Blut und wunden," was included in Johann Crüger's (LBW 23) *Praxis Pietatis Melica,* 1656.

Except for the first half of stanza 4, which is taken with alterations from *The Lutheran Hymnal,* 1941, the English text is by James Waddell Alexander. His translation was included in *The Christian Lyre,* 1830, a hymnal prepared by a Congregational minister, Joshua Leavitt (LBW 243).

Of Scottish ancestry, Alexander was born in Hopewell, Virginia, on March 13, 1804. He graduated from the College of New Jersey (now Princeton University) in 1820, and from Princeton Theological Seminary seven years later. After serving as pastor in Charlotte County, Virginia, and at First Presbyterian Church, Trenton, New Jersey, he was professor of belles-lettres and rhetoric at New Jersey College from 1833 to 1844. After serving five years as pastor of Duane Street Presbyterian Church in New York City, he went to Princeton Seminary as professor of ecclesiastical history and church government. From 1851 he ministered to Fifth Avenue Presbyterian Church, New York. He died July 31, 1859, at Sweet Springs, Virginia.

Alexander wrote many articles for *The Princeton Quarterly Review,* and more than thirty books for the American Sunday School Union alone. His translations, including "O sacred head," were included in *The Breaking Crucible, and other Translations,* 1861.

HERZLICH TUT MICH VERLANGEN (also "Passion Chorale") first appeared in Hans Leo Hassler's *Lustgarten neuer teutscher Gesäng, Balletti, Galliarden und Intraden,* 1601, as a setting for the secular text, "Mein Gmüt ist mir verwirret, das macht ein Jungfrau zart." In 1613, the tune was attached to Christoph Knoll's funeral hymn, "Herzlich thut mich verlangen"; in 1625 it appeared with Johann Hermann Schein's (LBW 123) "Ach Herr, mich armen Sünder"; and finally, in Johann Crüger's *Praxis Pietatis Melica,* 1656, it was used with the present text.

Hassler, son of a Nürnberg organist, was born October 25, 1564. In 1584 he went to Venice where he studied with Andrea Gabrielli and became a friend and colleague of Giovanni Gabrielli. The following year he became organist to Octavian II of the house of Fuggers in Augsburg. Octavian died in 1600 and Hassler went to Prague as court organist to Emperor Rudolph II. While in Prague he also manufactured and installed musical clocks. In 1601 he went to Nürnberg where he was organist to the Frauenkirche and chief *Kapellmeister* of the town. His reputation as a first-rate organist and composer spread rapidly. He was married in 1604 and went to live in Ulm. Four years later he accepted a position as organist to Christian II, Elector of Saxony, at Dresden. During the last years of his life he suffered from tuberculosis and he died June 8, 1612, while accompanying the Elector to the imperial election at Frankfurt.

Hassler's works include a large number of secular and sacred choral works, the latter including his *Psalmen und christliche Gesäng,* 1607, containing fifty-two elaborate motet-form settings of chorale melodies, and his *Kirchengesänge, Psalmen und geistliche Lieder,* 1608, with seventy simpler settings of chorale melodies. He also composed some organ works.

J. S. Bach (LBW 219) used this melody extensively in his works, including it five times in the *St. Matthew Passion,* twice in the *Christmas Oratorio,* and using it in five cantatas (24, 135, 153, 159, and 161). An organ setting by Bach can be found among his Miscellaneous Preludes. Johannes Brahms also included two settings for organ among his eleven chorale preludes.

Tune: Herzlich tut mich verlangen

See LBW 116 for the background of this hymn and the tune, which is given there in its original rhythmic form. The harmonization found here is a combination of that given for tune I, and a simplification of the Bach harmonization at tune II, in the *Service Book and Hymnal,* 1958 (#88).

118   SING, MY TONGUE *(Pange, lingua, gloriosi proelium)*

Tune: Fortunatus New

Born about 530 at Ceneda, near Treviso in northern Italy, Venantius Honorius Clemantianus Fortunatus spent most of his adult life in Gaul. He was converted to Christianity at an early age. He also began to write poetry when he was young, and later trained in oratory and poetry at Milan and Ravenna. According to legend Fortunatus developed a severe eye disease and was nearly blind, but recovered his sight after he had anointed his eyes with oil from a lamp burning before the altar of St. Martin of Tours in a church in Ravenna. Grateful for his restored sight, he did in fact set out on a pilgrimage to the shrine of St. Martin at Tours in 565. In Gaul he met Queen Rhadegunda who influenced him to take holy orders, and he entered the Abbey of St. Croix at Poitiers. (The Queen had been taken by the Frankish king Clothaire II as his wife, after he had captured her people in Thuringia. She had later separated herself from him and retired to the convent of St. Croix.) In 599 he became bishop of Poitiers, and remained in that post until his death in 609.

Fortunatus' numerous poetic writings range from insignificant rhymes repaying hosts for dinner, to some of the finest hymns of Christendom. A volume entitled *Hymns for all the Festivals of the Christian Year* is, unfortunately, lost. The present hymn consisted originally of ten stanzas (and in some manuscripts a doxology is added). As a Latin office hymn it was usually divided into two groups of five stanzas with the doxology following each group. Thus divided it was used at Matins (after midnight) and Lauds (sunrise) daily from Passion Sunday until Maundy Thursday.

John Mason Neale's (LBW 34) translation was included in his *Medieval Hymns,* 1851. The text has been considerably altered. Another translation of the hymn is given at LBW 155.

FORTUNATUS NEW appeared in *Spirit,* March, 1967, and two years later was included in the *Worship Supplement* to *The Lutheran Hymnal.*

The composer, Carl Flentge Schalk, was born September 26, 1929, in Des Plaines, Illinois. He received a Bachelor of Science degree from Concordia Teachers College, River Forest, Illinois, in 1952 and a Master of Music degree from Eastman School of Music, Rochester, New York, in 1957. In addition he holds a Master of Arts degree from Concordia Theological Seminary, St. Louis, Missouri. While a student at Concordia College, he served also as an instructor there for one year. After graduation he was teacher and director of music at Zion Lutheran Church, Wausau, Wisconsin, for six years, and from 1958 to 1965, was director of music for the International Lutheran Hour, St. Louis. He became assistant professor in 1965, and associate professor in 1968, at Concordia Teachers College. Married to Noel Donata Roeder, he is the father of three children.

Since 1965 Schalk has been a member of the music editorial advisory committee of Concordia Publishing House, and since 1966 has edited *Church Music.* From 1967 to 1978 he served on the hymn music committee of the Inter-Lutheran Commission on Worship. He is a member of The American Musicological Society, The Hymn Society of America, The Lutheran Society for Worship, Music and the Arts (president since 1976), and the Lutheran Education Association. He has been lecturer and leader at numerous church music workshops. Among his publications are *Planning the Wedding Service* (1963) and *The Roots of Hymnody in The Lutheran Church—Missouri Synod* (1965). He was editor of *Key Words in Church Music* and co-editor with Carl Halter of the *Handbook of Church Music,* both published in 1978. His articles have appeared in *Lutheran Education, Concordia Theological Monthly, Response, The Christian Century,* and *Church Music.* In addition to his hymn tunes, his musical publications include numerous collections and individual pieces for choirs, music for mixed choir with instruments, organ preludes, and instrumental works.

119 NATURE WITH OPEN VOLUME STANDS

Tune: Angelus

See LBW 39 for Isaac Watts. This hymn was included in his *Hymns and Spiritual Songs,* 1707.

ANGELUS. Georg Joseph was a musician in the employ of the Prince-Bishop of Breslau during the last half of the seventeenth century. Between 1657 and 1668, together with the poet, Johann Scheffler (LBW 455), he published five volumes of hymns. The melody by Joseph on which this tune is based is found in *Heilge Seelen-Lust oder Geistliche Hirten-Lieder,* Breslau, 1657. There, set to the text, "Du meiner Seelen güldne Ziehr," the melody appeared as given below.

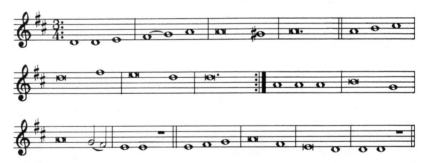

Its present form is from *Cantica Spiritualia,* Munich, 1847, with further slight rhythmic changes from the 1875 Revised Edition of *Hymns Ancient and Modern.*

120 OF THE GLORIOUS BODY TELLING
(Pange, lingua, gloriosi corporis)
Tune: Pange lingua

Thomas Aquinas, son of Landulph, Count of Aquino and a nephew of Emperor Frederick I, and of Theodora, a wealthy Neapolitan lady, was born in 1227, and sent at the age of five to be educated at the Benedictine monastery at Monte Cassino. Seven years later he was sent to the University of Naples, where he came to know some of the Fathers of the Dominican Order and decided to become a member of that order. The decision displeased his mother greatly, and she caused him to be apprehended on his way to Paris and held him a prisoner for over two years, until the Pope at last influenced Emperor Frederick to order his release. Thomas studied with Albertus Magnus, first at Cologne, then at Paris. In 1248 he was appointed second professor to a new Dominican school established at Cologne. He received a doctor's degree from the University of Paris in 1257, and thereafter had a series of important appointments. He was a member of Louis IX's Council of State, a member of the commission appointed to establish uniformity in the Dominican schools, and an aid to Urban IV in his project for uniting the Eastern and Western churches. He held a chair of theology in the Dominican College of Rome, and was sent as a "definitor" of the Roman Province first to London and then to Paris. Other positions he refused—offers of the patriarchate of Jerusalem, a cardinal's hat, and the archbishopric of Naples. In 1272 he became a lecturer at the University of Naples. Two years later he was summoned to the Second Council of Lyons on the differences of the Greek and Latin Churches. On the way, however, he became ill, and died at the Benedictine Abbey of Bossa Nuova, on March 7, 1274.

Thomas wrote voluminously. His principal work, the *Summa Theologiae,* carried such authority that it was placed alongside the Scriptures and papal decrees at the Council of Trent. In 1263 he was commissioned by Pope Urban IV to compose the special Mass and Offices for the Feast of Corpus Christi (the Thursday following Trinity Sunday in the Roman calendar). He also wrote several hymns for these services, two of which are included in the LBW—the present hymn, and "Adoro te devote" (LBW 199). The opening line and the meter of this Latin hymn are based on Fortunatus' hymn given at LBW 118.

The English text, based on translations from John Mason Neale's (LBW 34) *Medieval Hymns,* 1851, and Edward Caswall's (LBW 37) *Lyra Catholica,* 1849, is taken, with a few alterations in stanzas 2 and 4, from *The English Hymnal,* 1906.

PANGE LINGUA, the plainsong melody, Mode III, proper to "Pange lingua gloriosi proelium certaminis" (LBW 118), exists with many slight variations from one locality to another. The harmonization is by Carl Schalk (LBW 118).

121   RIDE ON, RIDE ON IN MAJESTY!

Tune: The King's Majesty

Of this hymn, Osborne* (#449) writes, "Objective, robust, confident and stirring, it possesses that peculiar combination of tragedy and victory which draws the singer into the very centre of the drama." "Ride on, ride on in majesty!" was one of thirteen hymns contributed by Henry Hart Milman to his friend Bishop Heber's (LBW 84) *Hymns Written and Adapted to the Weekly Church Services of the Year,* 1827. A few slight alterations have been made in the text.

The son of a physician to George III of England, Milman was born February 10, 1791, in London. At Brasenose College, Oxford, he received first class in classics, and prizes in poetry, English essay, and Latin verse and essay. He completed a Bachelor of Arts degree in 1814, a Master of Arts in 1816, and in 1849, a Doctor of Divinity. Ordained in 1816, he was appointed vicar of St. Mary's, Reading, the following year. In 1821 he was called to be professor of poetry at Oxford, and in 1827 was also Bampton lecturer. From 1835 to 1849 he was canon of Westminster and rector of St. Margaret's, after which he was dean of St. Paul's Cathedral. He died at Sunninghill near Ascot on September 24, 1868, and was buried at St. Paul's.

The list of Milman's works is impressive. Early in his career he wrote a number of successful plays. After 1827 he turned to the writing of scholarly prose works, mostly theological, including a *History of the Jews,* 1862; *Christianity from the Birth of Christ to the Abolition of Paganism in the Roman Empire,* 1840; and a *History of Latin Christianity,* 1854-1855.

THE KING'S MAJESTY was the setting for this hymn in *The Hymnal 1940* of the Episcopal Church. The composer, Graham George, writes, "It originated as a result of a choir practice before Palm Sunday in, I suppose, 1939, during which I had been thinking '*Winchester New* is a fine tune, but it has nothing whatever to do with the tragic trumpets, as one might theatrically call them, of Palm Sunday.' At breakfast the following morning I was enjoying my toast and marmalade when the first two lines of this tune sang themselves unbidden into my mind. This seemed too good to miss, so I went to my study, allowed the half-tune to complete itself—which it did with very little trouble—and there it was." (Osborne,* #449)

Graham George was born April 11, 1912, in Norwich, England, and emigrated in 1928 to Canada. During his undergraduate study he was a student of Alfred Whitehead. He graduated from the University of Toronto with a Bachelor of Music degree in 1936, and a Doctor of Music degree three years later. Further advanced studies included composition with Paul Hindemith at Yale University (1952–1953), orchestral conducting with Willem van Otterloo in Holland in 1956, and electronic music under François Bayle in Paris (1966 and 1967), as well as formal studies in philosophy from 1955 to 1963. After a year as director of music at West Hill High School, Montreal, George entered the Canadian Army and served overseas from 1941 to 1945. On his return, he taught briefly in the Montreal public schools before going to Queen's University in Kingston, Ontario, where he is professor of music and resident musician. As such he has prepared and conducted annual performances of operas, and symphonic and choral works from 1946 to 1972. He has served as organist of Mount Royal United, Montreal (1932–1934); Church of the Ascension, Montreal (1936–1937); St. Peter's, Sherbrooke (1937–1940); St. Matthew's, Montreal (1940–1941); St. James, Kingston (1946–1947); Sydenham Street, Kingston (1949–1954); St. Paul's, Kingston (1956–1959); Grace Church, Gananoque (1962–1966); and since 1968, Edith Rankin Memorial United Church, Collins Bay. He is married and is the father of four sons.

George is an associate of the Canadian College of Organists and of the Royal College of Organists, and a fellow of the Canadian College of Organists. He has served as president (1965–1968) of the Canadian Folk Music Society, a member of the council (1965–1968) of the College Music Society, secretary-general (1969–present) of the International Folk Music Council, and president (1972–1974) of the Royal Canadian College of

Organists. Over the course of the years he has founded and conducted the St. Francis Madrigal Singers of Sherbrooke, the Queen's Symphony Orchestra, the Kingston Choral Society, and the Kingston Symphony Orchestra. He has received numerous awards and commissions, and is the composer of an extensive list of compositions, including works for stage, orchestral works, choral works, works for chorus and orchestra, vocal solos, chamber music, part songs, organ and piano works, filmscores and radio music, and a number of hymn tunes. His *Tonality and Musical Structure* was published in 1970.

122   LOVE CONSECRATES THE HUMBLEST ACT
Tune: Twenty-fourth

Silas Bettes McManus was born in Rootstown, Portage County, Ohio, on September 17, 1845. His grandfather Bettes had been a captain in the Revolutionary War; his grandmother Bettes was a French woman who knew General LaFayette. Silas moved with his parents in 1863 to Marsh Brook Farm near Lima (Howe), Indiana, where he lived for the rest of his life. He was married in 1880 to Mary Hillegass of Huntertown, Indiana. He graduated from the Fort Wayne medical college and had one year of post-graduate study at the University of Michigan, but never practiced medicine. Instead he became an author, and wrote for *Puck, Boston Transcript, Detroit Free Press, New York Independent, Burlington Hawk Eye, Ram's Horn,* and others. Throughout his life he was a devout member of the Methodist Episcopalian Church. From 1893 to 1895 he was state senator, a position he is said to have held with honor and with fidelity to the interests of his constituency. He was most well-known as a poet who knew and lived the homespun life of his area and painted it with warmth. His *Rural Rhymes* was published in 1898. He died unexpectedly at Marsh Brook on April 15, 1917.

This hymn was first published in the *Church and Sunday School Hymnal* of the Mennonite Church, Elkhart, Indiana, 1902, and is given here with some alteration.

TWENTY-FOURTH (also called "Primrose") was included in two collections published in 1813—John Wyeth's (LBW 33) *Repository of Sacred Music, Part Second,* Harrisburg, Pennsylvania, and Robert Patterson's *Church Music,* Cincinnati. Since the registry of the Patterson collection with the district of Pennsylvania preceeded Wyeth's by seven months, it must, unless an earlier source is found, be considered the first published appearance of the tune. In Wyeth's collection it was the setting for Isaac Watts's (LBW 39) "Salvation! Oh, the joyful sound." In the index of the *Repository,* the tune is credited to "Chapin," a name which is found in several southern shape-note hymnals. There were no fewer than seven Chapins active in church music during the first quarter of the nineteenth century, two of whom have been credited with this tune: the brothers Amzi and Lucius Chapin. In his article in the Fall, 1960, issue of the *Journal of Research in Music Education,* Charles Hamm attributes the tune to Lucius.

Born in 1760 in Springfield, Massachusetts, Lucius Chapin was a fifth-generation descendant of deacon Samuel Chapin who came from England in 1636. His father was a deacon in the church who often led the singing. In 1775 he enlisted as a fifer in the Continental army in Boston. He re-enlisted the following year and served at Ticonderoga. Then for three more years as a volunteer he fought against General Burgoyne and at the battle of Stillwater, and spent the historic winter of 1777–1778 with Washington at Valley Forge, after which he fought in the battle of Monmouth. After his discharge he set himself up as a singing master and held classes in Vermont, New Hampshire, Massachusetts, and Connecticut. In 1787 he ventured into the new territory of the Shenandoah Valley in Virginia, and after a trip north in 1791 to marry Susan Rousseau of Staten Island, he returned to Virginia, teaching in Rockbridge, Augusta, and Rockingham counties. A staunch Presbyterian, Lucius considered himself a missionary of the causes of music and religion, especially after 1792, when on his way back to Virginia from New England his ship had nearly gone down in a storm. In 1794 he went into Kentucky, settling in Vernon in Flemming County. There he remained for the next forty years, ranging as far west as Greensburg, and as far north as Cincinnati, Bethel, West Union, and into eastern Indiana. For a time his brother, Amzi, joined him in Virginia and Kentucky, but returned in 1798 to New England. It seems possible that Ananias Davisson (LBW 220), who compiled the *Kentucky Harmony,* 1816, received his basic music education from one or both of the Chapin brothers. At least as early as 1800, Lucius also developed a system of subordinate schools, where his more talented students, under his supervision, held singing schools of their own. Eventually Lucius' success attracted other singing teachers to the area, and as he grew older the numbers in his classes decreased. In addition, he suffered constantly from the frostbite he had received at Valley Forge. In 1835 he retired from teaching and moved to Hamilton County, Ohio, where he remained until his death the day before Christmas in 1842.

This tune is closely related to "New Britain" (LBW 448), and is given here with a harmonization by Robert Leaf (LBW 184).

123 AH, HOLY JESUS *(Herzliebster Jesu)*
Tune: Herzliebster Jesu

Based on a Latin meditation by Jean de Fécamp (d. 1078) (the seventh in a group of *Meditationes* formerly attributed to St. Augustine of Hippo, but actually written by several Latin writers), this German hymn was included in Johann Heermann's *Devoti Musica Cordis, Hauss-und Hertz-Musica,* published in Breslau in 1630.

Heermann was born October 11, 1585, at Raudten near Wohlau, in Silesia. The son of a poor furrier, he was the only surviving child of five born to his parents. He himself was severely ill during his childhood, and his mother vowed that if he survived, she would somehow prepare him for the ministry. After studying at Fraustadt, Breslau, and Brieg, he entered the University of Strassburg in 1609, but was forced by eye trouble to discontinue after a year and return to Raudten. Through the recommendations of Baron Wenzel, he was appointed diaconus of Köben, a small town near his home, and in 1611 was promoted to the pastorate. There for a half-dozen years he was free from trouble and happy in his work, his marriage, his friendships, and his literary pursuits. In 1616, however, Köben was devastated by fire. In the following year his wife died, and in 1618 the Thirty Years' War broke out. Silesia, belonging to Roman Catholic Austria, was the scene of extensive fighting and terrorism, and Köben itself was plundered four times. Several times during these troubled years Heermann lost all his movable possessions. In

1631 the town was struck by the pestilence. Afflicted with throat trouble since 1623, Heermann was compelled to cease preaching in 1634. He retired to Lissa in Posen in 1638 and died there on February 17, 1647.

In the midst of his many trials Heermann wrote a great number of fine hymns. Regarded by some as second only to Paul Gerhardt (LBW 23), Heermann marks the transition from the objective hymns of the Reformation to the more subjective hymns of the following period.

Robert Bridges' translation was included in *The Yattendon Hymnal,* a collection of one hundred hymns published in four parts from 1895 to 1899. Although never intended for church use itself, this important collection served as a valuable source for later compilers of hymnals.

Robert Seymour Bridges was born October 23, 1844, at Walmer, Kent, in England, of a distinguished and wealthy family. After studying at Corpus Christi College, Cambridge, Bridges spent two years traveling abroad and, on his return home, made his plans for life. He would study medicine and retire from that profession at age forty to devote the rest of his life to poetry. Accordingly, he studied for five years at St. Bartholomew's Hospital, and then worked as a physician in several London hospitals. Lung disease forced him to retire in 1881, a few years short of his intended retirement date. In 1884 he married Mary Monica Waterhouse, daughter of an architect, and they lived for thirty years in Yattendon, during which time he edited *The Yattendon Hymnal* in collaboration with Harry Ellis Wooldridge. In 1907 he built Chilswell House, Boar's Hill, in Oxford, and there he lived with his family until his death on April 21, 1930.

Bridges' writing of poetry commenced long before his retirement from medicine and he had published several collections by that time. In 1913 he was appointed Poet Laureate, and in 1929, on the publication of his *The Testament of Beauty,* he received the Order of Merit. In 1924 he and his wife were guests of the University of Michigan for three months and he later received an honorary doctorate from that institution as well as from Oxford, St. Andrews, and Harvard.

HERZLIEBSTER JESU appeared with its harmonization in Johann Crüger's (LBW 23) *Newes vollkömliches Gesangbuch Augsburgischer Confession,* published in Berlin in 1640 (Zahn* #983). Forerunners of the tune seem to have been the setting of Psalm 23, "Mon Dieu me paist," included in the Genevan Psalter, *c.* 1543, and which came into Lutheran use in 1613 (Zahn* #3199),

and the tune "Gelieben Freund" from Johann Hermann Schein's *Cantional* of 1627 (Zahn* #981):

Schein, distinguished German musician, and contemporary of Heinrich Schütz (LBW 180) and Samuel Scheidt, was the son of a Lutheran pastor. Born at Grünhayn in Saxony on January 20, 1586, Johann moved in 1593 with his mother to Dresden after his father's death. There, from 1599 to 1603, he was a chorister in the court chapel of the Elector of Saxony and in 1603 he entered the Schulpforta School. From 1607 to 1611 he studied theology and philosophy at the University of Leipzig and for a while afterwards was a private tutor. In 1613 he became director of music at the court of Duke Johann Ernst of Saxe-Weimar, and two years later became one of J. S. Bach's most illustrious predecessors at St. Thomas' Church in Leipzig, where he devoted the rest of his life to the elevation and improvement of church music. There he died on November 19, 1630.

Schein's works, in Arthur Prüfer's edition (1902–1919), filled eight volumes. His best-known work is his *Cantional oder Gesangbuch Augspurgischer Confession.* First published in 1627, it contained 286 hymns and 206 tunes, of which fifty-seven were his own. A second edition in 1645 contained an additional twenty-two tunes of his composition. His thirty *Geistlicher Concerten* were based mostly on chorale tunes.

124   THE ROYAL BANNERS FORWARD GO *(Vexilla Regis prodeunt)*
Tune: Herr Jesu Christ, wahr Mensch und Gott

See LBW 118 for Fortunatus. This hymn, which reflects mystery and awe at Christ's death, also sounds the note of victory over that death. Written especially for the occasion, the hymn was first sung in procession on November 19, 568, when the relics of the Cross procured by Queen Rhadegunda from Emperor Justin II were brought to her new monastery at Poitiers. Fortunatus' text of eight stanzas is found in an eighth-century manuscript from St. Petersburg. In the eleventh century, two anonymous additional stanzas are found, including our stanza 6. The hymn was used as a Vesper (sunset) hymn during Passion Week.

Stanzas 1–3 and 6 of this English version are based on a translation by John Mason Neale (LBW 34) in his *Medieval Hymns,* 1851; stanzas 4 and 5 are from a text prepared by the hymnal commission for *The Hymnal 1940* of the Episcopal Church.

HERR JESU CHRIST, WAHR MENSCH UND GOTT. Johann Eccard was born at Mühlhausen in Thuringia in 1553. From 1567 to 1571 he was a pupil of David Köler in the court chapel school at Weimar, after which he went to Munich to study with Orlando di Lasso. By 1574 he had returned to Mühlhausen where in 1578 he became a musician in the household of Jacob Fugger. He entered the service of Margrave Georg Friedrich of Brandenburg at Königsberg in 1581, and five years later was called to Berlin as music director to the Elector of Bradenburg. There he died in the fall of 1611.

Eccard made an outstanding contribution to church music in the field of chorale melodies. Most important among his numerous publications was *Der Erste Theil Geistliche Lieder,* Königsberg, 1597, which was undertaken at the request of Margrave Georg Friedrich. Containing settings of well-known chorales, as well as tunes of Eccard's own composition, it was an attempt to produce a collection with artistic and musical, as well as religious worth.

This tune was included in the 1597 collection as a setting for Paul Eber's (LBW 303) "Herr Jesu Christ, wahr Mensch und Gott." Soon after its publication in Eccard's collection, it appeared with sundry variations in other sources, a fact which has led some to believe that the tune was "discovered" rather than written by Eccard. The harmonization was prepared by Paul Bunjes (LBW 38) for the *Worship Supplement,* 1969, to *The Lutheran Hymnal.*

125   THE ROYAL BANNERS FORWARD GO *(Vexilla Regis prodeunt)*
Tune: Vexilla Regis

See LBW 124 for a discussion of this hymn.

VEXILLA REGIS, given here in the Sarum (Salisbury, England) form, is the melody traditionally associated with this hymn, and is universally found with it in the Latin cycle (neither hymn nor tune appears in the Ambrosian or Mozarabic uses). Authorities believe the tune to be as old as the text.

The harmonization was prepared by Healey Willan for *The Hymn Book,* 1971, of the Anglican Church and the United Church of Canada.

Willan, a distinguished Canadian composer and organist, was born October 12, 1880, at Balham, in Surrey, England. Having begun his musical training in the resident choir school of St. Saviour's, Eastbourne, he later went on to advanced studies in organ and piano, and served as organist and choirmaster in Christ's Church, Wanstead, Essex, and St. John the Baptist, Kensington. In 1913 he came to Toronto as head of the theory department of Toronto University, and organist and choirmaster of St. Paul's Church. From 1914 to 1928 he also held the position of lecturer and examiner of the University of Toronto. Vice-principal of the Toronto Conservatory from 1920 to 1936, he became a professor of the faculty of music in 1937. He resigned in 1950, retaining the position of university organist for two more years. From 1921 until his death on February 16, 1968, he also served as precentor of the church of St. Mary Magdalene.

Willan's tenure at St. Mary Magdalene witnessed a steady flow of creativity. Deeply interested in the ancient liturgical modes, he was a renowned authority on plainsong and the music of the Eastern Church. A gifted improviser, he was also known among his students for his unwavering insistence upon liturgical fitness and beauty of church music, for his mastery of compositional technique, and for a fine sense of wit and humor. Among his sacred works are his adaptation of the Gradual and Antiphonale into English, fourteen settings of the Missa Brevis, eleven liturgical motets, and a number of hymn tunes. A fellow of the Royal College of Organists, he also composed numerous chorale preludes, preludes and fugues, and other works for organ. Musical director of the Hart House Players Club from 1919 to 1925, he wrote incidental music for fourteen classical plays. Among his other works are two symphonies, three operas, a piano concerto, cantatas, chamber music, and songs. Five Canadian universities honored him with degrees, as did Lambeth, in England, in 1956. He was the only composer outside Great Britain to be invited to write music for the coronation of Queen Elizabeth II.

126 WHERE CHARITY AND LOVE PREVAIL *(Ubi caritas et amor)*
Tune: Twenty-fourth

This Latin antiphon of unknown authorship is believed to date from the Carolingian era, or possibly earlier. In the pre-Vatican II rite it is the last and indispensable song to be sung during the washing of feet in the Maundy Thursday communion service. Under the pseudonym "J. Clifford Evers," Omer Westendorf's (LBW 221) translation was included in the *People's Mass Book,* Cincinnati, 1961.

For TWENTY-FOURTH see LBW 122.

127 IT HAPPENED ON THAT FATEFUL NIGHT
Tune: Bourbon

See LBW 39 for Isaac Watts. This hymn was included in his *Hymns and Spiritual Songs,* 1709. Originally beginning "'Twas on that dark and doleful night," the text has been considerably altered for the LBW.

BOURBON. This pentatonic melody first appeared with Watts's text in *Columbian Harmony,* compiled by William Moore (LBW 463) in Wilson County, Tennessee, and published in Cincinnati in 1825. There the tune is attributed to "Freeman Lewis." George Pullen Jackson in his *Spiritual Folk-Songs of Early America* notes that the same melody is used for "McFee's Confession," "Samuel Young," and "Come, Father build me," and that it is similar to "Lord Bateman." The tune is also related to "Consolation" (LBW 33), "Kedron" (LBW 420), and "Hiding Place" (LBW 537).

Little is known about Freeman Lewis. Born in 1780, he was a surveyor by profession and a musician by avocation. He lived in Uniontown, Pennsylvania, and in 1813 published a tune book entitled *The Beauties of Harmony* (second edition, 1816; third edition, 1818). He died in 1859.

The harmonization of the tune was prepared for the LBW by Philip Klepfer Gehring, professor of music and university organist at Valparaiso University, Valparaiso, Indiana. Born in Carlisle, Pennsylvania, on November 27, 1925, Gehring served in the United States Navy from 1943 to 1946, during which time he attended Franklin and

Marshall College for one year. He holds Bachelor of Arts and Bachelor of Music degrees (1950) from Oberlin College, Oberlin, Ohio; and Master of Music (1955) and Doctor of Philosophy (1963) degrees from Syracuse University, Syracuse, New York. He has studied organ with Arthur Poister, Fenner Douglass, and André Marchal, and composition with Herbert Elwell and Ernst Bacon. From 1950 to 1952 he was organist-choirmaster at Kimball Memorial Lutheran Church in Kannapolis, North Carolina, after which he served on the faculty of Davidson College for four years. Since 1958 he has held his present position at Valparaiso University.

Gehring was a recipient of the Selby-Huston Prize in organ and theory at Oberlin, as well as Southern Fellowships and Danforth Teacher Study grants. A second-prize winner in 1966 and first-prize winner in 1970 of the American Guild of Organists National Improvisation Contest, he was a participant by invitation at the International Organ Improvisation Competition, Haarlem, Holland, in 1971. He is charter member and former president of the Lutheran Society for Worship, Music, and the Arts, and has also been a national councillor for the American Guild of Organists and vice-president of Ecclesia Cantans, the international Lutheran church music association. His publications include organ and choral music, and articles in various music journals. With Donald Ingram, he was co-author of *The Church Organ—a Guide to its Selection,* 1974.

128   CHRIST THE LORD IS RISEN TODAY; ALLELUIA!
(Victimae Paschali, laudes)

Tune: Llanfair

For a discussion of this text, see LBW 137 where it appears with its original melody.

Jane Eliza Leeson's translation, which is found here with some alteration, was included in the Reverend Henry Formby's *Catholic Hymns,* 1851.

Leeson was born in London, England, in 1809 and spent most of her life there. During the early part of her life she was a member of the Catholic Apostolic Church, for which she produced a number of hymns, some as "prophetic utterances" improvised at services. Later she joined the Roman communion for which she wrote a number of hymns, especially hymns for children. She died at Leamington in Warwickshire, November 18, 1881.

LLANFAIR is described in Robert McCutchan's *Hymn Tune Names,* 1957, as the first eight letters of one of the longest words in any language: *Llanfairpwllgwyngyllgogerychwyrndrobwllllantysiliogogogoch* ("Church of St. Mary in the hollow of white hazel near the rapid whirlpool of the Church of St. Tysillio by the red cave"). It is the name of a Welsh village in Montgomery County where Robert Williams was born. Several persons have claimed to have written this tune, which was called "Bethel" when it first appeared in Williams' manuscript notebook, dated July 14, 1817. It was harmonized by John Roberts for J. Parry's *Peroriaeth Hyfryd,* 1837.

Robert Williams, a blind basketmaker who lived in Mynydd Ithel, Llanfechel, on the island of Anglesey in North Wales, is said to have sung well and to have been unusually gifted musically, having the ability to take down a tune perfectly after hearing it a single time. Born about 1781, he died a bachelor in 1821.

John Roberts (Ieuan Cwyllt) was born December 22, 1822, at Tanrhiwfelen near Aberystwyth. After studying music with Richard Mills, he became a school master at age sixteen. In 1852 he was chosen assistant editor of the most important Welsh paper of his day, *Amserau,* and he also later edited the *Gwladgarwr,* which had a wide circulation among the miners. He began preaching in 1856 and was ordained a Calvinistic Methodist minister three years later. After serving at Merthyr, Aberdare, he went in 1865 to Llanberis in North Wales, where he was pastor of Chapel Cock, and founded the Snowdon Temperance Union. In 1859 he founded the Welsh singing festival ("Cymanfâu Ganu") and the same year, published an important hymnal, the *Llyfr Tonau Cynulleidfaol,* which is said to have set a new standard for music in hymnals. He was editor of *Y Cerddor Cymreig,* a monthly music magazine, from 1861 to 1873; of *Telyn y Plant,* a publication for children, from 1859 to 1861; and of *Cerddor y Solffa,* from 1869 to 1874. He also prepared a translation of a collection of hymns by Dwight L. Moody and Ira Sankey in 1874. He died May 6, 1877, at Vron, near Carnarvon.

129 AWAKE, MY HEART, WITH GLADNESS
(Auf, auf, mein Herz, mit Freuden)
Tune: Auf, auf, mein Herz

See LBW 23 for Paul Gerhardt. This hymn was included in Johann Crüger's (LBW 23) *Praxis pietatis melica,* 1648.

Beginning *"Up, up, my heart with gladness,"* John Kelly's translation was given in his *Paul Gerhardt's Spiritual Songs,* London, 1867. Extensive alterations of Kelly's text are found in the *Evangelical Lutheran Hymn-Book,* 1912, with further changes being made in *The Lutheran Hymnal,* 1941, and the LBW. As found here, only the first stanza represents Kelly's work; the remaining stanzas are the work of many hands.

John Kelly was born at Newcastle-on-Tyne on October 5, 1833, and was educated at Glasgow University, 1849–1850. He studied theology at Bonn from 1852 to 1854 and, after two years as a private tutor, continued his theological studies at New College, Edinburgh (1856–1867), and at the College of the English Presbyterian Church in London, where he completed his theological curriculum in 1860. He was licensed by the Presbytery of Newcastle in 1860, and ordained and set apart for service in the India Mission of the English Presbyterian Church. Following the refusal of the medical advisor of the Foreign Mission Committee to pass him for service to India, however, Kelly accepted an invitation to undertake pioneer work at Tiverton. When he succeeded in establishing a congregation there, he served as its first pastor from 1864 to 1868. Thereafter he served at Hebburn-on-Tyne, 1868–1876, and Streatham, 1876–1880. He withdrew from the active ministry, and in 1881 became tract editor of the Religious Tract Society. In 1887 he went to reside at Croydon and became an elder of the church there. In addition to his translations of *Paul Gerhardt's Spiritual Songs,* and *Hymns from the Present Century from the German,* 1885, he published several other works. He suffered from cancer for several years and aggravated symptoms induced him, under medical advice, to go to Braemar, in Scotland, for the benefit of his health. There he died on July 19, 1890.

AUF, AUF, MEIN HERZ was written by Johann Crüger (LBW 23) for Gerhardt's text and is found together with it in *Praxis pietatis melica,* 1648.

130 CHRIST THE LORD IS RISEN TODAY!
Tune: Orientis partibus

See LBW 27 for Charles Wesley. This hymn was first published in the Wesley *Hymns and Sacred Poems,* 1739, and is given here with some alteration.

ORIENTIS PARTIBUS. In medieval France it became the custom to pay tribute to the donkey, the animal which had come to the manger in Bethlehem and later carried Mary and the Child Jesus on the flight into Egypt. The observance was first recorded at Rouen in the tenth century and continued as late as 1634 in Sens. On the Feast of the Circumcision, or another day shortly after Christmas, a woman carrying a child and seated on a donkey joined the procession of the clergy through the streets of the town and into the church. This tune, which was originally the setting for a combined medieval Latin and old French text beginning "Orientis partibus adventavis asinus" ("from the Eastern regions the donkey is now come"), is from the Office of the Circumcision written by Pierre de Corbeil.

Probably born during the last half of the twelfth century, Pierre de Corbeil went to the Academy of Paris at age ten. He was successively archdeacon of York, archdeacon of Evreux, assistant to the bishop of Lincoln, bishop of Cambrai (1199), and finally archbishop of Sens (1200). He died June 3, 1221 or 1222.

As it appears in the Sens manuscript, the tune is in mixolydian mode. (The LBW tune can be changed to mixolydian mode by reading the E's as E-flat.) The melody was adapted to its present form and brought into English hymnody in Richard Redhead's (LBW 109) *Church Hymn Tunes,* 1853. The harmonization is by Donald Busarow (LBW 30).

131 CHRIST IS RISEN! ALLELUIA!
Tune: Morgenlied

John Samuel Bewley Monsell, son of the archdeacon of Londonderry, Ireland, was born March 2, 1811, at St. Colomb's in Derry. He received a Bachelor of Arts degree from Trinity College, Dublin, in 1832, and an honorary Doctor of Laws degree in 1856. Ordained a deacon in 1834 and a priest the following year, he served successively as chaplain to Bishop Mant (LBW 176), chancellor of the diocese of Connor, and rector of Ramoan in Ireland. Going to England in 1853, he became vicar of Egham, Surrey, and finally in 1870, rector of St. Nicholas, Guildford. He died April 9, 1875, as a result of an accident which occurred when his church was being rebuilt.

Monsell published eleven volumes of poetry which included three hundred hymns. This hymn was included in his *Hymns of Love and Praise*, London, 1863, a collection dedicated to the memory of two of his children. Alterations to the text are very slight.

MORGENLIED was written for this text by Frederick C. Maker (LBW 107) and contributed to the 1881 supplement to *The Bristol Tune Book*.

132 COME, YOU FAITHFUL, RAISE THE STRAIN
(Ἄἴσωμεν πάντες λαοί)

Tune: Gaudeamus pariter

John of Damascus, whose Saracen name was Mansur, was one of the greatest of the poets of the Greek church. Born at the end of the seventh century of a good family in Damascus, he and his adopted brother, Cosmas the Melodist, were educated by a captive Italian monk, also named Cosmas. After holding an important office under the Caliph in Damascus for a number of years, John gave away all his possessions and he and his brother retired about 730 to the monastery of St. Sabas, located between Jerusalem and the Dead Sea. There he is said to have lived to a very old age. His death date is given in various sources as approximately 749, 754, or 780. In the West the day of his commemoration is March 27, and in the East, December 4.

At St. Sabas he was ordained a priest and spent his life writing his numerous works in prose and verse, including his πηγή γνώσεως ("fountain of knowledge") which contains a defense of orthodox faith. His writing embodies the theological thought of the early Greek church and was used extensively by the thirteenth-century Latin scholastics. In the field of hymnology he was a chief exponent of the new form, the canon (see pp. 6ff), and wrote a number of these for the great festivals of the church, along with other hymns. His role in liturgical music is somewhat parallel to that of Gregory I in the West (LBW 101), as he is credited with the setting down of the *Ocotechos,* a book of chants in the eight *echoi* or modes, for a cycle of eight Sundays. Legend credits him with the actual invention of the eight *echoi.*

"Come you faithful, raise the strain" is the first ode of the canon for St. Thomas' Sunday (the first Sunday after Easter). The customary reference of the first ode of a canon to the passage through the Red Sea, can be seen in the lines:

> Loosed from Pharoah's bitter yoke
> Jacob's sons and daughters,
> Led them with unmoistened foot
> Through the Red Sea waters.

The translation, which has been altered slightly, is from John Mason Neale's (LBW 34) *Hymns of the Eastern Church,* 1862.

GAUDEAMUS PARITER. Johann Horn, born in Domaschitz, Bohemia, about 1490, was ordained a priest of the Bohemian Brethren in 1518. Appointed an elder in 1529, he was consecrated a bishop four years later. In 1522 he accompanied Michael Weisse (LBW 37) to Wittenberg to discuss the views of the Brethren with Martin Luther (LBW 48). Horn's Czech hymn collection, *Písně chval božských,* published in Prague in 1541, far surpassed any contemporary songbook in size, containing 481 hymns with 300 melodies. He also prepared *Ein Gesangbuch der Brüder im Behemen und Merherrn,* Nürnberg, 1544, a revised edition of Weisse's 1531 *New Gesengbuchlen* containing thirty-two new hymns, some from his 1541 hymnal. For many years he served as pastor of the congregation at Jungbunzlau, Bohemia, where he died February 11, 1547.

Titled "Gaudeamus pariter omnes," this tune served as the setting for Horn's text, "Nun lasst uns zu dieser Frist" in his 1544 *Gesangbuch* (Zahn* #6285). The harmonization was prepared by Theodore Beck (LBW 33) for the *Worship Supplement,* 1969, to *The Lutheran Hymnal.*

133 JESUS LIVES! THE VICTORY'S WON!
(Jesus lebt, mit ihm auch ich)
Tune: Jesus, meine Zuversicht

This hymn was first published in Christian Fürchtegott Gellert's *Geistlichen Oden und Lieder,* Leipzig, 1757.

Born July 4, 1715, Gellert was the ninth of thirteen children born to the Lutheran pastor at Hainichen in the Saxon Harz near Freiberg. After studying theology at the University of Leipzig he became an assistant to his father, but was forced to give up the ministry because he could not trust his memory, and preaching sermons from manuscript was not tolerated in the Lutheran church of his day. In 1739 he became a domestic tutor to the sons of Herr von Lüttichau, and two years later returned to Leipzig to supervise the studies of one of his nephews. He completed a Master of Arts degree in 1744 and became a private tutor or lecturer in the philosophical faculty. Gellert took a personal interest in his students' well-being and conduct, and was very popular with his students, who included Johann Wolfgang von Goethe and Gotthold Ephraim Lessing. His lectures were highly regarded both for their content and for their charm of style. His spirited and humorous fables won for him universal esteem and a place among German classicists. In 1751 he was appointed assistant professor of philosophy, lecturing on moral philosophy and on poetry and rhetoric. Ten years later he was offered full professorship, but declined because he considered his health to be too poor. He died December 13, 1769.

The translation, with some alterations, is from *Sacred Hymns from the German,* 1841, prepared by Frances Elizabeth Cox. In that collection, with its second edition revised and enlarged in 1864, she published a total of fifty-six translations. Cox, who ranks highly among translators of German hymns, was born at Oxford, England, on May 10, 1812, and died at Headington, September 23, 1897.

For JESUS, MEINE ZUVERSICHT see LBW 340. The harmonization found here is from the *Neues Choralbuch,* 1970.

134 CHRIST JESUS LAY IN DEATH'S STRONG BANDS
(Christ lag in Todesbanden)
Tune: Christ lag in Todesbanden

See LBW 48 for Martin Luther. Based on the sequence "Victimae Paschali laudes" (LBW 137), this hymn was first included in the Erfurt

Enchiridia, 1524. The Easter Epistle (old pericopes), 1 Corinthians 5:6–8, is beautifully reflected in stanza 5.

Richard Massie's translation, beginning "Christ *lay awhile* in Death's strong bands," was included in his *Martin Luther's Spiritual Songs,* 1854, and is given here with only slight alteration.

A descendant of an ancient Cheshire family, Massie was born June 18, 1800, at Chester, the first of twenty-two children born to the rector of St. Bride's. He was married in 1834 to Mary Ann Hughes of Chester, but she died seven years later. A man of considerable wealth with two estates, Massie devoted himself to literature and published, in addition to *Luther's Spiritual Songs,* his *Lyra Domestica,* 1860 and 1864, which contained translations from German hymns, especially those of Karl Spitta (LBW 399). Massie had a keen interest in gardening and is said to have cultivated a fine rock garden, a rare thing in his day. He died at Pulford Hall, Coddington, Cheshire (one of his estates), on March 11, 1887.

CHRIST LAG IN TODESBANDEN. Two versions of this tune, which is a reconstruction of "Christ ist erstanden" (LBW 136), appeared in 1524—one in the Erfurt *Enchiridia,* and another in Johann Walther's (LBW 350) *Geystliche gesangk Buchleyn.* The latter is found here. Charles Sanford Terry (*Bach's Chorales,* III, Cambridge, 1929) believes that the revision was the work of Walther himself.

J. S. Bach (LBW 219) included two settings in his *Choralgesänge,* and used the melody in Cantata 4, where all seven movements are based on the tune, and in Cantata 158. Organ settings are included in his Miscellaneous Preludes and in the *Orgelbüchlein.*

135   THE STRIFE IS O'ER, THE BATTLE DONE
(Finita jam sunt praelia)

Tune: Victory

John Mason Neale (LBW 34), in the preface to his *Medieval Hymns,* 1851, considered this hymn to be from the twelfth century. The earliest date to which it has been traced, however, is 1695, when it appeared in a Jesuit Collection, *Symphonia Sirenum Selectarum, ex quatuor vocibus composita, Ad commodiorem usum Studiosae Juventutis,* published in Cologne.

Francis Pott translated the hymn about 1859 and it was included in his *Hymns Fitted to the Order of Common Prayer,* 1861.

Pott, born at Southward, England, on December 29, 1832, attended Brasenose College, Oxford, receiving a Bachelor of Arts degree in 1854 and a Master of Arts degree in 1857. He took holy orders in 1856 and ministered to Bishopsworth, Gloucestershire, 1856–58; Ardingly, Berkshire, 1858–61; Ticehurst, 1861–66; and Northhill, Bedfordshire, 1866–91. Deafness forced him to retire in 1891, and he spent his remaining days at Speldhurst, Kent, where he died October 26, 1909. In addition to publishing his hymnal mentioned above, he was a member of the committee for the Original Edition of *Hymns Ancient and Modern,* 1861, and also published *The Free Rhythm Psalter,* 1898, a guide to improved chanting.

VICTORY. Giovanni Pierluigi, born in Palestrina near Rome in 1525 or 1526, went to Rome in 1534 where he served as a chorister and received his music education at the basilica of Santa Maria Maggiore. In 1544 he returned to his native town, taking a position as organist and choirmaster of the cathedral there. Seven years later his bishop became Pope Julius II, and appointed Palestrina choirmaster of the Cappella Guilia at St. Peter's, Rome. Palestrina remained in Rome for the rest of his life, twice declining positions which would remove him from that city. After serving briefly as a singer in the Papal chapel (he was dismissed in 1555 because he was married), he became choirmaster at St. John Lateran, and in 1561, choirmaster at Santa Maria Maggiore where he remained for about seven years. From 1565 to 1571 he taught at the new Jesuit Seminary in Rome, and from 1571 until the end of his life he served again as choirmaster of the Cappella Guilia at St. Peter's. In 1580, having lost his wife, two sons, and two brothers, Palestrina for a while contemplated entering the priesthood, but instead married a wealthy widow of a furrier and leather merchant. He died February 2, 1594.

While it is only legend that Palestrina, with his *Mass of Pope Marcellus,* rescued polyphonic music from banishment in favor of plainsong, he did write much very fine church music, including 102 masses, 400 motets and other liturgical works, and fifty-six sacred Italian madrigals. Published by Breithopf & Härtel, 1862–1903, his works fill thirty-three volumes.

"Victory" is taken from the Gloria Patri from Palestrina's *Magnificat Tertii Toni,* 1591:

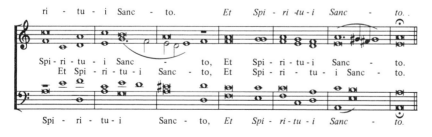

An adaptation appeared in the *Parish Choir, c.* 1850, and the present arrangement by William Henry Monk (LBW 272) was prepared for this text in the Original Edition of *Hymns Ancient and Modern,* 1861.

136 CHRIST IS ARISEN *(Christ ist erstanden)*
Tune: Christ ist erstanden

Martin Luther (LBW 48) once remarked, "After a time one tires of singing all other hymns, but 'Christ ist erstanden' one can always sing again." Based on the sequence "Victimae Paschali laudes" (LBW 137), this German Easter hymn and its tune date from around 1100. Wackernagel* quotes four versions found in twelfth-century sources. The hymn was used extensively during the following centuries and many variations in both text and tune can be found.

A translation by Martin Seltz (LBW 28) included in the *Worship Supplement,* 1969, to *The Lutheran Hymnal,* is given here with some alteration.

CHRIST IST ERSTANDEN is based on the plainsong melody proper to "Victimae Paschali laudes" (LBW 137). The form found here is from Joseph Klug's (LBW 85) *Geistliche Lieder,* 1533. J. S. Bach (LBW 219) used the tune in Cantata 66, and wrote an organ setting for his *Orgelbüchlein* and a harmonization for his *Choralgesänge.* The harmonization used here was prepared by Carl Schalk (LBW 118) for the *Worship Supplement,* 1969.

137 CHRISTIANS, TO THE PASCHAL VICTIM
(Victimae Paschali laudes)
Tune: Victimae Paschali

Both text and tune of this Latin sequence were included in an eleventh-century manuscript from Einsiedeln (Bäumker* I, #536–542). There it was ascribed to Wipo (died *c.* 1050), a Burgundian who served as chaplain to two German emperors, Konrad II and his son, Heinrich III, both of whose lives he recorded and to whom he presented collections of verses. The oldest of the five sequences retained after the Council of Trent (see p. 14), "Victimae Paschali laudes" also has the distinction of being the springboard from which liturgical drama came into existence. Liturgically, the hymn was used as a sequence during the Mass on Easter and daily throughout the following week, and also as a liturgical drama at Matins on Easter Day. Ryden*, p. 47, describes the following scene:

> This became a striking drama in which altar boys took the part of the two angels and three deacons represented the three Marys. In the dialogue which followed, the angels asked, "Whom seek ye?" to which the Marys replied, "Jesus of Nazareth." The angels thereupon removed the white altar-cloth representing the grave clothes, and answered, "He is not here." The Marys then turned toward the choir and sang, "Alleluia, the Lord is risen." At this point the officiating bishop or succentor entered the liturgical drama by asking questions, to which the Marys replied by singing in turn various stanzas of *Victimae paschali,* in which the entire choir finally joined. At the conclusion of the rite, the bishop intoned the *Te Deum* [LBW 3].

Among the Germans, vernacular stanzas were interpolated between the Latin ones, resulting in the development of the independent pre-Reformation chorale, "Christ ist erstanden" (LBW 136). Martin Luther's "Christ lag in Todesbanden" (LBW 134) is also based on "Victimae Paschali laudes."

The English version is a composite of several translations prepared for *The English Hymnal,* 1906.

VICTIMAE PASCHALI, the plainsong melody associated with this text from the beginning, was harmonized for the *Worship Supplement, 1969,* to *The Lutheran Hymnal,* by Carl Schalk (LBW 118).

138   HE IS ARISEN! GLORIOUS WORD!
(Han er opstanden! Store Bud!)
Tune: Wie schön leuchtet

See LBW 43 for Birgitte Katerine Boye. This single stanza hymn, to be sung before the reading of the Gospel from the pulpit, from Easter until Ascension, was first published in Ludvig Harboe and Ove Guldberg's *Psalmebog,* 1778. Translated in 1909 by George T. Rygh, the hymn was included in the *Lutheran Hymnary,* 1913, and is given here with slight alteration.

George Alfred Taylor Rygh, Lutheran pastor and teacher, was born in Chicago on March 21, 1860. Following his graduation in 1881 from Luther College, he studied for two years at Luther Seminary and Capital University, and during 1883 taught at Luther Seminary. From 1884 he was successively pastor in Portland, Maine, teacher at Wittenberg Academy (1889–1890), pastor at Grand Forks, North Dakota (1890–1891), teacher at North Dakota University (1891–1895), teacher at Mount Horeb, Wisconsin (1895–1898), pastor at Chicago (1899–1910), teacher at St. Olaf College (1910–1913), and pastor at Minneapolis (1920–1930). Thereafter, as pastor emeritus, he lived in Northfield, Minnesota. In addition to his pastoral and teaching work, he served from 1909 to 1914 as editor of the *United Lutheran,* as editor of the *American Lutheran Survey* from 1914 to 1921, and after 1925, editor of the *Lutheran Herald.* He translated a number of devotional books from Norwegian, and as a member of the committee on the *Lutheran Hymnary,* prepared several translations for that collection. Newberry College in Newberry, South Carolina, honored him with a Doctor of Letters in 1917. From 1919 to 1920 he was National Lutheran Council Commissioner to the Baltic States. He died July 16, 1942.

For WIE SCHÖN LEUCHTET see LBW 76. The harmonization used here is from the *Orgelchoralbuch,* 1952.

139   O SONS AND DAUGHTERS OF THE KING *(O filii et filiae)*
Tune: O filii et filiae

Written by Jean Tisserand, a Minorite friar who died in 1494, this hymn is patterned after a folk song with refrain, and is in the form of a trope (see p. 14) on the "Benedicamus Domino." The hymn, titled "L'alelueja du jour de Pasques," is found in a little book without title page, which was published sometime between 1518 and 1536, probably at Paris, France. It is now located in the Bibliothèque Nationale in Paris.

Tisserand, who was a man of considerable reputation in Paris, founded an order for penitent women and was the author of a history of some of his own order (the Minorites) who were martyred in Morocco in 1220.

John Mason Neale's (LBW 34) translation, which was included in his *Medieval Hymns,* 1851, opened as follows:

Ye sons and daughters of the King
Whom heavenly hosts in glory sing
Today the grave hath lost its sting.

The text as found here includes numerous alterations from several subsequent publications.

O FILII ET FILIAE belongs to this text and probably is contemporary with it, although so far the earliest known source for the tune is a Paris collection entitled *Airs sur les hymns sacrez, odes et noëls,* 1623. Samuel Webbe's *Collection of Motetts or Antiphons, c.* 1840 edition with Vincent Novello's accompaniments, contains the tune as it is found in the LBW. The harmonization was prepared for the *Worship Supplement,* 1969, to *The Lutheran Hymnal,* by Richard Hillert (LBW 63).

140 WITH HIGH DELIGHT LET US UNITE
(Mit Freuden zart zu dieser Fahrt)
Tune: Mit Freuden zart

This hymn by Vetter was one of six included in his *Kirchengesang darinnen die Heubtartickel des Christlichen Glaubens gefasset,* 1566.

Georg Vetter (or Strejc), was born in 1536 at Zabreh, Moravia. He entered the University of Königsberg in 1560 and the following year went to the University of Tübingen. Ordained a priest of the United Brethren in 1567, he went first to a congregation at Weisswasser in Moravia, and soon became a leader among the Brethren. By 1575 he had become pastor at Weisskirchen, but his excessive authoritarianism caused difficulty in the congregation, and in 1590 he moved to Gross-Seelowitz, promising at the Leipniker Synod in 1591 to amend his ways. He died at Gross-Seelowitz January 25, 1599.

In addition to his 1566 *Kirchengeseng,* Vetter prepared a Czech version of the Calvinist psalms with Claude Goudimel's settings in 1587, and had a large part in the Kralice Bible translation, a celebrated work similar in importance to Martin Luther's (LBW 48) German translation. Martin Franzmann's (LBW 233) translation was included in the *Worship Supplement,* 1969, to *The Lutheran Hymnal.*

MIT FREUDEN ZART served as the setting for Vetter's text in his *Kirchengeseng,* 1566. An earlier version of the tune (given below) is

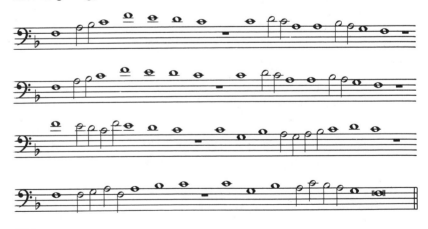

found with Psalm 138, "Il faut que de tous mes esprits," in *Trente*
quatre pseaumes de David, Geneva, 1551. A French secular song, "Une
pastourelle gentille," published by Pierre Attaingnant, 1529-1530, also
bears some similarity. According to Blüme* (p. 598), this tune originated
in the late Middle Ages. The harmonization was prepared by Carl Schalk
(LBW 118) for the *Worship Supplement,* 1969.

141   THE DAY OF RESURRECTION! ('Αναστάσεως ἡμέρα)
Tune: Herzlich tut mich erfreuen

This hymn by John of Damascus (LBW 132) is known as the "Golden
Canon for Easter" (see pp. 6ff). A translation of the entire canon was in-
cluded in John Mason Neale's (LBW 34) *Hymns of the Eastern*
*Church,*1862, with the present hymn (Ode I) beginning " '*Tis* the Day of
Resurrection." The text has been altered slightly.

At the Easter Eve midnight service it is customary in Eastern Churches
for worshipers to carry unlighted candles which are lighted on signal
while this hymn is sung, filling the church with their glow. In his *Hymns*
of the Eastern Church, Neale described a service in Athens where the
archbishop and priests and the King and Queen stood on a raised plat-
form with the crowd gathered around them with unlighted tapers. At
midnight the arrival of Easter was announced and a great shout went up,
" Χριστός ανέστι ," "Christ is risen!" The tapers were lighted, and during
the singing of this hymn drums and trumpets were sounded in the adjoining countryside.

HERZLICH TUT MICH ERFREUEN. The melody used with the
original Greek version of this hymn can be seen in Egon Wellesz' book,
A History of Byzantine Music and Hymnography, pp. 176–192. The
present German folk melody, originally associated with the secular text,
"Herzlich tut mich erfreuen die fröhlich Sommerzeit," was first printed
in Georg Rhau's (LBW 398) *Bicinia gallica, latina et germanica,* Wittenberg, 1544. In 1551 the tune appeared in Nürnberg with the secular
text "Papiers Natur ist Rauschen." Johann Walther (LBW 350) recast
the text, "Herzlich tut mich erfreuen," giving it a sacred character, and
the text and tune were published in his *Ein schöner Geistlicher und*
Christlicher newer Berckreyen, 1552. The LBW form of the melody is
that found in Walther's collection. The harmonization, from the *Wor-*
ship Supplement, 1969, to *The Lutheran Hymnal,* is by Theodore Beck
(LBW 33).

142   HAIL THEE, FESTIVAL DAY! *(Salve festa dies)*
Tune: Salve festa dies

See LBW 118 for Venantius Honorius Fortunatus. "Tempora florigero
rutilant distincta sereno," Fortunatus' 110-line poem on the Resurrection, is addressed to Felix, Bishop of Nantes, who died in 582. Ruth Ellis
Messenger, in her *Latin Hymns of the Middle Ages* (New York, 1948),
suggests that this is the earliest hymn to compare the Resurrection to
spring and the renewal of nature. The earliest source of the text is a St.

Petersburg manuscript of the eighth or ninth century. During the Middle Ages various portions of the poem—each beginning with lines 39 and 40:

Salve festa dies toto venerabilis aevo
Qua Deus infernum viciť et astra tenet

—came to be widely used as processionals for Easter, Ascension, Pentecost, and other festival days. These have often been translated as separate hymns for the various festivals.

In *Songs of Praise,* 1931, the hymns were combined into a single processional with optional lines for specific observances. This pattern, as well as much of the text from *Songs of Praise,* has served as the basis for the present version, prepared by the Inter-Lutheran Commission on Worship.

SALVE FESTA DIES, by Ralph Vaughan Williams (LBW 101), was marked "Anonymous" in *The English Hymnal,* 1906, but was later credited to the composer in *Songs of Praise,* 1931, and in the 1933 edition of *The English Hymnal.*

143 NOW ALL THE VAULT OF HEAVEN RESOUNDS
Tune: Lasst uns erfreuen

Written for the tune "Lasst uns erfreuen," Paul Zeller Strodach's Easter hymn was prepared for the *Service Book and Hymnal,* 1958. The text has been altered slightly for the LBW.

Born in Norristown, Pennsylvania, on March 27, 1876, Strodach attended Muhlenberg College, Allentown, Pennsylvania, where he received a Bachelor of Arts degree in 1896 and a Master of Arts degree three years later. In 1899 also, he graduated from the Lutheran Theological Seminary, Mt. Airy, Philadelphia, and was ordained. Between 1899 and 1912 he served congregations in Trenton, New Jersey; Easton and Washington, Pennsylvania; and Canton, Ohio. He was pastor at Grace Church, Roxborough, Philadelphia from 1912 to 1921 and at Holy Trinity, Norristown, Pennsylvania from 1921 to 1926, after which he served as literary editor of the United Lutheran Church Publication House in Philadelphia for twenty years.

A liturgical scholar and an author, he published *The Church Year,* 1924; *The Collect for the Day,* 1939; *The Road He Trod,* 1932; *Oremus: Collects, Devotions, Litanies from Ancient and Modern Sources,* 1925; *A Manual for Worship,* 1930 (revised edition, 1946); as well as sermons, other devotional material, and a collection of Christmas carols. Also an artist, he created magnificent illuminations in the medieval style. Strodach was a member of the Joint Committee that prepared the *Common Service Book,* 1917, and was on the Joint Commission for the *Service Book and Hymnal,* 1958, from its organization in 1945 until his death on May 30, 1947, in Easton.

LASST UNS ERFREUEN appeared in the *Ausserlesene Catholische Geistliche Kirchengesänge* printed by Peter von Brachel in Cologne, 1623, as given on page 239 (Bäumker*, I, #280). There it was the setting for the Easter hymn, "Last uns erfrewen hertzlich sehr."

The melody is possibly based on an earlier tune, perhaps a folk song, since the tune for Psalm 36 in *Aulcuns Pseaumes et Cantiques mys en chant,* Strasbourg, 1539, bears some resemblance, especially in the open-

ing phrase. Although the tune appeared in a number of Roman Catholic hymnals in Germany during the remainder of the seventeenth century, it never came into use among German Protestants. It entered *The English Hymnal,* 1906, with the present harmonization by Ralph Vaughan Williams (LBW 101) as a setting for Athelstan Riley's hymn, "Ye watchers and ye holy ones" (LBW 175). Percy Dearmer* has noted the economy of material used in this famous melody and comments on the "accumulating force of repetition when the repeated phrase, as here, is strong enough to bear it."

144 GOOD CHRISTIAN FRIENDS, REJOICE AND SING!

Tune: Gelobt sei Gott

Written for the tune, "Gelobt sei Gott," this hymn by Cyril Argentine Alington was included in *Songs of Praise,* published in London in 1931.

Alington, born October 23, 1872, in Candlesby in Lincolnshire, was a minister of the Church of England, as was his father before him. Educated at Trinity College, Oxford, he received a Bachelor of Arts degree in 1893 and a Master of Arts degree in 1895. In the following year he became a fellow of All Souls and assistant master at Marlborough College. He was ordained a deacon in 1899, and a priest in 1901. From 1899 to 1908 he was assistant master at Eton College, and from 1908 to 1916, head master of Shrewsbury School. In 1917 he received a Doctor of Divinity degree from Trinity College and returned to Eton College as head master, a post he held until 1933, when he became dean of Durham. From 1909 to 1910 and again from 1928 to 1929 he was select preacher at Oxford and from 1921 was chaplain to the King. A distinguished scholar and writer, Alington authored theological books, essays, novels, and poems. On May 16, 1955 he died at St. Weonards, Herefordshire.

GELOBT SEI GOTT (also "Vulpius"). This tune was included in Melchior Vulpius' *Ein schön geistlich Gesangbuch,* Jena, 1609, where it was the melody for "Gelobt sei Gott in höchsten Thron," a hymn by Michael Weisse (LBW 37) (Zahn* #283). The harmonization from the *Worship Supplement,* 1969, to *The Lutheran Hymnal,* is by Richard Hillert (LBW 63).

145 THINE IS THE GLORY *(A toi la gloire, o Ressuscité)*

Tune: Judas Maccabaeus

Written in French by Edmond L. Budry in 1884, this hymn was first published in *Chants Évangéliques,* Lausanne, 1885, and was included in

Cantate Domino, 1925, the hymnal of the World Student Christian Federation, along with a German translation by Johanna Meyer. The present text was prepared in 1923 by Richard Birch Hoyle. Paul Laufer has suggested that an Advent hymn by Friedrich-Heinrich Ranke (1798-1876), found with this tune by Handel in the *Evangelisches Gesangbuch für Elsass-Lothringern,* served as the basis for this hymn.

Budry, born August 30, 1854, was for thirty-five years the pastor of the Free Church at Vevey, Switzerland. Before going to Vevey, he had studied theology at Lausanne and served from 1881 to 1889 as pastor at Cully. He retired in 1923 and died November 12, 1932. In addition to original hymns, he prepared French versions of German, English, and Latin texts.

Hoyle, a Baptist minister born March 8, 1875, in Cloughfold, attended Regent's Park College, London, 1895-1900, and for twenty-six years served various churches in England. He then worked with the YMCA, and for a while was the editor of their publication, *The Red Triangle.* During this time he translated about thirty hymns from French. In 1934 he came to the United States and taught for two years at Western Theological Seminary in Philadelphia. On his return to England, he became pastor of the Baptist church in Kingston-upon-Thames. He died December 14, 1939, in London.

JUDAS MACCABAEUS is from the chorus, "See, the conquering hero comes," in George Frideric Handel's (LBW 39) oratorio *Judas Maccabaeus.* This chorus was not included in the original performance of the oratorio in 1747, but was transferred from *Joshua* in 1751. Very shortly thereafter it came into use as a hymn tune in Thomas Butts's *Harmonia Sacra, c.* 1760, where it was the melody for Charles Wesley's "Christ the Lord is risen today!" (LBW 130).

146 REJOICE, ANGELIC CHOIRS, REJOICE!
(Exultet iam angelica turba caelorum)
Tune: Wächterlied

This Latin hymn, attributed to Augustine, can be found in all the old rites—Roman, Gallican, Ambrosian, Mozarabic, and Sarum—sung by a deacon at the blessing of the Paschal candle.

Aurelius Augustine was born November 13, 354, at Tagaste, in Numidia, Africa. The son of a Christian mother, Monica, and pagan father, Patricius, he was reared a Christian. He attended the local school and then the school at nearby Madaura, but had to interrupt his studies at the age of sixteen because of a lack of funds. The following year, however, a benefactor made it possible for him to continue his education at Carthage. There he engaged in an active social life, and formed a liaison with a concubine who bore him a son, Adeodatus. A serious student continually in search of wisdom, Augustine at first embraced Manichaeism, attracted by their promise to provide him with comprehension of all that exists. After nine years, however, he abandoned the sect and went in 383 to Rome where he taught rhetoric for a year, and then moved to Milan where he became a professor. In Milan his encounters with Ambrose (LBW 28) and his reading of St. Paul brought about his conversion to orthodox Christianity. His mother joined him in Milan and insisted that he send the mother of his son, Adeodatus, back to Africa, and prepare for a good marriage to the woman she had

selected. In 386, however, Augustine abandoned his teaching career and
his proposed marriage, and retired to an estate at Cassiciacum near
Milan, for a life of prayer and study. Baptized the following year, he
went to his home at Tagaste in 388 where he sold his property, gave the
money to the poor, and retired to monastic life. Among his works written at this time is a dialogue with his sixteen-year-old son who died soon
afterward. In Hippo he attended a sermon by Bishop Valerius, and the
congregation there, recognizing Augustine, prevailed upon him to
become a priest. Consecrated a bishop in 395 he served in Hippo, the second city in Africa in ecclesiastical importance, for thirty-five years. During this time he traveled widely and wrote voluminously, many of his
works being a defense of the orthodox faith against Manichaeism,
Donatism, Pelegianism, and Arianism, struggles in which he engaged
throughout his time as bishop. He died at Hippo on August 28, 430.

Two English prose versions served as a basis for Joel Lundeen's versification, written June 4, 1974, for the LBW—one in *Holy Week and
Easter in Modern Speech,* 1969, and one in Godfrey L. Diekmann's *The
Easter Vigil,* 1953.

Joel Waldemar Lundeen, associate archivist for the Lutheran Church
in America since 1967, was born May 24, 1918, in Yuhsien, Honan,
China, where his parents were missionaries. After three years at
Augsburg College, Minneapolis, he went to Augustana College, Rock
Island, Illinois, where he completed a Bachelor of Arts degree in 1940.
He holds a Master of Divinity degree, 1945, from Augustana Theological
Seminary, Rock Island, and has pursued further graduate studies at
Union Seminary, New York, and at the University of Chicago. Ordained
in 1945, he first served for two years at Peace Lutheran Church, Arlington, Virginia. He was married in 1946 to Doris M. Nordling, a nurse, and
is the father of four sons. For a number of years he combined the parish
ministry with teaching—at First Lutheran, Clifton, New Jersey
(1947–1952) and Upsala College, East Orange (1948–1951); and at
Messiah, Lindsborg, Kansas (1952–1958) and Bethany College
(1952–1957). He was director of the library and church archivist at
Augustana Seminary from 1958 to 1967, and for nine years thereafter
was director of the library at the Lutheran School of Theology at
Chicago in addition to his present position as associate archivist. He also
teaches hymnology and worship courses at LSTC. Active in various
library, archival, and historical societies, he is past president of the
Augustana Historical Society and the Lutheran Historical Conference.
He was secretary of the Commission on Worship of the Augustana
Church from 1957 to 1962 and in 1965 became a member of the Hymn
Society of America. His publications include sermons, Bible studies and
devotional material, and articles on church music and Augustana Church
history, in addition to *The Archival Responsibility of the Seminary and
Church College Librarians,* 1962–1964, and *Preserving Yesterday for
Tomorrow: A Guide to the Archives of the LCA,* 1977. Throughout his
life, also, he has been a musician. Following studies at MacPhail School
of Music in Minneapolis, he won an organ scholarship with Wilbur
Swanson at Augustana College, and later studied briefly under Edward
Eigenschenk in Chicago. From the time he entered college he has served
as organist in various churches in Minneapolis, the Quad-Cities, and
Chicago.

WÄCHTERLIED ("aubade" or "morning song") was the melody of a
secular song, "Wolauf, wolauf mit lauter stimm'," one of thirty-eight

songs included in Christian Egenolff's *Reutterliedlin,* Frankfurt-am-Main, 1535.

Egenolff, a German publisher, was born July 22, 1502, at Hadamar, and in 1529 was a printer in Strasbourg. Later, in 1531, he set up the first publication house in Frankfurt, where he worked as an editor, printer, and distributor. His output covered a wide range of subjects, only a small percentage of which were music publications. Besides *Reutterliedlin,* he published two other collections of songs—*Gassenhawerlin,* also 1535, and *Grassliedlin* of unknown date. Many of the songs he published became the basis for *contra-facta* (secular songs adapted to sacred use). The present song was one of several reconstructed by Johann Walther (LBW 350) for his *Wittembergisch deudsch Geistlich Gesangbüchlein,* 1551. In 1551 Egenolff himself published a collection entitled *Gassenhawer-, Reiter-, und Bergliedlin . . .,* etc. The title translated by Blume* reads:

> Street songs, knightly and miners' songs, changed in a Christian, moral, and ethical manner, in order that the evil, vexatious melodies, the useless and shameful songs to be sung in the streets, fields, houses, and elsewhere, may lose their bad effects if they can have good, useful Christian texts and words.

Egenolff died at Frankfurt on February 9, 1555.

The present adaptation of the melody was prepared for the music edition of *Songs of Praise,* 1925, for "Lord Christ, when first thou cam'st to men" (LBW 421).

147 HALLELUJAH! JESUS LIVES! *(Halleluja! Jesus lebt!)*
Tune: Fred til Bod

Carl Bernhard Garve, the son of a farmer, was born January 24, 1763, at Jeinsen, near Hanover, Germany. Educated at Moravian schools in Zeist, Neuwied, and Niesky, and at the seminary at Barby, he served as a tutor, first at Niesky (from 1784) and then at Barby (from 1789). In 1797 he was sent to arrange documents in the archive at Zeist. Ordained a Moravian clergyman, he became a preacher in Amsterdam in 1799, and in 1801 went to Ebersdorf where he was both preacher and inspector of the training school. In 1809 he went to Berlin, and in 1816, to Neusalza an der Oder, ministering there until his retirement in 1836. He went to Herrnhut, where he died on June 21, 1841.

Garve published two collections of hymns: *Christliche Gesänge,* Görlitz, 1825, in which this hymn was published, and *Brüdergesänge,* published in 1827 at Gnadau.

The translation, by Jane Laurie Borthwick, is from *Hymns from the Land of Luther,* fourth series, 1862 (see LBW 25).

Jane and her sister, Sarah Borthwick Findlater (LBW 25), were daughters of the manager of the North British Insurance Office. Born in Edinburgh on April 9, 1813, she remained there until her death on September 7, 1897. She devoted herself to religious and social work and had a deep interest in the home and foreign missions of the Free Church of Scotland, of which she was a member. Under the initials "H. L. L." (derived from *Hymns from the Land of Luther*) she wrote several prose works, and contributed a number of hymns, both original and translated, to the *Family Treasury.* Many of these hymns were later collected and published in *Thoughts for Thoughtful Hours,* 1857. Sixty-one of the translations in *Hymns from the Land of Luther* were from Jane's pen.

FRED TIL BOD. For a discussion of this tune see LBW 338, where it appears with the text for which it was written.

148   NOW THE GREEN BLADE RISES
Tune: Noël Nouvelet

Written by John Macleod Campbell Crum for the French carol tune, "Noël nouvelet" (see comments below), this hymn was published in *The Oxford Book of Carols,* London, 1928.

Born at Mere Old Hall, Cheshire, England, on October 12, 1872, Crum completed a Bachelor of Arts degree in 1895 and a Master of Arts degree in 1901 at New College, Oxford. Ordained a deacon in 1897 and a priest in 1900, he served as assistant curate at St. John the Evangelist, Darlington (1897-1901); domestic chaplain to the bishop of Oxford, Francis Paget (1901-1910); assistant curate at Windsor (1907-1910); vicar of Mentmore with Ledburn (1910-1912); rector of Farnham (1913-1928); and canon of Canterbury (1928-1943). After 1943 he was canon emeritus of Canterbury. His publications include *Road Mending on the Sacred Way,* 1924; *What Mean ye by these Stones?* 1926; *The Original Jerusalem Gospel,* 1927; *Notes on the Old Glass of the Cathedral of Christ Church, Canterbury,* 1930; and *St. Mark's Gospel, Two Stages of its Making,* 1936; and together with Stephen Paget, the *Life of Francis Paget,* 1912. He died December 19, 1958 at Farnham, Surrey.

NOËL NOUVELET. This Dorian-mode melody was originally associated with the French carol, "Noël nouvelet." Marcel Dupré used the melody as the basis for his famous *Variations on a Noel.*

149   THIS JOYFUL EASTERTIDE
Tune: Vruechten

George Ratcliffe Woodward, a gifted translator of Latin, Greek, and German, was born December 27, 1848, at Birkenhead, England. Educated at Caius College, Cambridge, where he received a Bachelor of Arts degree in 1872 and a Master of Arts degree in 1875, he served as assistant curate of St. Barnabas, Pimlico, 1874 to 1882; vicar of Lower Walsingham, 1882 to 1888; rector of Chelmsondiston, 1888 to 1894; assistant curate of St. Barnabas, Pimlico, 1894 to 1899; licensed preacher in the London Diocese, 1899 to 1903; and from 1903 to 1906 was on the staff of St. Mark's, Marylebone Road. The latter part of his life was spent in Highgate. He died March 3, 1934, in St. Pancras.

Woodward edited a number of collections. The *Cowley Carol Book for Christmas, Easter and Ascension Tide* appeared in three series: the first in 1901 containing thirty-nine carols, the second in 1902 with sixty-five carols, and the third in 1919 with thirty-seven carols. "This Joyful Eastertide," the first stanza of which is found in the LBW, was published in the 1902 series of the *Cowley Carol Book.* Especially significant was his *Songs of Syon,* 1904, which included 414 authentic tunes from many lands. In this collection translations of foreign texts were given in their original meter (where good translations were not available Woodward provided them) and associated with their appropriate melodies. Tunes were included with their original harmonizations, or were given historically appropriate settings (plainsong tunes, for example, were not harmonized at all). In 1910 he published an edition of *Piae Cantiones* (1582) for the Plainsong and Mediaeval Music Society. Together with Charles Wood he prepared *An Italian Carol Book,* 1920, and *The Cambridge Carol Book,* 1924. A number of his translations, along with the original Greek texts, appeared in *The Christian East* from October, 1921, to July, 1922, and were collected into *Hymns from the Greek Church,* 1922. Woodward was honored with the Lambeth Doctor of Music degree in 1924.

VRUECHTEN. Woodward's hymn, "This Joyful Eastertide," was written for this tune when it was included in *The Cowley Carol Book.* The melody was originally the setting for the popular seventeenth-century Dutch song, "De Liefde Voortgebracht." In Joachim Oudaen's *David's Psalmen,* Amsterdam, 1685, it was used with "Hoe groot de Vruechten zijn"—hence its title. The harmonization was prepared by Alice Parker in 1966 for *The Mennonite Hymnal,* 1969.

Alice Stuart Parker, American composer and conductor, was born December 16, 1925, in Boston, Massachusetts. She holds a Bachelor of Arts degree (1947) from Smith College, and a Master of Science degree in composition (1949) from Juilliard School of Music, where she studied with Julius Herford, Vincent Persichetti (LBW 216), and Robert Shaw. Married in 1954 to Thomas Pyle, she is the mother of five children. From 1948 to 1967 she was an arranger for the Robert Shaw Chorale, and since 1951 she has taught music privately in New York City. Active as a conductor and lecturer, she was conductor at the Laurelville, Pennsylvania, Mennonite Church Center from 1961 to 1970, and lecturer at the Blossom Festival School in Ohio from 1969 to 1971 and at Aspen, Colorado, from 1970 to 1971. More recently she has appeared with the Texas Choral Directors Association, the Nova Scotia Choral Federation, the Illinois College Choral Festival, Southern Methodist University, and the Annual Convocation of the Hymn Society of America. She also teaches courses in choral arranging and composition and leads church music workshops. For three months in 1978 she was "in residence" with the Pittsburgh, Pennsylvania, Symphony. Among her compositions are works for women's choruses and orchestra; chorus and woodwind quartet; soprano solo, chorus and organ; vocal and string quartets; and for piano. Her third opera, *Singers Glen,* was premiered in 1978, and *The Family Reunion,* a one-act "back-yard" opera, has been performed by many church, college, and community groups. Her numerous arrangements of folk songs, hymns, and carols in collaboration with Robert Shaw are well-known in the United States and abroad. She is the author of a dictionary of music and of *Creative Hymn Singing,* and has received composer's grants from the National Endowment for the Arts and from the American Society of Composers, Authors, and Publishers; and commissions from the Atlanta Symphony, the North-Central and Texas divisions of the American Choral Directors Association, the Ohio State University, Mohawk Trail Concerts, the Franconia Foundation, and the Atlanta Opera Company. She is a member of the American Symphony Orchestra League, the National Opera Association, the American Choral Directors Association, and the Hymn Society of America; and is listed in *Who's Who of American Women,* the *World Who's Who of Women,* and the *Dictionary of International Biography.*

HYMN **151**

150 MAKE SONGS OF JOY *(Zpivejmež všickni vesele: Hallelujah)*
Tune: Zpivejmež všickni vesele

See LBW 96 for Juraj Tranovský. This hymn was included in the *Cithara Sanctorum* (Tranoscius), 1636. The translation was prepared in 1976 by Jaroslav J. Vajda (LBW 159) for this hymnal.

ZPIVEJMEŽ VŠICKNI VESELE. This tune was originally the setting for the Ascension hymn, "Vstoupil jest Kristus na nebe: Hallelujah." The harmonization is from the Chorvát, *Velka Partitura,* 1936.

151 JESUS CHRIST IS RISEN TODAY *(Surrexit Christus hodie)*
Tune: Easter Hymn

The Latin hymn on which this text is based is a trope (see p. 14) on the "Benedicamus Domino," found in three manuscripts of the fourteenth century from Prague, Engleberg, and Munich. The English translation first appeared in *Lyra Davidica, or a Collection of Divine Songs and Hymns, partly new composed, partly translated from German and Latin Hymns: and set to easy and pleasant tunes,* published by John Walsh, a famous music printer, in 1708. There the text read as follows:

> Jesus Christ is risen today, Halle-Halle-lujah.
> Our triumphant Holyday
> Who so lately on the Cross
> Suffer'd to redeem our loss.
>
> Haste ye females from your fright
> Take to Galilee your flight
> To his sad disciples say
> Jesus Christ is risen today.
>
> In our Paschal joy and feast
> Let the Lord of life be blest
> Let the Holy Trine be prais'd
> And thankful hearts to heaven be rais'd.

In John Arnold's *The Compleat Psalmodist,* issued in London in 1749, the first three stanzas of the hymn took their present shape. The fourth stanza, by Charles Wesley (LBW 27), comes from his *Hymns and Sacred Poems,* 1740, and was first attached to this hymn in the *Supplement* to Tate and Brady's *New Version* (LBW 452) around 1816.

EASTER HYMN (also called "Worgan") appeared with this hymn in *Lyra Davidica* in the form given on page 246. It is found in similar form in the *Collection of Tunes . . . as they are commonly Sung at the Foundery,* [1742], but underwent numerous changes as it passed through the last half of the eighteenth century. The basic shape comes from Arnold's *The Compleat Psalmodist* and several of the notes are appoggiaturas added later in the century. The tune seems to have been quite popular, appearing in a number of English and, later, American collections. It was sometimes ascribed to "Dr. Worgan," and Henry Edward

Dibdin in the preface to his *Standard Psalm Tune Book*, 1851, attributed it to Henry Carey.

152   LOOK, NOW HE STANDS!
Tune: Parsons

George Utech was born in 1931 in Le Mars, Iowa, and has received his education at Wartburg College, St. Olaf College, Wartburg Seminary, Lutheran Theological Seminary at Columbus, Ohio, the University of London in England, and the University of Iowa, Iowa City. Married to Kresite Lee of Aberdeen, South Dakota, he is the father of four children. His two hymns included in the LBW were written while he was serving as chaplain at Texas Lutheran College. Since 1968, he has lived in Pittsford, a suburb of Rochester, New York.

This hymn was written in 1963 and sung on Easter to a tune by Gerhard Cartford (LBW 466). It was included with the present tune, "Parsons," in *Contemporary Worship–1,* 1969.

PARSONS, by Carl Schalk (LBW 118), was first published as a setting for this hymn in *Contemporary Worship–1,* 1969.

153   WELCOME, HAPPY MORNING! *(Salve festa dies)*
Tune: Fortunatus

See LBW 142 for a discussion of this Latin hymn.

The translation of John Ellerton (LBW 262) was included in Robert Brown-Borthwick's *Supplementary Hymn and Tune Book,* 1868, and later in his own *Hymns, Original and Translated, 1888.*

FORTUNATUS was written for this hymn by Sullivan and included in Joseph Barnby's (LBW 280) *The Hymnary,* 1872.

Arthur Seymour Sullivan, well-known for his series of operettas written in association with the librettist W. S. Gilbert, was born at Bolwell Terrace, Lambeth, England, on May 13, 1842. He was a child of the Chapel Royal under Thomas Helmore. The first to hold a Mendelssohn scholarship (in 1856), he studied at the Royal Academy of Music under Sterndale Bennet and John Goss (LBW 549), and at the Leipzig Conservatory with Moritz Hauptmann, Ferdinand David, and Ignaz Moscheles.

246

At Leipzig he was a fellow-student of Edvard Grieg (LBW 314). Between 1861 and 1872 he was organist of St. Michael's, Chester Square, and of St. Peter's, Cranley Gardens, where he became a friend of Sir George Grove. After 1866 he was professor of music at the Royal Academy of Music. He directed a number of musical organizations, including the Glasgow Choral Union, Covent Garden Promenade Concerts, Leeds Festival, and the Philharmonic Society. Cambridge and Oxford Universities honored him with Doctor of Music degrees; he received the Legion of Honour in 1878, and was knighted in 1883. His works in church music include anthems and services as well as hymn tunes, and he was the editor of *Church Hymns with Tunes,* 1874. He died November 22, 1900, in Westminster.

154 THAT EASTER DAY WITH JOY WAS BRIGHT
(Claro paschali gaudio)
Tune: Erschienen ist der herrlich Tag

This hymn is a cento from the last part of "Aurora lucis rutilat," a very old Latin hymn of the fourth or fifth century which has sometimes been ascribed to Ambrose (LBW 28). It was, with "Ad coenam Agni" (LBW 210), the earliest hymn to be adopted for any special season. It is further noted by Arthur Sumner Walpole in his *Early Latin Hymns,* 1922, that, except for the hymns of Ambrose, this hymn and "Christe, qui lux es et dies" (LBW 273) are the only ones to be found both in ancient Irish hymnaries and in those outside Ireland. In many English uses the hymn was divided between Matins (after midnight) and Lauds (at sunrise) from the Sunday after Easter until Ascension.

John Mason Neale's (LBW 34) translation, included in his *Hymnal Noted,* 1851, began as follows:

> In this our bright and Paschal day
> The sun shines out in purer ray;
> When Christ, to earthly sight made plain,
> The glad Apostles see again.

His translation was extensively altered for the Original Edition of *Hymns Ancient and Modern,* 1861, and further changes have been made in many other hymnals, including the LBW.

ERSCHIENEN IST DER HERRLICH TAG. See LBW 47 for Nikolaus Herman. This tune served as the setting for three Easter hymns in Herman's *Die Sontags Euangelia,* 1560, the best-known of the texts being his "Erschienen ist der herrlich Tag." It is based on the Easter antiphon, "Ad monumentum venimus."

J. S. Bach (LBW 219) included a setting of the melody in his Cantata 145. Jan Bender's (LBW 396) harmonization was prepared for the *Worship Supplement,* 1969, to *The Lutheran Hymnal.*

155 PRAISE THE SAVIOR, NOW AND EVER
(Upp, min tunga, att lovsjunga)
Tune: Upp, min tunga

A discussion of Venantius Fortunatus' Latin hymn, "Pange, lingua, gloriosi proelium," can be found at LBW 118. Beginning "Upp, min tunga, att lovsjunga,'' the hymn appeared in Swedish translation in *Andeliga Psalmer och Wijsor,* 1614, and in G. Ollon's edition of the 1694 hymnal. Johan Olof Wallin (LBW 73) revised and shortened the hymn and moved it from the Passion section to the Easter section when he included it in the 1816 *Svenska Psalmboken.*

The English translation was prepared by the hymnal commission of the *Service Book and Hymnal,* 1958, and is given here with only slight alteration.

UPP, MIN TUNGA (also ''Riddarholm'') is an anonymous melody found in *Then Swenska Psalm-Boken,* 1697, as given below.

Earlier, in a different form (see p. 44), it was included in the *Riddarholmskyrkans handskrivna koralbok*, 1694. The harmonization is from the *Svenska Psalm-Boken*, 1884 edition.

156   LOOK, THE SIGHT IS GLORIOUS

Tune: Bryn Calfaria

While Thomas Kelly's more than 750 hymns have been described as somewhat uneven in value, the three contained in the LBW rank among the finest hymns of the English language. Kelly, who was to Ireland what Isaac Watts (LBW 39) was to England in the transition from psalmody to hymnody, was the son of a judge, born July 13, 1769, in Kellyville, County Queens. He graduated with highest honors from Trinity College, Dublin (Bachelor of Arts, 1789), and entered Temple for law study; but because of some of his readings, he underwent a spiritual change and decided instead to take holy orders. Ordained in 1792 in the Church of Ireland, Kelly was soon banned from preaching by the archbishop of Dublin due to his strong evangelical tendencies. He left the established church and became an independent preacher. About 1800 he married Miss Tighe of Rosanna, Wicklow. With his and his wife's combined wealth he built chapels in several places, including York Street in Dublin, and at Athy, Portarlington, Wexford, and Waterford. A generous and humble man, Kelly became a great friend of the poor in Dublin and was especially helpful during the Irish famine in the 1840s. He was also a man of high intellectual and scholastic achievements who daily read the Scriptures in their original language. His hymns were published in *A Collection of Psalms and Hymns,* 1800; *Hymns on Various Passages of Scripture,* 1804; and *Hymns Not Before Published,* 1815. Originally containing ninety-six poems, *Hymns on Various Passages of Scripture* went through numerous enlarged editions until the eighth, published in 1858, contained Kelly's total output of 765 hymns. ''Look, *ye saints,* the sight is glorious,'' based on Revelation 11:15 (''And he shall reign for ever and ever''), was included in the third edition, 1809. Except for the change in the opening line, the hymn is found in the LBW without alteration. Kelly suffered a severe stroke while preaching in Dublin, and died May 14, 1855.

BRYN CALFARIA, which has been described by Erik Routley (LBW 436) as "a piece of real Celtic rock," was originally the setting for "Gwaed y groes sy'n codi fynny," an intense hymn of Jesus and the cross. It was included in its present arrangement in *The English Hymnal,* 1906, with "Lord, enthroned in heavenly splendor" (LBW 172).

William Owen ("Prysgol" in Wales) was born in 1814 in Bangor, Carnarvonshire, in Wales. His father worked in the Penrhyn slate quarries, and William himself also worked there when he was growing up. Owen, who wrote his first hymn tune at age eighteen, later wrote a number of hymn tunes and anthems, many of which, including "Bryn Calfaria," were included in *Y Perl Cerddorol,* Vol. II, 1886. Most of his life was spent in Caeathrow, Carnarvon. He died in 1893.

157 A HYMN OF GLORY LET US SING! *(Hymnum canamus gloriae)*
Tune: Lasst uns erfreuen

This Latin hymn by the Venerable Bede is first found in an eleventh-century manuscript in the British Museum. Three other eleventh-century manuscripts, two at the British Museum and one at Durham, contain another variant beginning "Hymnum canamus Domino."

The Venerable Bede made contributions in many areas—scholarship, grammar, philosophy, poetry, biography, history, and religion. His *Historia Ecclesiastica* is an invaluable contribution to early English history. There is even some possibility that he contributed to the world of music. Gustave Reese, in his *Music in the Middle Ages* (New York, 1940), mentions a tract of disputed authenticity, *Musica Theoretica,* which has sometimes been attributed to Bede. His hymns, numbering a dozen at most, were possibly the first Christian hymns written on English soil. Born in 673 in a village at the mouth of the Tyne (now Jarrow in County Durham), Bede was orphaned when young. He received his education, first under Benedict Biscop and later under Ceolfrith, at Wearmouth and Jarrow monasteries, both of which were near his birthplace. At the age of nineteen he was ordained a deacon by St. John of Beverly and eleven years later was ordained a priest by the same prelate. The remainder of Bede's life was divided between the two monasteries and was spent in study. He died in Jarrow on May 26, 735.

The English text represents a combination of two translations—"A hymn of glory let us sing," by Elizabeth Rundle Charles (LBW 517) from her *Voice of Christian Life in Song,* 1858; and "Sing we triumphant hymns of praise," contributed by Benjamin Webb (LBW 88) to *The Hymnal Noted,* 1854—with some further revisions.

For LASST UNS ERFREUEN see LBW 143.

158 ALLELUIA! SING TO JESUS
Tune: Hyfrydol

See LBW 40 for William Chatterton Dix. Written to fill a need for Communion hymns in Church of England hymnals, this hymn was first included in Dix's *Altar Songs,* 1867, and a year later in the Appendix to the Original Edition of *Hymns Ancient and Modern.* With the omission of a stanza relating specifically to the Eucharist (the full text is included in *The Hymnal 1940* of the Episcopal Church), this hymn becomes appropriate for the Ascension or for general adoration and praise. The text is given here with some alteration.

HYFRYDOL (meaning "good cheer") was written before the composer, Rowland Hugh Prichard, was twenty years old, and was included in his *Cyfaill y Cantorion,* 1844.

Born at Craienyn near Bala, in North Wales, on January 14, 1811, Prichard spent most of his life there. His grandfather was the famous bard, Rowland Huw. Gifted with a good voice, Prichard was well-known as a precentor and wrote a number of good hymn tunes, many of which were included in Welsh periodicals. In 1880 he went to Holywell where he became a loom-tender's assistant at the Welsh Flannel Manufacturing Company's mills. Seven years later he died, on January 25.

159   UP THROUGH ENDLESS RANKS OF ANGELS
Tune: Ascended Triumph

This hymn, written in 1973, was published as an Augsburg Publishing House bulletin insert in 1974. The author, Jaroslav John (Jan) Vajda, was born April 28, 1919, in Lorain, Ohio, the son of a Lutheran pastor. Following his graduation from Concordia Junior College in 1938 he worked for a year in the Indiana Harbor steel mills to earn money for seminary studies. He entered Concordia Theological Seminary in St. Louis, Missouri, in 1939; served from 1942 to 1943 as vicar of Sts. Peter and Paul Lutheran Church in Central City, Pennsylvania; and graduated from the seminary with Bachelor of Arts and Bachelor of Divinity degrees in 1944. He remained at the seminary for an accelerated year of post-graduate studies in preparation for his Master of Sacred Theology degree. His first call was to Holy Trinity Lutheran Church, Cranesville, Pennsylvania (a bilingual, Slovak and English parish), where he ministered from 1945 to 1949. From 1949 to 1953 he served Our Blessed Savior Lutheran Church in Alexandria, Indiana. In 1953 he moved to Tarentum, Pennsylvania, where he supervised a relocation and building of a church in Brackenridge, Pennsylvania, concluding his ministry at St. John's Lutheran Church (also bilingual) in 1963. From 1959 to 1963, also, he was editor of *The Lutheran Beacon* of the Synod of Evangelical Lutheran Churches. He went to St. Louis, Missouri, in 1963, where he was editor of *This Day* magazine, a monthly family religious/cultural publication. Since 1971, when *This Day* ceased publication, he has been book editor and developer for Concordia Publishing House. Married to Louise Mastiglio of Milwaukee, Wisconsin, in 1945, he is the father of three children.

Vajda, whose original and translated hymns and poems have appeared in print in the United States and in Czechoslovakia, began writing poetry at the age of eighteen, and made his first translation from Slovak three years later. His Bachelor of Divinity thesis, "A History of the *Cithara Sanctorum* by Juraj Tranovsky," written in 1944, is being pursued in a project which will trace the origin of eleven hundred hymns in the Slovak Lutheran hymnals. His interest in poetry, hymnody, and music provided background for his work on the Commission on Worship of the Lutheran Church—Missouri Synod (1960-1978) and on the Inter-Lutheran Commission on Worship (1967-1978), on both of which commissions he worked particularly with hymn texts. Among his translations are *Bloody Sonnets,* 1950; *Slovak Christmas,* 1960; *Janko Kral,* 1972; *An Anthology of Slovak Literature,* 1977; and an opera, *Zuzanka Hrashkovie,* 1978. He is also the author of *They Followed the King,* 1965, and *Follow the King,* 1977, as well as a number of hymns and translations in the *Worship Supplement,* 1969, to *The Lutheran Hymnal,* and in the LBW. The recipient of a number of awards for *This Day,* he has also been commissioned to write two hymns—a Bicentennial hymn in 1975, and a hymn for the Hymn Society of America in 1978. He is listed in *Who's Who in the Midwest* (1968) and in *Who's Who in Religion* (1978).

ASCENDED TRIUMPH. "Up through endless ranks of angels" was originally written for a Swedish tune, and was published in the Augsburg Publishing House bulletin insert with a tune by Carl Schalk (LBW 118). "Ascended Triumph" was written in the summer of 1973 while the composer, Henry V. Gerike, was attending summer school at Concordia Seminary, St. Louis. It has also been used as the basis for a commissioned work by Walter Pelz (LBW 240), which has been published by Concordia Publishing House.

The son of a Lutheran pastor, Gerike was born August 17, 1948, in Parkers Prairie, Minnesota. At Concordia College, St. Paul, Minnesota, he studied with Paul Manz (LBW 50), graduating with a Bachelor of Arts degree in 1970. He has also studied organ with Herbert Gotsch, and composition with Richard Hillert (LBW 63). From 1970 to 1975 he taught at Concord Lutheran School, Pagedale, Missouri, during which time he was also music director at Unity Lutheran Church, Ben Nor, Missouri, and after 1972, was director of the St. Louis Lutheran Children's Choir. He was co-founder and first chairman of the St. Louis Lutheran Parish Musicians Guild. He has done graduate work at Concordia Teachers College, River Forest, Illinois, and since 1975, has served as teacher and music director of St. Paul's Lutheran Church and School, Aurora, Illinois. He is co-founder of the Fox Valley Lutheran Parish Musicians Guild.

160   FILLED WITH THE SPIRIT'S POWER
Tune: Sheldonian

Emphasizing the Holy Spirit's gift of fellowship and the church's unity, this hymn was first published in *100 Hymns,* 1969, and has since been included in various hymnals around the world.

The author, John Raphael Peacey, was born July 16, 1896, at Hove, Brighton, Sussex, in England. After attending St. Edmund's School, Canterbury, he enlisted in the armed forces in 1915 and served in France. He was mentioned in several dispatches and received the Military Cross. In 1919 he entered Selwyn College, Cambridge, to study for the ministry, and in 1921 graduated with honors in theology. He took holy orders and became assistant master at Wellington College, and two years later was appointed dean and chaplain of Selwyn College. In 1927 he went to Simla, India, where he was headmaster at Bishop Cotton School for nine years, and after that, principal of the school until 1945, when he returned to England. There he became canon residentiary of Bristol Cathedral. On his retirement in 1967 to Hurstpierpoint, Sussex, he served as rural dean until his death on October 31, 1971.

SHELDONIAN. Cyril Vincent Taylor was born in Wigan, Lancashire, England, on December 11, 1907. From 1918 to 1926 he attended Magdalen College School, Oxford, serving also as a chorister at Magdalen College Chapel until 1923. In 1929 he received a Bachelor of Arts degree from Christ Church, Oxford, and after graduate studies at Westcott House in Cambridge, was ordained a deacon in 1931 and a priest in 1932. He served as curate of St. Mary's, Hinckley, from 1931 to 1933, and of St. Andrew's, Kingswood, 1933 to 1936. From 1936 to 1939 he was precentor at Bristol Cathedral, after which he was employed for fourteen years as assistant to the head of religious broadcasting. In 1953 he was appointed warden and chaplain of the Royal School of Church Music, and in 1958, perpetual curate of Cerne Abbas. Since 1969 he has been precentor and residentiary canon at Salisbury Cathedral.

Both a theologian and a musician, Taylor served as one of the editors of the *BBC Hymn Book,* London, 1951, to which he contributed twenty tunes. "Sheldonian" is named for the Sheldonian Theater in Oxford, which was across the street from the room in which the compilers of the *BBC Hymn Book* held some of their meetings. It was first published in a leaflet by Novello in 1943 with the words "Lead us, O Father, in the paths of peace." Osborne* notes that Taylor's settings "reveal a richness of harmony and melody that many attempt and few attain."

161 O DAY FULL OF GRACE *(Den signede Dag)*
Tune: Den signede Dag

A pre-Reformation vernacular "day song" served as the basis for this hymn. The earliest source of the ancient folk hymn, which existed in a number of versions throughout Scandinavia, is a manuscript from about 1450 in the Uppsala University library. There it appears in Swedish with the opening line "Then signadhe dagh ther jak nw se." Revised for Protestant use, it first appeared in print in Danish, in Hans Thomissön's (LBW 227) *Den danske Psalmebog,* 1569. For the thousandth anniversary of the introduction of Christianity into Denmark, Grundtvig recast the hymn in 1826. A translation of Gruntvig's text was given in the *Concordia Hymnal,* 1932. A new translation of the older text has been prepared for the LBW by Gerald Thorson.

Thorson, who has been a professor of English at St. Olaf College, Northfield, Minnesota, since 1964, was born at Menomonie, Wisconsin, on June 8, 1921. Married to Anneliese Staub, he is the father of six children. His studies have included English, German, and Greek at Augsburg College (Bachelor of Arts, 1943); American studies at the University of Minnesota (Master of Arts, 1948); and English and comparative literature at Columbia University (Doctor of Philosophy, 1957); as well as linguistics and Scandinavian studies at the University of Wisconsin, French at Grenoble University, and Norwegian literature and history at Oslo University. After three years in the United States Infantry, he joined the faculty of Augsburg College in 1946, where he was chairman of the department of English from 1952 to 1964, chairman of

the humanities division from 1958 to 1964, and professor of English
from 1959 to 1964. At St. Olaf he has been professor of English and
chairman of the English department from 1964 to 1975, acting chairman
of the German department from 1975 to 1976, and chairman of the
language and literature division from 1973 to 1977. In addition he has
served as lecturer in English at Wagner College from 1951 to 1952,
visiting professor of American literature at the University of Iceland
from 1961 to 1962, and guest professor of American literature at
Konstanz University in Germany from 1970 to 1971.

Thorson is the author of a large number of articles, poems, reviews,
editorials, and essays, including fifteen articles on literature and the
teaching of English. He has served as Minnesota state chairman of the
National Council of Teachers of English Achievement Awards Program,
1958-1960; chairman of the Commission on Literature and Drama of the
Lutheran Society for Worship, Music, and the Arts, 1958-1961; member
of the International Board of Moderators of Lambda Iota Tau,
1959-1961; president of the Minnesota Council of Teachers of English,
1960-1961; associate editor of *Response* magazine, 1960-1970; chairman
of the board of publications of the Lutheran Society for Worship,
Music, and the Arts, 1962-1965; chairman of the Minnesota Association
of Department of English Chairmen, 1964-1970; and a member of the
hymn text committee of the Inter-Lutheran Commission on Worship,
1968-1977; and since 1977 has been a member of the editorial advisory
board of the *Journal* of the Society for the Study of Multi-Ethnic
Literatures in the United States. He has been the recipient of George
Sverdrup and Torger Thompson fellowships, a Fulbright Lectureship, an
American Lutheran Church Faculty Growth Award, a St. Olaf College
Humanities grant, and Augsburg College's Distinguished Alumnus
Citation.

DEN SIGNEDE DAG, one of Christoph Weyse's finest tunes and, indeed, one of the grandest church melodies to come out of Scandinavia,
was written in 1826 for this hymn by Grundtvig. It was included in
Weyse's *Koralbog,* 1839.

Christoph Ernst Friedrich Weyse, son of an herb peddler and captain
in the militia, was born March 5, 1774, at Altona, Denmark. When he
was seven years old, his father died, and his mother later remarried. His
mother was a pianist, and he received his earliest music training from his
maternal grandfather, C. B. Hauser, a violinist. He began piano lessons
in 1782, and soon came to be regarded as a prodigy. At ten he began
composing, and studied with a pupil of Carl Philipp Emanuel Bach.
When he was confirmed his parents discussed his future. His stepfather
wished for him to become a merchant, but his mother supported him in
his desire to become a musician. His mother died the same year,
however, and he yielded to his stepfather's wish and was apprenticed to a
merchant. It lasted for eight days. The merchant claimed the boy to be of
no use, and Weyse was thus rescued from pursuing that career. Through
the mayor of Altona, it was arranged for him to study with J. A. P.
Schulz (LBW 52) in Copenhagen, in whose home he lived as a son from
1790 to 1793. Through Schulz's influence he had violin lessons, and
organ lessons at Vor Frue Kirke, and was introduced to the court, where
he played his own compositions. He also appeared as a pianist in the
Harmonic Society and at the Royal Theater, but did not like the life of a
concert pianist and gave his last performance in 1802. From 1794 to 1805
he was organist of the Reformed church in Copenhagen. During these

years he composed a number of symphonies and piano pieces. When Schulz became ill and retired from teaching he was succeeded by F. L. Ae. Kunzen. Through Kunzen's wife, Weyse became interested in singing, and later, in 1809, taught singing to Princess Caroline. In 1799 he became a teacher to Peter Tutien's daughters, and fell in love with Julie, then sixteen. In 1801 he suffered a stroke which marked him for life, and was also refused Julie's hand in marriage. For several years thereafter he composed nothing. In 1805 the University of Copenhagen appointed him organist of Vor Frue Kirke, a position he held until his death. A performance of Mozart's *Don Giovanni* in 1807 inspired him to write again and he composed a number of successful *Singspielen*. In 1816 he was named a professor, a title he greatly cherished, and after 1819 he was town composer, writing music for occasions of church and state. In this capacity he wrote over thirty cantatas for the court church, and became well-known as a church composer. Of greatest significance for future generations were his romances and songs, some for texts by Bernhardt S. Ingemann (LBW 355), published after his death. Weyse had a number of other interests in addition to music. He could read English, French, Latin, and German, and had an extensive library. He loved the art of cooking. He had a medical collection and practiced medicine, and read also in linguistics, astronomy, geography, history, mathematics, and theology. Toward the end of his life he found a new home in Roskilde, where he practiced organ at the cathedral church, which he loved. He had a considerable ability to improvise, and when Franz Liszt visited Copenhagen in 1841, Weyse impressed him by improvising a five-voice double fugue a half-hour long. He was honored by the University of Copenhagen with a doctorate in 1842, and died the same year, on October 8.

162 LORD GOD, THE HOLY GHOST
Tune: Des Plaines

This hymn by James Montgomery (LBW 50) was published in Thomas Cotterill's (LBW 547) *Selection of Psalms and Hymns for Public and Private Worship*, 1819, and in a slightly altered version, in Montgomery's *Christian Psalmist*, 1825.

DES PLAINES, named for the town in which the composer was born and grew up, was written for the LBW. See LBW 118 for Carl Schalk.

163 COME, HOLY GHOST, GOD AND LORD
(Komm, Heiliger Geist, Herre Gott)
Tune: Komm, Heiliger Geist, Herre Gott

See LBW 48 for Martin Luther. The Latin antiphon, "Veni Sancte Spiritus: repletuorum corda fidelium," dates from the eleventh century. Out of this antiphon grew a single German stanza beginning "Komm, Heiliger Geist, Herre Gott," for which the earliest sources are two fifteenth-century manuscripts from Munich and the *Crailsheim Schulordnung* of 1480. It was well-known in Luther's day. Luther himself was fond of it, and in his table talks spoke of both the words and the music as having been composed by the Holy Ghost himself. Leaving the original German stanza nearly intact, Luther added two stanzas and published the whole in the Erfurt *Enchiridia,* 1524, and in Johann Walther's (LBW 350) *Geystliche gesangk Buchleyn,* 1524.

The composite English translation prepared for *The Lutheran Hymnal,* 1941, is given here with some alterations.

KOMM, HEILIGER GEIST, HERRE GOTT was included with Luther's text in the Erfurt *Enchiridia,* 1524. It is a simplified version of the plainchant melody associated with the German stanza.

J. S. Bach (LBW 219) employed this melody in Cantatas 59 and 175, and in an abbreviated form in Cantata 172. His motet, "Der Geist hilft," uses the tune, and two organ settings are found among the Eighteen Chorales.

164 CREATOR SPIRIT, BY WHOSE AID *(Veni, Creator Spiritus)*
Tune: All Ehr und Lob

See LBW 472 for "Veni, Creator Spiritus." This English text by John Dryden was included in a work published by Jacob Tonson in 1693: *Examen Poeticum: being The Third Part of Miscellany Poems, Containing Variety of New Translations of the Ancient Poets, Together with many Original Copies, by the Most Eminent Hands.*

Dryden was born August 9, 1631, at Aldwinkle, Northamptonshire, England, and was educated at Trinity College, Cambridge, receiving a Bachelor of Arts degree in 1654. He was born of Puritan parents, and expressed this background in his *Heroic Stanzas on the Death of Oliver Cromwell,* 1658, the first verses to bring him fame. In 1660, however, like many other Englishmen of the time, he became a Royalist, and celebrated the Restoration with two works, *Astraea Redux* and *A Panegyric on the Coronation.* His marriage in 1663 to Lady Elizabeth Howard was an unhappy one in which he seems to have been plainly unfaithful. In 1685 he became a member of the Roman Catholic Church for which he prepared a number of translations from Latin. He had become Poet Laureate and Historiographer Royal in 1670, but was stripped of these posts on the accession in 1688 of William, a Protestant. He died May 1, 1700, and is buried at Westminster Abbey beside Geoffrey Chaucer.

ALL EHR UND LOB is by an unknown composer and first appeared in the Strassburg *Kirchengesangbuch,* 1541. The harmonization was prepared for the LBW by Richard Hillert (LBW 63).

165 HOLY, HOLY, HOLY
Tune: Nicaea

This hymn by Reginald Heber (LBW 84) was first published in *A Selection of Psalms and Hymns for the Parish Church of Banbury,* third edition, 1826, and was included the next year in his posthumous *Hymns.*

NICAEA, which has become firmly bonded to Heber's Trinity text, is appropriately named for the Council of Nicaea (325 A.D.) which crystallized the doctrine of the Trinity. First published in the Original Edition of *Hymns Ancient and Modern,* 1861, the setting seems to have used John Hopkins' "Trinity," 1850, given below, as a starting point.

etc.

Similarity to "Wachet auf" (LBW 31) in the first and last phrases has also been noted. Although included in countless hymnals, both the melody and the harmony of "Nicaea" have remained unchanged.

Son of a banker, the composer, John Bacchus Dykes, was born March 10, 1823, at Kingston upon Hull in England. His musical talents became apparent when he was quite young, and at the age of ten he began to play the organ for his grandfather's church. In 1847 he received a Bachelor of Arts degree from St. Catherine's, Cambridge, where he was instrumental in founding the University Music Society. Ordained the same year, he served briefly at Malton, Yorkshire, after which he became minor canon and precentor at Durham Cathedral in 1849. Durham University bestowed an honorary Doctor of Music degree on him in 1861, and the following year he became vicar of St. Oswald's, Durham. During his years of ministry at St. Oswald's his personality and pastoral devotion won for him many friends and followers, but his high-church views conflicted with the low-church ideas of his bishop, who saw to it that Dykes had no assistance with his parish. The excessive burden of caring for a large parish alone, together with the strain of the controversy, took its toll, and Dykes died in his fifty-third year, on January 22, 1876, at Ticehurst, Sussex. His publications included sermons and articles on religion as well as services and anthems, but it is for his hymn tunes, numbering nearly three hundred, that he is remembered today.

166 ALL GLORY BE TO GOD ON HIGH
(Allein Gott in der Höh sei Ehr)
Tune: Allein Gott in der Höh

Nikolaus Decius' (LBW 111) rhymed version of the "Gloria in Excelsis" first appeared in 1525 in the Rostock *Gesang Buch* in Low German, beginning "Aleyn God yn der Höge sy eere," and was included in a High German version in Valentin Schumann's *Geistliche lieder auffs new gebessert und gemehrt,* published in Wittenberg in 1539.

A new translation was written for the LBW by Gilbert E. Doan (LBW 99).

256

ALLEIN GOTT IN DER HÖH was adapted by Decius for his High German text in Schumann's *Geistliche lieder* from the tenth-century plainsong "Gloria in Excelsis" used in the Roman Church at Easter time. The original plainsong can be found in *The Liber Usualis* (Tournai, 1963), p. 16. Decius began his melody where the Latin text begins "et in terra pax hominibus bonae voluntatis" ("and on earth, peace, good will to men").

J. S. Bach (LBW 219) used the melody in several of his works: in Cantatas 85, 104, 112, and 128, in his *Choralgesänge,* and in several organ movements—three in the *Clavierübung,* three in the Eighteen Chorales, and four among the Miscellaneous Preludes. Felix Mendelssohn (LBW 60) used it in his *St. Paul.* The LBW harmonization was prepared by Carl Schalk (LBW 118) for the LBW.

167   GLORY BE TO GOD THE FATHER!

Tune: Herr, ich habe misgehandelt

Written by Horatius Bonar especially for the English Presbyterian *Psalms and Hymns for Divine Worship,* 1867, this hymn first appeared in the author's *Hymns of Faith and Hope,* third series, 1866. Orginally the stanzas were six lines in length; the last two lines of each stanza are omitted here.

Bonar was a descendant of a family which had been represented in the Church of Scotland for over two centuries. Born December 19, 1808, in Edinburgh, he was the son of a solicitor of excise. He studied with Thomas Chalmers at the University of Edinburgh, and began his ministry as assistant at St. John's Parish, Leith. Ordained in 1837, he went to Kelso where he was in charge of the North Parish. At the time of the Disruption in the Church of Scotland in 1843, Bonar joined Dr. Chalmers and others in forming the Free Church of Scotland, and for many years was one of the editors of *The Border Watch,* the official Free Church paper. The University of Aberdeen honored him with a Doctor of Divinity degree in 1853. A trip to Egypt and Palestine from 1855 to 1856 aroused a great interest in the Jews and in prophecy. The second coming of Christ was much on Bonar's mind all of his life, and for many years he also edited *The Journal of Prophecy.* In 1866 he became the minister of the Chalmers Memorial Free Church, Grange, Edinburgh, and in 1883 he became moderator of the General Assembly of the Free Church of Scotland. He died in Edinburgh on July 31, 1889.

Bonar's life was one of devoted ministry to his church in all aspects—preaching, praying, visiting, and writing. Known as a man of broad and generous faith, and of wide scholarship and culture, he wrote voluminously—nearly one book a year. His hymns, some six hundred in all, were written quite casually so that a number of them possess poetical flaws. However, one or two have been claimed among the finest of English hymnody, and nearly one hundred entered common use in England and America. Five of his hymns are included in the LBW.

HERR, ICH HABE MISGEHANDELT. This tune was written by Johann Crüger (LBW 23) for Johann Franck's (LBW 224) hymn, "Herr, ich habe misgehandelt," in Crüger's *Geistliche Kirchen-Melodier*, Berlin, 1649 (Zahn* #3695). The melody in its original form (given above) and a translation of Franck's text can be found in *The Lutheran Hymnal*, 1941.

168   KYRIE, GOD FATHER *(Kyrie, Gott Vater)*

Tune: Kyrie, Gott Vater

The plainsong setting for a nine-fold Kyrie (from which the present melody is adapted) predates this text and formed the basis for it. The following example, giving the first portion of the plainsong melody, shows the melismatic setting of the text "Kyrie eleison," to which was added a trope (see p. 14), with one syllable for each note of the melody.

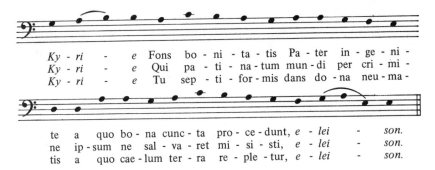

Willi Apel, in his book on *Gregorian Chant* (Bloomington, Indiana, 1958), cites Ekkehard IV of St. Gall (*c.* 980–1060) as attributing the trope to Tuotilo, a monk of St. Gall who died in 913.

During the sixteenth century the trope appeared in German translation as "Kyrie, Gott Vater in Ewigkeit," and was printed apparently in Wittenberg in 1541 (Wackernagel* III, #250). Although it is sometimes attributed to Johann Spangenberg (1484–1550), a pastor at Nordhausen and later superintendent at Eisleben, his authorship cannot be substantiated. Both the German Kyrie and the Latin original were sung on festivals from Trinity to Christmas.

The English translation was prepared in 1939 for *The Lutheran Hymnal*, 1941, by William Gustave Polack.

Polack, born December 7, 1890, at Wausau, Wisconsin, attended Concordia College, Fort Wayne, Indiana, and Concordia Seminary, St. Louis, Missouri. Ordained in 1914 by the Reverend C. A. Franck, founder and first editor of the *Lutheran Witness,* he succeeded Franck at Trinity Lutheran Church, Evansville, Indiana. In the same year, he was married to Iona Mary Gick of Fort Wayne, and later became the father of six children. In 1925 he was appointed professor of theology at Concordia Seminary, St. Louis, assuming chairmanship of the department of historical theology after a time. Named chairman of the Missouri Synod's Committee on Hymnology and Liturgics in 1929, he organized, the following year, the Intersynodical Committee on Hymnology and Liturgies for the Synodical Conference of North America, which prepared *The Lutheran Hymnal.* To this hymnal he contributed three original hymns and nine translations. For twenty-five years beginning in 1925 he was associate editor of the *Lutheran Witness,* and from 1928 to

1939 also edited the Concordia *Junior Messenger.* He served as secretary (1927-1937) and president (1945-1949) of the Concordia Historical Institute, and from 1927 to 1949 edited its quarterly. A list of his publications contains more than twenty-five items, including books of poetry—*Beauty for Ashes and Other Poems* (1935) and *Martin Luther in English Poetry* (1938)—as well as collections of hymns and works on the background of hymns. His major work on hymnology was *The Handbook to the Lutheran Hymnal,** 1942, which has gone through two revisions, 1947 and 1958, and is still in print. In the field of church history, his publications include *The Building of a Great Church: A Brief History of our Lutheran Church in America,* 1926, revised and enlarged in 1941; *David Livingstone,* 1929; *Into All the World: The Story of Lutheran Foreign Missions,* 1930; *The Story of C. F. W. Walther,* 1935, revised in 1947; and *The Story of Luther,* 1934. Valparaiso University, Valparaiso, Indiana, honored him with a Doctor of Divinity degree in 1942. He died at St. Louis on June 5, 1950.

KYRIE, GOTT VATER. As mentioned above, this melody is adapted from the plainsong "Kyrie fons bonitatis,"† which dates from early medieval times. Several adaptations of the melody are found in the sixteenth and seventeenth centuries. Of those quoted in Zahn,* the LBW version most closely resembles that found in *Das grosse Cantional: oder Kirchen-Gesangbuch,* Darmstadt, 1687 (Zahn* #8600d).

Carl Schalk (LBW 118) has prepared the harmonization for the LBW.

169 FATHER MOST HOLY *(O Pater sancte)*
Tune: Christe sanctorum

The annual commemoration of the Trinity was at first a votive office with no fixed date. Later, in England, it became customary to observe it on the Sunday after Pentecost, a custom which became general in the West. This Latin hymn in honor of the Trinity is first found in several tenth-century French manuscripts, and was translated by Percy Dearmer for *The English Hymnal,* 1906, which he edited with Ralph Vaughan Williams (LBW 101). The text given in the LBW, especially in the last two stanzas, represents extensive alteration.

Dearmer, born February 27, 1867, at Kilburn, Middlesex, England, received a Bachelor of Arts degree from Christ Church, Oxford, in 1892, and a Master of Arts degree in 1896. Ordained a deacon in 1891 and a priest in 1892, he served for the next several years in various parishes. From 1901 to 1915 he was vicar of St. Mary the Virgin, Primrose Hill, in London, where Martin Shaw (LBW 541) was organist. Together with Shaw and Vaughan Williams, Dearmer edited *Songs of Praise,* 1925, and the *Oxford Book of Carols,* 1928. Also active in social issues, he was from 1891 to 1912 secretary to the London Christian Social Union, and during World War I, was a chaplain of the British Red Cross in Serbia. From 1919 until his death on May 29, 1936, he was professor of ecclesiastical art at King's College, London, and from 1931 held the post of canon of Westminster as well. He wrote a number of books dealing with history, ecclesiastical arts, and social issues, and also prepared *Songs of Praise Discussed,** 1933, a handbook to the enlarged edition of *Songs of Praise,* 1931, of which he was also an editor.

†Although all tropes were ruled out at the Council of Trent (1545-1564), the first lines have remained with their respective chants as a convenient means of identification.

CHRISTE SANCTORUM. During the sixteenth and seventeenth centuries, concurrent with the "modernization" of the Breviaries (see p. 15), there arose in France a new kind of church tune. Although generally not clearly cast in a regular rhythmic meter, these tunes were more measured than the older plainchant and were also in the modern major and minor modes. Some of the tunes were adapted from older plainsong melodies, others from secular tunes, but the origins of most of the melodies have not been as yet discovered. These French melodies made their way into England when a number of them were taken from La Feillée's *Méthode de Plain-Chant* (published in 1750 and later in 1782 and 1808) into *The Hymnal Noted,* 1851, a work prepared by John Mason Neale (LBW 34) and Thomas Helmore. From there they entered *The English Hymnal,* 1906, and later English collections.

"Christe Sanctorum" first appeared in the *Paris Antiphoner,* 1681, where it was the setting for the hymn "Ceteri numquam." The harmonization was prepared for the *Worship Supplement,* 1969, to *The Lutheran Hymnal,* by Carl Schalk (LBW 118).

170 CROWN HIM WITH MANY CROWNS

Tune: Diademata

Stanzas 1–3 and 5–6 of this hymn are from Matthew Bridges' *Hymns of the Heart,* second edition, 1851. Stanza 4 is from a hymn beginning "Crown him with crowns of gold, All nations great and small," in Godfrey Thring's *Hymns and Sacred Lyrics,* 1874.

Bridges, born at Maldon, Essex, on July 14, 1800, was brought up in the Church of England, but because of the influence of John Henry Newman and the Oxford Movement, he entered the Roman Catholic Church in 1848. He published a number of prose and poetry works. In addition to *Hymns of the Heart,* he published another collection of hymns entitled *The Passion of Jesus,* 1852. Later he moved to Canada, where he lived in Quebec. Near the end of his life he returned to England and spent the rest of his days in a small villa at the Convent of the Assumption at Sidmouth, Devon. There he died on October 6, 1894.

Born March 25, 1823, in the rectory at Alford, Somerset, England, Thring was educated at Balliol College, Oxford, receiving a Bachelor of Arts degree in 1845. Ordained a deacon in 1846, and a priest the following year, he served as curate at Strathfield-Turgis, then at Strathfieldsaye, before succeeding his father at Laford in 1858. In 1867 he was appointed rural dean at Wells Cathedral, and in 1876 became prebend of East Harptree in Wells Cathedral. Besides his *Hymns and Other Verses* and *Hymns Congregational and Others,* both published in 1866, he was the editor of *A Church of England Hymn Book,* 1880, revised in 1882, a collection of extremely high quality which was an influential work, as well as the source of many alterations of texts found in later hymnals. Thring retired in 1893, and died ten years later at Shanley Green, Guildford, Surrey, on September 13.

DIADEMATA was written for this hymn when it was included in the Appendix to the Original Edition of *Hymns Ancient and Modern,* 1868.

Born at Canterbury on March 27 or 29, 1816, the composer, George Job Elvey, began his musical career under the cathedral organist, Highmore Skeats, whose daughter he later married. He also studied with his older brother, Stephen, and later attended the Royal Academy of

Music. In 1838 he received his Bachelor of Music degree at New College, Oxford, and two years later, by special dispensation, his Doctor of Music degree. At age nineteen, after deputizing briefly at Christ Church, Magdelan, and at New College, Oxford, Elvey applied for the position at St. George's Chapel, Windsor, and was appointed by King William IV over such other contestants as Samuel Sebastian Wesley (LBW 197) and Sir George Smart. There he served from 1835 to 1882, during which time he taught several members of the royal family and composed music for a number of royal events. Knighted in 1871, he died December 9, 1893, at Windlesham, Surrey.

171 REJOICE, THE LORD IS KING!

Tune: Laus Regis

See LBW 27 for Charles Wesley. This hymn was first published in John Wesley's *Moral and Sacred Poems,* 1744.

LAUS REGIS, originally called "Shamokin," was included in the Lutheran *Book of Worship with Hymns and Tunes,* Philadelphia, 1899, of which William E. Fischer was one of the music editors. There it was the setting for Samuel Crossman's (LBW 94) "Jerusalem on high My song and city is."

William Edward Fischer, born October 6, 1849, in Berlin, Germany, received a Bachelor of Arts degree from Pennsylvania College in 1872 and three years later graduated from the Lutheran Theological Seminary at Gettysburg. Ordained the same year, he accepted a call to Center Hall, where he remained until 1893 when he went to Shamokin, Pennsylvania. He was pastor of Trinity Lutheran Church, Shamokin, until his death on August 10, 1936.

Fischer held several prominent positions in the General Synod, including secretary and member of the hymnbook committee. From 1929 to 1931 he was on the hymnbook committee of the United Lutheran Church. As a representative of the Susquehanna Synod, he was for ten years a director of Gettysburg Seminary. During his ministry to Shamokin he was awarded a Doctor of Divinity degree by Susquehanna University. He was married and was the father of a son and two daughters.

172 LORD, ENTHRONED IN HEAVENLY SPLENDOR

Tune: Bryn Calfaria

Written by George Hugh Bourne, this hymn was included in *Seven Post-Communion Hymns,* 1874, a private publication for use at St. Edmund's College. Its first appearance in a hymnal was in the 1889 Supplement to *Hymns Ancient and Modern.*

The son of an Anglican clergyman, Bourne was born November 8, 1840, at St. Paul's Cray, Kent. He received a Bachelor of Arts degree from Christ Church College, Oxford, in 1863, a Bachelor of Civil Law degree in 1866, and a Doctor of Civil Law degree in 1871. Ordained a deacon in 1863 and a priest in 1864, he held his first position as assistant curate of Sandford-on-Thames from 1863 to 1865. In 1866 he was appointed headmaster of St. Andrew's, Chardstock, and in 1874 became warden of that school which had been transferred to St. Edmund's,

Salisbury. He was chaplain to the Bishop of Bloemfontein from 1879 to 1898. At Salisbury Cathedral he was sub-dean from 1887 until 1901 when he became treasurer and prebendary. Bourne died at St. Edmund's on December 1, 1925.

For BRYN CALFARIA see LBW 156. This harmonization is by Theodore Beck (LBW 33).

173 THE HEAD THAT ONCE WAS CROWNED
Tune: St. Magnus

See LBW 156 for Thomas Kelly. This hymn was included in the 1820 edition of his *Hymns on Various Passages of Scripture,* London.

ST. MAGNUS. A comtemporary of Henry Purcell, Jeremiah Clarke, whose birth has been dated variously from 1659 to 1673, was born in London and spent his life there. As a boy he was a chorister of the Chapel Royal under Dr. John Blow. He was organist of Winchester College from 1692 until 1695 when he succeeded John Blow at St. Paul's, London. It is probable that he sang for the coronation of James II, and that as the first organist of the new Cathedral of St. Paul's, he officiated at Father Smith's magnificent organ at the opening of Christopher Wren's masterpiece on December 2, 1697. Clarke was music master to Queen Anne for whom he composed some harpsichord pieces. In 1700, he and William Croft (LBW 320) became gentlemen of the Chapel Royal, and in 1704 both were appointed organists of the Chapel. Robert Bridges (LBW 123) called Clarke the inventor of the modern English hymntune; "his tunes are beautiful, and have the plaintive grace characteristic of his music and melancholy temperament. They are the first in merit of their kind, as they were first in time and they are truly national and popular in style, so that their neglect is to be regretted." Tragically, Clarke brought his own life to an end on December 1, 1707, because of an unfortunate romance.

Clarke wrote instrumental, operatic, and keyboard music, songs, and much church music including anthems, services, psalm tunes, and organ music. The well-known trumpet voluntary and trumpet tune once attributed to Purcell are also his.

This tune is first found in Henry Playford's *Divine Companion,* second edition, 1707, where it was set to a version of Psalm 117. Besides "St. Magnus," it has also been called "Nottingham," "Brentford," "Newborough," and "Buckingham."

174 FOR ALL THE SAINTS
Tune: Sine nomine

See LBW 77 for William Walsham How. This hymn, orginally beginning "For all *Thy* saints," was published in Earl Nelson's (LBW 177) *Hymns for the Saints' Days,* 1864.

SINE NOMINE, described by Dearmer* as "one of the finest hymntunes written during the present century," was written by Ralph Vaughan Williams (LBW 101) for this hymn and included in *The English Hymnal,* 1906, where it was marked "Anon."

Tune: Lasst uns erfreuen

John Athelstan Laurie Riley's hymn was written for the tune, "Lasst uns erfreuen," and included in *The English Hymnal,* 1906. Riley's studies of the Eastern churches are reflected in the imagery found in this text. Much of it is suggested by Greek liturgies, and the second stanza is actually a paraphrase of the *Theotokion,* the Hymn of Mary, sung in the early Greek church at the close of the choir office.

Riley, one of the editors of the 1906 *English Hymnal,* to which he contributed translations from Latin and Greek, as well as original hymns, was born in London on August 10, 1858. He received a Bachelor of Arts degree (1881) and a Master of Arts degree (1883) from Pembroke College, Oxford. During the 1880s he spent much time traveling in Persia, Turkey, and Kurdistan, out of which he published a number of pamphlets and articles on the Eastern Christian churches. In 1911 he published *The Religious Question in Public Education* and a revision of the Prayer Book, and four years later, *Concerning Hymn Tunes and Sequences.* For most of his life he was a member of the House of Laymen of the Province of Canterbury, and was an ardent supporter of the Anglo-Catholic movement. He was living on the Island of Jersey when it was invaded by the Germans during World War II, and there he died on November 17, 1945.

For LASST UNS ERFREUEN see LBW 143.

176   FOR ALL YOUR SAINTS, O LORD

Tune: Festal Song

Originally beginning "For all *Thy* saints, O Lord," this hymn was included in Richard Mant's *Ancient Hymns from the Roman Breviary, for Domestick Use . . . To which are added Original Hymns,* 1837.

The son of the rector at Southampton, England, Mant was born February 12, 1776. He received Bachelor of Arts (1797) and Master of Arts (1798) degrees from Trinity College, Oxford, and in 1801 became a fellow of Oriel. In 1811 he was Bampton Lecturer. Ordained a deacon of the Church of England in 1802 and a priest the following year, he traveled for some time before taking a post as curate of Buriton in Hamptonshire. Afterwards he served as curate of Crawley and then of Southampton before going as vicar to Coggeshill, Essex, in 1810. He became rector of St. Botolph's, Bishopsgate, London, in 1815, and of East Horsley, Surrey, in 1818. In 1820 he was consecrated bishop of Killaloe and Kilfenoragh in Ireland, and in 1823, of Down and Connor. Nine years later the see of Dromore was united with his diocese. Besides several collections of sacred poetry, and *The Book of Psalms in an English Metrical Version,* 1824, he was author of *The History of the Church in Ireland.* He died November 2, 1848, at Ballymoney in County Antrim.

FESTAL SONG was included in John Ireland Tucker's *The Hymnal with Tunes Old and New,* 1872, of the Episcopal Church, where it was set to William Hammond's "Awake and sing the song."

The composer, William Henry Walter, was born July 1, 1825, in Newark, New Jersey, and as a boy was organist at a Presbyterian Church and at Grace Episcopal Church in that city. He later studied with Edward

Hodges, and in 1842 became organist at the Church of the Epiphany in New York City. Thereafter he served at St. John's Chapel, St. Paul's Chapel, and Trinity Chapel until 1869. From 1865, also, he served as organist of Columbia University, which had honored him with a Doctor of Music degree the previous year. He composed sacred music, and published a *Manual of Church Music,* 1860; *Chorals and Hymns,* 1857; and *The Common Prayer, with Ritual Song,* 1868. He died in New York City in 1893.

The harmonization is by Paul O. Manz (LBW 50).

177   BY ALL YOUR SAINTS IN WARFARE
Tune: King's Lynn

Horatio Nelson, third Earl Nelson, was the son of Thomas Bolton of Burnham, Norfolk. (On succeeding to the title as second Earl, Thomas Bolton assumed the name of his uncle, the celebrated Admiral Viscount Nelson.) Horatio, born August 7, 1823, at Brickworth House in Wiltshire, attended Trinity College, Cambridge, receiving a Master of Arts degree in 1844. Succeeding to the title in 1835, he took his seat ten years later, and in the same year married Mary Jane Diana, daughter of the second Earl of Normanton. In 1909, he became the "father" of the Nelson House. He died of dropsy at Trafalgar House, and was buried March 1, 1913.

Earl Nelson published *A Form of Family Prayer,* 1852, and *A Calendar of Lessons for Every Day in the Year,* 1857. He was an active member of the Home Reunion Society and wrote extensively on the subject. Assisted by John Keble, Earl Nelson edited the *Salisbury Hymn-Book* in 1857, which was revised and published in 1868 as the *Sarum Hymnal.* The source of the present hymn is his *Hymns for Saints' Days, and other Hymns, By a Layman,* 1864. The design for the hymn, in which the first and last stanzas are suitable for any Saint's Day and intermediate stanzas are furnished for the persons specially commemorated, was suggested by a hymn of John S. B. Monsell's (LBW 131), "Ye saints! in blest communion," in his *Hymns of Love and Praise,* 1863. Originally the first line read: "*From* all *Thy* saints in warfare."

KING'S LYNN, a traditional English melody, is named after a town in Norfolk, England, where Charles Burney was organist of St. Margaret's Church from 1752 to 1759. Ralph Vaughan Williams (LBW 101) arranged the melody for G. K. Chesterton's "O God of Earth and Altar" (LBW 428) in *The English Hymnal,* 1906. Paul Bunjes' (LBW 38) harmonization was prepared for the *Worship Supplement,* 1969, to *The Lutheran Hymnal.*

178   BY ALL YOUR SAINTS IN WARFARE
Tune: King's Lynn

This hymn is a continuation of LBW 177.

179   AT THE NAME OF JESUS
Tune: King's Weston

Caroline Maria Noel, whose father was a Church of England clergyman and also a hymnwriter, was born in London April 10, 1817. She wrote some verses at the age of seventeen, but did not write again until the last twenty-five years of her life when increasing illness led her to do so. Her collection, which was published with the hope that it might be helpful to other invalids, was entitled *The Name of Jesus and other Verses for the Sick and Lonely,* 1861. "At the name of Jesus" was included in the 1870 enlarged edition of that work and has since been included in many hymnals. Noel died December 7, 1877, in Hyde Park.

KING'S WESTON was composed for this text by Ralph Vaughan Williams (LBW 101) and included in *Songs of Praise,* 1925.

180 MY SOUL NOW MAGNIFIES THE LORD

Tune: Ich heb mein Augen sehnlich auf

Based on the Magnificat (Luke 1:46–55), this hymn by Stephanie Kristin Frey was written in the summer of 1974 at the suggestion of Gracia Grindal (LBW 32). The author notes:

> There are no great stories of inspiration or insight to tell about my work on this text. The challenge technically was to preserve some of the richness of the biblical language, and at the same time have the syntax reflect contemporary sentence structure. Mary's song has always been a special one to me because it is such a moving declaration of praise and thanksgiving spoken with deep humility on the part of a woman whose life was to be radically changed by the work of the Creator.

Frey was born October 8, 1952, in Waterloo, Iowa, where her family lived. During her elementary years the family moved to Madison, Wisconsin, and she graduated from James Madison Memorial High School there. In 1974 she received a Bachelor of Arts degree in English, cum laude, from Luther College, Waverly, Iowa, and later that year she joined the staff at Augsburg Publishing House in Minneapolis as an editorial assistant. She has since taken a part-time position as an assistant editor in Educational Resources at Augsburg to allow her to enroll in 1978 at Luther Seminary in the Master of Divinity program.

ICH HEB MEIN AUGEN SEHNLICH AUF. One hundred years before the birth of J. S. Bach (LBW 219), another giant of sacred music was born. On October 8, 1585, Heinrich Schütz was born at Köstritz, Saxony. In 1599 he became a chorister in the chapel of the Landgrave Maurice of Hesse-Cassel, where he received thorough musical training and a good general education. Proceeding to the University of Marburg, he took up the study of law, but under sponsorship of the landgrave went the following year to Venice (then the capital of the music world) to study with Giovanni Gabrielli. Gabrielli died in 1612, and Schütz returned to Germany in 1613, continuing his law studies at Leipzig, and taking a position as organist to the landgrave. In 1617 he was appointed director of the chapel to the Elector Johann Georg of Saxony, a position he held for the remainder of his life. Two years later he was married to Magdalene Wildeck. The untimely death of his wife only six years later deeply influenced him, and he dedicated the rest of his life to composing church music. Turning in 1628 to his constant source of inspiration, the Psalms, he composed melodies with simple four-part harmonization for some of the rhymed Psalm paraphrases of Dr. Cornelius Becker. His *Psalmen Davids, in Teutsche Reimen gebrachte durch D. Cornelium Beckern* ("Becker Psalter") was published in Freiberg in 1628. Later, at the request of Elector Johann Georg II who succeeded his father in 1655, Schütz revised and enlarged the "Becker Psalter" and it was published in Dresden in 1661. From 1628 to 1629 Schütz again lived in Italy, this time to study with Claudio Monteverdi. During much of his career the Thirty Years' War disrupted Schütz's work, greatly reducing the number of musicians available to him and money for salaries, including his own. In 1622 he obtained leave to accept an invitation to Copenhagen extended by King Christian IV of Denmark. For the next several years he went back and forth between different courts, spending time at Copenhagen, Hanover, and Brunswick, and returning occasionally to Dresden, where he was still officially in the service of the elector. Finally in 1641 he returned to Dresden and spent the next three years reorganizing his music program. After 1657 he went to live with his sister at Weissenfels while continuing to render occasional service to the elector. During the later years of his life Schütz's health, especially his sense of hearing, began to fail. He spent much of his time in the study of Scriptures and spiritual books, and wrote his final masterpieces, the Passion settings according to Matthew, Luke, and John. He died in Dresden, November 6, 1672.

As the setting for Psalm 121, "Ich heb' mein' Augen sehnlich auf," this tune appeared in the "Becker Psalter," 1628, and the setting was included in the 1661 publication. Both tune and harmonization are given in simplified form, as found in George R. Woodward's (LBW 149) *Songs of Syon,* 1904.

181 GREET NOW THE SWIFTLY CHANGING YEAR
(Rok nový zase k nám přišel)
Tune: Rok nový

This very old and popular Slovak hymn appeared in the 1636 edition of the "Tranoscius" (LBW 96). The English translation was prepared in 1968 by Jaroslav Vajda (LBW 159) for the *Worship Supplement,* 1969, to *The Lutheran Hymnal.*

ROK NOVÝ, an anonymous Slovak melody, was first published in Tobias Závorka's *Kancional,* 1602, but may have been in existence as early as the fifteenth century. The harmonization was prepared by Theodore Beck (LBW 33) for the *Worship Supplement,* 1969.

182 RISE, O CHILDREN OF SALVATION
(Auf! ihr Christen, Christi Glieder)
Tune: Unser Herrscher

Justus Falckner, the first Lutheran pastor ordained in America, was an early representation of the later blending of the European background in American Lutheranism. Himself a German, Falckner was ordained by Swedish pastors. His first charge was a Dutch congregation in New York and along the Hudson River. His ordination is also of special interest, in that it is the earliest recorded instance of the use of an organ in church services in the United States. A group of German Pietists in the Wissahickon valley in Pennsylvania provided an orchestra and a small organ for the service.

Born November 22, 1672, in Langenreinsdorf, Crimmitschau in Zwickau, Saxony, Falckner was the son of a Lutheran pastor, and studied theology under the pietist, August Hermann Francke, at the University of Halle. Feeling inadequate for the ministry, he accepted a power of attorney in Rotterdam in 1700, and for a while was selling William Penn's lands in Pennsylvania. He was persuaded to accept a pastoral call to New York, however, and on November 24, 1703, was ordained in the Swedish Gloria Dei Church located in Wicacoa in the Philadelphia area. For a time he ministered to Dutch settlers on the Manatawny near New Hannover. Then he became pastor to congregations in New York and Albany, and ministered as well to three congregations in New Jersey—at Hackensack, in Bergen County, and on the Raritan River—and to two in New York, Loonenburg and Neuburg. He left the New York ministry either by death or retirement in 1723.

This hymn was published in Germany in Francke's *Geistreiches Gesang Buch,* Halle, 1697, and entered Johann Freylinghausen's *Gesangbuch* (LBW 32) in 1704, which resulted in its becoming widespread. It was translated in Emma Frances Bevan's *Songs of Eternal Life,* 1858.

Emma Frances Shuttleworth, whose father later became bishop of Chichester, was born at Oxford, England, on September 25, 1827. In 1856 she was married to R. C. L. Bevan of the Lombard Street banking firm. She prepared a number of translations from German which were published in her *Songs of Eternal Life,* and in *Songs of Praise for Christian Pilgrims,* 1859. She died at Cannes, France, on February 13, 1909.

UNSER HERRSCHER (also "Neander"). Joachim Neander's hymn, "Unser Herrscher, unser König," was first published with this tune in his *Alpha und Omega, Glaub- und Liebesübung,* Bremen, 1680. The last line originally read (Zahn* #3735a):

It was brought closer to its present form in Freylinghausen's 1704 *Gesangbuch.*

Although he died at the age of thirty, Neander wrote some sixty hymns, including "Praise to the Lord, the Almighty" (LBW 543), besides his hymn tunes, and has been called the "Paul Gerhardt [LBW 23] of the Calvinists." Born in 1650 at Bremen, Germany, he attended the Gymnasium Illustre there. During his youth he took religion quite lightly and—like many other seventeenth-century students—led a rather carefree and unruly existence. Pastor Theodore Under-Eyck of St. Martin's Church in Bremen led him to change his ways. After tutoring five young men in Frankfurt-am-Main, Neander accompanied them to the University of Heidelberg. Through friends of his pupils he came to know two ardent Pietists—Jakob Spener and Johann J. Schütz (LBW 542)—and was stirred by their faith and their godly example. In 1674 he was appointed head master of the grammar school at Düsseldorf, and five years later he went as unordained assistant to Pastor Under-Eyck at St. Martin's Church, Bremen. Tuberculosis cut his life short; he died May 31, 1680.

Neanderthal, the valley of the Düssel near Mettmann where Neander used to take long walks, was named for him. It was in this valley that the skeleton of the *Homo neanderthalensis,* Neanderthal man, was discovered in 1856.

183 THE SON OF GOD GOES FORTH TO WAR
Tune: All Saints New

See LBW 84 for Reginald Heber. This hymn for St. Stephen's Day was published in Heber's posthumous *Hymns,* 1827.

ALL SAINTS NEW was included with this text in John Ireland Tucker's *The Hymnal with Tunes Old and New,* 1872.

The composer, Henry Stephen Cutler, was born in Boston, Massachusetts, on October 13, 1824, and had lessons there with the organist of Trinity Church before going to Frankfort-am-Main in 1844 to study music. While in Europe he visited the English cathedrals and became interested in their choirs. On his return he took a position as organist at Grace Church, Boston (no longer in existence), but found no opportunity to carry out his ideas; so he moved to the Church of the Advent in 1852, where he organized a fine choir of men and boys, the first surpliced choir in this country. In 1858 he went to Trinity Church in New York City where he removed the women from the choir and introduced choir vestments and the choral service. (He was succeeded at Trinity in 1866 by Henry Arthur Messiter [LBW 553].) In 1865 Cutler went on a concert tour for a month and when he returned, was terminated for absence without leave. He subsequently held several positions in New York City, Brooklyn, Providence, and Philadelphia, with his final position being at St. Paul's Church in Troy, New York, whence he retired in 1885 and returned to Boston to live. He died December 5, 1902.

Cutler published a considerable amount of sacred music, much of which he had used in his services, including twenty-two anthems, services, organ compositions, and the *Trinity Psalter.* In 1864 he was honored with a Doctor of Music degree from Columbia University.

184 IN HIS TEMPLE NOW BEHOLD HIM
Tune: Lindsborg

Henry John Pye, born about 1825 at Clifton Hall, Staffordshire, England, received a Bachelor of Arts degree from Trinity College, Cambridge, in 1848 and a Master of Arts four years later. Having taken holy orders he became rector in 1851 of Clifton-Campville, Staffordshire. In 1868 he and his wife joined the Roman Catholic Church. In addition to sermons and works on the church and its history, Pye published a book of *Hymns* in 1851 for the use of his congregation at Clifton-Campville. It was in that hymnal that this hymn first appeared. He died January 3, 1903.

LINDSBORG is named for Lindsborg, Kansas, where the composer was visiting at the time he wrote the tune.

Robert Leaf, born February 20, 1936, holds a Bachelor of Music

Education degree from MacPhail College of Music, Minneapolis. He studied composition with Paul Fetler and has published nearly one hundred choir anthems. He has taught public school music, and resides in Minneapolis, where he continues to compose.

185 GREAT GOD, A BLESSING FROM YOUR THRONE
Tune: Lob sei dem allmächtigen Gott

A native of Germany, Conrad Hermann Louis Schuette was born June 17, 1843, at Vorrel in Hanover. Nine years later his family came to the United States, where he attended Capital University, Columbus, Ohio, and was ordained in 1865. The same year, also, he was married to Victoria M. Wirth of Columbus. After serving as pastor of St. Mark's Lutheran Church, Delaware, Ohio, he joined the faculty of Capital University in 1872 as professor of mathematics and natural philosophy, and later became a professor of theology. For a number of years he was president of Capital University, while serving also as pastor of Grace Lutheran Church in Columbus. In 1881 he was called as pastor of Christ Lutheran Church, Pleasant Ridge (now Bexley), Ohio, and in 1894, was elected president of The Joint Synod of Ohio and Other States, a position he held for thirty years. During this time he collected over $400,000 for educational work, and in 1898 was honored with a Doctor of Divinity degree from Capital University. As one of the founders and molders of The National Lutheran Council, he served as its president from 1923 to 1925. In addition to *The Church Member's Manual; Church, State, and School; Before the Altar*; and *Exercises Unto Godliness,* he contributed a number of articles to various church papers of the Ohio Synod. He died in Columbus on August 11, 1926.

Schuette wrote five original hymns and several translations from German for the *Evangelical Lutheran Hymnal,* Columbus, 1880, of the Ohio Synod. One of his German translations, "O blessed, holy Trinity," was taken into *The Lutheran Hymnal,* 1941. "Great God, a blessing from your throne," also included in the 1880 hymnal, has gone halfway around the world and back for its present form. The Australian *Lutheran Hymnal,* 1973, included the hymn with some alterations—extensive in the final stanza—and some slight further revisions of the text were made for the LBW.

LOB SEI DEM ALLMÄCHTIGEN GOTT. This tune was included in Johann Crüger's (LBW 23) *Newes vollkömliches Gesangbuch Augsburgischer Confession,* Berlin, 1640, as a setting for Michael Weisse's (LBW 37) hymn, "Lob sei dem allmächtigen Gott."

186 HOW BLESSED IS THIS PLACE, O LORD
Tune: Solothurn

Ernest Edwin Ryden, born of Swedish parentage on September 12, 1886, in Kansas City, Missouri, graduated from Manual Training High School there. In 1907 he entered Augustana College, graduating in 1910. For three years before college he had worked on the newspaper and in the general offices of the Kansas City Railway, and for a year after, he worked as a telegraph editor on a newspaper in Moline, Illinois. After studies at Augustana Seminary, he was ordained in 1914, and the same year was married to Agnes E. Johnson, also a graduate of Augustana College, who at the time was organist at the Lutheran Church in Wakefield, Nebraska. His first parish was Grace Lutheran Church, Jamestown, New York, the first English-speaking church of the Augustana Synod east of Chicago. When Holy Trinity Lutheran Church of the General Council, also in Jamestown, called Ryden to be their pastor, the two congregations merged in 1915, with the Holy Trinity congregation joining the Augustana Synod and the Grace Church congregation adopting the *Church Book* with the Common Service which was in use at Holy Trinity Church. (A stained glass window in the new Holy Trinity Church building is dedicated to Ryden.) During World War I, he also served as a camp pastor at Camp Wadsworth, New York. From 1920 to 1934 he was pastor of Gloria Dei Lutheran Church in St. Paul, Minnesota, and during those years the church became one of the largest and most influential in the city. While in St. Paul, he also presented weekly programs on the hymns of the church on radio KSTP; was head of the English Association of Churches of the Augustana Synod; and was president of the Board of Christian Service, an organization which built three orphanages (in Duluth, Mankato, and Red Wing) and Bethesda Hospital in St. Paul. In 1934 he was called to Rock Island, Illinois, to serve as editor of *The Lutheran Companion,* a position he held until 1961 when the publication was discontinued. For five years during this time he was also editor of the *Lutheran Outlook* of the American Lutheran Church. From 1934 to 1942 he was president of the American Lutheran Conference. He was also on the Board of Directors of Augustana College for twenty years, serving as president for many of those years. In 1935 he was a delegate to the Lutheran World Convention in Paris, and in 1948, was a representative at the World Council of Churches Assembly in Copenhagen. Augustana College bestowed on him a Doctor of Divinity degree in 1930, and in 1948 Sweden honored him with the Royal Order of the North Star. In 1964 Ryden became pastor, and later pastor emeritus, of Emmanuel Lutheran Church, North Grosvenor Dale, Connecticut. He and Mrs. Ryden were the parents of a son and three daughters. Ryden died January 1, 1981.

Author and translator of many hymns, Ryden was a co-editor of *The Hymnal,* 1925, of the Augustana Synod; editor of the *Junior Hymnal;* and from 1945 to 1958, secretary of the joint commission for the *Service Book and Hymnal,* 1958. His hymns and translations have also found their way into hymnals of other denominations, including *The Hymnal of the Evangelical Convenant Church,* 1950, and *The Methodist Hymnal,* 1964. His hymnological writings include two books, *The Story of Our Hymns,* 1935, and *The Story of Christian Hymnody,* 1958, and an article, "Lutheran Hymnbooks Since the Reformation," in the *Lutheran Encyclopedia,* 1964. The present hymn, based on Jacob's experience at Bethel (Genesis 28:10–22) and intended for church dedications, was written in 1924 and included in *The Hymnal,* 1925, of the Augustana Synod.

SOLOTHURN. Named for a canton and its capital in northwest Switzerland, this delightful Swiss melody has been included in a number of twentieth-century hymnals with various texts. In 1826 it was included in *Sammlung von schweizer Kahreihen und Volksliedern,* titled "Dursli und Babeli." Ludwig van Beethoven (LBW 551) was fond of the tune, and around 1790, wrote a set of *Six Easy Variations on a Swiss Air* for harp or pianoforte. In an article contributed to *The Hymn,* January, 1962, Robert L. Sanders notes that the tune was quoted in Johann Friedrich Reichart's *Frohe Lieder für deutscher Männer,* Berlin, 1781, as having the qualities desirable in a folksong. Sanders further gives three sixteenth-century variants, the earliest of which comes from a manuscript "Kleber's Codex" believed to date between 1515 and 1524.

The harmonization is by Stanley L. Osborne, member of the committee which prepared *The Hymn Book,* 1971, of the Anglican Church and the United Church of Canada (to which he contributed four tunes and a descant), and author of *If Such Holy Song,** 1976, a handbook to *The Hymn Book.*

Born January 6, 1907, near Bowmanville, in Clarke Township, Ontario, Osborne received a Bachelor of Arts degree in 1921 and a Bachelor of Divinity degree in 1932 from Victoria University. Following his ordination he served as pastor at Paradise Valley in Alberta, and at Coe Hill and Hay Bay in Ontario until 1938 when he went as assistant minister to Eaton Memorial Church, Toronto. Called in 1941 to First United Church in Port Credit, he served there until 1948, when he was appointed principal of Ontario Ladies' College in Whitby. In 1965 he became secretary of the joint committee for *The Hymn Book,* and three years later, full-time secretary. He has retired and lives in Oshawa.

Throughout his ministry, Osborne has also been a student of liturgy and music. At the University of Toronto he completed a Bachelor of Music degree in 1936 and a Doctor of Music degree in 1945. He holds a Doctor of Theology degree, 1954, from Victoria University and has received honorary doctorates from Victoria University in 1971 and from Queen's University in 1974. He was co-editor of the music in *The Canadian Youth Hymnal,* 1939, and edited *Jubilate Deo* from 1956 to 1959. His book, *The Strain of Praise,* appeared in 1974. He has written a number of instrumental and choral works, most of which are still in manuscript.

187   DEAREST JESUS, WE ARE HERE *(Liebster Jesu, wir sind hier)*
Tune: Liebster Jesu, wir sind hier

The son of a Lutheran pastor, Benjamin Schmolck was born at Brachitzchdorf, Leignitz, in Silesia, on December 21, 1672. Known throughout his life as a fine preacher, he delivered his first sermon at his father's church at the age of sixteen, and so impressed one of the influential members that he was given a three-year allowance to study theology. At the University of Leipzig he came under the influence of Johannes Olearius (LBW 29) and others, and for the rest of his life maintained the character of their teaching, described by Julian* as "a warm and living practical Christianity, but Churchly in tone and not Pietistic." He was ordained in 1701 as his father's assistant at Brachitzchdorf, and the following year, married Anna Rosina Rehwald, and became pastor of the Friedenskirche at Schweidnitz. Because of the Counter Reformation and the terms of the Peace of Westphalia, one church and three clergymen were allowed for the entire district which consisted of thirty-six villages. To this parish Schmolck ministered for the rest of his life, his last years complicated by strokes and partial paralysis, as well as cataracts. He died February 12, 1737.

Schmolck, who had supported himself during his final year at the university with his poetry and was crowned poet laureate in 1697, wrote some 900 hymns during his lifetime. The present hymn, which has the same first line as Tobias Clausnitzer's hymn found at LBW 248, was included in Schmolck's collection of fifty hymns, *Heilige Flammen der himmlisch-gesinnten Seele,* 1704.

Catherine Winkworth's (LBW 29) translation, beginning "Blessed Jesus, here we stand," was included in her *Lyra Germanica,* second series, 1858, and has been considerably altered. The present opening line, "Dearest Jesus, we are here," and much of the fifth stanza are from a translation by Matthias Loy (LBW 490) included in the *Evangelical Lutheran Hymnal,* 1880, of the Ohio Synod. Extensive alterations were made for *The Lutheran Hymnal,* 1941, and further revisions by the Inter-Lutheran Commission on Worship have brought the text to its present form.

LIEBSTER JESU, WIR SIND HIER. Born December 24, 1625, at Mühlhausen in Thuringia, Johann Rudolph Ahle was educated at the Universities of Göttingen and Erfurt. He served as cantor of St. Andreas' Church and director of the music school in Erfurt from 1646 until 1654, when he became organist at St. Blasius' Church, Mühlhausen. (His son, who succeeded him at Mühlhausen was J. S. Bach's [LBW 219] predecessor there.) In 1655 he was elected to the town council, and in 1661 he became mayor. He died in Mühlhausen on July 8, 1673.

Ahle published a number of hymnals, as well as a treatise on singing. Influenced by Heinrich Schütz (LBW 180) he, along with Heinrich Albert (LBW 266) and others, was instrumental in bringing a new style of music into the church which reflected Italian opera. Indeed, Albert and Ahle referred to their church melodies as "sacred arias." This tune was first published in *Neue geistliche auf die Sonntage,* Mühlhausen, 1664, as the setting for Franz Joachim Burmeister's Advent hymn, "Ja, er ists, das Heil der Welt." There it appeared as given below (Zahn* #683).

It was later reconstructed and associated with the present hymn in *Das grosse Cantional: oder Kirchen-Gesangbuch,* published in Darmstadt in 1687.

In addition to a harmonization included in the *Choralgesänge,* J. S. Bach (LBW 219) wrote various settings of this tune for organ which are included in his *Orgelbüchlein* and Miscellaneous Preludes.

188 I BIND UNTO MYSELF TODAY *(Atomriug indiu)*

Tune: St. Patrick's Breastplate

Tradition ascribes this *lorica* to St. Patrick. By 690, when Tirechan wrote his *Collections,* it was directed to be sung in all the monasteries and churches throughout Ireland and was apparently universally attributed to Patrick. Our earliest sources of the hymn are two eleventh-century manuscripts, which were published in 1897 as *The Irish Liber Hymnorum.*

St. Patrick, whose birthdate is given variously as about 372, 381, or 389, was born in Britain, a descendant of a Christian family of at least three-generations' standing. In his *Confession,* he gives the place of birth as "Bannavem Taberniæ," the location of which is uncertain. His father was a Roman, and Patrick himself was a freeman and of noble birth. When he was sixteen, he was captured by raiders from Ireland and carried away to be sold as a slave. During the next six years he was obliged to feed livestock, but also had opportunity to devote himself to prayer and to become acquainted with the Irish language. He eventually escaped, and seems to have studied at Lerins from 412 to 415, after which he was ordained by Amator. In 431 he returned to Ireland to assist Palladius in his missionary efforts, and the following year was consecrated bishop of Ireland by Germanus. From that time on he spent his life in converting the Irish people to Christianity, organizing churches, and contending with the Druids. He died March 17, 461 (some sources give 466). In addition to his *Confessions,* his most important writings include the *Letter to Coroticus.*

According to legend Patrick and the Druid king Loegaire met at Tara Hill, where a festival of the Druid fire-worshipers was about to begin with the extinction of all fires through the country. Patrick, however, defiantly lighted a Paschal fire on the Hill of Slane in full view of the King, who then set out to kill Patrick. In the pursuit, Patrick and his companions were miraculously transformed into deer and recited this hymn in flight; hence its title, "Faeth Fiada," or "The Deer's Cry." A translation of the preface to the hymn which is found in the eleventh-century manuscripts mentioned above reads:

> Patrick made this hymn; in the time of Loegaire mac Neill, it was made, and the cause of its composition was for the protection of himself and his monks against the deadly enemies that lay in ambush for the clerics. And it is a lorica of faith for the protection of body and soul against demons and men and vices: when any person shall recite it daily with pious meditation on God, demons shall not dare to face him, it shall be a protection to him against all poison and envy, it shall be a guard to him against sudden death, it shall be a lorica for his soul after his decease.
>
> Patrick sang it when the ambuscades were laid for him by Loegaire, in order that he should not go to Tara to sow the Faith, so that on that occasion they were seen before those who were lying in ambush as if they were wild deer having behind them a fawn, viz. Benen; and 'Deer's Cry' is its name.

The English verse paraphrase was made by Cecil Frances Alexander (LBW 114) for use on St. Patrick's Day, 1889. First printed on a leaflet and sung throughout Ireland on that day, it was included the same year in the *Writings of St. Patrick,* edited by C. H. H. Wright.

ST. PATRICK'S BREASTPLATE. This Irish air is given in George Petrie's *Collection of Irish Music,* edited by C. V. Stanford (LBW 189), 1903, where it is headed, "The Hymn of St. Bernard. Jesu dulcis memoria [LBW 316]. From Mr. Southwell." The present form of the tune is from *The English Hymnal,* 1906, and the harmonization is by Carl Schalk (LBW 118) from the *Worship Supplement,* 1969, to *The Lutheran Hymnal.*

189 WE KNOW THAT CHRIST IS RAISED
Tune: Engelberg

Of this hymn, written for the tune "Engelberg," the author, John Browlow Geyer, writes:

> "We know that Christ was raised" was written in 1967, when I was tutor at Cheshunt College, Cambridge, U. K. At that time a good deal of work was going on round the corner (involving a number of American research students) producing living cells ("the baby in the test tube"). The hymn attempted to illustrate the Christian doctrine of baptism in relation to those experiments. Originally intended as a hymn for the Sacrament of Baptism, it has become popular as an Easter hymn.

Based on Romans 6, the hymn appeared in *Hymns and Songs,* 1969, a supplement to the Methodist hymnal. It has since been included in *Contemporary Worship-4,* 1972, as well as several other publications. The second stanza has been considerably revised.

Geyer was born May 9, 1932, in Wakefield, Yorkshire, England. Among his antecedents he counts Rebecca Strong O.B.E., a pupil of Florence Nightingale, and Adolf Hanns Geyer, pastor of the Austrian Unierte Kirche. While a student at Queen's College, Cambridge, 1953–1956, he was awarded the Kennett Hebrew Exhibition; and in his middle year at Mansfield College, 1956–1959, he was granted a leave of absence to study under Professor Gerhard von Rad of Heidelberg, Germany, then resident at the Oekumenisches Studentenwohnheim. Ordained to the ministry of the Congregational Union of Scotland in 1959, he first served as chaplain to the Congregational students at the University of St. Andrews, and in 1963 was inducted as minister of the Congregational Church, Drumchapel, Glasgow. Two years later he was married to Margaret Lochhead Young, the daughter of a Scottish Congregational minister, and they have become the parents of three children. In 1965 he also took a position as tutor of Cheshunt College, Cambridge, and two years later was appointed a tutor of Westminster College as well. Since 1969 he has been minister of the Little Baddow Congregational Church, which in 1973 associated with the United Reformed Church.

Geyer's principal interest is the Old Testament; he is a member of the Society for Old Testament Study and has taught in this field in both Oxford and Cambridge. His publications include a commentary on *The Wisdom of Solomon,* 1973, and various articles in *Vetus Testamentum,* the *British Weekly,* and *Reform.* Twice he has acted as chaplain to conferences sponsored by the Royal School of Church Music. His hymns have appeared in *Dunblane Praises I,* 1964, and *New Songs for the Church,* 1969. "We know that Christ is raised" was also published in 1974 in *Cantate Domino,* along with French and German translations.

ENGELBERG was written by Charles Villiers Stanford for *Hymns Ancient and Modern,* 1904, to carry the text "For all the saints" (LBW 174).

Stanford, one of the most distinguished of modern composers, was born September 30, 1852, at Dublin. His musical talents were evident early, and before he was ten, one of his compositions was played in the Dublin Royal Theatre. In 1870 he became a choral scholar at Queen's College, Cambridge, and three years later, was appointed organist of Trinity College, Cambridge, where he received a Bachelor of Arts degree in 1874 and a Master of Arts degree in 1877. The years 1874–1876 were spent in Leipzig and Berlin, where he studied with Carl Reinecke and Friedrich Kiel. When the Royal College of Music opened in 1883 he was appointed professor of composition and orchestral playing, and in 1887 he became professor of music at Cambridge as well, holding both positions until his death. He resigned as organist to Trinity College in 1892 and went to London. Director of the Cambridge Musical Society from 1872 to 1893, the London Bach Choir from 1885 to 1902, and the Leeds Festival from 1901 to 1910, he also appeared as conductor in many cities in Europe and America. Among his pupils were Walford Davies, Ralph Vaughan Williams (LBW 101), and Gustav Holst. He was the recipient of honorary Doctor of Music degrees from Oxford (1883) and Cambridge (1888), a Doctor of Civil Law from Durham (1894), and Doctor of Laws from the University of Leeds (1904). Knighted in 1902, he was elected two years later to the Royal Academy of Arts in Berlin. His compositions number nearly two hundred works, including symphonies, concertos, operas, songs, and choral compositions; and his work with Irish melodies assisted in the revival of interest in folk music. He wrote a treatise on *Musical Composition,* 1911, and with Cecil Forsyth was co-author of a *History of Music,* 1916. He died March 29, 1924, in Marylebone, London, and is buried in Westminster Abbey.

190   WE PRAISE YOU, LORD

Tune: St. Magnus

This hymn was written in 1955 for the congregation of College Church, Parkville, in Melbourne, Australia, to fill a need for a baptism hymn. The author revised it in 1971 for use in *The Hymn Book,* 1971, of the Anglican Church and the United Church of Canada, and it has since appeared in hymn books of various denominations in Canada, the United States, and Australia.

Judith Beatrice O'Neill was born June 30, 1930, in Melbourne, Australia, and grew up in the country town of Mildura. She took an honors Bachelor of Arts degree and a Master of Arts degree in English language and literature, following which she studied at the London University Institute of Education on a Rotary Foundation Fellowship from 1952 to 1953. Returning to Australia in 1953 she became a tutor in English literature at the University of Melbourne and the following year was married to John O'Neill, a Presbyterian minister. Between 1956 and 1959 the O'Neills lived in Göttingen, Germany, and Cambridge, England, where John pursued post-graduate studies. They returned to Australia until 1964, when they went with their three daughters to Cambridge. There Dr. O'Neill is professor of New Testament studies in Westminster College and Judith is head of the English department at St. Mary's School.

From 1967 to 1970 Judith O'Neill edited a series of readings in literary criticism on John Keats, Charlotte and Emily Brontë, Alexander Pope, Christopher Marlowe, Jane Austin, and William Blake. She has written two school books for Cambridge University Press: *Martin Luther,* 1975 (now reprinted and also translated into Dutch, and selling particularly to Lutheran schools and churches in the United States), and *Transported to Van Diemen's Land,* 1977, a true story of two of her great-grandparents transported to Australia for petty theft in the 1840s.

For ST. MAGNUS see LBW 173.

191 PRAISE AND THANKSGIVING BE TO GOD

Tune: Christe sanctorum

In the fall of 1969, while having lunch with Stanley Osborne (LBW 186), Frank J. Whiteley mentioned the scarcity of hymns on Christian Baptism, and Osborne suggested that Whiteley himself write a baptism hymn. The content of "Praise and thanksgiving be to God" (which grew out of a Master's thesis that Whiteley was writing at the time) had been outlined by the following day, and was later arranged in poetic form by Harold Francis (Frank) Yardley. The hymn of five stanzas is included in an order of baptism which has been in use at the author's church, Devine Street United Church in Sarnia, Ontario, since 1971; and the first three stanzas were published in *The Hymn Book,* 1971, of the Anglican Church and the United Church of Canada.

Born in Sheffield, England, on December 22, 1914, Whiteley immigrated with his parents to Canada in 1920, settling in Dryden, Ontario. Upon completing high school he worked for a time at the Pulp and Paper Company in Dryden, and then graduated from Peterborough Normal School (1941) and taught sixth grade and school music at Bobcaygeon, Ontario, for a year. He became a candidate for ministry in the United Church of Canada in 1942, received Bachelor of Arts (1944) and Bachelor of Divinity degrees from Queen's University in Kingston, and was ordained in 1946. In 1970 he received a Master of Divinity degree from Toronto University. He has served several churches, all in Ontario: Parham, 1943–1946; Coe Hill, 1946–1948; Center Street in Oshawa, 1948–1952; Picton, 1952–1960; and Knox United in Peterborough, 1960–1967. Since 1967 he has been at Devine Street Church. He has served as Chairman of Presbytery on three occasions, has been a commissioner to the General Council of the United Church of Canada, and has been a member of several national church committees. He looks forward to retirement, when he hopes to complete a doctoral program with Toronto University, with a thesis on the "Theology of Housing."

Yardley was also born in England, in Salford, Lancashire, on March 11, 1911. His mother died a few months after he was born, and his father, a poor casual laborer then sixty years of age, employed housekeepers to look after him until he was eight. From 1919 to 1925 he was educated at Nicholls Hospital, a charitable institution, after which he worked for four years, first as an office boy and then as a farm laborer. At the age of eighteen he went to Ontario, going briefly to Grimsby, near Niagara, as a fruit-picker, then to Toronto where he worked in the magazine and book wholesaling trade. With the arrival of the depression he was steadily unemployed from 1931 to 1936. Through the years between 1929 and 1936 he lived as a boarder with an English couple who, though poor, became loving foster parents to him. As a child in England, Yardley went to a Socialist Sunday school, and at Nicholls Hospital, attended Anglo-Catholic services. Beyond that he had little to do with religion until he became associated with the Rhodes Avenue United Church in Toronto. Convinced by his friends that he should go into the ministry, he went from 1936 to 1938 as a lay supply minister to the dust bowl of Saskatchewan, where from 1928 to 1936 the people had not seen a decent crop. He went on to complete high school and graduated with honors from the shorter course in Arts and Theology at Victoria University. Following his ordination he went as pastor to Gainsborough, Saskatchewan, 1943; Ganonoque East, Ontario, 1945; Courtice, 1947; Embro, 1950; Wesley United, Brantford, 1954; St.

Paul's, Sarnia, 1960; and finally to Claresholm in Alberta, 1970. A series
of illnesses forced his retirement in 1962, and he resides in Calgary,
Alberta. He began his hymn-writing partly as a reaction against what he
calls "the morbidity of the Moody and Sankey era," and frequently used
his poems as a summary at the end of his sermons.

CHRISTE SANCTORUM is given at LBW 169.

192 BAPTIZED INTO YOUR NAME MOST HOLY
(Ich bin getauft auf deinen Namen)
Tune: O dass ich tausend Zungen hätte

Johann Jakob Rambach, son of a German cabinetmaker, was born in
Halle on February 24, 1693. He entered the University of Halle as a
medical student in 1712, but soon turned to theology. Especially interested in Old Testament studies, he became an assistant in 1715 to J. H.
Michaelis who was preparing an edition of the Hebrew Bible. In 1719 he
was invited to lecture to a group of students at Jena, and the following
year he received a Master of Arts degree at Halle. From 1723 he was on
the faculty of the theological school at the University of Halle, as well as
inspector of the orphanage, and after 1727, preacher at the Schulkirche.
He left Halle in 1731, receiving a Doctor of Divinity degree from the
university that year, and went to Giessen where he was superintendent
and first professor of theology. A year later, he also became director of
the *Paedogogium* at Giessen. A fever cut his life short; he died April 19,
1735.

Rambach, who became a very popular preacher and professor, wrote
voluminously in the field of practical theology and composed more than
180 hymns. Among his publications which included these hymns were
Geistliche Poesien, 1720, which also contained seventy-two cantata texts
based on the Gospels for Sundays and festivals; *Poetische Fest-
Gedancken,* 1723–1729; and *Geistreiches Haus-Gesang-Buch,* 1735. The
present hymn was one of eight included in *Erbauliches Handbuchlein
für Kinder,* Giessen, 1734.

Catherine Winkworth's (LBW 29) translation, included in her *Chorale
Book for England,* 1863, is given here with considerable alteration.
Three stanzas from a translation by Charles William Schaeffer (LBW
455) were included in the *Service Book and Hymnal,* 1958, #293.

O DASS ICH TAUSEND ZUNGEN HÄTTE (Dretzel) appeared in
Kornelius Heinrich Dretzel's *Des Evangelischen Zions Musicalische Harmonie,* Nürnberg, 1731, as the setting for "Weil nichts gemeiner ist alls
sterben" (Zahn* #2858). It was also one of the several tunes associated
with Johann Mentzer's hymn, "O dass ich tausend Zungen hätte" (LBW
560).

The son of an organist, Dretzel was born in Nürnberg in 1698 and at
the age of fourteen took his first position as organist of the Frauenkirche
there. He became organist of St. Ägydien in 1719, of St. Lorenz in 1743,
and finally, in 1764, of St. Sebald, where Johann Pachelbel later served
as organist. His 1731 chorale collection was the most complete published
up to that time. He died May 7, 1775.

193 CRADLING CHILDREN IN HIS ARM
(Herren strækker ud sin Arm)

Tune: Gaudeamus pariter

An English hymn of unknown authorship, which appeared in Edward Henry Bickersteth's (LBW 491) *Christian Psalmody,* 1834, formed the basis for this Danish hymn by Nicolai Grundtvig (LBW 62). The Danish hymn has in turn been translated to English by Johannes H. V. Knudsen. The original English hymn, based on Isaiah 40:11, reads as follows:

> Welcome to the Saviour's breast,
> Children of the Saviour's love:
> By Him may they now be bless'd;
> From Him never, never rove.
>
> We baptize them at thy word;
> Wash their souls from sin's deep stain,
> And in thy compassion, Lord,
> Grant them to be born again.

Grundtvig's Danish version was included in his *Sang-Värk til den Danske Kirke,* 1837. Knudsen's English translation, prepared at the request of the Inter-Lutheran Commission on Worship, was first published in *N. F. S. Grundtvig, Selected Writings,* 1976.

Johannes Knudsen was born in Nebraska in 1902 and grew up in Minnesota. He holds a degree from the University of Copenhagen and a Doctor of Philosophy degree from Hartford Seminary in Connecticut. His special emphasis has been in church history. An ordained Lutheran pastor, he has served for seven years in the parish ministry, but chiefly he has been an educator. He has been president of Grand View College and dean of Grand View Seminary, as well as dean of graduate studies at the Lutheran School of Theology in Chicago where he was a member of the faculty for seven years. He holds the title Professor Emeritus of the Lutheran School of Theology at Chicago, and lives in retirement in Des Moines. Married in 1934 to Ellen Paulsen, he is the father of two daughters.

Knudsen's essays and articles are legion, and his name is on the title page of eight books. He is editor of *Kirke og Folk,* a bilingual journal (Danish-English) published by the Danish Interest Conference, an agency of the Lutheran Church in America. He has been knighted by the King of Denmark, and has attended numerous ecumenical and international conferences (church and theological). He has been a lecturer at Danish universities and a Lutheran World Federation lecturer in Argentina.

For GAUDEAMUS PARITER see LBW 132.

194 ALL WHO BELIEVE AND ARE BAPTIZED
(Enhver, som tror og bliver döbt)

Tune: Es ist das Heil

See LBW 102 for Thomas Kingo and LBW 138 for George A. T. Rygh. This hymn, one of the favorite baptism hymns in Denmark and Norway, was first published in Kingo's 1689 hymnal and also in the official

Salmebog, 1699, where it was specified for use after baptism. The translation, originally beginning "He that believes and is baptized," was prepared by Rygh in 1909 and included in *The Lutheran Hymnary,* 1913.

For ES IST DAS HEIL (also "St. Paul") see LBW 297, where the tune appears in its original rhythmic form and with its original text.

195   THIS IS THE SPIRIT'S ENTRY NOW
Tune: Perry

This hymn, written at White Bear Lake, Minnesota, was partly inspired by the upcoming baptism of the author's first child in 1965, and was included as a part of his master's thesis (a study of Christology and the Sacraments in the hymnal) at Luther Theological Seminary. It was first published in *Contemporary Worship–4,* 1972. A few alterations have been made with the author's approval. The hymn, with its tune, "Perry," was published in 1979 as a chorale concertato by Kevin Norris.

Thomas Edmond Herbranson was born December 3, 1933, at Bagley, Minnesota, and grew up in a small town hotel in Warren, Minnesota. During his years at St. Olaf College, where he completed a Bachelor of Arts degree in history, he toured with the St. Olaf Choir and Quartet, and sang also for two summer seasons with the Aqua Follies. Afterwards he spent a year studying in Heidelberg, Germany, during which he traveled throughout Egypt and the Holy Lands on a motorcycle. He graduated from Luther Theological Seminary in 1960 following a year of internship in Maracaibo, Venezuela, in a tri-lingual congregation. From 1960 to 1962 he served as campus minister at Winona State College, Winona, Minnesota, and from 1963 to 1967 worked with the home mission church at White Bear Lake. In 1967 he went to Mexico City, where he served a bilingual congregation and worked among the Americans at Guadalajara and Cuernavaca, and among poor Mexicans in San Fernando. Returning to the United States in 1969 he completed a Master of Theology degree at Luther Seminary and pursued studies in speech-communications. In 1971 he joined Lutheran Brotherhood in Minneapolis as associate for program evaluation and development of the fraternal and public affairs department, and in 1973 he became executive secretary of the division of public relations at Lutheran Brotherhood. In 1979 he was appointed special projects coordinator in the office of Minnesota governor Albert H. Quie. He is completing a Master of Arts degree at the University of Minnesota.

PERRY was composed in July, 1962, for James A. Blaisdell's "Beneath the forms of outward rite," included in *The Book of Hymns* of the United Methodist Church, Nashville, 1964. It was written at Put-in-Bay, Ohio, the bay from which Commodore Oliver Hazard Perry went forth to his victory on Lake Erie during the War of 1812.

Leo Sowerby, for many years head of the theory and composition department at the American Conservatory, and organist-choirmaster at St. James's Episcopal Church, Chicago, was born May 1, 1895, in Grand Rapids, Michigan. After completing a Master of Music degree at the American Conservatory in 1918, Sowerby enlisted in World War I and served with the 332nd Field Artillery Band in England and France. He received a scholarship for three years' study in Italy in 1921, and participated in the Salzburg Festival of Contemporary Music in 1923. On his return to Chicago he taught at the American Conservatory, and in addition went to St. James's Church in 1927, remaining in both positions until 1963. From 1962 until his death he was director of the College of Church Musicians, Washington Cathedral. He died July 7, 1968, at Cleveland, Ohio.

Sowerby's compositions include symphonies, concertos, organ works, cantatas, anthems, and service music. His oratorio, *Canticle of the Sun,* based on a text by Francis of Assisi (LBW 527), won him the Pulitzer Prize in 1946. He served on the tunes committee in the preparation of *The Hymnal 1940* (Episcopal), and was a member of the joint commission on the revision of that hymnal.

196 PRAISE THE LORD, RISE UP REJOICING

Tune: Alles ist an Gottes Segen

Originally published in *Hundred Hymns for Today,* 1969, this hymn was included in *Contemporary Worship-4,* 1972.

H. C. A. Gaunt, an Anglican clergyman born in 1902, served from 1929 to 1937 as assistant master at Rugby School, after which he was headmaster of Malvern College until 1953. For ten years he was chaplain and head of the English department at Winchester College, and for another ten years, sacrist and precentor at Winchester Cathedral, retiring in 1973.

ALLES IST AN GOTTES SEGEN, with its harmonization by Jan Bender (LBW 396), was also used as the setting for this hymn in *Contemporary Worship-4.* Background of the tune is given at LBW 447 where it appears with its original text.

197 O LIVING BREAD FROM HEAVEN *(Wie wohl hast du gelabet)*

Tune: Aurelia

This hymn by Johann Rist was included in his *Neüer Himlischer Lieder,* 1651. Given the impulse to hymn writing by Josua Stegmann (LBW 263) at the University of Rinteln, Rist wrote in all about 680 hymns covering every aspect of theology. He was a highly respected writer in his day and received a number of honors. Emperor Ferdinand III crowned him poet in 1644, and in 1653 made him a member of the nobility. His works include: *Himlische Lieder,* 1641-1643; *Neuer himlischer Lieder sonderbahres Buch,* 1651; *Sabbahtische Seelenlust,* 1651; *Frommer und Gottseliger Christen alltägliche Haussmusik,* 1654; *Neue musikalische Fest-Andachten,* 1655; and *Neue musikalische Katechismus Andachten,* 1656. In addition to his hymns, Rist was the author of historical writings and two plays depicting the sufferings brought about by the Thirty Years' War.

The son of a pastor, Rist was born March 8, 1607, at Ottensen, near Hamburg, Germany, and studied at Hamburg and Bremen before entering the University of Rinteln in 1626 as a student of theology. While tutoring for a family in Hamburg he attended the University of Rostock where he studied Hebrew, mathematics, and medicine; and prior to his ordination he also studied briefly at the universities of Leyden, Utrecht, and Leipzig. In 1633 he went to tutor for the family of Heinrich Sagen, a lawyer at Heide in Holstein. There he became engaged to Elisabeth Stapfel, sister of Judge Franz Stapfel, and it seems to be through her influence that he secured the pastorate at Wedel near Hamburg. Although, like many other hymnwriters, Rist felt the effects of the Thirty Years' War (including the loss of his personal property—especially his scientific and musical instruments—and the destruction of the organ in his church), and he himself contracted the pestilence during his time at the University of Rostock, Rist's life generally seems to have been one of contentment. In spite of numerous calls to more prestigious positions, he remained at Wedel until his death on August 31, 1667, ministering both to the spiritual needs of his people as a pastor and to their physical needs as a physician.

Catherine Winkworth's (LBW 29) translation, which appeared in her *Lyra Germanica,* second series, 1858, originally consisted of eight stanzas of twelve lines, the opening lines reading as follows:

> O Living Bread from heaven,
> How richly hast Thou fed Thy guest!
> The gifts Thou now hast given
> Have filled my heart with joy and rest.

The original form of the translation was used in *The Lutheran Hymnal,* 1941. The altered form found in the *Service Book and Hymnal,* 1958, was from the *Church Book,* 1868, published in Philadelphia. The text has been further altered for the LBW.

AURELIA was originally written in 1864 for John Keble's wedding hymn, "The voice that breathed o'er Eden." It was included the same year in *A Selection of Psalms and Hymns,* edited by Charles Kemble and Samuel Sebastian Wesley, as the setting for three centos from John Mason Neale's (LBW 34) translation of *Hora novissima:* "Jerusalem the Golden" (LBW 347), "Brief life is here our portion," and "For Thee, oh dear, dear country." In his *Hymn Tune Names,* 1958, Robert McCutchan points out that the name "Aurelia," taken from the Latin "aurum" meaning "gold," refers to "Jerusalem the *golden.*" The tune was used with "The Church's one foundation" (LBW 369) in the Appendix to the Original Edition of *Hymns Ancient and Modern,* 1868, and has become firmly associated with that text.

Born in London, England, on August 14, 1810, Samuel Sebastian Wesley, grandson of Charles (LBW 27), was the first of several children born to Samuel Wesley and his housekeeper, Sarah Suter. Beginning his musical career as a chorister of the Chapel Royal in 1820, he held his first organ position at age sixteen and served several churches before becoming, in 1832, organist at Hereford Cathedral. Thereafter he was organist at Exeter Cathedral (1835–1842), Leeds Parish Church (1842–1849), Winchester Cathedral (1849–1865), and Gloucester Cathedral (1865–1876). Music study was undertaken at Oxford University where he received a Doctor of Music degree in 1839. Having an extreme penchant for fishing, Samuel Sebastian sometimes let fishing possibilities influence his choice of communities he would serve as organist. He died at Gloucester on April 19, 1876, and was buried at Exeter according to his own wish.

Highly regarded as a performer and composer, S. S. Wesley devoted his lifetime to bettering conditions, salaries, and status of church music and musicians, and was among the first organists to advocate the use of a full pedal board on English organs. Many of his ideas were included in *A Few Words on Cathedral Music and the Musical System of the Church, with a Plan of Reform,* 1849. He contributed much fine music to the church in the form of services, anthems, chants, and hymn tunes. His *European Psalmist* contained over 700 hymn tunes of which 130 were his own.

198   LET ALL MORTAL FLESH KEEP SILENCE
(Σιγησάτω πᾶσα σὰρξ βροτεία)
Tune: Picardy

This beautiful hymn is the "Prayer of the Cherubic Hymn" from the Liturgy of St. James, where it is used at the beginning of the Liturgy of the Faithful, when the bread and wine are brought to the table. Celebrated on St. James's Day, October 23, the liturgy is believed to have been composed by St. James the Less, first Bishop of Jerusalem, where it was probably first used, and is the original rite from which all other Syrian rites were derived. The Greek original is also found in the Liturgy of St. Basil as the Troparion for Holy Saturday morning. Gerard Moultrie's paraphrase in English meter was first published in the second edition of *Lyra Eucharistica,* 1864.

Gerard Moultrie, born September 16, 1829, at Rugby Rectory in England, attended Exeter College, where he received a Master of Arts degree in 1856. Following his ordination he served as chaplain to Shrewsbury School, to the Dowager Marchioness of Londonderry (1855–1859), curate at Brightwaltham (1859–1860) and Brinfield, Berkshire (1860–1864), and chaplain to the Donative of Barrow Gurney, Bristol (1864–1869). From 1869 he was vicar of Southleigh, and after 1873, warden of St. James's College, Southleigh. He died at Southleigh on April 25, 1885.

In addition to a number of original hymns, Moultrie prepared translations from Greek, Latin, and German.

PICARDY, a French folktune named for a province in northern France, probably dates from the seventeenth century. "Jesus Christ s'habille en pauvre," the folksong originally set to this tune, is an interesting take-off on the story of the rich man and Lazarus; it presents Christ going about in rags looking for charity and receiving crumbs from the rich man's table, while the dogs have rabbits to eat. One of the few French folksongs of a religious nature, it is taken down as sung by Mme. Pierre Dupont in Champfleury-Wekerlin, *Chansons populaires des provences de France,* IV, Paris, 1860. It was first adapted to this text in *The English Hymnal,* 1906. The present harmonization was prepared for the LBW by Ronald Nelson (LBW 258).

199   THEE WE ADORE, O HIDDEN SAVIOR
(*Adoro te devote, latens Deitas*)
Tune: Adoro te devote

This hymn by Thomas Aquinas (LBW 120) may well have been written at the time he was writing on the Eucharist and preparing the Office and

Mass for the festival of Corpus Christi. Regarding the poem, John Mason Neale (LBW 34), in his *Medieval Hymns,* 1851, wrote, "It is worthy of notice how the Angelic Doctor, as if afraid to employ any pomp of words on approaching so tremendous a Mystery, has used the very simplest expressions throughout." The text has never entered into breviaries or missals as a hymn, but has been included in missals since 1570 as a poem of personal devotion.

James Russell Woodford prepared this translation in 1850 and it was included in *Hymns arranged for the Sundays and Holy Days of the Church of England,* 1852.

Woodford, born at Henley-on-Thomas in England on April 30, 1820, received a Bachelor of Arts degree from Pembroke College, Cambridge, in 1842. Ordained the following year, he served successively as second master at Bishop's College, curate at St. John the Baptist Church in Bristol, rector of Kempsford in Gloucestershire from 1855, and vicar of Leeds from 1868, before becoming bishop of Ely in 1873, where he remained until his death on October 24, 1885. He also was honorary chaplain to the Queen and several times was select preacher at Oxford. In addition to the hymnal mentioned above, he published sermons and lectures, and was also joint-editor of *The Parish Hymn Book,* 1863.

ADORO TE DEVOTE, the melody proper to this hymn, is much newer than the hymn itself. It is one of the genre of French church melodies discussed at LBW 83. The earliest source in which it has been found is the Paris *Processionale,* 1697, where it was the setting for a variant of this hymn beginning "Adoro te supplex," designated to be sung in procession on the feast of Corpus Christi. The harmonization was prepared for the LBW by Frederick Jackisch (LBW 236).

200 FOR THE BREAD WHICH YOU HAVE BROKEN
Tune: Omni Die

Written November 18, 1924, this hymn was included in Benson's *Hymns Original and Translated,* 1925. The text has been altered for the LBW.

Louis FitzGerald Benson, a Presbyterian clergyman who did extensive work in hymnology, first trained at the University of Pennsylvania for law, which he practiced for seven years. He then entered Princeton Theological Seminary, was ordained in 1886, and served for six years as minister of the Church of the Redeemer, Germantown, Pennsylvania. A thorough scholar, Benson also lectured on liturgics at Auburn Theological Seminary, and on hymnology at Princeton. Together with Henry van Dyke (LBW 551) he edited *The Book of Common Worship of the Presbyterian Church in the United States.* He was also editor or co-editor of a number of hymnals, including *The Hymnal,* 1895, of the Presbyterian Church (and also its 1911 revision), *The Hymnal for Congregational Churches, The Chapel Hymnal* (1898), and *The School Hymnal* (1899). He was author of a comprehensive work on *The English Hymn: its Development and Use,* 1915. His hymnological library was bequeathed to Princeton Seminary. Born July 22, 1855, in Philadelphia, he died there October 10, 1930.

OMNI DIE was included in the 1631 edition of the *Gross Catolisch Gesangbuch* (first edition, 1625), published in Nürnberg. There it was set to "Omni die dic Mariae," one of the many *Marienlieder* (songs to and about the Virgin Mary) which were popular among Roman Catholics in Germany.

David Gregor Corner, compiler of the hymnal, was born in 1585 in Hirschberg, Silesia. He received a Master of Arts degree in Prague in 1609, and continued his studies at Graz and Vienna until 1614. For nine years he served as a Roman Catholic priest at several churches, including Rötz and Mautern; then in 1625, he entered the Benedictine monastery at Göttweig, where in 1631 he became prior. The University of Vienna bestowed the Doctor of Theology degree on him in 1624, and in 1638 he became rector of the university. He died at Göttweig on January 9, 1648. Both Corner's *Gross Catolisch Gesangbuch* and his *Geistliche Nachtigal*, 1631, were important collections of Roman Catholic hymns and tunes. The melodies in his hymnbooks were collected from many sources. Since many of the *Marienlieder* were set to folk tunes, there is a possibility that this tune is a folk melody.

The harmonic setting is by William Smith Rockstro (originally Rackstraw), who was born January 5, 1823, at North Cheam, Surrey, England. He studied with John Purkis and Sterndale Bennett, and at the Leipzig Conservatory from 1845 to 1846. A noted teacher and pianist who was also accompanist at the Exeter Hall Concerts, Rockstro was highly regarded in his day as an authority on ancient church music. From 1867 he served as organist and precentor at All Saints' Church, Babbacombe. Among his publications were textbooks on harmony and counterpoint; several essays, including one on George Frideric Handel (LBW 39) and one on Felix Mendelssohn (LBW 60); and articles in *Grove's Dictionary of Music and Musicians.* He died in London on July 2, 1895.

201   O GOD OF LIFE'S GREAT MYSTERY
Tune: Cannock

See LBW 61 for Royce J. Scherf. This hymn is published here for the first time.

CANNOCK is one of twenty-six tunes contributed by Walter Kendall Stanton to *The BBC Hymn Book,* London, 1951, where it was the setting for "Fight the good fight" (LBW 461).

Born at Dauntsey, Wiltshire, England, on September 29, 1891, Stanton was educated at the choristers' school at Salisbury and became a chorister at the cathedral at the age of ten. After attending Lancing College he was an organ scholar at Merton College, Oxford, from 1909 to 1913. He received Master of Arts and Bachelor of Music degrees in 1915 and a Doctor of Music degree in 1935. He served as director of music at St. Edward's School, Oxford, for nine years, after which he went to Wellington College, and in addition, to the University of Reading in 1927. In 1937 he resigned both positions and for eight years was musical director of the Midland BBC. In 1945 he became the first professor of the newly-created music department at Bristol University. During the next eleven years he laid the foundations for, and built up, a very fine music department, and also made a great impact on the musical life of the city. Following his retirement in 1956, his influence at the university continued to be felt, and the affection and regard held by many of his former students led them often to visit him and write to him. After his retirement he founded the North Hills Orchestra, and inaugurated the very successful Salisbury Concerts for Children of the counties of Wiltshire, Hampshire, and Dorset, and also was organist of the village church in the Wiltshire valley in which he lived. In 1975 he moved to a home for the elderly at Sedgehill, Shaftesbury, Dorset, and there he died on June 30, 1978.

Stanton's compositions display an assured mastery of technique. In addition to his hymn tunes, his works include two important motets for double choir, "The spacious firmament" and "Sing we triumphant hymns." He was governor of Clifton College, Bristol (1947-1958), and on the governing bodies of St. Andreis School, Somerset (1949-1967) and Lancing College, Sussex (1943-1971). He was on the management committee of the Bournemouth Symphony Orchestra from 1954 to 1968.

202 VICTIM DIVINE, YOUR GRACE WE CLAIM

Tune: Das neugeborne Kindelein

See LBW 27 for Charles Wesley. This hymn was included in Wesley's *Hymns on the Lord's Supper,* 1745.

DAS NEUGEBORNE KINDELEIN was the setting for Cyriacus Schneegass' text, "Das neugeborne Kindelein," in Melchior Vulpius' (LBW 115) *Ein schön geistlich Gesangbuch,* Jena, 1609 (Zahn* #491).

203 NOW WE JOIN IN CELEBRATION

Tune: Schmücke dich

See LBW 146 for Joel Lundeen. This hymn was included in *Contemporary Worship-4,* 1972.

For SCHMÜCKE DICH, see LBW 224. The harmonization found here is from the *Orgelchoralbuch,* 1952.

204 CUP OF BLESSING THAT WE SHARE

Tune: Torshov

Bernard Mischke was born at Little Falls, Minnesota, on March 18, 1926. He attended the Crosier Seminary at Onamia, Minnesota, and studied philosophy and theology at the seminary in Hastings, Nebraska, from 1944 to 1951. Ordained a Roman Catholic priest in 1951, he taught German and English at the Crosier Seminary in Onamia, Minnesota, from 1951 to 1969 (taking a year's leave to complete a Master of Arts degree in English and American literature at the University of Notre Dame, Indiana, in 1957) and again from 1971 to 1973. While continuing to teach part-time at the seminary in Onamia, he served as parish pastor of St. James Church, Aitken, Minnesota from 1969 to 1970, and St. Louis Church, Foreston, Minnesota from 1970 to 1971. From 1973 to 1977 he was pastor of St. Joseph's parish in Browerville, Minnesota, and from 1977 to 1979 he was on the road giving talks on mission and parish renewal throughout the Midwest. In 1979 he returned to St. Louis Church in Foreston.

"Cup of Blessing" was written in 1966 at the request of the World Library of Sacred Music, and published in the *People's Mass Book.* Mischke has also written the texts for *Psalms in Song,* 1965, and his books include *Meditations on the Psalms* (1963), *Meditations on the Mass* (1964), *Spreading the Word* (1973), and (with his uncle, Father Fritz Mischke) *Pray Today's Gospel* (1980).

TORSHOV, composed by Knut Nystedt, was the setting for this text in *Contemporary Worship-4,* 1972.

Nystedt, Norwegian composer, organist, and choral conductor, was born in Oslo on September 3, 1915. He studied music in his native city—organ with A. Sanvold, composition with P. Steenberg and B. Brustad, and orchestra conducting with Ø. Fjeldstad. In addition he studied composition with Aaron Copland and organ with Ernest White in the United States. He began his career as an organist in Oslo in 1938, and as a director in 1945. Since 1946 he has been organist of Torshov Church in Oslo. He has directed the Arioso Orchestra (1941–1943 and 1947–1957), the Hanches Chorale (1948–1950), and the Norwegian Soloists Choir since its founding in 1950. Since 1954 he has also been a teacher of choral conducting at the University of Oslo. Between 1962 and 1972 he traveled several times to the United States as a guest conductor and leader of choral workshops, and many of his compositions were written specifically for different workshops in the United States. With the Norwegian Soloists Choir he has toured throughout Scandinavia, Germany, and France, and in the years 1960, 1973, and 1975, made extensive tours of the United States. In 1978 they also toured the Far East.

Nystedt's early compositions had the stamp of neo-Classicism and were inspired by folk music. In the late 1950s and early 1960s he progressed to serial technique and cluster technique. His *De profundis* (1964) which combines Gregorian chant with cluster technique is a central work in Norwegian church music, and was selected for performance at the International Society for Contemporary Music in Stockholm in 1966. He has written a long series of sacred choral works, some of which, such as *Cry Out and Shout,* have become widely disseminated in the United States. His two masses (1970 and 1972) were written for use in the church service. His compositions also include a symphony for strings, chamber music, organ works, vocal solos, and an opera. Through the years he has been active in a number of church music organizations. In 1957 he received an award for his directorship of the Norwegian Soloists Choir, and in 1966 he was made a knight of the first class of the Order of St. Olaf.

205 NOW THE SILENCE

Tune: Now

See LBW 159 for Jaroslav J. Vajda and LBW 118 for Carl F. Schalk. The author of this hymn writes:

> The hymn text originated while I was shaving one morning (a time when I get a lot of original ideas). I was editor of *This Day* magazine at the time. Since my teenage years I have been writing and translating poetry, so many poetic

phrases run through my mind, some of them ending up on paper. Somewhere in the back of my mind, during my previous eighteen years in the full-time parish ministry, I was accumulating reasons and benefits in worship. I have felt that we often get so little out of worship because we anticipate so little, and we seldom come with a bucket large enough to catch all the shower of grace that comes to us in that setting. Suddenly the hymn began to form in my mind as a list of awesome and exciting things that one should expect in worship, culminating in the Eucharist and benediction. The introit or entrance hymn resulted.

Subconsciously I was producing a hymn without rhyme or without worn clichés, depending entirely on rhythm and repetition to make it singable. The reversal of the Trinitarian order in the benediction was made not only to make the conclusion memorable, but to indicate the order in which the Trinity approaches us in worship: The Spirit brings us the Gospel, by which God's blessing is released in our lives.

The poem first appeared in the May, 1968, issue of *This Day* magazine.

NOW was written for the text when it was included in the *Worship Supplement,* 1969, to *The Lutheran Hymnal.*

206   LORD, WHO THE NIGHT YOU WERE BETRAYED
Tune: Song 1

Written early in 1881, this hymn by William Henry Turton was sung on June 22 of that year for the English Church Union Anniversary Service at St. Mary Magdalene's in Munster Square. Originally reading "O thou, who at thy first Eucharist didst pray" in *Altar Hymns,* 1884, the first line was changed to "Thou, who at thy first Eucharist didst pray" in the 1889 Supplement to *Hymns Ancient and Modern.* Further alterations are found in the LBW.

Son of an English army officer, Turton was born in Peshawur, India, on December 30, 1856. He attended Clifton College, Bristol, England, where he received the school's gold medal of the Royal Geographical Society; and the Royal Military Academy, Woolwich, where he was a Pollock medalist. Commissioned in 1876 in the Royal Engineers, he served in the South African War from 1900 to 1902, and retired to Bristol with the rank of lieutenant colonel in 1905. He was decorated on several occasions and was made a Companion of the Distinguished Service Order. Included in his publications were *Hymns written by a Layman between the Festivals of All Saints,* 1880–1881 and 1881–1882; *Truth of Christianity* (which went through twelve editions), *The Plantagenet Ancestry,* 1928; and *The Marine Shells of Port Alfred,* 1932. (The collection on which the last work is based is now at the National Museum, Washington, D.C.) Turton died June 16, 1938, at North Lew, Devon.

SONG 1. Born in Oxford, England, in December of 1583 (baptized Christmas Day at St. Martin's Church), Orlando Gibbons became a chorister in 1596 at King's College Chapel, Cambridge, where his older brother, Edward, was a lay clerk. In 1605 he became organist of the Chapel Royal, a position he held for the rest of his life; and in 1619, he became King's musician for virginals. He received a Bachelor of Music degree from Cambridge in 1606, and in 1622, the Doctor of Music degree from Oxford University. In 1623 he was appointed organist of Westminster Abbey, and as such officiated at the funeral of James I two years later. He himself died suddenly of a stroke at Canterbury on Pentecost, June 5, 1625, having gone there under Charles I to provide the music for the arrival of Charles' bride, Henrietta Maria, from France. He is buried in Canterbury Cathedral.

Gibbons' works include secular vocal and instrumental music and especially masterful madrigals and virginal pieces, but it was his fine music for the Anglican Church, particularly his anthems, which led the old polyphonic style to its last high point in England.

George Wither's collection for which Orlando Gibbons prepared sixteen tunes with figured bass was never published. Wither obtained a patent from the King authorizing the publication of his book, titled *The Hymns and Songs of the Church*, 1623, bound up with the Old Version Psalter. However, the Company of Stationers strenuously and successfully opposed the printing of the book, as it contained hymns at a time when metrical psalmody was the only form of congregational song generally accepted in the church. It remained for Ralph Vaughan Williams (LBW 101) to discover these fine tunes and to introduce them in *The English Hymnal*, 1906. Since then they have attained great popularity. "Song 1" was composed for "Now shall the praises of the Lord be sung," a text based on the Song of Moses (Exodus 15) and intended to be sung at baptism. The last two phrases were originally repeated.

207 WE WHO ONCE WERE DEAD *(Midden in de Dood)*
Tune: Midden in de Dood

"Muus Jacobse" is the pen-name used by the Dutch poet, Klaas Hanzen Heeroma. Born September 13, 1909, at Hoorn on Terschelling, Heeroma grew up in Zwolle and studied Dutch literature under Albert Verway at Leiden. Before World War II he belonged as a poet and critic to the group called "Young Protestants" who published the periodicals *Opwaartsche Wegen* and *De Werkplaats*. During the war years he wrote sacred poetry, and afterwards, psalm versifications and hymns for the church. From 1936 to 1937 he was a teacher in Wassenaar, and from 1937 to 1948 was an editor for the *Woordenboek der Nederlandsche Taal* (a dictionary of the Netherlands language). In 1949 he went to Indonesia where for three years he was a professor at the University of Djakarta. From 1953 until his death he was a professor at the State University of Groningen. He died of an unsuccessful heart operation on November 21, 1972.

The hymn, written in 1961, was first published in *102 Gezangen*, The Hague, 1964. The translation was prepared by Forrest Ingram and David Smith.

Forrest Ingram is the author of *Steps Beyond Impasse: a Chronicle of the Dutch Church*, 1969, and of *Representative Short Story Cycles of the Twentieth Century*, 1971.

David Smith (N. D. Smith), born April 23, 1923, in London, England, completed a Bachelor of Arts degree at the University of London in 1950. He has taught full time for nine years and served for five years in the armed forces in the Middle East and in Europe. Since 1960 he has worked as a translator, and except for some part-time teaching of French, is "an almost full-time, self-employed translator." He has written four books for young readers: *The Battle of Britain*, 1962; *Winston Churchill*, 1963; *The Royal Air Force*, 1962; and *Discovering Flight*,

1966. He has published a large number of books, articles, and papers translated from French, Dutch, and German, covering a wide range of subjects. He is married, and the father of three children.

MIDDEN IN DE DOOD. Originally this hymn was sung to a tune by Tera de Marez Oyens-Wansink. The LBW tune by Rik Veelenturf was written for White Thursday, 1960. Carl Schalk (LBW 118) has prepared the harmonization, which was included in *Contemporary Worship-4*, 1972.

Henricus Joseph Veelenturf was born January 18, 1936, in Vlaardingen, Holland. Following *Gymnasium* studies, he entered the Society of Jesus in 1955. In 1966 he left the Society. He had completed his philosophical and theological studies, but was not ordained. From 1960 to 1966, as a member of the "Werk-groep Volkstaalliturgie," it was his job to introduce the new Dutch liturgy in local Roman Catholic parishes throughout Holland. He married in 1967, and started a liturgical center in Amsterdam, but two years later, disappointed with the atmosphere and regression in the Catholic church in Holland, he discontinued his work at the center, and started another job in community organization. He has since become a teacher in the social academy in Amsterdam.

Veelenturf, who refers to himself as "not a real composer of music, but an ordinary 'music-maker,'" has written some ten songs.

208 LORD JESUS CHRIST, YOU HAVE PREPARED
(Herr Jesu Christ, du hast bereit't)
Tune: Du Lebensbrot, Herr Jesu Christ

This hymn by Samuel Kinner first appeared in Jeremias Weber's *Gesang Buch,* 1638.

Kinner was born in 1603 at Breslau, Germany (now in Poland), and practiced medicine there for some time. He later entered the service of the Duke of Liegnitz-Brieg as counselor and court physician, and remained in that position until his death on August 10, 1668, at Brieg.

The English text was prepared for the LBW by the Inter-Lutheran Commission on Worship.

DU LEBENSBROT, HERR JESU CHRIST first appeared with that communion hymn by Johann Rist (LBW 197) in *Praxis Pietatis Melica* (LBW 23), Frankfurt am Main, 1668. The composer, Peter Sohren (Sohr, Sohrer), was born in Germany about 1630, and was possibly the son of Daniel Sohren, pastor in Lenzen, near Elbing. Little is known of him until he published his edition of *Praxis Pietatis Melica.* There on the title page he is noted to be the "Best old school and mathematics teacher of the Christian congregation of Heilige Leichnam in the Royal City of Elbing in Prussia." In his 1683 *Musikalischer Vorschmack* he is given as the cantor and organist of the Elbing congregation. His death date is not known, but is believed to be around 1692 since the 1693 edition of *Praxis Pietatis Melica* was prepared by someone else. Sohren's 1668 edition contained some 220 melodies of his own, and his *Musikalischer Vorschmack* is said to contain between 240 and 250 of his tunes.

The harmonization was prepared for the LBW by Paul B. Bouman, who since 1953 has served as teacher and director of music at Grace Lutheran Church, River Forest, Illinois. A native of Hamburg, Minnesota, Bouman was born in 1918 and received a Bachelor of Science in Education degree at Concordia Teachers College, and a Master of Music degree at Northwestern University. Further study was undertaken at Westphalian Church Music School in Herford, Germany. Before coming to his present position, he was teacher and director of music at Ebenezer Lutheran Church, Milwaukee, Wisconsin (1939–1945) and at St. Paul Lutheran Church, Melrose Park, Illinois (1945–1953). He has also served as guest instructor at Valparaiso University, Concordia Teachers College, River Forest, and at various local workshops. While living in Milwaukee he was a member of the Lutheran A Capella Choir, and for a time was also assistant conductor. His children's choir has won numerous awards, and he has presented rehearsal demonstrations to various chapters of the American Guild of Organists and other conferences in the area. He is the composer of several choral compositions, and is represented by organ pieces in the *Parish Organist*. Married to Victoria Bartling of Milwaukee, he is the father of five children.

209   COME, RISEN LORD

Tune: Knickerbocker

Based on Luke 24:28–31, this hymn was one of the sixteen contributed by George Wallace Briggs to *Songs of Praise,* London, 1931.

Briggs, born in Kirkby, Northamptonshire, England, on December 14, 1875, graduated from Emmanuel College, Cambridge, where he gained high honors in classical studies. Ordained in the Church of England, he went briefly to one of the poorer parishes in Wakefield, Yorkshire, then served as a chaplain in the Royal Navy from 1902 to 1909. Thereafter he was vicar of St. Andrew's, Norwich, 1909–1918; rector of Loughborough, 1918–1927; canon of Leicester Cathedral, 1927–1934; and canon of Worcester Cathedral from 1934 until his retirement in 1956. He died at Hindhead, Surrey, on December 30, 1959.

Briggs was much involved in educational work and published a number of books of hymns and prayers for children, including *Prayers and Hymns for Use in Schools,* 1927; *Little Bible,* 1931; *Daily Service,* 1936; and *Songs of Faith,* 1945. In addition he is noted for a number of single prayers, one of which was used on August 10, 1941, when Franklin Delano Roosevelt and Winston Churchill met for the adoption of the Atlantic Charter. He was one of the founders of the Hymn Society of Great Britain and Ireland, and in 1950 came to the United States where he lectured at Berkeley, California, and New Haven, Connecticut, and before the Hymn Society of America in New York City. In addition to his hymns, he wrote several hymn tunes.

KNICKERBOCKER. Written while the composer was at St. Paul's Church, Minneapolis, this tune was named for the rector there, Addison E. Knickerbocker. It was included as a setting for this hymn in *The Hymnal 1940* of the Episcopal Church.

Frank Kingston Owen, who is organist and choirmaster at St. Margaret's Church in Palm Desert, California, and organist emeritus of St. Paul's Cathedral, Los Angeles, was born June 6, 1902, at Manchester, England. He began music study at age four with his father, and appeared at an early age as a concert pianist. At the age of eight he became a chorister at Manchester Cathedral, and from age seventeen was organist in churches of several denominations. In 1923 he came to Pawtucket, Rhode Island. In the course of the next four years he served as organist of Central Falls Methodist Church, and played for Evensong at the chapel of the Episcopal Home for Incurable Women in Providence. He was married in 1929 to Elsie Anderson, of Fall River, Massachusetts, a nurse at the home. On occasion, also, he assisted at Grace Church, Providence, and during the week he substituted at several theaters in Pawtucket and Providence. He became organist at Christ Church, St. Paul, Minnesota in 1927, and nine years later accepted a similar post at St. Paul's Church, Minneapolis. After 1939 he was also supervisor of music at Breck School for boys and, for ten years while living in the Twin Cities area, was organist for the Bach Society at the University of Minnesota. From 1944 to 1953 he was organist and choirmaster at St. Luke's Church, Kalamazoo, Michigan, and also taught music theory at Kalamazoo College. In 1953 he began twenty-one years as director of music at St. Paul's Cathedral, Los Angeles, where he founded the Cathedral Choir School based on those of England.

Owen holds a Bachelor of Music degree from MacPhail College of Music, which is now a part of the University of Minnesota, and for over fifty years has been active in the American Guild of Organists. In addition he is a fellow of the Incorporated Guild of Church Musicians and a founding member of the Association of Anglican Musicians, and has participated in several other music organizations. Among his publications are various articles on the training and development of boys' voices, a twenty-two-month series on all the Anglican Cathedrals in England for *The Diapason,* and *A Choirboy's Handbook.* His anthem, "We Give Thee Thanks," was written in 1978 for the dedication of the organ at St. Margaret's Church.

210   AT THE LAMB'S HIGH FEAST WE SING *(Ad regias Agni dapes)*
Tune: Sonne der Gerechtigkeit

The original Latin hymn, "Ad coenam Agni providi," is dated by various authorities as originating sometime between the fourth and ninth centuries. Widely disseminated, it was found not only in England and in the Roman rite, but also in Mozarabic and Ambrosian use, and was sung as a daily Vesper (sunset) hymn from Saturday in Easter week to Ascension. Frost* notes: "The hymn abounds in references to the Pascal services, especially those of Easter Even, when the catechumens, clothed in white, were first baptized and then confirmed, and so went to their first communion on Easter morning." The commemoration of the deliverance of Israel from Egypt was also part of these services, and can be noted especially in stanza 3.

"Ad coenam Agni providi" was one of the hymns "revised" under the influence of humanism in the sixteenth and seventeenth centuries (see p. 15), and in the Roman Breviary completed in 1631 under Pope Urban VIII, it became "Ad regias Agni dapes." Robert Campbell's translation of "Ad regias Agni dapes" was prepared in 1849 and published in his *Hymns and Anthems for Use in the Holy Services of the Church within the United Diocese of St. Andrews, Dunkeld, and Dunblane* (the "St. Andrews Hymnal").

Campbell was a Scottish lawyer born December 19, 1814, at Trochraig, Ayrshire. He entered Glasgow University when he was still very young and later studied law at the University of Edinburgh. Originally a Presbyterian, he became a member of the Episcopal Church of Scotland at an early age, and later, in 1852, a member of the Roman Catholic communion. Always a devoted churchman, he directed much attention to young people and the poor. He died in Edinburgh, December 29, 1868.

SONNE DER GERECHTIGKEIT. "At the Lamb's high feast we sing" has been sung to a number of different melodies. The present combination is the work of Edward W. Klammer, manager of the music department of Concordia Publishing House. He notes that he first came across the melody while serving as "meter man" of the Hymn Committee of the Commission on Worship of the Lutheran Church—Missouri Synod, in which his job was to find new or better tunes for some of the hymns. When the Inter-Lutheran Commission on Worship was formed, Klammer was a member of the hymn music committee. The combination of text and tune was used in the *Worship Supplement,* 1969, to *The Lutheran Hymnal.*

Originally a fifteenth-century folksong, "Der reich Mann war geritten aus," the tune was included in the 1566 *Kirchengeseng* of the Bohemian Brethren. This hymnal, which was edited by Petrus Herbert, Johannes Geletzky, and Michael Tham, was the third edition of Johann Horn's 1544 hymnal (LBW 132).

The harmony by Jan Bender (LBW 396) is from the *Worship Supplement,* 1969.

211   HERE, O MY LORD, I SEE THEE

Tune: Farley Castle

See LBW 167 for Horatius Bonar. Written at the request of his older brother, Dr. John James Bonar of Greenock, Scotland, this hymn was read after communion in the author's church in October of 1855, and printed later that year as a leaflet for St. Andrew's Free Church, Greenock. It was included in the first series, 1857, of Bonar's *Hymns of Faith and Hope.*

FARLEY CASTLE, composed by Henry Lawes, appeared in George Sandys' *Paraphrase upon the Psalms of David,* 1637–1638, where it was the setting for Psalm 72.

Born at Dinton, Wiltshire, England, in December of 1595, Lawes was baptized January 5, 1596. A pupil of Giovanni Coperario (John Cooper, who was music master of the children of James I), Lawes was appointed an epistoler (one who reads the Epistle at the Communion service) of the Chapel Royal, January 1, 1626, and a gentleman of the Chapel in November of the same year. He became music master to the family of the Earl of Bridgewater, and was commissioned by the earl to write and direct a masque in honor of the festivities when he became lord president of Wales. Lawes asked his friend, John Milton (LBW 318), to prepare the text, and on Michaelmas night, September 29, 1634, *Comus* was given its first performance at Ludlow Castle. His best writing is found in his stage productions and in his 300 or more songs. He was highly esteemed by his contemporaries, especially by poets, because of his careful attention to text-setting, and he developed a style known as *aria parlante,* a style of melody midway between aria and recitative. Included in his church music are about twenty anthems. His hymn tunes were contributed to Sandys' *Psalms,* and to *Choice Psalms put into Musick for three Voices,* 1648, published with his brother, William (1602–1645), for use of the Chapel and the Royal Court of Charles I. During the Protectorate, Lawes lost all his court appointments, but regained them in 1660 with the Restoration, and wrote an anthem for the coronation of Charles II. He died October 21, 1662, in London. Ralph Vaughan Williams (LBW 101) brought Lawes's tunes into circulation in England and America when he included five of them in *The English Hymnal,* 1906.

The harmonization by Carl Schalk (LBW 118) was included in the *Worship Supplement,* 1969, to *The Lutheran Hymnal.*

212 LET US BREAK BREAD TOGETHER
Tune: Break Bread Together

Originally this spiritual seems not to have been associated with communion at all, but rather to have been a gathering song. Group protests and attempted escapes by Africans in slavery date from as early as the sixteenth century. At first these secret meetings were called by means of a drum or a horn as they had been in Africa. In 1676, however, the Colony of Virginia took the lead in prohibiting the assembling of Africans by drum beat, and songs such as this came to be used instead. Miles Mark Fisher, in *Negro Slave Songs in the United States* (1953), notes, "It relates hardly at all to holy communion, which does not necessarily require early morning administration or a devotee who faces east. Here it seems was a signal song of Virginia Negroes of the eighteenth century who used it and similar ones to convene their secret meetings." Apparently after the Civil War the first two stanzas were added and it came to be used as a communion hymn.

BREAK BREAD TOGETHER shares the history of the text. Leland Sateren (LBW 100) prepared the harmonization.

213 I COME, O SAVIOR, TO YOUR TABLE
(Ich komm' zu deinem Abendmahle)
Tune: Ich sterbe täglich

This German hymn by Heyder was included in the *Kirchengesangbuch für Evangelisch-Lutherische Gemeinden,* St. Louis, 1848, dated 1734. Polack* notes that Wetzel gives Blumberg's *Gesangbuch,* Zwickau, 1710, as the source. The translation was prepared by the editors of *The Lutheran Hymnal,* 1941. Alteration is limited to updated second-person pronouns.

Little is known about Friedrich Christian Heyder (1677–1754). From 1699 he served as a deacon in Merseburg, Germany, the city of his birth, and for thirty-five years beginning in 1706 he was pastor in Zörbig near Halle, where he died as pastor emeritus.

ICH STERBE TÄGLICH was included in the *Emskirchner Choral-Buch,* 1756, a manuscript collection from the municipal library in Leipzig, containing 295 melodies with four-part settings. It contains, in addition to some of the well-known melodies of the sixteenth and seventeenth centuries, many tunes from Johann Freylinghausen's *Gesangbuch* (LBW 32) and some from the Bayreuth *Melodienbüchlein* of 1733. The tune originally was the setting for Benjamin Schmolck's (LBW 187) burial hymn, "Ich sterbe täglich."

The harmonization was prepared for the LBW by Paul Frederick Foelber. Born June 11, 1926, in Fort Wayne, Indiana, Foelber holds Bachelor of Arts (1947) and Master of Divinity (1950) degrees from Concordia Seminary, St. Louis, Missouri; a Master of Music degree (1949) from Northwestern University, Evanston, Illinois; and a Doctor of Philosophy degree (1961) from the Catholic University of America, Washington, D.C. He has studied also at the University of Michigan. Foelber has been a teacher in the areas of humanities, music, worship, hymnology, and liturgics at Concordia Teachers College, Seward, Nebraska, 1950–1952; at St. John's College, Winfield, Kansas, 1956–1963; and since 1963, at Concordia College, Ann Arbor, Michigan, where he is chairman of the Division of Humanities. From 1952 to 1956 he was pastor of the Lutheran Church of St. Andrew, Silver Spring, Maryland. In addition he has been engaged in summer school teaching at Concordia Seminary, St. Louis. In 1970 he began five years as conductor of the Ann Arbor Cantata Singers and Orchestra. He served on the Commission on Worship for the Lutheran Church—Missouri Synod (1970–1977, chairman after 1976), and on the Inter-Lutheran Commission on Worship (1970–1978, vice chairman after 1973). He has written several articles in relation to the LBW, as well as others dealing with music, and with the role of literature, visual arts, and music in the life of the church.

214 COME, LET US EAT *(A va de laa mioo)*
Tune: A va de

Both text and tune of this Liberian hymn are by Billema Kwillia. Born about 1925, Kwillia learned to read Loma, his own language, as a young adult, when the church's literacy program reached his town. In the early 1960s he applied for a job as literacy teacher, and worked in that capacity for a number of years. During this time he became a Christian and was baptized. For a time he was an evangelist, conducting services and leading the Christians in his home town. Margaret D. Miller, translator of the hymn, notes that it was while Kwillia was a literacy teacher-evangelist that he sang this hymn for a meeting, and it was recorded on tape.

The hymn was first published in *Laudamus,* the hymnal for the Lutheran World Federation, fourth edition (1970), in the original Loma dialect, as well as in a German translation by Ulrich S. Leupold (LBW 516), and in this English translation, prepared in 1969 by Margaret Miller.

Miller, born March 23, 1927, at Clifton Springs, New York, was the daughter of missionaries to Liberia. Her father died at sea of a tropical disease in 1935, and her mother returned alone two years later to continue missionary service in Liberia, while Margaret and her sister attended Lankenau School for Girls in Philadelphia. Margaret won a scholarship to Wilson College, Chambersburg, Pennsylvania, and upon completion of a Bachelor of Arts degree in 1949, she went to Liberia for the Committee on World Literacy and Christian Literature, working from 1950 to 1953 to develop the literacy program sponsored jointly by the government and the missions. After a year of graduate work at the Kennedy School of Missions of the Hartford Seminary Foundation, Hartford, Connecticut, she was commissioned in New York in 1954 for service in Liberia. Since that time she has served at the literacy center in Wozi, a mud-hut village 180 miles inland, returning in 1956–1957, 1959–1960, and 1964–1965 for graduate studies in linguistics and anthropology at the Hartford Seminary Foundation in Connecticut. The language-literature-literacy program in which she works functions to put the Scriptures and other Christian materials in the hands of the people in their own language. Occasionally, also, she serves as a writer and an artist. She is editor of the *Loma Weekly,* a bilingual (Loma and English) newspaper.

Originally beginning "Come, let us see now the feast spread," in *Laudamus,* the translation has been altered, and the meter changed. Gilbert E. Doan (LBW 99) has provided the fourth stanza.

A VA DE, adapted by Leland Sateren (LBW 100) for *Contemporary Worship-4,* 1972, was given in triple meter in *Laudamus:*†

215   O LORD, WE PRAISE YOU *(Gott sei gelobet und gebenedeiet)*
Tune: Gott sei gelobet und gebenedeiet

Stanza 1 of this hymn was a *Leise,* dating from pre-Reformation times, when it was sung in processions and at Mass as a post-communion hymn. During the annual Corpus Christi procession it was sung by the congregation between the stanzas of the Latin sequence, Lauda Sion Salvatore (see p. 14). Martin Luther (LBW 48) added two stanzas of his own and the hymn was included in the Erfurt *Enchiridia,* 1524. As a hymn that had been and continued to be sung by the laity at communion, it was a special favorite of Luther's.

The composite translation, prepared for *The Lutheran Hymnal,* 1941, has been altered slightly for the LBW.

GOTT SEI GELOBET UND GEBENEDEIET has been associated with this text since pre-Reformation times and can be found in the *Miltenberger Processionale* which dates from the end of the fifteenth century (Bäumker,* I, p. 719f). The LBW form of the melody was included with Luther's hymn in Johann Walther's (LBW 350) *Geistliche Gesangbüchlein,* 1524. Carl Schalk (LBW 118) prepared the harmonization for the LBW.

†"A Va De," *Laudamus* (4th edition, 1970), the hymnal for the Lutheran World Federation: Geneva, Switzerland. Reprinted by permission of the Lutheran World Federation.

216 FOR PERFECT LOVE SO FREELY SPENT

Tune: Venerable

The author, Louise Marshall McDowell, describes the origins of this poem as follows:

> In my family there are many theological viewpoints—Catholic, several kinds of Protestant, Fundamentalists and Liberals. I wanted to write a hymn which could be sung with enthusiasm by all of them, and by Christians everywhere, but which would nevertheless be a strong expression of faith. I prayed to this effect, then fell into a deep reverie, reflecting on the many ways in which Communion is celebrated around the world. Emerging from this reverie, I discovered that I had, without any conscious awareness of writing, somehow written the words:
>
> > "For perfect love so freely spent,
> > For fellowship restored—"
>
> I have always felt that these two lines were truly inspired, in a different way from anything else I have written.

The hymn was first published in the Presbyterian *Worshipbook,* Philadelphia, 1972.

Louise Marshall McDowell, born April 11, 1923, in Geneva, Alabama, grew up an orphan and attended Huntingdon College in Montgomery, Alabama. For thirty-six years she has been the wife of a Presbyterian clergyman, and notes, "I have received no significant honors, other than my husband's statement that he doesn't think he could have made it without me." Their son, adopted at age ten, is now a Wesleyan Methodist missionary to the Indians in South Dakota. She has written verse occasionally since the age of ten and is currently writing a novel.

VENERABLE. Born June 6, 1915, in Philadelphia, Vincent Persichetti began the study of piano at age five, and later took lessons in organ, double bass, tuba, theory, and composition. By age eleven, he was performing professionally as an accompanist, radio staff pianist, orchestra member, and church organist; and at age sixteen he was appointed organist and choir director at Arch Street Presbyterian Church in Philadelphia, where he remained for twenty years. At Combs College of Music he studied composition with Russell King Miller. After his graduation in 1935, he was simultaneously head of the theory department of Combs College, a conducting major with Fritz Reiner at the Curtis Institute, and a piano major with Olga Samaroff at the Philadelphia Conservatory, while studying composition with several important American composers. He holds a diploma in conducting from Curtis Institute, and Master of Music (1939) and Doctor of Music (1945) degrees from the Philadelphia Conservatory. In 1941 he became head of the theory and composition departments at the Philadelphia Conservatory, and was married the same year to pianist Dorothea Flanagan. They are the parents of two children. Joining the faculty of the Juilliard School of Music in 1947, he became chairman of the composition department in 1963. Since 1952 he also has been director of the Elkan-Vogel music publishing firm. Among his many recognitions are honorary doctorates from Combs College, Bucknell University, and Baldwin-Wallace College; three Guggenheim Fellowships, two grants from the National Foundation on the Arts and Humanities, and one from the National Institute of Arts and Letters. He has received over seventy commissions from various orchestras and organizations, and has appeared as guest conductor, lecturer, and composer at over 200 universities. The list of his works is extensive and includes compositions for orchestra, band, chamber ensembles, organ, piano, chorus, and solo voice. In addition to his work as a composer, he is highly regarded as a teacher and has written one of the definitive books on modern compositional techniques: *Twentieth Century Harmony,* 1961. His *Hymns and Responses for the Church Year,* published in Philadelphia in 1956, is the source for the tune "Venerable." In that work it was a setting for a text by Peter the Venerable (1092–1156), "The gates of death are broken through." The composer notes, "This Easter hymn is effective when sung in unison with a rich organ background—or when sung by the choir in parts, a cappella (often transposed up a major second)." The tune was later used in the climactic statement of his Symphony No. 7 ("Liturgical Symphony").

217   WE PLACE UPON YOUR TABLE, LORD

Tune: Distress

This hymn was included in *100 Hymns for Today,* 1969. Originally opening "Upon thy table, Lord, we place these symbols of our work and thine," the text has been considerably altered.

The author, Maurice Frank Campbell Willson, was born November 21, 1884, son of the curate of St. Saviour's Church, Croydon, Surrey, in England. He attended Fettes College, Edinburgh, Scotland. During World War I he was a captain in the 20th London Regiment and served in France, Salonika, Palestine, and Mesopotamia. He was married to Frances K. Castens by 1922, and lived for a time in Weybridge, Surrey. He then moved with his family to Bedford, where for many years he was chief clerk in the filing offices of the Royal Court of Justice. The Willsons have been described as a musical family and "a happy one, full of fun and good humour, and always ready to help in 'Church do's.'" Active in St. Pauls Church in Bedford until his death, Willson became a sidesman in 1927 and a scoutmaster the same year, and was known as a friend of all the boys in the parish. He was also a member of the parish church council and a leader of the church dramatic club. He was of Irish extraction. When he died on November 17, 1944, after a long battle with cancer, the London *Times* printed the announcement with the addition, "Belfast papers please copy." His son preceded him in death in a military aircraft accident in World War II. His wife and daughter later moved to California.

DISTRESS, a pentatonic folk melody, was included in William Walker's (LBW 30) *Southern Harmony,* 1835, where it was the setting for Anne Steele's (LBW 240) "So fades the lovely blooming flower." With "Bourbon" (LBW 127) and "Kedron" (LBW 420), it is one of a group of tunes used with solemn texts. It is related to "Detroit" (LBW 240), and in his *Down-East Spirituals,* 1939, George Pullen Jackson quotes a very old Scottish tune, "Laird O' Cockpen," which is possibly the prototype of both melodies.

The harmonization was prepared by Ludwig Lenel (LBW 399) for *Contemporary Worship–4,* 1972.

218 STRENGTHEN FOR SERVICE, LORD (نيبلا هدن أبزا وهقهس)
[*Hayyel Maran 'idh dephshat*]

Tune: Wir dienen, Herr

This ancient communion hymn is believed by some to be based on a prayer by Ephraim the Syrian, a famous theologian, poet, and hymn-writer. Ephraim was born about 307 in Northern Mesopotamia and spent most of his days at Edessa, where he died in 373. The prayer is from the ancient Liturgy of Malabar, part of the Nestorian rite used by the Christians of the St. Thomas Church of South India. It is said by the deacon while the people are communing. (Of the three basic liturgy groups—Roman, Byzantine, and Asian—the liturgy of Malabar belongs to the Asian group, which includes also the liturgies used in Syria, Upper Mesopotamia, and Western Persia.)

John Mason Neale (LBW 34) in his *Liturgies of S. Mark, S. James. S. Clement, S. Chrysostom, and the Church of Malabar,* 1859, gave a prose translation of the prayer:

> Strengthen, O Lord, the hands which are stretched out to receive the Holy Thing: vouchsafe that they may daily bring forth fruit to thy divinity; that they may be worthy of all things which they have sung to thy praise within thy sanctuary, and may ever laud thee. Grant, moreover, my Lord, that the ears which have heard the voice of thy songs, may never hear the voice of clamor and dispute. Grant also that the eyes which have seen thy great love, may also behold thy blessed hope; that the tongues which have sung the *Sanctus* may speak the truth. Grant that the feet which have walked in the church may walk in the region of light; that the bodies which have tasted thy living Body may be restored in newness of life. On this congregation also, which adores thy divinity, let thy aides be multiplied, and let thy great love remain with us and by thee may we abound in the manifestation of thy glory, and open a door to the prayers of all of us. We all then, who have drawn near by the gift of the grace of the Holy Ghost, and to whom it has been vouchsafed to become fellow participators in the reception of these mysteries, most excellent, holy, divine, and quickening, let us all praise and exult in God, the Giver of them.

C. W. Humphreys prepared a hymn based on Neale's translation which was partly rewritten by Percy Dearmer (LBW 169) for *The English Hymnal,* 1906. That text has been considerably reworked for the LBW; the last two stanzas are basically new.

WIR DIENEN, HERR was written by Hans-Friedrich Micheelsen for Rudolf Alexander Schröder's (1878-1962) text, "Wir dienen, Herr, um keinen Lohn," in *Neue Gemeinde Lieder,* 1938.

The son of a teacher and music director in Hennstedt, Dithmarschen, Germany, Micheelsen was born June 9, 1902. On his father's suggestion he trained as a teacher for two years. Later, while employed as a private tutor, he studied organ and theory with Paul Kickstat. In 1932, he became a student of Paul Hindemith at the Musikhochschule in Berlin and took a position as organist of St. Matthew's Church. Called as director of the newly-established Landeskirchliches Kirchenmusik-Schule in Hamburg in 1938, he remained there until 1954 when he became director of church music at the Hamburg Musikhochschule. In 1962 he retired on a pension and went to live in Sasbachwalden, Schwarzwald. He died November 23, 1973, at Glüsing, near Heide in Holstein.

Micheelsen's compositions include oratorios, cantatas, and songs, as well as pieces for orchestra, organ, piano, and chorus. Strongly influenced by the music of Heinrich Schütz (LBW 180) and by his teacher, Paul Hindemith, his works have made a great impact for objectivity in church music.

219   COME WITH US, O BLESSED JESUS
Tune: Jesu, Joy of Man's Desiring

Published in the second edition of Hopkins' *Carols, Hymns, and Songs,* 1872, this hymn is the first of four stanzas entitled "Retrocessional for Christmas Day." A few slight alterations have been made in the text.

John Henry Hopkins Jr., who also wrote the text and tune for "We three kings of Orient are," (included in his first edition of *Carols, Hymns and Songs*, 1863) was born October 28, 1820, at Pittsburgh, Pennsylvania. Following his graduation in 1839 from the University of Vermont, he worked for a while in New York City as a reporter while studying law. In 1845 he took his Master of Arts degree from the University of Vermont, and in 1850 graduated from General Theological Seminary, New York City where he later served as the first instructor in church music (1855–1857). During the 1850s and 1860s he was active in the New York Ecclesiological Society, the American counterpart of John Mason Neale's (LBW 34) Cambridge Society, and designed stained glass windows, episcopal seals, and so forth. From 1853 to 1868 he edited the *Church Journal,* which he had founded. One of the leaders in the development of hymnody in the Episcopal church in the mid-eighteenth century, Hopkins wrote a number of hymns and hymn tunes and published, in addition to his *Carols,* etc., *Canticles Noted with Accompanying Harmonies,* 1866. In 1887 he edited Bishop John Freeman Young's (LBW 65) *Great Hymns of the Church.* Ordained a priest in 1872, he was rector of Trinity Church, Plattsburg, New York, from 1872 to 1876, and of Christ Church, Williamsport, Pennsylvania, until 1887. He died August 14, 1891, near Hudson, New York.

JESU, JOY OF MAN'S DESIRING. Originally "Come with us, O blessed Jesus" appeared with one of Hopkins' own tunes. The present setting is a form of "Werde munter" (see LBW 440), which was included in Johann Rist's (LBW 197) *Himmlische Lieder,* in the third group of ten hymns published in 1642. There it was the setting for his "Werde munter mein Gemüte" (Zahn* #6551). Each phrase of the melody began with two eighth-notes, thus:

The composer, Johann Schop, born probably in Hamburg sometime at the end of the sixteenth century, became a member of the court band at Wolfenbüttel in 1615, and later became a violinist at the Danish court. In 1621 he was appointed director of the town council music at Hamburg, and later also was organist to the town and to St. James's Church.

Schop had a reputation as an excellent performer on the organ, violin, lute, trumpet, and zinke. A close friend of Johann Rist, he provided musical settings for Rist's *Himmlische Lieder,* 1641–1643, and his *Geistliche Koncerte* also appeared in 1643. All copies of his *Newe Paduanen, Galliarden, Allemanden* published sometime between 1633 and 1640 seem to be lost. His secular airs are said to have influenced some melodies composed by Thomas Kingo (LBW 102). Schop died around 1665 in Hamburg.

J. S. Bach used the melody in Cantatas 46, 55, and 154 and twice in the *St. Matthew Passion.* Two harmonizations are also included in his *Choralgesänge.* The familiar "Jesu, joy of man's desiring," is from Cantata 147 for the Feast of the Visitation, "Herz und Mund und That und Leben."

Johann Sebastian Bach needs no introduction. His sacred works—the nearly 200 cantatas, the large choral works (B-minor Mass, *Magnificat,* Christmas and Easter Oratorios, motets), the organ works—communicate a deep Christian faith, and together with his secular music—cantatas, keyboard and orchestral works—bespeak his great genius. Numerous accounts of Bach's life have been written. Briefly told, he was born in Eisenach, Germany, on March 21, 1685. His father died before Bach was ten and the boy went to live with his elder brother, Johann Christoph, at Ohrdruf, where he attended the *Lyceum.* In Ohrdruf also he sang in the church and school choirs and received clavier lessons from his brother. At fifteen he went to Lüneberg where he was enrolled in the select choir of St. Michael's Church School. In that city he came to know Georg Böhm and more than once walked thirty miles to Hamburg to hear Adam Reinken. In 1703 he took his first organ position at St. Boniface Church in Arnstadt, where he remained until 1707. During this period, in 1705, he made his four-month visit to Lübeck where he went to learn from Dietrich Buxtehude. He married his cousin, Maria Barbara Bach, in 1707, and for a year was organist at the Church of St. Blasius in Mühlhausen. From 1708 to 1717 he held his first major position—that of court organist, and later in 1714, concertmaster of the Duke's chamber orchestra in Weimar. Bach became very well known as an organist and for the rest of his life was frequently called upon to inspect new organs. At Cöthen, from 1717 to 1723, Bach was court *Kapellmeister* to Prince Leopold. It was during this period that a number of his chamber and keyboard works were written, as the Court belonged to the Reformed Church and Bach did not play or compose for church services. His first wife died in 1720 and in the following year he was married to Anna Magdalena Wülcken. The last twenty-seven years of Bach's life were spent at Leipzig where he was cantor of St. Thomas' School and music director of the other Leipzig churches. There he composed his great choral works as well as harpsichord and organ music. Although there were often difficulties with the various authorities at Leipzig, Bach remained there until his death on July 28, 1750. Significantly, many of his manuscripts were signed "Soli Deo gloria"—"To God alone be the glory."

220 O JESUS, BLESSED LORD *(O Jesus, söde Jesus, dig)*
Tune: Tender Thought

See LBW 102 for Thomas Kingo. This hymn of thanksgiving after the Sacrament of the Altar was first published in *En Ny Kirke-Psalme-Bog,*

1689, the so-called "*Winter-Parten,*" and was repeated in Kingo's 1699 hymnal.

Arthur James Mason translated this hymn for the Supplemental Edition of *Hymns Ancient and Modern,* 1889. There have been some alterations for the LBW.

Mason was born in England on May 4, 1851, and attended Trinity College, Cambridge, receiving a Bachelor of Arts degree with honors in 1872, and in 1890, a Doctor of Divinity degree. Ordained in 1874, he served at Truro, then at All-Hallows, Barking, in London. In 1895 he became canon of Canterbury, professor of divinity at Cambridge, and a fellow of Jesus College. From 1903 to 1912 he was master of Pembroke College, and from 1908 to 1910 was also vice-chancellor of Cambridge University. He was the author of many theological works, the best-known of which is *The Faith of the Gospel,* and in addition prepared A. D. Walpole's *Early Latin Hymns* for publication after Walpole's death in 1920. Mason died eight years later, April 24, 1928, at Canterbury.

TENDER THOUGHT, an anonymous hexatonic melody, was included in Ananias Davisson's *Kentucky Harmony,* 1816, as the setting for "Arise, my tender thoughts, arise," a hymn by Philip Doddridge (LBW 35).

Davisson was born in 1780, and like the Chapins (LBW 122) was a staunch Presbyterian. He seems to have studied with one of the Chapins after 1794, and in 1818 is found in Knoxville, Tennessee. He died in 1857.

221 SENT FORTH BY GOD'S BLESSING
Tune: The Ash Grove

Under the pseudonym "J. Clifford Evers" this hymn was included in the *People's Mass Book,* 1964. Several alterations were made in the text when it entered *Contemporary Worship-4,* 1972, and a few further changes have been made for the LBW.

A life-long resident of Cincinnati, the author of this hymn, Omer Westendorf, was born February 24, 1916. He received a Bachelor of Music degree, and in 1950, a Master of Music degree from the College-Conservatory of Music of the University of Cincinnati. At the age of twenty he began his career as church organist and choirmaster of St. Bonaventure Church, a position he has held for over forty years. His Bonaventure Choir, a free-lance chorale, appears on a dozen recordings of religious music, and can be heard frequently in concert, both live and on television and radio. He has been a music instructor at several Cincinnati schools, and for a brief period, also, he was director of the Bishop's Choir at the Cathedral in Covington, Kentucky. In 1950 he founded the World Library of Sacred Music, and in 1957, World Library Publications, of which he served as chairman and president for many years. Since his resignation from World Library Publications in 1976, he has established a consultation agency on liturgical music, and lectures and conducts seminars on church music. He has written over thirty-five hymn texts, many under pseudonyms, and has compiled four successive hymnals, culminating in the *People's Mass Book,* the first vernacular hymn and service book to implement the Catholic liturgies decreed by Vatican

Council II. He has also served as a consultant for the most recent edition of the *Armed Forces Hymnal*. His hymn, "Gift of Finest Wheat," was the official hymn of the 41st Eucharistic Congress (Philadelphia, 1976), having won first prize for that honor in an international contest. His book titled *Music Lessons for the Man in the Pew* is aimed at teaching the art of sight reading choral music. Westendorf is married and the father of three children.

For THE ASH GROVE see LBW 557. This harmonization of the tune was prepared for *Contemporary Worship-4, 1972*, by Leland Sateren (LBW 100).

222   O BREAD OF LIFE FROM HEAVEN *(O Esca viatorum)*
Tune: O Welt, ich muss dich lassen

This Latin hymn, which first appeared in the *Maintzisch Gesangbuch, 1661*, is believed to be the work of a German Jesuit of the seventeenth century. The English text is a combination, with alterations, of translations by Philip Schaff (*Christ in Song*, 1868) and H. T. Henry (*American Catholic Hymnal,* 1913).

Schaff, renowned theologian of the Reformed Church, was born in Chur, Switzerland, January 1, 1819, and studied at the Universities of Tübingen, Halle, and Berlin. He came to the United States where he taught at the German Reformed Theological Seminary at Lancaster, Pennsylvania. From 1870 until his death on October 20, 1893, he was professor of sacred literature at Union Theological Seminary, New York City. The list of his theological works is extensive. In addition he made a valuable contribution to hymnody with his *Christ in Song,* and as editor of the *Deutsches Gesangbuch,* Philadelphia, 1859, and others.

Hugh Thomas Henry, born in Philadelphia on November 27, 1862, was educated at LaSalle College, the University of Pennsylvania, and St. Charles Seminary in Overbrook, Pennsylvania. Ordained in 1889 he remained at the seminary, teaching English and Latin until 1894, and music and literature until 1917. The seminary choir, of which he was director, became noted for its Holy Week performances in Philadelphia Cathedral. He served as rector of the Philadelphia Catholic High School for Boys from 1902 until 1919 when he was appointed professor of homiletics at The Catholic University of America, Washington, D.C., a position he held until 1937. In addition he lectured at the Catholic Summer School in Cliff Haven, New York, and twice served as president of the American Catholic Historical Society of Philadelphia, for which he wrote an annual section of the *Records.* Also a composer, he edited a journal, *Church Music,* for nine years beginning in 1905. He published a number of collections of verse, as well as works on preaching and *Catholic Customs and Symbols.* In 1902 the University of Pennsylvania honored him with a Doctor of Letters degree, and he was made a monsignor in 1915. He died at Jessup, Pennsylvania, March 12, 1946.

O WELT, ICH MUSS DICH LASSEN (also "Innsbruck"). This sublime melody was first printed in Georg Forster's *Ein Augzug guter alter und neuer Teutschen Liedlein,* Nürnberg, 1539, where it was the setting for a secular song, "Insbruck, ich muss dich lassen." Given in the top of a four-voice setting by Heinrich Isaac, it had the form given below.

The melody itself is believed to be a borrowed one, possibly dating from before the middle of the fifteenth century. It is found in a manuscript from 1505 where it is used with a hymn for St. Anne and St. Joachim. In the 1598 Eiselben *Gesangbuch* the tune was associated with Johann Hesse's hymn on death, "O Welt, ich muss dich lassen." Later it became associated also with Paul Gerhardt's (LBW 23) hymn, "Nun ruhen alle Wälder" (LBW 276).

Heinrich Isaac, whose works—along with those of Josquin des Prez, Ludwig Senfl, and Johann Walther (LBW 350)—Martin Luther (LBW 48) admired and often had performed in his home, was born a Netherlander around 1450. A truly international composer whose compositions absorbed the styles of Italy, France, Germany, and the Netherlands, Isaac was also prolific, writing in all forms current in his day, including sacred and secular songs, instrumental works, masses, and motets. Chief among his sacred works was his *Choralis Constantinus* which contained musical settings of the Propers for the entire church year. In his *Music in the Renaissance,* 1959, Gustave Reese refers to this work as "the most imposing musical creation of the entire pre-Reformation period in Germany." Around 1484 Isaac entered the service of Lorenzo de'Medici as court organist and director of music, and in this position taught Lorenzo's sons, one of whom was later to become Pope Leo X. In 1497 he became court composer to Emperor Maximilian I in Vienna and Innsbruck. The latter years of his life were spent in Florence where he died in 1517.

J. S. Bach (LBW 219) used the melody in both the St. Matthew and the St. John Passions, as well as in Cantatas 13, 44, and 97, and included four harmonizations in the *Choralegesänge.*

223 IN THE QUIET CONSECRATION

Tune: Kingdom

This hymn was written in 1910. First published in the author's *At His Table*, 1913, it was included four years later in *The Church Hymnal for the Christian Year.*

The author, Constance Headlam, was born in England December 30, 1844. In 1879 she married the Reverend Algernon Coote, who later was known as the Reverend Sir Algernon when he became eleventh baronet. She was his second wife, the first having been Cecilia Matilda Plumptre. Sir Algernon Coote died at Ballyfin, Ireland, in 1899, having held his title for four years. Constance then returned to Tunbridge Wells, Kent, where she had lived before her marriage. She died at Tunbridge Wells, August 16, 1936.

KINGDOM takes its title from the last line of the hymn "For the bread, which Thou hast broken" (LBW 200) for which it was written in 1959. It was used at the National Convocation of Methodist Youth in 1960, and was published as an anthem before it appeared in *The Book of Hymns,* 1964, of the Methodist Church.

Vicar Earle Copes was born August 12, 1921, at Norfolk, Virginia, and received a Bachelor of Arts degree in 1940 from Davidson College, Davidson, North Carolina. At Union Theological Seminary in New York City he received a Master of Sacred Music degree in 1944, and a Bachelor of Divinity degree the following year. An ordained Methodist clergyman, he has served as minister of music at Highland Park Methodist Church, Dallas, Texas (1946-1949), professor of organ and church music at Hendrix College, Arkansas (1949-1956), and Cornell College, Mount Vernon, Iowa (1956-1958). At the General Board of Education of the Methodist Church in Nashville, Tennessee, from 1958 to 1967, he edited the monthly periodical, *Music Ministry.* From 1967 to 1973 he was head of the department of organ and church music at Birmingham Southern College. Since 1973 he has been the musician member of a distinctive team ministry at Christ United Methodist Church in Dayton, Ohio, and serves also as a part-time faculty member of Wright State University in Dayton. He is a member of the promotion committee of the Hymn Society of America.

224 SOUL, ADORN YOURSELF WITH GLADNESS
(Schmücke dich, O liebe Seele)
Tune: Schmücke dich

Johann Franck, who ranks second only to Paul Gerhardt (LBW 23) as a hymnwriter, was one of the writers who marked the transition from the objective German "church song" to a more personal and mystical kind of poetry. He was also a writer of secular poetry of some renown during his time, but it is his hymns, finished in form and of earnest faith and simplicity, that have survived. Of these he wrote 110.

Born June 1, 1618, at Guben, Brandenburg, Germany, Franck was two years old when his father died and he was adopted by an uncle. He received his education at the University of Königsberg, the only German university not disrupted by the Thirty Years' War. There he formed a friendship with Simon Dach and Heinrich Held (LBW 478). He became a lawyer, as was his father, and after some travel, returned to Guben, where he became a councillor, a mayor, and finally a representative of the province to the Diet of Lower Lusatia. He died June 18, 1677.

This hymn was included in Johann Crüger's (LBW 23) *Geistliche kirchen Melodien,* Berlin, 1649. A translation by Catherine Winkworth (LBW 29) published in her *Lyra Germanica,* second series, 1858, and rewritten for her *Chorale Book for England,* 1863, has served as the basis for this text prepared by the Inter-Lutheran Commission on Worship.

SCHMÜCKE DICH, by Johann Crüger (LBW 23), made its first appearance in the same collection as the text.

304

Tune: Grace Church

Henry Eyster Jacobs, grandfather of Edward Traill Horn III (LBW 478), was born November 10, 1844, at Gettysburg, Pennsylvania. He graduated from Pennsylvania College, Gettysburg, and attended Gettysburg Lutheran Seminary during the Civil War years, spending his vacations caring for wounded Union soldiers. Following graduation from seminary in 1864, he taught at Pennsylvania College for two years and served as home missionary in Pittsburgh for a year before his appointment in 1868 as pastor at Philipsburg, Pennsylvania, and principal of Thiel Hall. From 1870 he was Latin professor at Pennsylvania College, until succeeding Charles Porterfield Krauth (LBW 62) in 1883 as professor of systematic theology at the Evangelical Lutheran Seminary at Philadelphia. In 1895 he became dean of the seminary. Also a scholar and an author, Jacobs translated the Lutheran Confessions into English and contributed to a number of reference works and journals, and from 1883 to 1896 was editor-in-chief of the *Lutheran Church Review*. His writings include a *History of the Evangelical Lutheran Church in the United States*; *Martin Luther: the Hero of the Reformation*; *German Emigration to America;* and *A Summary of Christian Faith*. He died July 7, 1932.

This hymn was written in 1910 and included in the *Common Service Book,* 1917.

GRACE CHURCH was included in William Gardiner's (LBW 356) *Sacred Melodies,* 1815, where it served as the setting for Ottiwell Heginbothom's "Father of mercies, God of love," and was said to be taken from the works of Ignaz Joseph Pleyel.

Pleyel, the twenty-fourth child of the village schoolmaster at Ruppersthal near Vienna, Austria, was born June 1, 1757. Musically gifted, he was a student of Franz Joseph Haydn (LBW 358) for five years and also studied for some years in Italy. He was assistant director of music at the Strasbourg Cathedral for several years and became director of music in 1789; but his stay was interrupted by the French Revolution. In 1791 he went to London to conduct the Professional Concerts, and later went to Paris, where he opened a music-selling and publishing business and in 1807 established the piano factory, Pleyel, Wolff & Company. He was a prolific composer, primarily of instrumental works. On November 14, 1831, he died in Paris.

226   DRAW NEAR AND TAKE THE BODY OF THE LORD
(Sancti, venite, Christi Corpus sumite)
Tune: Coena Domini

According to Irish legend, this hymn was first sung by angels. St. Patrick and his nephew Sechnall had a serious argument, with Sechnall accusing Patrick of preaching charity too little and Patrick threatening to ride his chariot over Sechnall. When the two men came together and were reconciled in the graveyard of their church, they immediately heard angels within the church singing this hymn. What is known for fact about the hymn is that it is very ancient and exists in the *Bangor Antiphonary,* which was written between 680 and 691 at the Monastery of Bangor,

County Down, Ireland. The manuscript is said to have been carried to Bobbio, a famous monastery founded in Italy by the Irish missionary Columbanus after he had been driven out of Burgundy by the reigning powers there. From Bobbio the manuscript traveled to the Ambrosian Library in Milan. It was discovered there and first published by Muratori in 1697–1698.

Winfred Douglas in his *Church Music in History and Practice* (Rev. Ed. 1962) notes the tendency of the Roman Church during the early centuries to admit no Eucharist hymns not found in Scriptures—a tendency not so prevalent among the Gallican, Mozarabic, and Celtic rites. It was only natural, therefore, that the "earliest metrical hymn, in the modern sense" should appear in one of these rites, namely in Ireland. The hymn was sung during the receiving of Communion, a use which seems to have been restricted mostly to Ireland.

John Mason Neale's (LBW 34) translation was published in his *Medieval Hymns,* 1851, where the final stanza read:

> Alpha and Omega, to whom shall bow
> All nations at the Doom, is with us now.

COENA DOMINI was written by Arthur Sullivan (LBW 153) for this text in his *Church Hymns with Tunes,* 1874.

227 HOW BLEST ARE THEY WHO HEAR GOD'S WORD
(O salig den, Guds Ord har hört)
Tune: Om Himmeriges Rige

Published in 1786 in Brun's *Evangeliske Sange,* a small collection of sixty-five hymns intended to serve as a supplement to Ove Guldberg's *Salmebog,* 1778, this hymn reflects an emphasis on the Word of God. It was based on the last portion of the Gospel for the third Sunday in Lent (old pericopes) "Blessed are those who hear the Word of God and keep it" (Luke 11:28).

Johan Nordahl Brun was born March 21, 1745, in Bynesset, Norway, the son of a farmer who was formerly a merchant. At the age of twelve he was enrolled in the mountain ski-patrol, but an older half-brother who was a theology student insisted that Brun study theology. Johan entered the prestigious school in Trondhjem in 1760, and following his graduation three years later, became the family tutor to Councillor Meinche and accompanied his son to Sor, Denmark. There, after three months' preparation, he took the theological and homiletic exams, receiving a very poor mark in the first. He returned to Trondhjem where he spent three years as an instructor, preacher, and writer, and then went back to Denmark. In 1767 he went to Copenhagen, studied frantically for three months, and passed his theological exams. He returned to work as a tutor but spent much time writing poetry, greatly influenced by the Norwegian nationalistic feeling of the time. In 1771 he was appointed private secretary to Bishop Gunnerius and accompanied him to Copenhagen on official business, but soon had to resign because he had no knowledge of the German language. Instead, he entered the contest for the best Danish tragedy and won with his *Zarine.* He had achieved a great personal victory, but his and the bishop's national cause, a Norwegian University, had suffered defeat. Brun wrote the first play on a subject from Norwegian history the following year and soon became a leader among Norwegian students in Copenhagen. His nationalistic songs were greatly loved. One of his songs, prohibited by the Danish police, is considered to be the first Norwegian national anthem. In spite of his success as a poet, however, his future ambitions were within the church. Ordained in 1772, he became assistant pastor at Bynesset, and two years later was appointed senior pastor of Korskirken in Bergen. A very active and imaginative minister, he later was consecrated bishop of the diocese of Bergen in 1804. He died July 26, 1816.

Brun was a powerful preacher with a strong emotional appeal. In his fight against the rationalists, he was sympathetic to H. M. Hauge and the Pietists. His hymns are an outstanding testimony of great Christian enthusiasm and inspiration.

The translation is from the *Service Book and Hymnal,* 1958.

OM HIMMERIGES RIGE (also "Island") is an anonymous tune which first appeared in Hans Thomissön's *Den danske Psalmebog,* 1569, as the setting for "Om himmeriges rige, saa ville vi tale."

Born in Hygom, Denmark, in 1532, Thomissön was the son of a pastor. Educated at the University of Copenhagen, he went in 1553 to Wittenberg as tutor for three young noblemen of the Venstermond family, and completed a Master of Arts degree there in 1555. He became rector of the school at Ribe, Denmark, where he was in charge of the student choir which sang at the cathedral. Four years later he was appointed to the faculty of the University of Copenhagen, as well as pastor of Vor Frue Kirke and dean of the Sokkelund district. In 1569 he issued *Den danske Psalmebog,* the finest hymnal of the period (noted by Julian* to be a reproduction, enlarged and somewhat altered, of the 1529 Rostock hymnbook [LBW 432]). Commanded by the king to be used in all churches, the hymnal remained in use in Denmark and Norway for well over a century. Thomissön died December 22, 1573, in Copenhagen, and was buried at Vor Frue Kirke.

228   A MIGHTY FORTRESS IS OUR GOD
(Ein feste Burg ist unser Gott)
Tune: Ein feste Burg

Based on Psalm 46, "God is our Refuge and Strength, a very present help in trouble," this great hymn of Martin Luther's (LBW 48) was written, in the words of Leupold* "to interpret and apply [this Psalm] to the church of his own time and its struggles." Perhaps the exact date and circumstances for its writing will never be known. Julian* and Ronander and Porter* give as a possible inspiration the Diet of Speyer (Spires) in 1529 at which German princes protested against the revocation of their liberties, giving rise to the term "Protestant." Julian then gives Joseph Klug's (LBW 85) 1529 *Geistliche Lieder* of Wittenberg as a possible first publication; Ronander and Porter give Michael Blum's *Enchiridion,* Leipzig, 1528–29. According to Leupold* the hymn is believed to have been in Klug's 1529 Wittenberg hymnal and also in Hans Weiss's Wittenberg hymnal of 1528, both of which are now lost. If the hymn appeared in a 1528 hymnal, perhaps it was written in response to persecutions which occurred in 1527, during which Luther's friend, Leonhard Kaiser was burned at the stake. One thing is certain; the hymn is one of the great hymns of the Church and deserves the widespread popularity it has achieved. The hymn spread rapidly over Germany. Luther sang it daily at Coburg; Philipp Melanchthon, Justus Jonas, and Caspar Cruciger (see LBW 86), during their banishment in 1547, were comforted by hearing a young girl sing it in Weimar; Gustavus Adolphus caused it to be sung by his army before the battle of Leipzig in 1631; and it was adopted by the Salzburg Emigrants of 1732 as their traveling hymn.

Widespread English usage came only in the nineteenth century. An early version by Miles Coverdale (1539) is quoted in *The Hymnal Companion** as follows:

> Oure God is a defence and towre
> A good armour and good weapen,
> He hath ben ever oure helpe and sucoure
> In all the troubles that we have ben in.
> Therefore wyl we never drede
> For any wonderous dede
> By water or by londe
> In hilles or the sea-sonde.
> Our God hath them al i his hond.

Another version was given in *Lyra Davidica,* 1708 (LBW 151). By 1900 there were over eighty translations in fifty-three languages (including sixty-three versions in English, listed in Julian* p. 324f); today the hymn can be sung in some two hundred tongues. The present English version is the work of the Inter-Lutheran Commission on Worship.

EIN FESTE BURG, by Martin Luther, is assumed to have been included in Klug's hymnal of 1529, but no copy of that collection exists. The earliest printed version remaining today is in *Kirche gesang, mit vil schönen Psalmen vnnd Melodey, gantz geendert uñ gemert,* Nürnberg, 1531. With one rhythm change (the first note in line 7 was a half note) the present form of the melody is identical with that found in the 1531 collection. The harmonization is from the *Neues Choralbuch,* 1956.

"Ein feste Burg" served as the basis for J. S. Bach's (LBW 219) Cantata 80, and the tune was given two settings in the *Choralgesänge.* Other composers have also used the melody, including Felix Mendelssohn (LBW 60) in his Fifth Symphony; Giacomo Meyerbeer, in his opera *Les Huguenots;* and Alexander Glazunoff in his *Finnish Fantasy.*

229 A MIGHTY FORTRESS IS OUR GOD
(Ein feste Burg ist unser Gott)
Tune: Ein feste Burg

This is the same hymn as given at LBW 228. The form of the tune here is based on the version given in Johann König's (LBW 22) 1738 *Harmonischer Lieder-Schatz* (Zahn* #7477d).

230 LORD, KEEP US STEADFAST IN YOUR WORD
(Erhalt uns, Herr, bei deinem Wort)
Tune: Erhalt uns, Herr

In 1541 it appeared as if Sultan Suleiman and his Turkish army might overrun Germany; they had already taken Hungary and were threatening

Vienna. The Elector requested the pastors to offer prayers for Germany's protection, and in response to this Martin Luther (LBW 48) prepared a special service in which he included this hymn. The original first stanza translated to English reads thus:

> Lord, keep us in Thy Word and work,
> Restrain the murderous Pope and Turk,
> Who fain would tear from off Thy throne
> Christ Jesus, Thy beloved Son.

Clearly, Luther saw the Church threatened spiritually and physically by the Pope as well as by the Mohammedan Turks. Later, when neither group posed such a threat, the text was changed in hymnals to include enemies of the Word in general.

The hymn, which was first published on a broadsheet at Wittenberg in 1542, also appeared that year in Low German in the *Magdeburg Gesangbuch,* and the following year in Joseph Klug's (LBW 85) *Geistliche Lieder* in High German. Leupold* mentions that it might also have been contained in a 1542 hymnal published in Zwichau, but no copy of that exists today.

Catherine Winkworth's (LBW 29) translation was included in her *Chorale Book for England,* 1863, and is given here with some alteration.

ERHALT UNS, HERR (also called "Preserve us, Lord," "Reading," "Spires," and "Wittenberg"). Believed by some authorities to be the work of Luther, this melody was included first in Joseph Klug's *Geistliche Lieder,* Wittenberg, 1543. It is patterned after a twelfth-century plainsong, "Veni Redemptor gentium" (LBW 28), which in the fifteenth century had the form given below (quoted from Konrad Ameln, *The Roots of German Hymnody of the Reformation Era,* 1964).

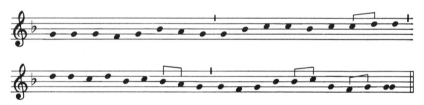

J. S. Bach (LBW 219) based his Cantata 126 on "Erhalt uns, Herr."

231   O WORD OF GOD INCARNATE

Tune: Munich

See LBW 77 for William Walsham How. This hymn was included in the 1867 Supplement to How and Morrell's *Psalms and Hymns,* first published in 1854.

MUNICH (also called "Meiningen") appeared as the setting for "O Gott, du frommer Gott" (LBW 504) in the *Neu-vermehrtes und zu Ubung Christl. Gottseligkeit eingerichtetes Meiningisches Gesangbuch,* Meiningen, 1693, as given below (Zahn* #5418).

The melody seems to have been made up of lines from various tunes by Hieronymous Gradenthaler included in *Lust und Arztneigarten,* a psalter

published in Regensburg by Wolf Helmhard von Hohenberg in 1675. It appeared in many varied forms after 1693 and by the nineteenth century was known all over Germany. The present form of the tune is from Felix Mendelssohn's (LBW 60) "Cast thy burden upon the Lord," in *Elijah,* 1847. The tune is included together with Mendelssohn's harmonization at LBW 305 and 503.

232 YOUR WORD, O LORD, IS GENTLE DEW
(Dein Wort, O Herr, ist milder Tau)
Tune: Af Himlens

This hymn, perhaps Carl B. Garve's finest, was included in *Christliche Gesänge,* published at Görlitz in 1825. Catherine Winkworth's translation included in the first series, 1855, of *Lyra Germanica* was cast in 8.6. 8.6. 888 meter. The present text is an altered form of the version she included in her *Chorale Book for England,* 1863.

See LBW 147 for Garve and LBW 29 for Winkworth.

AF HIMLENS was included in *Then Swenska Psalm-Boken,* 1697, as the setting for "Min siäl skal vthaf hiertans grund," and earlier, in Jesper Svedberg's 1694 collection (LBW 440), with Jacob Arrhenius' hymn, "Ditt namm, o Gud, jag lova will." It receives its name from its association with Johan Wallin's (LBW 73) "Af himlens här den Högstes makt" based on Psalm 19.

Leland Sateren (LBW 100) prepared the harmony for the *Service Book and Hymnal,* 1958.

233 THY STRONG WORD
Tune: Ebenezer

Written in 1954 for Concordia Seminary, St. Louis, Missouri, this hymn is based on the seminary motto, "Anothen to Phos," and was used in chapel services on campus. It was included in the *Worship Supplement,* 1969, to *The Lutheran Hymnal.*

Martin Hans Franzmann was born January 29, 1907 at Lake City, Minnesota, and received a Bachelor of Arts degree in 1928 from Northwestern College, Watertown, Wisconsin. Following his studies at Wisconsin Lutheran Seminary in Thiensville, Wisconsin, he returned to Northwestern College in 1936 as a professor. In 1946 he went as a professor to Concordia Seminary, St. Louis, where nine years later he was appointed chairman of the department of exegetical theology. Concordia Seminary, Springfield, Illinois, honored him with a Doctor of Divinity degree in 1958. A scholar throughout his life, Franzmann continued with graduate work at the University of Chicago for over twenty years, and also went to Greece on a Daniel L. Shorey Traveling Fellowship. On October 4, 1969, he was ordained at Westfield House in Cambridge, England, and became a tutor in a theological training program there. He died at Cambridge on March 28, 1976. He and his wife, Alice B. Bentzin, were the parents of three children.

Franzmann served the church in various capacities—as a member of the Synodical Advisory Committee on English Bible Version from 1950 to 1956; chairman of the synodical conference, 1952–1956; vice chairman of the Committee on Doctrinal Unity, 1950–1962; Lutheran Church —Missouri Synod representative to the Lutheran World Federation in 1962; and a member of the Commission on Theology and Church Relations from 1962 to 1969. He was the author of numerous theological and devotional books and articles including *Ha! Ha! Among the Trumpets* (1966); *Concordia Commentary: Romans* (1968); *Pray for Joy* (1970); *Alive with the Spirit* (1973); and *The Revelation to John* (1976). He was the editor of the *Concordia Bible with Notes: The New Testament,* 1971.

EBENEZER ("Ton-y-Botel") is taken from the second movement of a memorial anthem by Thomas John Williams entitled "Gloeu yn y Glyn" ("Light in the Valley") and was first published as a hymn tune in 1890 in *Llaw lyfr Moliant.* The name "Ton-y-botel" is derived from a tale that the tune was found in a bottle which had been washed onto the Welsh coast during a storm.

Thomas Williams, who studied composition under David Evans (LBW 339), was born in Wales in Ynsmeudwy, Swansea Valley, Glamorganshire, in 1869. An organist and choirmaster, he served at Zion Church in Llanelly from 1903 to 1913, and afterwards at Calfaria Church, Llanelly. He died there in 1944. Williams wrote a large number of hymn tunes and some anthems.

The harmonization was prepared by Richard Hillert (LBW 63) for the *Worship Supplement,* 1969, to *The Lutheran Hymnal.*

234 ALMIGHTY GOD, YOUR WORD IS CAST

Tune: St. Flavian

Written in 1815, this hymn was first published in Thomas Cotterill's (LBW 547) *Selection of Psalms and Hymns for Public and Private Use,* eighth edition, 1819.

The author, John Cawood, was born March 18, 1775, at Matlock, Derbyshire, England. His parents were farmers on a small scale, so during childhood his formal education was limited. At age eighteen he entered into menial service to a clergyman in Nottinghamshire. After three years of study under the Reverend Edward Spencer, rector of Wingfield, Wiltshire, however, he entered St. Edmund's Hall, Oxford, where he received a Bachelor of Arts degree in 1801, and was ordained the same year. Six years later he received a Master of Arts degree. Following his ordination he was curate to the adjacent parishes of Ribbesford and Dowles, and in 1814 he became perpetual curate of St. Ann's Chapel of Ease, Bewdley, in Worcestershire. There he remained until his death on November 7, 1852.

ST. FLAVIAN is the first half of the tune which was set to Psalm 132 in the English Psalter of 1562, published by John Day. Originally the tune appeared as given below.

The present form of the tune and most of the harmonization are from Richard Redhead's (LBW 109) *Church Hymn Tunes,* 1853. In the 1875 Revised Edition of *Hymns Ancient and Modern* it was given the name "St. Flavian."

John Day (Daye or Daie) was an artist of the printing trade when it was still relatively young; his musical type was well-set, he devised fine new Anglo-Saxon, Italic, Roman, and Greek type, and many of his publications were beautifully illustrated with woodcuts. A large number of first editions and important works were issued by Day, including the first church music book in English, *Certain Notes Set Forth in Four and Three Parts to Be Sung,* 1560.

Born in 1522 in St. Peter's Parish, Dunwich, on the Suffolk coast of England, Day went to London during his youth. There he learned his trade, and began to print in 1546. Three years later he moved his shop to Aldersgate, one of the old city gates, from whence came his many fine works, including numerous psalters. In 1561 he was admitted to the Livery of the Stationers' Company and later served as warden four times and became master in 1580. He died at Walden, Essex, on July 23, 1584, having had two wives, each of whom bore him thirteen children.

235 BREAK NOW THE BREAD OF LIFE

Tune: Bread of Life

Written in 1877 and originally beginning "Break *thou* the bread of life," this hymn was included the following year in *Chautauqua Carols,* a book published in New York in 1878 and designed as "A collection of favorite songs suitable for all Sunday school services."

The author, Mary Artemisia Lathbury, was a partner with Bishop John H. Vincent in the promotion of the Chautauqua Assembly from the time of its inception on what had been a Methodist camp meeting. Born August 10, 1841, in Manchester, New York, Lathbury was the daughter of a Methodist preacher, and two of her brothers were also ministers in that denomination. Although a professional artist, she contributed frequently to religious periodicals and was at one time general editor of the

publications of the Methodist Sunday School Union. She died in East
Orange, New Jersey, October 20, 1913.

BREAD OF LIFE was written in 1877 for Lathbury's hymn and included
with it in *Chautauqua Carols,* 1878.

William Fiske Sherwin, born March 14, 1826, at Buckland, Massachusetts, studied under Lowell Mason (LBW 353) in Boston, and later
became a teacher at the New England Conservatory there. He was closely
associated with Vincent at Chautauqua, and had charge of the musical
program there. For some time also he was musical editor for Century and
Company, and for Bigelow and Main. He died in Boston, April 14, 1888.

236   WHEN SEED FALLS ON GOOD SOIL
Tune: Walhof

Norman Peter Olsen was born February 15, 1932, at Union City, New
Jersey. His parents were Norwegian immigrants. After completing a
Bachelor of Arts degree at Concordia College, Moorhead, Minnesota, in
1954, he received a Bachelor of Theology degree from Luther Theolog-
ical Seminary, St. Paul, Minnesota, in 1959. During his theological
studies he served a two-year internship at First Lutheran Church,
Decorah, Iowa. He has served pastorates at Cyrus and Noral Lutheran
Parish, Cyrus and Kensington, Minnesota, 1959–1963; Our Redeemer's
Lutheran Church, Benson, Minnesota, 1963–1965; Christ Lutheran
Church, Glencoe, Minnesota, 1965–1973; and in 1973 went to Grace
Lutheran Church, Luverne, Minnesota. He married Ramona M. Dalen
of Benson, Minnesota, and they have four children.

Olsen's hymn-writing is of recent origin. In 1975, at the suggestion of
the senior choir director, Dolly Talbert, he wrote a Lenten hymn,
"Follow me," which was set to music by Mrs. Talbert. Other hymns
followed: "Break gently, O dawn" and "The first day" for Easter;
"Unto God my rock" for the congregation's centennial celebration; and
"When seed falls on good soil," another hymn for Lent. Mrs. Talbert
prepared tunes for each of these hymns, and in 1976 they were included
in a private publication for Grace Church entitled *Sing.* Since then he has
written other hymns, and notes, "Our venture into hymn-writing has
taken on an added dimension—beyond our own personal enjoyment: we
hope to encourage others and revive the Church's gift of hymnody, so
that along with the grand old hymns of the Christian community, the
Twentieth Century church may also sing of HER faith, and HER mission, and HER times."

The tune WALHOF was written in 1976 while the composer, Frederick
F. Jackisch, was waiting for a flight at the Minneapolis airport following
a meeting of the Inter-Lutheran Commission on Worship. The name
"Walhof" was chosen "to honor Karen Walhof who served as secretary,
score-keeper, policewoman, paper-pusher, mail-sender, encourager,
critic, all of the above and then some, for the music committees of
ILCW. Without her attention to detail we all would have been hopelessly
lost in a morass of hymnological materials."

Jackisch is professor of church music, university organist, and director
of graduate study at Wittenberg University in Springfield, Ohio. The
Wittenberg University Chapel Choir is also under his direction. Born in

Chicago in 1922, he graduated from Concordia Teachers College, River Forest, Illinois, and received his Master of Music degree from Northwestern University. In 1964 he was awarded a Lutheran World Federation grant for study of church music in Germany, and was invited to play recitals in Stuttgart, Herford, and Berlin. His Doctor of Philosophy degree was earned at Ohio State University in 1966, and in the fall of 1968 he served as an exchange professor of organ at the Berliner Kirchenmusikschule. He has served as director of music at St. John Lutheran Church, New Orleans, Louisiana, and Emmaus Lutheran Church in Fort Wayne, Indiana. A member of the American Guild of Organists, and past dean of the Fort Wayne Chapter, he has served as recitalist for several chapters and has concertized widely throughout the Midwest. He has also served as organ consultant for numerous churches in the Midwest. He is a member of the Lutheran Society for Worship, Music and the Arts, and of the Phi Mu Alpha music fraternity, and is a contributing editor of the *Journal of Church Music.* He served as chairman of the hymn music committee of the Inter-Lutheran Commission on Worship.

237   O GOD OF LIGHT

Tune: Atkinson

Entitled "The Divine Gift," this hymn was chosen from over 550 entries to the Hymn Society of America's contest for a new hymn expressing the spiritual significance of the Bible. It was written in 1952, and published the same year in the Hymn Society's *Ten New Hymns on the Bible.* On September 30, 1952, it was sung by two million people in thousands of communities in observance of the publication of the Revised Standard Version of the Bible.

Sarah Ellen Taylor was born in Stockport, England, on December 30, 1883. Her father, a lay preacher, once said that he had delivered six hundred sermons and traveled three thousand miles during twenty years of preaching in that country. In 1892 the family came to the United States where Sarah's father served for many years as the pastor of the Lonsdale Primitive Methodist Church, Cumberland, Rhode Island. Sarah began teaching a church school class at the church at age fifteen, and in later years remained very active in the congregation. After receiving a Bachelor of Arts degree in 1904 from Pembroke College of Brown University, Providence, and a Master of Arts degree from Brown University in 1910, Taylor taught Latin, Greek, and English Literature in mission schools in Alabama and Virginia. She then returned to Rhode Island, where she taught Latin, English, and ancient history at Cumberland High School from 1917 to 1930, and at Central Falls High School from 1930 until her retirement in 1949. She died October 5, 1954.

Taylor was the author of several hymns, and her anthem written for the tune "Duke Street" (LBW 352) was voted the Rhode Island State Anthem in 1933.

"The tune ATKINSON," writes the composer, "was written, like many such tunes, on an impulse when I happened to feel in the hymn-tune mood! It is named for Gordon Atkinson, a life-long friend and fellow Australian who lives in London, Ontario, and is presently National President of the Royal Canadian College of Organists."

Harold Barrie Cabena, distinguished Canadian organist, composer, and teacher, was born August 12, 1933, in Melbourne, Australia, and studied music privately under Bernard Clarke and A. E. H. Nickson. At the Royal College of Music in London, England, where he received the senior prize in organ, his teachers were John Dykes Bower, Herbert Howells (LBW 491), Eric Harrison, and W. E. Lloyd Webber. He came to Canada in 1957 and was appointed director of music at First-St. Andrew's United Church, London, Ontario, where he remained until 1975 when he resigned to move to Waterloo. At First-St. Andrew's he established the festival "The Church and the Arts" presenting, among other things, an annual opera and weekly organ recitals. Appointed to the faculty of Wilfrid Laurier University (then Waterloo Lutheran) in 1970, he is associate professor of church music and organ there. From 1967 to 1969 he was national president of the Royal Canadian College of Organists, and for many years was chairman of the examination committee. As an organ recitalist he has played widely in Canada, the United States, Australia, and England, as well as on C.B.C., A.B.C., and B.B.C. broadcasts and at conventions of the American Guild of Organists and the Royal Canadian College of Organists. He has received numerous commissions as a composer. His more than one hundred compositions include organ works, masses, anthems, piano pieces, choral works, songs, and an opera for children, in addition to a liturgical setting for the *Catholic Book of Worship,* 1972, and hymn tunes. In 1972 he was awarded the silver medal of L'Academie Française—Arts, Sciences, Lettres for services to French music. He is an honorary fellow of the Royal Canadian College of Organists.

238 GOD HAS SPOKEN BY HIS PROPHETS

Tune: Carn Brea

See LBW 209 for George Wallace Briggs. This hymn was included in *Ten New Hymns on the Bible,* printed in 1952 by the Hymn Society of America for the celebration of the publication of the Revised Standard Version of the Bible.

CARN BREA was composed at the request of the compilers of *The Hymn Book,* 1971, of the Anglican Church and the United Church of Canada, where it was the setting for "God who stretched the spangled heavens" (LBW 463). The composer describes Carn Brea as a granite hill near Cornwall, England, "topped by stone-age remains, a nineteenth-century monument, and a castle of no very great antiquity."

Derek Holman was born at Cornwall, England, on May 16, 1931, and holds Bachelor of Music and Doctor of Music degrees from the Royal Academy of Music in London. There he studied with Eric Thiman, York Bowen, and Sir William McKie, and received prizes in composition. In addition he is a fellow of the Royal College of Organists and has been made an honorary fellow of the Royal Academy of Music and the Royal School of Church Music. From 1954 to 1955 he was music master at Westminster Abbey Choir School, and from 1956 to 1965 was tutor, and later warden, of the Royal School of Church Music. After 1958 he was also organist at Croydon Parish Church. Since 1965, when he came to Canada, he has served as organist of Grace Church-on-the-Hill, Toronto, in addition to which he is an associate professor in the department of theory and composition at the University of Toronto.

Highly regarded in Canada and internationally as a composer, lecturer, and teacher, Holman has written a considerable amount of choral music, much of it for use in the church, and his works are frequently heard over C.B.C. He was a member of the subcommittee on tunes for *The Hymn Book,* 1971.

239 GOD'S WORD IS OUR GREAT HERITAGE
(Guds Ord det er vort Arvegods)

Tune: Ein feste Burg

First printed in *Salmer ved Jubelfesten,* 1817, Nicolai Grundtvig's (LBW 62) hymn, "Gods Kirke er vor Klippe-Borg," consisted of five stanzas. The first four were a Danish version of Luther's "Ein feste Burg" (LBW 228); the fifth stanza was Grundtvig's own. This final stanza, beginning "Guds Ord det er vort Arvegods," came into use as a separate hymn in Norway and Denmark as a closing hymn or a hymn for church festivals.

The translation is by Ole Gulbrand Belsheim, who was born August 26, 1861, at Vang, Valdres, Norway. His family came to the United States when he was five years old. After attending Luther College at Decorah, Iowa; Northfield Seminary; and Augsburg Seminary in Minnesota, he served as pastor at Milwaukee, Wisconsin; Albert Lea, Minnesota; Grand Meadow, Minnesota; and Mandan, North Dakota. For many years he served on the committee for *The Lutheran Hymnary,* 1913, for which this translation was prepared in 1909. In addition, he translated Nils J. J. Laache's *Catechism* into English in 1894 and edited *Christian Youth* for two years. He died February 12, 1925.

The alterations in lines 7 and 8 are from the *Service Book and Hymnal* 1958.

For EIN FESTE BURG see LBW 228.

240 FATHER OF MERCIES, IN YOUR WORD

Tune: Detroit

Anne Steele, daughter of an English timber merchant and unsalaried Baptist minister, was born in Broughton, Hampshire, in 1716 and showed poetic ability at an early age. Her life was greatly effected by a physical handicap resulting from a childhood hip injury, and by the accidental death by drowning of her fiancé a few hours before the time set for their marriage. Her hymns, including this one, were first published in 1760 in *Poems on Subjects chiefly Devotional* under the pseudonym "Theodosia." In all, her works comprised 144 hymns, thirty-four metrical psalms, and thirty poems. Following the lead of Isaac Watts (LBW 39), she was an early writer of English hymns (as distinguished from metrical Psalms), and the first among women. She died November 11, 1778.

DETROIT appeared anonymously in the 1820 *Supplement to Kentucky Harmony* (see LBW 220 for *Kentucky Harmony*); and in *Virginia Harmony,* 1831, and *Southern Harmony,* 1835 (LBW 30), it is credited to "Bradshaw." Some similarities can be seen between this tune and

"Distress" (LBW 217), and a likeness to "The wife of Usher's well" has also been noted.

Harmonization of the tune is by Walter L. Pelz, who has been a member of the music faculty of Bethany College, Lindsborg, Kansas, since 1969. A native of Chicago, born December 30, 1926, he received a Bachelor of Science in Education degree in 1948 from Concordia Teachers College, River Forest, Illinois, and a Master of Music degree three years later at Northwestern University. For fourteen years he taught elementary and junior high school at Seymour, Indiana (1948-1953), and at St. Joseph, Michigan (1953-1962). In 1962 he went to Minneapolis as minister of music at Christ Lutheran Church, and from 1967 until his appointment at Bethany was a graduate assistant at the University of Minnesota, where in 1970 he received a Doctor of Philosophy degree. While at the university, he composed his cantata "Genesis to a Beat" for four choirs, orchestra, tape-recorder, and optional audience participation, which had its premiere performance at Bethany in November of 1970. He continues to compose anthems, sacred works, and other music. His five-movement choral symphony, "Lord of the Land," written to commemorate the nation's Bicentennial, was premiered in November of 1976 at Bethany. Pelz is also director of the Chapel Choir at Bethany and organist at Messiah Lutheran Church, Lindsborg. He is a member of the American Guild of Organists, the American Society of University Composers, and the College Music Society. During the 1977-1978 sabbatical leave of Dr. Elmer Copley, he was appointed director of the Bethany College Choir and conductor of the Bethany Oratorio Society, whose nationally famous Christmas and Easter performances of Handel's *Messiah* have been held annually since 1882.

241   WE PRAISE YOU, O GOD
Tune: Kremser

Written at the end of the sixteenth century to celebrate the freedom of Holland from Spanish oppression, the anonymous Dutch text, "Wilt heden nu treden voor God den Heere," was included in Adrian Valerius' *Nederlandtsch Gedenckclanck,* a collection of Dutch songs published in Harlem in 1626. In 1877 Edward Kremser, director of a male singing society of Vienna, published a collection of works for male chorus and orchestra, the *Sechs Altniederländische Volkslieder* (all drawn from Valerius' collection), in which he included a German translation of the text together with the melody for the folk song, "Heij wilder dan wild." This tune, also from the Valerius collection, is here called KREMSER because of its appearance in his book.

"Wilt heden nu treden voor God den Heere," which has been translated by Theodore Baker as "We gather together to ask the Lord's blessing," is very "Old Testament" in its concepts of oppressing the wicked and upholding the righteous, and reflects the circumstances under which the hymn was written. The present text, which is a new hymn by Julia Cady Cory, was written for the tune "Kremser" in 1902. It was sung on Thanksgiving of that year at Brick Church and the Church of the Covenant in New York City, and in 1910 was included in *Hymns of the Living Church,* published in New York.

Julia Bulkely Cady, daughter of J. Cleveland Cady, an outstanding

New York City architect, was born November 19, 1882, and educated at Brearley School and Reynolds School in New York City. She was a member of the Brick Presbyterian Church, and later, when she lived in Englewood, New Jersey, of First Presbyterian Church in that city. Married to Robert Haskell Cory on March 28, 1911, she became the mother of three sons. She died May 1, 1963, at Englewood, New Jersey.

242 LET THE WHOLE CREATION CRY
Tune: Salzburg

Stopford August Brooke was born November 14, 1832, at Glendoen, Letterkenny, in Donegal County, Ireland. He received a Bachelor of Arts degree from Trinity College, Dublin, in 1856, and a Master of Arts degree two years later. Ordained in 1857, he served at St. Matthew's, Marylebone (1857–1859), and St. Mary Abbott's, Kensington (1860–1863), and from 1863 to 1865 was chaplain to the British Embassy at Berlin, Germany. When he returned to London he leased St. James's Chapel, which soon was crowded with those who came to hear him. In 1876 he leased Bedford Chapel where he ministered until his retirement in 1894. For some time he was also chaplain to the Queen. She was eager to make him canon of Westminster, but his liberal views did not allow it. He seceded from the Church of England in 1880, and although leaning towards Unitarianism in his ideas, he chose to remain independent of any denomination. His *Christian Hymns,* in which this hymn was included, was published in 1881. He died at The Four Winds, Surrey, March 18, 1916.

For SALZBURG see LBW 90.

243 LORD, WITH GLOWING HEART
Tune: Pleading Savior

This hymn was written in 1819 and included in the Episcopalian collection, *Church Poetry,* 1823, edited by William Augustus Muhlenberg.

Francis Scott Key, also the author of "The Star-Spangled Banner," was a lawyer who served for many years as United States District Attorney. Born at Pipe Creek, Frederick County, Maryland, on August 9, 1779, he graduated from St. John's College, Annapolis, in 1796. He was very active in the Episcopal Church, serving as vestryman and lay reader of St. John's Church, Georgetown, D.C., and later vestryman of Christ Church, Georgetown, and had at one time considered taking holy orders. From 1814 to 1826 he was a delegate to the General Convention. He died in Baltimore on January 11, 1843. His poems were published in Miller and Osbourn's *Lyra Sacra,* 1832, and in his collected poems, 1857.

PLEADING SAVIOR is an anonymous tune first found in Joshua Leavitt's *Christian Lyre,* 1830, as the setting for John Leland's "Now the Saviour standeth pleading." The pentatonic melody bears some similarity to "Jefferson" (LBW 30). Unlike many early American hymntunes which have been rediscovered only within the past twenty years or so, this tune was included already in *The English Hymnal,* 1906, and was taken from there into *The Hymnal 1940* (Episcopal).

Edited by Joshua Leavitt and published by Jonathan Leavitt in two volumes with a supplement, the *Christian Lyre* contained a number of good tunes and attained immediate success. Joshua Leavitt (1794–1873), born in Heath, Massachusetts, graduated from Yale. After serving for a time as preceptor of Wetherfield Academy, he studied law and practiced in Heath, and in Putney, Vermont. He returned to Yale in 1823 for theological studies. Ordained in 1825, he was minister of the Congregational Church in Stratford, Connecticut, for three years, after which he went to New York City as secretary of the Seamen's Friend Society and editor of the *Sailor's Magazine*. During the next several years he founded sailors' missions in various cities and worked with anti-slavery and temperance societies. He lived in Boston from 1837 to 1848 when he returned to New York City to work as editor of *The Independent*. There he remained until his death.

The harmonization of the tune was prepared by Gerald Near for the LBW. Born May 23, 1942, in Minneapolis, Minnesota, Near studied at the University of Michigan, Ann Arbor, and at the American Conservatory of Music in Chicago. After serving briefly as organist and choir master at St. Clement's Episcopal Church in St. Paul, Minnesota, he went to Calvary Episcopal Church, Rochester, Minnesota, in 1969, and from 1973 to 1976 was at Zumbro Lutheran Church, also in Rochester. He returned to the University of Michigan in 1977 and completed a Master of Music degree the following year. While at the university he held a teaching fellowship, and was the first student to conduct a major opera production there. In 1980 he became director of the New Sinfonia chamber orchestra in Rochester.

Near has studied organ with Rupert Sircom, Gerald Bales, and Robert Glasgow; composition with Gerald Bales, Leo Sowerby, and Leslie Bassett; and conducting with Gerald Bales, Elizabeth Green, and Gustav Meier. He has given organ recitals at various places in the United States and Europe, including the Cathedral of St. John the Divine in New York City and Canterbury Cathedral in England. He has published more than sixty works for organ, chorus, chamber orchestra, and symphony orchestra. His music has been performed on radio in Switzerland, West Germany, England, and Canada, and on National Public Radio in the United States. A harpsicord concerto was commissioned by Larry Palmer for the 1980 national convention of the American Guild of Organists in Minneapolis-St. Paul. One of his hymn tunes was included in *Hymns II*, 1976 (Episcopal), and a second appeared in *Hymns III*, 1979.

244 LORD OUR GOD, WITH PRAISE WE COME
(Herre Gud, dit dyre navn og aere)
Tune: Gud er Gud

Petter Dass, son of a Norwegian merchant who possibly immigrated from Scotland, was born in 1647 at Nord-Herø in the parish of Alstahaug. When Petter was six or seven years old his father died and the five children were parceled out among relatives. Petter went to live with his mother's sister, the wife of a pastor, until 1660 when he was moved to the home of an uncle in Bergen, where he attended the cathedral school. He entered the University of Copenhagen in 1666. There he was poor, lonely, and without relatives, and after three years of study he returned to Helgeland to earn his living as a tutor to the resident chaplain in Vefson, Jacob Wirthmond. He later applied for a position as house chaplain to the resident chaplain in the neighboring parish, and in 1673 was ordained, and was also married to Margrethe Andersdatter. After years of poverty he finally, in 1689, became senior pastor of Alstahaug, a large and wealthy parish in northern Norway. In this position he became a patriarchal ruler, feared and loved by his parishioners. To serve this vast parish, it was often necessary for him to make long, dangerous voyages on the open sea. He also became a successful fish dealer, and during the bad years of 1696–1698 was able to support and be of great assistance to the farmers of Helgeland. Due to illness he applied for retirement and in 1704 was succeeded by his son. He died three years later.

Dass, who has been described as the first poet of any consequence in Norway, wrote verse that was humorous and earthy—rich in symbolism from the daily life of the farmers and fishermen of his parish. None of his sacred poems were published during his lifetime, but he arranged them in four collections: *Aandelig Tidsfordriv eller Bibelske Visebog*; *Trende Bibelske Bøger, nemlig Ruth, Esther og Judith*; *Evangelie-Sange*, containing a singable text for each Sunday of the Church Year; and *Katechismus-Sange*, in which Martin Luther's catechism was set to verse. In addition he prepared *Nordske Dale-Viise*, ballads inspired by folk lore and set to existing melodies, and his chief work, *Norlands Trumpet*, which is still among the standard works of Norwegian literature today.

The present hymn was included in *Katechismus-Sange*. The translation by Peter A. Sveeggen (LBW 69) was first published in 1951 as an anthem (see below).

GUD ER GUD was written for this text by Leland Sateren (LBW 100) as an anthem and published in 1951. In 1970 the composer rearranged the first stanza of the anthem and it was included in *The Worshipbook* (Presbyterian). That arrangement was altered very slightly for the LBW.

245   ALL PEOPLE THAT ON EARTH DO DWELL
Tune: Old Hundredth

This text first appeared in 1561. Frost* notes that in two copies of *Four Score and Seven Psalmes of David in English Mitre* (Anglo-Genevan Psalter), one located in the library of St. Paul's Cathedral, and one in the British Museum, Thomas Sternhold is given as the author in the first, and William Kethe in the second. In a copy of *Psalmes of David in English Metre* (English Psalter), printed by John Day (LBW 234) in London of the same year, the text appears anonymously. The Scottish Psalter, 1564–1565, also attributes it to Kethe, however, and the evidence seems to be in his favor. Stanza 1, line 3 originally read "Him serve with *fear*," and was altered to "Him serve with *mirth*" in the Scottish Psalter of 1650. Dearmer* notes that the doxology, which is a later addition, is a nineteenth-century adaptation of the Common Meter doxology from the Tate and Brady *Psalter* (LBW 452), which originally read:

> To Father, Son, and Holy Ghost,
> The God whom we adore,
> Be glory, as it was, is now,
> And shall be evermore.

Nothing is known about the date of William Kethe's birth, or the exact place, although he is believed to have been a Scotsman. He is known to have been in exile in Frankfurt and Geneva during the Marian persecutions of 1555–1558. In 1563 and again in 1569 he served as chaplain to the forces of the Earl of Warwick, and from 1561 was rector of Childe Okeford near Blandford, where he seems to have remained until his death (dated variously from about 1593 to about 1608).

Twenty-five of his Psalm versions were included in the Anglo-Genevan Psalter, 1561, all of which made their way also into the Scottish Psalter, 1564–1565. Nine were in the Sternhold and Hopkins Psalter, 1562.

OLD HUNDREDTH, composed or adapted by Louis Bourgeois (LBW 29), was first included in the *Trente Quatre Pseaumes de David* (Genevan Psalter), 1551. There it was the setting for Psalm 134, "Or sus, serviteurs du Seigneur," a text by Theodore Beza. When William Kethe's version of Psalm 100 was included in the Anglo-Genevan Psalter and the English Psalter in 1561 this tune was associated with it in both collections (hence the title "Old Hundredth") and has been inseparably connected with the text ever since.

246   THE FIRST DAY OF THE WEEK

Tune: Kentucky 93rd

Frederick Pratt Green was born at Liverpool, England, on September 2, 1903, and was educated at Rydal School, Colwyn Bay. After four years in business, he entered the Wesleyan Methodist ministry in 1924, having trained at Didsbury College, Manchester. He served various churches, chiefly in Yorkshire and London, until his retirement in 1969. During his ministry he was for seven years bishop of York and Hull. For five years he was superintendent of the Dome Mission in Brighton, at a time when the evening congregation in that historic Free Church building was probably the largest in Britain. Since his retirement he has lived in Norwich.

Although he began to write poetry comparatively late in life (at the age of forty), he is represented in many anthologies, notably in the *Oxford Book of Twentieth Century English Verse,* and in many periodicals, including *The New Yorker.* He has published three collections of verse, the latest being *The Old Couple,* 1976; and is a member of P. E. N. International. He did not begin writing hymns, except for a few occasional pieces, until he was over sixty years of age. In 1966 the committee responsible for preparing *Hymns and Songs,* 1969 (supplement to the Methodist Hymn Book), requested that he write some hymns for that collection. "The first day of the week" was written in 1967 to speak to the relationship of Sabbath and Sunday. Since 1966 he has been a major contributor to *Cantate Domino* (the international hymnal of the World Council of Churches) and was the author of the hymn authorized to be sung in churches of all denominations in celebration of the Silver Jubilee of Queen Elizabeth II in 1977. He has been commissioned to write a number of hymns for special occasions at Norwich Cathedral, and was commissioned in 1978 to write a hymn in celebration of the centenary of the bells of St. Paul's Cathedral in London. Pratt Green writes, "Coming to hymn-writing after experience as a poet, I have learned to distinguish between these two activities. One writes poetry to please oneself, one writes hymns as a servant of Christ and his Church. Only one thing matters: that the hymn shall be right for use in worship."

KENTUCKY 93RD is an anonymous tune included in Ananias Davisson's *Kentucky Harmony,* 1816, (LBW 220) titled simply "Ninety-third" and used as the setting for "My Saviour and my King, Thy beauties are divine." The harmonization found here was prepared in 1973 by John Ferguson for *The Hymnal* of the United Church of Christ, 1974.

Ferguson, who since 1978 has been director of music at Central Lutheran Church in Minneapolis, was born January 27, 1941, in Cleveland, Ohio. He received a Bachelor of Music degree from Oberlin College Conservatory of Music, a Master of Arts degree from Kent State University, and a Doctor of Musical Arts degree from Eastman School of Music of the University of Rochester, New York, where his organ study was with Russell Saunders. He has established a fine reputation as a concert artist and clinician with many appearances throughout the country, and has been especially active in concerts and workshops sponsored by the American Guild of Organists. An active and dynamic advocate of the cause of good sacred music, he lectures and conducts workshops on music for worship and hymnody, and was music editor of the United Church of Christ hymnal published in 1974. He is especially interested in the art of creative hymn playing and has published arrangements to be used in congregational singing. Before going to Central Lutheran he was professor of music at Kent State University and organist-choirmaster at Kent United Church of Christ.

247 HOLY MAJESTY, BEFORE YOU *(Höga Majestät, vi alla)*
Tune: Wachet auf

The son of an impoverished Swedish soldier, Samuel Johan Hedborn was born at Heda, Östergötland Province, on October 14, 1783. Financial difficulties prevented his entering school until he was sixteen years of age, and he finally enrolled at Uppsala University at age twenty-three. He began to develop his poetic skills while at the university, and wrote lyric poetry and folk songs representing the new romantic school of writers. After serving periodically as a tutor, he was ordained in 1809 at Kinköping, and served for a time as assistant pastor in Normlösa and Hult, but had to request a leave. During the years 1810–1814 he experienced considerable indecision and depression. His studies at the university had aroused in him a desire to enter an academic career, but this was out of reach financially. He followed the path to ordination instead, but had misgivings about his ability to preach to others of light and hope when he himself was in such darkness. It was during this time, however, that he wrote many of his hymns, which give personal witness to both distress and grace and which, with their Christ-centered note, influenced Johan Wallin's (LBW 73) hymns. He published two collections, in 1812 and 1813, and ten of his hymns were later included in the 1819 *Svenska Psalm-Boken.* Wallin appointed him as a teacher at the school for the poor in 1813. In 1820 he became pastor to the congregations in Åskeryd and Bredestad in Linköping diocese, where he remained until his death on the day after Christmas, 1849.

"Höga Majestät, vi alla," one of our loftiest hymns of praise, was printed in *Psalmer av Hedborn,* 1812. A relationship can be seen between this hymn and Gerhard Tersteegen's (LBW 249) "O Majestät, wir fallen nieder," and like it, the hymn draws on Isaiah 6, Ezekiel 10, and Revelation 15. Kjellstrand's translation was included in *The Hymnal,* 1925, of the Augustana Synod.

August William Kjellstrand was known affectionately as "Kelly" among his students at Augustana College, where he was professor of Christianity and English from 1906 to 1930. He was highly respected for his fine teaching of English at a time when there were many Swedish-speaking students at the school. Born February 10, 1864, in Skoefde, Västergötland, Sweden, he came with his parents to the United States in 1870. He graduated from Augustana College, Rock Island, Illinois, in 1885, and went as an organist and school teacher to Chicago before receiving an appointment to Bethany College, Lindsborg, Kansas, as a teacher of Latin in 1886. He soon reached the level of full professor, and the college honored him with master's and doctor's degrees and granted him a leave for a year's study at Yale University. Returning to Bethany in 1893 he was head of the Latin department until 1897. He graduated from Augustana Theological Seminary the same year and served for two years as pastor of the Swedish Evangelical (now Emanuel) Lutheran Church in Fitchburg, Massachusetts, and three years at Gloria Dei Lutheran Church, Providence, Rhode Island, returning to Davenport in 1902. In 1906 he went to Augustana College and Academy, where from 1923 he was principal of the academy. From 1908 to 1921 he also was pastor of Grace Lutheran Church, Davenport. He died suddenly of a heart attack on October 29, 1930.

Kjellstrand translated several important works from German, Swedish, and Danish. His English translation of Frederik Hammarsten's sermons in *The Good Seed* are said to be so well-done that it is difficult to imagine that they were not originally written in English.

For WACHET AUF see LBW 31.

248 DEAREST JESUS, AT YOUR WORD *(Liebster Jesu, wir sind hier)*
Tune: Liebster Jesu, wir sind hier

Tobias Clausnitzer, born probably on February 5, 1619, at Thum near Annaberg in Saxony, studied at several universities and finally received a Master of Arts degree from Leipzig in 1643. The following year he became chaplain to the Swedish regiment at Leipzig (the Swedes having won two victories at that city in 1631 and 1642 during the Thirty Years' War) and as such preached the thanksgiving sermon at St. Thomas' Church, Leipzig, on the accession of Queen Christina to the Swedish throne. At the end of the Thirty Years' War he preached a thanksgiving sermon on January 1, 1649, at the peace celebration of General Wrangel's army at Weiden. In that year also he was appointed first pastor of Weiden, and later became a member of the consistory and inspector of the district. He died May 7, 1684.

The first three stanzas of this text were included in the *Altdorffisches Gesang-Büchlein,* 1663, as a hymn before the sermon. The Nicene Creed, which preceded the sermon hymn, is reflected briefly in the third stanza. The translation by Catherine Winkworth (LBW 29), included in her *Lyra Germanica,* second series, 1858, originally opened, "Blessed Jesus, at Thy word, We are gathered all to hear Thee," and has been extensively revised here. The doxology, of unknown authorship, comes from the

Berliner Gesangbuch, 1707, and is found here in an anonymous translation.

For LIEBSTER JESU, WIR SIND HIER, see LBW 187.

249 GOD HIMSELF IS PRESENT (Gott ist gegenwärtig)
Tune: Wunderbarer König

Gerhard Tersteegen, who ranks with Joachim Neander (LBW 182) and Friedrich Adolph Lampe as one of the three most important hymnwriters of the Reformed Church in Germany, was born November 25, 1697, at Mörs (Meurs) in Westphalia. He was intended by his parents to become a Reformed Church minister, but his father's death in 1703 made it financially impossible for him to be educated beyond Latin school. After serving for a short time as an apprentice to a merchant, he underwent an emotional religious experience and moved to a small cottage outside town where he supported himself by weaving silk ribbons. Eating only one small meal a day, he gave whatever else he had to the poor. Prolonged self-deprivation resulted in a severe depression which lasted for five years, at the end of which he became convinced of the grace of Christ, and began to speak at prayer meetings. Having already ceased to attend regular church services, he began to draw more and more people to himself until it was eventually necessary to give up his trade entirely and devote himself to prayer, preaching, visiting the poor, translating the works of medieval mystics, writing devotional material, and carrying on extensive correspondence. By this time, he was supported physically by his many followers. From 1732 to 1755 he traveled annually to Holland to preach, as the ban on conventicles was strictly enforced in his home country. Although Tersteegen himself remained outside the Reformed Church, his followers did not form a new sect when he died on April 3, 1769, at Mühlheim, but for the most part returned to the communion.

This hymn was first published in Tersteegen's Geistliches Blumengärtlein, 1729. The English version of stanzas 1 and 2 is from a translation prepared by Frederick William Foster and John Miller in the Moravian Hymn Book, 1789, and altered in William Mercer's (LBW 281) The Church Psalter and Hymn Book, 1855. Further alterations have been made, including changing the opening line, which read "God reveals his presence" in both collections. The translation of stanzas 3 and 4, which is also altered somewhat, was prepared in 1923 by Herman Brueckner for the American Lutheran Hymnal, 1930.

Frederick William Foster, born in England on August 1, 1760, was educated at the Moravian Brethren educational center, Fulneck, Yorkshire, and at the Moravian College in Saxony, at Barby near Magdeburg. He returned to England where he was a minister of the Moravian Church, finally becoming provincial superintendent. A translator of German hymns as well as composer of original English ones, Foster was also editor of the Moravian Hymn Book, 1801, its supplement in 1808, and the revised edition in 1826. Death came April 12, 1835, at Ockbrook near Derby.

John Miller (Johannes Müller) was born in Germany, at Groshennersdorf near Herrnhut, Saxony, in 1756. His parents were Lutheran but he was educated at the Moravian grammar school, and later attended the Moravian Theological College at Barby, as did Foster. He also went to

England, going to Fulneck in 1781 as assistant preacher and chaplain. Seven years later he married and went to Pudsey. He died of tuberculosis in 1790. With Foster, he contributed a number of translations to *The Moravian Hymn Book,* 1789.

Herman H. M. Brueckner, son of a Lutheran pastor, was born in Grundy County, Iowa, on March 11, 1866. Ordained in 1888, he served pastorates in Illinois, Michigan, Kentucky, and Wisconsin before going to Iowa City. There he remained for fifteen years and received a Master of Arts degree from the State University of Iowa in 1917. For the next nine years he worked part time at the university and continued graduate studies. In 1926 he went to Hebron College, an American Lutheran College (now closed) located in Hebron, Nebraska, where he taught French, German, English, and Christianity. He studied at the University of Nebraska in the summer of 1927, and took courses yearly during the summers from 1926 to 1934 at the University of Wisconsin. In 1938 he received an honorary Doctor of Divinity degree from Wartburg Seminary. He was married in 1899 to Leonore Schneider and was the father of five children. After his first wife's death in 1920, he was married in 1922 to Dorothy Staehling of Waverly. He retired professor emeritus from Hebron College in 1941 and died on January 25, 1942.

WUNDERBARER KÖNIG (also "Arnsberg"), was attributed to Joachim Neander (LBW 182) in his *Alpha und Omega. Joachimi Neandri Glaub- und Liebesübung,* published in Bremen in 1680. There it was the setting for his hymn "Wunderbarer König."

250 OPEN NOW THY GATES OF BEAUTY
(Tut mir auf die schöne Pforte)
Tune: Unser Herrscher

See LBW 187 for Benjamin Schmolck and LBW 29 for Catherine Winkworth. This hymn was included in Schmolck's *Kirchen-Gefährte,* 1732, and was translated in Winkworth's *Chorale Book for England,* 1863. The text is altered slightly.

For UNSER HERRSCHER see LBW 182.

251 O DAY OF REST AND GLADNESS
Tune: Ave Maria, klarer und lichter Morgenstern

Suggested by Psalm 118:24, "This is the day which the Lord has made; let us rejoice and be glad in it," this hymn was included in Christopher Wordsworth's (LBW 90) *Holy Year,* 1862.

AVE MARIA, KLARER UND LICHTER MORGENSTERN (also "Ellacombe") seems to be derived from a melody found with that text in the *Gesangbuch . . . der Herzogl. Wirtembergischen katholischen Hofkapelle* (a collection used in the private chapel of the Duke of Württemberg), 1784 (see first example, page 327).

A number of German variants are found in the nineteenth century. In 1833 it appeared in Xavier L. Hartig's *Vollständige Sammlung der*

gewöhnlichen Melodien zum Mainzer Gesangbuche as the setting for "Der du im heil'gen Sakrament" (Bäumker,* IV, #145), in a form much closer to the present one.

The version of the tune in use today was included in the 1868 Appendix to the Original Edition of *Hymns Ancient and Modern,* with John Jeremiah Daniell's "Come, sing with holy gladness."

252 YOU SERVANTS OF GOD

Tune: Lyons

See LBW 27 for Charles Wesley. This hymn was published in *Hymns for Times of Trouble and Persecution,* 1744.

LYONS. This tune is found in William Gardiner's (LBW 356) *Sacred Melodies,* volume II, published in London in 1815. There Gardiner gave no more clues to his source than "Subject Haydn." It is not known for sure whether he took his tune from the works of Franz Joseph Haydn (LBW 358) or from those of his younger brother, Johann Michael Haydn. There are a number of themes in the works of both men that could have suggested the opening line (which is the same as "Hanover" [LBW 548]), but so far the source does not seem to have been identified further.

Johann Michael Haydn was born September 14, 1737, in Rohrau, Austria, and was a chorister at St. Stephen's Church, Vienna, as was his brother, from 1745 to 1755. There also he studied organ and violin, and sometimes served as substitute organist. He developed a remarkable voice range of three octaves and when his brother's voice changed, Johann Michael replaced him on the solo parts. In 1757 he became *Kapellmeister* at Grosswardein to the Bishop Count Firmian, whose uncle, Archbishop Sigismund, later appointed him as *Konzertmeister* at Salzburg in 1762. He remained in Salzburg for over forty years, serving after 1777 as organist at the churches of Holy Trinity and St. Peter. When the French took Salzburg in 1800, Haydn lost all his property. Hearing of his misfortune, the Empress Maria Theresa (LBW 535) commissioned him to write a mass for which she paid handsomely. He directed its first performance at Laxenburg Palace with the empress herself singing the soprano arias. He died at Salzburg August 10, 1806.

A devout Roman Catholic, Johann Michael Haydn composed over three hundred works for the church, including a hundred pieces for organ and orchestra and a number of oratorios. Like J. S. Bach (LBW 219), he dedicated his manuscripts to the glory of God, signing them "O. A. M. D. Gl" ("Omnia ad Majorem Dei Gloriam"). The bulk of his work is still unpublished.

253 LORD JESUS CHRIST, BE PRESENT NOW
(Herr Jesu Christ, dich zu uns wend)
Tune: Herr Jesu Christ, dich zu uns wend

The earliest source of this hymn is the *Cantionale Sacrum,* second edition, 1651. It was not ascribed to Wilhelm II until 1676 in the *Altford Liederfreud,* so his authorship is somewhat uncertain.

Born April 11, 1598, in the castle of Altenburg, Wilhelm II, Duke of Saxe-Weimar, studied music and mathematics at the University of Jena. During the Thirty Years' War he was twice severely wounded, the second time being left for dead and then taken as a prisoner by Johann, Count of Tilly. Released in 1625, he assumed the government of Weimar, and ten years later was one of the parties signing the Peace of Prague. He devoted himself to the rebuilding of his regions, and after the Peace of Westphalia in 1648, found more time to devote to poetry and music. He died at Weimar on May 17, 1662.

Catherine Winkworth's (LBW 29) translation from her *Chorale Book for England,* 1863, is given here with considerable alteration.

HERR JESU CHRIST, DICH ZU UNS WEND. This tune first appeared in the *Cantionale Germanicum,* Gochsheim, 1628, and was published with the present text when it appeared in 1651. One tradition traces the melody back to John Huss.

In addition to a harmonization in *Choralgesänge,* J. S. Bach (LBW 219) wrote four organ settings of this tune, which are included in the *Orgelbüchlein,* the Eighteen Chorales, and the Miscellaneous Preludes.

254 COME, LET US JOIN OUR CHEERFUL SONGS
Tune: Nun danket all

See LBW 39 for Isaac Watts. This hymn was included in his *Hymns and Spiritual Songs,* 1707.

NUN DANKET ALL was composed by Johann Crüger (LBW 23) as a

setting for Paul Gerhardt's (LBW 23) "Nun danket all und bringet ehr" in Crüger's *Praxis Pietatis Melica,* second edition, 1647.

255   LORD, RECEIVE THIS COMPANY
Tune: Union

Pierre Teilhard de Chardin, French paleontologist, was born May 1, 1881, in the castle of Sarcenat, Orcines, Puy-de-Dôme. His father was a gentleman farmer and student of paleography; his mother, a noblewoman and great-grandniece of Voltaire. The young Teilhard studied with the Jesuits of Mongré, where the abbot Bremond was his professor, before entering, in 1899, the novitiate at Aix-en-Provence. While in Jersey from 1902 to 1905 he became interested in geology. From 1905 to 1908 he studied physics and chemistry at Claire, and from 1908 to 1912, theology at Hastings. In 1912 he was ordained and also began two years of study at the Museum of Natural History in Paris, during which time he was a student of Marcellin Boulle and, in 1913, worked in the Piltdown excavations. During World War I he served for four years at the front, at Ypres and Verdun, and was decorated for gallantry. In 1922 he received a doctorate at Sorbonne, and the following year became a professor of geology at the Catholic Institute in Paris. He did research in geology and paleontology in China from 1923 to 1945 and was one of the discoverers of the "Peking man." In addition he went on numerous other expeditions: the French expedition of Harar in the Gobi Desert, 1928; the Central Asian expedition of the American Museum, 1930; and the Harvard-Carnegie Expedition to Burma and Java, 1937–1938. He was elected to the Academy of Sciences in 1950, and was also associated with an anthropological research foundation in New York City. On Easter Sunday, April 10, 1955, he died in New York, having just returned from a mission in South Africa.

Teilhard proposed a new and controversial theory of evolution reconciling science and religion. His principal works include *Le Phenomene humain,* 1955; *L'Apparition de l'homme,* 1956; *Le Milieu divin,* 1957; *L'Avenir de l'homme,* 1959; and many volumes of letters.

The text on which this hymn is based is from "La Messe sur le Monde," written in 1923 and included in Teilhard's *Hymne de l'Universe,* Paris, 1961. In an English translation prepared by Simon Bartholomew (*Hymn of the Universe,* New York, 1961), it reads:

> Receive, O Lord, this all-embracing host which your whole creation, moved by your magnetism, offers you at this dawn of a new day.

George Utech's (LBW 152) adaptation was included in *Contemporary Worship–1,* 1969.

UNION, by Leland Sateren (LBW 100), was included with this text in *Contemporary Worship–1,* 1969.

256   OH, SING JUBILEE TO THE LORD
(Al verden nu raabe for Herren med fryd)
Tune: Guds Menighed, syng

Ulrik Vilhelm Koren was the first Norwegian pastor to settle west of the Mississippi. Born in Bergen, Norway, December 22, 1826, he attended the Bergen cathedral school, and entered the University of Christiania in 1844. He taught school for a year before being called to an Iowa parish. Ordained in 1853, he came with his wife, Else Elisabeth *née* Hysing, to his parish in Little Iowa (later Washington Prairie), Iowa. He served first as secretary, then as vice president of the Norwegian Synod from 1855 to 1874. He was president of the Iowa district from 1874 until 1894 when he became president of the Norwegian Lutheran Synod of America, a position he held until his death in 1910. All the while he ministered to his parish at Washington Prairie, near Decorah, preaching his fiftieth Christmas sermon there in 1903.

Also intensely interested in church music, Koren was a leader in the compilation of the *Norwegian Synod Hymn Book,* 1874, in which this hymn appeared, and it was at his suggestion that the *Rythmisk Koralbog,* which influenced the composition of *The Lutheran Hymnary,* 1913, was published.

The translation was prepared for the LBW by the Inter-Lutheran Commission on Worship.

GUDS MENIGHED, SYNG (also "Hoff") was composed about 1860, and was included in Erik Christian Hoff's 1878 *Melodibog* as the setting for "Guds menighed, syng."

Hoff, the son of a smith, was born in Bergen, Norway, January 21, 1832. He entered Stord seminary at a very early age and graduated in record time at the top of his class. At the seminary he also received a good introduction to music. While teaching in Bergen he became a lead singer in the choir at Korskirken. He studied organ and music theory at Vogel school of music and graduated with distinction. In 1860 he obtained a teaching job in Halmestrand. Two years later he accepted a teaching position in Oslo and became the conductor of several choirs there, and in 1864 he assumed the post of organist at the Garnisonkirke. These early years in the capital proved to be his most productive; despite his many responsibilities he composed and was in great demand as a teacher. His published works included organ works, songs for male chorus, and collections of children's songs. After 1870 he resigned from his teaching to devote his time to Norwegian choral music. As an organist he was very highly regarded. His improvisations and preludes contributed to the large attendance at the services, and King Oscar frequently visited the Garnisonkirke to hear him play. During a conversation with the king following one service, Hoff was encouraged to prepare a chorale book, a task which was to occupy all of his time until it was completed. After much research Hoff created a collection which contained not only tunes for the newly-authorized Magnus Landstad (LBW 310) *Kirkesalmebog,* but also for all other hymnals in use in Norwegian churches, including Thomas Kingo's (LBW 102) and the hymnal of the Norwegian Synod in America. In supporting the use of the original rhythmic forms of the chorales, as they had been sung during the Reformation, Hoff was in direct opposition to Ludvig Lindeman (LBW 285). His collection of tunes, the *Melodibog til samtlige authorisered Salmeboger,* eventually lost out to Lindeman's for authorization and financial support, and was published privately in 1878. The *Melodibog,* with its 265 tunes, drew upon both Swedish and Danish traditions, and also contained a number of new tunes, including sixty-one by Hoff, who was exceptionally gifted as a harmonizer. He died December 8, 1894.

257 HOLY SPIRIT, TRUTH DIVINE
Tune: Song 13

Samuel Longfellow, brother of Henry Wadsworth (LBW 279), was born June 18, 1819, in Portland, Maine, and received a Bachelor of Arts degree from Harvard in 1839. After graduation from Harvard Divinity School in 1846 he was ordained, and became minister to the Unitarian Church at Fall River, Massachusetts, in 1848. He toured Europe for two years, following which he went in 1853 to the Second Unitarian Church, Brooklyn, New York, and from 1860 to 1883 was at the Unitarian Church in Germantown, Pennsylvania. Thereafter he retired to prepare the biography of his brother which was published in 1886. He died in Portland, Maine, on October 3, 1892.

Longfellow published *Vespers,* 1859, and *A Book of Hymns and Tunes,* 1860, and in conjunction with Samuel Johnson, a fellow student at Harvard, he edited *A Book of Hymns for Public and Private Devotion,* 1846, and *Hymns of the Spirit,* 1864, in which this hymn was included.

SONG 13 appeared in George Wither's *Hymns and Songs of the Church,* 1623, where it was set to a text from the Song of Songs, "O my Love, how comely now." The rhythm has been considerably simplified from the original.

See LBW 206 for Orlando Gibbons.

Tune: Nilsson

See LBW 84 for Reginald Heber. This hymn for the first Sunday in Advent is based on Matthew 21, and was first printed in the *Christian Observer,* October, 1811. The LBW uses the revised form from Heber's *Hymns,* 1827.

NILSSON, newly-written for the LBW and published here for the first time, is named for the composer's father whose "official" name on citizenship papers is Nils Axel Nilsson.

Ronald Nelson, composer of the second setting of the Communion service in the LBW, was born April 29, 1927, in Rockford, Illinois. He completed a Bachelor of Music degree, summa cum laude, at St. Olaf College in 1949 and ten years later received a Master of Music degree from the University of Wisconsin. From 1949 to 1952 he taught vocal music in the Rockford public schools while serving as organist-choirmaster at Tabor Lutheran Church there. The position at Tabor was expanded to full-time in 1952 and he organized a Saturday choir school program, in addition to which he taught piano and voice privately, and from 1954 to 1955 was also part-time choir director and choir school director at Our Saviour's Lutheran Church. Since 1955 he has been director of music at Westwood Lutheran Church, St. Louis Park, Minnesota. There he has developed the music program to include eight choirs, a choir school program with a summer camp, and a voice and organ scholarship program. His compositions are available from a number of publishers, and he has served as guest lecturer and clinician at Luther Seminary in St. Paul and St. Olaf College, as well as church music camps, festivals, and workshops throughout the country. He is a member of the board of directors of the Choristers Guild and of the Southeast Minnesota District Commission on Worship of the American Lutheran Church. He has also served on the board of directors of the Twin Cities Chapter American Guild of Organists and was a member of the hymn music committee of the Inter-Lutheran Commission on Worship. In 1967 St. Olaf College honored him with a Distinguished Alumnus Award. Married to Betty Lou Oleson, he is the father of four children.

259 LORD, DISMISS US WITH YOUR BLESSING

Tune: Sicilian Mariners

Julian* lists four hymns beginning with this first line and includes a discussion of each. The present hymn appeared anonymously in *A Supplement to the Shawbury Hymn Book,* printed in 1773 at Shrewsbury, and in several later hymnals. The first indication of its authorship was in the *Selection of Psalms for Social Worship,* York, 1786, where it was marked with an "F." In J. Harris's *A Collection of Psalms and Hymns,* seventh edition, York, 1791, the full name, "Fawcett," first appeared. Stanza 1, which originally opened, "Lord, dismiss us with *Thy* blessing," has been altered in the last line. Godfrey Thring (LBW 170) rewrote the first three lines of stanza 3, and these have been further changed for the LBW.

John Fawcett was born in England on January 6, 1740, at Lidget

Green near Bradford, Yorkshire. At age sixteen he came under the influence of George Whitefield (LBW 522), and a few years later joined the
Baptist Church. He was ordained a Baptist minister in 1765 at Wainsgate
near Hebden Bridge, Yorkshire. Seven years later he was called to a London parish, and accounts relate that he had preached his farewell sermon
at Wainsgate and was packed to leave, but the congregation so prevailed
upon him to remain, that he did so. Later, in 1793, he also declined an invitation to become president of the Baptist Academy at Bristol. In 1811
Brown University, Providence, Rhode Island, honored him with a Doctor of Divinity degree. He died July 25, 1817, at Hebden Bridge.

In addition to his *Devotional Commentary on the Holy Scriptures,*
Fawcett published a number of poetical works. His hymns, numbering
over 160, were written largely for use after his sermons, and appeared as
*Hymns adapted to the Circumstances of Public Worship and Private
Devotion,* 1782.

SICILIAN MARINERS. This tune appeared in *The European Magazine
and London Review,* November, 1792, as the setting for "The Sicilian
Mariner's Hymn to the Virgin":

> O sanctissima, O piissima,
> Dulcis virgo Maria!
> Mater amata, intemerata,
> Ora, ora pro nobis.

Shortly thereafter the tune appeared on both sides of the Atlantic—in
Ralph Shaw's *The Gentleman's Amusement,* Philadelphia, 1794–1795,
as the setting for "O sanctissima," and in James Merrick and William
Lechair Tattersall's *Improved Psalmody,* volume I, London, 1794,
where it was the setting for a metrical version of Psalm 19, "God the
Heav'ns aloud proclaim." Titled "Dismission," the tune is found with a
single stanza of the present hymn in William Smith and William Little's
Easy Instructor, 1817, a collection which, in its 1801 edition, had introduced shape-note hymnody in America. In Germany, the melody is
associated with the Christmas hymn "O du Fröhliche, O du Selige." The
present-day Negro spiritual, "We shall overcome," also uses a version of
this tune.

The origins of this melody are not known. In his article in the July,
1976, issue of *The Hymn,* Byron E. Underwood quotes from *The European Magazine* that the hymn was "sung in unison by the whole crew of
the Sicilian seamen on board their ships when the sun sets . . . ," and also
mentions an 1866 source which calls it "a favorite of the gondoliers in
Venice, who sing it in solemn chorus, . . . especially on the morning of
St. Mary's Day."

The harmonization was prepared for the LBW by John Becker, who
since 1974 has served on the Division of Parish Services of the Lutheran
Church in America as Secretary for Church Music. Born in
Cooperstown, New York, March 11, 1927, Becker attended the public
schools there before serving in the United States Naval Reserve in Japan.
He attended Duke University, Durham, North Carolina, and graduated
from Hartwick College, Oneonta, New York, in 1949. In 1954 he received a Master of Sacred Music degree from Union Theological
Seminary, New York City, where he studied with Searle Wright. He then
went to study with Helmut Walcha at the Hochschule für Musik, Frankfurt-am-Main, Germany. He served as organist and choirmaster in
several New York churches, including Holy Trinity Lutheran Church in

Buffalo, where he directed an extensive music program for eighteen
years. He was dean of the Buffalo Chapter, American Guild of Organists
and served as general chairman of the national convention of AGO held
in Buffalo in 1970. Formerly a member of the Commission on Worship
of the Lutheran Church in America and chairman of the music committee, he is also an editor of the *Church Music Memo* and has presented articles in various professional journals.

HYMN **261**

260 ON OUR WAY REJOICING

Tune: Hermas

Designated for the first Sunday after Trinity, this hymn first appeared in
John S. B. Monsell's *Hymns of Love and Praise,* 1863, and was rewritten, using the first part of stanza 1 as a refrain, in his *Parish Hymnal,*
1873. See LBW 131 for Monsell.

HERMAS was first published in Havergal's *Psalmody,* London, 1871, as
the setting for "Jesus, I will trust thee."

Frances Ridley Havergal, youngest child of William H. Havergal
(LBW 406), was born at Astley, Worcestershire, in England on
December 14, 1836, and later went with her family to Worcester when
her father became the pastor of a church there. Although poor health did
not allow her to study regularly as a child, she started writing verses at an
early age and showed a gift for learning languages, acquiring a
knowledge of French, German, Italian, Latin, Greek, and Hebrew. In
addition to her writing of verse, she carried on a considerable correspondence and was involved in religious and philanthropic work. She
died at Oystermouth, Glamorganshire, near Swansea in Wales, on June
3, 1879. Her *Poetical Works* were published in 1884, and *Memorials,*
which contained a partial autobiography, in 1882.

The harmonization is by Robert Leaf (LBW 184).

261 ON WHAT HAS NOW BEEN SOWN

Tune: Darwall's 148th

The present form of this hymn comes from the *Irish Hymnal,* 1873. Stanza 1 is the sixth stanza of "What contradictions meet," from *Olney
Hymns,* book two (quoted in full at Polack* #43), and stanzas 2 and 3
are a separate hymn from *Olney Hymns,* book three, beginning "To
Thee our wants are known."

An inscription at St. Mary Woolnoth, London, written by Newton
himself, reads:

> John Newton, Clerk,
> Once an infidel and libertine,
> A servant of slaves in Africa,
> Was, by the rich mercy of our Lord
> And Saviour Jesus Christ,
> Preserved, restored, pardoned,
> And appointed to preach the Faith
> He had long labored to destroy,
> Near sixteen years at Olney in Bucks,
> And twenty-eight years in this church.

333

Newton, whose father was a ship master and whose mother was a God-fearing woman, was born July 24, 1725, in London. His mother died when he was seven years old and he was sent away to boarding school for a while, and then at the age of eleven he went away to sea with his father. When he was seventeen, he was taken into the navy and soon became a midshipman, but having overstayed a leave, he was flogged and degraded as a deserter. He got onto a ship which was bound for the African coast, where he came into the employ of a slave trader who half-starved him and treated him badly. During this time Newton felt that his morality sank to a very low level. In 1747 opportunity for escape came when the ship *The Greyhound* put in and departed for London. On the way the seeds for his conversion were sown. Aboard ship, with nothing to do, Newton read a part of *The Imitation of Christ* (see LBW 88), and later was confronted with death when a heavy storm broke in the side of the ship, and it would surely have sunk except that the cargo, being part dyewood and part beeswax, kept the vessel afloat. For six years thereafter, he was a slave dealer. Before he had gone into the navy, Newton had met Mary Catlett, then only fourteen. His love for her remained through all his difficulties in the navy and later in Africa, and in 1750 he was married to her. In 1754 he gave up the slave trade, which had become more and more distasteful to him, and became a tidesurveyor at Liverpool, where he had come to know George Whitefield (LBW 522) and the Wesleys (LBW 27 and 302). He studied Hebrew and Greek in preparation for becoming a clergyman, and in 1764 became curate of Olney, in a Buckinghamshire village. There he remained, working among mostly poor and ignorant people, until 1780 when he went to St. Mary Woolnoth in London where he built up a large congregation. In 1792 the College of New Jersey (now Princeton University) honored him with a Doctor of Divinity degree. Blind for the last years of his life, he died in London on December 21, 1807.

While at Olney, Newton became a friend of William Cowper (LBW 483) and together they prepared *Olney Hymns,* published in 1779, and consisting of three books: I, "On select Texts of Scripture"; II, "On occasional subjects"; and III, "On the Progress and changes of the Spiritual Life." *Olney Hymns* exerted an immense influence among the Evangelicals and many of the hymns soon took an important place in hymnody. From a negative standpoint, *Olney Hymns* completely disregarded the Church Year, and was somewhat overhung with the shadow of Cowper's depression and Newton's distress over former sins. The hymn "Glories of your name are spoken" (LBW 358) is one of the few hymns of praise included. Positively speaking, many of the best hymns are a fine expression of faith in the grace and love of the Savior.

DARWALL'S 148TH. John Darwall was born in Haughton, Staffordshire, England in January of 1731. After receiving a Bachelor of Arts degree at Brasenose College, Oxford, in 1756, he was ordained in 1761 and appointed curate of St. Matthew's Church in Walshall, Staffordshire, and in 1769, vicar of the same church. There he remained until his death on December 18, 1789.

Although he was a clergyman, Darwall composed two volumes of piano sonatas, and settings for all 150 psalms of the New Version (see pp. 64f). This tune was included in Aaron Williams' *New Universal Psalmodist,* published in London in 1770, with the text "Ye boundless realms of joy," Psalm 148.

Tune: Ellers

Born in Clerkenwell, London, England, on December 16, 1826, John
Ellerton was educated at King William's College on the Isle of Man and
at Trinity College, Cambridge. He received a Bachelor of Arts degree in
1849 and a Master of Arts degree five years later. Ordained a deacon in
1850 and a priest in 1851, he served at Eastbourne, Midhurst in Sussex,
and St. Nicholas in Brighton, before going in 1860 as vicar of Crewe
Greene and chaplain to Lord Crewe. He was appointed rector at
Hinstock in 1872, and four years later, rector of Barnes in Surrey. His
health failed while he was there, and he went for a while to Switzerland
and Italy to recover. When he returned in 1886, he became rector at
White Roding in Essex, where he remained until shortly before his death.
In 1892 he was offered the canonry of St. Alban's in Hertfordshire, but
was unable to accept it because of his paralysis. He died June 15, 1893,
while on a visit to Torquay in Devonshire.

Ellerton began his hymn-writing and edited *Hymns for Schools and
Bible Classes* (1859) while serving at Brighton. Later he was co-editor
with Bishop William How (LBW 77), and others, of *Church Hymns,*
published by the Society for the Promotion of Christian Knowledge,
1871. (The musical edition of this work, 1874, was prepared by Arthur
Sullivan [LBW 153], and was the source of several tunes and harmonizations found in the LBW.) In 1881 Ellerton published his *Notes and Illustrations of Church Hymns.* He contributed to Carey Brock's
Children's Hymn Book, 1882, and to the 1889 Supplement to *Hymns
Ancient and Modern,* and was also co-editor of *Children's Hymns and
School Prayers,* 1874, and the *London Mission Hymn Book,* 1885. His
own hymns were published in *Hymns, Original and Translated,* 1888.

Written in 1866 for the Festival of the Malpas, Middlewich, and Nant-
wich Choral Association, this hymn was later revised and shortened from
six to four stanzas for the Appendix to the Original Edition of *Hymns
Ancient and Modern,* 1868. The last stanza was sung at Ellerton's
funeral on June 20, 1893.

ELLERS. Edward John Hopkins was born in Westminster, London,
England, on June 30, 1818. At the age of eight he became a child of the
Chapel Royal, St. James's, and as such later sang for the coronation of
William IV. Young Edward also sang at St. Paul's Cathedral, and on a
typical Sunday would be shuttled back and forth between the two places
for one service or another for the entire day. Further, as were most
choristers in his day, he was poorly treated and scantily fed. He left the
Chapel Royal at fifteen and took the opportunity to hear James Turles at
Westminster Abbey, who on occasion allowed him to play parts of the
services there. At the age of sixteen Hopkins took his first organ position
at Mitcham Church, where Joseph Barnby (LBW 280) also began his
career. After four years there, he served at St. Peter's, Islington, and St.
Luke's, Berwick Street, Soho, before going in 1843 to Temple Church.
There he remained until 1898, when he was succeeded by Henry Walford
Davies. He died in London, February 4, 1901.

Hopkins was a pioneer in the establishment of several musical institutions, including the Royal College of Organists, and was a member of the
Royal Society of Musicians and an honorary member of the Royal
Academy of Music. Two honorary Doctor of Music degrees were
bestowed on him, one by the archbishop of Canterbury and one by Trin-

ity College in Toronto. He composed a large amount of church music, but it is for his hymn tunes and chants that he became most widely known. In addition to his own *Temple Service Book,* Hopkins served as music editor to a number of other hymnals of the Free Church of Scotland, the Wesleyan and Congregational churches, and the Presbyterian churches of England and Canada. With Dr. E. F. Rimbault he published *The Organ: its History and Construction,* long a standard work on the subject, and he also contributed articles to *Grove's Dictionary of Music and Musicians.*

"Ellers" first appeared in *The Supplemental Hymn and Tune Book, Compiled by Rev. R. Brown-Borthwick,* third edition, 1869. There it was written for unison voices with a varied organ accompaniment for each stanza. The composer provided a four-part setting for the Appendix to the *Bradford Tune Book,* 1872, edited by Samuel Smith.

The harmonization is by Arthur Sullivan (LBW 153).

263 ABIDE WITH US, OUR SAVIOR *(Ach bleib mit deiner Gnade)*
    Tune: Christus, der ist mein Leben

This German hymn by Josua Stegmann was published in the third edition of *Suspiria Temporum,* Rinteln, 1628. There is a possibility that it appeared in one or both of the previous editions, but neither is extant today. Stanzas 1, 2, and 4 are from the *Church Book,* Philadelphia, 1868, of the Pennsylvania Synod, marked "Unknown, Tr. 1848." Stanza 3 is from a translation prepared in 1890 by Frederic W. Detterer and published the following year in *Offices of Worship and Hymns.* Each of the stanzas has been slightly altered.

Son of a Lutheran pastor, Stegmann was born on September 14, 1588, at Sülzfeld near Meiningen, Germany. After receiving a Master of Arts degree from the University of Leipzig in 1611, he remained there as an adjunct of the philosophical faculty and completed a Doctor of Divinity degree in 1617. In that year he became superintendent of the district of Schaumburg, pastor at Stadthagen, and first professor of the *Gymnasium* at Stadthagen. In 1621 the *Gymnasium* was made into a university and moved to Rinteln, and Stegmann became professor of theology there. The Thirty Years' War soon interrupted his work there when he was forced to flee Rinteln in 1623. Two years later he returned and was appointed overseer of the Lutheran clergy of Hesse-Schaumburg. Following the Edict of Restitution issued by the emperor in 1629, Stegmann was much harassed. Benedictine monks settled in Rinteln in 1630 claiming to be the rightful professors of the new university and demanding that lands devoted to the payment of stipends for the university professors be turned over to them. Soldiers were sent to Stegmann's home to search it and seize his salary. In July of 1632 the monks compelled him to hold a disputation at which they planted men to jeer him. The pressure was too much, Stegmann's health failed, and he died August 3, 1632.

A Moravian clergyman, Detterer was born in Utica, New York, in 1861, and from 1884 to 1886 was a teacher at the Moravian Boys' School, Nazareth Hall. Later he became a professor at Moravian College. He died June 20, 1893, at Jamaica, West Indies.

CHRISTUS, DER IST MEIN LEBEN (also "Ach bleib mit deiner Gnade"). This tune by Melchior Vulpius (LBW 115) served as the setting for "Christus, der ist mein Leben," an anonymous hymn included in Vulpius' *Ein Schön Geistlich Gesangbuch,* Jena, 1609. (A translation of "Christus, der ist mein Leben" was included in *The Lutheran Hymnal,* 1941, #597.) J. S. Bach (LBW 219) based his Cantata 95 on "Christus, der ist mein Leben," and two harmonizations are also given in his *Choralgesänge.*

264   WHEN ALL YOUR MERCIES, O MY GOD

Tune: Winchester Old

This hymn was included in the Saturday, August 9, 1712, issue of the *Spectator* at the end of an article on gratitude.

Born May 1, 1672, Joseph Addison was the son of the rector of Milston near Amesbury in Wiltshire, England. After receiving a Bachelor of Arts degree in 1691, and a Master of Arts degree in 1693 from Magdalen College, Oxford University, he spent some years traveling on the continent. From 1698 to 1711 he was a fellow of Magdalen College. Although he was expected to become an Anglican clergyman, he chose instead to enter the fields of law and politics and held several important posts, being successively a commissioner of appeals, an undersecretary of state, secretary to the Lord Lieutenant of Ireland, and chief secretary for Ireland. He was married to the Dowager Countess of Warwick in 1716. Three years later, at the age of forty-seven, he died at Holland House in Kensington on June 17. He is buried at Westminster Abbey.

Also a writer, Addison collaborated with Richard Steele on the *Spectator* which appeared in 1712 and contained several of his hymns, and contributed also to *The Tatler, The Guardian,* and *The Freeholder.* His tragedy *Cato* was highly regarded. Samuel Johnson said of him: "Whoever wishes to attain an English style, familiar but not coarse, and elegant but not ostentatious, must give his days and nights to the volumes of Addison."

WINCHESTER OLD is found in *The Whole Book of Psalms* printed by Thomas Este in 1592. As with "Windsor" (LBW 114), this tune is felt to be based on a melody in Christopher Tye's *Actes of the Apostles,* this tune being similar to chapter eight.

The arrangement included in the Este psalter is attributed to George Kirbye, who was born around 1560, possibly in Suffolk, England. He seems to have lived at Rushbrooke near Bury St. Edwards, where he was a musician in the service of Sir Robert Jermyn, and perhaps also church warden of St. Mary's. He prepared most of the harmonizations in *The Whole Book of Psalms,* and in 1597 published his *First Set of English Madrigals.* He died in October of 1634 at Bury St. Edmunds.

Thomas Este (also Est, Easte, East), born perhaps in 1540, was a famous printer and music publisher who with his *Musica Transalpina,* a group of Italian madrigals, laid the groundwork for the English madrigal school. It was he who printed and published most of the musical works printed in England under the patent granted by Queen Elizabeth to Thomas Tallis (LBW 278), William Byrd, and Thomas Morley. In 1591 he published the second of William Daman's psalters (LBW 114). Este is also credited with establishing with his 1592 psalter the practice in England of calling psalm tunes by the names of places. Also, the 1592 psalter is believed to be the earliest example in which parts are printed on opposite pages rather than in separate books. For an unknown reason, Este changed his name in 1609 to Snodham. His death date is unknown.

265   CHRIST, WHOSE GLORY FILLS THE SKIES
Tune: Ratisbon

See LBW 27 for Charles Wesley. This hymn was included in John and Charles Wesley's *Hymns and Sacred Poems,* 1740.

RATISBON was included in Werner's *Choralbuch zu den neuen fächsichen Gesangbüchern vierstimmig für die Orgel,* Leipzig, 1815, where it was the setting for "Jesu meines Lebens Leben" (LBW 97) (Zahn* 6801). The tune for "Jesus, meine Zuversicht" (LBW 340) seems to have been the basis for this tune. Ratisbon, a German city dating from the first century, is now known as Regensburg.

Johann Gottlob Werner, born at Hayn, near Leipzig, Germany, in 1777, was organist at Frohburg in 1798, and in 1808 was assistant to Christian Tag, cantor of Hohenstein, Saxony. In 1819 he became organist and director at Merseburg. He died July 19, 1822.

266   MAKER OF THE EARTH AND HEAVEN
(Gott des Himmels und der Erde)
Tune: Gott des Himmels

Both text and tune of this hymn are by Heinrich Albert. Albert, a nephew and student of Heinrich Schütz (LBW 180), was born June 28, 1604, at Lobenstein, Saxony, in Germany. At the insistance of his parents he studied law at the University of Leipzig (his father was a tax collector) and also studied literature there. On his way from Königsberg to Warsaw with an embassy in 1626 he was captured by the Swedes (who later won a decisive victory at Leipzig in 1631 during the Thirty Years' War). After two years and much hardship he returned to Königsberg and continued his music study with Stobäus. On his appointment as organist of the Cathedral in Königsberg in 1631 he gladly gave up law and devoted himself entirely to music. Also a poet, he was made a member of the Poetical Union in Königsberg in 1639. He was married the same year to Elisabeth Starck. He remained as organist to the Königsberg Cathedral until his death on October 6, 1651.

Heinrich Albert's "Morgen-Lied" of seven stanzas, together with this tune, in a five-voice setting, appeared in his *Arien etliche theils geistliche, theils weltliche.* . . . The hymn was included in part five of the eight-part work published between 1638 and 1650.

The English version was prepared by the Inter-Lutheran Commission on Worship, based on two earlier translations—one by Catherine Winkworth (LBW 29) from her *Lyra Germanica,* first series, 1855, and another by Arthur Tozer Russell (LBW 86) from his *Hymns for Public Worship,* Dalton Hospital, London, 1848 (which in turn was founded on an English text by John Christian Jacobi in *A Collection of Divine Hymns,* London, 1720).

The harmonization of the tune is by Philip Gehring (LBW 127).

267 FATHER, WE PRAISE YOU *(Nocte surgentes vigilemus omnes)*
Tune: Christe sanctorum

The origins of this hymn are not certain. Although it is generally ascribed to Gregory the Great (LBW 101), it has also been suggested that it is from the Carolingian period, possibly written by Alcuin, since it is known that he wrote a few sapphics not unlike this hymn. It is preserved in a number of eleventh-century manuscripts. In the various breviaries—Roman, Sarum, York, Aberdeen, and others—it is usually assigned to Matins (after midnight) or Nocturns (at night) during the Trinity Season.

The translation was prepared by Percy Dearmer (LBW 169) and included in *The English Hymnal,* 1906, with the first line "Father, we praise *Thee.*" Other alterations are slight.

For CHRISTE SANCTORUM see LBW 169. The harmonization found here was done by Carl Schalk (LBW 118) for the *Worship Supplement,* 1969, to *The Lutheran Hymnal.*

268 NOW THAT THE DAYLIGHT FILLS THE SKY
(Jam lucis orto sidere)
Tune: Laurel

This Latin hymn of unknown authorship has been dated variously from the fourth to the eighth century. It is found uniformly for the Office of Prime (at sunrise) in nearly all medieval breviaries—Sarum, York, Aberdeen, Mozarabic, Roman, and Paris. Since the Office of Prime, the first of the Hour Services for the day, was instituted in the fifth century, it cannot be older than that, and some sources suggest that it may have been written in the fifth century for that office. Others feel that its tendency to rhyme would place it not earlier than the seventh or eighth century. It is found in several manuscripts of the eighth through the eleventh centuries.

Many translations of the hymn have been written. A translation by John Henry Newman beginning "Now that the daystar glimmers bright" was included in the *Service Book and Hymnal,* 1958. The present translation is by John Mason Neale (LBW 34) and was given in *The Hymnal Noted,* 1851. The final stanza is extensively altered.

LAUREL, by Dale Wood, was named for the composer's niece, and included in *Young Children Sing,* 1967, as the setting for "Good morning, Sun!" The soprano and tenor voices are in canon.

Wood, of Finnish-Polish parentage, was born February 13, 1934, in Glendale, California. At age thirteen, with no formal music training, he entered a hymn-writing contest sponsored by the Luther League, and his entry was selected from fifty-four hymns submitted by youth and adults in the nationwide competition. His first anthem was published in 1951 when he was serving as organist and choirmaster at Hope Lutheran Church in Hollywood, California. In 1951 also he was the recipient of a scholarship to Occidental College in Los Angeles, but chose instead to attend Los Angeles City College for two years, after which he studied for a year at the Los Angeles Institute for the Arts. In 1959 he published an anthem, "Christ is made the sure foundation" (LBW 367), for the seventy-fifth anniversary of Eden Lutheran Church, Riverside, California, where he served until 1968. From 1968 to 1976 he was organist and choirmaster at the Episcopal Church of St. Mary the Virgin in San Francisco, during which time he was also music director for the San Francisco Cathedral School for Boys, 1973–1974. He has written numerous articles on worship, liturgy, and church music and has conducted choral festivals throughout the United States and Canada. He has been an editorial consultant for several hymnals and has made numerous contributions to the Inter-Lutheran Commission on Worship and the international Choristers Guild. There are over three hundred published compositions to his credit, ranging from his first hymn to a major music drama scored for symphony orchestra. He continues his work as a composer and editor of church music from his home at The Sea Ranch in Northern California.

269 AWAKE, MY SOUL, AND WITH THE SUN

Tune: Morning Hymn

Born at Little Berkhampstead, Hertfordshire, England, in July of 1637, Thomas Ken was nine years old when his parents died and he went to live with his brother-in-law, Izaak Walton. He entered Winchester College in 1652 and Hart Hall, Oxford, in 1656. Becoming a fellow at New College, Oxford, the following year, he completed a Bachelor of Arts degree in 1661, and a Master of Arts degree three years later. He was ordained in 1662 and served for three years as curate of Little Easton in Essex, and for one year as domestic chaplain to Bishop Morley, a friend of Izaak Walton. Elected a fellow of Winchester in 1666, he was curate of Brightstone on the Isle of Wight from 1667 to 1669. For ten years he was prebendary of Winchester Cathedral and College, and chaplain to the bishop. While he was there he prepared *A Manual of Prayers for Use of the Scholars of Winchester College,* 1674, in which he suggested the use of three hymns for "Morning," "Evening," and "Midnight." He later wrote such hymns, publishing them separately in 1692, and including them in the Appendix to the second edition of *A Manual of Prayers,* 1695. Two of these hymns, "Awake, my soul," and "All praise to Thee" (LBW 278), have come into widespread use in English hymnals, and the doxology with which he closed both is the very familiar one used most often with the tune "Old Hundredth" (LBW 564, 565). In 1679 he went to The Hague as chaplain to Princess Mary, later Queen Mary, wife of William II of Orange, but was dismissed after a year for speaking out against a case of immorality at the Court. In 1683 he was a member (along with Samuel Pepys) of Lord Dartmouth's expedition to Tangier. Appointed bishop of Bath and Wells by Charles II in 1685, he later attended Charles' deathbed. James II, who succeeded Charles, declared Ken to be the most eloquent Protestant preacher of his time, but nevertheless imprisoned him along with six other bishops at the Tower of London for their refusal to subscribe to the Declaration of Indulgence. All seven were later acquitted. Deprived of his See for refusing to take the coronation oath to William of Orange in 1691, he retired to the home of his friend, Lord Weymouth, at Longleat, Wiltshire, where he died on March 19, 1711.

Both the Morning and Evening hymns underwent several alterations by Ken. The 1709 version of "Awake, my soul," from which the LBW text is taken, consisted originally of fourteen stanzas. Julian* pp. 618-619, gives the texts before and after revision.

MORNING HYMN. Although we know that Ken sang his three hymns to the viol or spinet, we do not know the tunes he used. The present tune was composed by François Barthélémon at the request of Jacob Duché (1737-1798), a native of Philadelphia, who was chaplain of the Female Orphan Asylum, Westminster Bridge Road, London. It was first published in the Supplement to *Hymns and Psalms Used at the Asylum for Female Orphans,* which appeared in 1789 or before.

François Hippolite Barthélémon, born at Bordeaux on July 27, 1741, was the oldest of sixteen children. His father was a French army officer; his mother, an Irish lady of a wealthy family. A perfect gentleman, well-educated in the diverse fields of music, fencing, and modern languages and Hebrew, he served for some time as an officer in the Duke of Berwick's regiment of the Irish brigade, but was persuaded to give up his military career in order to pursue music. He became an accomplished violinist, and served as the director of the Opera orchestra in London and later of the orchestra at Vauxhall Gardens (1770-1776). His compositions included operas, string quartets, a violin concerto, and catches and glees. When Franz Joseph Haydn (LBW 358) visited London in 1791 and 1794, he came to know Barthélémon and a warm friendship developed between the two, with Haydn later giving lessons to Barthélémon's daughter, Cecilia. Barthélémon died in London, July 23, 1808.

270 GOD OF OUR LIFE, ALL-GLORIOUS LORD
Tune: Grosser Gott

This hymn by Paul Zeller Strodach (LBW 143) was written for the *Service Book and Hymnal,* 1958.

GROSSER GOTT is found at LBW 535.

271 O SPLENDOR OF THE FATHER'S LIGHT
(Splendor Paternae gloriae)
Tune: Splendor Paternae

There is very little question among scholars that this hymn is definitely the work of Ambrose (LBW 28). It is ascribed to him by Fulgentius, Bishop of Ruspe, North Africa, who died in 533, and it is found in manuscripts as early as *c.* 700. Described by James Mearns in Julian* as

"A beautiful morning hymn, to the Holy Trinity, but especially to Christ as the Light of the World, and a prayer for help and guidance throughout the day," this hymn was used from very ancient times for Lauds (sunrise) on Monday.

A new translation has been prepared for the LBW by Gracia Grindal (LBW 32).

SPLENDOR PATERNAE, the Sarum (Salisbury, England) melody for this text, was not limited to this hymn, but served also as a setting for several other Latin hymns.

272 ABIDE WITH ME
Tune: Eventide

It is not known for sure when this hymn was written. An article in the *Spectator,* October 3, 1925, cited evidence that Henry Lyte composed it in 1820, after visiting a dying friend. In a letter to his daughter, Julia, written in August of 1847, Lyte included a copy which he referred to as "my latest effusion." According to tradition, he handed the hymn, together with a tune he had written, to a near relative on September 4, 1847, after preaching and administering communion to his congregation for the last time. Possibly Lyte wrote the hymn in 1820 and recalled it in 1847 with the approach of his own death.

Henry Francis Lyte, born June 1, 1793, at Ednam, Kelso, in Scotland, received a Bachelor of Arts degree at Trinity College, Dublin, in 1814. There he received the prize for an English poem three times. Having first considered entering the medical profession, he chose instead to take holy orders, and first served at Taghmon, near Wexford. After being "jostled from one curacy to another," he became perpetual curate in 1823 of Lower Brixham, Devon, a fishing village, where he remained for the rest of his life. Never of robust health, Lyte suffered from asthma and tuberculosis later in his life, and found the labors of his parish to be undermining his strength. He went to the Continent to regain his health, but to no avail, and died in Nice on November 20, 1847. He published three volumes of poetry during his lifetime.

EVENTIDE was written by William Henry Monk for this hymn for the Original Edition, 1861, of *Hymns Ancient and Modern.* One account relates that Monk realized at the end of one of the meetings for the preparation of that hymnal that there was no tune for the text, so he immediately sat down and, in spite of piano lessons in session in the room, wrote the tune in ten minutes. His widow, however, described it as having been written in her presence, while the couple were watching a sunset at a time of sorrow.

William H. Monk, editor of the *Parish Choir* and of several hymnals, is chiefly famous for his service as music editor of the Original Edition, 1861, of *Hymns Ancient and Modern* (a title he suggested), as well as of two subsequent editions, 1875 and 1889, of that hymnal.

Born at Brompton, London, March 16, 1823, Monk became an organist and served successively at Eaton Chapel, Pimlico; St. George's Chapel, Albemarle Street; Portman Chapel, Marylebone; and finally after 1852, at St. Matthias' Church, Stoke Newington, where he promoted congregational singing and established a daily choral service. At King's College, London, he served as choirmaster from 1847, as organist from 1849, and from 1874, as professor of vocal music. For some time also he was professor of music at the School for the Indigent Blind and at Bedford College, London. He received an honorary Doctor of Music degree from Durham University in 1882, and died seven years later, on March 1, in London.

273 O CHRIST, YOU ARE THE LIGHT AND DAY
(Christe, qui lux es et dies)
Tune: Christe, der du bist Tag und Licht

This Latin hymn by an unknown author is first found cited in the Rule of St. Caesarius, about 502, and is called "Ambrosian" (see LBW 28 for Ambrose) by Hincmar, Archbishop of Rheims, in his ninth-century treatise, *Contra Godeschalcum . . . Dê una et non Trinâ Deitate.* It had exceptionally wide use, being found not only in the usual Lenten cycle of the West, but in the Mozarabic and Ambrosian rites as well. During the sixteenth century a German version, possibly prepared by Martin Luther's friend and pupil, Erasmus Alberus, was included in the Erfurt *Enchiridia,* 1524, and Miles Coverdale included an English version in his *Goostly Psalmes,* 1539. In Dutch hymnody it occupied a unique position, being the only hymn to pass uninterrupted from the ancient office books into use in the Reformed Church. At a time when hymns were forbidden and only metrical psalms were allowed, this hymn was appended to the authorized metrical psalter of Peter Datheen, 1566. From later Dutch sources it became universally popular in South Africa.

Stanzas 1-3 are from a translation by William John Copeland included in his *Hymns for the Week, and Hymns for the Seasons,* London, 1848, and are given here with some alteration. Stanza 4 is from Isaac Watts's (LBW 39) *Psalms of David,* 1719, and is also slightly altered.

Born at Chigwell in England on September 1, 1804, Copeland attended Trinity College, Oxford, receiving successively a Bachelor of Arts degree (1829), a Master of Arts degree (1831), and a Bachelor of Divinity degree (1840). He was a fellow, and later dean, of his college. Following his ordination he served as curate of Hackney, and later of Littlemore. In 1849 he was appointed rector of Farnham in Essex, and rural dean of Newport. He died at Farnham on August 25, 1885.

Copeland's *Hymns for the Week* consisted mostly of translations from the Roman Breviary, and preceded those of Edward Caswall (LBW 37) by a year. He was also the editor of Cardinal John Newman's *Sermons.*

CHRISTE, DER DU BIST TAG UND LICHT is an adaptation of the plainsong melody proper to this hymn, which appeared with Wolfgang Meuslin's German version of the hymn in Joseph Klug's *Geistliche Lieder,* 1533 (LBW 85). The harmonization found here is from the *Neues Choralbuch,* 1956.

274 THE DAY YOU GAVE US, LORD, HAS ENDED
Tune: St. Clement

John Ellerton (LBW 262) wrote this hymn in 1870 for *A Liturgy for Missionary Meetings* and revised it for *Church Hymns,* 1871. The first line has been altered from "The day *Thou gavest,* Lord, *is* ended."

ST. CLEMENT was written for this text and appeared in *Church Hymns with Tunes,* 1874.

Clement Cotterill Scholefield, who composed many hymn tunes, was the son of a member of parliament. He was born June 22, 1839, at Edgbaston in Birmingham, England, and attended St. John's College, Cambridge, receiving a Bachelor of Arts degree in 1864 and a Master of Arts degree in 1867. Ordained the same year, he served parishes at Hove, Brighton, 1867; St. Peter's, South Kensington, 1869; and St. Luke's, Chelsea, 1879. In 1880 he became chaplain at Eton College, and from 1890 until his retirement in 1895, was vicar of Holy Trinity, Knightsbridge. He died September 10, 1904, at Godalming.

275 O TRINITY, O BLESSED LIGHT *(O lux beata, Trinitas)*
Tune: O heilige Dreifaltigkeit

This hymn is ascribed to Ambrose (LBW 28) in Hincmar of Rheims's treatise *De unâ et non Trinâ Deitate,* written in 857, and is one of twelve hymns regarded by the Benedictine editors as undoubtedly the work of Ambrose. Some sources question the attribution to Ambrose, since it is found in universal use in the West except in the early Milan liturgy. It can be found in various manuscripts beginning with the eighth century. Generally it was sung at Vespers (sunset) on Saturday, and sometimes also at Lauds (sunrise) or Vespers on Trinity Sunday.

Martin Luther's (LBW 48) last hymn was a translation of this Latin text to German, as "Der du bist drei in Einigkeit." The English translation has been prepared for the LBW by Gracia Grindal (LBW 32).

O HEILIGE DREIFALTIGKEIT was composed by Nikolaus Herman (LBW 47) for his text, "Wer hie für Gott will sein gerecht," in his *Die Sontags Euangelica vber das gantze Jar,* Wittenberg, 1560 (Zahn* #376). Three years later Herman transferred the tune to "Freut euch, ihr Christen alle gleich," and thereafter the tune was used with various texts until it came to be used with "O heilige Dreifaltigkeit" in Johann Stötzel's *Harfen- und Psalterspiel,* published in 1744 in Stuttgart. Originally the melody had the form given below.

276 NOW ALL THE WOODS ARE SLEEPING
(Nun ruhen alle Wälder)
Tune: O Welt, ich muss dich lassen

See LBW 23 for Paul Gerhardt. This masterpiece of hymnody, noted in Julian* to have been a special favorite of Johann C. F. von Schiller's mother, as well as of the poet himself, was first printed in the 1648 edition of Johann Crüger's (LBW 23) *Praxis Pietatis Melica*. Robert Bridges' (LBW 123) English version, "The duteous day now closeth," was included in the *Service Book and Hymnal*, 1958. A new text, using the opening line of Catherine Winkworth's (LBW 29) translation, and some material from Robert Bridges, was prepared for the LBW by the Inter-Lutheran Commission on Worship.

For O WELT, ICH MUSS DICH LASSEN see LBW 222.

277 TO YOU, BEFORE THE CLOSE OF DAY *(Te lucis ante terminum)*
Tune: Jam lucis

This ancient hymn has been in universal use at the daily service of Compline (at nightfall) throughout the Western Church. It is found in the earliest Ambrosian manuscripts, but is not attributed to Ambrose (LBW 28).

Many have translated this popular hymn. John Mason Neale's (LBW 34) translation, "Before the ending of the day," was included in his *The Hymnal Noted*, 1851, and has been adapted for use in the LBW.

JAM LUCIS, a Benedictine plainsong, is one of several tunes associated with "Jam lucis orto sidere" (LBW 268). It has frequently been set in Anglican chant in four parts, and is given thus in *The Church Hymnary*, London, 1927.

The harmonization found here was prepared by Carl Schalk (LBW 118) for the *Worship Supplement*, 1969, to *The Lutheran Hymnal*.

278 ALL PRAISE TO THEE, MY GOD, THIS NIGHT
Tune: Tallis' Canon

See LBW 269 for Thomas Ken. The LBW text is selected from the two versions of Ken's "Evening Hymn," published in 1696 and 1709.

TALLIS' CANON. Spanning the entire period in English music from Robert Fayrfax to Orlando Gibbons (LBW 206), Thomas Tallis' career touched the reign of several monarchs, both Roman Catholic and Protestant. His sacred compositions, like those of William Byrd and Christopher Tye (LBW 114), included settings of both Latin and English texts. Born around 1505, probably in Leicestershire, Tallis served for several years as organist at Waltham Abbey before it was dissolved in 1540. Beginning about that time he also became a gentleman of the Royal Chapel, serving jointly for a time with Byrd, remaining in that position until his death. In 1575 Queen Elizabeth issued a twenty-one-year patent on printing music and music paper to Tallis and Byrd, the earliest such monopoly issued in England. Tallis was married in 1552, and was living at Greenwich at the time of his death on November 23, 1585.

About 1560 Archbishop Matthew Parker prepared *The whole Psalter translated into English Metre, which contayneth an hundreth and fifty Psalmes.* This book, the first versification of the entire book of Psalms to be done by one person, is also probably the first psalter printed by

John Day (LBW 234). For this psalter Thomas Tallis provided nine tunes, with the nature of the first eight (one in each of the ecclesiastical modes) described in the *Psalter* as follows:

> The first is meeke: devout to see,
> The second is sad: in maiesty,
> The third doth rage: and roughly brayth,
> The fourth doth fawne: and flattry playth,
> The fyfth deligth: and laugheth the more,
> The sixth bewayleth: it weepeth full sore,
> The seventh tredeth stout: in froward race,
> The eighth goeth milde: in modest pace.

"Tallis' Canon" is the eighth of these tunes, and originally was set to Psalm 67.

279   OH, GLADSOME LIGHT (Φῶς ἱλαρὸν ἀγίας δόξης)
Tune: Elizabeth

"Oh, gladsome light" is an ancient Greek hymn which provides us with a link with the early Church. Sung as a part of the Greek Vesper office which was held at the time of lighting of lamps, this "Candlelight Hymn" has continued to be used for the same office in the Greek Church until the present day. Nothing is known of the authorship of the hymn, but it is known to have existed before the fourth century, for St. Basil (*c.* 370) referred to it as "ancient."

A translation by Robert Bridges (LBW 123) was included in the *Service Book and Hymnal*, 1958 (#220). The present text comes from Longfellow's *Christus, A Mystery*, Part II, 1893, with slight alterations.

Henry Wadsworth Longfellow, brother of Samuel (LBW 257), who counted four of the Pilgrims—including John Alden, Priscilla Mullens, and Elder Brewster—among his ancestors, was born February 27, 1807, in Portland, Maine. At the age of fifteen he entered Bowdoin College, Brunswick, Maine, as a sophomore, and there met Nathaniel Hawthorne with whom he later became close friends. Following his graduation in 1825 he accepted a projected professorship of modern languages on the condition that he study abroad, and from 1826 to 1829 he traveled in France, Spain, Italy, and Germany, laying the foundation for his mastery not only of those languages, but of Swedish, Finnish, Dutch, Portuguese, Old English, and Provençal as well. While serving as professor at Bowdoin from 1829 to 1835, he was married in 1831 to Mary Storer Potter of Portland. In 1835 he was appointed professor of modern languages and belles lettres at Harvard and left again for a period of study abroad. His wife, who had accompanied him there, died suddenly of a fever in Rotterdam. He returned to America in 1836 and lectured brilliantly at Harvard until he resigned in 1854 to devote himself totally to writing. He was married in 1843 to Frances Elizabeth Appleton, and they became the parents of six children. His second wife died in 1861, of burns received when her dress caught fire. Longfellow's later years were filled with many honors and good friendships. On a trip to Europe with his family in 1868-1869, he was honored with a Doctor of Letters degree from Cambridge, and Doctor of Civil Laws degree from Oxford, and was given a private audience by the Queen. He died in Cambridge, Massachusetts, on March 24, 1882, and two years later a bust of him was unveiled in the Poets' Corner of Westminster Abbey. He was the first American to be so honored.

Many of Longfellow's works are familiar to all—*The Village Blacksmith* (1840), *Evangeline* (1847), *The Song of Hiawatha* (1855), and *The Courtship of Miles Standish* (1858), to name a few. His translation of Alighieri Dante's *Divine Comedy* helped introduce American readers to that work, and *The Poets and Poetry of Europe* (1845) was an important step toward cosmopolitanism in American literature.

ELIZABETH was written by Allan Mahnke for Longfellow's translation and is published here for the first time.

Mahnke, born June 16, 1944, in St. Louis, Missouri, received a Bachelor of Arts degree from Concordia Senior College, Fort Wayne, Indiana, in 1966. On completion of a Master of Divinity degree at Concordia Seminary, St. Louis, he served from 1970 to 1973 as minister of music at Jehovah Lutheran Church, St. Paul, Minnesota. In 1972 he received a Master of Fine Arts degree from the University of Minnesota, where he was an instructor in organ, working as a teaching assistant to Dr. Heinrich Fleischer. Since 1972 he has been director of music development at Augsburg Publishing House, Minneapolis, and since 1973, has also served as minister of music at Cross View Lutheran Church, Edina, Minnesota. He has published a number of choral works.

280   NOW THE DAY IS OVER

Tune: Merrial

Sabine Baring-Gould, writer of a prodigious amount of literature in the fields of religion, travel, fiction, and verse, is said to have more works attached to his name in the British Museum catalogue than any other writer of his time. Especially important among his works are his *Lives of the Saints* (fifteen volumes, 1872–1877), *Curious Myths of the Middle Ages,* (two series, 1866–1868), *The Origin and Development of Religious Belief* (two volumes, 1869–1870), and two collections of folk songs, *Songs and Ballads of the West* (in collaboration with H. Fleetwood Shepherd, 1889–1891) and *A Garland of Country Song,* 1894.

Born at Lew-Trenchard, the 3,000-acre family estate at Exeter, England, on January 28, 1834, Baring-Gould spent much of his early life in Germany and France. He received a Bachelor of Arts degree from Clare College, Cambridge, in 1854 and a Master of Arts degree two years later. Ordained a deacon in 1864 and a priest in 1865, he served Horbury and Dalton in Yorkshire, and East Mersea, Colchester, in Essex. In 1881 he became rector of the family estate which he inherited from his father, which had been in the family for three hundred years. Although he was an aristocrat, he was democratic in his ideas. He fell in love with Grace Taylor, a girl of fine character who worked as a mill-hand, and supported her education at a boarding school. They were married in 1868, and the marriage, to which fifteen children were born, was an ideally happy one. Baring-Gould lived to be nearly ninety years old; he died January 2, 1924, at Lew-Trenchard.

"Now the day is over" was written for the children of Horbury Bridge during Baring-Gould's ministry in that parish and was first published in *The Church Times,* February 16, 1867. The hymn was repeated the following year in the Appendix to the Original Edition of *Hymns Ancient and Modern.*

MERRIAL. Barnby's tune was written in 1868, and included with this text in Barnby's *Original Tunes to Popular Hymns,* 1869. Robert McCutchan in his *Hymn Tune Names* notes that in Charles Robinson's *Laudes Domini,* 1884, the tune was called "Emmelar." "Emmelar," which represented "M. L. R.," Dr. Robinson's daughter's initials, was later changed to "Merrial" for "Mary L."

Joseph Barnby, born August 12, 1838, at York in England, was the son of an organist. He was a chorister at St. George's, Windsor, and later studied at the Royal Academy of Music. By the time he was twelve years old he was an organist and choirmaster, and after several lesser positions, he went to St. Andrew's, Wells Street, where from 1863 to 1871 he developed the music program to one of high reputation. From 1871 to 1886 he was at St. Anne's, Soho, where he established annual Lenten performances of the *St. John Passion.* In 1871, also, he conducted at Westminster Abbey the first performance of J. S. Bach's (LBW 219) *St. Matthew Passion* in an English church. He was precentor and director of musical instruction at Eton College from 1875, and remained there until he became principal of the Guildhall School of Music in 1892.

Barnby was musical advisor to Novello, Ltd., from 1861 to 1867. In 1867 he became conductor of "Barnby's Choir," which had been formed by Novello. This group was joined in 1872 by Charles Gounod's choir at Albert Hall, creating the Royal Albert Hall Choral Society. Barnby was also first conductor of the London Musical Society. He conducted the first performances in England of Anton Dvořák's *Stabat Mater* (1883) and Richard Wagner's *Parsifal* (1884). He was a fellow of the Royal Academy of Music, and was knighted in 1892. He died suddenly, a few hours after conducting a rehearsal of G. F. Handel's (LBW 29) *Judas Maccabaeus,* on January 28, 1896. His compositions include an oratorio (*Rebekah*), a number of part songs and vocal solos, as well as a large number of services and anthems, and 246 hymn tunes. He was editor of *The Hymnary,* 1872; *The Congregational Mission Hymnal,* 1890; *The Congregational Sunday School Hymnal,* 1891; and *The Home and School Hymnal,* 1893; and was one of the editors of *The Cathedral Psalter,* 1873.

281   GOD, WHO MADE THE EARTH AND HEAVEN

Tune: Ar hyd y nos

This hymn has come to us in stages. Reginald Heber's (LBW 84) hymn of a single stanza, beginning "God that madest earth and heaven," was one of two evening hymns included in his *Hymns,* 1827. It was included with a second stanza (our third stanza) by Richard Whately in *Sacred Poetry adapted to the Understanding of Children and Youth,* Dublin, 1838. Whately's stanza is a free translation of the Antiphon for the Nunc Dimittis at Compline:

> Salve nos, Domine, vigilantes; custodi nos dormientes;
> ut vigilemus in Christo, et requiescamus in pace.

For his *Church Psalter and Hymn Book,* 1864, William Mercer added two stanzas of his own. Each of the four stanzas has been altered slightly for the LBW.

Whately was born in St. Marylebone, London, on February 1, 1787, and educated at Oriel College, Oxford, receiving successively Bachelor of Arts (1808), Master of Arts (1812), and Bachelor and Doctor of Divinity (1825) degrees. Ordained a priest in 1814, he was appointed Bampton Lecturer in 1822, and three years later became principal of St. Alban's Hall, Oxford. In 1832 he founded a chair of political economy at Trinity College, Dublin. After 1831 he was bishop of Dublin, where he died October 8, 1863. He was a member of the Royal Irish Academy, and in 1833 took a seat in the House of Lords.

Although his hymns were few, Whately wrote extensively in the field of polemics. He wrote an interesting work entitled *Historic Doubts Relative to Napoleon Bonaparte* in response to some German critics who were at the time denying that Christ had ever lived, and is also credited with the *Letters on the Church by an Episcopalian* which helped initiate the Tractarian Movement.

Born in 1811 at Barnard Castle, Durham, England, William Mercer studied at Trinity College, Cambridge, receiving a Bachelor of Arts degree in 1836 and a Master of Arts degree five years later. In 1840 he was appointed to the parish of St. George's Sheffield,† where he remained for thirty-three years. During his ministry there the Day and Sunday Schools were erected and the church was filled to capacity. He died suddenly at Leavy Greave, Sheffield, August 21, 1873.

Mercer's chief claim to fame lies in the work he edited with James Montgomery (LBW 50) and John Goss (LBW 549), *The Church Psalter and Hymn Book, comprising The Psalter, or Psalms of David, together with the Canticles, Pointed for Chanting; Four Hundred Metrical Hymns and Six Responses to the Commandments; the whole united to appropriate Chants and Tunes, for the use of Congregations and Families,* 1854. For many years this collection was the most widely-circulated and influential hymnal in the Church of England; by 1864 its annual sale is said to have been 100,000.

AR HYD Y NOS, a traditional Welsh melody whose title literally means "on length of night," or "the livelong night," is first found in Edward Jones's *Musical Relicks of the Welsh Bards,* Dublin, 1784. There it was arranged for solo voice and harp variations as can be seen in the facsimile included in *The Hymnal Companion,* page 126. Reginald Heber is said to have written his hymn after hearing a harper play this tune in a Welsh home one evening. In Joshua Leavitt's (LBW 243) *The Christian Lyre,* New York, 1830, the tune was set to "There's a friend above all other," and bears the note, "This is a favorite piece among the Welch [*sic.*] and much used in their revivals. It was sent in manuscript from Bristol to a gentleman in New York, who kindly gave it to the Lyre." In some of Lowell Mason's (LBW 353) collections the tune was set to "When the spark of life is waning, Weep not for me." It is also well-known with the secular song, "All through the night."

The harmonization by Ralph Vaughan Williams (LBW 101) was included in *The English Hymnal,* 1906.

---

†Closed in 1978.

282 NOW REST BENEATH NIGHT'S SHADOW
(Nun ruhen alle Wälder)

Tune: O Welt, ich muss dich lassen

This is the same hymn as that given at LBW 276. The translation here is a composite one prepared for *The Lutheran Hymnal,* 1941.

For O WELT, ICH MUSS DICH LASSEN see LBW 222.

283 O GOD, SEND HERALDS

Tune: Intercessor

Written in connection with the celebration of the 100th anniversary of the founding of the Pacific School of Religion in Berkeley, California, this hymn was published in *Ten New Hymns on the Ministry,* 1966, of the Hymn Society of America. The opening line has been altered from "O God, send men whose purpose will not falter," and several other changes have been made for the LBW as well.

Elisabeth Havens Burrowes was born January 13, 1885, in Detroit, Michigan, and was educated at home until she was ten years old. She attended Peddie Institute, a coeducational Baptist boarding school near Princeton, New Jersey, where she met her future husband, Paul deNysse Burrowes. For a year she studied at Vassar College, but a temporary ebb in the family finances made it impossible for her to continue. She was married in 1908 and, as the wife of a civil engineer, moved frequently during the first ten years of her married life. After 1918 the family, which included five children, went to live in Englewood, New Jersey. Although she had completed only one year at college, Mrs. Burrowes continued a life-long pursuit of knowledge and employed her gift for writing. She was the author of two children's books, *Little Thunder* and *Good Night;* and a number of hymns and poems, several of which were published in *Christian Century.* During the Depression she turned from writing to teaching music to provide a more dependable income. At Dwight School she contributed translations of many folk songs, and the texts for two or three complete music dramas. After her husband's death in 1948 she became one of the first two women elders in the First Presbyterian Church of Englewood. In 1957 she moved to Berkeley, California, to be with her sister. There she was active in St. John's Presbyterian Church, and later in South Berkeley Community Church, where she found great strength in the interracial fellowship. For the congregation's twentieth anniversary she prepared a hymn, "Almighty God, we pray thee still to guide us." During her years in California she "studied Greek, had a crusading interest in nutrition, revelled in a course led by Pablo Casals, and followed the course of the Giants and Willie Mays with gusto." She died in Berkeley on March 27, 1975.

INTERCESSOR was written for Ada Rundall Greenaway's hymn, "O word of pity," in the 1904 edition of *Hymns Ancient and Modern.*

The composer, Charles Hubert Hastings Parry, was born at Bournemouth, England, on February 27, 1848. He took the Oxford Bachelor of Music degree while still a student at Eton, and later graduated from Exeter College, Oxford, Bachelor of Arts, in 1870. His father opposed his devoting himself to music, and for three years beginning in 1871 he held a post at Lloyd's, but found it did not suit him. Returning to music he became professor of composition and lecturer in music history at the Royal College of Music in 1883, succeeding Sir John Stainer (LBW 56). In 1894 he became director of the Royal College of Music, following Sir George Grove, who had earlier invited Parry to assist him in the compilation of the *Dictionary of Music and Musicians.* He was honored with Doctor of Music degrees by Cambridge in 1883, Oxford in 1884, and Dublin in 1891, and in 1894 Durham University conferred on him the Doctor of Civil Law degree. Knighted in 1898, he was later also created a baronet. He died October 7, 1918, at Rustington, Littlehampton, Sussex, and is buried at St. Paul's Cathedral.

Parry was a man of many and varied interests. He was a gifted lecturer and teacher and a masterly writer on musical subjects. His books include *The Art of Music,* 1893; Volume II of the *Oxford History of Music,* 1902; *Style in Musical Art,* 1911; and a work on *Bach.* Also highly regarded as a composer, he wrote five symphonies, an opera, cantatas, and organ works as well as a number of hymn tunes.

284 CREATOR SPIRIT, HEAVENLY DOVE *(Veni, Creator Spiritus)*
Tune: Komm, Gott Schöpfer

See LBW 472 for a discussion of this Latin hymn. Martin Luther (LBW 48) prepared a German translation beginning "Komm, Gott Schöpfer heiliger Geist," which was published in the Erfurt *Enchiridia,* 1524. The English translation of stanzas 1 and 3 is from Richard Massie's (LBW 134) *Martin Luther's Spiritual Songs,* 1854; stanzas 2, 4, 6, and 7 are from Edward Caswall's (LBW 37) *Lyra Catholica,* 1849; and stanza 5 is from Robert Campbell's (LBW 210) *Hymns and Anthems,* 1850.

KOMM, GOTT SCHÖPFER, based on the plainsong melody proper to "Veni, Creator Spiritus" (LBW 472), was included with Luther's translation, "Komm, Gott Schöpfer heiliger Geist," in Joseph Klug's (LBW 85) *Geistliche Lieder,* 1533. (See illustration, p. 352.)

285 SPIRIT OF GOD, SENT FROM HEAVEN ABROAD
(Du, som gaar ud fra den levende Gud)
Tune: Du, som gaar ud

See LBW 62 for Nicolai Grundtvig. James Montgomery's "O Spirit of the Living God" (LBW 388) served as the basis for this Danish hymn published in Grundtvig's *Sang-Värke til den Danske Kirke,* 1837. It has in turn been translated to English by Johannes H. V. Knudsen (LBW 193) for the LBW.

DU, SOM GAAR UD was composed by Ludvig Lindeman.

Ludvig Matthias Lindeman, the most famous of a family of Norwegian musicians, was born in Trondhjem on November 28, 1812. His grandfather, Christopher Madsen, who had studied medicine in London when G. F. Handel's (LBW 39) career was at its prime, changed his name to Lindeman when he set up medical practice in Trondhjem. Ludvig's father, Ole Andreas Lindeman, was a successful concert pianist; organist at Vor Frue Kirke, Trondhjem, for fifty-seven years; and editor of the first Norwegian chorale book, the 1835 *Choralebog.* Ludvig

widderbracht haft / auff das wir von der gewalt des Teuffels erlöset / inn dem reiche leben / Verleihe vns / das wir solches von gantzem hertzen gleuben / vnd inn solchem glauben bestendig / dich allzeit loben vnd dir dancken / Durch den selbigen deinen Son Jhesum Christum vnsern Herrn / Amen.

Der Hymnus / Veni creator spiritus.

Martinus Luther.

Kom

fo. m.

Kom got schöpffer heiliger geist / besuch

das hertz der menschen dein / Mit gna-
(den er-

fol wie du weist / das dein geschepff vor-
(hin fein

Denn du bist der tröster genand / des aller höchsten gabe thewr / Ein geistlich salb an vns gewand / ein lebend brun lieb vnd fewr.

fünd

fo. 12.

fünd vns ein liecht an jn verstand / gib vns jns hertz der liebe brunst / Das schwach fleisch inn vns dir bekand / erhalt fest dein krafft vnd gunst.

Du bist mit gaben siebenfalt / der finger an Gotts rechter hand / Des Vaters wort gibstu gar bald / mit zungen jnn alle land.

Des feindes list treib von vns fern / den fried schaff bey vns deine gnad / Das wir dein leiten folgen gern / vnd meiden der selen schad.

Ler vns den Vater kennen wol / das zu Jhesum Christ seinen son / Das wir des glaubens werden vol / Dich beyder geist zuuersehon.

Gott Vater sey lob vnd dem son / der von den todten aufferstund / Dem Tröster sey dasselb gethon / jnn ewigkeit alle stund. Amen.

C iij   Veni

studied music with his father and substituted at the organ for him at the age of twelve. When he went to Oslo to study theology (his father had not encouraged music as a profession), he often substituted for his brother as organist at Vor Frelsers Kirke, and also played cello in the theater orchestra. He soon realized that he had to choose music as a vocation, however, and in 1839, succeeded his brother at Vor Frelsers Kirke. This position he held for the rest of his life, becoming a virtuoso organist and improviser. For twenty-seven years he served together with Wilhelm A. Wexels (LBW 351), with whom there was some rivalry at times—Lindeman felt that Wexels' sermons were too long; Wexels, in turn, suggested that Lindeman's playing took over the service. In 1871 Lindeman was invited to play a series of recitals for the dedication of the new organ in the Royal Albert Hall, London. He was married in 1848 to Aminda Magnhilde Brynie, and with his son, Peter, in 1883, established what is today the Oslo Conservatory, the first music conservatory established in Norway. He was known as an excellent teacher and his influence was felt in Norwegian organ playing for generations to come. He also taught liturgical music at the theological seminary. He died May 23, 1887.

Lindeman published much music, including organ music, as well as hymn collections and liturgical works. His two major contributions were his *Koralbog, indeholdende de i Landstads Salmebog forekommende Melodier,* and his collecting of Norwegian folk tunes. The *Koralbog,* a book of melodies for Magnus B. Landstad's (LBW 310) hymnal, was completed in 1871, and in 1877 was authorized in preference to Erik C. Hoff's *Melodibog* (see LBW 256). Lindeman recorded some 2500 folk melodies for posterity, a large number of which were published in his *Ældre og Nyere Norske Fjeldmelodier,* 1853.

Roger Petrich (LBW 64) has prepared the harmonization.

286 BOW DOWN YOUR EAR, ALMIGHTY LORD

Tune: Herr Jesu Christ, meins

Written in 1864, this hymn was included in Thomas Edward Powell's *Hymns, Anthems, &c., for Public Worship,* a compilation that was begun in 1855 and gradually expanded during the next quarter century to ninety-seven hymns. Originally the first line read "Bow down *thine* ear, almighty Lord."

Powell was born at Hampstead, Middlesex, England, on August 22, 1823, and received a Bachelor of Arts degree in 1845. Ordained the following year, he served first as curate of Cookham-Dean, near Maidenhead, and after 1848 was vicar of Bisham. In addition to *Hymns, Anthems, &c.,* he published *The Holy Feast* in 1868. He died February 8, 1901.

HERR JESU CHRIST, MEINS (also "Breslau") is originally found in the mid-fifteenth century as a folksong, "Ich fahr dahin," in the *Lochamer Liederbuch* (see LBW 86). In 1602 it appeared in a manuscript in Königsberg, Prussia. It was the setting for Martin Behm's text, "Herr Jesu Christ, meins Lebens Licht," in *As hymnodus sacer,* a collection of twelve texts and eight tunes published in Leipzig in 1625 (Zahn* #5339). Felix Mendelssohn (LBW 60) used the melody in his oratorio *St. Paul,* and J. S. Bach (LBW 219) included harmonizations in his *Choralgesänge.*

287 O PERFECT LOVE
Tune: O Perfect Love

Dorothy Frances Blomfield, the daughter of the rector of St. Andrew's, Undershaft, was born at Finsbury Circus, London, England, on October 4, 1858. She was married in 1897 to Gerald Gurney, a onetime actor who was later ordained in the Church of England. In 1919 both were received into the Roman Catholic communion at Farnborough Abbey. She died in Kensington, London, on June 15, 1932. From one of her two volumes of poems, *A Little Book of Quiet,* come the lines:

> The kiss of the sun for pardon,
> The song of the birds for mirth;
> One is nearer God's heart in a garden
> Than anywhere else on earth.

Blomfield wrote "O perfect Love" one Sunday evening in 1884 at Pull Wyke, Ambleside, near Windermere, for her sister's wedding. John B. Dykes's (LBW 165) tune, "Strength and Stay" (see the *Service Book and Hymnal,* 1958, #219), was a favorite of her sister's and she desired a hymn for her wedding which would fit that tune. The author later commented, "The writing of it (in fifteen minutes) was no effort whatever after the initial idea had come to me of the two-fold aspect of perfect union, love and life, and I have always felt that God helped me write it."

O PERFECT LOVE was originally an anthem composed by Joseph Barnby (LBW 280) for the marriage of the Duke and Duchess of Fife in 1889. It was included in its present form in *The Hymnal* (Episcopal) edited by Charles Hutchins, 1892.

288 HEAR US NOW, OUR GOD AND FATHER
Tune: Hyfrydol

Harry Norman Huxhold, pastor of Our Redeemer Lutheran Church, Indianapolis, wrote the first two stanzas of this hymn to provide a congregational hymn invoking God's blessing on the marriage of his son Timothy to Pamela Jo on August 14, 1971. This is the first appearance of the hymn in print.

Born December 21, 1922, at Oak Park, Illinois, Huxhold attended Concordia College, Milwaukee, 1936–1942; Concordia Seminary, St. Louis, 1942–1947; and Concordia Teachers' College, River Forest, Illinois, during the summers of 1944 and 1945, receiving a Bachelor of Arts degree in 1944, and a Master of Divinity degree in 1947. Further studies included work in social and industrial relations at Loyola University, Chicago, 1950–1953; and studies at Chicago Theological Seminary, 1957; Luther Seminary, St. Paul, 1964–1965 (Master of Theology degree, 1968); and Christian Theological Seminary, Indianapolis, 1971–1972 (Doctor of Ministry degree *summa cum laude,* 1972). Beginning in 1947, he was pastor for two years at Trinity Lutheran Church, Darien, Wisconsin, and then worked for four years with the Lutheran Child Welfare Association at Addison, Illinois. From 1953 to 1960 he was pastor of Good Shepherd Lutheran Church, Palos Park, Illinois, during which time he was also an instructor of religion at Luther High School, Chicago, 1955–1956, and at Valparaiso University, 1958–1959. While ministering as campus pastor at University Lutheran Chapel, University of Minnesota, 1960–1965, he also served from 1963 to 1964 as vacancy pastor of Trinity First Lutheran, Minneapolis. Since 1965 he has been at Our Redeemer Church, and in the fall of 1973, was also appointed instructor of homiletics at Christian Theological Seminary.

He has held numerous offices in the church and served on many boards and committees within the church and the community. Most recently he has served as the chairman of the Evangelical Lutherans in Mission task force on higher education, and of the special ministries committee of the Indianapolis Church Federation. In 1974 he became president of the Lutheran Child Welfare Association, and in 1976, first vice president of the English Synod. He has published a large number of books and pamphlets, including *Christian Education and the Urban Parish* (editor), 1968; *The Church in Our House,* 1971; and *Power for the Church in the Midst of Chaos,* 1972; and his articles have appeared in a wide variety of journals. He is listed in the 1975 *Who's Who in Religion,* and was honored with the Eddy Hall Award from the University of Minnesota in 1965, and the Rabbi Morris Feuerlicht Hebrew Award from Chicago Theological Seminary, 1972. Married to Lucille Edythe Koerber, he is the father of five children.

The third stanza, based on 2 Corinthians 13:14, is by John Newton (LBW 261). Written to be sung after the sermon, it was published in *Olney Hymns,* 1779.

For HYFRYDOL see LBW 158. The harmonization is by Gerald Near (LBW 243).

289 HEAVENLY FATHER, HEAR OUR PRAYER
Tune: Name of Jesus

This hymn was written by Barbara E. Adam when she was asked to sing for a friend's wedding. It was later printed on a Lutheran Church in America weekly church bulletin on June 15, 1975. This is its first appearance in a hymnal.

Adam was born June 21, 1939, in Evanston, Illinois, and majored in piano at Western Illinois University, Macomb, Illinois, for a year and a half before transferring to the Lutheran Lay Training Institute, Milwaukee, Wisconsin. Upon graduation from the institute she took a position as a teacher in a newly-opened pre-kindergarten program at Ebenezer Lutheran parochial school in Milwaukee, teaching four year olds of many different faiths music, art, and "anything else [she] saw fit." In addition she and her husband, who was in his second year of training at the institute, undertook some personal evangelism in the city. At the end of a year they went to Regina, Saskatchewan, where her husband served as a lay assistant in the absence of a pastor and she directed the junior and senior choirs at Grace Lutheran Church, the largest Missouri Synod church in Western Canada. When a vacancy occurred in the church at Swift Current, Saskatchewan, they moved there. Since then the vacancy has been filled and she and her husband have worked at secular positions in Swift Current. She is also director of the junior choir at the local congregation of the Evangelical Lutheran Church of Canada.

A musician and an author, Adam has been teaching piano for twenty-five years. She held her first position as a junior choir director at the age of fifteen at Bethany Lutheran Church, Crystal Lake, Illinois, and has since directed choirs off and on at various other churches. She served for one year as organist of Immanuel Lutheran Church in Crystal Lake, and three years at Mt. Calvary Lutheran, Swift Current. She also notes that she has "dabbled in writing all of my life since early grade school." She has written a great deal of devotional material for various publications, including *My Devotions, The Home Altar,* and *Light for Today,* and has published poetry, testimonials, and articles in various journals. She is included in *Who's Who in Poetry,* 1978. Three other hymns have appeared on LCA bulletin covers.

NAME OF JESUS, by Ralph Alvin Strom, was included in the *Service Book and Hymnal,* 1958. There it was the setting for John Mason Neale's (LBW 34) translation of a hymn by Theoctistus of the Studium, "Jesus, Name all names above."

Strom, born October 31, 1901, at St. Paul, Minnesota, was married in 1926 to Mildred Olivia Johnson and became the father of four children. After attending Augsburg College and the University of Minnesota, he graduated from St. Olaf College with a Bachelor of Music degree in 1939, and in 1941 received a Bachelor of Music Education degree at the Minneapolis College of Music. He received a doctorate in 1974. From 1941 to 1944 he taught in the Minneapolis public schools, and after teaching a summer session at Gustavus Adolphus College in 1945, became superintendent of music and choral director at Columbia Heights High School, a position he held until 1967. He began his service as an organist in 1920 at Trinity Lutheran Church in Stillwater, Minnesota, and served also at St. Ansgars Lutheran Church, Cannon Falls, Minnesota, before going in 1924 to Gloria Dei Church in St. Paul where he remained for twelve years. Following nine years at Augustana Lutheran Church in Minneapolis he went in 1945 to Gustavus Adolphus Lutheran Church in St. Paul, where he stayed until his retirement in 1972. Remaining in the Twin Cities area, he served for a time at St. Andrew's Lutheran Church, Mahtomedi. He died January 25, 1977.

Also active in community music affairs, Strom was founder of the Bethesda Hospital Nurses Choir in 1926 and directed the group until 1972. He was a member of the American Guild of Organists and a member and past president of the Twin City Choirmasters Association. In 1957 he was one of a committee which made the arrangements for the Lutheran World Federation in Minneapolis. His compositions include the choral works "O Crimson Flood" and "God is our Refuge and Strength." Four of his hymn tunes were included in *The Hymnal,* 1925, of the Augustana Synod.

290 THERE'S A WIDENESS IN GOD'S MERCY

Tune: Lord, Revive Us

These stanzas are from Faber's hymn beginning "Souls of men, why will ye scatter?" first published in *Oratory Hymns,* 1854.

Frederick William Faber, born in Calverley, Yorkshire, in England on June 28, 1814, was of Huguenot ancestry and was brought up in strict Calvinism. He studied at Balliol and University Colleges, Oxford, where he received a Bachelor of Arts degree in 1836. Appointed a fellow of University College in 1837, he completed a Master of Arts degree two years later. At Oxford he came under the powerful influence of John

Henry Newman and the Oxford Movement. Ordained an Anglican deacon in 1837 and a priest in 1839, he served from 1843 to 1846 at Elton, Huntingdonshire. But in 1846 he, like many others caught up in the Oxford Movement, joined the Roman Catholic Church. In 1849 in London he founded the "Priests of the Congregation of St. Philip Neri," a branch of Newman's order in Birmingham. This London Oratory was moved in 1854 to Brompton, where Faber died September 26, 1863.

Faber wrote a total of 150 hymns, to correspond to the number of the Psalms. While some of these hymns are of poor quality, overly sentimental, or too heavily infused with Roman Catholic theology for use in Protestant hymnals, many of his hymns are of good quality and have come into extensive use. In the preface of his collection, *Jesus and Mary,* 1849, he stated his intention of providing "English Catholic hymns fitted for singing" and recognized the influence of the hymns of William Cowper (LBW 483), John Newton (LBW 261), and the Wesleys (LBW 27 and 302) in his hymn-writing.

LORD, REVIVE US, an anonymous tune, was the setting for John Newton's (LBW 261) "Savior, visit thy plantation" in *The Revivalist: a collection of choice revival hymns and tunes, original and selected,* Troy, New York, 1868, a Methodist collection compiled by Joseph Hillman. The tune name derives from the refrain, which repeats "revive us" five times. Dr. Leonard Ellinwood notes that the second line of Newton's text reads "Grant us, Lord, a gracious rain," and that as early as 1792 someone added the refrain, "Lord, revive us; All our help must come from Thee." The melody is one of many versions of "Holy Manna" (LBW 463) and is related to "Pleading Savior" (LBW 243).

The harmonization was prepared by Theodore Beck (LBW 33) for the *Worship Supplement,* 1969, to *The Lutheran Hymnal.*

291   JESUS SINNERS WILL RECEIVE *(Jesus nimmt die Sünder an)*
Tune: Meinen Jesum lass ich nicht

Erdmann Neumeister, author of cantata texts used by J. S. Bach (LBW 219) and other German composers writing after 1700, was born May 12, 1671, at Üchteritz, near Weissenfels. After receiving a Master of Arts degree from the University of Leipzig in 1695 he remained as university lecturer until 1697 when he took a position as assistant pastor at Bibra. The following year he became full pastor, and assistant superintendent of the Eckartsberg district. In 1704 he went to Weissenfels where he became tutor to the only daughter of Duke Johann George and assistant court preacher. Less than two years later his pupil died and Neumeister went to Sorau as senior court preacher, member of the consistory, and superintendent. In 1718 he published his *Evangelische Nachklang,* and later in his life, also composed tunes to some of his earlier hymns. From 1715 until his death on August 18, 1756, he was pastor of St. James's Church, Hamburg. A defender of High Lutheranism, and strongly opposed to Pietism, he was known in his day as a sincere and eloquent preacher.

This hymn, first published in *Evangelische Nachklang,* is given here in a composite translation prepared for *The Lutheran Hymnal,* 1941.

MEINEN JESUM LASS ICH NICHT was written by Johann Ulich for Christian Keymann's hymn, "Meinen Jesum lass ich nicht," in *M. Michael Schernacks von Treuen Britzen aus der Marke . . . Siebenfache Welte- und Himmels Capell,* Wittenberg, 1674. Originally the tune appeared as given below (Zahn* #3451a).

Adagio

Ulich, who was born in 1634, was organist in Torgau, Germany, from 1654 to 1660. Later he became choirmaster and director of the "Chori musici" in Wittenberg. Considered to be a well-educated musician, he would gladly have had his five collections of sacred cantatas, motets, and so on, published but could not find a publisher. "Meinen Jesum lass ich nicht" is one of seven tunes included in the 1674 collection, which was published by his music-minded pastor at Wittenberg, Michael Schernack. Ulich died in 1712.

The harmonization is from the *Neues Choralbuch,* 1956.

292   GOD LOVED THE WORLD *(Also hat Gott die Welt geliebt)*
Tune: Die helle Sonn leucht

There are numerous German hymns based on John 3:16 which begin "Also hat Gott die Welt geliebt." The origins of the present hymn are unknown. Polack* (LBW 168) lists the earliest known source as the *"Bollhagen Gesangbuch,"* 1791. Dr. August Suelflow of the Concordia Historical Institute has found the hymn in an earlier edition of this hymnal, which is undated, but published together with a prayer book dated 1778. The complete title of this Pomeranian hymnal, published in Stettin, is *Heiliges Lippen- und Herzens-Opfer einer gläubigen Seele oder Vollständiges Gesang-Buch.* Including two supplements and an additional section of new hymns, the book contained a total of 1313 hymns, and was still in print nearly a century later—in 1869. This hymn was published in German in the United States in the *Kirchengesangbuch für Evangelisch-Lutherische Gemeinden,* St. Louis, 1848. August Crull's (LBW 24) English translation was given in the *Evangelical Lutheran Hymn-Book,* 1889. Originally beginning "Our God so loved the world that He," the text is given here with some alterations.

DIE HELLE SONN LEUCHT. In the German hymnals mentioned above, the tune specified for this hymn is "Herr Jesu Christ, meins Lebens" (LBW 286). The present tune was composed by Melchior Vulpius (LBW 115), and included in his *Geistliches Gesangbuch,* Jena, 1609, as the setting for Nikolaus Herman's (LBW 47) "Die helle Sonn' leucht't jetzt herfür" (translated in *The Lutheran Hymnal,* 1941, as "The radiant sun shines in the skies").

Richard Hillert (LBW 63) prepared the harmonization for the LBW.

Tune: The Solid Rock

Edward Mote, born in London, England, on January 21, 1797, was a cabinetmaker by trade. Converted in 1813 by the preaching of the Rev. John Hyatt, he joined the Baptist church two years later. At the age of fifty-five he became a Baptist minister and was pastor of the Horsham Church, Sussex, for over twenty years. He died November 13, 1874.

Originally beginning "Nor earth, nor hell my soul can move," this hymn was written around 1834, and was first sung when Mote went to visit a dying woman in his congregation. He had it printed in the *Spiritual Magazine* and in 1836 Rees of Crown Street, Soho, published it. Later that same year, Mote himself published it with several alterations in *Hymns of Praise: A New Selection of Gospel Hymns, combining all the Excellencies of our Spiritual Poets, with many Originals,* which included a total of one hundred of Mote's originals.

THE SOLID ROCK was composed for this text in 1863 and included in William Batchelder Bradbury's *Devotional Hymn and Tune Book,* Philadelphia, 1864.

A native of York, Maine, born on October 6, 1816, Bradbury went to Boston when he was seventeen years old, where he studied under Lowell Mason (LBW 353) and George J. Webb (LBW 389) at their Boston Academy of Music. For the next few years he alternated between Boston and Maine, teaching singing and giving piano lessons, until he went to New York where he was organist at the Baptist Temple and held free singing classes for children. Following a trip to England, then to Germany where he remained to study music for two years, he returned to the United States. He held his first music convention in Somerville, New Jersey, in 1851 and later joined with Mason, Thomas Hastings (LBW 327), and George Root in their Normal Institutes. From 1854 he, in partnership with his brother, was engaged in building and selling pianos. He died January 7, 1868, in Montclair, New Jersey.

Although the amount of Bradbury's work was great (he published fifty-nine volumes) the quality was not high.

294 MY HOPE IS BUILT ON NOTHING LESS
Tune: Melita

See LBW 293 for a discussion of this hymn.

For MELITA see LBW 467.

295 OUT OF THE DEPTHS I CRY TO YOU
(Aus tiefer Not schrei ich zu dir)

Tune: Aus tiefer Not

Psalm 130 was a favorite of Martin Luther's (LBW 48), and this hymn is one of the finest of German Psalm versifications. Four stanzas, written in 1523, were in circulation on a broadsheet in Magdeburg by May 6 of the following year, and appeared also in 1524 in the Wittenberg *Etlich*

Christlich lider, and in the Erfurt *Enchiridia.* With the second stanza expanded to two stanzas, the hymn appeared in Johann Walther's (LBW 350) *Geystliche gesangk Buchleyn,* Wittenberg, 1524, and later, in 1542, in Luther's *Christliche Geseng zum Begrebnis,* Wittenberg. The hymn was sung in 1525 at the funeral of Elector Friedrich the Wise in the court church in Wittenberg, and at Halle, on February 20, 1546, it was sung at Luther's own funeral.

A new English translation has been prepared for the LBW by Gracia Grindal (LBW 32).

AUS TIEFER NOT. Several different tunes have been associated with this text. *Etlich Christlich lider* used "Es ist das Heil" (LBW 297); one of the Erfurt *Enchiridia* used the tune "Ach Gott vom Himmel;" and the Strassburg *Teutsch Kirchenampt mit lobgesengen,* 1525, included the melody found with this text in the *Service Book and Hymnal,* 1958. The present Phrygian-mode melody is possibly the work of Luther himself, and appeared in Walther's *Geystliche Gesangk Buchleyn,* 1524. The plaintive melody is especially well-suited to the text. J. S. Bach (LBW 219) based his Cantata 38 on this hymn.

296 JUST AS I AM, WITHOUT ONE PLEA
Tune: Woodworth

Charlotte Elliott was born March 18, 1789, at Clapham, England. She suffered an illness in 1821 which resulted in her becoming a permanent invalid, so that all her work was done with great effort against her physical weakness. In 1822 she met César Malan, an evangelist from Geneva, and through his influence devoted her life to religious pursuits. She maintained correspondence with him for the next forty years. After 1823 she lived in Brighton, where she died on September 22, 1871.

This hymn, based on John 6:37, was written in 1834 and published the following year in a leaflet, and was included in Elliott's *Invalid's Hymn Book,* 1838. She wrote the hymn one day when she had to remain at home while the rest of the family went to a bazaar to raise funds for a college for daughters of the poorer clergy at Brighton.

WOODWORTH by William Bradbury (LBW 293) first appeared in the *Mendelssohn Collection,* 1849, as the setting for "The God of love will sure indulge."

297 SALVATION UNTO US HAS COME
(Es ist das Heil uns kommen her)
Tune: Es ist das Heil

Both text and tune of this hymn appeared in *Etlich Christlich lider,* 1523/1524 (see LBW 48). The text is by Paul Speratus who assisted Martin Luther (LBW 48) in the preparation of the collection.

Speratus was born December 13, 1484, in Swabia, possibly at the castle of Röthlen near Ellwangen. His name seems originally to have been Paul Hoffer or Offer, which was later Latinized, as was the custom during the sixteenth century, to "Paulus Speratus." He entered the University of

Freiburg in 1502, and is believed to have studied also at Paris and in Italy. By 1518 he had become a preacher at Dinkelsbühl in Bavaria. In 1519 he went to Würzburg and in 1520, to Salzburg, but was asked to leave both places for expressing his evangelical views too openly. In the autumn of 1520 he went to Vienna, where he received his Doctor of Divinity degree. By this time he had already married, being one of the first priests to dare to take this step. A sermon which he preached in January, 1522, defending marriage and clearly setting forth the doctrine of justification by faith brought on him the condemnation of the theological faculty of the University of Vienna and he was forced to leave. He became a preacher at Iglau in Moravia, winning an enthusiastic following among the people there. King Ludwig, however, summoned him to Olmütz, where he was imprisoned in 1523. Three months later he was released, probably through the influence of Queen Maria of Hungary and Margrave Albrecht of Brandenburg (LBW 519). Based on Romans 3:28, this hymn seems to have been written during the author's imprisonment or after his arrival in Wittenberg at the end of 1523. On Luther's recommendation Speratus was appointed court preacher to Margrave Albrecht at Königsberg in May of 1524, and had charge also of the Alstadt church until the arrival of Johann Gramann (LBW 519) in October of 1525. He seems to have had a great deal to do with drawing up the Liturgy and Canons—the *Kirchenordnung*—for the Prussian church, and in 1526 he was chosen clerical commissioner to visit the parish churches of Prussia to see that the new arrangements were carried out. At the end of 1529 he became Lutheran bishop of Pomesania, taking up residence in Marienwerder. There he remained until his death on August 12, 1551.

The translation is from *The Lutheran Hymnal,* 1941. Stanza 3 is altered extensively, the others only slightly.

ES IST DAS HEIL (also "St. Paul"), the anonymous melody which appeared in *Etlich Christlich lider,* was also printed in 1524 in the Erfurt *Enchiridia* and Johann Walther's (LBW 350) *Geystliche Gesangk Buchleyn* (Zahn* #4430). It was one of four tunes included in *Etlich Christlich lider.* In the Erfurt *Enchiridia,* where it was used with "Nun freut euch, lieben Christen-gemein" (LBW 299), it is said to be the melody for the pre-Reformation Easter hymn, "Frewt euch, yhr frawen und yhr man, das Christ ist auferstanden."

J. S. Bach (LBW 219) used the tune in Cantatas 9, 86, 117, 155, and 186 and included a chorale prelude in the *Orgelbüchlein.*

298   ONE THERE IS, ABOVE ALL OTHERS

Tune: Amen sjunge hvarje tunga

This hymn is from book one of *Olney Hymns.* See LBW 261 for John Newton and *Olney Hymns.*

AMEN SJUNGE HVARJE TUNGA (also "Dana") was combined with Newton's text in the *Common Service Book,* 1917. Written in 1849 for Hans A. Brorson's (LBW 52) hymn, "Amen raabe hver en Tunge," Berggren's tune was included in his *Melodier til Salmebog for Kirke og Hus-Andagt,* Copenhagen, 1853.

Andreas Peter Berggren (also spelled Berggreen), born March 2, 1801, in Copenhagen, studied law at the university by his parents' decision, but studied music besides, for a time with C. E. F. Weyse (LBW 161), and devoted his life to that profession. He composed a number of larger works early in his life, most of which are forgotten. His major contributions were an eleven-volume collection of *Folkesange og Melodier,* 1842–1871; a fourteen-volume set of songs for use in schools, 1834–1876; and especially his *Melodier til Salmebog,* published in 1853, which contained a number of his own tunes. From 1838 he was organist at the Church of the Trinity in Copenhagen. He also became a professor of singing at the Metropolitan School in 1843, and after 1859 was superintendent of vocal music in the schools. He died November 9, 1880, in Copenhagen.

299 DEAR CHRISTIANS, ONE AND ALL
(Nun freut euch, lieben Christen gmein)
Tune: Nun freut euch

In 1523 Martin Luther (LBW 48) wrote his first hymn, a ballad on the martyrs' death of two of his followers, Johann Esch and Heinrich Voes (see *The Lutheran Hymnal,* 1941, #259). Shortly thereafter he wrote this, his first congregational hymn, which was published with its tune on a broadsheet in 1523, and in *Etlich Christlich lider,* 1523/1524 (see LBW 48).

The translation by Richard Massie (LBW 134) in his *Martin Luther's Spiritual Songs,* 1854, was included with some alterations in *The Lutheran Hymnal,* 1941, and has been further altered for the LBW.

NUN FREUT EUCH, based on the fifteenth-century secular folksong, "Sie gleicht wohl einem Rosenstock," was included in *Etlich Christlich lider*, 1524. Two other tunes have been used with this text, "Es ist das Heil" (LBW 297) and "Est ist gewisslich" (LBW 321).

The harmonization found here is by Carl Schalk (LBW 118).

300 O CHRIST, OUR HOPE *(Jesu, nostra redemptio)*
Tune: Lobt Gott, ihr Christen

This anonymous Latin hymn of the seventh or eighth century was used from Ascension to Pentecost—at Compline (nightfall) in Sarum (Salisbury), at Lauds (sunrise) in York, and at Vespers (sunset) in Roman use. It is found in several eleventh-century manuscripts.

The LBW version is adapted from a translation by John Chandler (LBW 22) which appeared in his *Hymns of the Primitive Church,* 1837.

LOBT GOTT, IHR CHRISTEN is at LBW 47.

301 COME TO CALVARY'S HOLY MOUNTAIN
Tune: Naar mit Öie

This hymn was first published in Thomas Cotterill's (LBW 547) *Selection of Psalms and Hymns for Public and Private Use,* 1819. See LBW 50 for James Montgomery.

NAAT MIT ÖIE, also called "Consolation" and "Holy Mountain," was composed for Hans A. Brorson's (LBW 52) hymn "Naar mit Øie, traet af Møie" and included in Lindeman's *Koralbog,* 1871. For Ludvig Lindeman see LBW 285.

302 JESUS, YOUR BLOOD AND RIGHTEOUSNESS
(Christi Blut und Gerechtigkeit)

Tune: O Jesu Christe, wahres Licht

Count Nicolaus Ludwig von Zinzendorf, founder of the new Moravian or newly organized United Brethren church, was born May 26, 1700, at Dresden, Germany. A member of a noble and wealthy family, he acquired all the accomplishments appropriate to his station and went to Wittenberg University to study law. Following his graduation in 1719 he married, and accepted a government position at the Saxon office in Dresden. Zinzendorf had been brought up in a religious family. When he met a carpenter of the Moravian Brethren who expressed the desire to have his persecuted fellow-believers move to Protestant Germany, Zinzendorf offered the group asylum on one of his own estates at Dresden. There, in 1722, the settlement named "Herrnhut" was established and five years later Zinzendorf joined them as superintendent. He determined to become a clergyman, and in 1734 received a license to preach from the University of Tübingen. Four years later he was consecrated a Moravian bishop. Some of his opponents, however, who looked with disfavor on the development of the Brethren, procured an edict in 1737 for the banishment of Zinzendorf on charges of preaching false doctrine. During the ten years until he could return to Saxony, he traveled widely, preaching and establishing Moravian missions at St. Petersburg, and in Germany, Holland, England, America (including work among the African slaves), and the West Indies. After his banishment was lifted he returned to Herrnhut which he made his headquarters for further mission work. Having spent his entire fortune for his church, he died a poor man at Herrnhut on May 9, 1760.

From the time he was twelve years old until a few days before his death Zinzendorf wrote hymns; his total output numbered in the neighborhood of two thousand. This hymn, originally thirty-three stanzas long, was written in 1739 when Zinzendorf was returning from a mission to St. Thomas in the West Indies, and was published that year in the eighth appendix to his *Das Gesang-Buch der Gemeine in Herrn-Huth,* a collection first published in 1735. The first stanza is based on "In Christi Wunden schlaf ich ein," a hymn ascribed to Paul Eber (LBW 303) (see *The Lutheran Hymnal,* 1941, #585).

Translation of the hymn is by John Wesley who had come to know a group of Moravians in 1735 while en route to Georgia. It was included in *Hymns and Sacred Poems,* 1740.

John Wesley was born at Epworth rectory, Lincolnshire, England, on June 17, 1703, and received his education at Charterhouse and Christ Church, Oxford, taking a Bachelor of Arts degree in 1724 and a Master of Arts degree, 1726–1727. He became a fellow of Lincoln College in 1727, and the following year was ordained and returned to Lincolnshire to assist his father at Epworth and Wroot. In 1729 he was called back to Oxford to teach, and a small band calling themselves "Oxford Methodists" immediately placed themselves under his leadership. Under the sponsorship of the Society for the Propagation of the Gospel, he and his brother Charles (LBW 27), went as missionaries to Savannah, Georgia, in 1735, meeting en route a group of Moravians with whom John was deeply impressed. His work in Georgia was not successful and he returned in 1737 to London. There, on May 24, 1738, he attended a meeting of the Moravians, where one of the members read Martin Luther's preface to the Epistle to the Romans, and he "felt [his] heart strangely warmed." In 1739 he purchased an old foundry in London which he converted into a chapel. For the rest of his life (more than half a century) he was an itinerant minister, traveling thousands of miles on horseback, delivering sermons and writing a large number of books and many hymns and hymn translations. He died in London on March 2, 1791.

In John Wesley's *A Collection of Thirty-six tunes, set to music, as they are sung at the Foundry,* London, 1742, this hymn was set to "Canon Tune" ("Tallis' Canon," LBW 278).

O JESU CHRISTE, WAHRES LICHT (also "O Jesu Christ, meins Lebens Licht") is an anonymous tune which appeared with Martin Behm's hymn, "O Jesu Christ, mein's Lebens Licht," in the *Andächtige Haus-Kirch . . . Gesängen* published in Nürnberg in 1676. It was originally in quadruple meter as given below (Zahn* #535).

The harmonization is by David Herman (LBW 97).

303   WHEN IN THE HOUR OF DEEPEST NEED
(Wenn wir in höchsten Nöten sein)

Tune: Wenn wir in höchsten Nöten sein

Considered to be second only to Martin Luther (LBW 48) among the Wittenberg poets, Paul Eber was born November 8, 1511, the son of a master tailor at Kitzingen, Bavaria. A fall from a horse in 1523 resulted in his being permanently deformed; nevertheless, he graduated from the University of Wittenberg in 1536, where he studied with Luther and Philipp Melanchthon. Thereafter he became a tutor in the philosophical faculty, and in 1544, a professor of Latin. In 1557 he was appointed professor of Hebrew and preacher of the Castle Church, and the following year, succeeded Johannes Bugenhagen (LBW 103) as pastor of the City Church and superintendent of the district. He received a Doctor of Divinity degree from the university in 1559. A close friend of Melanchthon's, he conducted the greater part of his correspondence, and on Melanchthon's death in 1560, became the leader of his party. He died December 10, 1569.

This hymn is based on a Latin hymn, "In tenebris nostrae et densa caligine mentis," by Eber's former teacher, Joachim Camerarius of

Nürnberg. The exact date and circumstances of its composition are unknown. It has been suggested, without proof, that it was written on Ascension Day in 1547 when, after the battle of Mühlberg, the Wittenbergers had received a message from the captive elector to deliver their city to Emperor Charles V. It was printed in Nürnberg on a broadsheet around 1560, and published in 1566 in the *Naw Betbüchlein,* Dresden.

Catherine Winkworth's (LBW 29) translation, "When in the hour of utmost need," was included in her *Lyra Germanica,* second series, 1858. A few alterations have been made for the LBW.

WENN WIR IN HÖCHSTEN NÖTEN SEIN, believed by some to be by Louis Bourgeois (LBW 29), was possibly included in the Genevan Psalter of about 1543, although no copies of that edition remain today. In the 1545 edition it was the setting for Clément Marot's metrical version of the Ten Commandments, "Leve le coeur, ouvre l'oreille." It was published with the present text in *Das Gebet Josaphat,* Wittenberg, 1567. In addition to his organ settings in the *Orgelbüchlein* and the Eighteen Chorales, J. S. Bach (LBW 219) prepared several four-part settings of the tune. The LBW harmonization is from the *Württembergische Choralbuch,* 1953.

304 TODAY YOUR MERCY CALLS US
Tune: Anthes

Oswald Allen was born in 1816 at Kirkby Lonsdale, Westmoreland, in England. He was an invalid all his life, suffering from a diseased spine. In 1843 he went to Glasgow, but was forced to return home after three years because of his poor health. Five years later he took a position at his father's bank, where after a time he succeeded his father as manager. He became well known as a friend of the poor and needy. He died October 2, 1878.

Allen's *Hymns of the Christian Life,* London, 1861, in which this hymn was included, were mostly written during the severe winter of 1859–1860. The singular pronouns in the original hymn have been changed to plural in a number of collections.

ANTHES was composed by Friedrich Konrad Anthes, the son of a seminary professor. Born at Weilburg in Nassau, Germany, May 2, 1812, he studied theology and served first as assistant pastor at Herborn and later as pastor at Haiger and Ackerbach. In Wiesbaden, in 1846, he published two works: *Die Tonkunst im evangelischen Kultus* and *Allgemeine fassliche Bemerkungen.* Forced to retire in 1857 because of poor health, he seems to have spent the rest of his life in Wiesbaden. The date of his death is not known.

305 I LAY MY SINS ON JESUS
Tune: Munich

See LBW 167 for Horatius Bonar. Published in *Songs in the Wilderness,* Kelson, 1843, this hymn was written a number of years earlier when Bonar was assistant at St. John's Church, Leith, to provide something the children could sing and appreciate.

For MUNICH see LBW 231. The present harmonization was prepared by Felix Mendelssohn (LBW 60) as the setting for "Cast thy burden upon the Lord" in his *Elijah*.

306 CHIEF OF SINNERS THOUGH I BE

Tune: Gethsemane

Born in Coleraine County, Londonderry, Ireland, in 1793, William McComb was for many years a bookseller in Belfast. His *The Dirge of O'Neill*, 1816, and *The School of the Sabbath*, 1822, along with some smaller pieces, were collected and published in 1864 as *The Poetical Works of William McComb*, which also included this hymn. He died about 1870.

For GETHSEMANE see LBW 109.

307 FORGIVE OUR SINS AS WE FORGIVE

Tune: Detroit

Of this hymn the author writes: "The idea of writing the 'Forgiveness' hymn came to me some years ago when I was digging up docks in a long-neglected garden. Realizing how these deeply-rooted weeds were choking the life out of the flowers in the garden, I came to feel that deeply-rooted resentments in our lives could destroy every Christian virtue and all joy and peace unless, by God's grace, we learned to forgive." First published in two collections in 1969, *100 Hymns for Today* (supplement to *Hymns Ancient and Modern*) and *Hymns and Songs* (supplement to the *Methodist Hymnbook*), the hymn has since entered several hymnbooks in England and North America.

Born of British parents on June 22, 1905, in Masuri in North India, Rosamond E. Herklots was educated at Leeds Girls' High School and Leeds University. She trained as a teacher, but soon gave up teaching for secretarial work. For more than twenty years she was secretary to an eminent neurologist. Presently she is working in the head office of the Association for Spina Bifida and Hydrocephalus in London. Although she has written verse since childhood, Herklots did not begin writing hymns until relatively recently. She has written some sixty or seventy hymns "intended to express in simple words the faith, hope and dedication of the ordinary Christian." In 1968 two of her hymns reached the finals in the Hymns for Britain contest and were sung on television. A number of others, especially her hymns for children, are used in Sunday schools and elsewhere.

For DETROIT see LBW 240. This harmonization was prepared for the LBW by Charles R. Anders (LBW 386). Because of its association with this hymn, this tune is called "Forgive our Sins" in some collections.

Tune: Gott der Vater wohn uns bei

This hymn is a revision by Martin Luther (LBW 48) of a medieval litany invoking the aid of the angels, prophets, patriarchs, apostles, and so on. The litany, which dates back to the fourteenth century, was used in some parts of Germany as a procession on St. Mark's Day and in Rogation Week. Several versions appeared during the fifteenth century, beginning "Sanctus Petrus won uns bey," "Sancta Maria won uns bey," "Du lieber Herr S. Niclas won uns bey," and so on. Using some lines of the original text, Luther created a hymn of invocation of the Holy Trinity, which was first printed in Johann Walther's (LBW 350) *Geystliche gesangk Buchleyn,* Wittenberg, 1524.

The English text is an altered form of Richard Massie's (LBW 134) translation in his *Martin Luther's Spiritual Songs,* London, 1854.

GOTT DER VATER WOHN UNS BEI also dates from the fourteenth century, and was included with Luther's text in Walther's *Geystliche gesangk Buchleyn.* Leupold* notes that the first two lines of this tune contain the germ of "Jesus, meine Zuversicht" (LBW 340). J. S. Bach (LBW 219) included a setting of this tune in his *Choralgesänge.*

The harmonization was done by Carl Schalk (LBW 118) for the LBW.

309 LORD JESUS, THINK ON ME (Μνώεο Χριστέ)

Tune: Southwell

Synesius of Cyrene (an ancient Greek city in Northern Africa) was born of an illustrious family whose pedigree was said to have extended back for seventeen centuries. He is described as an eloquent and brilliant man of high character. Seeing the threat of an invasion by the Goths he went to the court of Arcadius in Constantinople and for three years tried to warn them of the danger but, while the court admired his eloquence and zeal, his advice was not heeded. At first he was a pagan and studied at Alexandria with Hypatia, the neoplatonic philosopher. Around the turn of the century, Synesius embraced Christianity and in 403 he married a Christian wife. He was elected bishop of Ptolemais in 409 or 410. His birth date is given variously as about 365 or 375, and his death date as approximately 414 or 430.

This hymn is from the last of ten odes written by Synesius at various periods in his life. Allen William Chatfield described his English version as "a paraphrase or amplification rather than an exact translation of the original." Some of the LBW stanzas are from Chatfield's *Songs and Hymns of the Earliest Greek Christian Poets,* 1876, and some are from a revised edition of that work, published twenty years later.

Chatfield was born at Chatteris, Cambridgeshire, England, on October 2, 1808. He had a brilliant career at Trinity College, Cambridge, and graduated with a Bachelor of Arts degree in 1831. Ordained in 1832, he served as vicar of Stotfold, Bedfordshire, from 1833 to 1847. From 1847 until his death on January 10, 1896, he was vicar at Much-Marcle, Herefordshire. Besides *Songs and Hymns* he published several sermons, and rendered various parts of the service of the English Church into Greek.

SOUTHWELL was the setting for Psalm 45 in William Daman's (LBW 114) *The Psalmes of Dauid in English meter, with Notes of foure partes set vnto them, by Guiliemo Daman, for Iohn Bull, to the vus of the godly Christians for recreatyng them selues, in stede of fond and vnseemely Ballades,* printed by John Day (LBW 234) in 1579. This collection was prepared for the "private delite" of Daman's friend, John Bull, a London goldsmith, who thought so highly of them that he had them published. Daman, however, did not feel that the simple note-against-note four-part settings were worthy of his abilities and promptly withdrew the collection, destroying as many copies as he could, with the result that the book is a very rare item today. Originally the melody was in Dorian mode, which can be reconstructed here by sharping the C's in the soprano line.

310 TO YOU, OMNISCIENT LORD OF ALL
(Jeg staar for Gud, som alting ved)
Tune: Vater unser

Born October 7, 1802, in Måsøy, Finnmarken, in the extreme north of Norway, Magnus Brostrup Landstad was one of ten children born to the parish pastor there. His father was transferred to Øksnes in 1804, to Vinje in 1811, and finally to Seljord in 1819. The family was extremely poor; in the harsh climate the crops often froze before they matured, and there was war and depression. Landstad's father tutored him until he was ready to enter the University of Christiania (Oslo) in 1822. After working for a year in 1825 as a tutor at Gran, he returned to the university and completed his theological studies in 1827. Two years later he was married to Vilhelmine M. Lassen of Gran. In 1828 he was appointed resident vicar of the Lutheran church in Gausdal, and in 1834, senior pastor at Kviteseid. He succeeded his father at Seljord in 1839, remaining there for nine years. Thereafter he served successively at Fredrikshald (1848–1854), Borgesyssel (1854–1859), and Sandeherred (1859–1877). After his retirement in 1877 he moved to Christiania, where he died on October 8, 1880.

Landstad had a keen interest in folk lore and songs of Norway and published, in 1853, a large and impressive work entitled *Norske Folkeviser*. His interest in hymn-writing was aroused while he was still a student, when he chanced to pass a house where a book sale was in progress. A new shipment of old books had just arrived, and for four cents he purchased two leather-bound volumes. One was *Freuden-Spiegel des ewigen Lebens* by Philipp Nicolai (LBW 31), and the other was Bishop A. Arrebo's *Hexaemeron*. Thus he became acquainted with two splendid hymn collections, one German and the other Danish-Norwegian. Nicolai's hymns made a deep impression on Landstad, and he at once set about to translate them. He wrote his first hymn in 1825, and through the years his work with folk songs and folk lore developed and matured his poetic talents. During the 1840s he was requested by the Norwegian church ministry to revise the hymnal. He declined because of his parish duties; but when he went to Fredrikshald, he was given an assistant so that he might have more time available, and in 1852 he set to work on his hymnbook. By 1861, Landstad's *Udkast til Kirkesalmebog* was ready. At first it met with considerable criticism because of its "radical" language (the use of Norwegian rather than the conventional Danish), but in its revised version, 1869, the *Kirkesalmebog* was authorized as the official Norwegian hymnbook. The book was widely used and was the hymnal brought with the Norwegian immigrants to America. It was revised in the first quarter of the twentieth century. Ludvig Lindeman (LBW 285) issued a companion book containing melodies—the *Koralbog,* 1877. In addition to his original hymns, Landstad also prepared masterly translations of Latin and German texts. He wished for his hymnal to be a national one, and included many Norwegian poets. He was the first to use poems by Petter Dass (LBW 244). All hymns from the rationalistic era were excluded except those of Johan Nordahl Brun (LBW 227). When Landstad retired, the Norwegian parliament voted unanimously to grant him a pension in honor of his service in the church and his achievements as poet and publisher of hymns.

This hymn was first included in Landstad's *Udkast til Kirke-Salmebog,* 1861. Each of the three stanzas is based on a specific passage of Scripture; stanza 1 is based on Ezra 9:6; stanza 2, on Psalm 51:11; and stanza 3 on Luke 18:14.

The translation, originally beginning "Before Thee, God, who knowest all," was prepared in 1909 by Carl Doving (LBW 43) for *The Lutheran Hymnary,* 1913. Several alterations have been made in the text.

For VATER UNSER see LBW 442. The harmonization used here was prepared by Paul Bunjes (LBW 38) for the *Worship Supplement,* 1969, to *The Lutheran Hymnal.*

311 WONDROUS ARE YOUR WAYS, O GOD!

Tune: Wennerberg

Between the years 1861 and 1890 the Swedish composer, Gunnar Wennerberg, published his *Ur Davis Psalmer,* settings of the Psalms for solo voice and choir with piano accompaniment. Psalm 139, "Herre, du utransakar mig," was published in 1882. WENNERBERG is the final four-part chorale for verses 23 and 24 of Psalm 139, beginning "Utransaka mig, min Gud." In 1924 Claus August Wendell prepared an English paraphrase of verses 23 and 24, beginning "Search me, God, and know my heart," and the single stanza, together with the tune "Wennerberg," was included in *The Hymnal,* 1925, of the Augustana Synod. For the LBW Joel Lundeen (LBW 146) has written an additional stanza, stanza 1, "Wondrous are your ways, O God," also based on Psalm 139.

Claus August, son of Lars Gustaf Anderson, a Swedish farmer, was born April 24, 1866, at Södia Ving, Västergötland. (As a young man, Claus changed his name first from Anderson to Wingquist, then to Wendell.) When he was three years old he came with his family to the United States and they settled in Sycamore, Illinois, where Claus attended country school. He entered the Academy of Augustana College and persuaded his parents also to live and find work in Rock Island. In 1893 he received a Bachelor of Arts degree from Augustana College, and immediately the following year filled the chair of English literature and philosophy at the college while the professor was on leave of absence. He received a Master of Arts degree in 1897 and in that year was married to Anna Charlotte Norlin. From 1897 to 1902 he taught history at Rock Island High School and for two years thereafter spent some time in journalism. Wendell's theological training was undertaken for the most part by correspondence under the direction of Dr. Conrad Lindberg, and he was ordained a Lutheran pastor in 1905. After serving at Emmanuel Church, Rockford, Illinois, and Immanuel Church, Evanston, Illinois, he spent the remainder of his ministry, from 1914 to 1947, at Grace Lutheran Church, Minneapolis, Minnesota. He died September 18, 1950.

Wendell published several works, including *Little Journies in His Kingdom, The Larger Vision, Our Catechism,* and *Out of the Fog,* and was staff correspondent of the *Lutheran Companion,* in which position he became the voice of English Lutheranism in his synod. In addition to serving as chairman of the Association of English Churches, he was on the board of directors of the Augustana Book Concern, and a member of *The Hymnal,* 1925, Committee, the Hymnal Revision Committee, the Board of Christian Education and Literature, and the Board of Parish Education. He received a Doctor of Literature degree from Gustavus Adolphus College, and a Doctor of Divinity degree from Augustana in 1939. Wendell is described as a much-loved man who was highly regarded as a preacher, lecturer, and author.

Gunnar Wennerberg, a humorous and patriotic poet who served for many years as a member of the Swedish legislature, studied philosophy and esthetics at the University of Uppsala. Afterwards he took a teaching post at Skara, but his interest in music led him to undertake study of the piano and violoncello. In addition to a number of hymn tunes, several of which were included in a 1934 Swedish chorale book, he composed some duets, three oratorios, and sacred choral pieces. He was born October 2, 1817, at Linköping, and died August 24, 1901, at Läckö.

312 ONCE HE CAME IN BLESSING *(Gottes Sohn ist kommen)*
Tune: Gottes Sohn ist kommen

See LBW 132 for Johann Horn. This hymn was first published in *Ein Gesangbuch der Brüder inn Behemen und Merherrn,* Nürnberg, 1544. Catherine Winkworth's (LBW 29) translation was given in her *Chorale Book for England,* 1863. Stanzas 3 and 4 have been altered.

GOTTES SOHN IST KOMMEN (Zahn* #3294) is sometimes ascribed to Michael Weisse (LBW 37) and was included in his *Ein New Gesengbuchlen,* 1531, as the setting for his "Menschenkind, merk eben." It was associated with the present text in the 1544 hymnal. The tune appears to be based on the fifteenth-century Bohemian song, "Ave hierarchia."

The harmonization was prepared for the LBW by Jan Bender (LBW 396).

313 A MULTITUDE COMES FROM EAST AND WEST
(Der mange skal komme fra Öst og fra Vest)
Tune: Der mange skal komme

See LBW 310 for Magnus Brostrup Landstad. Based on the parable of the great banquet, Luke 14: 15–24, this hymn was included in Landstad's 1861 *Kirkesalmebog.* In 1858 Landstad wrote, "For me, whenever we gather to pray, we sing a psalm of penance. I believe it is right to do so as long as we are in this world." Accordingly, each stanza of this hymn ends, "Miskunne dig over oss, Jesus" ("Have mercy upon us, Jesus").

Peer Olson Strömme (LBW 102) prepared the translation in 1909 for *The Lutheran Hymnary,* 1913. Stanza 1 originally began *"There many shall come* from the east and the west," and stanzas 2 and 3 also contain a few alterations.

DER MANGE SKAL KOMME (also "Stockholm") is an anonymous tune which was first included in the *Riddarholmskyrkan handskrivna Koralbok,* 1694, and later, in *Then Swenska Psalmboken,* 1697. It was associated in Sweden with the hymn, "Himmelriket liknas widt tijo jungfruer." Landstad's folk-like hymn is well-suited to this tune. Originally the rhythm was a combination of 3/4 and 4/4 as given below.

etc.

Paul Bunjes (LBW 38) has prepared the harmonization for the LBW.

314 WHO IS THIS HOST ARRAYED IN WHITE
(Den store hvide Flok, vi se)
Tune: Den store hvide Flok

See LBW 52 for Hans Adolf Brorson.

This hymn, one of seventy written in the last year of Brorson's life, was included in his *Svanesangen* published in 1765, the year after his death. It has been made known in the United States by the St. Olaf College Choir. Indicative of the popularity of this jubilant hymn of triumph is the large number of translations in which it exists in Lutheran hymnals. The *Hymnal for Church and Home,* 1938, used a translation by J. C. Aaberg (LBW 75); *The Concordia Hymnal,* 1932, included one by Carl Doving (LBW 43). A "composite" translation used in *The Lutheran Hymnary,* 1913, was taken into *The Lutheran Hymnal,* 1941, and a different "composite" translation was provided for the *American Lutheran Hymnal,* 1930. A new translation was prepared for the *Service Book and Hymnal,* 1958, by the Hymnal Commission. The LBW translation was done by Gracia Grindal (LBW 32), with assistance from her father, Harold K. Grindal.

DEN STORE HVIDE FLOK (also "Behold a Host" and "Great White Host"). In his *Dansk Salms-Leksikon* (Copenhagen, 1930), O. E. Thuner lists nineteen tunes which have been attached to this hymn. The present tune is the one used in all American hymnals and in the *Norsk Koralbok,* 1936. A folk melody from Heddal, this tune is very popular in Norway and is known by all school children. The similarities between this tune and another from Heddal are noted at LBW 330. Ludvig Lindeman's (LBW 285) *AEldre og Nyere Norske Fjeldmelodier* included this tune.

Greig's harmonization is from his Opus 30, #10, an arrangement for four-part male chorus with baritone solo.

Edvard Hagerup Grieg was born in Bergen, Norway, June 15, 1843.

His father, a merchant and British consul at Bergen, was of Scottish ancestry. Edvard began his piano study with his mother at the age of six, and in 1858 entered the Leipzig Conservatory, where his teachers included Ignace Moscheles (piano) and Carl Reinecke (composition). Arthur Sullivan (LBW 153) was a fellow student at the conservatory. In 1863 he went to Copenhagen, Denmark (at that time the musical and cultural center of Norwegian as well as Danish life), where he met Hans Christian Anderson whose poems he set to music in his *Melodies of the Heart.* Introduced to Norwegian folk music by Ole Bulle in 1864, Grieg determined to direct his future efforts towards Norwegian national music. Unable to secure a church appointment or a post as director of the Christiania Theater, he presented a program in 1866 made up entirely of Norwegian music, assisted by his cousin Nina Hagerup, a singer to whom he was engaged, and violinist Wilhelmine Norman-Neruda. As a result of the success of this concert, he was accepted as one of the leading young musicians of Norway and was launched on his career. He obtained students and was appointed conductor of the Harmonic Society. The following year he established the Norwegian Academy of Music, and was married. His Piano Concerto in A minor, written in 1868, received hearty acclaim from Franz Liszt. In 1868 also he became acquainted with Lindeman's *Fjeldmelodier* which gave him new insight into Norwegian folk song, and on which he based twenty-five piano pieces. He helped found the Christiania Musical Society for promotion of orchestral music in 1871, and in 1876 his incidental music for Henrik Ibsen's *Peer Gynt* was first performed. The following year, led by his ever-growing love of the beauty of his native land, he moved to upper Børve in Ullensvang, located in the scenic Hardanger district, and from 1880 to 1882 he held his last official appointment, that of conductor of the Bergen Harmonic Society. In 1884 he build a home for his family at Troldhaugen in the Westland. For some twenty years thereafter he regularly spent his spring and early summer months composing new works or revising older ones; the late summer hiking in the mountains, often with Frants Beyer, Julius Röntgen, or Percy Grainger; and the fall and winter months on extended concert tours which took him to Denmark, France, Germany, Poland, Czechoslovakia, Holland, and England. Grieg had suffered from a respiratory problem since his student days, and after 1900 his health deteriorated considerably. Nevertheless, he continued his annual concert tours, and was actually planning to set out for England when he was ordered to a hospital on April 3, 1907, where he died the next day. His last work, written towards the end of 1906, was his *Four Psalms,* Opus 74, based on traditional melodies, one of which is found at LBW 330.

315   LOVE DIVINE, ALL LOVES EXCELLING
Tune: Hyfrydol

See LBW 27 for Charles Wesley. This hymn was first published in *Hymns for those that Seek, and those that have Redemption,* 1747.

For HYFRYDOL see LBW 158. The harmonization found here is from the *Service Book and Hymnal,* 1958.

316 JESUS, THE VERY THOUGHT OF YOU
(Jesu, dulcis memoria)

Tune: St. Agnes

"Jesu, dulcis memoria" is the opening line of an extended poem from which three hymns in the LBW are derived (see also LBW 356 and 537). Although this twelfth-century poem in its evangelical and devout character reflects the spirit of Bernard of Clairvaux (LBW 116), it has not been unanimously ascribed to him by scholars of Latin hymnody. Samuel W. Duffield is among those who do attribute the hymn to Bernard. Joseph Connelly, however, feels that it is perhaps the work of an English Cistercian; and Matthew Britt believes that the poem originated in England, doubtless from the Order of Citeaux, and that it moved to France and later to Italy and Germany. Others also support the idea that the hymn originated in England and later moved to the Continent. An eleventh-century manuscript ascribing the hymn to a Benedictine abbess, reported to have been discovered by Dom Poithier, has not been accepted as genuine by many writers. Originally forty-two stanzas long, the poem was extended to fifty-one stanzas during the fifteenth century. From about 1500, when the Feast of the Holy Name of Jesus came into general use, various portions of the total hymn were used in its observance.

The translation is by Edward Caswall (LBW 37) and was included in his *Lyra Catholica,* 1849. There are several alterations in the first three stanzas, and stanza 4 has been completely rewritten.

ST. AGNES was the setting composed by J. B. Dykes (LBW 165) for this hymn in J. Grey's *A Hymnal for use in the English Church, with accompanying tunes,* 1866.

317 TO GOD THE HOLY SPIRIT LET US PRAY
(Nun bitten wir den Heiligen Geist)

Tune: Nun bitten wir

The first stanza of this hymn is a German *Leise,* or sacred vernacular folk song ending with "Kyrie eleison." Probably suggested by the sequence "Veni Sancte Spiritus," it reads as follows:

> Nû biten wir den heiligen geist
> umbe des rechten glouben allermeist,
> daz er uns behijete an unsrem ende,
> sô wir heim suin var ûs disem ellende.
> Kyrieleis.

Our earliest source of "nun bitten wir" is a sermon by the famous medieval preacher, Brother Berthold of Regensburg (d. 1272), in which he quotes the hymn and encourages the people to sing it. One of few examples of vernacular hymns used by the congregation in pre-Reformation times, it was sung on Pentecost after the choir had sung the Latin "Veni Sancte Spiritus." During the Middle Ages it was customary in some churches to lower a wooden dove, or release a live dove, from the ceiling of the chancel while the hymn was sung.

Martin Luther (LBW 48) regarded this hymn highly and added three stanzas of his own. In 1524 it was included only in Johann Walther's (LBW 350) *Geystliche gesangk Buchleyn,* but very soon thereafter it was found in every Lutheran hymnal.

A translation prepared in 1965 by the Commission on Worship of the Missouri Synod, beginning "Now let us pray to God the Holy Ghost," and included in the *Worship Supplement,* 1969, to *The Lutheran Hymnal,* has been adapted for the LBW.

NUN BITTEN WIR is a pentatonic melody, which suggests that it is a very old folk tune, probably as old as the original first stanza. It was included with Luther's hymn in Walther's 1524 *Geystliche gesangk Buchleyn.* J. S. Bach (LBW 219) used the melody in Cantatas 169 and 197.

The harmonization is from the *Württembergische Choralbuch,* 1953.

318 THE LORD WILL COME AND NOT BE SLOW
Tune: Old 107th

John Milton was born in London, England, on December 9, 1608. His father, a well-educated man and a talented musician, is said to have contributed at least one harmonization to the Ravenscroft Psalter of 1621. After receiving a Bachelor of Arts degree in 1628, and a Master of Arts degree, 1632, from Christ's College, Cambridge, Milton spent several years with his father at Horton, Buckinghamshire. There he wrote *Comus, Il Penseroso, L'Allegro,* and *Lycidas.* In 1638 he toured France and Italy, visiting, among other people, Galileo, who was imprisoned at the time. On his return to London he set up a small school on Aldersgate Street and in 1643 was married to Mary Powell who was then only seventeen. She left him after a month, and after Milton made several attempts to recover her, she finally returned, bringing the rest of her family to live in Milton's house also. In 1649 he was appointed Latin secretary to the Council of State of Oliver Cromwell, a position he held for ten years. He lost his sight in 1652, and in the following year his wife died, leaving him with three children. His second marriage lasted only fifteen months; his wife, Catherine Woodchock, died in childbirth in 1657. With the Restoration in 1660, Milton might have been sent to the scaffold, had it not been for his fame and reputation. His third wife, whom he married in 1663, was devoted to him and restored order to his household. His *Paradise Lost,* which he had begun soon after the death of his second wife, was published in 1667, and *Paradise Regained* and *Samson Agonistes* followed in 1671. He died November 8, 1674, and was buried in St. Giles's Church, Cripplegate.

Milton's contributions to hymnody were limited to nineteen Psalm versifications. "The Lord will come and not be slow" consists of selections from Psalms 82, 85, and 86, all written in 1648, and published in his *Poems, etc. upon Several Occasions,* 1673. The selection of stanzas to make up this hymn has been attributed to W. Garrett Horder (*Worship Song,* 1905) and to the editors of *The English Hymnal,* 1906. Josiah Miller (*Our Hymns: Their Authors and Origin*) in 1866, however, wrote that this hymn "is made up of verses taken from his version of Psalms lxxxii, lxxxv, and lxxxvi." The cento may well date back to the mid-nineteenth century.

OLD 107TH is an anonymous Dorian-mode melody which was included in the *Pseavlmes Cinqvante de David,* Lyons, 1547, of which Louis

Bourgeois (LBW 29) was music editor. There it was the setting for Clément Marot's Psalm 107, "Donnez au Seigneur gloire," as given below.

When the tune was taken into *The Forme of Prayers and Ministration of the Sacraments* (Scottish Psalter), 1564, as the setting for William Kethe's (LBW 245) version of Psalm 107, it was altered to its present rhythm.

319   OH, SING, MY SOUL, YOUR MAKER'S PRAISE
(Herrasta veisaa kieleni)
Tune: Wächterlied

This hymn was included in the fourth Finnish hymnal, authorized in 1886.

Julius Leopold Fredrik Krohn, born in 1835, was for many years professor of Finnish language and literature at the University of Helsinki. An important member of the committee (1876–1880) which prepared the 1886 hymnal, Krohn also published the first history of Finnish hymnals in 1880. Many of his original, translated, or revised hymns are in use in Finland today. In addition to his work with hymnody, he was a prominent pioneer in the scholarly study of Finnish folk poetry. He died in 1888.

The translation was prepared in 1962 by Ernest Edwin Ryden (LBW 186) and Toivo Harjunpaa for *Laudamus,* the Lutheran World Federation hymnal, Helsinki, 1963.

Toivo K. I. Harjunpaa was born June 2, 1910, in Rauma, Finland. He holds a Bachelor of Divinity degree from the University of Helsinki; Master of Theology and Doctor of Theology degrees from the University of Abo, Finland; and a Master of Arts degree from the University of California, Berkeley. Ordained in 1936 at the Cathedral of Turku, Finland, he served first as assistant pastor at a church near Turku and as secretary of the Evangelical Student Association of Helsinki. From 1938 to 1945 he was seamen's chaplain and church liaison in London, and for three years thereafter he served as chaplain to the archbishop of Finland. In 1948 he immigrated to the United States where from 1949 to 1953 he was pastor of St. John's Lutheran Church, New Bedford, Massachusetts, and after 1951 also served as hospital chaplain in New Bedford. In

1953 he received a call to Shepherd of the Hills Lutheran Church in Berkeley, California, where he also became a part-time faculty member at the Pacific Lutheran Theological Seminary. After 1961 he was full-time professor of church history and liturgies, and dean of the chapel of Pacific Lutheran Seminary, and in 1962 was named professor of church history at the Graduate Theological Union, Berkeley, as well. He retired professor emeritus in 1977.

Harjunpaa has held numerous offices, including secretary of the Anglo-Scandinavian Christian Fellowship in England, secretary of the reconstruction committee of the Church of Finland, secretary of the Finnish National Committee of the Lutheran World Federation, president of the Hymnological Society of California, president of the West Coast branch of the American Society on Church History, and founding member of the North American Academy of Ecumenists. He has been associated with several professional theological societies in the United States and abroad—member of the editorial councils of the *Lutheran Quarterly* and *Una Sancta,* the United Lutheran Church in America consulting committee on worship, the Commission on the Liturgy and Hymnal, the Inter-Lutheran Commission on Worship, the committee on the Lutheran World Federation hymnal (*Laudamus*), and of the Societas Sanctae Birgittae of Sweden, and consultant for the World Council of Churches hymnal and for the liturgical and hymnal committees of the Church of Finland. His extensive publications include works in Finnish, Swedish, and German, as well as English. Among them are *Christians of Vision and Venture, Education and the Schools in Russian Alaska, Niceta of Remesiana and the Te Deum, Pastors' Self-Communion in the Lutheran Church,* and *Preaching in England during the Later Middle Ages.* He has also published articles in various periodicals and year books—"Historical Outline of Hymnody in Finland," "Jacob Tengström: First Archbishop of Finland," "Lex orandi—Lex credendi," "St. John Chrysostom in the Light of his Catechetical and Baptismal Homilies," and many others. He has been guest lecturer at the American Academy of Religion and at various colleges, universities, and professional societies in England, Finland, Germany, Italy, Scotland, Sweden, and the United States. He has attended, in various official capacities, the Lutheran World Federation assemblies in Lund (1947), Minneapolis (1957), and Helsinki (1963), and the World Council of Churches in Uppsala (1968). He is a corresponding member of the Historical Association of Turku, recipient of a *Festschrift—Ecclesia-Leiturgia-Ministerium*—published by Luther-Agricola Society in Helsinki (1977), and a commander of the Finnish Order of the Lion.

For WÄCHTERLIED see LBW 146.

320   O GOD, OUR HELP IN AGES PAST
Tune: St. Anne

See LBW 39 for Isaac Watts. Originally beginning "*Our* God, our help in ages past," this hymn is Psalm 90, first part, of the *Psalms of David,* 1719.

ST. ANNE. "St. Anne's Tune" was published anonymously as a new tune in *A Supplement to the New Version of the Psalms by Dr. Brady and Mr. Tate,* sixth edition, published in London in 1708, where it was set to Psalm 42, "As pants the Hart for cooling Streams." William Croft's name is attached to the tune by two of his contemporaries: Philip Hart, in his *Melodies Proper to be sung to any of ye versions of the Psalms of David, c.* 1720, and John Church, in *An Introduction to Psalmody,* 1723. Originally each phrase began and ended with a whole note, while the rest moved in half notes. The first phrase of this tune is one which appears several times in the seventeenth and eighteenth centuries. It is the first phrase of two tunes by Henry Lawes in Sandys' *Paraphrase upon the Psalms of David,* 1637, and is found in the first chorus of George F. Handel's (LBW 39) sixth Chandos anthem, "O praise the Lord," 1734. There is also the famous example of J. S. Bach's (LBW 219) Fugue in E-flat major ("St. Anne fugue"), which appears at the end of his Catechism chorales for organ.

Croft was born in Nether Ettinton, a village which no longer exists, located a few miles southeast of Stratford-on-Avon, in England. He was baptized there December 30, 1678. All that is known of his childhood is that he was a child of the Chapel Royal when Dr. John Blow was master and that he was a pupil of Blow's. From 1700 to 1711 he was probably the first organist of St. Anne's, Soho. Jeremiah Clarke (LBW 173) and Croft became joint organists to the Chapel Royal in 1704, and on Clarke's death in 1707 Croft remained as sole organist. A year later he succeeded John Blow as organist of Westminster Abbey and as master of the children and composer at the Chapel Royal, positions he held for the remainder of his life. In 1713 he received a Doctor of Music degree from Oxford University, and in 1725 was one of the founders of the Academy of Vocal Musick. He died August 14, 1727, at Westminster Abbey.

Croft wrote a variety of secular music earlier in his life, but it is for his sacred music—hymn tunes, anthems, services, and especially his burial service—that he is remembered. Of special interest also is his *Musica Sacra,* 1724, a collection of thirty anthems, which is the earliest example of English church music in score, engraved and stamped on plates. In the preface of the work, Croft sets forth the advantages of score over part books.

321 THE DAY IS SURELY DRAWING NEAR
(Es ist gewisslich an der Zeit)

Tune: Es ist gewisslich

The Latin hymn, "Dies irae, dies illa," served as the basis for an anonymous German hymn, "Es ist gewisslich an der Zeit," one of *Zwey schöne Lieder* published separately about 1565. Bartholomäus Ringwaldt revised the German hymn and included it in his *Handbuchlein: geistliche Lieder und Gebetlein, Auff der Reiss,* Frankfurt-an-der-Oder, 1586. The hymn was much used during the Thirty Years' War (1618–1648) when people often were convinced that the Last Day was at hand.

Bartholomäus Ringwaldt (Ringwalt, Ringwald) was born in Germany on November 28, 1522, and was ordained in 1557. After serving two other parishes, he settled in 1566 as pastor of Langfeld near Sonnenburg, Brandenburg, where he was still living in 1597. He seems to have died there in 1599 or 1600.

As a poet of the people, Ringwaldt had considerable influence on his contemporaries. Two of his collections, which contained lively pictures of people of various walks of life in his time, went through numerous editions until 1700. He was a prolific hymnwriter and, in addition to his

Handbüchlien, published *Der 91 Psalm neben Siben andern schönen Liedern,* 1577, and *Evangelia, Auff alle Sontag unnd Fest,* about 1581.

Philip Adam Peter's translation, written in 1872, was included in the *Evangelical Lutheran Hymnal,* 1880, of the Ohio Synod. It has been considerably altered for the LBW.

Born January 2, 1832, at Homburg-vor-der-Hohe, Hesse-Nassau, Germany, Philip A. Peter attended the common schools and the Corydon Academy of Indiana. In 1857 he was married to Mahala Rhodes. Trained by the Reverend E. S. Henkel in Corydon, he was ordained a pastor of the Joint Synod of Ohio and Other States in 1858. He went in 1869 to St. Paul's Lutheran Church, Olean, Indiana. In 1874 he received a call to a three-point parish made up of St. Matthew's Lutheran Church near Ithaca, Dark County; Trinity Lutheran Church in Franklin Township, Dark County; and Immanuel near Philipsburg, Montgomery County— all in Indiana. There he served for many years until ill health impeded his work. A separate pastor was called to Philipsburg in 1900, who assisted him during the last years of his ministry. Peter retired in 1908 and died February 9, 1919.

Besides his parish ministry, Peter served for nine years as secretary of the Southern District, and another eight as secretary of the Western District. His publications include a *History of the Reformation of the Sixteenth Century,* 1889; a German history of the Joint Synod of Ohio and Other States, 1900; and *St. Paul, the Great Apostle to the Gentiles,* 1901; as well as translations of several hymns.

ES IST GEWISSLICH (also "Nun freut euch"). According to one tradition, Martin Luther (LBW 48) wrote this tune down after hearing it sung by a traveling artisan. The tune dates from the fifteenth century and was originally associated with the secular text, "Wach auf, meins Herzens schöne." It was published in 1555 as given below.

The LBW form of the melody was included in Joseph Klug's (LBW 85) *Geistliche lieder,* Wittenberg, 1529, as the setting for Luther's "Nun freut euch lieben Christen gmein" (LBW 299).

J. S. Bach (LBW 219) used the melody in his *Christmas Oratorio* and in Cantata 70, and included a setting in his *Choralgesänge.* His organ settings are among his Miscellaneous Preludes.

The harmony is from the *Württemburgische Gesangbuch,* 1953.

322   THE CLOUDS OF JUDGMENT GATHER
(Hora novissima, tempora pessima)

Tune: Durrow

Here, as at LBW 316, an extended Latin poem is the source of more than one hymn. This hymn and "Jerusalem the Golden" (LBW 347) are from

Bernard of Cluny's *De Contemptu Mundi,* a poem of nearly three thousand lines describing the evils and vices of his time (including those within the church), and setting them in contrast to portrayals of heaven. The original poem was written in dactylic hexameters, with internal rhyme as well as rhymes at the ends of lines. A short quotation will illustrate the meter:

Hora noviss*ima*   tempora pess*ima*   sunt: vigil*emus!*
Ecce mina*citer*   imminet arb*iter*   ille supr*emus*

The difficulty of sustaining this form for 2,966 lines can well be imagined; Bernard remarked after completing the poem, "Unless the Spirit of wisdom and understanding had flowed in upon me, I could not have put together so long a work in so difficult a meter."

The monastery of Cluny, founded in 910 on the site of a hunting lodge belonging to William Duke of Aquitaine, was by the twelfth century extremely wealthy and famous throughout Europe. It had beautiful buildings with the finest church in France, its services were resplendent, and its influence was felt in all of Europe. Already a century earlier the powerful abbey had prodded French nobles to join the Spaniards in a holy war against the Moslems in Spain. At its peak it controlled a large number of monasteries in France, Italy, Germany, England, Scotland, and Poland. It was to this abbey that Bernard came during the time that Peter the Venerable was abbott (between 1122 and 1156), and it was to Peter that Bernard dedicated his poem *De Contemptu Mundi.*

Little is known about Bernard except for his poem. His birth and death dates are not recorded. He was born in France of English parents sometime early in the twelfth century. His exact birthplace has not been ascertained. Earlier writers felt that Bernard was born in Morlaix in Brittany, but later sources consider "Morlaix" to be an erroneous spelling of Murles or Morlas which is in the Pyrenees. It is generally assumed that Bernard remained at Cluny until his death.

Based on a translation from *The Rhythm of Bernard of Morlais,* 1858, by John Mason Neale (LBW 34), this English text was prepared for the LBW by the Inter-Lutheran Commission on Worship.

DURROW is an Irish folk melody associated with a County Limerick sea-song, "Captain Thomson." The harmonization was prepared for *The Hymn Book,* 1971, of the United Church and Anglican Church of Canada by William France.

The son of a Baptist minister, France was born April 12, 1912, near New Liskeard, Ontario. He received his first music lessons from his mother, and in 1929 he became organist at the Avondale United Church, Tillsonburg. He continued music study—piano, organ, and composition —with Gertrude Huntly, Frederick Horwood, Eugene Hill, Charles Peaker, and Healy Willan (LBW 125), and graduated from the University of Toronto with a Bachelor of Music degree in 1941. Since 1932 he has held several posts as organist and choirmaster: Devine Street United Church in Sarnia, 1932–1934; Central United Church in Sault Ste. Marie, 1934–1938; Dublin Street United Church in Guelph, 1938–1942; and Knox Presbyterian Church in Stratford, 1942–1950. In 1950 he became organist of Dominion-Chalmers United Church in Ottawa. He served as a member of the subcommittee on tunes for *The Hymn Book,* and has published over seventy compositions including songs, part songs, anthems, and works for organ and for piano.

323 O LORD OF LIGHT, WHO MADE THE STARS
(Creator alme siderum)
Tune: Conditor alme siderum

The Latin hymn, "Conditor alme siderum," sung at Vespers (sunset) during Advent, dates from the early Middle Ages. It is found in a ninth-century manuscript at Bern, and a tenth-century hymnal at Canterbury. One of the hymns "revised" (see p. 15) during the sixteenth and seventeenth centuries, it was included in altered form, beginning "Creator alme siderum," in the Roman Breviary, sponsored by Pope Urban VIII who ruled from 1623 to 1644.

The translation is by Melvin Farrell, and was included in *The People's Hymnal,* second edition, Cincinnati, 1961.

Born in 1930 in St. Paul, Minnesota, Farrell moved with his family to Seattle, Washington, in 1941. After attending minor seminary at St. Edward's Seminary in Kenmore, Washington, he went to Washington, D.C. for major seminary studies as a Basselin student at Theological College. In 1953 he obtained a Master of Arts degree in philosophy at Catholic University and, after further work during summer sessions, received a Master of Arts degree in literature from the University of Washington in 1956. The following year he completed an S. T. L. degree from Catholic University and was ordained. The first ten years of his ministry were spent in the minor seminary in Seattle, St. Edward's Seminary, where in 1962 he became principal of the high school department. In 1968 he returned to Catholic University for two years to complete a doctorate in theology. Beginning in 1970 he served for one year as president of St. Thomas Seminary College in Seattle, two years as rector of the major seminary in San Francisco (St. Patrick's Seminary, Menlo Park), and two years as director of formation for the Sulpician Province. In 1975 he became president-rector of St. Thomas Seminary in Seattle, and in 1977 was appointed research secretary for a special task force commissioned by the Archdiocese of Seattle to study the feasibility of a newly-designed theology program of priestly formation.

Farrell has published several works, including *First Steps to the Priesthood* (1960), *Getting to Know Christ* (1963), *Theology for Parents and Teachers* (1973), *Teaching the Good News Today* (1974), *The Christian Message at a Glance* (1975), and *A Catechism for Parents and Teachers* (1977). In addition he has been a regular author for *Hi-Time* (a weekly religion text for high school), has contributed various articles to theological and cathechetical periodicals, and has written many hymns, especially for *The People's Massbook,* 1966. He has conducted numerous workshops around the country in religious education and in continuing education for priests, and for five years has taught in the field of religious education at Seattle University summer sessions.

CONDITOR ALME SIDERUM is the plainsong melody universally associated with this text. The harmonization is by Carl Schalk (LBW 118).

324 O LOVE THAT WILL NOT LET ME GO
Tune: St. Margaret

George Matheson was born in Glasgow, Scotland, on March 27, 1842. Although he had suffered poor vision from his childhood, and by age eighteen was nearly totally blind, his sisters learned Latin, Greek, and Hebrew to assist him in his studies, and he won high honors at the University of Glasgow, receiving a Bachelor of Arts degree in 1861 and a Master of Arts degree the following year. In 1866 he was licensed to preach, and for a short time was assistant minister in Sandyford Church, Glasgow, before going in 1868 to Innellan, Argyllshire. He went to St. Bernard's, Edinburgh, in 1886 and remained there until failing health forced his resignation in 1889. He died August 28, 1906, in North Berwick. His extensive writings include one volume of verse, *Sacred Songs,* 1890.

According to Matheson's account, the hymn was written in five minutes on June 6, 1882. He was alone at the manse of Innellan at the time, the rest of the family having gone to Glasgow for his sister's marriage. It was included in *Life and Work, the record of the Church of Scotland,* January, 1883, and soon thereafter, in *The Scottish Hymnal,* 1885.

ST. MARGARET was written for this text by Albert Lister Peace for *The Scottish Hymnal,* 1885, of which he was editor. The composer's harmony has been retained.

Born January 26, 1844, in Huddersfield, England, Peace showed exceptional musical ability at a very young age and by age nine became organist of Holmfirth Parish Church in Yorkshire. After serving a number of other churches he was appointed organist to Glasgow Cathedral in 1879 and remained there until 1897 when he went to St. George's Hall, Liverpool. There he remained until his death March 14, 1912.

Peace had a wide reputation as an organist, and in the quarter-century following 1865, when the Church of Scotland lifted its ban on the use of organs in worship, he dedicated two-thirds of the organs built in Scotland. In addition to *The Scottish Hymnal,* Peace was editor of two other hymnals and a book of anthems for the Church of Scotland.

325   LORD, THEE I LOVE WITH ALL MY HEART
(Herzlich Lieb hab' ich dich, o Herr)
Tune: Herzlich Lieb

Based on Psalms 18 and 73, this German hymn has been a favorite of many, including Christian Gellert (LBW 133). Written about 1567, it was first published in *Kurtze und sonderliche Newe Symbola etlicher Fürsten,* Nürnberg, 1571.

Martin Schalling, son of the pastor at Strassburg, was born April 21, 1532, and entered the University of Wittenberg where he was a favorite student of Philipp Melanchthon and Nicolaus Selnecker (LBW 490). After receiving a Master of Arts degree he remained at Wittenberg for a short time as a lecturer before going in 1554 as pastor to Regensburg. Although described as a moderate and peace-loving man, Schalling lived and worked in a time of great turmoil and controversy in Protestant Germany, and found himself frequently at odds with various factions. He was forced to give up his first post after four years because of his preaching against the tenants of Matthias Flach, and went to Amberg, Bavaria. There he remained for ten years until Elector Friedrich III, of the Palatinate, decided to adopt the Calvinistic order of service and all

Lutheran clergy who did not conform, including Schalling, were expelled. He was allowed by Duke Ludwig, son of the elector, who remained a Lutheran, to minister to the Lutherans at Vilseck near Amberg. When Ludwig became regent of the Oberpfalz, he recalled Schalling in 1576 to Amberg as court preacher and superintendent, and when Friedrich III died and Ludwig became Elector of the Pfalz, he made Schalling general superintendent of the Oberpfalz and court preacher of Heidelberg. Later, however, when the clergy of Oberpfalz were pressed to sign the Formula of Concord, Schalling hesitated because he felt it dealt too harshly with the followers of Melanchthon, and for this he was banished from the court at Heidelberg and confined to his house from 1580 until 1583, when he was finally deprived of his offices. He stayed for a time at Altdorf and in 1585 was appointed pastor of St. Mary's Church in Nürnberg, where he remained until blindness forced his retirement. He died December 19, 1608, at Nürnberg.

Originally beginning "Lord, all my heart is fixed on Thee," Catherine Winkworth's (LBW 29) translation of this hymn was included in her *Lyra Germanica,* second series, 1858, and was altered to the original meter of the German hymn for the *Chorale Book for England,* 1863. The text has been extensively altered.

HERZLICH LIEB, the melody associated with this hymn, is by an unknown composer. It was included in Bernhard Schmid's *Zwey Bücher einer neuen Künstlichen Tabulatur auff Orgel und Instrument,* published in Strassburg in 1577. J. S. Bach (LBW 219) employed the melody in his St. John Passion.

Bernhard Schmid was born around 1520 (some sources give 1535), probably in Strassburg, and was married in 1552 to Catharina Klein. In 1562 he succeeded Franz Durst as organist of the Strassburg Cathedral, a position he held for thirty years. In 1592 he accepted a post in the Jung St. Peter Kirche, but he died less than a year later. His son, Bernard, the Younger, succeeded him at the cathedral. Schmid encouraged the use of instrumental music in the church. His 1577 tabulature, published for musical amateurs, is an important collection of early organ music, and contains French, German, and Italian secular songs, and a number of motets and dances. One of the pieces contained in the tabulature, the "Corante du roy," is the earliest example of a *courante.*

The harmonization of the tune was prepared by Friedrich Zipp and included in *Das Wochenlied,* 1950.

Zipp, who descends from a long line of teachers and organists, was born June 20, 1914, in Frankfurt-am-Main, Germany. He studied at Dr. Hoch's Konservatorium and the University of Frankfurt as well as the Hochschule für Musikerziehung und Kirchenmusik and the University of Berlin, working with Armin Knab from 1934 to 1938. In 1938 he became an organist and choirmaster in Frankfurt, and in 1940 he also became a teacher at the *Gymnasium* in Frankfurt. From 1941 to 1945 he was in military service, during which time he was taken prisoner by the Americans. Appointed a lecturer at the Hochschule für Musik in Frankfurt in 1947, he was forced by illness to interrupt his teaching from 1948 to 1950. He was made a professor at the Hochschule in 1962. He has also worked as a music critic. His compositions, which number more than three hundred, are predominantly sacred works.

MY HEART IS LONGING *(O, at jeg kunde min Jesus prise)*
Tune: Princess Eugenie

The Norwegian form of this hymn, "O, at jeg kunde min Jesus prise," is a free rendition by Lars Oftedal of a Swedish hymn, and was included in the supplement to the ninth edition of *Basunröst og Harpetoner,* 1875. The original Swedish text, *"Vi äro köpta och återlösta,"* was given in *Lofsånger och andeliga Wisor i nådene,* 1872, edited by Fredrik Engelke (1848–1906). The Swedish hymn was attributed to Princess Eugenie in a collection published by Birger Hall in 1887, but a search through the royal library in Stockholm of all the princess' writings has shown that the hymn was not among them.

Born in Stavanger, Norway, in 1838, Oftedal was a well-known preacher and newspaper editor, who later became a pastor in the Church of Norway. Also a politician, he was a member of the city council of Stavanger, and for some time served as a member of the Norwegian parliament. He died in 1900.

Peter Andrew Sveeggen's (LBW 69) English translation was prepared in 1931 for *The Concordia Hymnal.* The first five stanzas are unaltered except for updated second-person pronouns; stanza 6 is altered considerably.

PRINCESS EUGENIE is a Norwegian folk melody named for the Swedish princess, Eugénie Augusta Amalia Albertina (1830–1889), to whom this text was attributed in *Lofsånger och andeliga Wisor,* 1872. Jan Aasgaard of the Oslo University Library has located the melody in a manuscript by Arne Bjørndal, 1916, in which the source is given as *Den lille Harpe,* 1878. He further notes that the title is listed in Alfred Nielsen's *Sang-Katalog* (Copenhagen, 1924) where the source is given as *Hjemlandstoner,* and the composer as "Bjærum."

327 ROCK OF AGES, CLEFT FOR ME
Tune: Toplady

Augustus Montague Toplady was born in Farnham, Surrey, England, on November 4, 1740. His father, a major in the British army, was killed within the first year of Augustus' life. His mother later moved to Ireland, and there he received a Bachelor of Arts degree at Trinity College, Dublin, in 1700. He came under the influence of a Wesleyan lay preacher, James Morris, and was converted at a service held in a Dublin barn, but because of his extreme views and volatile temper he came into conflict with John Wesley (LBW 302), and the resulting bitterness lasted for many years. Ordained in 1762, he ministered for a time as curate of Blagdon, in the Mendips near Wells; and after 1768 as vicar of Broad Hembury, Devon. After 1775 he was minister of the Chapel of the French Calvinists in Leicester Fields, London. He died August 11, 1778.

In the October, 1775, *Gospel Magazine* appeared the lines:

> Rock of Ages, cleft for me
> Let me hide myself in thee!
> Foul, I to the fountain fly;
> Wash me, Saviour, or I die.

and the following March the same magazine carried the complete hymn. The LBW text is from Toplady's *Psalms and Hymns for Public and*

Private Worship, 1776, where stanza 4 was slightly revised. In addition to his *Psalms and Hymns,* Toplady published *Poems on Sacred Subjects,* 1769, and *Historic Proof of the Doctrinal Calvinism of the Church of England,* 1774.

TOPLADY was written for this text in Hastings' and Mason's *Spiritual Songs for Social Worship,* 1832, where it was called "Rock of Ages."

The composer, Thomas Hastings, was born October 15, 1784, in Washington, Connecticut. When he was twelve, his family moved to Clinton, New York. He received a country school education, and at age eighteen was leading the village choir. In 1823 he went to Utica where he edited a weekly religious paper, *The Western Recorder,* and nine years later he was called to New York City by twelve churches to lead their choirs. A Presbyterian, he was for many years director of the choir at Bleeker Street Presbyterian Church. The University of New York City conferred on him an honorary Doctor of Music degree in 1858. Hastings wrote a total of six hundred hymns, nearly one thousand tunes, and either alone or with others such as Lowell Mason (LBW 353) and William Bradbury (LBW 293), edited about fifty collections of music. Very few of his tunes or hymns, however, have remained in use. He died May 15, 1872, in New York City.

328   ALL HAIL THE POWER OF JESUS' NAME!

Tune: Coronation

In the November, 1779, issue of the *Gospel Magazine* the first stanza of this hymn appeared, together with the tune "Shrubsole" ("Miles Lane" —LBW 329). The following April, the stanza was repeated with six additional stanzas by Edward Perronet titled "On the Resurrection, the Lord is King." In 1787 the hymn appeared in John Rippon's *A Selection of Hymns, from the Best Authors intended to be an Appendix to Dr. Watts's Psalms and Hymns* with some of the stanzas either altered or replaced completely. There each stanza was titled: Angels, Martyrs, Converted Jews, Believing Gentiles, Sinners of Every Age, Sinners of Every Nation, Ourselves. The LBW takes the first five stanzas from the original seven stanzas and the last two from Rippon's *Selection.* Alterations are few and very minor.

Edward Perronet, of Swiss Huguenot ancestry, and son of a close friend and advisor of the Wesleys (LBW 27 and 302), was born in Sundridge, Kent, England, in 1726. Edward himself was for many years an ardent worker for Methodism, at times suffering physical abuse for his preaching. Differences arose between Perronet and the Wesleys, however, about whether itinerant preachers should also administer the sacraments and over Perronet's attacks on the Church of England. In 1771 he became one of the ministers to the Countess of Huntingdon, but came into conflict because of his negative feelings about the Church of England, and spent the final years of his life as an Independent or Congregational minister of a small church near Canterbury. He died there on January 2, 1792.

John Rippon, born April 29, 1751, at Tiverton in Devonshire, England, graduated from the Baptist College in Bristol and went in 1772 to preach at Carter's Lane Baptist Church, Tooley Street (later moved to New Park Street), in London. What originally was to be a temporary pastorate turned out to be a long, successful ministry terminated only by Rippon's death on December 17, 1836. Rippon wrote, in all, over a thousand hymns and published two collections—his *Selection* mentioned above, and in 1791, a *Selection of Psalm and Hymn Tunes from the Best Authors.*

As early as *The Village Harmony,* published in 1806, both tunes, "Miles Lane" and "Coronation," were included in one hymnal.

CORONATION was first included in Oliver Holden's *The Union Harmony or Universal Collection of Sacred Music,* published in Boston in 1793. This work consisted of two volumes, to which Holden contributed a total of thirty-five tunes. (In that collection the author of the hymn was erroneously given as "the Rev. Mr. Medley.") Interestingly, when the hymn appeared two years later in *The Massachusetts Compiler,* edited by Holden, Hans Gram, and Samuel Holyoke, it was set to Shrubsole's tune and not to "Coronation." In the original four-part setting, the melody moved about among the three upper parts.

Oliver Holden was born September 18, 1765, in Shirley, Massachusetts, and moved with his family to Charlestown when he was twenty-one. There his trade as a carpenter found ready use when he helped to rebuild the town which had been burned by the British. He became a large operator in real estate, and in addition opened a general store and conducted a singing school. He built a Puritan Church and ministered to its congregation and was also a prominent Freemason. For eight sessions (1818–1833) he was a member of the Massachusetts House of Representatives. Holden edited several collections, either alone or with others: *The American Harmony,* 1792; *Union Harmony* and *The Massachusetts Compiler* (see above); *The Worcester Collection* (sixth edition, revised), 1797; *Sacred Dirges, Hymns and Anthems,* 1800; *The Modern Collection of Sacred Music,* 1800; *Plain Psalmody,* 1800; and *The Charlestown Collection of Sacred Songs,* 1803. A small pipe organ which he used in the preparation of these collections is now kept by the Bostonian Society at the Old State House in Boston. Also a writer of poetry, he composed both the text and the tune of a piece in honor of the visit of George Washington to Boston in 1789. Death came September 4, 1844.

329   ALL HAIL THE POWER OF JESUS' NAME!

Tune: Miles Lane

See LBW 328 for discussion of this text.

MILES LANE, which first appeared (called "Shrubsole") with Edward Perronet's single stanza in the November, 1779, *Gospel Magazine,* was written in three parts with the tune in the middle. In the refrain, each "Crown him" is sung alone, first by the bass, then by the treble, then by the tenor, and the final "Crown him Lord of all" is in four parts with the melody in the tenor. A facsimile is given in the April, 1902, edition of *The Musical Times.*

William Shrubsole, son of a blacksmith, was born in January, 1760, in Canterbury. From 1770 to 1777 he was a chorister at Canterbury Cathedral and afterwards went to London to teach music. He became organist at Bangor Cathedral in 1782, but was dismissed two years later for "frequenting conventicles." From 1784 until his death on January

18, 1806, he was organist at Spa Fields Chapel of Lady Huntingdon's Connexion. Shrubsole and Perronet were close friends, so close in fact that Perronet named Shrubsole one of his executors and willed to him some property.

330 IN HEAVEN ABOVE *(I Himmelen, i Himmelen)*
Tune: I Himmelen, i Himmelen

This Swedish hymn, which was translated into Norwegian twice (once by Magnus Landstad [LBW 310] and once by Wilhelm Wexels [LBW 351]), is included in American hymnals in a translation by a Scotsman, William Maccall. The original hymn of five stanzas was written by Laurentius Laurentii Laurinus for the funeral of his wife on July 30, 1620. It was printed two years later in *En Christeligh Lijkpredikan,* together with two other Laurinus hymns and the lengthy sermon preached by a fellow pastor at the funeral. Subsequently the hymn was extended, with many of the additional stanzas no doubt also written by Laurinus himself, and in a 1651 *Manuale* it was eighteen stanzas in length. In 1814 and 1816 Johan Åström selected and considerably revised seven stanzas, which were given in the 1819 *Swenska Psalm-Boken.* The English translation was published in Maccall's *Hymns of Sweden Rendered into English,* 1868.

Laurinus, born in 1573 (Lövgren* gives 1577) in Söderköping, Sweden, studied first at Uppsala before going to Wittenberg, where he completed his Master's degree in 1603. The same year he was ordained and became assistant rector of Söderköping, and in 1608, rector. In 1609 he was appointed pastor of Häradshammar, and later also of Jonsberg, and he remained with these congregations for forty-six years. In 1620 he became rural dean. He lost his eyesight in his later years, and died on November 29, 1655 (some sources give November 22, 1656).

Laurinus wrote scholarly works in Latin, Swedish, and German. Among his diverse publications are his *Musica rudimenta,* the first Swedish textbook on singing; his *Haffenrefferi Compendium Locorum Theologicorum,* to which he appended several of his hymns; and *Plausus Seucicus,* 1650, a Swedish poem on the Thirty Years' War.

Åström was born November 20, 1767, in Gäfle, Sweden. When Johan was thirteen, his father died, but his mother provided his early education while working at her spinning wheel. He received a Master of Philosophy degree from Uppsala University in 1794. Ordained the previous year, he served for a short time as vice-pastor of the cathedral, as well as chaplain in a mental hospital in Uppsala. Thereafter he served as pastor of the German church in Norrköping, as rector of the archbishopric in Tuna and Stavby from 1805, and in Sigtuna and Altuna after 1821. He received an honorary Doctor of Theology degree in 1809, and was also a fellow of the Order of the North Star. During the years 1816–1818 he assisted Johan Wallin (LBW 73) in the preparation of the *Swenska Psalm-Boken.* The 1819 edition contained eleven original texts and many translations by Åström. He died in 1844.

Maccall was born February 25, 1812, in Largs, Ayrshire, Scotland, and died in England, at Bexley Heath, a suburb of London, on November 19, 1888. After receiving his Master of Arts degree from the University of Glasgow in 1833, he went to a theological academy in Geneva to prepare for the Presbyterian ministry. Instead, he became a

Unitarian minister, and served churches at Bolton, Lancaster (1837–1840), and Credton, Devonshire (1841–1846), and afterwards moved to London, where he wrote for several periodicals. His publications, in addition to *Hymns of Sweden* mentioned above, include a book of translations from Danish published as *Hymns of Denmark by Gilbert Tait; Russian Hymns,* 1879; and *Christian Legends,* 1884.

I HIMMELEN, I HIMMELEN (also "Hauge"), associated with Laurinus' hymn in Norwegian use, is a folk melody from Heddal, copied by Ludvig Lindeman (LBW 285) and included in his *Fjaeldmelodier.* (Note the resemblance of this melody to another melody from Heddal at LBW 314. Both emphasize the major triad, employ repetitions of motifs within a phrase, and use the same rhythmic patterns.) A setting for baritone solo and four-part chorus was included in Edvard Greig's (LBW 314) *Four Psalms,* Op. 74, the last music he wrote. Another tune, from *Then Svenska Psalm-Boken,* 1697, is used with this text in Sweden (see the *Service Book and Hymnal,* 1958, #146, first tune).

The harmonization is based on a setting by Elmer T. R. Hanke included in the *Hymnal for Church and Home,* 1942.

Hanke, who for thirty-five years was director of music at Carthage College, was born in St. Paul, Minnesota on July 31, 1901. He completed a bachelor's degree at Augustana College Conservatory and another at Carthage College. Further studies included a master's degree (1937) from the State University of Iowa, and work in Paris, France; the University of Minnesota; and Northwestern University. In 1926 he was married to Eudora Peterson. The Carthage College A Capella Choir, which he founded and directed for thirty-two years, was one of the oldest college touring choirs in the United States. It toured through many states and was heard on radio networks coast to coast. In 1958, Hanke was hospitalized with a blood clot, and his wife took the choir on its annual tour through the Midwest. He died on April 27, before the choir returned.

Hanke was a member of the College Music Association, composer of a number of choral and instrumental works, and together with Howard R. Runkel was editor of *Scandinavian Chorales,* 1940.

331   JERUSALEM, MY HAPPY HOME
Tune: Land of Rest

Entitled "A Song Made by F. B. P. To the tune of Diana," this hymn of twenty-six stanzas is included in a manuscript kept at the British Museum. It is undated but considered to be of the late sixteenth or early seventeenth century. The fact that another version exists (forty-four stanzas long) dated 1585, has led W. T. Brooke in Julian* to conclude that both must have had an earlier common source. The hymn seems to be based on *Liber Meditationum,* published in Venice in 1553 and sometimes ascribed to Augustine (LBW 146). The identity of F. B. P. is unknown. There have been several speculations, including a suggestion that it might have been Francis Baker, Pater (or priest), who was for a time imprisoned at the Tower of London.

LAND OF REST. Originally the tune "Diana" was suggested for this hymn (see above) and *The Hymnal 1940* (Episcopal) included a sixteenth-century folk song, "Diana and her darlings deare," as one of the settings. "Land of Rest," an anonymous hexatonic melody, was harmonized by Annabel Morris Buchanan in her *Folk Hymns of America,* New York, 1938, and headed "Heard as a child from my grandmother, Mrs. S. J. (Sarah Ann Love) Foster." Buchanan believes that it is a variant of some old folk air, probably of Scottish or Northern English origin, and that her grandmother's version was no doubt brought to Texas from South Carolina, via Tennessee. She notes that Anne G. Gilchrist has located two similar versions which she considers to be of the Lord Thomas and Fair Ellinor ballad-group, and that Phillips Barry of Massachusetts includes a Maine version with the Little Musgrave and Lady Barnard group. Many similarities can be seen between "Land of Rest" and "Swing low, sweet chariot," and Buchanan states that "Sweet Chariot" is obviously derived from the Scottish tune. In his *Soul Music Black and White* [p. 35f], however, Johannes Riedel presents evidence that "Sweet Chariot" derives from Rhodesia.) Titled "New Prospect" and attributed to W. S. Turner, a version of the tune was included in *The Sacred Harp* (1844) as the setting for "O land of rest! for thee I sigh."

Annabel Morris was born in Groesbeck, Texas, October 22, 1888, and studied music at the Landon Conservatory in Dallas, graduating in 1907. She studied piano in Philadelphia with Dr. H. A. Clarke, and in New York City was a student at the Guilmant Organ School and studied piano and composition with Cornelius Rybner. Married in 1912 to John Preston Buchanan, a lawyer and writer, she is the mother of four children. She has taught piano, organ, theory, and composition in colleges in Oklahoma, Texas, and Virginia, and from the time of her graduation from college, has given recitals in piano, organ, and folk music. Her work with American folk music and with music clubs has been extensive. From 1927 to 1930 she was president of the Virginia Federation of Music Clubs, and in 1931 she was co-organizer of the White Top Folk Festival which she directed until 1940. She has held offices in the National Federation of Music Clubs and the National League of American Pen Women, and has been a member of the American Guild of Organists. Publications include *Adventures in Virginia Folkways, American Folk Music, Book of American Composers, American Folk Music Booklet,* an article in Thompson's *International Cyclopedia,* and numerous contributions to periodicals. She has collected much valuable material in the area of folk music and has also written a large number of original compositions, many of which are influenced by folk music. In 1955 she was honored at a Town Concert in New York City for her work in collecting and creating folk music. She had her own apartment until 1976, when a broken hip made it necessary for her to move to Parkview Convalescent Center in Paducah, Kentucky. Her distinguished collection of books, photographs, recordings, and manuscripts was donated in 1978 to the University of North Carolina at Chapel Hill.

332 BATTLE HYMN OF THE REPUBLIC

Tune: Battle Hymn

Shortly after the beginning of the Civil War, Julia Ward Howe heard Union troops singing "John Brown's body lies a-mouldering in the grave," a song about a farmer (1800–1859) hanged in Charleston for his fight against slavery. Desiring to set better words to the tune, she wrote this text which was published in the February, 1862, issue of *The Atlantic Monthly.*

Mrs. Howe, a pioneer in woman suffrage and an ardent abolitionist, was born in New York on May 27, 1819. Her husband, Samuel Gridley Howe, an idealist and philanthropist, had served in the Greek civil war and devoted his life to work with the blind, the mute, and the mentally ill. A Unitarian, Mrs. Howe was a parishioner, along with her husband, of Theodore Parker, a Boston reformer and abolitionist. She was the author of two volumes of verse as well as other writings. She died October 17, 1910.

BATTLE HYMN, in existence long before the Civil War, has been used with a variety of texts by infantrymen as a marching song, by firemen, and in revival meetings.

Although attributed to William Steffe since the 1880s, this tune seems to be of unknown origin. Steffe, a Philadelphian who died in 1911, claimed that he wrote it in 1855 or 1856 for "Say, bummers, will you meet us," and later used it with a song of the Goodwill Fire Company of Philadelphia. The claim is generally regarded as a myth, however.

333 LORD, TAKE MY HAND AND LEAD ME
(So nimm denn meine Hände und führe mich)
Tune: So nimm denn meine Hände

Born in 1825 or 1826 in Riga, Latvia, Julie Hausmann moved shortly afterward to Mitau, where her father taught in the *Gymnasium.* She was one of seven sisters. Her family was of German background, but made their home in the Russian Baltic province. She studied with private tutors, although migraine headaches made her work difficult. After her mother died in 1859 she had to attend to her father who was in poor health. He was by then a town councillor, which in Russia at that time made him part of the aristocracy; consequently the name was changed to von Hausmann. They moved to Riga in 1861, where her father died. From 1866 to 1870 she stayed with a younger sister who was organist in the English church at Biarritz in southwestern France. In 1870 they went together to visit an older sister, Elizabeth, in St. Petersburg. Elizabeth was director of St. Anna school, to which was connected a pension house. There four of the sisters worked happily together for many years. Two of the sisters died in 1896 and 1898. The other two went to a seaside resort at Wössö in Estonia, where Julie died August 15, 1901.

Despite advanced age and bad eyesight she had continued to work at writing and doing volunteer work among the poor. She published a devotional book, *Hausbrot,* but did not publish her poetry. While she was caring for her father in Riga, her friend Olga von Karp saw some of her poetry and sent it to pastor Gustav Knak in Berlin. He liked it so much that he asked for the whole collection. The author consented to their publication only when it was agreed that it would be for the benefit of a hospital and orphanage in Hong Kong, and without her name. The collection was titled *Maiblumen, Lieder einer Stillen im Lande, dargereicht von G. Knak.* The first volume, which included "So nimm denn meine Hände," was published in 1862. Three other volumes followed, the last published by Knak's son.

The English version was prepared by the Inter-Lutheran Commission on Worship. Stanza 1 is from a translation by Herman Brueckner (LBW 249), written in 1925 and included in the *American Lutheran Hymnal,* 1930. Stanzas 2 and 3 are based on a text prepared in 1912 by Rudolph A. John.

Rudolph John was born March 26, 1859, in Washington, Missouri, where his father was pastor of St. Peter's Evangelical Church. After studying at Washington University and Eden Theological Seminary, he was ordained in 1878 and went to serve a group of mission churches in southern Illinois. Thereafter he ministered for a time to Evangelical churches in Sedalia, Missouri, and at St. John's Evangelical Church, Richmond, Virginia, before beginning a forty-four-year pastorate at St. Paul's Church, Chicago. He died in Chicago on July 17, 1938.

In addition to his parish duties he was also a journalist and a poet, and for a time after 1886 an editor of the *Christliche Kinderzeitung,* a German Sunday school paper. He founded the St. Paul's Church Home for the aged, serving as its superintendent after 1926, and held several official positions in the Evangelical Church.

SO NIMM DENN MEINE HÄNDE was given in Friedrich Silcher's *Kinderlieder für Schule und Haus,* III, published in Tübingen in 1842, set to "Wie könnt ich ruhig schlagen."

Silcher, born June 27, 1789, at Schnaith near Schorndorf, Württemberg, Germany, studied music first with his father who was an organist, and later at Auberlen. He taught at various places, including Ludwigsburg, and later became a conductor in Stuttgart. In 1817 he became director of music and organist at the University of Tübingen, where he remained until his retirement in 1860. While teaching at the university he took the time also to earn a Doctor of Philosophy degree which he received in 1852. He died at Tübingen on August 26, 1860.

In addition to an important collection of German folk songs—the *Sammlung deutscher Volkslieder*—he also published the *Württemberg Choralbuch,* the *Geschichte der evangelischen Kirchengesänge,* (1844), and other collections of hymns, collections of songs for children, and a text book on harmony and composition.

334 JESUS, SAVIOR, PILOT ME
Tune: Pilot

Edward Hopper, born in New York City February 17, 1818 (1816?), attended New York University and graduated from Union Theological Seminary in 1842. Ordained a Presbyterian minister, he served Greenville, New York; Sag Harbour, Long Island; and finally the Church of Sea and Land, New York, where many of his congregation were sailors. He died April 23, 1888.

This hymn was published anonymously in *The Sailor's Magazine,* March 3, 1871, and in *The Baptist Praise Book* of the same year.

PILOT was written for Hopper's hymn in *The Baptist Praise Book,* 1871. John Edgar Gould, born in Bangor, Maine, in 1822, operated a music store on Broadway in New York City, and later, about 1868, became a partner of William Gustavus Fischer (LBW 390) in a piano and music business in Philadelphia. He published several hymn books alone or in conjunction with Edward L. White. He undertook a trip to southern Europe and Northern Africa in hope of regaining his health, but died in Algiers on March 4, 1875.

The harmonization is by Walter Pelz (LBW 240).

335 MAY GOD BESTOW ON US HIS GRACE
(Es wolle Gott uns gnädig sein)
Tune: Es wolle Gott uns gnädig sein

It was Martin Luther's (LBW 48) suggestion that his *Formula Missae et Communionis* (Wittenberg, 1523) should close with the Aaronic Benediction or Psalm 67:6–7. Accordingly, this hymn, Luther's paraphrase of Psalm 67, was included at the end of Paul Speratus' (LBW 297) German translation of Luther's *Formula Missae,* published in January of 1524. Written in 1523, it has been described as the first missionary hymn of Protestantism.

Julian* lists three English translations of this hymn from the sixteenth century in addition to many later ones. The LBW text is an altered form of that given by Richard Massie (LBW 134) in his *Martin Luther's Spiritual Songs,* 1854.

ES WOLLE GOTT UNS GNÄDIG SEIN. This Phrygian-mode melody appeared together with Luther's hymn on a broadsheet (*Der Lxvj. Deus Misereatur*) printed by Hans Knappe the Younger in Magdeburg in 1524. Apparently this was also printed early in the year, for Leupold* notes that on May 6 a man was arrested in Magdeburg for singing and selling the hymns "Aus tiefer Not" (LBW 295) and "Es wolle Gott uns gnädig sien."

The tune is based on a fifteenth-century *Marienlied,* "Maria, du bist genadenwoll." Carl Schalk (LBW 118) prepared the harmonization for the LBW.

"Es wolle Gott uns gnädig sein" was sung by Gustavus Adolphus' army before the battle of Lützen in 1632, and Christian Frederick Schwartz, Lutheran missionary to India, chose the hymn for the opening service of the mission church in Trichinopoli, South India, on July 11, 1792.

336 JESUS, THY BOUNDLESS LOVE TO ME
(O Jesu Christ, mein schönstes Licht)
Tune: Ryburn

Founded on a prayer in Johann Arndt's *Paradiesgärtlein,* Paul Gerhardt's hymn of sixteen stanzas was included in Johann Crüger's (LBW 23) *Praxis Pietatis Melica,* Berlin, 1653. John Wesley's translation is from his *Hymns and Sacred Poems,* 1739. See LBW 23 for Gerhardt and LBW 302 for Wesley.

RYBURN served as the setting for W. E. Gladstone's "O lead my blindness by the hand" in the *BBC Hymn Book,* London, 1951. The composer, Norman Cocker, was born at Sowerby Bridge in England in 1889, and became a chorister at Magdalen College, Oxford. Later he received his training as an organist from Henry Ley who considered him to be one of his most brilliant students. He was appointed organist and choir-master of St. Philip and St. James, Oxford, in 1909, and three years later became music master at Magdalen College School. While at Oxford he also directed the Oxford University Light Music Orchestra. For four years during World War I he served in the armed forces, after which he became sub-organist at Manchester Cathedral in 1919, advancing to organist-choirmaster on the death of Dr. Wilson in 1943. He gave himself entirely to his service at the cathedral, where he was known as a first-class choir trainer and a gifted improviser. Knowledgable also in the field of organ construction, he designed the new organ at Manchester Cathedral on novel lines. His compositions include many organ works, of which his *Tuba Tune* is the best-known, as well as several symphonies written especially for school orchestras. In 1951 Manchester University honored him with a Master of Arts degree. He died in Manchester on November 15, 1953.

337 OH, WHAT THEIR JOY *(O quanta qualia)*
Tune: O quanta qualia

Peter Abelard, one of the founders of the University of Paris, was born in 1079 in Pailais in Brittany. He has been described by Charles Homer Haskins (*The Renaissance of the Twelfth Century,* 1955) as "daring, original, brilliant, one of the first philosophical minds of the whole Middle Ages." Although designed for the military profession he abandoned his heritage and became a wandering student, determined to devote his life to the pursuit of knowledge. He soon overshadowed his teachers and was drawing great crowds to himself. He became a tutor to Heloïse, niece of Canon Fulbert of Notre Dame, a remarkable woman known throughout the kingdom for her learning. Although Abelard was at this time a priest, the two went to Brittany where they were secretly married and became the parents of a son. On their return to Paris, Abelard was emasculated by ruffians hired by Canon Fulbert, and subsequently entered the Abbey of St. Denis as a monk; Heloïse became a nun at Argenteuil. In 1120, however, Abelard returned to teaching, gathering throngs as before. His emphasis on questioning and reasoning in his approach to Scripture drew a great deal of animosity from some of his fellow clergy. Twice he was tried for heresy, first in 1121 at the Council of Soissons, and again in 1141 at the Council of Sens, when the great mystic, Bernard of Clairvaux (LBW 116), clashed with Abelard and procured his condemnation. On his way to Rome to appeal the decision, Peter Abelard died at St. Marcel near Chalons-sur-Saone, April 21, 1142.

Abelard's hymns are from a collection of hymns and sequences which he sent for the use of Heloïse and the nuns in her convent. John Mason Neale's (LBW 34) translation is from the *Hymnal Noted,* 1851. Stanza 2 has been extensively altered and stanza 4 has been completely rewritten.

O QUANTA QUALIA (also "Regnator orbis") is one of the French tunes discussed at LBW 83, and has its origin in the *Paris Antiphoner,* 1681. There it was set to "Fumant Sabaeis," a hymn for the Feast of the

Purification. When Neale included his translation in *The Hymnal Noted* it was given with an adaptation of a later form of the melody as found in La Feillée's *Methode de Plain Chant,* 1808, where it was the setting for J. B. Santeüil's "Regnator orbis." The *Hymnal Noted* form of the melody is used in the LBW, with a harmonization prepared by David Evans (LBW 339) for *The Church Hymnary,* 1927.

338 PEACE, TO SOOTHE OUR BITTER WOES
(Fred til Bod for bittert Savn)
Tune: Fred til Bod

See LBW 62 for Nikolai Grundtvig and LBW 138 for George A. T. Rygh. A hymn by Grundtvig beginning "Fred er Jorderiges Savn" was given in an unpublished *Psalme-Blade til Kirke-Bod,* 1843. The revised form of the hymn, beginning "Fred til Bod for bittert Savn," was published in *Kirkesalmer til Prøve,* 1845. Rygh's translation, prepared in 1908, was given in an altered form in the *Lutheran Hymnary,* 1913.

FRED TIL BOD (also "Easter Glory") was included in Ludvig Lindeman's (LBW 285) *Koralbog for den Norska Kirke,* 1871.

339 O LORD, NOW LET YOUR SERVANT
Tune: Kuortane

This hymn by Ernest Edwin Ryden (LBW 186) was written in 1924 and included in *The Hymnal,* 1925, of the Augustana Synod. Alterations are limited to updated second-person pronouns.

KUORTANE (also "Nyland") is a folk melody from the parish of Kuortane in Ethalapohjanmaa (South Ostrobothnia) in Finland. It was included in the Appendix to the 1909 edition of *Suomen Evankelis Luterilaisen Kirken Koraalikirja,* and was introduced to English hymnody when David Evans harmonized it for Anna Warring's "In heavenly love abiding" in *The Church Hymnary,* 1927.

Evans, music editor and representative of Wales on the committee of the revised *Church Hymnary,* 1927, was born February 6, 1874, at Resolven, Glamorganshire. He was educated at Arnold College, Swansea; University College, Cardiff; and Oxford University (Doctor of Music, 1895). After serving as organist and choirmaster of Jewin Street Welsh Presbyterian Church in London, he went to University College, Cardiff, where from 1903 to 1939 he served as professor of music, organizing a large music department. He also became a senior professor of the University of Wales. Evans was a prolific composer (his works include cantatas, anthems, and services) and a leading adjudicator at the National Eisteddfod. For five years, 1916–1921, he was editor of *Y Cerddor,* a Welsh music journal. An enthusiastic advocate of congregational singing, he published a collection of hymn tunes titled *Moliant Cenedl.* He died May 17, 1948, shortly after conducting a singing festival at Rhosllannerchrugog near Wrexham.

340 JESUS CHRIST, MY SURE DEFENSE *(Jesus, meine Zuversicht)*

Tune: Jesus, meine Zuversicht

This hymn, which has been described as "of first rank" and "an acknowledged masterpiece of Christian poetry," is of unknown authorship. It was first published in Christoph Runge's *D. M. Luthers und anderer vornehmen geistreichen und gelehrten Männer Geistliche Lieder und Psalmen,* Berlin, 1653, a hymnal directed by Luise Henriette von Brandenburg as a means of bringing together the Lutheran and Reformed communions. It has sometimes been attributed to Luise Henriette. Runge stated in his preface to *Geistliche Lieder* that she contributed four hymns, but her name was not given with any of them in the hymnal, and was first found with this hymn only as late as 1769. Possibly the hymns had been written for her and she contributed them because they were favorites; or perhaps she wrote them herself in Dutch and they were reset by another person, since she herself did not have the command of High German necessary to have written the hymns as they stand in that language.

Luise Henriette, daughter of the Prince of Nassau-Orange and Stadtholder of the United Netherlands, was born at The Hague on November 27, 1627. She was brought up in the Christian faith of the Reformed communion. In 1646 she was married to Elector Friedrich Wilhelm of Brandenburg. Of the four sons born to her, the first died in infancy, and the second at the age of twenty-four. The third later became King Friedrich I of Prussia. From the birth of the fourth, in 1666, she never recovered, and died the following year, on June 18, in Berlin.

Christoph Runge, born September 10, 1619, in Berlin, was the son of a book publisher and followed his father's profession. Especially significant among his publications was Johann Crüger's (LBW 23) *Praxis Pietatis Melica.* He died in Berlin in 1681.

The first three stanzas of the English text are, with slight alterations, from Catherine Winkworth's (LBW 29) *Chorale Book for England,* 1863. The last two stanzas are from the *Evangelical Lutheran Hymn-Book,* 1912, and were altered for *The Lutheran Hymnal,* 1941.

JESUS, MEINE ZUVERSICHT ("Ratisbon") appeared anonymously with this text in Crüger's *Praxis Pietatis Melica* issued by Runge in 1653 (Zahn* 3432b). Crüger's name has been attached to the tune since the 1668 edition of *Praxis Pietatis Melica,* and he possibly either wrote it or adapted it from an older melody. According to Haeussler* some historians state that Crüger's name was given with the tune in part two of *Psalmodia Sacra (Geistliche Lieder),* Berlin, 1658, edited by Ambrosius Lobwasser, but no copy of that collection is available. Zahn* suggests that the tune was perhaps written by Princess Luise Henriette to whom the book was dedicated.

Another form of the melody (given above), published in Runge's *Geistliche Lieder und Psalmen*, is felt to have served as a suggestion for the tune "Ratisbon" (LBW 265).

J. S. Bach (LBW 219) used the tune in Cantata 145 and an organ setting is included among the Miscellaneous Preludes. A harmonization is also given in his *Choralgesänge*.

The harmonization is from the *Orgelchoralbuch*, 1952.

341 JESUS, STILL LEAD ON *(Jesu, geh voran)*
Tune: Seelenbräutigam

See LBW 302 for Nicolaus von Zinzendorf, LBW 147 for Jane Borthwick.

The German hymn from which this is translated appeared in Christian Gregor's *Gesangbuch zum Gebrauch der evangelischen Brüdergemeinen*, Barby, 1778, and was made up of selected stanzas from two hymns written in 1721 by Zinzendorf: "Seelenbräutigam, O du Gottes-Lamm" and "Glanz der Ewigkeit." The translation by Jane Borthwick was included in the *Free Church Magazine*, 1846, and repeated, slightly revised, in her *Hymns from the Land of Luther*, first series, 1854. The extensive alteration of stanza 3 is from the *Church Book*, 1868, and some further slight alterations have been made for the LBW.

SEELENBRÄUTIGAM was written by Adam Drese for his hymn "Seelenbräutigam, Jesu Gotteslamm," and was given in the Darmstadt *Geistreiches Gesangbuch*, 1698.

Adam Drese was born in December of 1620 in Darmstadt, Germany, and was sent in 1655 by Duke Wilhelm IV of Weimar to Warsaw to study under the Italian Marco Sacchi. On his return to Weimar he became *Kapellmeister* to the duke. When Duke Wilhelm died, Drese went with the duke's son, Bernhard, to Jena in 1662, and was in his employ until 1667. In 1672 he became town mayor of Jena, and in 1683 was appointed *Kapellmeister* at Arnstadt, where he died February 15, 1701.

From 1667 he devoted much of his time to the study of Philipp Jakob Spener and of Martin Luther's (LBW 48) commentary on Romans, and from about 1680 his home became a meeting place for the Pietists. He is said to have written operas and instrumental works but these are no longer extant; the operas are believed to have been destroyed by him when he became a Pietist. A dissertation on theory also no longer exists. A number of his hymn tunes remain in the *Muskalisches Lustwäldlein*, 1652–1657, of Georg Neumark (LBW 453) whose acquaintance Drese had made in Weimar.

J. S. Bach's (LBW 219) settings of the tune are included in the *Choralgesänge* and in *Schemelli's Gesangbuch*.

342 I KNOW OF A SLEEP IN JESUS' NAME
(Jeg ved mig en Sövn i Jesu Navn)
Tune: Den Signede Dag

See LBW 310 for Magnus Brostrup Landstad. This hymn is believed to have been written on Easter morning, 1851. Landstad's ten-year-old daughter had died of typhus in January of that year, and on Easter Eve an eight-year-old son died of the same disease. The hymn was included in his *Udkast til Kirke-Salmebog,* 1861.

Translated to English by K. A. Kasberg, O. H. Smeby, and Carl Doving (LBW 43), the hymn was included in *The Lutheran Hymnary,* 1913. The few alterations are from the *Service Book and Hymnal,* 1958.

For DEN SIGNEDE DAG see LBW 161.

343   GUIDE ME EVER, GREAT REDEEMER
(Arglwydd, arwain trwy'r anialwch)
Tune: Cwm Rhondda

William Williams is said to have been to Wales what Paul Gerhardt (LBW 23) was to Germany, and Isaac Watts (LBW 39) to England. Born February 11, 1717 at Cefn-y-Coed, in the parish of Llanfair-y-bryn a few miles northeast of Llandovery, Williams was the son of a well-to-do farmer and received a good education. Although he at first entered Llwynllwyd Academy at Carmarthen to study medicine, he was deeply stirred by the preaching of Howell Harris and determined to enter the ministry. In 1740 he was ordained a deacon of the Established Church and served for a while as a curate at Llanwrtyd and Llanddewi-Abergwesyn, but was refused ordination as a priest because of his evangelistic views. Eventually he associated himself with the Calvinistic Methodist movement and for over half a century threw himself into evangelistic work, traveling extensively throughout Wales, often accompanied by his wife who was a singer. He wrote a total of over eight hundred Welsh hymns as well as more than a hundred in English, and some other poetry and prose works. Williams died January 11, 1791, at Pantycelyn, a farm three miles east of Llandovery, and is buried in the churchyard of Llanfair church, an ancient and curious church set in the midst of Roman earthworks.

This hymn of five stanzas, first written in Welsh, was published in Williams' *Alleluia,* Bristol, 1745. The present English form takes the first stanza from Peter Williams' translation of stanzas 1, 3, and 5, included in his *Hymns on Various Subjects,* 1771. The other two stanzas are from a version made either by Williams himself or by his son John in 1772, retaining the first stanzas of the 1771 text, translating a new stanza 3 and 4 of the original, and adding a fourth stanza. This version was first published as a leaflet and then in Lady Huntingdon's *Collection of Hymns,* fifth edition (1772 or 1773). The opening line originally read "Guide me, *O thou* great *Jehovah,*" and there are a few other alterations in the LBW as well.

Peter Williams, a prominent figure in the Methodist Revival in Wales, was born at Llansadurnin, Carmarthenshire, on January 7, 1772. While at the Carmarthen Grammar School he was converted by the preaching of George Whitefield (LBW 522). Ordained in 1744, he was first appointed to the parish of Eglwys Cymmyn and served several curacies in the Established Church, but was forced to leave because of the fervency of his preaching. In 1746 he joined the Calvinistic Methodists, becoming an itinerant preacher. They later also expelled him on grounds of heresy. Finally he established a chapel on his own lands in Waterstreet, Carmarthen. An eloquent preacher, he did great service with his Welsh Bible with annotations (1767–1770) and concordance (1773) and also published a Welsh hymn book (1759) in addition to his 1771 *Hymns.* He died at Llandyfeilog on August 8, 1796.

CWM RHONDDA, named for the valley of the Rhondda in the heart of the coal mining industry, was written by John Hughes for a Baptist *Cymanfa Ganu* (singing festival) at Capel Rhondda, Pontypridd, Wales. The date of its composition is given as 1905 or 1907 in various sources. During the next quarter-century it was used at some five thousand such festivals. In 1918 "Cwm Rhondda" appeared as the setting for James Montgomery's "Angels, from the realms of glory" (LBW 50) in *Cân a Mawl: Song and Praise,* a bilingual hymnal of the Calvinistic Methodist Church of the United States of America, published in Chicago.

John Hughes was born at Dowlais in Wales in 1873, and in the next year moved with his family to Llantwit Vardre, Glamorganshire, where he lived for the rest of his life. There at the age of twelve he became a door boy at the Glyn Colliery and eventually came to have an official post in the traffic department of the Great Western Colliery Company. He was active in the Salem Baptist Church where he was a life-long member and where he succeeded his father as deacon and precentor. He wrote a number of hymn tunes as well as two anthems and some Sunday school songs. Death came May 14, 1932.

344   WE SING THE PRAISE OF HIM WHO DIED
Tune: Windham

See LBW 156 for Thomas Kelly. This hymn first appeared in *Hymns by Thomas Kelly, not before Published,* 1815. In later editions of the book the last two lines of the hymn were altered to their present form.

WINDHAM, attributed to Daniel Read, appeared in numerous American collections as the setting for Isaac Watts's (LBW 39) "Broad is the road that leads to death." It was first published in Read's *The American Singing Book,* New Haven, Connecticut, 1785. Early hymnals printed the tune in duple rhythm as shown below; only later was it recognized as a triple-meter tune.

etc.

Daniel Read, born November 16, 1757, in Rehobeth, near Attleboro, Massachusetts, served as a soldier during the Revolutionary War, going in 1777 and 1778 with John Sullivan's expeditions into Rhode Island. Near the end of the war he went to New Haven. There he set up a partnership with Amos Doolittle, an engraver, and the two published and sold books. He was married in 1785 to Jerusha Sherman. In addition to his book publishing Read was active in public affairs, sold ivory combs, was a stockbroker in a New Haven bank, and was a director of the library. Among his own publications, in addition to *The American Singing Book,* were *An Introduction to Psalmody,* 1790; *The Columbian Harmonist,* 1793; *The New Haven Collection of Sacred Music,* 1817; and the *American Musical Magazine,* 1786, a monthly which was the first of its kind in America. In 1832 he compiled *Musica Ecclesia,* offering the proceeds from its publication to the American Home Missionary Society. His offer was not accepted and the book was never published. He died at New Haven on December 4, 1836.

345 HOW SWEET THE NAME OF JESUS SOUNDS
Tune: St. Peter

See LBW 261 for John Newton. This hymn, included in *Olney Hymns,* 1779, is considered by Louis F. Benson to be one of Newton's classics (along with "Glorious things of thee are spoken" [LBW 358]), and Julian* also ranks it with the first hymns in the English language. There are several slight alterations in the text.

ST. PETER. Alexander Robert Reinagle was born August 21, 1799, at Brighton in East Sussex, England, and was of Austrian descent. His grandfather, Joseph Reinagle Sr., was "trumpeter to the king"; his father, Joseph Jr., was a noted cellist and friend of Franz Joseph Haydn (LBW 358) under whom he played in Johann Peter Saloman's orchestra in London; and his uncle (also Alexander Reinagle) came to the United States in 1786 and for twenty years was a leading conductor, composer, and teacher in Philadelphia and Baltimore. Alexander very likely received his musical training from his father, and served as organist at St. Peter-in-East, Oxford (hence the name of this tune) for over twenty years, beginning in 1822. Thereafter he went to Kidlington near Oxford, where he spent the remainder of his days. He died April 6, 1877.

Reinagle was an outstanding organ teacher, and among his pupils were Sir John Stainer (LBW 56) and Mrs. Stainer, who also studied with Mrs. Reinagle, herself a pianist. He composed a number of sacred works, and published several books of instruction for violin and cello, as well as two collections of hymn tunes (1836 and 1840).

This tune was first written as a solo with piano accompaniment and included in *Psalm Tunes for the Voice and Piano Forte, c.* 1830, where it was the setting for Psalm 118. In 1840 it appeared with the name "St. Peter" in Reinagle's *A Collection of Psalm and Hymn Tunes, Chants, and other Music, as sung in the Parish Church of St. Peter's in the East, Oxford.* It was reharmonized by the composer for the Original Edition of *Hymns Ancient and Modern,* 1861.

346 WHEN PEACE, LIKE A RIVER
Tune: It Is Well

On the advice of the family physician, Horatio G. Spafford planned a European trip for his family, for his wife's health. At the last minute he had to remain in Chicago, but sent his wife and four daughters ahead as planned on the S. S. *Ville du Havre,* intending to follow them in a few days. The *Ville du Havre,* however, was struck by the English ship *Lochearn* on November 22, 1873, and sank within twelve minutes, taking the lives of his four daughters. Mrs. Spafford and the other survivors landed at Cardiff, Wales, on December 1, and Spafford wrote this hymn aboard ship as he sailed to meet her.

Spafford, born in North Troy, New York, on October 20, 1828, went to Chicago in 1856, where he established a successful legal practice and became a professor of medical jurisprudence at Lind University (later

Chicago Medical College). An active Presbyterian layman, he served as a Sunday school teacher and as a director and trustee for McCormick Theological Seminary. He also took part in YMCA work. During a visit to England and Scotland in 1870 he came to know Dr. Piazza Smith, Astronomer Royal for Scotland, and became interested in Biblical archaeology. He met with several tragedies during his lifetime. Two years prior to the loss of his daughters he suffered heavy real estate losses in the Chicago fire and in 1880 his son also died. In 1881 the Spaffords decided to follow their interest in the Holy Land and, with a group of friends, went to Jerusalem where they established the American Colony. There he died on October 16, 1888.

IT IS WELL was composed for this text by Philip P. Bliss and both text and tune appeared in *Gospel Hymns No. 2,* 1876, compiled by Ira D. Sankey and Bliss.

Philip Paul Bliss was born in a log cabin in Clearfield County, Pennsylvania, July 9, 1838. He left home at age eleven to work on farms and in lumber camps, gaining some formal grammar school education along the way. At age twelve he joined the Baptist church. His first musical instruction was received from J. G. Towner, and at a music convention. In 1859 he married Lucy J. Young and for a year he worked on the farm for his father-in-law. Thereafter, with his horse and a twenty-dollar melodeon, he took to the road as an itinerant musician, teaching singing schools in the winter months and attending the Normal Academy of Music in Geneseo, New York, in the summers. For four years beginning in 1864 he worked for Root and Cady music publishers in Chicago, who published a number of his collections. In 1874 he joined Dwight L. Moody as a singing evangelist, traveling throughout the South, Middle West, and East. He and his wife were among the one hundred persons who lost their lives in a train wreck near Ashtabula, Ohio, on December 29, 1876.

347 JERUSALEM THE GOLDEN *(Urbs Sion aurea, patria lactea)*
Tune: Complainer

A discussion of this hymn is given at LBW 322. In 1849 Archbishop Richard C. Trench published ninety-six lines of the Latin poem in his *Sacred Latin Poetry* and from this portion John Mason Neale (LBW 34) made his translation of one hundred forty lines, given in his *Medieval Hymns,* 1851, from which this text is taken.

COMPLAINER served as the setting for "I am a great complainer that bears the name of Christ" in William Walker's *Southern Harmony,* New Haven, 1835 (LBW 30). The tune may either be by Walker himself, or may be one of the many spiritual folk songs he collected in the South.
The harmonization is by Roger Petrich (LBW 64).

348 JERUSALEM, WHOSE TOWERS TOUCH THE SKIES
(Jerusalem, du hochgebaute Stadt)
Tune: Jerusalem, du hochgebaute Stadt

Johann Mattäus Meyfart, son of the pastor of Wahlwinkel near Gotha in Germany, was born on November 9, 1590, at his grandfather's house in

Jena where his mother had gone to visit. He attended the universities of Jena and Wittenberg, receiving from Jena a Master of Arts degree in 1611 and a Doctor of Divinity in 1624. For some time he was on the philosophical faculty at Jena. In 1616 he became a professor at the *Gymnasium* in Coburg, and in 1623 was appointed director. A dissertation he published in 1633 met with disfavor among his colleagues at Coburg and he left there to become a professor of theology at the University of Erfurt, and in 1634 was appointed rector of the university. After 1636 he was also pastor of the Prediger Church. He died January 26, 1642.

This hymn was included in the *Tuba Novissima,* 1626, one of the several devotional works for which Meyfart was noted. The work contained four sermons preached at Coburg on Death, Last Judgement, Eternal Life, and Eternal Punishment. "Jerusalem, du hochgebaute Stadt" formed the conclusion of the third sermon, based on Matthew 17:1–9. The English text was prepared for the LBW by Gilbert E. Doan (LBW 99).

Of JERUSALEM, DU HOCHGEBAUTE STADT, Polack* has written, "Too much cannot be said of the beauty and effectiveness of this melody, which breathes the spirit of joyous triumph over death and the grave. . . . It ranks with the best gems of our Evangelical hymnodical treasures."

Melchior Franck, whose birth date has been given variously as 1573, 1575, and 1580, was born in Zittau (Oberlausitz), Germany, and was a student of Hans Leo Hassler (LBW 116). He held a position at St. Egidien in Nürnberg for a short time. By 1603 he was *Kapellmeister* at Coburg, remaining there until his death on June 1, 1639.

Franck ranks with Hassler and Michael Praetorius (LBW 36) as a master of his period. His compositions include both sacred and secular works, especially many fine lied and chorale motets, and were published in various collections, the best-known of which is probably *Geistlicher Musicalischer Lustgarten,* 1616. On the death of his daughter, a victim of the Thirty Years' War, he composed "Ist Gott für uns, wer mag wider uns sein." The present tune is possibly from a set of motets based on the Sunday Gospels, 1623. It was included in the *Christlich-Neu-vermehrt und gebessertes Gesangbuch,* Erfurt, 1663, where the first line read (Zahn* #6141):

349 I LEAVE, AS YOU HAVE PROMISED, LORD
Tune: Mit Fried und Freud

This versification of the Song of Simeon, or Nunc dimittis, (Luke 2:29–32) was prepared for the LBW by Gilbert E. Doan Jr. (LBW 99).

MIT FRIED UND FREUD. Martin Luther (LBW 48) prepared a German hymn based on the Song of Simeon, "Mit Fried' und Freud' ich fahr' dahin," which was included in Johann Walther's (LBW 350) *Geystliche gesangk Buchleyn,* Wittenberg, 1524. (An English translation of Luther's hymn was given in *The Lutheran Hymnal,* 1941, #137). This

Dorian-mode melody appeared together with Luther's hymn in 1524 and is very possibly his own composition. The form of the melody found here is, with some slight rhythmic variation, from Joseph Klug's (LBW 85) *Geistliche Lieder,* 1533. Harmonization of the tune is from the *Orgelchoralbuch,* 1952.

J. S. Bach's (LBW 219) settings of the tune include two for cantatas—Cantata 83 and one now lost—and an organ setting in the *Orgelbüchlein.*

350 EVEN AS WE LIVE EACH DAY *(Mitten wir im Leben sind)*
Tune: Mitten wir im Leben sind

This hymn has its origins in a Latin antiphon, "Media vita in morte sumus," which was enormously popular during the Middle Ages. According to tradition the monk Notker Balbulus (d. 910) of St. Gall in Switzerland was watching workmen build a bridge at the Martinstobel, across the yawning gorge of the Goldach, and was inspired to write this hymn. There seems to be no support for the legend, however, since the text is found in two eleventh-century English manuscripts, while the earliest source from St. Gall dates from the fourteenth century. The second part of the hymn, beginning "Holy and righteous God," is based on the *Trisagion* of the Greek liturgy, which dates from the fifth century, and Leupold* notes that "its melody is not unrelated to the music of the same words in the *Improperia* for Good Friday."

[handwritten margin note: Close paraphrase of Leupold without acknowledgement]

Several German versions were in existence by the fifteenth century. In his rendition, Martin Luther (LBW 48) altered the character of the hymn from an almost frantic cry for help to a positive statement of faith, and added two stanzas of his own. This text first appeared in the Erfurt *Enchiridia,* 1524, and has long held a foremost place among German hymns for the dying.

[handwritten margin note: LBW 350 is Luther's rendition (see Leupold) Confusing]

The English text, based on translations found in Leupold* and in *The Lutheran Hymnal,* 1941, was prepared by Eugene Brand.

Born in Richmond, Indiana, on November 22, 1931, Brand graduated from Capital University in Columbus, Ohio (Bachelor of Arts, 1953). There he was a pre-seminary and music major. He received a Bachelor of Divinity degree in 1957 from Lutheran Theological Seminary in Columbus, Ohio, and two years later completed a Doctor of Theology degree (magna cum laude) at the University of Heidelberg, Germany. He has pursued further studies at Cambridge University in England, and at Union Theological Seminary in New York City. Ordained to the American Lutheran Church in 1960, he served for eleven years as professor of theology and worship at Lutheran Theological Seminary. In 1971 he transferred to the Lutheran Church in America, and was successively director of the Commission on Worship (1971-1973), coordinator for worship of the Division for Parish Services (1973-1975), and project director of the Inter-Lutheran Commission on Worship (1975-1978). In 1977 he was appointed director of the Office of Studies of Lutheran World Ministries.

Brand has served on the Inter-Lutheran Commission on Worship, where he was a commission member and chairman of the liturgical texts committee from 1966 to 1971; the International Consultation on English Texts (1969-1976); and the USA Consultation on Common Texts, of which he was chairman from 1971 to 1977. He was Lutheran World

Federation Observer to the Vatican Consilium on the Sacred Liturgy
from 1968 to 1970, and was on the USA/LWF Advisory Committee on
Studies from 1969 to 1976, and the Liturgical Conference board from
1972 to 1976. In 1979 he was appointed to the academy committee and
chairman of the membership committee of the North American
Academy of Liturgists, and a council member of the Societas Liturgica.
Other memberships include the Lutheran Society for Worship, Music
and the Arts; the American Guild of Organists; and the Hymn Society of
America. Among his publications are *Thoughts on Music used in Worship* (1966), *The Rite Thing* (1970), and *Baptism: A Pastoral Perspective*
(1975). His articles have been included in *Una Sancta, The National
Lutheran, Response, Sacred Music, Church Music, Lutheran Quarterly,
Dialog,* and *Worship,* and he has also contributed to *The Encyclopedia
of the Lutheran Church* (ed. J. Bodensieck, 1965), *Interpreting Luther's
Legacy* (ed. Meuser and Schneider, 1969), and *A Dictionary of Liturgy
and Worship* (ed. J. G. Davies, 1972). He has lectured widely in the
United States, and also in Germany. In 1978 Lutheran Theological
Seminary in Columbus honored him with a Doctor of Divinity degree.

MITTEN WIR IM LEBEN SIND was adapted by Johann Walther from
the melody associated with the medieval Latin text. The original tune is
first found in a thirteenth-century gradual. Walther's version was included in his *Geystliche gesangk Buchleyn,* Wittenberg, 1524.

Johann Walther, a friend of Martin Luther and one of the earliest
Lutheran composers, was born in a village near Cola (Kahla?) in Thuringia in 1496. In 1524 he was a bass singer in the court of Friedrich the
Wise, Elector of Saxony, at Torgau. A year later he was made *Kapellmeister* or *Sängermeister* to Elector Johann of Saxony. The Electoral orchestra was disbanded in 1530 and reconstituted by the town, and four
years later Walther became cantor to the school in Torgau. In 1548 he
went to Dresden as *Kapellmeister* to Elector Moritz of Saxony. There he
remained until 1554 when he received a pension and returned to Torgau,
where he died April 24, 1570.

For three weeks in 1524 Walther lived in Luther's home in Wittenberg,
assisting him in adapting music for the German Mass, and preparing his
Geystliche gesangk Buchleyn. The following year, on October 29, he was
present in the Stadtkirche at Wittenberg when the German Mass was
celebrated for the first time. He published several collections, the last of
which, *Das christliches Kinderlied Dr. Martin Luthers,* 1566, contained
several of his hymn texts, as well as his musical settings. Bishop Bang has
said of him, "On the whole it may be said that Walther together with
Luther laid the foundation for evangelical church song."

351   OH, HAPPY DAY WHEN WE SHALL STAND
(O taenk naar engang samles skal)
Tune: Lobt Gott, ihr Christen

Written by Wilhelm Andreas Wexels for the general convention of the
Norwegian Mission Society, July 6 and 7, 1846, this hymn was first sung
as the closing hymn of the morning service at Our Saviour's Church,
Christiania (Oslo), on July 6. Dahle* observes that, since then, scarcely
has there been a mission service in Norwegian Lutheran congregations
where this hymn was not used. First published in a pamphlet, *Nogle Mis-*

sionssalmer, produced for the occasion, the hymn later appeared in *Tillaeg Til den Evangelisk-christelige Psalmbog,* 1853.

When, at the close of the Napoleonic wars, Norway was separated from Denmark and given over to Sweden, the era of Danish-Norwegian hymnody came to an end. It was Wexels who made the earliest efforts to create a national hymnbook for Norway. Yet, in spite of the fact that he published several hymnals (the last one, published in 1859, containing 850 hymns), none of them was ever accepted as an official hymnal. Ryden* attributes their failure to gain acceptance to the fact that Wexels' orthodox Christianity did not appeal to the Rationalists and was too "high church" for the Pietists.

Born March 29, 1797, in Copenhagen, Denmark, Wexels attended the Metropolitan School of Copenhagen and the University of Christiania, Norway. In 1816 he began theological studies, and two years later became catechist at Our Saviour's Church in Christiania. He was made residing curate of the congregation in 1846, and ministered there until his death on May 14, 1866, refusing even the bishopric of Bergen in order to remain with his congregation. For some time he was also preacher to the theological students at the University of Christiania.

Gracia Grindal's (LBW 32) translation was prepared for the LBW.

For LOBT GOTT, IHR CHRISTEN see LBW 47. This harmonization is from the *Württemburgishe Choralbuch,* 1953.

352 I KNOW THAT MY REDEEMER LIVES!
Tune: Duke Street

Samuel Medley, born June 23, 1738, in Cheshunt, Hertfordshire, England, was apprenticed to an oilman in London, but did not like the business and so joined the navy. In 1759, off Port Lagos, he received a severe leg wound and was obliged to return home where he lived with his grandfather. A sermon by Isaac Watts (LBW 39) read to him by his grandfather made a profound impression on him. He joined the Baptist Church on Eagle Street (now Kingsgate Church) in London, and often heard the preaching of George Whitefield (LBW 522) in whose *Psalms and Hymns,* twenty-first edition, 1775, this hymn appeared. In 1762 he married and moved to Soho, where he set up a school which he had established earlier near the Seven Dials. He began to preach in 1766 and a year later became a pastor of the Baptist Church at Watford, Hertford-shire. When in 1772 he went to Byron Street Baptist Church in Liverpool, his earlier experience with the sea gave him a special line of communication with his seafaring listeners, and during his twenty-seven years there the congregation increased considerably, so that a new meeting house was built. Medley's war injury had impaired his health for the rest of his life, and after a long illness he died July 17, 1799. During his lifetime he published several collections of hymns.

DUKE STREET first appeared anonymously as a setting for Joseph Addison's (LBW 264) Psalm 19 in Henry Boyd's *A Select Collection of Psalm and Hymn Tunes,* published in Glasgow in 1793. In William Dixon's *Euphonia,* 1805, it was called "Duke Street" and attributed to John Hatton. The harmonization is that prepared by David Evans (LBW 339) for *The Church Hymnary,* 1927.

All that is known about John Hatton is that he was born in Warrington, England, and that he lived for a time on Duke Street, St. Helen's, in Windle Township, Lancaster, England. His funeral sermon was preached in the Presbyterian Church in St. Helen's, December 13, 1793.

353 MAY WE YOUR PRECEPTS, LORD, FULFILL
Tune: Meribah

Born January 30, 1798, at Falmouth, England, Edward Osler trained as a physician and from 1819 to 1836 was house surgeon at the Swansea Infirmary. Thereafter he turned to literary pursuits and for some time worked with the Society for Promoting Christian Knowledge in London and Bath. He went to Truro in 1841 and became editor of the *Royal Cornwall Gazette,* a position he held until his death, March 7, 1863.

Osler's publications include works on religion and natural history, and a biography. Together with William Hall he produced *Psalms and Hymns adapted to the Services of the Church of England,* 1836 (the "Mitre Hymn Book"), to which he contributed fifteen metric Psalms and fifty hymns, including this hymn.

MERIBAH was published by Lowell Mason in 1839.

Born January 8, 1792, in Medfield, Massachusetts, Mason was the descendant of early settlers in the United States. As a child he learned to play whatever instruments were available to him and at age sixteen was directing a church choir. In 1812 he moved to Savannah, Georgia, where he worked for a number of years as a bank clerk. There, also, he studied harmony and composition with a German musician, F. L. Abel, with whom he collaborated in compiling what was to become the first edition of *The Boston Handel and Haydn Society Collection of Church Music.* This hymnal, based on William Gardiner's *Sacred Melodies* (LBW 356), was sponsored by the Handel and Haydn Society and published in 1822. It subsequently ran through seventeen editions, selling over fifty thousand copies. While in Savannah, Mason organized singing schools and taught music. A charter member of the First Presbyterian Church, he was also active in Sunday school and mission society work. In 1818 he married Abigail Adams of Westboro, Massachusetts. Owing to the success of his 1822 collection Mason returned to Massachusetts in 1827, settling in Boston. After serving three other churches briefly as music director, Mason served for fourteen years at the Bowdoin Street Church where Lyman Beecher, father of Harriet Beecher Stowe, was minister. There he achieved a high reputation. He was also president and conductor of the Handel and Haydn Society from 1827 until 1832, when he resigned to establish, with George Webb (LBW 389), the Boston Academy of Music. A few years later he succeeded in establishing music education in the public schools of Boston and also set up the teacher training sessions in his academy. On his travels to Europe he studied with Johann G. Nägeli (LBW 370) whose music served later as the basis for several of Mason's hymn tunes. He published a number of hymnals, either alone or together with Thomas Hastings (LBW 327) and George Webb. New York University conferred on him an honorary doctorate in 1855—one of the very earliest such degrees bestowed in the United States. He died at his home in Orange, New Jersey, on August 11, 1872. Mason's entire library was given to Yale University and is located there in the music school library.

Tune: Invocation

See LBW 186 for Ernest E. Ryden. This hymn of invocation of the Holy Trinity was written for the tune "Finlandia" in 1941, and dedicated to the class of Augustana Seminary ordained that year, of which the author's son-in-law was a member.

INVOCATION was composed for this text in the *Service Book and Hymnal*, 1958.

The composer, Carl Wilfred Landahl, was born September 1, 1908, in Taipingtien, Hupeh Province, China, of Swedish missionary parents. He attended the American School at Kikungshan, Honan, China, after which he studied at St. Olaf College, Northfield, Minnesota, and graduated from the University of Minnesota School of Music in 1931. Two years later he completed a Master's degree at Columbia School of Music in Chicago. After teaching piano privately in Chicago, he went to Dakota Wesleyan University at Mitchell, South Dakota, where he taught piano and theory. In 1942 he was called to the military service. He served as a chaplain's assistant and was in Germany with the Occupation Army. While in Europe, he studied briefly at the Royal Scottish Academy of Music in Glasgow. On his return to the United States in 1946 he was married to Ragnbild Nelson. He taught for some time at Northwestern College in Minneapolis, and did some theological studies in the Psalms at Luther Seminary, and also composed some choral works. He pursued further theological studies at Southern Baptist Seminary in Los Angeles (Bachelor of Divinity, 1950), and while in California did some organ playing and choral directing. Returning to Minneapolis in 1952, he joined the faculty of Augsburg College and also Bethel College in St. Paul, teaching piano, theory, hymnology, and music appreciation. He also held organ and choral directing positions in various churches, and did a great deal of accompanying. He died October 26, 1961, in Minneapolis.

Landahl was the composer of a number of anthems and organ and piano works, including the American Guild of Organists' Prize Anthem, 1949, and a tune which was awarded honorable mention in the Herbert Memorial Psalm Tune Contest, 1952. He was a member of the American Guild of Organists and of the music committee of the Lutheran World Federation General Assembly, 1955–1957.

355 THROUGH THE NIGHT OF DOUBT AND SORROW
(Igjennem Nat og Traengsel)
Tune: Ebenezer

This Danish hymn for the second Sunday in Advent (old pericopes) has, through its translation by Sabine Baring-Gould (LBW 280), come into widespread use in the English-speaking Church. Written by Bernhardt Severin Ingemann in 1825, it was first published in *Høimesse-Psalmer, Anden Udgave med et Tillaeg*, Copenhagen, 1843. Baring-Gould's translation was published in 1867 in *The People's Hymnal*, and in altered form, in the Revised Edition, 1875, of *Hymns Ancient and Modern*.

Born May 28, 1789, the son of the Lutheran pastor at Thorkildstrupp on the Island of Falster, Ingemann entered the University of Copenhagen in 1806. The following year, when the British attacked Copenhagen to prevent Napoleon from taking the Norwegian-Danish navy, Ingemann helped to defend the city. His apartment and his early works were burned in the siege. In 1809 he lost his mother, three brothers, and a niece in an epidemic, a tragedy which made itself felt in much of his later poetry. Three years later he was engaged to Lucie Madie, and in 1813, graduated from the university and became a private tutor at Walkendorf's Collegium. Ingemann was a sensitive, soft-spoken man with few friends. His first published works were tragic in nature and full of flaming idealism. His poetry soon gained many admirers and one collection followed another. In 1817 he was sent with government funds to study and travel in Germany, France, Italy, and Switzerland. When he returned to Copenhagen in 1819, Nicolai Grundtvig (LBW 62) was one of the poets to greet him with a poem. In 1822 he was appointed professor of literature at the academy at Sorö on the Island of Sjaelland, and in 1842 he became director of the academy, a position he held until the school closed in 1849. He died February 24, 1862.

A close friend of Grundtvig, Ingemann, through his epic poems and historical novels, contributed greatly to the upsurge of Danish national feeling, as did the works of Grundtvig. As a writer of children's stories, he was second in popularity only to Hans Christian Andersen, whom he also counted among his friends. In all, his published works fill thirty-four volumes. The success of his *Morgensalmer,* 1822, and *Høimesse-Psalmer,* first edition, 1825, led to his being commissioned to prepare a new *Psalmebog,* 1855, for the Church of Denmark.

For EBENEZER see LBW 233.

356 O JESUS, JOY OF LOVING HEARTS *(Jesu, dulcedo cordium)*
Tune: Walton

A cento beginning "Jesu dulcedo cordium," made up of stanzas 4, 3, 20, 28, and 10 of "Jesu dulcis memoria" (LBW 316) as it appears in Herman A. Daniel's *Thesaurus Hymnologicus* (1841-1855), was selected and freely translated by Ray Palmer (LBW 479) as "Jesus, thou Joy of loving hearts" and included in the *Sabbath Hymn Book,* 1858.

WALTON (also "Germany," "Fulda," "Beethoven," and "Melchizedec"). William Gardiner's *Sacred Melodies from Haydn, Mozart, and Beethoven adapted to the best English Poets and Appropriated to the use of the British Church,* published in London, consisted of six volumes, the first published in 1812, the remainder in 1815. Volumes I and II contained hymns with tunes with a "view of forming a more elevated system of Psalmody than any before in use." The last four volumes contained anthems by a number of nineteenth-century composers. *Sacred Melodies* served as an important source of hymn tunes and was heavily drawn upon by Lowell Mason (LBW 353). "Walton" was included in Volume II of *Sacred Melodies* where it originally began without an upbeat, thus:

Gardiner marked the tune "Subject from Beethoven," but noted later in his *Music and Friends,* 1838, that the melody was somewhere in Beethoven's works, but he could not point out where. Ellinwood* notes that the opening and closing lines of the tune bear some resemblance to the *Allegretto ma non troppo* of Beethoven's (LBW 551) Piano Trio, Opus 70, No. 2, 1809:

William Gardiner, born March 15, 1770, in Leicester, England, carried on a successful stocking manufacturing business which he had taken over from his father. On the side, however, he devoted himself ardently to music, and through his business travels and contacts met a number of musicians, including Franz Joseph Haydn (LBW 358) and Ludwig van Beethoven. He died November 16, 1853, in Leicester.

Published in three volumes, Gardiner's *Music and Friends; or Pleasant Recollections of a Dilettante,* 1838–1853, contains accounts of his travels and contacts with various musicians. Other works included a translation from French of Marie-Henri Beyle's *Lives of Haydn and Mozart,* and a landmark book on the science of acoustics, *The Music of Nature,* 1832.

357   OUR FATHER, BY WHOSE NAME

Tune: Rhosymedre

This hymn for families, with its second stanza based on Luke 2:52, was written by F. Bland Tucker in 1939 and printed in 66.66.88 meter in the 1940 Report of the Joint Committee on the Revision of the Hymnal (Episcopal). The author subsequently changed the meter of the hymn to fit this tune, and in this form it was included in *The Hymnal 1940.*

The son of an Episcopalian bishop and brother of a former presiding bishop of the Church, Francis Bland Tucker was born in Norfolk, Virginia, on January 6, 1895. He received a Bachelor of Arts degree from the University of Virginia in 1914, and Bachelor of Divinity (1920) and Doctor of Divinity (1944) degrees from Virginia Theological Seminary. After serving in World War I as a private in Evacuation Hospital no. 15 of the American Expeditionary Forces, he was ordained a deacon in 1918 and a priest two years later. From 1920 to 1925 he was rector of Grammer Parish, Brunswick County, Virginia, and for twenty years thereafter was rector of St. John's Georgetown, Washington, D.C. In 1945 he was appointed rector of old Christ Church, Savannah, Georgia, where he remained until his retirement in 1967. He still lives in Savannah. He was a member of the Joint Commission on the Revision of the Hymnal, and was active in the creation of *The Hymnal 1940.* Still going strong, he continues to write hymns, and now serves on a committee of the commission which is preparing a new hymnal. In 1980 he was made a Fellow of the Hymn Society of America.

For RHOSYMEDRE see LBW 94. The harmonization is by Richard Hillert (LBW 63).

358 GLORIES OF YOUR NAME ARE SPOKEN

Tune: Austria

See LBW 261 for John Newton. Originally beginning *"Glorious things of thee* are spoken," this hymn was included in *Olney Hymns,* 1779. It is based on Isaiah 33:20–21.

AUSTRIA (also "Austrian Hymn"). During Haydn's visits to England in 1791 and 1794 he was impressed with the singing of "God save the King" and felt the lack of such an expression of nationalism in Austria. In 1797 the poet Lorenz Leopold Hauschka was commissioned to write the words for an Austrian national hymn, and Haydn was requested to write the music. The Austrian Hymn, "Gott erhalte Franz den Kaiser," was sung for the first time on February 12, 1797, the Emperor's birthday, at the National Theater in Vienna and in many other theaters in the provinces. Later Haydn used the tune as the theme for a masterly set of variations in the slow movement of his Quartet in C, Opus 76, number 5. William Henry Hadow, in *A Croation Composer,* points to a Croation folksong, "Vjatvo rano se ja vstanem," as the basis for Haydn's melody. He quotes several variants. The form most likely to have been used is the one from Čembe, as given below.

The son of a wheelright, Franz Joseph Haydn was born March 31, 1732, at Rohrau near the Hungarian border in Eastern Austria. He received his first musical training from his uncle and later was a choirboy at the Cathedral of St. Stephen in Vienna until his voice changed. For a while thereafter he supported himself with odd jobs and teaching, meanwhile teaching himself counterpoint and receiving a few lessons in composition from an Italian composer, Nicola Porpora. After two years of service at the chapel of the Bohemian nobleman, Count von Morzin (for whose orchestra Haydn wrote his first symphony), he entered the service of Prince Paul Anton Esterházy, head of a wealthy and powerful Hungarian noble family in 1761. Prince Nicholas succeeded to the title the following year, and Haydn spent almost thirty years in nearly ideal circumstances, composing music for the court orchestra, theaters, chamber groups, and so on. During the 1770s and 1780s Haydn's fame spread throughout Europe. In 1790 Prince Nicholas died, and his son Nicholas II who succeeded him cared more for the glory of having such a famous man as Haydn in his service than he cared for his music. Haydn made two visits to England, where he received a Doctor of Music degree from Oxford, and spent two seasons (1791–1792 and 1794–1795), mostly under the management of Johann Peter Salomon, conducting concerts and composing many new works. Still nominally in the service of the prince he composed six masses for him between the years 1796 and 1802. He spent the last years of his life in Vienna, where he died May 31, 1809.

Haydn's prodigious output includes 104 symphonies, 83 string quartets, 52 piano sonatas, 18 operas, and 14 masses in addition to other chamber music, songs, arias, oratorios, cantatas, and other liturgical music. He made an extensive contribution in terms of the development of the classical sonata form and of symphonic orchestration. A devout Christian who regarded himself as the steward of his God-given musical abilities, he prefaced each of his scores with "In nomine Domini" and closed them with "Laus Deo."

359   IN CHRIST THERE IS NO EAST OR WEST

Tune: McKee

"John Oxenham" was a pseudonym taken by William Arthur Dunkerley from Charles Kingsley's *Westward Ho!* which had been given to him by his Sunday school teacher many years earlier. Dunkerley was born November 12, 1852, at Cheetham in Manchester, England, and was educated at Victoria University in Manchester. His father was a wholesale provision merchant, and after his graduation William took over the French branch of his father's business. After five years there he was married to a Scottish woman, Margery Anderson, and the couple came to live for a while in the United States, where he opened a branch of his father's business in New York. While in this country he became interested in the *Detroit Free Press,* and when he returned in 1881 to London he published an edition there for several years, and also entered other publishing ventures. His first attempt at fiction was a serial for one of his newspapers. He met with such success as a writer that he soon devoted the remainder of his life to that profession, giving much of his effort to works of a religious nature. He left London in 1913 and moved to Hanger Hill Farm at Ealing, where he began writing fiction under the pseudonym John Oxenham. In all, he wrote over forty novels and twenty other volumes of prose and poetry. He died January 24, 1941.

This hymn was part of "The Pageant of Darkness and Light" written by Dunkerley for the London Missionary Exhibition held in the Agricultural Hall, Islington, London, in 1905. The pageant soon became the chief attraction at the exhibition and was performed for several succeeding years in Europe and America. The hymn was published in *Bees in Amber,* 1913.

MCKEE is based on the black spiritual, "I know the angel's done changed my name," which was included in the Fisk University *Jubilee Songs,* 1884, compiled by Theodore F. Seward and George L. White.

It was adapted by Harry T. Burleigh for this hymn in 1939, and is named for the Reverend Elmer M. McKee, rector of St. George's Church, New York City (1936–1946), where Burleigh sang for many years. First published as a leaflet, it was included in *The Hymnal 1940* (Episcopal), and has since been used with this hymn in a number of other hymnals.

Harry Thacker Burleigh was born December 2, 1866, in Erie, Pennsylvania, and became a choir boy at St. Paul's Cathedral there. In 1892 he entered the National Conservatory of Music in New York on a four-year scholarship, and joined the choir of St. Philip's Protestant Episcopal Church in Haarlem. Two years later he was selected for the choir of St. George's Protestant Episcopal Church, Stuyvesant Square, where he remained for over fifty years. From 1900 to 1925 he also sang at Temple Emmanu-El. His rich voice was admired by many. Booker T. Washington arranged many appearances for him. He often sang for Anton Dvorak, and may well have been the one to give Dvorak the themes for his *New World Symphony.* Twice he sang command performances for King Edward VII. In 1911 he became music editor for the G. Ricordi music publishing firm in New York. In 1917 the National Association for the Advancement of Colored People awarded him the Spingarn Medal for highest achievement during 1916 by an American citizen of African descent. A charter member of the American Society of Composers, Authors, and Publishers, he wrote many spirituals, songs, and anthems, including "Deep River" and "Little Mother of Mine." He was honored with a Master of Arts degree from Atlanta University and a Doctor of Music degree from Howard University. He died in Stamford, Connecticut, September 11, 1949.

360 O CHRIST, THE HEALER, WE HAVE COME
Tune: Distress

See LBW 246 for Frederick Pratt Green. This hymn was first published in *Hymns and Songs,* London, 1969.

For DISTRESS see LBW 217. This setting is by Ludwig Lenel (LBW 399).

361 DO NOT DESPAIR, O LITTLE FLOCK
(Verzage nicht, du Häuflein klein)
Tune: Kommt her zu mir

The earliest source of this hymn, a pamphlet entitled *Epicedion,* published in Leipzig probably at the end of 1632, called it the "Königlicher Schwanengesang." "So ihre Majest. vor dem Lützenschen Treffen inniglichen zu Gott gesungen" ("The King's Swansong. Thus his majesty sang fervently to God before his fall at Lützen"). This hymn, as well as "A mighty fortress" (LBW 228) and "May God bestow on us his grace" (LBW 335), was sung by the army of Gustavus Adolphus before the historic battle of Lützen on November 5, 1632. During the battle, which was a decisive one for Protestantism in the Thirty Years' War, King Gustavus Adolphus of Sweden lost his life. The fact that Gustavus sang the hymn on the day of his death led some to believe that he wrote the hymn, or that the idea was communicated to his chaplain, Dr. Jacob Fabricius, who later wrote it as a hymn. Most likely, however, Johann Michale Altenburg was the author of the hymn. Jeremias Weber's *Leipzig Gesangbuch,* 1638, attached his name to it. The hymn has been used extensively among Swedish Lutherans, especially on Reformation Sunday and Gustavus Adolphus Day (November 6).

Altenburg was born at Alach near Erfurt, Germany, on Trinity Sunday, 1584. After serving for a while as teacher and precentor in Erfurt, he became pastor at Ilversgehofen and Marbach near Erfurt in 1608, of Trochtelborn in 1611, and of Gross-Sommern (Sömmerda) near Erfurt in 1621. He suffered many hardships at Gross-Sommern during the Thirty Years' War, with troops continually passing through, plundering as they went and pressing houses into service as their quarters. Altenburg once served as involuntary host to some three hundred soldiers and a horse. In 1631 he fled to Erfurt where he remained for six years without a charge, until he was appointed diaconus of St. Augustine's Church in 1637, and pastor of St. Andrew's Church the following year. He died February 12, 1640, in Erfurt.

This hymn is believed to have been inspired by the news of the victory at Leipzig on September 17, 1631. Altenburg was a good musician as well as a hymnwriter, and also composed some hymn tunes.

The English version, prepared by the Inter-Lutheran Commission on Worship, uses some lines from a translation included in Catherine Winkworth's (LBW 29) *Lyra Germanica, 1855.*

KOMMT HER ZU MIR is a fifteenth-century German folksong, a *Lindenschmied-Ton,* which was associated with the texts, "Es ist nicht lang, dass es geschah," "Was wölln wir aber heben an" and "Sankt Ottilia, die war blind geborn." From 1490 on it was found with a ballad-style folksong about a robber knight. It appeared in various forms around 1530 attached to Georg Grünwald's hymn, "Kommt her zu mir, spricht Gottes Sohn." Published singly as *Ain schöns newes Christlichs lyed* in 1530, the tune appeared as given below. It is found four years later in *Der erst teil. Hundret vnd ainundzweintzig newe Lieder,* published in Nürnberg by Hieronymus Formschneyder.

The original *Lindenschmied-Ton* had five lines of music. The tune was expanded to six lines for Grünwald's hymn by repeating the fourth line.

J. S. Bach (LBW 219) used the tune in Cantatas 74 and 108.

362 WE PLOW THE FIELDS AND SCATTER
(Wir pflügen und wir streuen)
Tune: Wir pflügen

Matthias Claudius, son of a Lutheran pastor at Reinfeld, about ten miles west of Lübeck in Holstein, Germany, was born August 15, 1740. He studied theology at the University of Jena from 1759 to 1763, but an illness, together with the rationalistic thinking at the university, caused him to shift his attention to law and languages. In 1771 he became literary editor of *Der Wandsbecker Bote,* and the following year he was married to Anna Rebecca Behn, a carpenter's daughter. From 1776 to 1777 he was a commissioner of Agriculture and Manufactures of Hesse-Darmstadt. He had become acquainted with Johann Wolfgang von Goethe, and for a time associated with a group of free-thinking philosophers. A severe illness in 1777, however, caused him to return to the faith of his youth, and he relinquished his position at Hesse-Darmstadt to return to Wandsbeck to edit the *Bote* in a Christian spirit. The Crown Prince of Denmark appointed him auditor of the Schleswig-Holstein Bank at Altona in 1788. His last days were spent in his daughter's house in Hamburg, where he died January 21, 1815.

Especially well-versed in the writings of William Shakespeare and Isaac Newton, Claudius did a great service to the common people by bringing them the finer things of cultural life with his *Wandsbecker Bote.* Henry Wadsworth Longfellow (LBW 279) included some of Claudius' works in his *Poets and Poetry of Europe.*

The German poem from which this hymn is taken was first published in 1782 and begins "Im Anfang war's auf Erden." It is the Peasants' Song in Claudius' sketch, *Paul Erdmann's Feast,* where the peasants are pictured as singing it on the way to Paul's house for a harvest-thanksgiving celebration. Jane Campbell's free translation of selected stanzas was first published in the Reverend C. S. Bere's *A Garland of Songs,* 1861.

Jane Montgomery Campbell, born in 1817, was the daughter of an Anglican clergyman who was for many years vicar of St. James's, Paddington, London, and for the last four years of his life, prebendary of St. Paul's. She enjoyed music and taught singing to the children in her father's parish, and published a handbook for use in her work with London children. She assisted Charles S. Bere in the compilation of *Garland of Songs,* and with his *Children's Chorale Book,* 1869. She was involved in a carriage accident, and died at Bovey-Tracey, Devon, on November 15, 1878.

WIR PFLÜGEN. See LBW 52 for Johann A. P. Schulz. This tune first appeared anonymously with Claudius' poem in A. L. Hoppenstedt's *Melodien für Volksschulen,* 1800, and was attributed to Schulz eight years later in Lindner's *Jugenfreund.*

363 CHRIST IS ALIVE! LET CHRISTIANS SING

Tune: Truro

This hymn by Brian Arthur Wren was included in *New Church Praise,* 1975 (supplementary hymnal of the United Reformed Church of England and Wales). Alterations to the text are minor and very few.

Born June 3, 1936, at Romford, Essex, England, Wren enlisted in national service before entering New College, Oxford, in 1957. He received a Bachelor of Arts degree in 1960. Five years later he graduated from Mansfield College and was ordained a minister of the Congregational Church at Hockley, Essex. He became secretary in 1970 to Churches' Action for World Development, an ecumenical committee sponsored by the British Council of Churches, the Conference of British Missionary Societies, the Roman Catholic Mission Commission, and the

Roman Catholic Justice and Peace Commission. He is the author of a number of hymns.

TRURO appeared anonymously in Thomas Williams' *Psalmodia Evangelica: A Collection of Psalms and Hymns in Three Parts for Public Worship,* Part II, 1789, where it was the setting for Isaac Watts's (LBW 39) "Now to the Lord a noble song." Although attributed to the well-known music historian, Charles Burney, in nearly all the hymnals of the nineteenth century, as well as in some twentieth-century hymnals, the tune is by an unknown composer. Nothing is known of Thomas Williams who compiled *Psalmodia Evangelica.* The tune is named for an ancient town in southwestern Cornwall, England, which is well-known for its cathedral and its pottery.

364   SON OF GOD, ETERNAL SAVIOR
Tune: In Babilone

Written in 1893 by Somerset Thomas Corry Lowry, this hymn was first published in *Goodwill,* February, 1894, and included the following year in the *Christian Social Union Hymn Book.*

The son of a lawyer, Lowry was born in Dublin, Ireland, on March 21, 1855. He received Bachelor of Arts (1877) and Master of Arts (1880) degrees from Trinity Hall, Cambridge, and was ordained a deacon in 1879 and a priest the following year. He served at Doncaster, Yorkshire, and North Holmwood (where this hymn was written) before his appointment as vicar of St. Augustine's, Bournemouth in 1900. In 1911 he became rector of Wonston, and from 1914 to 1919, was vicar of St. Bartholomew's, Southsea. He died at Torquay, January 29, 1932.

Lowry was the author of *The Work of the Holy Spirit,* 1894; *Convalescence,* 1897; *Lessons from the Passion,* 1899; *The Days of our Pilgrimage,* 1900; and *Hymns and Spiritual Songs,* 1910.

IN BABILONE was included in *Oude en Nieuwe Hollantse Boerenlities en Contradansen,* a collection of some one thousand tunes without accompaniment published in Amsterdam about 1710. Many of these melodies were published in Julius Röntgen's *Old Dutch Peasant Songs and Country Dances Transcribed for the Piano,* London, 1912. Ralph Vaughan Williams (LBW 101) was aware of Röntgen's work during his preparation of *The English Hymnal,* 1906, and included Röntgen's harmonization of "In Babilone" as the setting for Christopher Wordsworth's (LBW 90) "See the Conqueror mounts in triumph." The *Service Book and Hymnal,* 1958, used a setting by T. Tertius Noble; the LBW harmonization is Röntgen's as found in *The English Hymnal.*

Julius Röntgen, distinguished Dutch pianist, composer, conductor, musicologist, editor, and professor, was born May 9, 1855, in Leipzig, Germany. He studied music at Leipzig with Franz Lachner, Moritz Hauptmann, Ernst Frederich Edward Richter, and Carl Reinecke, and in 1877 went to Amsterdam. After eight years as professor at the Amsterdam Conservatory, he became conductor of the Society for the Advancement of Musical Art in 1886, succeeding Verhulst. In 1918 he was appointed director of the Amsterdam Conservatory, but he retired in 1924 to devote himself entirely to composition. He died at Utrecht September 13, 1932.

Röntgen's compositions included twelve symphonies, three piano concertos, three operas, chamber music, and film scores. A friend of Franz Liszt, Johannes Brahms, and Edvard Grieg (LBW 314), he published a biography of Grieg in 1930. In the same year he was nominated by Sir Donald Tovey for an honorary degree at the University of Edinburgh.

365 BUILT ON A ROCK *(Kirken den er et gammelt Hus)*
Tune: Kirken den er et gammelt Hus

This hymn by Nicolai Grundtvig (LBW 62), a great favorite among Scandinavian Christians, originally consisted of seven stanzas, and was included in that form in *Sang-Värk til den Danske Kirke,* 1837. It appeared later in *Festsalmer,* 1854, revised and abbreviated by Grundtvig.

Translated into English by Carl Doving (LBW 43) in 1909, the hymn was included in *The Lutheran Hymnary,* 1913. The LBW version of the text is a revision of Doving's translation, prepared by Fred C. M. Hansen for the *Service Book and Hymnal,* 1958.

Hansen was born June 25, 1888, at Vejle, Denmark, and came with his family to the United States in 1890. He graduated in 1910 from Dana College and in 1914 from Trinity Seminary, both in Blair, Nebraska, and studied also at the University of Nebraska in Lincoln. After his ordination he served the Danish Evangelical Lutheran Church, Davenport, Iowa, 1914–1918; Our Savior's Lutheran, Audubon, Iowa, 1918–1928; Kingo Lutheran Church, Milwaukee, 1928–1936; Our Saviour's Lutheran, Council Bluffs, Iowa, 1936–1943; and Golgotha Lutheran Church, Chicago, 1943–1958. In the United Evangelical Lutheran Church he was president of the Iowa district from 1939 to 1943 and of the Illinois district from 1944 to 1948. He retired in 1958 to Blair, Nebraska, where he died April 4, 1965.

During Hansen's pastorate at Audubon, Iowa, he and Pastor P. E. Jensen helped to found the Lutheran Bible Camp at Lake Okoboji, Iowa. The two pastors also published a monthly paper entitled *Kirketidende,* and Hansen edited a similar parish paper in each of the churches he served. From 1922 to 1926 he also edited *Our Lutheran Youth. I was Sick,* a greeting to the sick translated from Christian physicians in the Scandinavian countries, was published in 1953. In addition to serving on a committee for the *Service Book and Hymnal,* 1958, he served earlier in the same capacity for the *Hymnal for Church and Home* and the *Junior Hymnal* of the Evangelical Lutheran Church. Hansen contributed original hymns as well as translations to each of these.

KIRKEN DEN ER ET GAMMELT HUS (also "Kirken"). See LBW 285 for Ludvig Lindeman. This tune, Lindeman's first, was written in 1840 for this hymn, and included that year in Wilhelm Wexels' (LBW 351) *Christelige Psalmer.*

366 LORD OF OUR LIFE *(Christe, du Beistand deiner Kreuzgemeine)*
Tune: Iste Confessor

Son of a saddler, Matthäus Apelles von Löwenstern was born at Neustadt in Oppeln, Silesia, on April 20, 1594. In 1625 he went to Bernstadt as music director and treasurer to Duke Heinrich Wenzel of

Münsterberg, and the following year was appointed director of the princely school at Bernstadt. He became counsellor, secretary, and director of finance in 1631, and later entered the service of Emperors Ferdinand II and Ferdinand III who ennobled him. His final position was that of *Staatsrath* at Öls to Duke Karl Friedrich of Münsterberg. He died April 11, 1648, at Breslau.

This hymn was one of Löwenstern's thirty hymns which were bound up with the Breslau *Kirchen und Haus-Music,* 1644. Philip Pusey's English version was published in Alexander Reinagle's (LBW 345) *Psalm and Hymn Tunes,* Oxford, 1840.

Pusey, described by Benjamin Disraeli as "both by his lineage, his estate, his rare accomplishments and fine abilities, one of the most distinguished country gentlemen who ever sat in the House of Commons," was born June 25, 1799, at Pusey, Berkshire, England, and educated at Christ Church, Oxford. At Oxford his brother, Edward Bouverie Pusey, was one of the leaders of the Tractarian movement. After leaving Christ Church without completing a degree, Philip settled on his estate, devoting himself to public service and to agriculture, becoming one of the most progressive agriculturists of his time, writing extensively on the subject, and helping to establish the Royal Agricultural Society. He was a connoisseur and collector of art, and was one of the founders of the London Library. He died July 9, 1855, at Kensington.

ISTE CONFESSOR is one of the French Church melodies discussed at LBW 83. In the Poitiers Antiphoner of 1746 it was the setting for the eighth-century Latin hymn "Iste confessor Domini sacratus." The melody is sometimes called "Rouen" because it is also found in the Rouen *Processionale,* 1763.

The harmonization is by Paul Bunjes (LBW 38).

367 CHRIST IS MADE THE SURE FOUNDATION
(Angularis fundamentum)
Tune: Eden Church

The Latin hymn "Urbs beata Jerusalem" consisted of eight stanzas and a doxology. It is of unknown authorship and has been dated variously from the sixth to the eighth centuries. Some writers, such as Herman A. Daniel and John Mason Neale (LBW 34), considered the seventh and eighth stanzas (stanzas 2 and 3 of the present hymn) to have been written later, while Richard C. Trench in his *Sacred Latin Poetry* (London, 1864) noted that the hymn "coheres intimately in all its parts" and must surely have been written at one time. Based on 1 Peter 2:5, Revelation 21, and Ephesians 2:20, the hymn was included in most medieval rites as the proper Office hymn for the dedication of a church. The hymn has been traditionally divided; the first four stanzas and the doxology were used at Vespers (sunset) and the last four stanzas and the doxology, for Lauds (sunrise). The present hymn consists of stanzas 5 (beginning "Angularis fundamentum") and 7–9 of the original Latin hymn.

Neale's translation was included in his *Medieval Hymns,* 1851, and in *The Hymnal Noted* of the same year. The first half of Neale's text, beginning "Blessed city, heavenly Salem," was included in the *Service Book and Hymnal,* 1958, #245. The LBW stanzas contain a number of alterations.

EDEN CHURCH was adapted by Dale Wood (LBW 268) from his anthem, "Christ is made the sure foundation," written for the seventy-fifth anniversary of Eden Lutheran Chruch, Riverside, California, in 1959.

368   I LOVE YOUR KINGDOM, LORD
Tune: St. Thomas

Timothy Dwight, under whose presidency Yale College grew to great renown, was a grandson of Jonathan Edwards. Born May 14, 1752, at Northampton, Massachusetts, Dwight graduated from Yale in 1769, and remained six years thereafter as a tutor. For some time he was chaplain in the Revolutionary War, during which he came to be a friend of George Washington. He was appointed minister to the Congregational Church in Fairfield, Connecticut, in 1783, and to supplement his income, also conducted an academy. From 1795 he was professor of theology as well as president of Yale, and in addition taught ethics, metaphysics, logic, literature, and oratory. During this time he undertook, at the request of the General Association of the Presbyterian Churches of Connecticut, a revision of Isaac Watts's (LBW 39) *Psalms and Hymns.* The resulting *Psalms of David by Isaac Watts* was published in 1800 at Hartford, Connecticut. From this volume comes "I love thy kingdom, Lord," which is the third and last part of Psalm 137 entitled "Love to the Church." Dwight's *Psalms* remained in widespread use among Congregational and Presbyterian congregations over thirty years. Although plagued for his last forty years by poor eyesight resulting from early morning reading by candlelight and a smallpox innoculation (he could not read for more than about fifteen minutes without experiencing great pain), Dwight managed to lead a distinguished and varied life, including, in addition to his other activities, small farming and service in the Massachusetts legislature. He died in Philadelphia on January 11, 1817.

ST. THOMAS, which very soon came into extensive use in the United States with many different texts, first appeared as "Holborn" in Aaron Williams' *The Universal Psalmist,* London, 1763. "Holborn" was an extended tune, the setting for four stanzas of Charles Wesley's (LBW 27) "Soldiers of Christ, arise." "St. Thomas" is the part of the melody which was the setting for the second stanza. In 1770 the shortened version, called "St. Thomas," appeared in Isaac Smith's *A Collection of Psalm Tunes,* and in Williams' *New Universal Psalmodist,* fifth edition, London, where it was the setting for Psalm 48 ("Great is the Lord our God").

Aaron Williams (1731–1776) was a music engraver and publisher, and a teacher of music in West Smithfield, London, England. For a time he was also clerk of London Wall Scots Church. He compiled a number of collections, including *The Royal Harmony,* 1766; *Harmonia Coelestis (or the harmony of heaven imitated, a collection of scarce and much esteemed anthems),* sixth edition 1775; and *Psalmody in Miniature, in 3 books, containing the tenor and bass of all the tunes generally used in churches, chapels or dissenting congregations,* 1778. His *Universal Psalmodist* appeared in an American edition as Daniel Bailey's *The American Harmony,* Newburyport, Massachusetts, 1769.

Tune: Aurelia

Samuel John Stone, born April 25, 1839, at Whitmore, Staffordshire, England, received a Bachelor of Arts degree from Pembroke College, Oxford, in 1862, and a Master of Arts degree ten years later. After serving as curate of Windsor (1862–1870) and then of St. Paul's, Haggerston, he succeeded his father as vicar of St. Paul's, Haggerston, in 1874. He and his father built the parish into a fully-equipped one (it had had neither church, nor school, nor vicarage, when his father had come there as vicar). In 1890 he became rector of All Hallows-on-the-Wall, in London, where he remained until his death, November 19, 1900, at the Charterhouse.

Stone published several collections of poems and hymns, and was a member of the committee of *Hymns Ancient and Modern*.

In 1866 Bishop John William Colenso of Natal, South Africa, wrote a book entitled *The Pentateuch and Book of Joshua, Critically Examined,* in which he challenged the historicity of many of the Old Testament accounts. He was severely criticized and was deposed by Bishop Gray of Capetown. When Bishop Colenso appealed to higher ecclesiastical authorities in England a great debate ensued, in which Stone was involved. Out of this he composed a set of hymns on the Apostles' Creed, which he published in 1866 as *Lyra Fidelium; Twelve Hymns on the Twelve Articles of the Apostles' Creed.* "The Church's one foundation" is based on the ninth article, "The holy Catholic Church; The Communion of Saints."

For AURELIA see LBW 197.

370   BLEST BE THE TIE THAT BINDS
Tune: Dennis

This hymn by John Fawcett (LBW 259) was published in his *Hymns adapted to the circumstances of Public Worship and Private Devotion,* Leeds, 1782.

DENNIS. Johann or Hans Georg Nägeli was born May 26, 1773 (some sources give 1768), at Wetzikon near Zurich, Switzerland. There in 1792 he established a music publishing firm which issued a number of important first editions, including the first printing of Ludwig van Beethoven's (LBW 551) sonatas, Opus 31. A pioneer in music education, he founded the *Zurcherische Singinstitut* and applied the principles of Johann Heinrich Pestalozzi to music instruction. Lowell Mason (LBW 353) was much influenced by his methods and applied them in the United States. Nägeli died December 26, 1836, in Wetzikon (or Zurich).

In addition to a number of vocal and instrumental works, Nägeli published some theoretical works, and was a music editor.

"Dennis" was included in Mason's and Benjamin Webb's (LBW 389) *The Psaltery,* 1845, where it was the setting for Philip Doddridge's (LBW 35) "How gentle God's commands." Mason ascribed the tune to Nägeli, but did not give the source. Ellinwood* gives as a possible source the melody for "O selig, selig, wer vor dir" which was included in Nägeli's *Christliches Gesangbuch,* 1828, as given below.

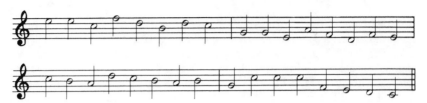

The harmonization is by Donald Busarow (LBW 30).

371   WITH GOD AS OUR FRIEND *(Med Gud och hans vänskap)*
Tune: Ack, saliga stunder

This hymn by Carl Olof Rosenius, which has been called "the revivalist Marseillaise of all middle-Sweden," first appeared in the *Pietisten,* number 1, in 1851, and was repeated later that year in Ahnfelt's *Andeliga Sånger* (see below) with music. It has been noted to be similar in strophic form and in content to the German hymn, "O selige Studen." A translation by Ernst W. Olson (LBW 474) beginning "With God and his mercy" was included in the *Hymnal,* 1901, of the Augustana Synod. The present English version was prepared by the Inter-Lutheran Commission on Worship for the LBW.

The son of a parish pastor with Pietistic leanings, Rosenius was born February 3, 1816, at Nysätra, Västerbotten, Sweden. Dedicated for the ministry by his parents from the time of his birth, he began at the age of fifteen to attend conventicles. He was a mystic and spoke of a "voice" that warned and guided him. After studying at Piteå, Umeå, and Härnösand, he went to Uppsala University, but never completed his entrance examinations. Instead he took a position as a tutor at the Lanna Estate near Stockholm. For a while he became disenchanted and entered a period of doubt and agnosticism. At this point in his life he met George Scott, a Methodist revivalist preacher in Stockholm, and on New Year's Day, 1840, preached his first sermon as a lay preacher. With Scott he joined in editing the *Missionstidning* (1840) and in starting the publication of *Pietisten* (1842). When Scott was deported to England because of opposition to his preaching, Rosenius continued as editor of *Pietisten* and as leader of Scott's followers. Although influenced by the separatists, Rosenius remained within the Lutheran Church. He died February 24, 1868.

ACK, SALIGA STUNDER (also "Med Gud och hans vänskap"). Oskar Ahnfelt, a Swedish pastor's son, was born May 21, 1813, at Gallup, Skåne Province, and grew up in a cultured home, surrounded by good music and literature. After receiving most of his elementary education from his older brothers, he entered Lund University in 1829, with the intention of entering the ministry. He lost interest in his studies, however, and for several years worked as a tutor in the cities of Karlshamn and Jönsköping before going in 1840 to Stockholm to pursue the study of music. There he came in contact with Rosenius and became active in the conventicle movement. Singing and playing his ten-string guitar, he traveled over much of Sweden, as well as to Denmark and Norway. Due to an edict against conventicles, Ahnfelt frequently found himself in trouble with the law, and was involved in a court case when the edict was repealed in 1858. He set many of the texts of Rosenius and Lina Sandell (LBW 474) to music. His first edition of *Andeliga Sånger,* 1850, which contained twelve songs with accompaniment for piano or guitar, was financially underwritten by the well-known singer, Jenny Lind, also a follower of Rosenius. He published eleven more volumes, the last in 1877. In 1851 he settled in Karlshamn, where he died October 22, 1882.

The tune name, "Ack, saliga stunder," refers to a text written by Ahnfelt's wife for this tune several years later. The harmonization was prepared by David Wikander and included in *Den Svenska Koralboken,* 1941.

Born in Sweden July 21, 1884, Wikander graduated from the Academy of Music as an organist, cantor, and music teacher in 1909-1910. He served from 1920 to 1952 as organist of the Cathedral of Stockholm. In addition, he was a member of the committee of church music in the divine service founded in 1936, the Missal Committee founded in 1940, and the Royal Academy of Music from 1941. In 1952 he was honored by the King of Sweden with the medal "Litteris et artibus." Among his many sacred and secular compositions are a mass for a capella mixed chorus, and settings of the poems "Kung Liljekonvalje" and "Förvårs-kväll." He died on November 15, 1955.

372   IN ADAM WE HAVE ALL BEEN ONE
Tune: The Saints' Delight

See LBW 233 for Martin H. Franzmann. This hymn was written in 1961 and included in *A New Song,* 1963.

THE SAINTS' DELIGHT. This is a shortened version of an anonymous tune which appeared in William Walker's (LBW 30) manuscript collection of anthems, fuguing tunes, and hymn tunes, titled *Miss Elizabeth Adams' Music Book,* 1832,[†] and in 1835 was included in *Southern Harmony* as the setting for Isaac Watts's (LBW 39) "When I can read my title clear To mansions in the skies."

Leland B. Sateren (LBW 100) prepared the harmonization for *Contemporary Worship-1,* 1969.

373   ETERNAL RULER OF THE CEASELESS ROUND
Tune: Song 1

Written during the Civil War, this hymn was composed by John White Chadwick for his June 19, 1864, graduation from Harvard Divinity School.

Chadwick was born in Marblehead, Massachusetts, October 19, 1840. His family was poor and he was severely handicapped in getting a formal education. In 1858 he managed to enter the Normal School at Bridgewater, and he later entered Harvard Divinity School, graduating in 1864.

†For a full description of this collection, see Milburn Price, "Miss Elizabeth Adams' Music Book: A Manuscript Predecessor of William Walker's *Southern Harmony,*" *The Hymn,* XXIX, 2 (April, 1978) pp. 70-75.

Ordained the same year to the Second Unitarian Church in Brooklyn, New York, he served there until his death on December 11, 1904. He was buried in Marblehead beside his father, one of the last of the old-time fishermen of the town.

Chadwick was the author of a number of works, including *A Book of Poems,* 1876; *In Nazareth Town and Other Poems,* 1883; *A Legend of Good Poets,* 1885; *Old and New Unitarian Beliefs,* 1894; *Theodore Parker,* 1900; *A Few Verses,* 1900; and *William Ellery Channing,* 1903. He also made contributions to *Harper's Magazine* and other periodicals.

For SONG 1 see LBW 206.

374 WE ALL BELIEVE IN ONE TRUE GOD
(Wir glauben all an einen Gott/Schöpfer)
Tune: Wir glauben all

The single-stanza medieval hymn based on the creed, dating from the fourteenth century, is first found with Latin and German words in a Breslau manuscript of 1417. Using the first two lines of this medieval German hymn, Martin Luther (LBW 48) expanded it to three stanzas, paraphrasing the three articles of the creed. Luther's text was first published in Johann Walther's (LBW 350) *Geystliche gesangk Buchleyn,* Wittenberg, 1524. In the Strassburg *Kirchenamt,* 1524/1525, and in Luther's German Mass of 1526, this hymn was given as a substitute for the Latin Credo of the mass, a use which soon became universally accepted in the Lutheran liturgy.

The English text found in the LBW is a composite translation from *The Lutheran Hymnal,* 1941.

WIR GLAUBEN ALL. Originating in the plainsong setting of the creed, "Credo in unum Deum," the melody associated with the medieval German hymn was adapted for Luther's text, and published with it in Walther's *Geystliche gesangk Buchleyn.* It is not known for sure whether the tune was revised by Luther or by Walther. The melody is in Dorian mode; the original form does not include the four C#'s or the G# used here.

The harmonization was prepared for the LBW by Carl Schalk (LBW 118).

375 ONLY-BEGOTTEN, WORD OF GOD ETERNAL
(Christe cunctorum dominator alme)
Tune: Iste confessor

This anonymous Latin Office hymn for the consecration of a church is first recorded in a Bern manuscript dating from the ninth century. Sometimes also found with the first line "Christe *sanctorum* dominator alme," this hymn was in use for Matins (after midnight) in all the major western liturgies.

Based on an altered form of the hymn as found in the Roman Breviary, 1632, Maxwell Julius Blacker's translation was made for use at St. Barnabas' Church, Pimlico, England, in 1884.

Blacker was born May 17, 1822, and received a Master of Arts degree from Merton College. Ordained in 1848, he held a number of curacies, including St. Barnabas', Pimlico. A number of his translations from Latin were included in the *Hymner* of the Plainsong and Mediaeval Music Society. He died June 11, 1888.

For ISTE CONFESSOR see LBW 366. This harmonization is by Paul Bunjes (LBW 38).

376   YOUR KINGDOM COME!

Tune: Old 124th

Written for the 1940 convention of the Women's Missionary Society of the United Lutheran Church in America, this hymn was first published in the November 1940 issue of *Lutheran Woman's Work*. The first line originally read, "*Thy* kingdom come," and there are several other slight alterations.

The daughter of a professor of English at Gettysburg College, Margaret Rebecca Himes was born July 5, 1875, at Gettysburg, Pennsylvania. She attended Gettysburg College, where she received a Bachelor of Arts degree in 1894 and a Master of Arts degree three years later. In 1897 also she was married to Julius F. Seebach, a Lutheran pastor with whom she had graduated from college, and she later became the mother of two sons. Very active in mission work of the church, she was from 1912 to 1913 president of the Lutheran Women's Missionary Society of the Susquehanna Synod. In 1917 she became editor of *Lutheran Woman's Work,* a position she held for twenty years. She published several books including *That Man Donaleitis,* 1909; *Missionary Milestones,* 1912; *An Eagle in the Wilderness* (a story of Henry Melchior Muhlenberg), 1924; *The Mystery of Jordan Green,* 1933; *Martin of Mansfield,* 1916; and *Land of All Nations,* 1924. In 1935 Carthage College in Illinois honored her with a Doctor of Letters degree, and her alma mater followed suit in 1943. She died October 10, 1948.

OLD 124TH first appeared in the Genevan Psalter of 1551 (LBW 29), where it was the setting for Psalm 124, "Or peut bien dire Israël maintenant." It soon came into English use, also with Psalm 124, hence the title "Old 124th." A shortened version, omitting the third line of the melody, is called "Toulon" and can also be found in many hymnals.

377   LIFT HIGH THE CROSS

Tune: Crucifer

This hymn, a revision by Michael Robert Newbolt of lines written earlier by George William Kitchin, was first published in the 1916 Supplement to *Hymns Ancient and Modern.*

Kitchin, son of the rector of St. Stephen's, Ipswich, was born at Naughton Rectory, Suffolk, England, on December 7, 1827. He attended King's College School and College, and Christ Church, Oxford, graduating in 1846. In 1863 he became censor and tutor at Oxford, and five years later, censor of the non-collegiate students. An Anglican clergyman, he was appointed dean of Winchester in 1883, dean of Durham in 1894, and in 1909, chancellor of Durham University. He published works in the fields of history, biography, and archaeology. He died October 13, 1912, at Durham.

Newbolt was born in England in 1874 and received Bachelor of Arts (1895) and Master of Arts (1912) degrees from St. John's College, Oxford. Ordained a deacon in 1899 and a priest the following year, he was assistant curate of Wantage, 1899–1905; vicar of St. Mary's, Iffley, 1905–1910; principal of the Missionary College, Dorchester, 1910–1916; perpetual curate of St. Michael and All Angels, Brighton, 1916–1927; and canon of Chester Cathedral, 1927–1946. In 1946 he was licensed to officiate in the diocese of Oxford. He died at Bierton, Buckinghamshire, February 7, 1956.

CRUCIFER was written for this text and included with it in the 1916 Supplement to *Hymns Ancient and Modern.*

The composer, Sydney Hugo Nicholson, was born in London, England, on February 9, 1875, the son of Sir Charles Nicholson, a founder and first chancellor of the University of Sydney. He received Master of Arts and Doctor of Music degrees from New College, Oxford. At the Royal College of Music he studied under Walter Parratt and Charles V. Stanford (LBW 189) and while a student there, served as organist at Barnet Parish Church beginning in 1897. He became organist of Lower Chapel, Eton College, in 1903 and assistant organist at Carlisle Cathedral the following year. In 1908 he was appointed organist of Manchester Cathedral and ten years later went to Westminster Abbey. He resigned in 1927 to devote himself to the School of English Church Music at St. Nicholas College, Chislehurst, which he founded that year, and of which he was director until his death on May 30, 1947. In 1945 the school became the Royal School of Church Music and was transferred to Canterbury, and in 1954 it was moved to Addington Palace, Croydon.

Nicholson had an important part in the later history of *Hymns Ancient and Modern,* becoming musical editor under Dr. W. H. Frere in 1913. In 1928 he became a proprietor, the first layman to hold the post, and from 1938 to 1947 he was chairman. His compositions include some operettas and various forms of church music, including anthems and some hymn tunes. Among his other publications are *Boys' Choirs,* 1922; *Church Music, a practical handbook,* 1927; *Quires and Places where they sing,* 1932; *Principles and recommendations of the School of English Church Music,* 1941; *Peter—The Adventures of a Chorister,* 1944; and with George L. H. Gardner, *A Manual of English Church Music,* 1923. He toured the United States in 1938, and was knighted the same year for his services to church music.

378   AMID THE WORLD'S BLEAK WILDERNESS
Tune: Granton

This hymn was written for the LBW by Jaroslav Vajda (LBW 159). The author has employed *terza rima,* a verse form in which the second of three lines rhymes with lines 1 and 3 of the following stanza—*aba, bcb, cdc,* etc. This scheme was used by Alighieri Dante in his *Divine Comedy.*

GRANTON, named for the composer's birthplace, was written at the suggestion of Theodore DeLaney of the Inter-Lutheran Commission on Worship hymn text committee. The composer, Richard Hillert (LBW 63), notes:

The exceptional structure (*terza rima*) of the text is reflected in the structure of the melody. There are three phrases, so constructed as to allow (in the last stanza) the second phrase to form a satisfactory conclusion to the whole. The third phrase, with its lowered seventh, employs a mixolydian characteristic.

379 SPREAD, OH, SPREAD, ALMIGHTY WORD
(Walte, walte nah und fern)

Tune: Gott sei dank

Described in Julian* as "one of the best and most useful of hymns for Foreign Missions," this hymn was first printed separately in 1827, and was included the following year in the *Kern des deutschen Lieder-schatzes,* published in Nürnberg.

Jonathan Friedrich Bahnmaier, a principal member of the committee which prepared the *Württemberg Gesangbuch,* 1842, was born at Oberstenfeld near Württemberg, Germany, on July 12, 1774. His father was town preacher of Oberstenfeld. Following theological studies at Tübingen, he served for eight years as an assistant to his father before going to Marbach on the Neckar in 1806, and to Ludwigsburg in 1810. In 1815 he was appointed professor of education and homiletics at Tübingen, and in 1819 became dean and town preacher at Kirchheim-unter-Teck. There he served for twenty-one years. A distinguished preacher, and a supporter of the causes of education, missions, and Bible societies, Bahnmaier published two volumes of hymns and songs for various occasions. He suffered a stroke while inspecting a school at Brucker, and died at Owen on August 18, 1841.

The English text was prepared for this hymnal by the Inter-Lutheran Commission on Worship.

GOTT SEI DANK appeared in Johann Freylinghausen's 1704 *Geistreiches Gesangbuch* (LBW 32) where it was set to Heinrich Held's (LBW 478) hymn, "Gott sei dank durch alle Welt" (Zahn* #230). (A translation of that hymn can be found in *The Lutheran Hymnal*, 1941, #91.) In its original form the tune was as given below.

The present form of the melody is from Gottfried Heinrich Stölzel's hymnal of 1744.

380 O CHRIST, OUR LIGHT, O RADIANCE TRUE
(O Jesu Christe, wahres Licht)

Tune: O Jesu Christe, wahres Licht

This hymn by Johann Heermann (LBW 123) was included in his *Devoti musica cordis,* published in Breslau in 1630, in a section titled "In the time of the persecution and distress of pious Christians.'' Polack* quotes Philipp Wackernagel, who notes, ''When we consider the many kinds of trials, sufferings of body and soul, under which many would have lost courage and given up in despair, then Heermann's hymns will loom up before us as among the most exalted of spiritual poems.''

Catherine Winkworth's (LBW 29) translation, beginning ''O Christ, our true and only Light,'' was included in her *Lyra Germanica,* second series, 1858. Stanza 2, with some alterations, is from that text. The remaining four stanzas were prepared by Gilbert E. Doan (LBW 99) for the LBW.

For O JESU CHRISTE, WAHRES LICHT see LBW 302. This harmonization is from the *Neues Choralbuch,* 1956.

381 HARK, THE VOICE OF JESUS CALLING
Tune: Galilean

When Daniel March preached to the Christian Association in his Clinton Avenue Church in Philadelphia on October 18, 1868, he entitled his sermon, based on Isaiah 6:8, ''Here am I; send me.'' Finding no hymn appropriate to his text, he wrote these words, which were sung from manuscript. The hymn was included in Robert Lowry's *Bright Jewels for the Sunday School,* New York, 1869, where it was marked ''Words by V. A.''

Daniel March, born in Millbury, Massachusetts, on July 21, 1816, received a Bachelor of Arts degree from Yale in 1840 and was ordained a Presbyterian minister in 1845. He later became a Congregationalist and ministered to several parishes of that denomination, including Woburn, Massachusetts, where he died on March 2, 1909.

The author of several religious works, including *Night Scenes in the Bible,* 1868, *Our Father's House,* 1870, *Home Life in the Bible,* 1873, and *From Dark to Dawn,* 1878, he is remembered today for this hymn.

GALILEAN is by Joseph Barnby (LBW 280), 1883.

382 AWAKE, O SPIRIT OF THE WATCHMEN
(Wach auf, du Geist der ersten Zeugen)
Tune: Dir, dir, Jehova

Born September 7, 1690, in Jantkawe (Hansdorf) near Milisch, Karl Heinrich von Bogatzky was the son of an army officer of a noble Hungarian family. At age fourteen he became a page in the court of the Duke of Sachsen-Weissenfels, after which his father sent him to Breslau to train for the army. During a long illness, however, he came to feel that God had other plans for him, and he gave up a military career and joined the Pietists—a decision which resulted in his father's disowning him. He studied law at the Universities of Jena and Halle; then in 1716 he took up theological studies. His health was so poor that he was unable to take up the parish ministry, but he devoted much time to religious writing and speaking at private meetings. Having access to the higher ranks of society, he was influential in the conversion of a number of persons of nobility in Bohemia, Silesia, and Saxony. He left Silesia in 1740 and lived for five years in Saalfeld, where he wrote a number of his works. His last twenty-eight years were spent in the orphanage at Halle, where his friend G. A. Franck gave him a room. He died June 15, 1774.

In addition to his *Meditations and Prayers on the New Testament,* which appeared in seven volumes between 1755 and 1761, his publications included a German version of an English work: *Das güldene Schatzkästlein der Kinder Gottes,* 1718, a recast of John Berridge's popular devotional work, *The Golden Treasury.*

This hymn was included in *Die Übung der Gottseligkeit in allerley Geistlichen Liedern,* Halle, 1750. The translation by C. Winfred Douglas (LBW 498) and Arthur William Farlander was prepared for *The Hymnal 1940* of the Episcopal Church. The only alterations are those made for the sake of updating the second-person pronouns.

Farlander, a member of the committee for *The Hymnal 1940* and *The Hymnal 1940 Companion,* was born in Germany on April 21, 1898. He came to the United States in 1919 and studied at James Millikin University, the University of Chicago Divinity School, the Evangelical Theological Seminary in Chicago, and the Church Divinity School of the Pacific. Ordained a deacon in 1926 and a priest the following year, he was rector of All Saints' Church, San Francisco (1927–1930); dean of St. James's Cathedral, Fresno, California (1930–1936); and from 1936 until his death on January 23, 1952, rector of the Church of the Incarnation, Santa Rosa, California.

DIR, DIR, JEHOVA (also "Crasselius"). The earliest form of this anonymous tune appeared in Georg Wittwe's *Musicalische Hand-buch der geistlichen Melodien,* Hamburg, 1690. There it was the setting for Georg Neumark's "Wer nur den lieben Gott lässt walten" (LBW 453) as given below.

Very popular in Germany, the tune was also introduced into England, adjusted to Long Meter and called "Swift German Tune," in John Wesley's (LBW 302) *A Collection of Tunes, Set to Music, as they are commonly Sung at the Foundery,* 1742. The melody was later called "Frankfort," and also "Winchester New," which is the name by which it is known in many hymnals today. The reconstruction of the tune to the form found in the LBW is from Johann Freylinghausen's *Geistreiches Gesangbuch,* 1704 (LBW 32), where it was the setting for Bartholomäus Crasselius' hymn, "Dir dir, Jehovah, will ich singen" (see *The Lutheran Hymnal,* 1941, #21, for this text).

383   RISE UP, O SAINTS OF GOD!

Tune: Festal Song

Written in 1977 for this tune, Norman O. Forness' hymn is published here for the first time.

Forness was born January 5, 1936, in Minot, North Dakota, and grew up in Sumner, Washington. He received a Bachelor of Arts degree, cum laude, from Pacific Lutheran University in Tacoma, Washington; a Master of Arts in history from Washington State University, Pullman, Washington; and a Doctor of Philosophy degree in American history from The Pennsylvania State University. In the fall of 1964 he joined the history faculty of Gettysburg College, Gettysburg, Pennsylvania, where he has remained except for two years, 1966–1968, when he served as assistant dean of the college. He holds the rank of associate professor of history, and has recently completed a book on the early history of the United States.

For FESTAL SONG see LBW 176. This harmonization is by Paul Manz (LBW 50).

384 YOUR KINGDOM COME, O FATHER *(Suo, Herra valtakuntas)*
Tune: Noormarkku

Three stanzas of this hymn were from a Swedish original, "Tillkomme dit rike, O Herre vår Gud," written by Lina Sandell-Berg (LBW 474). Kauko-Veikko Tamminen translated the hymn to Finnish, adding a stanza of his own, and his hymn was published in *Siionin Kannel,* Helsinki, 1910.

Tamminen (1882–1946) was a Finnish Lutheran clergyman and the executive director of The Finnish Lutheran Gospel Association. A member of The Finnish Church's General Assembly, he also served from 1928 to 1938 on the committee which prepared the 1938 hymnal of the Church of Finland. To this collection he contributed several revisions of earlier hymns and a number of original texts. He was the author of many sacred poems and songs, and his widely-heard radio sermons were published in several volumes.

The English text, originally beginning "*Thy* kingdom come," was prepared in 1962 by Ernest E. Ryden (LBW 186) for *Laudamus,* 1970, the hymnal of the Lutheran World Federation. Alterations are minor.

NOORMARKKU, the Finnish folk tune associated with this text, uses an interesting alternation of $\frac{5}{4}$ and $\frac{4}{4}$ meter. Named for a parish in southwestern Finland, near the city of Pori, it is one of the sacred folk melodies collected in that part of the country by Mikael Nyberg (LBW 485). The harmonization is by Richard Hillert (LBW 63).

385 WHAT WONDROUS LOVE IS THIS
Tune: Wondrous Love

Both text and tune of this nineteenth-century American hymn are of unknown origins. The text is first found in Stith Mead's *A General Selection of the Newest and Most Admired Hymns and Spiritual Songs Now in Use*, published in Lynchburg, Virginia in 1811. The text and tune first appeared together in William Walker's (LBW 30) *Southern Harmony,* published in 1843, and both were also included in B. F. White's (LBW 423) *The Sacred Harp,* 1844.

The hymn is one of several which used the so-called "Captain Kidd meter," found in a ballad about a wild pirate executed in England in 1701:

My name was Robert Kidd, when I sailed, when I sailed;
My name was Robert Kidd, when I sailed;
My name was Robert Kidd, God's laws I did forbid,
So wickedly I did when I sailed, when I sailed
So wickedly I did when I sailed.

Anne G. Gilchrist, in George Pullen Jackson's *Down-East Spirituals* (New York, *c.* 1939), traces this unique meter to a sixteenth-century song, "My luve is lyand seik, send him joy, send him joy," in *Complaynt of Scotland,* 1549.

WONDROUS LOVE first appeared in William Walker's *Southern Harmony,* 1843, as noted above. In several early collections it was attributed to "Christopher" or, in one case, to "James Christopher of Spartanburg, South Carolina." Another book gives it to the Rev. Alex Means, Oxford, Ohio. "Wondrous Love" is basically a new tune, distinct from the melody of the Captain Kidd ballad.

Donald Busarow (LBW 30) has prepared the LBW harmonization.

386 CHRIST IS THE KING!

Tune: Beverly

Written at the suggestion of Percy Dearmer (LBW 169) for the Welsh tune Llangoedmor, this text was included in the enlarged edition of *Songs of Praise,* 1931, as a hymn for the Feast of St. Simon and St. Jude (October 28). Originally the text consisted of four stanzas of six lines without alleluias. There are some alterations in each of the LBW stanzas.

The author, George Kennedy Allen Bell, oldest son of Canon J. Allen Bell, vice-dean of Norwich Cathedral in England, was born on Hayling Island in 1883, and educated at Christ Church, Oxford (Bachelor of Arts, 1905; Master of Arts, 1910; Doctor of Divinity, 1924). He won the Newdigate Prize for Poetry at Oxford in 1904 and continued to write poetry for the rest of his life. Ordained in 1907, he was curate of Leeds, 1907–1910; tutor and lecturer in classics and English at Christ Church, Oxford, 1910–1914; resident chaplain to the archbishop of Canterbury, 1914–1924; and from 1924 to 1929, was dean of Canterbury, where he introduced a number of improvements. In 1929 he became bishop of Chichester. He died at his home in Canterbury on October 3, 1958.

Bell served as assistant secretary of the Lambeth Conference in 1920 and as episcopal secretary in 1930. A leader in the ecumenical movement, he edited *Documents on Christian Unity* from 1920 to 1948, and invited nonconformists to preach at Canterbury Cathedral, which shocked many at the time. From 1948 to 1954 he was chairman of the Central Committee of the World Council of Churches, and from 1954 until his death was honorary president of that organization. He was also interested in religious drama and was president of the Religious Drama Society of Great Britain from its inception. It was he who invited T. S. Eliot to write *Murder in the Cathedral* and encouraged Christopher Fry to write *The Boy with a Cart.* Bell was outspoken in his condemnation of Nazism, and after World War II advocated a humane treatment of Germany. Among his writings on social and religious subjects are the *Biography of Randall Davidson, Archbishop of Canterbury,* 1935; and *The Church and Humanity,* 1946. A Doctor of Letters degree received in 1945 from the University of Southern California was one of several such honors bestowed on him.

BEVERLY, written for this text and published here for the first time, is named for the composer's wife, whom he describes as "a darn good violinist and my manuscript scribe."

Charles Richard Anders Jr., pastor of All Saints Lutheran Church, Tamarac, Florida, was born in Frederick, Maryland, July 29, 1929. He holds a Bachelor of Arts degree (1950) from Wittenberg University, a Bachelor of Music degree (1951) from St. Olaf College, a Bachelor of Divinity degree (1954) from Hamma School of Theology, and a Master of Music degree in musicology from Indiana University (1962). Ordained in 1954, he was assistant pastor of the Lutheran Church of the Redeemer, Atlanta, Georgia, from 1954 to 1957, and pastor of Advent Lutheran Church, Greenwood, Indiana from 1957 to 1962. From 1963 to 1967 he was assistant director of the Commission on Worship (LCA), after which he turned to college teaching as associate professor of music first at Thiel College (1967–1968), then at St. Olaf College (1968–1972). He served as an editor at Augsburg Publishing House in Minneapolis for two years, 1973–1975, before going to All Saints, Tamarac. He is a contributing editor of *Church Music* and the *Journal of Church Music,* and the composer of a number of choral works. From 1967 to 1975 he served on the hymn music committee of the Inter-Lutheran Commission on Worship.

387   SPIRIT OF GOD, UNLEASHED ON EARTH
Tune: Donata

This hymn was included in *Contemporary Worship-4,* 1972.

The author, John W. Arthur, was born March 25, 1922, in Mankato, Minnesota, and received both Bachelor of Arts and Bachelor of Music degrees from Gustavus Adolphus College in 1944. From January to September of that year he also studied at Wartburg Theological Seminary. He completed a Bachelor of Divinity degree at Augustana Theological Seminary and was ordained in 1946 as pastor of Zion Lutheran Church, Duquesne, Pennsylvania. In 1949 he completed a Master of Theology degree at Western Theological Seminary (Pittsburgh Theological Seminary) and began six years of service at an Augustana Board of American Missions congregation, St. Paul Lutheran Church, Floral Park, Queens, New York. From 1957 to 1958 he was Lutheran Campus Pastor at Stanford University and San Jose State College in California, and from 1958 to 1960, part-time executive director of the Lutheran Student Foundation of Northern California. Between 1960 and 1967 he was Western Regional Secretary for the Division of College and University Work of the National Lutheran Council, and also served as an unpaid assistant pastor of First Evangelical Lutheran Church, Palo Alto, California. During this time also, in 1964 and 1965, he studied at Pacific Lutheran Theological Seminary and Stanford University. He was appointed assistant professor of liturgics and director of worship at the Lutheran School of Theology at Chicago in 1967, and from 1970 to 1976 was pastor of First Lutheran Church, Palo Alto. Ill health forced his retirement in 1976, and he died August 15, 1980, at Palo Alto.

Arthur served on many worship committees, including the liturgical text committee of the Inter-Lutheran Commission on Worship, the Committee on Common Texts, the Liturgical Conference, the board of directors of the Center for Contemporary Celebration, and the Illinois Synod

(LCA) Committee on Worship. In addition, he was a member of the American Association of University Professors. His publications include *Oremus: a Book of Worship for Corporate and Private Prayer*, 1963; *Folk Song Feast*, 1966; and *Table of the Lord*, 1968; and with Daniel Moe (LBW 427), *Contemporary Liturgy*, 1963. Married to Mary E. Hulslander in 1945, he had four children.

DONATA, meaning "gift of God," is the middle name of the composer's wife, Noel Donata (Roeder) Schalk. See LBW 118 for Carl Schalk. This tune was included with this hymn in *Contemporary Worship–4*.

388   O SPIRIT OF THE LIVING GOD
Tune: Melcombe

See LBW 50 for James Montgomery. This hymn was written in 1823 for the public meeting of the Auxiliary Missionary Society for the West Riding of Yorkshire, Salem Chapel, Leeds, June 4, 1823. Published first on a fly-sheet for that meeting and later in the *Evangelical Magazine,* the hymn was revised for its inclusion in Montgomery's *Christian Psalmist,* 1825.

MELCOMBE. Samuel Webbe was born in 1740 in London, England. His father, a government official newly appointed to Minorca, died there before his wife and son could join him. Samuel was apprenticed at the age of eleven to a cabinetmaker, but left that occupation at the end of his apprenticeship and earned enough money copying music to take music lessons. During the time that he was studying with Carl Barbandt of the Bavarian embassy chapel in London, he also learned several foreign languages. A Roman Catholic, he served as organist at the Portuguese, Sardinian, and Spanish embassies in London, and made a valuable contribution to English Roman Catholic church music with his masses, motets, and especially his hymn tunes. He was also a good composer of catches and glees and was active in organizations for their performance. His publications include *A Collection of Sacred Music As Used in the Chapel of the King of Sardinia in London, c.* 1793; *A Collection of Masses for Small Choirs,* 1792; and *A Collection of Motetts and Antiphons,* 1792. He probably also edited *An Essay on the Church Plain Chant,* 1782, in which this tune was included. With his son, Samuel Webbe the Younger (LBW 35), he compiled *Antiphons in Six Books of Anthems,* 1818. He died in London March (May?) 25, 1816.

389   STAND UP, STAND UP FOR JESUS
Tune: Webb

George Duffield Jr. was the father of Samuel Augustus Willoughby Duffield, author of two important works, *English Hymns; their Authors and History,* 1886, and *Latin Hymn Writers and their Hymns,* 1889. Haeussler* notes that the Duffield family were descendants of Richard de Duffield, a bailiff in York in 1315, and of George Duffield of Lancaster County, Pennsylvania, who was born in Ireland in 1690. Born

September 12, 1818, at Carlisle, Pennsylvania, George graduated from Yale College and Union Theological Seminary. He served Presbyterian churches in Brooklyn, New York (1840–1847); Bloomfield, New Jersey (1847–1852); Philadelphia (1852–1861); Adrian, Michigan (1861–1865); Galesburg, Illinois (1865–1869); Saginaw City, Michigan (1869); and Ann Arbor and Lansing, Michigan (1869–1884). He was a member of the board of regents of the University of Michigan for seven years, and the recipient of an honorary Doctor of Divinity degree from Knox College. He died in Bloomfield, New Jersey, on July 6, 1888.

During the great revival of 1858, the Reverend Dudley Atkins Tyng, minister of Epiphany Episcopal Church in Philadelphia, preached to a large congregation of the Young Men's Christian Association and the ministers associated with them. A few days later he died suddenly of an accident. His parting message had been "Stand up for Jesus." Duffield wrote this hymn after Tyng's funeral and incorporated it into his sermon the following Sunday. It was first published in full in the *Lyra Sacra Americana,* 1868.

WEBB was originally included in *The Odeon: A Collection of Secular Melodies,* published by George James Webb and Lowell Mason (LBW 353) in 1837. (The collection was named for the Odeon, an unused theater in Boston which Mason and Webb used for their Boston Academy of Music.) There it was the setting for "'Tis dawn, the lark is singing."

Webb was born in England, at Rushmore Lodge, Salisbury, on June 24, 1803. His father was a farmer of some means. Some consideration was given to George's entering the ministry, but he chose to enter the music profession and for a while served as organist at Falmouth. In 1830 he immigrated to Boston, where he was very shortly engaged as organist to Old South Church, a position he held for forty years. He also soon met Lowell Mason, with whom he was a professor of the Boston Academy of Music and published a number of collections. From 1840 he was president of the Handel and Haydn Society. He went to Orange, New Jersey, in 1870, and a few years later, to New York City, where he gave singing lessons. Two years before his death on October 7, 1887, he returned to Orange.

Webb composed a number of anthems and hymn tunes, and arranged the musical service for the Swedenborgian Church. Among his publications are *Vocal Technics; The Massachusetts Collection of Psalmody,* 1840; *The American Glee Book,* 1841; and with Lowell Mason, *The National Psalmist,* 1848, and *Cantica Laudis,* 1850.

390   I LOVE TO TELL THE STORY

Tune: Hankey

Anabella Katherine Hankey, the daughter of a banker, was born in Clapham, England, in 1834. A member of the Clapham Sect of Evangelicals, she began teaching Sunday school in Croydon and at age eighteen established a Bible class for girls in London's West End. Some of these girls kept in contact with her for the rest of her life. Her interest in missions was spurred by a trip to South Africa, where she went to nurse and bring home an invalid brother, and she devoted the proceeds of her writings to mission work. She died in London, May 9, 1911.

In 1866 Hankey wrote an extended poem on the life of Jesus, in two parts: "The Story Wanted," from which "Tell me the old, old story" is taken, and "The Story Told," which includes the present hymn. It was published in 1867 as a leaflet. Although she very much opposed the addition of a refrain, it was tacked on and seems destined to stay as the text and Fischer's tune have become so strongly associated.

HANKEY was first published in a Methodist pamphlet, *Joyful Songs,* Philadelphia, 1869.

William Gustavas Fischer, born in Baltimore, Maryland, October 14, 1835, worked at bookbinding at J. B. Lippincott's in Philadelphia and studied music in the evenings. He later taught music at Girard College, Philadelphia, for ten years, after which he established a retail piano business and music house with John E. Gould (LBW 334). He wrote a large number of gospel tunes, influenced by Lowell Mason (LBW 353) and Thomas Hastings (LBW 327). He died August 12, 1912, in Philadelphia.

391   AND HAVE THE BRIGHT IMMENSITIES
Tune: Kingsfold

Written by Howard Chandler Robbins, this hymn was first printed in the *Living Church,* April 4, 1931.

Born in Philadelphia on December 11, 1876, Robbins received a Bachelor of Arts degree from Yale University in 1899, and a Bachelor of Divinity degree from the Episcopal Theological Seminary in 1903. Ordained a deacon in 1903 and a priest in 1904, he served as curate of St. Peter's, Morristown, New Jersey, 1903–1905; rector of St. Paul's, Englewood, New Jersey, 1905–1911; and rector of the Church of the Incarnation, 1911–1917. From 1917 to 1929 he was dean of the Cathedral of St. John the Divine, after which he resigned to become a professor at General Theological Seminary until he retired in 1941. He was visiting preacher at St. John's, Lafayette Square, Washington, D.C., from 1942 to 1944. In 1937 Robbins was a delegate to the World Conference on Faith and Order. A member of the Joint Commission on the Revision of *The Hymnal 1940,* he made a special contribution to that hymnal both in terms of numbers and of high calibre of his hymns. He was the recipient of a number of honorary degrees, and the author of several theological books, including a biography of Bishop Slattery, 1931; *Preaching the Gospel Today,* 1939; and with Burton Scott Easton, *The Eternal Word in the Modern World,* 1937. Robbins died March 20, 1952, in Washington, D.C.

KINGSFOLD. This Aeolian-mode melody is one of the many fine English folksongs introduced to twentieth-century hymnody by Ralph Vaughan Williams (LBW 101) in *The English Hymnal,* 1906. There it was the setting for Horatius Bonar's "I heard the voice of Jesus say" (LBW 497). Noted by Alfred J. Hipkins in Westminster, it was set to the English ballad, "Dives and Lazarus," in *English County Songs,* 1893, edited by Lucy E. Broadwood and J. A. Fuller Maitland. In *The Oxford Book of Carols,* 1928, it appears in a slightly different form with "Come all you worthy Christian men." "Kingsfold" is the name of a village in Surrey where Vaughan Williams heard a variant of the tune. The melody is known as "The Star of County Down" in Ireland.

The LBW harmonization is by Richard Hillert (LBW 63).

392 O LORD, SEND FORTH YOUR SPIRIT
Tune: Wedlock

This text has been adapted for the LBW from a hymn beginning "Speak forth thy word, O father," by Charles Joseph Jeffries. The hymn first appeared on a church bulletin, and in 1969 was included in the *Worship Supplement* to *The Lutheran Hymnal*.

Born May 7, 1896, in Lewisham, London, England, Jeffries attended Malvern College (of which he later became a governor), and later Magdalen College, Oxford, where he studied classics. He enlisted in the Wiltshire Regiment during World War I, but in 1917 was gassed and wounded and returned home as an invalid, his voice permanently damaged. The same year he joined the Colonial Office, and in 1947, became Joint Deputy Under-Secretary of State. He instituted Overseas Service training courses at Farnham Castle and established Queen Elizabeth House as a Commonwealth center in Oxford. On his retirement in 1956 he was knighted by the Queen for his efforts at unifying various branches of the Colonial Civil Service. Jeffries was an avid reader and a devout Christian. He served on the governing board of the Society for the Promotion of Christian Knowledge and on the general committee of the British and Foreign Bible Society, and from 1950 to 1955 was a member of the House of Laity of the Church of England. He contributed a number of articles to *The Times* and other periodicals. *Who's Who* lists fifteen publications of his. He died December 11, 1972, at Bromley, Kent.

WEDLOCK. This pentatonic tune is given in George Pullen Jackson's *Down-East Spirituals* (New York, *c.* 1939), where he lists the source as Cecil J. Sharp and Maud Karpeles, *English Folk-Songs from the Southern Appalachians,* London, 1932. The melody, which Sharp and Karpeles took down in North Carolina in 1918, is suggested by Jackson to be related to the Irish chantey, "The Banks of Newfoundland." The original text, "When Adam was created," which speaks of the subservience of a woman in marriage, is discussed in some detail by Jackson. (Coming from England, this text seems to be based on lines from Chaucer's "Parson's Tale" in the *Canterbury Tales,* which in turn has antecedents in Latin sermons of the twelfth, thirteenth, and fifteenth centuries.) A variant of the tune, titled "Creation," was included in *The Sacred Harp,* Philadelphia, 1844 (LBW 423).

The harmonization is based on one prepared by Austin C. Lovelace for *The Book of Hymns,* 1964, of the Methodist Church. Austin Cole Lovelace, a leader in Methodist and interdenominational music, was born in Rutherfordton, North Carolina, March 26, 1919. After completing a Bachelor of Arts degree in 1939 at High Point College, High Point, North Carolina, and a Master of Sacred Music degree in 1941 from Union Theological Seminary, New York City, he taught at the University of Nebraska and Queens College in Charlotte, North Carolina. He also served churches in Lincoln, Nebraska, and Charlotte and Greensboro, North Carolina. From 1952 to 1962 he was minister of music at First Methodist Church, Evanston, Illinois, and was associate professor of church music at Garrett Theological Seminary. For two years thereafter, while lecturing in hymnology at Union Theological Seminary, he served as minister of music at Christ Church Methodist in New York City. From 1964 to 1970 he was minister of music at Montview Boulevard Presbyterian Church, Denver, and after 1968, also taught at Temple Buell College (Colorado Women's College) in Denver. In 1970 he became minister of music at Lover's Lane Methodist Church, Dallas, Texas, and since 1977, has served at Wellshire Presbyterian Church, Denver.

Lovelace was organizing chairman and first president of the National Fellowship of Methodist Musicians, 1955-1957, is active in the Hymn Society of America and the American Guild of Organists, and is a member of the Choristers' Guild board. He has conducted numerous church music workshops in forty states, and in Suva, Fiji. In 1954 he was organist for the Second Assembly of the World Council of Churches, and ten years later, director of music for the General Conference of the Methodist Church in Pittsburgh. He has written over 350 works for choir, organ, and solo voice, and is the author of *The Organist and Hymn Playing,* 1962; *The Anatomy of Hymnody,* 1965; and (with William C. Rice) *Music and Worship in the Church,* 1960. He was chairman of the subcommittee on hymn tunes for *The Book of Hymns* (Methodist), 1964; and with Fred D. Gealy and Carlton R. Young (LBW 469) prepared the *Companion to the Hymnal,* 1970. High Point College honored him with a Doctor of Music degree in 1963.

393 RISE, SHINE, YOU PEOPLE!

Tune: Wojtkiewiecz

This hymn was written at the request of Wilson Egbert of Augsburg Publishing House in Minneapolis, and was first published in an APH bulletin insert in 1973.

The author, Ronald Allan Klug, was born June 26, 1939, in Milwaukee, Wisconsin, and received a Bachelor of Science in Education at Dr. Martin Luther College, New Ulm, Minnesota, in 1962. For three years thereafter he taught at St. Matthew Lutheran School, Oconomowoc, Wisconsin. From 1965 to 1968 he did graduate work in English and worked as a teaching assistant at the University of Wisconsin in Milwaukee. He worked as an advertising copywriter at Concordia Publishing House, St. Louis, Missouri, from 1968 to 1969, and as a book editor at Augsburg Publishing House from 1970 to 1976. Since that time he has been an English teacher at the American School in Fort Dauphin, Madagascar. He has written other texts for music, as well as articles, book reviews, and poetry, and has published a book for children, *The Strange Young Man in the Desert,* 1970, and one for teenagers, *Lord, I've Been Thinking,* 1978.

WOJTKIEWIECZ. See LBW 268 for Dale Wood. This tune was commissioned for Ronald Klug's hymn, and published together with it as a bulletin insert. The tune bears the composer's family name, Wojtkiewiecz, which was lost early in this century when an immigration official suggested it be changed to Wood.

394 LOST IN THE NIGHT *(Seklernas väkter saa dröjande skrida)*

Tune: Lost in the Night

A Finnish folksong has served as the basis for this hymn. The tune, here called LOST IN THE NIGHT, comes from the province of Carelia, now in Russia, and is found in a collection of Finnish folk melodies published in 1857 by K. Collan and R. Lagi. The original text was secular and quite erotic, with a last line, "Will he not come soon?" Several Scandinavian hymns have used the tune, including Lina Sandell's (LBW 474) "Herre fördölj ej ditt ansikteför mig," a hymn about Christ's second coming, which keeps the last line, "Will he not come soon?" The English text found here was prepared by Olav Lee in 1929, and included in the *Concordia Hymnal,* 1932. There it was noted to be a "translation of a Norwegian rendering of a Finnish song." Joel Lundeen (LBW 146) has suggested that at least the last two stanzas are a translation of the Swedish hymn, "Seklernas väkter saa dröjande skrida," by Olga Maria Kullgren. This hymn, written for an all-Scandinavian mission meeting held in Gothenburg, Sweden, September 6–8, 1885, was printed in *Sanningsvittnet* on October 22 of that year.

Olga Maria Virginia Holmén was born February 12, 1849, in Skarstad, Västergötland Province in Sweden. She went to Gothenburg in the early 1870s as a folk school teacher, receiving room and board from the Kullgren family. In 1884 she was married to L. Kullgren, his first wife having died the year before. She wrote texts for a number of songs, and in 1883 published a collection of poetry titled *Harpolek.* Together with her husband she took part in various Christian activities. She died on her sixtieth birthday, February 12, 1909.

Born May 29, 1859, at Trysil, Østerdalen, Norway, Olav Lee entered the Hamar Normal School in 1876, and the following year immigrated to the United States. He studied at Luther College, 1878–1883; Luther Seminary, 1883–1885; Capital University, 1885–1886; and Wisconsin University, 1904. Ordained in 1886, he was pastor at Northwood, North Dakota, 1886–1890; Canton, South Dakota, 1891–1892; Holden and Dale, Minnesota, 1899; Kenyon, Minnesota, 1909; Grand River, South Dakota, 1910; Hayfield, Minnesota, 1911–1912; Lyle, Minnesota, 1912–1913; Northfield, Minnesota, 1917–1918; and Coon Valley, Wisconsin, 1920. In addition, he taught at Augustana College, Canton, South Dakota, from 1890 to 1894, and from 1894 was professor of Hebrew, Latin, and religion at St. Olaf College, Northfield, Minnesota. He retired professor emeritus in 1933, and died in Northfield on May 22, 1943. Married in 1887 to Bertha M. Schmidt, he was the father of six children.

Lee served on the committee for Deaf and Blind Missions (1899–1900) and on the planning committee for Charities (1906–1908), and from 1917 to 1933 was secretary of the St. Olaf faculty. He was author of *The Religious Training of our Children,* 1915, and *The Second Coming of Christ,* 1931; translator of *Ibsen Studies* by P. J. Eikeland, 1934; editor of a *History of St. John's Church* (where he was a member of the board of trustees), 1920; and interim editor in 1903 and 1907 of *Lutheraneren.* Some of his hymn translations, submitted to the committee of the 1913 *Lutheran Hymnary,* came to the attention of F. Melius Christiansen, who asked him to translate some hymns and songs for the St. Olaf Choir. Lee prepared some forty translations, most of which were incorporated into the *St. Olaf Choir Series,* 1918—, and seven were also included in *The Concordia Hymnal,* 1932.

395 I TRUST, O CHRIST, IN YOU ALONE
(Allein zu dir, Herr Jesu Christ)
Tune: Allein zu dir

This hymn first appeared in an undated Nürnberg broadsheet around 1540. In 1542 it was published in Low German in the Magdeburg *Gesangbuch* and three years later it was included by Martin Luther (LBW 48) in Valentin Babst's *Geystliche Lieder,* Leipzig, 1545.

No author's name was given in these early publications, and sources are not in complete agreement regarding the hymn's authorship. Wackernagel* and subsequently Julian* attribute it to Johannes Schneesing (also Chionusus or Chyonusus), a native of Frankfurt-am-Main, Germany. Appointed assistant, before 1524, to Johann Langenhayn, pastor of St. Margaret's Church in Gotha, who had embraced the doctrines of the Reformation, Schneesing later became pastor in Friemar, near Gotha. There he died in 1567. The hymn was claimed for Schneesing in 1597 by one of his pupils, Marx Wagner, who noted that Schneesing had inserted the hymn into the liturgy which he composed for the church in Friemar. (Konrad Hubert is then credited only with some revisions to the text.)

Other sources, including the *Handbuch zum Evangelischen Kirchengesangbuch,* edited by Christhard Mahrenholz and Oskar Söhngen (Göttingen, 1953-) ascribe the text to Hubert alone.

The son of an artisan, Konrad Hubert was born in 1507 in Bergzabern, Pfalz, and spent his school years in Heidelberg. He attended the University of Basel, where he was won over to the cause of the Reformation. In 1531 he is found in Strassburg as a deacon and private secretary to Martin Bucer. (He has been described as a virtuoso in the difficult art of deciphering his master's handwriting.) He edited Bucer's large hymn collection of 1541 and took care of the Strassburg editions of 1560 and 1572. He also prepared a book of Latin song for children. Following Bucer's departure from Strassburg in 1549, Hubert came on bad times. His loyalty to Bucer's theology caused him to be expelled from the church in 1562 and to lose his position as assistant at St. Thomas Church the following year. He continued to work on Bucer's sacred writings, receiving a helping hand from Johan Sturm and from the English archbishop, Edmund Grindell. He died with his pen in hand on April 13 (23?), 1577.

The English translation was prepared by Gilbert E. Doan (LBW 99) for the LBW.

ALLEIN ZU DIR is an anonymous melody which first appeared, as a setting for this text, on a broadsheet titled *Eyn schönn Lied von vnser heiligenn Tauff,* Wittenberg, 1541. Four years later it was included in Valentin Babst's *Geystliche Lieder,* Leipzig. The harmonization was prepared for the LBW by Jan Bender (LBW 396).

396 O GOD, O LORD OF HEAVEN AND EARTH
Tune: Wittenberg New

This hymn by Martin H. Franzmann (LBW 233) was written for the 450th anniversary of the Reformation in 1967.

WITTENBERG NEW was written for Franzmann's text when it was included in the *Worship Supplement,* 1969, to *The Lutheran Hymnal,* and is named for Wittenberg University, Springfield, Ohio.

The composer, Jan O. Bender, was born in Haarlem, Holland, in 1909. His mother was German and his father was Dutch. After his father's death, his family moved in 1922 to Lübeck, Germany. Music studies included work with Karl Straube in Leipzig, and with Hugo Distler at Amsterdam and Lübeck. From 1934 to 1960 he served as organist and choirmaster at several places in Germany, including seven years from 1953 to 1960 at St. Michael's Church in Lüneberg, where Johann Sebastian Bach (LBW 219) had once been a choirboy. In 1960 he came to the United States and for five years was assistant professor of music at Concordia Teachers College, Seward, Nebraska. From 1965 to 1976 he was first associate professor, then full professor at the School of Music, Wittenberg University, Springfield, Ohio. He then went back to Germany, where he lived at Hanerau in Holstein. He returned to the United States, and went to teach at Valparaiso University, Valparaiso, Indiana, in January of 1979, and in the fall of that year went to Gustavus Aldolphus College, St. Peter, Minnesota.

Bender's music publications are legion. Opus numbers 1–76 contain over 1100 single pieces published in Germany and the United States. In 1975 he received an honorary Doctor of Letters degree from Concordia College in Seward, the Canticum Novum award from Wittenberg University in Springfield, and a Fellowship in the American Hymn Society. He is represented by a number of harmonizations in the LBW.

397 O ZION, HASTE

Tune: Angelic Songs

Mary Ann Thomson was born in London, England, on December 5, 1834, and grew up in England. She came to the United States and was married to John Thomson, who was the first librarian of the Free Library in Philadelphia. For many years she was a member of the Church of the Annunciation in Philadelphia, where her husband was the accounting warden. She contributed a number of hymns and poems to *The Churchman,* New York, and *The Living Church,* Chicago. She died in Philadelphia on March 11, 1923.

"O Zion, haste" is one of over forty hymns written by Thomson. It was begun one night in 1868 when she was sitting up with one of her children who had typhoid fever. Being especially fond of the tune for Frederick W. Faber's (LBW 290) "Hark, hark, my soul! angelic songs are swelling," she determined to write a missionary text for it. The refrain did not immediately take shape in her mind, however, and was written about three years later. The hymn was included in Charles Hutchins' *The Church Hymnal* (Episcopal), 1892.

ANGELIC SONGS (also "Tidings") was written in 1875 or 1876 for "Hark, hark, my soul! angelic songs are swelling" since the composer did not like either of the existing tunes, one by Henry Smart (LBW 50) and one by John B. Dykes (LBW 165). (It is not known which of the tunes Thomson had in mind when she wrote "O Zion, haste.") "Angelic Songs" was first published in *The Hymnal Companion to the Book of Common Prayer,* second edition, London, 1877. Included in Charles

Hutchins' *The Church Hymnal,* New York, 1892, with the present text, it has since become firmly associated with it.

James Walch was born at Edgerton, near Bolton in England, on June 21, 1837, and studied music with his father, and later with Henry Smart. In 1851 he was appointed organist of Duke's Alley Congregational Church, Bolton. He then served two churches simultaneously, taking a position at Walmsley Church in 1857 and at Bridge Street Wesleyan Chapel in 1858. He became organist to St. George's Parish Church in Bolton in 1863. From 1874 to 1877 he conducted the Bolton Philharmonic Society, and from 1877 until his death in 1901, was honorary organist at a parish church in Barrow-in-Furness, where he had a music business. He died at Llandudno, Caenarvonshire, in Wales on August 31, 1901.

398   "TAKE UP YOUR CROSS," THE SAVIOR SAID

Tune: Nun lasst uns den Lieb begraben

This hymn, written when the author was nineteen years old, was included in his *Visions of Death, and Other Poems,* 1833. Originally beginning "Take up *thy* cross," the text has been included in many hymnals with frequent variations. The LBW form represents considerable alteration.

Charles William Everest was born at East Windsor, Connecticut, on May 27, 1814, and graduated from Trinity College, Hartford, in 1838. Ordained an Episcopalian clergyman in 1842, he served as rector at Hamden, Connecticut from 1842 to 1873, and was also an agent for the Society for the Increase of the Ministry. He died January 11, 1877, at Waterbury, Connecticut.

NUN LASST UNS DEN LIEB BEGRABEN is found in Georg Rhau's *Newe deudsche geistliche Geseng,* Wittenberg, 1544. There it was the setting for "Nun lasst uns den Lieb begraben," a text attributed to Michael Weisse (LBW 37) (translated in *The Lutheran Hymnal,* 1941, #596).

Rhau (1488–1548), printer and composer, and friend of Martin Luther (LBW 48), taught for a time at Leipzig University, and also served as *Kantor* at St. Thomas' School in Leipzig, a position later held by J. S. Bach (LBW 219). The first and greatest music publisher of the Reformation, he established a business in Wittenberg, and set for himself the task of providing all the necessary music for Lutheran churches, schools, and choruses. Among his own compositions is a twelve-part mass for the debate between Luther and Eck at Leipzig in 1519. Rhau's *Newe deudsche geistliche Geseng,* an anthology of the works of nineteen different composers, was one of the most important early Lutheran collections.

Harmonization of the tune is by Jan Bender (LBW 396).

399   WE ARE THE LORD'S
(Wir sind des Herrn, wir leben oder sterben)
Tune: We Are the Lord's

Karl Johann Philipp Spitta was one of the leading hymnwriters of the revival period in Germany—a period in which the Lutheran church removed itself from the rationalism of the previous century and returned to what Julian* calls a period of "evangelical theology, piety and hymnody."

Of Huguenot ancestry, Spitta was born August 1, 1801, in Hannover, the son of a bookkeeper and teacher of French. When Karl was only four years old, his father died, and he himself was in such poor health for most of his childhood that his mother decided that he should be apprenticed to a watchmaker, rather than enter a professional career. He remained with this occupation, telling no one of his dislike for it until after the death of his older brother who had been studying for the ministry. Karl was then offered the opportunity to take up his brother's profession. He gladly accepted, and after a year of hard study gained admission to the *Gymnasium* at Hannover in 1819, and in 1821, to the University of Göttingen, where he studied under professors of strong rationalistic tendencies. He completed his course in 1824. Near the end of his university career he underwent a profound spiritual change and in 1826, while serving as tutor to the family of a judge at Lüne, near Lüneberg, he wrote to a friend, "In the manner in which I formerly sang I sing no more. To the Lord I consecrate my life and my love, and likewise my song. . . . He gave to me song and melody. I give it back to him." From this point until 1847 he wrote most of his hymns. In 1828 he was ordained and thereafter served for two years at Sudwalde near Hoya before becoming assistant chaplain to the garrison and to the prison at Hameln on the Weser. His pietistic attitudes prevented his succeeding as permanent chaplain there in 1837 and he went instead as pastor to Wechold near Hoya. In 1837, also, he was married to Joanna Mary Magdalene Hotzen. There were seven children. One son, Friedrich, was a theologian noted for his works on liturgics; another, Johann August Philipp, for his important biography of J. S. Bach (LBW 219). Spitta was appointed Lutheran superintendent at Wittingen in 1847, at Peine in 1853, and finally at Burgdorf in 1859. Death came unexpectedly on September 28, 1859, as he sat at his writing table.

The majority of Spitta's hymns were published in *Psalter und Harfe,* published at Pirna in 1833, and in its successor, *Psalter und Harfe: Zweite Sammlung,* 1843. The present hymn, founded on Romans 14:8, was included in the latter volume. These two volumes were immensely popular. The first passed through fifty-five editions by 1889; the second, through 42 editions by 1887.

Charles Tamberlane Astley's translation was published in his *Songs in the Night,* 1860, a collection containing both original poems and translation from German.

Astley was born May 12, 1825, at Cwmllecoediog, near Mallwyd, in North Wales, and was a scholar of Jesus College, Oxford (Bachelor of Arts, 1847; Master of Arts, 1849). Ordained in 1849, he became evening lecturer at Bideford. Thereafter he served as incumbent of Holwell, Oxford, 1850–1854; vicar of Margate, 1854–1864; and rector of Brasted, 1864–1878. He died in 1878.

WE ARE THE LORD'S. Ludwig Lenel's setting for this text was written in 1960 and published in *Four Hymns for Choir,* 1964.

Lenel, composer-in-residence at Muhlenberg College, Allentown, Pennsylvania, was born May 20, 1914, in Strasbourg, France. He is now an American citizen. In 1932 he became an artist pupil of Albert Schweitzer in Guensbach, Alsace, and served as his assistant on two concert tours through South Germany (1932) and Switzerland (1936).

Following studies at the Hochschule für Musik in Cologne, Germany (diploma, 1935), the Conservatory of Music in Basel, Switzerland (diploma, 1938), and the Schola Cantorum Basiliensis, he came to the United States where he completed a Master of Music degree at Oberlin Conservatory of Music in 1940. He remained at Oberlin for a year to teach composition, then taught organ, theory, composition, and choral conducting at Monticello College, Alton, Illinois, from 1941 to 1944; Westminster College, New Wilmington, Pennsylvania in 1945; and Elmhurst College, Elmhurst, Illinois, from 1945 to 1948. From 1951 to 1952 he served as organist and choir director at Christ Lutheran Church, Allentown, Pennsylvania, and presented a series of lectures on Romanticism for the New School for Social Research in New York City. In 1952 he was appointed professor of music at Muhlenberg College.

Lenel has been a faculty member at numerous church music and composers' institutes and has appeared often as a conductor and as an organist on both sides of the Atlantic. A charter member of the Lutheran Society for Worship, Music and the Arts, he conducted J. S. Bach's (LBW 219) *St. John Passion* for their first annual convention at the University of Minnesota. Also a member of the American Guild of Organists, he became an associate in 1947 and a fellow in 1956. He served for several years as a member of the hymn music committee of the Inter-Lutheran Commission on Worship. The list of his compositions, both published and unpublished, is extensive and includes organ and piano works, choral music, songs, chamber music, and works for larger instrumental groups. Two operas are based on libretti prepared by his wife, Jane Harman Lenel. His articles and interviews have been included in *The Precentor, Response,* and *Church Music.* He is the father of three children.

400 GOD, WHOSE ALMIGHTY WORD
Tune: Italian Hymn

Based on Genesis 1:3 and written about 1813, this hymn was quoted by the Reverend Thomas Mortimer, lecturer of St. Olave's, Southwark, at a meeting of the London Missionary Society on May 12, 1825. It was published the following month in the *Evangelical Magazine.* The first line originally read, "*Thou* whose *eternal* word," and there have been a few other alterations in the text.

The author, John Marriott, son of the rector of Cottesbach near Lutterworth, England, was baptized on September 11, 1780. He attended Christ Church, Oxford, where he was one of two to receive honors in the first year there were public examinations for honors at Oxford. He completed a Bachelor of Arts degree in 1802 and a Master of Arts in 1806. He was ordained in 1804 and for a while was private tutor and domestic chaplain to the family of the fourth Duke of Buccleuch, who in 1808 appointed him to the rectory of Church Lawford in Warwickshire. He retained this position until his death, although his wife's ill health made it necessary for them to live in Devonshire, where he was curate of three parishes—St. James's and St. Lawrence in Exeter, and Broad Clyst. Ossification of the brain developed in 1824, and he died March 31, 1825, at St. Giles in the Fields, Middlesex. Only after his death were his hymns published, as he would not permit it during his lifetime.

Marriott was a good friend of Sir Walter Scott. Scott dedicated the second canto of his *Marmion* (1808) to Marriott and included some of Marriott's ballads in his *Minstrelsy of the Scottish Border,* 1802–1805.

For ITALIAN HYMN see LBW 522, where it appears with its original text. This harmonization is by Charles William Ore.

Ore, born December 18, 1936, at Winfield, Kansas, studied with Theodore Beck (LBW 33) at Concordia College, Seward, Nebraska, completing a Bachelor of Science degree in 1958. After further studies with Myron Roberts at the University of Nebraska and with Thomas Matthews at Northwestern University, he received a Master of Music degree in 1960. From 1961 to 1966 he taught at Concordia Teachers College, River Forest, Illinois, and in 1966 he was appointed associate professor of music at Concordia Teachers College, Seward, Nebraska. In 1975 he also took a position as director of music at Pacific Hills Lutheran Church in Omaha, Nebraska. He has written a number of works for organ, as well as *Lisbon Psalms* for voice and organ and for voice and piano.

401 BEFORE YOU, LORD, WE BOW
Tune: Darwall's 148th

See LBW 243 for Francis Scott Key. Published in 1832, this hymn was probably written for the Fourth of July celebration of that year. Originally beginning "Before *the* Lord we bow," the text has been altered only slightly.

For DARWALL'S 148TH see LBW 261.

402 LOOK FROM YOUR SPHERE OF ENDLESS DAY
Tune: Gonfalon Royal

Written in 1840, this hymn was included five years later in a private collection of nineteen hymns. The text has been considerably altered for the LBW.

Earliest of the famous New England poets, William Cullen Bryant was born November 3, 1794, at Cummington, Massachusetts. Educated at Williams College, he was admitted to the bar in 1815 and practiced law for a time at Great Barrington. In 1825 he turned to journalism, moving to New York where he founded the *New York Review,* and for many years edited the *New York Evening Post.* His first literary work was published when he was fourteen, and his well-known *Thanatopsis* appeared in 1817. Over one hundred of his poems dealt with the subject of nature. He was also an early writer against slavery. His twenty hymns, some of which were inspired by those of Isaac Watts (LBW 39), were written at intervals during his life. In the course of his lifetime Bryant was a member of Congregational, Episcopalian, Presbyterian, and Baptist churches. He died on Long Island, New York, July 12, 1878.

GONFALON ROYAL, originally the setting for "The royal banners forward go" (LBW 124), was written by Percy Carter Buck for the boys at Harrow School. It first appeared in *Fourteen Hymn Tunes,* 1913. "Gonfalon" is an old Norman-English word meaning "banner."

Percy Buck was born March 25, 1871, at West Ham, Essex, England. He went to the Royal College of Music on an organ scholarship, where he studied with Walter Parratt, Charles Harford Lloyd, and C. H. H. Parry (LBW 283), receiving a Bachelor of Arts degree in 1891. From 1891 to 1894 he was organist at Worcester College, Oxford, and from 1894 to 1896, organist at Wells Cathedral. During this time, in 1897, he received both his Doctor of Music and Master of Arts degrees. He went to Bristol as organist in 1899, and then on to Harrow School in 1901, where he was director of music for twenty-six years. In addition, from 1910 to 1920 he occupied the chair of music at Dublin University, and from 1925 to 1930 held the post of King Edward professor of music at the University of London. A fellow of Worcester College, Oxford, and of the Royal College of Music, he was honored with knighthood in 1936. He died October 3, 1947.

Buck's publications include *The Scope of Music,* 1924; *The History of Music,* 1929; and *Psychology for Musicians,* 1944. In addition, he edited, with E. C. Bairstow, the *English Psalter,* 1925, and the *Oxford Song Book,* 1931. He was a member of the committee which published the *Tudor Church Music* series which began in 1923.

403 LORD, SPEAK TO US, THAT WE MAY SPEAK

Tune: Canonbury

See LBW 260 for Frances Ridley Havergal. Written April 28, 1872, at Winterdyne, this hymn was printed that same year as one of William Parlane's musical leaflets, and was included in 1874 in *Under the Surface.* The text was originally in first-person singular, and was altered for the LBW.

CANONBURY is adapted from the fourth piano piece in Schumann's *Nachtstücke,* Opus 23, written in 1839, which begins as given below.

Robert Alexander Schumann was born at Zwickau, Saxony, on June 8, 1810, the son of a bookseller and editor. When Schumann was sixteen his father died, and his mother decided he should become a lawyer. At Leipzig, however, he devoted much more time to mystical literature and the study of piano with his future father-in-law, Friedrich Wieck, than to the study of law. His mother sent him away to Heidelberg, and then to Italy, but he continued his interest in piano, and in 1840 was married to Clara Wieck. Clara was herself one of the leading pianists of her day and did much to make Robert's pieces known. (After her husband's death she was from 1878 to 1892 head of the piano department of the Hoch Conservatory in Frankfurt-am-Main.) Schumann, whose music fully embodies the Romantic spirit, was turned by a finger injury from a career as a concert pianist to that of a composer. His compositions include a large number of piano works and songs, as well as chamber music, symphonies, choral works, and a piano concerto. For ten years beginning in 1834 he was editor of the Leipzig *Neue Zeitschrift für Musik,* a journal of great importance and influence on the Romantic movement, in which Schumann was one of the first to recognize the genius of Frédéric Chopin and Johannes Brahms. Accounts of his life describe Schumann as a man of high ideals and greatness and generosity of spirit. During the later part of his life he experienced increasingly severe depression and following an attempt in 1854 to drown himself in the Rhine, he was placed at his own request in an asylum at Endenich, near Bonn. There he died on July 29, 1856.

404   AS SAINTS OF OLD

Tune: Regwal

With the opening line "As *men* of old their first fruits brought," this hymn first appeared in *Ten New Stewardship Hymns,* 1961, of the Hymn Society of America.

Frank von Christierson was born on Christmas Day, 1900, in Lovisa, near Helsinki, Finland, and in 1905 came with his parents and five brothers and sisters to the United States. Following graduation from Stanford University with a Bachelor of Arts degree in psychology, he served for three years as youth work director in San Luis Obispo, California. In 1929 he graduated from San Francisco Theological Seminary and was ordained to the Presbyterian ministry. The following year he received a Master of Arts degree. After serving at Calvary Presbyterian Church in Berkeley for fourteen years, he became the founding pastor of Trinity Community Presbyterian Church, North Hollywood, where he remained for sixteen years. Thereafter he was pastor of the newly-organized Celtic Cross United Presbyterian Church of Citrus Heights, California, for five years. Since his retirement in 1965 he has held five interim pastorates in north California and Nevada, and since 1970 has served as part-time pastor of the First Presbyterian Church in Roseville, California, where he ministers especially to the sick and elderly.

Through the years Christierson has held many important offices, including moderator of the San Francisco and Los Angeles Presbyteries. He was also chairman of Christian education for the Los Angeles Presbytery for six years, and chairman of radio and television for the Sacramento Presbytery and the Sacramento Council of Churches for three years. The television program which he inaugurated in 1962, "Capitol and Clergy," is still running. He has traveled extensively—to Europe, Asia, Asia Minor, and Alaska. Married to Frances May Lockhart in 1925, he is the father of two children.

Of the author's nearly fifty hymns, fifteen have been published by the Hymn Society of America, and many have found their way further into other hymnals: the Methodist *Book of Hymns,* 1964; *The Hymnal* of the United Church of Christ, 1974; the Presbyterian *Worshipbook,* 1970; the hymnals of the United States Armed Forces and of the Church of Scotland; a Portuguese hymnal used in the United States and in Brazil; and an Armenian hymnal published in California. The author writes of the present hymn:

As pastor of two new churches, with small memberships and great financial needs, I have been deeply concerned with stewardship, also because I am deeply concerned about missions and the outreach of the church to "all the world," also because stewardship is a very important phase of the Christian life. No one is deeply Christian until he is a "good steward."

With the tune REGWAL by Leland B. Sateren (LBW 100), this hymn was published in 1963 by Augsburg Publishing House as an anthem, and in 1970 appeared in R. Harold Terry's (LBW 557) *Sing!*

405 LORD OF LIGHT

Tune: Abbot's Leigh

This hymn by Howell Elvet Lewis, contributed to *The Congregational Hymnary,* 1916, was written to declare that "in doing God's will, active co-operation is as much needed as humble resignation." Some alterations have been made for the LBW.

Lewis, born at Conwil Elvet in Carmarthenshire, Wales, on April 14, 1860, received a Master of Arts degree from the University of Wales in 1906. After attending the Presbyterian College in Carmarthen he entered the Congregational ministry and held pastorates at Buckley, Flintshire (1880-1884); Fish Street, Hull (1884-1891); Park Chapel, Llanelly, Carmarthenshire (1891-1898); Harecourt, Canonbury, London (1898-1904); and the Welsh Tabernacle, King's Cross, London (1904-1940). As a poet, he received the bardic crown at the National Eisteddfod in Wales in 1888 and from 1923 to 1927 was archdruid of Wales. He was president of the National Free Church Council from 1926 to 1927 and chairman of the Congregational Union of England and Wales from 1933 to 1934. The University of Wales conferred on him the honorary Doctor of Divinity degree in 1933 and an honorary Doctor of Laws degree in 1949. In 1948 the King conferred upon him the Order of the Companion of Honour. A lifelong student of hymnology, Lewis was one of the earliest members of the Hymn Society of Great Britain and Ireland and was a member of the editorial committee of the *Congregational Hymnary.* He wrote numerous books of poetry, devotion, and sermons in both English and Welsh. Though nearly blind in his later years, he remained vigorous, and after his ninetieth birthday was still preaching every Sunday. He died at Penwith on December 10, 1953.

ABBOT'S LEIGH was composed one Sunday morning in the spring of 1941 at Abbot's Leigh, a village just across the Clifton suspension bridge from Bristol, England. The composer, Cyril Vincent Taylor (LBW 160), was working there in the wartime headquarters of the religious broadcasting department of the BBC. First printed in a leaflet, the tune was selected as the setting for "Glorious things of thee are spoken" (LBW 358) in the 1950 edition of *Hymns Ancient and Modern.*

406 TAKE MY LIFE, THAT I MAY BE

Tune: Patmos

See LBW 260 for Frances Ridley Havergal. Written February 4, 1874, this hymn originated in December, 1873, when the author made a five-day visit to Areley House in Worcestershire. Of this visit she later wrote:

> There were ten persons in the house, some unconverted and long prayed for, some converted but not rejoicing Christians. He gave me the prayer, "Lord, give me *all* in this house." And He just *did*. Before I left the house everyone had got a blessing. The last night of my visit I was too happy to sleep, and passed most of the night in praise and renewal of my own consecration, and these little couplets formed themselves and chimed in my heart, one after another till they finished "ever, only, all, for Thee."

Originally beginning "Take my life, and let it be Consecrated, Lord, to Thee," the hymn was first published in the Appendix of Charles B. Shepp's *Songs of Grace and Glory*, 1874. Julian* notes that the hymn has been translated into French, German, Swedish, Russian, and other European languages, as well as several from Africa and Asia; and that it was the family's wish that the hymn be sung to her father's tune, "Patmos."

PATMOS, taken from an unpublished manuscript dated 1869, was published in Havergal's *Psalmody*, 1871.

William Henry Havergal, born at Chipping, Wycombe, Buckinghamshire, England, on January 18, 1793, attended St. Edmund's Hall, Oxford, where he received a Bachelor of Arts degree in 1815, and a Master of Arts degree in 1819. He was ordained a deacon in 1816 and a priest the following year. After two curacies in Gloucestershire, he became rector of Astley near Bewdley in 1829. Forced to resign because of a carriage accident the same year, in which he sustained a brain concussion and permanent eye injury, he spent his time in studying music, and began to compose anthems and services. English church music was at a low ebb during the first half of the nineteenth century, and Havergal set out to bring about some reform. By 1842 he was able to resume the ministry and he became rector of St. Nicholas, Worcester, and three years later became honorary canon of Worcester Cathedral. Failing health made it necessary for him to move to a quieter parish, and from 1860 to 1867 he was vicar of Shareshill near Wolverhampton. He died April 19, 1870, at Leamington, Warwickshire.

Havergal published a reprint of the *Ravenscroft Psalter*, a *History of the Old Hundredth Psalm Tune*, 1854; *A Hundred Psalm and Hymn Tunes*, 1859; and his best-known work, *Old Church Psalmody*, 1847.

407 COME, YOU THANKFUL PEOPLE, COME

Tune: St. George's, Windsor

This hymn first appeared in Alford's *Psalms and Hymns*, 1844. It was subsequently altered in his *Poetical Works*, 1865, and again in his *Year of Praise*, 1867. The final stanza, especially, has undergone revisions. In *Psalms and Hymns* it read as follows:

> Then, thou Church triumphant come
> Raise the song of harvest Home;
> All are safely gathered in,
> Free from sorrow, free from sin,
> There for ever purified,
> In God's garner to abide:
> Come, ten thousand angels, come.
> Raise the song of harvest-home.

The LBW text, with very slight changes to update the second-person pronouns, is from *Year of Praise.*

Henry Alford, son of the rector of Aston Sandford, Buckinghamshire, was born in London, England, October 7, 1810. He graduated with honors from Trinity College, Cambridge, in 1832, and was ordained the following year to the curacy of Ampton. Thereafter he was vicar of Wymeswold, Leicestershire (1835–1853) and incumbent at Quebec Chapel in London (1853–1857) before going to Canterbury as dean in 1857. He died at Canterbury on January 12, 1871.

Julian* lists some eighteen poetical and hymnological works by Alford, including those mentioned above. Prime among his literary works was a four-volume commentary on the Greek New Testament, a work which required some twenty years in the preparation, and which served as a standard during the last half of the nineteenth century. In addition he was a member of the New Testament Revision Committee. He held several important appointments, including a fellowship of Trinity College, and the Hulsean Lectureship, 1841–1842.

ST. GEORGE'S, WINDSOR, is named for the church where George J. Elvey (LBW 170) was organist for forty-seven years. It was first included in E. H. Thorne's *A Selection of Psalm and Hymn Tunes,* London, 1858—a collection of tunes to complement T. B. Morrell and W. W. How's *Psalms and Hymns* (LBW 77)—where it was set to James Montgomery's (LBW 50) "Hark, the song of jubilee."

408   GOD, WHOSE GIVING KNOWS NO ENDING

Tune: Rustington

Regarding this hymn, the author has written:

> "God, whose giving knows no ending" was written in the White Mountains of New Hampshire while we were summering at our cottage in the tiny town of Randolph in 1961. At that time the Hymn Society of America, of which my father was then President, was sponsoring a competition for stewardship hymns. In our family we were in the habit of listening to hymns on records from time-to-time during those days of leisure. One of them was set to the tune of Hyfrydol [LBW 158], a tune unknown to me until that time. In some way the idea of writing a hymn text to that music gradually slipped into my mind, and in about a month I had my hymn.

The text was first published in *Ten New Stewardship Hymns,* 1961, of the Hymn Society of America.

Robert Lansing Edwards was born in Auburn, New York, on August 5, 1915. He attended Deerfield Academy, and received a Bachelor of Arts degree from Princeton University in 1937. He completed a Master of Arts degree at Harvard University the following year, and went on to do work toward a Doctor of Philosophy degree in history. During World War II he served from 1941 to 1946 as a captain of intelligence for the Army. Continuing his education at Union Theological Seminary in New York City, he received a Master of Divinity degree and was ordained in 1949. He was minister of First Congregational Church, Litchfield, Connecticut, from 1949 to 1956, and since that time has been minister of Immanuel Congregational Church in Hartford. In 1975 he completed a research fellowship at Yale Divinity School.

Edwards has held positions as president of the Greater Hartford

Council of Churches, 1966–1968; president of the Connecticut Institute for the Blind, 1967–1977; member of the executive committee of the Connecticut Prison Association; and moderator (1972–1974) and trustee (since 1974) of the Pastoral Union of the Hartford Seminary Foundation. Three times a delegate to the International Congregational Council, he also served in 1968 as a delegate of the United Church of Christ to the World Council of Churches Assembly in Uppsala, Sweden. His publications include three hymns, a book of Advent verse, and *Nairobi Notebook,* an account of the Fifth Assembly of the World Council of Churches. His wife, Sarah Alexander Edwards is presently completing studies for a Doctor of Philosophy degree, and is an ordained minister-at-large of the United Church of Christ. They are the parents of two children.

Named RUSTINGTON for the town in Sussex, England, where the composer, Charles Hubert Hastings Parry (LBW 283) lived for several years, this tune was first included in *The Westminster Abbey Hymn-Book,* 1897, as the setting for Benjamin Webb's (LBW 88) "Praise the Rock of our salvation."

409 PRAISE AND THANKSGIVING

Tune: Bunessan

Albert Frederick Bayly was born September 6, 1901, at Bexhill-on-Sea, Sussex, England, and was educated at St. Mary Magdalen School in St. Leonards and at Hastings Grammar School. While training at the Royal Dockyard School at Portsmouth he received a Bachelor of Arts degree with honors from London University. In 1925 he entered Mansfield College in Oxford to study for the ministry. Upon graduation in 1928 he became assistant minister at Whitley Bay Congregational Church, and also took charge of Fairway Hall, Monkseaton, Northumberland, a new branch church established by the Whitley Bay Congregation. Thereafter he served at Morpeth Congregational Church, 1938–1946; Hollingreave Church in Burnley, 1946–1950; Swanland Congregational Church in East Yorkshire, 1950–1956; Eccleston Congregational Church at St. Helens in Lancashire, 1956–1962; and Thaxted Congregational Church in Essex from 1962 until his retirement in 1972. He was made an honorary fellow of Westminster Choir College, Princeton, New Jersey, in 1968, and on May 31, 1978, was honored at a special service in Westminster Abbey.

Bayly wrote his first hymn, "Rejoice, O people, in the mounting years," for the Triple Jubilee of the London Missionary Society in London in 1945. Published in his booklet, *Rejoice, O People,* 1951, the hymn was revised for general use and included also that year in *The BBC Hymn Book* and *Congregational Praise.* Encouraged by the success of his first hymn, Bayly wrote more, publishing *Again I Say, Rejoice* in 1967, *Rejoice Always* in 1971, and *Rejoice in God* in 1977. In addition to his hymns, he has prepared libretti for three of W. L. Lloyd Webber's cantatas. Of the present hymn, which was included in *Again I Say, Rejoice,* he notes:

> This was written to meet the need for harvest thanksgiving hymns which remind us that we can thank God for his gifts rightly only if we are ready to do His will by sharing those gifts with others, so they can rejoice with us. The

only other words I know set to the tune "Bunessan" are "Morning is broken," so that by using this very attractive and popular Scottish tune, I have sought to give it a wider usefulness.

BUNESSAN is a Gaelic melody taken down from a wandering Highland singer by Alexander Fraser, who published it in *Songs and Hymns of the Gael,* 1888. In the Irish *Church Hymnal,* 1917, it was used as the setting for Mary Macdonald's "Child in the Manger." John Becker (LBW 259) has prepared the harmonization for the LBW.

410 WE GIVE THEE BUT THINE OWN
Tune: Heath

Written by William W. How (LBW 77) around 1858, this hymn was included in the revised and enlarged edition of T. B. Morrell and How's *Psalms and Hymns,* published in 1864.

HEATH (also called "Schumann") appeared in Lowell Mason's (LBW 353) and George Webb's (LBW 389) *Cantica Laudis,* New York, 1850, where it was called "White." Used as the setting for "Thou shalt, O Lord, descend," the tune was there marked "Arr. from Schumann" (LBW 403). Clara Schumann expressed doubt, however, that the tune was taken from any of her husband's works. The tune has been called "Heath" because of its association with George Heath's "My soul, be on thy guard."

411 LORD OF ALL GOOD
Tune: Morestead

See LBW 409 for Albert F. Bayly. Written for a Christmas Fair at Eccleston Congregational Church where Bayly was pastor, this hymn was first printed in *Again I Say, Rejoice,* 1967. Originally beginning "Lord of all good, our gifts we bring *to Thee,*" the text has been altered only slightly.

MORESTEAD was composed for Butler's "Lift up your hearts" in *Hymns for Church and School,* 1964. The composer, Sydney Watson, notes that he often names his hymn tunes for places where he has worked or with which he has had pleasant associations. Morestead is a village through which he used to bicycle on his way to Winchester and "it seemed appropriate to recall this association and to remember the lovely country in that part of Hampshire."
Born at Denton, Lancashire, England, on September 3, 1903, Watson was educated at the Royal College of Music and entered Keble College, Oxford, as an organ scholar in 1922. Following his graduation in 1925 he became assistant master at Stowe School, and four years later, precentor at Radley College. In 1933 he was appointed organist at New College, Oxford, and conductor of the Oxford Harmonic Society. He succeeded Sir George Dyson as master of music at Winchester College in 1938, and from 1946 to 1955 was precentor and director of music at Eaton. Returning to Oxford in 1955, he served as organist of Christ Church Cathedral, and conductor of the Oxford Bach Choir and the Oxford Orchestral Society until his retirement in 1970. Since 1970 he has lived at Aynho,

near Oxford, and works as an examiner for the Associated Board of the Royal School of Music. He holds a Doctor of Music degree from Oxford and a fellowship in the Royal College of Organists.

412 SING TO THE LORD OF HARVEST
Tune: Wie lieblich ist der Maien

John Samuel Bewley Monsell (LBW 131) included this hymn in the second edition of his *Hymns of Love and Praise,* 1866.

WIE LIEBLICH IST DER MAIEN, by Johann Steurlein, was originally the setting for the secular song, "Mit Lieb bin ich umfangen," in 1575. In *Dauids Himlische Harpffen,* published in Nürnberg in 1581 by Gregor Gunderreitter, the tune was associated with a sacred text.

Steurlein (also Steuerlein), lawyer, poet, and musician, and son of the first Lutheran pastor of Schmalkalden, was born July 5, 1546. Following his law studies, in about 1569 he was appointed town clerk of Wasungen, where he encouraged the music efforts of the young Melchior Vulpius (LBW 115). In 1589 he went to Meiningen, where he was secretary in the chancery, a notary public, and about 1604, mayor of Meiningen. Also a writer of verse (his "The old year now hath passed away" was included in *The Lutheran Hymnal,* 1941, #125), he was crowned as a poet by the Emperor Rudolph II for his rhyming of the Old and New Testaments in German. His musical works include German motets, passion settings, and melodies with four-part settings for his poetical works. His *Geistliche Lieder,* 1575, and *Sieben und Zwantzigk neue geistliche Gesenge,* 1588, apparently had wide circulation. He died at Meiningen on May 5, 1613.

Regarding the association of this tune with Monsell's text, Edward Klammer, manager of the music department of Concordia Publishing House, writes:

> Back in the 1950's I was studying the contents of *Handbuch der deutschen evangelischen Kirchenmusik* edited by Konrad Ameln, Christhard Mahrenholz, Wilhelm Thomas, and Carl Gerhardt . . . . I came across the melody and four-part setting of "Wie lieblich ist der Maien." The text is by Martin Behm (1557–1622). We (Concordia Publishing House) needed a new Thanksgiving anthem, and that "May-melody" struck me as being a good tune for a Thanksgiving anthem. So I proceeded to look for a text which would fit the meter and the spirit of the melody. I sent both to Healey Willan who composed "Sing to the Lord of Harvest" © 1954, which turned out to be one of our all-time best sellers.

The hymn with the present harmonization by Jan Bender (LBW 396) appeared in the *Worship Supplement,* 1969, to *The Lutheran Hymnal.* The combination appears also, with a harmonization by Healey Willan (LBW 125), in *The Hymn Book,* 1971, of the Anglican Church and the United Church of Canada.

413 FATHER ETERNAL, RULER OF CREATION
Tune: Langham

Written in 1919 at the request of Dr. H. R. L. Sheppard of St. Martin's in the Fields, London, for the Life and Liberty Movement, this hymn was later included in *Songs of Praise,* 1925. The Life and Liberty Movement was a group formed at the end of World War I to promote world peace. The alterations to the text, made for the LBW, are few and slight.

Laurence Housman, brother of the poet A. E. Housman, was born at Bromsgrove, Worcestershire, England, on July 18, 1865. Following his education at Bromsgrove School and South Kensington, he worked first as a book-illustrator. He turned to writing, however, and in 1893, while working as art critic for the *Manchester Guardian,* published *The Writings of William Blake.* A playwright, poet, and author, he wrote over eighty books, including the immediately famous *An English Woman's Love-Letters,* 1900, and numerous plays, the best known of which were two series, *Little Plays of St. Francis* (1922-1931) and *Victoria Regina* (1934). The later series, banned from the English stage, had a successful run in New York during the 1935-1936 season with Helen Hayes in the leading role. Confirmed in the Church of England, Housman was for a time attracted to Roman Catholicism, and in later years, because of his pacifist views, was drawn to the Quakers. He died February 20, 1959, at Glastonbury, Somersetshire, and on that day the *Manchester Guardian* published, with comments and explanation, an obituary notice he himself had written earlier and sold to the paper.

LANGHAM, written for these words in 1919, was first sung at a meeting of the Life and Liberty Movement at Queen's Hall, London, and was published together with the hymn in *Songs of Praise,* 1925.

Geoffrey Turton Shaw, younger brother of Martin (LBW 541), was born November 14, 1879, in Clapham, England. He was a chorister at St. Paul's Cathedral, and later studied organ at Gonville and Caius, Cambridge, where his teachers included C. V. Stanford (LBW 189) and Charles Wood. From 1902 to 1910 he was music-master of Gresham's School, Holt. Later, after holding several organ posts, he became inspector of music for the London schools. In 1920 he succeeded his brother as organist of St. Mary's, Primrose Hill. Together with his brother, he was honored in 1932 with a Doctor of Music degree from the archbishop of Canterbury. He retired in 1940 and died in London, April 14, 1943.

Like his brother, Geoffrey did much to promote interest in folk song in England, and was active in creating popular interest in good music and in raising the standards of church music. He was chairman of the BBC music committee for schools and conductor of the League of Arts Choir. Composer of numerous unison and part songs, hymn tunes, and descants, he also wrote an opera, and with his brother, edited several collections.

414 O GOD OF LOVE, O KING OF PEACE

Tune: Ack, bliv hos oss

This hymn by Henry W. Baker was included in the Original Edition of *Hymns Ancient and Modern,* 1861.

Henry Williams Baker, who had a major responsibility for the creation of the earliest edition of *Hymns Ancient and Modern,* was the first chairman of the committee, a post he held for twenty years. In addition he edited and/or contributed to several other hymnals. The oldest son of Admiral Henry Loraine Baker, Bart., he was born May 27, 1821, at Belmont House, Vauxhall, London. He received a Bachelor of Arts degree in 1844 and a Master of Arts degree in 1847 from Trinity College, Cambridge. Ordained in 1844, he became vicar of Monkland in Herefordshire in 1851, where he remained for the rest of his life. In 1859 he succeeded to the baronetcy. Haeussler* notes that the hymnal he edited, *Hymns Ancient and Modern,* broke all existing sales records, with sixty million copies sold between 1861 and 1912. A high churchman, Baker believed firmly in celibacy of the clergy, and died unmarried on February 12, 1877, at Monkland.

ACK, BLIV HOS OSS was the setting for that Swedish hymn in *Then Swenska Psalm-Boken,* Stockholm, 1697. There it appeared as given below.

The tune has also been called "Pax." The setting is by Carl Schalk (LBW 118).

415   GOD OF GRACE AND GOD OF GLORY

Tune: Cwm Rhondda

Harry Emerson Fosdick, who was pastor of Riverside Church in New York City from 1926 to 1946, was born May 24, 1878, in Buffalo, New York. He received a Bachelor of Arts degree in 1900 from Colgate University, a Bachelor of Divinity degree from Union Theological Seminary in 1904, and in 1908, a Master of Arts degree from Columbia University. Ordained a Baptist minister in 1903, he was minister of the First Baptist Church in Montclair, New Jersey, from 1904 to 1915, and during World War I, served as a chaplain to the American troops. In 1919 he became pastor of the First Presbyterian Church of New York City, but soon became embroiled in the Fundamentalist-Modernist controversy, and resigned in 1925. A few months later he was called to Park Avenue Baptist Church in New York City. At his request the congregation constructed a larger, interdenominational church (Riverside Church) near Columbia University, using funds from John D. Rockefeller Jr., a trustee. In the summer of 1930, while vacationing at his summer home in Boothbay Harbor, Maine, Fosdick wrote "God of grace and God of glory" for the opening of Riverside Church on October 5, 1930. The hymn was also sung February 8, 1931, for the dedication service, and was published in H. Augustine Smith's *Praise and Service,* New York, 1932.

From 1908 to 1915 Fosdick was also a teacher of homiletics, and from 1915 to 1924, professor of practical theology at Union Theological Seminary. He became a very influential figure in Protestant America. In addition to his posts at Riverside Church and Union Seminary, he was preacher on the National Vespers nationwide radio broadcasts from 1926 to 1946, and was the author of thirty-two books. He was also an early supporter of pastoral counselling and of the Church's cooperation with psychiatry. Among his works are *The Second Mile,* 1919; *The Secret of Victorious Living,* 1934; *A Guide to Understanding the Bible,* 1938; *On Being a Real Person,* 1943; *The Man from Nazareth,* 1949; and *A Faith for Tough Times,* 1952. His autobiography, *The Living of These Days,* was published in 1956. He died at Bronxville, New York, on October 5, 1969.

For CWM RHONDDA see LBW 343. Originally this hymn was sung to the tune "Regent Square" (LBW 50), a favorite of Fosdick's. Its association with "Cwm Rhondda" dates from *The Methodist Hymnal,* 1935. The present harmonization is by Paul Bunjes (LBW 38).

416   O GOD OF EVERY NATION

Tune: Tuolumne

In 1958 this hymn by William Watkins Reid Jr. won first place in a national hymn-writing contest sponsored by the Hymn Society of America in cooperation with the Department of International Affairs of the National Council of Churches. Published in the Hymn Society's *Twelve New World Order Hymns,* it was sung by the six hundred delegates at the opening session of the interdenominational Fifth World Order Study Conference at Cleveland, Ohio, November 18–21, 1958. The hymn is given here with a few slight alterations.

Reid was born November 12, 1923, in New York City. He completed a Bachelor of Arts degree in botany at Oberlin College, Oberlin, Ohio, and five years later received a Bachelor of Divinity degree at Yale Divinity School. From 1943 to 1945 he served in the United States Army Medical Corps, during which time he earned three battle stars, and for eight months was a prisoner of war in Germany. He was married in 1946 to Margaret Amelia Latsha (who also holds a Bachelor of Divinity degree from Yale), and is the father of three children. During the summer of 1949 he and his wife were in charge of a pastorate of three Congregational churches in North Dakota. He ministered to Methodist Church Circuits at Camptown, Pennsylvania, 1950–1957, and Caverton (Wyoming), Pennsylvania, 1957–1967, and from 1967 to 1978 was pastor of Central United Methodist Church, Wilkes-Barre, Pennsylvania. In 1978 he was appointed superintendent of the Wilkes–Barre district of the United Methodist Church, making his residence in Kingston, Pennsylvania.

Reid is a member of the Hymn Society of America and has published several hymns. He has also contributed articles to several journals. He has participated in a wide variety of community organizations and affairs, including the Queens County (New York) bird club, the Wilkes–Barre little theater, the Heart Association, youth work, civil defense, a study on housing, and ecumenical activities. In 1971 he was Republican candidate for city councilman in Wilkes–Barre.

TUOLUMNE was commissioned by the Inter-Lutheran Commission on Worship for this hymn in 1968, and was included with it in *Contemporary Worship–1,* 1969. "Tuolumne" is an American Indian name for a region of the California Sierra Nevada, where the composer, Dale Wood (LBW 268), wrote the tune.

417 **IN A LOWLY MANGER BORN**
(Mabune no naka ni) [まぶねのなかに]
Tune: Mabune

This hymn first appeared in Koh Yuki's *Poems on the Life of Jesus,* 1929, as a prologue. In some English translations the hymn is titled "Behold the Man," and Pauline Smith McAlpine, whose work on Japanese hymns was published in 1974, notes that these words appear in the Japanese original over and over again, like a recurring theme.

Koh Yuki was born April 16, 1896, at Sakaiminato, Tottori Prefecture, Japan, and has a Literary Doctorate from Kwansei Gakuin University, Osaka, where he studied Biblical science, theology, and French literature. For fifty years beginning in 1921 he was pastor of the Tokyo Futaba Independent Church, which later became the Kyodan Higashi Nakano Church, a part of the Church of Christ in Japan. Since 1971 he has been pastor emeritus of the church. In addition, he has held positions as lecturer at Tokyo Women's College and Aoyama Gakuin University, and served as a member of the board of the Christian School of Music and of the committee of the Christian Education Society. He is an authority on the works of Pascal and on Christian art, and his translations include several of Pascal's works, and also *The Imitation of Christ* (see LBW 88). His original works include a *History of Hymns, Theology and Music of Hymns, Introduction to Christian Worship, The Japanese and Christianity,* and others. Twice he has been involved in the compilation of the Japanese Common Hymnal, and his original and translated hymns number over five hundred.

Several English translations of this hymn have been written. The present English text, which was prepared for the LBW, is based on versions by Arthur Gamblin and Vern Rossmann, both missionaries to Japan.

MABUNE, which means "manger," is a tune name taken from the Japanese first line of this hymn. Written for this text in 1930, the tune was published the following year in the *Sambika.* McAlpine notes that in Japan this is one of the best-loved and most widely sung of all indigenous hymns.

Seigi Abe was born May 18, 1890 (1891?), in Sendai, Japan. Following his graduation in 1911 from Tohoku Gakuin College, he came to the United States and in 1913 entered the New England Conservatory of Music in Boston. There he studied piano with F. Stuart Mason, 1913–1920, voice with Charles A. Bennett, 1921–1926, sacred music, and composition. Upon graduation in 1926 he returned to Japan, and from 1927 was the head of the music department of Meiji Gakuin, a Presbyterian boys' school in Tokyo. In 1948 he became a professor at the Christian School of Music. He has composed or arranged many hymns and songs, and other sacred music, including an oratorio, *Job.* He died in 1974.

Harmonization of the tune was prepared by Richard Hillert (LBW 63) for the LBW.

418 **JUDGE ETERNAL, THRONED IN SPLENDOR**
Tune: Rhuddlan

Born at Ledbury, Hereford, England, on January 27, 1847, Henry Scott Holland received a Bachelor of Arts degree in 1870 and a Master of Arts degree in 1873 from Balliol College, Oxford. Ordained a deacon in 1872 and a priest in 1874, he served as select preacher at Oxford from 1879 to 1880, and from 1894 to 1896, and as censor of Christ Church from 1882 to 1884. In 1884 he was appointed a canon, and two years later, a precentor, at St. Paul's, London, where he remained until 1910. In 1911 he returned to Oxford as a lecturer and regius professor of divinity. He died at Oxford, March 17, 1918.

A founder and strong supporter of the Christian Social Union, Holland was editor of *The Commonwealth,* the organ of the Union, from its inception in 1896 to 1912. His only hymn, "Judge eternal, throned in splendor," first appeared in the July, 1902, issue of *The Commonwealth,* and four years later was included in *The English Hymnal,* which he helped to edit. Other publications include an important essay on "Faith" in *Lux Mundi,* 1889; *So as by fire; notes on the war,* 1916; and *Our place in Christendom,* 1916. He was joint author of *Jenny Lind, the artist,* 1891, and an editor of the *Christian Psalter.* His sermons and some autobiographical material are included in *A Bundle of Memories,* 1915. The University of Aberdeen honored him with a Doctor of Divinity degree in 1903.

RHUDDLAN, named for a village near the mouth of the river Clwyd in Flintshire, North Wales, was arranged for this text in *The English Hymnal,* 1906. A traditional Welsh melody, "Dowch i'r Frwydr" ("Come to battle"), it is found in Edward Jones's *Musical Relicks of the Welsh Bards,* 1794. It is one of over sixty Welsh folk songs set by Franz Joseph Haydn (LBW 358) for voices, violin, and piano (harp), 1799–1805.

419 LORD OF ALL NATIONS, GRANT ME GRACE
Tune: Beatus vir

Based on Philippians 2:1–18, this hymn was written for the Lutheran Human Relations Association of America and sung at their Eleventh Annual Institute at Valparaiso University, July 29–31, 1960. Since then the hymn has been traditionally sung during the banquet of the annual institute, as well as at worship services and meetings of various chapters of the LHRAA. First printed in *Christians, Awake,* the LHRAA institute proceedings for 1960, the hymn was given with the present tune, "Beatus vir," in *A New Song,* a supplement to *This Day* magazine, October, 1967, and in the *Worship Supplement,* 1969, to *The Lutheran Hymnal.* It can be found in several other Concordia Publishing House collections, as well as in the hymnals of the United Presbyterian Church and the Reorganized Church of Latter Day Saints.

Born January 23, 1916, in St. Louis, Olive Wise graduated at the top of her class from Normandy High School, and went on to attend Brown's Business College (where her father was principal) and Washington University, St. Louis, where she majored in English and Latin. From 1937 to 1939 she was secretary to the principal at Ward Junior High School, University City, Missouri, and in 1939 she was married to Pastor Ruben Edward Spannaus of Woodland, California. They are the parents of a daughter and three sons. In 1942 the family moved to Seattle, Washington, and in 1957, to Elmhurst, Illinois, where Pastor Spannaus was executive director of Lutheran Child and Family Services. "Retired—but still *doing,*" she and her husband returned to Seattle in 1978.

Olive Wise Spannaus has assumed leadership roles in many church and community organizations. The first woman elected, she has served since 1972 on the board of directors of the synodical English District of the Lutheran Church—Missouri Synod. In addition she has been a member of the LCMS Task Force on Women (1973–1977), and held offices at various levels of the English District of the Lutheran Women's Missionary League, the league of women voters, and the Valparaiso Guild, and served on the board of directors of the Lutheran Women's Caucus and on the Inter-Lutheran Commission on Worship committee which produced the new marriage service. She was co-author of the 1973 Mustard Seeds series, *The Spirit and Me,* mini-Bible studies published by the International Lutheran Women's Missionary League; and with her husband, she authored *The Total Woman versus The Shalom Woman,* 1976. Among her other hymns is one written and sung for the 1977 convention of the International LWML, "Sisters and brothers, look upward."

BEATUS VIR, a very popular and much-used melody, was the setting for "O blahoslavený člověk" in the *Šamotulsky Kancionál,* 1561. The tune was named "Beatus vir" by the compilers of the *Worship Supplement,* 1969, using the Latin first line of Psalm 1, which was the basis of the original Czech text. The Kucharik Partitura, *Duchovna Citara,* published in America in 1933, credits the tune to Matthias Kunwaldsky (Konwaldsky), a bishop of the Unity who was born in 1442 at Kunwald, near Lititz, and died January 23, 1500, at Leipnik. He contributed four hymns to the 1501 Bohemian hymn book, and five others to the 1561 edition. The harmonization is by Richard Hillert (LBW 63).

420 LORD, SAVE YOUR WORLD

Tune: Kedron

See LBW 409 for Albert Frederick Bayly. This hymn was written in November of 1947, and included in the author's *Rejoice, O People,* 1951.

KEDRON, named for the river which flows between Jerusalem and the Mount of Olives, was included in Amos Pilsbury's *United States Sacred Harmony,* 1799. There it was the setting for the following stanza from Charles Wesley's (LBW 27) hymn, "Ye that pass by, behold the man":

> Thou man of grief remember me,
> Thou never canst thyself forget
> Thy last mysterious agony,
> Thy fainting pangs and bloody sweat.

The tune name no doubt refers to John 18:1, "When Jesus had spoken these words, he went forth with his disciples across the Kidron valley, where there was a garden, which he and his disciples entered." (RSV) This powerful Aeolian-mode melody was one of the most popular tunes of the rural South in pre-Civil War days, and is one of a group of tunes—see also "Bourbon" (LBW 127) and "Distress" (LBW 217)—which were used with extremely solemn texts. George Pullen Jackson, in his *Down-East Spirituals* (1939), suggests that both "Kedron" and "Distress" have a prototype in a very old Scottish tune, "Laird o' Cockpen." The editor of *United States Sacred Harmony,* Amos Pilsbury, was a singing master active in Charleston, South Carolina.

421 LORD CHRIST, WHEN FIRST YOU CAME TO EARTH
Tune: Mit Freuden zart

Born October 8, 1882, in Richmond, Virginia, Walter Russell Bowie received a Bachelor of Arts degree from Harvard in 1904, and a Master of Arts degree the following year. He graduated from Virginia Theological Seminary in 1909, and in 1919 received its Doctor of Divinity degree. He was married in 1909 to Jean Laverack. Ordained a deacon in 1908 and a priest in 1909, he was rector of Emmanuel Church, Greenwood, Virginia, 1908–1911; St. Paul's Church, Richmond, 1911–1923; and Grace Church, New York City, 1923–1939. During World War I he served as a hospital chaplain in France. He was professor of practical theology and dean of students at Union Theological Seminary from 1939 until 1950 when he returned to Virginia Theological Seminary (now the Protestant Episcopal Theological Seminary in Virginia) as professor of homiletics. He retired in 1955 and died at Alexandria, Virginia, April 23, 1969.

Bowie also lectured at General Theological Seminary, Yale Divinity School, and Seabury-Western Divinity School in Evanston, Illinois. He was for some years editor of the *Southern Churchman* and president of the Churchman Associates of New York City. He served on the Commission on Faith and Order of the World Council of Churches and was one of the committee which prepared the Revised Standard Version of the Bible. His publications are numerous, including *Thy Master, A Life of Jesus Christ,* 1928, and *The Story of the Bible,* 1951 and 1952. He was honored with a Doctor of Sacred Theology degree from Syracuse University in 1933.

Dean Dwelly of Liverpool Cathedral, one of the editors of *Songs of Praise,* asked Bowie to write an Advent hymn in the *Dies Irae* mode. Written in 1928, this hymn was included in *Songs of Praise,* 1931. A few alterations have been made for the LBW.

For MIT FREUDEN ZART see LBW 140. The harmonization is by Carl Schalk (LBW 118).

422 O GOD, EMPOWER US
Tune: Wellington Square

Inspired by the author's life-long interest in world peace and non-violent change, this hymn is published here for the first time.

Born in Jacksonville, Illinois, October 6, 1906, Lee McCullough Baldwin was educated in the Jacksonville schools and graduated from Illinois College, Jacksonville (Bachelor of Arts, 1928). In 1940 he received a Master of Divinity degree at Garrett Theological Seminary, Evanston, Illinois. Joining what is now the Central Illinois Conference of the United Methodist Church in 1940, he was pastor of a number of Methodist churches in central Illinois until his retirement in 1972. Married in 1946 to Mary Jean Talbot, a teacher and graduate of Illinois State

A page from *The Sacred Harp,* Philadelphia, 1860, showing the tune "Beach Spring" (LBW 423). The melody is in the middle line. The variously-shaped noteheads—triangles, circles, squares, and diamonds—were intended to aid in note reading.

University, Normal, Illinois, he is the father of two children, a son and a daughter.

WELLINGTON SQUARE. The composer, Guy Warrack, writes:

> If I have any small claim to a place in English hymnology it must be said to have germinated in Chelsea about 1925 when the first edition of *Songs of Praise* was becoming known in the land, refreshed by such names as Vaughan Williams [LBW 101], Martin Shaw [LBW 541], and many such composers. Among a new generation of hymn writers could be found the name of Jan Struther [LBW 469], a writer versatile in many fields. Our two families had long been close friends, both living at that time in Chelsea enjoying the comparative peace of Wellington Square half-a-century ago.

This tune, named after a part of London's Chelsea, was written for Jan Struther's hymn, "When Stephen, full of power and grace," and included with it in the enlarged edition of *Songs of Praise,* 1931. Influenced by English folk song, the tune makes repeated use of the opening four-note motif.

Born February 3, 1900, in Edinburgh, Scotland, Guy Douglas Hamilton Warrack attended Magdalen College, Oxford. He went on to study at the Royal College of Music, where he was a pupil of Ralph Vaughan Williams, and where he became an excellent timpani player. Following his graduation in 1925, he joined the teaching staff of the Royal College of Music, and in 1926 he organized a small orchestra for the performance of some of the forgotten classics, especially those of English composers. He held many conducting posts, including an appointment in 1934 to the Handel Society, and in 1935 to the BBC Scottish orchestra in Edinburgh. He is now retired and lives in London.

Warrack's compositions, mostly for orchestra, include a set of *Variations for Orchestra,* 1924, and a *Symphony in C minor,* 1932.

423 LORD, WHOSE LOVE IN HUMBLE SERVICE
Tune: Beach Spring

See LBW 409 for Albert Frederick Bayly. This hymn was included in *Seven New Social Welfare Hymns,* published by the Hymn Society of America for the Second National Conference on Churches and Social Welfare, October 23–27, 1961. The text has been altered for the LBW.

BEACH SPRING. Attributed to B. F. White, this tune was included in *The Sacred Harp,* Philadelphia, 1844, as the setting for Joseph Hart's "Come, ye sinners, poor and wretched."

Benjamin Franklin White, brother-in-law to William Walker (LBW 30), was born September 20, 1800, one of fourteen children born to a farmer and his wife who lived near Spartanburg, South Carolina. He attended school for three terms, and with a self-acquired training in music, gained considerable success as a singing school teacher. In 1825 he married Thurza Golightly, and they also became the parents of fourteen children, five of whom died as infants or small children. Together with William Walker he prepared the manuscript for *Southern Harmony* (1835), which was published, however, with only Walker's name on the title page. White moved around 1840 to Hamilton in Harris County, Georgia, and in 1844, together with Elisha James King, published *The Sacred Harp.* In 1852 he became the first editor of the Harris County weekly newspaper, *The Organ.* A member of the Georgia militia, he attained the rank of major before the Civil War. He was appointed clerk of the Inferior Court in 1858 and elected mayor of Hamilton in 1865. He died December 5, 1879, in Atlanta, Georgia.

The Sacred Harp, an oblong collection of "Old Baptist Tunes," has gone through numerous editions to the present, and *Sacred Harp* singings are still held in some southern communities.

424   LORD OF GLORY, YOU HAVE BOUGHT US
Tune: Hyfrydol

Written in 1864, this hymn by Eliza S. Alderson was included in the Appendix to the Original Edition of *Hymns Ancient and Modern.* John B. Dykes composed the tune "Charitas" for the hymn, and also added the fifth stanza which takes its first four lines from stanza 1. Originally beginning "Lord of glory, *who hast* bought us," this hymn is given here with a number of slight alterations.

Eliza Sibbald Dykes, sister of John B. Dykes (LBW 165), was born at Hull, England, August 16, 1818. She was married in 1850 to the Reverend W. T. Alderson, who from 1833 to 1876 was chaplain to the West Riding House of Correction. Gifted in painting and in language, she began writing poetry early in her life, and as a young girl, wrote hymns for Sunday School festivals and missionary meetings at St. John's Church, Hull, where her grandfather, Thomas Dykes, was pastor. She wrote many hymns, but only twelve were published, titled simply *Twelve Hymns* [N.D.]. During the last two or three years of her life she was an invalid and suffered a great deal. She died March 18, 1889, at Heath, near Wakefield, where her husband had ministered for many years.

For HYFRYDOL see LBW 158.

425   O GOD OF MERCY, GOD OF LIGHT
Tune: Just as I Am

See LBW 170 for Godfrey Thring. Written in 1877, this hymn first appeared in Thring's *Church of England Hymn Book,* 1880 and 1882. There it was included as an offertory hymn, under Luke 10:36–37, "Which now of these three was neighbor unto him that fell among the thieves?" The first line originally read "O God of mercy, God of *might.*" The present form includes several alterations, especially in the second stanza.

JUST AS I AM, also known as "Barnby," was written by Joseph Barnby (LBW 280) for Charlotte Elliott's hymn, "Just as I am, without one plea" (LBW 296), and was included in the *Home and School Hymnal* published in London in 1892.

Harmonization of the melody is by Larry Jon Houff, who has served as assistant pastor and director of music at First Lutheran Church, Springfield, Ohio, since his ordination in 1972. Houff was born July 1, 1944, in Lorain, Ohio. At Wittenberg University he studied organ with Frederick Jackisch (LBW 236) and Elmer Blackmer, and composition with Jan Bender (LBW 396), and received a Bachelor of Music degree in 1966. In 1971 he completed a Master of Divinity degree at Waterloo Lutheran Seminary, Waterloo, Ontario. Previous to taking his present post he held positions as part-time lecturer in church music at Waterloo Lutheran University, Waterloo Lutheran Seminary, and Wittenberg University, and as organist at parishes in Waterloo, Kitchener, and St. Jacob's, Ontario, and in Springfield, Ohio. He was a member of the Hymn Music Committee of the Inter-Lutheran Commission on Worship. Married to Gundula Glüer, he is the father of two children.

426 O SON OF GOD, IN GALILEE
Tune: Lewis-Town

Anna Bernardine Dorothy Hoppe was born May 7, 1889, in Milwaukee. Her parents were German immigrants. After completing an eighth-grade education, she was employed throughout her life as a stenographer in various business offices. Her gift for poetry revealed itself when she was still a child. At the age of twenty-four she began to write spiritual poetry, most of which was composed on-the-run—on her way to and from church and from work, and during her lunch hours. Some of her poems were published in the *Northwest Lutheran,* a periodical of the Wisconsin Synod, and came to the attention of Dr. Adolf Hult of Augustana Seminary, who influenced her to write her *Songs for the Church Year,* 1928. Several hymnals have contained her work, including *The Hymnal,* 1925, of the Augustana Synod (where she is represented by twenty-three hymns); the *American Lutheran Hymnal,* 1930, and a collection called *Selah.* She died in Milwaukee, Wisconsin on August 2, 1941.

The present hymn, originally beginning "O *Thou who once* in Galilee," was given with the tune "Tallis' Ordinal" in the *American Lutheran Hymnal.* In the *Worship Supplement,* 1969, to *The Lutheran Hymnal,* the words were sung to "Salem," a tune by Richard Hillert (LBW 63).

William Billings' LEWIS-TOWN is found in *The Continental Harmony,* 1794, where it was the setting for "How vast must their advantage be," Psalm 133, from the Tate and Brady (LBW 452) *New Version,* 1696. The tune is in three sections; the LBW uses only the middle section.

The composer was born October 7, 1746, in Boston, and worked as a tanner and, after 1787, as a "sealer of leather" (inspector of tanned leathers) for the town of Boston. He is said to have received his first regular music instruction from John Barry, a tenor in the choir of New South Church, where he and his family were members. For the most part, however, his music education, including his composition training, was on his own. When working on his first publication, *The New England Psalm-Singer,* 1770, he availed himself of material in other such collections at hand, including Aaron Williams' (LBW 368) *The Universal Psalmodist* and William Tans'ur's (LBW 483) *The Royal Melody Complete.* (Among those engaged in the production of *The New England Psalm-Singer* was the engraver Paul Revere.) By 1769 Billings had established himself as a singing teacher, and thereafter held numerous singing schools in Boston and the surrounding towns. For a while he taught music in Providence, Rhode Island, during which time, in 1774, he was married to Lucy Swan of Stoughton, Massachusetts. By 1778 Billings could refer to his "long experience" as a teacher of singing. Having returned to Boston, he taught singing in a number of churches there, conducted public concerts, and published several collections: *The Singing Master's Assistant,* 1778, with a second edition in 1779, and a third in 1781; *Music in Miniature,* 1779; *The Psalm Singer's Amusement,* 1781; and in 1786, *The Suffolk Harmony.* His music had become very well-known, especially in New England, and could be found on programs together with the works of George Frideric Handel (LBW 39). Like many others in early America, Billings was busy with a number of diverse activities. In addition to his music and his position as sealer of leather, he dabbled in literature, and held other public offices, such as an inspector of police, inspector of trade, and "scavenger" (one who inspected the dimensions of baskets used for measuring coal). Although he reached the height of his fame in the late 1780s, for reasons unknown to us today, his financial state worsened around 1790, and he was eventually forced to mortgage his house on Newbury Street. Hoping to improve his financial situation with the sale of another book, he submitted the manuscript for his last collection to a printer in 1791. Publishers were reluctant to take a risk, however, and only in 1794 did *The Continental Harmony* finally come out. The following year his wife died, and by 1798 he had moved from his Newbury Street house. He continued in favor as a teacher of singing schools in Boston and the surrounding towns until his death on September 26, 1800. (For more complete biographical material see Hans Nathan's *William Billings: Data and Documents,* Detroit, 1976.)

The harmonization was prepared for the LBW by Donald Busarow (LBW 30).

427 O JESUS CHRIST, MAY GRATEFUL HYMNS BE RISING
Tune: City of God

This hymn by Bradford Gray Webster was the Hymn Society of America's first choice of the hymns submitted for the Convocation on Urban Life in America, called by the Council of Bishops of the Methodist Church. It was one of *Five New Hymns on the City* published by the Hymn Society for the convocation in Columbus, Ohio, February 24-26, 1954. The hymn was included in *Contemporary Worship-1,* 1969. It has also been included in *The Australian Hymn Book*, an ecumenical collection published in 1977.

Webster was born October 30, 1898, in Syracuse, New York. (His twin sister, Alice Southwarth Webster Goldschmidt, went as a missionary to South America, and still resides in Montevideo, Uruguay.) He attended Amherst College, Amherst, Massachusetts, interrupting his sophomore year to earn a second lieutenant commission at Camp Lee, Virginia, in 1919, and graduated from Boston University School of Theology in 1925. After serving a student charge in New Hampshire, he was a minister in the Central New York Conference of the Methodist Church for ten years, and in the Old Geneseo (now Western New York) Conference for thirty years, including churches in Gowanda (1939–1946), Syracuse, and Buffalo, New York. He is now retired and lives in Bloomsburg, Pennsylvania.

Webster has been active in a number of civic organizations, and is now active in the American Association of Retired Persons, and various national, conference, district, and local church organizations. His wife, Irene Anderson Stryker, attended Syracuse University and Boston

University School of Religion, and for many years taught music in the Buffalo public schools. They are the parents of a son and a daughter. Another son died in an airplane crash off the coast of Newfoundland.

CITY OF GOD. Originally the tune "O Perfect Love" (LBW 287) was used with this hymn. Daniel Moe's fine, strong setting found here was written in 1956. The following year the composer expanded it into a choir anthem, and the tune and anthem were published as a unit by Augsburg Publishing House. In 1969 it was included in *Contemporary Worship-1*.

Moe, who teaches at the Oberlin College Conservatory of Music in Oberlin, Ohio, also conducts the Oberlin College Choir, Oberlin College Chorus, and Musical Union. He was born November 2, 1926, at Minot, North Dakota. He completed a Bachelor of Arts degree at Concordia College in Moorhead, Minnesota; a Master of Arts at the University of Washington; and a Doctor of Philosophy at the University of Iowa; and did further graduate study at Hamline University; the Kirchenmusikschule in Hanover, Germany; and the Aspen School of Music. From 1953 to 1959 he was director of choral activities at the University of Denver, after which he was director of choral music at the University of Iowa. There he developed a nationally-recognized graduate program in choral literature and conducting. He has also been a visiting professor at the University of Southern California. In 1972 he was appointed to the Oberlin faculty. He is married to Doris Tanner of Minnesota, and they have three sons.

In addition to his work as a conductor, Moe has published over forty compositions, including works for orchestra, chorus, and chamber groups. Among his commissioned works are *Cantata of Peace* for the Fellowship of Methodist Musicians, 1971; *Exhortations from Proverbs* for the inauguration of John D. Rockefeller IV as president of West Virginia Wesleyan College, 1973; *Magnificat* (for chorus and orchestra) for the Wyoming Music Education Association, 1974; and *Chief Seattle's Psalm* for the University of Alabama's Bicentennial Church Music Workshop, 1976. Known throughout the country for his work as a guest conductor and choral clinician, he has directed All-State choruses in seventeen states and presented workshops and lectures in many high schools and colleges. In 1972 he served as consulting director of the third International University Choral Festival at Lincoln Center. In 1976 Gustavus Adolphus College honored him with a Doctor of Music degree and with its first Gustavus Adolphus College Fine Arts Award. He has also received the 1974 Canticum Novum award from Wittenberg University, a fellowship from the Danforth Foundation, and other awards. He served on the Inter-Lutheran Commission on Worship and is past president of the Lutheran Society for Worship, Music, and the Arts. His publications include *Problems in Conducting,* 1968, and *Basic Choral Concepts,* 1972, and a chapter on twentieth-century choral music in *Choral Conducting: A Symposium* (edited by Harold A. Decker and Julius Herford, 1973). Together with John Arthur (LBW 387) he produced *Contemporary Liturgy,* 1963.

428   O GOD OF EARTH AND ALTAR

Tune: King's Lynn

Gilbert Keith Chesterton, a colorful and controversial figure in English literature, was born in Kensington, London, on May 29, 1874. He attended St. Paul's School and the Slade School of Art in London. Through his work in art reviews and criticism in *The Spectator, The Bookman,* and other London periodicals, he found his way into journalism. He had a remarkable facility with words, and was able to dictate 13,000–14,000 words a week while maintaining "a schedule of lectures that would have floored an ordinary man." Yet, although he wrote some one hundred stories, novels, plays, biographies, and volumes of verse during his lifetime, he was totally dependent on his wife, Frances *née* Blogg, to whom he was married in 1901, for all practical matters. In 1922, through the influence of Hilaire Belloc, he was converted to Roman Catholicism. He became convinced that the Middle Ages were the golden age of history; he looked on the medieval trade system as the cure for the industrial ills and saw the return to Roman obedience as a means of destroying what remained of Puritanism and bringing back "merrie England." A number of his works, including his *Short History of England,* 1917, were infused with this thinking. In America he is most widely known as the author of a series of detective stories in which the priest, Father Brown, is the hero. A man of enormous size (he weighed between 300 and 400 pounds) as well as energy, Chesterton suffered a complete physical breakdown in the winter of 1914–1915, brought on in part by his intemperate habits and his concern over a libel suit brought against his younger brother, Cecil. Following his recovery, however, his literary pursuits were even heavier than before. He died June 14, 1936, at Topmeadow, Beaconsfield.

This hymn, originally written for the tune "Aurelia" (LBW 197), was contributed to *The Commonwealth* of which Henry Scott Holland (LBW 418) was editor, and was included in *The English Hymnal,* 1906.

For KING'S LYNN see LBW 177. The harmonization found here is that used in the *Service Book and Hymnal,* 1958.

429   WHERE CROSS THE CROWDED WAYS OF LIFE
Tune: Walton

Written by Frank Mason North at the request of Caleb T. Winchester, a member of the committee which prepared *The Methodist Hymnal,* New York, 1905, this hymn took shape in the author's mind as he prepared a sermon on Matthew 22:9. Printed in *The Christian City,* June 3, 1903, it entered *The Methodist Hymnal* two years later.

Born in New York City on December 3, 1850, North graduated from Wesleyan University, Middletown, Connecticut, receiving a Bachelor of Arts degree in 1872 and a Master of Arts degree three years later. Ordained a Methodist minister in 1873, he served churches in Florida, New York, and Middletown, Connecticut until 1892. From 1892 to 1912 he was editor of *The Christian City* and secretary to the New York City Missionary Society of the Methodist Episcopal Church; and from 1912 to 1924, he was corresponding secretary of the Methodist Board of Foreign Missions. Also, from 1916 to 1920 he was president of the Federal Council of Churches of Christ in America. His alma mater presented him with a Doctor of Divinity degree in 1894 and a Doctor of Laws degree in 1919, and he was elected to the French Legion of Honor in 1919 and to the Greek Royal Order of George I the following year. He belonged to the governing boards of a number of institutions of higher learning, including several in the Far East. In 1874 he married Fannie Laws Stewart of Philadelphia, who died four years later, and in 1885 he married Louise Josephine McCoy of Lowell, Massachusetts. He was the father of one son by each marriage. He died at Madison, New Jersey, on December 17, 1935, a few days short of his golden wedding anniversary (December 23).

For WALTON see LBW 356.

430 WHERE RESTLESS CROWDS ARE THRONGING
Tune: Llangloffan

Written in October of 1953, this hymn was one of five obtained by the Hymn Society of America for use at a convocation on Urban Life in America held at the Methodist Church in Columbus, Ohio, in 1954. It was included four years later in the *Service Book and Hymnal.*

Thomas Curtis Clark was born in Vincennes, Indiana, January 8, 1877. His father, a minister of the Christian Church, later took a parish at Bloomington, Indiana, and in that city Thomas attended the University of Indiana, securing a Bachelor of Arts degree in 1899 and following it with postgraduate work. After a brief period in which he taught high school, and worked as a singing evangelist and in the piano business, he embarked in 1906 upon his life's vocation, that of editorial work for Christian publications. He was poetry editor of *The Christian Century* from 1912 to 1948 and editor of the *Twentieth Century Quarterly* after its founding in 1919. From 1929 he was also on the staff of *The Christian Century Pulpit.* Among his several collections of original poems were a number devoted to Abraham Lincoln whom he greatly admired. In 1910 he was married to Hazel P. Davis whom he described as "the most devoted Christian I have ever known." He died on December 7, 1953.

LLANGLOFFAN, a Welsh tune of unknown origin, was included in Daniel Evans' *Hymnau a Thônau,* 1865. David Evans' (LBW 339) harmonization, prepared for *The Church Hymnary,* 1927, is given here with passing tones removed.

431 YOUR HAND, O LORD, IN DAYS OF OLD
Tune: Old 107th

Edward Hayes Plumptre, born in Bloomsbury, London, England, on August 6, 1821, attended King's College, London, and University College, Oxford. He graduated Bachelor of Arts with high honors in 1844 and completed a Master of Arts degree three years later. For some time he was a fellow of Brasenose College. He took holy orders in 1846 and soon gained prominence as a theologian and preacher, holding positions at King's College as chaplain, 1847–1868; professor of pastoral theology, 1853–1863; and professor of New Testament exegesis, 1864–1881. He also served as assistant preacher at Lincoln's Inn, dean of Queen's College, Oxford, and prebendary of St. Paul's. At Oxford University he delivered the Boyles Lectures in 1866 and the Grinfield Lectures from 1872 to 1874. From 1869 to 1874 he was a member of the Old Testament Company of Revisers of the Bible. In 1869 he was appointed rector of

Pluckley, Kent, and in 1873 he exchanged parishes with E. J. Selwyn, vicar of Brickley in Kent. From 1881 until his death on February 1, 1891, he was dean of Wells in Somersetshire.

Plumptre's extensive writings include *Lazarus, and other Poems,* 1864; *Master and Scholar,* 1866; and a *Life of Bishop Ken* (LBW 269), 1888; as well as translations of Sophocles, Æschylus, and Dante. In 1875 Glasgow University honored him with a Doctor of Divinity degree.

The present hymn, originally beginning "*Thine arm, O Lord, in days of old,*" is given here with several alterations. Written in 1864, it was published as a leaflet, *A Hymn used in the Chapel of King's College Hospital,* and was included in the Appendix to the Original Edition of *Hymns Ancient and Modern,* 1868.

For OLD 107TH see LBW 318. Barrie Cabena's (LBW 237) harmonization was prepared for the LBW.

432 WE WORSHIP YOU, O GOD OF MIGHT
(Vi lova dig, o store Gud)
Tune: Vi lova dig, o store Gud

See LBW 73 for Johan Olof Wallin. This Swedish version of the *Te Deum laudamus* (see Canticle #3) is based on an earlier hymn, "Dig vare lov och pris, o Krist," which was in the 1695 *Swenska Psalm-Boken.* Both the older hymn and Wallin's recast were included in the 1811 *Psalmer.* A new translation by Joel Lundeen (LBW 146) is given here with some alteration. Two other hymns based on the *Te Deum* are LBW 535 and 547.

VI LOVA DIG, O STORE GUD (also "Ter Sanctus") was included in *Een ny Handbog, med Psalmer oc aandelige Lofsange,* published in Rostock in 1529. *Een ny Handbog* was an enlarged edition of the earliest Danish-Norwegian Lutheran hymnal, brought out by Klaus Mortensen Tönderbinder at Malmö in 1528. With some changes and additions it later became Hans Thomissön's *Salmebog,* 1569 (LBW 227).

The harmonization was prepared for the *Worship Supplement,* 1969, to *The Lutheran Hymnal,* by Richard Hillert (LBW 63).

433 THE CHURCH OF CHRIST, IN EVERY AGE
Tune: Wareham

See LBW 246 for Frederick Pratt Green. This hymn was written in 1967 at the request of the committee for *Hymns and Songs,* 1969, in which it first appeared. The author notes, "They wanted a hymn which tackled the relationship of Sabbath and Sunday. The changes asked for by *your* [LBW hymn text] committee have improved it!"

WAREHAM is named for the composer's birthplace in Dorsetshire, England. Little is known about William Knapp since the records of the parish where he was born were lost in a fire that destroyed the parish church in 1762. Believed to have been of German descent, he was born in 1698 or 1699, and possibly served as an organist in Wareham and in Poole. He was also known as a "country psalm-singer." For thirty-nine years he was parish clerk of St. James's Church in Poole, where he died September 26, 1768. He and George Savage, sexton of St. James's Church, were the subjects of a humorous poem by H. Price of Poole, which appeared in the *London Magazine* in 1742:

> From pounce and paper, ink and pen,
>   Save me, O Lord, I pray;
> From Pope and Swift and such-like men,
>   And Cibber's annual lay;
> From doctors' bills and lawyers' fees,
>   From ague, and gout and trap;
> And what is ten times worse than these,
>   George Savage and Will Knapp.

In addition to his 1738 collection mentioned below, Knapp prepared *The New Church Melody,* 1753.

"Wareham tune," which was the setting for Psalm 36:8–10 in Knapp's *A Sett of New Psalm-Tunes and Anthems in four parts,* London, 1738, was somewhat more florid in its original form. When the tune appeared with the same text in *Psalms, Hymns, and Anthems,* 1774, of the London Foundling Hospital, the alterations to the present form had already occurred. The melody, which is made up almost entirely of step-wise motion, was used extensively in American and British collections of the late eighteenth and the nineteenth centuries, nearly always with the name "All Saints."

434   THE SON OF GOD, OUR CHRIST

Tune: Sursum Corda

Originally published in *Three more new hymns for Youth by Youth,* 1957, this text was the first choice of the hymns obtained by the Hymn Society of America at the request of the United Christian Youth Movement of the National Council of the Churches of Christ in the U.S.A. for use during National Youth Week, January 27–February 3, 1957. The third stanza contains a number of alterations.

Edward M. Blumenfeld was born in Chicago, one of twins, on September 23, 1927. His family later moved to Cincinnati, Ohio, and then to Milwaukee, Wisconsin, where he completed high school. After serving from 1945 to 1946 in the United States Navy, he attended Carroll College in Waukesha, Wisconsin, and graduated in 1949. He studied medicine at Marquette University School in Milwaukee until he experienced a call to prepare for the ministry. Before he was able to enter seminary, however, he served in the United States Army and worked in steel mills until 1952. He received a Bachelor of Divinity degree from Hartford Theological Seminary in 1955 and a Master of Arts degree from Garrett Theological School (Northwestern University) in 1961. Ordained to the ministry of the Congregational-Christian Churches (now the United Church of Christ) in East Burke, Vermont, in 1955, he was called to the yoked parish of First Congregational Church, Swanton, and Union Congregational Church, Alburg, Vermont. He has since ministered to congregations in Illinois and Wisconsin and is presently pastor of Bethany United Church of Christ, Milwaukee. Married in 1954 to Flora Merriam, who was also a student at Hartford Seminary, he is the father of one son.

Although he had written poetry for his high school paper, and for his own enjoyment for years, Blumenfeld had not written a hymn before 1957 when he composed "The Son of God, Our Christ." Since that time he has written several other hymns, and continues also to write poetry for his sermons, for holiday greetings, for a service club newsletter, and so forth.

SURSUM CORDA was written in 1941 for Henry Montagu Butler's "Lift up your hearts!" and submitted anonymously for use in *The Hymnal 1940* of the Episcopal Church.

The composer, Alfred Morton Smith, was born May 20, 1879, in Jenkintown, Pennsylvania. After completing a Bachelor of Science degree at the University of Pennsylvania in 1901, he entered Philadelphia Divinity School, where he received a Bachelor of Divinity degree in 1905, and in 1911, a Bachelor of Sacred Theology degree. Ordained an Episcopalian deacon in 1905 and a priest in 1906, he served for a short time at St. Peter's Church, Philadelphia, then St. Luke's Church, Long Beach, California. He was called in 1906 to Los Angeles, where he ministered for ten years to St. Matthias' Church, and also worked for two years in the City Mission. During World War I he was a chaplain in the United States Army and was sent to France, and later to Germany with the Army of the Occupation. Returning to Philadelphia in 1919, he became a member of the staff of the Episcopal City Mission, and was also chaplain to the Eastern State Penitentiary, Sleighton Farm School, and the city hospitals. In addition he served as an assistant at St. Clement's Church, 1920–1928; chaplain at Valley Forge Military Academy, 1928–1930; and associate priest at St. Elisabeth's Church, 1930–1933. He retired in 1955, and in 1963 entered Druim Moir, a retirement residence for elderly clergy and/or their families in the Chestnut Hill area of Philadelphia. After 1968 he lived in Brigantine, New Jersey, until his death on February 26, 1971.

As an adult Smith studied harmony with Frederick M. Schlieder and violoncello with Bertrand Austin. Besides some hymn tunes and carols he composed two masses, *Missa de Sancto Matthia,* 1936, and *Missa de Sancto Clemente,* 1948.

435 O GOD, WHOSE WILL IS LIFE AND GOOD

Tune: Leupold

Hardwicke Drummond Rawnsley, the son of an Anglican clergyman, was born September 28, 1851, at Shiplake, Henley-on-Thames, England. He received his early education under his godfather, Edward Thring (brother of Godfrey—LBW 170), and attended Balliol College, Oxford, completing a Bachelor of Arts degree in 1875 and a Master of Arts degree in 1883. Ordained in 1875, he was curate of St. Barnabas', Bristol, 1875–1878; vicar at Low Wray, Lancashire, 1878–1883; vicar at Crosthwaite, 1883–1917; and honorary canon of Carlisle, 1893. His published works include some hymns and a number of books of poetry. A lover of nature and beauty, he also published twelve books on the English Lake District, and organized the National Trust for Places of Historic Interest and Natural Beauty. Following his death at Grasmere on May 28, 1920, the National Trust acquired property on Lord's Island and a segment of the Great Wood on the shore of Derwent Water in his memory.

Originally beginning "*Father,* whose will is life and good," this hymn was included in *A Missionary Hymn Book,* London, 1922, a publication of the Society for the Promotion of Christian Knowledge.

LEUPOLD has been adapted by the composer, Leland Sateren (LBW 100), from his anthem, "Turn not thy face," 1964. An earlier 4-part setting was published in 1956.

436   ALL WHO LOVE AND SERVE YOUR CITY
Tune: Birabus

In October, 1966, a working party of authors and composers took up residence at Scottish Churches House in Dunblane to explore and compose new music for use in the church. One day in a working session, having been asked to compose a piece of music, Erik Routley fell to thinking about the riots that had just broken out in Oakland, California. At the time he had also been searching for words to be sung to Peter Cutts's tune, "Birabus" (see below). He began writing and this hymn, his first, was the result.

Routley was born October 31, 1917, at Brighton, England, and received a Bachelor of Arts degree from Magdalen College, Oxford, in 1940. Following studies at Mansfield College, he was ordained in 1943 at Trinity Congregational Church, Wednesbury, Dartford, in Edinburgh, and two years later he became pastor of Dartford Congregational Church. In 1946 he received his Bachelor of Divinity degree and in 1948, was appointed tutor and lecturer in church history at Mansfield College. When he completed his Doctor of Philosophy degree at Oxford in 1952 his thesis was *The Music of Christian Hymnody,* which was published in 1957. He became minister of Augustine-Bristo Congregational Church in Edinburgh in 1959, and of St. James's Congregational Church, Newcastle-upon-Tyne, in 1967. In 1970 he was elected to a one-year term as president of the Congregational Church of England and Wales. He came to the United States in January of 1975 and was appointed visiting professor and director of music at Princeton Theological Seminary. In September of 1975 he became professor of church music at Westminster Choir College in Princeton, and in 1978 also took the post of director of chapel.

Well-known and highly regarded in the fields of hymnody and church music, Routley has published extensively, including *The Church and Music,* 1950; *The English Carol,* 1958; *Church Music and Theology,* 1959; *Music Sacred and Profane,* 1960; *Hymns Today and Tomorrow,* 1964; *Twentieth Century Church Music,* 1964; *The Musical Wesleys* and *Words, Music, and the Church,* 1968; *Exploring the Psalms,* 1975; and *Church Music and the Christian Faith,* 1978. He was secretary of the committee that prepared *Congregational Praise,* 1951; principal editorial consultant of *Cantate Domino,* third edition, 1974, the hymnal of the World Council of Churches; and editor of *Westminster Praise,* 1976, and its companion, 1977. From 1948 to 1974 he was editor of the *Bulletin* of the Hymn Society of Great Britain. He has published numerous articles, as well as hymn texts, hymn tunes, and some other musical works. He also lectures widely.

BIRABUS was written by Peter Cutts in the fall of 1962 for use the following January with "In the cross of Christ I glory" (LBW 104), sung at the Student Christian Movement Congress in Bristol, England. The composer writes, the "tune-title has significance purely within the S. C. M., being the nickname [of] the vehicle in which I and a number of others returned to Britain from an international conference in Austria, summer 1962." The melody was first published in *Dunblane Praises II,* and thence in *New Songs for the Church.* The present, more accurate, version is from *Hymns and Songs,* published in London in 1969.

A native of Birmingham, England, Peter Warwick Cutts was born June 4, 1937. He received a Bachelor of Arts degree with honors in music from Clare College, Cambridge, in 1961. After completing a Bachelor of Arts degree in theology from Mansfield College, Oxford, in 1963, he returned to Clare College for a Master of Arts degree, completed in 1965. He has held teaching posts in the music department of Huddersfield College of Technology and in the music and religious studies departments of Oastler College of Education in Huddersfield, and since 1969 has been a lecturer in music at Bretton Hall College, Wakefield, Yorkshire. He has held various joint organist/assistant organist positions, and is director of chapel music at Bretton Hall College. In addition to his hymn tunes, which have appeared in various hymnals in the United States and England, Cutts has published articles for several magazines.

437 NOT ALONE FOR MIGHTY EMPIRE

Tune: Geneva

William Pierson Merrill was born in Orange, New Jersey, on January 10, 1867. Following his education at Rutgers College (Bachelor of Arts, 1887; Master of Arts, 1890), and at Union Theological Seminary (Bachelor of Divinity, 1890), he was ordained to the Presbyterian ministry. He became the pastor of Trinity Church in Chestnut Hill, Philadelphia (1890–1895) and of Sixth Church, Chicago (1895–1911), and from 1911 was minister of Brick Presbyterian Church, New York City, retiring pastor emeritus in 1938. He was honored with Doctor of Divinity degrees from Rutgers College (1905) and from New York University (1923), a Doctor of Sacred Theology degree from Columbia University in 1927, and a Doctor of Humanities degree from Rollins College. Merrill was a preacher of note and published a number of theological works, among them *Christian Internationalism,* 1919; *The Common Creed of Christians,* 1920; *The Freedom of the Preacher,* 1922; *Liberal Christianity,* 1925; *Prophets of the Dawn,* 1927; *The Way,* 1933; and *We See Jesus,* 1934. From 1915 he was president of the trustees of the Church Peace Union. Married in 1896 to Clara Dwymour Helmer, he was the father of three sons. He died June 19, 1954.

This hymn was written in 1909 after a Thanksgiving service where Merrill was impressed by a prayer made by Jenkin Lloyd Jones emphasizing the spiritual blessings America had received. It was later rewritten and was included in a Presbyterian publication, *The Continent,* in 1911, and the Presbyterian *Hymnal,* 1933.

GENEVA, named for Geneva, New York, where the composer served for many years as organist and choirmaster, was written in 1940 and included that year in *The Hymnal* of the Episcopal Church.

George Henry Day was born September 13, 1883, in New York City. Music study was begun early with his parents and at age eight he joined the choir at Trinity Chapel. In 1903 he became G. Edward Stubbs's student and assistant at St. Agnes' Chapel, and in 1911 he was appointed organist and choirmaster at St. Peter's Episcopal Church in Chelsea Square. Although he had been involved with music since childhood, Day studied accounts and commercial law when he attended New York University and for a time held a position as an assistant auditor of a manufacturing company. He chose music as his life's work, however, and graduated from the New York College of Music in 1913. In 1916 he was married to Anna Fredericka Hanken and went to Youngstown, Ohio, as organist and choirmaster of St. John's Church. The following year he went to St. John's Church in Wilmington, Delaware. During his years there he studied with Edward Shippen Barnes (LBW 71) and Orlando Mansfield, and won the Doctor of Music degree from Lincoln-Jefferson University by examination in 1923. In 1925 he was appointed organist and choirmaster of Christ Church, Rochester, New York, and in 1935 he went to Trinity Church, Geneva, New York. There he remained until his death on November 23, 1966.

Day was active in the American Guild of Organists, holding a fellowship in that organization, and serving as a member of the council, 1915-1916; national treasurer, 1913-1916; president of the Delaware Chapter, 1921-1925; and dean of the Western New York Chapter, 1925-1930. His compositions, which numbered some four hundred, included cantatas, anthems, motets, organ works, and hymn tunes.

438   LORD, TEACH US HOW TO PRAY ARIGHT
Tune: Song 67

See LBW 50 for James Montgomery. Written in 1818 and first printed on a broadsheet for use in the Sheffield Nonconformist Sunday school, this hymn was included the following year in Thomas Cotterill's (LBW 547) *Selection of Psalms and Hymns* and in Edward H. Bickersteth's (LBW 491) *Treatise on Prayer.*

SONG 67 was originally the setting for Psalm 1 in E. Prys's *Llyfr y Psalmau,* 1621. In 1623 it was given with a bass by Orlando Gibbons (LBW 206) in George Withers' *Hymnes and Songs of the Church.* There it was Song 67, the setting for a hymn for St. Matthias' day which began:

> When one among the twelve there was,
>   That did thy grace abuse;
> Thou left him, Lord, and in his place,
>   Didst just Matthias choose.

Originally the tune opened with a half note, the first three phrases ended with a half note and quarter rest, and the final note was a whole note.

439   WHAT A FRIEND WE HAVE IN JESUS
Tune: Converse

Written by Joseph Medlicott Scriven in 1855 and sent to his mother in Ireland to comfort her in a time of sorrow, this hymn was included in Horace Hastings' *Social Hymns, Original and Selected,* Boston, 1865.

Scriven was born September 10, 1819, in Seapatrick, County Down, in Ireland. His father was a captain in the Royal Marines, and after two years at Trinity College, Joseph also decided on a military career, and entered Addiscombe Military College, Surrey, in 1837. Poor health forced him to abandon the course, however, and he returned to Trinity College to complete a Bachelor of Arts degree in 1842. His fiancée was accidentally drowned on the eve of their wedding, and in 1844 he emigrated to Canada, teaching school for a while at Woodstock and Brantford, Ontario, before moving to Bewdley, near Rice Lake. His plans for marriage were cut short a second time when his fiancée, Eliza Roche, died suddenly following a brief illness. A member of the Plymouth Brethren, Scriven attempted to follow in a literal way the teachings of the Sermon on the Mount, and gave all his time and property to Christian service, doing work for the sick and poor. In later years his tendency toward depression, noticeable already when he left Ireland, increased greatly as a result of failing health, poverty, and his fear of becoming a burden to others. He died October 10, 1886, by drowning in Rice Lake. Whether his death was accidental or not is not known.

CONVERSE (also "Erie", named for the city in Pennsylvania where the composer lived for many years) was written in 1868 and published two years later in his *Silver Wings* under the pseudonym Karl Reden. The tune has also been called "Friendship."

Born in Warren, Massachusetts, on October 7, 1832, Charles Crozat Converse was the son of one of the early settlers of Woburn, Massachusetts. He went to Leipzig in 1855 where he studied law and philosophy, as well as music theory and composition under Moritz Hauptmann, E. Friedrich Richter, and Louis Plaidy at the Leipzig Conservatory. There also he made the acquaintance of Franz Liszt and Louis Spohr. He returned to the United States in 1859 and graduated from the Albany, New York, Law School two years later. From 1875 he practiced law in Erie, Pennsylvania, where he was also in charge of the Burdetta Organ Company. He composed a number of hymn tunes, as well as larger works. A Doctor of Music degree was offered him by Sterndale Bennett of Cambridge University in England for the five-voice double fugue at the end of his Psalm-Cantata on Psalm 126, but he declined the offer. In 1895 Rutherford College honored him with a Doctor of Laws degree. He spent his last years in Highwood, New Jersey, where he died October 18, 1918.

440   CHRISTIANS, WHILE ON EARTH ABIDING
(Du som fromma hjartan vaarder)
Tune: Werde munter

Stanza 2 of this hymn, written by Jesper Svedberg, is a paraphrase of the Aaronic benediction (Numbers 6:24–26), originally beginning "Herre, signe du och raade." In 1816 Johan Olof Wallin (LBW 73) revised the hymn slightly and expanded it to six stanzas, with the first line, "Du som fromma hjartan vaarder." The present two stanzas are the fifth and sixth stanzas of an English version, beginning "Guardian of pure hearts, and hearer," which was included in the *Hymnal,* 1901, of the Augustana

Synod. The translation is by an unknown poet. Several changes were made for the LBW.

Jesper Svedberg, Sweden's first important hymnwriter, was born on Sveden Estate near Falun on August 28, 1653. The son of a miner, as was Martin Luther (LBW 48), he was a descendant of a respected mining family in the Kopparberg mining district. He entered Uppsala University but unfortunate experiences with poor teachers caused him to move for a time to Lund University. Later he returned to Uppsala, and was ordained in 1683. As chaplain of the royal cavalry regiment in Stockholm, he so impressed King Karl XI that he was soon elevated to court preacher. In 1690 he became dean and pastor in Vingåker, and two years later, theological professor and dean of the cathedral at Uppsala. In 1691 he was commissioned by the king to prepare a new hymnbook. After two years the work was submitted to the archbishop and the theological faculty for examination and, with a few minor revisions, was approved. Containing 482 Swedish hymns and a few in Latin, it was printed in 1694. Soon afterwards, however, it met with violent criticism, especially from Bishop Carl Carlsson, who condemned it as containing "innumerable heresies of a theological, anthropological, Christological, soteriological, and eschatological nature." Ryden* relates that the book was promptly confiscated and sent by the authorities in large quantities to the Swedish colonists along the Delaware River, who used it for their worship for many years. The king at once appointed a commission to revise the hymnal. The resulting collection, printed in 1695, omitted seventy-five hymns, mostly ones by Svedberg and Haquin Spegel, and added six new ones. The revised hymnal remained in use until the issue of Wallin's *Svenska Psalm-Boken* in 1819. Although Svedberg was humiliated over the rejection of his hymnal, the revised edition clearly bore his stamp, nevertheless, and the *Psalmbok* of 1937 still included thirty-three of his texts. Svedberg lived to receive high honors from his countrymen and the Church. In 1703 he was consecrated bishop of Skara, a position he held until his death on July 26, 1735. Emmanuel Swendenborg, the famous mystic and philosopher, was his son.

WERDE MUNTER is a rhythmic variant of the tune found at LBW 219.

441 ETERNAL SPIRIT OF THE LIVING CHRIST
Tune: Adoro te devote

Frank von Christierson (LBW 404), author of this hymn, writes:

> "Eternal Spirit of the Living Christ" is a deeply devotional hymn, the outpouring of my heart to Christ, who is the center and life of my faith. It just came to me one morning, and I wrote as I felt led. I have often felt that Paul's frequent use of the expression "in Christ" is entirely typical of him, and should be typical of every Christian life. Also this hymn expresses my strong feeling that I can't begin to say to God what is really in my heart, but I think He understands.

The hymn appeared on the front cover of *The Hymn,* January, 1947, a publication of the Hymn Society of America.

For ADORO TE DEVOTE see LBW 199. The harmonization was prepared by Leland Sateren (LBW 100) for the LBW.

442   O THOU, WHO HAST OF THY PURE GRACE

Tune: Vater unser

Written by Martin H. Franzmann (LBW 233), this hymn was included in the *Worship Supplement,* 1969, to *The Lutheran Hymnal.*

VATER UNSER, as it appears here, was adapted by Martin Luther (LBW 48) for his versification of the Lord's Prayer included in Valentin Schumann's *Geistliche lieder auffs new gebessert und gemehrt,* Wittenberg, 1539. Other forms of the melody can be found in earlier sources —in a manuscript part book which Johann Walther (LBW 350) gave to Luther in 1530, and in Michael Weisse's (LBW 37) *Ein New Gesengbuchlen,* 1531, where it was set to "Begeren wir mit jnnikeit." There is a possibility that all were based on an older prototype.

The tune was also used in the English Psalter of 1560 with an English versification of the Lord's Prayer, and was set to Psalm 112 in the Anglo-Genevan Psalter of 1561. It was commonly found in English and Scottish psalters thereafter.

J. S. Bach (LBW 219) used the melody in Cantatas 10, 101, and 102, and in the *St. John Passion,* and included a harmonization in the *Choralgesänge.* His organ settings can be found in the *Orgelbüchlein,* the *Clavier Übung,* and among the Miscellaneous Preludes.

The present harmonization is from the *Württembergische Choralbuch,* 1953.

443   RISE, MY SOUL, TO WATCH AND PRAY
(Mache dich, mein Geist, bereit)
Tune: Straf mich nicht

Johann Burkhard Freystein, son of the vice-chancellor to Duke August of Saxony and inspector of the *Gymnasium* at Weissenfels, was born at Weissenfels on April 18, 1671. He studied law, mathematics, philosophy, and architecture at the University of Leipzig, and then lived for some time at Berlin and Halle before going to Dresden as an assistant to a lawyer. After receiving a Doctor of Laws degree at Jena in 1695, he set up his own practice in Dresden. He became Counselor at Gotha in 1703, but returned six years later to Dresden as a member of the court council and counselor of justice, and was also, in 1713, appointed a member of the Board of Works. He died of dropsy in Dresden on April 1, 1718.

Freystein's hymn was included in the *Geistreiches Gesang-Buch,* published in Halle in 1697. The English form given here is an adaptation of Catherine Winkworth's (LBW 29) translation given in her *Chorale Book for England,* 1863.

STRAF MICH NICHT was the melody used with Johann Georg Albinus' text, "Straf mich nicht in deinem Zorn," in *Hundert ahnmüthig- und sonderbahr geistlicher Arien,* 1694, an appendix to *Geist- und Lehr-reiches Kirchen- und Hauss-Buch,* published in Dresden the same year. The tune appeared earlier as a "Lamente," in a manuscript collection of dance music written down before 1681. J. S. Bach (LBW 219) included a setting in his Cantata 115. The present harmonization is from the *Orgelchoralbuch,* 1952.

444 WITH THE LORD BEGIN YOUR TASK
(Fang dein Werk mit Jesu an)

Tune: Fang dein Werk

This German hymn by an unknown author is found in *Morgen- und Abend-segen,* published in Waldenburg in 1734. William Gustave Polack's (LBW 168) translation was prepared in 1937 for *The Lutheran Hymnal,* 1941. Except for one line in the fourth stanza, alterations consist only of updated second-person pronouns.

FANG DEIN WERK. This tune is found with the hymn "Schwing dich auf zu deinem Gott" in Kornelius Dretzel's (LBW 192) *Des Evangelischen Zions Musicalische Harmonie,* Nürnberg, 1731 (Zahn* #6352). There it appeared as given below.

Some sources attribute the tune to Peter Frank (Franck), a German merchant's son born September 27, 1616. Frank studied theology at Jena around 1636, and in 1640 was at the University at Altorf. He worked as a private tutor from 1643 to 1645, after which he served as a pastor in churches in Thüngen, Rossfeld, Rodach, Gleussen, and Herreth. He died June 22, 1675.

The harmonization was prepared for the LBW by Donald Busarow (LBW 30).

445 UNTO THE HILLS

Tune: Sandon

Written in 1877, this paraphrase of Psalm 121 was included in Campbell's *Book of Psalms* the same year. The hymn has gained a place of prominence in Canada, and during World War II was a favorite with the Canadian soldiers.

John Douglas Sutherland Campbell, Marquis of Lorne and later ninth Duke of Argyll, was born in Staffordhouse, London, England, on August 6, 1845. Educated at Eton, St. Andrew's, and Trinity College, Cambridge, he became the liberal member of Parliament for Argyll in 1868. In 1871 he was married to Princess Louise, daughter of Queen Victoria. He served for three years as private secretary to his father who was secretary of state for India, and from 1878 to 1883 was governor-general of Canada. At the end of his term in office he returned to England where from 1895 to 1900 he represented Manchester for the Unionists in Parliament. He died May 2, 1914, of double pneumonia, while vacationing on the Isle of Wight.

Campbell's writings included several books about Canada, a book of reminiscences titled *Pages from the Past* (1907), and some poetry.

SANDON was written for John Henry Newman's "Lead, kindly light," and included in Purday's *The Church and Home Metrical Psalter and Hymnal,* 1860.

The composer, Charles Henry Purday, was the son of a bookseller. Born in Folkstone, England, on January 11, 1799, he had a fine voice, and was for many years the precentor of the Scottish Church, Crown Court, Drury Lane, in London. In 1837 he sang for the coronation of Queen Victoria. He was a popular music lecturer and one of the pioneers in the area of the use of program notes. A music publisher and a strong advocate of the reform of music copyright laws, he issued his *Copyright, a Sketch of its Rise and Progress* in 1877. Among his other publications were *The Sacred Musical Offering,* 1833; *Crown Court Psalmody,* 1854; *A few directions for chanting,* 1855; and with Frances Havergal (LBW 260), *Songs of Peace and Joy,* 1879. With John Thomas he edited a large volume of Welsh airs. He died April 23, 1885, in Kensington, London.

446 WHATEVER GOD ORDAINS IS RIGHT
(Was Gott tut, das ist wohlgetan,/es bleibt)
Tune: Was Gott tut

Samuel Rodigast, son of a German Lutheran pastor, was born October 19, 1649, at Gröben, near Jena. He received a Master of Arts degree from the University of Jena in 1671 and five years later became an adjunct, or instructor, of the philosophical faculty there. From 1680 to 1698 he was joint rector of the Greyfriars *Gymnasium* in Berlin, and after 1698, full rector. A fine scholar and educator, he was offered a professorship at the University of Jena and rectorships at the schools in Stade and Stralsund, but he chose to remain at his post in Berlin, where he died March 29, 1708.

Based on Deuteronomy 32:4, this hymn has some reminiscences of an older hymn by Johann Altenburg (LBW 361) which has the same opening line. The hymn was written in 1675 to comfort the author's friend, Severus Gastorius (see below), during a serious illness. Published the following year in the Appendix to *Das Hannoverische Gesangbuch,* it was sung frequently by the members of the choir school in Gastorius' charge, and soon became widespread. It was a favorite hymn of Friedrich Wilhelm III of Prussia, who requested that it be sung at his funeral.

The translation was prepared for the LBW by Gracia Grindal (LBW 32).

WAS GOTT TUT was composed for this hymn by Severus Gastorius, who was cantor of Jena about 1675. The melody was suggested by Carl von Winterfeld in the 1880s to have been the work of the distinguished organist and composer, Johann Pachelbel, but that ascription was later considered by Zahn* to be unfounded. It first apeared in the *Ausserlesenes Weimarisches Gesangbuch,* 1681, and was altered to its present form in the 1690 *Nürnbergisches Gesang Buch.* J. S. Bach (LBW 219) used the tune in Cantatas 12, 69, 75, 98, 100, and 144, and in the first of his three wedding cantatas.

Tune: Alles ist an Gottes Segen

This anonymous text first appeared in the *Andächtige Haus-Kirch . . . Gesängen* published in Nürnberg in 1676, and possibly dates from around 1673. In her *Lyra Germanica,* second series, 1858, Catherine Winkworth (LBW 29) included a translation beginning "All things hang on our possessing." The present form of the hymn includes alterations from several sources.

ALLES IST AN GOTTES SEGEN is based on a tune by Johann Löhner written for Heinrich Arnold Stockfleth's hymn, "Wunderanfang! herrlichs Ende!" and published in *Der Geistlichen Erquick-Stunden . . . Poetischer Andacht-Klang,* Nürnberg, 1691. There it appeared as given below. Numerous musical settings of "Alles ist an Gottes Segen" appeared through the years, including several forms of Löhner's tune.

Revisions in Johann Balthasar König's *Harmonischer Lieder-Schatz,* Frankfurt-am-Main, 1738 (LBW 22), and Johann Adam Hiller's *Allgemeines Choral-Melodienbuch für Kirchen und Schulen,* Leipzig, 1793, brought the tune to its present form. The harmonization given here is from the *Orgelchoralbuch,* Württemberg, 1952.

Johann Löhner, fellow-organist and contemporary of Johann Pachelbel in Nürnberg, was born in that city on December 21, 1645. Orphaned at an early age, he went to live with his sister, whose husband, Georg Kaspar Wecker, became Löhner's second father, and later, his teacher and example in organ playing. After traveling to Vienna, Salzburg (where he played successfully for the archbishop), and Leipzig to study music, he returned to his home town of Nürnberg. There he served as organist of the Frauenkirche, Heilige Geistekirche, and finally of St. Lorenzkirche. Löhner's works include church music, a large number of hymn tunes, songs, and operas of the *Singspiele* variety based on sacred subjects. He died in Nürnberg April 2, 1705.

Hiller, whose father was also a musician, was born on Christmas Day, 1728, at Wendisch-Offing near Görlitz. He attended the University of Leipzig, and from 1754 to 1760 was private tutor to Count Brühl. In 1763 he established the large weekly concerts in Leipzig. He was appointed director of music at the Paulinerkirche in 1779, and at the new church in 1784. In 1789 he became *Kantor* at St. Thomas' Church in Leipzig, where J. S. Bach (LBW 219) had served. His compositions include a large number of sacred and secular vocal and instrumental works. He retired in 1801, and died in Leipzig on June 16, 1804.

448 AMAZING GRACE, HOW SWEET THE SOUND

Tune: New Britain

See LBW 261 for John Newton. This hymn was included in *Olney Hymns,* 1779.

NEW BRITAIN, a pentatonic melody which is also known as "Amazing Grace," "Harmony Grove," "Symphony," "Solon," and "Redemption," appeared in *Virginia Harmony,* 1831, compiled by James P. Carrell and David S. Clayton. Its origin is unknown. In earlier sources the third line read as follows:

The present form of the tune is credited to Edwin Othello Excell (1851–1921) and was included in *Make His Praise Glorious,* Chicago, 1900. "Twenty-fourth" (LBW 122) is closely related to this tune. Austin C. Lovelace (LBW 392) has prepared the harmonization, which was included in *The Book of Hymns,* 1964, of the Methodist Church.

449 THEY CAST THEIR NETS

Tune: Peace of God

William Alexander Percy's poem, "His Peace," was included in *Enzio's Kingdom and Other Poems,* 1924, beginning:

> I love to think of them at dawn
>   Beneath the frail pink sky,
> Casting their nets in Galilee
>   And fish-hawks circling by.
>
> Casting their nets in Galilee
>   Just off the hills of brown;†

and continuing as in the LBW.

The son of United States Senator LeRoy Percy, William was born in Greenville, Mississippi, on May 14, 1885. After receiving a Bachelor of Arts degree in 1904 from the University of the South, and a Bachelor of Laws degree from Harvard University in 1908, he practiced law with his father until World War I. During the war he distinguished himself first by his work for the Belgian Relief, 1916–1917, and then as a captain of the 37th Division from 1918 to 1919, receiving the Croix de Guerre with gold and silver stars. After the war he returned to Mississippi and settled on the family estate, Trail Lake Plantation, near Greenville. In 1927 he was again involved in relief work during an extensive flood in the Greenville area. He began writing poetry in 1911 and continued throughout most of his life. His autobiography, *Lanterns on the Levee, Recollections of a Planter's Son,* was published in 1941, and in August, 1952, *The*

---

†Reprinted by permission of LeRoy P. Percy, Executor of the Estate of William A. Percy.

Reader's Digest carried his life story in "The most unforgettable character I've met." He died January 21, 1942, in Greenville.

PEACE OF GOD. Herbert Gustav Draesel Jr. was born in Jersey City, New Jersey, on March 14, 1940. He completed a Bachelor of Arts degree at Trinity College, Hartford, Connecticut, in 1961, and a Bachelor of Divinity degree at General Theological Seminary, New York City, three years later. Since that time he has served as curate (1964–1965) and rector (1965–1972) of the House of Prayer in Newark, New Jersey; rector of the Church of St. Mary the Virgin, Chappaqua, New York, 1972–1975; and rector of Grace Church, White Plains, New York, since 1975.

In 1963, while he was at General Seminary, Draesel wrote a mass and this hymn tune for a liturgical conference, and both were published the following year in *Rejoice! Music for the Worship of God in the Twentieth Century*. He has also composed various anthems for children, and has written and composed several children's shows which have been produced in the New York City area.

The harmonization is by Jerry Evenrud, Director for Parish Music and the Arts for the American Lutheran Church. Born June 14, 1929, in Preston, Minnesota, Evenrud graduated in 1951 from St. Olaf College, where he majored in church music and organ, and was a member of the Blue Key Honorary Society. Two years later he received a Master of Sacred Music degree from Union Theological Seminary, New York. Upon graduation, he served for two years in the United States Army. In 1955 he became director of the ministry of music at Grace Lutheran Church, Eau Claire, Wisconsin, and in 1962 became assistant professor of music at the University of Wisconsin. During the summers from 1957 to 1960 he studied at Syracuse University, Syracuse, New York, where he was summer organist at Hendricks Chapel. Active in the American Guild of Organists, he has twice served as dean of the Chippewa Valley Chapter. He is a member and past treasurer of the Lutheran Society for Worship, Music, and the Arts, and for ten summers he has been the August music director at Holden Village, Chelan, Washington. He has served as director of the Eastern District of the Choral Union of the Evangelical Lutheran Church, Secretary to the Commission on Worship and Church Music of the American Lutheran Church, and from 1969 to 1972, chairman of the University Artists Course Committee of the University of Wisconsin. In 1976 he joined the Inter-Lutheran Commission on Worship as a member of the hymn music committee. He has conducted numerous church music conferences and institutes across the country, and his articles have appeared in the *Church Music Memo, Journal of Church Music, Acts 76,* and *Acts 77.* Married in 1956 to Avis Holmgren, he is the father of three children.

450 WHO TRUSTS IN GOD, A STRONG ABODE
(Wer Gott vertraut, hat wohlgebaut)
Tune: Was mein Gott will

Fortunately Joachim Magdeburg found in God a strong abode, for he certainly had none on this earth. Born around 1525 at Gardelegen in the Altmark, Germany, he entered Wittenberg University in 1544. Two years later he was appointed rector of the school at Schöningen, near Helmstädt, Brunswick. In 1547 he became pastor of Dannenberg in

Lüneberg, but was unable to exist on the meager salary and moved after two years to Salzwedel in the Altmark. For his refusal to adopt the Roman ceremonies prescribed by the Act of the Interim he was banished from the Electorate of Brandenburg in 1552. His friend, superintendent Johann Aepinus, secured his appointment to St. Peter's Church in Hamburg, but the following year Aepinus died, and his successor, Eitzen, was not so sympathetic to him. When Magdeburg published a tract on communion in 1558 without first submitting it to Eitzen for revision, he was removed from his post. He went to the city of Magdeburg, where with Matthias Flach (Illyricus Flacius), whom he had met in Hamburg, he compiled the Church history known as *The Magdeburg Centuries.* For a time he was pastor of Ossmanstedt in Thuringia, but was dispossessed as a follower of Flach in 1562. He stayed with Count von Mansfeld, Baron von Schönburg, and others until the Emperor Maximilian II once more permitted Protestant preachers in Austria. In 1564 he was appointed a military chaplain at Raab in Hungary where he ministered to German-speaking troups, living first at Raab until his house was burnt, and then at the castle of Gräfenworth. After joining with nineteen other Evangelical clergy in Austria to present a Confession of Faith to the Austrian Diet, he was compelled to leave and by 1571 was living in Erfurt. Back in Austria once again, he was a pastor in Efferding in 1581, but two years later was expelled as an adherent to the ideas of Flach. Beyond that point his life story is unknown.

His single stanza, which has much in common with "Ein feste Burg" (LBW 228), was included in his *Christliche und tröstliche Tischgesenge,* Erfurt, 1572. Two additional stanzas are found in Seth Calvisius' *Harmonia cantionum ecclesiasticarum,* Leipzig, 1597. The translation, originally given in first-person singular, was included in Benjamin Hall Kennedy's *Hymnologia Christiana,* 1863. There are several alterations.

Born November 6, 1804, at Summer Hill near Birmingham, England, Kennedy received a Bachelor of Arts degree with honors from St. John's College, Cambridge, in 1827. From 1828 to 1836 he was a fellow of St. John's College, after which he was head master of Shrewsbury School for thirty years, and in 1867 became Regius Professor of Greek at Cambridge University, and canon of Ely. Ordained in 1829, he also served for some time as prebendary in Lichfield Cathedral and rector of West Felton, Salop. In 1880 he was elected an honorary fellow of St. John's College. His publications included works in Latin, editions of some of the Classics, sermons, and *The Psalter,* 1860. His *Hymnologia Christiana* contained nearly two hundred translations from German, recasts of other hymns, Psalm paraphrases, and original hymns. He died April 6, 1889.

WAS MEIN GOTT WILL. This tune, widely-known in Germany, also appeared in Magdeburg's *Tischgesenge,* but as the setting for "Was mein Gott will, das g'scheh allzeit," a hymn ascribed to Margrave Albrecht of Brandenburg (LBW 519). Originally it was attached to the French love song, "Il me suffit de tous mes maulx," in *Trente et quatre chansons musicales,* a collection published in Paris by the first French music publisher, Pierre Attaignant, between 1529 and 1534. It was included in the *Souter Liedekens Thantwerpen* in 1540 as a setting for Psalm 140.

Claude (Claudin) de Sermisy, to whom the tune is ascribed, was born about 1490, probably in France. We first hear of him in 1508 when he became *clerc musicien* at Sainte-Chapelle du Palais, Paris. In 1515 he was among the singers of the Royal Chapel present for the funeral of

Louis XII, and in that same year he accompanied François I to a meeting with Pope Leo X at Bologna, where the French chapel singers vied with the papal choir. In 1520 he went with François I to meet Henry VIII at the Field of Cloth of Gold; and in 1532 he was present when the two kings met at Boulogne. He became *sous-maître* of the chapel, responsible for maintaining the singing-boys there, and in 1533, was made a canon of Sainte-Chapelle, a position which gave him a residence and a large salary. He retained his post as *sous-maître,* however, sharing it with Louis Hérault in 1547 at the time of François I's death and under Henri II, probably resigning soon after 1554. His name appears on the rolls at Sainte-Chapelle until 1561. He died in Paris October 13, 1562.

Sermisy composed a wide variety of music, including masses, motets, and some two hundred chansons. His works were very popular judging from the number of times they were published both before and for many years after his death.

The melody was a special favorite of J. S. Bach's (LBW 219); he used it more than any other tune. It is found in Cantatas 65, 72, 92 (in five movements), 103, 111, and 144, and in the St. Matthew Passion.

The harmonization is from the *Orgelchoralbuch, 1952.*

451 THE LORD'S MY SHEPHERD

Tune: Brother James's Air

This version of Psalm 23 is from *The Psalms of David in Meeter* (Scottish Psalter), Edinburgh, 1650. The text is made up of lines from a number of earlier versions (see Julian* p. 1154 and Millar Patrick, *Four Centuries of Scottish Psalmody* [1949] p. 103).

BROTHER JAMES'S AIR. Brother James is the name by which James Leith Macbeth Bain was known. Born in Scotland around 1840, Brother James was a mystical writer, poet, and spiritual healer. He passed from orthodox religious belief to agnosticism to a revelation of an all-pervading Divine Love, and felt that his introduction to the Christo Theosophic Society restored his lost simplicity of faith. In this "rapture of faith restored" he wrote many poems and melodies, including apparently "Brother James's Air." He formed a Brotherhood of Healers for treating both physical and spiritual illness, often singing to his patients as part of the healing process. He published *The Brotherhood of Healers. Being a Message to all Practical Mystics . . . and an Introduction to the Study of the Essential Principles of Spiritual, Psychic and Mental Healing,* 1906, and a number of similar works. During the latter part of his life he worked in the slums of Liverpool and at a children's home. He died September 19, 1925.

The LBW setting of the tune is adapted from a choral arrangement written by Gordon Jacob and published in London in 1934.

Gordon Percival Septimus Jacob was born at Norwood, near London, England, on July 5, 1895. He attended Dulwich College, interrupting his studies in 1914 to enlist in the armed forces. From 1917 to 1918 he was a prisoner of war. He studied at the Royal College of Music under Charles V. Stanford (LBW 189), Herbert Howells (LBW 491), and Sir Adrian Boult. In 1926 he was appointed professor of composition at the Royal College of Music. His *Orchestral Technique,* published in 1931, quickly became famous. He received a Doctor of Music degree in 1935 at London University, and was honored with the John Collard Fellowship of the Worshipful Company of Musicians, 1943–1946; the Fellowship of the Royal College of Musicians in 1946; and an appointment to the Royal Academy of Musicians in 1947. He was named editor of Penguin Scores in 1948. Known as a brilliant teacher, he has also composed two symphonies, four orchestral suites, and six concerti, as well as chamber music and vocal works. In 1968 he was made a Commander of the British Empire. Now retired, he lives at Saffron Walden in Essex.

452 AS PANTS THE HART FOR COOLING STREAMS
Tune: Martyrdom

This metrical paraphrase of Psalm 42 was included in Tate and Brady's *New Version of the Psalms of David*, London, 1696 (see also pp. 64ff). The most extensive alterations are found in stanza 5.

Son of a major in the king's army, Nicholas Brady was born October 28, 1659, at Bandon, County Cork, Ireland. At the age of twelve he was sent to England where he attended Westminster, and Christ Church, Oxford. Returning to Ireland he completed a Bachelor of Arts degree in 1685 at Dublin University, and was ordained in 1688. He served for a few months as prebendary of Kinaglarchy, Cork, after which he was presented with the livings of Killmyne and Drinah. He was also chaplain to Bishop Wetenhall. He upheld the cause of William of Orange during the revolution, and was later sent by the people of Bandon to the English Parliament to ask for compensation for their losses. While in London he was much admired for his preaching, and was appointed lecturer at St. Michael's, Wood Street. In 1691 he went to the church of St. Catherine Cree where he prepared, together with Nahum Tate (below), the *New Version*. He resigned in 1696 to go to Richmond, Surrey, a post he held until his death on May 20, 1726. In addition, he was rector of Stratford-on-Avon, 1702–1705; and of Clapham, 1705–1706. In 1699 the University of Dublin honored him with both Bachelor of Divinity and Doctor of Divinity degrees. He was chaplain to William III, to Mary, and to Anne, both as Princess of Wales and as queen. Although his pastoral posts brought him an adequate income, his expensive habits made it necessary for him also to keep a school at Richmond. Married to Letitia Synge, daughter of the archbishop of Cork, he was the father of four daughters and four sons.

Besides the *New Version,* his publications included a tragedy—*The Rape, or the Innocent Impostors*—and an *Ode for St. Cecilia's Day,* 1692; a partial translation of Virgil's *AEneid,* 1726; and two volumes of sermons.

Nahum Tate, son of an Irish clergyman, was born in Dublin in 1652, and educated at Trinity College, Dublin (Bachelor of Arts, 1672). He went to London in 1668, where he made his living writing for the stage. Much of Tate's work consisted of adaptations or translations of the works of others, or was done as a colleague or one of a company. His only really successful work was an adaptation of Shakespeare's *King Lear,* which opened in 1681 and held the stage until nearly 1840. He was appointed poet laureate in 1692, and on Anne's accession in 1702 was reappointed and also named historiographer-royal, holding the post until the accession of George I in 1715. Described as an honest and quiet man, given somewhat to "fuddling," Tate had a problem with intemperance and improvidence, and was poverty-stricken throughout much of his life.

He died in London at Suffolk House, Southwark, a debtor's refuge, on August 12, 1715.

Tate's most significant contribution was his collaboration with Brady on the *New Version*. Authorized by the king to be used in all the churches, the *New Version* had the support of the Whigs, although it met with some opposition from the stronger Tories among the clergy. In 1698 the two authors prepared a supplement containing paraphrases of the Lord's Prayer, Apostles' Creed, Commandments, Canticles, etc., which was authorized by the queen in 1703. Bound up with *The Book of Common Prayer,* Tate and Brady's work was in use well into Victorian times.

For MARTYRDOM see LBW 98. The present harmonization was done for the LBW by David Herman (LBW 97).

453 IF YOU BUT TRUST IN GOD TO GUIDE YOU
(Wer nur den lieben Gott lässt walten)
Tune: Wer nur den lieben Gott

Georg Neumark wrote both the text and the musical setting of this beautiful hymn, and included them in his *Musikalisch-poetischer Lustwald,* published in Jena in 1657.

Catherine Winkworth (LBW 29) gave a translation beginning "Leave God to order all thy ways, And hope in Him whate'er betide" in her *Lyra Germanica,* first series, 1855. In her *Chorale Book for England,* 1863, she included a revised version beginning "If thou but suffer God to guide thee." Stanzas 1, 3, and 4 are altered from that version. Stanza 2 has been prepared for the LBW by Jaroslav Vajda (LBW 159).

Born March 16, 1621, three years after the beginning of the Thirty Years' War, Neumark was the son of a clothier at Langensalza in Thuringia. He received a *Gymnasium* education and then set out in a caravan of merchants (it was necessary in those times to travel under guard from one city to another) intending to go by way of Leipzig and Lübeck to Königsberg to attend the only university not disrupted by the war. Outside of Magdeburg, however, the caravan was plundered by highwaymen who stripped Neumark of everything but his prayer book and a bit of money he had sewn into his clothing. He returned to Magdeburg but found no employment; neither did he find any in Lüneberg, Winsen, or in Hamburg. Finally in Kiel the chief pastor, Nicolaus Becker, befriended him; and when the position of tutor to Judge Stephen Henning became available, Becker secured it for Neumark. It was at this time of relief from his anxieties that he wrote this hymn. After two years he had accumulated enough money to go to Königsberg University, where he remained five years studying law, and also poetry under Simon Dach, supporting himself as a family tutor. During these years he again lost all his possessions, this time by fire. In 1648 he left Königsberg and from then until 1651 he spent time in Warsaw, Thorn, Danzig, and Hamburg, before finally going to Thuringia. There he became court poet, librarian, and registrar to Duke Wilhelm II of Sachse-Weimar, and later was secretary of the Ducal Archives. In 1653 he was admitted to the principal literary association in Germany of the time—the Fruit-bearing Society. During the last few months of his life he was blind but was allowed to keep his positions in Weimar until his death on July 18, 1681.

J. S. Bach (LBW 219) used this tune in Cantatas 21, 27, 84, 88, 93, 166, 179, and 197, and in his *Choralgesänge.* Organ settings are found in his *Orgelbüchlein,* in the *Schübler Chorales,* and among his Miscellaneous Preludes.

In some hymnals this tune is called "Neumark."

454 IF GOD HIMSELF BE FOR ME *(Ist Gott für mich, so trete)*
Tune: Ist Gott für mich

For Paul Gerhardt see LBW 23. Founded on Romans 8, this heroic hymn —bearing the watchword of the Lutheran church, "If God be for us, who can be against us?"—has been described as worthy of a place alongside "A mighty fortress" (LBW 228). The final stanza, originally the fifteenth, has been a special favorite of many Christians. The hymn was first printed in Johann Crüger's *Praxis pietatis melica,* Frankfurt, 1656 (LBW 23).

The English text is taken from *The Lutheran Hymnal,* 1941, with some alteration. Stanzas 1, 2, and 4 are based on a translation by Richard Massie (LBW 134) which was contributed to William Mercer's (LBW 281) *The Church Psalter and Hymn Book,* 1857. The translator of stanza 3 is unknown.

IST GOTT FÜR MICH. This tune is first found in London on January 14, 1590, associated with the ballad of Lord Willoughby of Eresby (1555–1601). The first stanza read:

> The fifteenth Day of July,
> with glistering Spear and Shield,
> A famous Fight in Flanders,
> was foughten in the field;
> The most couragious Officers,
> was English Captains three;
> But the bravest man in Battel
> was brave Lord Willoughby.

In 1594 it was used in the musical drama *Rowland and Margaret,* and in 1596 we hear of its being sung by an English actor in Frankfurt-am-Main. It soon became very popular, and was known throughout much of Europe as "Roland's tune." The English composer, William Byrd (1546–1623), wrote a setting for virginal entitled *Lord Willobies Welcome Home,* and the German composer, Samuel Scheidt (1587–1654), composed a *Canzon à 5 voc. super O nachbar Roland.*

In 1609 the tune was combined with Bader David Spaiser's text, "O Gott, ich tu dirs klagen," in his *Vier vnd zwantzig Geystliche Lieder Sambt jhren aignen Welsch- vnd Teutschen Melodeyen,* published in Augsburg.

The LBW harmonization is from the *Württembergische Choralbuch,* 1953.

455 "COME, FOLLOW ME," THE SAVIOR SPAKE
(Mir nach, spricht Christus, unser Held)
Tune: Machs mit mir, Gott

Johann Scheffler was born in 1624 in Breslau in Silesia. His father, of Polish nobility, had been forced to leave his homeland because of his adherence to Lutheranism. Johann studied medicine at the universities of Breslau, Strassburg, Leyden, and Padua, and in 1649 he became private physician to Duke Sylvius Nimrod of Würtemberg-Oels. During his studies in Holland he had sought the acquaintance of disciples of Jakob Böhme whose writings had interested him as a boy, and at Würtemberg also he associated with Böhme's followers and became introduced, through a large library bequeathed to him, to the works of other mystics. Eventually he found his thought more compatible with that of the Roman Catholic Church, which he joined in 1653, later adopting the name Angelus Silesius after a Spanish mystic, Juan ab Angelis. In the following year he was given the honorary title of Court Physician to Emperor Ferdinand III, but remained in Breslau. In 1661 he gave up his profession entirely and was ordained a priest. From 1664 he was counsel and court marshal to Sebastian von Rostock, newly-created Prince Bishop of Breslau, but on the bishop's death in 1671, Scheffler entered St. Matthias, a Jesuit monastery in Breslau, where he died July 9, 1677.

Scheffler began writing poetry at age sixteen. Nearly all his hymns were written while he was still a Lutheran, although they were published later—in *Heilige Seelenlust,* 1657, and in *Cherubinischer Wandersmann,* 1675. "Come, follow me," based on Matthew 16:24, was included in *Heilige Seelenlust,* 1668. Stanza 4, of unknown authorship, was included in Freylinghausen's *Geistreiches Gesangbuch,* 1704 (LBW 32). Scheffler's hymns were promoted especially by Gerhard Tersteegen (LBW 249), also a mystic, who included a number of them in his hymn collections.

Schaeffer's translation was included in the *Evangelical Lutheran Hymn-Book,* 1912. Extensive changes in all but the first stanza were made for *The Lutheran Hymnal,* 1941, and that form of the hymn is found here, with further alterations of the last two lines of the hymn.

Charles William Schaeffer was born in Hagerstown, Maryland, on May 5, 1813. When Charles was only a year old, his father, a Lutheran pastor, died of a fever contracted while visiting a camp of soldiers near Hagerstown, and his mother went to Carlisle, Pennsylvania, where she later married the Reverend Benjamin Keller. In 1829 the family moved to Germantown, Pennsylvania, and there Charles attended Germantown Academy. He graduated with honors from the University of Pennsylvania in 1832, and went on to Gettysburg Theological Seminary. In 1835 he became the first resident pastor to two congregations in Montgomery County, Pennsylvania—St. Peter's in Barren Hill and Union Church, White Marsh. From 1840 to 1849 he was pastor of the first Lutheran church established in Harrisburg, Pennsylvania, and for twenty-five years after that, ministered to St. Michael's Church, Germantown. During those years he received a Doctor of Divinity degree from the University of Pennsylvania. When the Philadelphia Seminary was opened in 1864, he was appointed a professor and later became chairman of the faculty, retiring as professor emeritus in 1894. From 1859 until his death he was also a trustee of the university. He served as treasurer and later president of the Pennsylvania Synod, and was president of the General Council and of the General Synod. Among his publications were a *History of the Lutheran Church in Harrisburg* and an *Early History of the Lutheran Church in America.* He died March 15, 1896.

MACHS MIT MIR, GOTT. This tune first appeared in Bartholomäus Gesius' *Das ander Theil des andern newen Operis Geistlicher Deutscher*

Lieder, Frankfurt an der Oder, 1605. There it was the setting for "Ein wahrer Glaub' Gottes Zorn stillt." The present form of the tune was prepared by Johann Hermann Schein (LBW 123) for his hymn, "Machs mit mir, Gott." Published on a broadsheet in 1628, it was included in the second edition (1645) of his *Cantional* (see below). The tune has had various names, including "Eisenach," "Schein," "Leipsig," and "Stuttgart." J. S. Bach (LBW 219) used the melody in the *St. John Passion* as well as in Cantatas 139 and 156. A setting was also included in the *Choralgesänge.*

Gesius, whose family name was originally Göss or Gese, was born in Müncheberg, near Frankfurt, Germany, around 1555, and studied theology at Frankfurt. He also studied music, and first served as a *Kantor* in Wittenberg before going in 1592 to Frankfurt an der Oder. There he remained until his death of the plague in 1613.

Gesius was a prolific composer and published ten collections of hymns, as well as liturgical music and motets, a Passion according to St. John, and a theoretical work, *Synopsis musicae practicae,* with editions in 1609, 1615, and 1618.

Schein was the writer of both hymns and tunes, and his best-known work was his *Cantional Oder Gesang-Buch Augsburgischer Confession,* published in Leipzig in 1627. He wrote a vast amount of music including songs, German and Latin motets, occasional pieces for weddings and funerals, and a collection of thirty *Geistlicher Concerten* mostly based on chorale tunes.

456 THE KING OF LOVE MY SHEPHERD IS
Tune: St. Columba

For Henry W. Baker see LBW 414. Described by John Ellerton (LBW 262) as "perhaps the most beautiful of all the countless versions of Psalm 23," this hymn was included in the Appendix to the Original Edition of *Hymns Ancient and Modern,* 1868. The last words of the author at his death were from the third stanza.

ST. COLUMBA is named for the Irish saint who "carried the torch of Irish Christianity to Scotland" (and who also has the dubious distinction of being the first to report a sighting of the Loch Ness monster, in 546). The tune is one of the Irish melodies collected by George Petrie (1789–1866) and given in Charles Villiers Stanford's (LBW 189) *Complete Collection of Irish Music as noted by George Petrie,* 1902. There it is said to have been sung at the dedication of a chapel in the county of Londonderry. A simpler form of the melody was given in the *Irish Church Hymnal,* 1874, with John Newton's (LBW 261) "Great Shepherd of thy people, hear," where it is said to be a "Hymn of the Ancient Irish Church." Winfred Douglas (LBW 498), in *A Brief Commentary on Selected Hymns and Carols,* suggests that the melody, "a masterpiece of Irish folksong," is probably from the eighteenth century. The association of the tune with this text, and also its harmonization, are from *The English Hymnal,* 1906.

Tune: Jesu, meine Freude

See LBW 224 for Johann Franck. Modeled on a song, "Flora, meine Freude, Meiner Seele Weide," in Heinrich Albert's (LBW 266) *Arein, Part IV,* 1641, this hymn was given first in Johann Crüger's (LBW 23) *Praxis Pietatis Melica,* 1653. Catherine Winkworth's (LBW 29) translation was included in her *Chorale Book for England,* 1863, and is given here with a few alterations.

JESU, MEINE FREUDE was included in Crüger's *Praxis Pietatis Melica,* 1653, together with the text.

Besides his motet which uses this hymn, J. S. Bach (LBW 219) included the tune in Cantatas 12, 64, 81, and 87, and also prepared organ works which are found in the *Orgelbüchlein* and Miscellaneous Preludes.

458   JESUS, PRICELESS TREASURE *(Jesu, meine Freude)*

Tune: Gud skal alting mage

This text is the same as that given at LBW 457.

GUD SKAL ALTING MAGE . This tune by Ludvig Lindeman (LBW 285), a setting for "Gud skal alting mage," has also been called "Lindeman."

459   O HOLY SPIRIT, ENTER IN *(O Heilger Geist, kehr bei uns ein)*

Tune: Wie schön leuchtet

Described by James Mearns in Julian* as "a beautiful New Testament paraphrase of Isaiah 11:2," this hymn was contributed by Michael Schirmer to Johann Crüger's (LBW 23) *Newes vollkömliches Gesangbuch Augspurgischer Confession,* 1640. The English version is adapted from a translation by Catherine Winkworth (LBW 29) given in her *Chorale Book for England,* 1863.

Schirmer, son of an inspector of wine casks at Leipzig, Germany, was born in July (baptized July 18) of 1606. Entering the University of Leipzig in 1619, he completed a Master of Arts degree in 1630. He was the author of a Scriptural play (*Der verfolgte David*) and of a number of poems, including versions of the songs of the Old and New Testaments (*Biblische Lieder und Lehrsprüche,* 1650) and a metrical version of Ecclesiasticus (*Das Buch Jesus Sirach*). In 1637 he was crowned a poet. His five hymns, which came into extensive use in Germany, are described in Julian* as "practical, clear, objective, churchly hymns, somewhat related to those of Gerhardt [LBW 23]; and still more closely to those of Johann Heermann [LBW 123]." Schirmer's German version of Virgil's *AEneid* in alexandrine meter was published in 1668.

Schirmer's life was full of trials and disappointments, and from 1644 to 1649, and again after his wife's death, he suffered from depression. Like many others, he endured the effects of the Thirty Years' War and the pestilence and poverty which accompanied it. His wife and two sons preceded him in death, and his own health was poor, so that although he had served as subrector of the Greyfriars *Gymnasium* from 1636, and conrector from 1651, other younger men were always preferred for the rectorship. He resigned his post in 1668 and remained in Berlin until his death on May 4, 1673.

For WIE SCHÖN LEUCHTET see LBW 76. This harmonization is from the *Orgelchoralbuch*, 1952.

460 I AM TRUSTING YOU, LORD JESUS
Tune: Stephanos

Francis R. Havergal (LBW 260) wrote this hymn in September of 1874 at Ormont Dessons. It was included four years later in her *Loyal Responses*. Except for the last line of stanza 1, which read "Great and free," alterations are limited to the use of "you" in place of "thee."

STEPHANOS by Henry W. Baker (LBW 414) was written for John Mason Neale's (LBW 34) "Art thou weary, Art thou languid" which was included in the Appendix to the Original Edition of *Hymns Ancient and Modern*, 1868. The tune is named after St. Stephen the Sabaite, to whom Neale originally attributed the Greek hymn from which he made his translation.

The harmonization by Thomas E. Gieschen was prepared for the LBW.

Gieschen, born July 11, 1931, at Wauwatosa, a suburb of Milwaukee, Wisconsin, attended Wisconsin Conservatory of Music and Wisconsin State Teachers College, Milwaukee. In 1952 he completed a Bachelor of Science degree in education at Concordia Teachers College, River Forest, Illinois, where he studied organ with Paul Bunjes (LBW 38). At the University of Michigan he was a student of Barrett Spach (Master of Music, 1958; Doctor of Music, 1968). He was teacher and director of music at Gethsemane Ev. Lutheran Church, Milwaukee, from 1952 to 1955, and at Emmaus Ev. Lutheran Church, Milwaukee, from 1955 to 1957. Since that time he has been a member of the faculty of Concordia Teachers College in River Forest, where he is now professor of music and chairman of the music department. He was also organist and choirmaster at Our Redeemer Ev. Lutheran Church in Chicago from 1957 to 1971, and associate organist of the Ev. Lutheran Church of St. Luke, Chicago, from 1976 to 1978. In addition to serving as organ recitalist and organ consultant, he has also composed, arranged, and edited choral and organ music, and is a contributing editor of *Church Music*. Married in 1952 to Roselyn Newman, he is the father of four children.

461 FIGHT THE GOOD FIGHT
Tune: Grace Church, Gananoque

Based on 1 Timothy 6:12, this hymn was included in John Samuel Bewley Monsell's (LBW 131) *Hymns of Love and Praise for the Church's Year,* 1863, for the nineteenth Sunday after Trinity. The hymn originally began "Fight the good fight with all *thy* might." Stanzas 3 and 4 of this hymn were altered for *The Hymnal 1940* (Episcopal), and the text has been further revised for the LBW.

GRACE CHURCH, GANANOQUE. Named for the church, located on the St. Lawrence Seaway, where the composer, Graham George (LBW 121), served from 1962 to 1966, this tune began to take shape around 1950. Revised in 1962, it was first published in *The Book of Hymns* (Methodist), 1964. Osborne* (#175) includes the following comment from the composer:

> There are two things wrong with the way this fine hymn is usually sung. One is that people don't recognize the fight is that of the Happy Warrior, though the words say it quite clearly; and the other is [the tune] *Pentecost,* which sings well, partly because the singer has only to establish and hold tight. I don't in fact deny the validity of very simple tunes which have this roof-raising capacity. I was brought up a Baptist, and anyone who has ever heard a churchfull of Baptists roaring their battlesong "Blest be the tie that binds," [LBW 370] must be incurably obstinate if he denies that something is going on. But "Fight the good fight," as to a lesser degree "Blest be the tie that binds," has more in it than to serve merely as a sort of religious "Sieg Heil," and my purpose in *Grace Church, Gananoque* was to design a tune sufficiently obvious to have some chance of competing with the obviousness of *Pentecost,* which would yet catch something of that "more-than-that."

462   GOD THE OMNIPOTENT!

Tune: Russian Hymn

A hymn of four stanzas, "God the all-terrible! King, who ordainest," written by Henry Chorley for this tune, was included in John Hullah's *Part Music,* I, 1842. From these the LBW uses stanzas 1 and 3 as the first two stanzas, with slight alterations in each stanza. LBW stanzas 3 and 4 are from a hymn written by John Ellerton (LBW 262) based on Chorley's hymn and beginning, "God, the Almighty one, wisely ordaining." Written during the Franco-German war, in 1870, Ellerton's hymn was included in Brown-Borthwick's *Select Hymns for Church and Home,* 1871. Here the only alteration is the substitution of "we have" for "man hath" in stanza 3, line 2. Selected stanzas from both hymns were combined to form one hymn as early as *Church Hymns,* 1871.

Henry Fothergill Chorley, a friend of Charles Dickens, was born in Blackley Hurst, Lancashire, England, on December 15, 1808. He was self-taught except for some time spent at the Royal Institute in London. After a short time in business he recognized that his real interests were literary. He secured a post with *The Athenaeum* in 1830 and remained on the staff for thirty-eight years, writing musical criticism and book reviews. He also served as music critic for *The Times* for several years until his death on February 16, 1872. In the field of music he supported the ideas of Felix Mendelssohn (LBW 60) and Louis Spohr, but openly attacked those of Frédéric Chopin, Robert Schumann (LBW 403), and Richard Wagner. In addition to his work for *The Athenaeum* and *The Times,* he wrote voluminously, including novels, drama, and opera libretti.

RUSSIAN HYMN, "God save the Czar," was written by Alexander Lvov in 1833 by order of Czar Nicholas I to take the place of the English tune, "God save our gracious King" (LBW 568), which up to that time had been used with a Russian text as the national anthem. It has also been called "Russia," Russian Anthem," and "Rephidim."

Alexis Feodorovich Lvov (Lwoff) was born in Reval (now Tallinn),

Estonia on June 5 or 6, 1799. His father, an authority on church music and folksong, was a student of Dmitri Bortniansky and his successor at the imperial court chapel in St. Petersburg. He also served at the Institute of Road Engineering. Alexis, who received some music training at home, pursued a career in the Russian army. Highly favored, he was major-general adjutant to the Czar at the time he retired in 1836 to succeed his father at the imperial court chapel, where he remained for twenty-four years. An excellent violinist, Lvov established a string quartet which became well-known throughout Europe. He composed a violin concerto, works for strings, operas, and a considerable amount of church music. In addition he prepared a violin method and a work on early Russian chants, which became an authoritative work. Retiring from his various posts in 1867 due to deafness, he died on December 16 or 28, 1870, at Romanovo, near Kovno, Lithuania.

463   GOD, WHO STRETCHED THE SPANGLED HEAVENS
Tune: Holy Manna

Dr. Catherine Arnott Cameron was born March 27, 1927, in Canada and has become a naturalized United States citizen. The daughter of Dr. John Sutherland Bonnell, a noted New York minister, she is married to Dr. Stuart Oskamp, professor of social psychology at the Claremont graduate school, Claremont, California, and is the mother of two children. She is associate professor of social psychology at the University of La Verne, La Verne, California.

"The hymn," the author notes, "was written over a period of several months at a time when I was experiencing a new sense of direction, growth, and creativity in my life. I wrote it to go with the tune 'Austria' [LBW 358] by Haydn." First published in *Contemporary Worship–1,* 1969, the text has been altered for the LBW, extensively so in the last stanza.

HOLY MANNA, a rousing pentatonic melody found frequently in early American collections, first appeared in William Moore's *The Columbian Harmony,* 1825 (LBW 127), where it was the setting for a hymn some-times attributed to George Atkins, "Brethren, we have met to worship." "Holy Manna" is one of eighteen tunes claimed by William Moore in the collection. Little is known of Moore except that he lived in "West Tennessee, Wilson County" on March of 1825, and compiled *The Columbian Harmony,* which was registered in Washington, D.C., the following month. A number of related melodies exist, including "Lord, revive us" (LBW 290) and "Pleading Savior" (LBW 243), and two Negro spirituals, "Weepin' Mary," and "Don't get weary." The harmonization was prepared by Charles Anders (LBW 386) for *Contemporary Worship–1,* 1969.

464   YOU ARE THE WAY
Tune: Dundee

Based on John 14:6, this hymn was written by George Washington Doane and published in his *Songs by the Way,* 1824. It was the only

American hymn to be included in the Original Edition of *Hymns Ancient and Modern,* 1861. Initially beginning *"Thou art* the way," the first stanza of the hymn has been rewritten.

Born May 27, 1799, in Trenton, New Jersey, Doane spent some of his childhood in New York City, and at the age of ten moved with his family to Geneva, New York. In 1818 he completed a Bachelor of Arts degree with high honors at Union College, Schenectady, New York, and after practicing law for two years, entered General Theological Seminary in New York City as one of its earliest students. Ordained a deacon in 1821 and a priest two years later, he served from 1821 to 1824 as assistant pastor of Trinity Church, New York City, and for four years thereafter as professor of rhetoric and belles-lettres at Trinity College, Hartford, Connecticut. He became assistant rector (and later rector) of Trinity Church in Boston in 1828, and in 1832, New Jersey's second bishop, taking residence in Burlington. The following year he also became rector of St. Mary's Church there. In 1837 he founded St. Mary's Hall for women, and in 1846, Burlington College for men. He died in Burlington on April 27, 1859.

Described as a man of great energy and personal warmth, Doane was also a very capable administrator. Hauessler* notes that during his years as bishop the number of the clergy in the diocese increased from 18 to 99; the number of parishes, from 30 to 84; and communing members, from 657 to over 5,000; with an increase in income from $400 to $50,000. One of the early American writers of hymns and supporters of hymn-singing as distinguished from psalmody, he published the first American reprint of John Keble's *Christian Year* in 1834. His collected works, published in 1860 by his son, filled four volumes.

DUNDEE is one of the twelve "common tunes" which were included in the 1615 Scottish Psalter, *The CL Psalms of David,* published by Andro Hart in Edinburgh. There it was called "French Tune" although no French source has so far been identified. In Thomas Ravenscroft's *Whole Booke of Psalmes,* 1621, a collection of tunes compiled for use with the Old Version in England, the tune was called "Dundy Tune," and set to Psalm 36. In Scotland the tune continued to be called "French," and another tune, known in England as "Windsor" (LBW 114), was called "Dundie," a situation which has resulted in some confusion.

465 EVENING AND MORNING
(Die güldne Sonne voll Freud und Wonne)
Tune: Die güldne Sonne

This hymn by Paul Gerhardt (LBW 23) was first published in the third set of Ebeling's *Pauli Gerhardi Geistliche Andachten,* 1666 (see below).

The first two stanzas given here are from a translation of stanzas 4 and 8–12 of the original hymn, prepared by Richard Massie (LBW 134) and contributed to William Mercer's (LBW 281) *The Church Psalter and Hymn Book,* 1857 edition. Stanzas 3 and 4 are from an English text beginning "The sun ascending, To us is lending," done by Herman Brueckner (LBW 249) in 1918 and included in the *American Lutheran Hymnal,* 1930.

DIE GÜLDNE SONNE was composed by Ebeling for this hymn and published together with it.

Johann Georg Ebeling, a prominent Lutheran musician of the seventeenth century, was born July 8, 1637, in Lüneburg, Germany. In 1662 he succeeded Johann Crüger (LBW 23) as director of music at St. Nicholas Church, and cantor and faculty member at the Greyfriars *Gymnasium* in Berlin. While in Berlin he came to know Paul Gerhardt, whose hymns he published in *Pauli Gerhardi Geistliche Andachten, bestehend in 120 Liedern mit 4 Singstimmen, 2 Violinen und General-bass,* 1666-1667. A second collection of hymns, *Evangelischer Lustgarten Herrn Pauli Gerhard's,* was published in 1669. In 1668 he became professor of Greek, poetry, and music, as well as cantor at the Caroline *Gymnasium* in Stettin, Pomerania, and remained in that city until his death on December 4, 1676.

The harmonization is from the *Württembergische Choralbuch,* 1953.

466 GREAT GOD, OUR SOURCE

Tune: Great God, Our Source

Suggested by the Cuban missile crisis, and the paradox of the atomic age, this hymn was written while the author, George Utech (LBW 152), was chaplain at Texas Lutheran College. It was included in *Contemporary Worship-1,* 1969.

GREAT GOD, OUR SOURCE was written for Utech's hymn and published with it in *Contemporary Worship-1.*

The composer, Gerhard M. Cartford, was born March 21, 1923, at Fort Dauphin, Madagascar. After serving in the United States Army from 1943 to 1946 he completed a Bachelor of Music degree at St. Olaf College in 1948, and a Master of Sacred Music degree at Union Theological Seminary. The following year was spent in Norway, where he studied folk music and hymnody under a Fulbright scholarship. His studies were continued at Luther Seminary, 1954-1955; St. John's University, Collegeville, Minnesota, 1955; and the University of Minnesota (Doctor of Philosophy, 1961). He served as choir director of Zion Lutheran Church, Staten Island, 1948-1950; organist and choir director at Grace Lutheran Church, Eau Claire, Wisconsin, 1951-1954; and director of music, Bethel Lutheran Church, Minneapolis, 1955-1960. At Luther College he was choir director from 1954 to 1958, and also served as assistant to Dr. H. Preus in liturgics from 1955, and as organist from 1956. From 1961 to 1974 he was a member of the music department of Texas Lutheran College, Seguin, Texas, where he was chairman of the department for eleven years. For three years thereafter he was assistant professor of liturgy, church music, and the arts at Luther-Northwestern Seminaries, St. Paul, Minnesota, since which time he has lived in South America, where he is assisting in the production of a Lutheran liturgy. He has also taught summer school at Concordia Seminary, St. Louis; the University of Minnesota; and at various summer church music institutes.

Cartford has published a number of choral and liturgical pieces, including a musical setting for the communion rite in *Contemporary Worship-2,* and has made original and editorial contributions to Setting 3 of the Holy Communion and to Evening Prayer in the LBW. For seven years he served as editor of *Response,* the journal of the Lutheran Society for Worship, Music and the Arts. He has contributed to two books— *Cantors at the Crossroads* (1967) and volume 22 of *Norwegian-American Studies* (1965)—and has written articles for the *Encyclopedia of the Lutheran Church* (edited by Julius Bodensiek, 1965) and various American and foreign periodicals. From 1967 to 1977 he served on the liturgical music committee of the Inter-Lutheran Commission on Worship, and was its chairman after 1975. He is a member of the Lutheran Society for Worship, Music and the Arts; Ecclesia cantans (an international church music society); the Norwegian-American Historical Association; and the American Musicological Society.

Married to Pauline F. Ferguson of Lowell, Massachusetts, he is the father of three children.

467   ETERNAL FATHER, STRONG TO SAVE
Tune: Melita

This hymn was submitted in 1860 for the Original Edition of *Hymns Ancient and Modern.* Originally the first stanza read:

> O Thou who bidd'st the ocean deep
> Its own appointed limits keep,
> Thou Who dost bind the restless wave,
> Eternal Father, strong to save;
> > O hear us when we cry to Thee
> > For all in peril on the sea.

The hymnal compilers revised the hymn, giving the first stanza its present form, and it was published the same year in the text edition of *Hymns Ancient and Modern.*

There is some uncertainty about the date of William Whiting's birth, although November 1, 1825, is the generally-accepted date. The son of a grocer, he was baptized January 22, 1826, at Kensington, England, and moved with his family in 1829 to Clapham, where he attended school. In 1841 he entered the Winchester Training Institute, and the following year, became master of the Winchester College Choristers' School, a position he held until his death on May 3, 1878. He was married to Fanny Lucas at Salisbury Cathedral in 1850. In addition to his position at the school he was active in civic and church affairs, and was appointed honorary secretary to the Winchester-Hursley branch of the English Church Union (an organization founded to further the cause of the Catholic wing in the Church of England). He published two collections of verse, *Rural Thoughts,* 1851, and *Edgar Thorpe, or the Warfare of Life,* 1867, and wrote several other hymns which were included in various collections. A biography of William Whiting with detailed information on the location and times in which he lived and worked has been published by Patricia Hooper (Southampton, 1978).

MELITA was written for this text by John B. Dykes (LBW 165) and first published in the original music edition of *Hymns Ancient and Modern,* 1861. "Melita" is the Roman name for the island of Malta where Paul was shipwrecked while traveling as a prisoner to Rome (Acts 28:1-2). The hymn and tune are used in Benjamin Britten's *Noyes Fludde.*

468 FROM GOD CAN NOTHING MOVE ME
(Von Gott will ich nicht lassen)

Tune: Von Gott will ich nicht lassen

Ludwig Helmbold, son of a woolen manufacturer, was born January 13, 1532, at Mühlhausen, Thuringia, in Germany. He attended the universities of Leipzig and Erfurt, receiving a Bachelor of Arts degree in 1550, and served for two years thereafter as headmaster of St. Mary's School in Mühlhausen. Returning to Erfurt, he completed his Master of Arts degree in 1554 and remained there as lecturer until his appointment in 1561 as associate rector of the St. Augustine *Gymnasium* in Erfurt. In 1563 a pestilence broke out in Erfurt, killing four thousand inhabitants. Those who were able left the city, including Pancratius and Regine Helbich, rector of the university and his wife, who were close friends of Helmbold and his wife. To console and strengthen the two women for the parting, Helmbold prepared this hymn, based on Psalm 73:23, and it was first printed as a broadsheet dedicated to Regine Helbich, godmother to the Helmbolds' oldest daughter. Later, in 1569, it was included in *Hundert Christenlich Haussgesang,* published in Nürnberg. When the university was reopened in 1565 after the plague, Helmbold was appointed dean of the philosophical faculty, and the following year was crowned a poet by the Emperor Maximilian II. His determined Protestantism forced him to resign in 1570, however, and he entered the parish ministry, serving first at St. Mary's Church in Mühlhausen, and beginning in 1586, at St. Blasius' Church and as superintendent of Mühlhausen. He died April 8, 1598.

Helmbold wrote four hundred hymns, both in Latin and German. Among his publications were his *Geistliche Lieder,* 1575, and *Neue Geistliche Lieder,* 1595.

The translation was prepared for the LBW by Gerald Thorson (LBW 161).

VON GOTT WILL ICH NICHT LASSEN is related to "Une jeune pucelle" at LBW 72. The earliest source of the melody is a French collection, *Recueil de plusieurs chansons divisé en trois parties,* Lyons, 1557, with the text "Une jeune fillette." Also found in Holland, the tune appeared in Germany in 1560 with the hunting song, "Einmal tät ich spazieren." Helmbold was the first to associate the tune with a sacred text when he used it with the present hymn in 1563, and it later appeared with his text in Joachim Magdeburg's (LBW 450) *Christliche und Tröstliche Tischgeseng,* Erfurt, 1572.

J. S. Bach (LBW 219) included an organ setting among his Eighteen Chorales, and used the tune in Cantata 73. The setting here is from the *Württemburgische Choralbuch,* 1953.

469 LORD OF ALL HOPEFULNESS

Tune: Slane

Daughter of Henry Torrens and Eva Anstruther, Joyce Torrens wrote under the pseudonym Jan Struther, which she derived from her mother's maiden name. Born in London on June 6, 1901, and educated privately, she was married in 1923 to Anthony Maxtone Graham. She began writing articles, short stories, and poems for periodicals at age sixteen, and her several volumes of poetry include *Betsinda Dances and Other Poems,* 1931; *Sycamore Square and Other Poems,* 1932; *Try Anything Twice,* 1938; and *The Glass-Blower,* 1941. Her best-known work is a novel, *Mrs. Miniver,* 1940, which describes life in an English middle class family before World War II. During the war she lived with her two children in New York City, where she was in much demand as a lecturer. In 1948 she was married to A. K. Placzek. Cancer cut her life short; she died July 20, 1953, in New York City.

Written for this tune, "Lord of all hopefulness" was one of twelve hymns contributed by Jan Struther to the enlarged edition of *Songs of Praise,* 1931.

SLANE is the name of a hill some ten miles from Tara, County Meath, in Ireland, where St. Patrick is said to have challenged King Loegaire by lighting the Easter Eve fire (see LBW 188). The tune was included in Patrick W. Joyce's *Old Irish Folk Music and Songs,* 1901, with the ancient ballad "With my love come on the road." It was used as a setting for the old Irish hymn, "Be thou my vision," in *The Church Hymnary,* 1927.

The harmonization was adapted by Carlton R. Young from that found in *Congregational Praise,* 1951.

Carlton Raymond Young, professor of church music at the Chandler School of Theology in Atlanta since 1978, was born April 25, 1926, in Hamilton, Ohio. After serving in the United States (Army) Air Force from 1944 to 1946, he received a Bachelor of Science degree in music education in 1950 from the University of Cincinnati College of Music. Further studies included a Bachelor of Sacred Theology degree, 1953, at Boston University School of Theology (where he was a church music major), a summer session in 1955 at Union Theological Seminary in New York City, and a research leave in 1970, during which he studied hymnology and choral literature in Vienna and Prague. Ordained an elder of the Methodist Church in 1953, he was minister of music at the Church of the Saviour, Cleveland Heights, Ohio, 1953–1956, and at Trinity Methodist Church, Youngstown, Ohio, 1956–1959. From 1959 to 1964 he was editor and director of music publications at Abingdon Press, after which he became associate professor, and in 1970, professor, of church music at Perkins School of Theology and School of the Arts, Southern Methodist University, Dallas, Texas. He also served as director of music at Casa View Church, Dallas, from 1971 to 1974. In 1975 he became professor of church music and director of the Master of Arts program of study in church music education at Scarritt College, Nashville, Tennessee, and since 1971, has been editorial consultant with Hope Publishing Company.

Young has written numerous articles on Christian education, worship, and hymnody, and is the composer of some one hundred choral works. He was editor of *The Methodist Hymnal,* 1966; a co-author of the *Companion to the Hymnal,* 1970; and executive editor of *Ecumenical Praise,* 1977. In 1969 Ohio Northern University honored him with a Doctor of Music degree.

Married to Marjorie Lindner, he is the father of four children.

470 PRAISE AND THANKS AND ADORATION
(Lov og Tak og evig Aere)
Tune: Freu dich sehr

See LBW 102 for Thomas Hansen Kingo. This hymn first appeared in *En Ny Kirke-Psalmebog*, 1689, and was altered for the *Kirke Psalmebog*, 1699. The translation was prepared for the LBW by the Inter-Lutheran Commission on Worship.

FREU DICH SEHR is given at LBW 29. This harmonization by J. S. Bach (LBW 219) is the closing chorale of Cantata 32, "Liebster Jesu, mein Verlangen."

471 GRANT PEACE, WE PRAY, IN MERCY, LORD
(Verleih uns Frieden gnädiglich)
Tune: Verleih uns Frieden

The Latin antiphon, "Da pacem, Domine," based on 2 Kings 20:19; 2 Chronicles 20:12, 15; and Psalm 122:7, dates from the sixth or seventh century. In 1279 Pope Nicholas III ordered it sung at every mass before the "Agnus Dei." Martin Luther (LBW 48) prepared a German prose version in 1527, and it is believed that the hymn version came in 1528 in response to the threat of the Turks who terrified all Christendom by moving unhindered as close as Vienna. Luther called on young and old to overcome the enemy with prayer. The verse form is presumed to have been included in Joseph Klug's *Geistliche Lieder*, 1529 (LBW 85). In many regions of Germany this hymn was sung immediately after the sermon, either separately, or appended to "Lord, keep us steadfast in your word" (LBW 230).
The English translation is from *Laudamus*, 1952, the hymnal of the Lutheran World Federation.

VERLEIH UNS FRIEDEN in its opening line resembles the traditional plainchant melody for "Da pacem, Domine." The rest of the tune more strongly recalls "Erhalt uns Herr" (LBW 230) and "Nun komm, der Heiden Heiland" (LBW 28). It was first published in Jobst Gutknecht's *Kirchen gesenge*, Nürnberg, 1531. The harmonization is by Carl Schalk (LBW 118).

472 COME, HOLY GHOST, OUR SOULS INSPIRE
(Veni, Creator Spiritus)
Tune: Veni, Creator Spiritus

The author of this well-known and important Latin hymn is not known with certainty. Among those credited with possible authorship are Charlemagne, Ambrose (LBW 28), Gregory the Great (LBW 101), and Rhabanus Maurus. The great theologian and scholar, Rhabanus Maurus, is most widely accepted as the possible writer. Born of a noble family at Mainz, Germany, in 776, Rhabanus was educated at Fulda, after which he entered the Benedictine order. He was ordained a deacon in 801 and went to Tours to study under Alciun, who gave him the surname Maurus, after St. Maur, a disciple of Benedict. In 803 he was appointed head of the school at Fulda, which became famous because of his teaching. Ordained a priest in 814, he became abbot of Fulda in 822. Twenty years later he resigned and retired to the cloister of St. Peter to devote himself to literature. He was archbishop of Mainz from 847 until his death at Winkel on the Rhine, February 4, 856. Among his voluminous writings are a Latin-German glossary on the Bible, *De Universo Libri XXII,* and commentaries on the Old and New Testaments, as well as a number of poems.

The earliest use of the hymn was at Vespers during the week of Pentecost, and it came also to be used at Terce (9 a.m.—the hour which the Apostles received the Holy Ghost—Acts 2:15) in the late tenth century. In addition, it has been used through the centuries on any special occasion when invocation of the Holy Spirit was appropriate, especially at ordinations. The earliest mention of the hymn is of its use in 1049 at the Synod of Rheims. In 1307 is was included with the English coronation rite in the *Liber Regalis,* and has been used continuously at English coronation ceremonies ever since. Martin Luther (LBW 48) included a translation, "Komm, Gott Schöpfer, heiliger Geist," in the Erfurt *Enchiridia,* 1524, and an English translation was included in the 1549 *Book of Common Prayer,* where it was the only hymn specifically prescribed.

John Cosin's paraphrase was included in *A Collection of Private Devotions in the Practice of the Ancient Church, Called the Hours of Prayer,* 1627. Based on the primers (prayer books) which were widely used at the time, *A Collection* was simple enough for ordinary people to understand and parts of it were used in teaching children to read. (The *New England Primer,* Cambridge, 1540, was an American descendant.) The translation was also included in the 1662 publication of the *Book of Common Prayer* with which John Cosin assisted in the final revision.

Cosin, an Anglican clergyman, was born at Norwich, England, November 30, 1594, and graduated from Caius College, Cambridge. Following his ordination he was appointed prebendary at Durham in 1624 and archdeacon of East Riding, Yorkshire, the following year. He became master of Peterhouse, Cambridge, in 1634, and vice-chancellor of the university in 1640. Two years later he was deprived of all his appointments by the Puritans and fled to France, where he was chaplain to the exiled members of the royal family. With the restoration of Charles II in 1660 he returned to England and became dean and later bishop of Durham. He died at Westminster, January 15, 1672.

VENI, CREATOR SPIRITUS originally served as the setting for the Ambrosian Easter hymn, "Hic est diesverus Dei," but has been associated with "Veni, Creator Spiritus" since it came into existence. The form of the tune found here is the Mechlin version from the *Vesperale Romanum,* published in 1848 at Malines, Belgium. The harmonization is by Healy Willan (LBW 125).

473 COME, HOLY GHOST, OUR SOULS INSPIRE
(Veni, Creator Spiritus)
Tune: Komm, Gott Schöpfer

This text is the same as LBW 472.

For KOMM, GOTT SCHÖPFER see LBW 284. The harmonization found here is from the *Orgelchoralbuch,* 1952.

474 CHILDREN OF THE HEAVENLY FATHER
(Tryggare kan ingen vara)
Tune: Tryggare kan ingen vara

Karolina Wilhelmina Sandell, a pastor's daughter, was born October 3, 1832, at Fröderyd, Småland. When she was twelve years old she was stricken with a paralysis and, although she was declared incurable by physicians, later recovered her health. When she was twenty-six her father fell from a boat on a trip from Jönköping to Gothenburg, and drowned before her eyes. In the fall of 1860 her mother also died. The next year she joined the editorial staff of the Evangelical National Foundation where she came to know Carl Rosenius (LBW 371) and was frequently a guest in his home. In 1867 she was married to C. O. Berg, a temperance man and wealthy Stockholm merchant, and became an assistant to him with his literary work. She died July 26, 1903.

Lina Sandell began writing hymns at an early age. The present text was written while she was still in her teens and appeared in her *Andeliga daggdroppar* in 1855. The Evangelical National Foundation's *Sionstoner,* with which she assisted, contained 126 of her originals or translations. Her collected works, published between 1882 and 1892, contain 650 poems.

The translation, by Ernst William Olson, was published in *The Hymnal,* 1925, of the Augustana Synod.

Olson, born in Finja parish, Skåne, Sweden, on March 16, 1870, emigrated to the United States with his parents when he was five years old. The family first settled on the prairie near Wahoo, Nebraska, and later moved to Texas. In 1891 he graduated from Augustana College, Rock Island, Illinois, and for the next seven years served as editor of various Swedish weekly publications. From 1906 to 1911 he was office editor for the Engberg-Holmberg Publishing Company in Chicago, and thereafter held a similar position with the Augustana Book Concern until his retirement in 1949. He died October 6, 1958.

Well-known for his abilities as a writer and poet, both in English and Swedish, Olson was awarded a prize in 1922 for Swedish poetry, and in 1926 was honored with a doctorate from Augustana College. Among his several works was *A History of the Swedes in Illinois,* 1908. He was on the committees for *The Hymnal,* 1925 (which included four original hymns and twenty-eight translations by him), and the *Service Book and Hymnal,* 1958. He was also one of the board of editors of the Augustana Historical Society.

TRYGGARE KAN INGEN VARA. Lina Sandell did not use this melody originally. The hymn was first associated with this tune in Fredrik Engelke's *Lofsånger och andeliga wisor,* 1873.

Sources differ on the origins of this tune. The Methodist Hymnal *Companion** quotes Gerald Göransson, director of the Royal School of Music in Stockholm, who believes that it may have originated in England and come to Sweden in the pietistic revivalism which flourished during the second half of the nineteenth century, and which brought many English gospel song tunes to Sweden. Åke Lilliestam of the Swedish national library feels that the tune "goes back to an old Scandinavian, probably Swedish folk song; there are several tunes of a closely related character." Lövgren* calls it a Swedish folksong discovered by Engelke, which has German origins. He quotes three related songs:

1) "Und wir sitzen so fröhlich," a German song lampooning Napolean

I, which was sung around 1812-1813. Quoted in *Hessische Blätter für Volkskunde,* 1910.

2) "Es kann ja nicht immer so bleiben," a German soldier's song from 1813, and the War of 1870. Quoted in Ludwig Erk and Franz M. Böhme, *Deutscher Liederhort,* II, 1893.

3) "En vacker huster hette Tora," a Swedish song of the early 1800s, of which the text is apparently an addition to an earlier song.

With so many variants in at least two countries at the beginning of the nineteenth century, it seems very possible that the tune has antecedents in the 1700s, which perhaps remain to be discovered.

475 COME, GRACIOUS SPIRIT, HEAVENLY DOVE
Tune: Wareham

This hymn was first included in Simon Browne's *Hymns and Spiritual Songs,* book I, 1720. Originally beginning "Come, Holy Spirit, Heavenly Dove, My sinful maladies remove," it has undergone frequent and considerable alterations, which are fully discussed in Julian.* The form found in the LBW represents selections from the original and from the version in the 1769 *Bristol Collection* published by Ash and Evans. Stanza 4 is from William Mercer's (LBW 281) *The Church Psalter and Hymn Book,* 1864.

Browne was born around 1680 at Shepton Mallett, Somersetshire, England. He studied for the Independent Ministry at the academy at Bridgewater, and served an Independent congregation in Portsmouth until 1716 when he became pastor of the Independent Chapel in Old Jewry, London. In London he lived as a near neighbor to Isaac Watts (LBW 39). On one occasion Browne was attacked by a highwayman, and in the struggle that followed, accidentally killed his assailant. This incident was followed by the death of his wife and, shortly thereafter, of his son. These misfortunes no doubt had a bearing on the depression—accompanied by the delusions that he had lost all his mental faculties and was forgotten by God—which he suffered later in life. In spite of this burden, he retired to Shepton Mallet where he continued to work, translating classical authors, compiling a dictionary, and writing books for children and hymns. A volume of sermons was published in 1722, and his Exposition of the First Epistle to the Corinthians was included in Matthew Henry's *Commentary on the Old and New Testament,* 1710. He died at Shepton Mallet in 1732.

For WAREHAM see LBW 433.

476 HAVE NO FEAR, LITTLE FLOCK
Tune: Little Flock

Marjorie Ann Jillson was born in Detroit, Michigan, on October 29, 1931, and completed a Bachelor of Arts degree in religion in 1953 at the College of Wooster, Wooster, Ohio. For some time she was employed by the United States government at Gallaudet College, a liberal arts college for the deaf in Washington, D.C., and since 1973 she has been working as a dental secretary in Detroit. A member of Grosse Pointe Memorial

Church (United Presbyterian), she has written the texts for *Three Simple Melodies,* 1972, and *Five Hymns,* 1973, both collections set to music by Heinz Werner Zimmermann.

Jillson's first stanza, based on Luke 12:32, was set to music by Zimmermann in 1971. The author was requested to write three more stanzas, and the work was included in *Five Hymns,* St. Louis, 1973. The two-stave version of the music was prepared by William J. Reynolds when the hymn was included in the *Baptist Hymnal,* 1975.

Born August 11, 1930, in Freiburg, Germany, Zimmermann studied composition with Julius Weismann from 1946 to 1948. He continued his education at the Heidelberg School of Sacred Music where he studied composition with Wolfgang Fortner from 1950 to 1954, and at Heidelberg University, where he studied musicology with Thrasyboulos Georgiades. He received a state diploma for composition and music theory at the State Music Academy in Freiburg. From 1954 to 1963 he taught music theory and composition at the Heidelberg School of Sacred Music. Thereafter he served as director of the Berlin School of Sacred Music in West Berlin (Johannesstift Spandau) until 1975 when he was appointed full professor of composition and music theory at the State Music Academy in Frankfurt am Main. During the years that he was at the Berlin School of Sacred Music he also made two lecture tours of the United States; taught at Wittenberg University, Springfield, Ohio, for one term on a Fulbright grant; and lectured for a summer term at New College, Oxford University, in England. Since his first composition appeared in print in 1957, he has published a large number of works, especially choral works, with a variety of instrumental accompaniments. He has received a number of composition prizes and commissions, and was honored with a Doctor of Music degree from Wittenberg University in Springfield in 1967. His article, "Word and Tone in Modern Hymnody," appeared in the May, 1971, issue of the *Diapason.*

William Jensen Reynolds was born April 2, 1920, in Atlantic, Iowa. Five months later the family moved to Oklahoma, where his father was a church music director and evangelistic singer. He received his education at Oklahoma Baptist University, Southwest Missouri State College (Bachelor of Arts, 1942), Southwestern Baptist Theological Seminary (Master of Sacred Music, 1945), North Texas State College (Master of Music, 1946), Westminster Choir College, and George Peabody College for Teachers (Doctor of Education, 1961), serving for seven years as a part-time church musician during his student days. After serving as minister of music at First Baptist Church, Ardmore, Oklahoma (1946-1947) and First Baptist Church, Oklahoma City, Oklahoma, (1947-1955), he joined the church music department of the Baptist Sunday School Board in Nashville, Tennessee, working in various editorial capacities. In 1971 he became head of the department.

Reynolds is the author of *A Survey of Christian Hymnody* (1963), *Hymns of Our Faith* (1964), *Christ and the Carols* (1967), *Congregational Singing* (1975), and the *Companion to the Baptist Hymnal* (1976). He was a member of the hymnal committee for the *Baptist Hymnal,* 1956, and chairman of the hymnal committee and general editor for the *Baptist Hymnal,* 1975, and has served as president of the Hymn Society of America. He is a composer and arranger of sacred choral music and has published a wide variety of materials. He has served as music director for meetings of the Southern Baptist Convention, the Baptist World Alliance, and the Baptist Youth World Conference.

Tune: St. Peter

Originally beginning "O God of *Bethel*, by whose hand," this hymn was written by Philip Doddridge (LBW 35) to follow his sermon, preached on January 16, 1737, on "Jacob's Vow." When he included it in his *Hymns Founded on Various Texts in the Holy Scriptures*, 1755, he changed the opening line to "O God of *Jacob*, by whose hand." The present form of the hymn is based on a revision included in the Scottish *Translations and Paraphrases*, 1781. Julian* gives a complete discussion of the various versions of the hymn.

For ST. PETER see LBW 345.

478   COME, OH, COME, O QUICKENING SPIRIT
(Komm, O komm, du Geist des Lebens)

Tune: Komm, O komm, du Geist des Lebens

This hymn by Heinrich Held was first printed in Johann Niedling's *Neuerfundener geistlicher Wasserquelle*, published in Frankfurt an der Oder, 1658. A translation prepared by Charles Schaeffer (LBW 455) in 1866 was published in the Pennsylvania Synod *Church Book* two years later, and included in nearly all major United States Lutheran hymnals after that time. The present translation by Edward Traill Horn III was prepared for the *Service Book and Hymnal*, 1958.

Held, one of the best of the Silesian hymnwriters, came from a prestigious family in Guhrau. Born July 21, 1620, he went to school in Guhrau until the plague struck the town and his father sent him to Glogau for safety. In 1628 he moved with his parents to Fraustadt, then a part of Poland, to escape Roman Catholic persecutions. There he learned Polish and studied music. In 1637 he entered the *Gymnasium* at Thorn, where his poetic inclination blossomed. After studying law for two years at Königsberg, he worked as a tutor in East Prussia until his father's death, at which time he returned to Fraustadt. In 1642 he entered the University of Frankfurt an der Oder, where he published his only extant collection of poems, *Deutscher Gedichte Vortrab*, in 1643. For four years thereafter he lived in Stettin with a relative, the Pomeranian chief judge, to practice law. He continued to read law at Rostock, where he also studied and lectured in poetry under a subsidy from Queen Christine of Sweden. After serving once more as a tutor in East Prussia he traveled to Holland, England, and France under financial assistance from Duke Gustav Adolph of Mechlenberg. Finally he settled in Fraustadt to practice law, but the political upheavals of the Thirty Years' War forced him to leave, and he returned to Stettin to live with his relatives. In Altdamm, a suburb of Stettin, he became city clerk in 1657 and chamberlain and councillor in 1658. The following year Altdamm was besieged. Held fell ill and was taken to Stettin where he died August 16, 1659.

Edward Traill Horn III (grandson of E. T. Horn, one of the chief architects of the Common Service of 1888) was born in Philadelphia on July 4, 1909. Early education was in the public schools of New York City and Ithaca, New York, after which he remained in Ithaca to complete a Bachelor of Arts degree from Cornell University. Graduate study in the fields of economics and sociology was pursued at Cornell University from 1930 to 1931, and at the University of Pennsylvania from 1944 to 1948. In the interim he attended the Lutheran Theological Seminary at Philadelphia and was ordained in 1934, in which year also he was married to Sophie W. Oldach of Hilton, New York. For nine years after his ordination he served as Lutheran university chaplain at Cornell University, where he also served as acting chaplain from 1932 to 1934 and from 1943 to 1944. In 1943 he became assistant professor of preaching and church administration, and director of field work at the Lutheran Theological Seminary at Philadelphia. He served as pastor of Trinity Lutheran Church, Germantown, in Philadelphia from 1945 until his retirement in 1977.

The list of committees, commissions, and so on, on which Horn has served is extensive. He has served as a trustee of the Philadelphia Seminary, Muhlenberg College, and Gettysburg Seminary. He was a member of the *Common Service Book* committee from 1939 to 1952 (chairman from 1950 to 1952) and from 1945 to 1958 was on the commission which prepared the *Service Book and Hymnal.* He was a member of the Inter-Lutheran Commission on Worship until 1972. He has also served on numerous committees on worship, liturgy, the sacrament of the altar, confirmation, worship and arts, etc. From 1955 to 1965 he served on the National Council of Churches. Lectureships include: Swope Lecturer at Gettysburg Seminary; Reu Lecturer, Wartburg Seminary; visiting lecturer, Union Theological Seminary School of Sacred Music, 1955–1969; and visiting lecturer in Finland, England, and Germany for the Lutheran World Federation, 1961. He has preached at many colleges, universities, and seminaries. Publications include *Altar and Pew,* 1951; *The Christian Year,* 1956; and *The Church at Worship,* 1957, as well as articles in church publications.

KOMM, O KOMM, DU GEIST DES LEBENS. Dated 1680 in Conrad Kocher's (LBW 82) *Zionsharfe,* this tune has sometimes been attributed to Johann Christoph Bach. It was included in the *Neu-vermehrts und zu Übung Christliche Gottseligkeit eingerichtetes Meiningisches Gesangbuch,* 1693 (Zahn* #3651), set to J. C. Werner's "Ich begehr nicht mehr zu leben." There it had the form given below.

In the *Geistreiches Gesang Buch,* 1698, it was associated with the present hymn.

479 MY FAITH LOOKS UP TO THEE

Tune: Olivet

Written in 1830, this hymn was published in 1831 in Thomas Hastings' (LBW 327) and Lowell Mason's *Spiritual Songs for Social Worship,* Utica, New York.

Ray Palmer, son of a Rhode Island judge, was born at Little Compton, Rhode Island, on November 12, 1808. He went to Boston where he worked for some time as a store clerk before going to Phillips Academy. In 1830 he graduated from Yale and became, in 1835, pastor of Central Congregational Church, Bath, Maine, where he served until he was appointed pastor of First Congregational Church in Albany in 1850. From 1865 until his retirement in 1878 he was corresponding secretary to the American Congregational Union. He died March 29, 1887, in Newark, New Jersey. His publications include: *Spiritual Improvement,* 1839; *What is Truth?,* 1860; *Remember Me, or The Holy Communion,* 1865; *Hymns and Sacred Pieces, with Miscellaneous Poems,* 1865; *Hymns of my Holy Hours, and Other Pieces,* 1868; *Home, or the Unlost Paradise,* 1873; and *Voices of Hope and Gladness,* 1881.

OLIVET, Lowell Mason's (LBW 353) familiar setting of Palmer's first hymn, appeared in three parts in *Spiritual Songs for Social Worship,* 1831. The opening phrases of the earliest form of the tune read as given below.

Mason later altered the phrase to what it is today.

480 OH, THAT THE LORD WOULD GUIDE MY WAYS
Tune: Evan

Based on Psalm 119, this tune was included in Isaac Watts's (LBW 39) *Psalms of David Imitated,* 1719.

EVAN. See LBW 406 for William Henry Havergal. This tune, originally published in 1847 as a setting of Robert Burns's poem, "O Thou dread power, who reign'st above," was arranged for Lowell Mason's (LBW 353) *New Carmina Sacra,* 1850, where it was called "Eva," and set to "In mercy, Lord, remember me." Havergal considered that form a "sad estrangement" of the original tune and reconstructed it himself, giving us the present form of the tune.

481 SAVIOR, LIKE A SHEPHERD LEAD US
Tune: Her vil ties

Dorothy Ann Thrupp, daughter of an Anglican clergyman and hymnwriter, wrote a number of hymns which were included in various collections. Born in London, June 26, 1779, she died there December 14, 1847.

"Savior, like a shepherd lead us" was given anonymously in her *Hymns for the Young,* fourth edition, 1836. It was later attributed to "Lyte" (LBW 272) and to a "D. A. T." in various hymnals, but the authorship really is not known.

HER VIL TIES, called "Our Lady, Trondhjem" in the *Service Book and Hymnal,* 1958, was written in 1860 for Hans Brorson's (LBW 52)

501

"Her vil ties, her vil bies," and was first published in Lindeman's *Koralbog* of 1871. It has also been associated with Nicolai Grundtvig's (LBW 62) "Påskemorgen slukker sorgen." See LBW 285 for Ludvig Lindeman.

482 WHEN I SURVEY THE WONDROUS CROSS
Tune: Rockingham Old

Based on Galatians 6:14, this hymn first appeared in Isaac Watts's (LBW 39) *Hymns and Spiritual Songs,* 1707.

ROCKINGHAM OLD was named for the Marquis of Rockingham who was twice prime minister of Great Britain and Edward Miller's friend and patron. When included in Miller's *The Psalms of David for the use of Parish Churches,* 1790, the tune was marked "Part of the melody taken from a hymn tune." The hymn tune from which it was taken remained unidentified for over a century. In the May, 1909, issue of the *Musical Times* the original melody was identified as "Tunbridge" which appeared as given below.

This anonymous tune was a setting for Charles Wesley's (LBW 27) "All ye that pass by" in Aaron Williams' (LBW 368) *A Second Supplement to Psalmody in Miniature, c.* 1780. In the copy of that collection owned by Miller is a notation in his own hand that it would make a good long meter tune. Called "Rockingham," it was set to the present text in William Mercer's (LBW 281) *The Church Psalter and Hymn Book,* 1854.

Born in Norwich, England, in 1731, Edward Miller was apprenticed to his father's profession, that of a paver, but ran away and studied music with Dr. Charles Burney at Lynn, and at one time played flute in George

Frideric Handel's (LBW 39) orchestra. From 1756 to 1807 he was organist of Doncaster Parish Church. In addition to *The Psalms of David* mentioned above, he also published *The Psalms of David Set to new Music*, 1774; *Thoughts on the Present Performance of Psalmody*, 1791; *The Psalms of Watts and Wesley*, 1801; *Sacred Music*, 1802; and *Elements of Thorough-bass and Composition*, 1787. *Psalms of David*, 1790, was a very popular collection, acknowledged by a gift of £25 from King George II. At Ramsey, in the Isle of Man, a large barrel organ was erected in the church to play a number of Miller's tunes. In 1786 he received a Doctor of Music degree from Cambridge. In addition to hymn tunes, he wrote a number of other smaller works, including six sonatas for harpsichord. He died September 12, 1807.

483   GOD MOVES IN A MYSTERIOUS WAY

Tune: Bangor

Written in 1773, this hymn was first published in John Newton's (LBW 261) *Twenty-six Letters on Religious Subjects; to which are added Hymns*, London, 1774.

William Cowper was born November 15, 1731, at Berkhampstead, Hertfordshire, England. His father was rector of Great Berkhampstead and a chaplain to George II. His mother, to whom he was closely attached, died when he was six years old. Following his education at Westminster, he was apprenticed to an attorney at age eighteen and called to the Bar in 1754. From 1759 to 1763 he was commissioner of bankrupts. When he was offered a position as clerk to the journals of the House of Lords, his dread of appearing before the House for the examination worsened a depression he had experienced since his school days, and he attempted suicide. After some time at a hospital at St. Albans, he went to Huntingdon where he was near his brother John who was at Cambridge. There he became lifelong friends with the Reverend Morely Unwin and his family. He chanced to meet John Newton when Unwin died in 1767 and Newton came to give his condolences. Cowper and Mrs. Unwin moved to Olney where Newton had a curacy, and there Cowper worked as a lay assistant, visiting the parishioners; and there, with Newton, he wrote the *Olney Hymns*. His depression returned, however, and Cowper became convinced that God had commanded him to kill himself, and that by failing to do so he had incurred God's wrath. In 1794 he was granted an annual pension of £300, and the following year, moved with Mrs. Unwin, who was by then a helpless invalid, to East Dereham. During the last twenty years of his life Cowper wrote a good bit of poetry, with his greatest work, *The Task*, coming from a brighter period afforded by his fascination with Lady Austin's wit and written at her instigation. He died April 25, 1800.

BANGOR was included in William Tans'ur's *A Compleat Melody or Harmony of Zion*, London, 1734, as the setting for Psalm 11, "In God the Lord I put my trust." A popular Scottish psalm tune, it was mentioned by Robert Burns in his poem, "The Ordination":

> Mak haste an' turn king David owre,
>   An' lilt wi' holy clangor;
> O' double verse come gie us four,
>   An' skirl up the Bangor.

This tune was included in most late eighteenth-century and early nineteenth-century American collections of psalm and hymn tunes. Osborne* relates a story in which the Reverend Seth Noble went to Boston in 1791 to arrange for the village of Sunbury, Maine, to be incorporated as a town. Waiting for the clerk to fill out the necessary papers, Noble was humming this tune. When the clerk unexpectedly asked him the name, he replied "Bangor," and thus the town was called Bangor.

Little is known of Tans'ur's life. Born in Dunchurch, Warwickshire, England, he was baptized November 6, 1706. His parents were German, with the name Tanzer, and it was William who changed his name to the present spelling. The son of a laborer, he became an itinerant musician, going from town to town teaching music and psalmody, playing the organ, and collecting materials for his books of psalm tunes and anthems. Eventually he settled in St. Neots as a bookseller and music teacher. There he died October 7, 1783.

A Compleat Melody went through numerous editions, becoming the *Royal Melody Compleat* in 1755. Tans'ur also published a *New Musical Grammar,* 1746, renamed *Elements of Musick Displayed* in 1772 and reprinted as late as 1826. His theoretical works show more than the usual skill for his day, and were an early influence on William Billings (LBW 426).

484 GOD, MY LORD, MY STRENGTH
(Pán Bůh jest má sila i doufání)
Tune: Pán Bůh

This anonymous hymn was included in the "Tranoscius," 1636 (LBW 96). The tune, PÁN BŮH, first appeared in the Prague *Gradual* of 1567. Jaroslav Vajda (LBW 159), translator of the text, notes that the melody "has a stirring Reformation quality with typical Slavic progressions, well-suited to a text of Christian trust." Theodore Beck (LBW 33) prepared the harmonization for the *Worship Supplement,* 1969, to *The Lutheran Hymnal.*

485 LORD, AS A PILGRIM *(Oi Herra, jos mä matkamies maan)*
Tune: Oi Herra, jos mä matkamies maan

Wilhelmi Malmivaara, a provost and leader of the pietistic movement in Ostrobothnia in northern Finland, came from a family of leading Lutheran pastors. His father, Miilo Kustaa Malmberg (the name was later changed to the Finnish form), became one of the greatest preachers of Finnish church history. Wilhelmi's son became bishop of Oulu, and several other members of the family still are also clergymen. Wilhelmi, in addition to succeeding his father as pastor of the Lapua parish, also founded a publishing house, edited a monthly religious journal, wrote devotional books and hymns, served as a member of the legislature, and helped to establish folk high schools for rural youth. In 1918 the Church Assembly established a committee under the chairmanship of Malmivaara to prepare a supplement to the 1886 hymnal. When the proposed supplement appeared five years later, however, it was rejected because of a strong desire for a thorough revision of the 1886 hymnal.

Work on the new hymnal began in 1928, and the resulting 1938 Finnish hymnal contained a number of Malmivaara's hymns and translations. Born at Lapua on February 13, 1854, he died January 12, 1922, in Helsinki.

First published in 1903, this poignant hymn was written after the author had lost two children and his wife within the space of a few weeks. Malmivaara's expression of his struggles and Christian hope struck a responsive note among the Finns during the Russo-Finnish conflict of the second World War, when this hymn could be heard in every corner of the land.

The English text is by Gilbert E. Doan (LBW 99).

OI HERRA, JOS MÄ MATKAMIES MAAN. Berndt Mikael Nyberg, Swedish-Finnish Lutheran composer and teacher, was born February 7, 1871, in Helsinki. He was a music teacher at Rauma (1896–1898) and Sordavala (1898–1920) teachers' colleges, and for the last twenty years of his life was principal of the Christian folk high school in Jamilahti in eastern Finland. His works, which number about two hundred, were chiefly sacred compositions—cantatas, choral and solo pieces, and chorale preludes to be used with Richard Faltin's chorale book (1888; rev. ed., 1903). He also published some textbooks on music pedagogy. With Ilmari Krohn he traveled in central and southwest Finland, while they were yet students, and collected sacred folk tunes. He also made several journeys alone, and in all, collected some 572 sacred and secular folk tunes. His foremost work was assisting as translator and member of the music committee for *Andeliga Sånger och Psalmer,* 1900 and 1903, a Swedish-language hymnal published by The Finnish Missionary Society in Helsinki. He composed the present tune, "Oi Herra, jos mä matkamies maan," for this text in the enlarged edition, 1920, of *Andeliga Sånger.* (Two years later, *Andeliga Sånger,* containing exactly the same hymns and melodies, was published in Finnish as *Hengellisiä Lauluja,* and the resulting bilingual hymnal was the most widely-used "unofficial" hymnal in Finland.) Nyberg also contributed a number of tunes to Krohn's *Suomen Kansan Sävelmiä I Hengellisiä Sävelmiä,* 1898, a collection of religious folk melodies and German chorale tunes and their variants. He died January 19, 1940, in Äänekoski.

Walter Pelz (LBW 240) prepared the harmonization for the LBW.

486 SPIRIT OF GOD, DESCEND UPON MY HEART

Tune: Morecambe

This is one of four hymns by George Croly included in Charles Rogers' *Lyra Britannica,* 1867.

Croly, born August 17, 1780, in Dublin, Ireland, received a Master of Arts degree from the University of Dublin in 1804. The same university conferred a Doctor of Laws degree on him in 1831. He was ordained to the Church of Ireland, and ministered in Ireland until 1810, when he went to London. There he devoted himself very successfully to literature, writing in many forms—drama, poetry, novels, satires, and others. He was a strong conservative both in religion and in politics. After 1835 he returned to the ministry, serving a united parish of St. Bene't, Sherehob, and St. Stephen's, Walbrook, where his bold preaching drew large congregations. In 1854 he published *Psalms and Hymns for Public Worship,* a collection which included a number of his own hymns. He died suddenly while walking down a street in Holborn, England, November 24, 1860.

MORECAMBE, written in 1870 for "Abide with me" (LBW 272), was first printed in a leaflet and titled "Hellespont." It is named for Morecambe, a well-known watering place on Morecambe Bay, West England, not far from Bradford where the composer, Frederick Cook Atkinson, served as organist at the time the tune was written. In 1887 it was published in G. S. Barrett's and E. J. Hopkins' (LBW 262) *Congregational Church Hymnal,* London.

Born August 21, 1841, at Norwich, England, Atkinson was chorister and assistant organist from 1849 to 1860 at the Norwich Cathedral. There he studied under Dr. Zechariah Buck. He received a Bachelor of Music degree from Cambridge in 1867, after which he served as organist and choirmaster at St. Luke's Church, Manningham, Bradford, and from 1881 to 1885, of Norwich Cathedral. His final post was at St. Mary's Parish Church, Lewsham. His compositions included a number of services, anthems, and hymn tunes, as well as songs and piano pieces. He died at East Dereham, November 30, 1896.

487 LET US EVER WALK WITH JESUS *(Lasset uns mit Jesu ziehen)*
Tune: Lasset uns mit Jesu ziehen

Based on Luke 18:31–43 and intended for Passiontide, this hymn was first published in *Heilige Karwochen,* Nürnberg, 1653. See LBW 115 for Sigismund von Birken. The English text was prepared for the LBW by the Inter-Lutheran Commission on Worship.

LASSET UNS MIT JESU ZIEHEN (Zahn* #7916) was composed in 1788 by Georg Gottfried Boltze for Paul Gerhardt's (LBW 23) hymn of thanksgiving, "Sollt ich meinem Gott nicht singen," and was included in Johann Kühnau's *Vierstimmige alte und neue Choralgesänge,* 1790.

Little is known of Boltze's life except that he was cantor and school teacher at the orphanage in Potsdam in 1750, and was still living in 1789.

Harmonization of the tune is by Frederick Jackisch (LBW 236).

488 BREATHE ON ME, BREATH OF GOD
Tune: Durham

First published in a pamphlet entitled *Between Doubt and Prayer,* printed privately in 1878, this hymn was included in Henry Allon's *Congregational Psalmist Hymnal,* 1886, and published posthumously in Hatch's *Towards Fields of Light,* 1890.

Edwin Hatch was born at Derby, England, on September 4, 1835. He was brought up a Nonconformist, but in 1853 he joined the Church of England and attended Pembroke College, Oxford, where he received a Bachelor of Arts degree with honors in 1857. He took holy orders in 1859 and ministered in the East End of London for three years before coming to Canada where he was professor of classics at Trinity College, Toronto. Returning to England in 1867, he became vice-principal of St.

Mary Hall, Oxford. He became Bampton and Grinfield lecturer in 1880, university reader in ecclesiastical history in 1885, and rector of Purleigh, Essex, and Hibbert lecturer in 1888. He was awarded an honorary Doctor of Divinity degree in Edinburgh in 1883, and died six years later on November 10.

Hatch has been described as a thorough scholar and a man of great originality and force of character, who won a great reputation on the Continent as well as in England.

DURHAM, which has also been called "Dover" and "Hampton," comes from *Psalmody in Miniature,* a collection edited by Aaron Williams (LBW 368) and published about 1770. In the *Common Service Book,* 1917, the harmonization is attributed to Henry Gauntlett.

The son of the curate at Wellington, Shropshire, England, Henry John Gauntlett was born July 9, 1805. Although he spent thirteen years as a lawyer because his father had decided he would enter that profession, his first love was music. From age nine he had been organist at his father's church at Olney, Buckinghamshire, and from 1819 to 1825 he was choirmaster there. During the years he worked as a lawyer he continued to play at various churches. Between the years 1827 and 1863 he was organist at St. Olave's, Southwark; organist to the King of Hanover; honorary choirmaster of St. John's, Milton-next-Greavesend; organist at Union Chapel, Islington; and organist at St. Bartholomew the Less, Smithfield. He died at Kensington on February 21, 1876.

An accomplished musician, Gauntlett made many contributions in his sphere of church music. He wrote an enormous number of psalm and hymn tunes—he is said to have written ten thousand—and was music editor for a large number of hymnals, including *The Church Hymn and Tune Book* (with W. J. Blew, 1844-1851), *The Hallelujah* (with J. J. Waite, 1848-1866), and *The Congregationalist Psalmist* (with Henry Allon, 1851). He also wrote much organ music, as well as songs, glees, and anthems, and published *One Hundred and Fifty-six Questions on the Art of Music Making and the Science of Music,* 1864. He was a pioneer in introducing the extension of the compass of English organs and in 1852 took out a patent for an electromagnetic action to the organ. Felix Mendelssohn (LBW 60) wrote of him:

> His literary attainments, his knowledge of the history of music, his acquaintance with acoustical laws, his marvelous memory, his philosophical turn of mind, as well as his practical experience, rendered him one of the most remarkable professors of the age.

The Archbishop of Canterbury conferred on him the first Doctor of Music degree bestowed by an archbishop in two hundred years.

489 WIDE OPEN ARE YOUR HANDS *(Salve Jesu, pastor bone)*
Tune: Leominster

This hymn is from the same Latin poem as "O Sacred Head, now wounded" (LBW 116). Charles Porterfield Krauth's (LBW 62) translation was prepared in 1870.

LEOMINSTER, arranged by Arthur Sullivan (LBW 153), was included in his *Church Hymns,* 1874, as an "Old Melody, harmonized by Arthur

Sullivan.'' The collection of his *Hymn Tunes,* 1902, credits the tune to ''G. W. Martin.'' Martin's melody, entitled ''The Pilgrim's Song,'' first appeared in *The Journal of Part Music,* Vol. II, 1862.

George William Martin, born in London on March 8, 1828, was very gifted in training choirs of school children. After serving as chorister of St. Paul's Cathedral as a youth, he became professor of music in the Normal College for Army Schoolmasters, and later music master in St. John's Training College, Battersea (1845-1853). In 1849 he was also appointed organist of Christ Church in Battersea. The Metropolitan Schools Choral Society and the National Choral Society gained high reputations under his directorship. He was also a composer of glees, madrigals, and part-songs. From 1861 to 1862 he was editor of *The Journal of Part Music.* The story of his later life is one of tragic intemperance, which finally resulted in his death at Belingbroke House Hospital, Wandaworth, April 16, 1881.

Gerhard Cartford (LBW 466) harmonized the tune for the LBW.

490 LET ME BE YOURS FOREVER *(Lass mich dein sein und bleiben)*
Tune: Lob Gott getrost mit Singen

Nikolaus Selnecker, a favorite pupil of Philipp Melanchthon and one of the framers of the Formula of Concord, was born at Hersbruck near Nürnberg, Germany, on December 5, 1532. A musician as well as a clergyman, he first held a position as organist at the chapel in the Kaiserburg in Nürnberg at the age of twelve. During his stay at Leipzig, he built up the Motet Choir of St. Thomas Church which was later conducted by J. S. Bach (LBW 219). He received a Master of Arts degree from Wittenberg in 1554 and afterwards was second court preacher and tutor to the court at Dresden, during which time he was ordained at Wittenberg in 1558. His life as a theologian was full of the conflicts and disagreements over Communion which were raging between the Calvinists and Lutherans. More than once he was called to, or removed from, pastoral and university posts depending on the sentiments of the local rulers. For three years he was professor of theology at the University of Jena. Then in 1568 he was appointed to the same post at the University of Leipzig, and became also pastor of St. Thomas Church and superintendent of Leipzig. There, except for a few years when he was court preacher and general superintendent at Wolfenbüttel, he remained until 1589 when controversy again forced him to leave. He spent some time as superintendent at Hildesheim where he had many weighty matters to settle and was finally called upon to arbitrate matters of dispute in Augsburg in 1591. The trip was made in miserable winter weather and a resulting illness confined Selnecker to his room until April. When Elector Christian I died and Selnecker was recalled to Leipzig, he was there only a few weeks before his own death on May 24, 1592.

Selnecker was the author of some 175 works in German and Latin, many of which dealt with the controversies in which he was involved, and he also wrote a number of hymns. His single stanza beginning ''Lass mich dein sein und bleiben'' was published in *Passio. Das Leiden und Sterben unsers Herrn Jesu Christi, aus den Vier Evangelisten,* 1572, and was included with two additional anonymous stanzas in the *Rudolstädter Gesangbuch,* 1688. The translation by Matthias Loy, prepared in 1863, was included in the *Evangelical Lutheran Hymnal,* 1880, of the Ohio Synod.

Loy, born in Cumberland County, Pennsylvania, on March 17, 1828, received his Christian education from his mother. In 1834 he moved with his family to Hogestown, and at the age of fourteen he was apprenticed to Baab and Hummel, printers in Harrisburg. There he worked for six years, during which he also attended school. While in Harrisburg he came to the attention of Charles W. Schaeffer (LBW 455) who encouraged him to become a Lutheran pastor. He studied Greek and Latin under the principal of the Harrisburg Academy and later attended the academy as a regular student. In 1847 he moved to Circleville, Ohio, to publish a German semimonthly paper for the United Brethren Publishing House; but at the suggestion of the Lutheran pastor in Circleville, he secured a release from his contract and instead entered the theological seminary of the Evangelical Lutheran Synod of Ohio at Columbus. While at Columbus he was a reader for the *Lutheraner,* edited by C. F. W. Walther. In 1849 he was called to a congregation in Delaware, Ohio, and in 1860 he elected president of the Joint Synod of Ohio. Four years later he became editor of the *Lutheran Standard.* In 1865 he was appointed professor of theology at Capital University, where he served until 1878 when he also resigned as president of the Ohio Synod and took a post as professor of theology at Concordia Seminary, St. Louis, Missouri. Two years later he returned to Ohio as president of Capital University and, once again, as president of the Ohio Synod. He retired professor emeritus in 1902 and died on January 26, 1915.

In addition to editing the *Lutheran Standard* Loy started the *Columbus Theological Magazine* in 1881, and wrote four books: *The Doctrine of Justification,* 1868; *Sermons on the Gospels,* 1888; *Christian Church,* 1896; and *The Story of My Life,* 1905.

LOB GOTT GETROST MIT SINGEN was originally a secular German folk song, "Entlaubt ist uns der Walden gen disem Winter Kalt," popular as early as the fifteenth century. Hans Gerle, a leading lute player and composer who died in 1570, was the first to print it, in his *Musika Teutsch,* Nürnberg, 1532. Johann Horn (LBW 132) adapted it for his text, "Lob Gott getrost mit Singen," in *Ein Gesangbuch der Brüder inn Behemen und Merherrn,* Nürnberg, 1544; and it appeared the following year in Valentin Babst's *Geystliche Lieder,* published in Leipzig, with Johann Kolross' "Ich dank dir lieber Herre," by which title it is also known.

J. S. Bach (LBW 219) used the tune in his Cantata 37.

491 O GOD, I LOVE THEE *(O Deus, ego amo te)*
Tune: In manus tuas

The origins of this hymn are somewhat obscure. Julian* devotes articles to it on pages 826 and 1679. The Latin text "O Deus ego amo Te, Nec amo Te ut salves me," from which Edward Henry Bickersteth prepared his English translation is from *Caeleste Palmetum,* Cologne, 1669. An earlier Latin form, "Non me movet, Domine," is found in Joannes Nadassi's *Pretiosae occupationes merientium,* published in 1657 in Rome. It would appear that the hymn first existed as a Portuguese or Spanish sonnet. A Portuguese form of the sonnet in use in India in the seventeenth century was accredited to Francis Xavier. The earliest known source of the Spanish poem, "No me mueve, di Dios, Para querert," is the *Epitome de la vida y muerte de San Ignacio de Loyola,* Roermond, 1662, where it appears anonymously. In Johannes Caramuel's *Conceptus Evangelici,* also 1662, it is ascribed to Xavier.

Bickersteth's translation was printed by J. Townsend in "For use in the Diocese of Exeter," February 2, 1889, and in the Appendix to the 1890 edition of *Hymnal Companion* (see below). A translation by Edward Caswall (LBW 37) published in his *Lyra Catholica,* 1849, beginning "My God, I love Thee, not because I hope for heaven thereby," is in use in a number of hymnals.

Francis Xavier, Roman Catholic missionary to India and Japan, was born at the castle Xavier, near Sangüesa in Navarre, on April 7, 1506. He entered the College of Sainte-Barbe in Paris in 1525, and after completing a Master of Arts degree in 1530, served for four years as regent of Beauvais College. In 1534 he became one of the original seven members of the Society of Jesus (Jesuit Order) founded by Ignatius Loyola in the Church of St. Mary on Montmartre. He studied theology from 1534 to 1536 and received holy orders with Loyola at Venice in 1537. Appointed a minister to the Christians in southeast India, he departed from Portugal in April of 1541 and arrived at Goa, after a tedious and dangerous voyage, thirteen months later. For seven years he labored in India and at Malacca in Malaysia and Amboina in Indonesia. He and his congregation in India faced many trials and hardships—plundering and murder at the hands of neighboring peoples, as well as the greed and cruelty of the Portuguese merchants and officials. From 1549 to 1551 he worked in several cities in Japan, including Kagoshima, Kyoto, and Yamaguchi, leaving a Christian community of some two thousand in Japan. He returned to Goa in February of 1552 and sailed the following August for China. While waiting on the island of Shang-chwan to gain entrance into China, however, he became ill with a fever in November, and died December 3, 1552.

Bickersteth, son of an English surgeon who later entered the ministry and was himself a hymnwriter, was born January 25, 1825, at Barnsbury Park, Islington, London. Educated at Trinity College, Cambridge (Bachelor of Arts in 1847; Master of Arts in 1850), he was ordained a deacon in 1848 and a priest the following year. After serving as curate of Banningham, Norfolk, and Christ Church, Tunbridge Wells, he became rector of Hinton Martell. From 1855 to 1885 he was vicar of Christ Church, Hampstead, and from 1885 to 1890, dean of Gloucester and bishop of Exeter. He died May 16, 1906, at Westbourne Terrace in London.

In addition to a commentary on the New Testament and several collections of sermons and poems, Bickersteth was editor of *Psalms and Hymns,* 1858, based on his father's *Christian Psalmody,* 1833, and of *The Hymnal Companion to the Book of Common Prayer,* 1870.

IN MANUS TUAS, written by Herbert Howells, was commissioned for the *New Catholic Hymnal,* 1971, as the setting for Hamish Swanston's text, "This world, my God, is held within your hand."

The English composer Howells was born October 17, 1892, at Lydny, Gloucestershire. He became a student of Herbert Brewer at Gloucester Cathedral in 1905, and served as an apprentice from 1909 to 1911. Although he was entirely self-taught in the area of composition, the works he wrote in the ensuing few months gained him, in 1912, an open scholarship in composition at the Royal College of Music in London. There he studied with Charles V. Stanford (LBW 189). For a short time he was sub-organist at Salisbury Cathedral, but his health failed, and from 1917 to 1920 he spent his time alternately in Gloucestershire and at St. Thomas' Hospital. He was appointed a teacher of composition at the Royal College of Music in 1920, and in 1932 he became the first John Collard Fellow of the Worshipful Company of Musicians. In 1936 he took a position as director of music at St. Paul's Girls' School, succeeding Gustav Holst. The following year he received a Doctor of Music degree from the University of Oxford.

The list of Howells' compositions is extensive and includes works for chorus, organ, piano, and chamber ensembles, as well as songs and a large number of works for the church service. In 1920 he went to South Africa where he conducted in Cape Town, and in 1923 he toured the United States and Canada. He has been a very popular adjudicator at music competitions, and is also a gifted music critic. He now resides at Beverly Close in London.

492 O MASTER, LET ME WALK WITH YOU

Tune: Maryton

Washington Gladden, who wrote extensively on civic and social affairs of his day, composed this hymn in 1879. It first appeared in *The Sunday Afternoon,* March, 1879, a periodical of which he was editor. In the next year it was published in Charles H. Richards' *Songs of Christian Praise with Music,* New York.

Born in Pottsgrove, Pennsylvania, on February 11, 1836, Gladden graduated from Williams College in 1859. The following year he was ordained to the Congregational ministry, and was married to Jennie Cohoon of Brooklyn. After ministering for one year to a congregation in Brooklyn, New York, he served at Morrisania, New York, 1861–1866, and at North Adams, Massachusetts, 1866–1871. He was an editor for *The Independent* for three years, but returned to the parish ministry at North Church, Springfield, Massachusetts in 1874, and from 1882 until his death, was pastor of First Congregational Church in Columbus, Ohio. He died in Columbus on July 2, 1918.

Gladden, known as a distinguished preacher and lecturer, wrote a number of books and contributed to many religious and secular periodicals. Among his more than thirty works are: *From the Hub to the Hudson,* 1869; *The Christian Way,* 1877; *Who Wrote the Bible?* 1891; *Art and Morality,* 1897; *The Christian Pastor,* 1898; *Social Salvation,* 1901; *Christianity in Socialism,* 1905; and *The Labor Question,* 1911. He served as moderator of the National Council of Congregational Churches from 1904 to 1907. The University of Wisconsin and Roanoke College honored him with doctorates, and in 1895 the University of Notre Dame conferred on him a Doctor of Laws, probably the first such degree bestowed on a Protestant clergyman by a Roman Catholic School.

MARYTON was originally the setting for John Keble's "Sun of my soul, thou Saviour dear" in *Church Hymns with Tunes,* 1874.

The composer, Henry Percy Smith, was born on the island of Malta (some sources say in England) in 1825, and received Bachelor of Arts (1848) and Master of Arts (1850) degrees from Balliol College, Oxford. Ordained a deacon of the Church of England in 1849, and a priest the following year, he ministered to Eversley, Hamptonshire, 1849–1851; St.

Michael's, York Town in Surrey, 1851–1868; and Great Barton, Suffolk, 1868–1882. From 1882 to 1895 he was chaplain of Christ Church, Cannes, in France and in 1892 he became canon of Gibraltar. He died in England, at Bournemouth, Hampshire, on January 28, 1898.

The harmonization is one of a number prepared by Eric Harding Thiman for *Congregational Praise,* 1951. Thiman, chairman of the music committee, also contributed fifteen hymn tunes and several descants to that collection.

A native of England, Thiman was born at Ashford, Kent, on September 12, 1900, and attended the Guildhall School of Music. He became a Fellow of the Royal College of Organists in 1921 and the next year took a post as organist at Park Chapel, Crough End, London. He completed a Doctor of Music degree in 1927 and in 1930 became professor of harmony at the Royal College of Music, where he served for many years. In 1956 he was appointed dean of the faculty of music at London University, and in 1957, organist of London's City Temple. He died following an operation on February 13, 1975.

Thiman wrote a large number of works for the church—anthems, cantatas, and organ compositions—as well as *44 Hymn Tunes Freely Harmonized,* and a text book and its companion volume, *Varied Harmonies to 34 Well-known Hymn Tunes.* He also composed a number of part songs. Well-known as an examiner for the Royal College of Organists, and as a recitalist, he performed throughout England and in various parts of the Commonwealth.

493 HOPE OF THE WORLD

Tune: Donne secours

Georgia Harkness received inspiration for this hymn at the Second General Assembly of the World Council of Churches held at Evanston, Illinois, in the summer of 1954. It was published the same year by the Hymn Society of America in *Eleven Ecumenical Hymns.*

Born April 21, 1891, at Harkness, New York, Georgia Elma Harkness received a Bachelor of Arts degree from Cornell University in 1912. At Boston University she completed Master of Arts and Master of Religious Education degrees in 1920, and in 1923, a Doctor of Philosophy degree. Ordained a Methodist minister in 1926, she pursued further studies at Harvard in 1926, at Yale from 1928 to 1929, and at Union Theological Seminary from 1936 to 1937. She was professor of philosophy at Elmira College in New York from 1922 to 1927, and thereafter, at Mount Holyoke College for two years. From 1939 to 1950 she was professor of applied theology at Garrett School of Theology, Evanston, Illinois, the first woman in the country to hold a full professorship in a theological seminary. From 1950 to 1961 she was professor of applied theology at Pacific School of Religion, Berkeley, California, a position which allowed her six months a year for travel and writing. She also taught at Union Theological Seminary at Manila, and from 1956 to 1957, was a professor at the International Christian University at Mitaka, Japan. She died at Claremont, California, August 30, 1974.

Harkness was the recipient of a number of honors, including Churchwoman of the Year in 1958, and a Doctor of Letters degree from Elmira College in 1962. She exercised wide influence as a writer, teacher, and lecturer, and was active in various committees and conferences of the

Methodist Church, including the Methodist Commission on World Peace. Her writings include thirty-seven books, among them *Prayer and the Common Life,* 1947; *The Modern Rival of Christian Faith,* 1952; *Christian Ethics,* 1957; *The Providence of God,* 1960; *The Fellowship of the Holy Spirit,* 1966; *The Ministry of Reconciliation,* 1971; and *Women in Church and Society,* 1972.

DONNE SECOURS was composed or adapted by Louis Bourgeois (LBW 29) for Clément Marot's version of Psalm 12, "Donne secours, Seigneur, il en est heure," in *Trente quatre pseaumes de David,* Geneva, 1551. The melody, which is in Dorian mode, has been called one of the most beautiful and original in that psalter.

The harmonization is by Claude Goudimel, about whose life much is unknown. He was born in Besançon in southern France sometime during the first part of the sixteenth century, and was the composer of many works both sacred and secular, including chansons, masses, motets, and Magnificats. According to some writers he went to Rome before 1540 and opened a public school of music where his students included Giovanni Nanini and Giovanni Pierluigi da Palestrina (LBW 135). In 1549 he began his work in Paris as editor and composer for the publisher Nicolas Du Chemin, and later, the house of Ballard (Adrian Le Roy and Robert Ballard). At some point around 1560 he converted from Roman Catholicism to Protestantism, and is found as godfather to a child in the Protestant Church at Metz in 1565. His settings of the psalter began before his conversion, however, as the psalms were used both in the Roman Catholic and the Protestant churches until banned by the former. Fearing Roman Catholic persecutions he went to Besançon and later to Lyons. Unfortunately, the St. Bartholomew's Day massacre which had started in Paris on August 24 of 1572 spread to Lyons, and Goudimel was among those killed between August 27 and 31 of that year.

Besides his other music works, Goudimel produced three settings of the Genevan psalter. His *Les pseaumes . . . mis en musique à quatre parties,* finished in 1562 and published in Paris by François Jaqui in 1564, was the first complete psalter in an entirely homophonic setting. The music of this psalter was later used by Ambrosius Lobwasser for his German psalter in 1573, and both collections went through numerous editions. A second psalter, published in Paris in 1568, placed the melody in the top voice with a slightly more florid setting. The third work, published between 1551 and 1566 in eight volumes of from eight to ten pieces each, treated the psalm tunes in three- to eight-part motets. This psalter was not yet complete when the composer lost his life in Lyons.

494 JESUS CALLS US; O'ER THE TUMULT
Tune: Galilee

See LBW 114 for Cecil Frances Alexander. This hymn, based on Matthew 4:18–20, was included in *Hymns for Public Worship,* printed in 1852 by the Society for the Propagation of Christian Knowledge.

GALILEE was written by William Herbert Jude for these words in 1874 and included in George Barrett's and Edward J. Hopkins' (LBW 262) *The Congregational Church Hymnal,* London, 1887.

Born in September of 1851 in Westleton, Suffolk, England, Jude held two major positions as organist during his life, first at the Blue Coat Hospital, Liverpool, and then, beginning in 1889, at the Stretford Town Hall near Manchester. He traveled extensively as a lecture-recitalist in Great Britain and Australia, and was the editor of a number of works on hymnody and sacred music, including the *Music and the Higher Life,* 1904; *Mission Hymns,* 1911; *Festival Hymns,* 1916; the *Monthly Hymnal,* and *Minister of Music.* He also composed an operetta, *Innocents Abroad,* songs, and anthems. He died August 8, 1922, in London.

The harmonization was prepared by Dale Wood (LBW 268) for the LBW.

495 LEAD ON, O KING ETERNAL!
Tune: Lancashire

Ernest Warburton Shurtleff was born in Boston, Massachusetts, on April 4, 1862. He attended Harvard University and the New Church Theological Seminary (Swedenborgian) in Cambridge, Massachusetts, and in 1887, graduated from Andover Theological Seminary. "Lead on, O King Eternal" was written for the Andover graduation ceremonies and was included the same year in the author's *Hymns of Faith.* Ordained to the Congregational ministry, he served for four years in Ventura, California; from 1891 to 1898 in Old Plymouth, Massachusetts; and from 1898 to 1905 at First Congregational Church in Minneapolis, Minnesota. In 1905 he went to Frankfurt-am-Main, Germany, where he established the American Church. The next year he went to Paris to work among students and during the first World War he and his wife, Helen S. *née* Cramer of Cameron, Texas, did relief work there until his death on August 29, 1917.

Shurtleff's literary works include *Poems,* 1883; *New Year's Peace,* 1885; *Song of Hope,* 1886; *Shadow of the Angel,* 1886; and *Song on the Waters,* 1913.

LANCASHIRE. See LBW 50 for Henry T. Smart. Originally this tune was written as a setting for Reginald Heber's (LBW 84) "From Greenland's Icy Mountains," to be sung at a large missionary meeting held in Blackburn, Lancashire, on October 4, 1836. It was later published in *Psalms and Hymns for Divine Worship,* London, 1867.

496 AROUND YOU, O LORD JESUS *(O Jesu, än de dina)*
Tune: O Jesu, än de dina

Written in 1814 by Frans Mikael Franzén, this hymn was included in revised form in *Stockholms Posten,* July 1, 1817, and in the *Swenska Psalm-Boken,* 1819. The translation of stanza 1 was prepared for the LBW by Joel Lundeen. Stanzas 2 and 3 are from Olof Olsson's translation beginning "Thine own, O loving Saviour," included in the *Hymnal,* 1901, of the Augustana Synod. They are given here with several alterations.

See LBW 26 for Frans Mikael Franzén and LBW 146 for Joel Lundeen.

Olof Olsson, a beloved and esteemed Lutheran pastor, was born in Karlskoga, Värmland, Sweden, on March 31, 1841, and attended the parish school. Later he studied music with an organist in Västergötland. Following advanced education at Fjellstedt's Mission Institute, Uppsala; the Mission Institute in Leipzig, Germany; and Uppsala University, he was ordained in 1863, and served for six years in the diocese of Karlstad. Although he was a pietist and championed the free-church cause, he never left the state church. In 1869 he and his wife moved to America and settled in the valley of the Smokey Hill River in McPherson County, Kansas. There, in addition to ministering to his congregation at Lindsborg, he served for a short while in the Kansas legislature. After three calls, beginning in 1875, he went in 1877 to Augustana College, Rock Island, Illinois, as a professor of theology. Ill health and grief over the death of his wife forced him to resign in 1888, and he spent several months traveling in the United States and abroad. He accepted a call to Woodhull, Illinois (near Rock Island) in 1889, and from 1891 until his death on May 12, 1900, he served as president of Augustana College and Theological Seminary.

Olsson was author or editor of a number of publications, including the *Korsbaneret,* an annual which he took over in 1880, which went into its fifty-fifth edition in 1933 as the Swedish yearbook of the Augustana Synod. In addition, he was one of the leaders in producing the *Hymnal,* 1901, Augustana's first English-language hymnal.

O JESU, ÄN DE DINA, believed to be of Danish origin, appeared in 1569 in Hans Thomissön's (LBW 227) *Den danske Psalmebog.* There it was the setting for "Hielp Gud at ieg nu kunde," a Danish version of Heinrich Müller's German hymn, "Hilf Gott dass mirs gelinge." The melody is said to bear a similarity to the German secular melody, "Es wohnet Lieb bei Liebe." The LBW form of the tune and the harmony are those found in the *Koralbok för Svenska Kyrkan,* 1939.

497 I HEARD THE VOICE OF JESUS SAY
Tune: Third Mode Melody

Based on John 1:16, "Of his fullness have we all received, and grace for grace," this hymn by Horatius Bonar (LBW 167) was included in his *Hymns Original and Selected,* 1846.

THIRD MODE MELODY is the third of Thomas Tallis' (LBW 278) nine tunes included in Archbishop Parker's *Psalter,* 1560, where the melody was originally in the tenor. The beautiful and haunting Phrygian mode melody has served as the setting for various texts in English hymnals; the combination with Bonar's text is found in *The Hymnal 1940* of the Episcopal Church. Ralph Vaughan Williams' (LBW 101) *Fantasy on a Theme by Thomas Tallis* is based on this melody.

498 ALL WHO WOULD VALIANT BE
Tune: St. Dunstan's

John Bunyan, a tinker by trade, was born at Elstow, near Bedford, England, on November 30, 1628, and attended the village school. After some years in the Parliamentary Army, from which he was released in 1647, he married a woman whose only dowry was her piety and two religious books. Following a period of soul searching he joined a religious community founded by John Gifford, and began preaching in 1653. Two years later his wife died, leaving him with four children. He became a strongly influential Nonconformist preacher, for which he was imprisoned for twelve years beginning in 1660, and for a shorter time beginning in 1675. While in prison he spent his time making laces for the support of his children and writing voluminously. His autobiographical *Grace Abounding to the Chief of Sinners* appeared in 1666. The first part of *The Pilgrims' Progress,* published in 1678, was begun during his second imprisonment, and was followed by *The Life and Death of Mr. Badman,* 1680, and *The Holy War,* 1682. The second part of *Pilgrims' Progress,* published in 1684, contains the poem from which this hymn is taken. All in all Bunyan wrote more than sixty books and pamphlets. After his release from prison he returned to Bedford, where he ministered to a Baptist congregation. During his last years he was held in great esteem by his fellow Nonconformists and preached both in London and on circuit in the country. Champion of the singing of hymns in the church (in contrast to the General Baptists who disapproved of congregational psalmody), he published his *Solomon's Temple Spiritualized* in 1688. He died August 31, 1688, of a cold resulting from a long ride in the rain to reconcile a father and son.

Originally Mr. Valiant-for-Truth's song in part II of *The Pilgrims' Progress* opened:

> Who would true valour see,
> Let him come hither;
> One here will constant be,
> Come wind, come weather.

The three-stanza poem was reconstructed for *The English Hymnal,* 1906, where the opening line was "*He* who would valiant be." In the LBW the hymn has been further altered to read in plural form.

ST. DUNSTAN'S was written by Charles Winfred Douglas for this text and included in the 1918 edition of the Episcopal *Hymnal.* Douglas and his family moved in 1911 to a residence on the grounds of the Community of St. Mary in Peekskill, New York. There they lived in a stone house near the entrance to the grounds, which the school children called "The Castle," but which the Douglases called "St. Dunstan's." This tune was written on December 15, 1917, as Douglas rode home to Peekskill on the train. The composer has written:

> Bunyan's burly song strikes a new and welcome note in our *Hymnal.* The quaint sincerity of the words stirs us out of our easy-going dull Christianity to the thrill of great adventure. The ballad-like rhythm requires special musical treatment incompatible with a mechanical regularity of measures. The tune is, therefore, in free rhythm, following the words. It should have a quality of sturdiness which always reminds the writer of St. Paul valiantly battling through manifold disaster in "the care of all the churches." (From *The Hymnal 1940 Companion,** p. 331.)

Douglas, whose Scottish ancestors were settlers of Gloucester, Massachusetts, was born February 15, 1867, in Oswego, New York. Working as a store clerk, accompanist, and assistant organist at St. Paul's Cathedral, he made his way through Syracuse University, receiving a Bachelor of Music degree in 1891. For a year thereafter he served as a vocal instructor at the university before going as organist and choirmaster to Church of Zion and St. Timothy's Church, New York City.

Following studies at St. Andrew's Divinity School, Syracuse, he was ordained in 1893 and returned to New York City as curate of the Church of the Redeemer, with responsibility also for the music, and as a teacher at St. John's school. Because of poor health he went to Colorado in 1894, going first to Denver and then to Evergreen, a community with which the remainder of his life was identified although he traveled and held positions widely. In 1896 he was married to Mary Josepha Williams, a physician who had inherited a considerable fortune which financed much of his future career and publications. The next few years of his life were spent preaching, lecturing on music, and conducting missions throughout Colorado and as far away as Hastings, Nebraska. In 1901, following a trip to England, he suffered a severe physical and nervous breakdown and took his recovery living among the Hopi and Navajo Indians in the desert, the Hopis making him a blood brother. His knowledge of the Indian culture and arts soon made him a sought-after authority in the field, and president Theodore Roosevelt joined him in endeavoring to improve the methods of Indian education. At intervals from 1903 to 1906 he studied church music in England, France, and Germany, spending time with the Benedictines of Solesmes on the Isle of Wight and also making the acquaintance of Percy Dearmer (LBW 169) who was then engaged in the preparation of *The English Hymnal*, 1906. In 1906 he became director of music at the Community of St. Mary, Peekskill, New York, where the application of his plainsong studies led to his many adaptations for English use and to his becoming an outstanding authority in the field. In 1907 he also became canon residentiary of St. Paul's Cathedral, Fond du Lac, Wisconsin, and after 1911 was honorary canon residentiary. For many years he lectured and worked in the Chicago area, going in the summers to Colorado to teach and lecture on plainsong. Over the years he lectured in many American seminaries as liturgiologist, linguist, and musicologist. In 1925 he was sent on a "peace-making" mission to the various Episcopal missions in the Philippines and also visited Honolulu, Japan, Hong Kong, and Canton. In 1934, the year he "retired," he was made chaplain of the western province of the Community of St. Mary, Kenosha, Wisconsin, and was elected honorary canon of St. John's Cathedral, Denver. From 1937 to 1943 he was vicar of the Mission of the Transfiguration in Evergreen, a mission he had founded in 1897. His first wife died in 1938, and in 1940 he was married to Anne Woodward. He died January 18, 1944, having that day completed an organ setting of the hymn tune, "Stuttgart."

In addition to serving as a musical editor of *The Hymnal*, 1916 and 1940, of the Episcopal Church, Douglas edited a number of other hymnals, and published his lectures as *Church Music in History and Practice*, 1937.

499   COME, THOU FOUNT OF EVERY BLESSING

Tune: Nettleton

Although authorship of this hymn was at one point claimed for Selina Hastings, Countess of Huntingdon, it seems most likely to have been the work of Robert Robinson. (See Julian,* page 252.) An entry in Robinson's Church Book reads: "Mr. Wheatley of Norwich published a hymn beginning 'Come, Thou Fount of every blessing' (1758)." However, no such hymn has been found. The hymn of four stanzas appeared in 1759 in *A Collection of Hymns used by the Church of Christ in*

Angel-Alley, Bishopsgate. In several later collections it was credited to Robinson. The fourth stanza, beginning "O, that day when free from sinning," was omitted in Martin Madan's *Psalms and Hymns,* 1760, and has generally not been used since that time. The opening line of stanza 2, "Here I raise my Ebenezer," refers to 1 Samuel 7:12, "Then Samuel took a stone and set it up between Mizpah and Jeshanah, and called its name Ebenezer; for he said, 'Hitherto the LORD has helped us.'" The last half of stanza 1 has been rewritten.

Born of humble parentage on September 27, 1735, at Swaffham, in Norfolk, England, Robinson went with his family to Scarning, in the same county, at the age of eight. Shortly thereafter his father died. His mother, a godly woman, hoped to see her son enter the ministry of the Church of England, but this was financially impossible. Instead he was apprenticed at the age of fourteen to a barber and hairdresser in London, where he was often reprimanded for spending more time with his books than at his work. Three years later he and some companions plied an old woman fortune teller with alcohol to amuse themselves with her predictions, and later that evening, went to hear George Whitefield (LBW 522). The fortune teller's predictions that Robinson would live to see his children and grandchildren, together with Whitefield's disconcerting sermon on Matthew 3:7 and the "wrath to come," made a deep impression on him, and at the age of twenty he made his confession of faith in Christ. He remained in London, attending the meetings of John Wesley (LBW 302) and other evangelical preachers, until 1758 when he was invited as a Calvinistic Methodist to be minister of the chapel at Mildenhall in Norfolk. Within the year he moved to Norwich, where he established an Independent congregation, and in 1759 he was called to the pulpit of a Baptist church in Cambridge, having been first baptized by immersion. He had married by the time he went to Cambridge, and his family became so large that for some years he also managed a farm in order to provide for them. Although unschooled, he became a very popular preacher and later learned Latin and French. During the last twenty years of his life he authored several books, including *Arcana; or the Principles of the Late Petitioners to Parliament for Relief in the Matter of Subscription,* 1774; and in 1776, *A Plea for the Divinity of our Lord Jesus Christ in a Pastoral Letter to a Congregation of Protestant Dissenters at Cambridge,* which gained him the respect of clergy of the Church of England and the Nonconformists alike. His *The History and Mystery of Good Friday* appeared in 1777, and in 1790, after nine years of labor, he published his *History of the Baptists.* He retired in 1790 and died the same year, on June 9, "soft, suddenly, and alone" as he had wished.

NETTLETON appeared anonymously with this text in John Wyeth's *Repository of Sacred Music, Part Second,* 1813 (LBW 33), where it is identified as a new tune and appeared as given below.

It is there set in two parts and called "Hallelujah." It has also been named "Good Shepherd" in some collections. Its unfounded ascription to Ahasel Nettleton (1783–1844), nineteenth-century evangelist, has given it its present tune name. In his *White Spirituals in the Southern Uplands* (1933) George Pullen Jackson notes that the tune is one of a group related to the folk melody "Go tell Aunt Tabby (Aunt Rhody, Aunt Nancy, etc.) her old grey goose is dead."

500 FAITH OF OUR FATHERS
Tune: St. Catherine

See LBW 290 for Frederick W. Faber. This hymn first appeared in *Jesus and Mary,* 1849. It consisted of two separate poems, one set of four stanzas for England, in which stanza three began

> Faith of our Fathers! Mary's prayers
> Shall win our country back to Thee.

and a set of seven stanzas for Ireland, in which the third stanza read

> Faith of our Fathers! Mary's prayers
> Shall keep our country fast to Thee.

This hymn has been variously altered for use in Protestant hymnals.

ST. CATHERINE was included in Hemy's *Crown of Jesus Music,* Part II, 1864, where it was the setting for "Sweet Saint Catherine, maid most pure." The last eight measures which make up the refrain were added by James George Walton when he included the tune in his *Plainsong Music for the Holy Communion Office,* 1874.

Henri Frederick Hemy, the son of German parents, was born November 12, 1818, at Newcastle on Tyne in England. He served as organist at St. Andrew's Roman Catholic Church in Newcastle and later taught music at Tynemouth and at St. Cuthbert's College, Ushaw, Durham. In addition to his *Crown of Jesus Music,* which was popular in Roman Catholic churches, he published a book on piano playing, the *Royal Modern Tutor for the Pianoforte,* 1858, which went through many editions. He died June 10, 1888, at Hartlepool.

James Walton was born at Clitheroe, Lancashire, England, on February 19, 1821, and died September 1, 1905, at Bradford, York. Aside from the fact that he edited *Plainsong Music for the Holy Communion Office,* little is known about him.

Gerhard Cartford (LBW 466) prepared the harmonization for the LBW.

501 HE LEADETH ME: OH, BLESSED THOUGHT!
Tune: He Leadeth Me

Written in March of 1862 when Joseph Henry Gilmore delivered a lecture on Psalm 23 at a midweek service at the First Baptist Church in Philadelphia, this hymn was first printed without the author's knowledge in the Boston *Watchman and Reflector* (December 4, 1862), where it had been sent by Mrs. Gilmore.

Gilmore, born in Boston on April 29, 1834, graduated from Brown University and the Newton Theological Seminary, and taught Hebrew briefly at Newton Seminary. Ordained in 1862, he was pastor of the Baptist church in Fisherville, New Hampshire, for a year. From 1863 to 1864 he served as private secretary to his father, who was governor of New Hampshire, and also edited the Concord *Daily Monitor*. In 1865 he became pastor of the Second Baptist Church, Rochester, New York, and in 1867 also became acting professor of Hebrew at the Rochester Theological Seminary. He accepted a position as professor of rhetoric, logic, and English literature at the University of Rochester in 1868, and remained there until his retirement in 1911. He died July 23, 1918, in Rochester.

HE LEADETH ME (also "Aughton"). William Bradbury (LBW 293) altered Gilmore's text to include a refrain and published it with this tune in *The Golden Censor*, 1864.

502 THEE WILL I LOVE, MY STRENGTH
(Ich will dich lieben, meine Stärke)
Tune: Ich will dich lieben

This hymn was included in Johann Scheffler's (LBW 455) most important collection, the *Heilige Seelen-Lust oder Geistliche Hirten-Lieder,* published in Breslau in 1657. Scheffler's hymns had great influence on the pietistic hymnwriters of the next period, including Gerhard Tersteegen (LBW 249) and Benjamin Schmolk (LBW 187). The esteem in which his hymns were held by the Moravians and their hymnwriter, Nicolaus von Zinzendorf (LBW 302), probably led to their introduction to John Wesley (LBW 302) who translated this hymn for his *Hymns and Sacred Poems,* 1739.

ICH WILL DICH LIEBEN was included with this hymn in Johann König's (LBW 22) *Harmonischer Lieder-Schatz,* 1738 (Zahn* #2767). The tune has also been used for "Wer nur den lieben Gott lässt walten" (LBW 453).

503 O JESUS, I HAVE PROMISED
Tune: Munich

John Ernest Bode, son of the head of the foreign department of the post office, was born in St. Pancras, England, on February 23, 1816. He completed a Bachelor of Arts degree (1837) and a Master of Arts degree (1840) at Christ Church, Oxford. In 1835 he was the first to win the Hertford Scholarship and from 1837 to 1843 was tutor of Christ Church College. Ordained in 1841, he was appointed rector of Westwell, Oxfordshire, in 1847, and of Castle Camps, Cambridgeshire, in 1860, where he remained until his death on October 6, 1874.

Bode was Bampton Lecturer at Oxford in 1855, and published two collections of poems, *Ballads from Herodotus,* 1853, and *Short Occasional Poems,* 1858, as well as *Hymns from the Gospel of the Day, for Each Sunday and the Festivals of Our Lord,* 1860. In 1857, when the Oxford professor of poetry was elected, Bode lost by a single vote to Matthew Arnold.

"O Jesus, I have promised" was written in 1866 for the confirmation of Bode's daughter and two sons. First printed in a leaflet of the Society for Promoting Christian Knowledge in 1868, it was included in the Appendix to the S. P. C. K. *Psalms and Hymns for Public Worship* the following year under the text of Luke 9:57, "Lord, I will follow thee whithersoever thou goest."

For MUNICH see LBW 231.

504   O GOD, MY FAITHFUL GOD *(O Gott, du frommer Gott)*
Tune: Was frag ich nach der Welt

Given in his *Devoti musica cordis* published in Breslau in 1630, this hymn by Johann Heermann (LBW 123) was entitled "A daily prayer." It seems to have been written between 1623 and 1630 during the time of Heermann's greatest suffering. Catherine Winkworth's (LBW 29) translation, which was included in her *Lyra Germanica,* second series, 1858, is given here in an altered form.

WAS FRAG ICH NACH DER WELT (also "Darmstadt" and "O Gott, du frommer Gott"), by Ahasuerus Fritsch, was first included in *Himmels-Lust und Welt-Unlust* published in Leipzig in 1679 as given below (Zahn* #5206).

There it was set to Johann J. Schütz's (LBW 542) "Die Wollust dieser Welt." In the 1698 Darmstadt *Geistreiches Gesangbuch,* where it was the setting for Wolfgang Dessler's "Was frag ich nach der Welt," it took a form much closer to the present one. The fifth and seventh phrases of the LBW version are from J. G. Nicolai's *Volständiges Choralbuch,* 1765, and the sixth phrase, from Johann Balthasar König's (LBW 22) *Harmonischer Lieder-Schatz,* 1738.

Fritsch, born December 16, 1629, was the eighth of eleven children born to the mayor of Mücheln on the Geissel, near Merseburg, Germany. During his youth he and his family were forced many times to flee from plunderers and soldiers in the Thirty Years' War. When Ahasuerus was fourteen his father died, but his mother managed to see him through the

Gymnasium at Halle, and in 1650 he went to Jena to study under J. Georg Adam Stuve. He became tutor in 1657 to Count Albert Anton von Schwarzburg-Rudolstadt, whose family assisted him in his career. In 1661 he received a Doctor of Law degree from the University of Jena, and later became chancellor of the university and president of the consistory of Rudolstadt. He was married in 1662, and his wife, Dorothea Maria, bore nine children, seven of whom survived him. He died on August 24, 1701.

J. S. Bach (LBW 219) used this melody in Cantatas 45, 64, 94, and 133.

505   FORTH IN THY NAME, O LORD, I GO

Tune: Song 34

See LBW 27 for Charles Wesley. This hymn was included in *Hymns and Sacred Poems,* 1749.

SONG 34 (also "Angel's Song") by Orlando Gibbons (LBW 206) was included in George Wither's *Hymns and Songs of the Church,* 1623, where it was the setting for The Song of the Angels, Luke 2:13, "Thus angels sung, and thus sing we."

The harmonization is by Carl Schalk (LBW 118). The rhythm of the fourth and fifth notes of the first phrase has been altered from half to quarter notes, and a quarter-note rest has been added at the beginning of the second phrase.

506   DEAR LORD AND FATHER OF MANKIND

Tune: Rest

This hymn is taken from John Greenleaf Whittier's seventeen-stanza poem, "The Brewing of Soma," which was first published in the April, 1872, issue of the *Atlantic Monthly.* The opening lines of the poem described a rite of the priests of Indra (the chief god of early Hinduism) in which the intoxicating beverage Soma, brewed from honey and milk, was used to produce a drunken frenzy, out of which the worshipers hoped to begin a joyous new life:

> The fagots blazed, the caldron's smoke
> Up through the green wood curled;
> "Bring honey from the hollow oak,
> Bring milky sap," the brewers spoke,
> In the childhood of the world.

In later stanzas a parallel was drawn between the Hindu rite and some of Christian worship, especially the noisy, hysterical revivals and camp meetings which the poet found so offensive:

> And yet the past comes round again,
> And new doth old fulfill;
> In sensual transports wild as vain
> We brew in many a Christian lane
> The heathen Soma still!

The closing six stanzas of the poem, beginning with "Dear Lord and Father of mankind," portray Whittier's concept of true worship.

Whittier, of Puritan ancestry and Quaker parentage, was born near Haverhill, Massachusetts, December 17, 1807. Poverty in the family made it impossible for him to attend school beyond the primitive district school. He worked on the family farm until he was twenty and thereafter worked as a shoemaker and teacher, finally accumulating enough money to attend two sessions at the Haverhill Academy. Excited by a book of Robert Burns's poems which he had purchased from a peddler, Whittier was writing verse himself by the time he was fourteen. His first works were printed in the *Newburyport Free Press* in 1825. He was appointed editor of *The American Manufacturer* in Boston in 1828, and two years later went to Hartford to work on the *New England Review*. In 1831, however, he was forced to return home because of illness, and once more worked on the farm for five years, doing his writing at night. In 1836 he became editor of the *Pennsylvania Freeman*. Whittier was a strong supporter of the abolition of slavery and suffered much because of his stand, including physical abuse and, in 1838, the burning of his publication office. After 1840 he lived in Amesbury, Massachusetts, and in 1847, became the editor of the *National Era*. His last years were spent at Oak Knoll, Danvers, Massachusetts. He died at Hampton Falls, New Hampshire, September 7, 1892, and was buried at Amesbury.

Whittier was the author of a number of poems, including *Snowbound*, 1866; *The Tent on the Beach*, 1867; *Our Master*, 1866; and *The Eternal Goodness*, 1892.

REST (also "Elton") was composed by Frederick C. Maker (LBW 107) for this text and given in G. S. Barrett's and E. J. Hopkins' (LBW 262) *Congregational Church Hymnal*, London, 1887.

507 HOW FIRM A FOUNDATION

Tune: Foundation

John Rippon's (LBW 328) *A Selection of Hymns*, 1787, contained this hymn, attributed simply to "K---." The initial has sometimes been interpreted as Keen, Kirkham, or George Keith, but the author of the hymn really is not known. The alterations are slight.

FOUNDATION is an anonymous tune. Titled "Protection," it was the setting for this hymn in Joseph Funk's *A Compilation of Genuine Church Music*, Winchester, Virginia, 1832. William Walker's (LBW 30) *Southern Harmony*, 1835, called the tune "The Christian's Farewell," and *The Sacred Harp*, 1844 (LBW 423), credited the tune (there called "Bellevue") to "Z. Chambless."

Born April 6, 1778, Joseph Funk was the descendant of German Mennonites who a generation before had arrived in eastern Pennsylvania from the Rhine-Palatinate. Around 1780 the family moved to the Shenandoah Valley, settling not far from Harrisonburg, Virginia, in a community later called Singer's Glen. He was married to Elizabeth Rhodes (changed from "Roth") on Christmas Day, 1804, and cleared a plot of land and constructed a small log house. Elizabeth died in 1813, having given birth to five children, and Joseph married Rachel Britton the following year. She was the mother of nine more children. Amidst the struggles of maintaining a home and creating a farm from the virgin forest, Joseph found time to learn and teach music, and to complete his *Choral-Music* in 1816. In 1832 he published his *Genuine Church Music* which appeared in several subsequent editions as *Harmonia Sacra.* He also made English translations of a Mennonite *Confession of Faith* (1837) and his grandfather Henry Funk's *A Mirror of Baptism,* 1851. Around 1804 he had constructed a log schoolhouse on his property, where he taught school. In 1847 the schoolhouse was converted to a print shop, and in the same year he conducted seven singing schools east of the Blue Ridge Mountains. Together with his sons he had taught singing schools in eleven Virginia counties by 1858, and in 1859 established the *Southern Musical Advocate and Singer's Friend,* a monthly music journal devoted to rural music and singing schools. Suspended during the Civil War, the periodical resumed in the late 1860s, running until 1869. The *Advocate* was followed by a similar publication, *Musical Million,* produced by Funk's grandson, Aldine Kieffer. Funk died in 1862.

The harmonization is by Charles Huddleston Heaton, organist and choir director of East Liberty Presbyterian Church, Pittsburgh, Pennsylvania.

Born November 1, 1928, in Centralia, Illinois, Heaton received a Bachelor of Music degree from DePauw University, Greencastle, Indiana, in 1950. At Union Theological Seminary, New York, he completed a Master of Sacred Music degree in 1952 and a Doctor of Sacred Music degree in 1957. In the interim, he served from 1952 to 1954 in the United States Army. He was minister of music at Second Presbyterian Church, St. Louis, from 1956 to 1972, during which time he was also director of music at Temple Israel from 1959 to 1970, and lecturer in music at Eden Theological Seminary, 1968–1971. Since 1972 he has been in Pittsburgh.

Heaton is the editor of the *Hymnbook for Christian Worship,* 1970, and has published *How to Build a Church Choir,* 1958, and *A Guide to Worship Services of Sacred Music,* 1962, as well as articles in several periodicals. A fellow of the American Guild of Organists, he has served as national councillor and a regional chairman for that organization. He is also active in the Hymn Society of America. He is listed in several biographical dictionaries, including *Who's Who in the Midwest* and the *Dictionary of International Biography.* Married to Jane Pugh of Centralia, Illinois, he is the father of three children.

508 COME DOWN, O LOVE DIVINE *(Discendi, amor santo)*

Tune: Down Ampney

"Laudi," Italian vernacular hymns of praise and devotion, date from the period of Francis of Assisi (LBW 527) and during the thirteenth and fourteenth centuries were used especially by the "flagellants," groups of penitents who, frightened by the devastating wars and plagues of their time, sought atonement for the sins of the age by punishing themselves. Later, congregations (called "Companie de Laudesi" or "Laudisti") formed which cultivated devotional singing among the Italian people. Out of the musical and dramatic representations which occurred in their meetings the oratorio developed in the sixteenth century.

This hymn is taken from an extended poem in a collection of Bianco da Siena's *Laudi Spirituali,* published by Telesforo Bini at Lucca in 1851, and translated by Richard Littledale in the *People's Hymnal,* 1867.

Bianco da Siena (Bianco di Santi), whose birthdate is unknown, was born at Anciolina in the Val d'Arno in Italy. In 1367 he entered the newly-founded Order of the Jesuates, a group of laymen following the rule of St. Augustine. He lived a while in Venice and died there in 1434.

Richard Frederick Littledale, the son of a merchant, was born September 14, 1833, in Dublin, Ireland. He had a distinguished university career, receiving Bachelor of Arts (1858), Master of Arts (1858), and Bachelor of Laws and Doctor of Laws (1862) degrees from Trinity College, Dublin, and a Doctor of Civil Law degree from Oxford, also in 1862. Ordained a deacon in 1856 and a priest in 1857, he ministered in 1856 to St. Matthew's, Thorpe Hamlet, Norfolk, and from 1857 to 1861 at St. Mary the Virgin, Crown Street, Soho. Chronic ill health made it necessary for him to give up parish ministry, and he devoted the rest of his life to literature, publishing nearly fifty works in the fields of theology, history, liturgy, and hymnology. He contributed frequently to various periodicals, including the *Church Quarterly Review,* and following the death of John Mason Neale (LBW 34) completed his *Commentary on the Psalms from Primitive and Mediaeval writers,* II–IV, 1868–1874. He translated hymns from seven diffferent languages— Greek, Latin, Syriac, German, Italian, Danish, and Swedish—and compiled *Carols for Christmas and Other Seasons,* 1863. With James Edward Vaux he prepared the *Priest's Prayer Book,* 1864; *The People's Hymnal,* 1867; and *The Altar Manual,* 1863–1877. He died January 11, 1890.

DOWN AMPNEY was composed by Ralph Vaughan Williams (LBW 101) for this text in the 1906 *English Hymnal.* Named after Vaughan Williams' birthplace near Cirencester in Gloustershire, the tune was marked "Anon." when it first appeared. Well-suited both to the unusual meter and to the introspective character of the text, the tune is described in Parry and Routley* as "perhaps the most beautiful hymn tune composed since the 'Old Hundredth'" (LBW 245).

509 ONWARD, CHRISTIAN SOLDIERS
Tune: St. Gertrude

See LBW 280 for Sabine Baring-Gould. Written for a children's festival at Horbury Bridge, near Wakefield, in 1864, this hymn was printed the same year in the October 15 issue of *The Church Times.*

ST. GERTRUDE, written for Baring-Gould's text in *The Hymnary,* 1872, first appeared as one of four samples included in the December, 1871, *Musical Times* where the forthcoming hymnal was advertised. The tune was named in honor of Mrs. Gertrude Clay-Ker-Seymer, at whose home at Hanford, Dorsetshire, Sullivan was staying when he composed it. See LBW 153 for Arthur Seymour Sullivan.

510 O GOD OF YOUTH
Tune: Lynne

This hymn was written to be sung at a high school commencement in 1935 at Pontiac, Michigan. It was later adopted as the official hymn of the National Federation of Young People.

Bates Gilbert Burt, born in Wheeling, West Virginia, on December 21, 1878, was educated at Kenyon College, where he received a Master of Arts degree in 1901. He entered Seabury Divinity School for a year in 1902, and was ordained an Episcopalian deacon in 1903 and a priest the following year. His ministry as dean of St. Paul's Cathedral in Marquette, Michigan, from 1904 to 1917 and 1920 to 1922 was interrupted by two years' service as a chaplain in France during World War I. From 1922 until he retired in 1947 he was rector of All Saints' Church, Pontiac, Michigan. He died at Edgewood, Maryland, April 5, 1948.

Burt composed several hymn tunes and some chant settings and, together with his son, wrote a number of Christmas carols. In 1946 he became a member of the joint commission on the revision of *The Hymnal 1940* (Episcopal).

LYNNE. When this hymn was first sung in 1935, it was set to a tune entitled "Deus juvenum." Later, in 1940, Burt wrote this tune, named "Lynne" in honor of his granddaughter, and text and tune were included in the Episcopal *Hymnal 1940*. The harmonization is by Paul Bunjes (LBW 38).

511 RENEW ME, O ETERNAL LIGHT
(Erneure mich, o ewiges Licht)
Tune: Herr Jesu Christ, meins

Johann Friedrich Ruopp, the son of a shoemaker, was born the end of February, 1672, at Strassburg in Alsace-Lorraine. He was a student of theology and poetry at the universities of Strassburg and Jena from 1689 to 1692. After serving as a vicar at Lampertheim, he became pastor at Goxweiler, near Strassburg, in 1692. Seven years later he became assistant to his step-brother in the village of Breuschwickersheim, also near Strassburg, where he was held in high esteem for his scholarship. As a student he had turned to Pietism, and while he was at Lampertheim and later at Goxweiler, he secretly prepared a collection of hymns titled *Jesuslieder*. Together with his colleagues, and in 1704 with Johann Friedrich Haug, he attempted to spread a "living Christianity." Accused of sectarianism, he was defrocked and forced to leave Alsace-Lorraine. After considerable tribulation he made his way to Halle, then a center of Pietism, where he worked as a food inspector at the orphanage and became an assistant to the theological faculty. He died May 26, 1708.

This hymn was first included in *Jesuslieder*. The translation, by August Crull (LBW 24), was given in the *Evangelical Lutheran Hymn-Book,* 1889.

For HERR JESU CHRIST, MEINS see LBW 286. Except for the passing notes and an altered rhythm in the last phrase, the tune is given here as it originally appeared (Zahn* #533a).

512 OH, BLEST THE HOUSE *(Wohl einem Haus, da Jesus Christ)*
Tune: Wo Gott zum Haus

Apparently written for the First Sunday after the Epiphany, 1746, this hymn was included in the author's *Evangelisches Gesangbuch,* Memmingen, 1782.

526

Christoph Carl Ludwig, Baron von Pfeil, was born January 20, 1712, at Grünstadt, near Worms, Germany, where his father was then in the service of the Count of Leinigen. In 1728 he entered the University of Halle as a law student, and after completing his course at the University of Tübingen, he was appointed Württemberg secretary of legation at Regensburg in 1732. Beginning in 1745 he held a number of political offices, but he resigned in April of 1763, finding himself unable to cooperate in carrying out the absolutism of the Württemberg prime minister, Count Montmartin. He retired to his estate of Deufstetten, near Crailsheim, which he had purchased two years earlier. In September of 1763 he was appointed privy councillor and Prussian ambassador to the Diets of Swabia and Franconia by Frederick the Great. He was thereafter created Baron by Emperor Joseph II, and in 1765, received the cross of the Red Eagle Order from Frederick the Great. An intermittent illness confined him to his bed after August, 1783, and he died the following year on February 14.

Von Pfiel's hymn-writing began as a result of a spiritual change he experienced on the Tenth Sunday after Trinity in 1730, and continued throughout his life, with the number of his printed hymns reaching 950. In addition to *Evangelisches Gesangbuch,* his publications included *Lieder von der offenbarten Herrlichkeit,* 1741; a set of Psalm versions, 1747; and *Evangelische Glaubens-und Herzensgesänge,* 1783.

Catherine Winkworth's (LBW 29) translation was included in her *Chorale Book for England,* 1863. Alterations are not extensive.

For WO GOTT ZUM HAUS see LBW 85. The harmonization is by Frederick Jackisch (LBW 236).

513 COME, MY WAY, MY TRUTH, MY LIFE
Tune: The Call

Three weeks before his death George Herbert entrusted the manuscript of his most famous work, *The Temple,* to Nicholas Ferrar, requesting that he read it "and then, if he can think it may turn to the advantage of any dejected soul, let it be made public." This hymn was included in *The Temple,* which was published in 1633 after the author's death.

Born April 3, 1593, at Montgomery Castle in Wales, Herbert attended Trinity College, Cambridge, receiving a Bachelor of Arts degree in 1611. Four years later he completed his Master of Arts degree and became a major fellow of the college, and in 1619, became public orator for the university. Herbert, esteemed by Francis Bacon and a friend of other important poets, enjoyed the favor of King James I. After James's death, Herbert took holy orders and was appointed prebend of Leighton Ecclesia and to the parish of Leighton Bromswold in 1626. Ill-health forced his resignation three years later, and from 1630 until his death he was rector of the little parish of St. Andrew Bemerton in the parish of Fugglestone St. Peter, near Salisbury. He died of consumption on March 1, 1633 (some sources have 1632), and was buried beneath the altar of his own church.

Herbert's *Life* was written by his intimate friend, Isaak Walton. *Harmonia Sacra,* 1688, contains settings of his poems by Henry Purcell and John Blow.

THE CALL is from Ralph Vaughan Williams' (LBW 101) *Five Mystical Songs from George Herbert,* 1911.

514 O SAVIOR, PRECIOUS SAVIOR

Tune: Angel's Story

See LBW 260 for Frances Ridley Havergal. This hymn was written at Leamington, November, 1870, and published in *Under the Surface,* 1874.

ANGEL'S STORY, originally called "Watermouth," was composed for Emily Miller's "I love to hear the story Which angel voices tell" and appeared in *The Methodist Sunday School Hymnal,* London, 1881.

Arthur Henry Mann, born in Norwich, England, on May 16, 1850, was a chorister at the cathedral there, and occasionally assisted his teacher, Dr. Zechariah Buck. At New College, Oxford, he received a Bachelor of Music degree in 1874, and a Doctor of Music degree in 1882. He became organist of St. Peter's, Wolverhampton in 1870, Tettenhall Parish Church in 1871, and Beverly Minster in 1875, before going to King's College, Cambridge, where he remained for fifty-three years. Highly regarded as an organist and master of choristers, he contributed much to the fine musical traditions of the college. After 1897, he was also organist to the University of Cambridge, which awarded him an honorary Master of Arts degree in 1910. Death came November 19, 1929.

Mann was one of the early members of the Royal College of Organists, and a fellow of King's College. A composer of church music, he was also a great collector of early hymn books, and served as music editor of Charles D. Bell's *The Church of England Hymnal,* 1895. Much of his time was spent working over George F. Handel's (LBW 39) manuscripts.

515 HOW MARVELOUS GOD'S GREATNESS
(Hve dýrðlegur er dróttinn)

Tune: Den Blomstertid nu kommer

This hymn, which so beautifully reflects the rugged coasts and mountainous terrain of Briem's Iceland, is the only hymn in the LBW from that country. It was first published in *Sálmabok til Kirkju-og Heima-Söngs,* Reykjavík, 1886.

Valdimar Olafsson Briem, one of the best and most prolific of Icelandic hymnwriters, and the son of a distinguished family, was born February 11, 1848, on the Grund estate in northern Iceland. His parents died, and he was brought up by his uncle, a prominent clergyman in southern Iceland. He graduated in 1869 from the Latin School in Reykjavík, and three years later completed studies at the Theological Seminary there. For thirty-eight years beginning in 1880 he served as pastor of Stori-Napur, and was district superintendent for much of that time as well. From 1909 until his death on May 3, 1930, he was vice-bishop of the Skalholt diocese.

The Icelandic hymnal of 1886 included 102 original hymns and thirty-nine translations by Briem. In addition, he contributed lyrics to several journals, compiled *Frjettir frá Islandi,* 1871–1878, and published two major poetical works, *Biblíuljoð* (metrical pictures of Biblical events), 1896–1897, and *Ljóð úr Jobsbók* (a collection of songs based on the book of Job), 1908.

The English translation by Charles Venn Pilcher was given in his *The* very few.

Pilcher was born June 4, 1879, in Oxford, England, where his father was rector of St. Clement's Church. His mother's great-aunt was Charlotte Elliott (LBW 296) and her aunt was Emily E. S. Elliott. At Hertford College, Oxford, he completed a Bachelor of Arts degree in 1902, and later received Master of Arts (1905) and Bachelor of Divinity (1909) degrees. In 1921 he completed a Doctor of Divinity degree at Oxford. He was ordained in 1903 and served for two years in the parish of St. Thomas, Birmingham, and one year as domestic chaplain to the bishop of Durham, Handley Carr Glyn Moule. In 1906 he was appointed teacher of New Testament Greek and patristics at Wycliffe College, Toronto, Ontario. After two years he became assistant curate to St. Alban's Cathedral and in 1910 took the same post at St. James Cathedral. From 1916 to 1919 he was precentor at the Church of the Resurrection. During these years also he was married and became the father of two children. In 1916 he returned to Wycliffe as a part-time lecturer, and in 1919 was appointed professor of Old Testament. From 1923 to 1936 he was professor of New Testament language and literature. In 1936 he went to Australia to become bishop-coadjutor of the diocese of Sydney, where he remained, preaching in the Cathedral Church of St. Andrew, teaching at Moore Theological College, and serving as a member of the Board of Studies for Divinity Degrees. He resigned in 1956 and died July 4, 1961.

Pilcher was an excellent teacher and preacher and published a number of Biblical and devotional works and articles in religious journals. A poet who inherited his mother's fascination with Iceland, he published a number of articles on the country and translated many hymns and classics. Translations from Greek, Latin, German, and Russian, as well as original hymns, can also be found among his writings. Also a musician, he played bass clarinet for ten years in the Toronto Symphony, and from 1931 to 1936 was canon precentor of the diocese of Toronto. With Healey Willan (LBW 125) and J. Campbell McInness he conducted church music summer schools in the diocese. He was a world traveler and took an active part in social issues.

DEN BLOMSTERTID NU KOMMER is a Swedish melody which appeared in the Roslagskulla manuscript, 1693. In *Then Swenska Psalm-Boken,* 1697, it was the setting for Israel Kolmodin's hymn, "Den blomstertid nu kommer" (a hymn which possibly traces its origins to the medieval Latin carol, "Tempus adest floridam"). J. Irving Erickson, in his *Twice-Born Hymns* (Chicago, 1976), notes that the folk melody is older, however, and was the setting for an extended *visa* about a Roman count captured by the Turks on his way to visit the grave of Christ, and released when his wife, disguised as a monk, sang for the Turkish king. Lövgren* places the tune, with "The Count of Rome," in Harold Olufsson's songbook of 1573.

516 ARISE, MY SOUL, ARISE! *(Nyt ylös, sieluni)*
Tune: Nyt ylös, sieluni

The Swedish hymn writer, Johan Kahl (1721–1746), was born in Visby on the island of Gotland in the Baltic Sea. The son of a merchant and member of the city council, he served as a civil servant in Stockholm, where he became a part of the Moravian movement which had taken root in Sweden. In 1743 the Swedish Moravians published their first edition of *Sions Sånger,* a collection of ninety religious songs for use in their conventicles. The enlarged edition, published in 1745, contained 223 songs, many of which were by Kahl. Neither edition had the official ecclesiastical authorization then required by law. In 1790 an anonymous collection of Finnish spiritual songs, *Halullisten Sjelujen Hengelliset Laulut,* was published in Turku. It included several translations from *Sions Sånger.* The same year the first complete edition of *Sions Sånger* in Finnish, translated by a parish priest, Elias Lagus, was published in Turku. Titled *Sionin Wirret,* the book became a great favorite among the conservative Pietists in southeast Finland.

"Arise, my soul, arise" was originally written in Swedish by Kahl. Beginning "Upp, upp, min själ! och sjung," it was included in the 1745 edition of *Sions Sånger.* It first appeared in Finnish in *Halullisten Sjelujen Hengelliset Laulut.* Ernest E. Ryden (LBW 186) prepared the English versification for the *Service Book and Hymnal,* 1958, from a literal translation of the Finnish form.

NYT YLÖS, SIELUNI, also called "Suomi," originated in Kalanti, near Uusikaupunki, in southwest Finland. The tune was discovered in the summer of 1890 by two university students, Berndt Mikael Nyberg (LBW 485) and Ilmari Krohn, son of Julius Krohn (LBW 319), who later became an internationally famous musicologist and teacher at Helsinki University. Out on a field trip collecting secular folk melodies, Nyberg and Krohn met an old sexton who belonged to the conservative Pietists—the Rukoilevaiset, or "Praying People"—of southwest Finland, who sang this melody for them. The tune was published in a collection of folk melodies titled *Kansan Lahja Kirkolle,* Jyväskylä, 1891.

The harmonization was prepared for the *Service Book and Hymnal,* 1958, by Ulrich S. Leupold.

Leupold was a native of Berlin, Germany, where his father was organist at St. Petri, and his mother was a singer and voice teacher. Born January 15, 1909, he received a Doctor of Philosophy degree in musicology from the University of Berlin in 1932. Following theological studies at the University of Berlin (1927-1934), the University of Zurich (1929), and the Seminary of the Confessing Church (1935-1937), he came to the United States in 1938, where he was minister of music at Augsburg Lutheran Church, Toledo, Ohio, for one year. Ordained in 1939, he was assistant pastor of St. Matthew's Lutheran Church, Kitchener, Ontario, until 1942. In 1942 he was married to Gertrude Daber at Kitchener, Ontario, and became pastor of Christ Lutheran Church, Maynooth, Ontario, where he remained until 1945. From 1945 until his death on June 9, 1970, he was professor of music and New Testament at Waterloo Lutheran University, and for most of those years was dean of the seminary.

The editor of volume 53 of *Luther's Works,* "Liturgy and Hymns," Leupold also translated Vilmos Vajta's *Luther on Worship,* 1958, and contributed countless articles to various publications. In the field of music he published organ works and anthems, a *Manual on Intoning,* and an edition of Max Reger's responses. He served on the Commission on Worship of the Lutheran Church in America, as well as on the Commission on the Liturgy and Hymnal; served on the board of directors of the Lutheran Society of Worship, Music, and Arts; and was a member of the Faith and Order Study Commission of the Canadian Council of Churches, and of the Spanish Hymnal Committee. He was also a lecturer at theological conferences in Europe. In 1967 he was the recipient of the Canadian Centennial Medal, and served as president of the Canadian Society of Biblical Studies. Knox Divinity College honored him with a doctorate in 1969.

517   PRAISE TO THE FATHER

Tune: Flemming

This hymn by Elizabeth Rundle Charles is unusual in that it does not use rhyme at the ends of the lines.

Elizabeth Rundle, born January 2, 1828, at Tavistock, Devonshire, in England, was the daughter of a member of Parliament, and the wife of Andrew Paton Charles, a barrister. Privately educated at home by tutors, she started writing at an early age and later, through her writings, became one of the best-known women of her day in England. Her very popular fiction works covered a wide range of historical interests, including early Christian life in Great Britain, the life and times of Martin Luther (LBW 48) and John Wesley (LBW 302), the English civil wars, and so on. Her *Chronicles of the Schönberg-Cotta Family,* 1863, the historical novel of Luther's times, was also widely-read in the United States. Her hymn-writing, which began in 1850 with a translation of a hymn by Joachim Neander (LBW 182), included original hymns as well as translations from Latin, German, and Swedish, and were published in *The Voice of Christian Life in Song,* 1864, and other publications. Besides being a writer she was also a musician and an artist. She died at Hampstead Heath near London. Her death date is given variously as March 28 or April 1, 1896.

FLEMMING (also "Integer Vitae") gained for its composer, a physician by vocation, a place in *Grove's Dictionary of Music and Musicians.* Friedrich Ferdinand Flemming, born at Neuhausen, Saxony, on February 28, 1778, studied medicine at the universities of Wittenberg, Jena, Vienna, and Trieste, and subsequently set up practice in Berlin. There he became involved in the musical life of the city and composed a number of songs for male chorus for the society founded in 1808 by Carl F. Zelter. He died in Berlin, May 27, 1813.

Written in 1811, "Flemming" was originally a setting for male chorus of Horace Ode XXII, "Integer vitae, scelerisque purus." Already in 1836 the music had been taken over into hymnody, when it was set to "Danket dem Schöpfer" in J. B. C. Schmidt's *Sammlung von Kirchengesängen fur katholische Gymnasien* (Bäumker,* IV, #341).

518   BEAUTIFUL SAVIOR *(Schönster Herr Jesu)*

Tune: Schönster Herr Jesu

Sometimes called the "Crusaders Hymn," a designation which is entirely unfounded, this hymn first appeared in a manuscript from Münster, Germany, dated 1662, and was first printed in the Roman Catholic *Munsterisch Gesangbuch* of 1677. Joseph A. Seiss's "Beautiful Savior" is a distinctly Lutheran translation; the anonymous "Fairest Lord Jesus," which first appeared in 1850 in Richard Storrs Willis' (LBW 54) *Church Carols and Choir Studies,* is the English form used in non-Lutheran hymnals. Seiss's translation was published in the *Sunday School Book for the use of Evangelical Lutheran Congregations,* Philadelphia, 1873.

Joseph August Seiss (originally "Seuss"), of Alsatian ancestry, was born at the German Moravian settlement of Graceham in Frederick County, Maryland, on March 18, 1823. He received his early education at the Moravian school and at the age of sixteen was confirmed a member of the Moravian church. Discouraged by his father and his bishop from entering the ministry, he nevertheless studied by night with his Moravian pastor and then, with the help of a few Lutheran clergymen, entered Pennsylvania College at Gettysburg in 1839. He pursued his theological course primarily in private, and in 1842 was licensed to preach by the Evangelical Lutheran Synod of Virginia. Thereafter he ministered to Martinsburg and Shepherdstown in Virginia (1844–1847); the English Lutheran Church in Cumberland, Maryland (1847–1852); and Second English Lutheran Church of Baltimore, Maryland (1852–1858). In 1858 he became pastor of St. John's Lutheran Church in Philadelphia, where he remained for sixteen years until he, with some of his members, established the Church of the Holy Communion in western Philadelphia. He remained in Philadelphia until his death on June 20, 1904.

Seiss was the author or editor of some eighty works, including *The Last Times,* 1856; *The Evangelical Psalmist,* [1859]; *The Assassination of a President,* 1865; *Ecclesia Lutherana,* 1868; *Lectures on the Gospels,* 1868–1872; and *Lectures on the Epistles,* 1885; as well as works on education and the Lutheran liturgy, and hymn collections.

SCHÖNSTER HERR JESU (also "Crusader's Hymn" and "St. Elizabeth"). The melody with which this hymn was first published is given as the first tune for hymn #346 in *The Hymnal 1940* of the Episcopal Church. The present melody, from the Glaz district of Silesia, was heard among the haymakers in 1839 and written down by August Heinrich Hoffmann von Fallersleben. Hoffmann von Fallersleben (1798–1874), a noted poet and scholar—together with Ernst Friedrich Richter (1808–1879), director of the St. Thomas school in Leipzig where J. S. Bach (LBW 219) had once served—collected a number of sacred and secular folksongs from Silesia. These were published in *Schlesische Volkslieder,* Leipzig, 1842, including this tune, which appeared with a considerably altered form of the hymn "Schönster Herr Jesu." A facsimile reproduction of the tune as first published is given in Haeussler,* page 234. By 1850 the tune had come to the United States in Willis' collection (see above). Named "Ascalon" in England, the melody has served there as a setting for Isaac Watts's (LBW 39) "How pleased and blest was I." It is also sung in Scandinavian churches. Franz Liszt used the tune in his oratorio, *Legend of St. Elizabeth,* 1862. In an arrangement by F. Melius Christiansen the hymn has been sung for many years by the St. Olaf Choir.

As with many folk melodies, this tune seems to have its roots in older melodies. A tune composed by Christian Ernst Graaf for "Laat ons Juichen, Batavieren," used at the installation of Willem V as Statholder in the Hague in 1766, was set the same year in eight variations (K. 24) by Wolfgang Amadeus Mozart, who was visiting the Hague at the time. The opening lines, given below, contain a similarity to "Schönster Herr Jesu."

etc.

519 MY SOUL, NOW PRAISE YOUR MAKER!
(Nun lob, mein Seel, den Herren)
Tune: Nun lob, mein Seel

Johann Gramann (also Graumann or Poliander) was born July 5, 1487, in Neustadt in the Bavarian Palatinate. Following his studies at Leipzig University where he received a Master of Arts degree in 1516 and a Bachelor of Divinity in 1520, he was appointed rector of St. Thomas' School in Leipzig, where J. S. Bach (LBW 219) was later *Kapellmeister.* In 1519 Gramann, as Johann Eck's secretary, attended a disputation between Eck, Martin Luther (LBW 48), and Andreas Bodenstein von Karlstadt. So impressed was he with Luther's Scriptural foundation for his opinions and his appeal to the dictates of conscience, as opposed to Eck's cleverness in the art of disputation, that he espoused the cause of the Reformation and left Leipzig in 1522, joining Luther and Philipp Melanchthon at Wittenberg. In 1523 he was appointed preacher at Würzburg, but left two years later because of the outbreak of the Peasants' War, and went to Nürnberg as preacher to the nunnery at St. Clara. On Luther's recommendation he was invited by Margrave Albrecht of Brandenburg to assist in furthering the Reformation in Prussia. Beginning his work in October of 1525 at the Altstadt Church in Königsberg, he labored with great zeal and success, refuting the Anabaptists and Schwenckfeldians, and establishing evangelical schools in the province. He died at Königsberg on April 29, 1541.

Martin Chemnitz, distinguished Lutheran theologian and one of the authors of the *Formula of Concord,* noted in 1575 that this hymn was written at the request of Margrave Albrecht, based on his favorite psalm, Psalm 103, and that it was joyfully sung by him on his deathbed. The hymn was also used by Gustavus Adolphus on April 24, 1632, at the first restored Protestant service in Augsburg, and was sung by the inhabitants of Osnabrück, Westphalia, as a thanksgiving at the close of the Thirty Years' War on October 25, 1648. It first appeared as a broadsheet in Nürnberg about 1540, and was printed in Kugelmann's *Concentus novi,* 1540 (see below).

Catherine Winkworth's (LBW 29) translation was included in her *Chorale Book for England,* 1863. Some alterations have been made for the LBW.

NUN LOB, MEIN SEEL is one of three sacred settings stemming from the fifteenth-century secular German folk song, "Weiss mir ein Blümlein blaue." It appeared with this hymn in Kugelmann's *Concentus novi, trium vocum,* printed in Augsburg in 1540. This publication was dedicated to Margrave Albrecht of Prussia—a Renaissance prince, statesman, humanist, lied poet, and perhaps also a melody composer—who influenced the creation of the collection and helped to finance it by ordering three hundred copies.

Johann (Hans) Kugelmann is first found as a trumpeter, then in 1536, as *Kapellmeister* in the court of Margrave Albrecht. From 1540 to 1543 Nikolaus Decius (LBW 111) was his assistant in Königsberg. His death date is possibly 1556.

The harmonization is from the *Württembergische Choralbuch,* 1953. J. S. Bach (LBW 219) used the tune in Cantatas 17 and 29.

520 GIVE TO OUR GOD IMMORTAL PRAISE!
Tune: Duke Street

This hymn by Isaac Watts (LBW 39) is from his Psalm 136 of the *Psalms of David,* 1719.

For DUKE STREET see LBW 352.

521 LET US WITH A GLADSOME MIND
Tune: Williams Bay

This paraphrase of Psalm 136 was written by John Milton (LBW 318) in 1623, when he was only fifteen. It appeared in the *Poems of Mr. John Milton, both English and Latin,* 1645, in twenty-four two-line stanzas with the refrain: "For His mercies aye endure, Ever faithful, ever sure." The text as given here contains some alterations.

WILLIAMS BAY was composed by Daniel Moe (LBW 427) and included in *The Contemporary Liturgy,* 1963, which he prepared with John Arthur (LBW 387) for the Lutheran Student Association of America.

522 COME, THOU ALMIGHTY KING
Tune: Italian Hymn

This hymn of unknown authorship was first published in a tract of unknown date, along with Charles Wesley's (LBW 27) "Jesus, let Thy pitying eye," and is bound up with the British Museum copy of George Whitefield's *Collection of Hymns for Social Worship,* sixth edition, 1757, and also with the 1759 and 1760 editions. In later editions the hymn was included in the body of Whitefield's collection. The only alteration is in stanza 2, where the last two lines originally read "Spirit of holiness, on us descend!"

George Whitefield was a great eighteenth-century English evangelical preacher who also made preaching tours of the American colonies, and was involved in the "Great Awakening" started by Jonathan Edwards in

Northhampton, Massachusetts, in 1734. Old South Presbyterian Church at Newburyport, Massachusetts, was founded by his followers. While Whitefield made use of the hymns of Charles and John Wesley (LBW 302) and Isaac Watts (LBW 39) in his meetings, he preferred those of Watts and was responsible for bringing about the "Era of Watts" in American churches. His *Collection of Hymns,* first published in 1753 for use at his Tabernacle on Tottenham Court Road, was reprinted several times in America.

Born December 16, 1714, in Gloucester, England, Whitefield was educated at Pembroke College, Oxford, where he joined the Oxford Holy Club along with the Wesleys in 1735. Ordained to the Church of England in 1736, he began preaching for the Methodists the following year, and two years later made the first of several trips to the American colonies. While remaining a friend of the Wesleys, he took a divergent theological position from theirs in 1741. For a time he served as chaplain to Selina Hastings, the Countess of Huntingdon. He died September 30, 1770, at Newburyport, Massachusetts, and is buried under the pulpit of Old South Presbyterian Church.

Here called ITALIAN HYMN in reference to the composer's place of birth, this tune has also been titled "Moscow" for his place of death. The name given the tune on its first appearance, in Martin Madan's *A Collection of Psalm and Hymn Tunes, Never published before,* 1769, was "Hymn to the Trinity." Madan's *Collection* was published for the benefit of Lock Hospital, at Hyde Park in London.

The composer, Felice de Giardini, was a brilliant Italian violinist. Born at Turin on April 12, 1716, he began his musical career as a chorister at Milan Cathedral, where he studied singing, clavier, and harmony. Afterwards he returned to Turin where he studied violin, and then played for the opera first at Rome and then at San Carlo, Naples. Following a tour of Germany, he arrived in London in 1750 where he was immediately successful, playing, teaching, and conducting. His efforts at managing the Italian Opera were, however, much less successful and he suffered great losses. He left England in 1784, resolved to retire and spend the rest of his life in Italy, but became restless and returned to London in 1790, starting a comic opera at Haymarket. The venture was a failure and he took his troupe to Russia where he died December 17, 1796, at Moscow.

Giardini was a prolific composer of operas, violin music, etc., and in addition to this hymn tune prepared, with another composer, an oratorio for use at Lock Hospital Chapel. "Italian Hymn" has entered the ranks of immortal hymn tunes and is found widely in collections of many denominations.

523   HOLY SPIRIT, EVER DWELLING

Tune: In Babilone

The author of this hymn, Timothy Rees, was born August 15, 1874, at Llain, Llanon, in Wales. After completing a Bachelor of Arts degree in 1896 at St. David's College, Lampeter, he went to St. Michael's College in Aberdeen. Ordained a deacon of the Church of England in 1897, and a priest the following year, he served from 1897 to 1901 as curate of Mountain Ash, and from 1901 to 1906 as chaplain to St. Michael's College. In 1907 he became a member of the Community of the Resurrection at Mirfield, and in the years that followed, went on several missions—to New Zealand in 1910 and 1913, to Canada in 1914, and to Ceylon in 1929. During World War I, from 1915 to 1919, he was a chaplain to the armed forces, and was awarded the Military Cross. He was appointed warden of the College of the Resurrection in 1922, where he remained until his consecration as bishop of Llandaff in 1931. He died April 29, 1939.

Written in 1922, this hymn was included in *The Mirfield Mission Hymn Book*.

For IN BABILONE see LBW 364. The harmonization found here was prepared for the *Worship Supplement*, 1969, to *The Lutheran Hymnal* by Carl Schalk (LBW 118).

524   MY GOD, HOW WONDERFUL THOU ART
Tune: Dundee

This hymn by Frederick William Faber (LBW 290) was included in his *Jesus and Mary*, 1849.

For DUNDEE see LBW 464.

525   BLESSING AND HONOR
Tune: American Hymn

This hymn is stanzas 8, 4, 5, and 7 of a poem beginning "Into the heav'n of the heav'ns hath He gone." Written by Horatius Bonar (LBW 167), it was included in his *Hymns of Faith and Hope*, third series, 1866. There are a few slight alterations in the text.

AMERICAN HYMN was included with this text in the *Common Service Book*, 1917.

The composer, Matthias Keller, was born at Ulm in Württemberg, Germany, on March 20, 1813, and showed an aptitude for music at an early age. His parents sent him to Stuttgart to study, and at age sixteen he became first violinist in the Royal Chapel, a position he held for five years. During this time, also, he began to compose. He studied harmony and counterpoint in Vienna for three years, after which he was band-master of the third Royal Brigade for seven years. A republican in politics, he expressed his views rather freely, which drew some criticism from his superior officers. After attending a celebration and dinner at which he met a Mr. Thorndyke from Boston, Massachusetts, he determined to immigrate to the United States, and in 1846, on his thirty-third birthday, took passage from Havre. He went first to Philadelphia, where he played first viol in the Walnut Street Theater, and later worked at the Chestnut Street Theater. He then moved to New York, where he saw an offer of five hundred dollars for an American Hymn. "American Hymn," along with the composer's own text, "Speed our republic, O Father on high!" was written for the contest. The five hundred dollars he won, however, along with three or four hundred dollars his brother had saved towards buying a house, went to pay the price of introducing the piece at a grand concert, for which their total receipts were forty-two dollars. He moved to Boston, where his "American Hymn" was much more successful. For a number of years it was played by the bands on the Boston Common on July 4, and in 1869 the music was used as a setting for Oliver Wendell Holmes's "Ode of Peace" at the First Peace Jubilee in Boston. Besides this piece, Keller wrote over one hundred songs, including a number of sacred songs. A year before his death he collected his literary work and published a collection entitled *Keller's Poems*. He died October 13, 1875, and was buried in the Dorchester district of Boston beside his wife who preceded him in death by several years.

526   IMMORTAL, INVISIBLE, GOD ONLY WISE
Tune: St. Denio

The hymns of Walter Chalmers Smith have been described as "rich in thought and vigorous in expression." Certainly that description fits this hymn, based on 1 Timothy 1:17, which was included in Smith's *Hymns of Christ and the Christian Life,* 1867. The text was subsequently altered by the author and published in W. Garrett Horder's *Congregational Hymns,* 1884. Stanza 4 was further changed for the LBW.

Born December 5, 1824, at Aberdeen, Scotland, Smith attended the University of Aberdeen and New College, Edinburgh. He was ordained to the Free Church of Scotland in 1850, and ministered to the Scottish Church at Chadwell Street, Islington, London; the Orwell Free Church, Milnathort; the Free Tron Church, Glasgow; the Roxburgh Free Church, Edinburgh; and the Free High Church, Edinburgh. The last charge was held from 1876 to 1894. In 1893 he was moderator of the Assembly of the Free Church in Scotland. He died at Kinbuck, Perthshire, on September 20, 1908.

Smith wrote a number of poetical works; poetry was to him "the retreat of his nature from the burden of his labours" and a source of relief and means of expressing what he could not fully express in his pulpit. Among his publications were *The Bishop's Walk,* 1860; *North Country Folk,* 1883; *A Heretic and Other Poems,* 1891; and *Poetical Works,* 1902.

ST. DENIO, also called "Joanna," is a traditional Welsh secular tune which was used with different songs, such as one about a cuckoo and another entitled "Can Mlyned i 'nawr" ("A hundred years from now"). There are many related tunes in England also, including one about a cuckoo. The *Journal of the Welsh Folk Song Society,* I (1911), gave the tune from a late eighteenth- or early nineteenth-century manuscript as follows:

As a hymn tune it first appeared in John Roberts' *Caniadau y Cyssegr,* 1839, beginning as given below.

The harmonization was prepared by Richard Hillert (LBW 63) for the *Worship Supplement,* 1969, to *The Lutheran Hymnal.*

527 ALL CREATURES OF OUR GOD AND KING
(Laudato si', mi Signor, con tutte le tue creature)
Tune: Lasst uns erfreuen

Francis of Assisi's love for all nature is beautifully set forth in his "Canticle of the sun, and hymn of creation." In 1225, very ill and temporarily blind, Francis took refuge from the summer heat in a straw hut at San Damiano. His discomfort was increased by a swarm of field mice which also occupied the hut. Under these circumstances he wrote this magnificent *lauda* (see LBW 508) praising God for all his creatures.

William Henry Draper paraphrased Francis' hymn, summoning the creatures themselves to the praise of God, sometime between 1899 and 1919. Written for a Pentecost festival for the children at Leeds, it was included in *Hymns of the Spirit,* a little book containing ten hymns, published in 1926. A number of slight alterations have been made for the LBW.

Born in Assisi in 1182, Giovanni Bernadone, more commonly known as Francesco, was the son of a wealthy Italian cloth merchant. From his mother he learned songs in French and Provançal, as well as his native Italian, and he studied Latin at the school near the church of St. George. In 1202 he served in the war between Assisi and Perugia, and was held prisoner for a year. After recovering from a serious illness he set out once again to join the forces of Walter of Brienne, but had a vision at Spoletto bidding him to return to Assisi. Following this he experienced a number of visions and episodes. On a visit to the ruined chapel of S. Damiano outside Assisi he heard a voice from the crucifix commanding him to "repair my house." Francis hurried home, gathered up much of the cloth in his father's warehouse and rode off to Foligno, where he sold not only the cloth, but the horse. His angry father first kept him at home, then took him before the civil authorities, and finally called him before the bishop. There Francis renounced material possessions and family ties and embraced a life of poverty. He repaired not only the church of S. Damiano, but also the chapel of St. Peter the Apostle, and the chapel of St. Mary, Porziuncola, where on St. Matthias' Day, February 24, 1208, he heard Christ's mission to the Apostles from Matthew 10:9-11 at Mass. Although a layman, he began preaching to the townspeople. For the group of disciples who joined him he composed a rule of life, aimed at following the teaching of Christ and walking in his footsteps, which was approved by Pope Innocent III. In 1212 he established an order for nuns, and later also formed the Third Order of Brothers and Sisters of Penance, a fraternity in which followers could carry out the principles of the order without withdrawing from the world or taking religious vows. The Franciscan Order grew rapidly and soon extended outside Italy. He set out in 1211 for the Holy Land, but was shipwrecked and forced to return. Illness prevented a trip to the Moors in Spain a year or two later, and a proposed journey to France was called off because he was needed to direct the order in Italy. He did go to Egypt. After 1221 he simplified and revised the rule, and in 1223 it was approved by Honorius III. Afterward he withdrew more and more from administrative demands and retired from the world to spend his time in prayer and singing. By tradition he had a vision in 1224, after which he bore the marks of the cross in his hands. During his last two years he was in constant pain, and nearly blind from an eye disease he had contracted in the east. Following unsuccessful medical treatment at Rieti, he was returned to Assisi, and died at Porziuncola on October 4, 1226. Two years later he was proclaimed a saint by Pope Gregory IX. Francis' writings include a number of sermons, poems, and letters.

Draper, born December 19, 1855, at Kenilworth, Warwickshire, England, first attended Cheltenham College, Oxford. He graduated from Keble College, Oxford, receiving a Bachelor of Arts degree in 1877 and a Master of Arts degree three years later. Ordained to the Church of England in 1880, he served as assistant curate at St. Mary's, Shrewsbury (1880-1883); vicar of Alfreton (1883-1889); Vicar of the Abbey Church, Shrewsbury (1889-1899); and rector of Adel in Yorkshire (1899-1919). From 1919 to 1930 he was Master of the Temple, and from 1930 until his death, vicar of Axbridge. He died August 9, 1933, at Clifton in Bristol.

The writer of over sixty hymns, of which some of his finest were translations from Latin and Greek, Draper published *The Victoria Book of Hymns,* 1897, and *Hymns for Holy Week,* 1899; he also edited *Seven Spiritual Songs by Thomas Campion,* 1919, and in 1925, *Hymns for the Tunes by Orlando Gibbons* (LBW 206).

For LASST UNS ERFREUEN see LBW 143.

528   ISAIAH IN A VISION DID OF OLD
(Jesaia, dem Propheten, das geschah)
Tune: Jesaia, dem Propheten

This hymn is Martin Luther's (LBW 48) German *Sanctus,* based on Isaiah 6:1-4, which was included in his *Deudsche Messe und ordnung Gottis diensts,* Wittenberg, 1526. In the rubrics to his service Luther suggested that this hymn, or his "Gott sei gelobet" (LBW 215), or the hymn by John Huss, "Iesus Christus, nostra salus" (see *The Lutheran Hymnal,* 1941, #311) be sung after the consecration of the bread and before the blessing of the cup. Following the blessing of the cup he recommended the use of the remainder of these hymns, or the German *Agnus Dei,* "Christe, du Lamm Gottes" (LBW 103). Leupold* notes that in later sixteenth-century agendas it was suggested that the part of the hymn beginning "Holy, Holy, Holy," be sung with special gravity and dignity, and that in city churches it was customary for three altar boys to intone that section while kneeling before the altar.

Originally prepared for *The Lutheran Hymnal,* 1941, Martin Franzmann's (LBW 233) translation is published here for the first time.

JESAIA, DEM PROPHETEN, was adapted by Luther from an eleventh-century plainsong *Sanctus* which was used on Sundays during

Advent and Lent. (The original plainchant can be seen in the *Liber Usualis,* Tournai, Belgium, 1963, under #XVII of the Ordinary Chants of the Mass.) Luther's adaptation appeared, along with his text, in his *Deudsche Messe.* The LBW form of the melody was included in *Geystliche Lieder,* published in Leipzig by Valentin Babst in 1545. The harmonization was prepared for the LBW by Carl Schalk (LBW 118).

529 PRAISE GOD. PRAISE HIM
(Tandanei tuthipoome, tiru sabhatyaare)
Tune: Tandanei

A. Chelladurai of Madras, India, writes:

> Madurai is an ancient, historical, and famous city from time immemorial, situated in the southern part of the Tamilnad state. Once it was the capital of Pandiya Kingdom, and was the seat of knowledge, and the birth place of the famous *Tamil Sangam.* There are ever so many legends connected with the city and its surroundings. It is a pride to all southerners that the late Rev. Masillamony was one who hailed from this place.

Vedamuthu Masillamony was born in or about 1858 at Silukkuvarpatti in the Madurai district in southern India. His ancestors were Christians even before 1800 when his grandfather, a Roman Catholic, became a Protestant. He attended boarding school at Batlagundu and Pasumali, Madurai, after which he took the theological course in the American Madurai Mission Theological Seminary at Pasumalai. For some time he was a boarding school teacher and evangelist without being a very zealous Christian. In 1890 he joined the Danish Lutheran Missionary Society as a teacher at Siloam and Ulundurpet, Tirukoilur; and two years later, through the influence of his friend, Visuvasam, and through an experience at a monthly meeting, he experienced a deepening of his faith. He returned to study at the American Madurai Mission from 1897 to 1906, during which time he was ordained a Lutheran pastor in 1901. Afterwards he rejoined the Danish Missionary Society as an evangelist at Kalluchurchi and a teacher at the Catechists' Training School at Nellicuppam, South Arcot District. He was pastor of two churches in Tiruvannamalai—at Sengalmedu from 1911 to 1915, and at Saron from 1915 until his retirement in 1929. He died two days before Christmas in 1932.

Masillamony Iyer (the "Iyer" means "Pastor") was regarded as an outstanding preacher and a good pastor. He was the author of a number of hymns, many of which were embodied in the common Tamil hymn book.

Originally written in Tamil, "Praise God. Praise Him" is a very popular hymn in the Madras area. It was first published in the 1950 edition of H. A. Popley's *Christava Keerthanaigal.* The English paraphrase, by Daniel Thambryajah Niles, was prepared for the *Hymnal* of the East Asia Christian Conference, Kyoto, 1963. A few alterations have been made for the LBW.

Niles, who contributed forty-four hymns, translations, and adaptations to the E.A.C.C. hymnal, was born in August of 1908 in Ceylon. The grandson of a Methodist minister, he at first intended to follow his father's profession and entered Ceylon University as a law student. He chose to live in a Hindu students' hostel where he might have opportunity to make a Christian witness, little knowing that the warden there, himself a devout Hindu, would convince him to enter the Christian ministry. Ordained in 1932 he served as superintendent of the Point Pedro and Jaffna Circuits, as principal of the Methodist Central College in Jaffna, and as secretary and later chairman of the North District of the Methodist Church in Ceylon. In 1968 he was elected president of the Ceylon Methodist Conference. He died at Vellore Christian Medical College in India on July 17, 1970.

Held in great esteem and affection in the World Council of Churches, Niles was co-preacher with John R. Mott at the inaugural meeting in 1948. When the East Asian Christian Conference was founded in 1957 he became its secretary, and in 1968 he was elected president. In Ceylon he served as secretary of the Student Christian Movement, the YMCA, and the National Christian Council. Internationally he served as evangelism secretary of the World YMCA in Geneva, chairman of the World Student Christian Federation, and director of evangelism in the World Council of Churches at Uppsala in 1968. A gifted leader, administrator, and writer, he was the author of a number of theological, devotional, and biblical books for young people, as well as articles in many worldwide religious publications. Among his works published in the United States are *That They May Have Life,* 1951; *The Preacher's Task and the Stone of Stumbling,* 1958; *As Seeing the Invisible,* 1961; *Upon the Earth,* 1962; *We Know in Part,* 1964; and *The Message and its Messengers,* 1966.

TANDANEI. Martin Kretzmann notes that with the Tamil version of this hymn the tune source is given as "English tune." He suggests that it is not authentic Carnatic music, which does not lend itself to group singing, but possibly an adaptation of a tune used in a movie. The melody was included in the East Asia Christian Conference *Hymnal* arranged by John Milton Kelly, music editor of the hymnal. It is given here with a harmonization prepared for *The Hymnal,* 1974, of the United Church of Christ by John Ferguson (LBW 246) and Mary Louise Enigson Van Dyke.

Van Dyke was born in 1927 in Rochester, Pennsylvania, and graduated from Oberlin College, Oberlin, Ohio, in 1947. She received a Master of Arts in Music Education at Western Reserve in 1953 and a Master of Arts in Sacred Music from Kent State University in 1967. Before joining the music staff of The First Church in Oberlin, she held a similar position at Kent United Church of Christ, Kent, Ohio.

530 JESUS SHALL REIGN
Tune: Duke Street

This hymn by Isaac Watts (LBW 39) is from Psalm 72, second part, "Christ's kingdom among the Gentiles," in the *Psalms of David,* 1719. The alterations are minor and very few.

For DUKE STREET see LBW 352.

531 BEFORE JEHOVAH'S AWESOME THRONE

Tune: Old Hundredth

The original first stanza of Isaac Watts's (LBW 39) paraphrase of Psalm 100, published in *Psalms of David*, 1719, read as follows:

> Sing to the Lord with joyful Voice;
> Let every Land his Name adore;
> The British Isles shall send the Noise
> Across the Ocean to the Shore.

Only stanza 3 in the LBW remains as written by Watts; the rest of the hymn is from a revision by John Wesley (LBW 302) included in the *Collection of Psalms and Hymns* which was published in the American colonies at Charlestown in 1735. Originally beginning "Before Jehovah's *awful* throne," Wesley's text is otherwise unaltered except for a slight change in stanza 4.

For OLD HUNDREDTH see LBW 245. The harmonization given here is from the *Württembergisches Choralbuch*, 1953.

532 HOW GREAT THOU ART *(O store Gud)*

Tune: O store Gud

Carl Gustaf Boberg was born August 16, 1859, at Mönsterås, Sweden. The son of a shipyard carpenter, he worked as a sailor for several years, after which he attended the craft school at Nybro and taught crafts in his hometown. Having undergone a conversion experience at age nineteen, he began preaching, and after two years at the Bible school in Kristinehamn, became a preacher in his hometown. From 1890 to 1916 he was editor of the weekly *Sanningsvittnet,* and from 1912 to 1931 he was a member of the Swedish parliament. An engaging speaker and gifted writer, he published several collections of poems. He died at Kalmar on January 7, 1940.

"O store Gud" was written one evening during the summer of 1885. The author, returning from a meeting in Kronobäck, was struck by the beauty of nature and the sound of church bells in the still of the evening. The hymn was included in the March 13, 1886, issue of *Mönsterås Tidningen.* Boberg included the poem in several other periodicals as well, but it was forgotten until one day when he heard it sung in Värmland with the Swedish folk melody to which it is now attached. He subsequently included it with the tune in *Sanningsvittnet,* 1891.

The English text by Stuart Wesley Keene Hine, which was popularized during a Billy Graham crusade, is a translation of a Russian version, which in turn had been translated from a German rendition of the original Swedish hymn. It has lost much of the original in the process and, except for a few lines, may well be considered a new text. The English version, which took shape during the late 1930s, with a fourth stanza added in 1948, was published in 1949 together with a Russian version in a Russian gospel magazine, *Grace and Peace.*

Born in London, England, on July 25, 1899, Hine attended the Coopers Company School in London. Although he passed the entrance examination for Oxford University, he did not continue his education. He served in France during World War I. He and his wife worked as missionaries from 1923 to 1932 in east Poland, and from 1932 to 1939 in Ruthenia in east Czechoslovakia. They also worked among East European displaced persons in Britain, and have published gospel literature in various languages. He has lived in Somerset in recent years.

O STORE GUD is a Swedish melody of unknown origin, first published in *Sanningsvittnet,* 1891. There it appeared in three-quarter time, as arranged by Erik Adolf Edgren, a musician who later came to America. In 1894 the melody was given in the *Svenska Missionsförbundets Sångbok* in quadruple meter, much as it appears in the LBW. The harmonization is by Stuart Hine (see above).

533 NOW THANK WE ALL OUR GOD *(Nun danket alle Gott)*
Tune: Nun danket alle Gott

Found in every German hymnal, this hymn by Martin Rinkart has also been used extensively in England and America in a translation by Catherine Winkworth (LBW 29) given in her *Lyra Germanica,* second series, 1858. Often called the German *Te Deum,* it has been used throughout the years at national festivals or occasions of thanksgiving, such as the completion of the cathedral at Cologne in 1880, or the Diamond Jubilee Celebration of Queen Victoria in 1897. Rinkart's German text is believed to have been included in his *Jesu Heartz-Büchlein,* 1636, as it is included in the 1663 edition, the earliest extant today. The earliest available source of the hymn is Johann Crüger's (LBW 23) *Praxis Pietatis Melica,* 1647.

Rinkart (also Rinckart), son of a cooper, was born April 23, 1586, in Eilenburg, Saxony. He was a foundation scholar and chorister at St. Thomas' School in Leipzig, and later a theological student at the university, receiving his Master of Arts degree in 1616. In 1610 he became master of the *Gymnasium* at Eisleben and cantor of St. Nicholas Church there, and after a few months became pastor of St. Anne's Church in the Neustadt of Eilenburg. Two years later he became pastor of Erdeborn and Lütjendorf nearby. In 1617 he was invited by the town council to become the archdeacon of Eilenberg, where he remained for thirty-two years. Much of the time was spent amidst the horrors of the Thirty Years' War. Since Eilenburg was a walled city, people from miles around sought refuge there, and overcrowding resulted in famine and pestilence. When in 1637 the superintendent left and two other clergymen died, Rinkart alone was left to minister to the city, sometimes preaching burial services for forty or fifty persons in one day. His wife also was taken by the pestilence, and he himself fell ill, but survived. Twice also he dissuaded the Swedish commander from imposing excessive tribute on the town. His services, however, were received with little gratitude by the city authorities, and in his later years he was much harassed by them. He died exhausted on December 8, 1649. In spite of his trials, he was a good musician, and also wrote extensively, including a number of hymns and seven dramas on the Reformation for the centenary in 1617.

NUN DANKET ALLE GOTT appeared with Rinkart's hymn in Johann Crüger's *Praxis Pietatis Melica,* 1647 edition, and has been ascribed to Crüger since Christoph Runge's (LBW 340) *Gesangbuch* of 1653. J. S. Bach (LBW 219) used the melody in Cantatas 79 and 192. It is also one of his Wedding Chorales and included in the *Choralgesänge,* and an organ setting is among his Eighteen Chorales. The LBW harmonization is from the *Orgelchoralbuch,* 1952.

534 NOW THANK WE ALL OUR GOD *(Nun danket alle Gott)*

Tune: Nun danket alle Gott

See LBW 533 for a discussion of this hymn and its tune. The form of the melody found here is a rhythmic variant. The harmonization is from *Den Svenska Koralboken*, 1939.

535 HOLY GOD, WE PRAISE YOUR NAME
(Grosser gott, wir loben dich)

Tune: Grosser Gott

This German versification of the *Te Deum laudamus* (LBW 3) by an unknown author appeared in the *Katholisches Gesangbuch,* published in Vienna in 1744 at the request of the Austrian empress, Maria Theresa (1717-1780). Described by one historian as "the most human of the Habsburgs," Maria Theresa was a devout Roman Catholic, and a key political figure in eighteenth-century Europe.

Dated 1853 in Hall and Lasar's *Evangelical Hymnal,* New York, 1880, Clarence Augustus Walworth's translation was included in the *Catholic Psalmist,* Dublin, 1858. The first line originally read, "Holy God, we praise *Thy* name."

Walworth was born on May 30, 1820, at Plattsburg, New York. After graduation in 1838 from Union College he read law at offices in Canandaigua and Albany, but left the profession and entered General Theological Seminary in 1842. Originally a Presbyterian, he studied for the Episcopal ministry. The Oxford Movement, strong in England at the time, also found its way to American schools and Walworth became a part of it. He was ordained a Roman Catholic priest in 1845, taking the name Clarence Alphonsus. A mission preacher of considerable influence, he was one of the founders of the Order of Paulists in the United States, and from 1866 to 1900 was rector of St. Mary's Church in Albany, New York. Blind for the last ten years of his life, he died in Albany on September 19, 1900.

Walworth was the author of a number of hymn paraphrases and translations, as well as *The Gentle Skeptic,* 1863; *Andiatorocte of the Eve of Lady Day and Other Poems,* 1888; and *The Oxford Movement in America,* 1895.

Other hymns based on the *Te Deum* are given at LBW 432 and 547.

GROSSER GOTT (also "Te Deum"), also anonymous, appeared together with the German text in the *Katholisches Gesangbuch,* as given below.

Many variants of the melody appeared during the first half of the nineteenth century, a full history of which can be found in Bäumker,* III, 285–287. Another form of the tune, "Hursley," is given at LBW 270.

536 O GOD OF GOD, O LIGHT OF LIGHT
Tune: O Grosser Gott

The author of this hymn, John Julian,* is especially noteworthy for his monumental *Dictionary of Hymnology,* first published in 1891. The second edition, which appeared in 1907, was reprinted in 1915 and 1925, and was published in a Dover edition in 1957.

Julian was born January 27, 1839, in St. Agnes, Cornwall, England. Educated privately, he was ordained a deacon in the Church of England in 1866, and a priest in 1867. In 1876 he became vicar of Wincobank, and in 1905, vicar of Topcliffe, Yorkshire. From 1901 he was also canon of Yorkshire. He was honored with a Master of Arts from Durham University in 1887, a Doctor of Divinity from Archbishop Benson of Canterbury in 1894, and a Doctor of Laws from Howard University in Washington, D.C., in 1894. In addition to his *Dictionary,* he published *Concerning Hymns,* 1874, and *Outgrowth of some Literary, Scientific and other Hobbies,* 1899. His vast collection of materials on hymnody was given to the Church House, Dean's Yard, London. He died January 22, 1913, at Topcliffe.

"O God of God, O Light of Light" was written for the Sheffield Church Choirs Union Festival, April 16, 1883, and was included the following year in Garrett Horder's *Congregational Hymns.* The text has been adapted by the Inter-Lutheran Commission on Worship for the LBW.

O GROSSER GOTT is an anonymous tune which appeared in the *Schlag-Gesang- und Notenbuch,* Stuttgart, 1744. The harmonization was prepared for the LBW by Paul Bouman (LBW 208).

537 O JESUS, KING MOST WONDERFUL! *(Jesu Rex, admirabilis)*
Tune: Hiding Place

This hymn is taken from the longer poem, "Jesu, dulcis memoria," discussed at LBW 316. The opening stanza is stanza 9 of the Latin original. The translation is marked for Matins in Edward Caswall's (LBW 37) *Lyra Catholica,* 1849, and follows "Jesus, the very thought of thee" (LBW 316).

HIDING PLACE, an anonymous hexatonic tune, is found in Joshua Leavitt's (LBW 243) *Christian Lyre,* 1830. There it is the setting for a hymn by Jehoiada Brewer, the first stanza of which reads:

> Hail, sovereign love that first began
> The scheme to rescue fallen man;
> Hail, matchless, free eternal grace
> That gave my soul a hiding-place.

The tune is related to "Consolation" (LBW 33) and to "Bourbon" (LBW 127), and in his *Down-East Spirituals,* 1939, George Pullen

Jackson notes its secular relatives to be "The Bailiff's Daughter of Islington," "Heart's Ease," and "Gernutus the Jew of Venice." The harmonization was prepared for the LBW by Roger Petrich (LBW 64).

538   OH, PRAISE THE LORD, MY SOUL!
Tune: Michael

This hymn by David Frank Wright was written for *Morning Praise and Evensong,* published at Notre Dame, Indiana, in 1973.

Wright was born May 18, 1941, at Eagle Grove, Iowa. After two years at Loras College in Dubuque, Iowa, he entered the Aquinas Institute School of Philosophy at River Forest, Illinois, where he completed a Bachelor of Arts degree in 1964 and a Master of Arts degree in 1966. He received a Master of Theology degree in 1969 from the Aquinas Institute School of Theology in Dubuque, and in 1977, a Doctor of Philosophy from the University of Notre Dame at South Bend, Indiana. A member of the Order of Preachers (Dominicans) since 1961, he was ordained a priest in 1968. Between 1969 and 1974 he did graduate work in liturgical studies at the University of Notre Dame, and served in a parish in the diocese of Kalamazoo, Michigan. Since 1974 he has been on the faculty of Aquinas Institute in Dubuque. With William G. Storey and Frank C. Quinn he published *Morning Praise and Evensong* in 1973. His doctoral dissertation was *A Medieval Commentary on the Mass: Particulae 2-3 and 5-6 of the "De missarum mysteriis" (ca. 1195) of Cardinal Lothar of Segni (Pope Innocent III),* 1977.

MICHAEL was written for the LBW by Charles R. Anders (LBW 386).

539   PRAISE THE ALMIGHTY *(Lobe den Herren, o meine Seele!)*
Tune: Lobe den Herren, o meine Seele

Johann Daniel Herrnschmidt was born April 11, 1675, at Bopfingen, in Württemberg, Germany, where his father was pastor. He received a Master of Arts degree from the University of Altdorf in 1698, and went in the autumn of that year to Halle. Three years later he became an assistant at his father's church and also at the Town Church. In 1712 he was appointed superintendent, court-preacher, and a member of the consistory at Idstein, and in the same year, completed a Doctor of Divinity degree at Halle. He was appointed professor of theology at Halle in 1715, and in 1716 he also became subdirector of the Pädagogium and the Orphanage, where August Hermann Francke was director. He died at Halle, February 5, 1723.

Nearly all of Herrnschmidt's hymns were written during his first residence at Halle, 1698–1702, and many were published in J. A. Freylinghausen's (LBW 32) *Geistreiches Gesang-Buch,* 1704. This hymn, based on Psalm 146, was included in the second part of Freylinghausen's book, 1714. The translation by Alfred Brauer was published in the *Australian Lutheran Hymn Book,* 1925. Slightly altered for *The Lutheran Hymnal,* 1941, the text has undergone a few more changes for the LBW.

Born near Birdwood (formerly Blumberg), South Australia, on August 1, 1866, Alfred Ernest Richard Brauer worked for a time as a clerk in an Adelaide office before entering Prince Alfred College (Wesleyan) in Adelaide as a law student. Turning to theology, he received preparatory theological instruction from Pastor Strempel of Hahndorf (later St. Michael's, Ambleside), and then came to the United States where he entered Concordia Seminary, Springfield, Illinois, in the fall of 1887. Upon graduation in 1890 he accepted a call from the Dimboola parish in the Australian state of Victoria and began ministering also to the new settlers who were taking up land in the Mallee districts, gathering and founding several congregations among them. He also filled the position of assistant teacher at Murtoa College until a full-time teacher could be appointed. In 1896 he was called to the Lutheran school in Hahndorf, where Pastor Strempel, now his father-in-law, was pastor of the congregation. When Strempel was elected Synod President, Brauer was appointed his secretary and called by the Hahndorf congregation as associate pastor. After Strempel's death, Brauer became pastor of the congregation. During his Hahndorf pastorate, he also conducted services among the new farming settlements in the Murray and Mallee districts, gathering or founding six congregations. In 1921 he accepted a call to St. John's, Melbourne, and its affiliates at Bacchus Marsh and Clarkefield. By request of Synod he also was home missionary in the metropolitan area, as well as in Gippsland and on the northeast railway line, and worked also among the migrants. In 1940 he celebrated the golden anniversary of his ordination, and three years later celebrated fifty years of marriage. He resigned in 1942 from the Melbourne parish, remaining for another six months as an assistant to his successor, and died on October 18, 1949, at Melbourne.

When the synod decided in 1912 to publish an English church paper, *The Australian Lutheran,* Brauer was chosen editor, with assistants in several states of the commonwealth; and when the synod resolved to publish their own English-language hymnal, he was appointed chairman of the committee which compiled the *Australian Lutheran Hymn-Book,* 1925. His chief literary endeavor, to which he devoted many years of his spare time and holidays, was the writing of the history of the Evangelical Lutheran Church of Australia. Post-war difficulties caused postponement of its publication; *Under the Southern Cross* finally appeared in 1956.

LOBE DEN HERREN, O MEINE SEELE, is an anonymous tune which appeared in the 1665 appendix to *New-vermehrte Christlich Seelenharpf,* Ansbach, 1664. It was the setting for "Lobet den Herren aller Herren." Originally it appeared as given below. The harmonization was written for the LBW by Carl Schalk (LBW 118).

540 PRAISE THE LORD! O HEAVENS

Tune: Austria

The London Foundling Hospital was a unique institution founded in 1738 by a Captain Coram for the care and education of orphans. Music and singing played an important role in the rehabilitation of the children and in the support of the orphanage through special concerts, which were attended by the fashionable society people of the day. From 1782 to 1877 choirs from the home sang at St. Paul's Cathedral. George Frideric Handel (LBW 39) gave a benefit concert at the hospital in 1749 to raise funds for the chapel, and later donated a pipe organ. (So many people attended the opening recital that it was necessary to repeat the performance.) In his later years, as his health permitted, he conducted annual performances of his *Messiah* in the chapel.

In 1774 a collection of sixteen hymns titled *Psalms, Hymns, and Anthems of the Foundling Hospital* was published in London. A second edition of twenty-two hymns appeared in 1796, and was followed by several subsequent editions. "Praise the Lord, ye heavens adore him," based on Psalm 148, is by an unknown poet. The earliest printing of the hymn, according to Frost,* seems to have been a four-page leaflet of four hymns found pasted in the back of a 1797 edition of the Foundling Hospital collection. A leaflet with two additional hymns, titled "Hymns of Praise. For Foundling Apprentices Attending Divine Service to return Thanks," was added to some copies of the 1796 and 1801 editions, where the indication for this hymn is "Music by 'Haydn.'" The hymn was incorporated into the body of *Psalms and Hymns* for Magdalen Chapel, 1804, and the 1809 edition of the Foundling Hospital colletion. Originally beginning "Praise the lord! *ye* heav'ns adore him," this hymn is altered only very slightly to update the text.

For AUSTRIA see LBW 358.

541 PRAISE THE LORD OF HEAVEN!

Tune: Nous allons

Thomas Briarly Browne was the son of Pryce Jones and changed his name to Thomas Browne when he was eighteen. Born on Christmas Day, 1805, at Mellington Hall, Montgomeryshire, Wales, he went to England where he attended Brasenose College, Oxford. From 1827 he was barrister at Lincoln's Inn, and from 1847 until his death on February 16, 1874, was Inspector of Union Schools.

This hymn was published in Browne's *National Bankruptcy and other Poems,* London, 1844. In addition to *National Bankruptcy* he published *Thoughts of the Times,* 1838, and *The Oxford Divines not Members of the Church of England,* 1839.

NOUS ALLONS is a French carol or noël which served as the setting for "Nous allons ma mie" and "Ah ma Voisine es tu fachée." It is found in several collections, including L. Eugène Grimault's *Noëls Angevins,* 1878, and J. L. Roque's *50 Noëls anciens,* 1897. An organ setting was written by the French organist, Claude Balbastre (1729–1799). The harmonization was prepared by Martin Shaw for the *Oxford Book of Carols,* 1928.

Martin Edward Fallas Shaw, who with Percy Dearmer (LBW 169) and Ralph Vaughan Williams (LBW 101) edited *Songs of Praise* (1925) and *Songs of Praise Enlarged* (1931), and *The Oxford Book of Carols* (1928), was the older brother of Geoffrey Shaw (LBW 413). Born March 9, 1875, at Kensington, London, he studied at the Royal College of Music under Charles V. Stanford (LBW 189), C. H. H. Parry (LBW 283), and Walford Davies. His musical career included four positions—organist at St. Mary's, Primrose Hill (1908-1920); organist at St. Martin-in-the-fields (1920-1924); master of music at the Guild House in London (1924-1935); and director of music for the diocese of Chelmsford (1935-1945). Having composed from childhood, he published many songs and much church music, the latter possessing "dignity, massiveness, and reserve," and having done much to "free English church music from a load of sentimentality" (Moffatt and Patrick,* p. 496). Many of the melodies written while he was at St. Mary's were published as *Additional Tunes,* 1915. His *Principles of English Church Music Composition* was published in 1921. Together with his brother and with Vaughan Williams he encouraged the revival of English folk music, and he published a number of collections of folk songs. His autobiography, *Up to Now,* was published in 1929. Both Martin and Geoffrey Shaw were honored in 1932 with the Lambeth degree of Doctor of Music. Martin died at Southwold, October 24, 1958.

542   SING PRAISE TO GOD, THE HIGHEST GOOD
(Sei Lob und Ehr dem höchsten Gut)
Tune: Lobt Gott den Herren, ihr

Johann Jakob Schütz, born September 7, 1640, at Frankfurt-am-Main, Germany, studied at Tübingen and became licensed to practice civil and canon law. Returning to Frankfurt, he practiced law there for the rest of his days, in later years achieving the title of *Rath,* or counsellor. His *Christliches Gedenckbüchlein,* which contained this hymn, was published in Frankfurt in 1675, and a second booklet, *Christliche Lebensregeln,* was published in 1677. Influenced by Philipp Jakob Spener and Johann Wilhelm Petersen, he eventually drifted from the Lutheran church and became a Separatist. Schütz had an interest in the Frankfurt company which purchased land in Germantown, Pennsylvania, from William Penn in 1683. He died at Frankfurt on May 22, 1690.

The translation by Frances Elizabeth Cox (LBW 133) was published in *Lyra Eucharistica* in 1864, and in her own *Hymns from the German,* second edition, of the same year. Four years later it entered the Lutheran *Church Book,* Philadelphia. Originally beginning "Sing praise to God *who reigns above,*" the text has been adapted for the LBW.

LOBT GOTT DEN HERREN, IHR was composed by Melchior Vulpius (LBW 115) for an anonymous Epiphany hymn based on Psalm 117, "Lobt Gott den Herren, ihr Heiden all." It was first published in his *Ein schön geistlich Gesangbuch,* Jena, 1609 (Zahn* #4533).

543 PRAISE TO THE LORD, THE ALMIGHTY
(Lobe den Herren, den mächtigen König)

Tune: Lobe den Herren

Based on Psalm 103:1-6 and Psalm 150, this hymn was written by Joachim Neander (LBW 182) and published in *A und Ω. Joachimi Neandri Glaub- und Liebesübung,* Bremen, 1680.

The translation by Catherine Winkworth (LBW 29) was included in her *Chorale Book for England,* 1863. Some alterations have been made for the LBW.

LOBE DEN HERREN appeared in 1665 with the text "Hast du den, Liebster, dein Angesicht gänzlich verborgen" in Part II of the Stralsund *Ernewerten Gesangbuch* as follows (Zahn* #1912):

When it was associated with Neander's text in 1680 it had a considerably different form:

The melody as it appears today is the 1665 version with alterations made in hymnals of 1692, 1701, and 1708.

There is a strong possibility that the tune was used with the secular text, "Seh ich nicht blinkende, flinkende Sterne aufgehen," before it was associated with a sacred text.

J. S. Bach (LBW 219) used the melody in Cantatas 57 and 137, and an unfinished cantata, "Herr Gott, Beherrscher aller Dinge," and in an organ setting, "Kommst du nun, Jesu," in the *Schübler Chorales.* The harmonization used here is from the *Orgelchoralbuch,* 1952.

544 THE GOD OF ABRAHAM PRAISE *(Yigdal Elohim Ḥai)*

Tune: Yigdal

The thirteen articles of the Hebrew Creed were drawn up by the great Hebrew scholar, Moses Maimonides. Son of the *dayyan* of Cordoba,

Spain, Maimonides was born in 1135. To escape religious persecutions by the Muslims, the family left Cordoba in 1148 and finally settled at Fez in Morocco around 1160. There he wrote treatises on the Jewish calendar and on logic, and continued his studies, especially in medicine. After living for a time in Israel the family lived in Alexandria, and later in Cairo, Egypt. For eight years Maimonides was free to devote himself to study and writing, supported by his brother, David, who dealt in precious stones. When David, on a business trip, drowned in the Indian Ocean, Maimonides became a physician to support himself. Appointed physician to al-Fadil (who at the time was virtual ruler of Egypt) in 1185, Maimonides became very famous. According to legend, Richard the Lionhearted at one time sought his services. Maimonides' two major works are the *Mishnah Torah,* which he compiled in 1180, and the *Guide,* 1190. He died December 13, 1204.

Authorship of the metrical form of the creed (the "Yigdal") has been attributed by some to Daniel ben Judah, a liturgical poet who lived in Rome in the mid-fourteenth century. Others ascribe it to Immanuel ben Solomon, a scholar and poet known in Italian as Manoello Giudeo. Born in Rome about 1261, Immanuel lived there until 1321. From 1321 until his death sometime after 1328, he lived in various Italian communities, probably working as a tutor in homes of wealthy families. Julian* (pp. 1149–1150) quotes the Hebrew text and gives the following literal translation:

> Extolled and praised be the living God, who exists unbounded by time.
> He is one of unparalleled unity, invisible and eternal.
> Without form or figure—incorporeal—holy beyond conception.
> Prior to all created things—the first, without date or beginning.
> Lo! He is Lord of the world and all creation, which evince his greatness and dominion.
> The flow of his prophetic spirit has he imparted to men selected for his glory.
> No one has appeared in Israel like unto Moses; a prophet, beholding his glorious semblance.
> God has given the true law to his people, by the hands of his trusty prophet.
> This law God will never alter nor change for any other.
> He perceives and is acquainted with our secrets—sees the end of all things at their very beginning.
> He rewards man with kindness according to his work; dispenses punishment to the wicked, according to his misdeeds.
> At the end of days by him appointed, will he send our Messiah, to redeem those who hope for final salvation.
> God, in his mercy, will recall the dead to life. Praised be his glorious name for evermore.

After hearing Leoni (Meyer Lyon) sing the Yigdal in the Great Synagogue, Duke's Place, London, Thomas Olivers (LBW 27) prepared a paraphrase, giving it a Christian character. Written, according to tradition, at the house of John Blakewell in Westminster, the twelve stanzas first appeared in a leaflet entitled *A Hymn to the God of Abraham.* The original publication is undated. The fourth and fifth editions appeared in 1772, and the sixth (London and Philadelphia), seventh, and eighth, in 1773.

YIGDAL, also named "Leoni" for Meyer Lyon (Meier Leoni) who sang the Yigdal and transcribed it for Olivers, seems no older than the seventeenth century. The LBW form of the melody is identical (with the omission of embellishing notes) with that found in Aaron Williams' (LBW 368) *British Psalmody,* published in the late 1770s. The tune has also been called "Judea" and "Jerusalem."

Meyer Lyon (1751-1797), a singer at Drury Lane or Covent Garden, was also cantor at various London synagogues, including the Great Synagogue from 1768 to 1772. After twelve years in Dublin, he returned briefly to London, and in 1787 became *chazan* of the Ashkenazic (English and German) Synagogue in Kingston, Jamaica. There he remained for the rest of his life.

545 WHEN MORNING GILDS THE SKIES *(Beim frühen Morgenlicht)*
Tune: O Seigneur

This German hymn, which was included in the *Katholisches Gesangbuch für den öffentlich Gottesdienst im Biszthume Würzburg,* 1828 (Bäumker* IV, #45), is found in several forms, also beginning "Wach ich früh Morgens auf," and "Wach' ich am Morgen auf." The existence of the hymn in such a variety of forms suggests the possiblity that it was written earlier than 1828.

Robert Bridges' (LBW 123) translation was included in his *Yattendon Hymnal,* 1899. There are some slight alterations. A translation by Edward Caswall (LBW 37), which has the same opening line, is also in common use.

O SEIGNEUR, described by Dearmer* as a "superbly robust and ardent tune," was the tune selected by Bridges for his translation in the *Yattendon Hymnal.* Composed or adapted by Louis Bourgeois (LBW 29), it was the setting for Clément Marot's version of Psalm 3, "O Seigneur, que de gens," in *Trente quatre pseaumes de David,* Geneva, 1551. In the notes to the *Yattendon Hymnal,* Bridges cites a tune, "Inventor rutili," in *Melodiae Prudentiae,* Leipzig, 1533, from which he feels this melody to be derived.

The harmonization was prepared for the LBW by Richard Hillert (LBW 63).

546 WHEN MORNING GILDS THE SKIES *(Beim frühen Morgenlicht)*
Tune: Laudes Domini

This hymn is the same as LBW 545.

LAUDES DOMINI was written by Joseph Barnby (LBW 280) for the Appendix to the Original Edition of *Hymns Ancient and Modern,* 1868, where it was the setting for Edward Caswall's (LBW 37) translation.

547 THEE WE ADORE, ETERNAL LORD! *(Te Deum laudamus)*
Tune: Mendon

This paraphrase of the *Te Deum laudamus* (LBW 3) was written by Thomas Cotterill and included in the 1815 appendix to his *Selection of*

Psalms and Hymns. Two other hymns based on the *Te Deum* are found at LBW 432 and 535.

Cotterill, son of a woolstapler, was born December 4, 1779, at Cannock, Staffordshire, England. He received a Bachelor of Arts degree in 1801 and a Master of Arts degree in 1805 from St. John's College, Cambridge, and was ordained to the Church of England in 1803. After serving as curate of Tutbury (1803–1808) and incumbent of Lane End, Staffordshire (1808–1817), he became perpetual curate of St. Paul's, Sheffield. In 1810 Cotterill published his first edition of *A Selection of Psalms and Hymns for Public and Private Use.* With James Montgomery's (LBW 50) assistance, he prepared the eighth edition in 1819, and introduced it to his congregation. Since the sixteenth century, metrical psalmody had been the only accepted congregational song in the Church of England. Cotterill's 1819 *Selection* came on the scene when there was both an increase in the use of hymns in Anglican churches, and a growing opposition by some to the use of these hymns. Cotterill's collection brought a storm of protest from his congregation, which was strengthened by outside feeling. Haeussler* remarks, "Occasionally there have been difficulties in churches over the introduction of a new hymnal, but seldom has the matter been carried to court, as was the case when a faction of his Sheffield church actually brought suit against Cotterill." Before the matter reached trial before the Diocesan Court of York, however, Bishop Harcourt suggested a compromise—that Cotterill withdraw the collection, and create another one, to be approved by and dedicated to the bishop. The resulting hymnal appeared in 1820, and went into several subsequent editions. It is the 1819 hymnal, however, which held an important influence on the hymnody of later generations. A number of hymns in present hymnals are used as they were altered by Montgomery and Cotterill in the 1819 *Selection.* Cotterill also prepared a volume of *Family Prayers,* which reached a sixth edition in 1824. He died December 29, 1823.

MENDON, named for a village in Worcester County, Massachusetts, is one of those tunes for which the ultimate source remains to be discovered. Referred to simply as a German melody, the tune appeared in a large number of nineteenth-century American hymnals with a wide variety of texts. Robert McCutchan, in his *Hymn Tune Names* (1957, p. 101), places it in *The Methodist Harmonist,* 1821. In the 1833 edition of that collection, the tune, called "German Air," appears in a form identical to that given here. In Francis D. Allen's *New York Selection of Sacred Music,* 1822, it was the setting for Isaac Watts's (LBW 39) "Far from my thoughts, vain world, be gone." Lowell Mason (LBW 353), who invariably altered the last phrase of the tune in his collections, prepared the harmonization for his *Sabbath Hymn and Tune Book,* 1859, from which the LBW harmonization is taken.

548 OH, WORSHIP THE KING

Tune: Hanover

A paraphrase of Psalm 104 by William Kethe (LBW 245) was recast in the same meter by Robert Grant (LBW 91) to create this hymn. The original first stanza read

> My soule praise the Lord, speake good of his Name,
> O Lord our great God, how doest thou appeare,

So passing in glorie, that great is thy fame,
Honour and maiestie, in thee shine most cleare.

Grant's version was included in Edward Bickersteth's (LBW 491) *Christian Psalmody,* 1833. There have been a few slight alterations, such as stanza 6, line 4, which originally read, ". . . shall *lisp* to thy praise."

HANOVER. Later attributed to William Croft (LBW 320), this tune, like "St. Anne," first appeared anonymously in the sixth edition of *A Supplement to the New Version of Psalms by Dr. Brady and Mr. Tate,* 1708. There it was the setting for a version of Psalm 67, "Our God, bless us all with mercy and love." The tune had a wide variety of names during the eighteenth century, including "Bromswick Tune," "Aliff (Ayliffe) Street," "St. Michael's Tune," and "Old 104th."

549 PRAISE, MY SOUL, THE KING OF HEAVEN
Tune: Praise, My Soul

This hymn is the second of two paraphrases of Psalm 103 published by Henry Francis Lyte (LBW 272) in his *Spirit of the Psalms,* 1834. There are a few slight alterations in the text. Line 5 originally read "Praise Him! Praise Him!" in all stanzas, but has been changed to "Alleluia! Alleluia!" in most hymnals today.

PRAISE, MY SOUL (also "Lauda anima") first appeared in Robert Brown-Borthwick's *Supplemental Hymn and Tune Book,* third edition, with New Appendix, 1869. There it had two forms—the first using unison voices with varying organ accompaniments in D major, and the second, a four-voice setting in E-major. (Organists wishing to use the other variations can find them in *The Hymnary,* 1927, published by Oxford, or in Austin C. Lovelace's [LBW 392] *Wedding Music for the Church Organist and Soloist,* published by Abingdon.)

The composer, John Goss, whose father was also an organist, was born December 27, 1800, at Fareham, Hampshire, England. He was a chorister at the Chapel Royal under John Stafford Smith, and later under Thomas Attwood, for whom he held deep affection and respect throughout his life. After three years at Stockwell Chapel (later St. Andrew's Church), he became, in 1824, organist of St. Luke's, Chelsea. In 1838 he succeeded Thomas Attwood at St. Paul's Cathedral in London, where he served with quiet distinction until his retirement in 1872, when he was followed by John Stainer (LBW 56). He was appointed professor of harmony at the Royal Academy of Music in 1827, a position he held for forty-seven years. During this time he published *An Introduction to Harmony and Thoroughbass,* 1833, which reached its thirteenth edition. In 1856 he was made one of the composers of the Chapel Royal. Goss, who wrote a number of fine anthems, never began one without first asking a blessing on his work; many of his compositions were initialed I. N. D. A.—"In Nomine Domini. Amen." He edited *Parochial Psalmody,* 1826 (for his congregation in Chelsea), and *Chants, Ancient and Modern,* 1841, and was musical editor of William Mercer's (LBW 281) *Church Psalter and Hymn Book,* 1856. Earlier in his life he wrote a number of secular glees, one of which, "There is beauty on the mountains," was made popular in the United States by William H. Cummings

(LBW 60). Knighted in 1872 by Queen Victoria, he was honored with a Doctor of Music degree from the University of Cambridge four years later. He died at Brixton in London on May 10, 1880, and was buried at St. Paul's.

550 FROM ALL THAT DWELL BELOW THE SKIES
Tune: Old Hundredth

These two stanzas by Isaac Watts (LBW 39) are the long meter version (he also included a short meter form) of Psalm 117, given in the *Psalms of David,* 1719.

For OLD HUNDREDTH see LBW 245. This harmonization is from the *Württembergische Choralbuch,* 1953.

551 JOYFUL, JOYFUL WE ADORE THEE
Tune: Hymn to Joy

Inspired by the Berkshire Mountains, this hymn was presented to President James Garfield at breakfast one morning in 1907, when the author, Henry van Dyke, was on a preaching visit at Williams College. It was included in 1911 in *Poems of Henry van Dyke* and *The Hymnal* of the Presbyterian Church.

Born November 10, 1852, in Germantown, Pennsylvania, van Dyke received a Bachelor of Arts degree in 1873 and a Master of Arts in 1876 from Princeton University. He completed his work at Princeton Theological Seminary the following year, and was ordained in 1879. His first charge was the United Congregational Church in Newport, Rhode Island, where he remained for four years. From 1883 to 1899 he was minister of Brick Presbyterian Church in New York City, after which he became professor of English at Princeton, a post he held for twenty-three years. He was succeeded at Brick Church by Maltbie Babcock (LBW 554). President Woodrow Wilson, while still president of Princeton University, came to know van Dyke well, and later appointed him United States Minister to the Netherlands and Luxembourg, where he served from 1913 to 1916. In 1917 he was a lieutenant commander in the United States Navy Chaplains Corps. After 1923 he retired and devoted himself entirely to literary work. He died April 10, 1933, at Princeton.

Van Dyke was highly regarded as a preacher and was the author of several books, including *The Reality of Religion,* 1884; *The Story of the Psalms,* 1887; *The Poetry of Tennyson,* 1889; *Sermons to Young Men,* 1893; *The Story of the Other Wise Man,* 1896; and *The Gospel for an Age of Doubt,* 1896. He served as moderator of the General Assembly of the Presbyterian Church, and was chairman of the committee for the *Book of Common Worship,* 1905, and its revision in 1932. Several honorary doctorates were bestowed on him in the United States, and in 1917 he received a Doctor of Civil Law degree from Oxford University. In 1909 he was American lecturer at the University of Paris, and the following year, was made a fellow of the Royal Society of Literature in England.

HYMN TO JOY. Ludwig van Beethoven, son and grandson of musicians, was baptized on December 17, 1770, in Bonn, Germany, and was probably born the day before. His home life was marked by poverty and his father's intemperance and abusiveness. Having begun his music study with his father, he continued with Christian Neefe, under whom he received careful training and valuable experience. Substitute court organist at eleven, accompanist for the court orchestra at twelve, and assistant court organist at fourteen, he played viola in the theater orchestra from 1788 to 1792. As a young man he went to Vienna, where he studied with Franz Joseph Haydn (LBW 358), Johann Schenk, Antonio Salieri, and Johann Georg Albrechtsberg. There he remained, becoming Europe's most renowned pianist and composer and establishing himself in the affections of the aristocracy with his playing and his improvisations. Beethoven's career as a composer spanned and helped to bring about the transition from the Classic to the Romantic eras of music history. Having inherited the forms of Mozart's and Haydn's generation, he greatly expanded both the forms and the materials of music. From 1798 Beethoven began to lose his hearing and by 1819 was almost totally deaf. Some of his greatest works, however, were written during this time—his Ninth Symphony, *Missa Solemnis, Diabelli* variations, and his last piano sonatas and string quartets. A complete list of Beethoven's works occupies twenty pages in *Grove's Dictionary of Music and Musicians.* He died March 26, 1827.

This tune, which evolved out of some two hundred sketches, was the setting for Johann Christop von Schiller's "An die Freude" (Ode to Joy) in Beethoven's ninth and last symphony. Written between 1817 and 1823 and published in 1826, the Ninth Symphony was first performed in Vienna on May 7, 1824. Beethoven, by then totally deaf, conducted the performance, and at its completion, one of the soloists had to turn him around so he could see the waving hats and handkerchiefs of the enthusiastic audience. It has been used as a hymn tune since 1846, when it appeared as the setting for three different texts in Elam Ives Jr.'s *The Mozart Collection,* published in New York.

Born in 1802 at Hamden, Connecticut, Ives seems to have started teaching in his early twenties, first near Hamden, then in Hartford. While in Hartford he edited *American Psalmody,* 1829, with Deodatus Dutton Jr. In 1830 he went to Philadelphia, where he worked as a teacher, author, and editor, and for four years, as principal of the Philadelphia Seminary. His *American Elementary Singing Book,* 1831, was perhaps the first music book published in America advocating Pestalozzian principles, and probably influenced Lowell Mason (LBW 353) to experiment with them. The same year, also, he and Mason edited the *Juvenile Lyre.* In the 1830s he moved to New York City, where he is believed to have remained until a year or two before his death. Highly regarded as a teacher and musician, he edited *The Music Review and Record of Musical Science, Literature, and Intelligence* from May 1838 to June 1839, and was the only professional musician to contribute to the columns of *The Harbinger.* He was one of three editors of *The Beethoven Collection,* 1844. His *The Mozart Collection,* which appeared two years later, is unique for its day in the inclusion of four chorales harmonized by J. S. Bach (LBW 219). *One Hundred Songs, Original and Selected,* which Ives published in the 1840s, advertises the Ives Academy of Music. In 1861 an American musical directory listed him as a teacher of piano, violin, and singing. His extensive and valuable library was sold at auction in New York City in 1851. He died in 1864 at Hamden, Connecticut.

Tune: In dir ist Freude

Johann Lindemann, son of a burgess of Gotha, in Thuringia, Germany, was born in 1549. He studied first at the *Gymnasium* in Gotha and attended the University of Jena from 1568 to 1570, when he completed a Master of Arts degree. From the 1570s he was a *Kantor* at Gotha, retiring from that post on a pension in 1631. He died November 6, 1631.

In his *Amorum Filii Dei Decades Duae,* published in 1598 in Erfurt, Lindemann included two sacred texts for melodies found in Gastoldi's *Balletti* (see below)—"Jesu, wollst uns weisen" for "Viver lieto voglio," and the present hymn, "In dir ist Freude," for "Alieta vita, Amor ciinuita." (See illustration on the following page.)

Catherine Winkworth's (LBW 29) translation was included in her *Lyra Germanica,* second series, 1858. A few changes have been made in the second stanza.

IN DIR IST FREUDE. Giovanni Giacomo Gastoldi, Italian priest and composer, was born about 1556 at Caravaggio, Italy. By 1581 he was a chorister in the court of Mantua, where his father also served. He was almost certainly a student of Giaches de Wert, and substituted for him often during his illnesses. In 1582 he became *maestro di cappella* at the church of Santa Barbara in Mantua. He remained, however, in the service of the duke of Mantua, and as a result, came in contact with all the musicians who came to Mantua during Claudio Monteverdi's rise to fame there. Gastoldi was especially famous for his ballettos—light-hearted, dancelike pieces, many of which have a fa-la-la refrain. His *Balletti a cinqve voce,* 1591, went through many editions in Italy and abroad until 1657. The influence of these pieces can be seen in the works of Monteverdi and Claudio Sartori in Italy, in Hans Leo Hassler's (LBW 116) *Lustgarten,* 1601, and in the ballets of Thomas Morley in England. He died about 1622.

The harmonization is by Jan Bender (LBW 396).

553 REJOICE, O PILGRIM THRONG!

Tune: Marion

This hymn by Edward Hayes Plumptre (LBW 431), based on Psalm 20:4 and Philippians 4:4, was written May, 1865, for the Peterborough Choral Festival at Peterborough Cathedral. The same year it was published in *Lazarus and other Poems,* second edition, and with a special music setting, by Novello and Company. Three years later it entered the Appendix to the Original Edition of *Hymns Ancient and Modern.* The opening line originally read, "Rejoice, *ye pure in heart.*"

MARION. Arthur Henry Messiter, born April 1, 1834, in Frome Selwood, Somersetshire, England, was apprenticed for four years, beginning at age seventeen, to a musician of talent and high local reputation. Afterwards he studied piano and voice privately and devoted himself to teaching piano. He came to the United States in 1863, and for a time sang in the choir of Trinity Episcopal Church in New York City. In the next few years he held several positions—organist to St. Mark's Church, Philadelphia; professor of music at the Female College in Poultney, Ver-

Above: Title page of Gastoldi's Balletti a cinqve voci, *Venice, 1593, which contained the song "Alieta vita" for which Johann Lindemann wrote his hymn, "In thee is gladness" (LBW 552). Below: Title page of the 1868 edition of Catherine Winkworth's* Lyra Germanica, *and page 167 of this lavishly-illustrated book giving "In thee is gladness."*

mont; and organist to St. Paul's, Calvary Chapel, and St. James the Less, all in Philadelphia. In 1866 he went to Trinity Church in New York City, a position held by Henry Stephen Cutler (LBW 183) a short time before, where he gained a considerable reputation for himself and his music program. He retired in 1897 and died July 2, 1916, in New York City.

"Marion," named for the composer's wife, was written for this hymn in 1883. It was sung at Trinity Church on June 19, 1887, for the jubilee service on the fiftieth anniversary of the accession of Queen Victoria, and also in May, 1897, for the bicentennial of Trinity Parish. It was included in the *Hymnal with Music as Used in Trinity Church,* 1893.

In addition to writing a number of anthems, Messiter edited a *Psalter,* 1889, and a *Choir Office Book,* 1891, and was the author of *A History of the Choir and the Music of Trinity Church,* 1906.

554 THIS IS MY FATHER'S WORLD

Tune: Terra Patris

Maltbie Davenport Babcock, a dynamic Presbyterian minister of many gifts—scholastic, dramatic, and athletic abilities, as well as poetic and musical talents—was born in Syracuse, New York, August 3, 1858. Following his graduation from Syracuse University in 1875 he went to Auburn Theological Seminary and was ordained into the Presbyterian ministry. He first served at Lockport, New York, after which he went to Brown Memorial Church in Baltimore in 1885. There his magnetic personality and his preaching drew people from all walks of life. In 1899 he succeeded Henry van Dyke (LBW 551) as pastor of the Brick Presbyterian Church in New York City. He died May 18, 1901, in Naples, Italy, while on a Mediterranean cruise.

This hymn was included in *Thoughts for Everyday Living,* a collection of sermons and poems published in 1901 after his death. The hymn originally consisted of sixteen stanzas of four lines, each beginning, "This is my Father's world." LBW uses stanzas 2–5 and 14 and 16.

TERRA PATRIS (also "Terra beata"). Born August 7, 1852, in Philadelphia, Franklin Lawrence Sheppard graduated at the head of his class of 1872 at the University of Pennsylvania, and was a charter member of the university's chapter of Phi Beta Kappa. Three years later he took charge of the foundry in Baltimore which was part of Isaac A. Sheppard and Co., his father's stove and heater company. He became a vestryman at Zion Episcopal Church in Baltimore. When he later joined the Presbyterian Church in Baltimore, he was active not only within the congregation, but on several occasions was a lay delegate to the General Assembly. Eventually he became a member of the Board of Publication and Sabbath-School Work, of which he was later president. His leadership did much to bring about the construction of the Witherspoon Building, the denominational headquarters in Philadelphia. Sheppard also studied music and at one time was an organist in the Episcopal Church. He was a member of the committee which prepared *The Hymnal,* 1911, of the Presbyterian Church. He died February 15, 1930, in Germantown, Pennsylvania.

Sheppard considered this tune to be an English melody he learned from his mother during his childhood days, and when the tune was included in *Alleluia,* the Presbyterian Sunday School hymnal which he edited in 1915, it was given as a ''Traditional English Melody arranged by S. F. L.'' The English folk tune, ''Rusper,'' found in *The English Hymnal,* 1906, as given below, is apparently the one he recalled, in somewhat altered form, in his later years.

The harmonization was prepared in 1929 by Stanley Oliver and included in *The Hymnary* of the United Church of Canada, 1930.

Oliver, outstanding New Zealand choral conductor, voice coach, and adjudicator, was born in Kent, England, in 1892 and attended the London College of Music. He came to Canada in 1912, taking a post as organist and choirmaster at St. James United Church and as director of the Mendelssohn Choir in Montreal. From 1934 to 1950 he was conductor of the Royal Wellington Choral Union in New Zealand. His Schola Cantorum, founded in 1930, sang throughout New Zealand and over the New Zealand Broadcasting Service until 1959. He was made an honorary fellow of Trinity College, London, in 1957, and the following year he was a judge at the Llangollen International Eisteddfod in Wales. In poor health from 1960, he died January 19, 1964.

555   WHEN IN OUR MUSIC GOD IS GLORIFIED
Tune: Fredericktown

Originally written for the tune ''Engelberg'' (LBW 189), this hymn by Frederick Pratt Green (LBW 246) was commissioned in 1971 for a Festival of Praise, and has been sung on many such occasions since then. It appeared on the front cover of *The Hymn,* July, 1973, and was included in *New Church Praise,* Edinburgh, 1975.

FREDERICKTOWN was written by Charles R. Anders (LBW 386) for this hymn and is published here for the first time. ''Fredericktown'' is the name by which the composer's birthplace was originally known.

556   HERALD, SOUND THE NOTE OF JUDGMENT
Tune: New Malden

The son of a Canadian physician who had founded and constructed the hospital in Ratham, India, Moir Alexander James Waters was born at

560

Ujjain in Central India, January 15, 1906. At the age of eleven he returned to Canada to attend school and in 1928, completed a Bachelor of Arts degree at University College of the University of Toronto. Following his graduation in 1931 from Emmanuel College, he was ordained and served for a year at Timothy Eaton Memorial Church in Toronto and another year at Newton-on-Ayr in Scotland before going in 1933 to First United Church in London, Ontario. First United Church merged with St. Andrew's in 1938 and Waters remained for two more years as co-pastor. In 1940 he went as a missionary to India, working for some time at Kharua and the surrounding villages, and teaching for three years at the Theological Seminary at Indore. Returning to Canada, he served briefly in 1945 as minister of Lawrence Park Community Church in Toronto before going the same year to First United Church in Victoria, British Columbia, where his morning services were heard on radio up and down the British Columbia coastline. After serving as president of the British Columbia Conference of the United Church from 1954 to 1955, he was pastor of Port Nelson United Church in Burlington, Ontario, 1955–1959, and Robinson Memorial United Church in London, Ontario from 1959 to 1969. He returned to First–St. Andrew's in London as associate pastor from 1969 to 1973. Waters served for a number of years on the senate of Victoria University, which honored him with a Doctor of Divinity degree in 1968. Following his retirement he lived in London, Ontario, where he died February 15, 1980.

This hymn was written in 1968 when Waters was minister of Robinson Memorial Church in London, Ontario. The occasion was the dedication of a new window with the subject of Jesus' baptism. Unable to find a hymn which carried the message of John the Baptist as the herald of Christ, he wrote this hymn, which was sung with trumpet and organ to the tune "Regent Square" (LBW 50). Stanza 2 reflects the prophecy of the coming of John the Baptist found in Isaiah 40:3. The hymn was published in the *Hymn Book*, 1971, of the Anglican Church and United Church of Canada.

NEW MALDEN. David McCarthy originally wrote this tune for use in a school chapel service with Frederik Herman Kaan's "God who spoke in the beginning." He then sent the tune to Frederick Pratt Green (LBW 246), with whom he has collaborated on a number of occasions, and within a week Pratt Green replied with a new hymn, "When our confidence is shaken." Text and tune were printed for the first time in Pratt Green's *Twenty-six Hymns,* 1971. The composer notes that New Malden is "a town in suburban Surrey where lived at the time one of the most far-sighted and devoted of Methodist musicians, Commander John Farmer, responsible above all for the establishment of the flourishing music weekend courses, Youth Makes Music. It was in his honor that the tune was named."

McCarthy was born April 2, 1931, at Pentre Broughton, near Wiescham in North Wales. At Downing College, Cambridge University, he completed a Bachelor of Arts in English and theology, and proceeded to a Master of Arts. He was appointed assistant English master at Woodhouse Grove School (Methodist foundation) near Bradford in Yorkshire, and since 1960 he has been director of music there.

557 LET ALL THINGS NOW LIVING

Tune: The Ash Grove

"Let all things now living" was written by K. K. Davis for this tune in the 1920s. It was published in 1939 under the pseudonym John Cowley in her four-part anthem with descant which became very popular.

Born June 25, 1892, in St. Joseph, Missouri, Katherine Kennicott Davis completed a Bachelor of Arts degree at Wellesley College, Wellesley, Massachusetts, in 1914, and pursued postgraduate study from 1916 to 1918. She studied piano, composition, and theory with Jessie L. Gaynor, Clarence C. Hamilton, Stuart Mason, and Nadia Boulanger. She taught in the music department at Wellesley College from 1916 to 1918, and from 1921 to 1929 taught in private schools in Concord, Massachusetts, and in Philadelphia. After 1929 she was engaged in freelance work—arranging, composing, editing, and so on. She has published nearly eight hundred separate items, mainly choral pieces and arrangements. A number of her texts (including "The Little Drummer Boy," 1941) appeared under pen names such as John Cowley or C. R. W. Robertson. In addition, she is the author and composer of *First Studies in Rhythm* (1920), the *Concord Piano Books* (1925–1928), the *Concord Duet Book* (1930), *Cinderella* (a folk operetta, 1933), the *Green Hill Choir Books* (1938–1940), the *Belfry Book* (1943), *This is Noel* (a Christmas cantata), *The Bow Street Books,* and the *Second Belfry Book,* as well as the *Galaxy Junior Chorus Book* (with A. T. Davisson and F. W. Kempf, 1942), *Songs of Freedom* (with Nancy Loring, 1948), and a one-act opera, *The Unmusical Impresario* (with Heddy Root Kent). Stetson University in Florida has honored her with a doctorate. She lived in Concord, Massachusetts, for a number of years, and continued to compose until 1977, when failing eyesight forced her to stop. She died at Concord April 20, 1980, and is buried there in the Sleepy Hollow Cemetary. Her music library was given to the Merrimac Valley Chapter of the Choristers Guild and has been given by them as a permanent loan to the University of Lowell.

THE ASH GROVE is a Welsh folk melody. K. K. Davis gave a small pamphlet, the *Book of National Songs,* published by Novello, as her source of the tune.

The present harmonization is by R. Harold Terry, who also suggests an optional six-measure pedal point on low D beginning in measure 17 (where stanza 1 reads "banners").

Born February 3, 1925, in Salisbury, North Carolina, Terry received a Bachelor of Arts degree in 1945 from Lenoir-Rhyne College, Hickory, North Carolina, and a Bachelor of Divinity degree three years later from the Lutheran Theological Southern Seminary, Columbia, South Carolina. His graduate study was at Union Theological Seminary in New York City (Master of Sacred Theology, 1955), and at Columbia University and Temple University. In 1973 Lenoir-Rhyne College honored him with a Doctor of Sacred Music degree. He served as assistant pastor of St. John's Lutheran Church, Salisbury, North Carolina, 1948–1950; and as pastor of Emanuel Lutheran Church, Ridgefield Park, New Jersey, 1950–1953, and St. Mark's Lutheran Church, China Grove, North Carolina, 1953–1959. From 1959 to 1977 he was editor for worship and music resources for the Board of Parish Education of the United Lutheran Church in America, which later became the Division for Parish Services of the Lutheran Church in America. In this capacity he compiled and edited *Church School Hymnal for Children* (1964), *Young Children Sing* (1967), *Music Resource Book* (1967), *Music in Christian Education* (1969), *Hymns: The Story of Christian Song* (1969), *Sing! Hymnal for Youth and Adults* (1970), and *Children Sing,* Book 1 (1972), Book 2 (1973), and Book 3 (1977). He was also editor, contributing editor, or editorial consultant for numerous educational resources, teachers' guides, pupil materials, recordings, films, and other curriculum aids, and from 1974 to 1977, edited the weekly worship aid, *Celebrate.* In 1977 he was called to be pastor of Peace Lutheran Church in Gibsonville, North Carolina.

From 1969 to 1972 Terry was a member of the commission on music of the Episcopal Diocese of Pennsylvania. Active in the Hymn Society of America, he has served on the national executive committee, as president of the Philadelphia chapter, and, since 1977, as a member of the research committee. He has frequently been a faculty member and program director of Lutheridge School of Church Music conducted by the Lutheridge summer assembly, Arden, North Carolina. Married to Kathryn L. Wagoner of Salisbury, North Carolina, he is the father of two daughters and a son. A third daughter died in 1971.

558   EARTH AND ALL STARS!

Tune: Earth and All Stars

This hymn was written for the 90th anniversary of St. Olaf College in 1964. The author, Herbert Brokering, comments, "I tried to gather into a hymn of praise the many facets of life which merge in the life of community. So there are the references to building, nature, learning, family, war, festivity."

The son of a Lutheran pastor, Herbert Frederick Brokering was born May 21, 1926, at Beatrice, Nebraska. Following his studies at Wartburg College, Waverly, Iowa, he attended Wartburg Seminary and the Lutheran Theological Seminary, Columbus, Ohio. He has completed a Master of Arts degree in child psychology at the University of Iowa, and has done additional graduate work in religious education at the University of Pittsburgh, and in theology at the Universities of Kiel and Erlangen in Germany. He has worked with the Lutheran World Federation, and with the World Council of Churches workcamp in Europe, and with the Lutheran Student Association at the University of Iowa. For ten years he was a parish pastor, serving in Cedarhurst, New York; Pittsburgh, Pennsylvania; and San Antonio, Texas. From 1960 to 1970 he was with the department of parish education of the national offices of the American Lutheran Church. Since that time he has been in freelance, or "tent" ministry, serving as a resource person and consultant for local, regional, and national seminars on creative worship and ministry in all denominations. He has also served as a part-time professor of creative worship and education in seminaries and military schools, and been on the Holden faculty for a number of years. A close friend of Dr. Roland Bainton, he has collaborated with him in Renaissance-Reformation festivals throughout the Midwest, and as tour guides of Reformation sites in 1978. He and his wife, Lois *née* Redelfs, a writer and early childhood teacher, are the parents of four children.

Brokering writes daily, and is the author of over thirty books, including *Lord, Be With,* 1969; *City and Country,* 1970; *Surprise Me,*

Jesus, 1973; and *Lord, If,* 1977. His texts for hymns and anthems have been set to music by more than thirty composers, and he has prepared the libretti for seventeen cantatas, including an Easter cantata by Dave Brubeck. He has also written a full-length musical, "Christ Carnival." He notes:

> Many of the images through which I visualize the rhyme and rhythm of the gospel came to me in Nebraska and Iowa. Season, emotions, death and resurrection, bread, wine, water, wind, sun, spirit—have made great impressions on my imagination. Words want to be seen. Words have their roots in visuals and images. We see what we know. We imagine the language of faith. The image power we have is an enormous gift from God. We are in God's image!

Both text and tune of this hymn were included in *Twelve Folksongs and Spirituals,* 1968, and were given also in *Contemporary Worship-1* the following year.

EARTH AND ALL STARS was composed by David N. Johnson, a native of San Antonio, Texas, born June 28, 1922. After receiving his Bachelor of Music degree from Trinity University, he went to Syracuse University, where he completed Master of Music and Doctor of Philosophy degrees. He also holds the associate degree from the American Guild of Organists. He has been chairman of the music department of St. Olaf College, university organist at Syracuse University, and organist/choir director of Trinity Episcopal Cathedral, Phoenix, and is presently professor of music at Arizona State University. In addition, he has given a number of lecture-demonstrations on new publications for organ and choir, and has presented lectures and prepared a recording on improvisation. His publications, which number well over three hundred compositions, include organ and choral works, most of them intended for church use.

The harmonization of the tune is by Jan Bender (LBW 396).

559   OH, FOR A THOUSAND TONGUES TO SING
Tune: Azmon

Written by Charles Wesley (LBW 27) on May 21, 1738, the first anniversary of his great spiritual change, this hymn was included in *Hymns and Sacred Poems,* 1740. Originally the hymn of eighteen stanzas opened with LBW stanza 5, "Glory to God, and praise, and love" (here altered in its first line).

AZMON is from a tune written in 1828 by Carl Gotthilf Gläser and included in Lowell Mason's (LBW 353) *Modern Psalmist,* 1839, where it was the setting for "Come, let us lift our joyful eyes." As it appeared in 1839, the tune was in 4/4 meter, but by 1850 it had been altered, both in *The New Carmina Sacra,* and in Mason's and George Webb's (LBW 389) *Cantica Laudis,* to the 3/2 rhythm used today.

Gläser, born May 4, 1784, in Weissenfels, Germany, was a chorister at St. Thomas' Church in Leipzig, where J. S. Bach (LBW 219) had earlier served. For a while he studied law at the University of Leipzig, but he eventually turned his efforts to music, and studied violin with the Italian master, Bartholomeo Campagnoli, who was teaching in Leipzig at the time. He went to Barmen, where he taught piano, violin, and voice, and also directed choruses and owned a music shop. He also composed a number of works, including motets, school songs, and instrumental music. He died April 16, 1829.

560 OH, THAT I HAD A THOUSAND VOICES
(O dass ich tausend Zungen hätte/und einen)
Tune: O das ich tausend Zungen hätte

The German hymnwriter, Johann Mentzer, was born July 27, 1658, at Jahmen, near Rothenburg in Silesia, and studied theology at Wittenberg. In 1691 he became pastor at Merzdorf, and two years later went to Hauswalde, near Bischofswerde. In 1696 he went to Kemnitz, near Bernstadt in Saxony, where he remained until his death on February 24, 1734. Among Mentzer's neighbors and good friends were three other hymnwriters: Johann Christoph Schwedler, Henriette Catherine von Gersdorf, and Nicolaus Ludwig von Zinzendorf (LBW 302).

Shortly after Mentzer arrived in Kemnitz a nearby farmhouse was destroyed by lightning. It has been suggested that this hymn, Mentzer's best, was written after this event to show that Christians have reason to give God thanks and praise in all circumstances. The hymn was first published in Johann A. Freylinghausen's *Neues Geistreiches Gesangbuch,* Halle, 1704 (LBW 32). A translation based on those in Henry Mills's *Horae Germanicae,* 1845, and Catherine Winkworth's (LBW 29) *Lyra Germanica,* first series, 1855, was included in *The Lutheran Hymnal,* 1941, and is given here with some alterations, especially in the final stanza.

O DASS ICH TAUSEND ZUNGEN HÄTTE, probably composed by Johann Balthasar König (LBW 22), appeared in his *Harmonischer Liederschatz,* Frankfurt, 1738, as the setting for Angelus Silesius' (LBW 455) hymn, "Ach sagt mir nichts von Gold und Schätzen" (Zahn* #2806). It later became firmly associated with the present hymn, and has remained so to the present. The harmonization is from the *Württembergische Choralbuch,* 1953.

561 FOR THE BEAUTY OF THE EARTH
Tune: Dix

Originally written as a Communion hymn, "For the beauty of the earth" was included in Orby Shipley's *Lyra Eucharistica,* second edition, 1864. Haeussler* writes: "Folliott Sanford Pierpoint wrote this one day in late spring near his native city of Bath, England, when violets and primroses were in full bloom and all the earth seemed to rejoice. He climbed up a hill and sat down to rest and meditate. The panorama before him inspired him to write these beautiful lines."

Born October 7, 1835, at Bath, England, Pierpoint graduated from Queens' College, Cambridge, in 1857. After serving for some time as headmaster of Somersetshire College, he lived in various places, mostly at Babbicombe, Devonshire, on a small inheritance supplemented occasionally with some teaching of classics. He was the author of numerous hymns and sacred poems. He died March 10, 1917, at Newport, Monmouthshire.

For DIX see LBW 82.

562 LIFT EVERY VOICE AND SING
Tune: Lift Ev'ry Voice and Sing

Two brothers, James Weldon Johnson and J. Rosamond Johnson, collaborated in writing "Lift every voice and sing," which has become the official song of the National Association for the Advancement of Colored People. The piece was published as sheet music in 1921.

The text is by James Weldon Johnson, author, lawyer, educator, and diplomat, born in Jacksonville, Florida, on June 17, 1871. A charter member of the American Society of Composers, Authors, and Publishers, he held Bachelor of Arts and Master of Arts degrees from Atlanta University, and served for a time as principal of Stanton School. He was founder and editor of the *Daily American,* the first Negro daily in the United States. Self-educated in law, he was admitted to the Florida bar. He was appointed United States consul to Puerto Cabello, Venezuela, and later to Corinto, Nicaragua. On his return to the United States he became assistant editor of the New York *Age.* He was a visiting professor of creative literature at Fisk University, a trustee of Atlanta University, and director of the American Fund for Public Service, and for fourteen years served as national secretary of the National Association for the Advancement of Colored People. His publications include *The Book of American Negro Poetry,* 1922; *God's Trombones,* 1927; *Black Manhattan,* 1930; *Negro Americans,* 1934; *St. Peter Relates an Incident,* 1935; and his autobiography, *Along This Way,* 1933. His translation of Enrique Grandos' opera, *Goyescas,* was produced by the Metropolitan Opera Company in 1915. With his brother, J. Rosamond, he collaborated in writing a number of songs (see below). He died at Wiscasset, Maine, on June 26, 1938.

LIFT EVERY VOICE AND SING. John Rosamond Johnson, composer, author, conductor, actor, and singer, was born in Jacksonville, Florida, on August 11, 1873. At the New England Conservatory in Boston, Massachusetts, he studied with Charles Dennee, Dietrich Strong, George Whiting, Carl Riessman, and David Bispham. He also held an honorary Master of Arts degree from Atlanta University. For some time he was supervisor of music for the public schools in Jacksonville. From 1896 to 1898 he toured in vaudeville in the United States and Europe. Later he was music director of the Hammerstein Opera House in London, and in 1914, of the Music School Settlement in New York City. During World War I he was a second lieutenant in the New York National Guard. In 1901 the Johnson brothers, together with Robert Cole, signed what was apparently the first contract ever made between black songwriters and a Tin Pan Alley publisher (Joseph W. Stern and Company). J. Rosamond became a member of the American Society of Composers, Authors, and Publishers in 1927. The author of *Rolling Along in Song,* 1937, he also edited an *Album of Negro Spirituals,* 1940. He wrote the Broadway stage scores for *Humpty Dumpty, Shoo-Fly Regiment, The Red Moon,* and *Mr. Load of Kole,* as well as songs for *Sleeping Beauty and the Beast.* His Broadway appearances included *Porgy and*

Bess, Mamba's Daughters, and *Cabin in the Sky.* With his brother, James Weldon (see above), he wrote a number of songs, including "Since You Went Away," "The Awakening," "Morning, Noon and Night," "Two Eyes," "The Maiden with the Dreamy Eyes," and "My Castle on the Nile." He died November 11, 1954.

The LBW harmonization is by Robert P. Schultz, who since 1965 has been president and recording engineer of his own recording studio, Voice Works, in Minneapolis, Minnesota. Born May 14, 1937, at St. Joseph, Michigan, Schultz completed a Bachelor of Arts degree at Valparaiso University, Valparaiso, Indiana, in 1960. He went to the Twin Cities where he taught at Concordia College in St. Paul from 1960 to 1965 and completed a Master of Arts degree at the University of Minnesota in 1964. From 1965 to 1976 he was also director of music at Resurrection Lutheran Church in Roseville, and since 1976 he has held the same position at Richfield Lutheran Church. His *Three Christmas Carols for Electronic Tape and Unison Voices* was published in 1976, and *Two Christmas Carols for Electronic Tape and Unison Voices* appeared two years later. Married to Carol Haugen, he is the father of three children.

563 FOR THE FRUIT OF ALL CREATION

Tune: Santa Barbara

This hymn by Frederick Pratt Green (LBW 246) was written in 1970 to bring Dr. Francis Jackson's tune, "East Ackliam," into use. It was first published in the Roman Catholic hymnal, *Praise the Lord,* 1972.

SANTA BARBARA. The tune name, "Santa Barbara," writes the composer, "seemed appropriate because of the text: 'For the fruits of his creation . . . ,' Santa Barbara being opulent witness to the beauties in nature and geography, and also my place of residence since 1971."

Born in Kansas City, Missouri, on November 24, 1927, Emma Lou Diemer studied composition, completing Bachelor of Music and Master of Music degrees at Yale School of Music, and a Doctor of Philosophy degree at Eastman School of Music, Rochester, New York. She has studied privately with Paul Hindemith, Howard Hanson, Roger Sessions, Bernard Rodgers, and Ernst Toch. A recipient of a Fulbright scholarship for study in Belgium, she has also been a participant in the Berkshire Music Center, and from 1959 to 1961 was composer-in-residence under a Ford Foundation Young Composers Project in the schools of Arlington, Virginia. She was professor of theory and composition at the University of Maryland from 1965 to 1970, and since 1971 has held the same post at the University of California in Santa Barbara. Since 1940 she has also served as organist in churches in various cities, including the Lutheran Church of the Reformation in Washington, D.C., from 1962 to 1971, and in 1973, was appointed organist for the First Church of Christ, Scientist, in Santa Barbara.

Diemer has received Creative Arts grants from the universities of Maryland and California, and awards from the American Society of Composers, Authors, and Publishers, and the National Federation of Music Clubs. Yale School of Music Alumni Association honored her with their Certificate of Merit (1977), and she has had commissions from the Kindler Foundation, Maryland State Teachers Association, the South Carolina Tricentennial, Wayne State University, the Lutheran

Church in America, Dallas Civic Chorus, Armstrong Flute Company, and various other church and school organizations. Numbering over one hundred, her compositions include works for orchestra, band, chamber ensemble, organ, piano, carillon, marimba, solo voice, and chorus (mixed, women's, and men's).

564 PRAISE GOD, FROM WHOM ALL BLESSINGS FLOW
Tune: Old Hundredth

This doxology is stanza 5 of LBW 269.

For OLD HUNDREDTH see LBW 245. The harmonzation found here is from the *Württembergische Choralbuch,* 1953.

565 PRAISE GOD, FROM WHOM ALL BLESSINGS FLOW
Tune: Old Hundredth

Both text and music are identical with LBW 564 except for a rhythmic variation at the beginning of the fourth phrase of music.

566 MY COUNTRY, 'TIS OF THEE
Tune: National Anthem

Samuel Francis Smith, born in Newton Centre, Massachusetts, October 21, 1808, graduated from Harvard in 1829 in the same class as Oliver Wendell Holmes, and from Andover Theological Seminary in 1832. He was editor of the *Baptist Missionary Magazine* for a year and a half, and from 1834 to 1842 was minister of a Baptist congregation in Waterville, Maine, and also professor of modern languages at Waterville College (now Colby College). He returned to Newton Centre, where he served the First Baptist Church from 1842 until 1854 when he became secretary to the American Baptist Missionary Union, a position he held until 1869. He died November 16, 1895, at Newton Centre.

Smith wrote nearly one hundred hymns, twenty-six of which were included in *The Psalmist,* 1843, which he edited with the Reverend Baron Stow. *The Psalmist,* which contained 1180 hymns, was the finest hymnbook the Baptists had created to that point and continued to influence American Baptist hymnals for many years after its publication. A great admirer of the work of Adoniram Judson, Smith toured the mission fields of Asia and Europe in 1880, and returned to write *Rambles in Mission Fields,* 1884. His son, Dr. A. W. Smith, was a Baptist missionary to Burma, where he served as president of the theological seminary at Rangoon.

In 1829, Smith's friend, William C. Woodbridge, returned from Europe with a number of German music books, which he gave to Lowell Mason (LBW 353). Since Mason couldn't read German, he passed the books along to Smith. Leafing through the books, Smith was struck with "Gott segne Sachsenland" (LBW 569) and its tune, which is here called "National Anthem." "I think," he later recalled, "I instantly felt the impulse to write a patriotic hymn of my own adapted to the tune. Picking up a scrap of waste paper which lay near me, I wrote at once, probably within half an hour, the hymn 'America' as it is now known everywhere.'' The hymn was first sung at a July 4 celebration at the Boston Sabbath School Union at Park Street Church in 1831, and was included in Mason's *Choir, or Union Collection of Church Music,* 1832.

For NATIONAL ANTHEM see LBW 568.

567 GOD OF OUR FATHERS
Tune: National Hymn

Written by Daniel Crane Roberts in 1876 for a Juy 4 Centennial celebration, and sung at Brandon, Vermont, to the tune, "Russian Hymn" (LBW 462), this hymn was included with the present tune in John Ireland Tucker's 1892 *Hymnal,* and in the same year in Charles Hutchins' *The Church Hymnal* with the tune "Pro Patria" by Horatio Parker.

Roberts was born in Bridgehampton, Long Island, New York, on November 5, 1841, and graduated from Kenyon College, Gambier, Ohio, in 1857. After serving in the army during the Civil War he was ordained an Anglican deacon in 1865 and a priest in 1866. During his lifetime he ministered to Christ Church, Montpelier, Vermont; St. John's Church, Lowell, Massachusetts; St. Thomas's Church, Brandon, Vermont; and finally, for twenty-three years, at St. Paul's Church, Concord, New Hampshire. He was for many years president of the New Hampshire State Historical Society, and in 1885 Norwich University honored him with a Doctor of Divinity degree. He died October 31, 1907, at Concord.

NATIONAL HYMN. This tune was published together with the text in Tucker's 1892 *Hymnal.*

The composer, George William Warren, was born in Albany, New York, August 17, 1828, and attended Racine College in Wisconsin. Beginning in 1846 he served twelve years as organist at St. Peter's Church, Albany; two years at St. Paul's, Albany; and ten years at Holy Trinity Church, Brooklyn. He was organist at St. Thomas' Church, New York City, from 1870 to 1900. In addition he composed a number of services and anthems, and hymn tunes which were included in his *Hymns and Tunes as Sung at St. Thomas' Church,* 1888. Racine College honored him with a Doctor of Music degree. He died in New York on March 17, 1902.

568 GOD SAVE OUR GRACIOUS QUEEN!
Tune: National Anthem

The origins of the text and tune of this hymn are very obscure and a number of theories have been advanced concerning them. Known for certain is the fact that both appeared in *Harmonia Angelicana,* probably published in 1743 or 1744, and in *Thesaurus Musicus,* dated variously from 1740 to 1745. In those collections two stanzas were included, from which the LBW uses the first, originally beginning "God save *the Lord our King.*" The second stanza in the LBW is a third stanza added in the October 1745 *Gentleman's Magazine* "as sung at both playhouses" [Drury Lane and Covent Garden]. Originally it opened "Thy choicest gifts in store On *George* be pleased to pour." At the same time as the text was published in English, a Latin version was used by John Tavers, organist of the Chapel Royal, in 1743 or 1744. This Latin version may well have been the one sung in the Stuarts' Catholic Chapel in 1688, and may have been translated at least in part by Henry Carey, to whom the text and tune have on occasion been attributed.

The tune NATIONAL ANTHEM (also "America"), which appeared with the text in *Harmonia Angelicana* (see above), was not confined to the British patriotic hymn. It also was held in honor in Denmark and Sweden, and served as the setting for "Dieu sauve la France" in France, "Heil dir im Siegerkranze" and "Gott segne Sachsenland" (LBW 569) in Germany, and for the Russian national anthem until 1833 (see LBW 462). In the July, 1934, issue of *The Musical Quarterly* (pp. 259–266) Edward Maginty suggested that the outline of the tune is contained in the plainsong Magnificat antiphon, "Unxerunt Salomonen Sadoc sacerdos" (see the *Liber Usualis,* Tournai, 1963, p. 987). Percy Scholes' *Oxford Companion to Music* (10th edition, London, 1970) devotes a number of pages to "God save the Queen," and notes that the melody has a galliard rhythm. Traces of the melody have been found in several works, including a keyboard piece by John Bull (*c.* 1562–1638) and two instrumental works by Henry Purcell (*c.* 1659–1695). Franz Joseph Haydn heard "God save the King" sung in England and was inspired to write "Austria" (LBW 358). The tune was used in Carl Maria von Weber's *Kampf und Sieg* and *Jubilee Overture;* Ludwig van Beethoven's (LBW 551) *Battle Symphony,* piano variations, and arrangement for chorus, piano, violin, and cello; and Johannes Brahms's *Triumphlied.*

The harmonization found here (but not at LBW 566 or 569) is by Ernest Campbell MacMillan.

Of Scottish ancestry, Ernest MacMillan was born in Mimico, Ontario, on August 18, 1893. His distinguished musical career began early. At ten he played the organ in Massey Hall in Toronto. At thirteen he won an award for advanced harmony at the University of Edinburgh. The next year he was appointed organist of Knox Church, Toronto, and in 1911 he was the highest-ranking candidate to become a fellow of the Royal College of Organists, and also received a Bachelor of Music degree from Oxford University. From 1919 to 1925 he was organist and choirmaster at one of Toronto's largest churches, the Timothy Eaton Memorial Church. In 1920 he was a teacher at the Canadian Academy of Music, and from 1927 to 1928 he served as president of the Royal Canadian College of Organists. He received a Bachelor of Arts degree from the University of Toronto in 1915. His career as a conductor began in a prison camp. While studying in Paris he went in the spring of 1914 to Bayreuth to hear Richard Wagner and was captured as an alien, spending the next four years in prison. There, in addition to conducting a group of his fellow musicians, he composed and submitted an exercise which was accepted for the requirements of Doctor of Music at Oxford University. Back in Canada, he conducted, with Richard Tattersall, one of the first complete performances of J. S. Bach's (LBW 219) *St. Matthew Passion* in Toronto, a performance which became an annual event. He later conducted a number of other first performances in Canada. He served as dean of the faculty of music at Toronto University from 1927 to 1952, and also was principal of the Toronto Conservatory of Music from 1926 to 1942. In addition he served as adjudicator at many festivals and worked for the encouragement of young musicians. From 1931 to 1956 he was conductor of the Toronto Symphony orchestra, and from 1942 to 1957 also conducted the Toronto Mendelssohn Choir. He was in great demand as a conductor and appeared in numerous cities in the United States, and in Jamaica, Brazil, and Australia. His compositions include music for organ and chamber groups, and he also set down and arranged a number of French Canadian and Indian songs. For his services to the music of Canada he was knighted in 1935, the first person outside the United Kingdom to receive the honor. He died May 6, 1973.

569   GOD BLESS OUR NATIVE LAND *(Gott segne Sachsenland)*
Tune: National Anthem

The German hymn on which this text is based was published in Gottfried Wilhelm Fink's *Zeitung für die elegante Welt,* 1815, and was first sung on November 13, 1815, in the presence of the King of Saxony. The English text by Charles Timothy Brooks was written while he was studying at Harvard Divinity School. The last two lines of stanza 1, and all of stanza 2 as found here are by John Sullivan Dwight. (See Julian* p. 1566 for a complete history of English texts.) The revised text was included in Lowell Mason's (LBW 353) and George Webb's (LBW 389) *The Psaltery,* 1845. There have been a few slight alterations for the LBW.

Siegfried August Mahlmann, author of the original German hymn, was born in Leipzig, Saxony, Germany, on May 13, 1771. After studying law at the University of Leipzig and traveling throughout Europe, he bought a book store in Leipzig in 1802. He edited the *Zeitung für die elegante Welt* from 1805 to 1816, and the *Leipziger Zeitung* from 1810 to 1818. He attained a reputation as a song writer, and a number of his children's songs are still known in Germany. He died December 16, 1826, in Leipzig.

Born at Salem, Massachusetts, on June 20, 1813, Brooks graduated from Harvard in 1832 and from the divinity school three years later. He was ordained a Unitarian minister. After serving parishes in Maine and Vermont, he became, in 1837, minister to a church in Newport, Rhode Island, where he remained until failing health and eyesight made it necessary for him to resign in 1871. He died June 14, 1883.

Dwight, born the same year as Brooks (1813) on May 13, in Boston, also graduated from Harvard College and Divinity School. He served briefly at a Unitarian church in Northampton, Massachusetts, but extreme shyness caused him to give up the ministry, and later even public worship. Founder of *Dwight's Journal of Music,* he edited that publication for nearly thirty years. He thought highly of German music and its standards, and in 1837 was involved in the organization of the Harvard Musical Association. He died September 5, 1893, in Boston.

For NATIONAL ANTHEM see LBW 568.

BIBLIOGRAPHY AND INDEXES

Bibliography

References cited in the book from this bibliography are marked with an asterisk (*).

Aaberg, Jens Christian. *Hymns and Hymnwriters of Denmark*. Des Moines: Committee on Publication of the Danish Evangelical Lutheran Church in America, 1945.

Bäumker, Wilhelm. *Das Katholische Deutsche Kirchenlied in seinen Singweisen*. Reprint of the 1883-1911 edition. Hildesheim: Georg Olms Verlagsbuchhandlung, 1962.

Blume, Friedrich, *et. al. Protestant Church Music: A History*. New York: W.W. Norton & Company, 1974. (A translation of Blume, *Geschichte der Evangelischen Kirchenmusik,* 1964, together with articles and revisions by Ludwig Finscher, Georg Feder, Adam Adrio, Walter Blankenburg, Torben Schousboe, Robert Stevenson, and Watkins Shaw.)

Bucke, Emory Stevens (gen. ed.), Fred G. Healy, Austin C. Lovelace, and Carlton R. Young. *Companion to the Hymnal: A Handbook to the 1964 Methodist Hymnal.* Nashville: Abingdon, 1970.

Dahle, John. *The Library of Christian Hymns*. Trans. by M. Caspar Johnshoy. 3 vols. Starbuck, Minnesota: The Luther Memorial Publishing Co., 1924.

Dearmer, Percy, compiler. *Songs of Praise Discussed.* London: Oxford University Press, 1933.

Douglas, Charles Winfred; Ellinwood, Leonard; and others. *The Hymnal 1940 Companion.* New York: The Church Pension Fund, 1951.

Frost, Maurice. *Historical Companion to Hymns Ancient and Modern.* London: Wm. Clowes and Sons, Ltd., 1962.

Haeussler, Armin. *The Story of Our Hymns.* St. Louis: Eden Publishing House, 1952.

Julian, John, editor. *A Dictionary of Hymnology.* Reprint of the 1907 edition. 2 vols. New York: Dover Publications, 1957.

Leupold, Ulrich Siegfried, editor. *Liturgy and Hymns.* Vol. LIII of *Luther's Works.* General editor, Helmut T. Lehmann. Philadelphia: Fortress Press, 1965.

Lövgren, Oscar. *Den Segrande Sången.* Stockholm: Missionsförbundets förlag, 1967.

Malling, Anders. *Dansk Salme Historie.* Copenhagen: J.H. Schultz Forlag, 1962-1972.

Moffatt, James, and Patrick, Millar, editors. *Handbook to the Church Hymnary.* With supplement. London: Oxford University Press, 1935.

Osborne, Stanley L. *If Such Holy Song: The Story of the Hymns in The Hymn Book 1971.* Whitby, Ontario: The Institute of Church Music, 1976.

Parry, K.L., and Routley, Erik. *Companion to Congregational Praise.* London: The Independent Press, 1953.

Polack, William G. *The Handbook to the Lutheran Hymnal.* Reprint of 1958 third and revised edition. St. Louis: Concordia Publishing House, 1975.

Reed, Luther D. *The Lutheran Liturgy.* Philadelphia: Fortress Press, 1947. Revised edition, 1960.

Reynolds, William J. *Companion to Baptist Hymnal.* Nashville: Broadman Press, 1976.

Ronander, Albert C., and Porter, Ethel K. *Guide to the Pilgrim Hymnal.* Philadelphia: United Church Press, 1966.

Ryden, Ernest Edwin. *The Story of Christian Hymnody.* Rock Island, Illinois: Augustana Press, 1959.

Seaman, William R. *Companion to the Hymnal of the Service Book and Hymnal.* Published by The Commission on the Liturgy and Hymnal, 1976.

Wackernagle, Philipp. *Das deutsche Kirchenlied vom der ältestan Zeit bis zu Anfang des XVIII Jahrhanderts.* 5 vols. Reprint of 1841 edition. Hildesheim: Georg Olms Verlagsbuchhandlung, 1964.

Zahn, Johannes. *Die Melodien der deutschen evangelischen Kirchenlieder, aus den Quellen geschäpft und mitgeteilt von Johannes Zahn.* 6 vols. Gütersloh: C. Bertelsmann, 1889-1893.

Hymns for the Church Year

Numbers listed refer to LBW hymn numbers.

The following list provides suggestions to assist in the selection of congregational hymns, as well as hymn-based choir music and organ works. Hymns appropriate for all three series—A, B, and C—are given first, followed by those which relate to the individual series. This list incorporates the list found on pp. 929-931 of the LBW, with the Hymn of the Day marked (H), and all others from that list marked §. Further suggestions appear in the order in which the items occur in the service:†

(Pr)   Reflecting the emphasis of the Prayer of the Day

(I)   Based on or reflecting the emphasis of the First Lesson

(PsP)   Psalm paraphrase

(Ps)   Based on or reflecting the emphasis of the Psalm

[Ps] Other than Old Testament Psalm suggested for the service

(II)   Based on or reflecting the emphasis of the Second Lesson

(G)   Based on or reflecting the emphasis of the Gospel

(Undesignated hymns at the end of the list either contain elements from all three lessons, or are generally appropriate to the day, or the season of the Church year.)

Where there is a choice of prayers or lessons the first is indicated with (a), the second with (b). Where there are multiple lections, each is specified. Sometimes a hymn ties in with an entire lesson; more often a single stanza of a hymn picks up a single verse of Scripture.

SUNDAYS AND PRINCIPAL FESTIVALS

1 Advent

Savior of the nations, come (H), 28
Wake, awake, for night is flying §, 31
Fling wide the door, unbar the gate §, 32
The advent of our God (G-a), 22
Lord our God, with praise we come (G-a), 244
Once he came in blessing (G-a), 312
The day is surely drawing near (G-a), 321
O Lord, how shall I meet you (G-b), 23
Come, O precious Ransom, come (G-b), 24
The King shall come when morning dawns, 33
O Savior, rend the heavens wide, 38

A

Grant peace, we pray, in mercy, Lord (Ps),   471
Hark! A thrilling voice is sounding! (II), 37

B

Do not despair, O little flock (Ps), 361
Look from your sphere of endless day (Ps), 402
Who trusts in God, a strong abode (Ps), 450
Savior, like a shepherd lead us (Ps), 481
Lord, as a pilgrim (Ps), 485

† A listing of prayers and lections is given in the LBW pp. 13ff, and in the *Ministers' Desk Edition,* pp. 121ff.

C

Oh, come, oh, come, Emmanuel (I), 34
O God of love, O King of peace (Ps), 414
Hark! A thrilling voice is sounding!
(G-a), 37
Through the night of doubt and sorrow
(G-a), 355
A stable lamp is lighted (G-b), 74

2 Advent

On Jordan's banks the Baptist's cry (H), 36
Prepare the royal highway §, 26
Comfort, comfort now my people §, 29
Hark, the glad sound! (I), 35
By all your saints in warfare (stanza 15)
(G), 178

A

Oh, come, oh, come, Emmanuel (I), 34
Lo, how a rose is growing (I), 58
Creator Spirit, by whose aid (I), 164
O Holy Spirit, enter in (I), 459
Come, Holy Ghost, our souls inspire (I),
472, 473
Jesus shall reign (PsP), 530

B

Rejoice, rejoice, believers (I), 25
Jesus sinners will receive (I), 291
My soul, now praise your maker! (I), 519
The Lord will come and not be slow (Ps),
318
Lord our God, with praise we come (II),
244
O God, our help in ages past (II), 320

C

Let us ever walk with Jesus (Ps), 487
Oh, that I had a thousand voices (Ps), 560

3 Advent

Hark! A thrilling voice is sounding! (H),
37
Hark, the glad sound! The Savior
comes §, 35
The only Son from heaven §, 86
Rejoice, rejoice, believers (I), 25
On Jordan's banks the Baptist's cry (G),
36
Herald, sound the note of judgment (G),
556

A

Hail to the Lord's anointed (I), 87
Praise the Almighty (PsP), 539

B

My soul proclaims the greatness of the
Lord [Ps], 6
My soul now magnifies the Lord [PsP],
180

C

Rejoice, O pilgrim throng (II), 553

4 Advent

Oh, come, oh, come, Emmanuel (H), 34
Savior of the nations, come §, 28
Come, thou long-expected Jesus §, 30
O Savior, rend the heavens wide (Pr), 38
My soul proclaims the greatness of the
Lord (G), 6
From east to west (G), 64
My soul now magnifies the Lord (G), 180
Lo! He comes with clouds descending, 27

A

Prepare the royal highway (Ps), 26
Fling wide the door, (Ps), 32
O God of God, O Light of Light (Ps), 536

B

Hail to the Lord's anointed (I), 87

C

O little town of Bethlehem (I), 41
Savior, like a shepherd lead us (Ps), 481

Christmas Eve

Joy to the world, the Lord is come!, 39
O little town of Bethlehem, 41
Infant holy, infant lowly, 44
Once again my heart rejoices, 46
From heaven above to earth I come, 51
Lo, how a rose is growing, 58
Hark! The herald angels sing, 60
The bells of Christmas chime once more,
62
From shepherding of stars, 63
Silent night, holy night!, 65
Away in a manger, 67
I am so glad each Christmas Eve, 69
Angels we have heard on high, 71

Christmas Day

From heaven above to earth I come (H)
(Luke), 51
Of the Father's love begotten (H) (John),
42
Once again my heart rejoices §, 46
All praise to you, eternal Lord §, 48
Rejoice, rejoice this happy morn (Luke),
43
Infant holy, infant lowly (Luke), 44
Angels, from the realms of glory (Luke),
50
Good Christian friends, rejoice (Luke), 55
The first Noel the angel did say (Luke), 56
Hark! The herald angels sing (Luke), 60
From shepherding of stars (Luke), 63
From east to west, from shore to shore
(Luke), 64
Come rejoicing, praises voicing (Luke), 66
He whom shepherds once came praising
(Luke), 68
Angels we have heard on high (Luke), 71
O Savior of our fallen race (John), 49
Let our gladness have no end (John), 57
Oh, come, all ye faithful, 45

When Christmas morn is dawning, 59
All hail to you, O blessed morn!, 73

A

Earth and all stars! (Ps), 558

C

Joy to the world! (PsP), 39

1 Christmas

Let all together praise our God (H), 47
The only Son from heaven §, 86
Your little ones, dear Lord, are we, 52
Cold December flies away, 53
It came upon the midnight clear, 54
Good Christian friends, rejoice, 55
Lo, how a rose is growing, 58
Hark! The herald angels sing, 60
The hills are bare at Bethlehem, 61
'Twas in the moon of wintertime, 72

A

All praise to you, eternal Lord §, 48
When Christ's appearing was made
  known (G), 85

B

All praise to you, eternal Lord §, 48
In his temple now behold him (G), 184
O Lord, now let your servant (G), 339
I leave, as you have promised, Lord (G),
  349
Our Father, by whose name (G), 357
In a lowly manger born (G), 417

C

In a lowly manger born §, 417
Our Father, by whose name (G), 357
Oh, blest the house (G), 512

2 Christmas

Of the Father's love begotten (H), 42
Let all together praise our God §, 47
Let all mortal flesh keep silence §, 198
I heard the voice of Jesus say (G), 497
What child is this, 40
Angels, from the realms of glory, 50
The first Noel, 56
He whom shepherds once came praising,
  68
Go tell it on the mountain, 70

Epiphany

O Morning Star, how fair and bright!
  (H), 76
Bright and glorious is the sky §, 75
Brightest and best of the stars of the
  morning §, 84
Jesus shall reign (PsP), 530
Hail to the Lord's anointed (PsP), 87
What child is this (G), 40
Angels, from the realms of glory (G), 50
The first Noel (G), 56

He whom shepherds once came praising
  (G), 68
O chief of cities, Bethlehem (G), 81
As with gladness men of old (G), 82
When Christ's appearing was made known
  (G), 85

1 Epiphany (Baptism of Our Lord)

To Jordan came the Christ, our Lord (H),
  79
From God the Father, virgin-born §, 83
When Christ's appearing was made
  known §, 85
On Jordan's banks the Baptist's cry (G),
  36
Oh, love, how deep (G), 88
Songs of thankfulness and praise (G), 90
I bind unto myself today (G), 188
Bright and glorious is the sky, 75
O chief of cities, Bethlehem, 81
As with gladness men of old, 82
Brightest and best of the stars of the
  morning, 84
All who believe and are baptized, 194
This is the Spirit's entry now, 195
Eternal Ruler of the ceaseless round, 373

2 Epiphany

The only Son from heaven (H), 86
Jesus, priceless treasure (H), 457, 458
Bright and glorious is the sky, 75
O chief of cities, Bethlehem, 81
As with gladness men of old, 82
Brightest and best of the stars of the
  morning, 84

A

Jesus calls us; o'er the tumult §, 494
Sing praise to God, the highest good (Ps),
  542
O Christ, thou Lamb of God (G), 103
Lamb of God, pure and sinless (G), 111
By all your saints in warfare (stanza 5)
  (G), 177
Eternal God, before your throne we bend
  (G), 354
O God of God, O Light of Light (G), 536

B

Jesus calls us; o'er the tumult §, 494
Lord, speak to us, that we may speak (I),
  403
May God bestow on us his grace (PsP),
  335
By all your saints in warfare (stanza 14)
  (G), 178

C

All praise to you, O Lord §, 78
Hark, the voice of Jesus calling (II), 381
When Christ's appearing was made known
  (G), 85
Songs of thankfulness and praise (G), 90

3 Epiphany

O Christ, our light, O Radiance true (H), 380
O God of light, your Word, a lamp unfailing §, 237
Hail to the Lord's anointed (Pr), 87
O Morning Star, how fair and bright!, 76
O one with God the Father, 77
From God the Father, virgin-born, 83
God, whose almighty word, 400

A

"Come, follow me," the Savior spake §, 455
Where charity and love prevail (II), 126
Lord of our life (II), 366
The Church's one foundation (II), 369
Eternal Ruler of the ceaseless round (II), 373
By all your saints in warfare (stanzas 8, 10) (G), 177
They cast their nets (G), 449
Jesus calls us; o'er the tumult (G), 494

B

"Come, follow me," the Savior spake §, 455
By all your saints in warfare (stanza 8) (G), 177
They cast their nets (G), 449
Jesus calls us; o'er the tumult (G), 494

C

Hail to the Lord's anointed §, 87
O Trinity, O blessed Light (Ps), 275
Through the night of doubt and sorrow (II), 355
The Church's one foundation (II), 369
O Christ, the healer, we have come (II, G), 360
Once he came in blessing (G), 312

4 Epiphany

Hope of the world (H), 493
Songs of thankfulness and praise §, 90
The only Son from heaven, 86

A

Son of God, eternal Savior §, 364
O Holy Spirit, enter in (Pr), 459
Dearest Jesus, at your word (I), 248
You are the way (I, II), 464
Your Word, O Lord, is gentle dew (Ps), 232
When I survey the wondrous cross (II), 482
How blest are those who know their need of God (G), 17
Jesus, the very thought of you (G), 316

B

Dear Christians, one and all, rejoice §, 299
Your Word, O Lord, is gentle dew (Ps), 232

O God, my faithful God (II), 504
O Christ, the healer, we have come (G), 360
God of our life, all-glorious Lord, 270

C

God of grace and God of glory §, 415
O God of youth (I), 510
Jesus, thy boundless love to me (II), 336
In Christ there is no east or west (II), 359
Come down, O Love divine (II), 508
Joyful, joyful we adore thee (II), 551
To God the Holy Spirit let us pray (II, G), 317

5 Epiphany

Hail to the Lord's anointed (H), 87
Your Word, O Lord, is gentle dew §, 232
O one with God the Father, 77
From God the Father, virgin-born, 83
Christ, whose glory fills the skies, 265

A

May we your precepts, Lord, fulfill §, 353
Lord, save your world (I), 420
Lord, whose love in humble service (I), 423
The Church of Christ, in every age (I), 433
Lord, with glowing heart (II), 243
Salvation unto us has come (II, G), 297
Lord of light (G), 405

B

O Christ, the healer, we have come §, 360
Jesus, still lead on (I), 341
God, my Lord, my strength (I, II), 484
What wondrous love is this (II), 385
I love to tell the story (II), 390
O Zion, haste (II), 397
Look from your sphere of endless day (II), 402
Rise, shine, you people! (II, G), 393
God, whose almighty word (G), 400
Your hand, O Lord, in days of old (G), 431
My soul, now praise your maker!, 519

C

Lord, speak to us, that we may speak §, 403
Let the whole creation cry (I), 242
Holy Majesty, before you (I), 247
God himself is present (I), 249
Hark, the voice of Jesus calling (I), 381
We worship you, O God of might (I), 432
Isaiah in a vision did of old (I), 528
Holy God, we praise your name (I), 535
Thee we adore, eternal Lord! (I), 547
The Lord will come and not be slow (Ps), 318
The Son of God, our Christ (G), 434
Jesus calls us; o'er the tumult (G), 494

6 Epiphany

O Christ, our hope, our heart's desire (H), 300

Oh, that the Lord would guide my ways §, 480

Eternal Spirit of the living Christ (Pr), 441

The only Son from heaven, 86

A

Lord Jesus, think on me §, 309

Come, gracious Spirit, heavenly dove (I), 475

Come, oh, come, O quickening Spirit (I), 478

Oh, that the Lord would guide my ways (I), 480

O one with God the Father (II), 77

Holy Spirit, truth divine (I, II), 257

Forgive our sins as we forgive (G), 307

B

O Jesus Christ, may grateful hymns be rising §, 427

God the Father, be our stay (II), 308

Fight the good fight (II), 461

Thee will I love, my strength (II), 502

Songs of thankfulness and praise (G), 90

O Christ, the healer, we have come (G), 360

Your hand, O Lord, in days of old (G), 431

O God, whose will is life and good (G), 435

C

O Jesus Christ, may grateful hymns be rising §, 427

Amid the world's bleak wilderness (I), 378

I am trusting you, Lord Jesus (I), 460

Your Word, O Lord, is gentle dew (Ps), 232

Christ is arisen (II), 136

Jesus Christ, my sure defense (II), 340

I know of a sleep in Jesus' name (II), 342

I know that my Redeemer lives! (II), 352

Arise, my soul, arise (II), 516

How blest are those who know their need, (G), 17

7 Epiphany

O God, O Lord of heaven and earth (H), 396

Oh, love, how deep, how broad, how high §, 88

Lord, keep us steadfast §, 230

A

Praise to the Lord, the Almighty (PsP), 543

Praise, my soul, the King of heaven (PsP), 549

Creator Spirit, by whose aid (II), 164

If God himself be for me (II), 454

O Holy Spirit, enter in (II), 459

B

Songs of thankfulness and praise (G), 90

O Christ, the healer, we have come (G), 360

C

Praise to the Lord, the Almighty (PsP), 543

Praise, my soul, the King of heaven (PsP), 549

Jesus lives! The victory's won! (II), 133

Now the green blade rises (II), 148

In Adam we have all been one (II), 372

Praise and thanks and adoration (II), 470

Forgive our sins as we forgive (G), 307

Lord of all nations, grant me grace (G), 419

8 Epiphany

Sing praise to God, the highest good (H), 542

As with gladness men of old §, 82

The only Son from heaven, 86

A

Jesus, priceless treasure §, 457, 458

I love your kingdom, Lord (I), 368

Praise, my soul, the King of heaven (I), 549

We plow the fields and scatter (G), 362

B

Salvation unto us has come §, 297

When in the hour of deepest need (I), 303

Son of God, eternal Savior (I), 364

O God of love, O King of peace (I), 414

Praise to the Lord, the Almighty (PsP), 543

Praise, my soul, the King of heaven (PsP), 549

C

O God of mercy, God of light §, 425

He is arisen! Glorious Word! (II), 138

With high delight let us unite (II), 140

Thine is the glory (II), 145

Make songs of joy (II), 150

Jesus Christ, my sure defense (II, G), 340

My hope is built on nothing less (G), 293, 294

If God himself be for me (G), 454

In thee is gladness (G), 552

Father eternal, ruler of creation (G), 413

The Transfiguration of Our Lord

Oh, wondrous type! Oh, vision fair (H), 80

How good, Lord, to be here! §, 89

O God of God, O Light of Light §, 536

O Morning Star, how fair and bright!, 76

Beautiful Savior, 518

B

Renew me, O eternal Light (II), 511

581

C

God, whose almighty word (II), 400

Ash Wednesday

Out of the depths I cry to you (H), 295
Savior, when in dust to you §, 91
O Lord, throughout these forty days §, 99
To you, omniscient Lord of all (Ps), 310
Today your mercy calls us (II), 304

1 Lent

God the Father, be our stay (H), 308
A mighty fortress is our God (H), 228, 229
Who trusts in God, a strong abode §, 450
Guide me ever, great Redeemer (Pr-a), 343
Lord, keep us steadfast (Pr-b), 230
Lord of our life (Pr-b), 366
Lord, thee I love with all my heart (G), 325
Jesus, still lead on (G), 341
If God himself be for me (G), 454
God, my Lord, my strength (G), 484

A

Out of the depths I cry to you (PsP), 295
In Adam we have all been one (I), 372
Praise and thanks and adoration (I), 470

B

Rise, O children of salvation (II), 182
In thee is gladness (II), 552

C

Lift every voice and sing (I), 562
Praise to the Lord, the Almighty (Ps), 543
Where charity and love prevail (II), 126
God loved the world (II), 292
Once he came in blessing (II), 312
All who would valiant be, 498

2 Lent

Lord, thee I love with all my heart (H), 325
Jesus, refuge of the weary §, 93
A Lamb goes uncomplaining forth, 105
Jesus sinners will receive, 291
We sing the praise of him who died, 344

A

O Jesus, joy of loving hearts §, 356
The God of Abraham praise (I, II), 544
Salvation unto us has come (II), 297
I heard the voice of Jesus say (G), 497

B

"Take up your cross," the Savior said §, 398
How blessed is this place, O Lord (I), 186
Only-begotten, Word of God eternal (I), 375

O God of Jacob (I), 477
One there is, above all other (II), 298
O Christ, our hope (II), 300
"Come, follow me," the Savior spake (G), 455
Let us ever walk with Jesus (G), 487
Around you, O Lord Jesus (G), 496
O God, my faithful God (G), 504

C

O Jesus Christ, may grateful hymns be rising §, 427
Lord Christ, when first you came to earth (I, G), 421
As pants the hart for cooling streams (PsP), 452

3 Lent

May God bestow on us his grace (H), 335
In the cross of Christ I glory §, 104

A

God, whose almighty word §, 400
Your kingdom come! (II), 376
O God, O Lord of heaven and earth (II), 396
O Jesus, king most wonderful! (II), 537
Father eternal, ruler of creation (II, G), 413
My song is love unknown (G), 94

B

O God of earth and altar §, 428
Oh, that the Lord would guide my ways (I), 480
Sing praise to God, the highest good (I), 542
Your Word, O Lord, is gentle dew (Ps), 232

C

Jesus, the very thought of you §, 316
The God of Abraham praise (I, II), 544
Oh, that I had a thousand voices (Ps), 560
Jesus, still lead on (II), 341
Guide me ever, great Redeemer (II), 343
Lord, as a pilgrim (II), 485
All who would valiant be (II), 498
O God, my faithful God (II), 504

4 Lent

I trust, O Christ, in you alone (H), 395
God loved the world so that he gave (H), 292
On my heart imprint your image §, 102
Your heart, O God, is grieved, 96
Christ, the life of all the living, 97
What wondrous love is this, 385
Give to our God immortal praise, 520

A

Lord of glory, you have bought us §, 424
Salvation unto us has come (II), 297

A lamb goes uncomplaining forth (G), 105

The Son of God goes forth to war (G), 183

Lord Christ, when first you came to earth (G), 421

B

God loved the world so that he gave §, 292

Amazing grace, how sweet the sound (II), 448

Deep were his wounds (G), 100

O Christ, our king, creator, Lord, 101

Wide open are your hands, 489

Give to our God immortal praise, 520

C

In Adam we have all been one §, 372

Nature with open volume stands (II), 119

When I survey the wondrous cross (II), 482

Jesus sinners will receive (G), 291

One there is above all others (G), 298

Today your mercy calls us (G), 304

5 Lent

My song is love unknown (H), 94

Glory be to Jesus §, 95

Christ, the life of all the living §, 97

Your heart, O God, is grieved, 96

Jesus, I will ponder now, 115

A

Breathe on me, breath of God (I), 488

Come, thou Fount of every blessing (II), 499

Let us ever walk with Jesus (G), 487

B

To you, omniscient Lord of all (Ps), 310

Renew me, O eternal Light (Ps), 511

A lamb goes uncomplaining forth (G), 105

Now the green blade rises (G), 148

My heart is longing, 326

We sing the praise of him who died, 344

C

Kyrie! God, Father (Ps), 168

Beneath the cross of Jesus (II), 107

We sing the praise of him who died (II), 344

When I survey the wondrous cross (II), 482

God loved the world (G), 292

Sunday of the Passion (Palm Sunday)

A lamb goes uncomplaining forth (H), 105

O sacred head, now wounded §, 116, 117

The royal banners forward go §, 124, 125

Jesus, still lead on (Ps), 341

At the name of Jesus (II), 179

Jesus, refuge of the weary (G), 93

My song is love unknown (G), 94

Christ, the life of all the living (G), 97

Of the glorious body telling (G), 120

Ah, holy Jesus (G), 123

Come, risen Lord, and deign to be our guest (G), 209

All glory, laud, and honor, 108

Ride on, ride on in majesty!, 121

The Son of God goes forth to war, 183

Monday in Holy Week

Beneath the cross of Jesus §, 107

Sing, my tongue (II), 118

Victim Divine, your grace we claim (II), 202

Tuesday in Holy Week

O Christ, our king, creator, Lord §, 101

When I survey the wondrous cross (II), 482

Wednesday in Holy Week

It happened on that fateful night §, 127

Chief of sinners though I be (G), 306

Maundy Thursday

O Lord, we praise you, bless you, and adore you (H), 215

We, who once were dead §, 207

Thee we adore, O hidden Savior, thee §, 199

My song is love unknown, 94

Of the glorious body telling, 120

It happened on that fateful night, 127

Lord Jesus Christ, you have prepared, 208

Around you, O Lord Jesus, 496

A

Love consecrates the humblest act §, 122

Where charity and love prevail (G), 126

B&C

O Lord, we praise you, 215

Good Friday

Sing, my tongue, the glorious battle (H), 118

Deep were his wounds, and red §, 100

O sacred head, now wounded §, 116, 117

Were you there, 92

In the hour of trial, 106

Go to dark Gethsemane, 109

At the cross, her station keeping, 110

Lamb of God, pure and sinless, 111

Jesus, in thy dying woes, 112, 113

There is a green hill far away, 114

Ah, holy Jesus, 123

The royal banners forward go, 124, 125

Easter Day

Christ Jesus lay in death's strong bands
(H), 134
Good Christian friends, rejoice and
sing §, 144
At the Lamb's high feast we sing §, 210
The day of resurrection! (Ps, G), 141
Christ the Lord is risen today; Alleluia!
(G), 128
Christ the Lord is risen today! (G), 130
The strife is o'er, the battle done (G), 135
Christians, to the paschal victim (G), 137
O sons and daughters of the King (G),
139
Hail thee, festival day! (G), 142
Thine is the glory (G), 145
Hallelujah! Jesus lives! (G), 147
Jesus Christ is risen today (G), 151
That Easter day with joy was bright (G),
154

B

Praise and thanks and adoration (II), 470

C

Come, you faithful, raise the strain (I-a,
G), 132

Easter Evening

Praise to the Lord, the Almighty (Ps), 543
Christ Jesus lay in death's strong bands
(II), 134
Lord, enthroned in heavenly splendor (II),
172
That Easter day with joy was bright (G),
154
Come, risen Lord (G), 209
Abide with us, our Savior (G), 263

2 Easter

O sons and daughters of the King (H),
139
Come, you faithful, raise the strain §, 132
That Easter day with joy was bright §,
154
Christ is risen! Alleluia! (G), 131
The first day of the week (G), 246
Awake, my heart, with gladness, 129
Jesus lives! The victory's won!, 133
Make songs of joy, 150

A

O Savior, precious Savior (II), 514

B

Praise the Lord! O heavens, adore him
(PsP), 540
Praise the Lord of heaven! (PsP), 541
Ye watchers and ye holy ones (Ps), 175
Let the whole creation cry (Ps), 242
All creatures of our God and King (Ps),
527

C

Look, oh, look, the sight is glorious (II),
156
The head that once was crowned (II), 173

3 Easter

With high delight let us unite (H), 140
Now all the vault of heaven resounds §,
143
Look, now he stands! §, 152
He is arisen! Glorious Word!, 138
This joyful Eastertide, 149
Welcome, happy morning!, 153
O Christ, our hope, 300

A

When all your mercies, O my God (Ps),
264
Forth in thy name, O Lord, I go (Ps), 505
May we your precepts, Lord, fulfill (II),
353
Come, risen Lord (G), 209
Abide with us, our Savior (G), 263

B

Jesus Christ, my sure defense (I), 340
Wondrous are your ways, O God! (Ps),
311
Here, O my Lord, I see thee (II), 211
O Lord of light, who made the stars (II),
323

C

By all your saints in warfare (stanza 11)
(I), 177
Oh, sing, my soul, your maker's praise
(Ps), 319
Come, let us join our cheerful songs (II),
254
Blessing and honor (II), 525

4 Easter

The King of love my shepherd is (H), 456
I know that my Redeemer lives! §, 352
O God of Jacob, by whose hand §, 477
Come, gracious Spirit, heavenly dove
(Pr-a & b), 475
May God bestow on us his grace (Ps), 335
Jesus, thy boundless love to me (Ps), 336
Who trusts in God, a strong abode (Ps),
450
Rejoice, angelic choirs, rejoice!, 146

A

The King of love my shepherd is (PsP) §
456
We sing the praise of him who died (II),
344
I trust, O Christ, in you alone (II), 395
With God as our friend (G), 371

B

The Lord's my shepherd; I'll not want
(PsP) §, 451

Eternal Ruler of the ceaseless round (I), 373
Praise the Lord, rise up rejoicing (G), 196
Built on a rock (G), 365
In Adam we have all been one (G), 372

C

Savior, like a shepherd lead us §, 481
Ye watchers and ye holy ones (II), 175
Come, let us join our cheerful songs (II), 254
Who is this host arrayed in white (II), 314
Arise, my soul, arise! (II), 516
Blessing and honor (II), 525
Holy God, we praise you name (II), 535

5 Easter

At the Lamb's high feast we sing (H), 210
Jesus, thy boundless love to me §, 336
Give to our God immortal praise, 520

A

You are the way; through you alone §, 464
When all your mercies, O my God (Ps), 264
Hallelujah! Jesus lives! (G), 147
Jesus, your blood and righteousness (G), 302
Jesus Christ, my sure defense (G), 340
I know that my Redeemer lives! (G), 352
You are the way (G), 464
Let us ever walk with Jesus (G), 487
Come, my way, my truth, my life (G), 513

B

Amid the world's bleak wilderness §, 378
We know that Christ is raised (I), 189
God of our life, all-glorious Lord (II), 270
To God the Holy Spirit let us pray (II), 317
Eternal Spirit of the living Christ (II), 441
Come down, O Love divine (II), 508
Chief of sinners though I be (G), 306

C

Lord of all nations, grant me grace §, 419
Before you, Lord, we bow (Ps), 401
All creatures of our God and King (Ps), 527
In heaven above (II), 330
Jerusalem, my happy home (II), 331
Oh, what their joy (II), 337
Jerusalem the golden (II), 347
Jerusalem, whose towers touch the skies (II), 348

6 Easter (Church Music Sunday)

Dear Christians, one and all, rejoice (H), 299
One there is, above all others §, 298
Son of God, eternal Savior §, 364
Rejoice, angelic choirs, rejoice!, 146

Let the whole creation cry, 242
Evening and morning, 465
How marvelous God's greatness, 515
Oh, praise the Lord, my soul!, 538
When in our music God is glorified, 555
Earth and all stars!, 558

A

Welcome, happy morning! (II), 153
All glory be to God on high (G), 166
Eternal God, before your throne (G), 354
Come, oh, come, O quickening Spirit (G), 478
Come down, O Love divine (G), 508

B

All creatures of our God and King (Ps), 527
This is my Father's world (Ps), 554
We sing the praise of him who died (II), 344
O Splendor of the Father's light (G), 271
O God, empower us (G), 422
Eternal Spirit of the living Christ (G), 441

C

May God bestow on us his grace (PsP), 335
Jerusalem, my happy home (II), 331
Jerusalem the golden (II), 347
Jerusalem, whose towers touch the skies (II), 348
Lord, dismiss us with your blessing (G), 259
Savior, again to your dear name (G), 262
Peace, to soothe our bitter woes (G), 338
Christians, while on earth abiding (G), 440
Grant peace, we pray, in mercy, Lord (G), 471
Thee will I love, my strength (G), 502

Ascension

Up through endless ranks of angels (H), 159
A hymn of glory let us sing! §, 157
Hail thee, festival day!, 142

A

Look, oh, look, the sight is glorious §, 156

B

Lord, enthroned in heavenly splendor §, 172

C

Alleluia! Sing to Jesus §, 158

7 Easter

Oh, love, how deep, how broad, how high (H), 88
Crown him with many crowns, 170
O Christ, our hope, 300

585

A

Lord, teach us how to pray aright §, 438
Hail thee, festival day! (I), 142
A hymn of glory let us sing! (I), 157
Up through endless ranks of angels (I), 159
And have the bright immensities (I), 391

B

Have no fear, little flock §, 476
By all your saints in warfare (stanza 12) (I), 177
O Christ, you are the light and day (G), 273
Lord, thee I love with all my heart (G), 325
I trust, O Christ, in you alone (G), 395
We worship you, O God of might (G), 432

C

Lord, receive this company §, 255
O Morning Star, how fair and bright! (II), 76
The King shall come (II), 33
Lord, who the night you were betrayed (G), 206
Son of God, eternal Savior (G), 364

Vigil of Pentecost

O God, our help in ages past (Ps, 33), 320
Out of the depths I cry to you (PsP, 130), 295
O day full of grace (I-b), 161
Spirit of God, sent from heaven abroad (I-b), 285
O Spirit of the living God (I-b), 388
O day of rest and gladness (I-b, G), 251
We all believe in one true God (II), 374
Eternal Spirit of the living Christ (II), 441
I heard the voice of Jesus say (G), 497

Pentecost

Come, Holy Ghost, God and Lord (H), 163
Lord God, the Holy Ghost §, 162
To God the Holy Spirit let us pray §, 317
Oh, worship the King (PsP), 548
Oh, praise the Lord, my soul! (Ps), 538
Come, Holy Ghost, our souls inspire *[Ps]*, 472, 473
O day full of grace (II), 161
Spirit of God, unleashed on earth (II), 387
O Spirit of the living God (II), 388
Come, oh, come, O quickening Spirit, 478
Holy Spirit, ever dwelling, 523

A

Come, Holy Ghost, our souls inspire §, 472, 473
The first day of the week (G), 246

B

Come, Holy Ghost, God and Lord §, 163
Breathe on me, breath of God (I), 488
O God, O Lord of heaven and earth (II), 396
We worship you, O God of might (II), 432

C

Filled with the Spirit's power, with one accord §, 160
Father eternal, ruler of creation (I), 413
O God, O Lord of heaven and earth (II), 396
We worship you, O God of might (II), 432

Holy Trinity

Creator Spirit, heavenly dove (H), 284
All glory be to God on high §, 166
Father most holy, merciful, and tender §, 169
Lord, keep us steadfast (Pr-b), 230
Holy, holy, holy, 165
Glory be to God the Father!, 167
Kyrie! God, Father, 168
O Trinity, O blessed Light, 275
Eternal God, before your throne, 354
We all believe in one true God, 374

A

Creator Spirit, by whose aid (I-a), 164
Thy strong word did cleave the darkness (I-a), 233
God, whose almighty word (I-a), 400
Alleluia! Sing to Jesus (G), 158
Spread, oh, spread, almighty Word (G), 379

B

May we your precepts, Lord, fulfill (I), 353
O God, I love thee (I), 491
Thee will I love, my strength (I), 502
O God, my faithful God (I), 504
My God, how wonderful thou art (I), 524
God loved the world (G), 292

C

Salvation unto us has come (II), 297
Come, Holy Ghost, God and Lord (G), 163
To God the Holy Spirit let us pray (G), 317

2 Pentecost

To God the Holy Spirit let us pray (H), 317

A

My hope is built on nothing less §, 293, 294
Lord of all nations grant me grace (Pr), 419

Holy Spirit, truth divine (I), 257
Maker of the earth and heaven (I), 266
Oh, that the Lord would guide my ways (I), 480
O Holy Spirit, enter in (I, G), 459
Jesus, still lead on (Ps), 341
Amazing grace, how sweet the sound (II), 448
Dear Christians, one and all, rejoice (II, G), 299
If God himself be for me (II, G), 454
In thee is gladness (G), 552

B

Holy Spirit, truth divine §, 257
The first day of the week (I, G), 246
O day of rest and gladness (I, G), 251
All depends on our possessing (II), 447
From God can nothing move me (II), 468
O God, my faithful God, 504

C

Lord, whose love in humble service §, 423
Built on a rock (I), 365
From all that dwell below the skies (PsP), 550
God the Father, be our stay, 308
How firm a foundation, 507

3 Pentecost

When in the hour of deepest need (H), 303
Dear Christians, one and all, rejoice (A, B), 299
To you, omniscient Lord of all (A, B), 310
Today your mercy calls us (A, B), 304

A

Jesus sinners will recieve §, 291
There's a wideness in God's mercy (I, G), 290
The God of Abraham praise (II), 544
By all your saints in warfare (stanza 18) (G), 178
One there is, above all others (G), 298
"Come, follow me," the Savior spake (G), 455

B

Oh, for a thousand tongues to sing §, 559
In Adam we have all been one (I), 372
Praise the Savior, now and ever (I, II), 155
O God, our help in ages past (Ps), 320
On our way rejoicing (II), 260
My heart is longing (II, G), 326

C

When in the hour of deepest need §, 303
Even as we live each day (I, G), 350
Oh, sing, my soul, your maker's praise (Ps), 319
From God can nothing move me, 468

4 Pentecost

O God, O Lord of heaven and earth (H), 396
Awake, O Spirit of the watchmen (A, B), 382
Your kingdom come, O Father (A, B), 384
Praise the Lord, rise up rejoicing, 196

A

Spread, oh, spread, almighty Word §, 379
All people that on earth do dwell (PsP), 245
Before Jehovah's awesome throne (PsP), 531
O God of light (Ps), 237
Oh, sing jubilee to the Lord (Ps), 256
Open now thy gates of beauty (Ps, G), 250
O Lord, we praise you (II), 215
Chief of sinners though I be (II), 306
What wondrous love is this (II), 385
Hark, the voice of Jesus calling (G), 381
The Son of God, our Christ (G), 434

B

Almighty God, your Word is cast §, 234
In heaven above, in heaven above (II), 330
Spirit of God, sent from heaven abroad (G), 285
Come, you thankful people, come (G), 407
Lord our God, with praise we come, 244

C

O Jesus, joy of loving hearts §, 356
Out of the depths I cry to you, 295
Dear Christians, one and all, rejoice, 299
Today your mercy calls us, 304

5 Pentecost

Lord of our life, and God of our salvation (H), 366
Who trusts in God, a strong abode (H), 450
Jesus, priceless treasure (Pr), 457, 458
A mighty fortress is our God, 228, 229
God, my Lord, my strength, 484

A

Let me be yours forever §, 490
In Adam we have all been one (II), 372
Praise and thanks and adoration (II), 470
Once he came in blessing (G), 312

B

Who trusts in God, a strong abode §, 450
We know that Christ is raised (II), 189
Love divine, all loves excelling (II), 315
Lord, take my hand and lead me (G), 333
Jesus, Savior, pilot me (G), 334
Eternal Father, strong to save (G), 467
I am trusting you, Lord Jesus, 460

C

Christ is made the sure foundation §, 367
Baptized into your name most holy (II),
192
In Christ there is no east or west (II), 359
"Take up your cross," the Savior said
(G), 398
Let us ever walk with Jesus (G), 487

6 Pentecost

Even as we live each day (H), 350
Jesus, thy boundless love to me, 336
O God, I love thee, 491
Joyful, joyful we adore thee, 551

A

O God, send heralds who will never
falter §, 283
We know that Christ is raised (II), 189
All who believe and are baptized (II), 194
Let us ever walk with Jesus (G), 487
"Take up your cross," the Savior said
(G), 398

B

O God of mercy, God of light §, 425
If you but trust in God to guide you (I),
453
I trust, O Christ, in you alone (I, II), 395
Oh, sing, my soul, your maker's praise
(Ps), 319
God, whose giving knows no ending (II),
408
Lord of all good (II), 411
O Christ, the healer, we have come (G),
360
Your hand, O Lord, in days of old (G),
431
How sweet the name of Jesus sounds, 345

C

O God, send heralds who will never
falter §, 283
When all your mercies, O my God (Ps),
264
O Jesus, I have promised (G), 503
Forth in thy name, O Lord, I go (Ps), 505
Spirit of God, descend upon my heart
(II), 486
In thee is gladness (II), 552
Lord, thee I love with all my heart (II,
G), 325
Your kingdom come, O Father (II, G),
384
"Come, follow me," the Savior spake
(G), 455

7 Pentecost

O Christ, our light, O Radiance true (H),
380
Rejoice, O pilgrim throng!, 553

A

Peace to soothe our bitter woes §, 338
Before you, Lord, we bow (Ps), 401

All creatures of our God and King (Ps),
527
Awake, my soul, and with the sun (II),
269
May we your precepts, Lord, fulfill (II),
353
Come, gracious Spirit, heavenly dove (II),
475
Oh, that the Lord would guide my ways
(II), 480
I heard the voice of Jesus say (G), 497
Forth in thy name, O Lord, I go (G), 505
Jesus shall reign (G), 530

B

God moves in a mysterious way §, 483
O God of light (I, G), 237
God has spoken by his prophets (I, G),
238
Jesus, still lead on (II), 341

C

Jesus shall reign where'er the sun §, 530
My soul, now praise your maker! (I), 519
Now thank we all our God (I), 533, 534
Praise, my soul, the King of heaven (I),
549
In the cross of Christ I glory (II), 104
Beneath the cross of Jesus (II), 107
The head that once was crowned with
thorns (II), 173
I trust, O Christ, in you alone (II), 395
When I survey the wondrous cross (II),
482
All who love and serve your city (II, G),
436
Hark, the voice of Jesus calling (G), 381
Awake, O Spirit of the watchmen (G),
382
Look from your sphere of endless day
(II), 402
The Son of God, our Christ, 434

8 Pentecost

Forth in thy name, O Lord, I go (H), 505
To God the Holy Spirit let us pray (Pr-a),
317
Eternal Spirit of the living Christ (Pr-a),
441
Your Word, O Lord, is gentle dew, 232

A

Almighty God, your Word is cast §, 234
Sent forth by God's blessing (G), 221
When seed falls on good soil (G), 236
Open now thy gates of beauty (G), 250
On what has now been sown (G), 261

B

The Son of God, our Christ, the Word,
the Way §, 434
The Lord will come and not be slow (Ps),
318
Dear Christians, one and all, rejoice (II),
299

O God, O Lord of heaven and earth (II), 396

From God can nothing move me (II), 468
God moves in a mysterious way (II), 483
O God of God, O Light of Light (II), 536

C

O God of mercy, God of light §, 425
O God of love, O King of peace (Ps), 414
How blest are they who hear God's Word (II), 227
Hope of the world (G), 493
Lead on, O King eternal! (G), 495
For the fruit of all creation, 563

9 Pentecost

O Holy Spirit, enter in (H), 459
Holy Spirit, truth divine (Pr-a), 257
Eternal God, before you throne (Pr-a), 354
Come, oh, come, O quickening Spirit (Pr-a), 478
Dear Lord and Father of mankind (Pr-b), 506
The God of Abraham praise (I), 544
How blest are they who hear God's Word, 227

A

On what has now been sown §, 261
There's a wideness in God's mercy (Ps), 290
The Lord will come and not be slow (Ps), 318
Eternal Spirit of the living Christ (II), 441
Come, you thankful people, come (G), 407

B

O God of light, your Word, a lamp unfailing §, 237
Praise the Lord, rise up rejoicing (I, G), 196
The Lord's my shepherd (PsP), 451
The King of love my shepherd is (PsP), 456
Jesus, thy boundless love to me (Ps), 336
Who trusts in God, a strong abode (Ps), 450
Lord, receive this company (II), 255
Through the night of doubt and sorrow (II), 355
Christ is made the sure foundation (II), 367
The Church's one foundation (II), 369
Whatever God ordains is right (II), 446
Lord, who the night you were betrayed (II, G), 206
A multitude comes from east and west (II, G), 313

C

Lord, thee I love with all my heart §, 325
Jesus, thy boundless love to me (II), 336
Praise and thanks and adoration, 470

10 Pentecost

From God can nothing move me (H), 468
Jesus, priceless treasure (H), 457, 458

A

O God, O Lord of heaven and earth §, 396
God of grace and God of glory (I), 415
Lord Jesus, think on me (Ps), 309
Whatever God ordains is right (II), 446
All depends on our possessing (II), 447
If God himself be for me (II), 454
Immortal, invisible, 526

B

Jesus, priceless treasure §, 457, 458
Before you, Lord, we bow (Ps), 401
All creatures of our God and King (Ps), 527
Praise and thanksgiving be to God (II), 191
Through the night of doubt and sorrow (II), 355
The Church's one foundation (II), 369
Blest be the tie that binds (II), 370
Come down, O Love divine (II), 508
Onward, Christian soldiers (II), 509
Break now the bread of life (G), 235

C

Lord, teach us how to pray aright §, 438
We know that Christ is raised (II), 189
We who once were dead (II), 207
Oh, for a thousand tongues to sing (II), 559
Come, Holy Ghost, God and Lord (G), 163
Forgive our sins as we forgive (G), 307
Oh, sing, my soul, your maker's praise (G), 319
Our Father, by whose name (G), 357
Your kingdom come! (G), 376
Your kingdom come, O Father (G), 384
Lord of light (G), 405
Father eternal, ruler of creation (G), 413
O thou, who hast of thy pure grace (G), 442

11 Pentecost

Jesus, priceless treasure (H), 457, 458
Lord of all good (Pr-b), 411

A

Praise and thanksgiving §, 409
I heard the voice of Jesus say (I), 497
Sing to the Lord of harvest (I), 412
Oh, worship the King (PsP), 548
Oh, praise the Lord, my soul! (Ps), 538
Jesus lives! The victory's won! (II), 133
Jesus, thy boundless love to me (II), 336
If God himself be for me (II), 454
From God can nothing move me (II), 468
Break now the bread of life (G), 235

589

B

O Bread of life from heaven §, 222
Glories of your name are spoken (I), 358
How sweet the name of Jesus sounds (I, G), 345
Love divine, all loves excelling (II), 315
Breathe on me, breath of God (II), 488
O God, my faithful God (II), 504
Renew me, O eternal Light (II), 511
O living Bread from heaven (G), 197
Here, O my Lord, I see thee (G), 211
Soul, adorn yourself with gladness (G), 224
Guide me ever, great Redeemer (G), 343
O Lord, send forth your Spirit (G), 392

C

Son of God, eternal Savior §, 364
May we your precepts, Lord, fulfill (II), 353
In Christ there is no east or west (II), 359
Eternal Ruler of the ceaseless round (II), 373
Oh, that the Lord would guide my ways (II), 480
O God, my faithful God (II), 504
Renew me, O eternal Light (II), 511
Son of God, eternal Savior (G), 364
God of grace and God of glory (G), 415
Lord, save your world, 420

12 Pentecost

If God himself be for me (H), 454
Evening and morning, 465

A

Eternal Father, strong to save §, 467
Dear Lord and Father of mankind (I), 506
The Lord will come and not be slow (Ps), 318
Lord, take my hand and lead me (G), 333
Jesus, Savior, pilot me (G), 334
Lord of our life and God of our salvation (G), 366
Jesus, priceless treasure (G), 457, 458
From God can nothing move me (G), 468

B

Guide me ever, great Redeemer §, 343
Draw near and take the body of the Lord (Ps), 226
Forgive our sins as we forgive (II), 307
Joyful, joyful we adore thee (II), 551
O living Bread from heaven (G), 197
We who once were dead (G), 207
O Bread of life from heaven (G), 222
Soul, adorn yourself with gladness (G), 224
O Jesus, joy of loving hearts (G), 356

C

Rise, my soul, to watch and pray §, 443
When all your mercies, O my God (Ps), 264
O God, our help in ages past (Ps), 320

Salvation unto us has come (II), 297
Jesus, your blood and righteousness (II), 302
My faith looks up to thee (II), 479
Wake, awake, for night is flying (G), 31
Soul, adorn yourself with gladness (G), 224
Do not despair, O little flock (G), 361
Have no fear, little flock (G), 476
Christ, whose glory fills the skies, 265
We worship you, O God of might, 432
How firm a foundation, 507

13 Pentecost

When in the hour of deepest need (H), 303
Lord, keep us steadfast in your Word (H), 230

A

When in the hour of deepest need §, 303
A multitude comes from the east and the west (I), 313
In Christ there is no east or west (I), 359
O Christ, the healer, we have come (I, G), 360
May God bestow on us his grace (PsP), 335
To you, omniscient Lord of all (G), 310
Rise, shine, you people! (G), 393
Lord, whose love in humble service (G), 423
Father, we praise you, 267

B

How blest are they who hear God's Word §, 227
Take my life, that I may be (II), 406
Now thank we all our God (II), 533, 534
When morning gilds the skies (II), 545, 546
When in our music God is glorified (II), 555
Let all things now living (II), 557
O living Bread from heaven (G), 197
We who once were dead (G), 207
O Bread of life from heaven (G), 222
Soul, adorn yourself with gladness (G), 224
O Jesus, joy of loving hearts (G), 356

C

Lord, keep us steadfast in your Word §, 230
The Lord will come and not be slow (Ps), 318
God the Father, be our stay (II), 308
If you but trust in God to guide you (II), 453
Fight the good fight (II), 461
Evening and morning (II), 465
God, my Lord, my strength (II), 484
Thee will I love, my strength (II), 502
How firm a foundation, 507

14 Pentecost

O Christ, our light, O Radiance true (H), 380
We worship you, 432
Jesus shall reign, 530
Holy God, we praise your name, 535
Thee we adore, eternal Lord!, 547

A

Built on a rock the Church shall stand §, 365
The God of Abraham praise (I), 544
Blessing and honor (II), 525
Immortal, invisible, God only wise (II), 526
By all your saints in warfare (stanza 10) (G), 177

B

Hope of the world §, 493
Our Father, by whose name (I, II), 357
Oh, blest the house (I, II), 512
For the beauty of the earth (I, II), 561
You are the way (G), 464
Let me be yours forever (G), 490
O Jesus, I have promised (G), 503

C

A multitude comes from the east and the west §, 313
From all that dwell below the skies (PsP), 550
Jesus, your blood and righteousness (II), 302
Oh, what their joy (II), 337
Oh, happy day when we shall stand (G), 351
All who believe and are baptized, 194
The Lord will come and not be slow, 318

15 Pentecost

To you, omniscient Lord of all (H), 310
Son of God, eternal Savior (H), 364
Maker of the earth and heaven, 266

A

If God himself be for me §, 454
God's Word is our great heritage (I), 239
We praise you, O God (Ps), 241
I love your kingdom, Lord (Ps), 368
Where charity and love prevail (II), 126
Hark, the voice of Jesus calling (II), 381
"Take up your cross," the Savior said (G), 398
"Come, follow me," the Savior spake (G), 455
Praise and thanks and adoration (G), 470

B

To you, omniscient Lord of all §, 310
You are the way (I), 464
Oh, that the Lord would guide my ways (I), 480
A mighty fortress is our God (II), 228, 229
Let the whole creation cry (II), 242

God the Father, be our stay (II), 308
We sing the praise of him who died (II), 344
Do not despair, O little flock (II), 361
Eternal Ruler of the ceaseless round (II), 373
Stand up, stand up for Jesus (II), 389
With the Lord begin your task (II), 444
Fight the good fight (II), 461

C

O God of earth and altar §, 428
We give thee but thine own (II), 410
Lord of all nations, grant me grace (II), 419
Where cross the crowded ways of life (II), 429
Lord, whose love in humble service, 423

16 Pentecost

Praise the Almighty, my soul, adore him! (H), 539
Lord of all nations, grant me grace (H), 419

A

Lord of all nations, grant me grace §, 419
Awake, O Spirit of the watchmen (I), 382
O God of earth and altar (II), 428
God of our fathers (II), 567
Built on a rock (G), 365
And have the bright immensities (G), 391

B

O Son of God, in Galilee §, 426
Look from your sphere of endless day (I), 402
Praise the Almighty, my soul, adore him! (PsP), 539
We give thee but thine own (II), 410
O God, my faithful God (II), 504
O Christ, our light, O Radiance true (G), 380
Son of God, eternal Savior, 364

C

Take my life, that I may be §, 406
"Take up your cross," the Savior said (G), 398
Let us ever walk with Jesus (G), 487
God, my Lord, my strength, 484

17 Pentecost

Forgive our sins as we forgive (H), 307
Jesus sinners will receive (H), 291
Holy Majesty, before you, 247
Praise to the Father, 517
My soul, now praise your maker!, 519
Give to our God immortal praise!, 520
Now thank we all our God, 533, 534
Sing praise to God, the highest good, 542

A

Forgive our sins as we forgive §, 307
Where charity and love prevail (I, G), 126

My soul, now praise your maker! (PsP),
519
Praise to the Lord, the almighty (PsP),
543
Praise, my soul, the King of heaven
(PsP), 549
We are the Lord's (II), 399
In thee is gladness (II), 552

B

Let me be yours forever §, 490
Lord of all nations, grant me grace (II),
419
Lord, whose love in humble service (II),
423
O God of mercy, God of light (II), 425
O Jesus Christ, may grateful hymns be
rising (II), 427
Where cross the crowded ways of life (II),
429
The Church of Christ, in every age (II),
433
By all your saints in warfare (stanza 10),
(G), 177
"Take up your cross," the Savior said
(G), 398
Lord, thee I love with all my heart, 325
Around you, O Lord Jesus, 496

C

Jesus sinners will receive §, 291
To you, omniscient Lord of all (Ps), 310
Lord, teach us how to pray aright (Ps),
438
Immortal, invisible, God only wise (II),
526
Chief of sinners though I be (II, G), 306
Lord, with glowing heart (G), 243
Amazing grace, how sweet the sound (G),
448
Come, thou Fount of every blessing (G),
499
Praise God. Praise him (G), 529

18 Pentecost

Salvation unto us has come (H), 297
The Son of God, our Christ (Pr), 434

A

Salvation unto us has come §, 297
For all your saints, O Lord (II), 176
We are the Lord's (II), 399
All who love and serve your city (G), 436
Lord of all hopefulness (G), 469

B

All depends on our possessing §, 447
A Lamb goes uncomplaining forth (I, G),
105
Where charity and love prevail (II), 126
Christ is alive! Let Christians sing (II),
363
O God of every nation (II), 416
Children of the heavenly Father (G), 474

I trust, O Christ, in you alone, 395
Lord Christ, when first you came to
earth, 421

C

Father eternal, ruler of creation §, 413
O Trinity, O blessed Light (Ps), 275
Your kingdom come, O Father (II), 384
Lord, teach us how to pray aright (II),
438
Son of God, eternal Savior, 364
Rise up, O saints of God!, 383
O God of every nation, 416

19 Pentecost

Lord, keep us steadfast in your Word
(H), 230
Maker of the earth and heaven (Pr), 266
Now that the daylight fills the sky (Pr),
268

A

O Master, let me walk with you §, 492
Wondrous are your ways, O God! (I), 311
O God of love, O King of peace (Ps), 414
Look, the sight is glorious (II), 156
At the name of Jesus (II), 179
Lord, whose love in humble service (II),
423

B

O Jesus, I have promised §, 503
Spirit of God, unleashed on earth (I), 387
O Spirit of the living God (I), 388
Come, oh, come, O quickening Spirit (I),
478
You servants of God (Ps), 252
Jesus, the very thought of you (II), 316
Where cross the crowded ways of life (G),
429
Come down, O Love divine, 508

C

Oh, praise the Lord, my soul! §, 538
Praise the Almighty (PsP), 539
God the Father, be our stay (II), 308
Fight the good fight (II), 461
Immortal, invisible, God only wise (II),
526
God, whose giving knows no ending, 408
Arise, my soul, arise! (II), 516

20 Pentecost

Our Father, by whose name (H), 357
The Church of Christ, in every age (H),
433

A

The Church of Christ, in every age §, 433
Come, gracious Spirit, heavenly dove (II),
475
Breathe on me, breath of God (II), 488
Lord Christ, when first you came to earth
(G), 421

Whatever God ordains is right (G), 446
May God bestow on us his grace, 335

B

Our Father, by whose name §, 357
Look, the sight is glorious (II), 156
Crown him with many crowns (II), 170
At the name of Jesus (II), 179
All hail the power of Jesus' name! (II),
328, 329
Dearest Jesus, we are here (G), 187
Cradling children in his arm (G), 193
Oh, blest the house, 512
For the beauty of the earth, 561

C

O Jesus, I have promised §, 503
Out of the depths I cry to you (I), 295
Lord, keep us steadfast in your Word (II),
230
Holy Spirit, truth divine (II), 257
Forgive our sins as we forgive (G), 307
Eternal Ruler of the ceaseless round, 373

21 Pentecost

All who believe and are baptized (H), 194
Son of God, eternal Savior (Pr), 364
Around you, O Lord Jesus, 496

A

A multitude comes from the east and the
west §, 313
At the Lamb's high feast we sing (I), 210
Who is this host arrayed in white (I), 314
Arise, my soul, arise (I), 516
The Lord's my shepherd (PsP), 451
The King of love my shepherd is (PsP),
456
Jesus, thy boundless love to me (Ps), 336
Rejoice, the Lord is king! (II), 171
Rejoice, O pilgrim throng! (II), 553

B

Thee will I love, my strength, my tower §,
502
Lord, save your world (I), 420
O God of earth and altar (I), 428
Where restless crowds are thronging (I),
430
O God, our help in ages past (PsP), 320
"Come, follow me," the Savior spake
(G), 455
Let me be yours forever, 490
Hope of the world, 493

C

Your hand, O Lord, in days of old § (G),
431
Once he came in blessing (II), 312
Let us ever walk with Jesus (II), 487
Faith of our fathers (II), 500
Thee will I love, my strength, my tower
(II), 502
Jesus, thy boundless love to me (G), 336
Give to our God immortal praise!, 520
Sing praise to God, the highest good, 542

22 Pentecost

Forth in thy name, O Lord, I go (H), 505

A

Father eternal, ruler of creation §, 413
Earth and all stars! (Ps), 558
Eternal God, before your throne (II), 354
Eternal Ruler of the ceaseless round (II),
373
Come, Holy Ghost, our souls inspire (II),
472, 473
Lord of glory, you have bought us (G),
424

B

God, who stretched the spangled
heavens §, 463
O Christ, our hope (I, G), 300
Love consecrates the humblest act (G),
122
The Son of God goes forth to war (G),
183
Lord, whose love in humble service (G),
423
O Master, let me walk with you (G), 492

C

Out of the depths I cry to you §, 295
O God of Jacob (I), 477
Unto the hills (PsP), 445
Sing praise to God, the highest good (Ps),
542
How blest are they who hear God's Word
(II), 227
O Word of God incarnate (II), 231
O God of light (II), 237
Lord, speak to us (II), 403
Christians, while on earth abiding (G),
440

23 Pentecost

Lord, teach us how to pray aright (H),
438
To you, omniscient Lord of all (H), 310

A

Oh, that the Lord would guide my
ways §, 480
Rise up, O saints of God! (I), 383
Your Word, O Lord, is gentle dew (Ps),
232
God of our life, all-glorious Lord (G), 270
Lord, thee I love with all my heart (G),
325
Jesus, thy boundless love to me (G), 336
Spirit of God, descend upon my heart
(G), 486
O God, I love thee (G), 491
Hope of the world (G), 493
Jesus calls us; o'er the tumult (G), 494
Thee will I love, my strength (G), 502
O Jesus, king most wonderful! (G), 537

B

Oh, praise the Lord, my soul! §, 538
O Son of God, in Galilee (G), 426

Your hand, O Lord, in days of old (G), 431

O God, whose will is life and good (G), 435

Amazing grace, how sweet the sound (G), 448

God, whose almighty word, 400

Sing praise to God, the highest good, 542

C

To you, omniscient Lord of all §, 310

Oh, praise the Lord, my soul! (I), 538

Draw near and take the body of the Lord (Ps), 226

Jesus Christ, my sure defense (II), 340

Fight the good fight (II), 461

Savior, when in dust to you (G), 91

24 Pentecost

Wake, awake, for night is flying (H), 31

Love divine, all loves excelling (H), 315

A

Wake, awake, for night is flying §, 31

The Lord will come and not be slow (I), 318

I know of a sleep in Jesus' name (II), 342

Oh, happy day when we shall stand (II), 351

Rejoice, rejoice, believers (G), 25

Soul, adorn yourself with gladness (G), 224

B

Lord of light, your name outshining §, 405

Oh, that the Lord would guide my ways (I), 480

My God, how wonderful thou art (I), 524

I know that my Redeemer lives! (II), 352

God of our life, all-glorious Lord (G), 270

Lord, thee I love with all my heart (G), 325

Jesus, thy boundless love to me (G), 336

Spirit of God, descend upon my heart (G), 486

O God, I love thee (G), 491

Hope of the world (G), 493

Jesus calls us; o'er the tumult (G), 494

Thee will I love, my strength (G), 502

O Jesus, king most wonderful! (G), 537

C

If you but trust in God to guide you §, 453

Before you, Lord, we bow (Ps), 401

All creatures of our God and King (Ps), 527

Jesus sinners will receive (G), 291

One there is, above all others (G), 298

Today your mercy calls us (G), 304

Chief of sinners though I be (G), 306

25 Pentecost

Rejoice, angelic choirs, rejoice! (H), 146

A

Forth in thy name, O Lord, I go §, 505

O God, our help in ages past (PsP), 320

Praise to the Lord, the Almighty (Ps), 543

We are the Lord's (II), 399

Rise, my soul, to watch and pray (II), 443

Lord of light (G), 405

God, whose giving knows no ending (G), 408

B

As saints of old their firstfruits brought §, 404

Lord our God, with praise we come (II), 244

Take my life, that I may be (G), 406

C

I know that my Redeemer lives! §, 352

Blessing and honor (I), 525

Praise the Lord! O heavens, adore him (PsP), 540

Praise the Lord of heaven! (PsP), 541

Ye watchers and ye holy ones (Ps), 175

Let the whole creation cry (Ps), 242

All creatures of our God and King (Ps), 527

Abide with us, our Savior (II), 263

If God himself be for me (II), 454

From God can nothing move me (II), 468

Now thank we all our God (II), 533, 534

26 Pentecost

The Lord will come and not be slow, 318

The day is surely drawing near, 321

The clouds of judgment gather, 322

O Lord of light, who made the stars, 323

Rise, my soul, to watch and pray, 443

Lead on, O King eternal!, 495

Lord our God, with praise we come before you, 244

A

O god of earth and altar (H), 428

Dear Lord and Father of mankind (I,G), 506

God, whose giving knows no ending (II), 408

God the Father, be our stay (G), 308

Lord Jesus, think on me (G), 309

Come down, O Love divine (G), 508

B

Through the night of doubt and sorrow (H), 355

When all your mercies, O my God (Ps), 264

Forth in thy name, O Lord, I go (Ps), 505

O Christ, our hope (II), 300

Jesus, your blood and righteousness (II), 302

Lord, keep us steadfast in your Word (G), 230

Lord Christ, when first you came to earth (G), 421

Come, oh, come, O quickening Spirit (G), 478

C

Fight the good fight with all your might (H), 461
Christ, whose glory fills the skies (I), 265
Judge eternal, throned in splendor (I), 418
All creatures of our God and King (Ps), 527
This is my Father's world (Ps), 554
Earth and all stars! (Ps), 558
Lord, keep us steadfast in your Word (G), 230
Lord Christ, when first you came to earth (G), 421
Come, oh, come, O quickening Spirit (G), 478

27 Pentecost

The day is surely drawing near (H), 321
Lord Christ, when first you came to earth (H), 421
Lo! He comes with clouds descending, 27
The Lord will come and not be slow, 318
The clouds of judgment gather, 322
O Lord of light, who made the stars, 323
Rise, my soul, to watch and pray, 443

A

Rise, O children of salvation §, 182
Herald, sound the note of judgment (I), 556
My hope is built on nothing less, 293, 294

B

Rejoice, rejoice, believers §, 25
Who is this host arrayed in white (I), 314
A multitude comes from east and west (II, G), 313

C

Wake, awake, for night is flying (I), 31
Jerusalem, my happy home (I), 331
Jerusalem the golden (I), 347

Jerusalem, whose towers touch the skies (I), 348
Christ Jesus lay in death's strong bands (II), 134
With high delight let us unite (II), 140
Thine is the glory (II), 145
Make songs of joy (II), 150

Christ the King

Rejoice, the Lord is king! §, 171
The head that once was crowned with thorns §, 173
Crown him with many crowns, 170
Lord, enthroned in heavenly splendor, 172
O Lord of light, who made the stars, 323
All hail the power of Jesus' name!, 328, 329
Lift high the cross, 377
Christ is the king!, 386
O Savior, precious Savior, 514
Give to our God immortal praise!, 520

A

The day is surely drawing near (H), 321
Come, let us join our cheerful songs (Ps), 254
Praise and thanks and adoration (II), 470
O God of mercy, God of light (G), 425

B

At the name of Jesus (H), 179
Immortal, invisible, God only wise (I), 52
You servants of God (Ps), 252
This is my Father's world (Ps), 554
Of the Father's love begotten (II), 42
Glory be to God the Father! (II), 167

C

O Jesus, king most wonderful!§, 537
Of the Father's love begotten (II), 42
Immortal, invisible, God only wise (II), 526
On my heart imprint your image (G), 102

LESSER FESTIVALS

St. Andrew, Apostle (November 30)

Wake, awake, for night is flying (I), 31
Holy Majesty, before you (Ps), 247
May God bestow on us his grace (II), 335
Spread, oh, spread, almighty Word (II), 379
By all your saints in warfare (stanza 5) (G), 177
Jesus calls us; o'er the tumult (G), 494
Dear Lord and Father of mankind (G), 506
For all the saints, 174
For all your saints, O Lord, 176
Rise, O children of salvation, 182
The Son of God goes forth to war, 183
The Son of God, our Christ, 434

St. Thomas, Apostle (December 21)

Give to our God immortal praise (Ps), 520
Let us with a gladsome mind (Ps), 521
O sons and daughters of the King (G), 139
By all your saints in warfare (stanza 6) (G), 177
I know that my Redeemer lives! (G), 352
You are the way (G), 464
Come, my way, my truth, my life (G), 513
For all the saints, 174
For all your saints, O Lord, 176
Rise, O children of salvation, 182
The Son of God goes forth to war, 183
The Son of God, our Christ, 434

St. Stephen, Deacon and Martyr (December 26)

By all your saints in warfare (stanza 7) (II), 177
For all the saints, 174
For all your saints, O Lord, 176
Rise, O children of salvation, 182
The Son of God goes forth to war, 183
Faith of our fathers, 500
Holy God, we praise your name, 535

St. John, Apostle and Evangelist (December 27)

Creator Spirit, by whose aid (I), 164
Thy strong word did cleave the darkness (I), 233
God, who stretched the spangled heavens (I), 463
Let us with a gladsome mind (I), 521
By all your saints in warfare (stanza 8) (G), 177
Praise and thanks and adoration (G), 470
For all the saints, 174
For all your saints, O Lord, 176
Rise, O children of salvation, 182
The Son of God goes forth to war, 183
The Son of God, our Christ, 434

The Holy Innocents, Martyrs (December 28)

When Christ's appearing was made known (G), 85
By all your saints in warfare (stanza 9) (G), 177
Holy God, we praise your name, 535

The Name of Jesus (January 1)

Lord, dismiss us with your blessing (I), 259
Christians, while on earth abiding (I), 440
At the name of Jesus (II-b), 179
All hail the power of Jesus' name!, 328, 329
How sweet the name of Jesus sounds, 345
O Savior, precious Savior, 514
Oh, for a thousand tongues to sing, 559

The Confession of St. Peter (January 18)

Christ is made the sure foundation (I), 367
How sweet the name of Jesus sounds (Ps), 345
God the Father, be our stay (Ps), 308
Thee will I love, my strength (Ps), 502
By all your saints in warfare (stanza 10) (G), 177
Built on a rock the Church shall stand (G), 365
For all the saints, 174
For all your saints, O Lord, 176
Rise, O children of salvation, 182
The Son of God goes forth to war, 183
The Son of God, our Christ, 434
O God, I love thee, 491

The Conversion of St. Paul (January 25)

May God bestow on us his grace (PsP), 335
By all your saints in warfare (stanza 11), (II), 177
Do not despair, O little flock (G), 361
For all the saints, 174
For all your saints, O Lord, 176
Rise, O children of salvation, 182
The Son of God goes forth to war, 183

The Presentation of Our Lord (February 2)

In his temple now behold him (G), 184
O Lord, now let your servant (G), 339
I leave, as you have promised, Lord (G), 349
Our Father, by whose name (G), 357
In a lowly manger born (G), 417

St. Matthias, Apostle (February 24)

By all your saints in warfare (stanza 12) (II), 177
For all the saints, 174
For all your saints, O Lord, 176
Rise, O children of salvation, 182
The Son of God goes forth to war, 183
The Son of God, our Christ, 434

The Annunciation of Our Lord (March 25)

Beautiful Savior (Ps), 518
Come, thou almighty King (Ps), 522
Of the Father's love begotten (II), 42
From east to west (G), 64
My soul proclaims the greatness of the Lord, 6
Ye watchers and ye holy ones, 175
My soul now magnifies the Lord, 180

St. Mark, Evangelist (April 25)

Awake, O Spirit of the watchmen (I), 382
All praise to thee, my God, this night (Ps), 278
To Jordan came the Christ, our Lord (G), 79
For all the saints, 174
For all your saints, O Lord, 176
By all your saints in warfare (stanza 13), 178

St. Philip and St. James, Apostles (May 1)

O Christ, our light, O Radiance true (I, II), 380
God, whose almighty word (II), 400
By all your saints in warfare (stanza 14) (G), 178
For all the saints, 174
For all your saints, O Lord, 176
Rise, O children of salvation, 182
The Son of God goes forth to war, 183
Look from your sphere of endless day, 402

596

The Son of God, our Christ, 434
Praise to the Father, 517

The Visitation (May 31)

Lo, how a rose is growing (I), 58
Come down, O Love divine (II), 508
My soul proclaims the greatness of the
  Lord (G), 6
My soul now magnifies the Lord (G), 180
The only Son from heaven, 86

St. Barnabas, Apostle (June 11)

Sing praise to God, the highest good (I),
  542
For all the saints, 174
For all your saints, O Lord, 176
Rise, O children of salvation, 182
The Son of God goes forth to war, 183
Lord, whose love in humble service, 423
The Son of God, our Christ, 434

The Nativity of St. John the Baptist (June 24)

Comfort, comfort now my people, 29
For all the saints, 174
For all your saints, O Lord, 176
By all your saints in warfare (stanza 15),
  178
Rise, O children of salvation, 182
The Son of God goes forth to war, 183

St. Peter and St. Paul, Apostles (June 29)

Jesus sinners will receive (I), 291
Look from your sphere of endless day (I),
  402
Before Jehovah's awesome throne (I), 531
Glories of your name are spoken (Ps), 358
Creator Spirit, by whose aid (II), 164
By all your saints in warfare (stanzas 10,
  11) (II), 177
O Holy Spirit, enter in (II), 459
"Take up your cross," the Savior said
  (G), 398
For all the saints, 174
For all your saints, O Lord, 176
Rise, O children of salvation, 182
The Son of God goes forth to war, 183
Built on a rock, 365
The Son of God, our Christ, 434

St. Mary Magdalene (July 22)

Lord, thee I love with all my heart (Ps),
  325
Who trusts in God, a strong abode (Ps),
  450
From God can nothing move me (Ps), 468
Hallelujah! Jesus lives! (G), 147
For all the saints, 174
For all your saints, O Lord, 176

St. James the Elder, Apostle (July 25)

Dear Lord and Father of mankind (I), 506
Faith of our fathers (II), 500

By all your saints in warfare (stanza 16)
  (II, G), 178
The Son of God goes forth to war (II, G),
  183
For all the saints, 174
For all your saints, O Lord, 176
Rise, O children of salvation, 182
The Son of God, our Christ, 434
Holy God, we praise your name, 535

Mary, Mother of Our Lord (August 15)

Hark, the glad sound! (I), 35
Jesus, your blood and righteousness (I),
  302
Our Father, by whose name (II), 357
My soul proclaims the greatness of the
  Lord (G), 6
My soul now magnifies the Lord (G), 180
Ye watchers and ye holy ones, 175

St. Bartholomew, Apostle (August 24)

For all the saints, 174
For all your saints, O Lord, 176
By all your saints in warfare (stanza 17),
  178
Rise, O children of salvation, 182
The Son of God goes forth to war, 183
The Son of God, our Christ, 434

Holy Cross Day (September 14)

Now the green blade rises (G), 148
Sing, my tongue, the glorious battle, 118
We sing the praise of him who died, 344
Lift high the cross, 377
When I survey the wondrous cross, 482

St. Matthew, Apostle and Evangelist (September 21)

Salvation unto us has come (II), 297
One there is, above all others (II, G), 298
By all your saints in warfare (stanza 18)
  (G), 178
For all the saints, 174
For all your saints, O Lord, 176
Rise, O children of salvation, 182
The Son of God goes forth to war, 183
The Son of God, our Christ, 434

St. Michael and All Angels (September 29)

Praise to the Lord, the almighty (Ps), 543
Ye watchers and ye holy ones, 175
God himself is present, 249
Hosanna to the living Lord!, 258
We worship you, O God of might, 432
Holy God, we praise your name, 535
Thee we adore, eternal Lord!, 547
Praise, my soul, the King of heaven, 549
Rejoice, O pilgrim throng!, 553

St. Luke, Evangelist (October 18)

O Christ, the healer, we have come (I), 360

O God, whose will is life and good (I), 435

Up through endless ranks of angels (II, G), 159

For all the saints, 174

For all your saints, O Lord, 176

By all your saints in warfare (stanza 19), 178

Rise, O children of salvation, 182

The Son of God goes forth to war, 183

St. Simon and St. Jude, Apostles (October 28)

Peace, to soothe our bitter woes (G), 338

Grant peace, we pray, in mercy, Lord (G), 471

Come, Holy Ghost, our souls inspire (G), 472, 473

For all the saints, 174

By all your saints in warfare (stanza 20), 178

For all your saints, O Lord, 176

Rise, O children of salvation, 182

The Son of God goes forth to war, 183

The Son of God, our Christ, 434

Reformation Day (October 31)

A mighty fortress is our God (PsP), 228, 229

O God of love, O king of peace (Ps), 414

Salvation unto us has come (II), 297

Dear Christians, one and all (II), 299

Lord, keep us steadfast in your Word, 230

God's Word is our great heritage, 239

Through the night of doubt and sorrow, 355

Do not despair, O little flock, 361

Built on a rock, 365

The Church's one foundation, 369

O God, O Lord of heaven and earth, 396

All Saints' Day (November 1)

Draw near and take the body of the Lord (Ps), 226

Jerusalem, my happy home (II), 331

Oh, what their joy (II), 337

Jerusalem the golden, 347

Jerusalem, whose towers touch the skies (II), 348

How blest are those who know their need of God (G), 17

For all the saints, 174

Ye watchers and ye holy ones, 175

For all your saints, O Lord, 176

By all your saints in warfare (stanza 4), 177

Who is this host arrayed in white, 314

In heaven above, 330

Oh, happy day when we shall stand, 351

OCCASIONS

Unity

Praise and thanksgiving be to God (II), 191

Through the night of doubt and sorrow (II), 355

The Church's one foundation (II), 369

Blest be the tie that binds (II), 370

Son of God, eternal Savior (G), 364

Come, Holy Ghost, God and Lord, 163

Sent forth by God's blessing, 221

Lord Jesus Christ, we humbly pray, 225

Lord, receive this company, 255

May we your precepts, Lord, fulfill, 353

In Christ there is no east or west, 359

O Christ, the healer, we have come, 360

Eternal Ruler of the ceaseless round, 373

Christ is the king!, 386

Lord of light, 405

God, whose giving knows no ending, 408

Let all things now living, 557

Dedication and Anniversary

Christ is made the sure foundation (II), 367

O Jesus, king most wonderful! (II), 537

Come, Holy Ghost, God and Lord, 163

Father most holy, 169

How blessed is this place, O Lord, 186

O God, our help in ages past, 320

Built on a rock, 365

I love your kingdom, Lord, 368

The Church's one foundation, 369

Only-begotten, Word of God eternal, 375

Christians, while on earth abiding, 440

Come, Holy Ghost, our souls inspire, 472, 473

Holy Spirit, ever dwelling, 523

Now thank we all our God, 533, 534

Laying of a cornerstone

Great God, a blessing from your throne, 185

Harvest

O Bread of life from heaven (II), 222

Come, you thankful people, come (G), 407

We plow the fields and scatter, 362

As saints of old, 404

Praise and thanksgiving, 409

Sing to the Lord of harvest, 412

Now thank we all our God, 533, 534

For the fruit of all creation, 563

Day of Penitence

Lord of all nations, grant me grace (Pr), 419
Thee we adore, O hidden Savior (II), 199
Here, O my Lord, I see thee (II), 211
Today your mercy calls us (G), 304
Out of the depths I cry to you, 295
When in the hour of deepest need, 303
Forgive our sins as we forgive, 307
To you, omniscient Lord of all, 310
Father eternal, ruler of creation, 413
O God of love, O King of peace, 414
God of grace and God of glory, 415
O God of every nation, 416
Judge eternal, throned in splendor, 418
Lord, save your world; in bitter need, 420

National Holiday

Rejoice, O pilgrim throng! (Ps), 553
We praise you, O God, 241
Before you, Lord, we bow, 401
O God of every nation, 416
Judge eternal, throned in splendor, 418
O God of earth and altar, 428
Not alone for mighty empire, 437
God the omnipotent! King who ordainest, 462
Lift every voice and sing, 562
My country, 'tis of thee (United States), 566
God of our fathers, 567
God save our gracious Queen! (Canada), 568
God bless our native land, 569

Peace

The Lord will come and not be slow (Ps), 318
O God, empower us (G), 422
Christ is alive! Let Christians sing, 363
Son of God, eternal Savior, 364
Lord of our life, 366
Father eternal, ruler of creation, 413
O God of love, O King of peace, 414
God of grace and God of glory, 415
O God of every nation, 416
Lord Christ, when first you came to earth, 421
God the omnipotent!, 462
Great God, our source, 466
Grant peace, we pray, in mercy, Lord, 471

Day of Thanksgiving

We praise you, O God, 241
When all your mercies, O my God, 264
Now all the woods are sleeping, 276
We plow the fields and scatter, 362
Not alone for mighty empire, 437
Now thank we all our God, 533, 534
Praise to the Lord, the Almighty, 543
Let all things now living, 557
Oh, that I had a thousand voices, 560
For the beauty of the earth, 561
For the fruit of all creation, 563

Stewardship of Creation

Oh, worship the King (Ps), 548
Arise, my soul, arise! (II), 516
We plow the fields and scatter, 362
Son of God, eternal Savior, 364
As saints of old, 404
God, whose giving knows no ending, 408
Praise and thanksgiving, 409
We give thee but thine own, 410
Lord of all good, 411
Judge eternal, throned in splendor, 418
How marvelous God's greatness, 515
All creatures of our God and King, 527
Praise the Lord of heaven!, 541
Joyful, joyful we adore thee, 551
This is my Father's world, 554
Let all things now living, 557
Oh, that I had a thousand voices, 560
For the fruit of all creation, 563

New Year's Eve

Greet now the swiftly changing year, 181
O God, our help in ages past, 320
All depends on our possessing, 447
Evening and morning, 465
From God can nothing move me, 468
Come, gracious Spirit, heavenly dove, 475
O God of Jacob, 477
Oh, that the Lord would guide my ways, 480
Lord, as a pilgrim, 485
I heard the voice of Jesus say, 497
Now thank we all our God, 533, 534
Let all things now living, 557

Holy Baptism

The Lord's my shepherd (PsP, 23), 451
The King of love my shepherd is (PsP, 23), 456
Jesus, thy boundless love to me (Ps, 23), 336
As pants the hart for cooling streams (Ps, 42), 452
You servants of God (Ps, 93), 252
This is my Father's world (Ps, 93), 554
Grant peace, we pray, in mercy, Lord (Ps, 122), 471
God, my Lord, my strength (I, Ezekiel), 484
Salvation unto us has come (II, Romans 5), 297
We know that Christ is raised (II, Rom. 6, 2 Cor.), 189
We all believe in one true God (II, Romans 8), 374
Praise and thanksgiving be to God (II, Ephesians), 191
The Church's one foundation (II, Ephesians), 369
O Jesus, king most wonderful! (II, 1 Peter), 537
Alleluia! Sing to Jesus (G, Matthew), 158
Baptized into your name most holy (G, Matthew), 192
Christ is alive! Let Christians sing (G, Matthew), 363

To Jordan came the Christ (G, Matthew, Mark 1), 79

Dearest Jesus, we are here (G, Mark 10), 187

Amid the world's bleak wilderness (G, John 15), 378

I bind unto myself today, 188

We praise you, Lord, 190

Cradling children in his arm, 193

All who believe and are baptized, 194

This is the Spirit's entry now, 195

Marriage

Creator Spirit, by whose aid (I, Genesis 1), 164

When all your mercies, O my God (Ps, 33), 264

O God, our help in ages past (Ps, 33), 320

All people that on earth do dwell (PsP, 100), 245

Oh, sing jubilee to the Lord (PsP, 100), 256

Before Jehovah's awesome throne (PsP, 100), 531

Open now thy gates of beauty (Ps, 100), 250

From all that dwell below the skies (PsP, 117), 550

Give to our God immortal praise! (PsP, 136), 520

Let us with a gladsome mind (PsP, 136; Genesis 1), 521

Praise to the Lord, the Almighty (Ps, 150), 543

O perfect Love (G, Matthew), 287

All praise to you, O Lord (G, John 2), 78

Abide with us, our Savior, 263

Hear us now, our God and Father, 288

Heavenly Father, hear our prayer, 289

Love divine, all loves excelling, 315

Eternal God, before your throne we bend, 354

Oh, blest the house, 512

Come, my way, my truth, my life, 513

Now thank we all our God, 533, 534

Praise the Lord! O heavens, 540

Sing praise to God, the highest good, 542

Joyful, joyful we adore thee, 551

In thee is gladness, 552

Oh, that I had a thousand voices, 560

For the beauty of the earth, 561

Burial of the Dead

The Lord's my shepherd (PsP, 23), 451

The King of love my shepherd is (PsP, 23), 456

Jesus, thy boundless love to me (Ps, 23), 336

O God, our help in ages past (PsP, 90), 320

The day of resurrection! (Ps, 118), 141

Out of the depths I cry to you (PsP, 130), 295

For all the saints (II, Revelation 14:13), 174

I know of a sleep in Jesus' name (II, Revelation 14:13), 342

As pants the hart for cooling streams (PsP, 42), 452

Unto the hills (PsP, 121), 445

I know that my Redeemer lives! (I, Job; G, John 14), 352

Jesus Christ, my sure defense (I, Job), 340

Out of the depths I cry to you (II, Romans 5:20-21), 295

If God himself be for me (II, Romans 8), 454

Who is this host arrayed in white (II, Revelation 7), 314

Love divine, all loves excelling (II, Revelation 7), 315

Jerusalem, whose towers touch the skies (II, Revelation 7), 348

I heard the voice of Jesus say (G, Matthew 11), 497

Hallelujah! Jesus lives! (G, John 14), 147

Jesus lives! The victory's won!, 133

A mighty fortress is our God, 228, 229

O Love that will not let me go, 324

Even as we live each day, 350

We are the Lord's, 399

All depends on our possessing, 447

If you but trust in God to guide you, 453

My faith looks up to thee, 479

Corporate Confession and Forgiveness

Who trusts in God, a strong abode (Ps, 73), 450

From God can nothing move me (Ps, 73), 468

O God, our help in ages past (PsP, 90), 320

Out of the depths I cry to you (PsP, 130), 295

Wondrous are your ways, O God! (Ps, 139), 311

My God, how wonderful thou art (I, Deuteronomy), 524

A lamb goes uncomplaining forth (I, Isaiah 53), 105

Amazing grace (II, Romans 3, Ephesians 2), 448

O Lord, we praise you (II, Romans 5), 215

Chief of sinners though I be (II, Romans 5), 306

Alas! And did my Savior bleed (II, Romans 12), 98

Hark! A thrilling voice is sounding!, (II, Romans 13), 37

We know that Christ is raised (II, 2 Corinthians), 189

Eternal Ruler of the ceaseless round (II, Ephesians 6), 373

We give thee but thine own (II, James), 410

The Church's one foundation (II, 1 Peter), 369

Jesus, priceless treasure (II, 1 Peter), 457, 458

Thee we adore, O hidden Savior (II, 1 John), 199

600

Here, O my Lord, I see thee (II, 1 John), 211

My hope is built on nothing less (II, 1 John), 293, 294

Oh, for a thousand tongues to sing (II, 1 John), 559

Come to Calvary's holy mountain (G, Matthew 11), 301

I heard the voice of Jesus say (G, Matthew 11), 497

O God of mercy, God of light (G, Matthew 25), 425

Today your mercy calls us (G, Luke 15), 304

Savior, when in dust to you (G, Luke 18), 91

To you, omniscient Lord of all (G, Luke 18), 310

O God, empower us (G, John 15:9-14), 422

Maker of the earth and heaven, 266

O Christ, our hope, 300

I lay my sins on Jesus, 305

Forgive our sins as we forgive, 307

God the Father, be our stay, 308

Lord Jesus, think on me, 309

I trust, O Christ, in you alone, 395

Come, oh, come, O quickening Spirit, 478

My faith looks up to thee, 479

Renew me, O eternal Light, 511

Origins of Tunes—
Chronological Listing

Numbers listed refer to LBW hymn numbers.

This index and the index at page 609 have been provided to assist in the augmentation of Christian education materials; preparation of courses of study, services, or programs on hymnody; selection of hymns for special observances such as anniversaries and commemorations; and so on.

A slash indicates a revision or adaptation of a melody. In the case of revisions or adaptations, the tune is listed at each date, with all but the original appearances indented. Isometric forms of melodies, which generally date from the eighteenth century, are not listed separately, but are indicated by italicized numbers. Plainsong melodies have been listed separately as it is not possible to locate most of them geographically. In the case of many plainsong and folk melodies, dates of origin are unknown and their placement in the chronological listings is approximate.

AUSTRIA

Grosser Gott (1744), 270, 535
Austria (1797), 358, 540
? Lyons (18th century/Eng., 1815), 252

BOHEMIA

(See under Czechoslovakia)

CANADA

The King's Majesty (1939), 121
Grace Church, Gananoque (1962), 461
Carn Brea (1971), 238
Atkinson (20th century), 237

CATALAN

Lo desembre congelat (?), 53

CZECHOSLOVAKIA

Gottes Sohn ist kommen (Boh., 15th century/1531), 312
Narodil se Kristus Pán (Boh., 15th century), 57
Rok nový (Slov., 15th century), 181
Freuen wir uns all in ein (1531), 37
  Gottes Sohn ist kommen (Boh., 15th century/1531), 312
Gaudeamus pariter (Boh., 1544), 132, 193
Beatus vir (Slov., 1561), 419
  Mit Freuden zart (Switz., 1551/Morav., 1566), 140, 421
  Sonne der Gerechtigkeit (Germ., 15th century/Boh., 1566), 210

Pán Bůh (Slov., 1567), 484
Známe to, Pane Bože náš (1636), 96
  Čas radosti (Latin carol, 12th century/Boh., 1674?), 66
Zpívejmež všickni vesele (1936), 150

DENMARK

Vi lova dig, o store Gud (1529), 432
O Jesu, än de dina (1569), 496
Om Himmeriges Rige (1569), 227
Her kommer dine arme Smaa (1789), 52
Den signede Dag (1826), 161, 342
Det kimer nu til Julefest (19th century), 62
Amen sjunge hvarje tunga (1849), 298

ENGLAND

Deo gracias (*c.* 1415), 80, 88
Winchester Old (1533/1592), 264
Windsor (1533/1591), 114
Tallis' Canon (1560), 278
Third Mode Melody (1560), 497
St. Flavian (1562/1853), 234
Southwell (1579), 309
Greensleeves (before 1580), 40
Ist Gott für mich (1590/Germ., 1609), 454
  Windsor (1533/1591), 114
  Winchester Old (1533/1592), 264
Song 1 (1623), 206, 373
Song 13 (1623), 257
Song 34 (1623), 505
Farley Castle (1637-1638), 211
The First Nowell (17th century?), 56
Yigdal (17th century?/1770), 544

St. Magnus (1707), 173, 190
Easter Hymn (1708), 151
Hanover (1708), 548
St. Anne (1708), 320
Bangor (1734), 483
Wareham (1738), 433, 475
Antioch (1742/U.S., 1836), 39
National Anthem (c. 1743), 566, 568, 569
Stabat Mater (Germ., 1661/Eng., c. 1743), 110
Judas Maccabaeus (1747/c. 1760), 145
St. Thomas (1763/1770), 368
Helmsley (1765), 27
Italian Hymn (1769), 400, 522
Darwall's 148th (1770), 261, 401
Durham (c. 1770), 488
St. Thomas (1763/1770), 368
Yigdal (17th century?/1770), 544
Miles Lane (1779), 329
Duke Street (18th century), 352, 520, 530
Rockingham Old (c. 1780/1790), 482
Melcombe (1782), 388
Morning Hymn (c. 1789), 269
Truro (1789), 363
Rockingham Old (c. 1780/1790), 482
Chesterfield (1792), 35
Sicilian Mariners (Sicily?, 18th century/Eng., 1792), 259
Truth from Above (17th or 18th century), 81
Grace Church (1815), 225
Lyons (Austria?, 18th century/Eng., 1815), 252
Walton (Germ., 19th century?/Eng., 1815), 356, 429
St. Peter (c. 1830), 345, 477
Lancashire (1836), 495
Evan (1847/U.S., 1850), 480
Franconia (Germ., 1738/Eng., 1847), 22
King's Lynn (folksong), 177, 178, 428
Kingsfold (folksong), 391
Terra Patris (folksong/U.S., 1915), 554
Victory (It., 1591/Eng., c. 1850), 135
Gethsemane (1853), 109, 306
Orientis partibus (Fr., c. 1200/Eng., 1853), 130
St. Flavian (1562/1853), 234
Potsdam (Germ., 1742/Eng., 1854), 89
St. George's, Windsor (1858), 407
Sandon (1860), 445
Eventide (1861), 272
Melita (1861), 294, 467
Nicaea (1861), 165
St. Christopher (1863), 107
Aurelia (1864), 197, 369
St. Catherine (1864), 500
St. Agnes (1866), 316
Regent Square (1867), 50
Ave Maria, klarer und lichter Morgenstern (Germ., 1784/Eng., 1868), 251
Diademata (1868), 170
Laudes Domini (1868), 546
Merrial (1868), 280
Stephanos (1868), 460
Ellers (1869), 262

Patmos (1869), 406
Praise, My Soul (1869), 549
Morecambe (1870), 486
Hermas (1871), 260
St. Gertrude (1871), 509
Fortunatus (1872), 153
Coena Domini (1874), 226
Leominster (1874), 489
Maryton (1874), 492
St. Clement (1874), 274
Angel's Story (1881), 514
Morgenlied (1881), 131
Galilean (1883), 381
Galilee (1887), 494
Rest (1887), 506
O Perfect Love (1889), 287
Just as I Am (1892), 425
Morning Star (1892), 84
Rustington (1897), 408
Thornbury (1898), 77
Engleberg (1904), 189
Intercessor (1904), 283
Down Ampney (1906), 508
Lasst uns erfreuen (Germ., 1623/Eng., 1906), 143, 157, 175, 527
St. Patrick's Breastplate (Ire., folksong/Eng., 1906), 188
Salve festa dies (1906), 142
Sine Nomine (1906), 174
The Call (1911), 513
Gonfalon Royal (1913), 402
Crucifer (1916), 377
Langham (1919), 413
King's Weston (1925), 179
Oakley (1925), 101
Wellington Square (1931), 422
Abbot's Leigh (1941), 405
Cannock (1951), 201
Ryburn (1951), 336
Sheldonian (1951), 160
Garelochside (1957), 78
Birabus (1962), 436
Morestead (1964), 411
In manus tuas (1971), 491
New Malden (1971), 556

(Several English forms of plainsong melodies are listed under Plainsong.)

FINLAND

Kuortane (folksong), 339
Lost in the Night (folksong), 394
Noormarkku (folksong), 384
Nyt ylös, sieluni (folksong), 516
Oi Herra, jos mä matkamies maan (1920), 485

FRANCE

? Vexilla regis (6th century), 125
Orientus partibus (c. 1200/Eng., 1853), 130
O filii et filiae (15th century), 139
Veni, Emmanuel (15th century), 34
Was mein Gott will (1529/Germ., 1572), 450

603

0

Lasset uns mit Jesu ziehen (1788), 487
Alles ist an Gottes Segen (1691/1793),
196, 447
Tryggare kan ingen vara (Swed., or
Germ., *c.* 1800/Swed., 1873), 474
Mendon (19th century?/U.S., 1821), 547
Walton (19th century?/Eng., 1815), 356,
429
Flemming (1811), 517
Stille Nacht (1818), 65
Wir hatten gebauet (1819), 59
Hymn to Joy (1823/U.S., 1846), 551
Azmon (1828/U.S., 1839), 559
Dix (1838), 82, 561
Canonbury (1839/?), 403
Schönster Herr Jesu (1839), 518
Mendelssohn (1840/U.S., 1855), 60
So nimm den meine Hände (1842), 333
Angelus (1657/1847), 119
Munich (1693/1847), 231, 305, 503
Wem in Leidenstagen (1847), 95
Anthes (19th century), 304
Wir pflügen (1880), 362
Wir dienen, Herr (1938), 218
Little Flock (1971), 476

HOLLAND

Kremser (1626), 241
Vruechten (17th century), 149
In Babilone (*c.* 1710), 364, 523
Midden in de Dood (1960), 207

INDIA

Tandanei (1963), 529

IRELAND

Durrow (folksong), 322
St. Columba (folksong/19th century), 456
St. Patrick's Breastplate (folksong/Eng.,
1906), 188
Slane (folksong/1901), 469

ITALY

In dir ist Freude (1591/Germ., 1598), 552
Victory (1591/Eng., *c.* 1850), 135

JAPAN

Mabune (1930), 417

LIBERIA

A va de (*c.* 1965), 214

MORAVIA

(See under Czechoslovakia)

NORWAY

Den store hvide Flok (folksong), 314
I Himmelen, I Himmelen (folksong), 330
Dejlig er den Himmel blaa (*c.* 1840), 75

Kirken den er et gammelt Hus (1840), 365
Jeg er saa glad (19th century), 69
Princess Eugenie (folksong), 326
Guds Menighed, syng (*c.* 1860), 256
Her vil ties (1860), 481
Fred til Bod (1871), 147, 338
Du som gaar ud (19th century), 285
Gud skal alting Mage (19th century), 458
Naar mit Öie (1871), 301
Torshov (1972), 204

PLAINSONG, LATIN ANTIPHONS AND CAROLS

Veni, Creator Spiritus (?, LBW form from
Belgium), 472
See also under German: Komm, Gott
Schöpfer, (1533), 284, 473
Splendor Paternae (?, LBW form from
England), 271
Christe, qui lux es et dies (?)
See under German: Christe, der du bist
Tag und Licht, (1533), 273
Pange lingua (?), 120
Vexilla regis (France ?, 6th century, LBW
form from England), 125
A solis ortus cardine (Anglo-Saxon times,
LBW form from England), 64
Jam lucis (?), 277
Kyrie fons bonitatis (early middle ages)
See under German: Kyrie, Gott Vater,
(16th century/1687), 168
Conditor alme siderum (?), 323
Gloria in excelsis (10th century)
See under German: Allein Gott in der
Höh, (1539), 166
Sanctus, Sanctus, Sanctus (11th century)
See under German: Jesaia, dem
Propheten, (1526), 528
Victimae paschali (Germany, 11th cen-
tury), 137
See also under German:
Christ ist erstanden, (c. 1100), 136
Christ lag in Todesbanden, (1524),
134
Credo in unum Deum
See under German: Wir glauben all,
(1524), 374
Ad monumentum venimus (middle ages)
See under German: Erschienen ist der
herrlich Tag, (1560), 154
Christe Redemptor (12th-13th century,
LBW form from England), 49
Divinum mysterium (*c.* 12th century), 42
Veni Redemptor gentium (*c.* 12th century)
See under German: Nun komm, der
Heiden Heiland, (1524), 28
Omnis mundus iucundetur (12th century),
66
See under Czechoslovakia: Čas radosti,
66
Agnus Dei (12th or 13th century)
See under German: O Lamm Gottes
unschuldig, (1522/1542), 111
Puer est natus nobis (?)
See under German: Lobt Gott, ihr
Christen, (1554), 47, 300, 351

Komm, Heiliger Geist, Herre Gott (*c.* 15th century/Germ., 1524), 163
Veni, Emmanuel (Fr., 15th century), 34

POLAND

Ẉ zlobie lezy (folksong), 44

RUSSIA

Russian Hymn (1833), 462

SCOTLAND

Dundee (1615), 464, 524
Caithness (1635), 99
Martyrdom (*c.* 1790/1825), 98, 452
Brother James's Air (19th century), 451
Bunessan (Gaelic folksong), 409
St. Margaret (1885), 324

SICILY

? Sicilian Mariners (18th century/Eng., 1792), 259

SLOVAKIA

(See under Czechoslovakia)

SWEDEN

Den Blomstertid nu kommer (1693), 515
Af himlens (1694), 232
Bereden väg för Herran (1694), 26
Der mange skal komme (1694), 313
Upp, min tunga (1694), 155
Ack, bliv hos oss (1697), 414
Ack, vad är dock livet här (1697), 112, 113
Tryggare kan ingen vara (Swed. or Germ., *c.* 1800/Swed., 1873), 474
Haf trones lampa färdig (folksong), 25
Ack, saliga stunder (1850), 371
 Tryggare kan ingen vara (Swed. or Germ., *c.* 1800/Swed., 1873), 474
Wennerberg (1882), 311
O store Gud (1891/1894), 532

SWITZERLAND

Solothurn (*c.* 1520/1826), 186
Herzliebster Jesu (1543/Germ., 1640), 123
Wenn wir in höchsten Nöten sein (1543/Germ., 1567), 303
Donne secours (1551), 493
 Freu dich sehr (Fr., 1505/Switz., 1551), 29, *470*
Mit Freuden zart (1551/Moravia, 1566), 140, 421
 O Seigneur (Germ.? 1553/Switz., 1551), 545
Old Hundredth (1551), 245, 531, 550, 564, 565
Old 124th (1551), 376
 Solothurn (*c.* 1520/1826), 186
Dennis (19th century/U.S., 1845), 370

UNITED STATES

Windham (1785), 344
Coronation (1793), 328
Lewis-Town (1794), 426
Kedron (1799), 420
Consolation (1813), 33
Nettleton (1813), 499
Twenty-fourth (1813), 122, 126
Kentucky 93rd (1816), 246
Tender Thought (1816), 220
Detroit (1820), 240, 307
 Mendon (Germ.,?/U.S., 1821), 547
Bourbon (1825), 127
Holy Manna (1825), 463
Hiding Place (1830), 537
Pleading Savior (1830), 243
New Britain (1831), 448
Olivet (1831), 479
Foundation (1832), 507
The Saints' Delight (1832), 372
Toplady (1832), 327
Complainer (1835), 347
Distress (1835), 217, 360
Jefferson (1835), 30
Prospect (1835), 61
 Antioch (Eng., 1742/U.S., 1836), 39
Webb (1837), 389
 Azmon (Germ., 1828/U.S., 1839), 559
Meribah (1839), 353
Battle Hymn (19th century), 332
Wondrous Love (1843), 385
Beach Spring (1844), 423
 Dennis (Switz., 19th century/U.S., 1845), 370
 Hymn to Joy (Germ., 1823/U.S., 1846), 551
Rathbun (1849), 104
Woodworth (1849), 296
American Hymn (*c.* 1850), 525
Carol (1850), 54
 Evan (Eng., 1847/U.S., 1850), 480
Heath (1850), 410
 Mendelssohn (Germ., 1840/U.S., 1855), 60
The Solid Rock (1863), 293
He Leadeth Me (1864), 501
Converse (1868), 439
Lord, Revive Us (1868), 290
St. Louis (1868), 41
Hankey (1869), 390
Pilot (1871), 334
All Saints New (1872), 183
Festal Song (1872), 176, 383
Angelic Songs (*c.* 1875), 397
Penitence (1875), 106
It Is Well (1876), 346
Bread of Life (1877), 235
Marion (1883), 553
Away in a Manger (1887), 67
National Hymn (1892), 567
Laus Regis (1899), 171
Wedlock (19th century?), 392
Break Bread Together (Negro spiritual) 212
Go Tell It (Negro spiritual), 70
Land of Rest (White spiritual), 331

WALES

Original Language
First Lines of Hymns—
Chronological Listing

Numbers listed refer to LBW hymn numbers.

This index and the index at page 602 have been provided to assist in the augmentation of Christian education materials; preparation of courses of study, services, or programs on hymnody; selection of hymns for special observances such as anniversaries and commemorations; and so on.

Except for Greek and Latin hymns, the language and the place of origin are the same when not otherwise indicated. Under "French," for example, "Les anges dans nos campagnes" comes from France, while "A toi la gloire, o Ressuscité" comes from Switzerland. For a few Greek and Latin hymns the place of origin can be given with some certainty, but in many cases it is difficult if not impossible to place these hymns geographically since Greek and Latin were used throughout the Eastern and Western Churches respectively. Where there are some clues, a possible place of origin has been included, followed by a question mark. The origins of English translations are also given. English hymns are listed under the countries in which they were written.

Dates separated by commas indicate more than one source for the hymn. Dates separated by a slash indicate that a hymn or translation has undergone a major revision or been recast. In the case both of multiple sources and of revisions, the hymn is listed at each date, with all but the original appearance indented. Where it is known, the date of writing has been used; otherwise, the dates are those of first publication.

For an alphabetical listing of first lines of all languages see p. 636.

AFRICAN

(*Hymns from Africa can be found under* Greek *and* Loma.)

AMERICAN

(*Hymns from the United States can be found under* English: United States *and under* Norwegian.)

AUSTRALIAN

(*A hymn from Australia can be found under* English: Australia.)

CANADIAN

(*Hymns from Canada can be found under* English: Canada.)

CATALONIAN

Lo desembre congelat (?), 53
Cold December flies away (U.S., 1978)

DANISH

Den signede Dag, som vi nu ser (Swed., c. 1450), 1569, 161
O day full of grace that we now see (U.S., 1978)

Enhver, som tror og bliver döbt (1689), 194
All who believe and are baptized (U.S., 1909)

Lov og Tak og evig Aere (1689), 470
Praise and thanks and adoration (U.S., 1978)

O Jesus, söde Jesus, dig (1689), 220
O Jesus, blessed Lord, to you (Eng., 1889)

Skriv dig, Jesus, paa mit Hjerte (1689), 102
On my heart imprint your image (U.S., 1898)

Her kommer, Jesus, dina smaa (1732), 52
Your little ones, dear Lord, are we (U.S., 1898)

Den store hvide Flok, vi se (1765), 314
Who is this host arrayed in white (U.S., 1978)

Han er opstanden! Store Bud! (1778), 138
He is arisen! Glorious Word! (U.S., 1909)

Os er idag en Frelser född (1778), 43
Rejoice, rejoice this happy morn (U.S., 1911)

Dejlig er den Himmel blaa (1810), 75
Bright and glorious is the sky (U.S., 1930, 1958)

Det kimer nu til Julefest (1817), 62
The bells of Christmas chime once more (U.S., 1867)

Guds Ord det er vort Arvegods (1817), 239
God's Word is our great heritage (U.S., 1909)

Du, som gaar ud fra den levende Gud (Eng., 1823), 1837, 285
Spirit of God, sent from heaven abroad (U.S., 1978)

Herren straekker ud sin Arm (1837), 193
Cradling children in his arm (U.S., 1976)

Igjennem Nat og Traengsel (1825), 355
Through the night of doubt and sorrow (Eng., 1867)

Kirken den er et gammelt Hus (1837), 365
Built on a rock the Church shall stand (U.S., 1978)

Fred til Bod for bittert Savn (1845), 338
Peace, to soothe our bitter woes (U.S., 1908)

DUTCH

Midden in de Dood (1961), 207
We who once were dead (Eng., 20th century)

(A hymn probably from Holland can be found under Latin.)

ENGLISH

Australia

We praise you, Lord (1955), 190

(A single English translation from Australia can be found at LBW 539.)

Canada

What a friend we have in Jesus (1855), 439
Herald, sound the note of judgment (1968), 556
Praise and thanksgiving be to God (1969), 191

(Another hymn from Canada can be found under Huron.)

England

All people that on earth do dwell (1561), 245
Jerusalem, my happy home (16th or 17th century), 331
Let us with a gladsome mind (1623), 521
Come, my way, my truth, my life (1633), 513
The Lord will come and not be slow (1648), 318
My song is love unknown (1664), 94
All who would valiant be (1684), 498
Praise God, from whom all blessings flow (1692), 564, 565
All praise to thee, my God, this night (1692), 278
Awake, my soul, and with the sun (1692), 269
As pants the hart for cooling streams (1696), 452
The first Noel the angel did say (17th century?), 56
Alas! And did my Savior bleed (1707), 98
Come, let us join our cheerful songs (1707), 254
Nature with open volume stands (1707), 119
When I survey the wondrous cross (1707), 482
It happened on that fateful night (1709), 127
When all your mercies, O my God (1712), 264
Before Jehovah's awesome throne (1719, 1735), 531
From all that dwell below the skies (1719), 550
Give to our God immortal praise! (1719), 520
Jesus shall reign where'er the sun (1719), 530
Joy to the world, the Lord is come! (1719), 39
O God, our help in ages past (1719), 320
Oh, that the Lord would guide my ways (1719), 480
Come, gracious spirit, heav'nly dove (1720), 475
Before Jehovah's awesome throne (1719, 1735), 531
O God of Jacob, by whose hand (1737), 477
Oh, for a thousand tongues to sing (1738), 559
Christ the Lord is ris'n today! (1739), 130
Hark! The herald angels sing (1739), 60
Christ, whose glory fills the skies (1740), 265
God save our gracious Queen! (c. 1743) 568
Come, thou long-expected Jesus (1744), 30
Rejoice, the Lord is king! (1744), 171
You servants of God, your master proclaim (1744), 252
Victim Divine, your grace we claim (1745), 202

Love divine, all loves excelling (1747), 315

Forth in thy name, O Lord, I go (1749), 505

Hark, the glad sound! The Savior comes (1755), 35

Come, thou almighty King (*c.* 1757), 522

Lo! He comes with clouds descending (1758), 27

Come, thou Fount of ev'ry blessing (1759), 499

Father of mercies, in your Word (1760), 240

God moves in a mysterious way (1773), 483

Lord, dismiss us with your blessing (1773), 259

Praise the Lord! O heav'ns, adore him (1774), 540

I know that my Redeemer lives! (1775), 352

Rock of Ages, cleft for me (1775, 1776), 327

All hail the pow'r of Jesus' name! (1779, 1787), 328, 329

Amazing grace, how sweet the sound (1779), 448

Glories of your name are spoken (1779), 358

How sweet the name of Jesus sounds (1779), 345

On what has now been sown (1779), 261

One there is, above all others (1779), 298

Blest be the tie that binds (1782), 370

    All hail the pow'r of Jesus' name! (1779, 1787), 328, 329

How firm a foundation, O saints of the Lord (1787), 507

Look, oh, look, the sight is glorious (1809), 156

Brightest and best of the stars of the morning (1811), 84

Hosanna to the living Lord! (1811), 258

God, whose almighty word (*c.* 1813), 400

Almighty God, your Word is cast (1815), 234

Savior, when in dust to you (1815), 91

We sing the praise of him who died (1815), 344

Angels, from the realms of glory (1816), 50

Lord, teach us how to pray aright (1818), 438

Come to Calv'ry's holy mountain (1819), 301

Lord God, the Holy Ghost (1819), 162

Abide with me, fast falls the eventide (1820?), 272

Go to dark Gethsemane (1820), 109

The head that once was crowned with thorns (1820), 173

Hail to the Lord's anointed (1821), 87

O Spirit of the living God (1823), 388

    (*See also* Danish: Du, som gaar ud fra den levende Gud [1817])

In the cross of Christ I glory (1825), 104

Holy, holy, holy, Lord God Almighty! (1826), 165

God, who made the earth and heaven (Eng., 1827; Ire., 1838; Eng., 1864), 281

Ride on, ride on in majesty! (1827), 121

The Son of God goes forth to war (1827), 183

In the hour of trial (1834), 106

Just as I am, without one plea (1834), 296

My hope is built on nothing less (*c.* 1834), 293, 294

Praise, my soul, the King of heaven (1834), 549

Welcome to the Savior's breast (1834) (*See* Danish: Herren straekker ud sin Arm [1837]), 193

May we your precepts, Lord, fulfill (1836), 353

Savior, like a shepherd lead us (1836), 481

For all your saints, O Lord (1837), 176

God the omnipotent! King who ordainest (1842, 1878), 462

I lay my sins on Jesus (1843), 305

Come, you thankful people, come (1844), 407

Praise the Lord of heaven! (1844), 541

I heard the voice of Jesus say (1846), 497

There is a green hill far away (1848), 114

Faith of our fathers, living still (1849), 500

My God, how wonderful thou art (1849), 524

Crown him with many crowns (1851, 1874), 170

In his temple now behold him (1851?), 184

Jesus calls us; o'er the tumult (1852), 494

There's a wideness in God's mercy (1854), 290

Here, O my Lord, I see thee face to face (1855), 211

We give thee but thine own (*c.* 1855), 410

As with gladness men of old (*c.* 1858), 82

Praise to the Father for his lovingkindness (19th century), 517

Eternal Father, strong to save (1860), 467

At the name of Jesus (1861), 179

O God of love, O King of peace (1861), 414

Today your mercy calls us (1861), 304

O day of rest and gladness (1862), 251

Songs of thankfulness and praise (1862), 90

All praise to you, O Lord (1863), 78

Christ is risen! Alleluia! (1863), 131

Fight the good fight with all your might (1863), 461

On our way rejoicing (1863), 260

Bow down your ear, almighty Lord (1864), 286

By all your saints in warfare (1864), 177, 178

For all the saints who from their labors rest (1864), 174

For the beauty of the earth (1864), 561
God, who made the earth and heaven (Eng., 1827; Ire., 1838; Eng., 1864), 281
Lord of glory, you have bought us (1864), 424
Onward, Christian soldiers (1864), 509
Your hand, O Lord, in days of old (1864), 431
What child is this, who, laid to rest (1865), 40
Blessing and honor and glory and pow'r (1866), 525
Glory be to God the Father! (1866), 167
I love to tell the story (1866), 390
O Jesus, I have promised (1866), 503
Savior, again to your dear name we raise (1866), 262
Sing to the Lord of harvest (1866), 412
The Church's one foundation (1866), 369
Alleluia! Sing to Jesus (1867), 158
Now the day is over (1867), 280
O Word of God incarnate (1867), 231
Spirit of God, descend upon my heart (1867), 486
The King of love my shepherd is (1868), 456
O Savior, precious Savior (1870), 514
Jesus, in thy dying woes (1871), 112, 113
O one with God the Father (1871), 77
Lord, speak to us, that we may speak (1872), 403
O Lord, throughout these forty days (1873; U.S., 1978), 99
Crown him with many crowns (1851, 1874), 170
I am trusting you, Lord Jesus (1874), 460
Lord, enthroned in heav'nly splendor (1874), 172
The day you gave us, Lord, has ended (1870), 274
Take my life, that I may be (1874), 406
O God of mercy, God of light (1877), 425
Unto the hills around do I lift up (1877), 445
Breathe on me, breath of God (1878), 488
God, the omnipotent! King who ordainest (1842, 1878), 462
Let the whole creation cry (1881), 242
Lord, who the night you were betrayed did pray (1881), 206
O God of God, O Light of Light (1883), 536
How good, Lord, to be here! (1888), 89
Son of God, eternal Savior (1893), 364
Judge eternal, throned in splendor (1902), 418
This joyful Eastertide (1902), 149
In Christ there is no east or west (1905), 359
O God of earth and altar (1906), 428
Ye watchers and ye holy ones (1906), 175
The King shall come when morning dawns (1907), 33
In the quiet consecration (1910), 223
Lift high the cross, the love of Christ proclaim (1916), 377

Father eternal, ruler of creation (1919), 413
O God, whose will is life and good (1922), 435
Now the green blade rises from the buried grain (1928), 148
Christ is the king! O friends, rejoice (1931), 386
Come, risen Lord, and deign to be our guest (1931), 209
Good Christian friends, rejoice and sing! (1931), 144
Lord of all hopefulness, Lord of all joy (1931), 469
Praise and thanksgiving (1945), 409
Lord, save your world; in bitter need (1947), 420
God has spoken by his prophets (1952), 238
Lord of light, your name outshining (1961), 405
Lord, whose love in humble service (1961), 423
Lord of all good, our gifts we bring you now (1967), 411
The first day of the week (1967), 246
We know that Christ is raised and dies no more (1967), 189
Filled with the Spirit's pow'r, with one accord (1969), 160
Forgive our sins as we forgive (1969), 307
O Christ, the healer, we have come (1969), 360
Praise the Lord, rise up rejoicing (1969), 196
The Church of Christ, in ev'ry age (1969), 433
We place upon your table, Lord (1969), 217
For the fruit of all creation (1970), 563
When in our music God is glorified (1971), 555
Christ is alive! Let Christians sing (1975), 363

(*A hymn from England can also be found under* Latin.)

Ireland

God who made the earth and heaven (Eng., 1827; Ire., 1838; Eng., 1864), 281
Chief of sinners though I be (1864), 306

(*Another hymn from Ireland can be found under* Latin.)

Scotland

The Lord's my shepherd (1650), 451
Immortal, invisible, God only wise (1867), 526
Beneath the cross of Jesus (1872), 107
O Love that will not let me go (1882), 324
All who love and serve your city (1966), 436

United States

I love your kingdom, Lord (1800), 368

What wondrous love is this, O my soul,
O my soul! (1811), 385
Lord, with glowing heart I'd praise thee
(1819), 243
For the bread which you have broken
(1824), 200
You are the way; through you alone
(1824), 464
My country, 'tis of thee (1829), 566
My faith looks up to thee (1831), 479
Before you, Lord, we bow (1832), 401
"Take up your cross," the Savior said
(1833), 398
It came upon the midnight clear (1849),
54
Stand up, stand up for Jesus (1858), 389
He leadeth me: oh, blessed thought!
(1862), 501
Mine eyes have seen the glory of the
coming of the Lord (1862), 332
Eternal Ruler of the ceaseless round
(1864), 373
Holy Spirit, truth divine (1864), 257
O little town of Bethlehem (1868), 41
Jesus, Savior, pilot me (1871), 334
O Zion, haste, your mission high fulfilling
(1871), 397
Come with us, O blessed Jesus (1872),
219
When peace, like a river, attendeth my
way (1873), 346
Break now the bread of life (1877), 235
O Master, let me walk with you (1879),
492
Great God, a blessing from your throne
(1880), 185
Away in a manger, no crib for his bed
(1885), 67
Lead on, O King eternal! (1889), 495
Love consecrates the humblest act (1902),
122
We praise you, O God, our redeemer,
creator (1902), 241
Where cross the crowded ways of life
(1905), 429
Joyful, joyful we adore thee (1907), 551
Not alone for mighty empire (1909), 437
Lord Jesus Christ, we humbly pray (1910),
225
Let all things now living (c. 1920), 557
Lift ev'ry voice and sing (1921), 562
How blessed is this place, O Lord (1924),
186
O Lord, now let your servant (1924), 339
They cast their nets in Galilee (1924), 449
Wondrous are your ways, O God (1924,
1978), 311
Lord Christ, when first you came to earth
(1928), 421
God of grace and God of glory (1930),
415
O Son of God, in Galilee (1930), 426
And have the bright immensities (1931),
391
Our Father, by whose name (1939), 357
Your kingdom come! O Father, hear our
prayer (1940), 376

Eternal God, before your throne we bend
(1941), 354
Eternal Spirit of the living Christ (1947),
441
Deep were his wounds, and red (1953),
100
Where restless crowds are thronging
(1953), 430
Hope of the world, thou Christ of great
compassion (1954), 493
Thy strong word did cleave the darkness
(1954), 233
God of our life, all-glorious Lord (1958),
270
Now all the vault of heav'n resounds
(1958), 143
O God of ev'ry nation (1958), 416
A stable lamp is lighted (c. 1959), 74
Lord of all nations, grant me grace
(1960), 419
As saints of old their firstfruits brought
(1961), 404
God, whose giving knows no ending
(1961), 408
In Adam we have all been one (1961), 372
From shepherding of stars that gaze
(1963), 63
Look, now he stands! Stones could not
hold him down for long (1963), 152
Earth and all stars! (1964), 558
Sent forth by God's blessing (1964), 221
This is the Spirit's entry now (1965), 195
Cup of blessing that we share (1966), 204
O God, send heralds who will never falter
(1966), 283
O God, O Lord of heav'n and earth
(1967), 396
Now the silence (1968), 205
God, who stretched the spangled heavens
(1969), 463
Great God, our source and Lord of space
(1969), 466
Lord, receive this company (1969), 255
O thou, who hast of thy pure grace (1969),
442
Have no fear, little flock (1971, 1973),
476
Hear us now, our God and Father (1971),
288
For perfect love so freely spent (1972),
216
Now we join in celebration (1972), 203
Spirit of God, unleashed on earth (1972),
387
Have no fear, little flock (1971, 1973),
476
Oh, praise the Lord, my soul! (1973), 538
The hills are bare at Bethlehem (1973), 61
Up through endless ranks of angels
(1973), 159
My soul now magnifies the Lord (1974),
180
Heav'nly Father, hear our prayer (1975),
289
When seed falls on good soil (1975), 236
Rise up, O saints of God! (1977), 383

Nun bitten wir den Heiligen Geist (13th century/1524), 317

Wir glauben all an einen Gott/Schöpfer (14th century/1524), 374

Allein Gott in der Höh sei Ehr (1525), 166
All glory be to God on high (U.S., 1978)

Jesaja dem Propheten das geschah (1526), 528
Isaiah in a vision did of old (U.S., 1941)

Verleih uns Frieden gnädiglich (1527), 471
Grant peace, we pray, in mercy, Lord (Switz., 1952)

Christe, du Lamm Gottes (1528), 103
O Christ, thou Lamb of God (?)

Ein feste Burg ist unser Gott (c. 1529), 228, 229
A mighty fortress is our God (U.S., 1978)

O Lamm Gottes, unschuldig (1531), 111
Lamb of God, pure and sinless (U.S., 1978)

Vom Himmel hoch da komm ich her (1535), 51
From heav'n above to earth I come (Eng., 1855/U.S., 1978)

Allein zu dir, Herr Jesu Christ (1540), 395
I trust, O Christ, in you alone (U.S., 1978)

Nun lob, mein Seel, den Herren (c. 1540), 519
My soul, now praise your maker! (Eng., 1863)

Christ unser Herr zum Jordan kam (c. 1541), 79
To Jordan came the Christ, our Lord, (U.S., 1978)

Erhalt uns, Herr, bei deinem Wort (1541), 230
Lord, keep us steadfast in your Word (Eng., 1863)

Gottes Sohn ist kommen (Boh., 1544), 312
Once he came in blessing (Eng., 1863)

Lobt Gott, ihr Christen allzugleich (c. 1554), 47
Let all together praise our God (U.S., 1969)

Wenn wir in höchsten Nöten sein (c. 1560), 303
When in the hour of deepest need (Eng., 1858)

Von Gott will ich nicht lassen (1563), 468
From God can nothing move me (U.S., 1978)

Es ist gewisslich an der Zeit (1565/1586), 321
The day is surely drawing near (U.S., 1872)

Mit Freuden zart zu dieser Fahrt (Morav., 1566), 140
With high delight let us unite (U.S., 1969)

Herzlich Lieb hab ich dich, o Herr (1567), 325
Lord, thee I love with all my heart (Eng., 1863)

Lass mich dein sein und bleiben (1572, 1688), 490
Let me be yours forever (U.S., 1863)

Wer Gott vertraut, hat wohlgebaut (1572, 1597), 450
Who trusts in God, a strong abode (Eng., 1863)

Es ist gewisslich an der Zeit (1565/1586), 321
Wer Gott vertraut, hat wohlgebaut (1572, 1597), 450

In dir ist Freude (1598), 552
In thee is gladness (Eng., 1858)

Wachet auf, ruft uns die Stimme (1599), 31
Wake, awake, for night is flying (Eng., 1858)

Wie schön leuchtet der Morgenstern/voll Gnad (1599), 76
O Morning Star, how fair and bright! (U.S., 1978)

O Heiland, reiss die Himmel auf (1623), 38
O Savior, rend the heavens wide (U.S., 1969)

Jerusalem, du hochgebaute Stadt (1626), 348
Jerusalem, whose towers touch the skies (U.S., 1978)

Ach bleib mit deiner Gnade (1628), 263
Abide with us, our Savior (U.S., 1848, 1891)

Herzliebster Jesu, was hast du verbrochen (1630), 123
Ah, holy Jesus, how hast thou offended (Eng., 1899)

O Gott, du frommer Gott (1630), 504
O God, my faithful God (Eng., 1858)

O Jesu Christe, wahres Licht (1630), 380
O Christ, our light, O Radiance true (Eng., 1858; U.S., 1978)

Verzage nicht, du Häuflein klein (1632), 361
Do not despair, O little flock (U.S., 1978)

Nun danket alle Gott (1636?), 533, 534
Now thank we all our God (Eng., 1858)

Herr Jesu Christ, du hast bereit't (1638), 208
Lord Jesus Christ, you have prepared (U.S., 1978)

Gott des Himmels und der Erde (c. 1640), 266
Maker of the earth and heaven (Eng., 1848, 1855)

O Heilger Geist, kehr bei uns ein (1640), 459
O Holy Spirit, enter in (Eng., 1863)

Jesu, meine Freude (1641/1653), 457, 458
Jesus, priceless treasure (Eng., 1863)

Macht hoch die Tür, die Tor macht weit (1642), 32
Fling wide the door, unbar the gate (U.S., 1978)

Komm, du wertes Lösegeld (1644), 24
Come, O precious Ransom, come (U.S., 1889)

Auf, auf, mein Herz, mit Freuden (1648), 129
Awake, my heart, with gladness (Eng. and U.S., composite)

Ein Lämmlein geht und trägt die Schuld (1648), 105
A Lamb goes uncomplaining forth (U.S., 1978)

Nun ruhen alle Wälder (1648), 276, 282
Now all the woods are sleeping (U.S., 1978)
Now rest beneath night's shadow (U.S., 1941)

Schmücke dich, o liebe Seele (1649), 224
Soul, adorn yourself with gladness (Eng., 1863)

Herr Jesu Christ, dich zu uns wend (1651), 253
Lord Jesus Christ, be present now (Eng., 1863)

Wie wohl hast du gelabet (1651), 197
O living Bread from heaven (Eng., 1858)

Frölich soll mein Herze springen (1653), 46
Once again my heart rejoices (Eng., 1858)

Jesu, deine Passion (1653), 115
Jesus, I will ponder now (U.S., 1889)

Jesu, meine Freude (1641/1653), 457, 458
Jesus, meine Zuversicht (1653), 340
Jesus Christ, my sure defense (Eng., 1863; U.S., 1912)

Lasset uns mit Jesu ziehen (1653), 487
Let us ever walk with Jesus (U.S., 1978)

O Jesu Christ, mein schönstes Licht (1653), 336
Jesus, thy boundless love to me (Eng., 1739)

Wie soll ich dich empfangen (1653), 23
O Lord, how shall I meet you (Eng., 1863)

Ist Gott für mich (1656), 454
If God himself be for me (Eng., 1857; U.S., 1941)

O Haupt voll Blut und Wunden (1656), 116, 117
O sacred head, now wounded (U.S., 1830)

Ich will dich lieben, meine Stärke (1657), 502
Thee will I love, my strength, my tow'r (Eng., 1739)

Wer nur den lieben Gott lässt walten (1657), 453
If you but trust in God to guide you (Eng., 1863; U.S., 1978)

Jesu, meines Lebens Leben (1658), 97
Christ, the life of all the living (Eng., 1863)

Komm, o komm, du Geist des Lebens (1658), 478
Come, oh, come, O quick'ning Spirit (U.S., 1958)

Schönster Herr Jesu (1662), 518
Beautiful Savior (U.S., 1873)

Liebster Jesu, wir sind hier, dich und (1663, 1707), 248
Dearest Jesus, at your word (Eng., 1858)

Christe, du Beistand deiner Kreuzgemeine (1664), 366
Lord of our life and God of our salvation (Eng., 1840)

Die güldne Sonne/voll Freud und Wonne (1666), 465
Evening and morning (Eng., 1857; U.S., 1930)

Mir nach, spricht Christus, unser Held (1668), 455
"Come, follow me," the Savior spake (U.S., 1912)

Tröstet, tröstet, meine Lieben (1671), 29
Comfort, comfort now my people (Eng., 1863)

Alles ist an Gottes Segen (c. 1673), 447
All depends on our possessing (Eng., 1858)

Sei Lob und Ehr dem höchsten Gut (1675), 542
Sing praise to God, the highest good (Eng., 1864)

Was Gott tut, das ist wohlgetan, les bleibt (1675), 446
Whatever God ordains is right (U.S., 1978)

Lobe den Herren, den mächtigen König der Ehren (1680), 543
Praise to the Lord, the Almighty, the King of Creation! (Eng., 1863)

Lass mich dein sein und bleiben (1572/1688), 490

Erneure mich, o ewigs Licht (c. 1690), 511
Renew me, O eternal Light (U.S., 1889)

Auf, ihr Christen, Christi Glieder (1697), 182
Rise, O children of salvation (Eng., 1858)

Mache dich, mein Geist, bereit (1697), 443
Rise, my soul, to watch and pray (Eng., 1863)

616

Ermuntert euch, ihr Frommen (1700), 25
Rejoice, rejoice, believers (Eng., 1854)

Liebster Jesu, wir sind hier, deinem Worte (1704), 187
Dearest Jesus, we are here (Eng., 1858; U.S., 1880)

O dass ich tausend Zungen hätte/und einen (1704), 560
Oh, that I had a thousand voices (Eng., 1845, 1855; U.S., 1941)

Liebster Jesu, wir sind hier, dich und (1663, 1707), 248

Ich komm zu deinem Abendmahle (1710?), 213
I come, O Savior, to your table (U.S., 1941)

Lobe den Herren, o meine Seele (1714), 539
Praise the Almighty, my soul, adore him! (Australia, 1925)

Jesus nimmt die Sünder an (1718), 291
Jesus sinners will receive (U.S., 1941)

Jesu, geh voran (Moravia, 1721), 341
Jesus, still lead on (Eng., 1846)

Gott ist gegenwärtig (1729), 249
God himself is present (Eng., 1789; U.S., 1930)

Tut mir auf die schöne Pforte (1732), 250
Open now thy gates of beauty (Eng., 1863)

Fang dein Werk mit Jesu an (1734), 444
With the Lord begin your task (U.S., 1937)

Ich bin getauft auf deinen Namen (1734), 192
Baptized into your name most holy (Eng., 1863)

Christi Blut und Gerechtigkeit (Moravia, 1739), 302
Jesus, your blood and righteousness (Eng., 1740)

Grosser Gott, wir loben dich (1744), 535
Holy God, we praise your name (U.S., 1853)

Wohl einem Haus, da Jesus Christ (1746), 512
Oh, blest the house, whate'er befall (Eng., 1863)

Wach auf, du Geist der ersten Zeugen (1750), 382
Awake, O Spirit of the watchmen (U.S., 1940)

Jesus lebt, mit ihm auch ich (1757), 133
Jesus lives! The vict'ry's won! (Eng., 1841)

Also hat Gott die Welt geliebt (c. 1778), 292
God loved the world so that he gave (U.S., 1889)

Wir pflügen und wir streuen (1782), 362
We plow the fields and scatter (Eng., 1861)

Gott segne Sachsenland (1815), 569
God bless our native land (U.S., c. 1834)

Stille Nacht, heilige Nacht (1818), 65
Silent night, holy night! (U.S., 1863)

Dein Wort, o Herr, ist milder Tau (1825), 232
Your Word, O Lord, is gentle dew (Eng., 1863)

Halleluja! Jesus lebt (1825), 147
Hallelujah! Jesus lives! (Eng., 1862)

Walte, walte nah und fern (1827), 379
Spread, oh, spread, almighty Word (U.S., 1978)

Beim frühen Morgenlicht (c. 1828), 545, 546
When morning gilds the skies (Eng., 1899)

Wir sind des Herrn, wir leben oder sterben (1843), 399
We are the Lord's. His all-sufficient merit (Eng., 1860)

So nimm denn meine Hände und führe mich (Latvia, 1862), 333
Lord, take my hand and lead me (U.S., 1912, 1925/1978)

(*Hymns from Germany can also be found under* Latin.)

GREEK

Σιγησάτω πᾶσα σάρξ βροτεία (Jerusalem, 1st century), 198
Let all mortal flesh keep silence (Eng., 1864)

Φῶς ἱλαρὸν ἁγίας δόξης (3rd century), 279
Oh, gladsome light of the Father immortal (U.S., 1893)

Μνώεο Χριστέ (Egypt?, 5th century), 309
Lord Jesus, think on me (Eng., 1876, 1896)

Αἴσωμεν πάντες λαοί (near Jerusalem, 8th century), 132
Come, you faithful, raise the strain (Eng., 1862)

'Αναστάσεως ἡμέρα (near Jerusalem, 8th century), 141
The day of resurrection! (Eng., 1862)

HURON (Canada)

Estennialon de tsonue Jesus ahatonnia (17th century), 72
'Twas in the moon of wintertime (Can., 1963; U.S., 1978)

617

HEBREW

Yigdal Elohim Hai (Italy?, 12th century/
c. 1300), 544
*The God of Abr'ham praise (Eng.,
c. 1770)*

*(Hymns from the Holy Land can be found
under Greek.)*

ICELANDIC

Hve dýrðhlegur er drottinn (1886), 515
*How marvelous God's greatness (Can.,
1913)*

IRISH

Atomriug indiu (5th century), 188
I bind unto myself today (Eng., 1889)

*(Hymns from Ireland can also be found
under English: Ireland.)*

ITALIAN

Laudato si', mi Signor, con tutte le tue
creature (1225), 527
*All creatures of our God and King (Eng.,
c. 1910)*

Discendi, amor santo (c. 1400), 508
Come down, O Love divine (Eng., 1867)

Giesù sommo conforto (1563), 93
Jesus, refuge of the weary (Ire., 1853)

Viva, viva, Gesù, che per mio bene (18th
century), 95
Glory be to Jesus (Eng., 1857)

*(Hymns from Italy can also be found
under Latin and Hebrew.)*

JAPANESE

Mabune no naka ni (1929), 417
In a lowly manger born (U.S., 1978)

LATIN

Te Deum laudamus (3rd or 4th century?),
547
*Thee we adore, eternal Lord! (Eng.,
1815)*
*(See also German: Grosser Gott, wir
loben dich [1744], 535)*
*(See also Swedish: Vi lova dig, o store
Gud [1695/1811], 432)*

O lux beata Trinitas (Italy?, 4th century),
275
O Trinity, O blessed Light (U.S., 1978)

Splendor Paternae gloriae (Italy?, 4th
century), 271
*O Splendor of the Father's light (U.S.,
1978)*

Veni, Redemptor omnium (gentium)
(Italy?, 4th century), 28
*Savior of the nations, come (U.S., 1850,
1969, 1978)*

Claro paschali gaudio (4th or 5th century),
154
*That Easter day with joy was bright
(Eng., 1851)*

Ad regias Agni dapes (4th-9th century/
1631), 210
*At the Lamb's high feast we sing (Scot.,
1849)*

Exultet iam angelica turba caelorum
(c. 400), 146
*Rejoice, angelic choirs, rejoice! (U.S.,
1978)*

A solis ortus cardine (Italy?, 5th century),
64
*From east to west, from shore to shore
(Eng., 1871)*

Christe, qui lux es et dies (5th century?),
273
*O Christ, you are the light and day (Eng.,
1719, 1848)*

Corde natus ex Parentis (5th century), 42
*Of the Father's love begotten (Eng.,
1851)*

Hostis Herodes impie (Italy?, 5th century),
85
*When Christ's appearing was made known
(Eng., 1851; Can., 1971)*

O sola magnarum urbium (5th century), 81
*O chief of cities, Bethlehem (Scot., 1879;
U.S., 1879, 1932)*

Jam lucis orto sidere (5th-8th century),
268
*Now that the daylight fills the sky (Eng.,
1851)*

En clara vox redarguit (5th-10th century/
1632), 37
*Hark! A thrilling voice is sounding!
(Eng., 1849)*

Nocte surgentes vigilemus omnes (6th
century?), 267
*Father, we praise you, now the night is
over (Eng., 1906)*

Pange, lingua, gloriosi proelium (France?,
6th century), 118
*Sing, my tongue, the glorious battle
(Eng., 1851)*
*(See also Swedish: Upp min tunga [1614/
1816], 155)*

Rex Christe, factor omnium (Rome?,
6th century), 101
*O Christ, our king, creator, Lord (U.S.,
1858)*

Vexilla Regis prodeunt (France, 568), 124,
125
*The royal banners forward go (Eng.,
1851; U.S., 1940)*

Stabat Mater dolorosa (13th century), 110
At the cross, her station keeping (Eng., 19th century)

Urbs Sion aurea, patria lactea (France, 13th century), 347
Jerusalem the golden (Eng., 1851)

In dulci jubilo (Germany, 14th century), 55
Good Christian friends, rejoice (Eng., 1853)

Nunc angelorum gloria (Germany, 14th century), 68
The glorious angels came today (U.S., 1969)

Quem pastores laudavere (Germany, 14th century), 68
He whom shepherds once came praising (U.S., 1940/1969)

Surrexit Christus hodie (c. 14th century), 151
Jesus Christ is ris'n today (Eng., 1708)

Caelestis formam gloriae (Eng., 15th century), 80
Oh, wondrous type! Oh, vision fair (Eng., 1851; U.S., 1940)

O amor quam exstaticus (Holland?, 15th century), 88
Oh, love, how deep, how broad, how high (Eng., 1854; U.S., 1962)

O filii et filiae (France, 15th century), 139
O sons and daughters of the King (Eng., 1851)

O Deus, ego amo te (16th century?), 491
O God, I love thee; not that my poor love (Eng., 1889)

Ad regias Agni dapes (4th-9th century/1632), 210
Christe cunctorum dominator alme (c. 9th century/1632), 375
En clara vox redarguit (5th-10th century/1632), 37

O Esca viatorum (Germany, 1661), 222
O Bread of life from heaven (U.S., 1868, 1913)

Instantis adventum Dei (France, 1736), 22
The advent of our God (Eng., 1837)

Jordanis oras praevia (France, 1736), 36
On Jordan's banks the Baptist's cry (Eng., 1837)

Adeste, fideles, laeti triumphantes (France, c. 1743), 45
Oh, come, all ye faithful (Eng., 1841)

LOMA (Liberia)

A va de laa mioo, diioo (c. 1965), 214
Come, let us eat, for now the feast is spread (Liberia, c. 1970)

NORWEGIAN

Herre Gud, dit dyre navn og aere (17th century), 244
Lord our God, with praise we come before you (U.S., 1951)

O salig den, Guds Ord har hört (1786), 227
How blest are they who hear God's Word (U.S., 1958)

O taenk naar engang samles skal (1846), 351
Oh, happy day when we shall stand (U.S., 1978)

Jeg ved mig en Sövn i Jesu Navn (1851?), 342
I know of a sleep in Jesus' name (U.S., 1913)

Der mange skal komme fra Öst og fra Vest (1861), 313
A multitude comes from the east and the west (U.S., 1909)

Jeg staar for Gud, som alting ved (1861), 310
To you, omniscient Lord of all (U.S., 1909)

Al verden nu raabe for Herren med fryd (U.S., 1874), 256
Oh, sing jubilee to the Lord, ev'ry land (U.S., 1978)

O, at jeg kunde min Jesus prise (1875), 326
My heart is longing to praise my Savior (U.S., 1931)

Seklernas väkter saa dröjande skrida (?, 1885), 394
Lost in the night do the people yet languish (U.S., 1929)

Jeg er saa glad hver Julekveld (c. 1900), 69
I am so glad each Christmas Eve (U.S., 1931)

POLISH

W zlobie lezy (?), 44
Infant holy, infant lowly (Eng., 1925)

LATVIAN

(A hymn from Latvia is the last entry under German.)

SCOTTISH

(Hymns from Scotland can be found under English: Scotland.)

SLOVAK-BOHEMIAN

Narodil se Kristus Pán, Veselme se (15th century), 57
Let our gladness have no end, Hallelujah! (?)

Pán Bůh jest ma síla i doufáni (1626), 484
God, my Lord, my strength, my place of hiding (U.S., 1969)

Rok nový zase k nám přišel (1636), 181
Greet now the swiftly changing year (U.S., 1968)

Známe to, Pane Bože náš (1636), 96
Your heart, O God, is grieved, we know (U.S., 1969)

Zpivejmež všickni vesele: Hallelujah (1636), 150
Make songs of joy to Christ, our head (U.S., 1976)

Čas radosti, veselosti (1674), 66
Come Rejoicing, praises voicing (U.S., 1960)

(Hymns from Bohemia and Moravia can also be found under German.)

SWEDISH

Den signede Dag (*c.* 1450/Denmark, 1569), 161
O day full of grace (U.S., 1978)

Upp, min tunga, at lovsjunga (1614/1816), 155
Praise the Savior, now and ever (U.S., 1978)

I Himmelen, i Himmelen (1620, 1651/1816), 330
In heav'n above, in heav'n above (Eng., 1868)

Du som fromma hjartan vaarder (*c.* 1695/1816), 440
Christians, while on earth abiding (U.S., 1901)

Vi lova dig, o store Gud (1695/1811), 432
We worship you, O God of might (U.S., 1978)

Bereden väg för Herran (1812), 26
Prepare the royal highway (U.S., 1978)

Höga Majestät, vi alla (1812), 247
Holy Majesty, before you (U.S., 1925)

O Jesu, än de dina (1814), 496
Around you, O Lord Jesus (U.S., 1901, 1978)

Du som fromma hjartan vaarder (*c.* 1695/1816), 440

Upp, min tunga, at lovsjunga (1614/1816), 155

Var hälsad, sköna morgonstund (1819), 73
All hail to you, O blessed morn! (U.S., 1901)

I Himmelen, i Himmelen (1620, 1651/1816), 330

Med Gud och hans vänskap (1851), 371
With God as our friend, with his Spirit and Word (U.S., 1901)

När Juldagsmorgon glimmar (1851), 59
When Christmas morn is dawning (U.S., 1978)

Tryggare kan ingen vara (1855), 474
Children of the heav'nly Father (U.S., 1925)

Vi äro köpta och aterlösta (1872)
(See under Norwegian: O, at jeg kunde min Jesus prise [1875], 326)

O store Gud (1885), 532
O Lord my God, when I in awesome wonder (Eng.?, 1948)

SWISS

(A hymn from Switzerland can be found under French.)

SYRIAC

Hayyel Maran 'idh daphshat (4th century), 218
Strengthen for service, Lord, the hands (Eng., 1906)

TAMIL (India)

Tandanei tuthipoome, tiru sabhatyaare (before 1932), 529
Praise God from whom all blessings flow. Praise him (Ceylon?, 1963)

WELSH

Arglwydd, arwain trwy'r anialwch (1745), 343
Guide me ever, great Redeemer (Wales, 1771, 1772)

Authors, Composers, and Sources of Hymns and Canticles

Numbers listed refer to LBW hymn numbers.

Aaberg, Jens C., 75
Abe, Seigi, 417
Abelard, Peter, 337
Adam, Barbara E., 289
Addison, Joseph, 264
Ahle, Johann R., 187, 248
Ahnfelt, Oskar, 371
Ain schöns newes Christliches lyed, 361
Albert, Heinrich, 266
Alderson, Eliza S., 424
Alexander, Cecil F., 114, 188, 494
Alexander, James W., *116, 117*
Alford, Henry, 407
Alington, Cyril A., 144
Allen, *New York Selections,* 547
Allen, Oswald, 304
Alte Catholische Geistliche Kirchengesäng, Köln, 58
Altenburg, Johann M., 361
Ambrose, 28, 271, 275
American, 332
American folk hymn, 331, 392
Andächtige Haus-Kirche Gesängen, Nurnberg, 302, 380, 447
Andelig Örtegård för Barn, Jököping, 59
Anders, Charles R., *307,* 386, *463,* 538, 555
Anthes, Friedrich K., 304
Anton, Christoph, 90, 242
Aquinas, Thomas, 120, 199
Arthur, John W., 7, 8, 9, 10, 11, 12, 387
As Hymnodus Sacer, Leipzig 286, 511
Astley, Charles T., *399*
Åström, Johan, 330
Atkinson, Frederick C., 486
Augustine, 146
Ausserlesenes Catholisches Kirchengesäng, Köln, 38, 143, 157, 175, 527

Babcock, Maltbie D., 554
Bach, J. S., 89, *90, 219, 242*
Bahnmaier, Jonathan F., 379
Bain, J. L. Macbeth, 451
Baker, Henry W., *42,* 414, 456, 460
Baldwin, Lee M., 422
Balle, C. C. N., 62
Baring-Gould, Sabine, 280, *355,* 509
Barnby, Joseph, 280, 287, 381, 425, 546
Barnes, Edward S., *71*
Barthélémon, François H., 269
Bayly, Albert F., 409, 411, 420, 423
Beadon, Hyde W., 78

Beck, Theodore A., *33, 132, 141, 172, 181, 193, 290, 484*
Becker, John W., *259, 409*
Bede, The Venerable, 157
Beethoven, Ludwig van, 551
Bell, George K. A., 386
Belsheim, Ole G., *239*
Bender, Jan O., *28, 48, 86, 154, 196, 210, 312, 395,* 396, *398, 412, 552, 558*
Benedictine plainsong, 277
Benson, Louis F., 200
Berg, Caroline V. Sandell, 474
Berggren, Andreas P., 298
Berliner Gesangbuch, 248
Bern, 375
Bernard of Clairvaux, 116, 117, 316, 356, 489, 537
Bernard of Cluny, 322, 347
Bevan, Emma F., *182*
Bickersteth, Edward H., *491*
Billings, William, 426
Birken, Sigismund von, 115, 487
Blacker, Maxwell J., *375*
Bliss, Philip P., 346
Blumenfeld, Edward M., 434
Boberg, Carl, 532
Bode, John E., 503
Bogatzky, Karl H. von, 382
Bohemian Brethren, *Kirchengeseng, 210*
Bohemian carol, 57, 66
Bollhagen, *Heiliges Opfer,* 292
Boltze, Georg G., 487
Bonar, Horatius, 167, 211, 305, 497, 525
Borthwick, Jane L., *147, 341*
Bouman, Herbert J. A., *68*
Bouman, Paul B., *208, 536*
Bourgeois, Louis, 29, 245, 303, 318, 431, 493, 531, 545, 550, 564, 565
Bourne, George H., 172
Bowie, W. Russell, 421
Bowring, John, 104
Boye, Birgitte K., 43, 138
Bradbury, William B., 293, 296, 501
Brady, Nicholas, 452
Brand, Eugene, *350*
Brauer, Alfred E. R., *539*
Brebeuf, Jean de, 72
Bridges, Matthew, 170
Bridges, Robert, *123, 545, 546*
Briem, Valdimar, 515
Briggs, George W., 209, 238

Italic numbers indicate translations or musical settings.

Tunes—Alphabetical

Indented lines indicate names by which some tunes in this book may also be known.

First Lines of Canticles

Numbers listed refer to LBW canticle numbers.

Agnus Dei, 1
All you works of the Lord, bless the
    Lord, 18

Benedicite, omnia opera, 18
Benedictus, 2
Blessed be the Lord, the God of Israel, 2

Cantemus Domino, 19
Christ Jesus, being in the form of God,
    20
Climb to the top of the highest mountain,
    7
Come, let us sing to the Lord, 4

Domine clamavi, 5

God, who has called you to glory, 12

How blest are those who know their need
    of God, 17

I called to my God for help, 9
I will sing the story of your love, O Lord,
    16
I will sing to the Lord, 19

Jesus, Lamb of God, 1

Keep in mind that Jesus Christ has died
    for us, 13

Let my prayer rise before you as incense,
    5
Listen! You nations of the world, 14

Magna et mirabilia, 21
Magnificat, 6
My soul proclaims the greatness of the
    Lord, 6

Now listen, you servants of God, 11

O Lord, I call to you, 5
O ruler of the universe, Lord God, 21

Quaerite Dominum, 15

Seek the Lord while he may be found, 15
Sing praise to the Lord, all the earth, 10

Te Deum laudamus, 3
The people who walked in darkness, 8

Venite exultemus, 4

You are God; we praise you, 3

First Lines of Hymns, Original and Translated— Alphabetical

Numbers listed refer to LBW hymn numbers.

A hymn of glory let us sing!, 157
A lamb goes uncomplaining forth, 105
A mighty fortress is our God†, 228, 229
A multitude comes from the east and the west, 313
A Patre Unigenitus, 83
A solis ortus cardine, 64
A stable lamp is lighted, 74
A toi la gloire, O Ressuscité, 145
A va de laa mioo, diioo, 214
  Abide, O dearest Jesus‡, 263
Abide with me, fast falls the eventide†, 272
Abide with us, our Savior, 263
Ach bleib mit deiner Gnade, 263
Ad regias Agni dapes, 210
Adeste, fideles, laeti triumphantes, 45
Adoro te devote, latens Deitas, 199
Ah, holy Jesus, how hast thou offended†, 123
Ἀίσωμεν πάντες λαοί, 132
Al verden nu raabe for Herren med fryd, 256
Alas! And did my Savior bleed, 98
All creatures of our God and King†, 527
All depends on our possessing, 447
All glory be to God on high†, 166
All glory, laud, and honor†, 108
All hail the pow'r of Jesus' name!†, 328, 329
All hail to you, O blessed morn!, 73
  All my heart this night rejoices, 46
All people that on earth do dwell†, 245
  All praise to God, who reigns above, 542
All praise to thee, my God, this night†, 278
All praise to you, eternal Lord, 48
All praise to you, O Lord, 78
All who believe and are baptized, 194
All who love and serve your city, 436
All who would valiant be, 498
Allein Gott in der Höh sei Ehr, 166
Allein zu dir, Herr Jesu Christ, 395
Alleluia! Sing to Jesus†, 158
Alles ist an Gottes Segen, 447
Almighty God, your Word is cast, 234
Also hat Gott die Welt geliebt, 292
Amazing grace, how sweet the sound†, 448
Amid the world's bleak wilderness, 378

Ἀναστάσεως ἡμέρα, 141
And have the bright immensities, 391
Angels, from the realms of glory†, 50
Angels we have heard on high†, 71
Angularis fundamentum, 367
Arglwydd, arwain trwy'r anialwch, 343
Arise, my soul, arise!, 516
Around you, O Lord Jesus, 496
  As men of old their firstfruits brought, 404
As pants the hart for cooling streams, 452
As saints of old their firstfruits brought, 404
As with gladness men of old†, 82
At the cross, her station keeping, 110
At the Lamb's high feast we sing, 210
At the name of Jesus†, 179
Atomriug indiu, 188
Auf, auf, mein Herz, mit Freuden, 129
Auf, ihr Christen, Christi Glieder, 182
Aus tiefer Not schrei ich zu dir, 295
Awake, my heart, with gladness, 129
Awake, my soul, and with the sun, 269
Awake, O Spirit of the watchmen, 382
  Awake, thou Spirit, who didst fire, 382
Away in a manger, no crib for his bed†, 67

Baptized into your name most holy, 192
Beautiful Savior†, 518
Before Jehovah's awesome throne†, 531
  Before the ending of the day, 277
  Before thee, God, who knowest all, 310
Before you, Lord, we bow, 401
  Behold, a branch is growing, 58
  Behold a host arrayed in white, 314
  Behold a host, like mountains bright, 314
Beim frühen Morgenlicht, 545, 546
Beneath the cross of Jesus, 107
Bereden väg för Herran, 26
  Blessed Jesus, at thy word, 248
Blessing and honor and glory and pow'r, 525
Blest be the tie that binds, 370
Bow down your ear, almighty Lord, 286
Break now the bread of life, 235
Breathe on me, breath of God, 488
Bright and glorious is the sky, 75
Brightest and best of the stars of the morning†, 84

†Hymns included on list prepared by Consultation on Ecumenical Hymnody.
‡Indented lines indicate first lines by which some hymns in this book may also be known.

Index to Essays

*Numbers refer to pages in the
Historical Essays section of this book.*

About the Author and Contributors

MARILYN KAY STULKEN, a native of Hastings, Nebraska, holds a Bachelor of Arts degree from Hastings College and Master of Music and Doctor of Musical Arts degrees from Eastman School of Music, Rochester, New York. Presently director of music at Trinity Lutheran Church, Kenosha, Wisconsin, she has served as director of music at St. Paul's Lutheran Church, Pittsford, New York, and as organist at St. Mark's Lutheran Church, Cedar Rapids, Iowa. She has taught at Coe College in Cedar Rapids, and as visiting assistant professor at the University of Iowa in Iowa City. She has given numerous lectures, workshops, and organ recitals in the Midwest and on the East Coast. Her articles and reviews have appeared in many musical journals. She is an active member of the American Guild of Organists, the Organ Historical Society, The Hymn Society of America, and is worship representative on the Southport District Cabinet of the Wisconsin-Upper Michigan Synod of the LCA.

M. ALFRED BICHSEL, formerly Director of Music of the Chapel at Valparaiso University, was chairman of the Department of Church Music at Eastman School of Music. He continues to serve in an advisory capacity at Eastman.

CARL F. SCHALK is the composer of five musical settings for hymns in the LBW and the arranger of many more. A complete biography can be found at LBW 118 in this book.

EDWARD A. HANSEN, formerly bishop of the Southwest Minnesota District of the ALC, is now teaching at Golden Valley Lutheran College, Minneapolis, in the Division of Biblical and Theological Studies.

MANDUS A. EGGE, after serving as a parish pastor, was Executive Director of the Commission on Worship and Church Music for the ALC. He lives in Edina, Minnesota, and is preparing a history of the ILCW.

SHIRLEY McCREEDY, a private piano teacher in Winnipeg, Manitoba, is business manager for the *Music Teachers' Journal*, a publication of the Canadian Federation of Music Teachers' Associations.

JOEL W. LUNDEEN is represented by a number of hymn texts in the LBW. A complete biography can be found at LBW 146 in this book.

TOIVO K. HARJUNPAA is represented in the LBW by his translation of LBW 319. His biography can be found at LBW 319 in this book.

JAROSLAV J. VAJDA is the author of three hymns and several translations in the LBW. His biography is given at LBW 159 in this book.

CAROL ANN DORAN serves as organist and choir director of Incarnation Episcopal Church in Penfield, New York. She is also director of music at Colgate Rochester/Bexley Hall/Crozer Theological Seminary in Rochester, New York.

STANLEY E. YODER, previously a parish pastor, is instructional media producer at Western Psychiatric Institute and Clinic of the University of Pittsburgh; and is organist and choir director at Zion Lutheran Church in Penn Hills, Pennsylvania.

R. HAROLD TERRY prepared the harmonization for the tune found at LBW 557. His biography is given at LBW 557 in this book.